THE NEW OXFORD ATLAS

PREPARED BY
THE CARTOGRAPHIC DEPARTMENT
OF THE OXFORD UNIVERSITY PRESS

OXFORD UNIVERSITY PRESS
1978

Oxford University Press, Walton Street, Oxford OX2 6DP
OXFORD LONDON GLASGOW
NEW YORK TORONTO MELBOURNE WELLINGTON
IBADAN NAIROBI DAR ES SALAAM CAPE TOWN
KUALA LUMPUR SINGAPORE JAKARTA HONG KONG TOKYO
DELHI BOMBAY CALCUTTA MADRAS KARACHI

ISBN 0 19 211572 3

The Oxford Atlas first published 1951
The New Oxford Atlas first published 1975
Revised edition 1978

Compiled by
THE CARTOGRAPHIC DEPARTMENT OF THE OXFORD UNIVERSITY PRESS

Printed in Great Britain
Introductory text and maps: Cook Hammond and Kell Ltd, Mitcham, Surrey
Gazetteer: Butler and Tanner Ltd, Frome, Somerset

PREFACE

THE New Oxford Atlas is a development rather than a straightforward second edition of the Oxford Atlas first published in 1951. The distinguished editors of the Oxford Atlas, Brigadier Sir Clinton Lewis and Colonel J. D. Campbell, assisted by Mr. D. P. Bickmore of the Clarendon Press and Mr. Kenneth Cook of Messrs. Cook, Hammond & Kell, planned a coverage of topographic and thematic maps and a general style of mapping which have stood the test of time and which, in the opinion of the publishers, cannot be fundamentally improved upon in an atlas of the present scope.

Thus the New Oxford Atlas retains the basic arrangement of its predecessor. In particular it retains the scales, projections, sheet lines, and general colouring of its topographic maps, whilst incorporating complete revision of all information liable to change and a re-styling of certain elements of map design in the interests of greater clarity. Its thematic or special subject maps, which are particularly concerned with the basic aspects of physical geography and demography, incorporate the results of modern research and latest available information and are presented by newly-evolved cartographic techniques. The latter enable such aspects of physical geography as structure, relief, climate, and vegetation to be shown for all areas of the earth's surface at an unusually large, consistent scale. Furthermore all of these aspects are shown in direct relationship with each other and against a background of human geography. Since the vast subject of economic geography cannot be dealt with adequately in supplementary maps, the reader is referred here to the companion Oxford Economic Atlas of the World.

The gazetteer has been completely revised in conjunction with the maps and has been reset. Again, the practical principles of construction used in the Oxford Atlas gazetteer have been largely continued.

Whilst accepting full responsibility for the content of the New Oxford Atlas the publishers gratefully acknowledge the advice and assistance of many individuals and organizations in its preparation. Furthermore they hope that the generous and helpful comments and criticisms which have often been received in the past from the many users of the Oxford Atlas will continue in respect of its successor.

Contents

Index to Topographic Maps

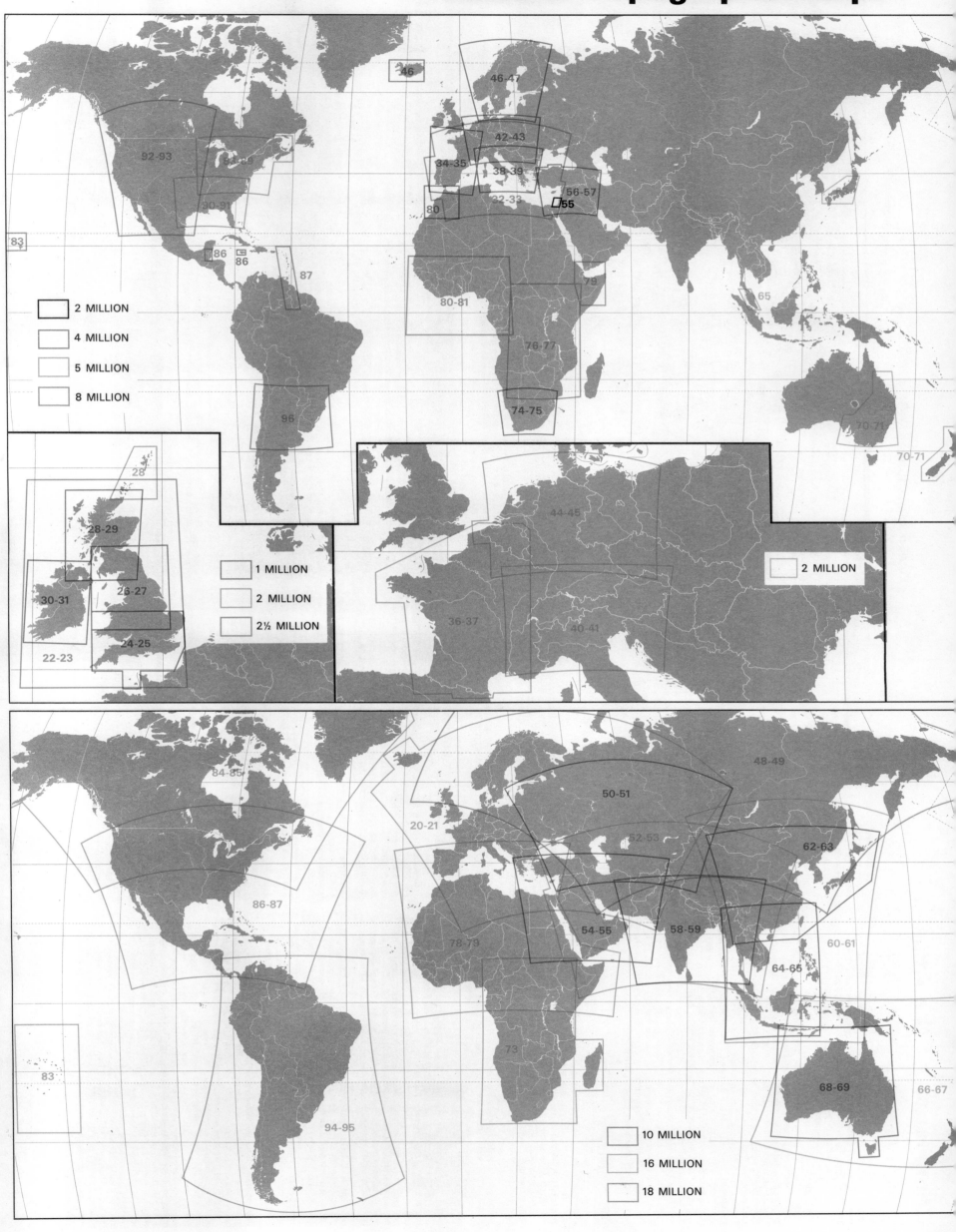

46

46-47

42-43

34-35

38-39

92-93

82-83

22-33

56-57

55

30-91

80

86

86

80-81

79

87

65

76-77

74-75

96

2 MILLION

4 MILLION

5 MILLION

8 MILLION

83

28

28-29

44-45

1 MILLION

2 MILLION

30-31

26-27

2 MILLION

22-23

24-25

36-37

40-41

2½ MILLION

84-85

48-49

50-51

20-21

52-53

62-63

86-87

54-55

58-59

60-61

78-79

64-65

83

73

68-69

66-67

94-95

10 MILLION

16 MILLION

18 MILLION

Compilation of the Atlas

Topographic maps

General sources The topography of the atlas has been taken from maps published mainly by British and American official and non-official bodies and at considerably larger scales than those of the atlas maps. A list of the principal maps used is given in The Oxford Atlas, First edition, page 8.

For the selection and grading of towns, the boundaries of subdivisions, the classification of communications, and other details of human geography, the most recent maps, census reports, official year-books, and other publications of the countries, and territories concerned have been consulted. The list of these is too long to include.

Frequent recourse has also been made to the following - U.N. Demographic Yearbook, Unesco Liste des Parcs Nationaux, U.S. Department of State International Boundary Studies and Geographic Notes. The Statesman's Year-Book. Whitaker's Almanack. Cartactual Map Service. Philip's Geographical Digest. Jane's World Railways. ABC World Airways Guide.

For the relief, on maps whose scale is 1:8M or smaller, great use has been made of the 1.5M series of Aeronautical Planning Charts published by the U.S. Coast and Geodetic Survey. For the larger scale maps relief has generally been based on the principal source maps noted above. Bathymetric information has been taken from the British Admiralty charts, from the International Hydrographic Bureau charts, and from recent hydrographic surveys.

Projections Notes on projections used and details of scale errors will be found at pages 114-115 to which the reader is referred.

Distances, areas and scales On each map there are figures in the borders. Those on the right show the area in square miles of each quadrilateral formed by the graticule. Those on the left show the distance in miles along each parallel of latitude (E.-W.) between two successive meridians. These enable areas to be estimated and the scale errors in different parts of the maps to be assessed (see p. 115). Comparisons of areas and distances are further facilitated by the arrangement of scales of most of the maps in a uniform sequence and at simple multiples of each other, i.e. 1:1M, 1:2M, 1:4M, 1:8M, 1:16M. 1:5M and 1:10M are substituted for 1:4M and 1:8M, certain cases, and some other variations in scale have been made, to enable particular regions or countries to be shown in one map.

Relief Actual contour lines have been omitted over most areas since they interfere with the smooth gradation of the layers and with the legibility of the lettering. The junctions of the layer tints in fact constitute contour lines. Faint blue contour lines have been inserted however between the two lowest land layers (green tints), and between bathymetric layers to enhance distinction.

For obvious reasons it is not desirable to adopt entirely uniform layer intervals (e.g. one particular tint representing the same range of altitude throughout the atlas). For each sequence of maps the layer intervals have been selected so as to show up the major physical features of the country or continent to the best advantage. In no case, however, does the light green tint extend above the 1,000 feet (305 metres) level.

Metrication Values of altitude layers are shown throughout in feet and metric equivalents whereas spotheights are in metres only. Scale-bars are, in most cases, graduated in miles and kilometres.

Place-names Country names have been given in their English forms, e.g. Germany, not Deutschland. Province and regional names are given, where they are well known, in their English form.
In general the policy with regards to foreign town names has been guided by practical considerations; versions have been employed which will be most familiar to readers of English language newspapers, periodicals, etc. This undoubtedly leads to inconsistencies. For example, in any one country the names of prominent towns will be in anglicized forms (e.g. Tripoli rather than Tarabulus) whereas the names of smaller places will be in locally accepted forms, but this is thought preferable to a thorough-going vernacularization of place-names. Where names have been officially changed however, e.g. in Central Africa or Tibet, the new names have of course been used. In Europe, and occasionally elsewhere, the vernacular forms of prominent place-names have been given in brackets, e.g. Vienna (Wien). Florence (Firenze). In Belgium where most towns have both Flemish and Walloon names only one of the official names has been given on the map.

For countries using non-Roman scripts, with the exception of China, transliterations have been based mainly on the practices of the British Permanent Committee on Geographical Names and the U.S. Board of Geographic Names. In China the familiar forms of the Chinese Post Office system have been used for larger towns whilst new names have been romanized according to the Wade-Giles system.

Geographical terms such as Lake, Island, Cape, Mountain, etc. except when they form part of the proper name, have generally been given in English instead of in the local terms; in certain cases, however, it is undesirable or impossible to translate the local term, e.g. Etang de Berre, Sierra Nevada, Cordillera Occidental, Rio Grande. All names, other than town or village names, are given topographic explanation in the Gazetteer, e.g. Garonne; riv., France.

The grading of town names and of town sites is based on the population and relative importance of the town (as obtained from the most recent census reports). A grading worked out solely on the basis of comparative population would have certain disadvantages. For example, in the map of the Middle East (pages 56-7) towns of comparatively small population in Turkey have a significance as great as many places of far larger population in the Nile delta. Thus a regional and not a worldwide basis for classification has been adopted, and extra emphasis is usually given where the town is an administrative capital or has some other special importance.

Users may find it of value to consult the map of World Population: Distribution and Growth (page 103) on which all towns of more than 100,000 inhabitants have been plotted by a series of graded circles.

Boundaries Since it is believed that the responsibility of the cartographer is to record geographical facts rather than opinions, the atlas aims to present only de facto situations and to take no side in arguments as to the political status of areas or boundaries. The latter may be said to indicate on the map change of authority on the ground. Major disputed boundaries have been separately shown, also cease-fire lines in the Middle and Far East. Internal boundaries are shown where information exists and scales permit.

Communications Railways are shown by black lines; gauges are distinguished where relevant. In Europe (except U.K.), North America, and other developed areas a system of main lines only has been shown.

Roads are shown in red. Again, in developed areas it has been possible to show only a selection of main roads. Elsewhere selection and classification have been based on the basis of regional importance rather than the physical characteristics of roads. Limited access roads ("motorways") are separately shown; main pack routes are shown where they form the only means of communication.

Gazetteer This has been compiled by listing all names on the maps. (References are to the 'squares' formed by the lines of latitude and longitude.) Please see page 116 for further details.

Thematic maps - sources

Oxford Economic Atlas of the World. 4th. Edition, Oxford University Press, London, 1972.
Oxford World Atlas, Oxford University Press, London, 1973.
The Atlas of Britain and Northern Ireland, Clarendon Press, 1963.
Census 1961, 1971 Great Britain and Northern Ireland (County Reports). H.M.S.O.
O.S. Administrative Areas maps, 1973, 1974.
Tectonic Map of Great Britain and Northern Ireland, The Institute of Geological Sciences, 1966.
O.S. 1:250,000 Fifth Series.
The Countryside Commission, Cambridge Gate, Regent's Park, London.
Climatic maps and graphs of U.K. are based on Crown copyright Meteorological Office maps and statistics used with the permission of the Controller of Her Majesty's Stationery Office.
The advice of Professor K. M. Clayton, University of East Anglia, in connection with the map of Superficial Deposits is gratefully acknowledged; the inset to the main map is adapted from a map in B. W. Sparks & R. G. West, The Ice Age in Britain, Methuen, London, 1972, by permission of the authors.

Ocean maps (pages 7-9)

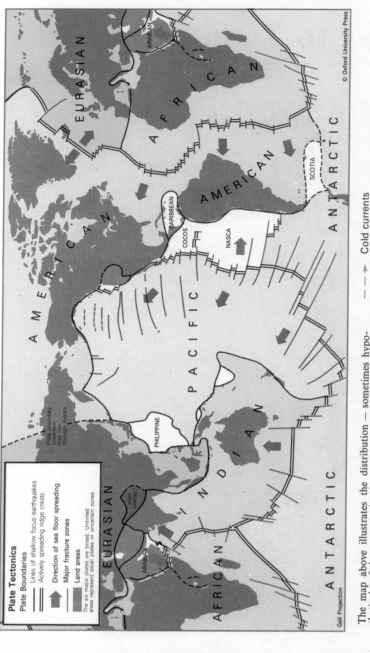

Plate Tectonics
Plate Boundaries
Lines of shallow focus earthquakes
Actively spreading ridge crests
Direction of sea floor spreading
Major fracture zones
Land areas
The six major plates are tinted. Untinted areas represent small plates or uncertain zones.

Gall Projection   © Oxford University Press.

The map above illustrates the distribution — sometimes hypothetical — of the geotectonic plates with which are associated the mid-ocean ridges, compression belts, and unstable areas shown on the ocean maps.

On these maps, and also on those at 1:25 million, a new series of altitude layer colours has been devised in which the value (strength) of the colours increases uniformly with height as the hues pass from yellow through buff to red. A three-dimensional effect is produced by a light blue hillshading pattern.

The chief fishing areas of the world are indicated by naming the main types of fish caught in each area, as measured by catch. The circulation of ocean currents is shown in a generalized way.

Explanation of symbols used on Ocean maps

Geotectonics

Rifted zones on land and 'mid-ocean ridges' in the sea along the axis of which the predominant movement of the lithosphere is outwards

Compression belts: land and ocean areas along the axis of which the predominant movement of the lithosphere is inwards

Faults: important scarp-forming faults and rift valley sides

Unstable areas

Andesite line distinguishing the primarily andesitic circum-Pacific volcanoes from the primarily basaltic oceanic volcanoes, also coinciding over large distances with the boundary of the Pacific geotectonic plate

★ Volcanoes active in historic time

Ocean currents

Size of arrow indicates importance or strength of current

Seasonality is indicated by the name of the month in which the current is strongest

Warm currents

Cold currents

Convergences: zones along which currents converge and descend

Divergences: zones along which currents upwell and diverge
The seasonal migration of convergences and divergences is shown by drawing two lines, representing their extreme positions in the months indicated

Other information

Sea Ice
Perennially unnavigable

Seasonally or perennially navigable. The extent of sea ice may vary widely from year to year

Relief

Icecaps

Seasonal rivers

International boundaries

Very small isolated islands

Cities with over 1 million inhabitants

Selected other cities

Heights and depths in metres

Sources

National Institute of Oceanography, Wormley, Surrey
The Oxford Atlas, Oxford University Press, London, 1970
Fiziko-Geografičeskij Atlas Mira, Academy of Sciences USSR, Moskva, 1964
Jørgsen Frimodt, Scandinavian Fishing Year Book, København, 1967

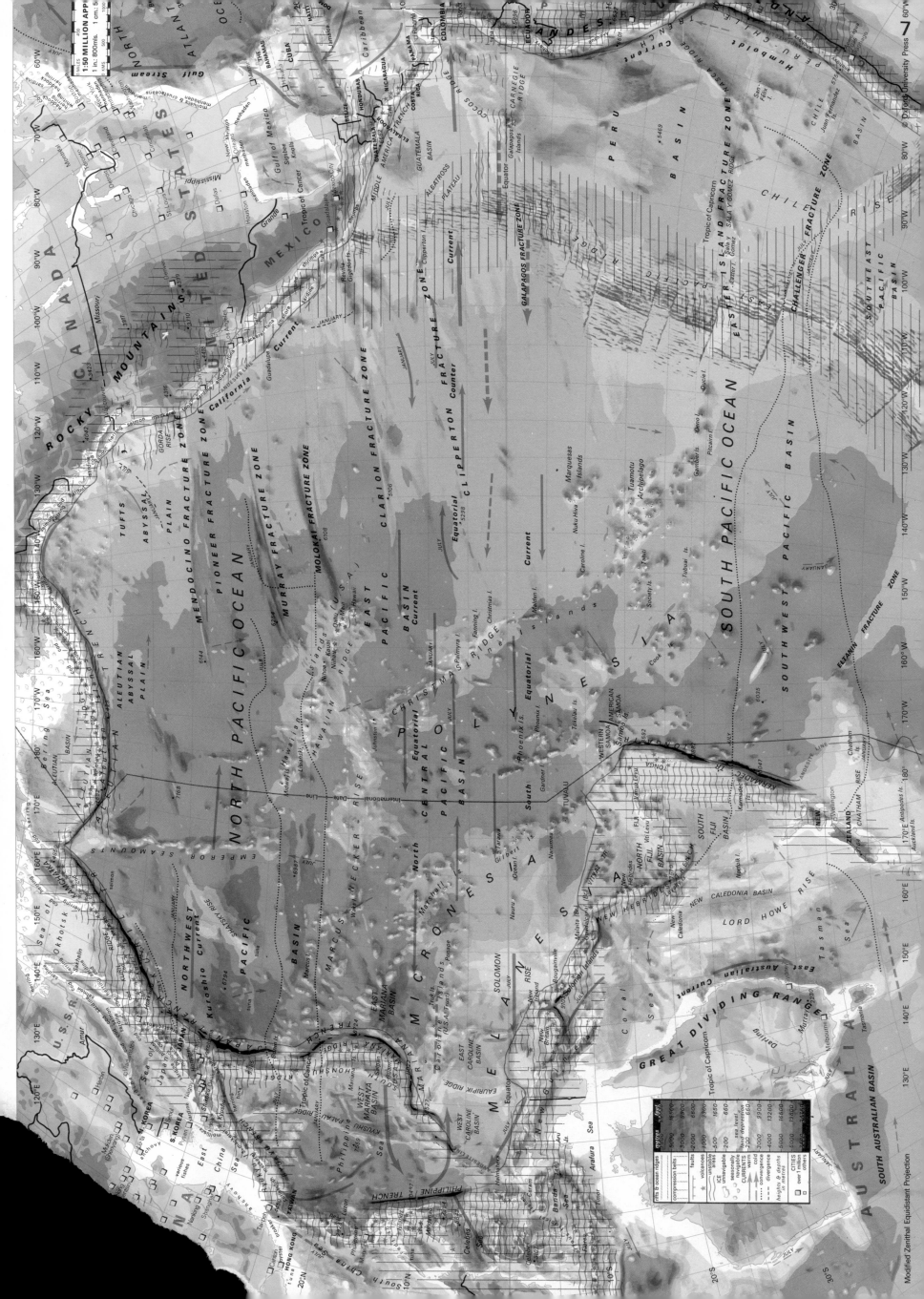

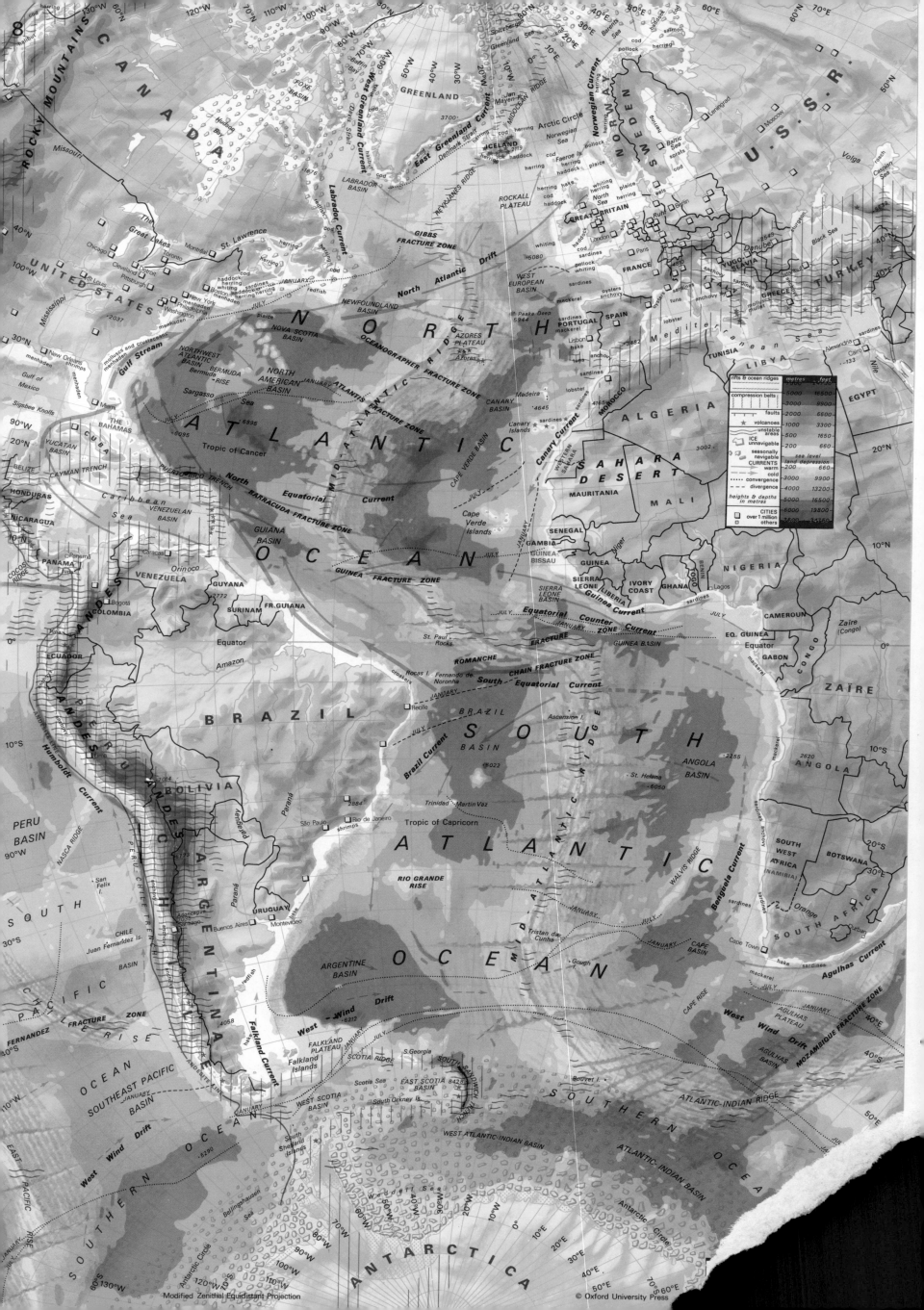

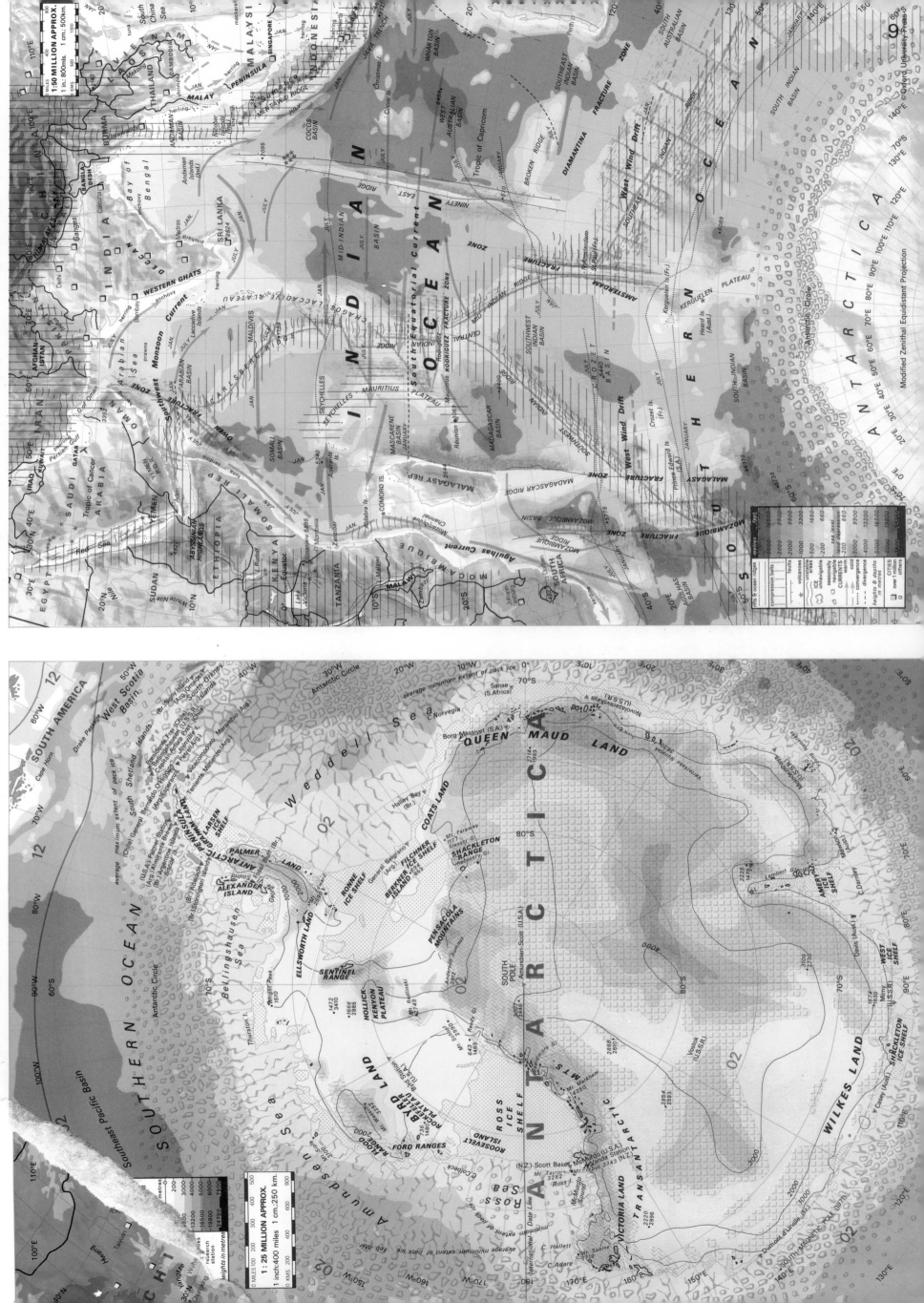

Physical Environment maps at approximately 1 : 25 million (pages 9-16)

Index to Physical Environment Maps

at a scale of
1:25 million approx.
(1 inch: 400 miles)

Numbers refer to pages in the atlas

THE SCALE OF THIS INDEX MAP IS 1:228 MILLION APPROX

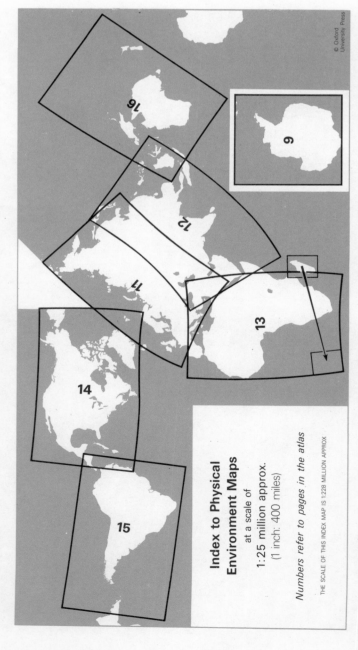

© Oxford University Press

The relationships of climate to relief and of relief to geology are rarely shown in map form. This series of maps which covers the whole land surface of the world employs the same altitude layer colouring as on the 1:50 million maps but combines in it with a simplification of geological information and a new climatic classification. Those elements of geology and structure most relevant to relief forms have been selected and a simple five-category rock-type classification based on this relationship has been devised. The depiction of all active volcanoes and important scarp-forming faults links these maps with the ocean maps.

The relationships of climate to relief and of relief to geology are rarely shown in map form. This series of maps which covers the whole land surface of the world employs the same altitude layer colouring as on the 1:50 million maps but combines in it with a simplification of geological information and a new climatic classification. Those elements of geology and structure most relevant to relief forms have been selected and a simple five-category rock-type classification based on this relationship has been devised. The depiction of all active volcanoes and important scarp-forming faults links these maps with the ocean maps.

As an alternative to temperature/rainfall as a basis for a world climatic classification as proposed by C. Troll (1958, 1964). The present classification by the late Professor D. L. Linton was devised as a modification of Troll's work with boundaries derived from actual isotherms and isohyets. The classification comprises two orders. The primary order forming the basis of the classification describes climate in terms of thermal conditions in the warmest month and the coldest month. Recognizing, with Köppen, that in middle and low latitudes lack of rain overrides considerations of temperature, a provision for arid and extremely arid climates is made. The secondary order of the classification recognizes that (a) in the middle latitudes, the seasonal range of temperature is significant, (b) in the tropics, the duration of wet and dry seasons is significant, and (c) certain areas of middle and low latitudes receive rainfall predominantly in winter (shown only on the world map). The extension of these categories over the oceans is one of the important features of this system of classification.

On the world map, the eleven main climatic types are given distinctive colours and two-digit numbers, and the secondary orders are shown by numbers and letters. On the maps at 1:25 million, the same data are shown in red outline form, with the areas identified by the key numbers and letters alone.

The map of the Antarctic on page 9 conforms to the 1:25 million series only in the depiction of climate, build (but in buff instead of grey), sea layers, sea ice and volcanoes. Special symbols and colours have been created to show the physical characteristics which are virtually confined to this continent. The altitude layers for the rock surface below the ice are shown in a grey/buff sequence while the continental ice surface itself is shown by means of fine black contour lines. The appearance is therefore of a transparent icecap through which may be seen the rock surface with its build character-istics below. Should the icecap be removed and no isostatic move-ment take place, the sea would flow into the areas coloured yellow, but not into the land-locked depressions coloured light green.

Explanation of symbols used on the Physical Environment maps

Seasonal Climate (See description of the classification above)

— Boundaries between regions

First two digits: Characteristics of warmest and coldest seasons

02 No summer (below 6°C), cold winter (below 2°C)

12 Very cool summer (6°-10°C), cold winter (below 2°C)

11 Very cool summer (6°-10°C), mild winter (2°-13°C)

22 Cool summer (10°-20°C), cold winter (below 2°C)

21 Cool summer (10°-20°C), mild winter (2°-13°C)

20 Cool summer (10°-20°C), no winter (over 13°C)

32 Full summer (over 20°C), cold winter (below 2°C)

31 Full summer (over 20°C), mild winter (2°-13°C)

30 Full summer (over 20°C), no winter (over 13°C)

X Arid (no more than 2.5 mm monthly for at least 10 months)

Z Extremely arid (no month receives as much as 50 mm. rainfall)

Third digit: Seasonal temperature range

For areas 21, 22 and 32 outside the tropics

1 Oceanic: seasonal range less than 12C°

2 Sub-continental: seasonal range 12-24C°

3 Continental: seasonal range 24-36C°

4 Very continental: seasonal range 36-48C°

5 Extremely continental: seasonal range more than 48C°

Small letters: Duration of wet and dry seasons

For areas 30 and 31 only

a All months rainy (more than 50mm rainfall)

b Rainy season predominant: 8-11 months with over 50 mm

c Rainy and dry seasons approximately equal: 5-7 months with over 50mm

d Dry season predominant: 1-4 months with over 50 mm

Other information

Sea ice

Perennially unnavigable

Seasonally or perennially navigable. The extent of sea ice may vary widely from year to year

Icecaps

Seasonal rivers

Lakes

Seasonal lakes

Salt pans (dry salt lakes)

Canals

Reefs

Marshes or bogs

Coniferous forests

Mixed forests

Deciduous forests

Tropical forests

Relief

metres   feet
sea level
—200   —660
—3000   —9900
—4000   —13200
—5200   —16500
—6000   —19800
—9000 & below —29400

sea level
—200   —660
—3000   —9900
—4000   —13200
5000   16500
6000   19800
9000 & below 29400

200   660
500   1650
1000   3300
2000   6600
3000   9900

Heights and depths in metres

Cities with over 1 million inhabitants

Cities with 100,000 to 1 million inhabitants

Selected other cities

International boundaries

Selected regional boundaries

Railways

The farthest limit of the Quaternary glaciation of the main polar icecap in the northern hemisphere is shown. Isolated glaciated areas are not shown.

Build (see map below)

Quaternary: later Tertiary and Quaternary sediments

Sedimentary cover: sedimentary cover rocks, flat-bedded or not strongly disturbed

Folded belts: strongly disturbed sedimentaries, meta-morphic zones of younger fold mountains and strongly re-elevated blocks of complex structure

Ancient platforms: areas of basement complex or peneplained fold mountains not strongly uplifted

Volcanic: plains or plateaux of relatively undisturbed Tertiary and Quaternary volcanics

Volcanoes active in historic time

Important scarp-forming faults and rift-valley sides

Sources

The Oxford Atlas, Oxford University Press, London, 1970
International Association of Volcanology, Catalogue of the active volcanoes of the world, Edinburgh, 1947
Climate: Professor D. L. Linton, University of Birmingham, UK
Fiziko-Geografičeskij Atlas Mira, Academy of Sciences, USSR, Moskva, 1964
The Antarctic: USGS Sketch Map Series, 1:500,000; Atlas Antarktiki, Volume I, MAGC, Moskva, 1966

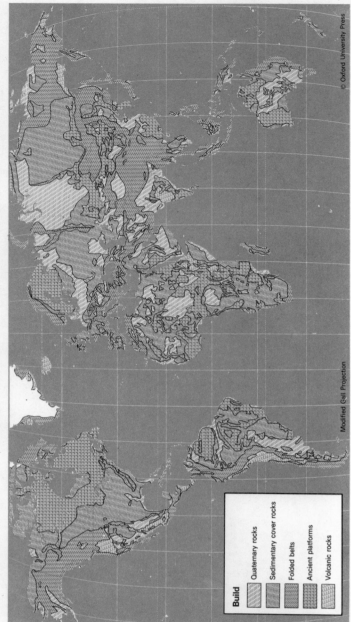

© Oxford University Press

Modified Gall Projection

Build

Quaternary rocks

Sedimentary cover rocks

Folded belts

Ancient platforms

Volcanic rocks

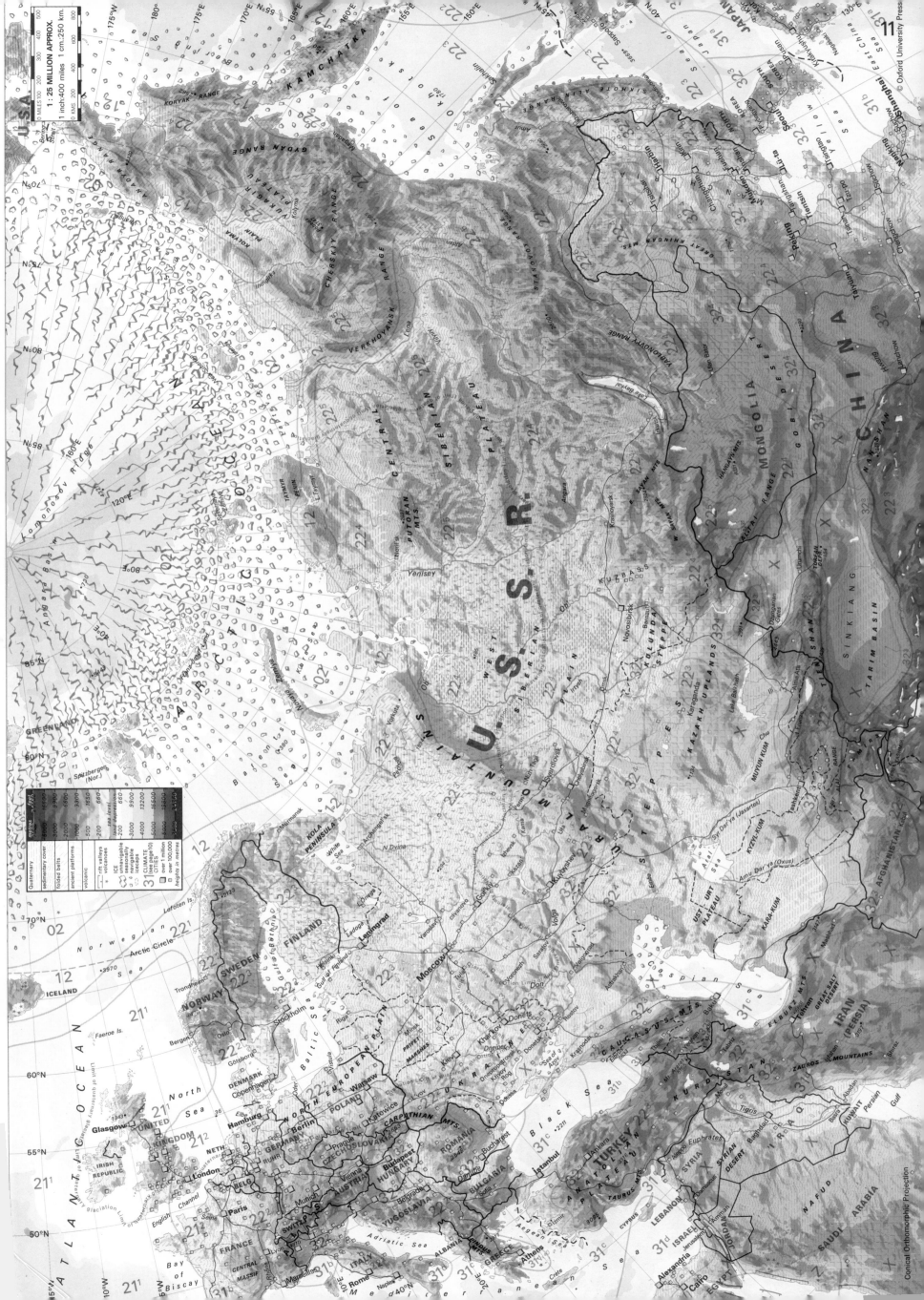

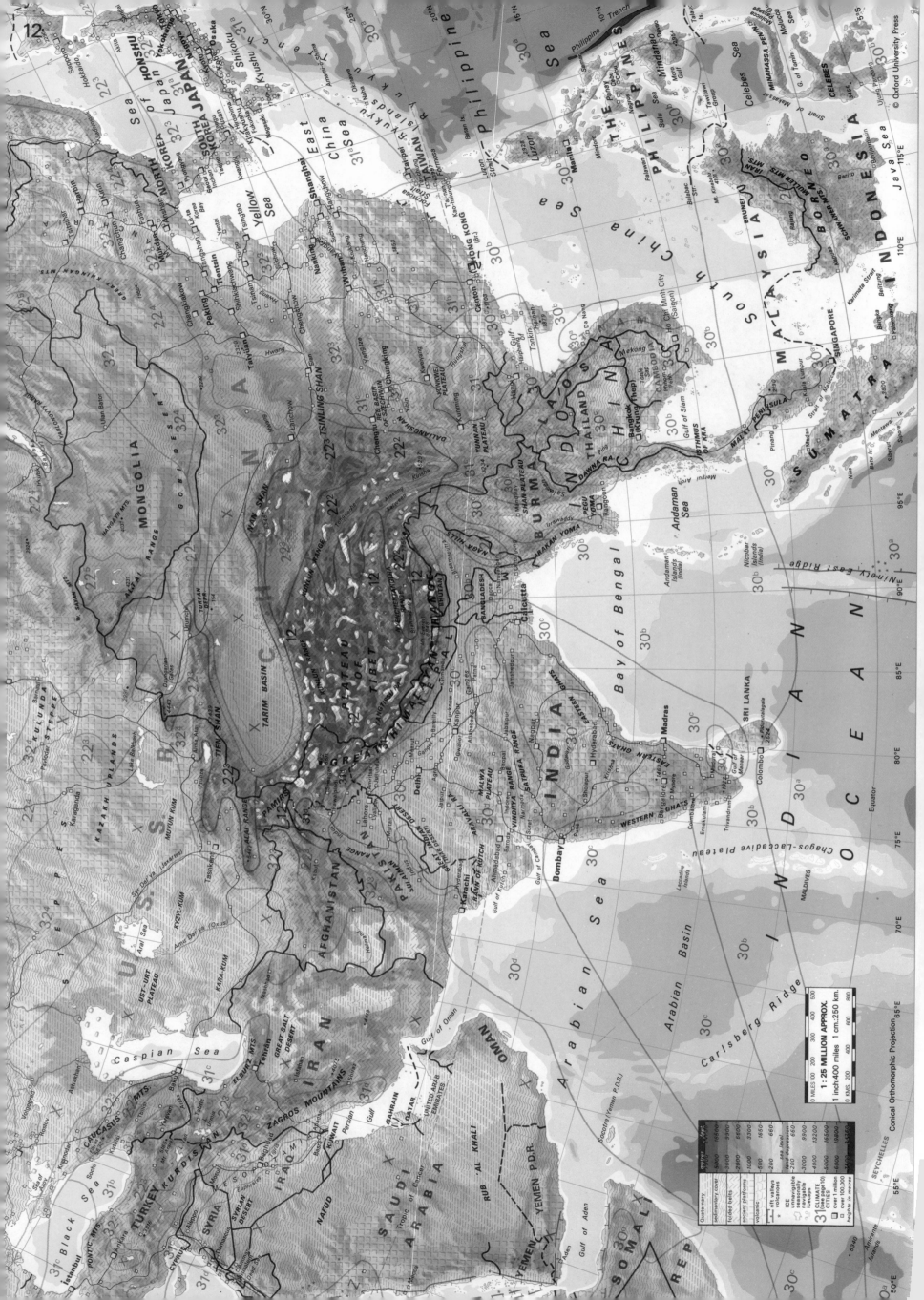

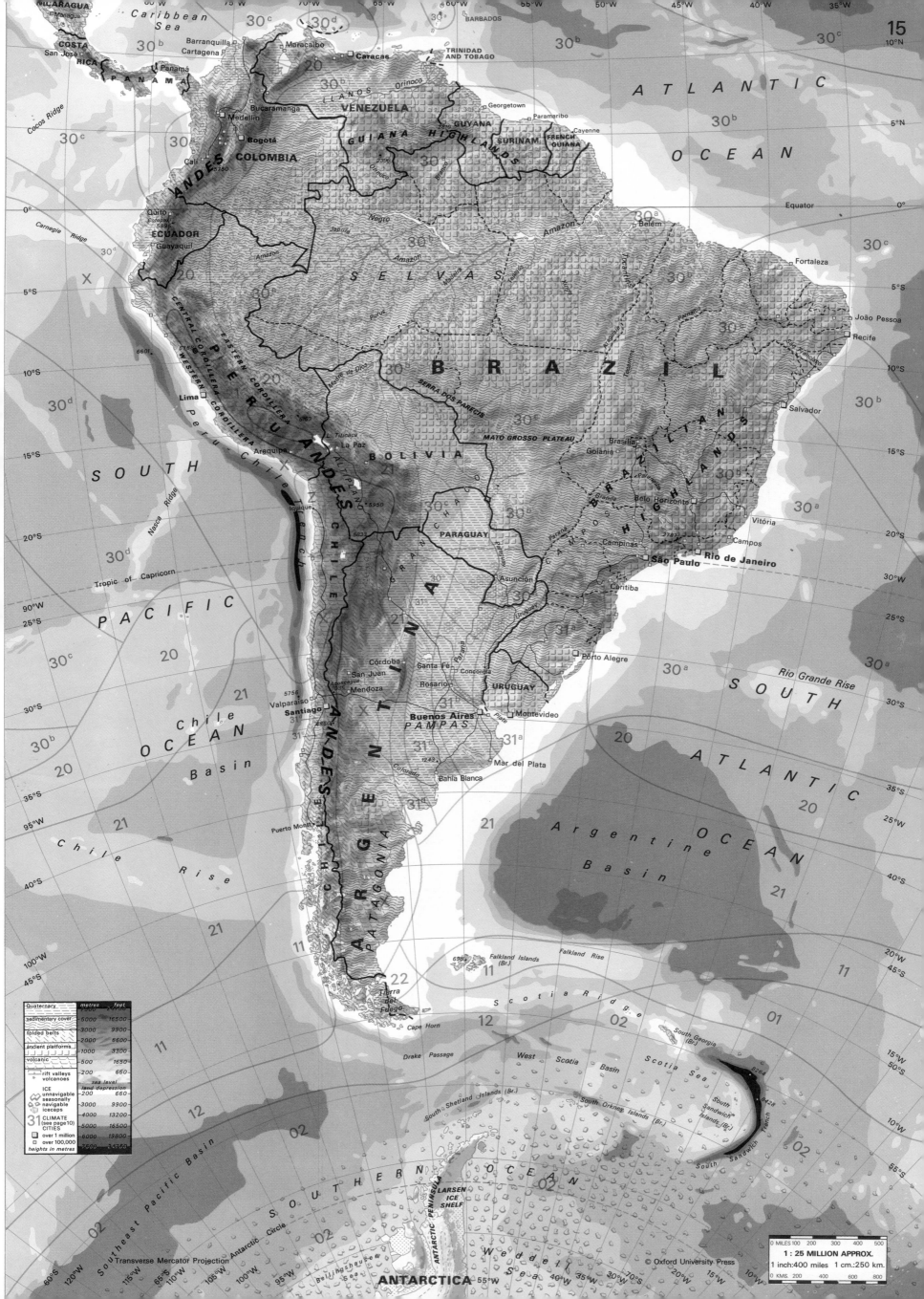

NICARAGUA
Managua
Caribbean Sea
COSTA
San José
RICA
PANAMA
Panamá
Cocos Ridge

Barranquilla
Cartagena
Maracaibo
Caracas
TRINIDAD AND TOBAGO
BARBADOS
LLANOS
Orinoco
VENEZUELA
Georgetown
Paramaribo
GUYANA
SURINAM
FRENCH GUIANA
Cayenne
GUIANA HIGHLANDS

Bucaramanga
Medellín
Bogotá
COLOMBIA
ANDES
Cali

ATLANTIC
OCEAN

Quito
Cotopaxi
ECUADOR
Guayaquil

Negro
Japurá
Amazon
Amazon

Belém

Equator

SELVAS

Fortaleza

BRAZIL

Madre de Dios
Purus
Madeira
Tapajós
Xingu
Tocantins
Araguaia

João Pessoa
Recife

Lima
PERU
ANDES
CENTRAL CORDILLERA
EASTERN CORDILLERA
WESTERN CORDILLERA
Peru-Chile Trench
L. Titicaca
La Paz
Arequipa
Iquique
ALTIPLANO

BOLIVIA
SERRA DOS PARECIS
MATO GROSSO PLATEAU
Brasília
Goiânia

Salvador

BRAZILIAN HIGHLANDS

SOUTH

PACIFIC

Nasca Ridge

OCEAN

Chile Basin

Tropic of Capricorn

PARAGUAY
Asunción
CHACO
Paraná
Paraguay
Pilcomayo

Belo Horizonte
Vitória
Campos
Campinas
São Paulo
Rio de Janeiro
Curitiba
CAMPOS HIGHLANDS

SOUTH

ATLANTIC

Rio Grande Rise

Córdoba
San Juan
Mendoza
Aconcagua
Valparaíso
Santiago
CHILE
ANDES
ARGENTINA
Santa Fé
Rosario
Concordia
URUGUAY
Buenos Aires
PAMPAS
Montevideo
Mar del Plata
Colorado
Bahia Blanca
Uruguay
Plate

OCEAN

Argentine Basin

Chile Rise

Puerto Montt

PATAGONIA

Falkland Islands (Br.)
Falkland Rise

Tierra del Fuego
Cape Horn
Scotia Ridge
Drake Passage
West Scotia Basin
South Georgia (Br.)
South Sandwich Islands (Br.)
South Sandwich Trench
South Shetland Islands (Br.)
South Orkney Islands (Br.)
Scotia Sea

Transverse Mercator Projection
Antarctic Circle
SOUTHERN OCEAN
Bellingshausen Sea
ANTARCTIC PENINSULA
LARSEN ICE SHELF
Weddell Sea
ANTARCTICA

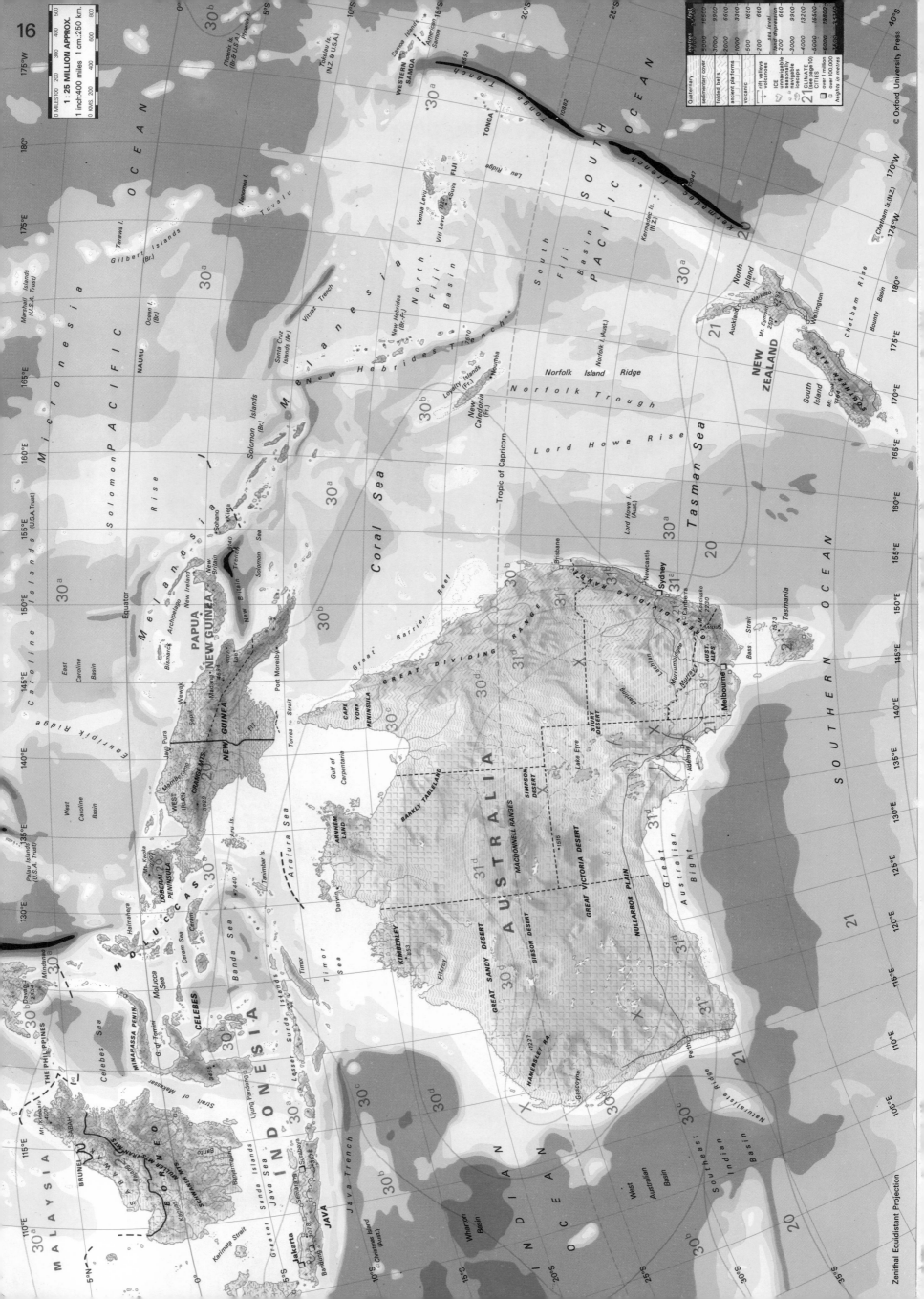

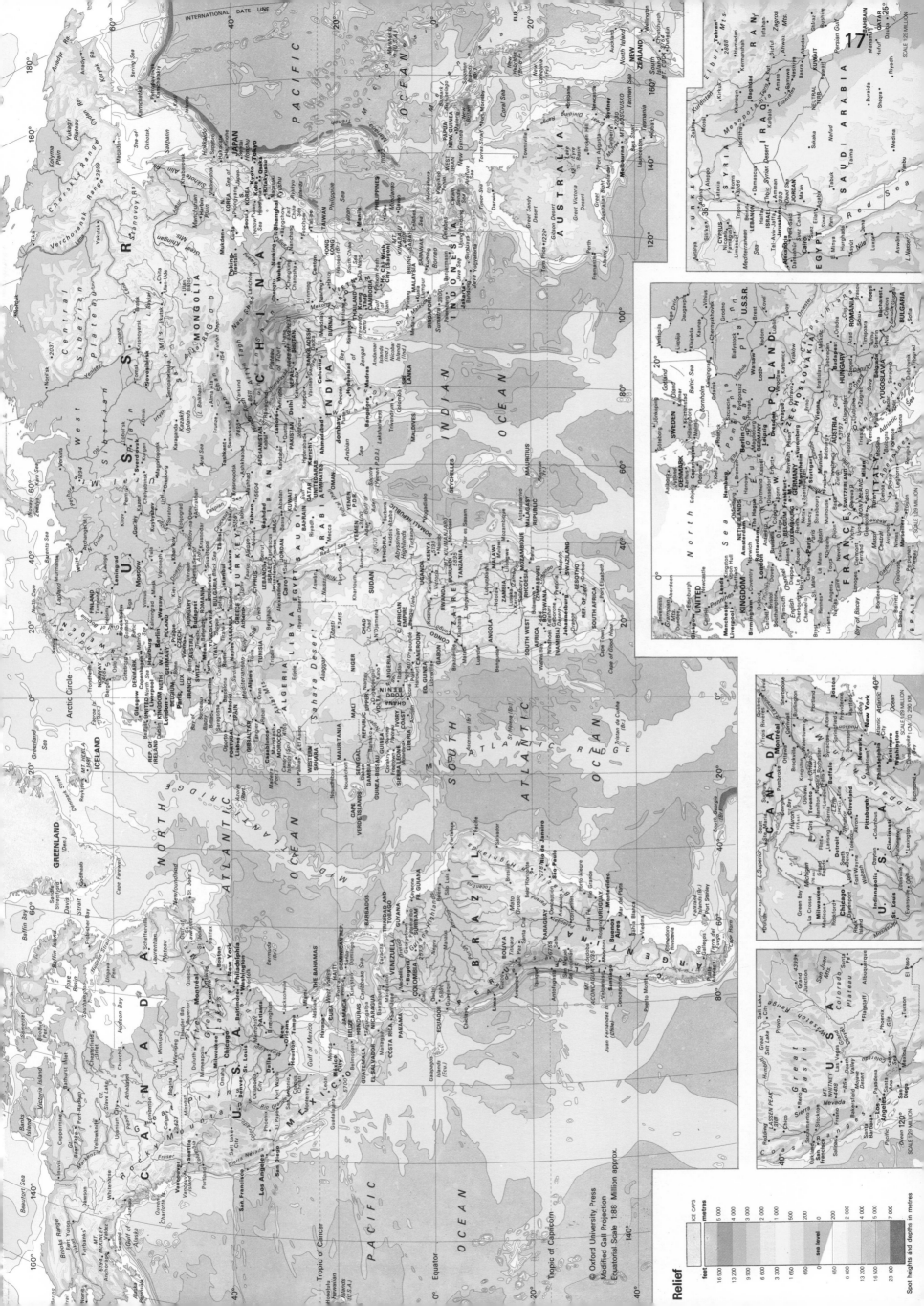

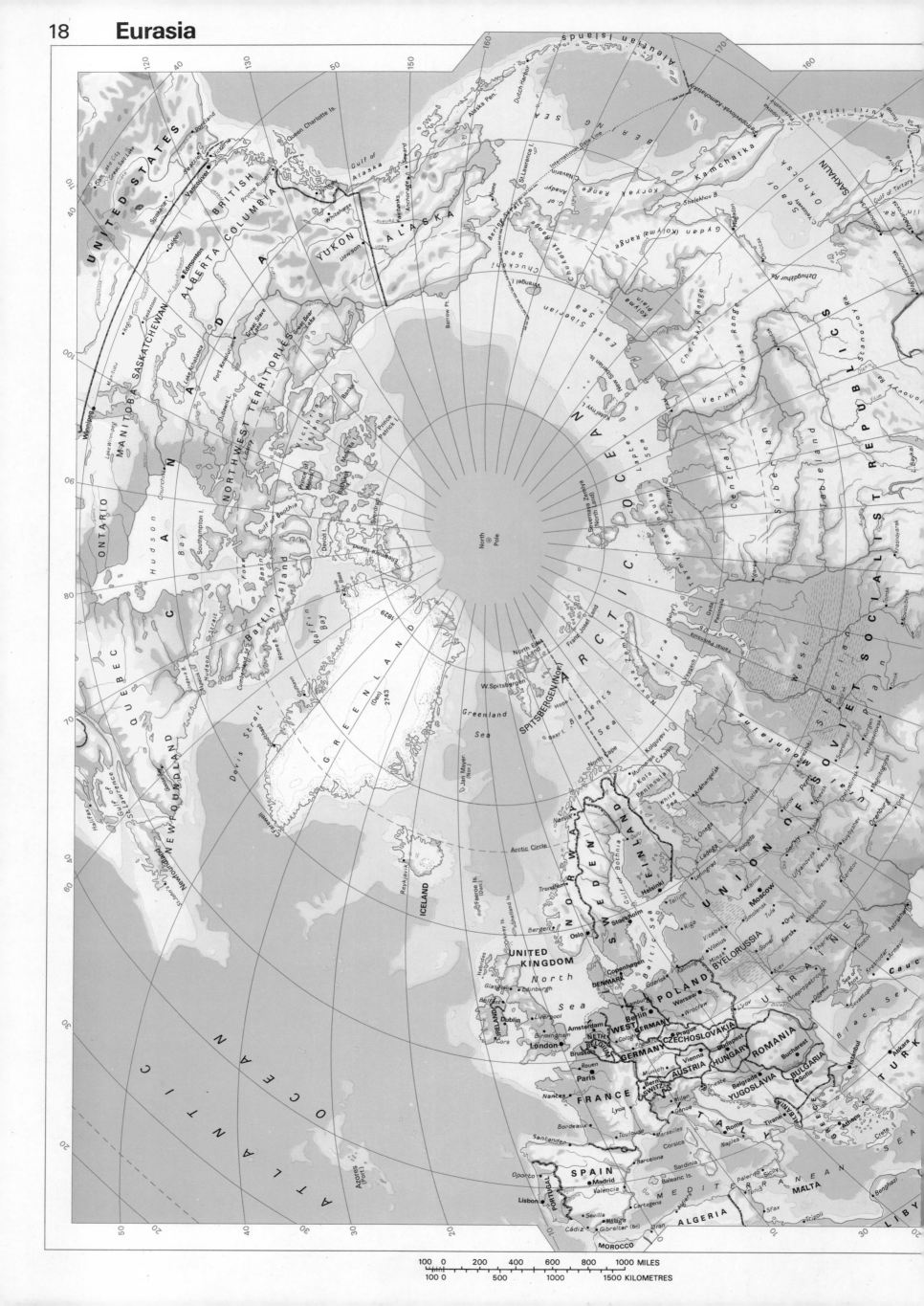

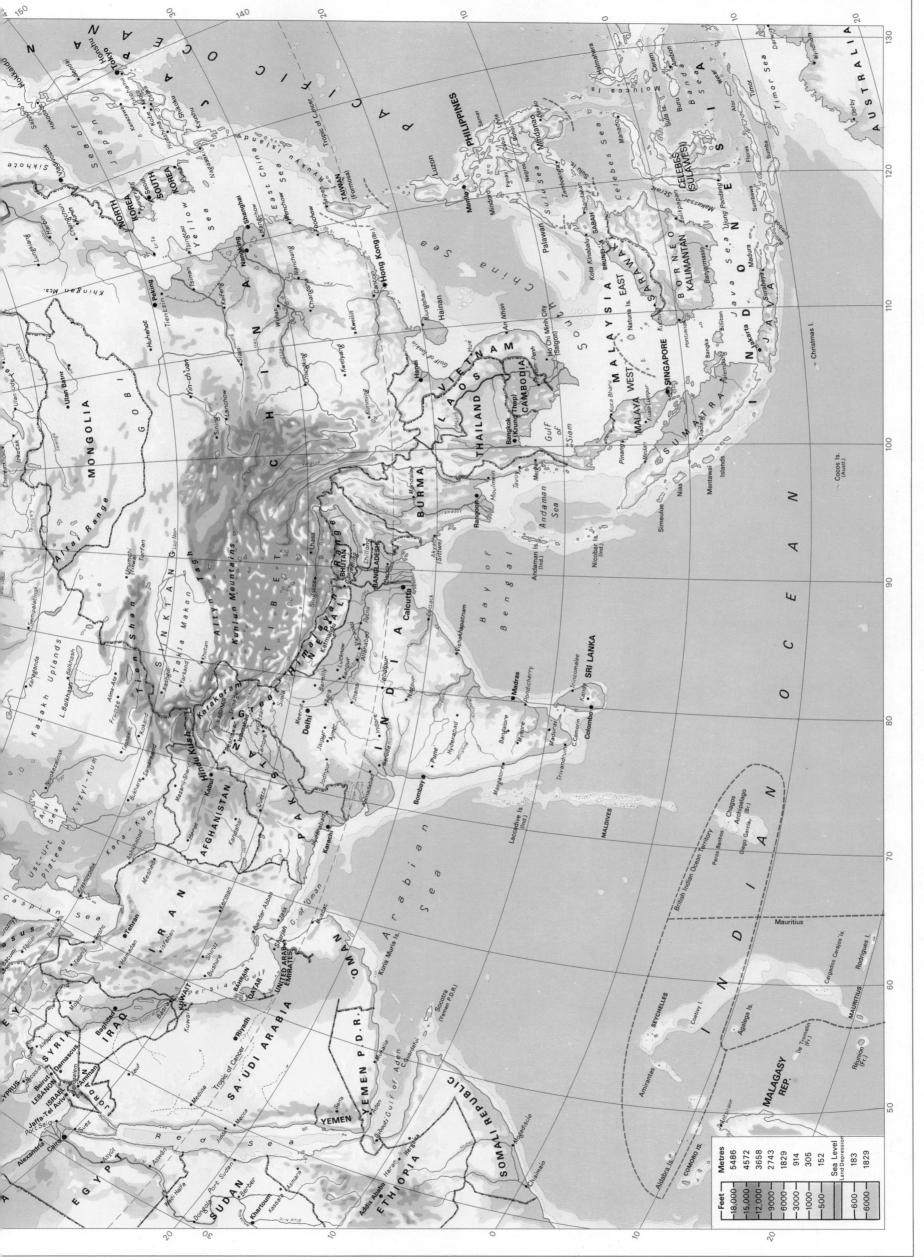

Feet	Metres
18,000	5486
15,000	4572
12,000	3658
9000	2743
6000	1829
3000	914
1000	305
500	152
Sea Level	
Land Depression	
600	183
6000	1829

Zenithal Equal-area Projection.
Origin 40°N, 95°E. For scale errors see p.115.

© Oxford University Press

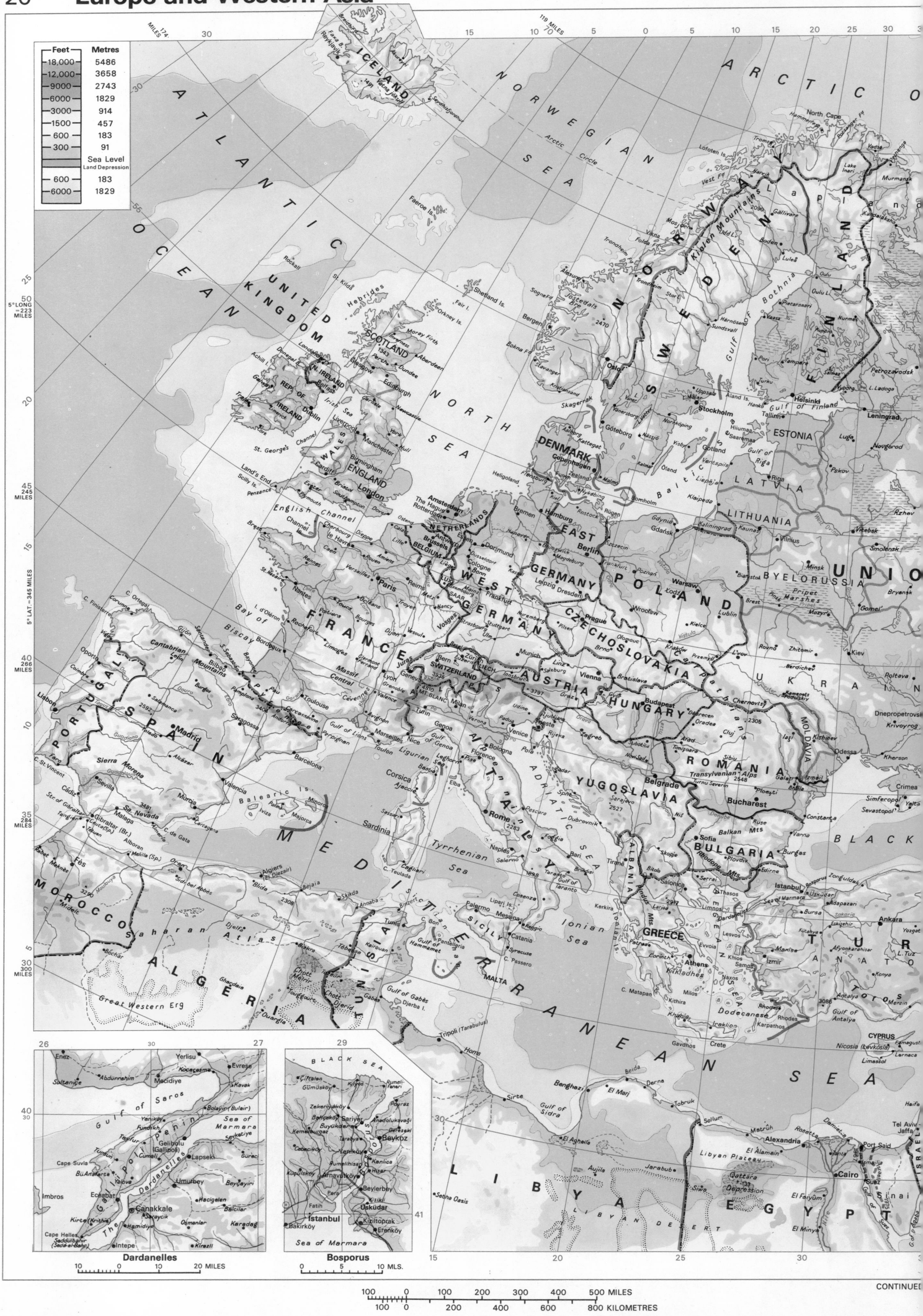

Feet	Metres
18,000	5486
12,000	3658
9000	2743
6000	1829
3000	914
1500	457
600	183
300	91
Sea Level	
Land Depression	
600	183
6000	1829

ARCTIC O

NORWEGIAN SEA

ICELAND

ATLANTIC OCEAN

NORTH SEA

UNITED KINGDOM
SCOTLAND
N. IRELAND
REP. OF IRELAND
WALES
ENGLAND
London

NORWAY
SWEDEN
FINLAND
Lapland
Helsinki
Stockholm
Oslo
Leningrad

DENMARK
Copenhagen

ESTONIA
LATVIA
LITHUANIA
BYELORUSSIA
UNION

NETHERLANDS
Amsterdam
Rotterdam
BELGIUM
Brussels
LUXEMBOURG

EAST GERMANY
Berlin
East Berlin
WEST GERMANY
SAAR

POLAND
Warsaw

CZECHOSLOVAKIA
Prague

FRANCE
Paris

SWITZERLAND
Bern
LIECH.
AUSTRIA
Vienna
HUNGARY
Budapest

ROMANIA
Bucharest

MOLDAVIA
UKRAINE
Kiev

PORTUGAL
Lisbon

SPAIN
Madrid

YUGOSLAVIA
Belgrade

BULGARIA
Sofia

ALBANIA
Tirana

GREECE
Athens

TURKEY
Ankara

MEDITERRANEAN SEA

MOROCCO

ALGERIA
Great Western Erg
Saharan Atlas

TUNISIA

LIBYA
Libyan Desert
Qattara Depression

EGYPT
Cairo

BLACK SEA

Tyrrhenian Sea

Ionian Sea

Adriatic Sea

SICILY
SARDINIA
CORSICA
MALTA
Rome
Naples

CYPRUS
Nicosia

Dardanelles	Bosporus
Gulf of Saros	BLACK SEA
Sea of Marmara	Sea of Marmara
Gallipoli	İstanbul
Çanakkale	Üsküdar

Dardanelles

Bosporus

CONTINUED

100	0	100	200	300	400	500 MILES
100	0	200	400	600	800 KILOMETRES	

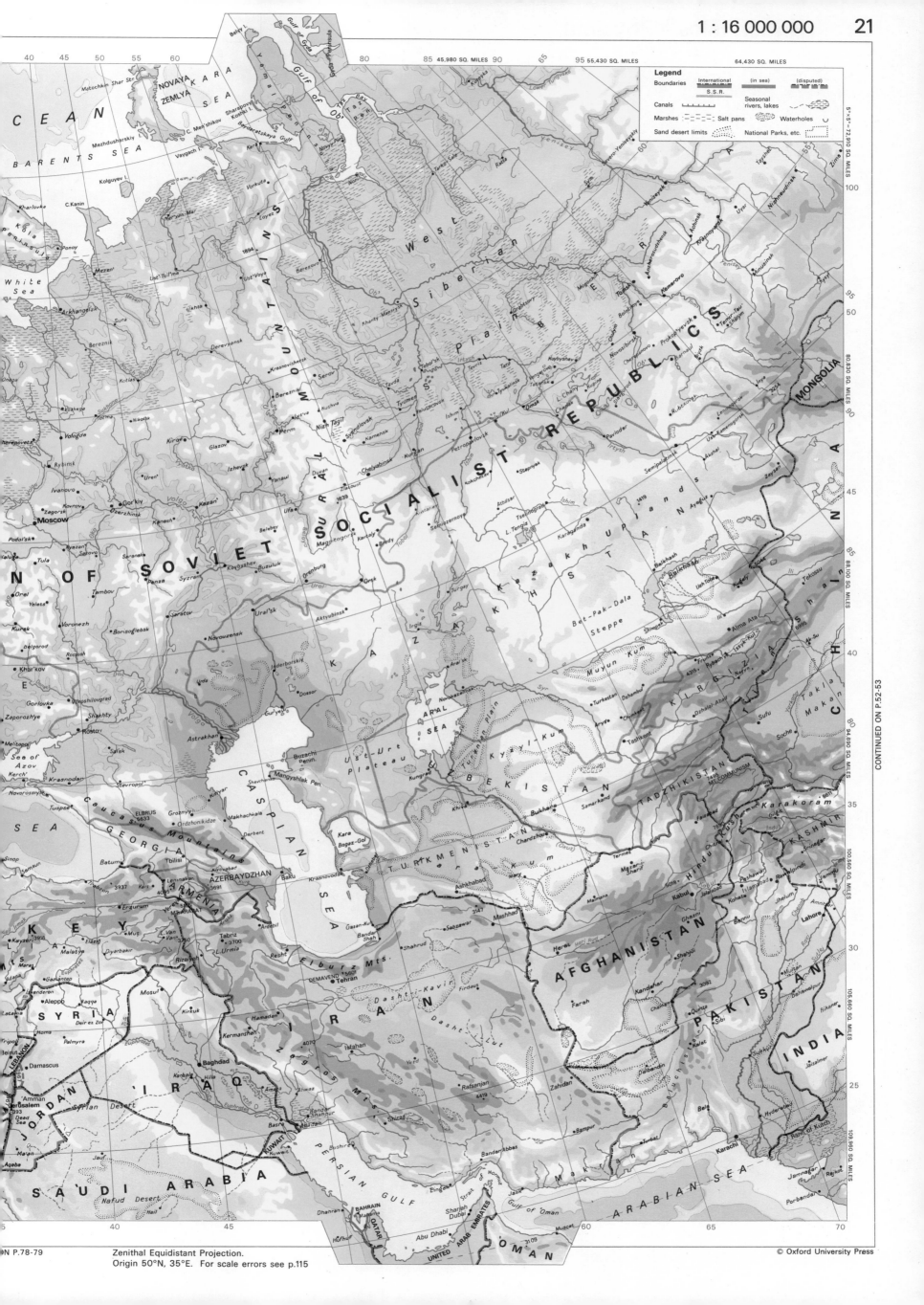

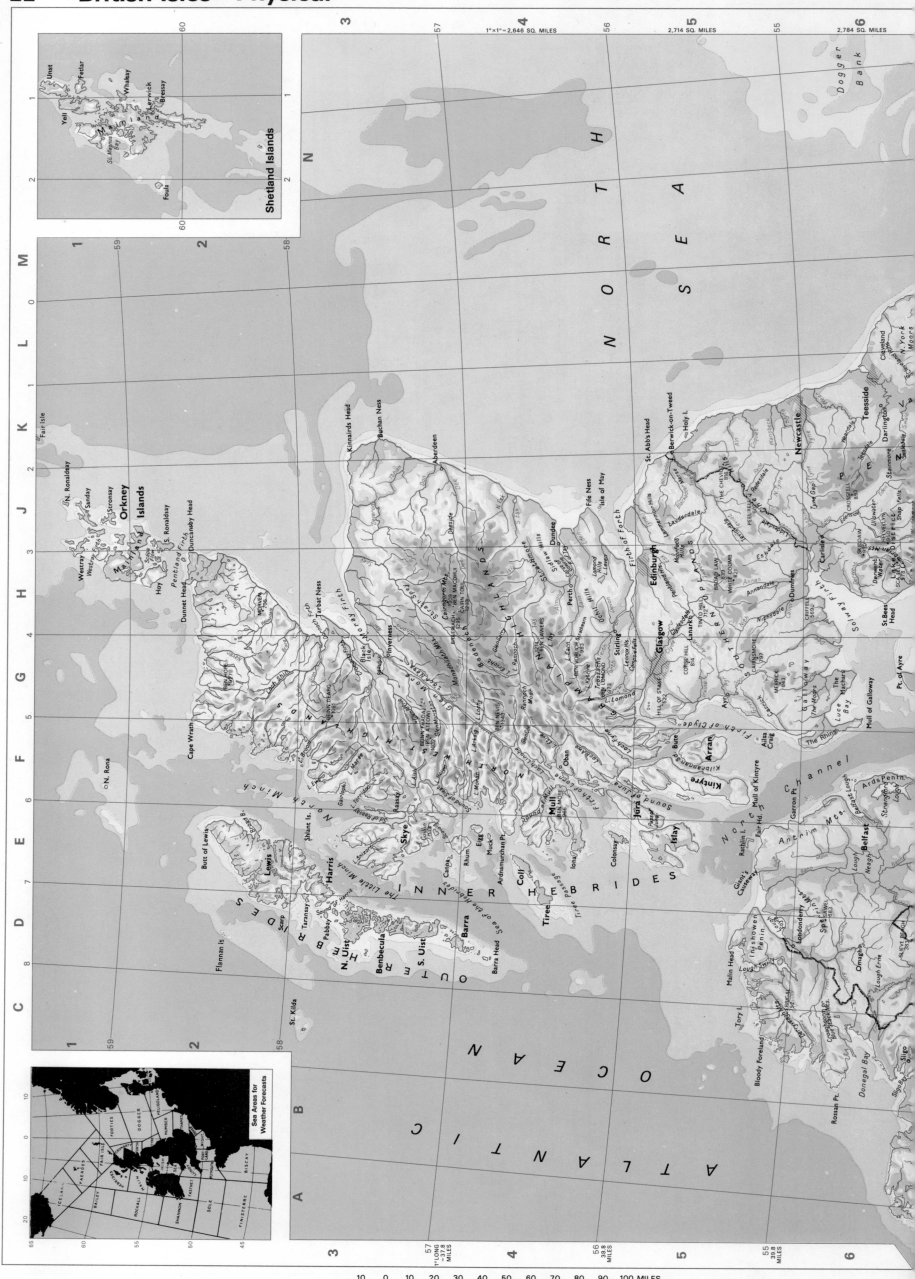

Shetland Islands

Sea Areas for Weather Forecasts

Conical Orthomorphic Projection. Origin 54°N.
Standard parallels 51½° & 56½°. Scale reduction 0.1%.
For scale errors see p.115.

© Oxford University Press

Legend

Chief urban areas

Canals

Feet	Metres
4000	1219
2800	853
2000	610
1200	366
800	244
400	122
200	61
Sea Level	18
60	37
120	91
300	

CARDIGAN BAY

GWYNEDD

National Park

CLWYD

SALOP (SHROPSHIRE)

STAFFORDS

POWYS

HEREFORD AND WORCESTER

GLOUCESTERSHIRE

DYFED

WEST GLAMORGAN

MID GLAMORGAN

SOUTH GLAMORGAN

GWENT

AVON

BRISTOL CHANNEL

SOMERSET

DEVON

DORSET

CORNWALL

Dartmoor National Park

Exmoor National Park

Brecon Beacons National Park

ENGLISH CHANNEL

Lyme Bay

Scale

Feet	Metres
2800	853
2000	610
1200	366
800	244
400	122
200	61
	Sea Level
60	18
120	37
300	91

Legend

Boundaries: International, Internal, (in sea), (disputed)
Roads: Motorways, Other roads, Tracks
Railways: (projected)
Canals
Airports: International, Domestic
Seasonal rivers, lakes
Waterholes
Marshes, Salt pans
Sand desert limits
National Parks, etc.

10 0 10 20 30 MILES
10 0 10 20 30 40 50 KILOMETRES

THE WASH

LINCOLNSHIRE

NORFOLK

Norwich

Great Yarmouth

Lowestoft

725 SQ. MILES   14

734 SQ. MILES   15

742 SQ. MILES   16

750 SQ. MILES   17

758 SQ. MILES   18

Boston

King's Lynn

Peterborough

CAMBRIDGESHIRE

Cambridge

SUFFOLK

Ipswich

Nottingham

W. Bridgford

Derby

Loughborough

Melton Mowbray

LEICESTERSHIRE

Leicester

Birmingham

Coventry

Market Harborough

Corby

Kettering

Northampton

Wellingborough

Rushden

Bedford

Huntingdon

Newmarket

Bury St Edmunds

Colchester

Harwich

Felixstowe

WARWICKSHIRE

Leamington

Warwick

Rugby

Stratford on Avon

Banbury

OXFORDSHIRE

Milton Keynes

Bletchley

Luton

Hitchin

Bishop's Stortford

Braintree

Chelmsford

ESSEX

Clacton on Sea

Oxford

Aylesbury

Berkhamsted

Hemel Hempstead

HERTFORDSHIRE

St Albans

Watford

Harlow

Southminster

Burnham on Crouch

High Wycombe

Amersham

BARNET

ENFIELD

WALTHAM FOREST

HAVERING

Brentwood

Billericay

Southend on Sea

Maidenhead

Slough

HARROW

BRENT

EALING

CAMDEN

HACKNEY

REDBRIDGE

BARKING

Grays

Thurrock

Swindon

Reading

Windsor

HOUNSLOW

RICHMOND

HAMMERSMITH

WANDSWORTH

LONDON

SOUTHWARK

LEWISHAM

GREENWICH

BEXLEY

Dartford

Gravesend

Sheerness

Margate

North Foreland

Broadstairs

Ramsgate

Newbury

KINGSTON

MERTON

SUTTON

CROYDON

BROMLEY

Rochester

Chatham

Gillingham

Sittingbourne

Faversham

Herne Bay

Whitstable

Canterbury

Woking

Farnborough

Aldershot

Guildford

Dorking

Reigate

Sevenoaks

Maidstone

KENT

Ashford

Deal

Dover

SURREY

Crawley

Tunbridge Wells

Tonbridge

Folkestone

Salisbury

Winchester

HAMPSHIRE

Horsham

WEST SUSSEX

EAST SUSSEX

Hastings

Bexhill

Southampton

Eastbourne

Brighton

Hove

Worthing

Bognor Regis

Chichester

Portsmouth

Newport

ISLE OF WIGHT

Bournemouth

The Needles

St Catherine's Point

STRAIT OF DOVER

Newquay

Truro

Camborne

Redruth

Falmouth

Land's End

Penzance

Isles of Scilly

St Mary's

Lizard Point

CHANNEL

Casquets

Alderney

C. de la Hague

GUERNSEY

Herm

Sark

JERSEY

St Helier

Channel Islands

Conical Orthomorphic Projection. Origin 54°N.
Standard parallels 51½° & 56½°. Scale reduction 0.1%.
For scale errors see p.115.

© Oxford University Press

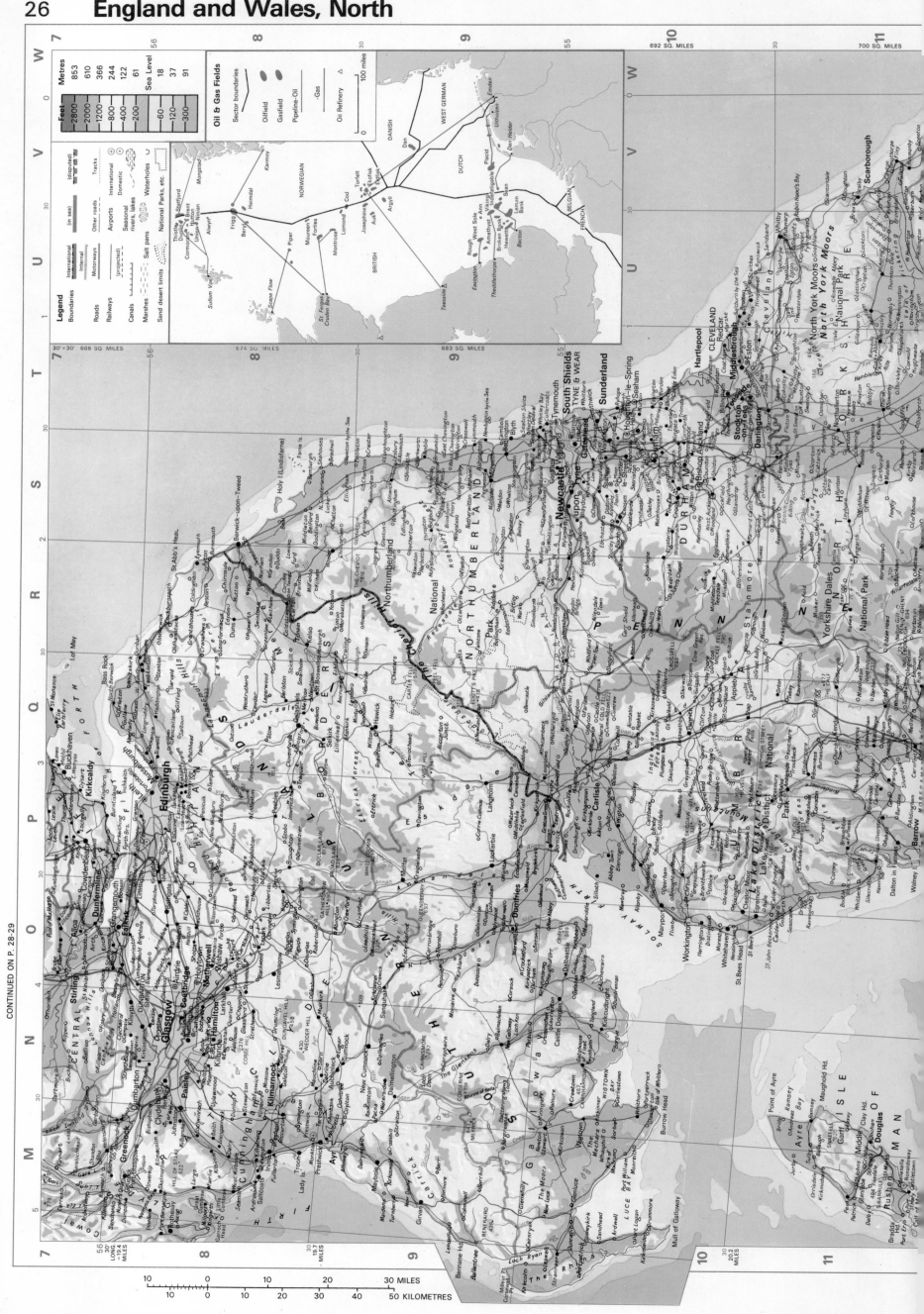

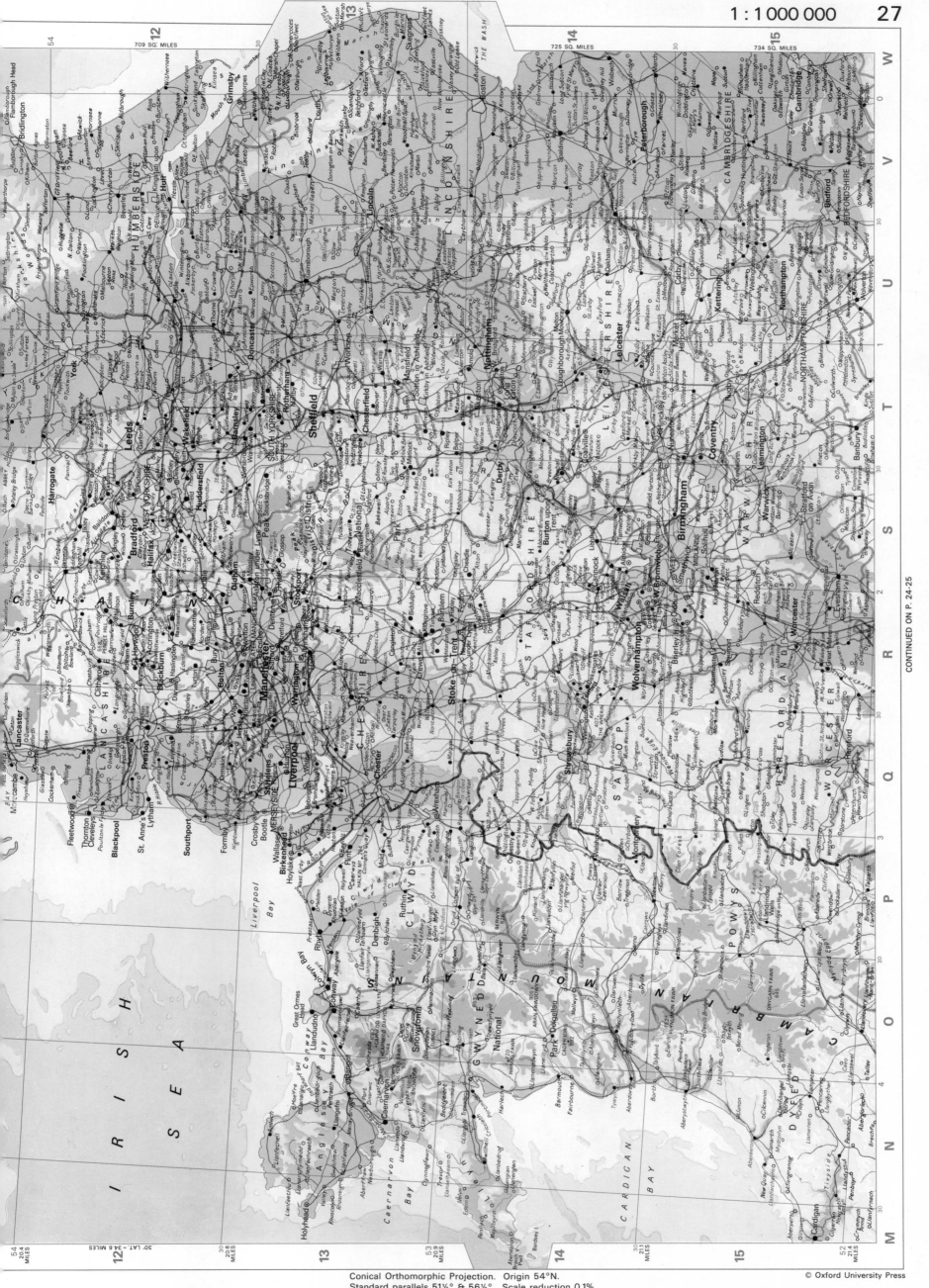

CONTINUED ON P. 24-25

Conical Orthomorphic Projection. Origin 54°N.
Standard parallels 51½° & 56½°. Scale reduction 0.1%.
For scale errors see p.115.

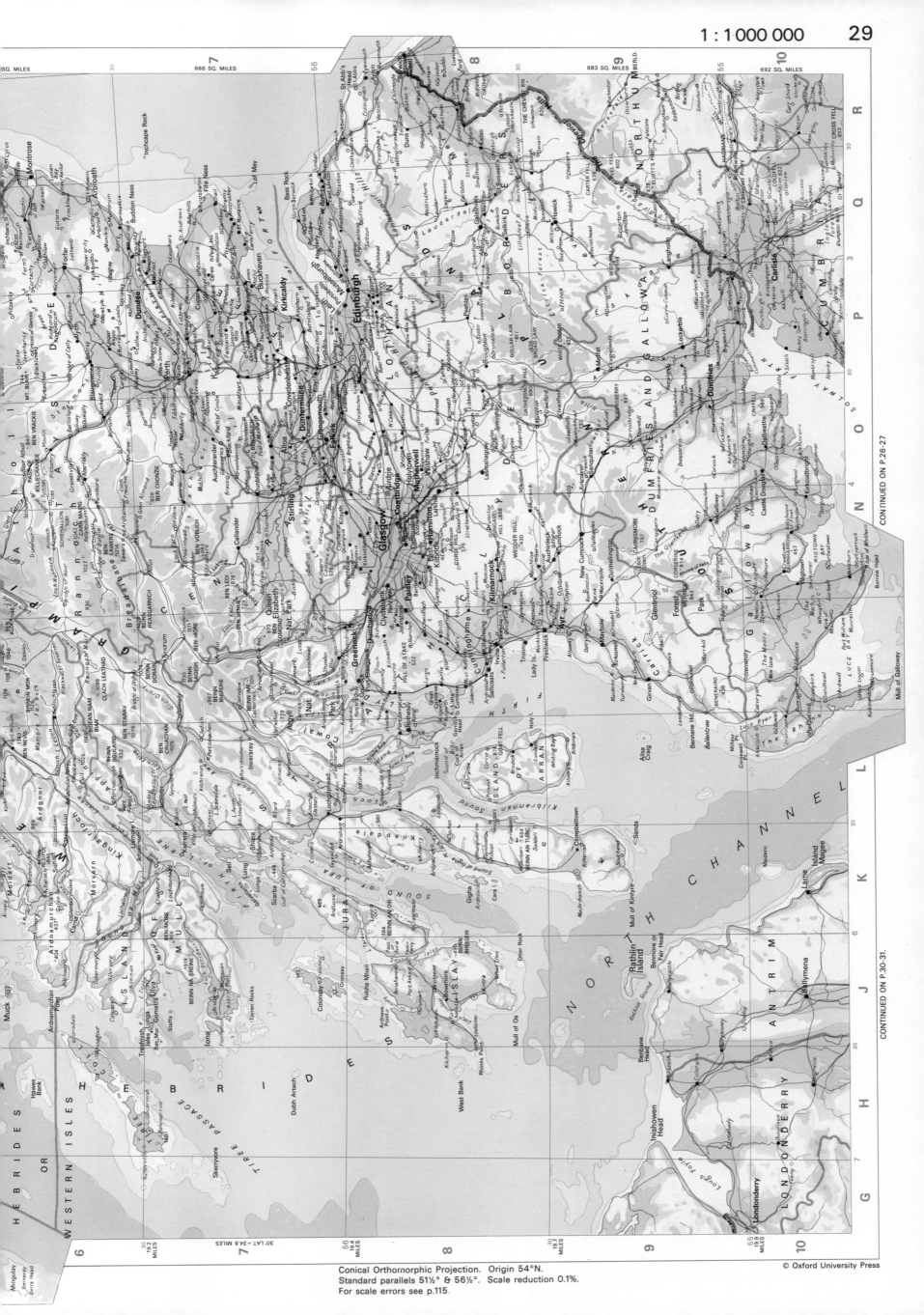

CONTINUED ON P.26-27

CONTINUED ON P.30-31.

Conical Orthomorphic Projection.   Origin 54°N.
Standard parallels 51½° & 56½°.   Scale reduction 0.1%.
For scale errors see p.115.

© Oxford University Press

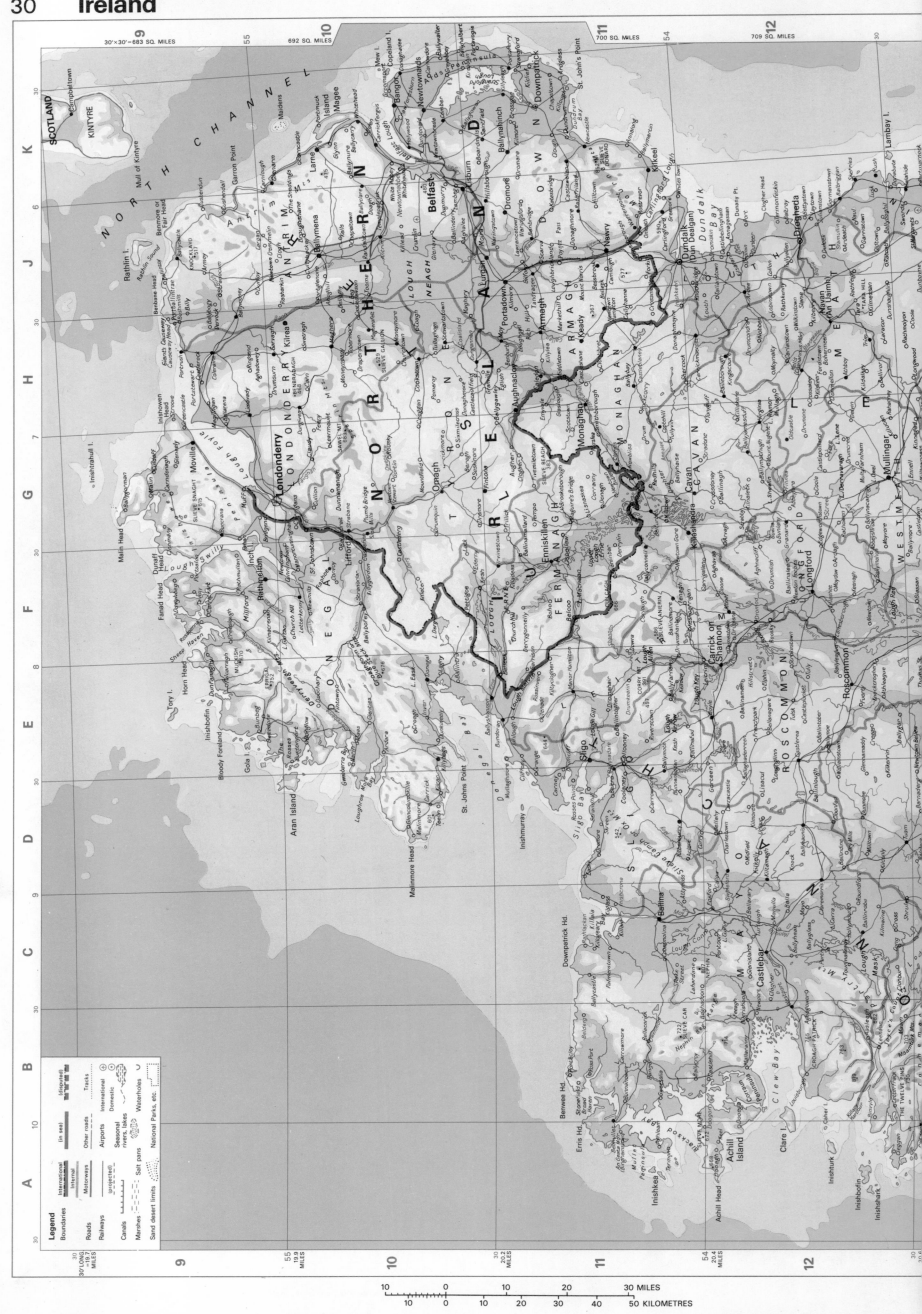

Legend

Boundaries
International
Internal
(disputed)
(in sea)

Roads
Motorways
(projected)
Other roads
Tracks

Railways

Canals

Marshes   Salt pans

Sand desert limits

Airports
International ⊕
Domestic ⊙

Seasonal
rivers, lakes

Waterholes

National Parks, etc.

30' × 30' = 683 SQ. MILES   692 SQ. MILES   700 SQ. MILES   709 SQ. MILES

30' LONG = 19.7 MILES   55 = 19.9 MILES   30 = 20.2 MILES   54 = 20.4 MILES

SCOTLAND

10   0   10   20   30 MILES
10   0   10   20   30   40   50 KILOMETRES

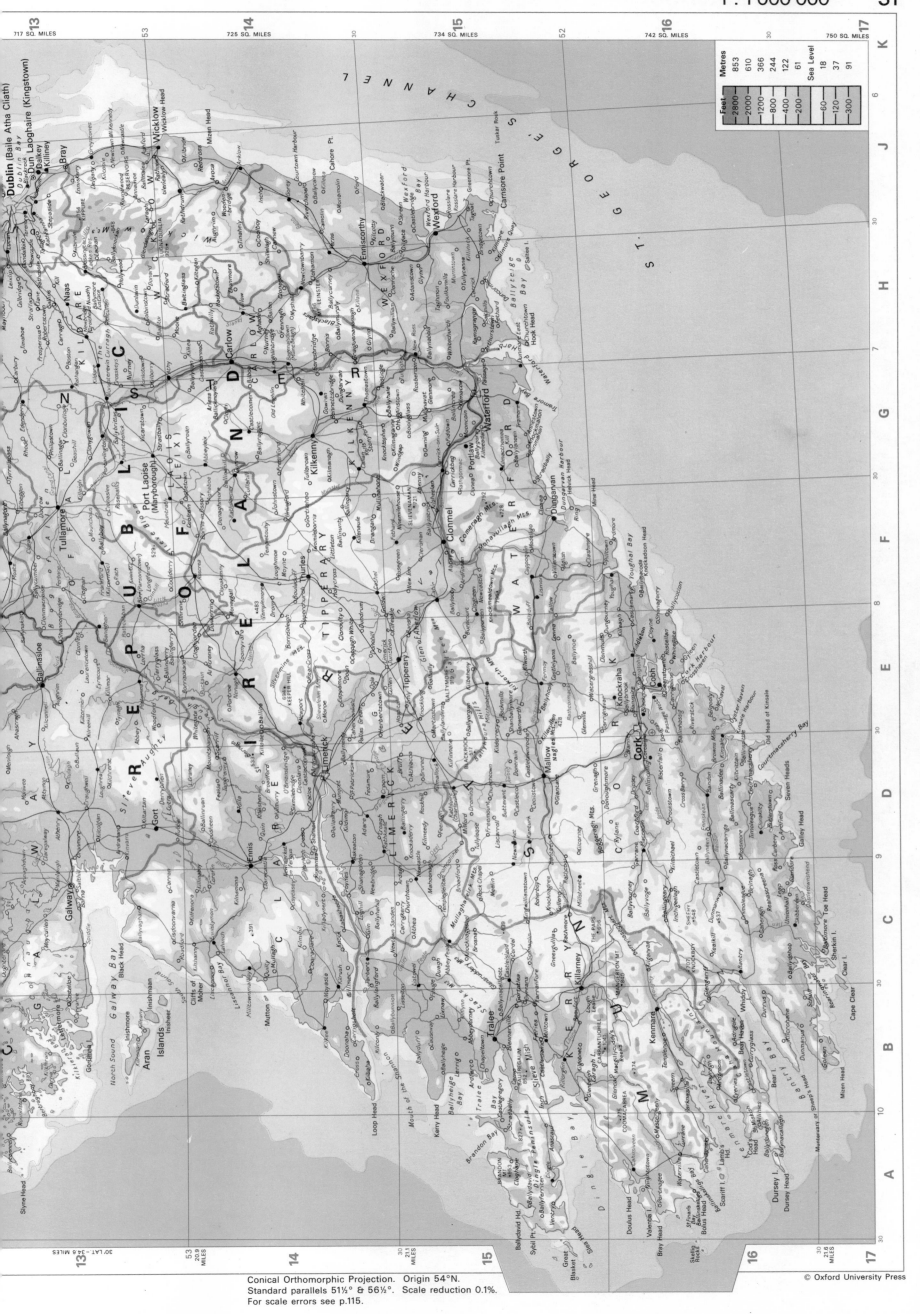

Metres
853
610
366
244
122
61
Sea Level
18
37
91

Feet
2800
2000
1200
800
400
200
60
120
300

Conical Orthomorphic Projection. Origin 54°N.
Standard parallels 51½° & 56½°. Scale reduction 0.1%.
For scale errors see p.115.

© Oxford University Press

Feet | **Metres**
12,000 | 3658
9000 | 2743
6000 | 1829
3000 | 914
1500 | 457
600 | 183
300 | 91
Sea Level
Land Depression
600 | 183
6000 | 1829

5° LONG. = 223 MILES
5° LAT = 345 MILES
45 245 MILES

ENGLAND
London
BAY OF BISCAY
ENGLISH CHANNEL
NETHERLANDS
BELGIUM
LUX
WEST GERMANY
EAST GERMANY
Berlin
Amsterdam
Brussels
Paris
FRANCE
NORMANDY
BRITTANY
GASCONY
PYRENEES
SWITZERLAND
AUSTRIA
ALPS
LOMBARDY
Milan
Turin
Genoa
PROVENCE
Marseilles
LIGURIAN SEA
CORSICA
SARDINIA
TUSCANY
Rome
ITALY
ABRUZZI
Naples
TYRRHENIAN SEA
PORTUGAL
SPAIN
Madrid
Lisbon
OLD CASTILE
NEW CASTILE
Barcelona
Valencia
Gulf of Valencia
BALEARIC ISLANDS
Minorca
Majorca
Iviza
ANDALUSIA
Sierra Morena
Sevilla
Córdoba
Granada
Málaga
Gibraltar (Br.)
Tangier
 Str. of Gibraltar
MOROCCO
Rabat
Fès
ALGERIA
Oran
Algiers (El Djezair)
ATLAS
Constantine
TUNISIA
Tunis
SICILY
Palermo
MALTA
MEDITERRANEAN SEA

Suez Canal
Port Said
EGYPT
Ismailia
Suez
Great Bitter Lake
Little Bitter Lake
1 : 2 000 000
0 5 10 15 20 MLS.

SPAIN
San Roque
La Línea
Algeciras
Gibraltar (Br.)
Tarifa
Strait of Gibraltar
Ceuta (Sp.)
MOROCCO
Tangier
1 : 1 000 000
0 5 10 MLS.

Gozo
Rabat (Victoria)
Comino (Kemmuna)
Malta
Valletta
Sliema
Feet | Metres
600 | 183
400 | 122
200 | 61
Sea Level
600 | 183
1 : 1 000 000
0 5 10 MLS.

Tripoli (Tarabulus)

100   0   100   200 MILES
100   0   100   200   300 KILOMETRES

F   20   G   25   H   30   J   35   K   40

50

POLAND

Warsaw
Siedice
Łódź
Tomaszów
Radom
Lublin

Pinsk
Stolin
Narovlya
Chernigov
Borzna
Sumy
Skorodnoye
Alekseyevka
Rossosh

U. S. S. R.

Kiev
Kharkov

C H O S L O V A K I A
ORAVIA
Brno

Vienna
Bratislava

HUNGARY

Budapest

R O M A N I A
Transylvanian Alps

Bucharest

Y U G O S L A V I A
Belgrade

BULGARIA
Sofia

Balkan Mts.

Dneprozerzhinsk
Dnepropetrovsk
Zaporozh'ye
Rostov
Taganrog

SEA OF AZOV

Krasnodar

Novorossiysk

Odessa

Sevastopol

B L A C K   S E A

45

ALBANIA
Tirane

MACEDONIA

G R E E C E
EPIRUS

Istanbul
Ankara

T U R K E Y

40

Athens
Piraeus
PELOPONNESE

Izmir

CYPRUS
Nicosia (Levkósia)

Beirut
Damascus

SICILY

I O N I A N
S E A

SEA OF CRETE

CRETE

S Y R I A

LEBANON
Tel Aviv-Jaffa
Jerusalem

JORDAN

M E D I T E R R A N E A N   S E A

Port Said

Alexandria
Cairo

Benghazi

L I B Y A

L I B Y A N   D E S E R T

E G Y P T

SINAI

F   20   G   25   H   30   J

Conical Orthomorphic Projection. Origin 42°N.
Standard parallels 35° & 49°. Scale reduction 0.7%.
For scale errors see p.115.

© Oxford University Press

CONTINUED ON P.42-43

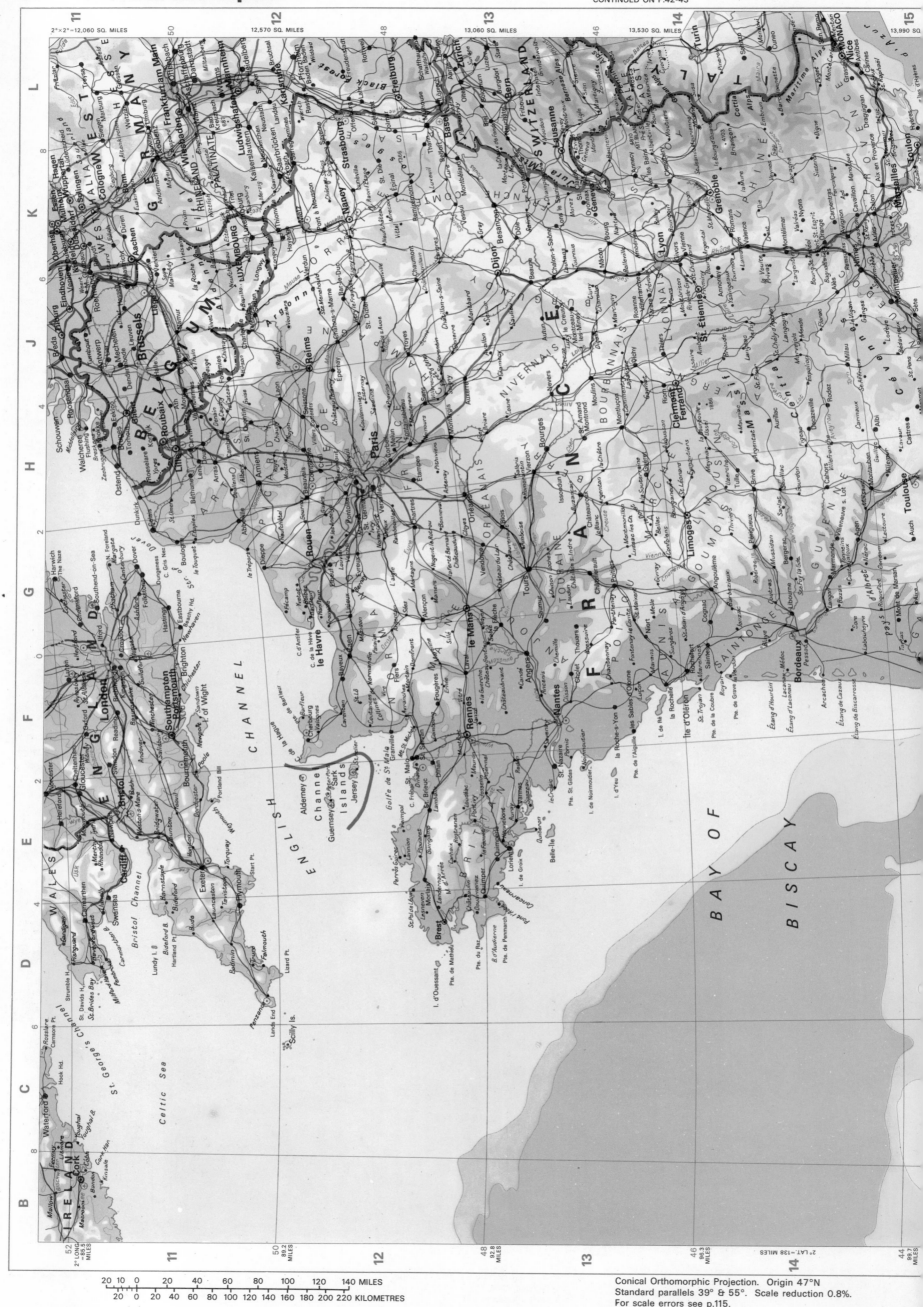

20 10 0   20   40   60   80   100   120   140 MILES
20 0   20   40   60   80 100 120 140 160 180 200 220 KILOMETRES

Conical Orthomorphic Projection. Origin 47°N
Standard parallels 39° & 55°. Scale reduction 0.8%.
For scale errors see p.115.

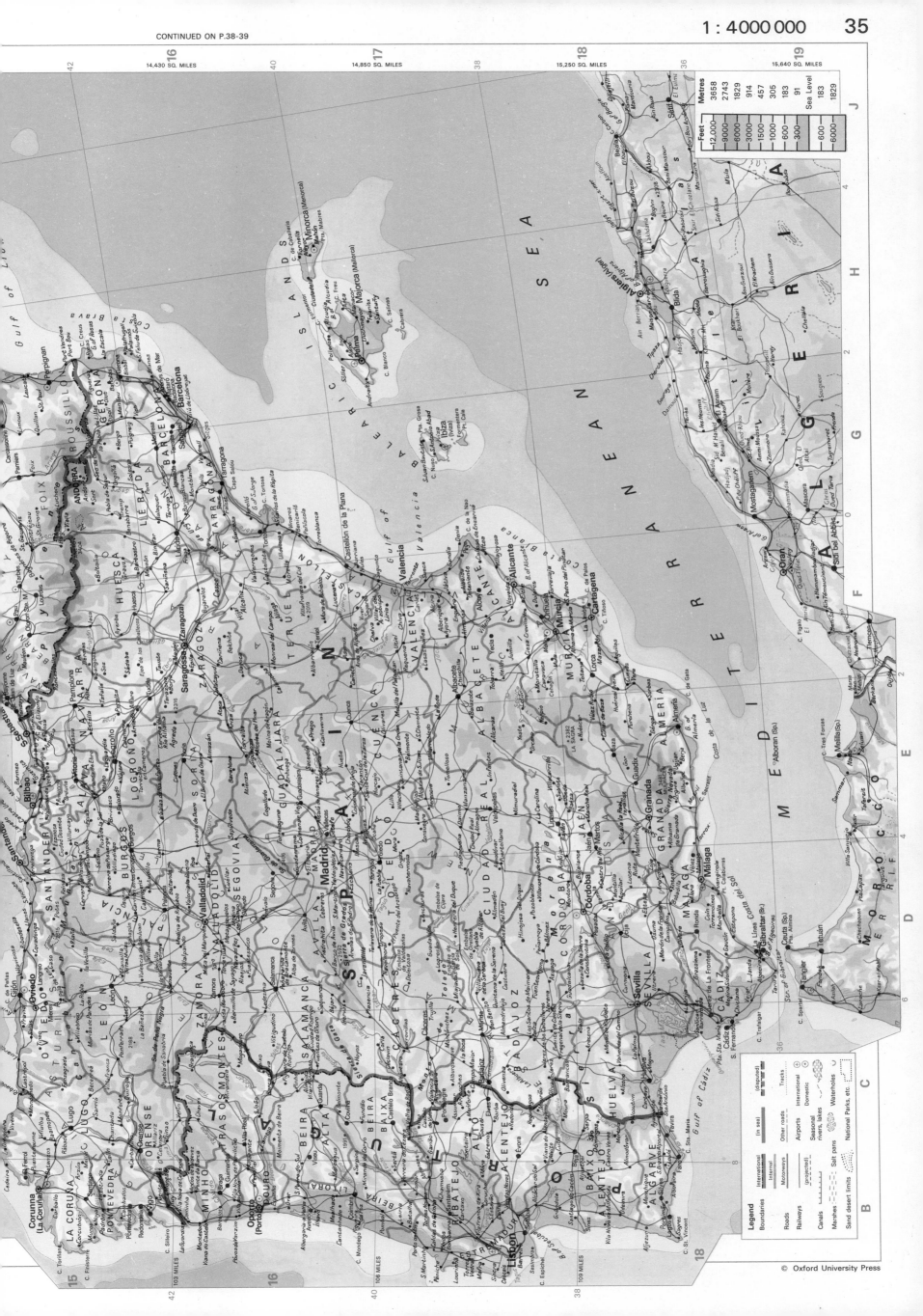

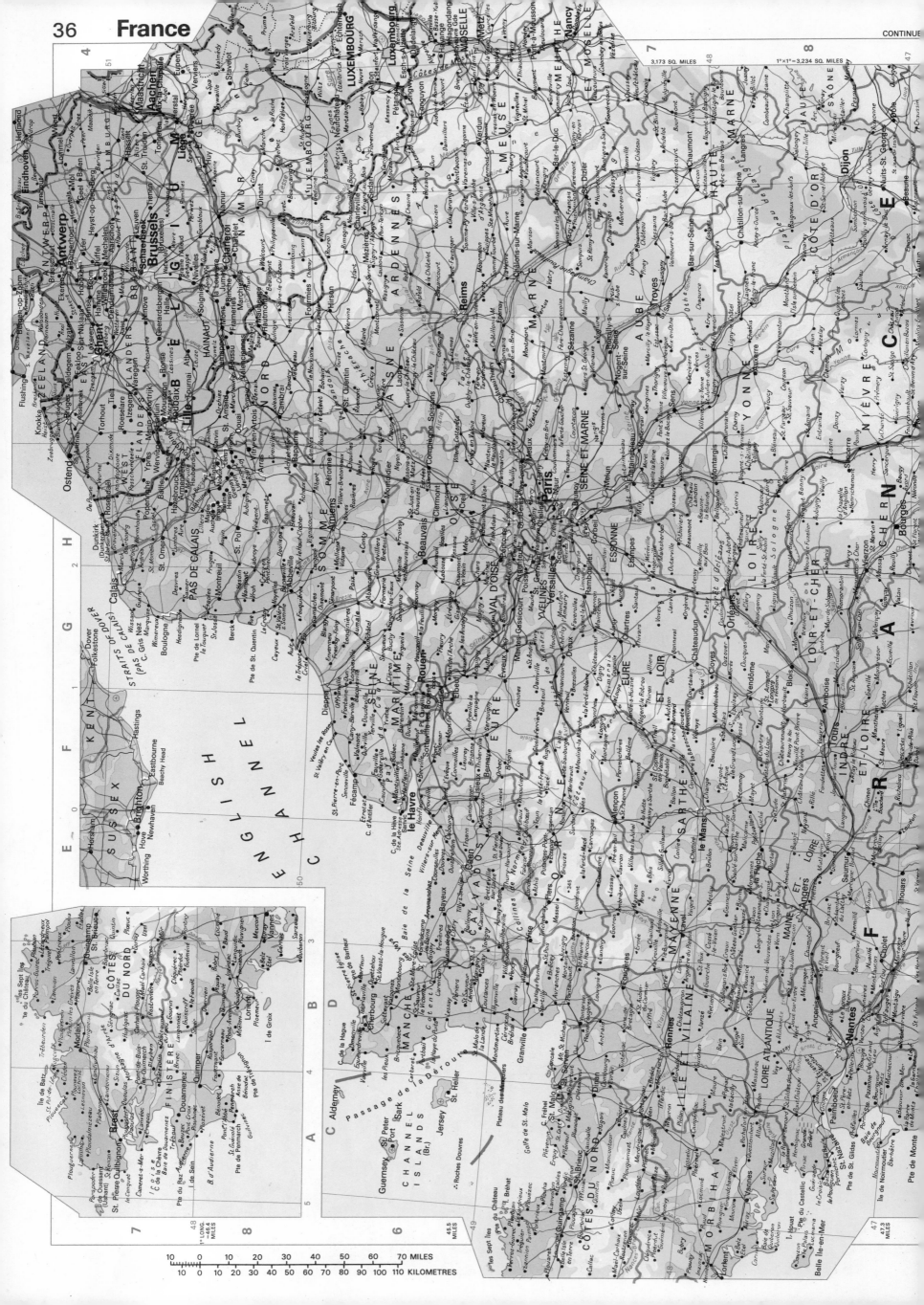

CONTINUE

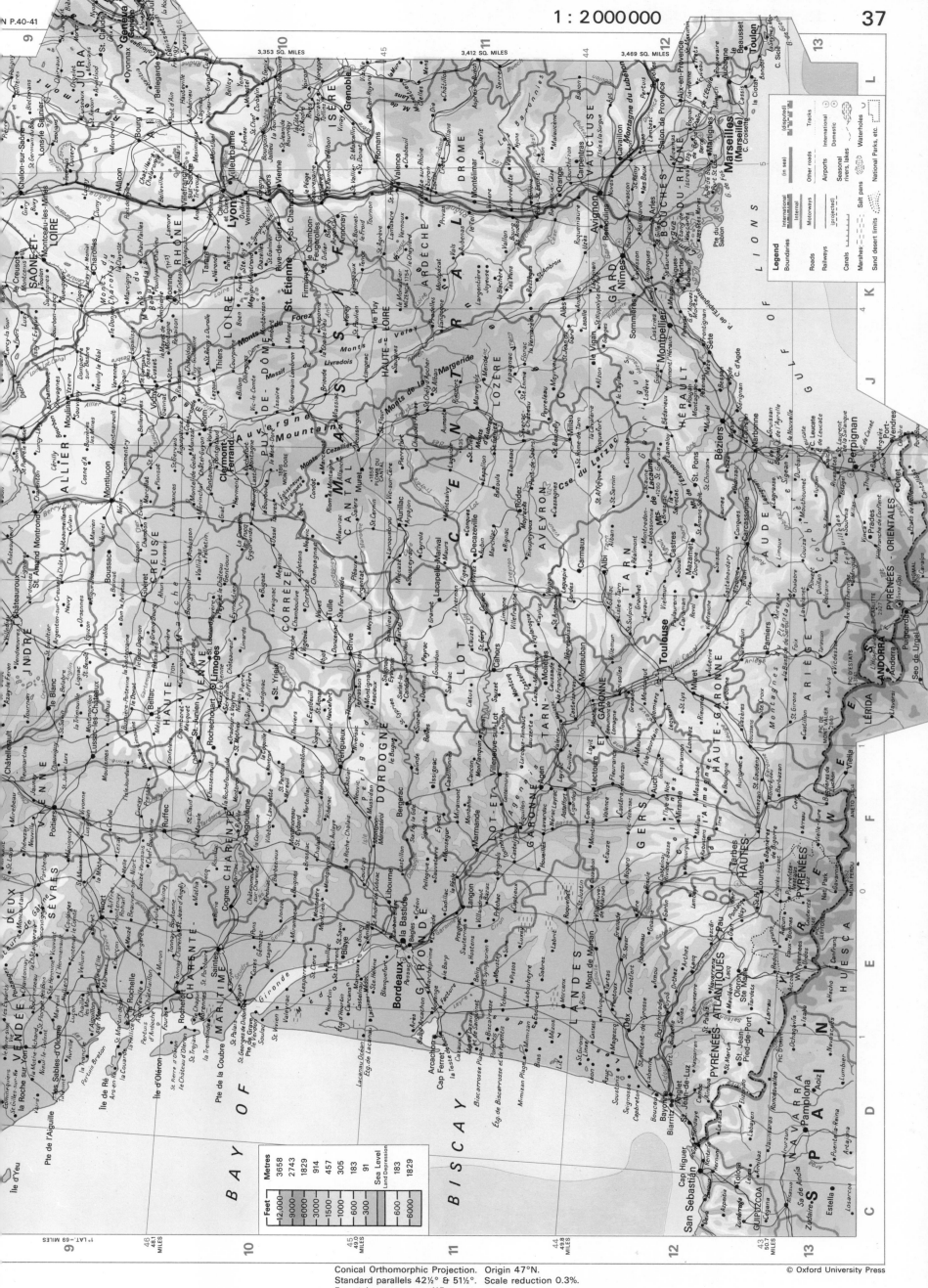

3,353 SQ. MILES

3,412 SQ. MILES

3,469 SQ. MILES

Legend

Boundaries	International ───
	Internal ───
Roads	Motorways
	(projected)
Railways ───
Canals ───

	International
	(disputed)
Other roads	Tracks
Airports	International ✈
	Domestic
Marshes ───	Salt pans
Sand desert limits	Waterholes
National Parks, etc.	Seasonal rivers, lakes

Feet	Metres
12,000	3658
9000	2743
6000	1829
3000	914
1500	457
1000	305
600	183
300	91
Sea Level	
Land Depression	
600	183
6000	1829

Conical Orthomorphic Projection. Origin 47°N.
Standard parallels 42½° & 51½°. Scale reduction 0.3%.
For scale errors see p.115.

CONTINUED ON P.42-43

CONTINUED ON P.34-35

20 10 0   20   40   60   80   100   120   140 MILES

-20 0   20 40 60 80 100 120 140 160 180 200 220 KILOMETRES

Q 20 R 22 S 24 T 26 U 28 V 30 W

HUNGARY

Budapest
Kecskemét
Szeged
Subotica
Novi Sad
Timişoara
Pécs
Osijek

ROMANIA

Cluj
Oradea
Arad
Sibiu
Braşov
Ploeşti
Bucharest (Bucureşti)
Craiova
Galaţi
Brăila
Constanţa

MOLDAVIA
Iaşi
Kishinev

U.S.S.R.
Odessa
BESSARABIA

Mouths of the Danube
Danube Delta Nat. Park

YUGOSLAVIA

Belgrade (Beograd)
Sarajevo
MONTENEGRO
Titograd
Dubrovnik
Priština
Skopje
MACEDONIA

ALBANIA
Tiranë
Durrës (Durazzo)
Vlorë

BULGARIA
Sofiya
Plovdiv (Philippopolis)
Varna
Burgas
Pleven
Turnovo
Stara Zagora

BLACK SEA

TURKEY
Istanbul
Üsküdar
Edirne (Adrianople)
KIRKLARELI
TEKIRDAĞ
Sea of Marmara
ÇANAKKALE
BALIKESIR
Bursa
İzmir (Smyrna)
MANISA
KÜTAHYA
AYDIN
MUĞLA
DENIZLİ

GREECE
Salonica (Thessaloníki)
Thessaly
Yannina (Ioánnina)
Lárisa
Vólos
EUBOEA (Évvoia)
Athens (Athínai)
Piraeus (Piraiévs)
Peloponnese (Morea)
Pátras
Trípolis
Kalámai (Kalamáta)
Spárti (Sparta)
Corfu (Kérkira)

Lesbos (Lésvos)
Chios (Khíos)
Sámos
CYCLADES (Kikládhes)
Náxos
Páros
DODECANESE
Rhodes (Ródhos)
CRETE (Kríti)
Candia (Iráklion)

AEGEAN SEA
IONIAN SEA
Sea of Crete
Mírtoön Sea
Sea of Marmara
Strait of Otranto

Legend

Boundaries	International	(in sea)	(disputed)
	Internal		
Roads	Motorways	Other roads	Tracks
Railways		Airports	
	(projected)	International	Domestic
Canals		Seasonal rivers/lakes	
Marshes	Salt pans	Waterholes	
Sand desert limits		National Parks, etc.	

Feet	Metres
12,000	3658
9000	2743
6000	1829
3000	914
1500	457
1000	305
600	183
300	91
Sea Level	Land Deprn.
600	183
6000	1829

Conical Orthomorphic Projection. Origin 47°N
Standard parallels 39° & 55°. Scale reduction 0.8%.
For scale errors see p.115.

© Oxford University Press

14 15 16 17 18 19

2°×2°=13,530 SQ. MILES
13,990 SQ. MILES
14,430 SQ. MILES
14,850 SQ. MILES
15,250 SQ. MILES
15,640 SQ. MILES

CONTINUED ON P.44-45

CONTINUED ON P.36-37

10   0   10   20   30   40   50   60   70 MILES

10   0   10   20   30   40   50   60   70   80   90 100 110 KILOMETRES

Conical Orthomorphic Projection. Origin 47°N.
Standard parallels 42½° & 51½°. Scale reduction 0.3%.
For scale errors see p.115.

© Oxford University Press

CONTINUED ON P.34-35

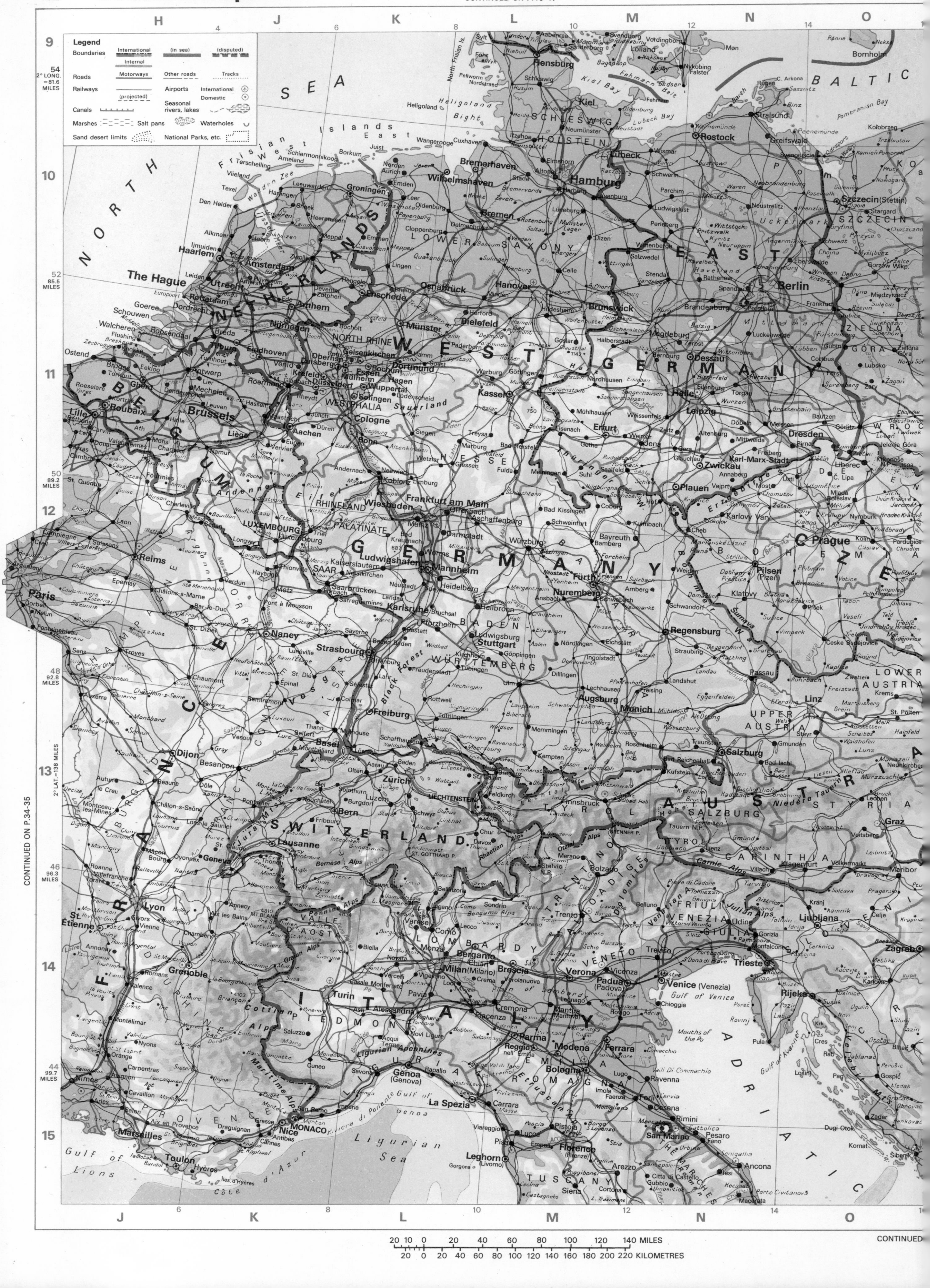

Legend

Boundaries	International	(in sea)	(disputed)
	Internal		
Roads	Motorways	Other roads	Tracks
Railways	(projected)	Airports	International ⊕
			Domestic ⊕
Canals		Seasonal rivers, lakes	
Marshes	Salt pans	Waterholes	
Sand desert limits		National Parks, etc.	

NORTH SEA

BALTIC SEA

West Frisian Islands · East Frisian Islands

NETHERLANDS
The Hague · Haarlem · Amsterdam · Utrecht · Rotterdam · Dordrecht · Arnhem · Enschede · Groningen · Den Helder · Alkmaar · Leeuwarden

BELGIUM
Brussels · Antwerp · Ghent · Bruges · Roubaix · Lille · Liège · Mechelen · Leuven · Namur

LUXEMBOURG
Luxembourg

WEST GERMANY
Flensburg · Kiel · Schleswig · Lübeck · Hamburg · Bremen · Bremerhaven · Wilhelmshaven · Hanover · Brunswick · Bielefeld · Münster · Osnabrück · Dortmund · Essen · Bochum · Wuppertal · Duisburg · Düsseldorf · Cologne · Bonn · Aachen · Kassel · Frankfurt am Main · Wiesbaden · Mainz · Darmstadt · Mannheim · Ludwigshafen · Heidelberg · Karlsruhe · Stuttgart · Würzburg · Nuremberg · Fürth · Regensburg · Augsburg · Munich · Freiburg · Saarbrücken · Koblenz

LOWER SAXONY · NORTH RHINE WESTPHALIA · HESSE · RHINELAND PALATINATE · SAAR · BADEN-WÜRTTEMBERG · BAVARIA · SAUERLAND

EAST GERMANY
Rostock · Stralsund · Greifswald · Schwerin · Berlin · Magdeburg · Dessau · Leipzig · Halle · Erfurt · Weimar · Jena · Gera · Dresden · Karl-Marx-Stadt · Zwickau · Plauen

POLAND
Szczecin (Stettin) · Zielona Góra

CZECHOSLOVAKIA (ČESKO...)
Prague · Pilsen (Plzeň) · Karlovy Vary · České Budějovice · Liberec

FRANCE
Paris · Reims · Metz · Nancy · Strasbourg · Dijon · Besançon · Lyon · St. Étienne · Grenoble · Troyes · Épinal · Mulhouse · Nîmes · Marseilles · Toulon · Nice · Menton · Avignon · Valence

SWITZERLAND
Basel · Bern · Zürich · Lausanne · Geneva · Lucerne · St. Gallen · Chur · Davos

LIECHTENSTEIN

AUSTRIA
Salzburg · Linz · Innsbruck · Graz · Klagenfurt · Villach · St. Pölten

LOWER AUSTRIA · UPPER AUSTRIA · SALZBURG · TYROL · CARINTHIA · STYRIA

ITALY
Turin · Milan (Milano) · Genoa (Genova) · Bergamo · Brescia · Verona · Padua (Padova) · Venice (Venezia) · Parma · Modena · Bologna · Ferrara · Ravenna · Florence (Firenze) · Leghorn (Livorno) · Pisa · San Marino · Rimini · Ancona · La Spezia · Carrara · Trieste · Bolzano · Trento · Como · Pavia · Cremona · Mantua · Piacenza · Reggio nell'Emilia

PIEDMONT · LOMBARDY · VENETO · EMILIA ROMAGNA · TUSCANY · TRENTINO ALTO ADIGE · FRIULI VENEZIA GIULIA · LIGURIA · MARCHE

YUGOSLAVIA
Ljubljana · Zagreb · Rijeka · Maribor · Celje

SLOVENIA

Adriatic Sea · Ligurian Sea · Gulf of Venice · Gulf of Lions

MONACO

| 20 10 0 | 20 | 40 | 60 | 80 | 100 | 120 | 140 MILES |
| 20 0 20 | 40 | 60 | 80 100 120 140 160 180 200 220 KILOMETRES |

CONTINUED

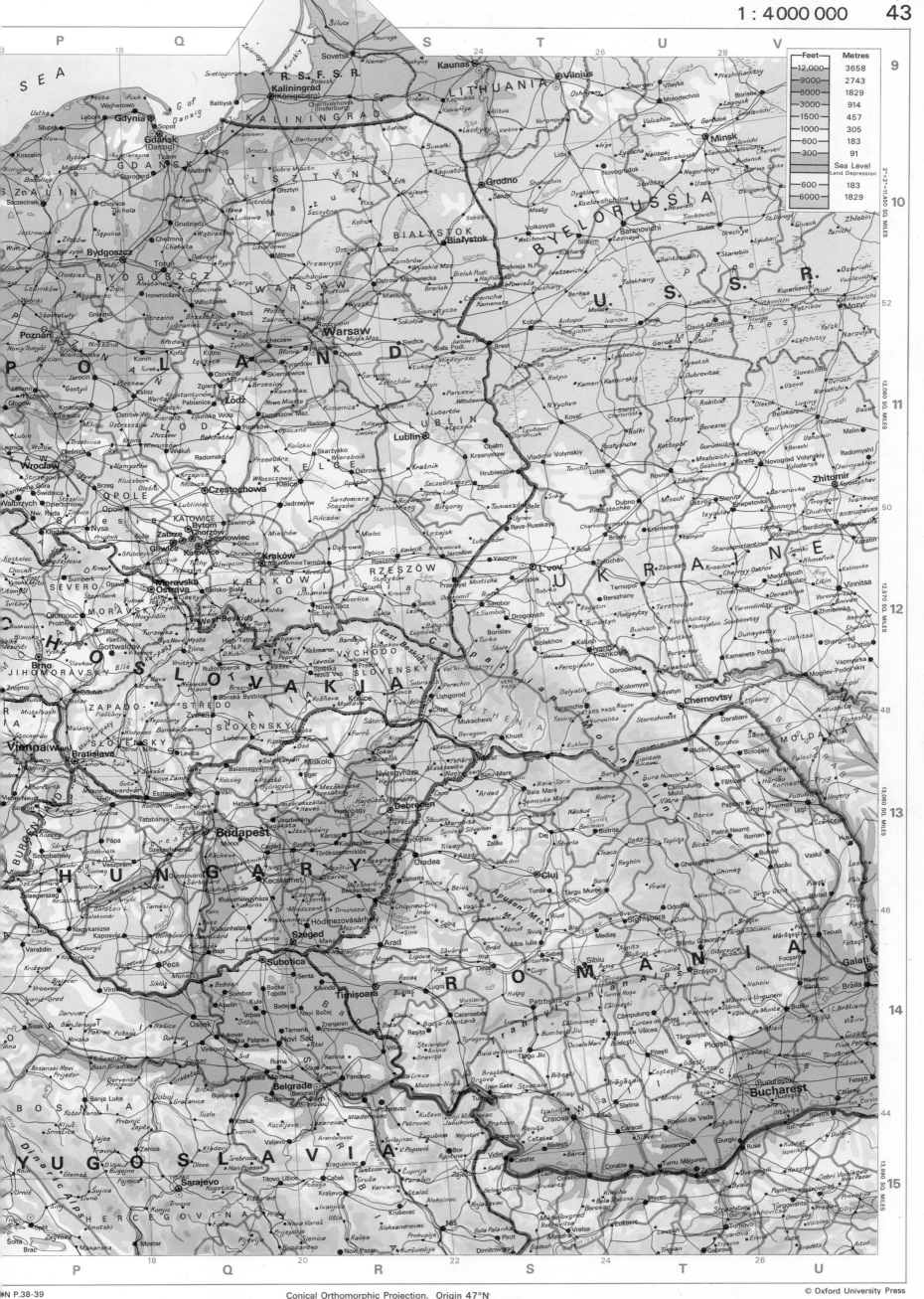

© Oxford University Press

Conical Orthomorphic Projection. Origin 47°N·
Standard parallels 39° & 55°. Scale reduction 0.8%.
For scale errors see p.115.

Feet	Metres
12,000	3658
9000	2743
6000	1829
3000	914
1500	457
1000	305
600	183
300	91
Sea Level	
Land Depression	
600	183
6000	1829

BALTIC SEA

KOSZALIN

P O L A N D

GERMANY

EAST

NEUBRANDENBURG

SCHWERIN

POTSDAM

FRANKFURT

Berlin
WEST

Potsdam

Frankfurt-
a-d-Oder

MAGDEBURG

Magdeburg

ZIELONA

GÓRA

POZNAŃ

Poznań

HALLE

LEIPZIG

Leipzig

COTTBUS

DRESDEN

Dresden

Görlitz

WROCŁAW

Wrocław

Legnica

ERFURT

GERA

Karl-Marx-Stadt

Zwickau

SEVEROČESKÝ

Liberec

VYCHODOČESKÝ

Plauen

Prague (Praha)

STŘEDOČESKÝ

Pilsen (Plzeň)

ZÁPADOČESKÝ

CZECHOSLOVAKIA

JIHOMORAVSKÝ

Brno
(Brünn)

MORAVIA

Nuremberg
(Nürnberg)

OBERPFALZ

JIHOČESKÝ

BAVARIA

MITTEL-FRANKEN

Regensburg

NIEDERBAYERN

LOWER AUSTRIA

Kiel

Hamburg

Lübeck

Neumünster

LESWIG

OLSTEIN

Rostock

Stralsund

Stettin / Szczecin

Hildesheim

Salzgitter

Brunswick
(Braunschweig)

Wolfsburg

Würzburg

Fürth

Conical Orthomorphic Projection. Origin 47°N.
Standard parallels 42½° & 51½°. Scale reduction 0.3%.
For scale errors see p.115.

© Oxford University Press

CONTINUED ON P.43

Transverse Mercator Projection.
Central meridian 18°E. Scale reduction 0.4%.
For scale errors see p.115.

© Oxford University Press

Legend

Feet	Metres
18,000	5486
14,000	4267
10,000	3048
6000	1829
3000	914
1500	457
1000	305
500	152
Sea Level	
Land Depression	
600	183
6000	1829

Boundaries: International, Internal, (in sea), (disputed)
Roads: Motorways, Other roads, Tracks
Railways: (projected)
Airports: International, Domestic
Canals
Marshes, Salt pans, Waterholes
Sand desert limits, National Parks, etc.
Seasonal rivers, lakes

NORWAY · SWEDEN · FINLAND · DENMARK · GERMANY · POLAND · ROMANIA · UKRAINE · BELORUSSIA · ESTONIA · LATVIA · LITHUANIA

RUSSIAN SOVIET FEDERATED

ARCTIC

BARENTS SEA · Kara Sea · White Sea · BALTIC SEA · Gulf of Bothnia · NOVAYA ZEMLYA · FRANZ JOSEF LAND · West Spitzbergen · North Cape

Moscow · Leningrad · Gorkiy · Kharkov · Kiev · Rostov · Volgograd · Kazan · Sverdlovsk · Chelyabinsk · Omsk · Novosibirsk · Barnaul · Kemerovo · NOVOSIBIRSK

West Siberian Plain · Ural Mountains · Ob Peninsula · Gyda Peninsula · Yamal

KAZAKHSTAN · UZBEKISTAN · TURKMENISTAN · KIRGIZIA · TADZHIKISTAN

CASPIAN SEA · Aral Sea · Lake Balkhash · BLACK SEA · Sea of Azov

GEORGIA · ARMENIA · AZERBAIDZHAN · Tbilisi · Baku · Tashkent · Alma-Ata · Ashkhabad · Samarkand · Bukhara · Frunze

Caucasus Mountains · Ust-Urt Plateau · Bet-Pak-Dala Steppe · Muyun Kum · Kyzyl Kum · Kara Kum · Takla Makan · Kun Lun Mountains · Tien Shan · Hindu Kush

TURKEY · IRAQ · IRAN · AFGHANISTAN · PAKISTAN · SINKIANG · TIBET · KASHMIR

Tehran · Tabriz · Baghdad · Mashhad · Kabul · Herat · Mazar-i-Sharif · Kandahar

Persian Gulf · BAHRAIN

Scale:
100 0 100 200 300 400 500 600 MILES
100 0 200 400 600 800 KILOMETRES

Conical Orthomorphic Projection.   Origin 56°N.
Standard parallels 46½° & 64½°   Scale reduction 1.25%
For scale errors see p.115.

© Oxford University Press

FINLAND

BALTIC SEA

ESTONIA
LATVIA
LITHUANIA
POLAND
BYELO-RUSSIA
U K R A I N E
MOLDAVIA

RUSSIAN SOVIET FEDERATED

Helsinki
Leningrad
Tallinn
Riga
Vilnius
Minsk
Smolensk
Vitebsk
Gomel'
Kiev
Vinnitsa
Zhitomir
Kishinev
Odessa
Nikolayev
Kirovograd
Krivoy Rog
Dnepropetrovsk
Dneprodzerzhinsk
Kremenchug
Cherkassy
Poltava
Kharkov
Kursk
Orel
Bryansk
Kaluga
Tula
Moscow
Moskva
Kalinin
Rybinsk
Yaroslavl
Kostroma
Ivanovo
Vladimir
Dzerzhinsk
Gorkiy
Kolomna
Ryazan
Tambov
Michurinsk
Penza
Ul'yanovsk
Kazan'
Izhevsk
Perm
Kirov
Kuybyshev
Tol'yatti
Syzran
Saratov
Engels
Balashov
Voronezh
Volgograd
Astrakhan'
Rostov-na-Donu
Taganrog
Zhdanov (Berdyansk)
Melitopol'
Kherson
Sevastopol'
Simferopol'
Novorossiysk
Krasnodar
Stavropol'
Pyatigorsk
Groznyy
Ordzhonikidze
Makhachkala
Baku
Tbilisi
Yerevan
Kirovabad
Batumi
Kutaisi
Sochi
Orenburg
Orsk
Magnitogorsk
Ufa
Ural'sk
Gur'yev

CRIMEA
BLACK SEA
Sea of Azov
Gulf of Taganrog
CAUCASUS
GEORGIA
ARMENIA
AZERBAYDZHAN
DAGESTAN
CASPIAN SEA
WEST KAZAKH
KALMYK
VOLGOGRAD
BASHKIR
TATAR
UDMURT
MARI
CHUVASH
MORDOV
KOMI
URAL MOUNTAINS

TURKEY
Ankara
Samsun
Trabzon
Erzurum
Kars
Tabriz
Resht
Tehran
Hamadan
Mosul
Aleppo
SYRIA
IRAQ
IRAN (PERSIA)

Ust-Urt Plateau
Kara-Bogaz-Gol
Mangyshlak Penin.
Buzachi Peninsula
Krasnovodsk
Ashkhabad
Elburz Mountains

100   0   100   200   300 MILES
100   0   100   200   300   400   500 KILOMETRES

CONTINUED ON P.54-55

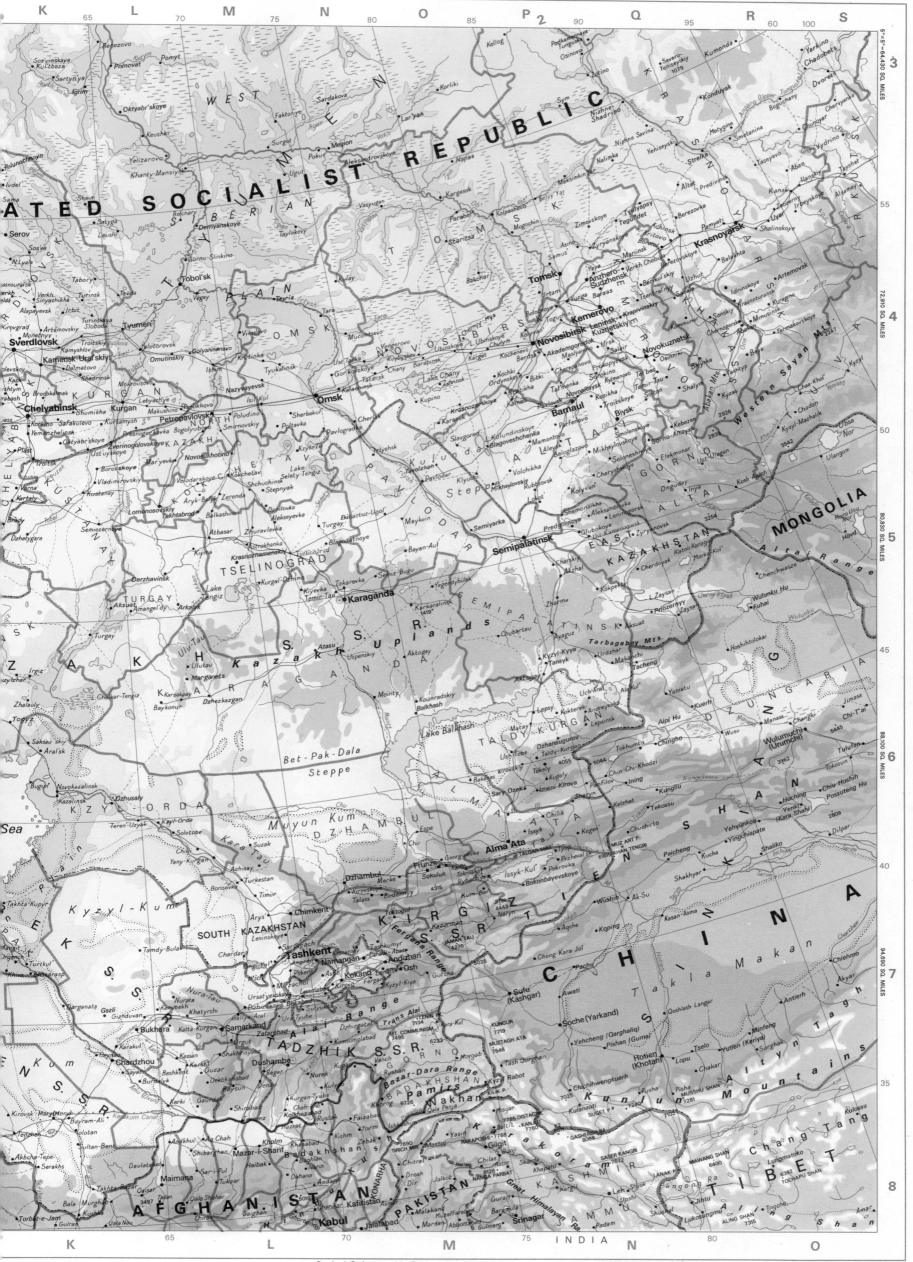

Conical Orthomorphic Projection. Origin 50°N,
Standard parallels 41° & 58½°. Scale reduction 1.25%.
For scale errors see p.115

CONTINUED ON P.58-59

© Oxford University Press

CONTINUED ON P78-79

BLACK SEA

U.S.S.R.

CASPIAN SEA

KAZAKH

Istanbul · Ankara · Krasnodar · Novorossiysk · Kerch · Astrakhan · Emba · Turgay · Karaganda · Balkhash · Lake Balkhash

TURKEY
Eskişehir · Afyonkarahisar · Konya · Kayseri · Sivas · Tokat · Trabzon · Erzurum · Diyarbakir · Malatya · Gaziantep · Urfa · Adana · Mersin · Tarsus · Antakya · Nicosia · Latakia · Aleppo · Homs

CYPRUS

SYRIA
Damascus · Beirut · Deir ez Zor

LEBANON

GEORGIA · Tbilisi · Batumi · Poti · Sochi

ARMENIA · Yerevan · MT. ARARA 5165

AZERBAYDZHAN · Baku · Kirovabad

Tabriz · Ardebil · Lake Urmia · Resht · Qazvin · Zenjan

IRAN
Tehran · MTS. DEMAVEND 5601 · Hamadan · Kermanshah · Khurramabad · Arak · Qum · Kashan · Isfahan · Yezd · Kerman · Shiraz · Bushire · Bandar Shahpur · Abadan · Ahwaz · Dizful · Amara

Elburz · Bandar Shah · Gurgan · Shahrud · Samnan · Mashhad · Birjand · Nehbandan · Zabula · Zahidan (Duzdab) · Dasht-i-Kavir · Dasht-i-Lut

IRAQ
Baghdad · Mosul · Kirkuk · Erbil · Hilla · Karbala · Najaf · Nasiriya · Basra · Ramadi

KUWAIT · Kuwait

JORDAN · Amman · Ma'an · Aqaba · Syrian Desert

ISRAEL · Tel Aviv · Jaffa · Jerusalem · Dead Sea

EGYPT · Port Said · Suez · Sinai Pen.

SUDAN · Port Sudan · Suakin

SAUDI ARABIA
Riyadh · Mecca · Medina · Jidda · Taif · Hail · Buraida · Anaiza · Laila · Hauta · Sulaiyil · Jabrin · Najd · Nafud · Hijaz · Hasa · Jauf · Sakaka

Tropic of Cancer

BAHRAIN · Manama · **QATAR** · Dauha · Huhuf · Ohahran

UNITED ARAB EMIRATES · Abu Dhabi · Dubai · Sharjah

PERSIAN GULF

Str. of Hormuz · Bandar Abbas · Jask · Lar

OMAN · Muscat · Khaburah · Ras al Hadd · Masira · C. Madraka · Salala

G. of Oman · Gwadar · Chahbar · **Makran**

AFGHANISTAN
Kabul · Herat · Farah · Kandahar · Chaman · Kalat · Quetta · Zabul · Hamun-i-Helmand · Mazar-i-Sharif · Maimana · Faizabad · Chitral · **Hindu Kush**

TURKMEN S.S.R. · Ashkhabad · Krasnovodsk · Kara-Bogaz-Gol · Gasan Kuli · Kizyl-Arvat · Kopet Dagh · Mary · Tedzhen · Chardzhou

UZBEK S.S.R. · Khiva · Turtkul · Bukhara · Samarkand · Karshi · Kara-Kalpak · Nukus · Kungrad · **Turan Plain** · **Kyzyl Kum** · **Kara Kum**

KIRGIZ · Tashkent · Namangan · Andizhan · Osh · Fergana · Kokand · Chimkent · Dzhambul · Frunze

TADZHIKISTAN · Dushambe · Samarkand · MT. COMMUNISM · **Pamirs**

Ust-Urt Plateau · Aral Sea · Aralsk · Kzyl-Orda

PAKISTAN
Peshawar · Rawalpindi · Islamabad · Kohat · Bannu · Lahore · Amritsar · Multan · Bahawalpur · Sukkur · Hyderabad · Karachi · Quetta · Kalat · Bela · **Baluchistan** · Srinagar · Jammu · Sialkot · Gujranwala · Ferozepore

Rann of Kutch · Bhuj · Jamnagar · Rajkot · Porbandar · Bikaner · Jaisalmer · Jodhpur · Ajmer · Udaipur

INDIA
Ahmadabad · Vadodara (Baroda) · Bharuch · Surat · Daman · Diu · Dhulia · Nasik · Bombay · Pune (Poona) · Satara · Ratnagiri · Kolhapur · Belgaum · Panaji · Karwar · Mangalore · Thana

Laccadive Is. (Ind.) · Minicoy

Nine Degree Chan. · **Eight Degree Chan.**

REPUBLIC OF MALDIVES · Male

ARABIAN SEA

INDIAN (OCEAN)

GULF OF ADEN
Aden · Djibouti · Zeila · Berbera · Sheikh · Burao

DJIBOUTI

ETHIOPIA · Harar · Dire Dawa · Jijiga · Hargeisa · Borama · Imi · Gabredare · Gerlogubi

SOMALI REP. · Las Anod · Bihen · Eil · Hafun · Bargal · Alula · C. Guardafui · Erigavo · Las Khoreh · Heis · Bossaso (Kassim)

YEMEN · Sana · Saiwun · Mukalla · **Hadhramaut**

YEMEN P.D.R. · Medinat ash-Sha'b · Perim · Mocha · Hodeidah · Zabid · Saida · Kamaran Is. · Farasan Is. · Qizan

Socotra (Yemen P.D.R.) · Abd al Kuri · The Brothers · Tamridah · Kuria Muria Is.

RED SEA · Asmara · Massawa · Dahlak Arch · Aden · Assab · Bab el Mandeb

Legend

Boundaries	International	(in sea)	(disputed)
	Internal		
Roads	Motorways	Other roads	Tracks
Railways	(projected)	Airports	International / Domestic
Canals		Seasonal rivers, lakes	
Marshes	Salt pans	Waterholes	
Sand desert limits	National Parks, etc.		

Feet	Metres
18,000	5486
14,000	4267
10,000	3048
6000	1829
3000	914
1500	457
1000	305
500	152
Sea Level Land Depr'n	
600	183
6000	1829

100   0   100   200   300   400   500 MILES
100   0   200   400   600   800 KILOMETRES

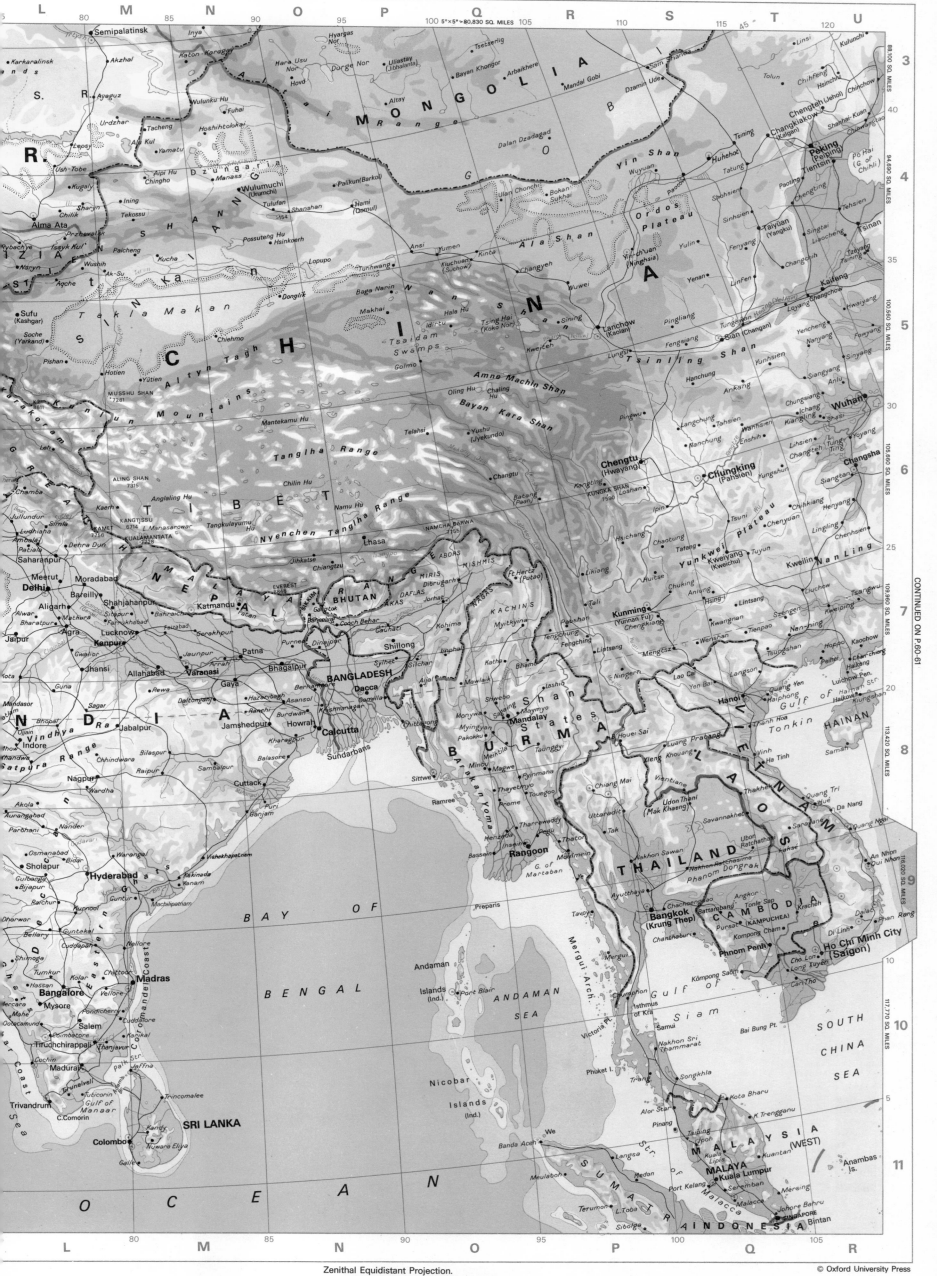

S. R.
R.
KIZIAE
ast

Semipalatinsk
Inye
Hara Usu Nor
Hyargas Nor
Durge Nor
Uliastay (Jibhalanta)
Tsetserlig
Linsi
Kulunchi
Karkaralinsk
Akzhal
Kaion-Karagay
Bayan Khongor
Arbaikhere
Mandal Gobi
Tolun
Chihfeng
Hsinchi
Ayaguz
Urdzhar
Tacheng
Hoshihtolokai
Hovd
Altay
Dalan Dzadagad
Dzamin Ude
Chengteh (Jehol)
Chinchow
Chankiakow (Kalgan)
Shanhai-Kuan
Lepsy
Wulunku Hu
Fuhai
Yin Shan
Wuyuan
Huhehot
Tatung
Peking Peiping
Tientsin
Po Hai (G. of Chihli)
Alma Ata
Chingho
Dzungaria
Ullan Chonchi
Bokan
Sukhai
Paoto
Shohsien
Paoting
Chengting
Tehsien
Wulumuchi (Urumchi)
Tulufan
Shanshan
Hami (Qomul)
Ordos Plateau
Yulin
Sinhsien
Taiyuan (Yangku)
Singtai
Sinan
Possuteng Hu
Hsinkoerh
Ansi
Yumen
Kinta
Changyeh (Suchow)
Tunhwang
Ninghsia
Yenan
LinFen
Liaocheng
Tzeyang Tsining
Sufu (Kashgar)
Soche (Yarkand)
Pishan
Hotien
Yütien
Donglik
Makhai
Idirtu
Tsing Hai (Koko Nor)
Sining
Lanchow (Kaolan)
Pingliang
Sian (Changan)
Yencheng
Nanyang
Siangyang
Singyang
Hwaiyang
Kweiteh Chengchow
Kaifeng
Leh
Golmo
Oling Hu
Chaling
Amne Machin Shan
Pingwu
Langchung
Tahsien
Wanhsien
Kiangling
Ichang
Tung Ting
Yoyang
Wuhan
Bayan Kara Shan
Yushu (Jyekundo)
Changtu
Batang (Paan)
Chengtu (Hwayang)
Kangting
KUNGKA SHAN 7590 Loshan
Ipin
Chungking (Pahsien)
Yungshun
Changteh
Changsha
Siangtan

MONGOLIA

CHINA

GREAT
TIBET
HIMALAYA
NEPAL
BHUTAN
INDIA
BANGLADESH
BURMA
THAILAND
LAOS
VIETNAM
CAMBODIA (KAMPUCHEA)
MALAYSIA (WEST)
MALAYA
SUMATRA
INDONESIA
SRI LANKA

BAY OF BENGAL
ANDAMAN SEA
SOUTH CHINA SEA
Gulf of Siam
INDIAN OCEAN

Delhi
Meerut
Moradabad
Bareilly
Aligarh
Shahjahanpur
Katmandu
Everest 8848
Bhutan
Kanpur
Lucknow
Patna
Varanasi
Allahabad
Gaya
Calcutta
Howrah
Dacca
Mandalay
Rangoon
Bangkok (Krung Thep)
Phnom Penh
Ho Chi Minh City (Saigon)
Hanoi
Haiphong
Kunming (Yunnan Fu)
Chengkiang
Madras
Bangalore
Hyderabad
Colombo

Andaman Islands (Ind.)
Nicobar Islands (Ind.)
Port Blair

Kuala Lumpur
Singapore

CONTINUED ON P.60-61

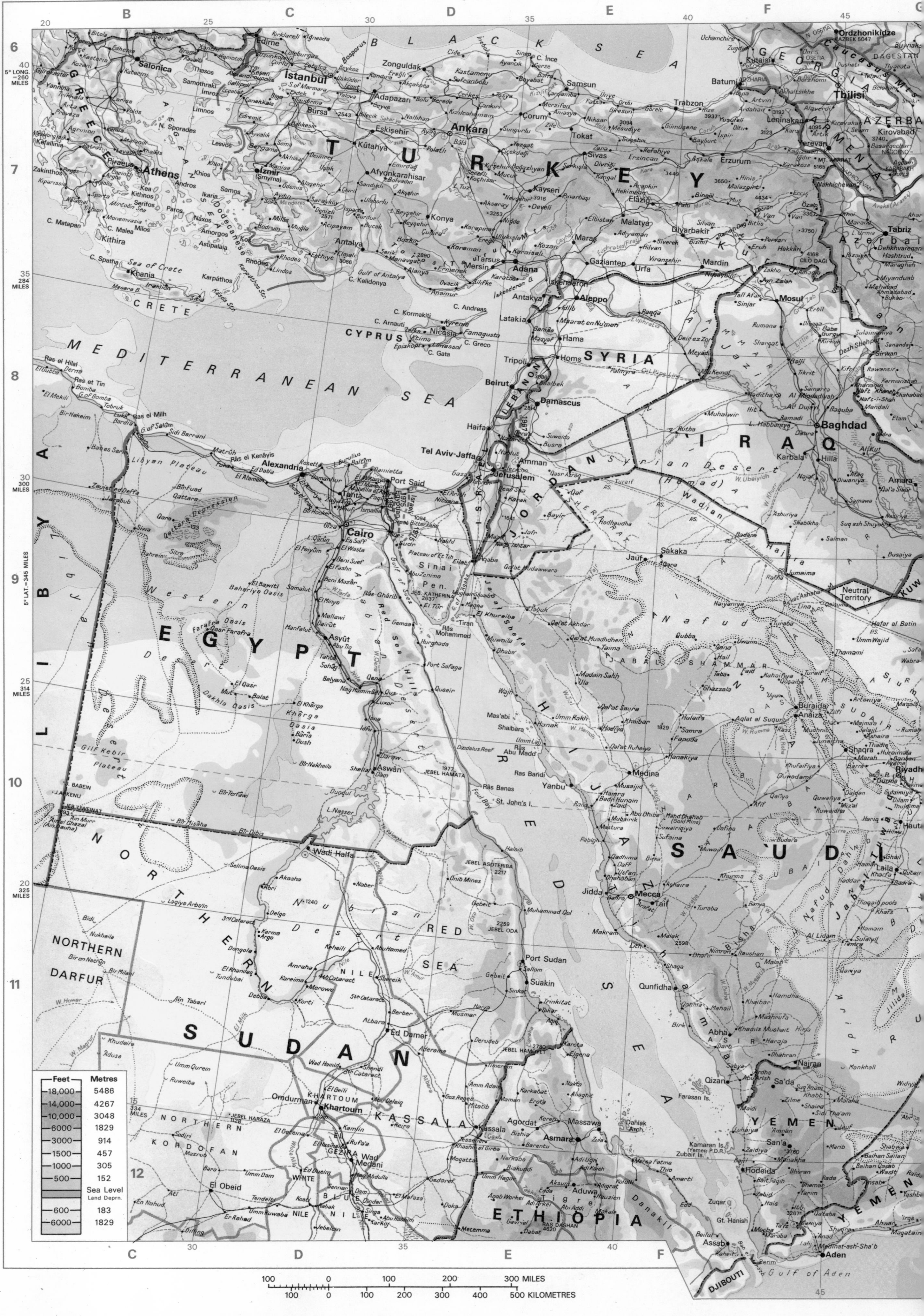

BLACK SEA

GREECE
Athens
Salonica
Istanbul

TURKEY
Ankara
İzmir (Smyrna)
Konya
Adana
Kayseri
Sivas
Erzurum
Trabzon

CYPRUS
Nicosia

MEDITERRANEAN SEA

CRETE

GEORGIA
Tbilisi
ARMENIA
Leninakan
Yerevan
AZERBAIJAN

Tabriz

SYRIA
Aleppo
Latakia
Homs
Hama
Beirut
LEBANON
Damascus
Haifa
Tel Aviv-Jaffa
Jerusalem
Amman
JORDAN
ISRAEL

IRAQ
Mosul
Baghdad
Karbala
Hilla

Syrian Desert (Hamad)

LIBYA
Tobruk

EGYPT
Alexandria
Port Said
Cairo
Asyût
Luxor
Aswân
L. Nasser
Wadi Halfa

Sinai Pen.
Gulf of Suez
Red Sea
RED SEA

SAUDI ARABIA
Medina
Mecca
Jidda
Taif
Riyadh
Buraida
Anaiza
Hail
Jauf
Sakaka
An Nafud

Port Sudan
Suakin

SUDAN
NORTHERN
Khartoum
Omdurman
KASSALA
Kassala
Asmara
Massawa

NORTHERN DARFUR
KORDOFAN
El Obeid
Wad Medani
GEZIRA
WHITE NILE
BLUE NILE

ETHIOPIA

YEMEN
San'a
Hodeida
Aden
DJIBOUTI
Gulf of Aden

Feet	Metres
18,000	5486
14,000	4267
10,000	3048
6000	1829
3000	914
1500	457
1000	305
500	152
Sea Level	Land Depnr.
600	183
6000	1829

100   0   100   200   300 MILES
100   0   100   200   300   400   500 KILOMETRES

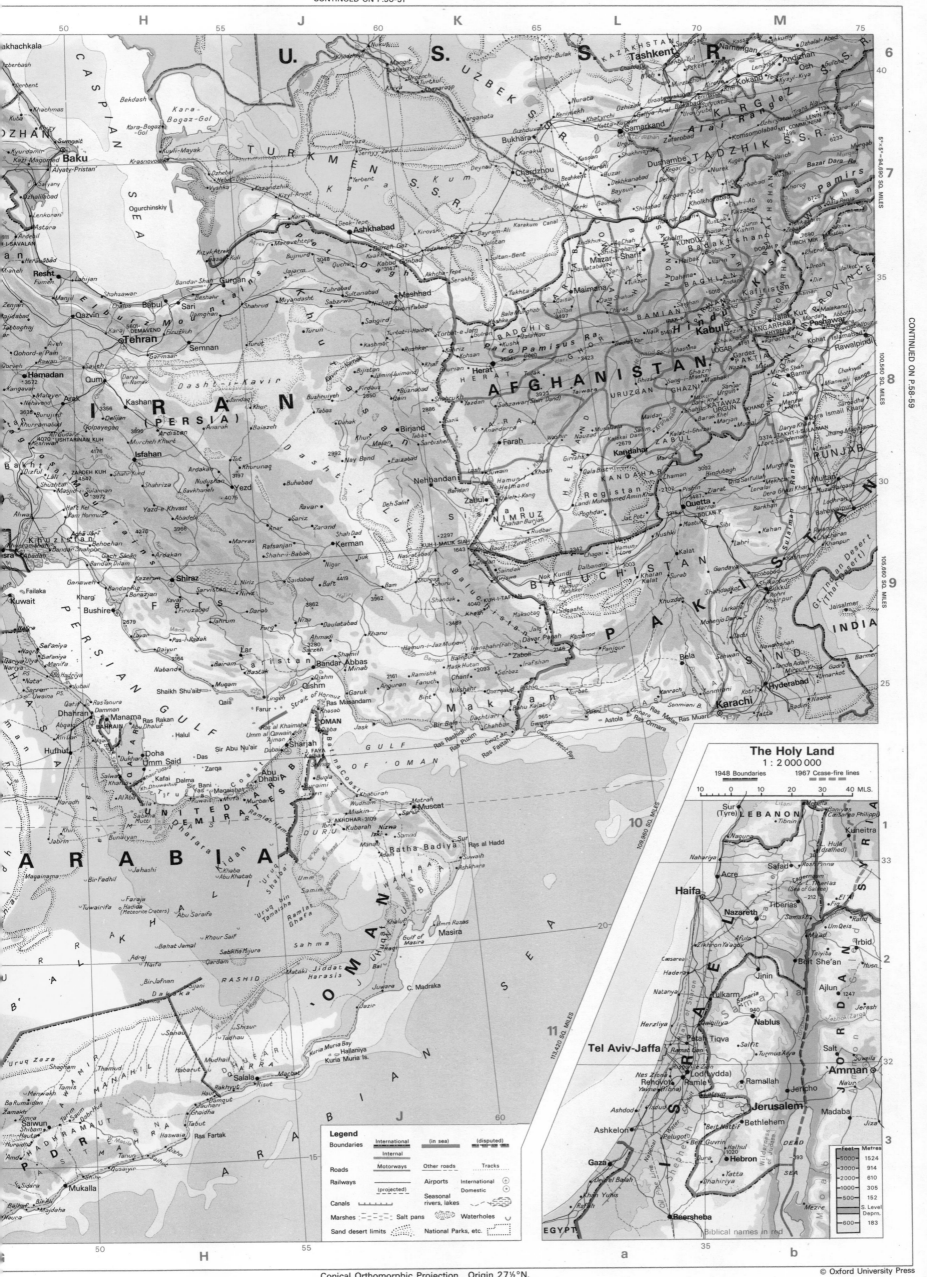

CONTINUED ON P.58-59

Conical Orthomorphic Projection. Origin 27½°N.
Standard parallels 16° & 38°. Scale reduction 2.0%.
For scale errors see p.115.

BLACK SEA

Sea of Marmara

İstanbul
Üsküdar

Zonguldak

KASTAMONU

SİNOP

Samsun

Ankara

T U R K E Y

Eskişehir

Kütahya

Afyonkarahisar

Konya

TOROS (TAURUS) MOUNTAINS

Antalya

Gulf of Antalya

Kayseri

Niğde

Adana (Seyhan)

Mersin (İçel)

Tarsus

Gaziantep

Urfa

Aleppo (Haleb)

CYPRUS

Nicosia (Levkosia)

Famagusta

Limassol

M E D I T E R R A N E A N   S E A

S Y R I A

Latakia (El Ladhiqiya)

Hama

Homs

Tripoli (Tarabulus)

Beirut

L E B A N O N

Damascus (Esh Sham)

Haifa

Tel Aviv-Jaffa

Jerusalem

I S R A E L

J O R D A N

Amman

Azraq Desert

National Park

S A U D I

Alexandria

Nile Delta

Port Said

Cairo (El Qâhira)

Suez

E G Y P T

S I N A I

Plateau of Et Tih

Gulf of Suez

Negeb

Feet	Metres
10,000	3048
6000	1829
3000	914
1500	457
1000	305
600	183
300	91
Sea Level	
Land Depr.	
600	183
6000	1829

20 10 0   20   40   60   80   100   120   140 MILES

20 0   20 40 60 80 100 120 140 160 180 200 220 KILOMETRES

CONTINUED ON P.51

CONTINUED ON P.55

AFGHANISTAN

PAKISTAN

I N D I A

Major places

Herat, Kabul, Kandahar, Quetta, Karachi, Hyderabad, Lahore, Amritsar, Srinagar, Jammu, New Delhi, Delhi, Jaipur, Jodhpur, Ahmadabad, Vadodara (Baroda), Bombay, Pune (Poona), Indore, Bhopal, Nagpur, Hyderabad, Sholapur, Bangalore, Mysore, Mangalore, Madras, Madurai, Trivandrum, Colombo

Regions / states

BADGHIS, HERAT, FARAH, GHAZNI, URUZGAN, BALUCHISTAN, MAKRAN, SIND, PUNJAB, KASHMIR, JAMMU, HIMACHAL PRADESH, RAJASTHAN, GUJARAT, MADHYA PRADESH, MAHARASHTRA, ANDHRA PRADESH, KARNATAKA, GOA, TAMIL NADU, SRI LANKA, OMAN

Water bodies

Gulf of Oman, ARABIAN SEA, G. of Kutch, G. of Cambay, G. of Manaar, Tropic of Cancer, Nine Degree Channel, Eight Degree Channel

LAKSHADWEEP, Laccadive Islands, REPUBLIC OF MALDIVES, C. Comorin

IRAN, U.S.S.R., Great Indian Desert (Thar Desert)

Feet	Metres
18,000	5486
14,000	4267
10,000	3048
6000	1829
3000	914
1500	457
1000	305
500	152
Sea Level	
600	183
6000	1829

100 0 100 200 300 MILES
100 0 100 200 300 400 500 KILOMETRES

CONTINUED ON P.62

CONTINUED ON P.64

Legend

Boundaries	International	(in sea)	(disputed)
	Internal		
Roads	Motorways	Other roads	Tracks
Railways	Metre	Broad	Narrow
	(projected)	Airports	
Canals		Seasonal rivers, lakes	
Marshes	Salt pans	Waterholes	
Sand desert limits		National Parks, etc.	

Conical Orthomorphic Projection. Origin 27½°N.
Standard parallels 16° & 38°. Scale reduction 2.0%.
For scale errors see p.115.

© Oxford University Press

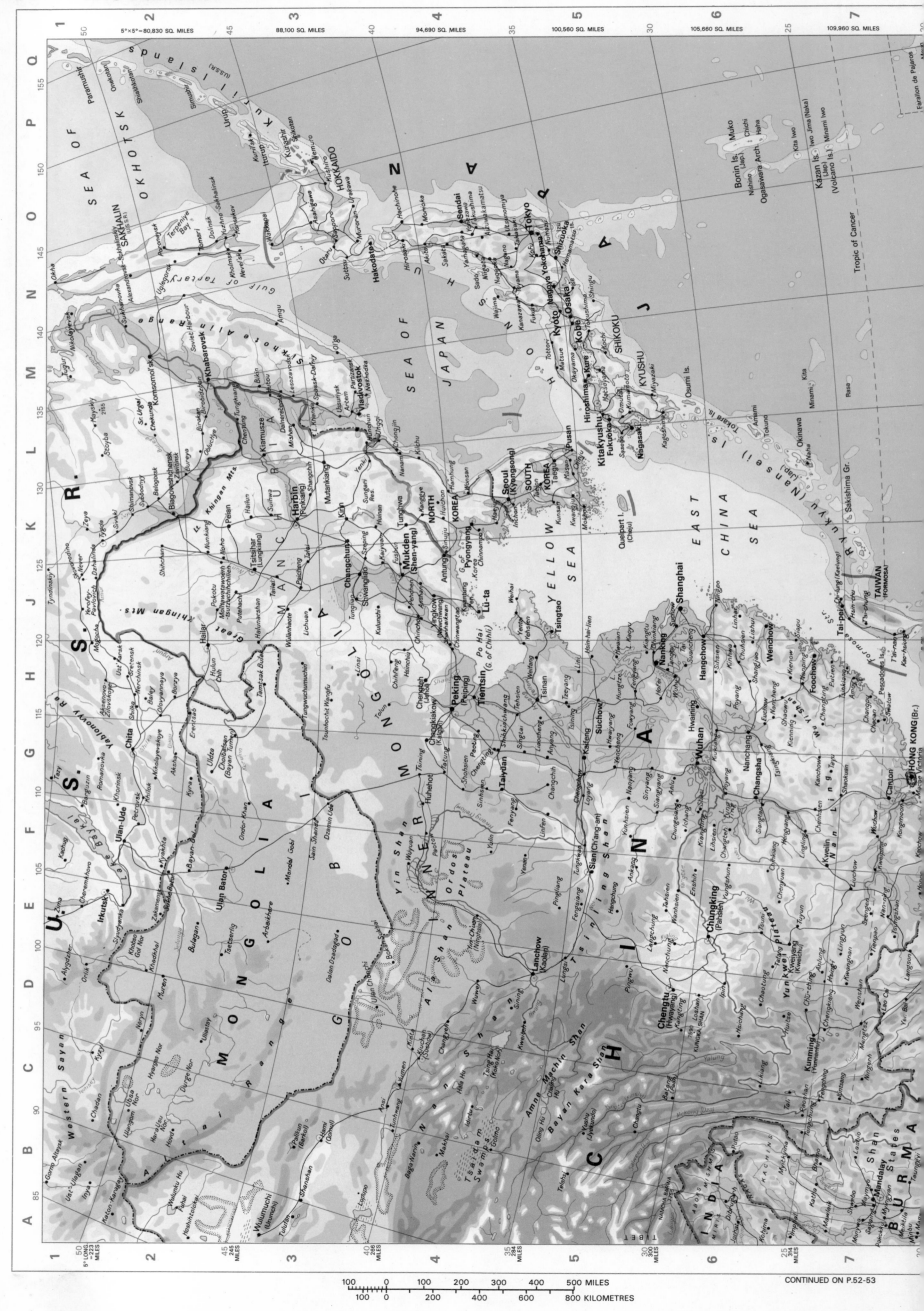

CONTINUED ON P.52-53

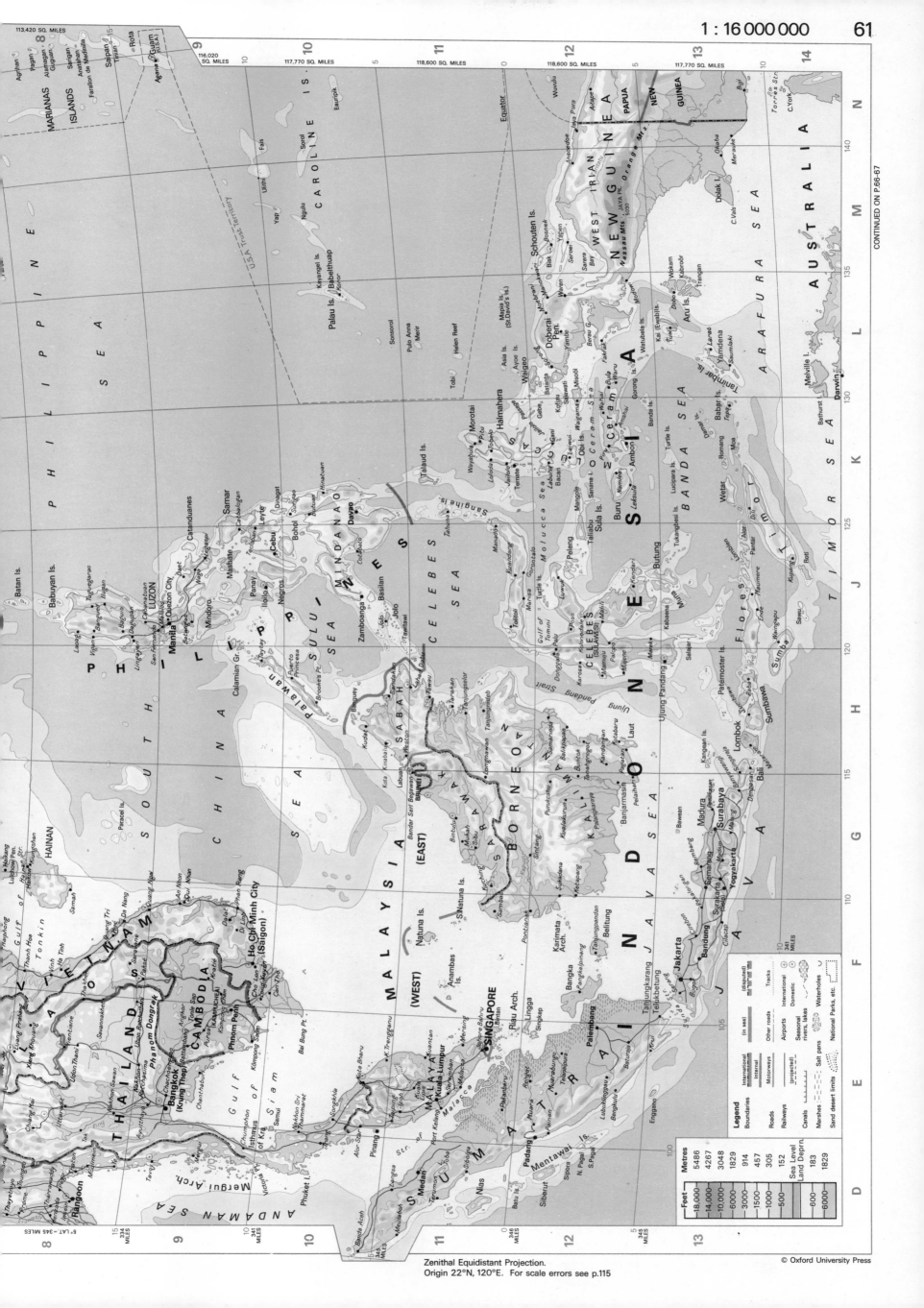

Zenithal Equidistant Projection.
Origin 22°N, 120°E. For scale errors see p.115

© Oxford University Press

CONTINUED ON P.66-67

Legend

Boundaries	
International	
Internal	

Roads	
Motorways	
(projected)	
Other roads	
Tracks	

Railways

Canals

Marshes — Salt pans

Sand desert limits

Airports
Seasonal
International
Domestic

Seasonal
rivers, lakes

Waterholes

National Parks, etc.

(in sea)

(disputed)

Feet	Metres
18,000	5486
14,000	4267
10,000	3048
6000	1829
3000	914
1500	457
500	305
Sea Level	152
Land Depn.	Sea Level
600	183
6000	1829

341
MILES

PHILIPPINE SEA

SOUTH CHINA SEA

CELEBES SEA

SULU SEA

BANDA SEA

CERAM SEA

MOLUCCA SEA

FLORES SEA

JAVA SEA

ARAFURA SEA

TIMOR SEA

ANDAMAN SEA

ARU SEA

CAROLINE IS.

MARIANAS ISLANDS

VIETNAM

THAILAND

CAMBODIA (KAMPUCHEA)

MALAYSIA (WEST)

MALAYSIA (EAST)

SINGAPORE

BRUNEI

SUMATRA

BORNEO

KALIMANTAN

SARAWAK

SABAH

INDONESIA

CELEBES (SULAWESI)

JAVA

LUZON

MINDANAO

PHILIPPINES

WEST IRIAN

PAPUA NEW GUINEA

AUSTRALIA

HAINAN

Rangoon

Bangkok (Krung Thep)

Phnom Penh

Ho Chi Minh City (Saigon)

Kuala Lumpur

Singapore

Medan

Padang

Palembang

Jakarta

Bandung

Surabaya

Yogyakarta

Manila

Quezon City

Cebu

Davao

Darwin

Gulf of Tonkin

Gulf of Siam

Strait of Malacca

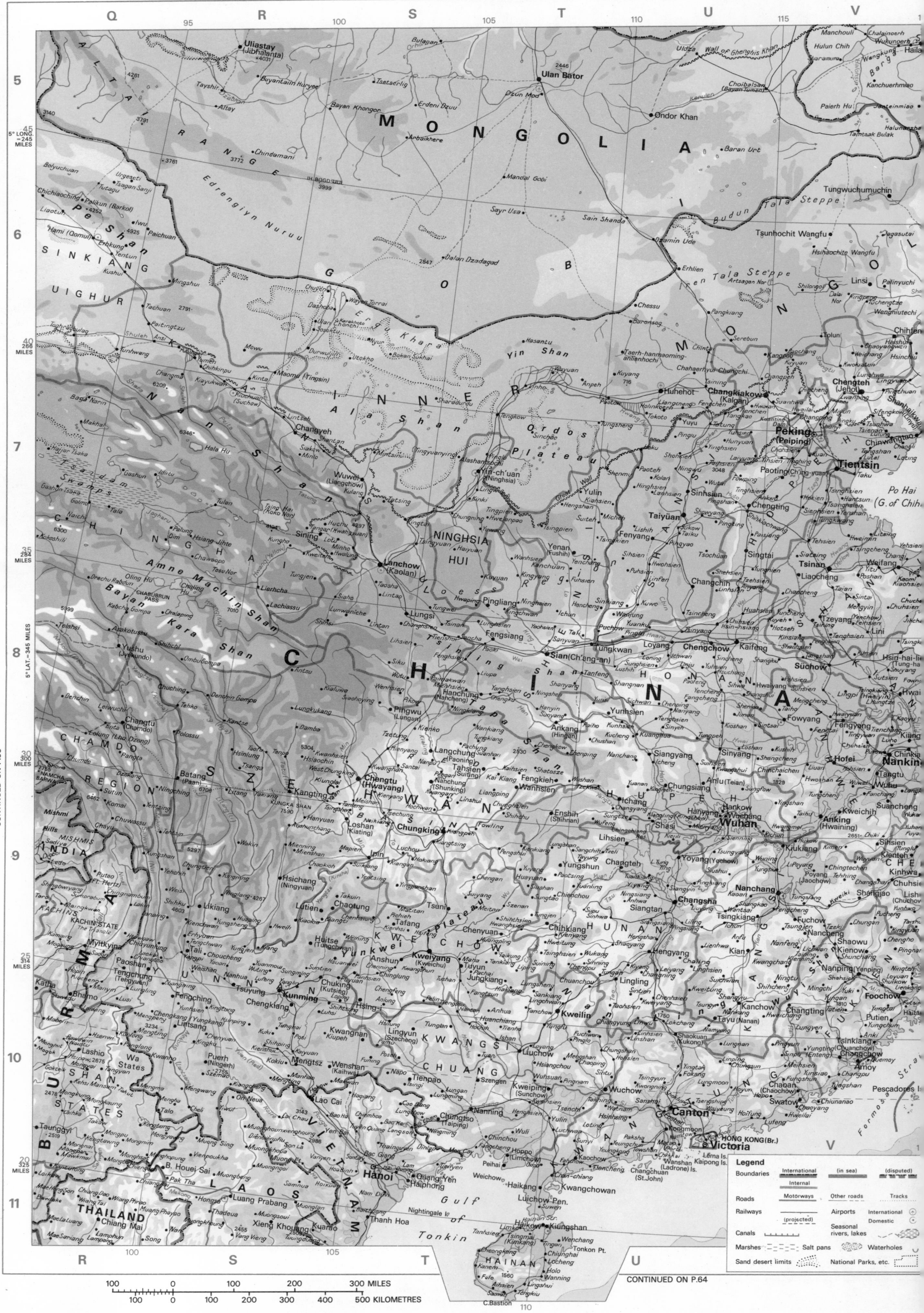

Q   R   S   T   U   V

MONGOLIA

Ulan Bator
Ondor Khan
Baran Urt
Manchouli
Choibalsan (Bayan Tumen)

SINKIANG
UIGHUR

G O B I

Budun Tala Steppe
Iren Tala Steppe

INNER MONGOLIA

Yin Shan
Ala Shan
Ordos Plateau

Hami (Qomul)
Huhehot
Changkiakow (Kalgan)
Chengteh (Jehol)

PEKING (Peiping)
TIENTSIN
Po Hai (G. of Chih)

NINGHSIA HUI

Lanchow (Kaolan)
Taiyüan
Singtai
Tsinan
Weifang

CHINGHAI

Amne Machin Shan
Bayan Kara Shan

Loyang Chengchow Kaifeng
Sian (Ch'ang-an)
HONAN
Suchow

CHINA

Chengtu (Hwayang)
Chungking
Hankow
Wuhan Anking (Hwaining)
Nanking

SZECHWAN

HUPEH

Yoyang (Yochow)
Nanchang
Changsha
HUNAN
CHEKIANG

Kunming
YUNNAN
Kweiyang (Kweichu)
KWEICHOW

Kweilin
KWANGSI CHUANG

Canton
HONG KONG (Br.)
Victoria
Swatow
Amoy
Foochow
FUKIEN
KWANGTUNG

BURMA
SHAN STATES

THAILAND
Chiang Mai

LAOS
Luang Prabang

VIETNAM
Hanoi
Haiphong

Gulf of Tonkin

HAINAN

Pescadores Is.
Formosa Str.

CONTINUED ON P.59
CONTINUED ON P.64

Legend

Boundaries	International	(in sea)	(disputed)
	Internal		
Roads	Motorways	Other roads	Tracks
Railways	(projected)	Airports	International
			Domestic
Canals		Seasonal rivers, lakes	
Marshes		Salt pans	Waterholes
Sand desert limits		National Parks, etc.	

100   0   100   200   300 MILES
100   0   100   200   300   400   500 KILOMETRES

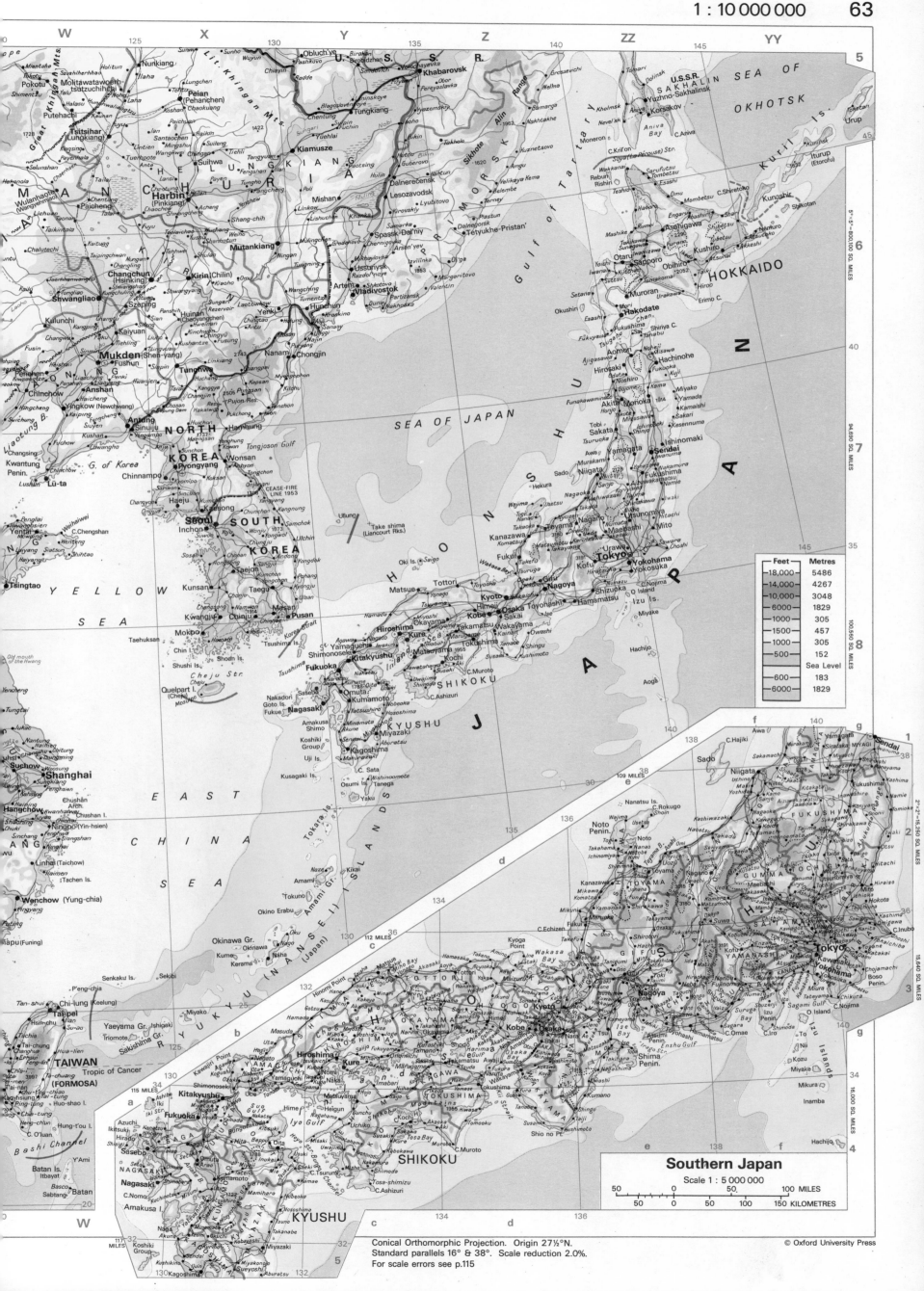

Southern Japan

Scale 1 : 5 000 000

Conical Orthomorphic Projection. Origin 27½°N.
Standard parallels 16° & 38°. Scale reduction 2.0%.
For scale errors see p.115

© Oxford University Press

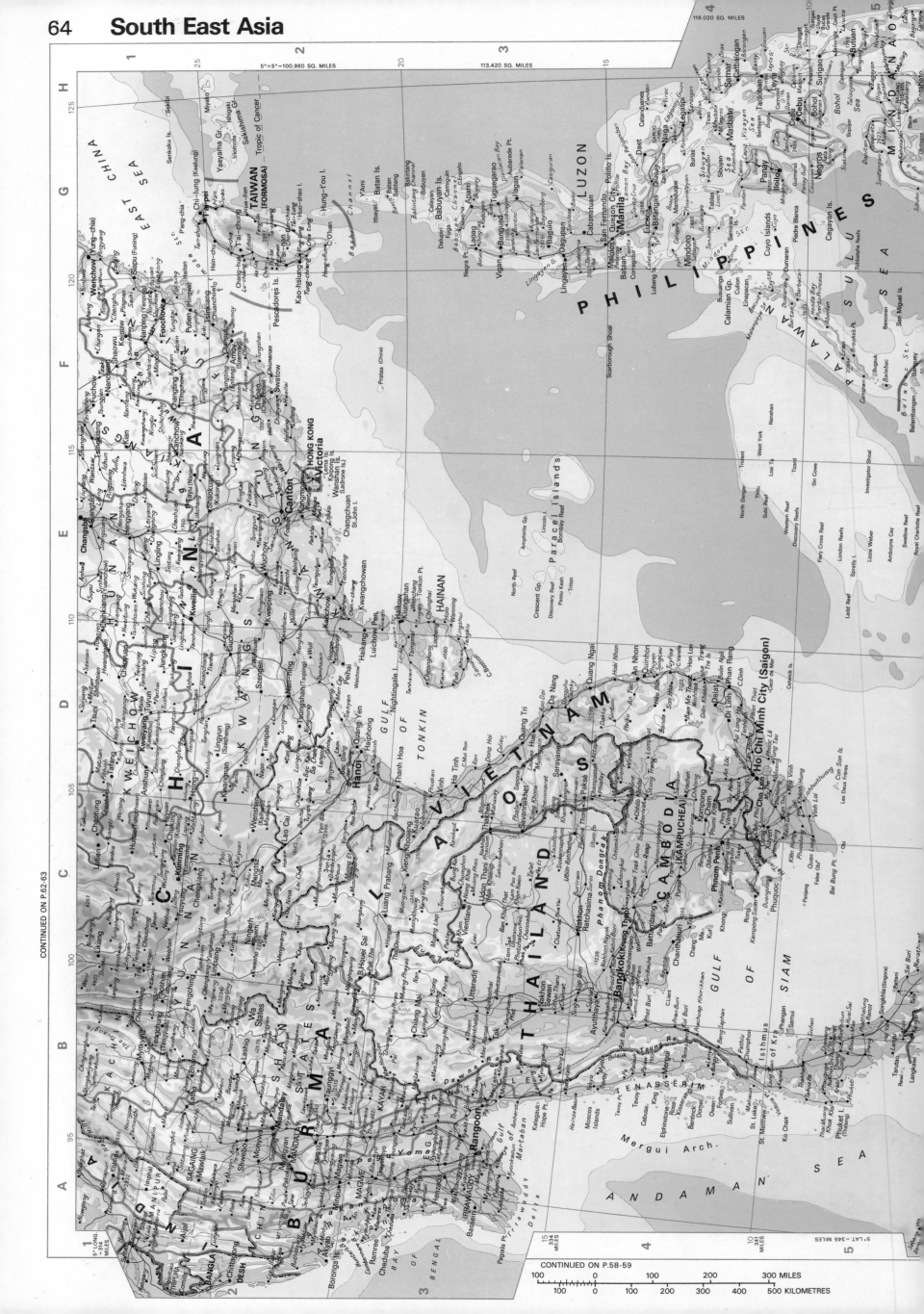

CONTINUED ON P.62-63

CONTINUED ON P.58-59

116,020 SQ. MILES

5°×5°=100,960 SQ. MILES

113,420 SQ. MILES

| 100 | | 100 | 200 | 300 MILES |
| 100 | 0 | 100 | 200 | 300 | 400 | 500 KILOMETRES |

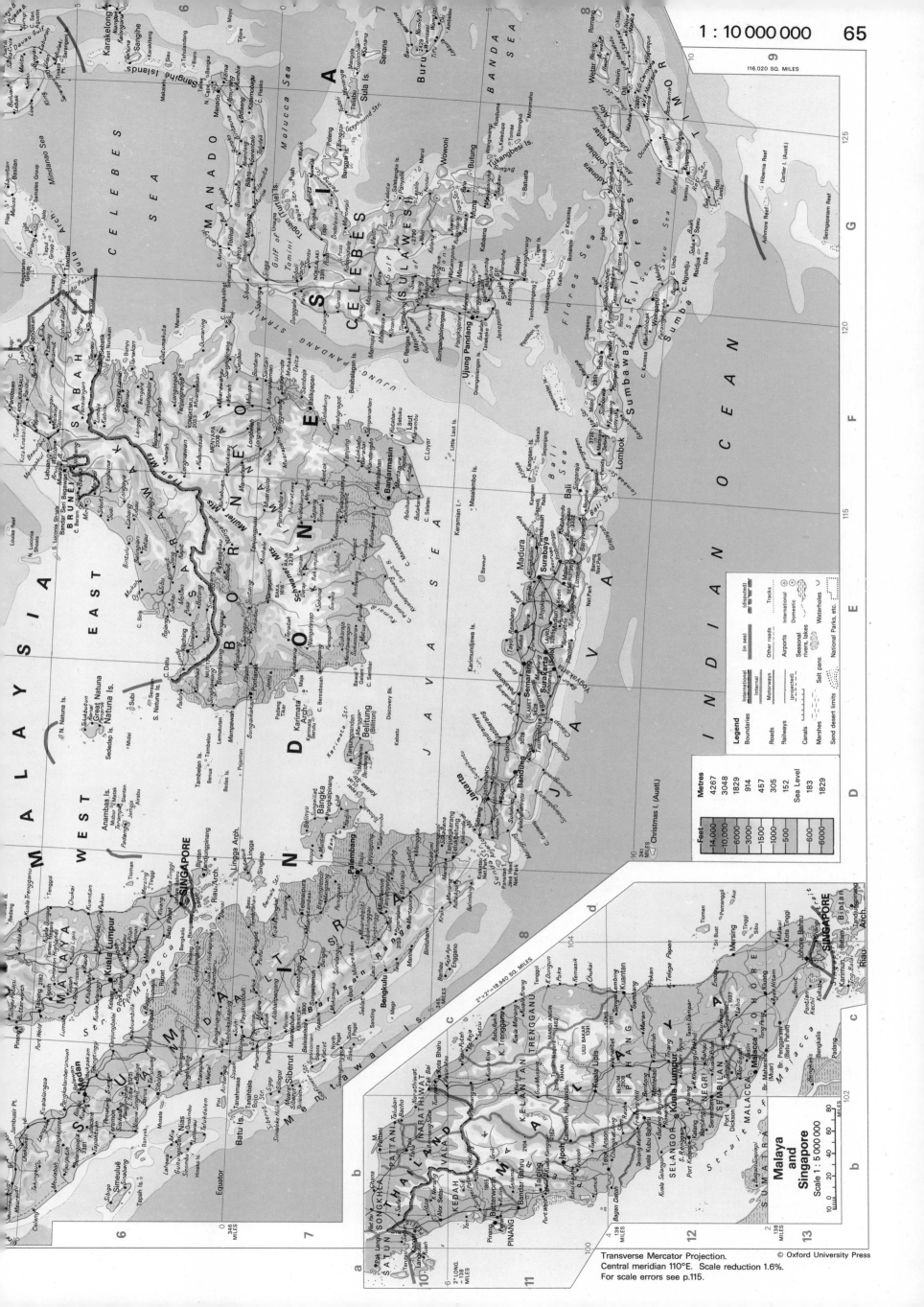

BORNEO (KALIMANTAN)

CELEBES (SULAWESI)

INDONESIA

MOLUCCA SEA

CERAM SEA

BANDA SEA

FLORES SEA

LESSER SUNDA IS.

Sumbawa Flores Sumba Timor Roti

WEST IRIAN

NEW GUINEA

PAPUA NEW GUINEA

BISMARCK ARCHIPELAGO

Nassau Mts. 5030 JAYA PK. Orange Mts.

Port Moresby

Gulf of Papua

ARAFURA SEA

Torres Strait C.York

TIMOR SEA

Melville I.

Bathurst

Darwin

Arnhem Land

Gulf of Carpentaria

Groote Eylandt

Wellesley Is.

Cape York Peninsula

Great Barrier Reef

Cairns

Townsville

INDIAN OCEAN

Joseph Bonaparte Gulf

C.Talbot

Wyndham

C.Leveque

Dampier Land

Derby

Broome

Halls Creek

NORTHERN TERRITORY

Newcastle Waters

Brunette Downs

Tennant Creek

Camooweal

Mount Isa

Cloncurry

Normanton

Croydon

Forsayth

Ingham

QUEENSLAND

Hughenden

Mackay

Proserpine

Great Sandy Desert

Port Hedland Goldsworthy

Dampier Roebourne Marble Bar

Barrow I.

Onslow

Tom Price

WESTERN AUSTRALIA

Gibson Desert

Tropic of Capricorn

Alice Springs

Macdonnell Range

Birdsville

Longreach

Barcaldine

Blackall

Augathella

Charleville

Quilpie

Carnarvon

Wiluna

Great Victoria Desert

SOUTH AUSTRALIA

Lake Eyre

Oodnadatta

Cunnamulla

Meekatharra

Mount Magnet Sandstone

Laverton

Cook

Tarcoola

Mt.Eba Lake Torrens Coondambo

Marree

Lake Frome

Flinders Range

Bourke

NEW SOUTH WALES

Wiluna

Malcolm Menzies

Kalgoorlie

Zanthus

Rawlinna Forrest

Eucla

Great Australian Bight

Ceduna

Lake Gairdner

Port Augusta Quorn

Cockburn Broken Hill

Cobar

Geraldton

Dongara

Mullewa

Southern Cross

Coolgardie

Esperance

Lake Lincoln Port Lincoln

Port Pirie

Peterborough

Wallaroo

Adelaide

Murray Bridge

Mildura

Swan Hill

Orange

Perth Fremantle

Northam

Narrogin

Katanning

Collie

Bunbury

C.Naturaliste

Albany

Recherche Arch.

Kangaroo I.

Bordertown

Horsham

Bendigo

Ballarat

VICTORIA

Melbourne

Geelong

Mt.Gambier

Portland

Warrnambool

Canberra

Albury

Wagga Wagga

Shepparton

Wonthaggi

King I.

Bass Strait

TASMANIA

Launceston

Hobart

Legend

Boundaries	International	(in sea)	(disputed)
	Internal		
Roads	Motorways	Other roads	Tracks
Railways	(projected)	Airports	International / Domestic
Canals		Seasonal rivers, lakes	
Marshes	Salt pans	Waterholes	
Sand desert limits		National Parks, etc.	

Feet	Metres
15,000	4572
10,000	3048
6000	1829
4000	1219
3000	914
2000	610
1000	305
500	152
Sea Level	
Land Deprn.	
600	183
6000	1829

100 0 100 200 300 400 500 MILES

100 0 200 400 600 800 KILOMETRES

P A C I F I C

O C E A N

GILBERT

Butaritari · Little Makin
Abaiang · Marakei
Tarawa
Maiana
Kuria · Abemama
Aranuka

ISLANDS

Ocean I.

Nonouti

Tabiteuea
Onotoa
Tamana · Arorae

Beru · Nikunau

Kingsmill Gr.

British

· NAURU

Tench I.
w Hanover
(vongai)
Kavieng · Tabar Is.
Lihir
Tanga Is.
New Ireland
Feni Is.
Mutiama
Kokopo
Bugumai
Green Is.

Lyra Reef

Nuguria Gr.

Nukumanu Is.

Nanomea

Buka
Sohano
Bougainville

Ontong Java Is.
or Lord Howe Atoll

Nanumanga · Niutao

TUVALU

Nui

Vaitupu

Nukufetau
Funafuti

Nukulailai

Kieta
Mawarena
Buin

Choiseul
Kimbatana

SOLOMON

usancay Is.
Trobriand Is.
Losuia
Kiriwina
Kulumadau
odenough
Fergusson
Woodlark I.
Laughlan Is.
D'Entrecasteaux Is.
Normanby I.
Basilaki
Samarai
Louisiade Arch.
Tagula
Rossel I.
Misima

Shortland Is.
Treasury Is.
(Mono Is.)
Vella Lavella
Ganongga
Kolombangara
New Georgia
Rendova
Vangunu
Russell Is.
Honiara
Guadalcanal

Santa Isabel

Stewart Is.

Florida Is.
Auki
Aola
Malaita
Ulawa

ISLANDS

Kira Kira
San Cristobal

Bellona

Rennell I.

Swallow Gr.
Duff Is.
Ndeni
Santa Cruz Is.
Utupua
Vanikoro · Peu
Tikopia

Cherry I.
(Anuda)
Mitre I.
(Fataka)

Rotuma

France

Nurakita

Indispensable Reefs

C O R A L

Willis Islets

inga Is.
Lihou Reef

Marion Reef

Mellish Reef

S E A

Torres Is.
Banks
Vanua Lava
Coso Lava
Santa Maria
Pellier
Espíritu Santo
Luganville
Oba (Maewo)
Aurora (Maewo)
Olpoin Dui
Pentecost
Malekula
Lamap
Ambrim
Lamenu
Epi
Ambrim

NEW HEBRIDES

France

Wallis Is. Uvea

Futuna · Horn Is.
Alofi

FIJI

Vanua Levu
Lombasa
Yasawa Gr.
Lautoka · Tavua
Viti Levu · Wandi
Vatulele

Taveuni
Korb
Ovalau
Suva · Ngau
Mbengga

Vanua Mbalavu

Niuafou

d'Entrecasteaux Reefs

Petrie Reef

Frederick Reef
Kenn Reef

Saumerez Reef

Wreck Reef

Avon I.
Sandy I.
Chesterfield Is.
Long I.

Bellona
Reefs

Fairway Reef

1628
Kone

Pegoumenes
Gatcha
Uvéa
Ponerihouen

d'Entrecasteaux Reefs

Efate
Vila

Eromanga

Tenakel
Tana

Aneityum

Moala
Kandavu
Matuku
Totoya
Lakemba
Kambara
Fulanga

Lau Group

Koro Sea

Vatoa

Ono-i-lau

Vavau Gr.
· Neiafu

Tofua
Haapai Gr.

T O N G A

Cato I.

**NEW
CALEDONIA**

Art I.

Nobut
Kutupari
Maré
Lifu
Uvéa

LOYALTY IS.

Noumea
I. des Pins
Walpole

Matthew I.
Hunter I.

Conway Reef

Nukualofa
Tongatapu
Eua

Ata

Tropic of Capricorn

Minerva Reefs

Rockhampton
Gladstone
Bundaberg
Maryborough
Gympie
Great Sandy I.

oowoomba
Brisbane
Ipswich
Warwick
Lismore
verell
Glen Innes
Grafton
Armidale
Coff's Harbour
Tamworth
Kempsey
Taree
Muswellbrook
Maitland
Newcastle
ithgow
Cessnock
Sydney
oomba
Wollongong

Middleton Reef

Elizabeth Reef

Norfolk I.

Lord Howe I.
Ball's Pyramid

New Zealand

Australia

T A S M A N

S E A

Kermadec Is.
France

Raoul I.

Macauley I.
Curtis I.

L'Esperance Rock

Three Kings Is.

Kaitaia
Dargaville · Whangarei

Auckland
Pukekohe
Hamilton
Thames
Tauranga
Whakatane
Rotorua

NORTH ISLAND

New Plymouth
Hawera
Wanganui
Palmerston
North
Napier
Hastings
Gisborne

SOUTH ISLAND

Westport
Nelson
Mabueka
Wellington

Greymouth
SOUTHERN ALPS

NEW

Christchurch

Queenstown
Timaru

Oamaru

Invercargill
Gore
Dunedin

Stewart I.

ZEALAND

Chatham Is.

Waitangi

Zenithal Equidistant Projection.
Origin 22°S, 150°E. For scale errors see p.115.

© Oxford University Press

5"×5"=118,600 SQ. MILES
117,770 SQ. MILES
118,020 SQ. MILES
113,420 SQ. MILES
109,960 SQ. MILES
105,660 SQ. MILES
100,560 SQ. MILES
94,690 SQ. MILES

CONTINUED ON P.65

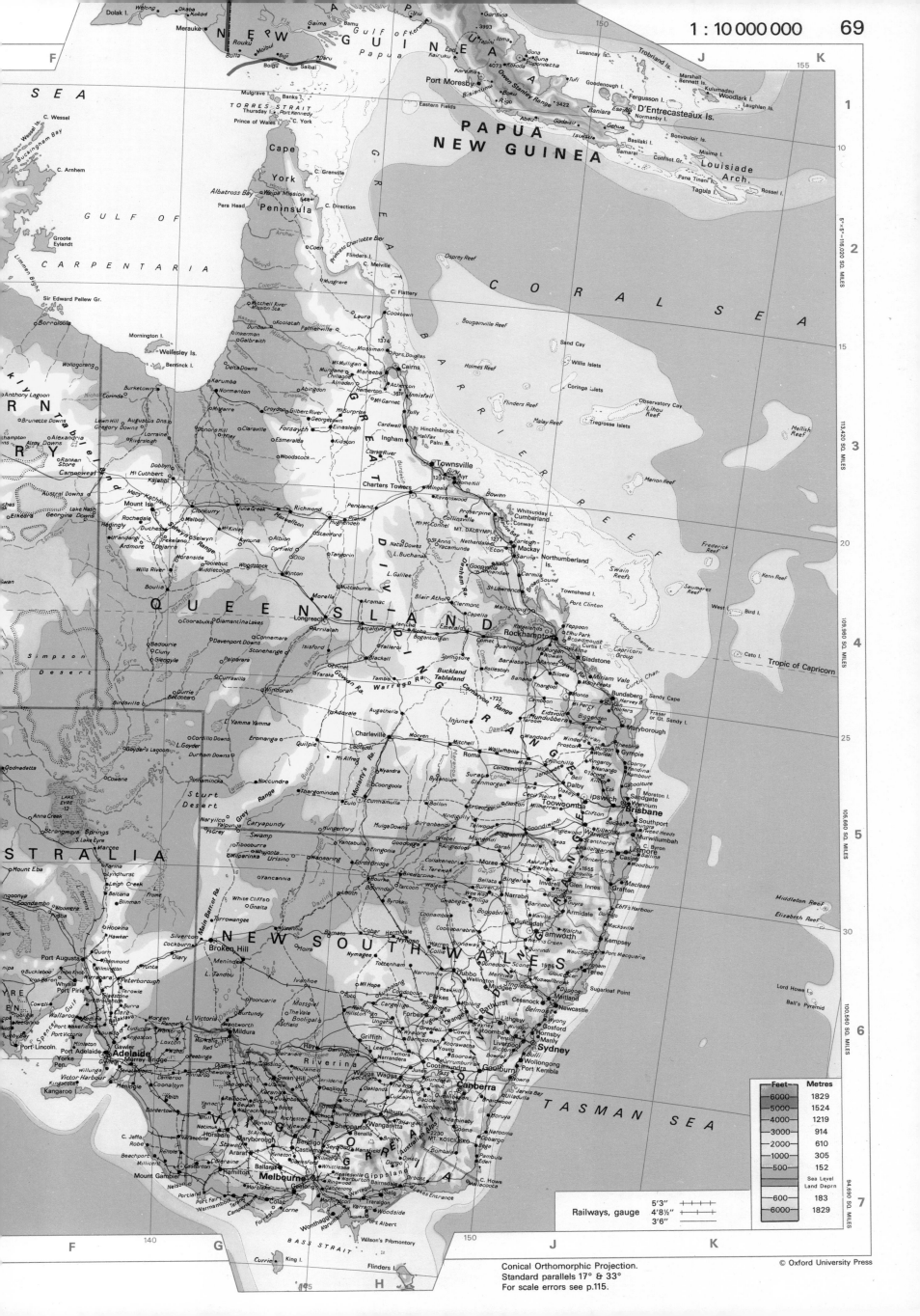

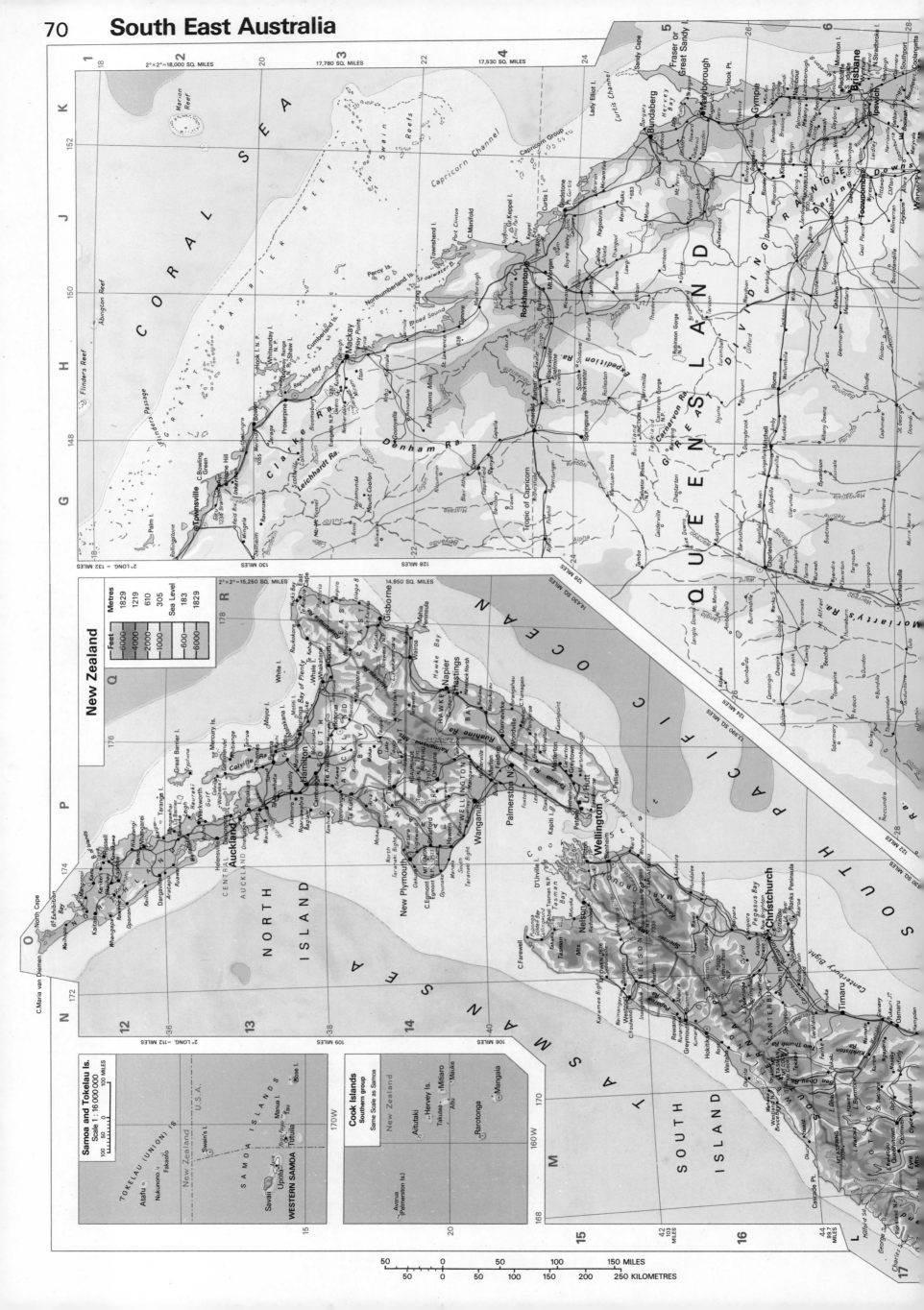

New Zealand

Feet	Metres
6000	1829
4000	1219
2000	610
1000	305
Sea Level	
600	183
6000	1829

2°×2°=15,250 SQ. MILES   14,850 SQ. MILES

Samoa and Tokelau Is.
Scale 1:16 000 000

Cook Islands
Southern group
Same Scale as Samoa

50   0   50   100   150 MILES
50   0   50   100   150   200   250 KILOMETRES

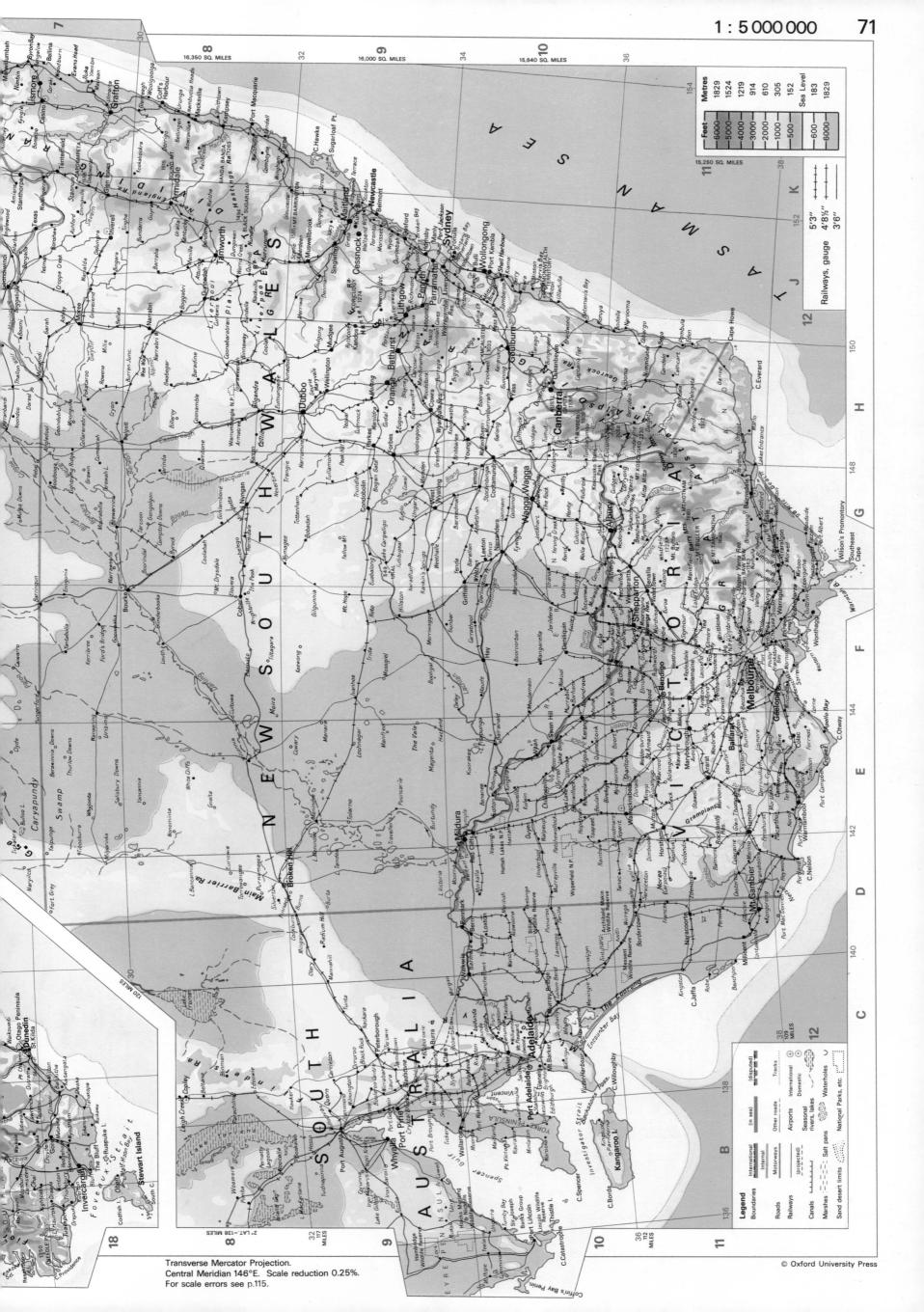

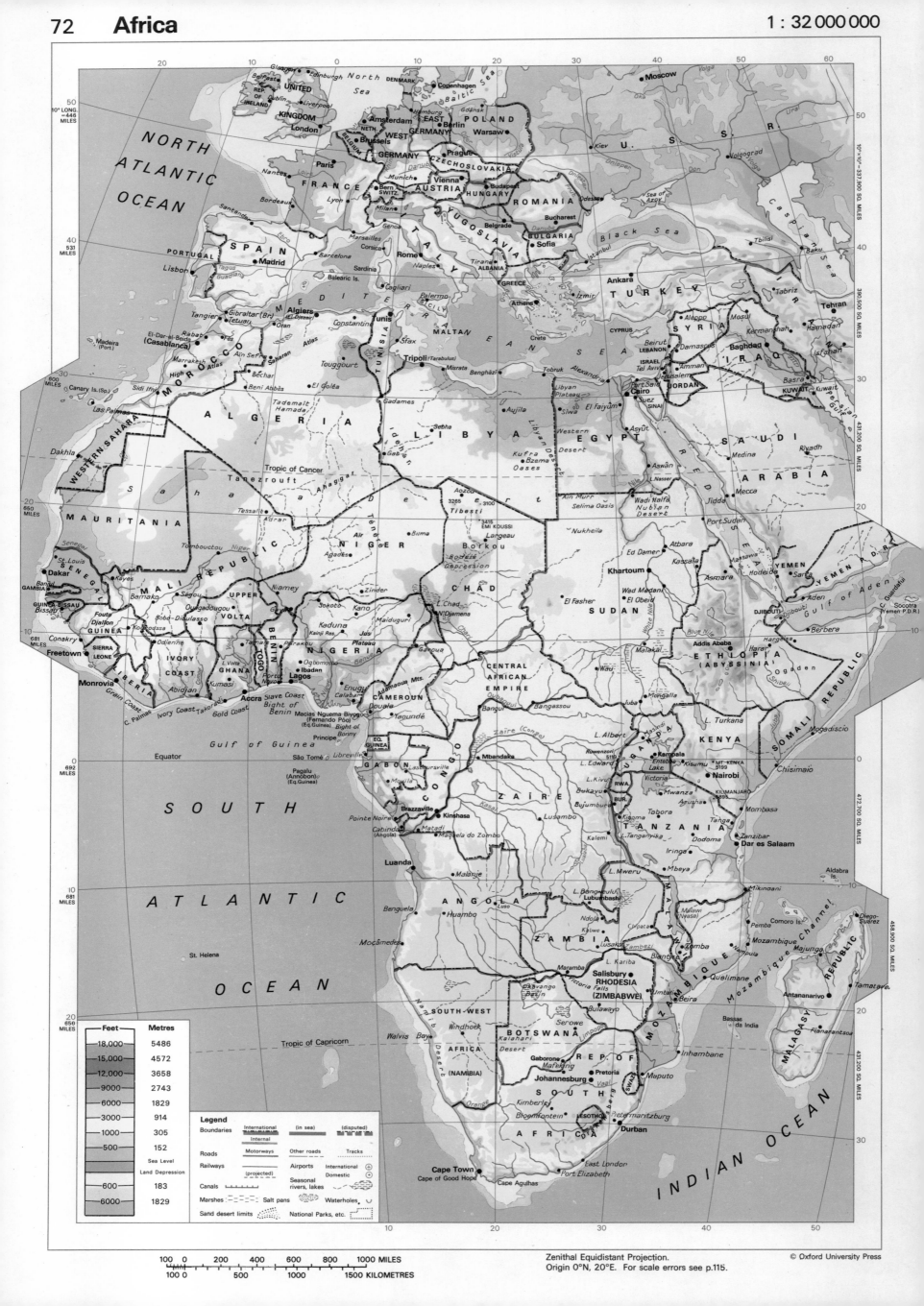

Zenithal Equidistant Projection.
Origin 0°N, 20°E. For scale errors see p.115.

© Oxford University Press

NIGERIA
CHAD
CAMEROUN
CENTRAL AFRICAN EMPIRE
SUDAN
ETHIOPIA (ABYSSINIA)
Addis Ababa
EQUATORIAL GUINEA
GABON
CONGO
Brazzaville
Kinshasa
ZAIRE
HAUT-ZAIRE
UGANDA
Kampala
Entebbe
KENYA
Nairobi
Equator
RWANDA
BURUNDI
KIVU
LAKE VICTORIA
KASAI ORIENTAL
KASAI OCCIDENTAL
BANDUNDU
TANZANIA
Dar es Salaam
ZANZIBAR
SHABA
Lubumbashi
L. TANGANYIKA
LAKE MALAWI (NYASA)
ANGOLA
Luanda
CABINDA
BAS ZAIRE
UIGE
MALANJE
LUNDA
KUANZA NORTE
KUANZA SUL
BENGUELA
HUAMBO
BIÉ
HUILA
CUNENE
CUANDO
CUBANGO
MOXICO
ZAMBIA
Lusaka
MALAWI
MOZAMBIQUE
RHODESIA
ZIMBABWE
Salisbury
Bulawayo
SOUTH-WEST AFRICA (NAMIBIA)
Windhoek
Walvis Bay
Tropic of Capricorn
KALAHARI DESERT
BOTSWANA
Gaborone
Pretoria
Johannesburg
TRANSVAAL
REP. OF SOUTH AFRICA
SWAZILAND
Maputo
NATAL
Durban
Pietermaritzburg
LESOTHO
Maseru
ORANGE FREE STATE
Bloemfontein
CAPE PROVINCE
TRANSKEI
Cape Town
Cape of Good Hope
Port Elizabeth
East London
ATLANTIC OCEAN
INDIAN OCEAN
MOZAMBIQUE CHANNEL

MADAGASCAR (MALAGASY REP.)
Antananarivo
TANANARIVE
Diego-Suarez
DIEGO SUAREZ
MAJUNGA
FIANARANTSOA
Same Scale

Feet	Metres
12,000	3658
9000	2743
7000	2134
5000	1524
3000	914
1000	305
500	152
Sea Level	
600	183
6000	1829

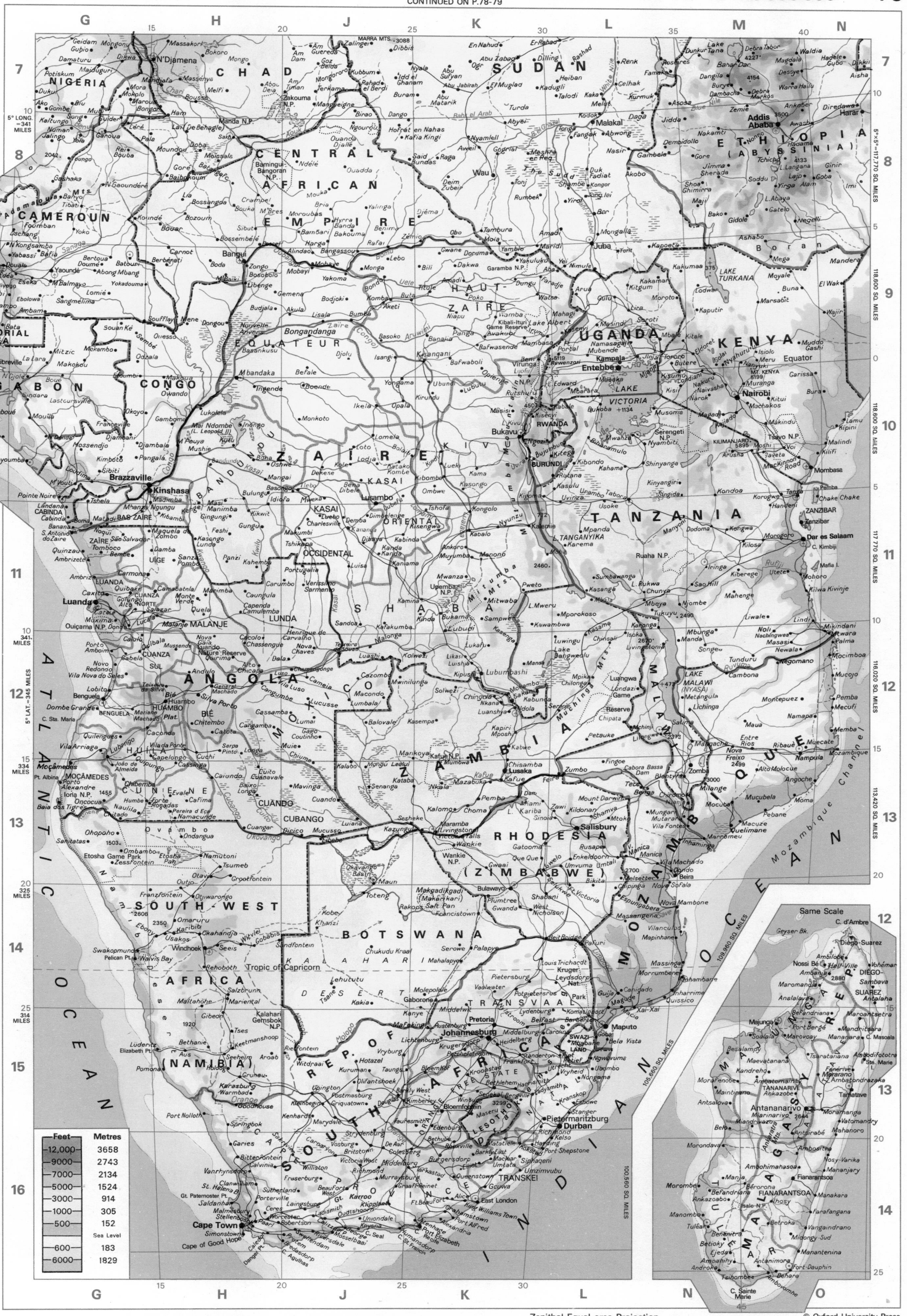

100 0 100 200 300 400 500 MILES
100 0 200 400 600 800 KILOMETRES

Zenithal Equal-area Projection.
Origin 15°N, 20°E. For scale errors see p.115.

© Oxford University Press

Rand Goldfields
Scale 1 : 1 000 000

Feet	Metres
6000	1829
5500	1676
5000	1524
4500	1372
4000	1219

5 0 5 10 15 MILES

SOUTH-WEST AFRICA (NAMIBIA)

BOTSWANA

KALAHARI DESERT

KGALAGADI

Windhoek

Krugersdorp JOHANNESBURG Germiston Boksburg Benoni Springs Brakpan Kempton Park Randfontein Roodepoort Florida Maraisburg Carletonville Dunnottar Nigel Heidelberg

Cape Town

CAPE PROVINCE

Cape Town

Scale 1 : 400 000

Feet	Metres
3000	914
2500	762
2000	610
1500	457
1000	305
500	152
S/L	S/L
100	30

0 2 4 6 MLS.

Table Mountain

Cape of Good Hope

Tropic of Capricorn

Worcester Paarl Stellenbosch Oudtshoorn George Mossel Bay Beaufort West Victoria West

20 10 0 20 40 60 80 100 120 140 MILES
20 0 20 40 60 80 100 120 140 160 180 200 220 KILOMETRES

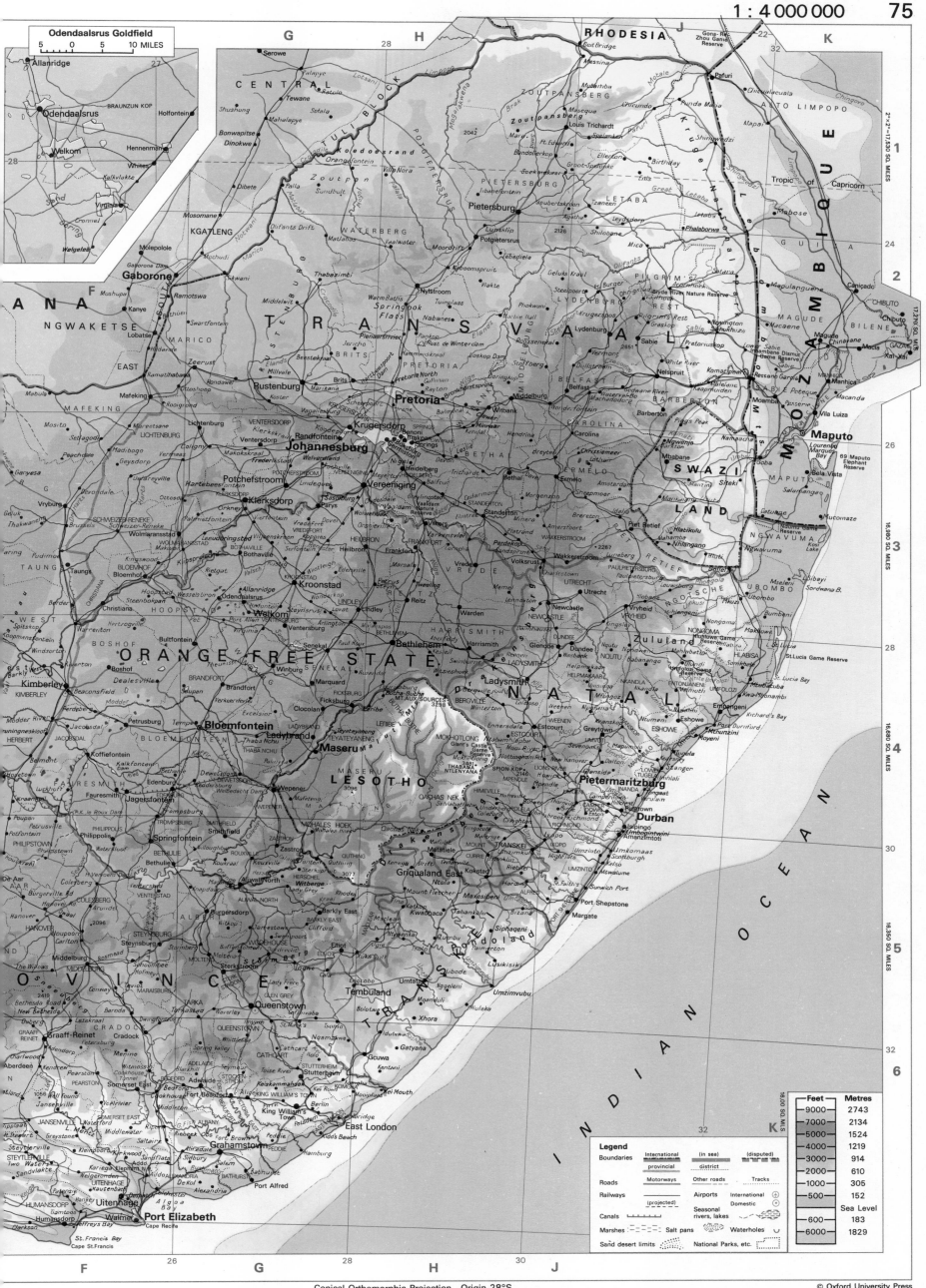

Odendaalsrus Goldfield

5   0   5   10 MILES

RHODESIA

CENTRAL

TRANSVAAL

ZOUTPANSBERG

Pietersburg

Gaborone

NGWAKETSE

KGATLENG

MOZAMBIQUE

Pretoria

Johannesburg

Krugersdorp

Vereeniging

Klerksdorp

Potchefstroom

Maputo

SWAZILAND

ORANGE FREE STATE

Kroonstad

Welkom

Kimberley

Bloemfontein

Maseru

Ladybrand

LESOTHO

Ladysmith

NATAL

Pietermaritzburg

Durban

TRANSKEI

Griqualand East

Tembuland

Queenstown

Graaff-Reinet

Uitenhage

Port Elizabeth

East London

Grahamstown

INDIAN OCEAN

Legend

Boundaries	International	(in sea)	(disputed)
	provincial	district	
Roads	Motorways	Other roads	Tracks
Railways	(projected)	Airports	International
			Domestic
Canals		Seasonal rivers, lakes	
Marshes		Salt pans	Waterholes
Sand desert limits		National Parks, etc.	

Feet	Metres
9000	2743
7000	2134
5000	1524
4000	1219
3000	914
2000	610
1000	305
500	152
Sea Level	
600	183
6000	1829

Conical Orthomorphic Projection. Origin 28°S.
Standard parallels 24° & 32°. Scale reduction 0.25%.
For scale errors see p.115.

© Oxford University Press

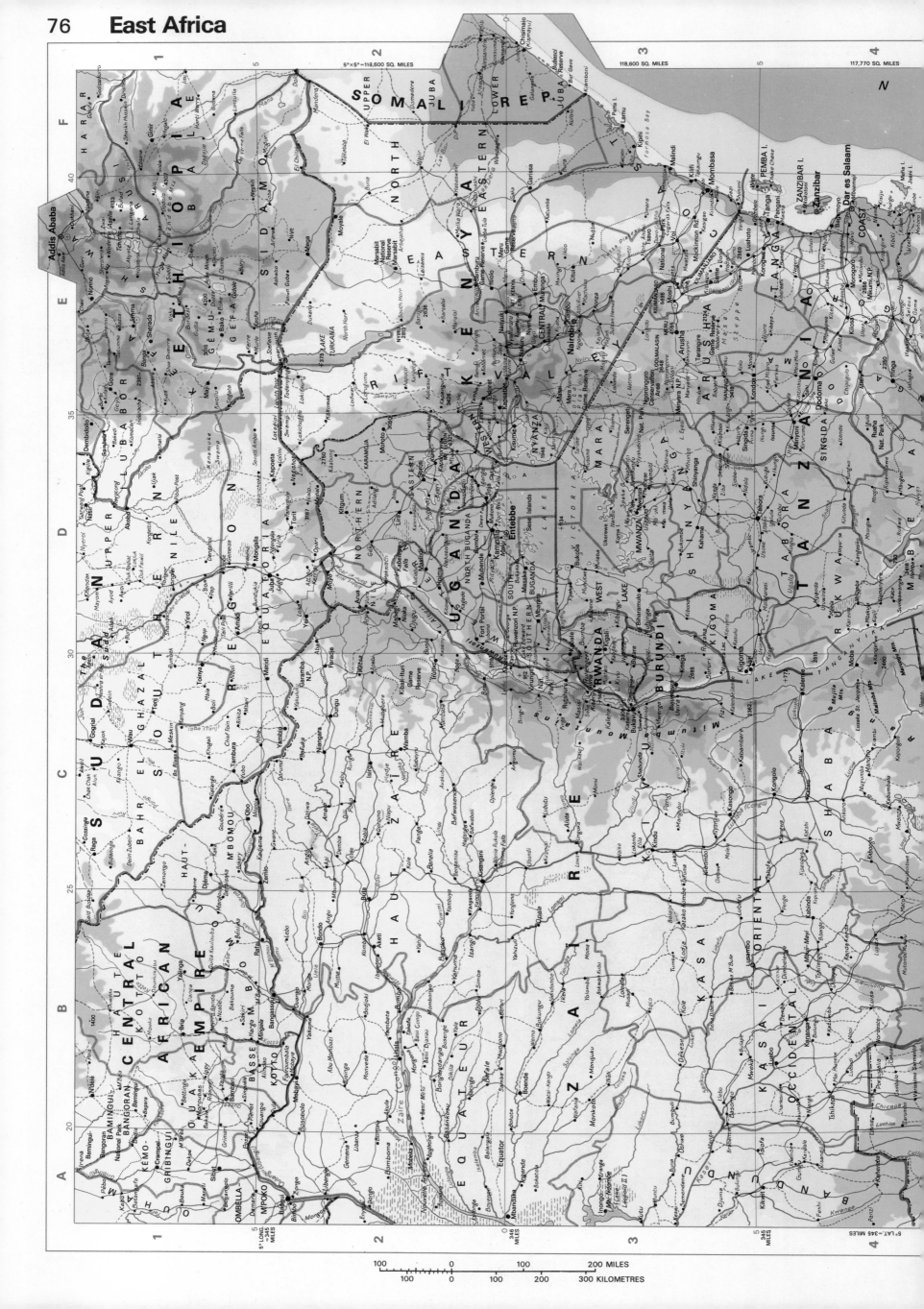

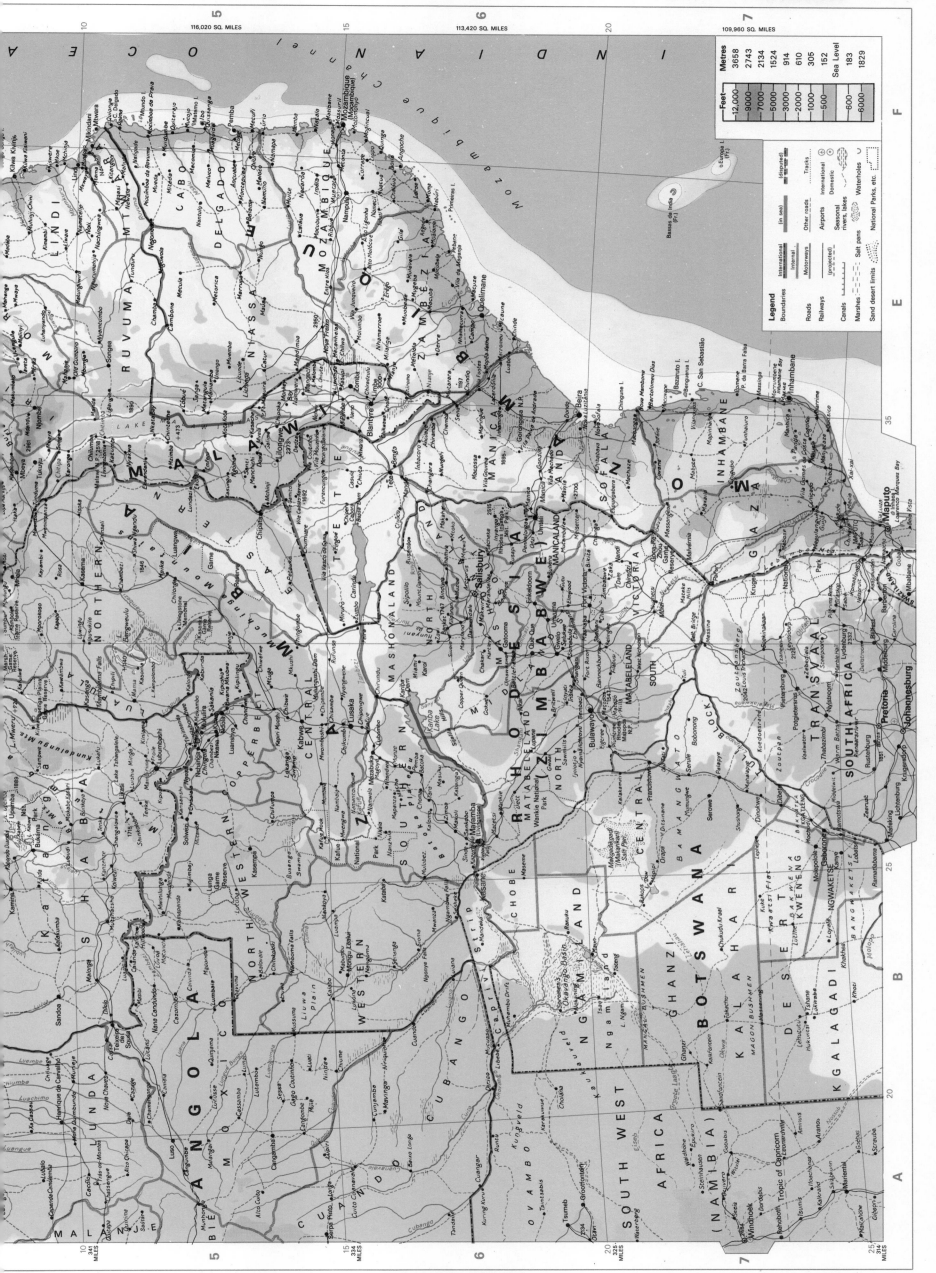

Transverse Mercator Projection.
Central meridian 30°E. Scale reduction 0.8%.
For scale errors see p.115.

© Oxford University Press

Azores (Portugal) Same Scale

Corvo, Flores, Graciosa, São Jorge, Terceira, Fayal, Pico, Horta, Angra Jo Heroismo, São Miguel, Ponta Delgada, Formigas, Santa Maria

ATLANTIC OCEAN

MADEIRA (Portugal), Funchal, Porto Santo, Desertas

CANARY ISLANDS (Spain), La Palma, Tenerife, Gomera, Hierro, Santa Cruz, Las Palmas, Gran Canaria, Fuerteventura, Lanzarote, Alegranza

5° LONG. = 300 MILES
5° LAT. = 345 MILES

SPAIN — Madrid, Lisbon, Oporto, Coimbra, Valladolid, Salamanca, Badajoz, Sevilla, Cádiz, Málaga, Granada, Murcia, Valencia, Barcelona, Zaragoza, Pamplona, Toledo, Córdoba, Gibraltar (Br.), Ceuta (Sp.), Tangier, Tetuan

PORTUGAL — Lisbon, Faro

FRANCE — Marseilles, Toulon, Nice, Turin, Milan, Genoa, Venice, Rome, Naples

CORSICA, SARDINIA, SICILY, MALTA, ITALY, YUGOSLAVIA, ALBANIA

MEDITERRANEAN SEA, Tyrrhenian Sea, Ionian Sea

MOROCCO — Rabat, Fès, Meknès, Casablanca, Marrakech, Agadir, Essaouira, Safi, High Atlas, Middle Atlas, Anti Atlas

ALGERIA — Algiers, Oran, Constantine, Mostaganem, Tlemcen, Biskra, Laghouat, Ghardaïa, Touggourt, El Oued, Saharan Atlas, Great Western Erg, Great Eastern Erg

TUNIS, TUNISIA, Sfax, Sousse, Kerkenna Is., Djerba Is., Gabès, Medenine

TRIPOLI, LIBYA, Misurata, Homs, Nalut, AL-JABAL AL-GHARBI, MISURATA

Tropic of Cancer

WESTERN SAHARA, Dakhla, C. Bojador, El Aaiún, Tarfaya

MAURITANIA — Nouadhibou, Nouakchott, Atar, TIRIS ZEMMOUR, INCHIRI, TRARZA, BRAKNA, TAGANT, HODH OCCIDENTAL, HODH ORIENTAL, ADRAR, ASSÀBA

SAHARA, SAHARA DESERT, Hoggar, Ahaggar, Tahat 3005, TASSILI, Tibesti, TIBESTI, EMI KOUSSI, BORKOU-ENNEDI, Djado Plateau

SENEGAL — Dakar, St Louis, Thiès, Kaolack, GAMBIA, Banjul, GUINEA-BISSAU, Bissau

MALI — Bamako, Tombouctou, Gao, Kayes, Ségou, Mopti, Nioro

GUINEA — Conakry, Kankan, Fouta Djalon Mts.

SIERRA LEONE — Freetown, Bo, Makeni

LIBERIA — Monrovia, Buchanan, Grain Coast

IVORY COAST — Abidjan, Bouaké, Man

UPPER VOLTA — Ouagadougou, Bobo Dioulasso, SIKASSO

GHANA — Accra, Kumasi, Tamale, Gold Coast

TOGO, BENIN, NIGER — Niamey, Maradi, Zinder, Tahoua, AGADÈS, Aïr, TAHOUA, ZINDER, DIFFA

NIGERIA — Lagos, Ibadan, Abuja, Kaduna, Kano, Sokoto, Maiduguri, Benin City, Enugu, Calabar, Ilorin, Abeokuta, Oshogbo, Zaria

CHAD — N'Djamena, KANEM, BATHA, GUÉRA, MOYEN CHARI, Lake Chad, BAGUIRMI

CAMEROUN — Yaoundé, Douala, Bamenda, Foumban

EQUATORIAL GUINEA — Bata, Malabo, Macias Nguema Biyogo (Fernando Poo), Pagalu (Annobon) (Eq. Guinea)

São Tomé, Principe, GABON — Libreville, CONGO, CENTRAL, Bangui

GULF OF GUINEA, Bight of Benin, Bight of Bonny, Slave Coast

Cape Verde Islands Same Scale — São Vicente, São Nicolau, Sal, Boa Vista, Santa Maria, São Tiago, Praia, Fogo, Brava, Maio, Porto Grande

Legend

Boundaries	International	(in sea)	(disputed)
	Internal		
Roads	Motorways	Other roads	Tracks
Railways	(projected)	Airports	International, Domestic
Canals		Seasonal rivers, lakes	
Marshes		Salt pans	
Sand desert limits		Waterholes	
		National Parks, etc.	

100 0 100 200 300 400 500 MILES
100 0 200 400 600 800 KILOMETRES

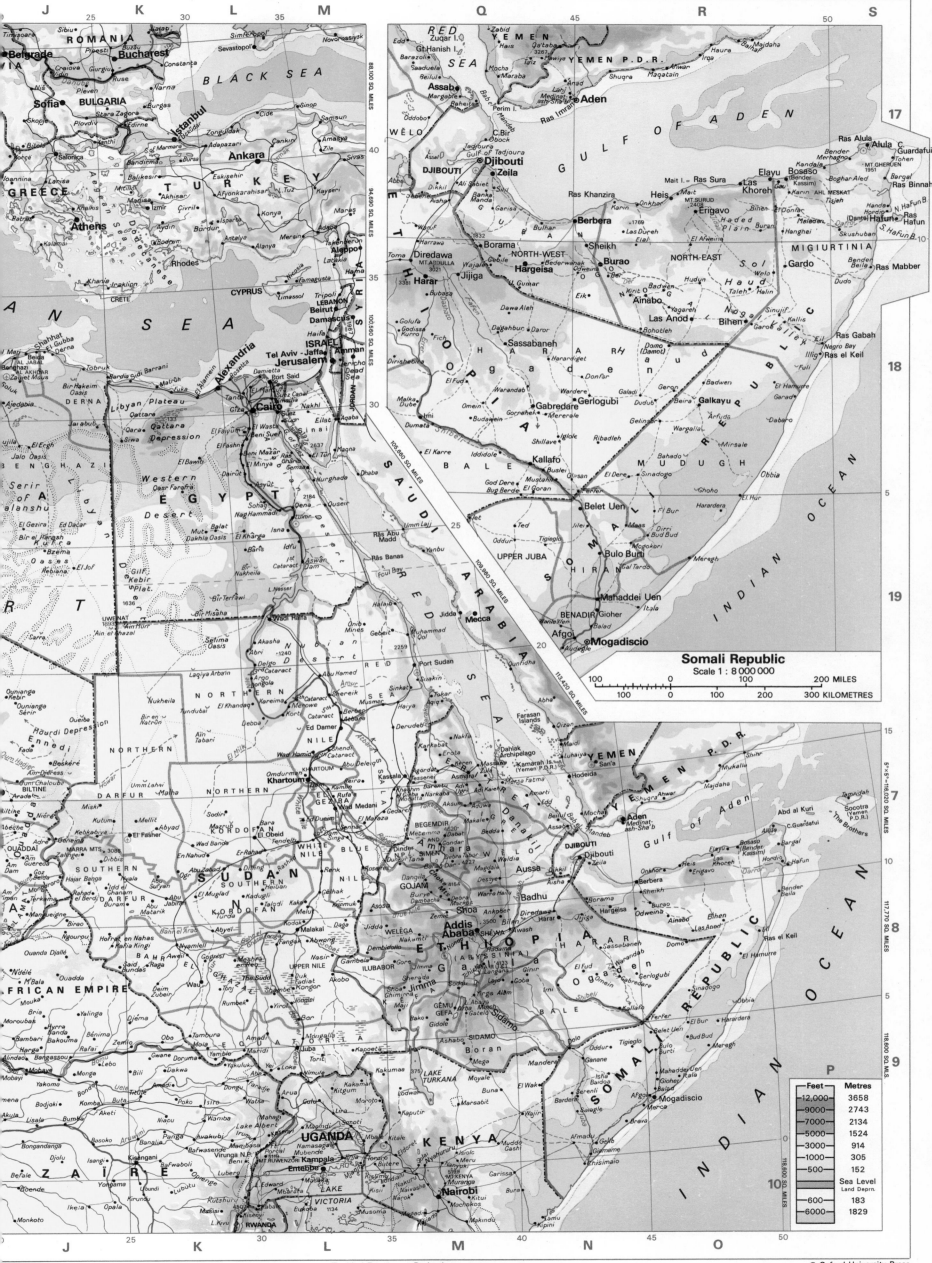

N P.73

Zenithal Equal-area Projection.
Origin 15°N, 20°E. For scale errors see p.115.

© Oxford University Press

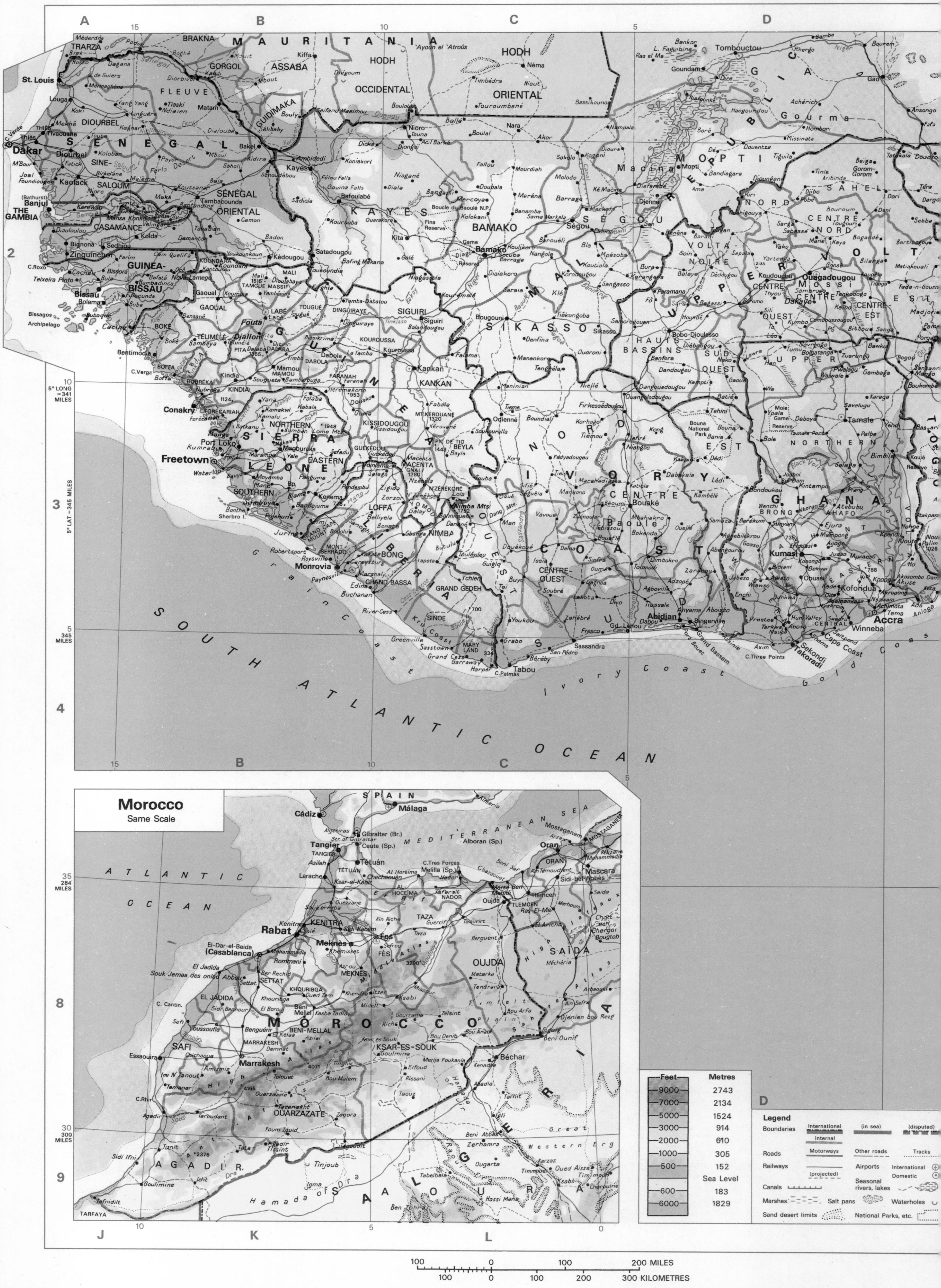

MAURITANIA
SENEGAL
THE GAMBIA
GUINEA-BISSAU
GUINEA
SIERRA LEONE
LIBERIA
IVORY COAST
MALI
UPPER VOLTA
GHANA
St. Louis
Dakar
Banjul
Bissau
Conakry
Freetown
Monrovia
Abidjan
Accra
Bamako
Ouagadougou
Kumasi
Tombouctou
SOUTH ATLANTIC OCEAN
Grain Coast
Ivory Coast
Gold Coast
Morocco
Same Scale
SPAIN
MEDITERRANEAN SEA
ATLANTIC OCEAN
MOROCCO
ALGERIA
Rabat
Tangier
Fès
Marrakesh
Casablanca
Feet
Metres
9000 2743
7000 2134
5000 1524
3000 914
2000 610
1000 305
500 152
Sea Level
600 183
6000 1829
Legend
Boundaries
International
(in sea)
(disputed)
Internal
Roads
Motorways
Other roads
Tracks
Railways
(projected)
Airports
International
Domestic
Canals
Seasonal rivers, lakes
Marshes
Salt pans
Waterholes
Sand desert limits
National Parks, etc.
100 0 100 200 MILES
100 0 100 200 300 KILOMETRES

CONTINUED ON P.76

Conical Orthomorphic Projection. Origin 6°N.
Standard parallels 1°S. & 13°N. Scale reduction 0.8%.
For scale errors see p.115.

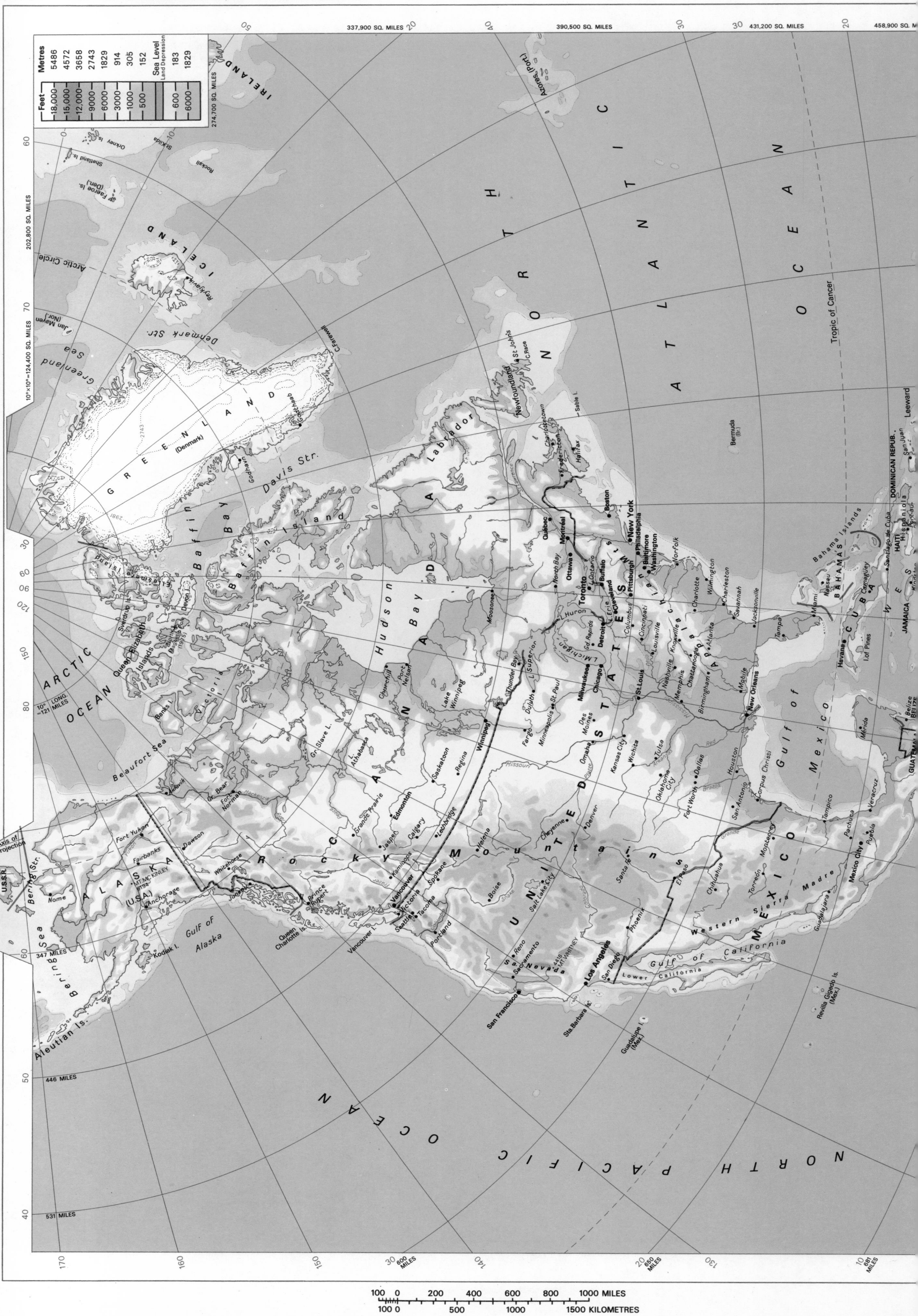

Feet	Metres
18,000	5486
15,000	4572
12,000	3658
9000	2743
6000	1829
3000	914
1000	305
500	152
Sea Level	
Land Depression	
600	183
6000	1829

337,900 SQ. MILES   390,500 SQ. MILES   431,200 SQ. MILES   458,900 SQ. MILES

274,700 SQ. MILES

202,800 SQ. MILES

10⁶×10⁶×124,400 SQ. MILES

IRELAND

Azores (Port.)

NORTH ATLANTIC OCEAN

Tropic of Cancer

Arctic Circle

Orkney Is.
Shetland Is.
St Kilda
Rockall
Faeroe Is.
Jan Mayen (Nor.)

ICELAND
Reykjavik

Denmark Str.
Greenland Sea

GREENLAND
(Denmark)
Godthåb
2743
1862

Davis Str.

Baffin Bay
Baffin Island
Ellesmere Is.
Devon I.
Queen Elizabeth Islands
Sverdrup Is.
Banks I.
Victoria
Gr. Bear L.

ARCTIC OCEAN

Beaufort Sea

Labrador

Hudson Bay

Newfoundland
St John's
C. Race
Sable I.
Halifax
Frederickton
Charlottetown

Bermuda (Br.)

Boston
New York
Philadelphia
Baltimore
Washington
Norfolk

Quebec
Montreal
Ottawa
North Bay
Toronto
L. Ontario
Buffalo
Pittsburgh
Cleveland
Detroit
L. Erie
L. Huron
L. Michigan
Columbus
Cincinnati
Louisville
Nashville
Knoxville
Charlotte
Wilmington
Charleston
Savannah
Jacksonville

CANADA
Moosonee
Churchill
Nelson
Lake Winnipeg
Gr. Slave L.
Athabasca
Fort Norman
Fort Yukon
Dawson
Whitehorse

UNITED STATES

St Louis
Memphis
Chattanooga
Birmingham
Atlanta
Mobile
New Orleans
Tampa
Miami

BAHAMA'S
Nassau
I. of Pines
CUBA
Havana
Santiago de Cuba
JAMAICA
HAITI
Hispaniola
DOMINICAN REPUB.
San Juan
Leeward

Gulf of Mexico

Milwaukee
Chicago
Duluth
Thunder Bay
L. Superior
Fargo
Minneapolis
St Paul
Des Moines
Omaha
Kansas City
Wichita
Tulsa
Oklahoma City
Dallas
Fort Worth
Houston
San Antonio
Corpus Christi
Brownsville
Monterrey
Tampico
Mexico City
Veracruz
Puebla
Pachuca
Guadalajara
Torreón
Chihuahua
El Paso
Santa Fe
Phoenix
Denver
Cheyenne
Salt Lake City
Helena
Boise
Spokane
Portland
Seattle
Tacoma
Victoria
Vancouver
Prince Rupert
Queen Charlotte Is.
Kamloops
Calgary
Edmonton
Lethbridge
Jasper
Prince George
Saskatoon
Regina
Winnipeg
Red Deer

Missouri
Red
Rio Grande
Brazos

ROCKY MOUNTAINS

Reno
Sacramento
San Francisco
Sta Barbara
Los Angeles
San Diego
Mt Whitney

Nevada

MEXICO
Western Sierra Madre
Gulf of California
Lower California

Guadalupe (Mex.)
Revilla Gigedo Is. (Mex.)

GUATEMALA
Belize
Mérida

ALASKA (USA)
Mt McKINLEY
Fairbanks
Anchorage
Nome
Kodiak I.
Gulf of Alaska
Juneau

Bering Sea
Bering Str.
U.S.S.R.
Aleutian Is.

Axis of projection

NORTH PACIFIC OCEAN

10° LONG. 121 MILES
347 MILES
446 MILES
531 MILES

| 100 | 0 | 200 | 400 | 600 | 800 | 1000 MILES |
| 100 | 0 | | 500 | | 1000 | 1500 KILOMETRES |

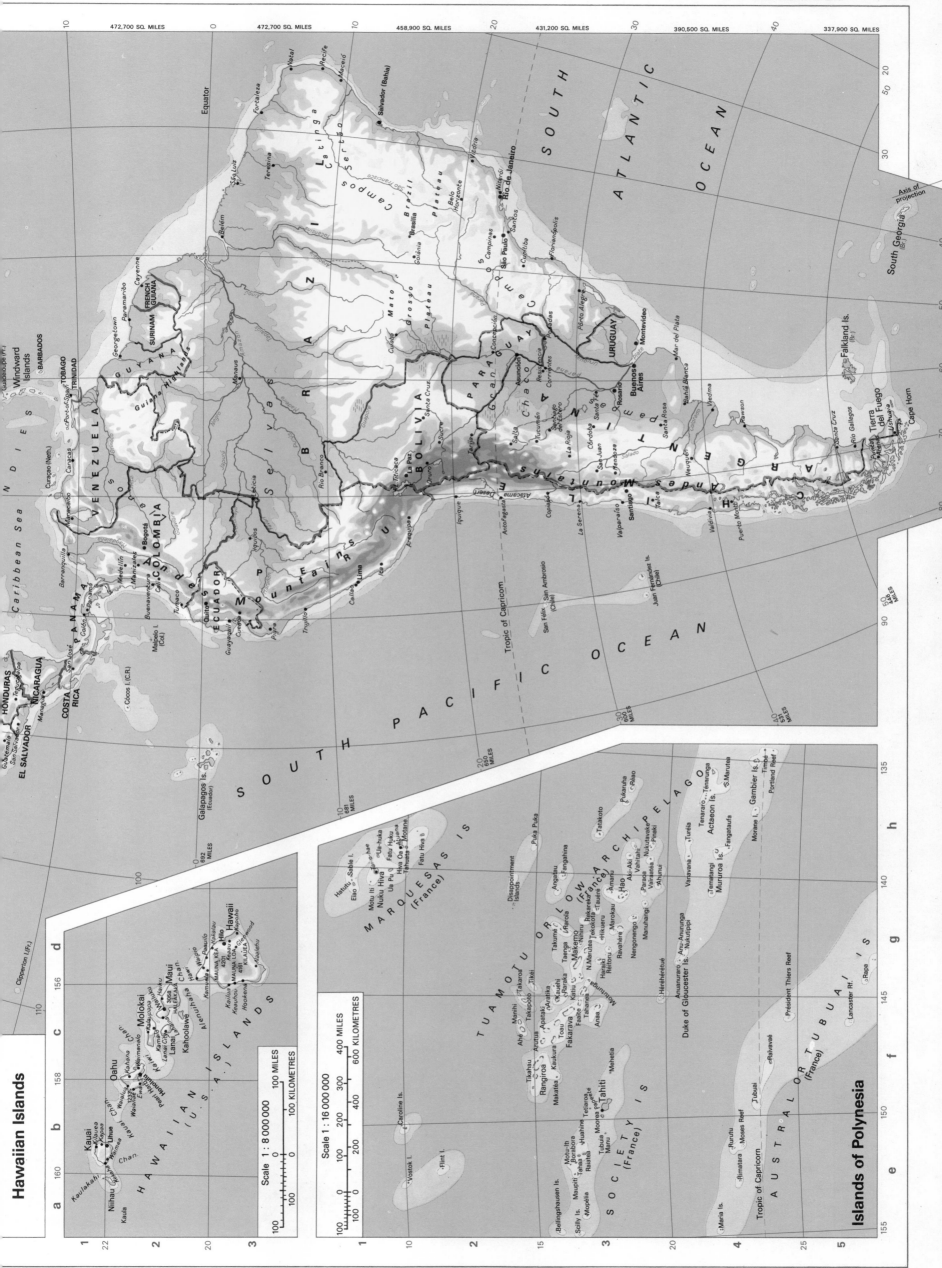

Hawaiian Islands

472,700 SQ. MILES   472,700 SQ. MILES   458,900 SQ. MILES   431,200 SQ. MILES   390,500 SQ. MILES   337,900 SQ. MILES

Equator

Axis of
projection

SOUTH

ATLANTIC

OCEAN

São Luís
Natal
Fortaleza
Recife
Teresina
Maceió
Salvador (Bahia)

B R A Z I L
Belém

Cayenne
FRENCH
GUIANA
SURINAM
Paramaribo
Georgetown
GUYANA

Campos
São Francisco
Brasília
Goiânia

Manaus
Mato
Grosso
Plateau
Cuiabá

Rio de Janeiro
Niterói
Belo
Horizonte
Campinas
São Paulo
Santos
Cuiabá

VENEZUELA
Guiana Highlands
Caracas

Manizales
COLOMBIA
Bogotá
Medellín

S e l v a s
Rio Branco

BOLIVIA
La Paz
Oruro
Sucre
Santa Cruz
Titicaca

PARAGUAY
Asunción
Gran Chaco
Corrientes
Resistencia

URUGUAY
Montevideo
Buenos
Aires
Rosario
Santa Fe
Córdoba

A n d e s
Mountains
Quito
ECUADOR
Cuenca
Guayaquil

Lima
Callao
Arequipa
Iquique
Atacama Desert
Antofagasta

A R G E N T I N A
Salta
Tucumán
La Rioja
San Juan
Mendoza
Santiago
Valparaíso

CHILE
La Serena
Copiapó

Bahía Blanca
Viedma

Puerto Montt
Valdivia

Neuquén
Santa Rosa

Tierra del Fuego
Cape Horn
Ushuaia
Río Gallegos
Punta Arenas
Santa Cruz

Falkland Is.
(Br.)

South Georgia
(Br.)

C a r i b b e a n   S e a
W I N D I E S
Windward
Islands
BARBADOS
TOBAGO
TRINIDAD
Port-of-Spain

Guadeloupe (Fr.)
Curaçao (Neth.)
Maracaibo
Barranquilla
PANAMA

HONDURAS
NICARAGUA
COSTA
RICA
EL SALVADOR
Guatemala
San Salvador
Tegucigalpa
Managua
San José

Galápagos Is.
(Ecuador)

Cocos
(C.R.)

Malpelo I.
(Col)

San Félix
San Ambrosio
(Chile)

Juan Fernández Is.
(Chile)

Tropic of Capricorn

S O U T H   P A C I F I C   O C E A N

Clipperton I. (Fr.)

Islands of Polynesia

MARQUESAS IS
(France)
Hatutu
Eiao
Motu Iti
Nuku Hiva
Ua Huka
Ua-huka
Ua Pou
Fatu Huku
Hiva Oa
Tahuata
Motane
Fatu Hiva

LOW ARCHIPELAGO
(France)
TUAMOTU
Puka Puka
Disappointment
Islands
Pukaruha
Reao

Manihi
Takaroa
Takapoto
Tikei
Angatau
Fangahina
Fakahina
Tatakoto

Caroline Is.
Vostok I.
Flint I.

SOCIETY IS
(France)
Scilly Is.
Bellingshausen Is.
Maupiti
Mopelia
Bora-Bora
Motu Iti
Tahaa
Raiatea
Huahine
Moorea
Tahiti
Mehetia
Tetiaroa

Abe
Arutua
Rangiroa
Tikahau
Makatea
Kaukura
Toau
Fakarava
Apataki
Aratika
Kauehi
Raraka
Taenga
Makemo
Marutea
Nihiru
Tekokota
Hikueru
Marokau
Ravahere
Reitoru
Haraiki
Anaa
Tahanea
Motutunga
Faaite
N. Marutea
Amanu
Hao
Nengonengo
Manuhangi
Paraoa
Vairaatea
Ahunui
Vahitahi
Pinaki
Nukutavake
Vanavana
Tureia
Anu-Anuraro
Anu-Anurunga
Nukutipipi
Hererétue
Duke of Gloucester Is.

Tenararo
Tenaruga
Actaeon Is.
S. Marutea
Fangataufa
Maria L.
Gambier Is.
Morane I.
Timoe
Portland Reef
Mururoa
Matureivavao
Tematangi

President Thiers Reef
Raivavae
AUSTRAL OR TUBUAI IS
(France)
Rurutu
Moses Reef
Rimatara
Tubuai
Rapa
Lancaster Rf.

Maria Is.
Tropic of Capricorn

Oblique Mercator Projection. Pole 20°N, 25°E.
Axis marked in border. Scale reduction 5.0%.
For scale errors see p.115.

© Oxford University Press

HAWAIIAN   (U.S.)   ISLANDS

Kauai
Kauai Chan.
Niihau
Kaula
Kaulakahi Chan.
Kekaha
Lihue
Kapaa

Oahu
Kahana
Kaena Pt.
Waianae
Wahiawa
Honolulu
Waialua
Waimea
Kailua

Molokai
Kamalo
Kaunakakai

Lanai
Lanai City

Kahoolawe
Alenuihaha Chan.

Maui
Lahaina
Wailuku
Kahului
Hana
Haleakala

Hawaii
Hilo
Hamakua
Honokaa
Waimea
Kailua
Kealakekua
Hookena
MAUNA KEA 4205
MAUNA LOA 4170
KILAUEA
Kapoho
Kalapana
Naalehu
Kona
Kawaihae

Scale 1 : 8 000 000
100 MILES
100 KILOMETRES

Scale 1 : 16 000 000
400 MILES
600 KILOMETRES

ARCTIC OCEAN

BEAUFORT SEA

BERING SEA

CHUKCHI SEA

U.S.S.R.

International Date Line

ALASKA

Alaska Range

Brooks Range

Gulf of Alaska

Kodiak Island

Fairbanks
Anchorage

YUKON

Mackenzie Mountains

Ogilvie Mts.

Dawson

Whitehorse

NORTHWEST TERRITORIES

District of Mackenzie

District of Keewatin

Great Bear Lake

Great Slave Lake

Victoria Island

Banks Island

Coppermine

Yellowknife

BRITISH COLUMBIA

ROCKY MOUNTAINS

Coast Mountains

Queen Charlotte Islands

Vancouver Island

Vancouver

Victoria

Prince Rupert

Kamloops

Alexander Archipelago

Juneau

Ketchikan

ALBERTA

SASKATCHEWAN

MANITOBA

Edmonton
Calgary
Lethbridge

Saskatoon
Regina

Winnipeg

Wood Buffalo Nat. Park

Lake Athabasca

Lake Winnipeg

PACIFIC OCEAN

WASHINGTON

Seattle
Tacoma
Spokane

OREGON

Portland

IDAHO

Boise

MONTANA

Helena

Great Falls

Billings

NORTH DAKOTA

Bismarck
Fargo

SOUTH DAKOTA

Pierre

Rapid City

WYOMING

Cheyenne

NEBRASKA

Lincoln
Omaha

NEVADA

Carson City
Reno

CALIFORNIA

San Francisco
Oakland
Sacramento

UTAH

Salt Lake City
Provo
Ogden

COLORADO

Denver
Colorado Springs

KANSAS

Topeka

UNITED STATES

MINNESOTA

Minneapolis
St. Paul

IOWA

Des Moines
Council Bluffs

Kansas City

Cape Mendocino

Aleutian Islands
Same Scale

BERING SEA

PACIFIC OCEAN

Attu
Agattu

NEAR ISLANDS

RAT ISLANDS

Kiska
Little Sitkin
Semisopochnoi
Amchitka
Amchitka Pass

Adak
Atka
Amlia
Seguam
Amukta

ANDREANOF ISLANDS

FOX ISLANDS

Unmak
Unalaska
Dutch Harbor

SANAK ISLANDS

SHUMAGIN ISLANDS

Feet	Metres
12,000	3658
7000	2134
5000	1524
3000	914
2000	610
1500	457
1000	305
500	152
Sea Level	
Land Depression	
600	183
6000	1829

| 100 | 0 | 100 | 200 | 300 | 400 | 500 MILES |

| 100 | 0 | 200 | 400 | 600 | 800 KILOMETRES |

CONTINUE

Newfoundland

0 20 40 60 80 100 MLS.
0   50   100 KILOMETRES

GREENLAND
(Denmark)

BAFFIN
BAY

Baffin
Island

HUDSON
BAY

DAVIS
STRAIT

LABRADOR

QUEBEC

Newfoundland

ATLANTIC
OCEAN

St. John's

UNITED   STATES

Chicago
Detroit
Cleveland
Pittsburgh
Philadelphia
Washington
Baltimore
New York
Boston
Buffalo
Toronto
Milwaukee

WISCONSIN
ILLINOIS
INDIANA
OHIO
WEST VIRGINIA
VIRGINIA
PENNSYLVANIA
NEW YORK
MAINE
VERMONT
NEW HAMPSHIRE
MASS.

Montréal
Ottawa
Québec
Halifax
NOVA SCOTIA
NEW BRUNSWICK
PRINCE EDWARD I.

Legend
Boundaries   International   (in sea)   (disputed)
              Internal
Roads   Motorways   Other roads   Tracks
Railways   Airports   International
              (projected)   Domestic
Canals   Seasonal
                              rivers, lakes
Marshes   Salt pans   Waterholes
Sand desert limits   National Parks, etc.

Zenithal Equidistant Projection.
Origin 45°N, 92½°W. For scale errors see p.115.

© Oxford University Press

P.86-87

Belize
Scale 1 : 8 000 000

Jamaica
Scale 1 : 4 000 000

Legend

Boundaries	International	(in sea)	(disputed)
	Internal		
Roads	Motorways	Other roads	Tracks
Railways	(projected)	Airports	International
			Domestic
Canals		Seasonal rivers, lakes	
Marshes		Salt pans	Waterholes
Sand desert limits		National Parks, etc.	

Bermuda Islands
Scale 1 : 1 000 000
0 2 4 6 8 10 MILES

Lesser Antilles
Scale 1 : 8 000 000
10 20 40 60 80 100 MILES

Trinidad and Tobago

Guyana
Scale 1 : 8 000 000
10 20 40 60 80 100 MILES

ATLANTIC OCEAN

CARIBBEAN SEA

THE BAHAMAS

VENEZUELA

COLOMBIA

BRAZIL

SURINAM

GUYANA

Tropic of Cancer

Feet	Metres
12,000	3658
7000	2134
5000	1524
3000	914
2000	610
1500	457
1000	305
500	152
Sea Level	
Land Depression	
600	183
6000	1829

Zenithal Equidistant Projection.
Origin 45°N, 92½°W. For scale errors see p.115

CONTINUED ON P.94-95

© Oxford University Press

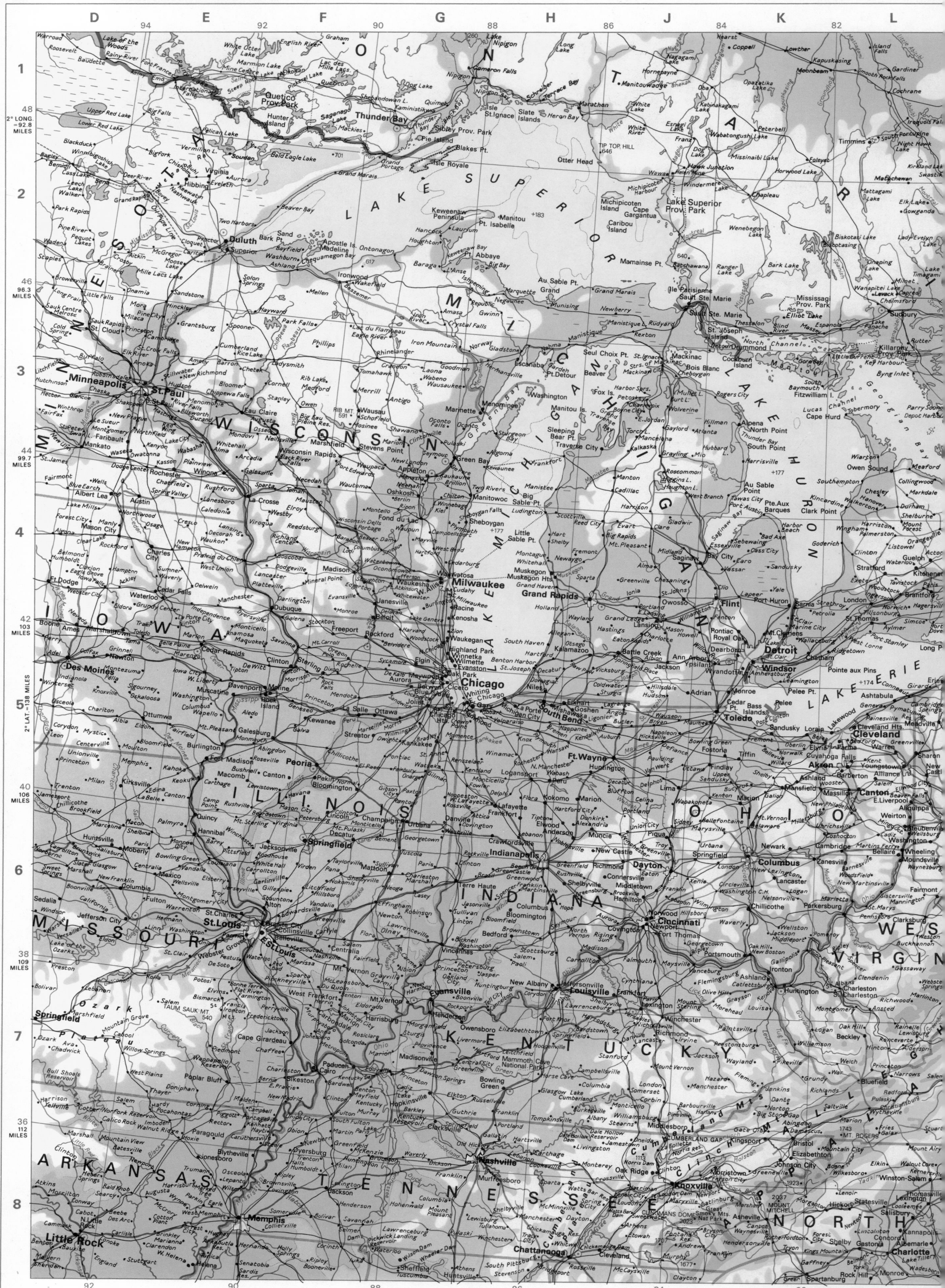

D 94 E 92 F 90 G 88 H 86 J 84 K 82 L

LAKE SUPERIOR

LAKE MICHIGAN

LAKE HURON

LAKE ERIE

MINNESOTA

WISCONSIN

MICHIGAN

ONTARIO

IOWA

ILLINOIS

INDIANA

OHIO

MISSOURI

KENTUCKY

WEST VIRGINIA

ARKANSAS

TENNESSEE

NORTH

Minneapolis · St. Paul · Duluth · Superior · Thunder Bay · Milwaukee · Madison · Chicago · Grand Rapids · Detroit · Windsor · Toledo · Cleveland · Akron · Canton · Columbus · Cincinnati · Indianapolis · Dayton · Fort Wayne · South Bend · Flint · Sault Ste. Marie · Des Moines · Springfield · St. Louis · Peoria · Louisville · Lexington · Nashville · Memphis · Little Rock · Knoxville · Chattanooga · Wheeling · Charleston · Sudbury

E 92 F 90 G 88 H 86 J 84 K 82 L

50   0   50   100   150 MILES
50   0   50 100 150 200 250 KILOMETRES

CONTINUED

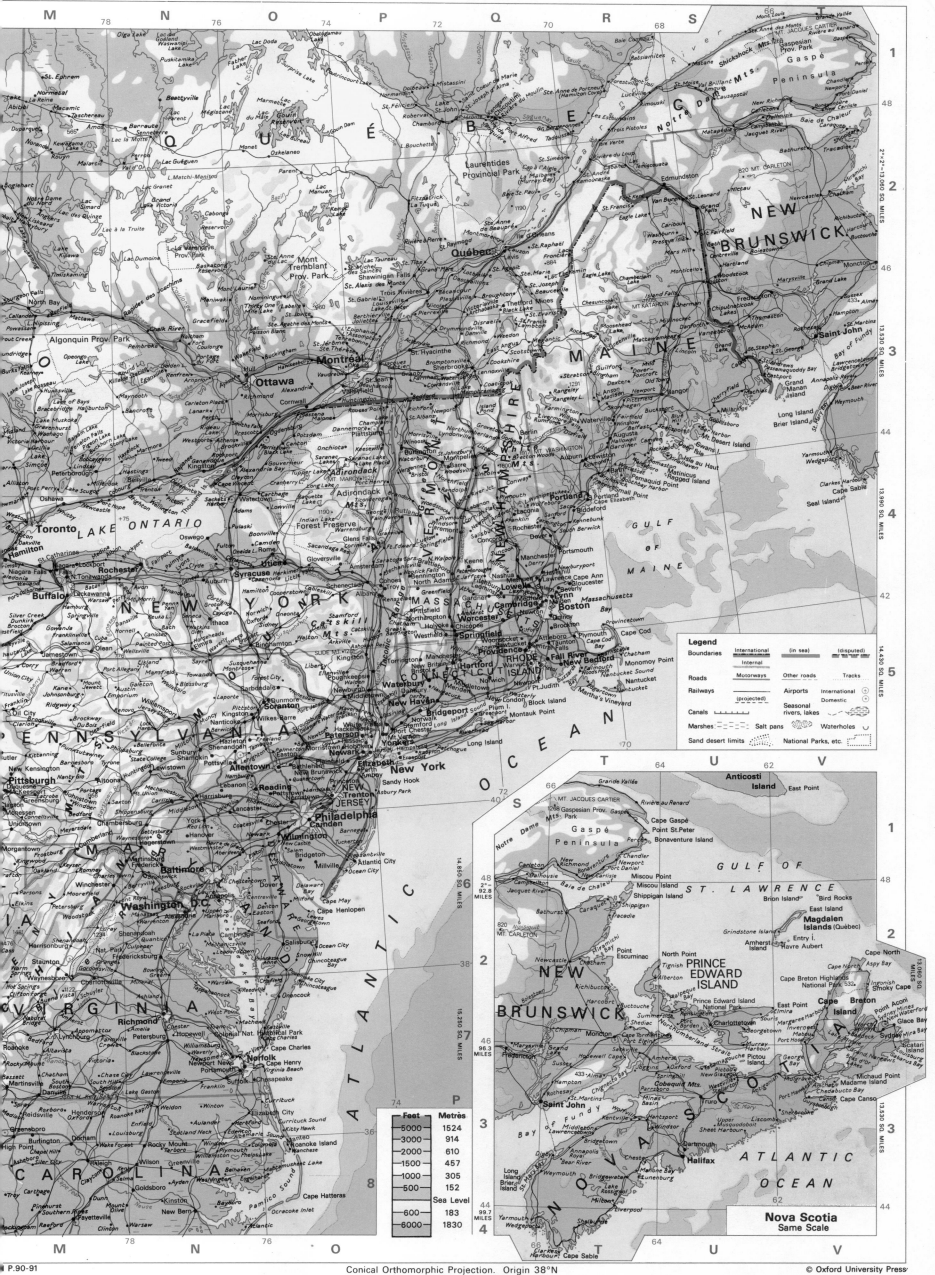

Legend
Boundaries   International   (in sea)   (disputed)
              Internal
Roads   Motorways   Other roads   Tracks
Railways   ——————   Airports   International ⊕
              (projected)   Domestic
Canals   Seasonal
                                   rivers, lakes
Marshes   Salt pans   Waterholes
Sand desert limits   National Parks, etc.

Nova Scotia
Same Scale

Feet	Metrès
5000	1524
3000	914
2000	610
1500	457
1000	305
500	152
Sea Level	
600	183
6000	1830

Conical Orthomorphic Projection. Origin 38°N
Standard parallels 32° & 44° Scale reduction 0·6%.

© Oxford University Press

Mississippi Delta
Scale 1 : 1 500 000

10 5 0   10   20 MILES

Feet	Metres
5000	1524
3000	914
2000	610
1500	457
1000	305
500	152
Sea Level	
600	183
6000	1829

50 0   50   100   150 MILES

50 0   50   100   150   200   250 KILOMETRES

Conical Orthomorphic Projection. Origin 38°N.
Standard Parallels 32° & 44°. Scale reduction 0.6%.
For scale errors see p.115

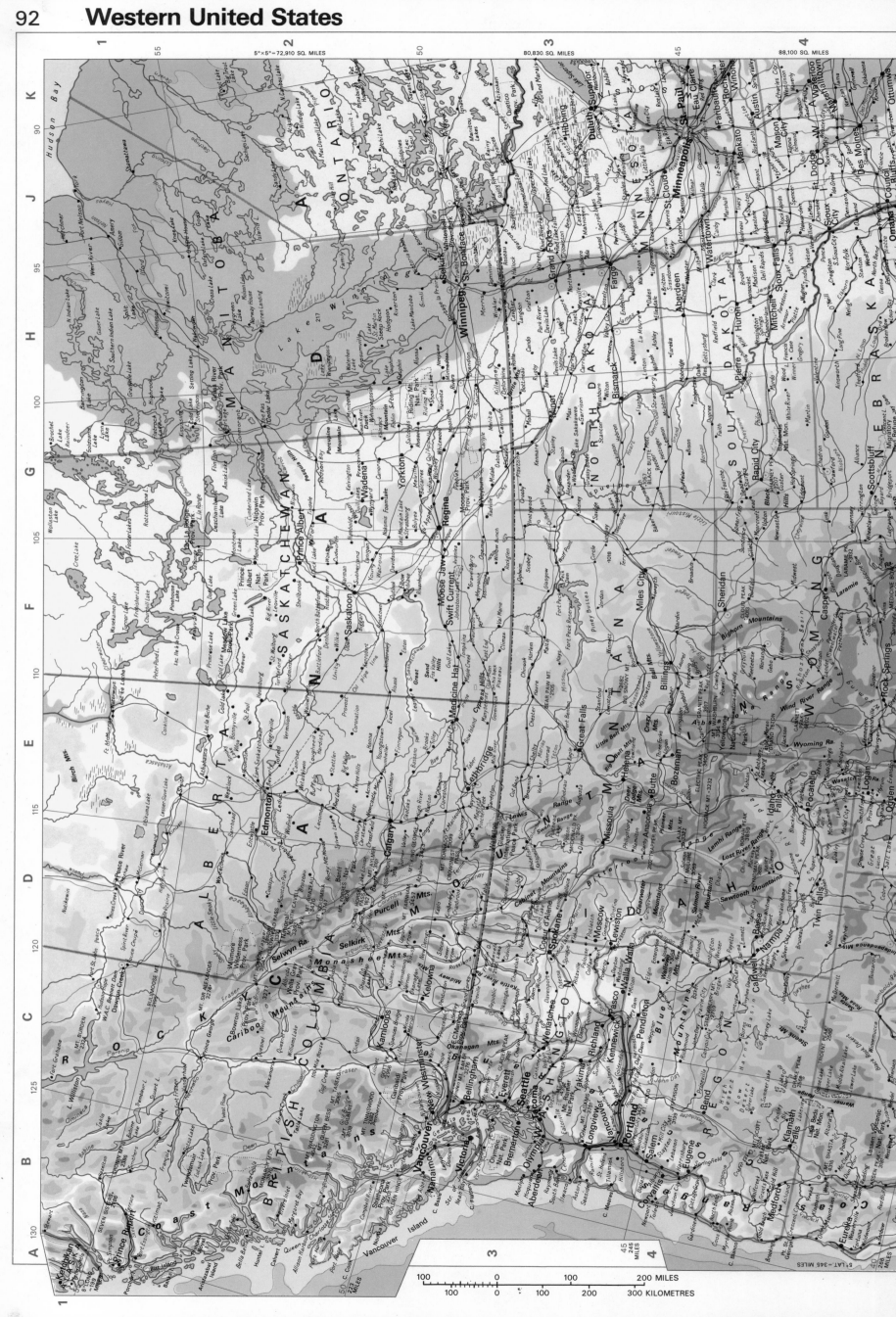

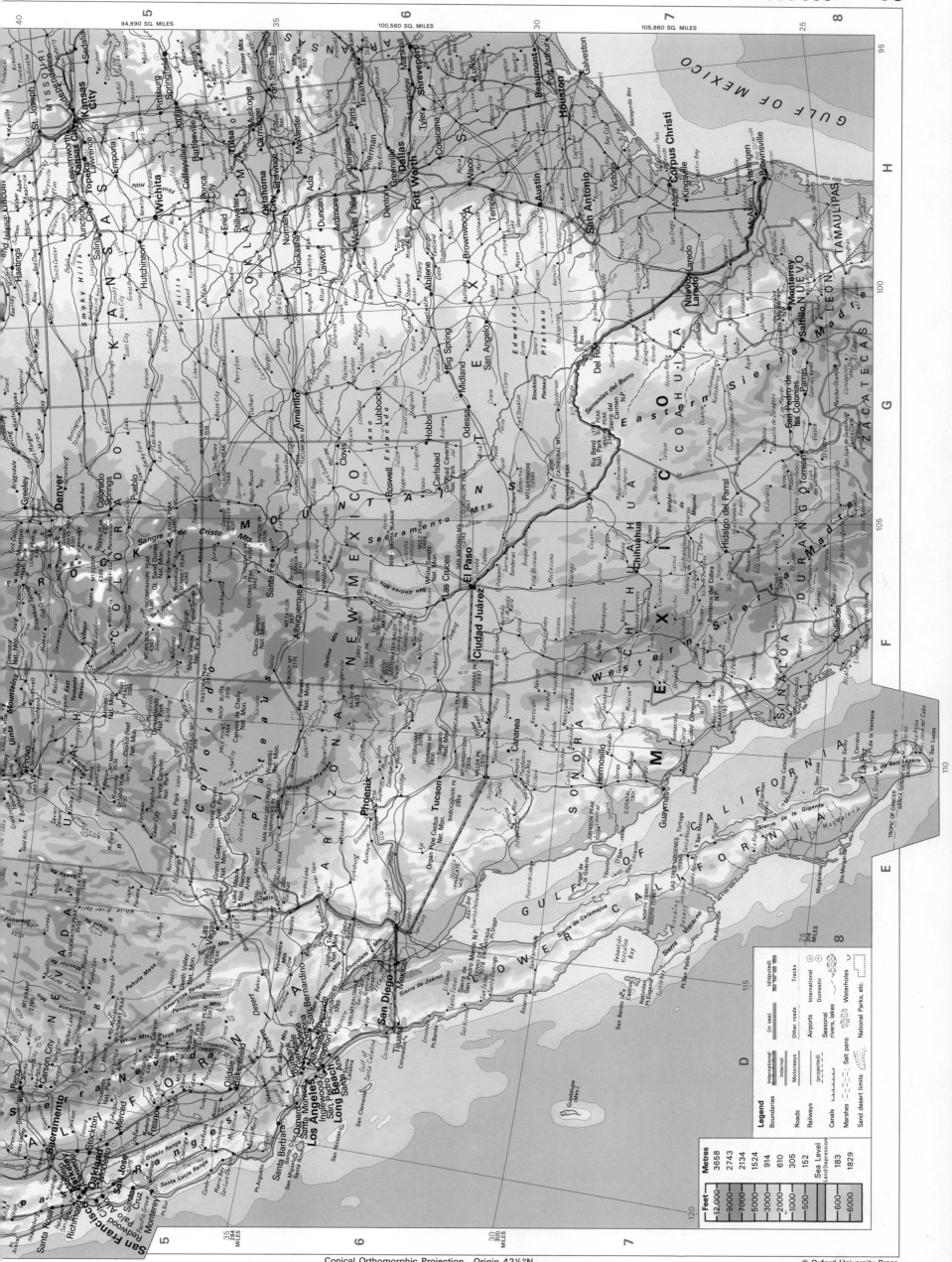

Conical Orthomorphic Projection. Origin 42½°N.
Standard parallels 32½ & 52½°. Scale reduction 1.5%.
For scale errors see p.115

Panama Canal

Scale 1 : 800 000

0 2 4 6 8 10 MILES

Layer intervals
300, 600, 1000 ft.

CARIBBEAN SEA

Cristóbal Colón

Gatún

Panamá

Balboa Ancón

La Boca

Panama Bay

CONTINUED ON P. 86-87

5°×5°=117,770 SQ. MILES

118,600 SQ. MLS.   117,770 SQ. MILES   116,020 SQ. MILES   113,420 SQ. MILES

118,600 SQ. MILES

Equator

ATLANTIC OCEAN

CARIBBEAN SEA

BARBADOS

TOBAGO

TRINIDAD

Port of Spain

Windward Islands

St. Vincent

Grenada

St. George's

PANAMA

COLOMBIA

Barranquilla
Cartagena
Sta. Marta
Maracaibo
Medellín
Bogotá
Cali
Manizales

VENEZUELA

Caracas
Barcelona
Ciudad Bolívar
Barinas
San Cristóbal
Mérida

GUYANA

Georgetown

SURINAM

Paramaribo

FRENCH GUIANA

Cayenne

ECUADOR

Quito
Guayaquil
Cuenca

PERU

Lima
Callao
Trujillo
Iquitos
Cuzco
Arequipa

BRAZIL

Belém
Fortaleza
Recife
Salvador (Bahia)
Belo Horizonte
Manaus
Brasília

MARANHÃO
CEARÁ
PERNAMBUCO
BAHIA
MATO GROSSO
RONDÔNIA
RORAIMA
AMAPÁ
PARÁ
AMAZONAS
ALAGOAS
SERGIPE

BOLIVIA

La Paz
Santa Cruz

ANDES

AMAZON

Equator

100 0 100 200 300 400 500 MILES

100 0 200 400 600 800 KILOMETRES

5° LONG.=341 MILES

5° LAT.=345 MILES

346 MILES   345 MILES   341 MILES   334 MILES

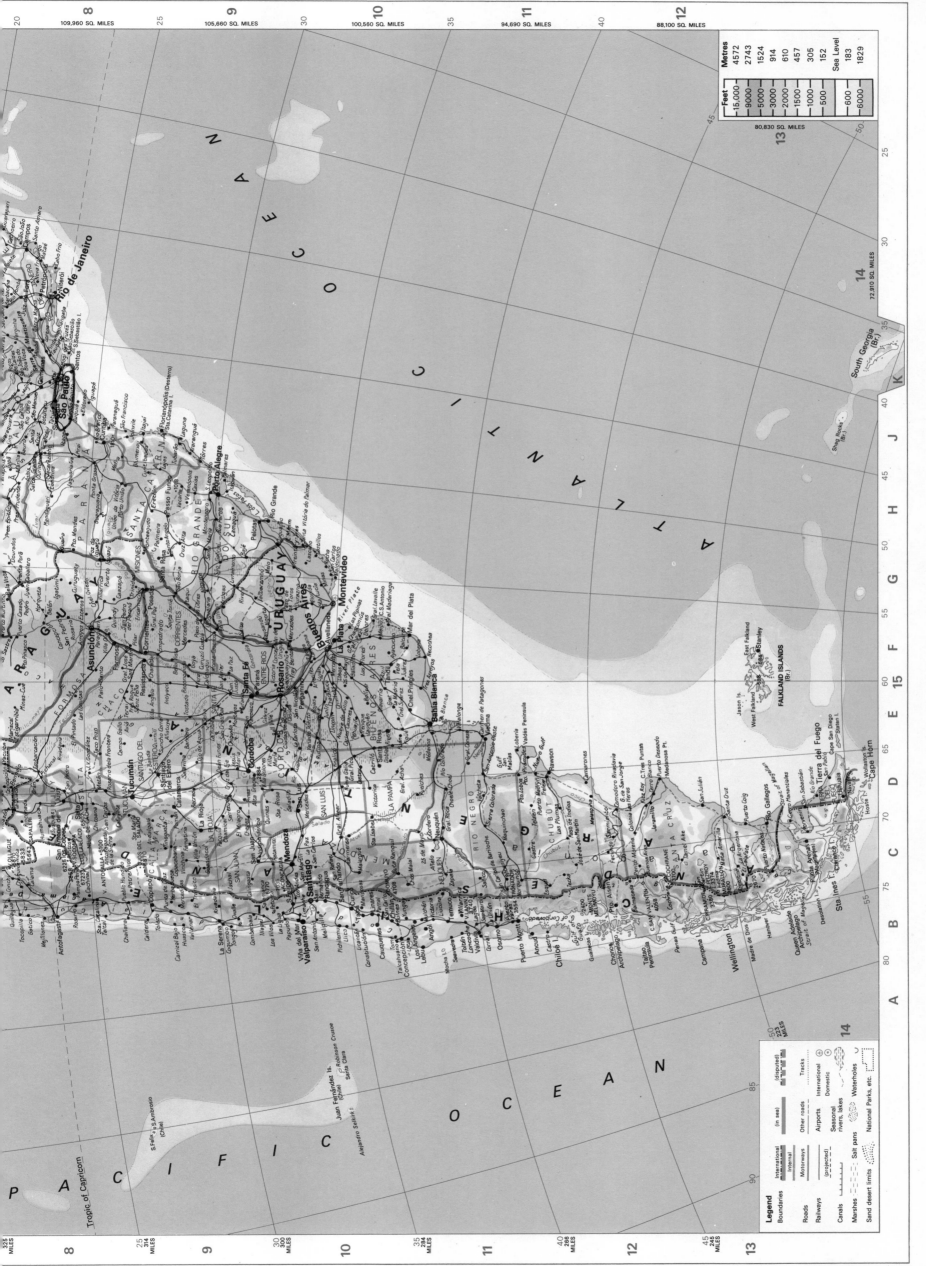

Transverse Mercator Projection.
Central meridian 60°W. Scale reduction 3.0%.
For scale errors see p.115

© Oxford University Press

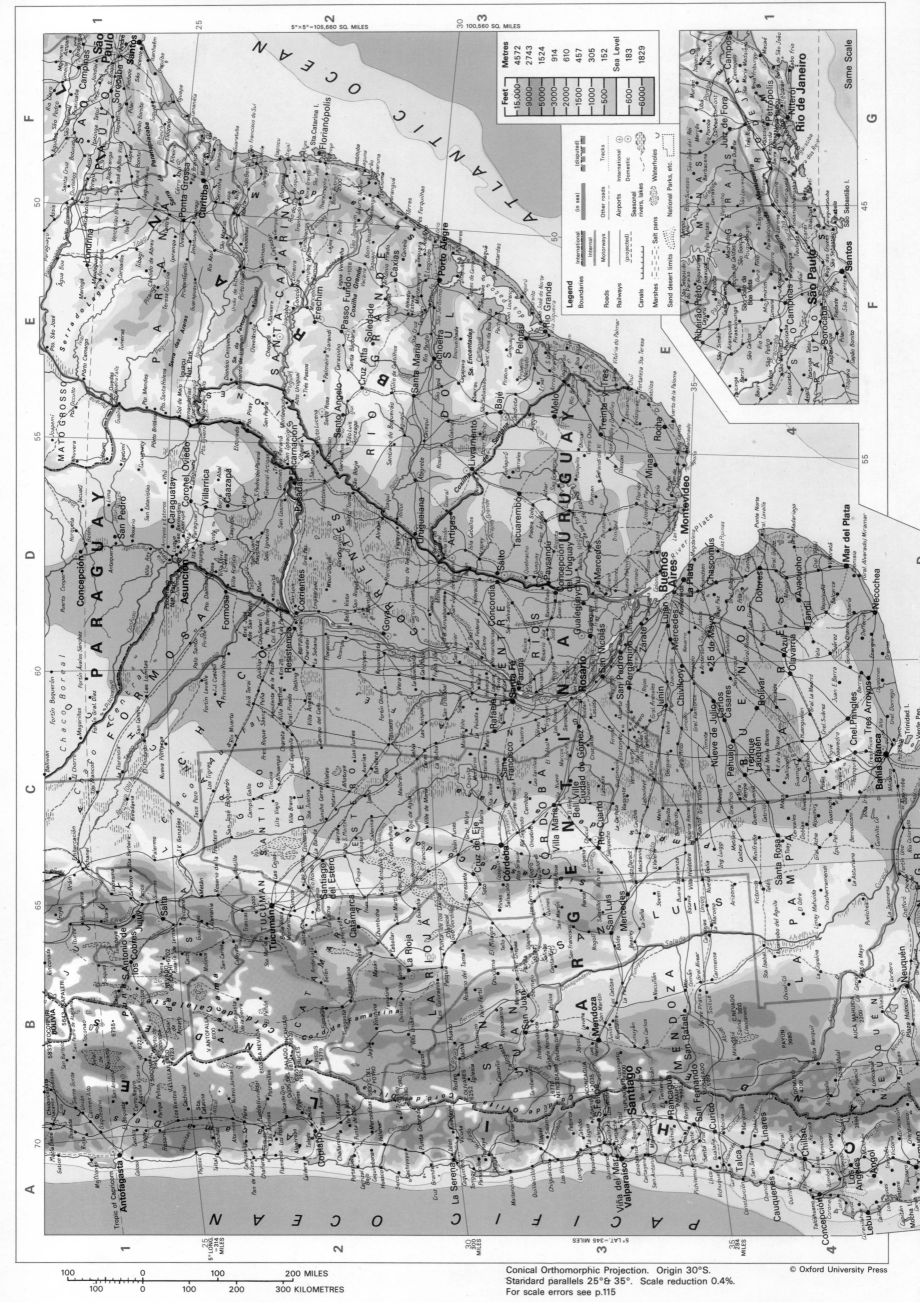

Conical Orthomorphic Projection. Origin 30°S.
Standard parallels 25° & 35°. Scale reduction 0.4%.
For scale errors see p.115

© Oxford University Press

100　0　100　200 MILES

100　0　100　200　300 KILOMETRES

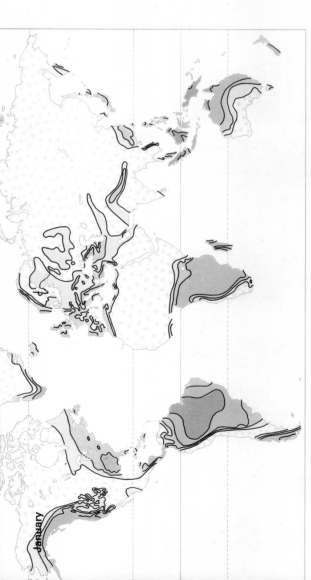

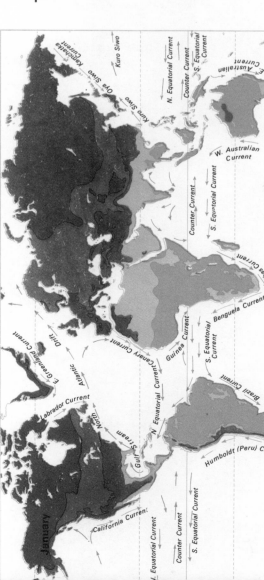

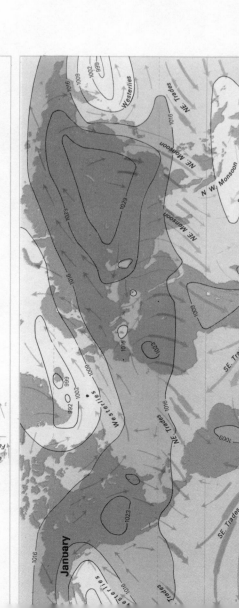

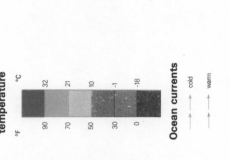

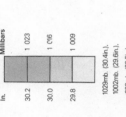

Rainfall
and other forms of precipitation

In.	Millimetres
10	254.0
4	101.6
2	50.8
1	25.4

Temperature/Ocean currents

Actual temperature

°F	°C
90	32
70	21
50	10
30	-1
0	-18

Ocean currents

cold

warm

Pressure/Winds

Atmospheric pressure

In.	Millibars
30.2	1 023
30.0	1 016
29.8	1 009

1029mb. (30.4in.), 1002mb. (29.6in.), 999mb. (29.5in.) isobars are also shown

Prevailing winds

Arrows indicate wind direction. The heavier the arrow the more regular (constant) the direction of the wind.

Modified Gall Projection

Frost Incidence

98

Frost-free period

Number of days with minimum temperature above 0°C (32°F)

- 60 — Summer frosts may occur where frost-free period is less than 90 days
- 90
- 120 — No summer frosts where frost-free period is more than 90 days
- 150
- 180
- 210
- 240
- 270

Frosts occur in some years only

Absence of frosts

Boundaries of frost probability

- 100%
- 50%

Modified Gall Projection

Equatorial Scale 1:88 Million approx.

Permafrost (perennially frozen ground) occurs extensively in Canada, Alaska and the U.S.S.R. It can be differentiated into 3 main zones: (a) continuous permafrost, where very little land is unfrozen and where permafrost may reach depths over 600 m. (approx 2 000 ft.); (b) discontinuous permafrost, where scattered patches of unfrozen land occur; and (c) sporadic permafrost, where patches of permafrost occur in a generally unfrozen area. Overlying permafrost is an 'active' layer of rock or soil which thaws in summer and freezes in winter. Permafrost creates both technical and financial problems for economic development. Melting of permafrost due to heat from buildings may lead to flooding and land subsidence, thus necessitating the careful siting of buildings and the use of effective insulation. Similarly, roads, railways, bridges, dams, sewerage and water-supply systems are affected by flooding, slumping and freezing, and maintenance is costly. Mining operations are hindered by the hardness of the ground, the thawing of permafrost in mine shafts and the formation of ice on machines. Agriculture is virtually negligible where permafrost near the ground surface limits the amount of soil available for plant growth. Also, apart from restrictions imposed by flooding and slumping, it is especially affected by the poorly developed soils and short growing season which are found in permafrost zones.

Plants vary quite considerably in their tolerance to low temperature conditions; some are killed when temperatures approach or reach freezing point whereas others can withstand such conditions although growth is negligible. In general, all plant activity is extremely low when temperatures are at or near freezing point and plant growth is not of economic significance when temperatures are below 4°C (approx. 40°F). The accompanying small world map indicates those areas where the mean monthly temperature is below 4°C for part or all of the year.

The length of the frost-free period gives a general indication of the length of the growing season and hence the suitability of different areas for the production of various crops. It may also serve to indicate whether double cropping is possible during the year. The length of the frost-free period is not, however, the only criterion for determining whether an area is suitable for the production of a particular crop. Other conditions may be equally important,

including the following: light intensity; photoperiod (number of daylight hours), for example in temperate rice growing areas; day and night temperature intensities, for example in the production of tomatoes and water regime. In some areas, where the occurrence of frosts threatens crops which are otherwise suited to the area, protective measures may be employed to avoid losses. Fruit crops are particularly susceptible to frosts, especially at blossom time. Consequently in some fruit growing areas, particularly the citrus groves of Florida and California, the use of smudge pots to create smoke palls, or of oil heaters, combats damaging frosts. The spreading of straw and mulch over early vegetable crops is another method of frost protection. Also, advances are being made in the development of crops which mature in a shorter, but favourable growing season, so permitting the extension of crop production in such areas as Alaska, Northern Canada and Siberia.

© Oxford University Press

Permafrost zones

North America

U.S.S.R.

Data for Mongolia not available

- Continuous permafrost
- Discontinuous permafrost

Sporadic permafrost and permafrost in mountain areas outside discontinuous zone excluded

Mean January and July temperatures

Mean monthly temperatures

- below 4°C (40°F) throughout the year
- below 4°C for part of the year
- above 4°C throughout the year

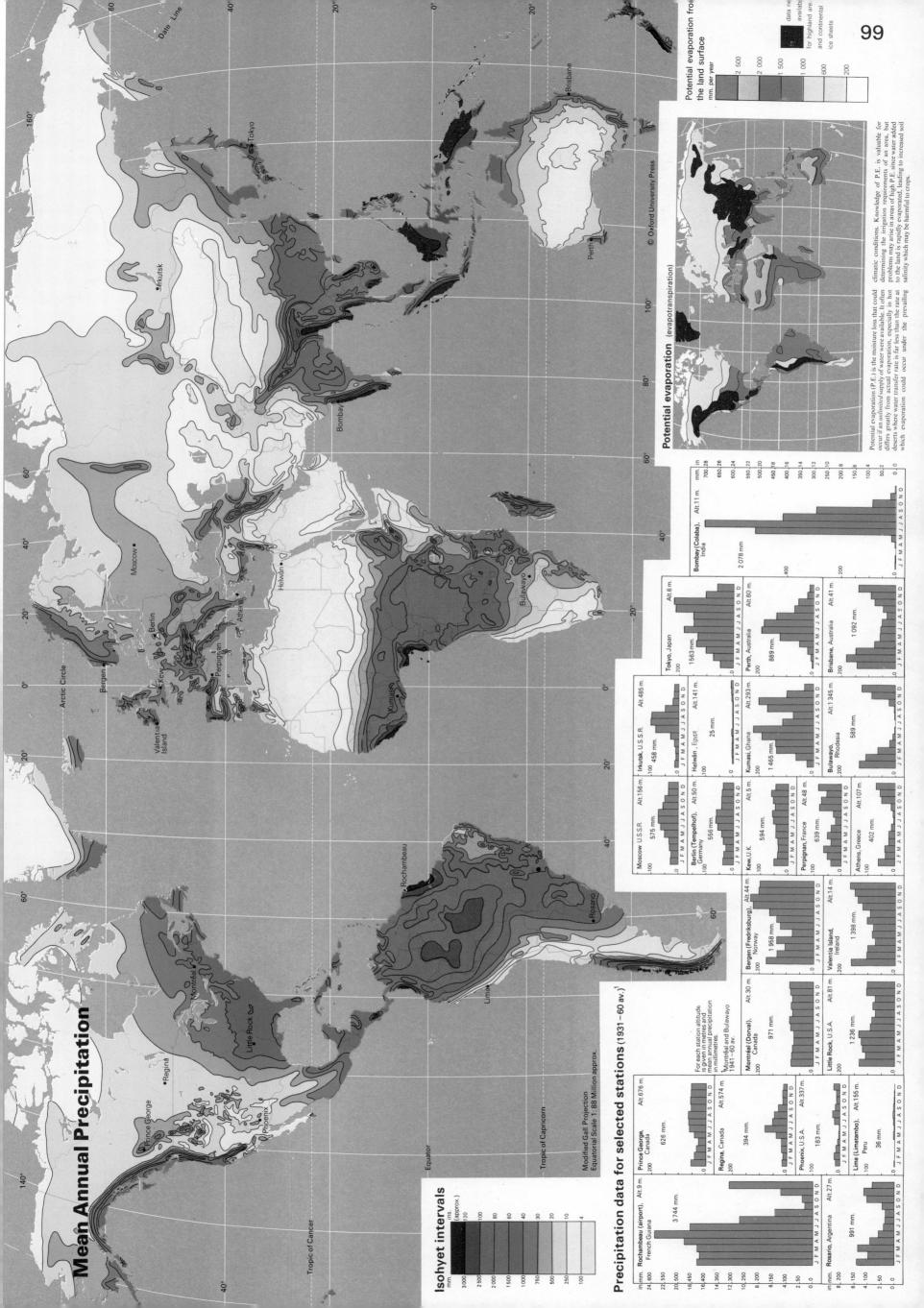

Mean Annual Precipitation

99

Isohyet intervals

mm.	ins. (approx.)
3000	120
2500	100
2000	80
1500	60
1000	40
750	30
500	20
250	10
100	4

Modified Gall Projection
Equatorial Scale 1:88 Million approx.

Precipitation data for selected stations (1931–60 av.)[1]

For each station altitude is given in metres and mean annual precipitation in millimetres.

[1] Montréal and Bulawayo 1941–60 av.

Rochambeau (airport), French Guiana, Alt.9 m. 3 744 mm.
Prince George, Canada, Alt.676 m. 626 mm.
Regina, Canada, Alt.574 m. 394 mm.
Phoenix, U.S.A., Alt.337 m. 183 mm.
Montréal (Dorval), Canada, Alt.30 m. 971 mm.
Little Rock, U.S.A., Alt.81 m. 1 236 mm.
Lima (Limatambo), Peru, Alt.155 m. 36 mm.
Rosario, Argentina, Alt.27 m. 991 mm.
Moscow, U.S.S.R., Alt.156 m. 575 mm.
Irkutsk, U.S.S.R., Alt.485 m. 458 mm.
Berlin (Tempelhof), Germany, Alt.50 m. 556 mm.
Helwân, Egypt, Alt.141 m. 25 mm.
Kew, U.K., Alt.5 m. 594 mm.
Kumasi, Ghana, Alt.293 m. 1 465 mm.
Perpignan, France, Alt.48 m. 639 mm.
Bulawayo, Rhodesia, Alt.1 345 m. 589 mm.
Athens, Greece, Alt.107 m. 402 mm.
Bergen (Fredriksberg), Norway, Alt.44 m. 1 968 mm.
Valencia Island, Ireland, Alt.14 m. 1 398 mm.
Bombay (Colaba), India, Alt.11 m. 2 078 mm.
Tokyo, Japan, Alt.6 m. 1 563 mm.
Perth, Australia, Alt.60 m. 889 mm.
Brisbane, Australia, Alt.41 m. 1 092 mm.

Potential evaporation from the land surface

mm. per year

	2 500
	2 000
	1 500
	1 000
	600
	200

data not available
for highland areas and continental ice sheets

© Oxford University Press

Potential evaporation (evapotranspiration)

Potential evaporation (P.E.) is the moisture loss that could occur if an unlimited supply of water were available. It often differs greatly from actual evaporation, especially in hot deserts where water transfer rate is far less than the rate at which evaporation could occur under the prevailing climatic conditions. Knowledge of P.E. is valuable for determining the irrigation requirements of an area, but problems may arise in areas of high P.E. since water added to the land is rapidly evaporated, leading to increased soil salinity which may be harmful to crops.

Seasonal Climates

Seasonal climates

This classification comprises eleven basic climatic types. Nine types are classified according to the temperature characteristics of summer and winter and two additional types are distinguished where aridity is the dominant influence.

Middle latitude climates are further subdivided according to seasonal temperature range. Tropical and certain subtropical climates are further subdivided according to the duration of wet and dry seasons.

A total of twenty – seven climatic types thus occurs. The extent of each type is shown by colours (on land only) and combinations of digits. The first digit indicates the summer characteristic and the second the winter. The third small digit, where present, indicates the seasonal temperature range, and a small letter indicates the duration of wet and dry seasons, explained opposite.

Summer and winter temperature characteristics

Summers are classified according to the mean temperature of the warmest month and designated 0, 1, 2 or 3.

		MEAN TEMPERATURE OF THE WARMEST MONTH
0	No summer	
1	Very cool summer	6°C (43°F) and under.
2	Cool summer	6°–10°C (43°–50°F)
3	Full summer	10°–20°C (50°–68°F) over 20°C (68°F)

Winters are classified according to the mean temperature of the coldest month and designated 0, 1 or 2.

		MEAN TEMPERATURE OF THE COLDEST MONTH
0	No winter	over 13°C (55°F)
1	Mild winter	2°–13°C (36°–55°F)
2	Cold winter	below 2°C (36°F)

Combinations of summer and winter conditions

02	No summer	Cool summer
	Cold winter	No winter
12	Very cool summer	Full summer
	Cold winter	Cold winter
11	Very cool summer	Full summer
	Mild winter	Mild winter
22	No winter	Cool summer
	Mild winter	Cold winter
21	Cool summer	
	Mild winter	

Arid climates

X	Arid
	Arid climates are those climates in middle and low latitudes in which no month receives as much as 60 mm. (2 in.) rainfall.
Z	Extremely arid
	Extremely arid climates are perennially rainless with no more than 2.5 mm. (0.1 in.) rainfall per month for at least 10 months of the year.

Seasonal temperature range

For areas 21, 22 and 32 outside the tropics

1	Oceanic	Seasonal range under 12°C (22° F)
2	Sub Continental	Seasonal range 12°–24°C (22°–43°F)
	Continental	Seasonal range 24°–36°C (43°–65°F)
3	Very Continental	Seasonal range 36°–48°C (65°–86°F)
4	Extremely Continental	Seasonal range over 48°C (86°F)

Duration of wet and dry seasons

For areas 30 and 31 only

a	All months rainy i.e. with over 50 mm. (2 in.) rainfall
b	Rainy season predominant 8-11 months with over 50 mm.
c	Rainy and dry seasons approx. equal 5, 6 or 7 months with over 50 mm.
d	Dry season predominant 1-4 months with over 50 mm.

Winter rain regions

Boundary of region where rainfall occurs predominantly in winter

Classification devised by Professor D.L. Linton

© Oxford University Press

Mean monthly temperatures for January and July (1931–60)

Selected stations (with altitude in metres)

	Jan.		July		Jan.		July	
	°C	°F	°C	°F	°C	°F	°C	°F
Coppermine (0)	-28.6	-19	9.3	49				
Verkhoyansk (137)	-46.8	-52	15.7	60	Chicago (190)	-3.3	26	24.3	76
Winnipeg (240)	-17.7	0	20.2	68	New York (16)	0.9	34	24.9	77
Moscow (156)	-9.9	14	19.0	66	Sydney (42)	21.9	71	12.3	54
Berlin (50)	-0.5	31	19.4	67	Rosario (27)'	23.8	75	9.9	50
Reykjavik (16)	-0.4	31	11.2	52	Pretoria (1400)'	21.0	70	10.3	51
Kew (5)	4.2	40	17.6	64	Rio de Janeiro (27)'	26.0	79	20.8	69
Hobart (54)	16.3	61	7.8	46	Kumasi (293)'	25.2	77	24.2	76
Quito (2812)	13.0	55	12.9	55	Madras (16)	24.5	76	30.7	87
Tokyo (6)	3.7	39	25.1	77	New Delhi (216)'	14.3	58	31.2	88
					Phoenix (337)	10.4	51	32.9	91

Temperatures decrease with increasing altitude at a rate of about 2°C (3.6°F) for every 300m. (1 000 ft).
Location, season and time of day all influence the actual rate.

1131-60 '1951-60

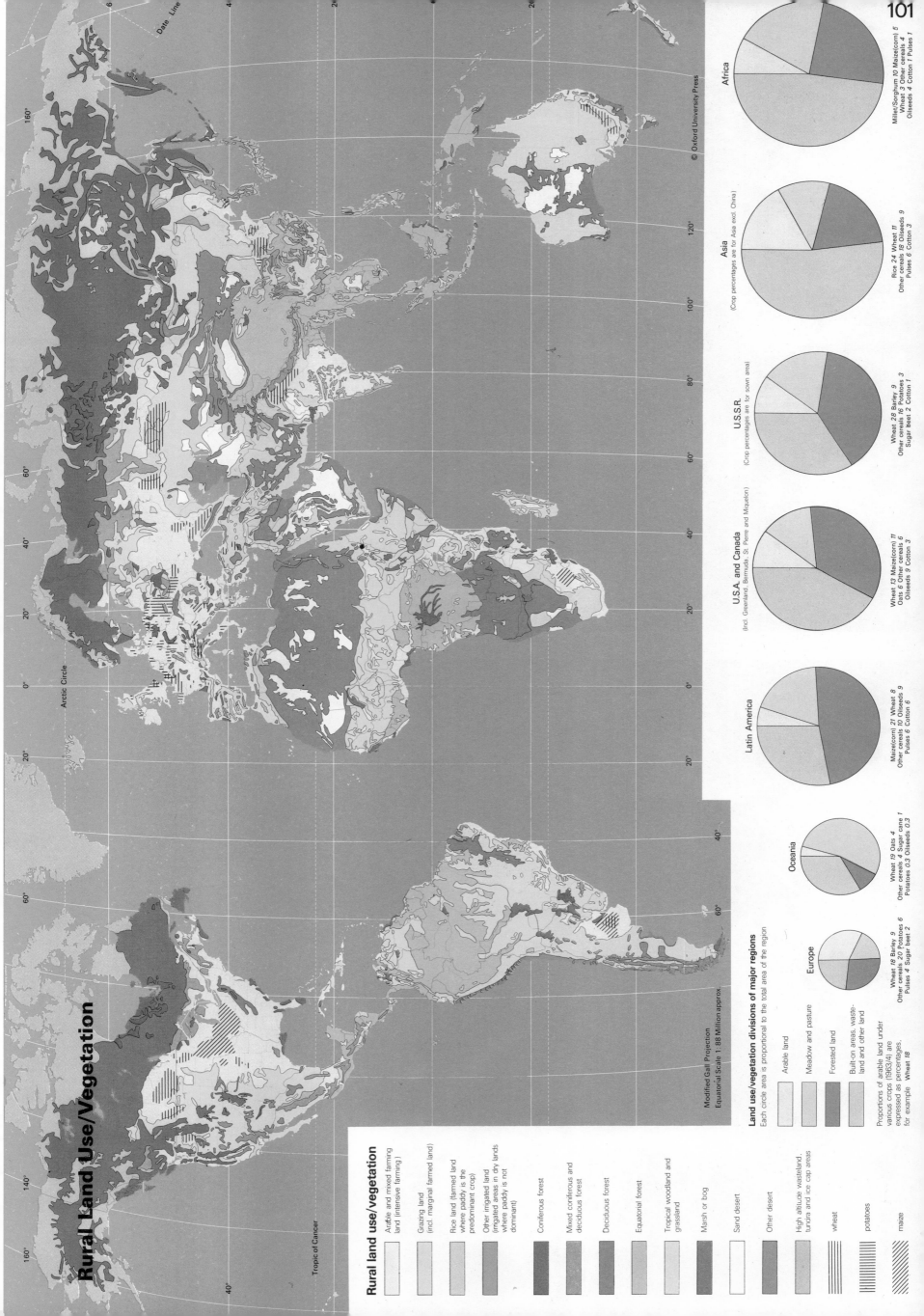

Rural Land Use/Vegetation

Rural land use/vegetation

Arable and mixed farming land (intensive farming)

Grazing land (incl. marginal farmed land)

Rice land (farmed land where paddy is the predominant crop)

Other irrigated land (irrigated areas in dry lands where paddy is not dominant)

Coniferous forest

Mixed coniferous and deciduous forest

Deciduous forest

Equatorial forest

Tropical woodland and grassland

Marsh or bog

Sand desert

Other desert

High altitude wasteland, tundra and ice cap areas

wheat

potatoes

maize

Land use/vegetation divisions of major regions

Each circle area is proportional to the total area of the region

Arable land

Meadow and pasture

Forested land

Built-on areas, wasteland and other land

Proportions of arable land under various crops (1963/4) are expressed as percentages, for example   Wheat 18

Europe

Wheat 18 Barley 9
Other cereals 20 Potatoes 6
Pulses 4 Sugar beet 2

Oceania

Wheat 19 Oats 4
Other cereals 4 Sugar cane 1
Potatoes 0.3 Oilseeds 0.3

Latin America

Maize(corn) 21 Wheat 8
Other cereals 10 Oilseeds 9
Pulses 6 Cotton 6

U.S.A. and Canada
(incl. Greenland, Bermuda, St. Pierre and Miquelon)

Wheat 13 Maize(corn) 11
Oats 6 Other cereals 6
Oilseeds 9 Cotton 3

U.S.S.R.
(Crop percentages are for sown area)

Wheat 28 Barley 9
Other cereals 16 Potatoes 3
Sugar beet 2 Cotton 1

Asia
(Crop percentages are for Asia excl. China)

Rice 24 Wheat 11
Other cereals 18 Oilseeds 9
Pulses 6 Cotton 3

Africa

Millet/Sorghum 10 Maize(corn) 5
Wheat 3 Other cereals 4
Oilseeds 4 Cotton 1 Pulses 1

© Oxford University Press

Modified Gall Projection
Equatorial Scale 1 : 88 Million approx.

Date Line

Arctic Circle

Tropic of Cancer

Population: Past and Future

1850

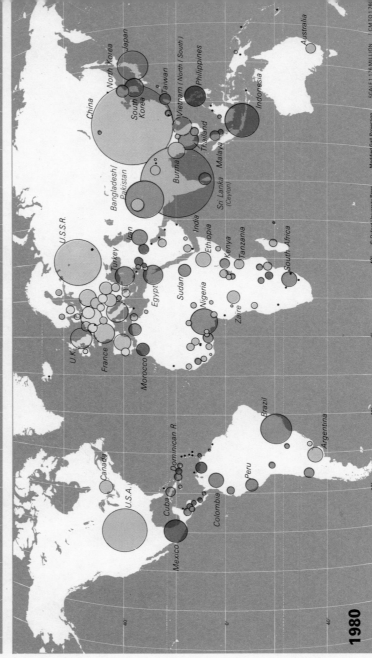

1920

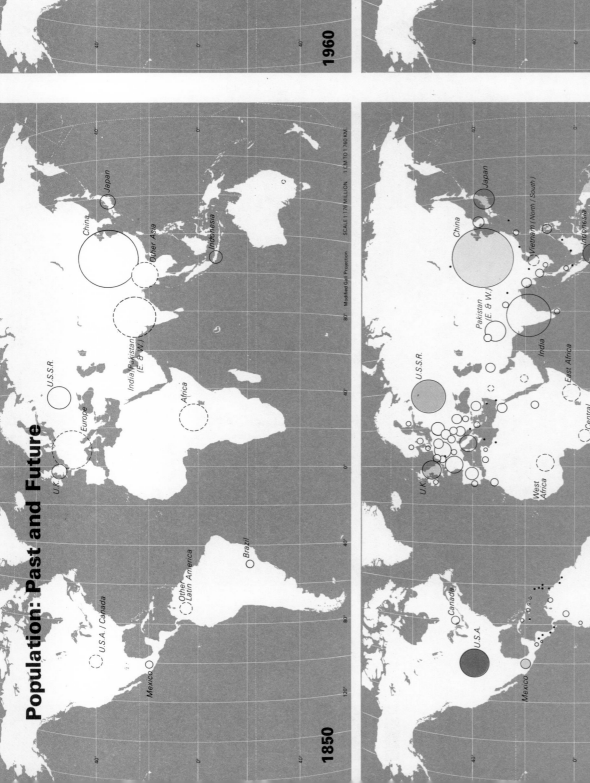

1960

1980

Population (historical distribution)

National population totals (in millions)

0.1 - 1.0

thereafter, population approximately equals $[r \cdot \frac{8}{3}]^2$ where r is the radius of the circle in millimetres
Thus:

144
64
4

Regional totals shown by heavy black line around colour

Data not available

Annual average rate of population change (percentage)

4.5 & OVER
3 - 4.5
1.5 - 3
0.75 - 1.5
0 - 0.75
DATA N A

Decrease shown by heavy black line around colour

This series of maps is intended to show the accelerating growth of the world's population since 1850 and its expected increase in the immediate future.

In 1850 the total population was about 1 000 million compared with the present figure of 3 500 million, and precise information about the population was scarce. At that time only a few nations had carried out national censuses. Most of the figures are based upon rough estimates made by various organizations and individuals. A large majority of the population lived in South and East Asia, where the agriculture-based economy was very similar to that found in many areas of the region today. It was only in Western Europe and North America that industrialization was leading to diversification in the employment of the labour force, making censuses more important for social planning.

By 1920 statistical information had improved considerably and only in tropical Africa and parts of the Middle East was there still an almost complete lack of demographic data. Thus, a general pattern of population distribution could be seen, major concentrations being in South and East Asia and Europe, with the U.S.A. having the fastest rate of increase (1850-1920) mainly because of large-scale immigration. This came first from

North and West Europe, and then, at the end of the nineteenth century and the beginning of the twentieth century, from South and East Europe, until the introduction of immigration restrictions, particularly after 1924.

The population distribution in 1960 was similar to that in 1920. It is estimated that the world population increased by 473 millions during the 1950's. At that time only a few nations maintained lower death rates. If current growth rates are maintained, the world population would be 7 000 million by the end of the century, and 12 000 million by 2030. Latin America showed the fastest rate of increase (1920-60). Other areas of rapid increase were a result of exceptional political situations, such as the creation of Israel as a Jewish state in 1948, and emigration from the Chinese mainland to Taiwan and Hong Kong after the revolution in 1949.

The forecast rates of increase (1960-80), based when possible on the 'medium' population projections of the 'UN Report on World Population Prospects as Assessed in 1963', are similar to those of 1920-60. Central America has particularly high growth rates while Europe has a low rate of increase, having reached a stable demographic equilibrium of low birth and death rates.

Population pyramids (% of population in each ten-year age group)

These pyramids show the structure of the population of selected countries in terms of age and sex. They are based on ten-year age groups up to the age of 80. The difference in age structures between nations is largely a result of their level of development. Thus Ghana, India and Venezuela have very large age groups of young people — the older people. On the other hand, the U.K. and France in particular have a nearly constant number of people in each age group up to 60, signifying a lower birth-rate and better medical standards. The pyramids also show that although more males than females are born, the females tend to live longer, as seen clearly in the U.K.

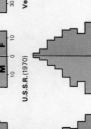

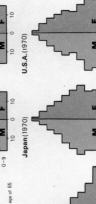

Ghana (1970)   Venezuela (1970)
E. Germany (1971)   France (1968)   U.S.S.R. (1970)
England and Wales (1971)   Japan (1970)   U.S.A. (1970)
India (1971)

Age groups: 80+, 70-79, 60-69, 50-59, 40-49, 30-39, 20-29, 10-19, 0-9

'Data for Venezuela, undifferentiated above the age of 65

Population by region

	PERCENTAGE OF WORLD TOTAL		
	1920	1960	1980
Europe	17.6	14.2	11.2
U.S.S.R.	8.3	7.2	6.5
North America	6.2	6.7	6.1
Latin America	4.8	7.1	8.8
East Asia*	29.7	26.5	24.4
South Asia	25.2	28.7	32.0
Africa	7.7	9.1	10.5
Oceania	0.5	0.5	0.5

*East Asia: China, Japan, Taiwan, Korea, Mongolia, Hong Kong, Macao, Ryukyu Is.

© Oxford University Press

Population Distribution and Growth

Modified Gall Projection   Equatorial Scale 1:88 Million approx.   © Oxford University Press

Population distribution

Towns of at least
100 000 population

- OVER 10 000 000
- 7 500 001 – 10 000 000
- 5 000 001 – 7 500 000
- 2 500 001 – 5 000 000
- 1 000 001 – 2 500 000
- 500 001 – 1 000 000
- 200 001 – 500 000
- 100 001 – 200 000

One dot per 100 000 population

Annual growth
(1963–72 av.)

PERCENTAGE

- 3–4
- 2–3
- 1–2
- 0–1
- DATA NA

Population statistics for selected countries

Latest census available in 1974

	CANADA	U.S.A.	MEXICO	BRAZIL	ARGENTINA	U.K.	FRANCE	NETHER-LANDS	W. GERMANY	SWEDEN	POLAND	YUGO-SLAVIA	TURKEY	SOUTH AFRICA	NIGERIA	ALGERIA	ETHIOPIA	EGYPT	SAUDI ARABIA	ISRAEL	IRAQ	INDIA	INDO-NESIA	PHILIP-PINES	CHINA	TAIWAN	JAPAN	U.S.S.R.	AUSTRALIA
Total population (thousands)	20 149	203 212	48 382	93 204	20 011	55 349	49 654	13 029	60 842	8 077	32 589	18 549	36 162	21 448	55 670	11 822	26 248	34 839	6 990	3 001	9 749	547 368	118 309	36 684	627 800	14 335	103 720	241 720	12 728
Population density (persons/sq.km.)¹	2	22	25	11	7	241	90	319	245	18	105	82	46	18	60	5	25	34	3	145	22	168	62	113	65	399	281	11	2
Percentage urbanized	74	74	59	56	74	77	70	78	38	82	52	9	37	48	16	39	10	43	9	82	59	20	17	32	14	62	72	56	86
Size of largest agglomeration (thousands)	2 553	11 571	7 314	5 186	8 352	7 379	7 369	1 063	2 134	1 344	1 308	565	2 052	1 969	900	943	796	4 961	225	838	1 657	7 005	4 576	1 377	10 820	1 155	11 454	7 172	2 717

¹ 1972

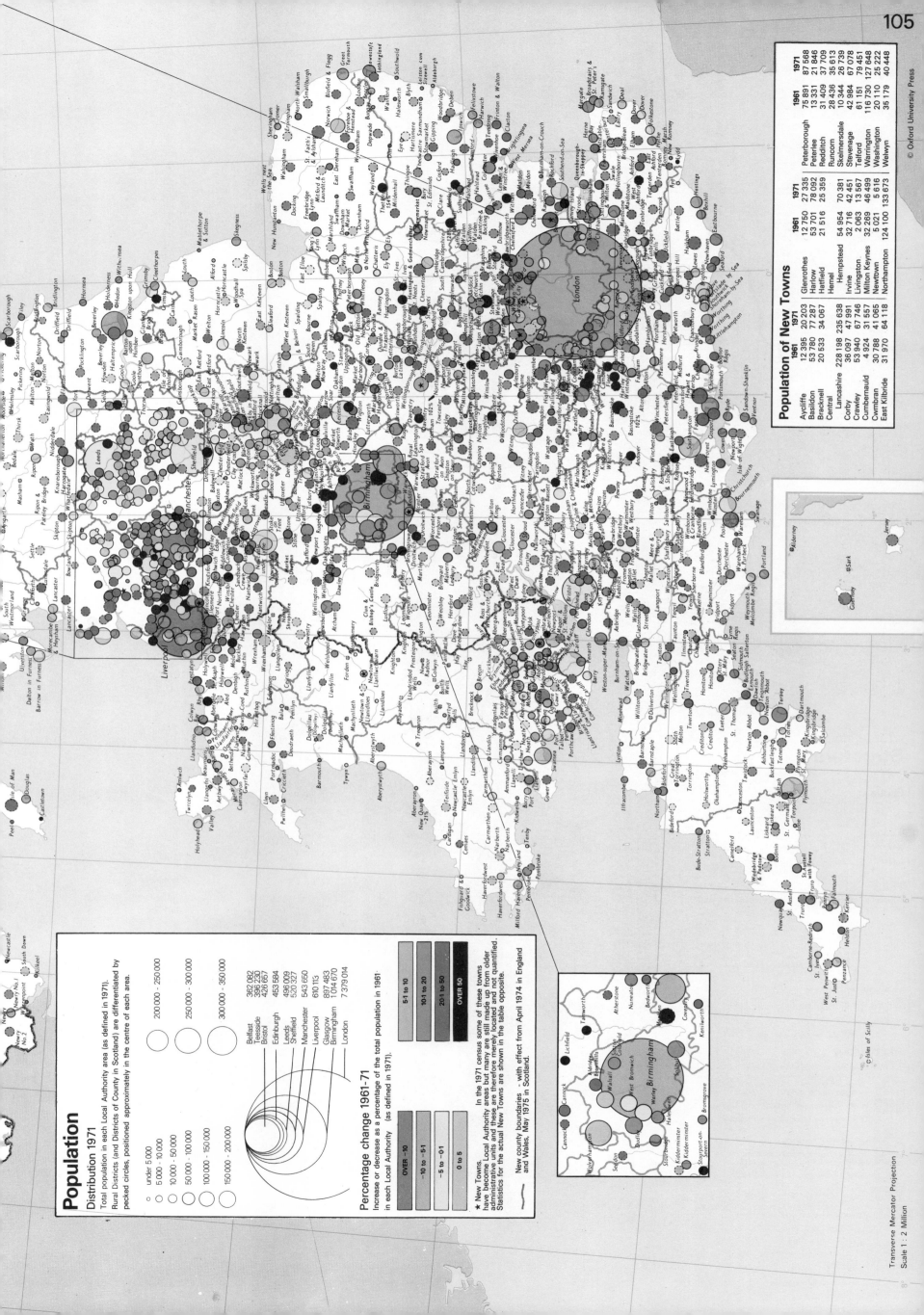

Population

Distribution 1971

Total population in each Local Authority area (as defined in 1971).

Rural Districts (and Districts of County in Scotland) are differentiated by pecked circles, positioned approximately in the centre of each area.

	under 5 000
	5 000 - 10 000
	10 000 - 50 000
	50 000 - 100 000
	100 000 - 150 000
	150 000 - 200 000
	200 000 - 250 000
	250 000 - 300 000
	300 000 - 350 000

Belfast	362 082
Teesside	396 230
Bristol	426 657
Edinburgh	453 584
Leeds	496 009
Sheffield	520 327
Manchester	543 650
Liverpool	610 113
Glasgow	897 483
Birmingham	1 014 670
London	7 379 014

Percentage change 1961-71

Increase or decrease as a percentage of the total population in 1961 in each Local Authority (as defined in 1971).

OVER -10	5·1 to 10
-10 to -5·1	10·1 to 20
-5 to -0·1	20·1 to 50
0 to 5	OVER 50

★ New Towns. In the 1971 census some of these towns have become Local Authority areas but many are still made up from older administrative units and these are therefore merely located and not quantified. Statistics for the actual New Towns are shown in the table opposite.

New county boundaries - with effect from April 1974 in England and Wales, May 1975 in Scotland.

Population of New Towns

	1961	1971		1961	1971		1961	1971
Aycliffe	12 395	20 203	Glenrothes	12 750	27 335	Peterborough	75 891	87 568
Basildon	53 780	77 287	Harlow	53 701	78 092	Peterlee	13 331	21 846
Bracknell	20 533	34 067	Hatfield	21 516	25 359	Redditch	31 409	37 709
Central Lancashire	228 198	235 638	Hemel Hempstead	54 954	70 381	Runcorn	28 436	35 613
Corby	36 097	47 991	Irvine	36 097	47 991	Skelmersdale	10 344	26 739
Crawley	53 940	67 746	Livingston	2 063	13 567	Stevenage	42 984	67 078
Cumbernauld	4 924	31 557	Milton Keynes	32 289	46 499	Telford	61 151	79 451
Cwmbran	30 788	41 065	Newtown	5 021	5 616	Warrington	116 730	127 648
East Kilbride	31 970	64 118	Northampton	124 100	133 673	Washington	20 110	25 222
						Welwyn	35 179	40 448

Transverse Mercator Projection

Scale 1 : 2 Million

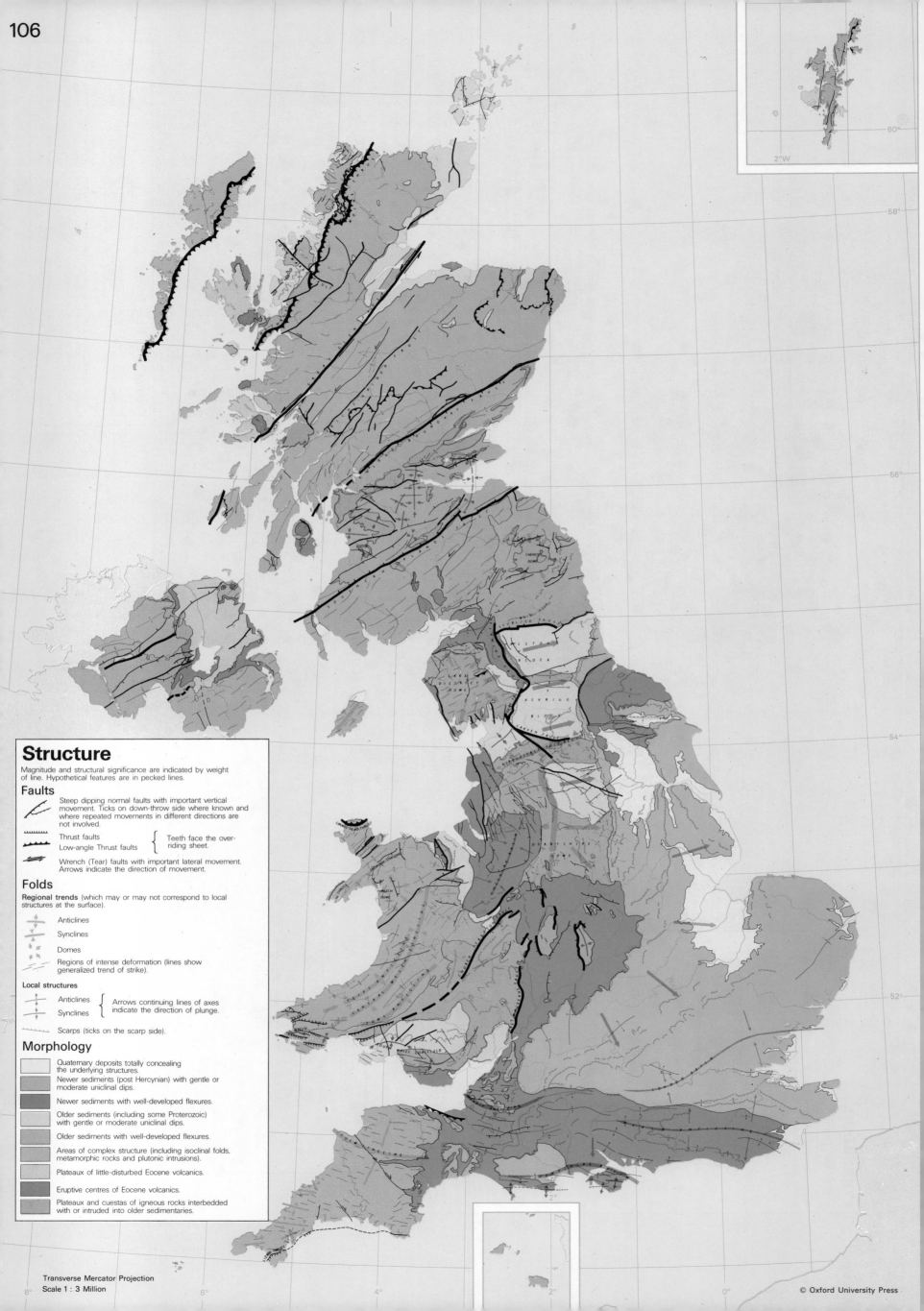

106

Structure

Magnitude and structural significance are indicated by weight of line. Hypothetical features are in pecked lines.

Faults

Steep dipping normal faults with important vertical movement. Ticks on down-throw side where known and where repeated movements in different directions are not involved.

Thrust faults
Low-angle Thrust faults } Teeth face the over-riding sheet.

Wrench (Tear) faults with important lateral movement. Arrows indicate the direction of movement.

Folds

Regional trends (which may or may not correspond to local structures at the surface).

Anticlines

Synclines

Domes

Regions of intense deformation (lines show generalized trend of strike).

Local structures

Anticlines } Arrows continuing lines of axes indicate the direction of plunge.
Synclines

Scarps (ticks on the scarp side).

Morphology

Quaternary deposits totally concealing the underlying structures.

Newer sediments (post Hercynian) with gentle or moderate uniclinal dips.

Newer sediments with well-developed flexures.

Older sediments (including some Proterozoic) with gentle or moderate uniclinal dips.

Older sediments with well-developed flexures.

Areas of complex structure (including isoclinal folds, metamorphic rocks and plutonic intrusions).

Plateaux of little-disturbed Eocene volcanics.

Eruptive centres of Eocene volcanics.

Plateaux and cuestas of igneous rocks interbedded with or intruded into older sedimentaries.

Transverse Mercator Projection
Scale 1 : 3 Million

© Oxford University Press

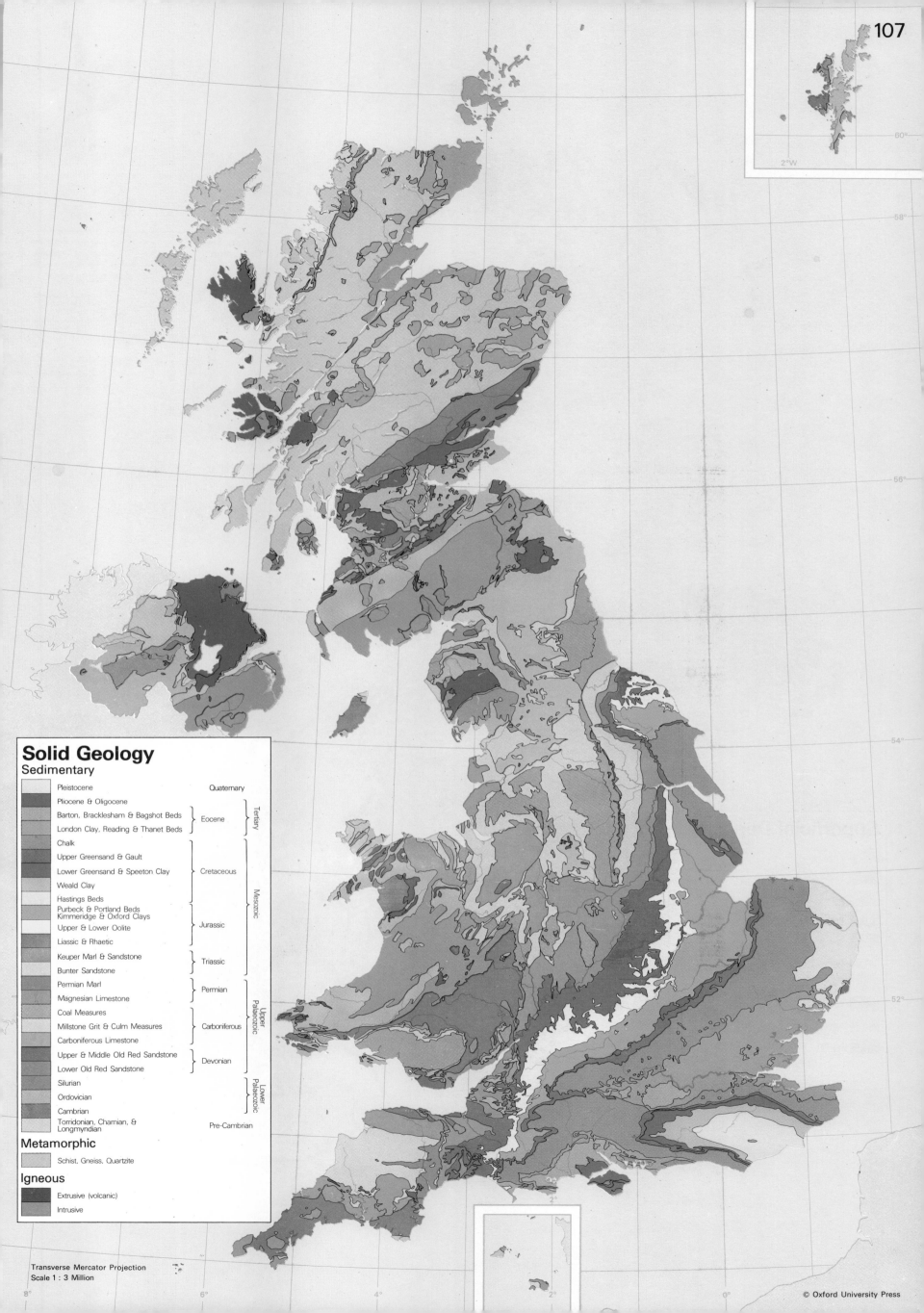

Solid Geology
Sedimentary

	Pleistocene	Quaternary
	Pliocene & Oligocene	
	Barton, Bracklesham & Bagshot Beds	Eocene / Tertiary
	London Clay, Reading & Thanet Beds	
	Chalk	
	Upper Greensand & Gault	
	Lower Greensand & Speeton Clay	Cretaceous / Mesozoic
	Weald Clay	
	Hastings Beds	
	Purbeck & Portland Beds Kimmeridge & Oxford Clays	
	Upper & Lower Oolite	Jurassic
	Liassic & Rhaetic	
	Keuper Marl & Sandstone	Triassic
	Bunter Sandstone	
	Permian Marl	Permian / Upper Palaeozoic
	Magnesian Limestone	
	Coal Measures	
	Millstone Grit & Culm Measures	Carboniferous
	Carboniferous Limestone	
	Upper & Middle Old Red Sandstone	Devonian
	Lower Old Red Sandstone	
	Silurian	Lower Palaeozoic
	Ordovician	
	Cambrian	
	Torridonian, Charnian, & Longmyndian	Pre-Cambrian

Metamorphic

	Schist, Gneiss, Quartzite

Igneous

	Extrusive (volcanic)
	Intrusive

Transverse Mercator Projection
Scale 1 : 3 Million

© Oxford University Press

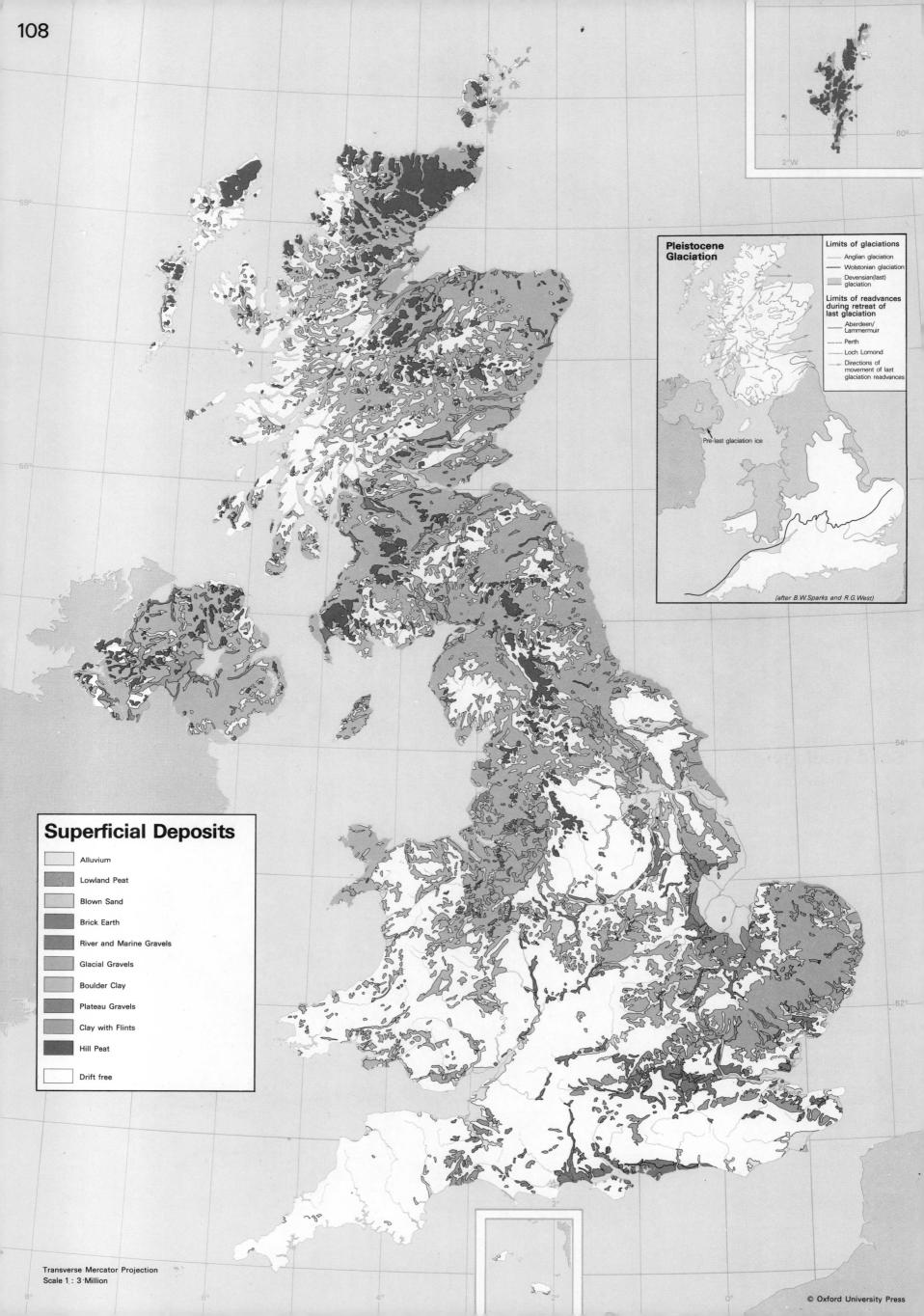

Superficial Deposits

	Alluvium
	Lowland Peat
	Blown Sand
	Brick Earth
	River and Marine Gravels
	Glacial Gravels
	Boulder Clay
	Plateau Gravels
	Clay with Flints
	Hill Peat
	Drift free

Pleistocene Glaciation

Limits of glaciations
- Anglian glaciation
- Wolstonian glaciation
- Devensian (last) glaciation

Limits of readvances during retreat of last glaciation
- Aberdeen/ Lammermuir
- Perth
- Loch Lomond
- Directions of movement of last glaciation readvances

Pre-last glaciation ice

(after B.W.Sparks and R.G.West)

Transverse Mercator Projection
Scale 1 : 3 Million

© Oxford University Press

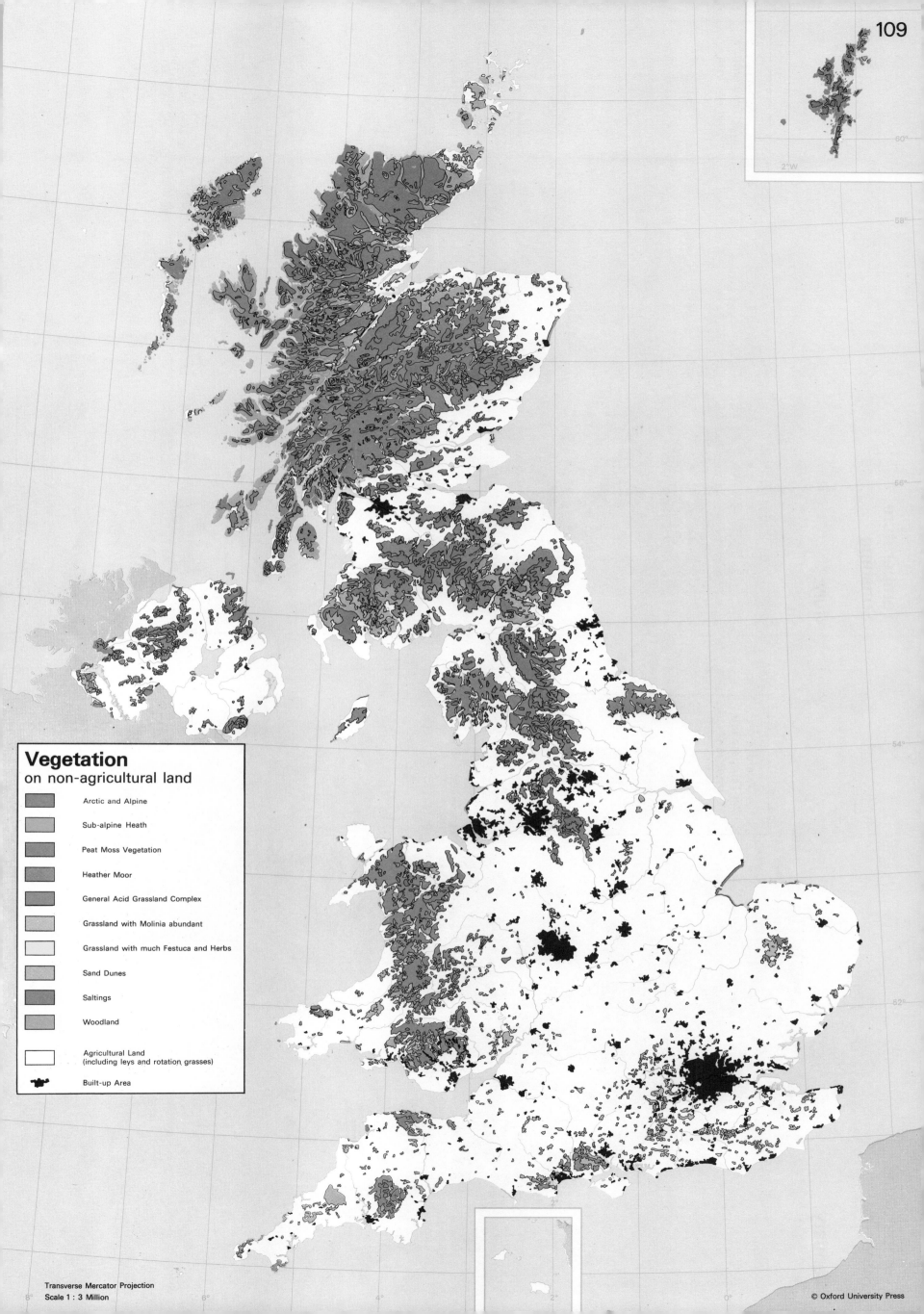

Vegetation
on non-agricultural land

- Arctic and Alpine
- Sub-alpine Heath
- Peat Moss Vegetation
- Heather Moor
- General Acid Grassland Complex
- Grassland with Molinia abundant
- Grassland with much Festuca and Herbs
- Sand Dunes
- Saltings
- Woodland

- Agricultural Land
  (including leys and rotation grasses)
- Built-up Area

Transverse Mercator Projection
Scale 1 : 3 Million

© Oxford University Press

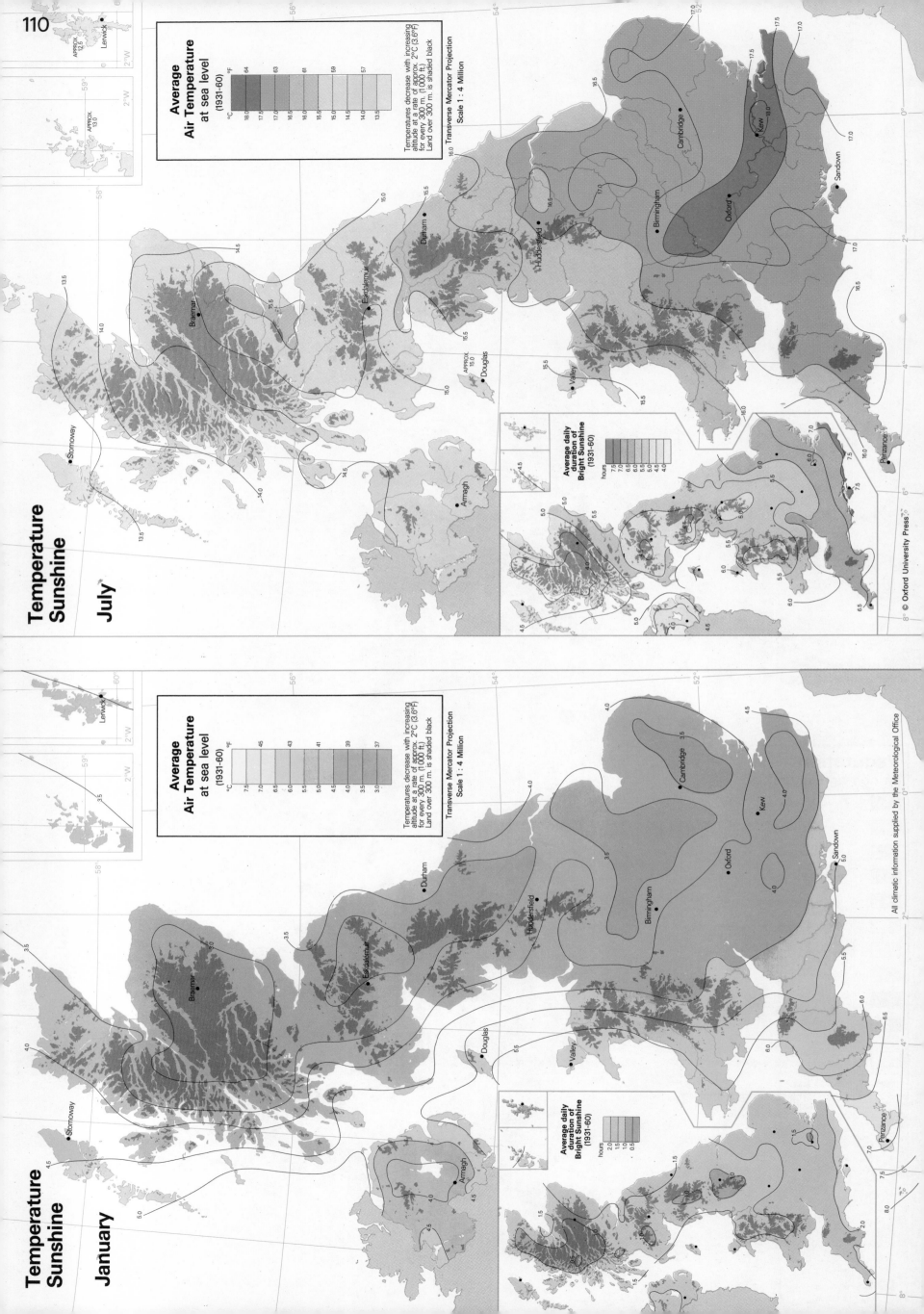

Temperature
Sunshine

July

Average
Air Temperature
at sea level
(1931-60)

°C   °F
18.0   64
17.5   63
17.0
16.5   61
16.0
15.5   59
15.0
14.5   57
14.0
13.5

Temperatures decrease with increasing
altitude at a rate of approx. 2°C (3.6°F)
for every 300 m. (1000 ft).
Land over 300 m. is shaded black

Transverse Mercator Projection
Scale 1 : 4 Million

Average daily
duration of
Bright Sunshine
(1931-60)

hours
7.5
7.0
6.5
6.0
5.5
5.0
4.5
4.0

© Oxford University Press

Temperature
Sunshine

January

Average
Air Temperature
at sea level
(1931-60)

°C   °F
7.5   45
7.0
6.5   43
6.0
5.5   41
5.0
4.5   39
4.0
3.5   37
3.0

Temperatures decrease with increasing
altitude at a rate of approx. 2°C (3.6°F)
for every 300 m. (1000 ft).
Land over 300 m. is shaded black

Transverse Mercator Projection
Scale 1 : 4 Million

Average daily
duration of
Bright Sunshine
(1931-60)

hours
2.0
1.5
1.0
0.5

All climatic information supplied by the Meteorological Office

Rainfall
Wind Direction

Averages of Temperature and Bright Sunshine 1931-60
(daily means of temperature; annual totals and daily means of bright sunshine.)

Averages of Rainfall 1916-50 (annual and monthly totals)

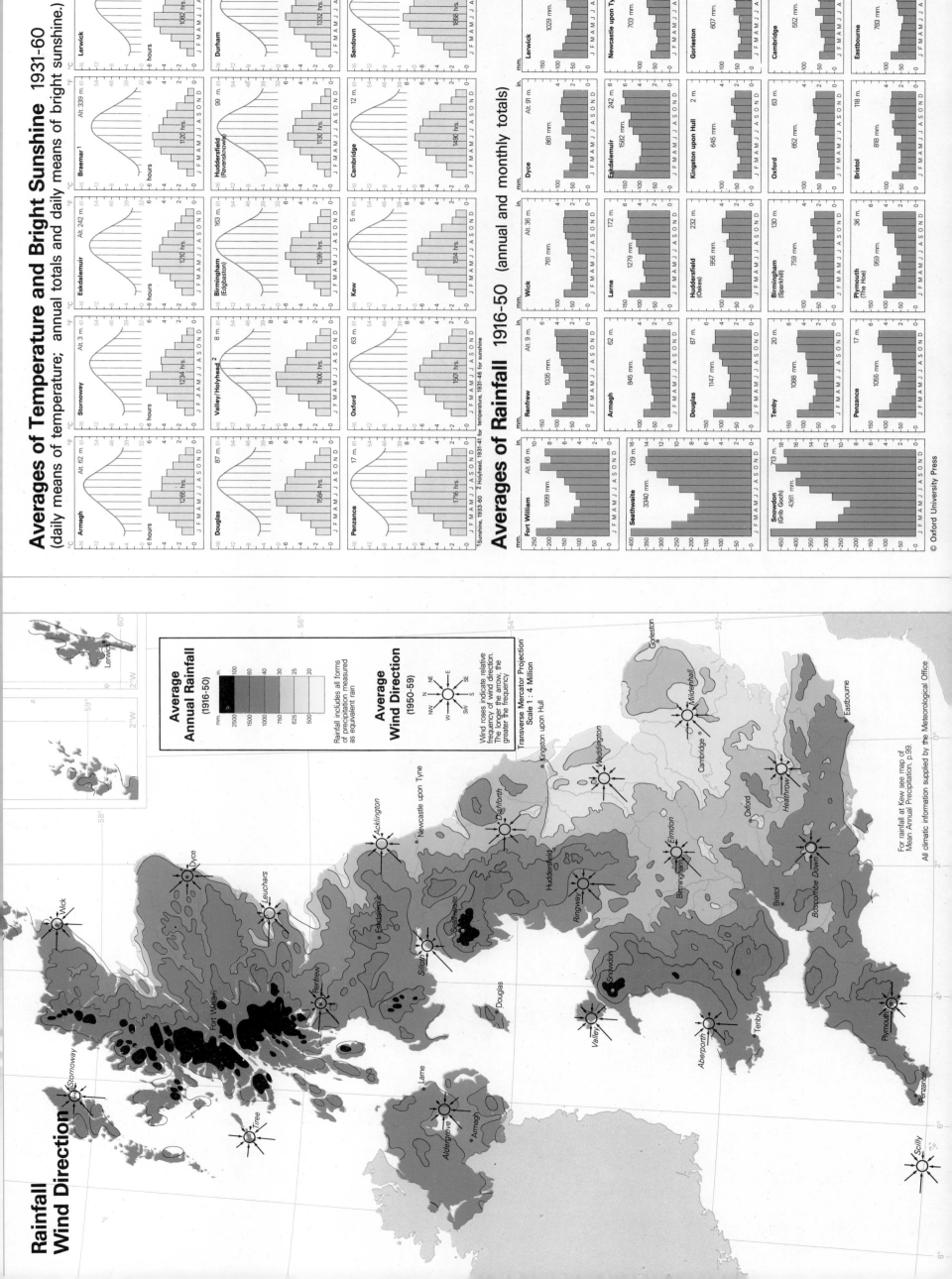

© Oxford University Press

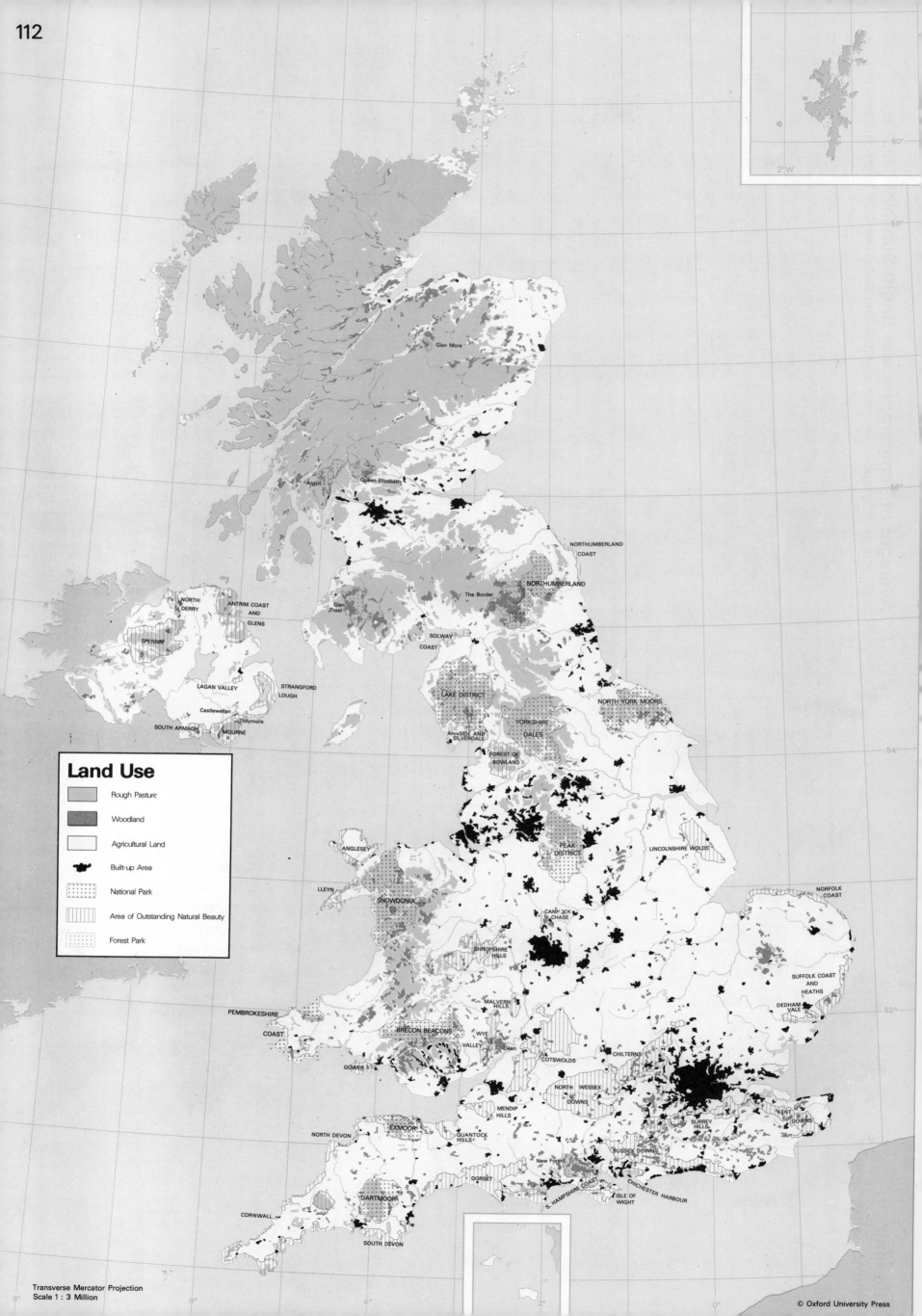

Land Use

	Rough Pasture
	Woodland
	Agricultural Land
	Built-up Area
	National Park
	Area of Outstanding Natural Beauty
	Forest Park

Glen More

NORTHUMBERLAND
COAST

NORTHUMBERLAND

The Border

Argyll

Queen Elizabeth

Glen
Trool

SOLWAY
COAST

NORTH
DERRY

ANTRIM COAST
AND
GLENS

SPERRIN

LAGAN VALLEY

STRANGFORD
LOUGH

Castlewellan

Tollymore

SOUTH ARMAGH

MOURNE

LAKE DISTRICT

NORTH YORK MOORS

YORKSHIRE
DALES

ARNSIDE AND
SILVERDALE

FOREST OF
BOWLAND

PEAK
DISTRICT

LINCOLNSHIRE WOLDS

ANGLESEY

LLEYN

SNOWDONIA

CANNOCK
CHASE

NORFOLK
COAST

SHROPSHIRE
HILLS

SUFFOLK COAST
AND
HEATHS

MALVERN
HILLS

DEDHAM
VALE

PEMBROKESHIRE
COAST

BRECON BEACONS

WYE
VALLEY

Dean

COTSWOLDS

CHILTERNS

GOWER

NORTH WESSEX
DOWNS

KENT
DOWNS

MENDIP
HILLS

SURREY
HILLS

EXMOOR

QUANTOCK
HILLS

NORTH DEVON

SUSSEX DOWNS

New Forest

DORSET

S. HAMPSHIRE COAST

CHICHESTER HARBOUR

ISLE OF
WIGHT

CORNWALL

DARTMOOR

SOUTH DEVON

60°

58°

56°

54°

52°

2°W

8°

6°

4°

2°

0°

Transverse Mercator Projection
Scale 1 : 3 Million

© Oxford University Press

Abbreviations

The list below serves two purposes: in the first place, it shows abbreviations used in the gazetteer. These gazetteer abbreviations are themselves of two types; abbreviations of proper names, e.g. 'Alb. — Albania' (official abbreviations, as for states in U.S.A., have been used as far as possible), and abbreviations of the topographical descriptions used in the gazetteer, e.g. 'geog. reg. — geographical region'. In the second place, abbreviations

are listed from the maps themselves, e.g. Ca. (It.) — Cima (peak). Abbreviations of the second word in a double name on the maps are not given, as the full name can be found in the gazetteer. As far as possible foreign topographical terms have been translated on the maps (e.g. Lübeck Bay), but in certain cases these terms are incorporated in the place-names and their abbreviated forms require explanation.

a. (Ger.)	am (upon the)	Eq. Guinea	Equatorial Guinea	Mal.	Malaysia, Malayan	S.	South, Southern
admin.	administrative	Erit.	Eritrea	Mald.	Maldives	S. (It., Sp.)	San (Saint)
Afg., Afghan.	Afghanistan	*est.*	estuary	Man.	Manitoba	S. (Port.)	São (Saint)
Afr.	Africa	Eth.	Ethiopia	*mand.*	mandate(d)	S., St. (Yugo.)	Stari (old)
Ala.	Alabama	Eur.	Europe	Mart.	Martinique	S. (Belg.)	Sint (Saint)
Alb.	Albania			Mass.	Massachusetts	s. (Fr.)	sur (on)
Alg.	Algeria	Falk. Is.	Falkland Islands	Maur.	Mauritania	Sa. (Port.)	Serra (range)
Alta.	Alberta	Fd. (Dan.,	Fiord	Md.	Maryland	Sa. (Sp.)	Sierra (range)
Ang.	Angola	Nor.)		Medit. Sea	Mediterranean Sea	S.A.	South America
Ant.	Antrim	*fed.*	federal	Mers.	Merseyside	S. Afr.	South Africa
Antarc.	Antarctica	Ferm.	Fermanagh	Mex.	Mexico	Sard.	Sardinia
Arab.	Arabia(n); Arabic	Fin.	Finland	Mich.	Michigan	Sask.	Saskatchewan
Arc.	Arctic	Fla.	Florida	Mid Glam.	Mid Glamorgan	Sau. Arab.	Saudi Arabia
Arch.	Archipelago	*for.*	forest	Minn.	Minnesota	S.C.	South Carolina
Arg.	Argentina	Fr.	France, French	Miss.	Mississippi	Scot.	Scotland
Ariz.	Arizona	Fr. Gu.	French Guiana	Mo.	Missouri	Sd.	Sound
Ark.	Arkansas	Ft.	Fort, Fortin	Mona.	Monaghan	S. Dak.	South Dakota
Arm.	Armagh			Mong.	Mongolia	Sen.	Senegal
A.S.S. Repub.	Autonomous Soviet	G.	Gulf, Golfe, Golfo	Mont.	Montana	S. Glam.	South Glamorgan
	Socialist Republic	G., Gr. (Ger.)	Gross (great)	Mor.	Morocco	Shet.	Shetland
Atl. O.	Atlantic Ocean	G. (Yugo.)	Gornji (upper)	Moz.	Mozambique	S.I.	South Island
Aus.	Austria	Ga. (U.S.A.)	Georgia (U.S.A.)	mt(s)., mtn(s).	mount(s), mountain(s)	S. Kor.	South Korea
Austl.	Australia	Gab.	Gabon			S.L.	Sierra Leone
Auton.	Autonomous	Gal.	Galway	N.	North, Northern	Som.	Somalia
		Gam.	Gambia	N., Nov.	Nov-yy, -aya (new)	Som. (Eng.)	Somerset
B.	Bay, Baie	Gd. (Fr.)	Grand (great)	(Russ.)		Sp.	Spain, Spanish
B. (Ger.)	Bad (spa)	Geb. (Egypt)	Gebel (mountain)	n. (Czech.)	nad (over)	Spits.	Spitsbergen
B. (Russ.)	Bolsh-oy, -aya (great)	Geb. (Ger.)	Gebirge (range)	N.A.	North America	Sra. (Arab.)	Sebkra (Salt Lake)
Bangl.	Bangladesh	*geog.*	geographical	*nat.*	national	S.S.R.	Soviet Socialist Republic
B.C.	British Columbia	Ger.	German	Nat. Mon.	National Monument	St(e).	Saint(e)
Beds.	Bedfordshire	*gey.*	geyser	N.B.	New Brunswick	St. (Eng.)	Street
Bel.	Belize	*glac.*	glacier	N.C.	North Carolina	St. (Russ.)	Star-yy, -aya (old)
Belg.	Belgium	Glos.	Gloucestershire	N. Dak.	North Dakota	Sta. (It., Port.,	Santa (Saint)
Berks.	Berkshire	Gob. (S.A.)	Gobernado (Governor)	Ndr. (Ger.)	Nieder (lower)	Sp.)	
Bj. (Arab.)	Bor(d)j (tower)	Gp.	Group (islands)	Nebr.	Nebraska	*Sta.*	Station
Bk.	Bank	Gral. (S.A.)	General	Nĕm. (Czech.)	Nĕmecky (German)	Staffs.	Staffordshire
Bol.	Bolivia	Gram.	Grampian	Nep.	Nepal	Sto. (Port.,	Santo (Saint)
Bord.	Borders	Grc.	Greece	Neth.	Netherlands	Sp.)	
Bots.	Botswana	Grn. (Bulg.)	Gorna (upper)	Nev.	Nevada	Str.	Strait(s)
Br.	British	Grnld.	Greenland	Newf.	Newfoundland	Strath.	Strathclyde
Br. (Mal.)	Bandar (harbour)	Gt.	Great, Greater	N.H.	New Hampshire	Sud.	Sudan
Braz.	Brazil	Gt. (S. Afr.)	Groot (great)	N.I.	North Island	Suff.	Suffolk
Bucks.	Buckinghamshire	Gt. Ldn.	Greater London	Nic.	Nicaragua	Sum.	Sumatra
Bulg.	Bulgaria	Gt. Man.	Greater Manchester	Nig.	Nigeria	Sur.	Surinam
Bur.	Burundi	Gu.	Guinea	Nizh. (Russ.)	Nizhn-iy, -aya (lower)	Sv. (Czech.,	Sveti (Saint)
		Guat.	Guatemala	N.J.	New Jersey	Yugo.)	
C.	Cape, Cap, Cabo, Capo	Guy.	Guyana	N. Kor.	North Korea	S. Viet.	South Vietnam
C. (S.A.)	Cerro (peak)	Gwyn.	Gwynedd	N. Mex.	New Mexico	S.W. Afr.	South West Africa
Ca. (It.)	Cima (peak)			Nor.	Norway, Norwegian	Swaz.	Swaziland
Calif.	California	Hants.	Hampshire	Norf.	Norfolk	Swed.	Sweden, Swedish
Cam.	Cameroun	Harb.	Harbour	Northants.	Northamptonshire	Switz.	Switzerland
Cambs.	Cambridgeshire	Hd.	Head	Northumb.	Northumberland	S. Yorks.	South Yorkshire
Can.	Canada	Hebr.	Hebrides	Notts.	Nottinghamshire	Syr.	Syria
Can. Is.	Canary Islands	Here. & Worcs.	Hereford & Worcester	N.S.	Nova Scotia	Szt. (Hung.)	Szent (Saint)
cap.	Capital	Herts.	Hertfordshire	N.S.W.	New South Wales		
Car.	Carlow	High.	Highland	N. Viet.	North Vietnam	Tas.	Tasmania
Carib. Sea	Caribbean Sea	Hond.	Honduras	Nw. (Pol.)	Nowy (new)	Tan., Tanzan.	Tanzania
Cen. Afr. Rep.	Central African Republic	Humb.	Humberside	N.W. Front.	North-West Frontier	Tay.	Tayside
Cen. Am.	Central America	Hung.	Hungary	Prov.	Province	Tenn.	Tennessee
Ch. (Arab.)	Chott (salt lake)	*i(s)., I(s).*	island(s), Island(s),	N.W.T.	Northwest Territories	Tex.	Texas
Chan.	Channel		Isle(s)	N.Y.	New York	Thai.	Thailand
Chan. Is.	Channel Islands	Î. (Fr.)	Île (island)	N. Yorks.	North Yorkshire	Tip.	Tipperary
Chât. (Fr.)	Château	Ice.	Iceland	N.Z.	New Zealand	Tng. (Mal.)	Tandjung (cape)
Ches.	Cheshire	Ill.	Illinois			Trans.	Transvaal
Chne. (Fr.)	Chaîne (chain)	Ind.	Indiana	O.	Ocean	Trin. & Tob.	Trinidad & Tobago
Ck., Cr.	Creek	Ind. O.	Indian Ocean	Ob. (Ger.)	Ober (upper)	Tun.	Tunisia
Cleve.	Cleveland	Indon.	Indonesia	Ofly.	Offaly	Tur.	Turkey
Cnel. (Arg.)	Coronel (Colonel)	Ing. (S.A.)	Ingeniero (Engineer)	O.F.S.	Orange Free State	Tyr.	Tyrone
Co.	County	*Ins.*	Inset	Okla.	Oklahoma		
col.	Colony	I. of M.	Isle of Man	Ont.	Ontario	U.A.E.	United Arab Emirates
Col. (Arg.)	Colonia (colony)	I. of W.	Isle of Wight	Oreg.	Oregon	Ug., Ugan.	Uganda
Colo.	Colorado	Irel.	Ireland	Ork.	Orkney	U.K.	United Kingdom
Colom.	Colombia	Isr.	Israel	Oxon.	Oxfordshire	U.N	United Nations
cond.	Condominium	*isth.*	isthmus			Unt. (Ger.)	Unter (lower)
Conn.	Connecticut	It.	Italy, Italian	P.	Pass	Up.	Upper
Cord. (S.A.)	Cordillera (range)	Iv. Cst.	Ivory Coast	Pa.	Pennsylvania	Up. V.	Upper Volta
Corn.	Cornwall			Pac. O.	Pacific Ocean	Uru.	Uruguay
Cors.	Corsica	J. (Arab.)	Jabal, Jebel (mountain)	Pak.	Pakistan	U.S.A.	United States of
C.P.	Cape Province	Jam.	Jamaica	Pan.	Panama		America
C.R.	Costa Rica	Jap.	Japan(ese)	Par.	Paraguay	U.S.S.R.	Union of Soviet
Cse. (Fr.)	Causse (limestone plateau)	Jor.	Jordan	P.E.I.	Prince Edward Island		Socialist Republics
Cumb.	Cumbria	Junct.	Junction	*penin.*	Peninsular		
Cyp.	Cyprus			Phil.	Philippines	V. (S.A.)	Vulcan (volcano)
Czech.	Czechoslovakia	K. (Mal.)	Kuala (river mouth)	Pk.	Peak	V. (Port., Sp.)	Villa, Vila
		Kans.	Kansas	*plat.*	plateau	V. (Yugo.)	Veliki (great)
D. (Tur.)	Dağ (mountain)	Ken.	Kenya	P.N.G.	Papua New Guinea	Va.	Virginia
D. (Czech.)	Dolni (lower)	Kg. (Mal.)	Kampong (village)	Pol.	Poland	*val.*	Valley
D. (Yugo.)	Doljni; Donji (lower)	Kild.	Kildare	Port.	Portugal, Portuguese	Vel. (Russ.)	Velik-iy, -aya (great)
Dah.	Dahomey	Kilk.	Kilkenny	P.R.	Puerto Rico	Ven., Venez.	Venezuela
Dan.	Danish	Km	Kilometre(s)	*Pref.*	Prefecture	Verkh. (Russ.)	Verkhn-iy, -aya (upper)
Dardan.	Dardanelles	Ky.	Kentucky	*princip.*	principality	Vict.	Victoria
D.C.	District of Columbia			Prot.	Protectorate	*volc.*	Volcano
Del.	Delaware	L.	Lake, Loch, Lough, Lac,	Prov.	Province	Vt.	Vermont
Den.	Denmark		Lago	Pt(e)	Point, Pointe		
Depend.	Dependency	La.	Louisiana	Pta. (Sp.)	Punta (point)	W.	West, Western
Dept.	Department	*lag.*	lagoon	Pto. (It.,	Porto, Pôrto, Puerto	War.	Warwickshire
Derby.	Derbyshire	Lancs.	Lancashire	Port., Sp.)	(port)	Wash.	Washington
Dist.	District (admin.)	Lat.	Latitude	Qat.	Qatar	Wat.	Waterford
dist.	district (topographical	Ld.	Land	Que.	Quebec	Wex.	Wexford
	term)	Leb.	Lebanon	Queens.	Queensland	W. Ger.	West Germany
Divis.	Division	Leics.	Leicestershire			W. Glam.	West Glamorgan
Dns.	Downs	Leit.	Leitrim	*ra.*	range	Wick.	Wicklow
Dodec.	Dodecanese	Les.	Lesotho	Rd.	Road	Wilts.	Wiltshire
Dol. (Pol.)	Dolovy (lower)	Lib.	Liberia	*Reg.*	Region (admin.)	Wis.	Wisconsin
Dom.	Dominion	Lim.	Limerick	*reg.*	region (geog.)	W. Mid.	West Midlands
Dom. Rep.	Dominican Republic	Lincs.	Lincolnshire	Rep., Repub.	Republic	Wmth.	Westmeath
Don.	Donegal	Lit.	Little	Res.	Reservoir	W. Sam.	Western Samoa
Dtsch. (Ger.)	Deutsch (German)	Lon.	Londonderry	Rhod.	Rhodesia	W. Va.	West Virginia
Dumf. & Gall.	Dumfries & Galloway	Long.	Longford, Longitude	R.I.	Rhode Island	Wyo.	Wyoming
Dz. (Tibet)	Dzong (fortified town)	Loth.	Lothian	*riv.*	river	W. Yorks.	West Yorkshire
		Lr.	Lower	*rlv.*	railway		
E.	East, Eastern	Lux.	Luxembourg	Rom.	Romania(n)	Yugo.	Yugoslavia(n)
É., Étg. (Fr.)	Étang (lagoon)	M. (It.)	Marittimo (maritime)	Rosc.	Roscommon		
Ec.	Ecuador	M. (Russ)	Mal-yy, -aya (little)	Russ.	Russian	Zam.	Zambia
E. Ger.	East Germany	M., Mt (e)	Mont(e) (mountain)	Rwa.	Rwanda	Zap. (Russ.)	Zapadn-yy, -aya (West)
El Sal.	El Salvador	Mad., Madag.	Madagascar				
Eng.	England	Maj.	Majorca				

Map projections

The choice of a map projection depends principally on the shape and size of the area to be covered, and to a lesser extent on any special purpose for which it may be required.

Large scale maps

Maps at such scales as 1:1M to 1:10M, which are large scales from the point of view of an atlas, necessarily cover fairly small areas of the globe; for them it is possible to use an Orthomorphic projection, that is, one which will everywhere be free from local distortion in shape, although the scale may vary slightly in different parts of the map. The best Orthomorphic projection for an area whose greatest extent is north and south is the Transverse Mercator. This has been used for Scandinavia 1:4M (pages 46-7), SE.Asia 1:10M (pages 64-5), SE.Australia and New Zealand 1:5M (pages 70-1), and E.Africa 1:8M (pages 76-7). The Conical Orthomorphic (or Lambert) projection is the best if the greatest extent of the area is east and west, and it has been used for all the other maps in the atlas between the scales of 1:1M and 1:10M, e.g. Mediterranean 1:8M (pages 32-3), Western U.S.S.R. 1:10M (pages 50-1), and W.Africa 1:8M (pages 80-1). For a square-shaped area either serves equally well, although the Conical Orthomorphic is preferable as being easier to draw. At scales of 1:2M or larger, both projections are substantially perfect, and the Conical Orthomorphic, the simpler one to produce, again takes preference. In both these projections the scale is 'true' only along the central parallel in the Conical Orthomorphic or the central meridian in the Transverse Mercator. On either side of this line it increases progressively. In order to make the average scale approximately correct a small over-all scale reduction has been applied to each map. Thus the scale along the central parallel or meridian (respectively) is too small by the stated amount, and at the long edges of the map it is too large by a rather greater amount, while it will be correct along two intermediate 'standard parallels' in the Conical Orthomorphic and along corresponding small circles in the Transverse Mercator. In each map in the atlas the latitude or the longitude of the central axis and the amount of its scale reduction is stated, and the scale error at any point of the map can be calculated as explained on page 115 (see Table 1). Note that in some cases several of the larger scale maps, e.g. Europe 1:4M, have been drawn all combined on a single projection, so maximum scale error does not necessarily occur at the edge of each component page.

Small scale maps

For maps at about 1:16M or smaller, the shorter edges of which represent a distance of 3,500 miles or more in a double page of this atlas, the change of scale in an Orthomorphic projection will be nearly 10 per cent. This begins to be excessive, and the enlargement of the outer areas is then best controlled by tolerating some local distortion instead. An Equidistant projection may be used, in which radial distances from the centre are true, with elongation only in directions perpendicular to the radius: or an Equal-area projection in which this elongation is accompanied by compression in the radial direction. In either case the maximum distortion is at the edges of the map. Table 2 shows the scale errors and distortions of these two projections. So long as distances from the centre do not exceed 3,000 miles (as in a 1:16M double-page map) the elongation round the edges in a Zenithal Equidistant is less than 10 per cent., and its distortion is less than that of the Equal-area, to which it is then preferable. At smaller scales, however, the greater distortion of the Equal-area may be preferred to the increasing enlargement of less important outer areas in the Equidistant projection.

In this atlas the projections for the maps of Europe, Asia, Australia, and N. America at 1:16M are Zenithal Equidistant, while an Equal-area projection has been used for Eurasia 1:32M (pages 18-19). In other cases, detailed below, special considerations have governed the choice of projection.

The map of Antarctica (1:25M, page 9) is on a Zenithal Equidistant projection. Equidistant projections have also been used for the maps of the Oceans (1:50M, pages 7-9) as enlargement of the bounding coast lines is preferable to their additional distortion by the Equal-area projection. The normal projection has, however, been modified to reduce the worst enlargement and distortion as follows: in a Zenithal Equidistant projection for the *Pacific Ocean*, which embraces 180° of longitude and 110° of latitude, Table 2 shows that the peripheral scale error and distortion in the centres of the important east and west edges of the map (Panama and East Indies) would be 57 per cent., while in the unimportant centre of the north edge (Bering Sea) it would be only 21 per cent. and in the centre of the south edge (Eltanin Fracture Zone) about 14 per cent. The projection has therefore been modified so as to give an equal stretching of 37 per cent. all round a bounding oval, while radial scales remain correct (Fig.5 illustrates the principle in respect of a Polar Zenithal Equidistant projection). Similarly, in the projection for the *Atlantic Ocean* the scale errors which would have been over 50 per cent. and 17 per cent. have been equalized at 22 per cent. In that for the *Indian Ocean* errors in the closely adjacent land areas have been kept down to 10 per cent. or less, at the expense of the unimportant Southern Ocean which has been stretched by up to 30 per cent.

On the map of U.S.S.R. at 1:18M (pages 48-9), since the important part of this area is a narrow belt of country running from east to west, it is possible to use the Conical Orthomorphic in spite of the small scale. Between 43° and 68° N. worst scale error is 1¼ per cent.

The large overlap between the two maps of Africa at 1:16M (pages 73 and 78-9) has made is convenient to draw these two maps as one map, and to use a Zenithal Equal-area instead of the two separate Equidistant projections which would otherwise be preferable.

In the case of the 1:32M map of the Americas (pages 82-3), the narrow width of the two continents makes it possible to find a great circle axis (marked in the margin of the map) such that no part of either continent lies more than 2,000 miles from it. An oblique Mercator (Orthomorphic) projection has consequently been possible with a scale error of −5 per cent. on the axis, and worst errors elsewhere of +7.8 per cent. in Lower California, +4.5 per cent. at San Francisco and Recife, +2 per cent. in Southern Chile and Newfoundland, and +11 per cent. in Eastern Greenland; small errors considering the size of the area.

The narrow width of South America (mapped at 1:16M on pages 94-5, and at 1:25M on page 15) makes a Transverse Mercator possible. The great circle used as the base line is the 60° W meridian, and the maps have a central scale error of −3 per cent. and maximum errors of +4 per cent. and +7 per cent. on the west and east coasts respectively. Very little of the land area of these maps has a scale error of over 3 per cent.

For the World maps (pages 17 and 97-103), horizontal parallels are desirable, coupled with an absence of any extreme local distortion. Gall's projection has consequently been adopted, modified by curving the meridians inwards slightly towards the poles in order to reduce undesirable scale exaggeration in high latitudes.

The choice for the thematic maps of the United Kingdom at scales of 1:2M, 1:3M, and 1:4M (pages 104-112) has been the Transverse Mercator projection as used by the Ordnance Survey with the central meridian at 2° W. Scale error over the whole area is less than +0.1 per cent. and may therefore be disregarded.

Map projections

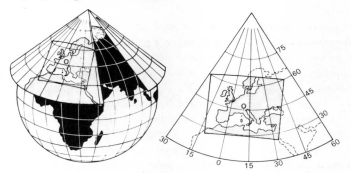

FIG. 1. Simple Conical projection; origin 45° N., 10° E.

The meridians are projected on to a cone which touches the sphere along a parallel through the origin O. In the Simple Conical (Equidistant), the Conical Orthomorphic, and the Conical Equal-area projections the parallels are then drawn as circles spaced respectively at true distances, gradually increasing distances, or gradually diminishing distances, as calculated to give the required property. Fig. 1 is at too small a scale to differentiate between the three types of this projection.

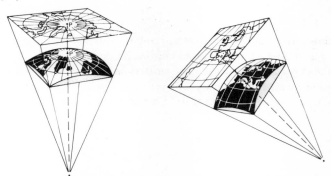

FIG. 2(a). Polar Zenithal projection.   FIG. 2(b). Oblique Zenithal projection; 'Pole' 40° N., 0°.

(For clarity, tangent planes have been raised above spheres.)

If the apex angle of the cone in the Conical projection is widened until it becomes 180°, the cone becomes a plane touching the sphere at P, and a Zenithal projection results. (a) **Polar.** The meridians are truly spaced radial lines and the parallels are concentric circles spaced (as in the Conical projections) so that radial distances are either true, or increased to give an Orthomorphic projection, or reduced to give equal areas. (b) **Oblique.** The projection need not be centred on the Pole. In such a case, the meridians and parallels are so plotted that radial *directions* from some central origin are correctly shown, while *distances* from the origin are either correct or appropriately increased or decreased as before.

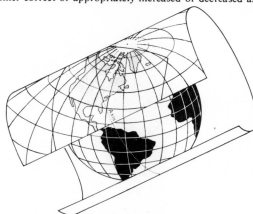

FIG. 3. Oblique Mercator projection—as map 82-3.

If the cone of the conical projection is elongated until it becomes a cylinder touching the sphere along the Equator, cylindrical projections result, the Cylindrical Orthomorphic being *Mercator's*. As with Zenithal projections, there is no need for the axis of the cylinder to be the Earth's polar axis. If the axis is taken in the plane of the equator the *Transverse Mercator* results: otherwise an *Oblique Mercator* (Fig. 3). Although scale errors are considerable on a Mercator's projection when used for a large part of the Earth's surface, they do not exceed 10 per cent. within 1,750 miles of whatever great circle is chosen as the axis.

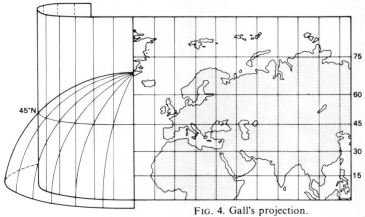

FIG. 4. Gall's projection.

Gall's projection (Fig. 4) is another cylindrical projection where the cylinder, instead of touching the sphere along the Equator (as in Mercator's), is supposed to cut the surface of the sphere mid-way between the Equator and the Poles, i.e. at 45° N and 45° S. The parallels are projected stereographically. Scale is true only along the 45th parallels: within them it is compressed, outside it is exaggerated.

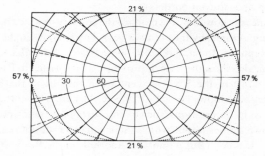

FIG. 5.

In Fig. 5 the full lines represent a Polar Zenithal Equidistant projection of a rectangular area, and the percentages represent scale errors in directions perpendicular to the radii. The broken lines show how the radii representing meridians may be curved so as to give approximately equal scale error all round a bounding oval. The same principle may be applied to Zenithal projections centred on any other point on the Earth (*see* page 114).

Scale errors

Table 1. *Conical Orthomorphic and Transverse Mercator Projections*

S in miles	Approximate error per cent.	S in miles	Approximate error per cent.
0	0.0	1,200	+4.6
200	+0.1	1,400	+6.3
400	+0.5	1,600	+8.2
600	+1.2	1,800	+10.4
800	+2.0	2,000	+12.8
1,000	+3.2		

S is the distance from the parallel through the origin in Conical projections or from the central meridian in the Transverse Mercator. From the tabulated error deduct the 'Scale Reduction' quoted on each map. Example: On map 33 the distance from Cairo to Jarabub is 418 miles by the map-scale and the mid point is 840 miles south of lat. 42°. The local scale error is therefore +2.2 per cent. −0.7 per cent., and the correct distance is 412 miles. There is, however, a simpler method of ascertaining scale error or true distances. Measure on the map-scale the distance along the nearest parallel between two adjacent meridians (interpolating between parallels if necessary) and compare this with the figure given in the left-hand border. In the above example the length between meridians along parallel 30° measures 304 miles and the true length is 300 miles. Proportionately, in 418 miles the error will be about +6 miles—the same as that determined from Table 1. For long distances, especially when crosssing the central parallel (or meridian in the Transverse Mercator), divide into two or four equal sections, compute the scale error in the centre of each section as above, and take the algebraic mean.

Table 2. *Zenithal Projections*

R Degrees	R Miles	Equidistant			Equal Area			Orthomorphic		
		M	P	D	M	P	D	M	P	D
0	0	0	0.0	0.0	0.0	0.0	0.0	0.0	0.0	0
10	700	0	+0.5	0.5	−0.4	+0.4	0.8	+0.8	+0.8	0
20	1,400	0	+2.1	2.1	−1.5	+1.5	3.0	+3.1	+3.1	0
30	2,100	0	+4.7	4.7	−3.4	+3.5	6.9	+7.2	+7.2	0
40	2,800	0	+8.6	8.6	−6.0	+6.3	12.3	+13.2	+13.2	0
50	3,500	0	+13.9	13.9	−9.4	+10.2	19.6	+21.7	+21.7	0
60	4,200	0	+20.9	20.9	−13.4	+15.3	28.7	+33.3	+33.3	0
70	4,900	0	+30.0	30.0	−18.1	+22.2	40.3	+49.0	+49.0	0
80	5,600	0	+41.7	41.7	−23.4	+30.4	53.8	+70.4	+70.4	0
90	6,300	0	+57.1	57.1	−29.3	+41.4	70.7	+100.0	+100.0	0

R is the distance of a point from the origin.
M is the percentage scale error at the point in a radial direction.
P is the percentage error in a direction perpendicular to the radius.
D = P − M is the local distortion, expressed as a percentage.

In non-Orthomorphic Zenithal projections true distances which are neither radial nor 'perpendicular' are not ascertainable as precisely as in Orthomorphic projections, but a rough approximation can be made by applying a scale correction suitably interpolated between the values of M and P according to the orientation of the distance to be measured.

The Gazetteer is an index of the towns and topographical features shown on the maps. Position is shown by reference numbers, then to the 'squares' formed on each map by the intersection of the lines of latitude and longitude; these are designated by numbers (shown in the side borders) and by letters (shown in the top and bottom borders).

Each place-name is followed by the name of the country in which it lies (or, in certain cases, e.g. Azores, by the ocean or sea). Town names in the United Kingdom, Irish Republic, India, Pakistan, South Africa, Australia, Canada, U.S.A., and China also show the state or province. Town names in Russia are followed by the name of the S.S.R. except when they lie in the Russian S.F.S.R., then they are followed only by U.S.S.R. All names other than town names are followed by descriptions, such as *riv., dist., plat.*: descriptions are also given for town names about which there might be doubt, e.g. 'West Point: *town*, Va., U.S.A.'. (But mountains and hills in the British Isles are gazetteered under Ben, Sgurr, Slieve, Mynydd, &c.)

Entries are in strict alphabetical order letter by letter; i.e. an entry of two or more words is alphabetized as if it were one word; a comma, however, between two words breaks the sequence: e.g. 'Burton' — 'Burton, North' — 'Burton Agnes'. Towns of the same name are given in alphabetical order of the country or province name which follows them: e.g. 'Amsterdam: Netherlands' — 'Amsterdam: N.Y., U.S.A.' — 'Amsterdam: Trans., S. Africa'. Finally, sequence is decided by alphabetical order of descriptive terms, as shown in the following example: 'Carmen: Mexico' — 'Carmen: Uruguay' — 'Carmen: *i.*, Mexico' — 'Carmen: *riv.*, Chile' — 'Carmen Alto: Chile' — 'Carmen del Parana: Paraguay' — 'Carmensa: Argentina'.

Places with alternative names are given under both names and cross-referenced. Foreign names preceded by the article (Le, La, El, Al, &c.), are gazetteered both under the name and the article, e.g. Le Havre: Havre, Le: El Alamein: Alamein, El.

Foreign letters have been alphabetized as if they were English letters, e.g. Å as A, Ã as A, Æ as AE, ð as dh, Ł as L, Ö as O, Ø as O.

Historical and Archaeological Place-names. Certain historical and archaeological place-names, not shown on the maps, have been included in the Gazetteer in italic type. The descriptions are by Dr. G. E. F. Chilver (Lecturer in Ancient History, Oxford University), and are located by reference to places shown on the map.

Countries, &c. Entries for countries, major dependencies, and areas of special sovereignty are in bold type, followed by brief description of status (if not included in name), capital, area, and population according to the latest available census report (*C*) or estimate (*E*).

Administrative Capitals. Capitals of countries are shown in large capital letters, e.g. ROME. Capitals of administrative divisions (e.g. counties in U.K.) and dependencies are shown in small capital letters, with the name of the division concerned. The entry for a province, country, &c. also shows the name of its capital. Thus 'ALBI: Tarn, France' — 'Tarn: *Dept.,* France (*cap.* Albi)'.

Gazetteer

Aa: *riv.*, France **36** H5
Aabenraa: Denmark **47** L9
Aachen (Aix-la-Chapelle): W. Germany **44** M5
Aachen: *Dist.*, North Rhine – Westphalia, West Germany **44** M5
Aalbæk Bay: Denmark **47** M8
Aalborg: Denmark **47** L8
Aalen: W. Germany **40** Q7
Aalst: Belgium **44** K5
Aalten: Netherlands **44** M4
Äänekoski: Finland **46** T5
Aansluit: S. Africa **74** E3
Aar, Mount: SW. Africa **74** B3
AARAU: Aargau, Switzerland **40** O8
Aarberg: Berne, Switz. **40** N8
Aarburg: Aargau, Switz. **40** N8
Aare: *riv.*, Switzerland **40** N8
Aargau: *Canton*, Switz. (*cap.* Aarau) **40** O8
Aarhus: Denmark **47** M8
Aarida, El: Lebanon **56** D4
Aars: Denmark **47** L8
Aarschot: Belgium **44** K5
Aasleagh: Mayo, Repub. of Ireland **30** B12
Aba: Nigeria **81** F3
Aba: Zaire **76** D2
Abacaxis: Brazil **94** F4
Abaco, Great and Little: *is.*, Bahamas **91** N12
Abadan: Iran **57** L6
Abadeh: Iran **55** H8
Abadla: Algeria **80** L8
Abaetetuba: Brazil **94** H4
Abaí: Paraguay **96** D2
Abaiang: *i.*, Gilbert Is. **67** O1
Abaji: Nigeria **81** F3
Abakaliki: Nigeria **81** F3
ABAKAN: Khakass, U.S.S.R. **51** Q4
Abakan Mtns.: U.S.S.R. **51** P4
Abala: *well*, Niger **81** E2
Abal Dufuf: *pump. station*, Saudi Arabia **57** G6
Abalemma: *well*, Niger **81** F1
Aban: U.S.S.R. **51** R3
Abancay: Peru **94** C6
Abancourt: France **36** G6
Abanga: *riv.*, Gabon **81** G4
Abano Bagni: Italy **41** R10
Abashiri: Japan **63** ZZ6
Abau: Papua/New Guinea **69** H2
Abaya, Lake: Ethiopia **76** E1
Abbabis: SW. Africa **74** B1
Abbach: W. Germany **41** S7
Abbaretz: France **36** D8
Abbaye, Point: *cape*, Mich., U.S.A. **88** G2
Abbe, Lake: Ethiopia **79** Q17
Abbert: *riv.*, Gal., Repub. of Ireland **31** D13
Abbeville: France **36** G5
Abbeville: Ala., U.S.A. **91** J10
Abbeville: La., U.S.A. **90** E11
Abbeville: S.C., U.S.A. **91** K8
Abbey: Galway, Repub. of Ireland **31** E13
Abbey: Tip., Repub. of Irel. **31** F15
Abbey Dore: Hereford & Worcester, England **24** Q16
Abbeydorney: Kerry, Repub. of Ireland **31** B15
Abbeyfeale: Lim., Repub. of Ireland **31** C15
Abbeylara: Long., Repub. of Ireland **30** G12
Abbeyleix: Laois, Repub. of Ireland **31** G14
Abbeyshrule: Long., Repub. of Ireland **30** F12
Abbeytown: Cumbria, Eng. **26** P10
Abbiategrasso: Italy **40** O10
Abbots: W. Australia **68** B5
Abbots Bromley: Staffs., England **27** S14
Abbotsbury: Dorset, Eng. **24** Q18
Abbotsford (House): Borders, Scotland **29** Q8
Abbotsley: Cambs., England **25** V15
Abbottabad: N.W. Front. Prov., Pakistan **58** M8
'Abd, Al: Saudi Arabia **55** H10
Abd al Kuri: *i.*, Somalia **79** P7
Abdera: Greek city on N. coast of Aegean between mouth of river Mesta and Pórto Lágo, Greece **39** T16
Abdulino: U.S.S.R. **50** H4
Abdulla, Mount: Ethiopia **79** Q18
Abdürrahim: Tur. (Dardan. *Inset*) **20** *Ins.*
ABÉCHÉ: Ouaddai, Chad **79** J7
Abelessa: Algeria **78** E5
Abel Tasman National Park: S.I., New Zealand **70** O15
Abemama: *i.*, Gilbert Is. **67** O1
ABENGOUROU: Est, Ivory Coast **80** D3
Abensberg: W. Germany **41** R7
ABEOKUTA: *Ogun*, Nigeria **81** E3
Abera: Ethiopia **76** E1
Aberaeron: Dyfed, Wales **24** N15
Aberaman: Mid. Glam., Wales **24** P16
Aberarder: High., Scotland **28** N6
Abercarn: Gwent, Wales **24** P16
Aberchirder: Gram., Scot. **28** Q4
Abercorn: Lothian, Scot. **29** P8
Aberdare: Mid. Glam., Wales **24** P16
Aberdaron: Gwynedd, Wales **27** M14
ABERDEEN: Gram., Scotland **28** R5
Aberdeen: Idaho, U.S.A. **92** E4
Aberdeen: Md., U.S.A. **89** N6
Aberdeen: Miss., U.S.A. **90** G9
Aberdeen: N.S.W., Austl. **71** J9
Aberdeen: *& Dist.*, S. Africa **75** F6
Aberdeen: S. Dak., U.S.A. **92** H3
Aberdeen: Wash., U.S.A. **92** C3
Aberdour: Fife, Scotland **29** P7
Aberdovey: Gwynedd, Wales **27** N14.
Aberdulais: W. Glam., Wales **24** O16
Aberedw: Powys, Wales **24** P15
Aberfan: Mid. Glam., Wales **24** P16
Aberfeldy: O.F.S., S. Africa **75** H4
Aberfeldy: Tayside, Scotland **29** O6
Aberffraw: Gwynedd, Wales **27** N13
Aberford: W. Yorks., England **27** T12
Aberfoyle: Central, Scotland **29** N7
Abergavenny: Gwent, Wales **24** P16
Abergele: Clwyd, Wales **27** O13
Abergorlech: Dyfed, Wales **24** N16
Abergynolwyn: Gwyn., Wales **27** O14
Aberhosan: Powys, Wales **27** O14
Aberlady: Lothian, Scotland **29** Q7
Abernethy: Tay., Scotland **29** P7
Aberporth: Dyfed, Wales **24** M15
Abersychan: Gwent, Wales **24** P16
Abert, Lake: Oreg., U.S.A. **92** C4
Aberthaw, E.: S. Glam., Wales **24** P17
Aberthaw, W.: S. Glam., Wales **24** P17
Abertillery: Gwent, Wales **24** P16
Aberuthven: Tayside, Scotland **29** O7
Aberystwyth: Dyfed, Wales **24** N15
Abez': U.S.S.R. **48** H4
Abha: Asir, Saudi Arabia **54** F11
Abhar: Iran **55** G7
Abi Addi: Ethiopia **54** E12
Ab-i-Diz: *riv.*, Iran **57** L6
ABIDJAN: Ivory Coast **80** D3
Abila: Hellenistic city near Rafid, Jordan **55** b2
Abilene: Kans., U.S.A. **90** C6
Abilene: Tex., U.S.A. **90** B9
Ab-i-Maima: *riv.*, Iran **57** K5
Abingdon: Ill., U.S.A. **88** F5
Abingdon: Oxon., England **25** T16
Abingdon: Queens., Austl. **69** G3
Abingdon: Va., U.S.A. **88** L7
Abinger: Surrey, England **25** V17
Abington: Strath., Scotland **29** O9
Abington Reef: Coral Sea **70** H2
Abiquaskolk: S. Africa **74** C4
Abisko: Sweden **46** Q2
Abitibi, Lake: Ont., Canada **89** M1
Abitibi: *riv.*, Canada **85** L7
Abkhaz A.S.S. Repub.: Georgia, U.S.S.R., (*cap.* Sukhumi) **50** F6
Ablis: France **36** G7
Åbo (Turku): Finland **47** S6
Aboisso: Ivory Coast **80** D3
ABOMEY: Centre, Benin **81** E3
Abong-Mbang: Cameroun **81** G4
Aborlan: Palawan, Phil. **64** F5
Abors: *tribe*, Arunachal Pradesh, India **59** Q9
Abou Deia: Chad **78** H7
Aboyne: Grampian, Scotland **28** Q5
Abqaiq: Saudi Arabia **55** G9
'Abr: Saudi Arabia **54** G11
Abraka: Nigeria **81** F3
Abrantes: Portugal **35** B17
Abrecjos, Point: *cape*, Mexico **93** E7
Abri: Sudan **54** D10
Abriachan: High., Scotland **28** N5
Abrolhos Arch.: Brazil **94** K7
Abrolhos (Houtman): *is.*, W. Australia **68** A5
Abrud: Romania **43** S13
Abruzzi Molise: *Reg.*, Italy (*cap.* L'Aquila) **38** N15
Abruzzo National Park: Italy **38** N16
Absaroka Range: Wyo., U.S.A. **92** F4
Absdorf: Austria **41** V7
Abu: Maharashtra, India **58** M10
Abu 'Arish: Saudi Arabia **54** F11
Abu Deleiq: Sudan **54** D11
ABU DHABI: U.A.E. **55** H10
Abu Dhaluf: Qatar **55** H9
Abu Dhiba': Saudi Arabia **54** E10
Abu Hadriya: Saudi Arabia **55** G9
Abu Hamed: Sudan **54** D11
Abu Hashim: Sudan **54** D12
Abu Hummus: Egypt **56** B6
Abuja: Nigeria **81** F3
Abu Jabirah: Sudan **79** K7
Abu Kemal: Syria **57** G4
Abu Khatab: *well*, Saudi Arabia **55** H10
Abukuma Range: *mtns.*, Japan **63** q2
Abu Matarik: Sudan **79** K7
Abumombazi: Zaïre **76** B2
Abu Nufuq: *well*, Iraq **57** G5
Abu Qîr: Egypt **56** B6
Abu Qîr Bay: Egypt **33** J5
Aburatsu: Japan **63** b5
Abu Rei: Chad **81** H2
Abu Saraifa: Saudi Arabia **55** H10
Abu Sufyan: Sudan **79** K7
Abu Sukhair: Iraq **57** J6
Abu Sultân: Egypt (Suez Canal. *Inset*) **32** *Ins.*
Abu Suweir: Egypt (Suez Canal. *Inset*) **32** *Ins.*
Abu Tabari: *well*, Sudan **54** C11
Abu Tig: Egypt **54** D9
Abu Zenima: Egypt **54** D9
Abwong: Sudan **79** L8
Åby: Sweden **23** P7
Abyad: Sudan **79** K7
Abyata Lake: Ethiopia **76** E1
Abydos: Egyptian city site W. of Balyana, Egypt **54** D9
Abydos: Greek city on E. side of narrowest point of Dardanelles W. of town Canakkale, Turkey **39** U16
Abyei: Sudan **79** K8
Abyssinia: *see under* Ethiopia.
Abyy: U.S.S.R. **49** q4
Acanthus: Greek city near Ierissós, Greece **39** S16
Acaponeta: Mexico **86** J13
Acapulco: Mexico **86** j14
Acará: Brazil **94** H4
Acarai, Sierra: *mtns.*, Guyana **87** e10
Acaraú: Brazil **94** J4
Acarigua: Venezuela **94** D2
Acarnania: ancient Greek district S. of G. of Amvrakia and W. of *Achelous* river, Greece **39** R17
Acatlán: Mexico **86** K14
Accous: France **37** E13
ACCRA: Ghana **80** D3
Accrington: Lancs., Eng. **27** R12
Aceguá: Uruguay **96** E3
Ace Ptolemais: Greek city, later Roman colony, at Acre, Israel **56** D5
Achaea: ancient district (including Patras and Aiyion) in N. Peloponnese, Greece **39** R17
Achaea: Roman province comprising most of modern Greece and S. Albania **39** R17
Achaguas: Venezuela **94** D2
Achahoish: Strath., Scotland **29** K8
Achair: U.S.S.R. **51** M4
Achalpur: Madhya Pradesh, India **58** N10
Achanalt: High., Scotland **28** M4
Achang: Sinkiang, China **48** K10
Achany Glen: High., Scot. **28** N4
Achar: Uruguay **96** D3
Acharacle: High., Scotland **29** K6
Acharnae: Greek village of central *Attica* (about 10 miles N. of Athens) **39** S17
Achavanich: High., Scot. **28** P3
Achelous: river rising in Pindus mtns. and flowing southwards to NW. end of G. of Patras, Greece **39** R17
Acheng: Heilungkiang, China **63** X5
Achenwald: Austria **41** R8
Achérich: Mali **80** D1
Achern: W. Germany **40** O7
Acheux: France **36** H5
Achiet-le-Grand: France **36** H5
Achikulak: U.S.S.R. **50** F6
Achill I.: *& cape*, Repub. of Ireland **30** A12
Achiltbuie: High., Scot. **28** L3
Achimota: Ghana **80** D3
Achinsk: U.S.S.R. **51** Q3
Achintraid: High., Scot. **28** K5
Achiras: Argentina **96** C3
Achisay: Kazakh., U.S.S.R. **51** L6
Achnacroish: Strath., Scot. **29** K6
Achnasheen: High., Scot. **28** L4
A'Chralaig: *mtn.*, Highland, Scotland **28** L5
ACI, Lake: Turkey **56** A3
Acil Barké: Mali **80** C2
Acıpayam: Turkey **56** A3
Acireale: Sicily **38** O18
Ackley: Iowa, U.S.A. **88** E4
Acklington: Northumb., England **26** S9
Acklins I: Bahamas **87** m13
Ackworth: W. Yorks., England **27** T12
Aclare: Sligo, Repub. of Ireland **30** D11
Acle: Norf., England **25** Z14
Acme: Alta., Canada **92** E2
Acomb: Northumb., Eng. **26** R10
Aconcagua: *mtn.*, Arg. **96** B3
Aconi, Point: *cape*, N.S., Can. **89** V2
Acornhoek: Trans., S. Afr. **75** J2
Acqui: Italy **40** O11
Acquigny: France **36** G6
Acragas: Greek city at Agrigento, Sicily **38** N18
Acre: Israel **55** b2
Acre: *State.*, Brazil (*cap.* Rio Branco) **94** C5
Actaeon Is.: Tuamotu Arch. **83** b4
Acte: Greek name of Áthos penin., Greece **39** T16
Actium: site of battle at tip of southern arm closing G. of Amvrakia, Greece **39** R17
Acton: Ont., Canada **88** L4
Acton Burnell: Salop, England **27** Q14
Acton Vale: Que., Canada **89** P3
Acumincum: Roman camp, later colony, at *Slankamen*, near confluence of Danube and Tisza, Yugo. **43** R14
Ada: Ghana **80** E3
Ada: Minn., U.S.A. **92** H3
Ada: Okla., U.S.A. **90** C8
Adair, Cape: N.W.T., Can. **85** m3
Adair Bay: Mexico **93** E6
Adak: *i.*, Aleutians **84** B7
Adala: Turkey **39** V17
Adam: Oman **55** J10
Adamaoua Mtns: Cameroun/Nigeria **81** G3
Adamello, Monte: *mtn.*, Italy **40** Q9
Adaminaby: N.S.W., Austl. **71** H11
Adams: N.Y., U.S.A. **89** N4
Adams, Mount: Wash., U.S.A. **92** C3
Adam's Bridge: *is. chain*, Sri Lanka/India **58** N13
Adamskraal: S. Africa **74** D6
Adamstown: Wex., Repub. of Ireland **31** H15
ADANA (Seyhan): *& Prov.*, Turkey **56** D3
ADAPAZARI: Sakarya, Turkey **56** B1
Adar: *watercourse*, Niger **78** F6
Adare: Lim., Repub. of Irel. **31** D14
Adare, Cape: Antarctica **9** 75S 170E
Adavale: Queens. Austl. **70** F5
Adayevskiy: Kazakh., U.S.S.R. **51** K4
Adda: *riv.*, Italy **40** P10
Adderbury: Oxon., England **25** T15
Addingham: W. Yorks., England **27** S12
ADDIS ABABA: Ethiopia **76** E1
Addis Alam: Ethiopia **76** E1
Addo: S. Africa **75** F6
Addo Elephant National Park: C.P., S. Africa **75** F6
Ad Dujayl: Iraq **57** J5
Adel: Ga., U.S.A. **91** K10
Adel: Iowa, U.S.A. **88** D5
Adelaide: *rsch. stn.*, Antarctica **9** 70S 70W
Adelaide: Bahamas **91** N13
Adelaide: *& Dist.*, S. Africa **75** G6
ADELAIDE: S. Australia **71** C10
Adelaide River: N. Territ., Australia **68** E2
Adelboden: Switzerland **40** N9
Adelong: N.S.W., Australia **71** H10
Adelsheim: W. Germany **44** P6
Adelzhausen: W. Germany **41** R7
Ademuz: Spain **35** F16
ADEN: Yemen P.D.R. **54** G12
Aden, Gulf of: Arabian Sea **79** R17
Adenau: W. Germany **44** M5
Adendorp: S. Africa **75** F6
Ader: *geog. reg.*, Niger **81** E2
Aderama: Sudan **54** D11
Aderbissinat: Niger **81** F1
'Adhaim: *riv.*, Iraq **57** J4
Adiabene (Media): ancient district NE. of Tigris around Nineveh, Iraq **57** H3
Adi Arkei: Ethiopia **54** E12
Adige: *riv.*, Italy **41** R10
Adigrat: Ethiopia **54** E12
Adi Kaieh: Ethiopia **54** E12
Adilabad: Andhra Pradesh, India **58** N11
Adilang: Uganda **76** D2
Adilcevaz: Turkey **57** H2
Adindan: Egypt **54** D10
Adirampattinam: Tamil Nadu, India **58** N12
Adirnaz: *riv.*, Turkey **56** A2
Adirondack Forest Preserve: N.Y./Vt., U.S.A. **89** O4
Adirondack Mtns.: N.Y., U.S.A. **89** O3
Adi Ugri: Ethiopia **54** E12
ADIYAMAN: *& Prov.*, Turkey **56** F3
Adjud: Romania **43** U13
Adler: U.S.S.R. **50** F6
Admiralty Inlet: N.W.T., Canada **85** L3
Admiralty I.: Alaska, U.S.A. **84** f6
Admiralty Is.: Bismarck Arch. **66** J2
Ado: Nigeria **81** E3
Ado Ekiti: Nigeria **81** F3
Adok: Sudan **76** D1
Adonara: *i.*, Indonesia **65** G8
Adoni: Andhra Pradesh, India **58** N11
Adorf: E. Germany **45** S5
Adoua: Cen. Afr. Rep. **76** B1
Adouda: Niger **78** F6
Adoumré: Cameroun **81** G3
Adour: *riv.*, France **37** D12
Adraj: *well*, Saudi Arabia **55** H10
Adramyttium: Greek city at Edremit, Turkey **39** U17
Adrano: Sicily **38** O18
Adrar: Algeria **78** D4
Adrar: *Dist.*, Mauritania (*cap.* Atar) **78** B5
Adrar of the Iforas: *highlands*, Mali **78** E6
Adre: Chad **79** J7
Adria: Italy **41** S10
Adrian: Mich., U.S.A. **88** J5
ADRIANOPLE (Edirne): Edirne, Turkey **39** U16
Adriatic Sea: S. Europe **38** O15
Adrigole: Cork, Repub. of Ireland **31** B16
Adur: *riv.*, W. Sussex, England **25** V18
Adusa: Sudan **54** C11
Aduwa: Ethiopia **54** E12
Advance: S. Africa **74** D5
Advie: Highland, Scotland **28** P5
Adwick le Street: S. Yorkshire, England **27** T12
Adygei: *Auton. Reg.*, U.S.S.R. (*cap.* Maykop) **50** F6
Adzharia: *A.S.S. Repub.*, Georgia, U.S.S.R. (*cap.* Batumi) **57** G1
Adzopé: Ivory Coast **80** D3
Ae: *riv.*, Dumf. & Gall., Scotland **29** O9
Æbeltoft: Denmark **47** M8
Aedui: Gallic tribe between rivers Saône and Allier, France **34** H13
Aegean Is.: Greece **39** T17
Aegean Sea: S. Europe **39** T17
Aegina: largest island of Saronic G., S. of Piraeus, Greece **39** S18
Aegospotami: beach on NW. side of Dardanelles opposite Lapseki, Turkey **39** U16
Aegosthena: ancient city of S. *Boeotia* at NE. corner of G. of Corinth, Greece **39** S17
Aenona: Roman town about 15 miles N. of Zadar on coast of Yugoslavia **38** O14
Aenus: Roman name of river Inn **41** T7
Aequi: ancient tribe in Sabini mtns. to E. and NE. of Rome **38** N15
Aequum: Roman colony about 5 miles N. of Sinj, Yugoslavia **38** P15
Aerzen: W. Germany **44** P3
Aesis: Roman name of river Esino, Italy **41** T12
Afaq: Iraq **57** J5

Afars & Issas, French Territory of the: *see* **Djibouti**
Affoltern: Switzerland **40** O8
Affric, Glen: High., Scotland **28** M5

Afghanistan: *Republic* **55** K8
Cap.: Kābul
Area: 251,000 sq. miles (650,090 sq. km.)
Pop.: 17,480,000 (*1971 E*)

Afgoi: Somalia **79** R19
Afia: Nias, Sumatra **65** B6
'Afif: Saudi Arabia **54** F10
Afikpo: Nigeria **81** F3
Åfjord: Norway **46** M5
Aflai Bani Kitab: *wells*, Oman **55** J10
Aflou: Algeria **78** E3
Afmadu: Somalia **76** F2
Afognak: *i.*, Alaska, U.S.A. **84** d6
Afsluitdijk: *dam*, Neth. **44** L3
Afton: Okla., U.S.A. **90** D7
Afuá: Brazil **94** G4
Afula: Israel **55** b2
Afweina, El: Somalia **79** R17
Afyon: *Prov.*, Turkey (*cap.* Afyonkarahisar) **56** B2
AFYONKARAHISAR: Afyon, Turkey **56** B2
Agab Workei: Ethiopia **54** E12
Agadem: *well*, Niger **81** G1
AGADÉS: *& Dept.*, Niger **81** F1
AGADIR: *& Prov.*, Morocco **80** K8
Agadir Tissint: Morocco **80** K9
Agaie: Nigeria **81** F3
Again: Sudan **76** C1
Agalega Is.: (Mauritius), Indian Ocean **19** 10S 50E
Agan: *riv.*, U.S.S.R. **51** N2
AGANA: Guam, Mariana Is. **61** N9
Agar: Madhya Pradesh, India **58** N10
AGARTALA: Tripura, India **59** Q10
Agata: U.S.S.R. **49** L4
Agatha: Trans., S. Africa **75** J1
Agatti: *i.*, Laccadive Is. **58** M12
Agattu: *i.*, Aleutians **84** A7
Agawa: Japan **63** b3
Agay: France **40** M12
Agbaja: Nigeria **81** F3
Agbede: Nigeria **81** F3
Agbor: Nigeria **81** F3
Agboville: Ivory Coast **80** D3
Agdam: Azer., U.S.S.R. **57** K2
Agdam: *riv.*, China **59** Q8
Agdash: Azer., U.S.S.R. **57** K1
Agde: *& Cap d'*, *town & cape*, France **37** J12
Agdzhabedzi: Azerbaydzhan, U.S.S.R. **57** K1
Agedincum: Roman name of Gallic centre at Sens, France **36** J7
AGEN: Lot-et-Garonne, Fr. **37** F11
Agenais: *geog. reg.*, France **37** F11
Agger: *riv.*, W. Germany **44** N5
Aghaboe: Laois, Repub. of Ireland **31** G14
Aghade: Carlow, Repub. of Ireland **31** H14
Aghadowey: Lon., N. Irel. **30** H9
Aghagower: Mayo, Repub. of Ireland **30** C12
Aghalee: Antrim, N. Ireland **30** J10
Aghavas: Leit., Repub. of Ireland **30** F12
Agheila, El: Libya **33** F5
Aghleam: Mayo, Repub. of Ireland **30** A11
Aghnacliff: Long., Repub. of Ireland **30** F12
Agincourt: battlefield about 14 miles NW. of St. Pol, France **36** H5
Agira: Sicily **38** O18
Aglish: Wat., Repub. of Irel. **31** F15
Agnebilékrou: Ivory Coast **80** D3
Agnita: Romania **39** T14
Agordat: Ethiopia **54** E11
Agordo: Italy **41** S9
Agostini, Cordillera de: *range*, Chile **95** C13
Agouma: Gabon **81** G5
Agout: *riv.*, France **37** H12
Agra: Uttar Pradesh, India **58** N9
Agrakhansk Penin.: U.S.S.R. **50** G6
Agras Junctas: SW. Africa **74** A3
Agreda: Spain **35** F16
Ağrı: *Prov.*, Turkey (*cap.* Karaköse) **57** H2
Agri: *riv.*, Italy **38** P16
Agrigento: Sicily **38** N18
Agrihan: *i.*, Mariana Is. **61** O8
Agrinion: Greece **39** R17
Agto: Greenland **85** o4
Agua Boa: Brazil **96** E1
Agua Clara: Brazil **94** G8
Aguadas: Colombia **94** B2
Aguas Belas: Brazil **94** K5
Aguascalientes: Mexico **86** j13
Agudos: Brazil **96** F1
Agueda: *riv.*, Spain **35** C16
Aguera, La: W. Sahara **78** A5
Agui: *riv.*, U.S.S.R. **51** R3
Aguilar: Spain **35** D18
Águilas: Spain **35** F18
Agulhas, Cape: S. Africa **74** D7
Agulhas Basin: Atlantic/Indian Ocean **9** 45S 20E
Agulhas Plateau: Indian O. **8** 40S 25E
Aguontum: Roman town at Lienz, Austria **41** S9
Agusan: *riv.*, Philippines **64** H5
Ahaggar: *highlands*, Algeria **78** F5
Ahar: Iran **57** K2
Ahascragh: Galway, Repub. of Ireland **31** E13
Ahaura: South I., N.Z. **70** N16
Ahaus: W. Germany **44** N3
Ahé: *i.*, Tuamotu Arch. **83** f2
Ahenny: Tip., Repub. of Irel. **31** G15
Aherlow, Glen of: Tip., Repub. of Ireland **31** E15
Ahir Daği: *mtn.*, Turkey **56** E3
Ahlainen: Finland **47** R6
Ahlat: Turkey **57** H2
Ahlen: W. Germany **44** N4
Ahlhorn: W. Germany **44** O3
Ahl Meskat: *mtn.*, Somalia **79** R17
AHMADABAD: Gujarat, India **58** M10
Ahmadabad: Iran **57** K3
Ahmadi: Iran **55** J9
Ahmadnagar: Maharashtra, India **58** M11
Ahoada: Nigeria **81** F3
Ahoghill: Antrim, N. Irel. **30** J10
Ahome: Mexico **93** E7
Ahr: *riv.*, W. Germany **44** M5
Ahram: Iran **55** H9
Ahrensburg: W. Germany **45** Q2
Ahrenshoop: E. Germany **45** S1
Ahrweiler: W. Germany **44** N5
Ähtäri: Finland **46** T5
Ähtärin Lake: Finland **46** T5
Ahtävä: Finland **46** S5
Ahuachapán: El Salvador **86** L15
Ahun: France **37** H9
Ahunui: *i.*, Tuamotu Arch. **83** g3
Ahvenanmaa (Åland) Is.: *is. & Prov.*, Finland (*cap.* Mariehamn) **47** R6
Ahwar: Yemen P.D.R. **54** G12
AHWAZ (Nasiri): Khuzistan, Iran **57** L6
Ai: Canaanite city about 2 miles ESE. of *Bethel* in mtns. about 10 miles N. of Jerusalem **55** b3
Aibling: W. Germany **41** S8
Aichach: W. Germany **41** R7
Aichi: *Pref.*, Japan (*cap.* Nagoya) **63** e3
Aichstetten: W. Germany **40** Q8
Aidenbach: W. Germany **41** T7
Aiffres: France **37** E9
Aigen: Austria **41** T7
Aigle: Switzerland **40** M9
Aigrefeuille: Charente-Maritime, France **37** E9
Aigrefeuille: Gironde, France **36** D8
Aigueperse: France **37** J9
Aigues-Mortes: *& Golfe d'*, France **37** K12
Aiguille, Pointe de l': *cape*, France **37** D9
Aiguilles: France **40** M11
Aiguillon: France **37** F11
Aiguillon, L': France **37** D9
Aiguillon-sur-Mer, l': Fr. **37** D9
Aigurande: France **37** G9
Aihsien: Hainan, China **62** T11
Aijal: Mizoram, India **59** Q10
Aiken: S.C., U.S.A. **91** L9
Aikton: Cumb., England **26** P10
Aileron: N. Territ., Austl. **68** E4
'Aili, Shaib: *wadi*, Saudi Arabia **56** F6
Aillevillers: France **40** M8
Ailly-le-Haut-Clocher: Fr. **36** G5
Ailort, Loch: High., Scotland **29** K6
Ailsa Craig: *i.*, Scotland **29** L9
Ailsh, Loch: High., Scot. **28** M3
Aim: U.S.S.R. **49** P6
Aimargues: France **37** K12
Aimere: Flores, Indonesia **65** G8
Aimorés: Brazil **94** J7
Aimorés, Serra dos: Brazil **94** J7
Ain: *Dept. & riv.*, Fr. (*cap. of Dept.* Bourg) **40** L9
'Ain: *wadi*, Oman **55** J10
Ainabo: Somalia **79** R18
Ain Aiche: Morocco **80** L8
'Ain 'Aissa: Syria **56** F3
'Ain 'Arus: Syria **56** F3
Ainazhi: Latvia, U.S.S.R. **47** T8
Ain Beida: Algeria **32** D4
Ain Benian: Algeria **35** H18
'Ain Dar: Saudi Arabia **55** G9
'Ain Dauha ('Ain el Ghazal): Libya **54** B10
'Ain Diyar: Syria **57** H3
Ain Draham: Tunisia **38** L18
Aine Galakka: Chad **78** H6

For Abbreviations see list on p.113. Italic type, e.g. *Ephesus*, refers to historical names not on maps. Capital letters, e.g. MADRID, show capitals of countries; small capital letters, e.g. CADIZ, show capitals of provinces, etc. General notes p.116.

118 'Ain el Beida—Althorpe

'Ain el Beida: Syria 56 E4
'Ain el Ghazal ('Ain Dauha): Libya 54 B10
Ainhoa: France 37 D12
'Ain Khasab: *well*, Iraq 57 H4
Ain Mlila: Algeria 32 D4
'Ain Murr: Sudan 54 C10
Aïn Oussera: Algeria 35 H19
Aïn Roua: Algeria 35 J18
Ain Salah: Algeria 78 E4
Ainsdale: Mers., England 27 P12
Ain Sefra: Algeria 80 L8
Ainslie, Lake: Cape Breton I., Canada 89 V2
Ainstable: Cumbria, England 26 Q10
Ainsworth: Nebr., U.S.A. 92 H4
Aïn Témouchent: Algeria 80 L7
Aintree: Mers., England 27 Q13
Ain Zalah: *oil field*, Iraq 57 H3
AÏOUNE EL ATROUS: Hodh Occidental, Mauritania 80 C1
Aipi Hu: *lake*, Sinkiang, China 51 O6
Aiquile: Bolivia 94 D7
Aïr (Azbine): *highlands*, Niger 78 F6
Airabu: *i.*, Anambas Is., Indonesia 65 D6
Airbangis: Sumatra 65 B6
Aird, The: *dist.*, High., Scot. 28 N5
Aird of Sleat: Inner Hebr., Scotland 28 K5
Airdrie: Strath., Scotland 29 O8
Aire: Landes, France 37 E12
Aire: Pas de Calais, France 36 H5
Aire: *riv.*, France 36 L6
Aire: *riv.*, England 27 T12
Airedale: *val.*, W. Yorks., England 27 S12
Airolo: Switzerland 40 O9
Airor: Highland, Scotland 28 K5
Airth: Central, Scotland 29 O7
Airvault: France 37 E9
Aisch: *riv.*, W. Germany 45 Q6
Aisha: Ethiopia 79 Q17
Aisne: *Dept. & riv.*, France (*cap. of Dept.* Laon) 36 J6
Aisne Lateral Canal: France 36 J6
Aitape: Papua/New Guinea 66 H2
Aitetsung: Tibet, China 59 Q8
Aitinen: *riv.*, Finland 46 U3
Aitkin: Minn., U.S.A. 88 E2
Aitolikón: Greece 39 R17
Aitos: Bulgaria 39 U15
Aitutaki: *i.*, Cook Is. 70 *Ins.*
Aiud: Romania 43 S13
Aivadzh: Tadzhik., U.S.S.R. 51 L7
Aiviekste: *riv.*, U.S.S.R. 47 U8
Aix-en-Othe: France 36 J7
Aix-en-Provence: France 40 L12
Aixe-sur-Vienne: France 37 G10
Aix-la-Chapelle (Aachen): W. Germany 44 M5
Aix-les-Bains: France 40 L10
'Aiyat, El: Egypt 56 B7
Aizuwakamatsu: Japan 63 f2
Ajabshir: Iran 57 J3
AJACCIO: *& gulf*, Corsica 38 L16
Ajana: W. Australia 68 A5
Ajanta: Maharashtra, India 58 N10
Ajax, Mount: Mont./Idaho, U.S.A. 92 E3
Ajdovščina: Yugoslavia 41 T10
Ajigasawa: Japan 63 ZZ6
Ajij: *riv.*, Iraq/Syria 57 G4
Ajlun: Jordan 55 b2
'Ajman: U.A.E. 55 J9
Ajmer: Rajasthan, India 58 M9
Ajo: Ariz., U.S.A. 93 E6
Ak: *riv.*, Kazakh., U.S.S.R. 51 N6
Ak: *riv.*, Turkey 56 B3
Akademgorodak: U.S.S.R. 51 O4
Akaho: Japan 63 e3
Akaishi Mtns.: Japan 63 f3
Akana: Japan 63 c3
Akaoka: Japan 63 c4
Akaroa: South I., N.Z. 70 O16
Akas: *tribe*, Arunachal Pradesh/Assam, India 59 Q9
Akasaki: Japan 63 c3
Akasha: Sudan 54 D10
Akashi: Japan 63 d3
Äkäslompolo: Finland 46 T3
Akatani: Japan 63 f2
Akbou: Algeria 35 J18
Ak-Bulak: U.S.S.R. 50 J4
Akçadağ: Turkey 56 E2
Akçakoca: Turkey 56 B1
Akdağ: *mtn.*, Tur. 56 B3
Akdağ: *mtn.*, Tur. 56 A3
Akdağmadeni: Turkey 56 D2
Aken: E. Germany 45 S4
Åkernes: Norway 47 K7
Akerre: Nigeria 81 F3
Akershus: *Co.*, Norway (*cap.* Lillestrøm) 47 M7
Aketi: Zaïre 76 B2
Akhalkaiaki: Georgia, U.S.S.R. 57 H1
Akhaltsikhe: Georgia, U.S.S.R. 57 H1
Akhchala, Lake: Azerbaydzhan, U.S.S.R. 57 L2
Akhcha-Tepe: Turkmen., U.S.S.R. 51 K7
Akhelóös: *riv.*, Greece 39 R17
Akhisar: Turkey 39 U17
Akhtopol: Bulgaria 39 U15
Akhtyrka: Ukraine 50 D4
Aki: Japan 63 c4
Akiak: Alaska, U.S.A. 84 c5
Aki-Aki: *i.*, Tuamotu Arch. 83 h3
Akimiski I.: N.W.T., Canada 85 I7
Akita: Japan 63 ZZ7
AKJOUJT: Inchiri, Mauritania 78 B6
Akkaraipattu: Sri Lanka 58 O13
Akkeshi: Japan 63 ZZ6
Akköy: Turkey 39 U18
Akkrum: Netherlands 44 L2
Aklavik: N.W.T., Canada 84 F4
Akniste: Latvia, U.S.S.R. 47 T8
Ako: Japan 63 d3
Ako: Nigeria 78 G7
Akoafim: Cameroun 81 G4
Akobo: *& riv.*, Sudan 76 D1
Akola: Maharashtra, India 58 N10
Akomolinga: Cameroun 81 G4
Akondjo: Gabon 81 F5
Akor: Mali 80 C1
Akosombo Dam: Ghana 80 E3
Akpatok I.: Que., Canada 85 N5
Akranes: Iceland 46 b4
Akritas, Cape: Greece 39 R18
Akron: Colo., U.S.A. 93 G4
Akron: Ohio, U.S.A. 88 L5
Akşakoca: Turkey 56 B1
Aksaray: Turkey 56 D2
Akşehir: *& lake*, Turkey 56 B2
Akseki: Turkey 56 B3
Aksenovo-Zilovskoye: U.S.S.R. 49 n7
Aksha: U.S.S.R. 49 N7
Ak-Su: Sinkiang, China 51 O6
Aksuat: (*Semipalatinsk*), Kazakh., U.S.S.R. 51 O5
Aksuat: (*Kustanai*), Kazakh., U.S.S.R. 51 K4
Aksubayevo: U.S.S.R. 50 H4
Aksum: Ethiopia 54 E12
Aktanysh: U.S.S.R. 50 H3
Aktash: U.S.S.R. 50 H4
Aktogay: Kazakh., U.S.S.R. 51 M5
Aktsek: Sweden 46 Q3
AKTYUBINSK: *& Reg.*, Kazakh., U.S.S.R. 50 J4
Akula: Zaïre 76 B2
Akun: *i.*, Aleutians 84 C7
Akune: Japan 63 b4
AKURE: Ondo, Nigeria 81 F3
Akureyri: Iceland 46 d4
Akuse: Ghana 80 E3
Akutan: *& i.*, Aleutians 84 C7
Akwana: Nigeria 81 F3
Akwanga: Nigeria 81 F3
AKYAB (Sitwe): Arakan, Burma 59 Q10
Akyar: Sinkiang, China 51 P7
Akzhal: Kazakh., U.S.S.R. 51 O5
Ål: Norway 47 L6
Al, El: Syria 55 b2
Ala: Italy 41 Q10
Alabama: *State & riv.*, U.S.A. (*cap.* Montgomery) 91 H9
Al 'Abd: Saudi Arabia 55 H10
Alaca: Turkey 56 D1
Aladağ: Turkey 56 C3
Ala Dağ: *mtn.*, Turkey 57 H2
Alaejos: Spain 35 D16
Alagez: *mtn.*, Armenia, U.S.S.R. 57 J1
Alagnon: *riv.*, France 37 J10
Alagoas: *State*, Braz. (*cap.*, Maceió) 94 K5
Alagoinhas: Brazil 94 K6
Alagón: Spain 35 F16
Alagón: *riv.*, Spain 35 C16
Alagóa Grande: Brazil 94 K5
Alahanpanjang: Sumatra 65 C7
Alai Range: Tadzhik./Kirgiz., U.S.S.R. 51 M7
Alajärvi: Finland 46 S5
Alakale: Turkey 57 H1
Alalakh: ancient city, site near Süveydiye, Turkey 56 D3
Ala Kul': *lake*, Kazakh., U.S.S.R. 51 O5
Alakylä: Finland 46 T3
Alamagan: *i.*, Mariana Is. 61 O8
Alamdo: Sinkiang, China 59 Q8
Alameda: Calif., U.S.A. 93 C5
'Alamein, El: Egypt 54 C8
Alamo: Nev., U.S.A. 93 D5
Alamo: Tex., U.S.A. 90 B12
Alamo, El: Mexico 93 D6
Alamogordo: N. Mex., U.S.A. 93 F6
Alamos: Mexico 93 F7
Alamos, Cerro: *mtn.*, Mex. 93 F7
Alamosa: Colo., U.S.A. 93 F5
Alanäs: Sweden 46 O4
Åland (Ahvenanmaa) Is.: *is. & Prov.*, Fin. (*cap.* Mariehamn) 47 R6
Åland, Sea of: Sweden 47 Q7
Alanya: Turkey 56 B3
Alapayevsk: U.S.S.R. 51 K3
Alaro: Maj., Balearic Is. 35 H17
Alas: *str.*, Indonesia 65 F8
Alaşehir: Turkey 39 V17
Ala Shan: *range*, Inner Mongolia, China 62 S7
Alashantsochi: Inner Mongolia, China 62 T7
Al Asimah: *Dist.*, Jordan, (*cap.* Amman) 56 E6
Alaska, G. of: N. America 84 e6
Alaska: *penin.*, Alaska, U.S.A. 84 D6
Alaska: *range*, N. America 84 d5
Alaska: *State*, U.S.A. (*cap.* Juneau) 84 —
Alaşkirt: Turkey 57 H2
Alassio: Italy 40 O12
Alatalo: Finland 46 V2
Ala-Tau: *mtns.*, Kazakh./Kirgiz., U.S.S.R. 51 N6
Alatri: Italy 38 N16
Alatyr': U.S.S.R. 50 G4
Alava: *Prov.*, Spain (*cap.* Vitoria) 35 E15
Alaverdy: Armenia, U.S.S.R. 57 J1
Alavus: Finland 46 S5
Alawoona: S. Australia 71 D10
Alayor: Minorca, Balearic Is. 35 J17
Alazan: *riv.*, Azerbaydzhan, U.S.S.R. 57 K1
Alazeya: *riv.*, U.S.S.R. 49 R4
Alba: Italy 40 O11
ALBACETE: *& Prov.*, Spain 35 F17
Alba de Tormes: Spain 35 D16
Alba Fucens: ancient Latin city N. of *Fucine* lake about 50 miles E. of Rome. 38 N16
Albaida: Spain 35 F17
Alba Iulia: Romania 43 S13
Alba Longa: ancient Latin city at *Castel Gandolfo* about 12 miles SE. of Rome 38 N16
Al Balqa: *Dist.*, Jordan (*cap.* Salt) 56 D5
Alban: France 37 H12

Albania: *Republic* 39 Q16
Cap.: Tiranë
Area: 11,100 sq. miles (28,749 sq. km.)
Pop.: 2,226,000 (*1971 E*)

Albanus: lake to E. of *Via Appia* about 13 miles SE. of Rome. 38 N16
Albany: Ga., U.S.A. 91 J10
Albany: Ky., U.S.A. 88 J7
ALBANY: N.Y., U.S.A. 89 P4
Albany: Oreg., U.S.A. 92 C4
Albany: Tex., U.S.A. 90 B9
Albany: W. Australia 68 B6
Albany: *Dist.*, S. Africa 75 G6
Albany: *riv.*, Canada 85 I7
Albany Downs: Queens., Australia 70 H6
Albarracin: Spain 35 F16
Albemarle Sd.: N.C., U.S.A. 89 N7
Albenga: Italy 40 O11
Alberga: *riv.* S. Australia 68 E5
Albergaria-a-Velha: Portugal 35 B16
Alberique: Spain 35 F17
Albert: France 36 H6
Albert: *Dist.*, S. Africa 75 G5
Alberta: *Prov.*, Canada (*cap.* Edmonton) 84 H6
Albert Canal: Belgium 44 L4
Albertinia: S. Africa 74 D7
Albert Lake: E. Africa 76 D2
Albert Lea: Minn., U.S.A. 88 E4
Albert Nile: *riv.*, Uganda 76 D2
Alberton: P.E.I., Canada 89 T2
Alberton: Trans., S. Africa 74 N *Ins.*
Albertville: Ala., U.S.A. 91 H8
Albertville: Zaïre 76 C4
Albertville: France 40 M10
ALBI: Tarn, France 37 H12
Albia: Iowa, U.S.A. 88 E5
Albina: Surinam 94 G2
Albina Point: *cape*, Angola 73 G13
Albion: Ill., U.S.A. 88 G6
Albion: Mich., U.S.A. 88 J4
Albion: N.Y., U.S.A. 89 M4
Albion: Queens., Australia 69 G4
Alboran: *i.*, Medit. Sea 35 E19
Albreda: B.C., Canada 92 D2
Albrighton: Salop, England 27 R14
Albuera, La: Spain 35 C17
Albufeira: Portugal 35 B18
Albula Pass: Switzerland 40 P9
Al Bu Muhammad: *tribe*, Iraq 57 K6
Albuñol: Spain 35 E18
Albuquerque: N. Mex., U.S.A. 93 F5
Albuquerque Cays: *is.*, Caribbean Sea 87 I15
Alburquerque: Spain 35 C17
Albury: N.S.W., Australia 71 G11
Alby: Sweden 46 O5
Alcácer do Sal: Portugal 35 B17
Alcalá de Henares: Spain 35 E16
Alcalá la Real: Spain 35 E18
Alcamo: Sicily 38 N18
Alcañices: Spain 35 C16
Alcañiz: Spain 35 F16
Alcántara: Spain 35 C17
Alcaraz: Spain 35 E17
Alcázar, Point: *cape*, Mor. (Gib. *Inset*) 32 *Ins.*
Alcázar de San Juan: Spain 35 E17
Alcazar Sequer: Morocco (Gib. *Inset*) 32 *Ins.*
Alcester: War., England 25 S15
Alchester: site of Roman town about 1½ miles S. of Bicester, Oxon., England 25 T16
Alcira: Spain 35 F17
Alcolea del Pinar: Spain 35 E16
Alconbury: Cambs., England 25 V15
Alcoota: N. Territ., Austl. 68 E4
Alcorta: Argentina 96 C3
Alcoutim: Portugal 35 C18
Alcoy: Spain 35 F17
Alcudia: *& bay*, Maj., Balearic Is. 35 H17
Aldabra Is.: Seychelles, Indian O. 19 OS 40E
Aldama: Chihuahua, Mex. 93 F7
Aldama: Tamaulipas, Mex. 86 K13
Aldamas, Los: Mexico 90 B12
Aldan: *& plat.*, U.S.S.R. 49 o6
Aldan: *riv.*, U.S.S.R. 49 p5
Aldbourne: Wilts., England 25 S17
Aldbrough: see *Isurium*.
Aldbrough: Humb., Eng. 27 V12
Alde: *riv.*, Suff., England 25 Y15
Aldeburgh: Suff., England 25 Z15
Alderholt: Dorset, England 25 S18
Alderley Edge: Ches., Eng. 27 R13
Aldermaston: Berks., Eng. 25 T17
Alderney: *i.*, Chan. Is. (Br.) 25 *Ins.*
Alderney, Race of: *str.*, Alderney/France 25 *Ins.*
Aldershot: Hants., England 25 U17
Alderson: W. Va., U.S.A. 88 L7
Aldford: Ches., England 27 Q13
Aldingham: Cumb., Eng. 26 P11
Aldridge: W. Mid., England 27 S14
Aldsworth: Glos., England 25 S16
Aledo: Ill., U.S.A. 88 F5
ALEG: Brakna, Mauritania 78 B6
Alegranza: *i.*, Canary Is. 78 B4
Alegrete: Brazil 96 D2
Alejandro Selkirk: *i.*, Juan Fernández Is. (Chile) 95 A10
Aleksandrovac: Yugoslavia 39 R15
Aleksandrov Gay: U.S.S.R. 50 G4
Aleksandrovka: Kazakh., U.S.S.R. 51 O4
Aleksandrovsk: Sakhalin, U.S.S.R. 49 Q7
Aleksandrovskoye: U.S.S.R 51 N2
Aleksandrów: Poland 43 Q10
Alekseyevka: Kazakh., U.S.S.R. 51 M4
Alekseyevka: U.S.S.R. 50 E4
Aleksinac: Yugoslavia 39 R15
Alemania: Argentina 96 B2
Ålen: Norway 46 M5
ALENÇON: Orne, France 36 F7
Alenquer: Brazil 94 G4
Alenuihaha Chan.: Hawaiian Is. 83 c2
ALEPPO (Haleb): *& Prov.*, Syria 56 E3
Aleria: Corsica 38 L15
Alès: France 37 K11
Ales: Sardinia 38 L17
Aleşd: Romania 43 S13
Alesia: Roman name of Gallic fort on plateau about 10 miles SE. of Montbard, Fr. 36 K8
Alessandra: Somalia 76 F2
Alessandria: Italy 40 O11
Ålesund: Norway 46 K5
Aletschhorn: *mtn.*, Switz. 40 N9
Aleutian Abyssal Plain: N. Pacific Ocean 7 45N 170W
Aleutian Basin: Bering Sea 7 50N 175E
Aleutian Is.: (U.S.A.), Pac. O. 84 *Ins.*
Aleutian Range: Alaska, U.S.A. 84 D6
Aleutian Ridge: Bering Sea 7 50N 180
Aleutian Trench: N. Pacific Ocean 7 50N 180
Alevin, Cape: U.S.S.R. 49 R6
Alexander: N. Dak., U.S.A. 92 G3
Alexander Arch.: Alaska, U.S.A. 84 F6
Alexander Bay: *town*, S. Africa 74 B4
Alexander City: Ala., U.S.A. 91 J9
Alexander Island: Antarctica 9 75S 75W
Alexandra: South I., N.Z. 70 M17
Alexandra: Vict., Australia 71 F11
Alexandra Land: Franz Josef Land 48 F1
Alexandretta: Westernized name of Iskenderon, Tur. 56 E3
Alexandria: B.C., Canada 92 C2
Alexandria: Egypt 56 B6
Alexandria: Ind., U.S.A. 88 J5
Alexandria: La., U.S.A. 90 E10
Alexandria: Minn., U.S.A. 92 H3
Alexandria: Ont., Canada 89 O3
Alexandria: Romania 39 T15
Alexandria: *& Dist.*, S. Africa 75 G6
Alexandria: Strath., Scot. 29 M8
Alexandria: Va., U.S.A. 89 N6
Alexandria Bay: *city*, N.Y., U.S.A. 89 O3
Alexandria Station: N. Territ., Australia 69 F3
Alexandrina, Lake: S. Austl. 71 C10
Alexandroúpolis (Dedeagach): Greece 39 T16
Alexis Creek: *town*, B.C., Can. 92 C2
Aleysk: U.S.S.R. 51 O4
Alfaro: Spain 35 F15
Alfarville: Algeria 80 M8
Al Fatha: *gorge*, Iraq 57 H4
Alfeld: W. Germany 45 P4
Alfiós: *riv.*, Greece 39 R18
Alfold: Surrey, England 25 U17
Alfonsine: Italy 41 S11
Alford: Gram., Scotland 28 Q5
Alford: Lincs., England 27 W13
Alfred: *Dist.*, Natal, S. Africa 75 H5
Alfredton: North I., N.Z. 70 P15
Alfreton: Derby., England 27 T13
Alfriston: E. Sussex, Eng. 25 W18
Alga: Kazakh., U.S.S.R. 50 J5
Ålgård: Norway 47 J7
Algarrobo: Argentina 96 C4
Algarrobo: Chile 96 A2
Algarrobo del Aguila: Arg. 96 B4
Algarve: *Prov.*, Portugal (*cap.* Faro) 35 B18
Algauer Alps: Austr./W. Ger. 40 Q8
Algeciras: *& bay*, Spain (Gib. *Inset*) 32 *Ins.*
Algezur: Spain 35 B18
Alghero: Sardinia 38 L16

Algeria: *Republic* 78 E4
Cap.: Algiers
Area: 919,951 sq. miles (2,382,673 sq. km.)
Pop.: 14,769,000 (*1971 E*)

Algiers, Bay of: Algeria 35 H18
ALGIERS (El Djezair): *& Dept.*, Algeria 35 H18
Algiers: La., U.S.A. 90 *Ins.*
Algoa Bay: S. Africa 75 F6
Algoma: Wis., U.S.A. 88 H3
Algona: Iowa, U.S.A. 88 D4
Algonquin Prov. Park: Ont., Can. 89 M3
Algorta: Uruguay 96 D3
Algrange: France 36 M6
Alhama de Granada: Spain 35 E18
Alhama de Murcia: Spain 35 F18
Alhambra: Calif., U.S.A. 93 D6
AL HOCEIMA: *& Prov.*, Morocco 80 L8
Alhuampa: Argentina 96 C2
Alia: Sicily 38 N18
Aliabad: Iran 57 K4
Aliaga: Spain 35 F16
Aliağa: Turkey 39 U17
Aliákmon: *riv.*, Greece 39 S16
Alibag: Maharashtra, India 58 M11
Alibori: *riv.*, Benin 81 E2
ALICANTE: *& Prov.*, Spain 35 F17
Alicante Bay: Spain 35 F17
Alice: Queens., Australia 69 H4
Alice: S. Africa 75 G6
Alice: Tex., U.S.A. 90 B12
Alicedale: S. Africa 75 G6
Alice Springs: N. Territ., Australia 68 E4
Alice Town: Bahamas 91 M13
Alicudi: *i.*, Lipari Is. (It.) 38 O17
Aligarh: Uttar Pradesh, India 58 N9
Ali Gharbi: Iraq 57 K5
Ali Gudarz: Iran 57 L5
Alijos Rock: Pacific O. 93 D7
Alima: *riv.*, Congo 81 H5
Alindao: Cen. Afr. Rep. 76 B2
Aling Shan: *mtn. & range*, Tibet, China 51 O8
Alingsås: Sweden 47 N8
Aliquippa: Pa., U.S.A. 88 L5
Ali Sabiet: Djibouti 79 Q17
Aliso: Roman fort probably near Hamm, W. Germany 44 N4
Alivérion: Euboea, Greece 39 T17
Aliwal North: *& Dist.*, S. Africa 75 G5
Al Jabal al Akhdar: *Prov.*, Libya (*cap.* Beida) 79 J3
Al-Jabal Al-Gharbi: *Prov.*, Libya (*cap.* Garian) 78 G4
Al Jazira: *geog. reg.*, Iraq 57 H4
Aljustrel: Portugal 35 B18
Alkamari: Niger 81 G2
Alkborough: Humb., Eng. 27 U12
Al Khalil: *Dist.*, Jordan (*cap.* Hebron) 56 D6
Al Khalis: Iraq 57 J5
Alkmaar: Netherlands 44 K3
Al Kut: Iraq 57 J5
Allada: Benin 81 E3
Allahabad: Uttar Pradesh, India 58 O9
Allaire: France 36 C8
Allakaket: Alaska, U.S.A. 84 d4
Allakh-Yun: U.S.S.R. 49 p5
Allanche: France 37 H10
Allanmyo: Burma 59 R11
Allansford: Vict., Australia 71 E12
'Allaqi: *& riv.*, Egypt 54 D10
Allariz: Spain 35 C15
Allata: Ethiopia 76 E1
Allauch: France 37 L12
Allegan: Mich., U.S.A. 88 J4
Allegheny: *riv.*, Pa., U.S.A. 89 M5
Allegheny Mtns.: U.S.A. 88 L7
Allen: Philippines 64 G4
Allen, Bog of: Offaly, Repub. of Ireland 31 F13
Allen, Lough: Leit./Rosc., Repub. of Ireland 30 E11
Allendale: S.C., U.S.A. 91 L9
Allendale Town: Northumb., England 26 R10
Allende: Mexico 93 G7
Allenheads: Dur., England 26 R10
Allentown: Pa., U.S.A. 89 O5
Allentsteig: Austria 41 V7
Alleppey: Kerala, India 58 N13
Aller: *riv.*, W. Germany 42 L10
Allevard: France 40 M10
Alley: Jamaica 86 *Ins.*
Allhallows: Kent, England 25 X17
Alliance: Nebr., U.S.A. 92 G4
Alliance, Ohio, U.S.A. 88 L5
Al Lidam: Saudi Arabia 54 F10
Allier: *Dept.*, France (*cap.* Moulins) 37 H9
Allier: *riv.*, France 37 J9
Alligator Point: *cape*, La., U.S.A. 90 *Ins.*
Alligator Pond Bay: *town*, Jamaica 86 j16
Allihies: Cork, Repub. of Ireland 31 A16
Allington, East: Devon, England 24 O19
Allison Harbour: B.C., Canada 92 B2
Alliston: Ont., Canada 89 M3
Alloa: Central, Scotland 29 O7
Allobroges: Gallic tribe in valley of Rhône E. of Vienne, France 40 L10
Allonby: Cumbria, England 26 P10
Allora: Queens., Australia 70 J7
Allos: France 40 M11
Alloway: Strath., Scotland 29 M9
Allstedt: E. Germany 45 R4
Alma: Ga., U.S.A. 91 K10
Alma: Mich., U.S.A. 88 J4
Alma: N.B., Canada 89 T3
Alma: Nebr., U.S.A. 93 H4
Alma: Wis., U.S.A. 88 F3
ALMA-ATA: *& Reg.*, Kazakhstan, U.S.S.R. 51 N6
Almaden: Queens., Australia 69 G3
Almadén: Spain 35 D17
Almagro: Spain 35 E17
Almansa: Spain 35 F17
Al Mansuriyah: Iraq 57 J4
Almazán: Spain 35 E16
Almedia: Portugal 35 C16
Almeirim: Brazil 94 G4
Almeley: Here. & Worcs., Eng. 24 Q15
Almelo: Netherlands 44 M3
Almendralejo: Spain 35 C17
ALMERÍA: *& Prov.*, Spain 36 E18
Almeria, G. of: Spain 35 E18
Almhult: Sweden 47 O8
Almina, Pta.: *cape*, Morocco 35 D19
Al Miqdadiyah: Iraq 57 J5
Almirante: Panama 87 I16
Almirante Brown: *rsch. stn.*, Antarctica 9 65S 65W
Almiropotamos: Euboea, Greece 39 T17
Almirós: Greece 39 S17
Almodóvar: Portugal 35 B18
Almodóvar: Spain 35 D17
Al Moktar: Niger 81 F2
Almond, Glen: *valley*, Tayside, Scotland 29 O7
Almondbury: W. Yorks., Eng. 27 S12
Almondsbury: Avon, Eng. 24 Q16
Almora: Uttar Pradesh, India 58 N9
Almuradiel: Spain 35 E17
Aln: *riv.*, Northumb., England 26 S9
Alness: Highland, Scot. 28 N4
Alnham: Northumb., Eng. 26 R9
Alnmouth: Northumb., Eng. 26 S9
Alnwick: Northumb., Eng. 26 S9
Alofi: *i.*, Horn Is., Pac. O. 67 Q4
Aloi: Uganda 76 D2
Alón (Iliodhrómia): *i.*, N. Sporades, Greece 39 S17
Alonsa: Man., Canada 92 H2
Alor: *i. & str.*, Indonesia 65 G8
Alora: Spain 35 D18
Alor Gajah: Malaya, Malaysia 65 c12
ALOR SETAR: Kedah, Malaya, Malaysia 65 b10
Alosno: Spain 35 C18
Alost: *see* Aalst.
Aloysius Mount: W. Austl. 68 D5
Alpachiri: Argentina 96 C4
Alpena: Mich., U.S.A. 88 K3
Alpes-de-Haute-Provence: *Dept.*, France (*cap.* Digne) 40 M11
Alpes Maritimes: *Dept.*, France (*cap.* Nice) 40 N12
Alpha: Queens., Australia 70 G4
Alpha: *riv.*, Queens., Australia 70 G5
Alphen: Netherlands 44 K3
Alpheus: river reaching sea S. of Katákolon, Greece 39 R18
Alphington: Devon, Eng. 24 O18
Alport: Derby., England 27 S13
Alps, Algauer: Austria/W. Germany 40 Q8
Alps, Bavarian: W. Germany 41 R8
Alps, Bergamo: Italy 40 P9
Alps, Bernese: Switzerland 40 N9
Alps, Carnic: Austria/Italy 41 S9
Alps, Cottian: France/Italy 40 N11
Alps, Dinaric: Yugoslavia 38 P14
Alps, Fischbach: Austria 41 V8
Alps, Glein: Austria 41 V8
Alps, Graian: France/Italy 40 N10
Alps, Julian: Italy/Yugo. 41 T9
Alps, Kitzbühel: Austria 41 S8
Alps, Lepontine: Switzerland/Italy 40 O9
Alps, Ligurian: Italy 40 O11
Alps, Ötztal: Austria 41 Q9
Alps, Pennine: Switz./Italy 40 N10
Alps, Provence: France 40 L12
Alps, Rhaetian: Switzerland 40 P9
Alps, Savoy: France 40 M10
Alps, Seetaler: Austria 41 U8
Alps, Stub: Austria 41 U8
Alps, Transylvanian: Rom. 39 S14
Alps, Venetian: Italy 41 S9
Al Quds: *Dist.*, Jordan (*cap.* Jerusalem) 56 D6
Alresford, New: Hants., Eng. 25 T17
Alrewas: Staffs., England 27 S14
Alroy: N. Territ., Australia 69 F3
Alsace: *Prov.*, France 34 K12
Alsager: Ches., England 27 R13
Alsask: Sask., Canada 92 F2
Alsasua: Spain 37 C13
Alsfeld: W. Germany 44 P5
Alsh, Loch: High., Scot. 28 K5
Alsten: *i.*, Norway 46 N4
Alsterbro: Sweden 47 O8
Alston: Cumbria, England 26 R10
Alstonfield: Staffs., Eng. 27 S13
Alta: Norway 46 S2
Altagracia: Venezuela 94 C1
Altai: *Territ.*, U.S.S.R. (*cap.* Barnaul) 51 O4
Altai Range: Mongolia 51 P5
Altamaha: *riv.*, Ga., U.S.A. 91 L10
Altamira: Brazil 94 G4
Altamira: Chile 96 B2
Altamira: Mexico 86 K13
Altamura: Italy 38 P16
Altano, Cape: Sardinia 38 L17
Altar: Mexico 93 E6
Altare: Italy 40 O11
Altares, Point: *cape*, Morocco (Gib. *Inset*) 32 *Ins.*
Altarnun: Corn., England 24 M18
Altat: U.S.S.R. 51 Q3
Altata: Mexico 93 F8
Altavista: Va., U.S.A. 89 M7
Altay: Mongolia 62 R5
ALTDORF: Uri, Switzerland 40 O9
Alte: *riv.*, Norway 46 S2
Altea: Spain 35 F17
Altenberg: E. Germany 45 T5
Altenberge: W. Germany 44 N3
Altenburg: E. Germany 45 S5
Altenkirchen: W. Germany 44 N5
Altenmarkt: Austria 41 V7
Altenmarkt: W. Germany 41 S8
Alt Gaarz: E. Germany 45 R1
Altharen: W. Germany 44 N3
Althofen: Austria 41 U9
Althorpe: Humb., England 27 U12

Altkirch—Aouinet Bel Egra 119

Altkirch: France 40 N8
Altmühl: riv., W. Germany 41 Q6
Altnaharra: High., Scot. 28 N3
Alto Alentejo: Prov., Port. (cap. Portalegre) 35 C17
Alto Araguaca: Brazil 94 G7
Alto Chicapa: Angola 77 A5
Alto Cuito: Angola 77 A5
Alto Gracia: Argentina 96 C3
Alto Ligonha: Mozambique 77 E6
Alto Molócuè: Mozambique 77 E6
Alton: Hants., England 25 U17
Alton: Ill., U.S.A. 88 F6
Alton: Queens., Australia 70 H6
Alton: Staffs., England 27 S14
Altona: W. Germany 45 P2
Altoona: Pa., U.S.A. 89 M5
Alto Parnaiba: Brazil 94 H5
Altopascio: Italy 40 Q12
Alt-Ötting: W. Germany 41 S7
Alto Uruguai: Brazil 96 E2
Altrincham: Gt. Man., Eng. 27 R13
Altstätten: Switzerland 40 P8
Altun Köpru: Iraq 57 J4
Alturas: Calif., U.S.A. 92 C4
Altus: Okla., U.S.A. 90 B8
Alty Agach: U.S.S.R. 57 L1
Altyn Tagh: range, China 51 O7
Alucra: Turkey 56 F1
Aluk: Sudan 76 C1
Alukosungmu: Tibet, China 58 N8
Alūksne: Latvia, U.S.S.R. 47 U8
Alula: Somalia 79 S17
Al 'Uzayr: Iraq 57 K6
Alva: Central, Scotland 29 O7
Alva: Okla., U.S.A. 90 B7
Alvarado: Mexico 86 K14
Alvdal: Norway 47 M5
Älvdalen: Sweden 47 O6
Alveley: Salop, England 24 R15
Alverdiscott: Devon, Eng. 24 N17
Alverstoke: Hants., England 25 T18
Alvesta: Sweden 47 O8
Alveston: War., England 25 S15
Alvie: Highland, Scotland 28 O5
Alvie: Vict., Australia 71 E12
Alvito: Portugal 35 C17
Älvsborg: Co., Sweden (cap. Vänersborg) 47 N7
Älvsby: Sweden 46 R4
Alwalton: Cambs., England 25 V14
Alwar: Rajasthan, India 58 N9
Alwinton: Northumb., Eng. 26 R9
Alyaty Pristan': Azerbaydzhan, U.S.S.R. 57 L2
Alyayom: U.S.S.R. 49 u4
Alygdzher: U.S.S.R. 49 I7
Alyn: riv., Clwyd, Wales 27 P13
Alyth: Tayside, Scotland 29 P6
Alytus: Lithuania, U.S.S.R. 47 T9
Alzamay: U.S.S.R. 51 R3
Alzey: W. Germany 44 O6
Alzon: France 37 J12
Alzonne: France 37 H12
Ama: Mali 80 D2
Ama: La., U.S.A. 90 Ins.
Amadeus, Lake: N. Territ., Australia 68 E4
Amadi: Sudan 76 D1
Amadi: Zaïre 76 C2
Amadia: Iraq 57 H3
Amadjuak: & lake, N.W.T., Canada 85 m5
Amagasaki: Japan 63 d3
Amahai: Moluccas, Indon. 61 K12
'Amairi: wadi, Oman 55 J10
Amakusa: i., Japan 63 b4
Åmål: Sweden 47 N7
Amaliás: Greece 39 R18
Amami Group: is., Ryukyu Is., China Sea 63 X9
Amami: i., Ryukyu Is., China Sea 63 X9
Amance: France 40 M8
Amangel'dy: Kazakh., U.S.S.R. 51 L4
Amantea: Italy 38 P17
Amanu: i., Tuamotu Arch. 83 g3
Amanus: mtns. (Giąous Dagh) NE. of head of G. of Iskenderon, Turkey 56 E3
Amanzimtoti: Natal, S. Afr. 75 J5
Amapá: Territ., Brazil (cap. Macapa) 94 G3
Amapá (Montenegro): Brazil 94 G3
Amar: Tibet, China 59 O8
Amara: Iraq 57 K6
Amarante: Brazil 94 J5
Amarante: Portugal 35 B16
Amarat: tribal area, Iraq 57 G5
Amargosa Range: U.S.A. 93 D5
Amarillo: Tex., U.S.A. 93 G5
Amarti: Ethiopia 54 F12
Amasa: Mich., U.S.A. 88 G2
Amasra: Turkey 56 C1
AMASYA: & Prov., Turkey 56 D1
Amatsu: Japan 63 g3
Amazon: riv., Brazil 94 G4
Amazonas: State, Brazil (cap. Manaus) 94 E4
Ambala: Haryana, India 58 N8
Ambalu: Borneo 65 E7
Amban: Cameroun 81 G4
Ambanja: Malagasy Rep. 73 O12
Ambarchik: U.S.S.R. 49 S4
Ambathalla: Queens., Austl. 70 F5
Ambato: Ecuador 94 B4
Ambatomainty: Malagasy Rep. 70 O13
Ambatondrazaka: Malagasy Repub. 73 O13
Ambazac: France 37 G10
Ambelau: i., Indonesia 65 H7
Amberg: W. Germany 45 R6
Ambergris Cay: i., Belize 86 Ins.
Ambérieu: France 40 L10
Amberley: W. Sussex, Eng. 25 U18
Ambert: France 37 J10
Ambes: France 37 E10
Ambeté: geog. reg., Gabon 81 G5
Ambidedi: Mali 80 B2
Ambierle: France 37 J9
Ambikapur: Madhya Pradesh, India 59 O10
Ambilobé: Malagasy Rep. 73 O12
Ambjörby: Sweden 47 N6
Ambla: Estonia, U.S.S.R. 47 T7
Amble: Northumb., Eng. 26 S9
Amblecote: W. Mid., England 24 R15
Ambleside: Cumbria, Eng. 26 Q11
Ambleston: Dyfed, Wales 24 M16
Amblève: riv., Belgium 44 L5
Ambohimahasoa: Malagasy Rep. 73 O14
Amboise: France 36 G8
Ambon: Indonesia 61 K12
Ambositra: Malagasy Rep. 73 O14
Ambovombe: Malagasy Rep. 73 O15
Amboyna Cay: i., S. China Sea 64 E5
Ambracia: Greek city near Árta in plain N. of G. of Amvrakia, Greece 39 R17
Ambrières: France 36 E7
Ambrim: i., New Hebrides 67 N5
Ambriz: Angola 73 G11
Ambrizete: Angola 73 G11
Amby: Queens., Australia 70 H6
Amchitka: i. & passage, Aleutians 84 a7
'Amd: Hadhramaut, Yemen P.D.R. 55 G11
Am Dam: Chad 79 J7
Amderma: U.S.S.R. 48 H4
Am-Djéress: well, Chad 79 J6
Ameland: i., W. Frisian Is. 44 L2
Amelia: Va., U.S.A. 89 N7
Amelia: i., Fla., U.S.A. 91 L10
Amelinghausen: W. Germany 45 Q2
Ameria: Roman city to E. of Tiber and about 15 miles W. of Terni, Italy 38 N15
American Falls: city, Idaho, U.S.A. 92 E4
American Samoa: U.S. Territ., (cap. Pago Pago) 70 Ins.
Americus: Ga., U.S.A. 91 J9
Amersfoort: Netherlands 44 L3
Amersfoort: Trans., S. Afr. 75 H3
Amersham: Bucks., England 25 U16
Amery: Man., Canada 92 J1
Amery: Wis., U.S.A. 88 E3
Amery Ice Shelf: Antarctica 9 70S 70E
Ames: Iowa, U.S.A. 88 E4
Amesbury: Wilts., England 25 S17
Amfíklia: Greece 39 S17
Amfípolis: Greece 39 S16
Ámfissa: Greece 39 S17
Amfreville-la-Campagne: Fr. 36 F6
Amga: & riv., U.S.S.R. 49 P5
Amganba: riv., Cam./Nig. 81 G2
Amgu: U.S.S.R. 63 Z5
Am Guereda: Chad 79 J7
Amgun': riv., U.S.S.R. 49 p7
Amhara: geog. reg., Ethiopia 79 M7
Amherst: Burma 59 R11
Amherst: Mass., U.S.A. 89 P4
Amherst: N.S., Canada 89 T3
Amherst: Va., U.S.A. 89 M7
Amherst: i., Magdalen Is., Canada 89 U2
Amherstburg: Ont., Canada 88 K4
Amiens: Queens., Australia 71 J7
AMIENS: Somme, France 36 H6
Amij: wadi, Iraq 57 G5
Amini: i., Laccadive Is. 58 M12
Amino: Japan 63 d3
Aminuis: SW. Africa 77 A7
Amirante Is.: Seychelles, Indian Ocean 19 OS 50E
'Amiriya, El: Egypt 56 A6
Amisk Lake: Sask., Canada 92 G2
Amisus: Greek city on S. coast of Black Sea near Samsun, Turkey 56 E1
Amite: La., U.S.A. 90 F10
Amiun: Lebanon 56 D4
Amizmiz: Morocco 80 K8
Åmli: Norway 47 L7
Amlia: i., Aleutians 84 b7
Amlwch: Gwynedd, Wales 27 N13
Amm Adam: Sudan 54 E11
Ammaedara: Roman camp near Kalaa Djerda (Tunisia) 38 L19
'AMMAN: Al Asimah, Jordan 55 b3
Ammanford: Dyfed, Wales 24 O16
Ammarnäs: Sweden 46 P4
Ammathus: Hellenistic city on W. coast of Lake Tiberias about 2 miles S. of Tiberias, Israel 55 b2
Ammerån: riv., Sweden 46 O5
Ammer See: lake, W. Germany 41 R8
Ammon: tribe, and region inhabited by them around 'Amman, Jordan. Old Testament traditional district name 55 b3
Amne Machin Shan: range, Chinghai, China 62 R8
Amöneburg: W. Germany 44 O5
Amorbach: W. Germany 44 P6
Amorgos: i., Cyclades (Grc.) 39 U18
Amory: Miss., U.S.A. 90 G9
Amos: Que., Canada 89 M1
Amou: France 37 E12
Amoy (Szeming): Fukien, China 62 V10
Ampacama: Argentina 96 B3
Ampanihy: Malagasy Rep. 72 N14
Amparo: Brazil 96 F1
Amper: riv., W. Germany 41 R7
Ampère: Algeria 32 D4
Ampezzo: Italy 41 S9
Amphitrite Group: is., Paracel Is. 64 E3
Ampleforth: N. Yorks., Eng. 26 T11
Amplepuis: France 37 K10
Ampthill: Beds., England 25 U15
Amqui: Que., Canada 89 S1
Amraha: Sudan 54 D11
'Amran: Yemen 54 F11
Amravati: Maharashtra, India 58 N10
Amreli: Gujarat, India 58 M10
Amritsar: Punjab, India 58 M8
Amroha: Uttar Pradesh, India 58 N9
Amroth: Dyfed, Wales 24 M16
Amrum: i., N. Frisian Is. 44 O1
Åmsele: Sweden 46 Q4
Amsteg: Switzerland 40 O9
AMSTERDAM: Neth. 44 K3
Amsterdam: N.Y., U.S.A. 89 O4
Amsterdam: Trans., S. Africa 75 J3
Amsterdam Fracture Zone: Indian Ocean 9 35S 75E
Amstetten: Austria 41 U7
AM-TIMAN: Salamat, Chad 79 J7
Amu (Oxus): riv., Kazakh., U.S.S.R. 51 K7
Amukta: i. & passage, Aleutians 84 b7
Amulree: Tayside, Scotland 29 O6
Amund Ringnes I.: N.W.T., Canada 84 K2
Amundsen Gulf: N.W.T., Canada 84 g3
Amundsen-Scott: rsch. stn., Antarctica 9 90S
Amundsen Sea: Antarctica 9 75S 135W
Amur: riv., U.S.S.R./China 49 p7
'Amur, Wadi: Sudan 54 D11
Amurang: Celebes 65 G6
Amurrio: Spain 35 E15
Amvrakia, G. of: Greece 39 R17
An: Burma 59 Q11
Anaa: i., Tuamotu Arch. 83 f3
Anab: wadi, Jordan 56 E6
Anabama: S. Australia 71 D9
Anabar: riv., U.S.S.R. 49 N3
Anaco: Venezuela 94 E2
Anaconda: Mont., U.S.A. 92 E3
Anacortes: Wash., U.S.A. 92 C3
Anactorium: Greek city on mainland NE. of N. end of Levkás, Greece 39 R17
Anad: Yemen P.D.R. 54 F12
Anadarko: Okla., U.S.A. 90 B8
Anadia: Brazil 94 K5
Anadolukavaği: Turkey (Bosporus Inset) 20 Ins.
Anadyr': U.S.S.R. 49 T5
Anadyr', Gulf of: U.S.S.R. 49 U5
Anadyr': riv., U.S.S.R. 49 T4
Anáfi: i., Cyclades (Greece) 39 T18
Anaghit: Ethiopia 54 E11
Anagnia: ancient Hernican city about 35 miles ESE. of Rome. 38 N16
Anah: Iraq 57 G4
Anai Mudi: mtn., Kerala, India 58 N12
'Anaiza: Saudi Arabia 54 F9
'Anaiza: tribal area, Iraq 57 G5
Anakapalle: Andhra Pradesh, India 59 O11
Analalava: Malagasy Rep. 73 O12
Anambas Is.: Indonesia 65 D6
Anambra: riv., Nigeria 81 F3
Anambra: State, Nigeria (cap. Enugu) 81 F3
Anamosa: Iowa, U.S.A. 88 F4
Anamur: Turkey 56 C3
Anandpur: Orissa, India 59 P10
Anantapur: Andhra Pradesh, India 58 N11
Anantnag: Jammu & Kashmir 58 N8
An'an'yev: Ukraine 50 D5
Anapa: U.S.S.R. 50 E6
Anapolis: Brazil 94 H7
Anar: Iran 55 J8
Anarak: Iran 55 H8
Anardarra: Afghanistan 58 K8
Anas: Roman name of river Guadiana (SW. Spain and Portugal) 35 C17
Anascaul: Kerry, Repub. of Ireland 31 A15
Anatahan: i., Mariana Is. 61 O8
Anatolia: penin., Asia 33 J4
Añatuya: Argentina 96 C2
Anavio (Brough): Roman fort about 3 miles N. of Hucklow, Derby., England 27 S13
Anaye: Niger 78 G6
Anbar: Prov., Iraq 57 G5
Anbyon: N. Korea 63 X7
Ancaster: Lincs., England 26 U14
Ance: riv., France 37 J10
Ancenis: France 36 D8
Anchorage: Alaska, U.S.A. 84 E5
Anchuras: Spain 35 D17
Ancohuma, Nevado de: mtn., Bolivia 94 D7
Ancón: Panama 94 Ins.
Ancón: Peru 94 B6
ANCONA: The Marches, Italy 41 T12
Anconcagua: volc., Arg. 96 B3
Ancrum: Borders, Scotland 29 Q8
Ancuabe: Mozambique 77 E5
Ancuaze: Mozambique 77 D6
Ancud: Chile 95 C12
Ancy-le-Franc: France 36 K8
Andacollo: Argentina 96 A4
Andalgalá: Argentina 96 B2
Åndalsnes: Norway 46 K5
Andalusia: Ala., U.S.A. 91 H10
Andalusia: old Prov., Spain 35 D18
Andam: wadi, Oman 55 J10
Andaman Basin: Indian O. 9 10N 90E
Andaman Is.: India, [cap.(with Nicobar Is.) Port Blair] Indian Ocean 59 Q12
Andaman Sea: Indian O. 59 R12
Andaraí: Brazil 94 J6
Andaral: Afghanistan 58 L7
Andelot: France 40 L7
Andelsbuch: Austria 40 P8
Andelys, Les: France 36 G6
Andenes: Vesterålen, Nor. 46 P2
Andenne: Belgium 44 L5
Anderida: Roman shore-fort at Pevensey, E. Sussex, Eng. 25 W18
Andermatt: Switzerland 40 O9
Andernach: W. Germany 44 N5
Anderson: Argentina 96 C4
Anderson: Ind., U.S.A. 88 J5
Anderson: S.C., U.S.A. 91 K8
Anderson, Cape: Que., Can. 85 M5
Anderson: riv., Canada 84 G4
Anderson Summit: mt., Antarctica 9 85S 95W
Andes: range, S. America 94 C6
And Fjord: Norway 46 P2
Andhra Pradesh: State, India (cap. Hyderabad) 59 O11
Andía, Sierra de: mtns., Sp. 37 C13
Andifli: Turkey 56 A3
Andikíthira: i., Greece 39 S19
Andırın: Turkey 56 E3
Ándissa: Lesbos, Greece 39 T17
Andizhan: Uzbek., U.S.S.R. 51 M6
Andkhui: Afghanistan 51 L7
Andoas: Peru 94 B4
Andong: S. Korea 63 X7
Andorf: Austria 41 T7

Andorra: Republic 37 G13
Cap.: Andorra
Area: 190 sq. miles (466 sq. km.)
Pop.: 19,000 (1971 E)

Andouille: France 36 E7
Andover: Hants., England 25 T17
Andover: N.H., U.S.A. 89 Q4
Andoversford: Glos., Eng. 24 S16
Andøy: i., Vesterålen, Nor. 46 O2
Andradina: Brazil 94 G8
Andraitx: Maj., Balearic Is. 35 H17
Andreanof Is.: Aleutians 84 B7
Andreas: I. of Man, U.K. 26 N11
Andreas, Cape: Cyprus 56 D4
Andrées Land: Greenland 85 R3
Andrews: N.C., U.S.A. 91 K8
Andrews: Oreg., U.S.A. 92 D4
Andrews: S.C., U.S.A. 91 M9
Andrews: Tex., U.S.A. 93 G6
Andreyevka: Kazakh., U.S.S.R. 51 O5
Andreyevka: U.S.S.R. 50 H4
Andria: Italy 38 P16
Andrijevica: Yugoslavia 39 Q15
Andrítsaina: Greece 39 R18
Androka: Malagasy Rep. 73 N14
Andros: & i., Cyclades (Grc.) 39 T18
Androscoggin: riv., U.S.A. 89 Q3
Andros I.: Bahamas 87 M13
Androth: i., Laccadive Is. 58 M12
Andrushevka: Ukraine 43 V11
Andryushkino: U.S.S.R. 49 R4
Andújar: Spain 35 D17
Andulo: Angola 73 H12
Anduze: France 37 J11
Anécho: Togo 81 E3
Anegada: i. (Br.), Virgin Is. 87 b1
Aneityum: New Hebrides 67 N6
Añelo: Argentina 96 B4
Aneta: N. Dak., U.S.A. 92 H3
Aneto: mtn., Pyrénées 35 G15
Anfo: Italy 40 Q10
Anfu: Kiangsi, China 62 U9
Angara: riv., U.S.S.R. 49 M6
Angaston: S. Australia 71 C10
Angatau: i., Tuamotu Arch. 83 g3
Angaur: i., Palau Is. 61 L10
Ånge: Sweden 46 O5
An Geata Mo'r (Binghamstown): Mayo, Repub. of Ireland 30 A11
Angel de la Guarda: i., Mex. 93 E7
Angeles, Los: Chile 96 A4
Angel Falls: Venezuela 94 E2
Ängelholm: Sweden 47 N8
Angeli: Finland 46 T2
Angelina: riv., Tex., U.S.A. 90 D10
Angellala: & riv., Queensland, Australia 70 G6
Angelo: Trans., S. Africa 74 N Ins.
Angera: Italy 40 O10
Ångerman: riv., Sweden 46 P5
Angermünde: E. Germany 45 U2
ANGERS: Maine et Loire, Fr. 36 E8
Angerville: France 36 H7
Ångesån: riv., Sweden 46 S3
Angical: Brazil 94 J6
Angicos: Brazil 94 K5
Angkor: ruins of ninth-century capital of Khmers, Khmer Rep. 64 C4
Anglaling Hu: lake, Tibet, China 59 O8
Angle: Dyfed, Wales 24 L16
Angledool: N.S.W., Austl. 71 G7
Anglesey: i., Gwynedd, Wales 27 N13
Anglet: France 37 D12
Angleton: Tex., U.S.A. 90 D11
Angliers: Que., Canada 89 M2
Anglin: riv., France 37 G9
Anglure: France 36 J7
Angmagssalik: Greenland 85 Q4
Angmering: W. Sussex, Eng. 25 V18
Ango: Zaïre 76 C2
Angoche: Mozambique 77 E6
Angol: Chile 96 A4

Angola: Republic 73 H12
Cap.: Luanda
Area: 481,351 sq. miles (1,246,699 sq. km.)
Pop.: 5,673,000 (1970 C)

Angola: Ind., U.S.A. 88 J5
Angola Basin: N. Atlantic Ocean 8 15S 00
Angostura: Mexico 93 F7
ANGOULÊME: Charente, Fr. 37 F10
Angouma: Gabon 81 G4
Angoumois: Prov., France 34 G14
ANGRA DO HEROISMO: Terceira I., Azores, Portugal 78 Ins.
Angra dos Reis: Brazil 96 G1
Angren: & riv., U.S.S.R. 51 M6
Angu: Zaïre 76 B2
Anguilla: i. see St. Christopher-Nevis Anguilla.
Angul: Orissa, India 59 P10
Angumu: Zaïre 76 C3
Anguran: Iran 55 J9
Angus, Braes of: hills, Tayside, Scotland 29 P6
Anholt: i., Denmark 47 M8
Anhua: Kwangsi Chuang, China 62 T9
Anhwa: Hunan, China 62 U9
Anhwei: Prov., China (cap. Hofei) 62 V8
Aniak: Alaska, U.S.A. 84 D5
Anie: Togo 80 E3
Animas, Las: Chile 96 A2
Animas Peak: N. Mex., U.S.A. 93 F6
Anio: tributary on left bank of river Tiber reaching latter about 2 miles N. of Rome. 38 N16
Anizy-le-Château: France 36 J6
Anjala: Finland 47 U6
Anjengo: Kerala, India 58 N13
Anjer Lor: Java 65 D8
Anjo: Japan 63 e3
Anjou: Prov., France 34 F13
Anju: N. Korea 63 X7
Anjum: Netherlands 44 M2
Anka: Nigeria 81 F2
Ankang (Hingan): Shensi, China 62 T8
ANKARA: & Prov., Tur. 56 C2
Ankara: riv., Turkey 56 C2
Ankarara Mtns.: Malagasy Rep. 73 O14
Ankarede: Sweden 46 O4
Ankazoabo: Malagasy Rep. 73 N14
Ankazobe: Malagasy Rep. 73 O13
Anki: Fukien, China 62 V9
Anking (Hwaining): Anhwei, China 62 V8
Anklam: E. Germany 45 T2
Ankober: Ethiopia 79 M8
Ankogel: mtn., Austria 41 T8
Ankoro: Zaïre 76 C4
Ankpa: Nigeria 81 F3
Ankwo: Hopeh, China 62 V7
Anloga: Ghana 80 E3
Anlu (Teian): Hupeh, China 62 U8
Anlung: Kweichow, China 62 T9
Ann, Cape: Mass., U.S.A. 89 Q4
Anna: Ill., U.S.A. 88 G7
Anna: U.S.S.R. 50 F4
ANNABA (Bône) & Dept., Algeria 38 K8
Annaberg: E. Germany 45 T5
Anna Creek: town, S. Austl. 69 F5
Annagassan: Louth, Repub. of Ireland 30 J12
Annaghdown: Gal., Repub. of Ireland 31 C13
An-Nahiya: Iraq 57 G4
Annai: Guyana 87 d9
Annalee: riv., Cavan/Monaghan, Repub. of Ireland 30 G11
Annalong: Down, N. Irel. 30 K11
Annamoe: Wick., Repub. of Ireland 31 J13
Annan: Dumf. & Gall., Scot. 29 P10
Annan: riv., Dumf. & Gall., Scot. 29 P9
Annandale: Queens., Austl. 70 H3
Annandale: val., Dumf. & Gall., Scotland 29 P9
Anna Plains: town, W. Austl. 68 C3
ANNAPOLIS: Md., U.S.A. 89 N6
Annapolis Royal: N.S., Can. 89 T3
Annapurna: mtn., Nepal 59 O9
Ann Arbor: Mich., U.S.A. 88 K4
Annbank: Strath., Scotland 29 M9
ANNECY: Haute-Savoie, France 40 M10
Annemasse: France 40 M9
Annestown: Wat., Repub. of Ireland 31 G15
Annet: i., Scilly Is., Eng. 25 J19
Annfield Plain: Dur., Eng. 26 S10
An Nhon: Vietnam 64 D4
Anningie: N. Territ. Austl. 68 E4
Anniston: Ala., U.S.A. 91 J9
Annobon (Pagalu): i. (Equatorial Guinea), G. of Guinea 81 F5
Annonay: France 37 K10
Annot: France 40 M12
Annotto Bay: town, Jamaica 86 Ins.
Annuello: Vict., Australia 71 E10
Anoka: Minn., U.S.A. 88 E3
Anou Izileg: Algeria 78 F5
Áno Viánnos: Crete 39 T19
Anpeh: Inner Mongolia, China 62 T6
Anröchte: W. Germany 44 O4
Ansâb: well, Iraq/Saudi Arabia 57 J7
Ansab: Yemen P.D.R. 54 G12
Ansbach: W. Germany 45 Q6
Anse: France 37 K10
Anshan: Liaoning, China 63 W6
Anshun: Kweichow, China 62 T9
Anshunchang: Szechwan, China 62 S9
Ansi: Kansu, China 62 R6
Ansoedoe: West Irian, Indonesia 61 M12
Anson: Tex., U.S.A. 90 B9
Anson, North: Maine, U.S.A. 89 R3
Ansongo: Mali 80 E1
Ansted: W. Va., U.S.A. 88 L6
Anstey: Leics., England 27 T14
Anston: S. Yorks., England 27 T13
Anstruther: Fife., Scotland 29 Q7
Anta: Heilungkiang, China 63 X5
ANTAKYA (Antioch): Hatay, Turkey 56 E3
Antalaha: Malagasy Rep. 73 P12
Antalya: gulf, Turkey 56 B3
ANTALYA: & Prov., Turkey 56 B3
ANTANANARIVO: & Prov., Malagasy Rep. 73 O13
Antandrus: Greek city on N. coast of Edremit G. about 10 miles W. of Edremit, Turkey 39 U17
Antanimora: Malagasy Rep. 73 O14
Antarctic Peninsula: Antarctica 9 70S 65W
Antas: riv., Brazil 96 E2
An Teallach: mtn., Highland, Scotland 28 L4
Antequera: Paraguay 96 D1
Antequera: Spain 35 D18
Anthedon: Graeco-Roman city on coast about 3 miles NW. of Gaza, Egypt 55 a3
Anthony: Kans., U.S.A. 90 B7
Anthony Lagoon Station: N. Territ., Australia 69 F3
Anti-Atlas: range, Morocco 80 K8
Antibes: & cape, France 40 N12
Anticosti I.: Canada 85 n8
Antierh: Sinkiang, China 51 O7
Antifer, Cap d': cape, France 36 F6
Antigo: Wis., U.S.A. 88 G3
Antigonish: N.S., Canada 89 V3
Antigua: Guatemala 86 k15

Antigua: Br. associated state 87 c2
Cap.: St. John's
Area: 171 sq. miles (443 sq. km.)
Pop.: 70,000 (1970 C)

Antigua Veracruz: Mexico 86 K14
Anti Lebanon (Jebel esh Sharqi): range, Syria 56 E4
Antilla: Argentina 96 C2
Antilles, Greater: arch., W. Indies 87 m14
Antilles, Lesser: arch., W. Indies 87 Ins.
ANTIOCH (Antakya): Hatay, Turkey 56 E3
Antioch-towards-Pisidia: Hellenistic and Roman town near Yalvac, Turkey 56 B2
Antipatris: Herodian city about 8 miles NE. of Jaffa, Israel 55 a2
Antipodes Is.: (N.Z.), Southern Ocean 7 50S 175E
Antisana, Cerro: mtn., Ec. 94 B4
Antitaurus Mtns.: E. of river Seyhan and N. of plain around Adana, Turkey 56 D3
Antler: riv., Sask., Canada 92 G3
Antlers: Okla., U.S.A. 90 D8
Antofagasta: Chile 96 A1
Antofagasta de la Sierra: Argentina 96 B2
Antofalla: volc., Argentina 96 B2
Antonina: Brazil 96 F2
Antonine Wall: Roman wall from about 3 miles W. of Clydebank to about Bo'ness, Central, Scot. 29 N8
Antonio Prado: Brazil 96 E2
Antonito: Colo., U.S.A. 93 F5
Antopol': Byelorussia 43 T10
Antou: Szechwan, China 62 S8
Antrain: France 36 D7
Antri: Madhya Pradesh, India 58 N9
Antrim: & Co., N. Ireland (co. town Belfast) 30 J10
Antrim Mtns.: N. Ireland 30 J9
Antsalava: Malagasy Rep. 73 N13
Antsirabe: Malagasy Rep. 73 O13
Antsirane: see Diego Suarez.
Antu: Kirin, China 63 X6
An Tuc: Vietnam 64 D4
Antung: Liaoning, China 63 W6
ANTWERP (Anvers): & Prov., Belgium 44 K4
Antwerpen: see Antwerp.
AN UAIMH (Navan): Meath, Repub. of Ireland 30 H12
Anuanuraro: i., Tuamotu Arch. 83 g4
Anu-Anurunga: i., Tuamotu Arch. 83 g4
Anuda (Cherry I.): Pacific O. 67 N4
Anundsjö: Sweden 46 Q5
Anupgarh: Rajasthan, India 58 M9
Anuppur: Madhya Pradesh, India 58 O10
Anuradhapura: Sri Lanka 58 O13
Anvers: see Antwerp.
Anvik: Alaska, U.S.A. 84 c5
Anvin: France 36 H5
Anwick: Lincs., England 27 V13
Anyang: Honan, China 62 U7
Anyuy, Great: riv., U.S.S.R. 49 s4
Anza: Colombia 94 B2
Anzhero-Sudzhensk: U.S.S.R. 51 P3
Anzio: Italy 38 N16
Ao: Japan 63 e3
Aoga: i., (Japan), Pacific O. 63 Z8
Aoiz: Spain 35 F15
Aoji: N. Korea 63 Y6
Aola: Solomon Is. 67 M3
Aomori: Japan 63 ZZ6
AOSTA: Valle d'Aosta, Italy 40 N10
Aouïnet: Algeria 78 C4
Aouinet Bel Egra: well, Algeria 78 C4

For Abbreviations see list on p.113. Italic type, e.g. *Ephesus*, refers to historical names not on maps. Capital letters, e.g. MADRID, show capitals of countries; small capital letters, e.g. CADIZ, show capitals of provinces, etc. General notes p.116.

120 Aouk—Ashford

Aouk: riv., Central African Republic/Chad 79 J8
Aoulef Arab: Algeria 78 E4
Aous: river rising in Pindus Mtns. and flowing NW. to sea just N. of Gryke, Albania 39 Q16
Aoya: Japan 63 c3
Aozu: Chad 78 H5
Apalachee Bay: Fla., U.S.A. 91 J11
Apalachicola: & bay, Fla., U.S.A. 91 J11
Apamea (Cibotus): Graeco-Roman city at Dinar, Turkey 56 B2
Apamea: Roman colony at Mudanya, Turkey 39 V16
Apamea: Graeco-Roman city about 50 miles NW. of Hama, Syria 56 E4
Apaporis: riv., Colombia 94 C3
Aparri: Luzon, Philippines 64 G3
Apataki: i., Tuamotu Arch. 83 f3
Apatin: Yugoslavia 39 Q14
Apatity: U.S.S.R. 46 X3
Apatzingán: Mexico 86 j14
Apeldoorn: Netherlands 44 L3
Apen: W. Germany 44 N2
Apennines: range, Italy 38 N15
Aperi: Karpáthos, Dodec. 39 U19
Aphek: city of ancient Israel at Fiq, Syria 55 b2
Aphetae: harbour at E. end of western arm closing G. of Pagasae, Greece 39 S17
Api: Zaïre 76 C2
Api: mtn., Nepal 58 O9
APIA: Western Samoa 70 Ins.
Apiacás, Serra Dos: range, Brazil 94 F6
Aplao: Peru 94 C7
Ap Long Ha: Vietnam 64 D4
Apo: mtn., Philippines 65 H5
Apolda: E. Germany 45 R4
Apollo Bay: S. Australia 71 E12
Apolo: Bolivia 94 D6
Apolyont, Lake: Turkey 39 V16
Apopka, Lake: Fla., U.S.A. 91 L11
Apostle Is.: Wis., U.S.A. 88 F2
Apóstoles: Argentina 96 D2
Apoteri: Guyana 87 d8
Appalachian Mtns.: U.S.A. 88 L7
APPENZELL: & Canton, Switzerland 40 P8
Appiano: Italy 40 O10
Appin: dist., Strath., Scot. 29 L6
Appingedam: Netherlands 44 M2
Appleby: Cumbria, Eng. 26 R10
Appleby: Humb., England 27 U12
Appleby Magna: Leics., England 27 S14
Applecross: Highland, Scotland 28 K5
Appledore: Devon, England 24 N17
Appledore: Kent, England 25 X17
Applethwaite: Cumbria, England 26 P10
Appleton: Oxon., England 25 T16
Appleton: Wis., U.S.A. 88 G3
Appleton City: Mo., U.S.A. 90 D6
Appley Bridge: Lancs., Eng. 27 Q12
Appomattox: Va., U.S.A. 89 M7
Apsheronskiy: U.S.S.R. 50 E6
Apsley: Tas., Australia 68 H8
Apt: France 40 L12
Apucarana: Brazil 96 E1
Apulia: Reg., Italy (cap. Bari) 38 P16
Apulum: Roman camp at Alba Iulia, Romania 43 S13
Apurimac: riv., Peru 94 C6
Apuşeni Mtns.: Romania 43 S13
Aq: Prov., Iran 57 J2
'Aqaba: Jordan 56 D7
'Aqaba, G. of: Red Sea 54 D9
'Aqarquf, Lake: Iraq 57 J5
Aq Chah: Afghanistan 51 L7
Aqche: Sinkiang, China 51 N6
Aqiq: Sudan 54 E11
Aqiq: wadi, Saudi Arabia 54 F10
Aq Kand: Iran 57 L3
Aqlat al Suqur: Saudi Arabia 54 F9
'Aqra: Iraq 57 H3
Aquae Sextiae: Roman city at Aix-en-Provence, France 37 L12
Aquae Sulis: Roman town at Bath, England 24 R17
Aquidauana: Brazil 94 F8
AQUILA, L': Abruzzi Molise, Italy 38 N15
Aquincum: Roman camp and town on right bank of river Danube N. of Budapest, Hungary 43 Q13
Aquinum: ancient city on borders of Latium and Samnium about 55 miles SE. of Rome. 38 N16
Aquitania: Roman province of SW. France, bounded on N. by river Loire (ethnographic Aquitania was S. of the Garonne) 34 G14
Arabah, Wadi: depression, Israel/Jordan 56 D6
Arabba: Italy 41 R9
Arabi: La., U.S.A. 90 Ins.
Arabia Felix (Eudaemon): Graeco-Roman name of (a) Sau. Arab., (b) Aden 54 —
Arabian Basin: Indian O. 9 10N 60E
Arabian Desert: Egypt 54 D9
Arabian Sea: Indian O. 58 L11
Arabia Petraea: Roman province of 'Amman, Negeb, and Sinai, extending E. to approximate line Damascus-Basra-'Aqaba 56 D6
Araç: Turkey 56 C1
ARACAJÚ: Sergipe, Brazil 94 K6
Aracati: Brazil 94 K4
Araçatuba: Brazil 95 G8
Aracena: Spain 35 C18
Arachosia: ancient Greek name of district of Baluchistan from Kandahar, Afghan., SE. towards Indus valley 58 L8
Araçuai: Brazil 94 J7
Arad: Romania 43 R13
Arada: Chad 79 J6
Arae Flaviae: Roman town at Rottweil, W. Germany 42 L12
Arafat: Saudi Arabia 54 F10
Arafura Sea: Australia 68 E2
Aragón: old Prov., Spain 35 F16
Aragón: riv., Spain 35 F15
Araguari: Brazil 94 H7
Araguaia: riv., Brazil 94 H5
Araguari: riv., Brazil 94 G3
Ara Hangay: Prov., Mongolia 62 S5
Araioses: Brazil 94 J4
Araiporanga: Brazil 96 E1
Arakaka: Guyana 87 c7
Arakan: state, Burma (cap. Sittwe) 59 Q10
Arakan Yoma: range, Burma 59 Q11
Araks (Araxes): riv., U.S.S.R./Iran 57 K2
Arakthos: riv., Greece 39 R17
Aral Sea: Uzbek., U.S.S.R. 50 J6
Aral'sk: Kazakh., U.S.S.R. 51 K5
Aral-Sor: lake, Kazakh., U.S.S.R. 50 G5
Aramac: Queens., Australia 69 H4
Aranda de Duero: Spain 35 E16
Arandelovac: Yugoslavia 39 R14
Aran I.: Don., Repub. of Ireland 30 D10
Aran Is.: Repub. of Ireland 31 B13
Aranjuez: Spain 35 E16
Aran Fawddwy: mtn., Gwynedd, Wales 27 O14
Aranos: S. W. Africa 77 A7
Aransas Pass: Tex., U.S.A. 90 C12
Arantangi: Tamil Nadu, India 58 N12
Aranuka: i., Gilbert Is. 67 O1
Arao: Japan 63 b4
Araouane: Mali 78 D6
Arapey: Uruguay 96 D3
Arapey Grande: riv., Uruguay 96 D3
Arapkir: Turkey 56 F2
Arar: Roman name of river Saône 37 K9
'Arar: wadi, Saudi Arabia 57 G6
Araranguá: Brazil 96 F2
Araraquara: Brazil 96 F1
Araras, Serra das: mtns., Brazil 96 E2
Ararat: Vict., Australia 71 E11
Ararat, Mount: Turkey 57 J2
Ararat Station: Armenia, U.S.S.R. 57 J2
Araro: Ethiopia 76 E2
Aras: riv., Turkey 57 H1
Arasanj: Iran 57 M4
Aras de Alpuente: Spain 35 F17
Aratapu: North I., N.Z. 70 O13
Aratika: i., Tuamotu Arch. 83 f3
Arauca: Colombia 94 C2
Arauca: riv., Venezuela 94 D2
Arauco: Chile 96 A4
Arausio: Roman city at Orange, France 37 K11
Araxá: Brazil 94 H7
Araxes (Araks): riv., U.S.S.R./Iran 57 K2
Arba, I': Algeria 35 H18
ARBA MINCH: Gēmu Gefa, Ethiopia 79 M8
Arbaouat: Algeria 80 M8
Arbatax: Sardinia 38 L17
Arbay Heere: Mongolia 62 S5
Arbela: ancient Persian city at Erbil, Iraq 57 J3
Arbesbach: Austria 41 U7
Arbirlot: Tay., Scotland 29 Q6
Arboga: Sweden 47 O7
Arbois: France 40 L9
Arbon: Switzerland 40 P8
Arbrå: Sweden 47 P6
Arbresle, l': France 37 K10
Arbroath: Tay., Scotland 29 Q6
Arbuckle: Calif., U.S.A. 93 C5
Arbuthnott: Gram., Scotland 28 R6
Arc: France 40 L8
Arc: riv., France 40 M10
Arcachon: France 37 D11
Arcachon, Bassin d': France 37 D11
Arcadia: Fla., U.S.A. 91 L12
Arcadia: Wis., U.S.A. 88 F3
Arcadia: district of central Peloponnese (including Megalopolis and Tripolis), Greece 39 S18
Arcassa: Karpáthos, Dodec. 39 U19
Arc-en-Barrois: France 36 L8
Arces: France 36 J7
Archelais: Herodian city about 8 miles N. of Jericho, Israel 55 b3
Archer: riv., Queens., Austl. 69 G2
Archer City: Tex., U.S.A. 90 B9
Archers Post: Kenya 76 E2
Arches Nat. Mon.: Utah, U.S.A. 93 F5
Archiac: France 37 E10
Archibald Makin Wildlife Reserve: S. Australia 71 D10
Archidona: Spain 35 D18
Arcis-sur-Aube: France 36 K7
Arco: Idaho, U.S.A. 92 E4
Arco: Italy 41 Q10
Arcola: battlefield N. of river Adige about 3 miles ESE. of Soave, Italy 41 R10
Arcos de Valdevez: Port. 35 B16
Arcot: Tamil Nadu, India 58 N12
Arctic Bay: town, N.W.T., Canada 85 L3
Arctic Red River: settlement, N.W.T., Canada 84 f4
Arctic Village: Alaska, U.S.A. 84 E4
Arcturus: Rhodesia 77 D6
Ardagh: Lim., Repub. of Ireland 31 C15
Ardagh: Long., Repub. of Ireland 30 F12
Ardahan: Turkey 57 H1
Ardakan: (NNW. of Yezd), Iran 55 H8
Ardakan: (NNW. of Shiraz), Iran 55 H8
Ardam: Azerbaydzhan, U.S.S.R. 57 K2
Ardara: Don., Repub. of Ireland 30 E10
Ardasa: Turkey 56 F1
Ardclach: High., Scotland 28 O5
Ardcroney: Tip., Repub. of Ireland 31 E14
Ardea: ancient Roman city in plain of Latium about 20 miles due S. of Rome. 38 N16
Ardeath: Meath, Repub. of Ireland 30 J12
Ardébé: Chad 81 H2
Ardebil: Iran 57 L2
Ardèche: Dept. & riv., Fr. (cap. of Dept. Privas) 37 K11
Ardee: Louth, Repub. of Ireland 30 H12
Arden, Forest of: West Midlands, England 25 S15
Ardencaple Fiord: Grnld. 85 S3
Ardennes: Dept., France (cap. Mézières) 36 K6
Ardennes: mtns., Belgium 44 L5
Ardentes: France 37 G9
Ardentinny: Strath., Scot. 29 M7
Ardeonaig: Tay., Scotland 29 N7
Ardessie: Highland, Scotland 28 L4
Ardfern: Strath., Scotland 29 K7
Ardfert: Kerry, Repub. of Ireland 31 B15
Ardfield: Cork, Repub. of Ireland 31 D16
Ardfinnan: Tip., Repub. of Ireland 31 F15
Ardglass: Down, N. Ireland 30 K11
Ardgour: dist., High., Scot. 29 L6
Ardgroom: Cork, Repub. of Ireland 31 B16
'Ardha: Saudi Arabia 54 F11
Ardhéa: Greece 39 S16
Ardila: riv., Spain/Portugal 35 C17
Ardino: Bulgaria 39 T16
Ardistan: Iran 55 H8
Ardlethan: N.S.W., Austl. 71 G10
Ardlui: Strath., Scotland 29 M7
Ardlussa: Inner Hebrides, Scotland 29 K7
Ardminish: Inner Hebr., Scotland 29 K8
Ardmolich Bridge: High., Scot. 29 K6
Ardmore: Okla., U.S.A. 90 C8
Ardmore: Wat., Repub. of Ireland 31 F16
Ardmory: Queens., Austl. 69 F4
Ardnacrusha: Clare, Rep. of Ireland 31 D14
Ardnamurchan: cape & dist., Highland, Scotland 29 J6
Ardnave Point: cape, Inner Hebr., Scotland 29 J8
Ardoch: Queens., Australia 70 F6
Ardoch: site of Roman camp about 1 mile N. of Braco, Tayside, Scotland 29 O7
Ardpatrick: Strath., Scot. 29 K8
Ardrahan: Galway, Repub. of Ireland 31 D13
Ardres: France 36 G5
Ardrishaig: Strath., Scotland 29 L7
Ardross: Highland, Scotland 28 N4
Ardrossan: Strath., Scotland 29 M8
Ards Penin.: Down, N. Irel. 30 K10
Ardtalnaig: Tay., Scotland 29 N6
Ardud: Romania 43 S13
Ardwell: Dumf. & Gall., Scot. 29 M10
Åre: Sweden 46 N5
Areavaara: Sweden 46 S3
Arebi: Zaïre 76 C2
Arecibo: Puerto Rico 87 N14
Areia Branca: Brazil 94 K4
Arelate: Roman city at Arles, France 37 K12
Ar(e)morica: Roman name of area in NW. France between Seine and Loire 34 H13
Arena, Point: cape, Calif., U.S.A. 93 C5
Arenas de San Pedro: Spain 35 D16
ARENDAL: Aust Agder, Nor. 47 L7
Arendsee: E. Germany 45 R3
Arends I.: Indonesia 65 E8
Arenosa: Panama 94 Ins.
Arenys de Mar: Spain 35 H16
Areópolis: Greece 39 S18
Arequipa: Peru 94 C7
Arès: France 37 D11
Arévalo: Spain 35 D16
Arezzo: Italy 38 M15
Arfuda: well, Somalia 79 R18
Arga: riv., Spain 35 F15
Argao: Philippines 64 G5
Argeles: France 37 H13
Argens: riv., France 40 M12
Argent: France 36 H8
Argenta: Italy 41 R11
Argentan: France 36 E7
Argentat: France 37 G10
Argenteuil: France 36 H7
Argentia: Newf., Canada 85 v3

Argentina: Republic 95 D11
Cap.: Buenos Aires
Area: 1,072,067 sq. miles (2,776,653 sq. km.)
Pop.: 23,552,000 (1971 E)

Argentine Basin: S. Atlantic Ocean 8 45S 50W
Argentina, La: Argentina 95 C14
Argentine Islands: rsch. stn., Antarctica 9 70S 65W
Argentino, Lake: Argentina 95 C14
Argenton-sur-Creuse: Fr. 37 G9
Argentorate: Roman camp at Strasbourg, France 40 N7
Argentre-du-Plessis: France 36 D7
Argeş: riv., Romania 39 T14
Arghandab: riv., Afghan. 58 L8
Arghanstan: riv., Afghanistan 58 L8
Arginusae: Islands off W. coast of penisula to N. of Çandarli G., Turkey 39 U17
Argo: Sudan 54 D11
Argolis: ancient name of peninsula running E. and S. from city of Argos, Greece 39 S18
Argonne: hills, France 36 L6
Argonne, Forêt d': for., Fr. 36 K6
Argos: Greece 39 S18
Argostolion: Cephalonia, Ionian Is. 39 R17
Argueil: France 36 G6
Arguello, Point: cape, Calif., U.S.A. 93 C6
Argun': riv., U.S.S.R./China 49 n7
Argungu: Nigeria 81 E2
Argyle Downs: W. Australia 68 D3
Argyll National Park: Strathclyde, Scotland 29 M7
Argyz: U.S.S.R. 50 H3
Arhavi: Turkey 57 G1
Aria: North I., N.Z. 70 P14
Ariano Irpino: Italy 38 O16
Ariano Polesine: Italy 41 S11
Aribinda: Upper Volta 80 D2
Arica: Chile 94 C7
Arica: Colombia 94 C4
Arica: Peru 94 B4
Aricha, El: Algeria 80 L8
Arichat: Cape Breton I., Canada 89 V3
Aricia: ancient city of Latium on Via Appia about 15 miles SE. of Rome 38 N16
Ariconium: Roman settlement at Weston-under-Penyard about 3 miles E. of Ross, Here. & Worcs., England 24 Q16
'Aridh: desert, Saudi Arabia 54 G11
'Aridh: geog. reg., Saudi Arabia 54 G10
Aridhglas: Inner Hebr., Scotland 29 J7
Ariège: Dept., France (cap. Foix) 37 G13
Ariège: riv., France 37 G12
Ariminum: Roman colony at Rimini, Italy 41 S11
Arinagour: Inner Hebr., Scotland 29 H6
Arinthod: France 40 L9
Aripo, Mount: Trinidad 87 c5
Aripuanã: riv., Brazil 94 E5
Aris: SW. Africa 74 B1
Arisaig: & dist., High., Scot. 28 K6
Arisaig, Sound of: Highland, Scotland 29 K6
Aristazabal I.: B.C., Canada 92 B2
Ariza: Spain 35 E16
Arizaro, Salar de: salt pan, Argentina 96 B1
Arizona: Argentina 96 B4
Arizona: State, U.S.A. (cap. Phoenix) 93 E6
Arizpe: Mexico 93 E6
Årjäng: Sweden 47 N7
Arjasa: Kangean Is., Indon. 65 F8
Arjeplog: Sweden 46 P3
Arka: U.S.S.R. 49 Q5
Arkabutla Reservoir: Miss., U.S.A. 90 F8
Arkadak: U.S.S.R. 50 F4
Arkadelphia: Ark., U.S.A. 90 E8
Arkaig, Loch: High., Scot. 28 L6
Arkalyk: Kazakh., U.S.S.R. 51 L4
Arkansas: State, U.S.A. (cap. Little Rock) 90 E8
Arkansas: riv., U.S.A. 93 G5
Arkansas City: Ark., U.S.A. 90 F9
Arkansas City: Kans., U.S.A. 90 C7
Arkhangelos: Rhodes, Dodecanese 39 V18
ARKHANGEL'SK (Archangel): Arkhangel'sk, U.S.S.R. 48 F5
Arkhangel'sk (Archangel): Reg., U.S.S.R. 50 F2
Arkle: mtn., High., Scot. 28 M3
Arklow: Wick., Repub. of Ireland 31 J14
Arkona, Cape: Rügen, E. Ger. 47 N9
Arkonam: Andhra Pradesh, India 58 N12
Arkösund: Sweden 47 P7
Arkticheskogo Institut Is.: U.S.S.R. 48 K2
Arkville: N.Y., U.S.A. 89 O4
Arlanc: France 37 J10
Arlberg Pass: Austria 40 Q8
Arlecdon: Cumbria, England 26 P10
Arles: France 37 K12
Arlesey: Beds., England 25 V15
Arless: Laois, Repub. of Irel. 31 G14
Arleuf: France 36 K8
Arlington: Devon, England 24 O17
Arlington: O.F.S., S. Afr. 75 G4
Arlington: Tex., U.S.A. 90 C9
Arlington: Wash., U.S.A. 92 C3
ARLON: Luxemburg, Belgium 44 L6
Arltunga: N. Territ., Austl. 68 E4
Arma: Kans., U.S.A. 90 D7
Armadale: High., Scotland 28 N2
Armadale: Lothian, Scot. 29 O8
Armadale Bay: village, Inner Hebr., Scotland 28 K5
ARMAGH: & Co., N. Ireland 30 H11
Armagnac, Collines de l': hills, France 37 F12
Armançon: riv., France 36 K8
Armatree: N.S.W., Australia 71 H8
Armavir: U.S.S.R. 50 F5
Armenia: Colombia 94 B3
Armenian S.S. Repub.: U.S.S.R. (cap. Yerevan) 57 J1
Armentières: France 36 H5
Armidale: N.S.W., Australia 71 J8
Armitage: Staffs., England 27 S14
Armoed: S. Africa 74 E6
Armorica: see Ar(e)morica.
Armour: S. Dak., U.S.A. 92 H4
Armoy: Antrim, N. Ireland 30 J9
Armstrong: B.C., Canada 92 D2
Armstrong: Ont., Canada 85 L7
Armstrong: riv., N. Territ., Australia 68 E3
Armthorpe: S. Yorks., Eng. 27 T12
Arnauti, Cape: Cyprus 56 C4
Arnavutköy: Turkey (Bosphorus Inset) 20 Ins.
Arnay-le-Duc: France 36 K8
Arncliffe: N. Yorks., England 26 R11
Arneburg: E. Germany 45 S3
Arnedo: Spain 35 E15
Arneiroz: Brazil 94 J5
Arnes: Iceland 46 c3
ARNHEM: Gelderland, Neth. 44 L4
Arnhem, Cape: Australia 69 F2
Arnhem Land Reserve: N. Territ., Australia 68 E2
Arnisdale: High., Scotland 28 K5
Arnish: Inner Hebr., Scot. 28 J5
Arnissa: Greece 39 R16
Arniston: S. Africa 74 D7
Arno: riv., Italy 40 Q12
Arnol: Outer Hebr., Scot. 28 H3
Arnold: Notts., England 27 T14
Arnoldstein: Austria 41 T9
Arnon: river flowing into approximately central point of E. coast of Dead Sea, Jordan 55 b3
Arnøy: i., Norway 46 R1
Arnprior: Ont., Canada 89 N3
Arnsberg: Dist., North Rhine-Westphalia, West Germany 44 N4
Arnsberg: W. Germany 44 O4
Arnsberger Wald: hills, W. Germany 44 O4
Arnside: Cumb., England 26 Q11
Arnstadt: E. Germany 45 Q5
Arnstein: W. Germany 45 P6
Arnstorf: W. Germany 41 S7
Aroab: SW. Africa 74 C3
Arolsen: W. Germany 44 P4
Aron: France 36 E7
Arona: Italy 40 O10
Aroostook: riv., U.S.A. 89 R2
Arorae: i., Gilbert Is. 67 P2
Arosa: Switzerland 40 P9
Arpa: riv., Turkey 57 H1
Arpaçay: Turkey 57 H1
Arpajon: France 37 H11
Arpinum: ancient Roman city in Liri valley about 60 miles ESE. of Rome. 38 N16
Arrah: Bihar, India 59 O9
Ar-Rahab: desert, Iraq 57 J6
Arraiján: Panama 94 Ins.
Arraias: Brazil 94 H6
Arran, I. of: Strath., Scotland 29 L8
ARRAS: Pas de Calais, France 36 H5
Arreau: France 37 F13
Arrecife: Canary Is. 78 B4
Arrecifes: Argentina 96 C3
Arrée, Monts d': hills, France 36 B7
Arribas: Spain 37 D12
Ar Rifa': Iraq 57 K6
Arrilalah: Queens., Australia 69 G4
Arrochar: Strath., Scotland 29 M7
Arroio Grande: Brazil 96 E3
Arronches: Portugal 35 C17
Arroux: riv., France 36 K8
Arrow: riv., Here. & Worcs., England 24 Q15
Arrow, Lough: Sligo, Repub. of Ireland 30 E11
Arrowhead: B.C., Canada 92 D2
Arroyos y Esteros: Paraguay 96 D2
Ars-en-Ré: Île de Ré, France 37 D9
Arsen'yev: U.S.S.R. 63 Y6
Arsia: river forming NE. boundary of Roman imperial Italy, flowing into Raše Chan., Yugoslavia 41 U10
Arsiero: Italy 41 R10
Arsikere: Karnataka, India 58 N12
Arsuk: Greenland 85 P5
Arta: Greece 39 R17
Artà: Majorca, Balearic Is. 35 H17
Artajona: Spain 37 D13
Artashat: Armenia, U.S.S.R. 57 J2
Artawiya: Saudi Arabia 54 G9
Artaxata: ancient city of Armenia on river Aras about 20 miles SW. of Yerevan borders of Turkey and U.S.S.R. 57 J1
Artem: U.S.S.R. 63 Y6
Artema: i., Azerbaydzhan, U.S.S.R. 57 M1
Artemisa: Cuba 87 I13
Artemisium: promontory at most northerly point of Euboea, Greece 39 S17
Artemovsk: Ukraine 50 E5
Artemovsk: U.S.S.R. 51 Q4
Artemovskiy: Irkutsk, U.S.S.R. 49 N6
Artemovskiy: Sverdlovsk, U.S.S.R. 51 K3
Artenay: France 36 G7
Artesia: see Mosomane
Artesia: N. Mex., U.S.A. 93 G6
Arthabaska: Que., Canada 89 Q2
Arthez: France 37 E12
Arthurs Pass National Park: S.I., New Zealand 70 N16
Arthurstown: Wex., Repub. of Ireland 31 H15
Artigas: Uruguay 96 D3
Artik: Armenia, U.S.S.R. 57 H1
Art I.: New Caledonia 67 M5
Artois: Prov., France 34 H11
Artova: Turkey 56 E1
Artsagan Nor: lake, Inner Mongolia, China 62 U6
Artsiz: Ukraine 39 V14
ARTVIN: & Prov., Turkey 57 G1
Aru: Zaïre 76 D2
Arua: Uganda 76 D2
Aruanã: Brazil 94 G6
Aruba I.: (Neth.), Caribbean Sea 94 C1
Aru Is.: Indonesia 61 L13
Arukua: i., Tuamotu Arch. 83 f3
Arun: riv., W. Sussex, England 25 U18
Arunachal Pradesh: Union Terr., India 59 Q8
Arundel: S. Africa 75 F5
Arundel: W. Sussex, England 25 U18
Arus: SW. Africa 74 C3
ARUSHA: & Reg., Tanzania 76 E3
Arusi: Prov., Ethiopia (cap. Aselle) 76 E1
Aruwimi: riv., Zaïre 76 B2
Arvad: Phoenician city & seaport N. of Tripoli, Lebanon 56 D4
Arvagh: Cavan, Repub. of Ireland 30 F12
Arverni: Gallic tribe in country of Auvergne mtns., France 37 J10
Arvida: Que., Canada 89 Q1
Arvidsjaur: Sweden 46 Q4
Arvika: Sweden 47 N7
Arwala: Wetar, Indonesia 65 H8
Aryk-Balyk: Kazakh., U.S.S.R. 51 L4
Arys': Kazakh., U.S.S.R. 51 L6
Aryta: U.S.S.R. 49 o5
Arzamas: U.S.S.R. 50 F3
Arzen: W. Germany 44 P3
Arzew: & gulf, Algeria 35 F19
Arzfeld: W. Germany 44 M5
Arzgir: U.S.S.R. 50 F5
Arzila: Morocco 80 K7
Arzua: Spain 35 B15
Aš: Czechoslovakia 45 S5
Asa: Japan 63 b3
Asab: SW. Africa 74 B2
Asaba: Nigeria 81 F3
Asadabad: Iran 57 L4
Asahigawa: Japan 63 ZZ6
Asakotussu: Chinghai, China 62 R8
Asandia: Madhya Pradesh, India 59 O10
Asansol: W. Bengal, India 59 P10
Åsarna: Sweden 46 O5
Asbestos Mtns.: S. Africa 74 E4
Asbury Park: city, N.J., U.S.A. 89 O5
Ascalon: see Ashkelon.
Ascensión: Mexico 93 F6
Ascensión Bay: Mexico 86 L14
Ascension I.: (Br.), S. Atlantic Ocean (cap. Georgetown) 8 10S 15W
Aschach: Austria 41 U7
Aschaffenburg: W. Germany 44 P6
Aschendorf: W. Germany 44 N2
Aschersleben: E. Germany 45 R4
Ascog: Strathclyde, Scotland 29 L8
Ascoli Piceno: Italy 38 N15
Ascot: Berks., England 25 U17
Asculum: Roman city at Ascoli Piceno, Italy 38 N15
Ascunción, La: Venezuela 94 E1
Åseda: Sweden 47 O8
Åsele: Sweden 46 P4
ASELLE: Arusi, Ethiopia 76 E1
Åsen: Sweden 47 N6
Asenovgrad: Bulgaria 39 T15
Asfeld: France 36 K6
Asfordby: Leics., England 27 U14
Asha: U.S.S.R. 50 J4
Ashabo: Ethiopia 76 E2
'Ashaira: Hijaz, Sau. Arab. 54 F10
'Ashaira: Najd, Sau. Arab. 54 G9
Ashanti: Reg., Ghana (cap. Kumasi) 80 D3
'Ashar: Iraq 57 K6
Ashbourne: Derby., England 27 S13
Ashburn: Ga., U.S.A. 91 K10
Ashburton: Devon, England 24 O18
Ashburton: South I., N.Z. 70 N16
Ashburton: riv., W. Austl. 68 B4
Ashbury: Oxon., England 25 S16
Ashby: Humb., England 27 U12
Ashby, West: Lincs., Eng. 27 V13
Ashby-de-la-Zouch: Leics., England 27 T14
Ashby Magna: Leics., Eng. 27 T14
Ashchi: Kazakh., U.S.S.R. 50 J5
Ashdod: Israel 55 a3
Ashdod: Philistine city at Isdud, Israel 55 a3
Ashdown: Ark., U.S.A. 90 D9
Ashdown Forest: dist., East Sussex, England 25 W17
Asheboro: N.C., U.S.A. 91 M8
Asher: Israelite tribe which lived on W. side of Galilean hills around Acre, Israel 55 b2
Asherton: Tex., U.S.A. 90 B11
Asheville: N.C., U.S.A. 91 K8
Ashfield: Central, Scotland 29 O7
Ashford: Derby., England 27 S13
Ashford: Gt. Ldn., Eng. 25 V17
Ashford: Kent, England 25 X17
Ashford: N.S.W., Australia 71 J7
Ashford: Wick., Repub. of Ireland 31 J13

Ashford Carbonell—Baarle Nassau 121

Ashford Carbonell: Salop, England **24** Q15
Ashfork: Ariz., U.S.A. **93** E5
Ash Grove: Mo., U.S.A. **90** E7
Ashi: *riv.*, Kazakh., U.S.S.R. **51** N5
Ashibe: Japan **63** a4
Ashikaga: Japan **63** f2
Ashill: Norf., England **25** X14
Ashington: Northumb., Eng. **26** S9
Ashio: Japan **63** f2
Ashizuri, Cape: Japan **63** c4
Ashkelon (Ascalon): Israel **55** a3
ASHKHABAD: Turkmenistan, U.S.S.R. **50** J7
Ashkelon: Philistine city at *Askalan*, 2 miles WSW. of Majdal, Israel **55** a3
Ashkara: Oman **55** J10
Ashkirk: Borders, Scotland **29** Q9
Ashland: Kans., U.S.A. **90** B7
Ashland: Ky., U.S.A. **88** K6
Ashland: Ohio, U.S.A. **88** K5
Ashland: Oreg., U.S.A. **92** C4
Ashland: Va., U.S.A. **89** N7
Ashland: Wis., U.S.A. **88** F2
Ashley: N. Dak., U.S.A. **92** H3
Ashley: N.S.W., Australia **71** H7
Ashley: Staffs., England **27** R14
Ashmore: Dorset, England **24** R18
Ashmore & Cartier I.: (Austl.), Indian Ocean **68** C2
Ashmûn: Egypt **56** B6
Ashokan Reservoir: N.Y., U.S.A. **89** O5
Ashover: Derby., England **27** T13
Ash Shan: *desert*, Iraq **57** K6
Asht: Tadzhik., U.S.S.R. **51** M6
Ashtabula: Ohio, U.S.A. **88** L5
Ashtarak: Armenia, U.S.S.R. **57** J1
Ashtead: Surrey, England **25** V7
Ashton: Idaho, U.S.A. **92** E4
Ashton in Makerfield: Greater Manchester, England **27** Q13
Ashton Keynes: Wilts., Eng. **24** S16
Ashton under Hill: Hereford & Worcester, England **24** R15
Ashton under Lyne: Greater Manchester, England **27** R13
Ashton upon Mersey: Greater Manchester, England **27** R13
Ashuanipi, Lake: Newf., Canada **85** N7
Ashuapmuchuan: *riv.*, Que., Canada **89** P1
Ashuriya: *well*, Iraq **57** H6
Ashwater: Devon, England **24** N18
Ashwell: Herts., England **25** V15
Ashwell: Leics., England **27** U14
Asiago: Italy **41** R10
Asia Is.: West Irian, Indon. **61** L11
Asia Minor: name in common use for area of Asiatic Turkey up to line of Euphrates **33** J4
Asila: *well*, Iraq **57** H5
Asilah: Morocco **35** D19
Asilik: *well*, Niger **81** F1
Asinara: *i.* & *gulf*, Sardinia **38** L16
Asino: U.S.S.R. **51** P3
Asir: *geog. reg.*, Saudi Arabia **54** F11
Aşkale: Turkey **57** G2
Askam: Cumbria, England **26** P11
Askanmäki: Finland **46** U4
Askeaton: Lim., Repub. of Ireland **31** D14
Asker: Norway **47** M7
Askern: S. Yorks., England **27** T12
Askersund: Sweden **47** O7
Askham: Cumbria, England **26** Q10
Askino: U.S.S.R. **50** J3
Askival: *mtn.*, Inner Hebr., Scotland **28** J6
Askja: *volc.*, Iceland **46** e4
Askrigg: N. Yorks., England **26** R11
Asluj: Israel **56** D6
Asmar: Afghanistan **58** M8
ASMARA: Eritrea, Ethiopia **79** M6
Åsnen, Lake: Sweden **47** O8
Asola: Italy **40** Q10
Asolo: Italy **41** R10
Asopus: river of E. *Boeotia* flowing into straight between *Delium* and *Oropus* (opposite Nea Psara). **39** S17
Aspang: Austria **41** W8
Aspatria: Cumbria, England **26** P10
Aspen: Colo., U.S.A. **93** F5
Aspendus: Greek city on right bank of *Eurymedon* near Serik, Turkey **56** B3
Aspern: Austria **41** W7
Aspres-sur-Buëch: France **40** L11
Aspy Bay: Cape Breton I., Canada **89** V2
Assab: Ethiopia **79** Q17
Assaba: *Dist.*, Mauritania (*cap.* Kiffa) **78** B6
As Sa'diyah: Iraq **57** J4
Assaikio: Nigeria **81** F3
Assal, Lake: Djibouti **79** Q17
Assam: *State*, India (*cap.* Shillong) **59** Q9
Assebroek: Belgium **44** J4
ASSEN: Drenthe, Netherlands **44** M3
Assens: Funen, Denmark **47** L9
Asshur: early Assyrian capital at Sharqat, Iraq **57** H4
Assi (Orontes): *riv.*, Syria/Lebanon **56** E4
Assiniboia: Sask., Canada **92** F3
Assiniboine: *riv.*, Man./Sask., Canada **92** H3
Assiniboine, Mount: B.C./Alta., Canada **92** D2
Assinie: Ivory Coast **80** D3
Assis: Brazil **96** E1
Assisi: Italy **38** N15
Asso: Italy **40** P10
Assomption, l': Que., Can. **89** P3
Assos: Cephalonia, Ionian Is. **39** R17
Assos: Greek city on N. coast of Edremit G. about 10 miles E. of westward end, Turkey **39** U17
Assumar: Portugal **35** C17
Assynt, Loch: High., Scot. **28** L3
Astaffort: France **37** F11
Astakós: Greece **39** R17
Astaneh: Iran **57** L5
Astara: Iran/U.S.S.R. **57** L2
Astbury: Ches., England **27** R13
Asti: Italy **40** O11
Astico: *riv.*, Italy **41** R10
Astigi: Roman town at Ecija, Spain **35** D18
Astin Tagh: *range, see* Altyn Tagh **51** O7
Astipálaia: *i.*, Dodecanese, Greece **39** U18
Astola: *i.*, Baluchistan, Pak. **58** K9
Aston: Herts., England **25** V16
Aston, Cape: N.W.T., Can. **85** N3
Aston Abbots: Bucks., Eng. **25** U16
Aston Clinton: Bucks., Eng. **25** U16
Astor: Jammu & Kashmir **58** M7
Astorga: Spain **35** C15
Astoria: Oreg., U.S.A. **92** C3
Åstorp: Sweden **47** N8
ASTRAKHAN: *& Reg.*, U.S.S.R. **50** G5
Astrakhanka: Kazakh., U.S.S.R. **51** L4
Åstrand: Sweden **47** N6
Ástros: Greece **39** S18
Astudillo: Spain **35** D15
Astura: Roman name of river flowing into Tyrrhenian Sea about 5 miles E. of Anzio, Italy **38** N16
Asturiana, La: Argentina **96** B4
Asturias: *old Prov.*, Spain **35** C15
Astwood: Bucks., England **25** U15
Astwood Bank: *village*, Here. & Worcs., England **24** S15
ASUNCIÓN: Paraguay **96** D2
Asuncion: *i.*, Mariana Is. **61** O8
Aswa: *riv.*, Uganda **76** D2
Aswad: *wadi*, Oman **55** J10
Aswan: Egypt **54** D10
Asyut: Egypt **54** D9
Ata: *i.*, Tonga Is. **67** Q6
Atacama Desert: Chile **96** B1
Atacama, Puna de: *geog. reg.*, Argentina **96** B1
Atacama, Salar de: *salt pan*, Chile **96** B1
'Ataiba: *tribal area*, Saudi Arabia **54** F10
Atakora Mtns.: Benin **81** E2
Atakpamé: Togo **80** E3
Atalándi: Greece **39** S17
Atalaya: Peru **94** C6
Atambua: Timor, Indon. **65** G8
Atami: Japan **63** f3
Atamisqui: Argentina **96** C2
Atangmik: Greenland **85** o5
ATAR: Adrar, Mauritania **78** B5
Atar: *geog. reg.*, Mauritania **78** B5
Atascadero: Calif., U.S.A. **93** C5
Atasu: Kazakh., U.S.S.R. **51** M5
Atauro: *i.*, Timor **65** H8
Atay: Kirgiz., U.S.S.R. **51** M6
Atbara: Sudan **54** D11
Atbara: *riv.*, Sudan **54** E11
Atbasar: Kazakh., U.S.S.R. **51** L4
Atchafalaya: *riv.*, La., U.S.A. **90** F10
Atchafalaya Bay: La., U.S.A. **90** F11
Atchison: Kans., U.S.A. **93** H5
At Daban: U.S.S.R. **49** o5
Atebubu: Ghana **80** D3
Ateca: Spain **35** F16
Ateste: Roman city at *Este* about 5 miles W. of Monselice, Italy **41** R10
Ath: Belgium **44** J5
Athabasca: Alta., Canada **92** E2
Athabasca: *riv.*, Alta., Can. **92** E1
Athabasca, Lake: Sask., Can. **84** J6
Athalmer: B.C., Canada **92** D2
Athboy: Meath, Repub. of Ireland **30** H12
Athea: Lim., Repub. of Irel. **31** C15
Athenry: Galway, Repub. of Ireland **31** D13
Athens: Ala., U.S.A. **91** H8
Athens: Ga., U.S.A. **91** K9
ATHENS (Athinai): Greece **39** S18
Athens: Ont., Canada **89** O3
Athens: Tenn., U.S.A. **91** J8
Athens: Tex., U.S.A. **90** D9
Atherstone: War., England **27** S14
Atherton: Gt. Man., Eng. **27** Q12
Atherton: Queens., Australia **69** H3
Athesis: Roman name of river Adige, Italy **41** R10
ATHIÉMÉ: Sud-Ouest, Benin **81** E3
ATHINAI (Athens): Greece **39** S18
Athi River: Kenya **76** E3
Athis: France **36** E7
Athlacca: Lim., Repub. of Ireland **31** D15
Athleague, Rosc., Repub. of Ireland **30** E12
Athlone: C.P., S. Africa **74** *Ins.*
Athlone: Westmeath, Repub. of Ireland **31** F13
Athni: Karnataka, India **58** N11
Athol: Mass., U.S.A. **89** P4
Atholl: *dist.*, Tay., Scotland **29** O6
Atholl, Forest of: *dist.*, Tayside, Scotland **29** N6
Áthos: *penin.*, Greece **39** T16
Athy: Kild., Repub. of Irel. **31** H14
ATI: Batha, Chad **81** H2
Ati: Sudan **54** C12
Atico: Peru **94** C7
Atienza: Spain **35** E16
Atikokan: Ont., Canada **88** F1
Atikup: Ont., Canada **92** J2
Atina: *wadi*, Saudi Arabia **55** H11
Atiu: *i.*, Cook Is. **70** *Ins.*
Atka: U.S.S.R. **49** R5
Atka: & *i.*, Aleutians **84** b7
Atkarsk: U.S.S.R. **50** G4
Atkins: Ark., U.S.A. **90** E8
ATLANTA: Ga., U.S.A. **91** J9
Atlanta: Mich., U.S.A. **88** J3
Atlanta: Tex., U.S.A. **90** D9
Atlantic: Iowa, U.S.A. **92** J4
Atlantic: N.C., U.S.A. **91** N8
Atlantic City: N.J., U.S.A. **89** O6
Atlantic-Indian Basin: Southern Ocean **8** 65S 20E
Atlantic-Indian Ridge: S. Atlantic Ocean **8** 55S 20E
Atlantis Fracture Zone: N. Atlantic Ocean **8** 30N 45W
Atlas, High: *range*, Morocco **80** K8
Atlas, Little: *range*, Algeria **35** H18
Atlas, Middle: *range*, Mor. **80** L8
Atlas, Saharan: *range*, Alg. **80** L8
Atlin: B.C., Canada **84** f6
Atmore: Ala., U.S.A. **91** H10
Atocha: Bolivia **94** D8
Atoka: Okla., U.S.A. **90** C8
Atranos: *riv.*, Turkey **56** A2
Atrek: *riv.*, Iran **55** J7
Atropatene: district of ancient Media S. of middle valley of Araxes in Azerbaijan, Iran **57** K2
Atsa: Tibet, China **59** Q8
Atsugi: Japan **63** f3
Atsumi Penin.: Japan **63** e3
Atsunai: Japan **63** ZZ6
Atsutoko: Japan **63** YY6
Attalla: Ala., U.S.A. **91** H8
Attawapiskat: *riv.*, Canada **85** L7
Attendorn: W. Germany **44** N4
Atter See: *lake*, Austria **41** T8
Attica: Ind., U.S.A. **88** H5
Attica: district surrounding Athens, Greece **39** S17
Attigu: Sudan **76** D2
Attikamagen, Lake: Newf., Canada **85** N7
Attleboro: Mass., U.S.A. **89** Q5
Attleborough: Norf., Eng. **25** Y14
Attopeu: Laos **64** D4
Attu: & *i.*, Aleutians **84** A7
Attunga: N.S.W., Australia **71** J8
Attymass: Mayo, Repub. of Ireland **30** C11
Attymon: Galway, Repub. of Ireland **31** D13
Atuana: Marquesas Is. **83** h1
Atuel: *riv.*, Argentina **96** B4
Atufa: *i.*, Tokelau Is. **70** *Ins.*
Atui: *watercourse*, W. Africa **78** A5
Åtvidaberg: Sweden **47** P7
Atwick: Humb., England **27** V12
Au: Austria **40** P8
Auadi: Western Sahara **78** B5
Aub: SW. Africa **74** B1
Aubagne: France **40** L12
Aubarede Point: *cape*, Luzon, Philippines **64** G3
Aube: *Dept.*, France (*cap.* Troyes) **36** J7
Aube: *riv.*, France **36** K7
Aubel: Belgium **44** L5
Aubenas: France **37** K11
Aubigny: France **36** H5
Aubigny-sur-Nère: France **36** H8
Aubin: France **37** H11
Au Bouleau, Lac: *lake*, Que., Canada **89** M2
Aubrac, Monts d': France **37** J11
Auburn: Ala., U.S.A. **91** J9
Auburn: Ind., U.S.A. **88** J5
Auburn: Maine, U.S.A. **89** Q3
Auburn: Nebr., U.S.A. **93** H4
Auburn: N.Y., U.S.A. **89** N4
Auburndale: Fla., U.S.A. **91** L11
Aubusson: France **37** H10
Aucá Mahuida: *mtn.*, Arg. **96** B4
AUCH: Gers, France **37** F12
Auchan: Nigeria **81** F2
Auchel: France **36** H5
Auchencairn: Dumfries & Galloway, Scotland **29** O10
Auchi: Nigeria **81** F3
Auchinblae: Gram., Scotland **28** R6
Auchinleck: Strath., Scotland **29** N9
Auchterarder: Tayside, Scot. **29** O7
Auchterderran: Fife, Scot. **29** P7
Auchtermuchty: Fife, Scotland **29** P7
AUCKLAND: Central Auckland, North I., New Zealand **70** P13
Auckland Is.: (N.Z.), Southern Ocean **7** 55S 165E
Auckland, West: Dur., Eng. **26** S10
Aucun: France **37** E13
Aude: *Dept.*, France (*cap.* Carcassonne) **37** H12
Aude: *riv.*, France **37** J12
Audegle: Somalia **79** Q19
Audenarde: *see* Oudenaarde.
Audenge: France **37** D11
Audierne: France **36** A7
Audierne, Baie d': *bay*, France **36** A8
Audincourt: France **40** M8
Audlem: Ches., England **27** Q14
Audley: Staffs., England **27** R13
Audley End: Essex, England **25** W15
Audruicq: France **36** H5
Audun-le-Roman: France **36** L6
Aue: E. Germany **45** S5
Aue: *riv.*, W. Germany **44** O3
Auerbach: W. Germany **45** R6
Auerstadt: battlefield in hills about 2 miles NW. of Bad Sulza, E. Germany **45** R4
Aufidus: Roman name of river Ofanto, Italy **38** O16
Augathella: Queens., Austl. **70** G5
Augher: Tyr., N. Ireland **30** G11
Aughnacloy: Tyr., N. Irel. **30** H11
Aughrim: Galway, Repub. of Ireland **31** E13
Aughrim: Wick, Repub. of Ireland **31** J14
Augpilagtoq: Greenland **85** O3
Augrabies Falls National Park: C.P., S. Africa **74** D4
Augsburg: W. Germany **41** Q7
Augusta: Ark., U.S.A. **90** F8
Augusta: Ga., U.S.A. **91** L9
Augusta: Kans., U.S.A. **90** C7
AUGUSTA: Maine, U.S.A. **89** R3
Augusta: Mont., U.S.A. **92** E3
Augusta: Sicily **38** O18
Augusta: W. Australia **68** B6
Augusta: Wis., U.S.A. **88** F3
Augusta, North: S.C., U.S.A. **91** L9
Augusta Praetoria: Roman colony at Aosta, Italy **40** N10
Augusta Taurinorum: Roman city at Turin, Italy **40** N10
Augusta Trevirorum: Roman city at Trier, W. Germany **44** M6
Augusta Victoria: Chile **96** B1
Augusta Vindelicorum: Roman town at Augsburg, W. Germany **41** Q7
Augustodunum: Roman city at Autun, France **36** K9
Augustonemetum: Roman settlement at Clermont-Ferrand, France **37** J10
Augustów: Poland **43** S10
Augustus, Mount: W. Austl. **68** B4
Augustus Downs: Queens., Australia **69** F3
Au Haut, Isle: *i.*, Maine, U.S.A. **89** R3
'Auja, El: Egypt **56** D6
Aujila: Libya **33** G6
Auki: Solomon Is. **67** M3
Aulander: N.C., U.S.A. **89** N7
Auldearn: High., Scotland **28** O4
Auldhouse: Strath., Scotland **29** N8
Aulis: ancient port on mainland opposite Chalcis, Greece **39** S17
Aulla: Italy **40** P11
Aulnay: France **37** E9
Aulnoye: France **36** J5
Ault: France **36** G5
Aultbea: Highland, Scot. **28** K4
Aulus: France **37** G13
Aumale: France **36** G6
Aumont: France **37** J11
Aunay-sur-Odon: France **36** E6
Auncanquilcha: *mtn.*, Chile **95** D8
Auneau: France **36** G7
Auneuil: France **36** H6
Aunis: *Prov.*, France **34** F13
Auob: *riv.*, SW. Africa **74** C2
Auponhia: Sula Is., Indon. **65** H7
Aur: *i.*, Maiaya, Malaysia **65** d12
Aura: Finland **47** S6
Aurangabad: Maharashtra, India **58** N11
Auranitis: ancient Greek name of W. portion of Hauran district, W. of Jebel Druz, Damascus, Syria **56** E5
Auray: France **36** C8
Aurburn Range: Queens., Australia **70** J5
Aurdal: Norway **47** L6
Aurich: W. Germany **44** N2
Aurich: *Dist.*, Lower Saxony, West Germany **44** N2
Aurignac: France **37** F12
AURILLAC: Cantal, France **37** H11
Auroman: Iran **57** K4
Auronzo: Italy **41** S9
Aurora: Ill., U.S.A. **88** G5
Aurora: Ind., U.S.A. **88** J6
Aurora: Minn., U.S.A. **88** E2
Aurora: Mo., U.S.A. **90** E7
Aurora (Maewo): *i.*, New Hebrides **67** N5
Aus: SW. Africa **74** B3
Au Sable: *riv.*, Mich., U.S.A. **88** K3
Au Sable Point: *cape* (Lake Huron), Mich., U.S.A. **88** K3
Au Sable Point: *cape* (Lake Superior), Mich., U.S.A. **88** H2
Ausangate: *mtn.*, Peru **94** C6
Aussa: *geog. reg.*, Ethiopia **79** N7
Aussee: Austria **41** T8
Aust Agder: *Co.*, Norway (*cap.* Arendal) **47** K7
Austefjord: Norway **46** K5
Austerlitz: battlefield about 12 miles ESE. of Brno, Czechoslovakia **43** P12
Austin: Minn., U.S.A. **88** E4
Austin: Nev., U.S.A. **93** D5
Austin: Pa., U.S.A. **89** M5
AUSTIN: Tex., U.S.A. **90** C10
Austin, Lake: W. Australia **68** B5
Austral Downs: N. Territ., Australia **69** F4
Australia: *Commonwealth* **68/9**
Cap.: Canberra
Area: 2,967,909 sq. miles (7,686,884 sq. km.)
Pop.: 12,959,000 (*1972 E*)
Australian Alps: Vict./N.S.W., Australia **71** H11
Australian Capital Territory: Australia **71** H10
Austral (Tubuai) Is.: (Fr.), Pacific O. **83** e4
Austrasia: eastern kingdom of the Franks in the basin of river Rhine in early Middle Ages (*cap.* Metz) **42** K12
Austria: *Republic* **40/1** U8
Cap.: Vienna (Wien)
Area: 32,374 sq. miles (83,849 sq. km.)
Pop.: 7,456,403 (*1971 C*)
Austvågøy: *i.*, Lofoten Is., Norway **46** O2
Austwick: N. Yorks., England **26** R11
Auterive: France **37** G12
Autheuil: France **36** G6
Authie: *riv.*, France **36** H5
Authon: Eure-et-Loir, Fr. **36** F7
Autlán: Mexico **86** j14
Autun: France **36** K9
Auve: France **36** K6
Auvergne: N. Territ., Austl. **68** D3
Auvergne: *Prov.*, France **34** H14
Auvergne Mtns.: France **37** J10
Auvézère: *riv.*, France **37** G10
Auvillar: France **37** F11
Aux Barques, Pointe: *cape*, Mich., U.S.A. **88** K3
AUXERRE: Yonne, France **36** J8
Auximum: Roman city about 10 miles S. of Ancona, Italy **40** T12
Auxonne: France **40** L8
Aux Pins, Pointe: *cape*, Ont., Canada **88** L4
Aux Sources, Mont: South Africa **75** H4
Auzances: France **37** H9
Ava: Mo., U.S.A. **88** E7
Availles-Limouzine: France **37** F9
Avakubi: Zaire **76** C2
Avallon: France **36** J8
Avalon Penin.: Newf., Can. **85** w3
Avanos: Turkey **56** D2
Avaré: Brazil **96** F1
Avaricum: Roman name of Gallic centre at Bourges, France **36** H8
Avaris (*Tanis*): Egyptian city near modern *San*, 25 miles NE. of Faqus, Egypt **56** B6
AVARUA: (Palmerston Is.) Cook Is. **70** *Ins.*
Avaviken: Sweden **46** Q4
Avebury: Wilts., England **25** S17
Aveh: Iran **57** L4
Aveiro: Portugal **35** B16
Avellaneda: Argentina **96** D3
Avellino: Italy **38** O16
Avenir: Fr. Guiana **94** G3
Avennio: Roman city at Avignon, France **37** K12
Aventicum: capital of Helvetii and (later) Roman colony in *Avenches*, about 12 miles NW. of Fribourg, Switz. **40** N9
Averias: Argentina **96** C2
Averøy: *i.*, Norway **46** K5
Aversa: Italy **38** O16
Aves (Bird) I.: (Ven.), Leeward Is. **87** b3
Avesnes: France **36** J5
Avesta: Sweden **47** P6
Aveyron: *Dept.* & *riv.*, France (*cap.* of *Dept.* Rodez) **37** H11
Avezzano: Italy **38** N15
Aviano: Italy **41** S9
Avia Terai: Argentina **96** C2
Avich, Loch: Strath., Scot. **29** L7
Aviemore: High., Scotland **28** O5
Avigliana: Italy **40** N10
AVIGNON: Vaucluse, France **37** K12
ÁVILA: & *Prov.*, Spain **35** D16
Avilés: Spain **35** D15
Avisio: *riv.*, Italy **41** R9
Avispas, Las: Argentina **96** C2
Avning: Denmark **47** M8
Avoca: & *riv.*, Vict., Austl. **71** E11
Avoca: & *riv.*, Wick., Repub. of Ireland **31** J14
Avoch: Highland, Scot. **28** N4
Avola: B.C., Canada **92** D2
Avon: *Co.*, England (*co. town* Bristol) **24** R16
Avon: N.Y., U.S.A. **89** N4
Avon: *riv.*, Avon/Wilts., England **25** S18
Avon: *riv.*, Devon, England **24** O19
Avon: *riv.*, War./Hereford & Worcester, England **24** S15
Avon, The Bristol: *riv.*, Eng. **24** R17
Avondale: Queens., Austl. **70** K5
Avon I.: Chesterfield Is. **67** L5
Avonlea: Sask., Canada **92** F2
Avonmouth: Avon, Eng. **24** Q17
Avon Park: *city*, Fla., U.S.A. **91** L12
Avontuur: S. Africa **74** E6
Avonwick: Devon, England **24** O19
Avord: France **36** H8
Avranches: France **36** D7
Avre: *riv.*, Eure, France **36** F7
Avre: *riv.*, Somme, France **36** H6
Avricourt: France **40** M7
Avrig: Romania **39** T14
Avrillé: France **37** D9
Awa: *i.*, Japan **63** f1
Awaji: *i.*, Japan **63** d3
Awamir: *tribe*, Yemen P.D.R. **55** G11
Awanui: North I., N.Z. **70** O12
Awash: Ethiopia **79** N8
Awash: *riv.*, Ethiopia **79** N7
Awasil: Iraq **57** H5
Awaso: Ghana **80** D3
Awatere: *riv.*, South I., New Zealand **70** O15
Awati: Sinkiang, China **51** N7
Awbeg: *riv.*, Cork, Repub. of Ireland **31** D15
Awe, Loch: Strath., Scotland **29** L7
Aweil: Sudan **76** C1
Awgu: Nigeria **81** F3
Awka: Nigeria **81** F3
Awkaka: Nigeria **81** E3
Awoi: Sudan **76** D1
Awusa, Lake: Ethiopia **76** E1
Axar Fiord: Iceland **46** e3
Axbridge: Som., England **24** Q17
Axdir: Morocco **35** E19
Axe: *riv.*, England **24** Q18
Axel: Netherlands **44** J4
Axel Heiberg I.: N.W.T., Canada **85** k2
Axim: Ghana **80** D4
Axiopolis: Greek city on river Danube at Cernavoda, Romania **39** V14
Axius: Greek name for river Vardar **39** S16
Ax-les-Thermes: France **37** G13
Axminster: Devon, England **24** Q18
Axmouth: Devon, England **24** P18
Ayacucho: Argentina **96** D4
Ayacucho: Colombia **94** C2
Ayacucho: Peru **94** C6
Ayaguz: Kazakh., U.S.S.R. **51** O5
Ayaina: Saudi Arabia **54** G10
Ayamonte: Spain **35** C18
Ayan: U.S.S.R. **49** p6
Ayancik: Turkey **56** D1
Ayangba: Nigeria **81** F3
Ayapel: Colombia **94** B2
Ayaş: Turkey **56** C1
Ayaviri: Peru **94** C6
Aycliffe: Durham, England **26** S10
Aydary: U.S.S.R. **51** M2
Ayden: N.C., U.S.A. **91** N8
AYDIN: & *Prov.*, Turkey **39** U18
Ayer: Switzerland **40** N9
Ayerbe: Spain **35** F15
Ayer Hitam: Malaya, Malaysia **65** c13
Ayers Rock National Park: N. Territ., Australia **68** E5
Áyi Dhéka: Crete **39** T19
Áyios Evstrátios: *i.*, Greece **39** T17
Áyios Miron: Crete **39** T19
Áyios Nikólaos: Crete **39** T19
Aylesbeare: Devon, England **24** P18
AYLESBURY: & *val.*, Bucks., England **25** U16
Aylesford: Kent, England **25** W17
Aylmer: Ont., Canada **88** L4
Aylmer: Que., Canada **89** O3
Aylmer, Lake: N.W.T., Canada **84** J5
Aylmer, Mount: Alta., Canada **92** D2
Aylon: Greece **39** S17
Aylsham: Norf., England **25** Y14
Aynho: Northants., England **25** T16
Ayod: Sudan **76** D1
Ayoe Is.: Indonesia **61** L11
Ayon I.: E. Siberian Sea, U.S.S.R. **49** s4
Ayora: Spain **35** F17
Ayos: Cameroun **81** G4
Ayr: Queens., Australia **70** G2
Ayr: Strathclyde, Scotland **29** M9
Ayr: *riv.*, Strath., Scotland **29** N8
Ayre: *dist.*, I. of Man, United Kingdom **26** N11
Ayre, Point of: *cape*, I. of Man, United Kingdom **26** N11
Ayrolle, Étang de l': *lag.*, France **37** J12
Aysgarth: N. Yorks., England **26** S11
Ayton: Borders, Scotland **29** R8
Ayton: N. Yorks., England **26** V11
Ayton, Great: N. Yorkshire, England **26** T11
Ayukai: Japan **63** g1
Ayutla: Mexico **86** K14
Ayutthaya: Thailand **64** C4
Ayvacık: Turkey **39** U17
Ayvalık: Turkey **39** U17
Aywaille: Belgium **44** L5
Ayzpute: Latvia, U.S.S.R. **47** R8
Azaouad: *geog. reg.*, Mali **78** D6
Azare: Nigeria **81** G2
Azay-le-Feron: France **37** G9
Azay-le-Rideau: France **36** F8
Azbine (Air): *highlands*, Niger **78** F6
Azeffoum: Algeria **35** J18
Azerables: France **37** G9
Azerbaijan: *geog. reg.*, Iran **57** K2
Azerbaijan-e Bakhtari: *Prov.*, Iran (*cap.* Rizaiyeh) **57** K3
Azerbaijan-e Khavari: *Prov.*, Iran (*cap.* Tabriz) **57** K2
Azerbaydzhan S.S. Repub.: U.S.S.R. (*cap.* Baku) **50** G6
Azghar: Sinkiang, China **51** N7
Azigui: *well*, Mali **81** E1
Azilal: Morocco **80** K8
Azizabad: Iran **57** K4
Azizia: Libya **32** E5
Aziziya: Iraq **57** J5
Azogues: Ecuador **94** B4
Azores: *is.* (Port.), Atlantic O. **78** *Ins.*
Azores Plateau: N. Atlantic Ocean **8** 35N 30W
Azotus: Graeco-Roman name of *Ashdod*, city at Isdud, Israel **55** a3
Azoum: *riv.*, Chad **79** J7
Azov: U.S.S.R. **50** E5
Azov, Sea of: U.S.S.R. **50** E5
Azovy: U.S.S.R. **48** H5
Azpeitia: Spain **37** C12
Azrou: Morocco **80** K8
Azua: Dominican Repub. **87** m14
Azuaga: Spain **35** D17
Azuchi: *i.*, Japan **63** a4
Azuero, Penin. of: Panama **87** l16
Azul: Argentina **96** D4
Azules: *riv.*, Panama **94** *Ins.*
Azur: France **37** D12
Baä: Roti I., Indonesia **65** G9
Baäh: Savu I., Indonesia **65** G9
Baalbek: Lebanon **56** E4
Baamonde: Spain **35** C15
Baarle Nassau: Netherlands **44** K4

For Abbreviations see list on p.113. Italic type, e.g. *Ephesus*, refers to historical names not on maps. Capital letters, e.g. MADRID, show capitals of countries; small capital letters, e.g. CADIZ, show capitals of provinces, etc. General notes p.116.

122 Baarn—Balzar

Baarn: Netherlands **44** L3
Bab, El: Syria **56** E3
Baba Cape: Turkey **39** U17
Babadag: Romania **39** V14
Babaeski: Turkey **39** U16
Babahoyo: Ecuador **94** B4
Babanango: Natal, S. Africa **75** J4
Babar: *i.*, Indonesia **68** D1
Babar Is.: Indonesia **61** K13
Babati: Tanzania **76** E3
Bab el Mandeb: *str.*, Red Sea **54** F12
Babelthuap: *i.*, Palau Is. **61** L10
Babenhausen: W. Germany **44** O6
Bab es Serir: Libya **33** G5
Babeyru: Zaïre **76** C2
Babimbi: Cameroun **81** G4
Babine: *riv.*, B.C., Canada **92** B1
Babine Lake: B.C., Canada **92** B2
Babo: West Irian, Indonesia **61** L12
Baboquivari Peak: Ariz., U.S.A. **93** E6
Baboua: Cen. Afr. Rep. **81** G3
Babul: Iran **55** H7
Babuyan Is.: & *chan.*, Phil. **64** G3
Babylon: N.Y., U.S.A. **89** P5
Babylon: *ruin*, capital of Babylonian Empire, site N. of Hilla, Iraq **57** J5
Babylon: Roman camp at *Old Cairo* on right bank of Nile about 8 miles S. of Cairo, Egypt **56** B7
Bacabal: Maranhão, Brazil **94** J4
Bacabal: Pará, Brazil **94** F5
Bacan: Moluccas, Indonesia **61** K12
Bacău: Romania **43** U13
Baccarat: France **40** M7
Bacchus Marsh: *town*, Vict., Australia **71** F11
Bacerac: Mexico **93** F6
Ba Cham: Vietnam **64** D2
Bac Giang: Vietnam **64** D2
Bacharach: W. Germany **44** N5
Bachau: Gujarat, India **58** M10
Bachíniva: Mexico **93** F7
Bacho: Thailand **65** b10
Back: *riv.*, N.W.T., Canada **84** j4
Back: Outer Hebr., Scotland **28** J3
Backaland: Eday, Orkney Is. **28** *Ins.*
Backan: Vietnam **64** D2
Bačka Palanka: Yugoslavia **39** Q14
Bačka Topola: Yugoslavia **39** Q14
Backe: Sweden **46** P5
Bäckefors: Sweden **47** N7
Backnang: W. Germany **40** P7
Backstairs Pass: *str.*, S. Austl. **71** B10
Backwell: Avon, England **24** Q17
Bac Mor: *i.*, Inner Hebr., Scotland **29** J7
Bacqueville: France **36** F6
Bacubirito: Mexico **93** F7
Bacuit: Palawan, Philippines **64** F4
Bacup: Lancs., Eng. **27** R12
Badachro: High., Scot. **28** K4
BADAJOZ: & *Prov.*, Spain **35** C17
Badakhshan: *geog. reg.*, Afghanistan **51** L7
Badakhshan: *prov.*, Afghanistan (*cap.* Faizabad) **55** M7
Badalona: Spain **35** H16
Badana: *pump. station*, Saudi Arabia **54** F8
Badanloch, L.: High., Scot. **28** N3
Badas: Brunei **65** E6
Badas Is.: Indonesia **65** D6
Bad Axe: Mich., U.S.A. **88** K4
Bad Bramstedt: W. Germany **45** P2
Badby: Northants., England **25** T15
Badcall: High., Scotland **28** L3
Baddeck: Cape Breton I., Canada **89** V2
Badderen: Norway **46** S2
Bad Driburg: W. Germany **44** P4
Bad Dürkheim: W. Germany **44** O6
Bad Ems: W. Germany **44** N5
Baden: Austria **41** W7
Baden: Switzerland **40** O8
Baden-Baden: W. Germany **40** O7
Badenoch: *dist.*, High., Scot. **28** N6
Baden Württemburg: *State.*, W. Germany (*cap.* Stuttgart) **40** O7
Badghis: *prov.*, Afghanistan (*cap.* Qala-Nau) **55** K7
Badhu: *geog. reg.*, Ethiopia **79** N7
Badi: Iraq **57** G4
Badia: Central African Rep. **76** A1
Badi'a: Saudi Arabia **54** G10
Badia Polesine: Italy **41** R10
Badin: Sind, Pakistan **58** L10
Bad Ischl: Austria **41** T8
Bad Kissingen: W. Germany **45** Q5
Bad Kreuznach: W. Germany **44** N6
Badlands: *geog. reg.*, U.S.A. **92** G3
Badlands Nat. Mon.: U.S.A. **92** G4
Bad Lauterberg: W. Germany **45** Q4
Badminton, Great: Avon, England **24** R16
Bad Nauheim: W. Germany **44** O5
Bad Oldesloe: W. Germany **45** Q2
Badon: Senegal **80** B2
Badonviller: France **40** M7
Badra: Iraq **57** J5
Bad Ragaz: Switzerland **40** P9
Badrallach: High., Scot. **28** L4
Bad Reichenhall: W. Germany **41** S8
Badr Hunain: Saudi Arabia **54** E10
Badrinath: Uttar Pradesh, India **58** N8
Bad Salzungen: E. Germany **45** Q5
Bad Schmiedeberg: E. Germany **45** S4
Bad Schwalbach: W. Germany **44** O5
Bad Schwartau: W. Germany **45** Q2
Bad Segeberg: W. Germany **45** Q2
Bad Sooden-Allendorf: W. Germany **45** P4
Bad Sulza: E. Germany **45** R4
Bad Sülze: E. Germany **45** S1
Badulla: Sri Lanka **58** O13
Bad Vöslau: Austria **41** W8
Badwen: Mudugh, Somalia **79** R18
Badwen: North East, Somalia **79** R18
Baetica: Roman province of S. Spain **35** D18
Baetis: ancient name of river Guadalquivir (S. Spain) **35** D18
Baéza: Spain **35** E18
Bafang: Cameroun **81** G3
Bafata: Guinea-Bissau **80** B2
Baffin Bay: Canada **85** N3
Baffin Bay: Tex., U.S.A. **90** C12
Baffin I.: N.W.T., Canada **85** M3
Bafia: Cameroun **81** G4
Bafing: *riv.*, Guinea/Mali **80** B2
Bafing Makana: Mali **80** B2
Bafoulabé: Mali **80** B2
BAFOUSSAM: Ouest, Cameroun **81** G3
Bafra: Turkey **56** D1
Bafra, Cape: Turkey **56** E1
Baft: Iran **55** J9
Bafuka: Zaïre **76** C2
Bafwaboli: Zaïre **76** C2
Bafwasende: Zaïre **76** C2
Bagalkot: Karnataka, India **58** N11
Bagamoyo: Tanzania **76** E4
Baga Narin: Chinghai, China **62** Q7
Baganga: Mindanao, Phil. **64** H5
Bagan Siapiapi: Sumatra **65** C6
Bagassi: Upper Volta **80** D2
Bagata: Zaïre **73** H10
Bagband: W. Germany **44** N2
Bagborough, West: Som., England **24** P17
Bagan Datoh: Malaya, Malaysia **65** b12
Bagara: Cen. Afr. Rep. **76** B1
Bagé: Brazil **96** E3
Bagenalstown (Muine Beagh): Carlow, Repub. of Ireland **31** H14
Bagenkop: Denmark **47** M9
Bages: France **37** H13
Bages, Étang de: *lag.*, France **37** H12
BAGHDAD: & *Prov.*, Iraq **57** J5
Bagheria: Sicily **38** N17
BAGLAN: & *Prov.*, Afghanistan **58** L7
Bagh nam Faoileann: *str.*, Outer Hebr., Scotland **28** G5
Bagigi: Nigeria **81** F3
Bagillt: Clwyd, Wales **27** P13
Bagley: Minn., U.S.A. **88** D2
Bagnell Dam: Mo., U.S.A. **88** E6
Bagnères-de-Bigorre: France **37** F12
Bagnères-de-Luchon: France **37** F13
Bagni di Lucca: Italy **40** Q11
Bagniewo: Poland **45** V3
Bagno di Romagna: Italy **41** R12
Bagnolo Mella: Italy **40** Q10
Bagnols-sur-Cèze: France **37** K11
Bagnone: Italy **40** P11
Bagoé: *riv.*, Mali **80** C2
Bagolino: Italy **40** Q10
Bagradas: Roman name of river Medjerda, Tunisia **38** L18
Bagshot: Surrey, England **25** U17
Baguio: Luzon, Philippines **64** G3
Bahado: *well*, Somalia **79** R18

Bahamas: *Commonwealth* **87** M12
Cap.: Nassau
Area: 4,404 sq. miles (11,406 sq. km.)
Pop.: 185,000 (*1971 E*)

Bahara: *well*, Kuwait **57** K7
Bahariya Oasis: Egypt **54** C9
Bahat Jamal: Saudi Arabia **55** H10
Bahau: Malaya, Malaysia **65** c12
Bahawalpur: Punjab, Pak. **58** M9
Bahçe: Turkey **56** E3
Bahi: Tanzania **76** E4
Bahia: *see* Salvador.
Bahia: *State*, Brazil (*cap.* Salvador) **94** J6
Bahía Blanca: Argentina **96** C4
Bahía de Caráques: Ecuador **94** A4
Bahía Negra: Paragay **94** F8
Bahra: Saudi Arabia **54** E10
Bahraich: Uttar Pradesh, India **58** O9

Bahrain: *Sheikhdom* **55** H9
Cap.: Manama
Area: 231 sq. miles (598 sq. km.)
Pop.: 220,000 (*1971 E*)

Bahr al Milh: *salt lake*, Iraq **57** H5
Bahrein: *depression*, Egypt **54** C9
Bahr el 'Arab: *riv.*, Sudan **79** K8
Bahr el Ghazal: *Prov.*, Sudan (*cap.* Wau) **76** C1
Bahr el Ghazal: *riv.*, Chad **78** H7
Bahr el Jebel: *riv.*, Uganda **76** D2
Bahr Salwa: *bay*, Sau. Arab. **55** H9
Bahu Kalat: Iran **55** K9
Bai: *well*, Oman **55** J11
Baia de Aramă: Romania **39** S14
Baia dos Tigres: Angola **73** G13
Baiae: port and settlement of Graeco-Roman period in territory of *Cumae*, 10 miles W. of Naples, Italy **38** O16
Baia Mare: Romania **43** S13
Baião: Brazil **94** H4
Baia-Sprie: Romania **43** S13
Baiazeh: Iran **55** J8
Baïbokoum: Chad **81** H3
Bai Bung Point: Vietnam **64** C5
Baïda: Cameroun **81** G3
Baidha: *well*, Saudi Arabia **56** E6
Baie Comeau: Que., Canada **89** R1
Baie de Chaleur: *bay*, N.B./Que., Canada **89** T2
Baie de la Seine: *bay*, France **36** E6
Baie du Lévrier: *Dist.*, Mauritania (*cap.* Nouadhibou) **78** A5
Baiersdorf: W. Germany **45** R6
Baie St. Paul: Que., Can. **89** Q2
Baignes: France **37** E10
Baigneux-les-Juifs: France **36** K8
Baihan Qasab: Yemen P.D.R. **54** G12
Baihan Sailan: Yemen P.D.R. **54** G11
Baiji: Iraq **57** H4
Baikha: U.S.S.R. **48** k5
Baildon: W. Yorks., England **27** S12
BAILE ÁTHA CLIATH (Dublin): Repub. of Ireland **31** J13
Bailén: Spain **35** E17
Băileşti: Romania **39** S14
Bailieborough: Cavan, Repub. of Ireland **30** H12
Bailleul: France **36** H5
Ba Illi: *riv.*, Chad **81** H2
Baillieston: Strath., Scotland **29** N8
Bain: France **36** D8
Bainbridge: Ga., U.S.A. **91** J10
Baing: Sumba, Indonesia **65** G9
Bairam: Iran **55** H9
Baird: Tex., U.S.A. **90** B9
Baird Mtns.: Alaska, U.S.A. **84** c4
Bairnsdale: Vict., Australia **71** G11
Bais: France **36** E7
Baise: *riv.*, France **37** F11
Baitadi: Nepal **58** O9
Bait Faqih: Yemen **54** F12
Baithuong: Vietnam **64** D3
Baixo Alentejo: *Prov.*, Port. (*cap.* Beja) **35** B18
Baixo Longa: Angola **77** A6
Baja: Hungary **43** Q13
Baján: Mexico **93** G7
Bajil: Yemen **54** F12
Baka: *mtn.*, Borneo **65** E7
Bakal: U.S.S.R. **50** J4
Bakala: Cen. Afr. Rep. **76** B1
Bakaly: U.S.S.R. **50** H3
Bakanas: Kazakh., U.S.S.R. **51** N6
Bakary: Cen. Afr. Rep. **76** C1
Bakchar: U.S.S.R. **51** O3
Bake: Mentawai Is., Indon. **65** C7
Bakedi: Ethiopia **76** D1
Bakel: Senegal **80** B2
Baker: Calif., U.S.A. **93** D5
Baker: Mont., U.S.A. **92** G3
Baker: Oreg., U.S.A. **92** D4
Baker, Mount: Wash., U.S.A. **92** C3
Baker Foreland: *cape*, Can. **85** k5
Baker Lake: & *settlement*, N.W.T., Canada **84** K5
Bakersfield: Calif., U.S.A. **93** D5
Bakewell: Derby., England **27** S13
Bakhatla: *tribal reserve*, Botswana **75** G2
Bakhmach: Ukraine **50** D4
Bakhtiari: *geog. reg.*, Iran **57** L5
Bakırköy: Turkey (Bosporus *Inset*) **20** *Ins.*
Bakka Bay: Iceland **46** f3
Bakkasel: Iceland **46** d4
Bako: & *geog. reg.*, Ethiopia **76** E1
Bakony Forest: Hungary **43** P13
Bakota: *geog reg.*, Congo/Gabon **81** G4
Bakota Mtns.: Congo **81** G5
Bakouma: Cen. Afr. Rep. **76** B1
Bakoven: C.P., S. Africa **74** *Ins.*
Bakoy: *riv.*, Guinea/Mali **80** C2
Baksay: Kazakh., U.S.S.R. **50** H5
BAKU: Azerbaydzhan, U.S.S.R. **57** L1
Bakumpai: Borneo **65** E7
Bakundi: Nigeria **81** G3
Bakuriani: Georgia, U.S.S.R. **57** H1
Bakwa M'Bule: Zaïre **76** B3
Bakwena: *tribal area*, Botswana **77** B7
Bala: Senegal **80** B2
Bâlâ: Turkey **56** C2
Bala: & *lake*, Gwyn., Wales **27** O14
Balaang: Celebes **65** G6
Balabac: Philippines **64** F5
Balabac: *i.* & *str.*, Phil. **64** F5
Balabalagan Is.: Indonesia **65** F7
Balad: Iraq **57** J4
Balad: Somalia **79** R19
Balad Ruz: Iraq **57** J5
Balagannakh: U.S.S.R. **49** o5
Balagannoye: U.S.S.R. **49** q6
Balaghat: Madhya Pradesh, India **58** O10
Balaguer: Spain **35** G16
Balaisalasa: Sumatra **65** C7
Balaitous, Pic: *mtn.*, Pyrénées **37** E13
Balakhta: U.S.S.R. **51** Q3
Balaklava: S. Austl. **71** C10
Balaklava: U.S.S.R. **50** D6
Balakovo: U.S.S.R. **50** G4
Balallan: Outer Hebr., Scot. **28** H3
Balama: Mozambique **77** E5
Balambangan: *i.*, Sabah, Malaysia **64** F5
Bala Murghab: Afghanistan **58** K7
Balandougou: Guinea **80** C2
Balanga: Luzon, Philippines **64** G4
Balangale: Zaïre **76** A2
Balashov: U.S.S.R. **50** F4
Balasore: Orissa, India **59** P10
Balassagyarmat: Hungary **43** Q12
Balat: Egypt **54** C9
Balaton Lake: Hungary **43** P13
Balaye: Upper Volta **80** D2
Balazote: Spain **35** E17
Balbeggie: Tay., Scotland **29** P7
Balboa: Panama **94** *Ins.*
BALBOA HEIGHTS: *city*, Canal Zone, Panama **94** *Ins.*
Balbriggan: Dublin, Repub. of Ireland **30** J12
Balcarce: Argentina **96** D4
Balcarres: Sask., Canada **92** G2
Balchik: Bulgaria **39** V15
Balcilar: Turkey (Dardan. *Inset*) **20** *Ins.*
Balclutha: South I., N.Z. **71** M18
Balcombe: W. Sussex, England **25** V17
Balde: Argentina **96** B3
Bald Eagle Lake: Minn., U.S.A. **88** F2
Balderton: Notts., England **27** U13
Bald Knob: *city*, Ark., U.S.A. **90** F8
Baldock: Herts., England **25** V16
Bald Peak: *see* Livermore, Mt.
Baldwin City: Kans., U.S.A. **90** D6
Baldwinsville: N.Y., U.S.A. **89** N4
Baldy Peak: Ariz., U.S.A. **93** F6
Bale: *Prov.*, Ethiopia (*cap.* Goba) **79** Q18
BÂLE (Basel): Switzerland **40** N8
Bale: Yugoslavia **41** T10
Balearic Is.: Spain (*cap.* Palma) **35** H17
Balemartine: Inner Hebr., Scotland **29** H7
Balen: Belgium **44** L4
Baler: Luzon, Philippines **64** G3
Balerno: Lothian, Scotland **29** P8
Baleshare: *i.*, Outer Hebr., Scotland **28** G4
Balestrand: Norway **47** K6
Baley: U.S.S.R. **49** n7
Balfour: Trans., S. Africa **75** H3
Balfron: Central, Scotland **29** N7
Balgray: Tayside, Scotland **29** Q6
Balhaf: Yemen P.D.R. **55** G12
Bali: *i.* & *str.*, Indonesia [*cap.* (with Lombok I.) Singaradja] **65** E8
Baliçeköy: Turkey (Bosporus *Inset*) **20** *Ins.*
Balige: Sumatra **65** B6
Baligród: Poland **43** S12
BALIKESIR: & *Prov.*, Turkey **39** U17
Balikh: *riv.*, Syria **56** F3
Balikpapan: Borneo **65** F7
Balimbing: Philippines **65** F5
Balimbing: Sumatra **65** C8
Baling: Malaya, Malaysia **65** b11
Balingen: W. Germany **40** O7
Balingian: Sarawak, Malaysia **65** E6
Balintang: *i.* & *chan.*, Phil. **64** G3
Balintore: High., Scot. **28** O4
Balipara: Assam, India **59** Q9
Bali Sea: Indonesia **65** F8
Baliza: Brazil **94** G7
Balkan Mtns.: Bulgaria **39** T15
Balkashino: Kazakh., U.S.S.R. **51** L4
Balkh: *prov.*, Afghanistan (*cap.* Mazar-i-Sharif) **55** L7
Balkhash: & *lake*, Kazakh., U.S.S.R. **51** N5
Balla: Bangladesh **59** Q10
Balla: Mayo, Repub. of Ireland **30** C12
Balla Balla: W. Australia **68** B4
Ballachulish: High., Scot. **29** L6
Ballachulish Ferry: Highland, Scotland **29** L6
Ballaghaderreen: Rosc., Repub. of Ireland **30** D12
Ballah, El: Egypt (Suez Canal *Inset*) **32** *Ins.*
Bal Lake: Norway **46** O3
Ballan: Vict., Australia **71** F11
Ballantrae: Strath., Scotland **29** L9
Ballantyne Str.: N.W.T., Canada **84** H2
Ballarat: Vict., Australia **71** E11
Ballard, Lake: W. Australia **68** C5
Ballasalla: I. of Man, U.K. **26** M11
Ballater: Gram., Scotland **28** P5
Ballaugh: I. of Man, U.K. **26** M11
Ballé: Mali **80** C1
Balleroy: France **36** E6
Ballësh: Albania **39** Q16
Ballevullin: Inner Hebr., Scotland **29** H7
Ballia: Uttar Pradesh, India **59** O9
Ballickmoyler: Laois, Repub. of Ireland **31** G14
Ballidu: W Australia **68** B6
Ballina: Mayo, Repub. of Ireland **30** C11
Ballina: N.S.W., Australia **71** K7
Ballina: Tip., Repub. of Ireland **31** E14
Ballinadee: Cork, Repub. of Ireland **31** D16
Ballinafad: Sligo, Repub. of Ireland **30** E11
Ballinagar: Offaly, Repub. of Ireland **31** G13
Ballinagh: Cavan, Repub. of Ireland **30** G12
Ballinakill: Laois, Repub. of Ireland **31** G14
Ballinalea: Wick., Republic of Ireland **31** J13
Ballinalee: Long., Repub. of Ireland **30** F12
Ballinamallard: Ferm., N. Ireland **30** F11
Ballinameen: Rosc., Repub. of Ireland **30** E12
Ballinamore: Leit., Repub. of Ireland **30** F11
Ballinascarty: Cork, Repub. of Ireland **31** D16
Ballinasloe: Galway, Repub. of Ireland **31** E13
Ballincollig: Cork, Repub. of Ireland **31** D16
Ballincrea: Kilk., Repub. of Ireland **31** G15
Ballinderry: Antrim, N. Irel. **30** J10
Ballinderry: Tip., Repub. of Ireland **31** E13
Ballindine: Mayo, Repub. of Ireland **30** D12
Ballindrait: Don., Repub. of Ireland **30** F10
Ballingarry: Lim., Repub. of Ireland **31** D15
Ballingarry: N. Rid., Tip., Repub. of Ireland **31** E13
Ballingarry: S. Rid., Tip., Repub. of Ireland **31** F14
Ballingeary: Cork, Repub. of Ireland **31** C16
Ballinger: Tex., U.S.A. **90** B10
Ballinhassig: Cork, Repub. of Ireland **31** D16
Ballinlough: Rosc., Repub. of Ireland **30** D12
Ballinluig: Tay., Scotland **29** O6
Ballinrobe: Mayo, Repub. of Ireland **30** C12
Ballinruan: Clare, Repub. of Ireland **31** D14
Ballinskelligs: & *bay*, Kerry, Repub. of Ireland **31** A16
Ballinspittle: Cork, Repub. of Ireland **31** D16
Ballintober: Rosc., Repub. of Ireland **30** E12
Ballintogher: Sligo, Repub. of Ireland **30** E11
Ballintoy: Antrim, N. Irel. **30** J9
Ballintra: Don., Repub. of Ireland **30** E10
Ballinunty: Tip., Repub. of Ireland **31** F14
Ballitore: Kild., Repub. of Ireland **31** H13
Ballivián: Argentina **96** C1
Ballivor: Meath, Repub. of Ireland **30** H12
Ballon: Carlow, Repub. of Ireland **31** H14
Ballon: France **36** F7
Balls Fiord: Norway **46** Q2
Ball's Pyramid: *i.*, Tasman Sea **67** L8
Ballybay: Monaghan, Repub. of Ireland **30** H11
Ballybofey: Don., Repub. of Ireland **30** F10
Ballyboghil: Dublin, Repub. of Ireland **30** J12
Ballybogy: Antrim, N. Irel. **30** H9
Ballyboy: Offaly, Repub. of Ireland **31** F13
Ballybrittas: Laois, Repub. of Ireland **31** G13
Ballybunnion: Kerry, Repub. of Ireland **31** B14
Ballycanew: Wex., Repub. of Ireland **31** J14
Ballycarney: Wex., Repub. of Ireland **31** H14
Ballycarry: Antrim, N. Irel. **30** K10
Ballycastle: Antrim, N. Irel. **30** J9
Ballycastle: Mayo, Repub. of Ireland **30** C11
Ballyclare: Antrim, N. Irel. **30** J10
Ballyconneely: Galway, Repub. of Ireland **31** A13
Ballyconnell: Cavan, Repub. of Ireland **30** F11
Ballycotton: Cork, Repub. of Ireland **31** E16
Ballycroy: Mayo, Repub. of Ireland **30** B11
Ballycumber: Offaly, Repub. of Ireland **31** F13
Ballydavid: & *cape*, Kerry, Repub. of Ireland **31** A15
Ballydehob: Cork, Repub. of Ireland **31** C16
Ballydonegan: Cork, Repub. of Ireland **31** A16
Ballyduff: Kerry, Repub. of Ireland **31** B15
Ballyduff: Wat., Repub. of Ireland **31** E15
Ballyfarnan: Sligo, Repub. of Ireland **30** E11
Ballyferriter: Kerry, Repub. of Ireland **31** A15
Ballygar: Galway, Repub. of Ireland **30** E12
Ballygawley: Tyr., N. Ireland **30** G11
Ballyglass: Mayo, Repub. of Ireland **30** C12
Ballygorey: Kilk., Repub. of Ireland **31** G15
Ballygorman: Don., Repub. of Ireland **30** G9
Ballygowan: Down, N. Irel. **30** K10
Ballyhahill: Lim., Repub. of Ireland **31** C14
Ballyhaise: Cavan, Repub. of Ireland **30** G11
Ballyhalbert: Down, N. Irel. **30** K11
Ballyhale: Kilk., Repub. of Ireland **31** G15
Ballyhaunis: Mayo, Repub. of Ireland **30** D12
Ballyhean: Mayo, Repub. of Ireland **30** C12
Ballyheige: & *bay*, Kerry, Repub. of Ireland **31** B15
Ballyhooly: Cork, Repub. of Ireland **31** E15
Ballyhoura Hills: Lim./Cork, Repub. of Ireland **31** D15
Ballyjamesduff: Cavan, Repub. of Ireland **30** G12
Ballyknockan: Wick., Repub. of Ireland **31** J13
Ballylanders: Lim., Repub. of Ireland **31** E15
Ballylaneen: Wat., Repub. of Ireland **31** G15
Ballyleague: Rosc., Repub. of Ireland **30** E12
Ballylongford: Kerry, Repub. of Ireland **31** C14
Ballylooby: Tip., Repub. of Ireland **31** F15
Ballylynan: Laois, Repub. of Ireland **31** G14
Ballymacelligott: Kerry, Repub. of Ireland **31** B15
Ballymachugh: Cavan, Repub. of Ireland **30** G12
Ballymacoda: Cork, Repub. of Ireland **31** F16
Ballymahon: Long., Repub. of Ireland **30** F12
Ballymartin: Down, N. Irel. **30** K11
Ballymena: Antrim, N. Irel. **30** J10
Ballymoe: Galway, Repub. of Ireland **30** E12
Ballymoney: Antrim, N. Irel. **30** H9
Ballymore: Westmeath, Repub. of Ireland **30** F13
Ballymore Eustace: Kild., Repub. of Ireland **31** H13
Ballymote: Sligo, Repub. of Ireland **30** D11
Ballymurn: Wex., Repub. of Ireland **31** J15
Ballymurphy: Carlow, Repub. of Ireland **31** H14
Ballynabola: Wex., Repub. of Ireland **31** H15
Ballynacallagh: Dursey I., Repub. of Ireland **31** A16
Ballynacarriga: Cork, Repub. of Ireland **31** C16
Ballynacarrigy: Westmeath, Repub. of Ireland **30** F12
Ballynagore: Westmeath, Repub. of Ireland **31** G13
Ballynahinch: Down, N. Irel. **30** K11
Ballynakill: Rosc., Repub. of Ireland **31** F13
Ballyneen: Cork, Repub. of Ireland **31** D16
Ballyneety: Lim., Repub. of Ireland **31** D14
Ballynoe: Cork, Repub. of Ireland **31** E15
Ballynure: Antrim, N. Irel. **30** K10
Ballyorgan: Lim., Repub. of Ireland **31** E15
Ballypatrick: Tip., Repub. of Ireland **31** F15
Ballyporeen: Tip., Repub. of Ireland **31** E15
Ballyragget: Kilk., Repub. of Ireland **31** G14
Ballyroan: Laois, Repub. of Ireland **31** G14
Ballysadare: Sligo, Repub. of Ireland **30** D11
Ballyshannon: Don., Repub. of Ireland **30** E10
Ballyteige Bay: Wex., Repub. of Ireland **31** H15
Ballyvaghan: Clare, Repub. of Ireland **31** C13
Ballyvoge: Cork, Repub. of Ireland **31** C16
Ballyvourney: Cork, Repub. of Ireland **31** C16
Ballywalter: Down, N. Irel. **30** K10
Ballywilliam: Wex., Repub. of Ireland **31** H15
Balma: Italy **40** O10
Balmaceda: Chile **95** C13
Balmaclellan: Dumfries & Galloway, Scot. **29** N9
Balme: Italy **40** N10
Balmedie: Gram., Scotland **28** R5
Balmerino: Fife, Scotland **29** P7
Balmoral: Tran., S. Africa **75** H2
Balmoral: Vict., Australia **71** D11
Balmoral Castle: Gram., Scot. **28** P5
Balmoral Forest: Gram., Scot. **28** P6
Balmorhea: Tex., U.S.A. **93** G6
Balonne: *riv.*, Queens., Australia **70** H6
Baloumbo: *geog. reg.*, Gabon **81** G5
Balovale: Zambia **77** B5
Balquidder: Central, Scot. **29** N7
Balrampur: Uttar Pradesh, India **58** O9
Balranald: N.S.W., Austl. **71** E10
Bals: Negros, Philippines **64** G5
Bals: Romania **43** T14
Balsam Lake: Ont., Canada **89** M3
Balsas: & *riv.*, Mexico **86** K14
Balsfjorden: Norway **46** Q2
Balsham: Cambs., England **25** W15
Baltanás: Spain **35** D16
Baltasound: Unst, Shetland Is. **28** *Ins.*
Baltic Sea: N. Europe **47** Q8
Baltîm: Egypt **56** B6
Baltimore: Cork, Repub. of Ireland **31** C17
Baltimore: Md., U.S.A. **89** N6
Baltinglass: Wick., Repub. of Ireland **31** H14
Baltistan: *geog. reg.*, Jammu and Kashmir **58** N7
Baltit: Gilgit, Jammu & Kashmir **58** M7
Baltiysk (Pillau): U.S.S.R. **47** Q9
Baltray: Louth, Repub. of Ireland **30** J12
Baltrum: *i.*, E. Frisian Is. **44** N2
Baluchistan: *geog. reg.*, Iran **55** K9
Baluchistan: *Prov.*, Pakistan (*cap.* Quetta) **58** L9
Balya: Turkey **39** U17
Balyana: Egypt **54** D9
Balygychan: U.S.S.R. **49** R5
Balyska: U.S.S.R. **51** P4
Balzar: Ecuador **94** B4

Bam: Iran 55 J9
Bama: Nigeria 81 G2
BAMAKO: & *Reg.*, Mali 80 C2
Bamangwato: *tribal area*, Botswana 77 C7
Bamba: Mali 80 D1
Bambadinca: Guinea-Bissau 80 B2
Bambafouga: Guinea 80 B2
BAMBARI: Ouaka, Cen. Afr. Rep. 76 B1
Bambatana: Solomon Is. 67 L3
Bambaya: Guinea 80 B2
Bamberg: W. Germany 45 Q6
Bamberg: S.C., U.S.A. 91 L9
Bambio: Central African Empire 81 H4
Bamboo Creek: *town*, W. Australia 68 C4
Bamburgh: Northumb., Eng. 26 S8
BAMENDA: Nord-Ouest, Cameroun 81 G3
BAMIAN: & *prov.*, Afghanistan 55 L7
Bamingui-Bangoran: *Pref.*, Cen. Afr. Rep. (*cap.* N'délé) 76 B1
Bamingui-Bangoran National Park: Cen. Afr. Rep. 76 A1
Bampton: Devon, England 24 P18
Bampton: Oxon., England 25 S16
Bampur: Iran 55 K9
Bampur: *riv.*, Iran 55 J9
Bamu: *riv.*, Papua-New Guinea 69 G1
Banagher: Offaly, Repub. of Ireland 31 F13
Banalia: Zaire 76 C2
Banam: Cambodia 64 D4
Banamba: Mali 80 C2
Banámichi: Mexico 93 E6
Banana: Queens., Australia 70 J5
Banana: Zaire 73 G11
Bananal I.: Brazil 94 G6
Banaras (Varanasi): Uttar Pradesh, India 59 O9
Banas: *riv.*, India 58 N9
Banat: *Prov.*, Romania 43 R14
Banat: *geog. reg.*, Yugo./Romania 43 R14
Banavie: High., Scotland 29 L6
Banaz: Turkey 56 A2
Banban: Saudi Arabia 54 G9
Banbridge: Down, N. Irel. 30 J11
Banbury: Oxon., England 25 T15
Bancannia, Lake: N.S.W., Australia 71 D8
Banchory: Gram., Scotland 28 R5
Banchory: Queens., Austl. 70 G4
Bancoran: *i.*, Philippines 64 F5
Bancroft: Ont., Canada 89 N4
Band: Romania 43 T13
Banda: Gabon 81 G5
Banda: Vietnam 64 D4
Banda Aceh: Sumatra 65 B5
Banda Atjeh: Sumatra 65 B5
Banda, La: Argentina 96 C2
Banda, Point: *cape*, Mexico 93 D6
Banda Banda: *mtn.*, N.S.W., Australia 71 K8
Banda Is.: Indonesia 61 K12
Banda Sea: Indonesia 66 E3
Bandajuma: Sierra Leone 80 B3
Bandak Lake: Norway 47 L7
Bandama: *riv.*, Ivory Coast 80 D3
Bandan: Iran 55 K8
Bandar: *see* Machilipatnam
BANDAR ABBAS: Saheli, Iran 55 J9
Bandar Bahru: Malaya, Malaysia 65 b11
Bandar Dilam: Iran 55 H8
Bandar Maharani (Muar): Malaya, Malaysia 65 c12
Bandar Ma'shur: Iran 57 L6
Bandar Penggaram (Batu Pahat): Malaya, Malaysia 65 c13
Bandar Rig: Iran 55 H9
BANDAR SERI BEGAWAN: Brunei 65 E6
Bandar Shah: Iran 55 H7
Bandar Shahpur: Iran 57 L6
Bandeirante: Brazil 94 G6
Bandera: Argentina 96 C2
Banderas: Mexico 93 F6
Banderas Bay: Mexico 86 J13
Bandiagara: Mali 80 D2
Bandikui: Rajasthan, India 58 N9
Band-i-Qir: Iran 57 L6
Bandirma: Turkey 39 U16
Bandol: France 40 L12
Bandolierkop: Trans., S. Africa 75 H1
Bandon: & *riv.*, Cork, Repub. of Ireland 31 D16
Bandra: Maharashtra, India 58 M11
BANDUNDU: & *Prov.*, Zaire 81 H5
Bandung: Java 65 D8
Bane: Iran 57 J4
Banes: Cuba 87 M13
Bañeza, La: Spain 35 D15
Banff: Alta., Canada 92 D2
Banff: Gram., Scotland 28 Q4
Banff Nat. Park: Alta., Can. 92 D2
Banfora: Upper Volta 80 D2
BANGALORE: Karnataka, India 58 N12
Bangalow: N.S.W., Austl. 71 K7
Banganapalle: Andhra Pradesh, India 58 N11
Bangar: Luzon, Philippines 64 G3
Bangassi: Mali 80 C2
BANGASSOU: M'Bomou, Cen. Afr. Rep. 76 B2
Banggai: Indonesia 65 G7
Banggai Is.: Indonesia 65 G7
Bangka: *i.*, Celebes 65 H6
Bangka: *i.* & *str.*, Indonesia 65 D7
Bangkalan: Java 65 E8
Bangkinang: Sumatra 65 C6
Bangko: Sumatra 65 C7
BANGKOK (Krung Thep): Thailand 64 C4

Bangladesh: *Republic* 59 P10
Cap.: Dacca
Area: 55,126 sq. miles (142,776 sq. km.)
Pop.: 60,675,000 (1970 E)

Bangor: Gwynedd, Wales 27 N13·
Bangor: Down, N. Ireland 30 K10
Bangor: Maine, U.S.A. 89 R3
Bangor: Mayo, Repub. of Ireland 30 B11
Bangor: Pa., U.S.A. 89 O5
Bangor-is-coed: Clwyd, Wales 27 Q14
Bang Phra: Thailand 64 C4
Bang Saphan: Thailand 64 B4
Bangson: Thailand 64 B4
Bangued: Luzon, Philippines 64 G3
Banguey: *i.*, Sabah, Malaysia 64 F5
BANGUI: Central African Republic 76 A2
Bangwaketse: *tribal reserve*, Botswana 75 F2
Bangweulu Lake: Zambia 77 D5

Banham: Norf., England 25 Y15
Ban Houei Sai (Fort Carnot): Laos 64 C2
Bani: *riv.*, Mali 80 C2
Bania: Ivory Coast 80 D3
Baniara: Papua-New Guinea 69 H1
Banifing: *riv.*, Mali 80 C2
Banikoara: Benin 81 E2
Bani Lam: *tribal area*, Iraq 57 K5
Baniyas: Syria 55 b1
Banja Luka: Yugoslavia 38 P14
Banjarmasin: Borneo, Indonesia 65 E7
BANJUL (Bathurst): The Gambia 80 A2
Bank: Trans., S. Africa 74 M*ins.*
Banka Banka: N. Territ., Australia 68 E3
Banka Manda: Somalia 79 Q17
Bankend: Dumfries & Galloway, Scotland 29 O9
Banket: Rhodesia 77 D6
Bankfoot: Tay., Scotland 29 O6
Ban Khut That: Thailand 64 C3
Bankor: Mali 80 D1
Banks: *i.*, Queens., Australia 69 G2
Banks I.: N.W.T., Canada 84 g3
Banks Is.: B.C., Canada 92 A2
Banks Is.: New Hebrides 67 N4
Banks Penin.: South I., N.Z. 70 O16
Bankura: W. Bengal, India 59 P10
Ban Me Thuot: Vietnam 64 D4
Bann: *riv.*, N. Ireland 30 H10
Bann: *riv.*, Wex., Repub. of Ireland 31 J14
Bannang Sata: Thailand 65 b10
Banningville: *see* Bandundu
Bannio: Italy 40 O10
Bannockburn: Central. Scot. 29 O7
Bannu: NW. Front. Prov., Pakistan 58 M8
Bañolas: Spain 35 H15
Banon: France 40 L11
Baños: Argentina 96 C2
Baños: Ecuador 94 B4
Bánovce: Czechoslovakia 43 Q12
Banovo Jaruga: Yugoslavia 38 P14
Ban Pong: Thailand 64 B4
Bansha: Tip., Repub. of Irel. 31 E15
BANSKÁ BYSTRICA:Stredoslovensky, Czech. 43 Q12
Banská Štiavnica: Czech. 43 Q12
Bansko: Bulgaria 39 S16
Banstead: Surrey, England 25 Y17
Banswara: Rajasthan, India 58 M10
Banta: *i.*, Indonesia 65 F8
Bantading: The Gambia 80 B2
Bantayan: *i.*, Philippines 64 G4
Banté: Benin 81 E3
Banteer: Cork, Repub. of Ireland 31 D15
Bantia: Roman city about 7 miles SE. of *Venusia*, It. 38 O16
Bantry: Cork, Repub. of Ireland 31 C16
Bantry Bay: Cork, Repub. of Ireland 31 B16
Banwell: Avon, England 24 Q17
Banyak: *i.*, Sumatra 65 B6
Banyo: Cameroun 81 G3
Banyumas: Java 65 D8
Banyuwangi: Java 65 E8
Banzyville: *see* Mobayi.
Bao: Karakelong Is., Indon. 65 H6
Bao Ha: Vietnam 64 D2
Baoulé: *geog. reg.*, Ivory Coast 80 C3
Baoulé: *riv.* (Senegal), Mali 80 C2
Baoulé: *riv.* (Niger), Mali 80 C2
Bapaume: France 36 H5
BAQUBA: Diyala, Iraq 57 J5
Baquedano: Chile 96 B1
Bar: Ukraine 43 U12
Bar: Yugoslavia 39 Q15
Bara: Sudan 54 D12
Bara: Buru, Indonesia 65 H7
Barabai: Borneo 65 F7
Barabinsk: U.S.S.R. 51 N3
Baraboo: Wis., U.S.A. 88 G4
Baradero: Argentina 96 D3
Baradine: N.S.W., Australia 71 H8
Baraga: Mich., U.S.A. 88 G2
Baragoi: Kenya 76 E2
Barahona: Dominican Repub. 87 m14
Barahona: Spain 35 E16
Baraka: *riv.*, Sudan 54 E11
Barak Khel: Afghanistan 58 L8
Barakula: Queens., Austl. 70 J6
Baralaba: Queens., Austl. 70 H5
Baram, Cape: Sarawak, Malaysia 65 E6
Barama: *riv.*, Guyana 87 d7
Baramanni: Guyana 87 d7
Baramati: Maharashtra, India 58 M4
Baramula: Jammu and Kashmir 58 M8
Baran: Rajasthan, India 58 N9
Barangbarang: Salajar, Indonesia 65 G8
Barani: Upper Volta 80 D2
Baranof I.: Alaska, U.S.A. 84 f6
Baranovichi: Byelorussia 43 U10
Baranovka: Ukraine 43 U11
Barashi: Ukraine 43 V11
Barataria: La., U.S.A. 90 *Ins.*
Barataria Bay: La., U.S.A. 90 *Ins.*
Barataria Pass: La., U.S.A. 90 *Ins.*
Barate: Timor, Indonesia 65 G8
Barazoli: Ethiopia 79 Q17
Barbacan: Palawan, Phil. 64 F4
Barbacena: Brazil 96 G1

Barbados: *Commonwealth* 87 c4
Cap.: Bridgetown
Area: 166 sq. miles (430 sq. km.)
Pop.: 239,000 (1971 E)

Barban: Yugoslavia 41 U10
Barbas, Cape: W. Sahara 78 A5
Barbastro: Spain 35 G15
Barbate: & *bay*, Spain (Gib. *Inset*) 32 *Ins.*
Barbâtre: Île de Noirmoutier, France 36 C9
Barbazan: France 37 F12
Barbezieux: France 37 E10
Barbon: Cumbria, England 26 Q11
Barbosa: Colombia 94 C2
Barbourville: Ky., U.S.A. 88 K7
Barbuda: *i.*, Leeward Is. 87 c2
Barby: Northants., England 25 T15
Barby: W. Germany 45 R4
Bârca: Romania 39 S15
Barca, La: Mexico 86 j13
Barca d'Alva: Portugal 36 C16
Barcaldine: Queens., Austl. 69 H4
Barcellona: Sicily 38 O17
BARCELONA: & *prov.*, Spain 35 H16
Barcelona: Venezuela 94 E1
Barcelonette: France 40 M11
Barcelos: Brazil 94 E4

Barcelos: Portugal 35 B16
Barcino: Roman town at Barcelona, Spain 35 H16
Barco de Avila, El: Spain 35 D16
Barcoo (Cooper's Creek): *riv.*, Queens., Australia 69 G4
Barcs: Hungary 43 P14
Barda: Azerbaydzhan, U.S.S.R. 57 K1
Barda do São Joâo: Brazil 96 G1
Barra do Corda: Brazil 94 H5
Barra do Quarai Brazil 96 D3
Barra Falsa, Pta. da: *cape*, Mozambique 77 E7
Barra Head: *cape*, Outer Hebr., Scotland 28 G6
Barra Mansa: Brazil 96 G1
Barranca: Peru 94 B4
Barrancabermeja: Colombia 94 O2
Barranca del Cobra Nat. Park: Mexico 93 E7
Barrancas: Venezuela 94 E2
Barrancos: Portugal 35 C17
Barranqueras: Argentina 96 D2
Barranquilla: Colombia 94 C1
Barras: Brazil 94 J4
Barre: Vt., U.S.A. 89 P3
Barre-de-Monts, La: France 36 C9
Barreiras: Brazil 94 J6
Barreirinha: Brazil 94 F4
Barreirinhas: Brazil 94 J4
Barreiro: Portugal 35 B17
Barrême: France 40 M12
Barren Is.: Alaska, U.S.A. 84 d6
Barretos: Brazil 94 H8
Barrhead: Alta., Canada 92 D1
Barrhead: Strath., Scotland 29 N8
Barrhill: Strath., Scotland 29 M9
Barrie: Ont., Canada 89 M3
Barrier Mtns.: South I., N.Z. 70 N17
Barrington: Som., England 24 Q18
Barrington, Mount: N.S.W., Austl. 71 J9
Barrington Lake: Man., Can. 92 G1
Barringun: N.S.W., Austl. 71 F7
Barrios, Los: Spain (Gib. *Inset*) 32 *Ins.*
Barrisdale: High., Scotland 28 K5
Barrock, High., Scotland 28 P2
Barro Colorado Is.: Panama 94 *Ins.*
Barron: Wis., U.S.A. 88 F3
Barrow: Alaska, U.S.A. 84 D3
Barrow: Argentina 96 C4
Barrow: Suff., England 25 X15
Barrow: *riv.*, Repub. of Irel. 31 H14
Barrow, Point: *cape*, Alaska, U.S.A. 84 D3
Barrow Creek: *town*, N. Territ., Australia 68 E4
Barrowden: Leics., Eng. 27 U14
Barrowford: Lancs., Eng. 27 R12
Barrow in Furness: Cumbria, England 26 P11
Barrow I.: W. Australia 68 B4
Barrow Str.: N.W.T., Can. 84 k3
Barrow upon Soar: Leics., England 27 T14
Barrule, South: *hill*, I. of Man, England 26 M11
Barry: Tayside, Scotland 29 Q6
Barry: S. Glam., Wales 24 P17
Barry: Ill., U.S.A. 88 F6
Barrydale: S. Africa 74 D6
Barry Mtns.: Vict., Australia 71 G11
Barsaloi: Kenya 76 E2
Barsi: Maharashtra, India 58 N11
Barstow: Calif., U.S.A. 93 D8
Bar-sur-Aube: France 36 K7
Bar-sur-Seine: France 36 K7
Bartan: Palawan, Phil. 64 F4
Bartenstein: W. Germany 45 P6
Barth: E. Germany 45 S1
Bartholomew Bayou: *riv.*, Ark., U.S.A. 90 P9
Bartibogou: Upper Volta 80 E2
Bartica: Guyana 87 d7
Bartin: Turkey 56 C1
Bartlesville: Okla., U.S.A. 90 D7
Bartlett: Tex., U.S.A. 90 C10
Bartlow: Cambs., England 25 W15
Barton: S. Australia 68 E6
Barton: Staffs., England 27 S14
Barton: N. Yorks., England 26 S11
Barton Bendish: Norf., Eng. 25 X14
Barton in the Clay: Beds., England 25 V16
Barton upon Humber: Humberside, England 27 V12
Bartoszyce: Poland 43 R9
Bartow: Fla., U.S.A. 91 L12
Barum: W. Germany 45 Q3
Ba Rumaîan: Saudi Arabia 55 G11
Barung: *i.*, Java 65 E8
Barus: Sumatra 65 B6
Baruth: E. Germany 45 T3
Barvas: Outer Hebr., Scot. 28 H3
Barwadih: Bihar, India 59 O10
Barwell: Leics., England 27 T14
Barwice: Poland 45 W2
Barwon: *riv.*, N.S.W., Austl. 71 G8
Barycz: *riv.*, Poland 43 P11
Barzan: Iraq 57 J3
Barzas: U.S.S.R. 51 P4
Basaki: Iran 55 H8
Basaluzzo: Italy 40 O11
Basankusu: Zaire 76 A2
Basavilbaso: Argentina 96 D3
Baschurch: Salop, England 27 Q14
Basco: Batan Is., Philippines 64 G2
Basdorf: E. Germany 45 T3
BASEL (Bâle): Switzerland 40 N8
Basel: *Canton*, Switzerland (*cap.* Liestal) 40 N8
Basey: Samar, Philippines 64 H4
Bashan: *Fertile district of ancient Palestine NE. of Sea of Galilee*, Syria 56 D5
Bashar: Nigeria 81 G3
Bashee: *riv.*, S. Africa 75 H6
Bashi Chan.: Phil./Taiwan 64 G2
Bashkir A.S.S. Repub.: U.S.S.R. (*cap.* Ufa) 50 J4
Basia: Bihar, India 50 O10
Basilaki: *i.*, Papua-New Guinea 69 J1
Basilan: *i.* & *str.*, Philippines 65 G5
Basildon: Essex, England 25 W16
Basilicata: *Reg.*, Italy (*cap.* Potenza) 38 P16
Basilio: Brazil 96 E3
Basim: Maharashtra, India 58 N10
Basing: Hants., England 25 T17
Basingstoke: Hants., Eng. 25 T17
Baskale: Turkey 57 J2
Baskanova: Krk, Yugoslavia 41 U11
Baskatong Res.: Que., Can. 89 O2
Bas Kouilou: Congo 81 G5
Basoko: Zaire 76 B2
Basongo: Zaire 76 B3
BASRA & *Prov.*, Iraq 57 K6
Basra: Syria 56 E5
Bass, Is. de: Austral Is. 83 g5
Bassac: *airfield*, Outer Hebr., Scotland 28 G5
Bassae: *site of ancient Greek temple in mtns. S. of Andritsaina*, Greece 39 R18

Bassano: Alta., Canada 92 E2
Bassano: Italy 41 R10
Bassari: Togo 80 E3
Bassas da India: *i.* (Fr.), Indian O. 77 E7
Bassas de Pedro: *i.*, Laccadive Is. 58 M12
Bassée, La: France 36 H5
Bassein: Maharashtra, India 58 M11
BASSEIN: Irrawaddy, Burma 59 Q11
Bassein: *riv.*, Burma 59 Q11
Basse-Kotto: *Pref.*, Cen. Afr. Rep. (*cap.* Mobaye) 76 B2
Basse Santa Su: The Gambia 80 B2
BASSE TERRE: Guadeloupe, Leeward Is. 87 c2
BASSETERRE: St. Christopher-Nevis-Anguilla, Leeward Is. 87 b2
Bassett: Va., U.S.A. 89 M7
Basse-Yurz: France 36 M6
Bassikounou: Mauritania 80 C1
Bassila: Benin 81 E3
Bassingbourn: Cambs., Eng. 25 V15
Bassingham: Lincs., England 27 U13
Bassira: Syria 57 G4
Bass Is.: Ohio, U.S.A. 88 K5
Bass Rock: Scotland 29 Q7
Bass Str.: Australia 66 E3
Bassum: W. Germany 44 O3
Bâstad: Sweden 47 N8
Bastak: Iran 55 H9
Bastar: Madhya Pradesh, India 58 O11
Bastetani: *ancient tribe near Murcia*, Spain 35 F18
Basti: Uttar Pradesh, India 59 O9
Bastia: Corsica 38 L15
Bastian Bay: La., U.S.A. 90 *Ins.*
Bastide, La: France 37 E11
Bastide-de-Sérou, La: France 37 G12
Bastion Cape: Hainan, China 62 T11
Bastogne: Belgium 44 L5
Baston: Lincs., England 25 V14
Bastrop: La., U.S.A. 90 F9
Bastrop: Tex., U.S.A. 90 C10
Basutråsk: Sweden 46 R4
Basu: *i.*, Sumatra 65 C7
Bas Zaire: *Prov.*, Zaire (*cap.* Matadi) 81 G6
Bata: Equatorial Guinea 81 F4
Bataan: *penin.*, Luzon, Phil. 64 G4
Batac: Luzon, Phil. 64 G3
Batakan: Borneo 65 E7
Batalha: Portugal 35 B17
Batam: *i.*, Riouw Arch., Indonesia 65 d13
Batanaea: *ancient Greek name of S. portion of Hauran district*, Syria 56 E5
Batang (Paan): Szechwan, China 62 R8
Batangafo: Cen. Afr. Rep. 76 A1
Batangas: Luzon, Phil. 64 G4
Batang Berjuntai: Malaya, Malaysia 65 b12
Batan Is. & *i.*, Philippines 64 G2
Batanta: *i.*, West Irian, Indon. 61 L12
Batavia: *see* Djakarta.
Batavia: Argentina 96 B3
Batavia: N.Y., U.S.A. 89 M4
Batchawana: Ont., Canada 88 J2
Batcombe: Som., England 24 R17
Bateman's Bay: *town*, N.S.W., Australia 71 J10
Batesburg: S.C., U.S.A. 91 L9
Batesville: Ark., U.S.A. 90 F8
Batesville: Miss., U.S.A. 90 G8
Bath: Avon, England 24 R17
Bath: Jamaica 86 *Ins.*
Bath: Maine, U.S.A. 89 R4
Bath: N.B., Canada 89 S2
Bath: N.Y., U.S.A. 89 N4
Batha: *Pref.*, Chad (*cap.* Ati) 81 H2
Batha: *riv.*, Chad 78 H7
Batha Badiya: *geog. reg.*, Oman 55 J10
Batha Lairi: *riv.*, Chad 81 H2
Bathford: Som., England 24 R17
Bathgate: Lothian, Scot. 29 O8
Bathoen: Botswana 75 F2
Bathurst: *see* Banjul.
Bathurst: N.B., Canada 89 T2
Bathurst: N.S.W., Australia 71 H9
Bathurst: & *Dist.*, S. Africa 75 G6
Bathurst: Tas., Australia 68 H8
Bathurst, Cape: N.W.T., Canada 84 G3
Bathurst Inlet (Burnside Harbour): N.W.T., Canada 84 j4
Bathurst I.: Australia 68 E2
Bathurst I.: N.W.T., Canada 84 j2
Batié: Upper Volta 80 D3
Batin: *watercourse*, Kuwait/Iraq 57 K7
Batina Coast: Oman 55 J10
Batiscan: *riv.*, Que., Canada 89 P2
Batkanu: Sierra Leone 80 B3
Batley: W. Yorks., England 27 S12
Batman: *riv.*, Turkey 57 G2
BATNA: Aurès, Algeria 32 D4
Bato: Japan 63 g2
Batoka: Zambia 77 C6
Batoka Plat.: Zambia 77 C6
BATON ROUGE: La., U.S.A. 90 F10
Batopilas: Mexico 93 F7
Batouri: Cameroun 81 G4
Batrun: Lebanon 56 D4
Battambang: Cambodia 64 C4
Batticaloa: Sri Lanka 58 O13
Battinga: Cen. Afr. Rep. 76 B1
Battle: E. Sussex, England 25 W18
Battle: *riv.*, Sask., Canada 92 E2
Battle Creek: *city*, Mich., U.S.A. 88 J4
Battlefields: Rhodesia 77 C6
Battleford: Sask., Canada 92 F2
Battleford, North: Sask., Canada 92 F2
Battle Harbour: Newf., Can. 85 O7
Battle Mountain: *city*, Nev., U.S.A. 92 D4
Batu Anam: Malaya, Malaysia 65 c12
Batu Gajah: Malaya, Malaysia 65 b11
Batu Is.: Sumatra 65 B7
Batukelau: Borneo 65 F6
Batulaki: Mindanao, Phil. 65 H5
Batumi (Batum): Adzhar, Georgia, U.S.S.R. 57 G1
Batu Pahat (Bandar Penggaram): Malaya, Malaysia 65 c13
Baturaja: Sumatra 65 C7
Batu Rakit: Malaya, Malaysia 65 c11
Baturetno: Java 65 E8
Batz: France 36 C8
Batz, Île de: *i.*, France 36 A7
Baubau: Butung, Indon. 65 G8
BAUCHI: & *State*, Nigeria 81 F2
Baud: France 36 B8

Baudette: Minn., U.S.A. 88 D1
Baudh: Orissa, India 59 O10
Baudó: Colombia 94 B2
Baugé: France 36 E8
Baúl, El: Venezuela 94 D2
Baule, La: France 36 C8
Baumber: Lincs., England 27 V13
Baume-les-Dames: France 40 M8
Baumholder: W. Germany 44 N6
Baunach: W. Germany 45 Q6
Bauple: Queens., Australia 70 K5
Baures: Bolivia 94 E6
Baurú: Brazil 96 F1
Bauska: Latvia, U.S.S.R. 47 T8
Bautregaum: mtn., Kerry, Repub. of Ireland 31 B15
Bautzen: E. Germany 45 U4
Bauxite: Ark., U.S.A. 90 E8
Bauya: Sierra Leone 80 B3
Bavaria: State, W. Germany [cap. Munich (München)] 45 Q6
Bavarian Alps: W. Germany 41 R8
Bavay: France 36 J5
Baviácora: Mexico 93 E7
Bavispe: Mexico 93 F6
Bawal: i., Borneo 65 E7
Baw Baw: mtn., Vict., Austl. 71 G11
Bawburgh: Norf., England 25 Y14
Bawdeswell: Norf., England 25 Y14
Bawdsey: Suff., England 25 Y15
Bawdwin: Burma 59 R10
Bawean: i., Indonesia 65 E8
Bawinkel: W. Germany 44 N3
Bawiti, El: Egypt 54 C9
Bawku: Ghana 80 D2
Bawlake: Burma 59 R11
Bawtry: S. Yorks., England 27 T13
Baxley: Ga., U.S.A. 91 K10
Baxter Springs: city, Kans., U.S.A. 90 D7
Bayamo: Cuba 87 M13
Bayana: Rajasthan, India 58 N9
Bayan-Aul: Kazakh., U.S.S.R. 51 N4
Bayanga: Cen. Afr. Rep. 81 H4
Bayan Kara Shan: range, Chinghai, China 62 R8
Bayan Tumen (Choibalsan): Mongolia 62 U5
Bayard: Nebr., U.S.A. 92 G4
Baybay: Philippines 64 G6
Bayble: Outer Hebr., Scot. 28 J3
Bayboro: N.C., U.S.A. 91 N8
Bayburt: Turkey 57 G1
Bay City: Mich., U.S.A. 88 K4
Bay City: Tex., U.S.A. 90 D11
Baydaratskaya Gulf: U.S.S.R. 48 h4
Baydon: Wilts., England 25 S17
Bayern: see Bavaria.
Bayeux: France 36 E6
Bayfield: Wis., U.S.A. 88 F2
Bayındır: Turkey 39 U17
Bayir: Jordan 56 E6
Bay Is.: Honduras 86 L14
Baykal Lake: U.S.S.R. 49 m7
Baykonur: Kazakh., U.S.S.R. 51 L5
Baymak: U.S.S.R. 50 J4
Bay Minette: Ala., U.S.A. 91 H10
Baymouth, South: Ont., Canada 88 K3
Bayombong: Luzon, Phil. 64 G3
Bayon: France 40 M7
Bayonne: France 37 D12
Bayovar: Peru 94 A5
Bayraktar: Turkey 57 H2
Bayram-Ali: Turkmen., U.S.S.R. 51 K7
Bayramiç: Turkey 39 U17
Bayreuth: W. Germany 45 R6
Bayrischzell: W. Germany 41 S8
Bay Roberts: Newf., Can. 85 w3
Bays, Lake of: Ont., Canada 89 M3
Bay St. Louis: Miss., U.S.A. 90 G10
Baystonhill: Salop, England 27 Q14
Baysun: Uzbek., U.S.S.R. 51 L7
Bayton: Hereford & Worcester, England 24 R15
Baytown: Tex., U.S.A. 90 D11
Bayuda: well, Sudan 54 D11
Bayunglencir: Sumatra 65 C7
Baza: Spain 35 E18
Baza Khatymi: U.S.S.R. 49 O6
Bazancourt: France 36 K6
Bazar: Ukraine 43 V11
Bazar-Dara Range: Tadzhik., U.S.S.R. 51 M7
Bazargechan: Armenia, U.S.S.R. 57 J1
Bazaruto I.: Mozambique 77 E7
Bazas: France 37 E11
Bazin: riv., Que., Canada 89 O2
Bazoche-Gouet, la: France 36 F7
Beach: N. Dak., U.S.A. 92 G3
Beachport: S. Australia 71 C11
Beachy Head: cape, E. Sussex, England 25 W18
Beaconsfield: Bucks., Eng. 25 U16
Beaconsfield: S. Africa 75 F4
Beaconsfield: Tas., Australia 68 H8
Beadlam: N. Yorks., England 26 U11
Beadnell: Northumb., Eng. 26 S8
Beal: Northumb., England 26 S8
Beal: N. Yorks., England 27 T12
Beale, Cape: B.C., Canada 92 B3
Beaminster: Dorset, Eng. 24 Q18
Bear: riv., Idaho, U.S.A. 92 E4
Beardmore Glacier: Antarctica 9 85S 170E
Beardstown: Ill., U.S.A. 88 F6
Bear Haven: Cork, Repub. of Ireland 31 B16
Bear I.: (Nor.), Arctic O. 48 c3
Bear I.: Repub. of Ireland 31 B16
Béarn: Prov., France 35 F15
Bear Paw Mount.: Mont., U.S.A. 92 F3
Bear River: city, N.S., Can. 89 T3
Bearsden: Strath., Scotland 29 N8
Bearsted: Kent, England 25 X17
Beas: riv., India 58 N8
Beatrice: Nebr., U.S.A. 93 H4
Beatrice: Rhodesia 77 D6
Beatty: Nev., U.S.A. 93 D5
Beaucaire: France 37 K12
Beauce: geog. reg., France 36 G7
Beauceville: Que., Canada 89 Q2
Beaudesert: Queens., Austl. 70 K7
Beaufort: France 40 M10
Beaufort: Kerry, Repub. of Ireland 31 B15
Beaufort: Gwent, Wales 24 P16
Beaufort: S.C., U.S.A. 91 L9
Beaufort: Sabah, Malaysia 65 F5
Beaufort: S.C., U.S.A. 91 L9
Beaufort: Vict., Australia 71 E11
Beaufort Sea: Arctic O. 84 F3
Beaufort West: & Dist., S. Africa 74 E6
Beaugency: France 36 G8
Beauharnois: Que., Canada 89 P3
Beaulieu: France 37 G11
Beaulieu: Hants., England 25 T18
Beauly: & firth, High., Scot 28 N5

Beauly: riv., High., Scotland 28 M5
Beaumaris: Gwynedd, Wales 27 N13
Beaumetz: France 36 H5
Beaumont: Belgium 44 K5
Beaumont: Manche, France 25 Ins.
Beaumont: Meurthe-et-Moselle, France 40 L7
Beaumont: Seine-et-Marne, France 36 H7
Beaumont: Tex., U.S.A. 90 D10
Beaumont-de-Lomagne: Fr. 37 F12
Beaumont Hill: N.S.W., Australia 71 F8
Beaumont-sur-Oise: France 36 H6
Beaumont-sur-Sarthe: France 36 F7
Beaune: France 36 K8
Beaune-la-Rolande: France 36 H7
Beaupréau: France 36 E8
Beauraing: Belgium 44 K5
Beaurepaire: France 37 L10
Beausset, Le: France 40 L12
BEAUVAIS: Oise, France 36 H6
Beauval: France 36 H5
Beauvoir-sur-Mer: France 36 C9
Beauvoir-sur-Niort: France 37 E9
Beaver: Alaska, U.S.A. 84 E4
Beaver: i., Mich., U.S.A. 88 J3
Beaver: riv., Sask., Canada 92 F2
Beaver Bay: city, Minn., U.S.A. 88 F2
Beaver City: Okla., U.S.A. 90 A7
Beaver Dam: city, Wis., U.S.A. 88 G4
Beaver Falls: city, Pa., U.S.A. 88 L5
Beaver Lake: Ont., Canada 92 K1
Beawar: Rajasthan, India 58 M9
Beazley: Argentina 96 B3
Bebington: Mers., England 27 P13
Bebra: W. Germany 45 P5
Bécancour: Que., Canada 89 P2
Beccles: Suff., England 25 Z15
Bečej: Yugoslavia 39 R14
Becerrea: Spain 35 C15
Béchar: Saoura, Algeria 78 D3
Bechenagskiy Pass: Armenia/Nakhichevan U.S.S.R. 57 J2
Bechyně: Czechoslovakia 45 U6
Becilla de Valderaduey: Sp. 35 D15
Beckham, West: Norf., Eng. 25 Y14
Beckingham: Lincs., Eng. 27 U13
Beckingham: Notts., Eng. 27 U13
Beckington: Som., England 24 R17
Beckley: W. Va., U.S.A. 88 L7
Beck Row: Suff., England 25 W15
Beckum: W. Germany 44 O4
Beclean: Romania 43 T13
Bécon: France 36 E8
Bečov: Czechoslovakia 45 S5
Bečváry: Czechoslovakia 45 V6
Bedale: N. Yorks., England 26 S11
Bédarieux: France 37 J12
Bedda: Ethiopia 79 N7
Beddgelert: Gwynedd, Wales 27 N14
Bédée: France 36 D7
Béderkesa: W. Germany 44 O2
Bederwanak: Somalia 79 Q18
BEDFORD: & Co., England 25 V15
Bedford: Ind., U.S.A. 88 H6
Bedford: Ohio, U.S.A. 88 L5
Bedford: Pa., U.S.A. 89 M5
Bedford: Que., Canada 89 P3
Bedford: Va., U.S.A. 89 M7
Bedford: & Dist., S. Africa 75 G6
Bedlington: Northumb., England 26 S9
Bednja: riv., Yugoslavia 41 W9
Bednodem'yanovsk: U.S.S.R. 50 F4
Bedourie: Queens., Austl. 69 F4
Bedous: France 37 E12
Bedout I.: W. Australia 68 B3
Bedrule: Bord., Scotland 29 Q9
Bedstone: Salop, England 24 Q15
Bedwellty: Gwent, Wales 24 P16
Bedworth: War., England 25 T15
Bedwyn, Great: Wilts., Eng. 25 S17
Beebe: Ark., U.S.A. 90 F8
Beechal: Queens., Australia 70 F6
Beechey Point: settlement, Alaska, U.S.A. 84 E3
Beech Grove: city, Ind., U.S.A. 88 H6
Beechworth: Vict., Australia 71 G11
Beeding, Lower: W. Sussex, Eng. 24 V17
Beeford: Humb., England 27 V12
Beeley: Derby., England 27 S13
Beelitz: E. Germany 45 S3
Beenleigh: Queens., Austl. 70 K6
Beerburrum: Queens., Austl. 70 K6
Beer Head: cape, Devon, England 24 P18
Beersheba: Israel 55 a3
Beeskow: E. Germany 45 U3
Beestekraal: Trans., S. Afr. 75 G2
Beeston: Ches., England 27 Q13
Beeston: Notts., England 27 T14
Beeswing: Dumfries & Galloway, Scotland 29 O9
Beetham: Cumbria, Eng. 26 Q11
Beetzendorf: E. Germany 45 R3
Beeville: Tex., U.S.A. 90 C11
Befale: France 76 B2
Befandriana: (E. of Majunga), Malagasy Rep. 73 O13
Befandriana: (N. of Tulear), Malagasy Rep. 73 N14
Befori: Zaire 76 B2
Beg, Lough: Lon./Antrim, N. Ireland 30 J10
Bega: N.S.W., Australia 71 H11
Begemdir & Simen: Prov., Ethiopia (cap. Gondar) 79 M7
Bègles: France 37 E11
Begna: riv., Norway 47 L6
Beguildy: Powys, Wales 24 P15
Behara: Malagasy Rep. 73 O15
Behbehan: Iran 55 H8
Behelve: Lothian, Scot. 29 Q8
Behelve: N.C., U.S.A. 91 N8
Behelvie: Gram., Scotland 28 R5
Beli: Cres, Yugoslavia 41 U10
Belin: France 37 E11
Belingwe: Rhodesia 77 C7
Belinyu: Bangka, Indonesia 65 D7
Belitung: i., Indonesia 65 D7

Beinn Bahn: mtn., Highland, Scotland 28 K5
Beinn Bheiger: mtn., Inner Hebr., Scotland 29 J8
Beinn Bhrotain: mtn., Grampian/Highland, Scotland 28 O5
Beinn Bhuidhe: mtn., Strath., Scotland 29 M7
Beinn Chlachair: Highland, Scotland 29 M6
Beinn Dearg: mtn., Highland, Scotland 28 M4
Beinn Dearg: mtn., Tayside, Scotland 28 O6
Beinn Dhorain: mtn., Highland, Scotland 28 O3
Beinn Dorain: mtn., Strathclyde, Scotland 29 M6
Beinn Edra: Inner Hebr., Scotland 28 J4
Beinn Eighe: mtn., Highland, Scotland 28 L4
Beinn Fhada (Ben Attow): mtn., Highland, Scot. 28 L5
Beinn Heasgarnich: mtn., Tayside, Scotland 29 M6
Beinn Ime: mtn., Strathclyde, Scotland 29 M7
Beinn Iutharn Mhor: mtn., Gram./Tay., Scotland 28 O5
Beinn Laoigh: mtn., Central, Scotland 29 M7
Beinn na Sreine: mtn., Strathclyde, Scotland 29 J7
Beinn Resipol: mtn., Strathclyde, Scotland 29 K6
Beinn Sgulaird: mtn., Strathclyde, Scotland 29 L6
Beinn Tharsuinn: mtn., Highland, Scotland 28 N4
BEIRA: Manica & Sofala, Mozambique 77 D6
Beira: well, Somalia 79 R18
Beira Alta: Prov., Portugal (cap. Viseu) 35 C16
Beira Baixa: Prov., Portugal (cap. Castelo Branco) 35 C16
Beira Litoral: Prov., Portugal (cap. Coimbra) 35 B16
BEIRUT: Lebanon 56 D5
Beit Bridge: Rhodesia 75 J1
Beit Guvrin: Israel 55 a3
Beith: Strath., Scotland 29 M8
Beit Nattif: Israel 55 a3
Beit She'an: Israel 55 b2
Beius: Romania 43 S13
Beja: Baixo Alentejo, Port. 35 C17
BÉJA: & Governorate, Tunisia 38 L18
Bejaia: & gulf, Algeria 35 J18
Béjar: Spain 35 D16
Bekabad: Uzbek., U.S.S.R. 51 L6
Bekdash: Turkmen., U.S.S.R. 50 H6
Bék éscsaba: Hungary 43 R13
Bek Pak Dala Steppe: Kazakh., U.S.S.R. 51 M5
Bekwai: Ghana 80 D3
Bela: Bulgaria 39 T15
Bela: Baluchistan, Pakistan 58 L9
Bela: Uttar Pradesh, India 58 O9
Belabre: France 37 G9
Bela Crkva: Yugoslavia 39 R14
Belaga: Sarawak, Malaysia 65 E6
Bela Palanka: Yugoslavia 39 S15
Bela Slatina: Bulgaria 39 S15
Bela Vista: Mozambique 75 K3
Bela Vista: Paraguay 95 F1
Belawan: Sumatra 65 B6
Belaya: riv., U.S.S.R. 50 H3
Belaya Glina: U.S.S.R. 50 F5
Belaya Kholunitsa: U.S.S.R. 50 H3
Belaya Tserkov': Ukraine 50 D5
Belcaire: France 37 G13
Belchatów: Poland 43 O11
Belcher Chan.: N.W.T., Can. 84 K2
Belcher Is.: Canada 85 M6
Belchford: Lincs., England 27 V13
Belchite: Spain 35 F16
Belclare: Galway, Repub. of Ireland 30 D13
Belcoo: Ferm., N. Ireland 30 F11
Belderg: Mayo, Repub. of Ireland 30 B11
Beleapani Reef: Laccadive Is. 58 M12
Belebey: U.S.S.R. 50 H4
BELÉM: Pará, Brazil 94 H4
Belembe: U.S.S.R. 63 Z5
Belen: Argentina 96 B2
Belen: N. Mex., U.S.A. 93 F6
Belén: Panama 87 I16
Belén: Paraguay 96 D1
Belén: Uruguay 96 D3
Beleşti Tirq: Romania 39 U13
Belev: U.S.S.R. 50 E4
BELFAST: N. Ireland 30 K10
Belfast: Maine, U.S.A. 89 R3
Belfast: & Dist., Trans., S. Africa 75 J2
Belfast Lough: N. Ireland 30 K10
Belfodio: Ethiopia 79 L7
Belford: Northumb., Eng. 26 S8
BELFORT: & Dept., France 40 M8
Belgaum: Karnataka, India 58 M11
Belgern: E. Germany 45 T4

Belgium: Kingdom 44 J5
Cap.: Brussels (Bruxelles)
Area: 11,779 sq. miles (30,508 sq. km.)
Pop.: 9,673,000 (1971 E)

Belgooly: Cork, Repub. of Irel. 31 E16
BELGOROD: & Reg., U.S.S.R. 50 E4
Belgorod Dnestrovskiy: Ukraine 50 D5
BELGRADE (Beograd): Yugoslavia 39 R14
Belhaven: Lothian, Scot. 29 Q8
Belhelvie: Gram., Scotland 28 R5
Beli: Cres, Yugoslavia 41 U10
Belin: France 37 E11
Belingwe: Rhodesia 77 C7
Belinyu: Bangka, Indonesia 65 D7
Belitung: i., Indonesia 65 D7

Belize: self-governing Colony of U.K. 86 Ins.
Cap.: Belmopan
Area: 8,866 sq. miles (22,963 sq. km.)
Pop.: 124,000 (1971 E)

Belize: Belize 86 Ins.
Bel'Kachi: U.S.S.R. 49 P6
Bell: Queens., Australia 70 J6
Bell: riv., Que., Canada 89 N1
Bella Bella: B.C., Canada 92 B2
Bellac: France 37 G9
Bellaco: Uruguay 96 D3
Bella Coola: B.C., Canada 92 B2

Bellaghy: Lon., N. Ireland 30 H10
Bellaire: Ohio, U.S.A. 88 L5
Bellanagare: Rosc., Repub. of Ireland 30 E12
Bellano: Italy 40 P9
Bellaria: Italy 41 S11
Bellary: Karnataka, India 58 N11
Bellata: N.S.W., Australia 71 H7
Bella Unión: Uruguay 96 D3
Bella Vista: Corrientes, Arg. 96 D2
Bella Vista: Tucumán, Arg. 96 B2
Bellbrook: N.S.W., Australia 71 K8
Belle Chasse: La., U.S.A. 90 Ins.
Belleek: Armagh, N. Ireland 30 J11
Belleek: Ferm., N. Ireland 30 E11
Bellefontaine: Ohio, U.S.A. 88 K5
Bellefonte: Pa., U.S.A. 89 N5
Belle Fourche: S. Dak., U.S.A. 92 G4
Bellegarde: Ain, France 40 L9
Bellegarde: Gard, France 37 K12
Bellegarde: Loiret, France 36 H8
Belle Glade: city, Fla., U.S.A. 91 L12
Belle Ile: i., France 36 B8
Belle Isle: str. of & i., Canada 85 v1
Belle-Isle-en-Terre: France 36 B7
Bellême: France 36 F7
Bellenaves: France 37 J9
Belleoram: Newf., Canada 85 v3
Bellerive: Tas., Australia 68 H8
Belleville: France 37 K9
Belleville: Ill., U.S.A. 88 G6
Belleville: Kans., U.S.A. 93 H5
Belleville: Ont., Canada 89 N3
Bellevue: Idaho, U.S.A. 92 E4
Bellevue: Nebr., U.S.A. 92 H4
Bellevue: Ohio, U.S.A. 88 K5
Belley: France 40 L10
Bellingen: N.S.W., Australia 71 K8
Bellingham: Northumb., England 26 R9
Bellingham: Wash., U.S.A. 92 B3
Bellingshausen: rsch. stn., Antarctica 9 65S 60W
Bellingshausen Is.: Society Is. 83 e3
Bellingshausen Sea: Antarctica 9 75S 85W
BELLINZONA: Ticino, Switz. 40 P9
Bell Island: town, Newf., Canada 85 w3
Belliyela: Liberia 80 B3
Bellnaves: France 37 J9
Bellona: i., Coral Sea 67 L4
Bellona Reefs: Coral Sea 67 L6
Bellovaci: Gallic tribe with centre at Beauvais, France 36 H6
Bell Peninsula: Canada 85 l5
Belluno: Italy 41 S9
Bell Ville: Argentina 96 C3
Bellville: & Dist., S. Africa 74 C6
Bellville: Tex., U.S.A. 90 C10
Bélmez: Spain 35 D17
Belmond: Iowa, U.S.A. 88 E4
Belmont: N.S.W., Australia 71 J9
Belmont: N.C., U.S.A. 91 L8
Belmont: S. Africa 75 F4
Belmonte: Brazil 94 K7
Belmonte: Portugal 35 C16
Belmonte: Spain 35 E17
BELMOPAN: Belize 86 Ins.
Belmullet: Mayo, Repub. of Ireland 30 B11
Belo: Malagasy Rep. 73 N13
Beloglazovo: U.S.S.R. 51 O4
Belogorsk: U.S.S.R. 49 o7
Belogradchik: Bulgaria 39 S15
BELO HORIZONTE: Minas Gerais, Brazil 94 J7
Beloit: Kans., U.S.A. 93 H5
Beloit: Wis., U.S.A. 88 G4
Belokany: Azerbaydzhan, U.S.S.R. 50 G6
Belokorovichi: Ukraine 43 V11
Belolutsk: U.S.S.R. 50 E5
Belopol'ye: Ukraine 50 D4
Belorado: Spain 35 E15
Beloretsk: U.S.S.R. 50 J4
Beloye, Lake: U.S.S.R. 50 E2
Belozersk: U.S.S.R. 50 E3
Belper: Derby., England 27 T13
Belsay: Northumb., England 26 S9
Belsdorf: E. Germany 45 R3
Belseln: Albania 39 Q16
Beltana: S. Australia 71 C8
Belterra: Brazil 94 G4
Belton: Humb., England 27 U12
Belton: Tex., U.S.A. 90 C10
Beltra: Sligo, Repub. of Ireland 30 D11
Bel'tsy: Moldavia, U.S.S.R. 43 U13
Belturbet: Cavan, Repub. of Ireland 30 G11
Beluran: Sabah, Malaysia 65 F5
Belvedere Maritimo: Italy 38 O17
Belvès: France 37 F11
Belvidere: Ill., U.S.A. 88 G4
Belvoir, Vale of: Notts., England 27 U14
Belvoir Castle: Leics., Eng. 27 U14
Belyando: riv., Queens., Australia 70 G4
Belyayevka: Ukraine 39 V13
Belyye: U.S.S.R. 50 D3
Belyy I.: U.S.S.R. 48 J3
Belyy' Yar: U.S.S.R. 51 P3
Belz: France 36 B8
Belz: Ukraine 43 S11
Belzig: E. Germany 45 S3
Belzoni: Miss., U.S.A. 90 F9
Bembe: Angola 73 G11
Bembesi: Rhodesia 77 C6
Bembridge: I. of Wight, England 25 T18
Bement: Ill., U.S.A. 88 G6
Bemidji: Minn., U.S.A. 88 D2
Bempton: Humb., England 27 V11
Bena: Minn., U.S.A. 88 E2
Benabarre: Spain 35 G15
Benacus: Roman name of Lake of Garda, Italy 40 Q10
Bena Dibele: Zaire 76 B3
Benadir: Reg., Somalia (cap. Merca) 79 R19
Ben Alder: mtn., High., Scot. 29 M6
Benalla: Vict., Australia 71 F11
Benares (Baranasi, Varanasi): Uttar Pradesh, India 59 O9
Bénat, Cap: cape, France 40 M12
Benavente: Spain 35 D15
Benavides: Tex., U.S.A. 90 B12
Ben Avon: mtn., Grampian, Scotland 28 P5
Benbane Head: cape, Antrim, N. Ireland 30 J9
Benbecula: i. & airfield, Outer Hebr., Scotland 28 G5
Benbow: Calif., U.S.A. 92 C4

Benbradagh: mtn., Lon., N. Ireland 30 H10
Ben Bragor: mtn., Outer Hebr., Scotland 28 H3
Benburb: Tyr., N. Ireland 30 H11
Bêncat: Vietnam 64 D4
Ben Chonzie: mtn., Tayside, Scotland 29 O7
Bencleuch: mtn., Central, Scotland 29 O7
Ben Cruachan: mtn., Strathclyde, Scotland 29 L7
Bencubbin: W. Australia 68 B6
Bend: Oreg., U.S.A. 92 C4
Bende: Nigeria 81 F3
Bendel: State, Nigeria (cap. Benin City) 81 F3
Bendemeer: N.S.W., Austl. 71 J8
Bendena: Queens., Australia 70 G6
Bender Beila: Somalia 79 S18
Bender Kassim: see Bosaso.
Benderloch: dist., Strathclyde, Scotland 29 L7
Bender Merhagno: Somalia 79 S17
Bendery: Moldavia, U.S.S.R. 39 V13
Bendigo: Vict., Australia 71 F11
Bendorf: W. Germany 44 N5
Bénéna: Mali 80 D2
Benenden: Kent, England 25 X17
Benenitra: Malagasy Rep. 73 N14
Beneraby: Queens., Austl. 70 J4
Beneraird: mtn., Strath., Scot. 29 M9
Beneshek: Nigeria 81 G2
Benešov: Czechoslovakia 45 U6
Benet: France 37 E9
Benevento: Italy 38 O16
Benfeld: France 40 N7
Benfleet, South: Essex, Eng. 25 X16
Bengal, Bay of: India 59 P12
Bengalia: N.S.W., Australia 71 J7
Bengamisa: Zaire 76 C2
Bengara: Borneo 65 F6
Ben Gardane: Tunisia 32 E5
Bengchroui: Cambodia 64 D4
BENGHAZI: & Prov., Libya 33 G5
Bengkalis: & i., Sumatra 65 c13
Bengkulu: Sumatra 65 C7
Ben Griam More: mtn., Highland, Scotland 28 M3
Bengtsfors: Sweden 47 N7
BENGUELA: & Prov., Angola 73 G12
Ben Guérin: Morocco 80 K8
Benguerua i.: Mozambique 77 E7
Benha: Egypt 56 B6
Ben Hope: mtn., Highland, Scotland 28 M3
Beni: Zaire 76 C2
Beni: riv., Bolivia 94 D6
Beni Abbès: Algeria 80 L8
Benicarló: Spain 35 G16
Bénima: Cen. Afr. Rep. 76 B1
Beni Mansour: Algeria 35 J18
Beni Mazar: Egypt 54 D9

Benin: Republic 81 E3
Cap.: Porto Novo
Area: 43,483 sq. miles (112,621 sq. km.)
Pop.: 2,760,000 (1971 E)

BENIN CITY: Bendel, Nigeria 81 F3
BENI-MELLAL: & Prov., Morocco 80 K8
Beni Ounif: Algeria 80 L8
Beni Saf: Algeria 80 L7
Beni Suef: Egypt 54 D9
Beni Ulid: Libya 32 E5
Benjamin Constant: Brazil 94 C4
Benkajang: Borneo 65 D6
Benkelman: Nebr., U.S.A. 93 G4
Ben Klibreck: mtn., Highland, Scotland 28 N3
Benkovac: Yugoslavia 41 V11
Ben Lawers: mtn., Tayside, Scotland 29 N6
Ben Ledi: mtn., Central, Scotland 29 N7
Ben Lomond: mtn., Central, Scotland 29 M7
Ben Loyal: mtn., Highland, Scotland 28 N3
Ben Macdhui: mtn., Grampian, Scotland 28 O5
Ben More: mtn., Central, Scotland 29 M7
Ben More: mtn., Inner Hebr., Scotland 29 J7
Benmore, Lake: res., New Zealand 70 N17
Ben More Assynt: mtn., Highland, Scotland 28 M3
Ben More Coigach: mtn., Highland, Scotland 28 L4
Benmore Head (Fair Head): cape, Antrim, N. Ireland 30 J9
Bennane Head: cape, Strathclyde, Scotland 29 L9
Bennett: U.S.S.R. 49 q2
Bennett: B.C., Canada 84 f6
Bennettsbridge: Kilk., Repub. of Ireland 31 G14
Bennettsville: S.C., U.S.A. 91 M8
Ben Nevis: mtn., High., Scot. 29 L6
Bennington: Vt., U.S.A. 89 P4
Bénodet: France 36 A8
Bénodet, Anse de: inlet, Fr. 36 A8
Ben Ohau Range: South I., New Zealand 70 N16
Benom: mtn., Malaya, Malaysia 65 c12
Benoue: riv., Cameroun 81 G3
Benque Viejo: Belize 86 Ins.
Ben Rinnes: mtn., Grampian, Scotland 28 P5
Bensane: Guinea 80 B2
Bensersiel: W. Germany 44 N2
Ben Sgriol: mtn., High., Scot. 28 K5
Bensheim: W. Germany 44 O6
Benson: Ariz., U.S.A. 93 E6
Benson: Minn., U.S.A. 92 H3
Benson: Oxon., England 25 T16
Ben Starav: mtn., Strathclyde, Scotland 29 L6
Benteng: Salajar, Indonesia 65 G8
Benthall: Salop, England 27 R14
Bentham, High & Lower: N. Yorks., England 26 Q11
Bentheim: W. Germany 44 N3
Bentimodia: Guinea 80 B2
Bentinck: i., Mergui Arch., Burma 59 R12
Bentley: Hants., England 25 U17
Bentley: S. Yorks., England 27 T12
Benton: Ark., U.S.A. 90 E8
Benton: Ill., U.S.A. 88 G7
Benton: Ky., U.S.A. 88 G7
Bentong: Malaya, Malaysia 65 b12
Benton Harbor: town, Mich., U.S.A. 88 H4
Bentonville: Ark., U.S.A. 90 D7
Bentworth: Hants., England 25 T17
Benua: i., Indonesia 65 D6

Benue: riv., Nigeria 81 G3
Benue: State, Nigeria (cap. Makurdi) 81 F3
Benut: Malaya, Malaysia 65 c13
Ben Venue: mtn., Tayside, Scotland 29 N7
Ben Vorlich: mtn., Tayside, Scotland 29 N7
Ben Vrackie: mtn., Tayside, Scotland 29 O6
Benwee Head: cape, Mayo, Repub. of Ireland 30 B11
Ben Wyvis: mtn., Highland, Scotland 28 M4
Ben Zohra: well, Algeria 80 L9
BEOGRAD (Belgrade): Yugoslavia 39 R14
Béoumi: Ivory Coast 80 C3
Bepara: Chad 81 H3
Beppu: Japan 63 b4
Bequia: i., Grenadines, Windward Is. 87 c4
Ber: Somalia 79 R18
Beragh: Tyr., N. Ireland 30 G10
Berar: geog reg., Maharashtra, India 58 N10
Berasbasah, Cape: Borneo 65 D7
Berat: Albania 39 Q16
Berau Gulf: West Irian, Indonesia 66 F2
Berau Penin.: West Irian, Indonesia 61 L12
Berawinnia Downs: N.S.W., Australia 71 E7
Berber: Sudan 54 D11
Berbera: Somalia 79 R17
BERBERATI: Haute-Sangha, Cen. Afr. Rep. 81 H4
Berbice: Co. & riv., Guyana 87 d8
Berceto: Italy 40 P11
Berching: W. Germany 45 R6
Berchogur: Kazakh., U.S.S.R. 50 J5
Berchtesgaden: W. Germany 41 T8
Berck: France 36 G5
Berdichev: Ukraine 43 V12
Berdsk: U.S.S.R. 51 O4
Berdyansk: Ukraine 50 E5
Berea: Ohio, U.S.A. 88 L5
Bere Alston: Devon, Eng. 24 N19
Béréby: Ivory Coast 80 C4
Bere Ferrers: Devon, Eng. 24 N19
Beregovo: Ukraine 43 S12
Bereku: Tanzania 76 E3
Berenice: Graeco-Roman port on W. coast of Red Sea south N. of Ras Banas, Egypt 54 E10
Bere Regis: Dorset, England 24 R18
Berestechko: Ukraine 43 T11
Berettyóújfalu: Hungary 43 R13
Beréza: Byelorussia 43 T10
Berezhany: Ukraine 43 T12
Berezino: Byelorussia 50 C4
Bereznik: U.S.S.R. 50 F2
Berezniki: U.S.S.R. 50 J3
Berezno: Ukraine 43 U11
Berezovka: Ukraine 50 E5
Berezovka: U.S.S.R. 51 Q3
Berezovo: U.S.S.R. 51 L2
Berezovskoye: U.S.S.R. 51 P3
Berga: Spain 35 G15
Berga: Sweden 47 P8
Bergama: Turkey 39 U17
Bergamo: Italy 40 P10
Bergamo Alps: Italy 40 P9
Berge: W. Germany 44 N3
Bergedorf: W. Germany 45 Q2
BERGEN: Hordaland, Norway 47 J6
Bergen: (NW. of Celle), Lower Saxony, W. Germany 45 P3
Bergen: (ESE. of Ulzen), Lower Saxony, W. Germany 45 Q3
Bergen: Rügen I., E. Germany 45 T1
Bergen aan Zee: Netherlands 44 K3
Bergen-op Zoom: Neth. 44 K4
Bergerac: France 37 F11
Bergfors: Sweden 46 Q2
Bergheim: W. Germany 44 M5
Bergholt, East: Suffolk, Eng. 25 Y16
Bergholt, West: Essex, Eng. 25 X16
Bergisch Gladbach: W. Germany 44 N4
Bergkvara: Sweden 47 P8
Bergsfjord: Norway 46 R1
Bergtheim: W. Germany 45 Q6
Berguent: Morocco 80 L8
Bergvik: Sweden 47 P6
Bergville: & Dist., Natal, S. Africa 75 H4
Bergzabern: W. Germany 44 O6
Berhala Str.: Sumatra 65 C7
Berhampore: W. Bengal, India 59 P10
Berhampur: Orissa, India 59 O11
Berikul'skiy: U.S.S.R. 51 P3
Bering Str.: & sea, U.S.S.R./U.S.A. 84 b5
Beringen: Belgium 44 L4
Berja: Spain 35 E18
Berka: E. Germany 45 Q5
Berkåk: Norway 46 M5
Berkane: Morocco 35 E19
Berkeley: Calif., U.S.A. 93 C5
Berkeley: & val., Glos., Eng. 24 R16
Berkeley, Cape: N.W.T., Canada 84 J3
Berkhamsted: Herts., Eng. 25 U16
Berkhamsted, Little: Herts., England 25 V16
Berkner Island: Antarctica 9 80S 55W
Berkovitsa: Bulgaria 39 S15
Berkshire: Co., England (co. town Reading) 25 T17
Berkshire Downs: hills, Oxfordshire/Berkshire, England 25 T16
Berlevåg: Norway 46 V1
Berlin: see East Berlin and West Berlin
Berlin: N.H., U.S.A. 89 Q3
Berlin: S. Africa 75 G6
Berlin: Wis., U.S.A. 88 G4
Bermejillo: Mexico 93 G7
Bermejo: & riv., Argentina 96 B3
Bermejo: Bolivia 95 E8
Bermejo: riv., Argentina 96 D2
Bermejo (old course): riv., Argentina 96 C1
Bermeo: Spain 35 E15
Bermillo de Sayago: Spain 35 C16

Bermuda: self-governing Colony of U.K., 87 Ins.
Cap.: Hamilton
Area: 20.6 sq. miles (53.3 sq. km.)
Pop.: 54,000 (1971 E)

Bermuda Rise: N. Atlantic Ocean 8 30N 65W
Bern: Canton, Switz. (cap. Bern) 40 N9
BERN (Berne): Switzerland 40 N9
Bernalillo: N. Mex., U.S.A. 93 F5
Bernam: riv., Malaya, Malaysia 65 b12
Bernardino: riv., Panama 94 Ins.
Bernardo de Irigoyen: Argentina 96 E2

Bernasconi: Argentina 96 C4
Bernaville: France 36 H5
Bernay: France 36 F6
Bernburg: E. Germany 45 R4
Bernera, Great: i., Outer Hebr., Scotland 28 G8
Bernera: i., Outer Hebr., Scotland 28 H3
Berneray: i., Outer Hebr., Scotland 28 G4
Berneray: i., Outer Hebr., Scotland 29 G6
Bernese Alps: Switzerland 40 N9
Bernicia: kingdom of Saxon England in Northumb. 22 E9
Bernie: Mo., U.S.A. 88 G7
Bernier I.: W. Australia 68 A4
Bernina: mtn., Switzerland 40 P9
Bernina Pass: Switzerland 40 Q9
Bernisdale: Inner Hebr., Scotland 28 J5
Bernkastel: W. Germany 44 N6
Bernsdorf: E. Germany 45 T4
Bernstadt: E. Germany 45 U4
Beroroha: Malagasy Rep. 73 O14
Beroubouaye: Benin 81 F2
Beroun: Czechoslovakia 45 U6
Berounka: riv., Czech. 45 T6
Berre: France 37 L12
Berre, Étang de: lag., France 37 L12
Ber Rechid: Morocco 80 K8
Berri: S. Australia 71 D10
Berridale: N.S.W., Australia 71 H11
Berriedale: High., Scotland 28 P3
Berriew: Powys, Wales 27 P14
Berrigan: N.S.W., Australia 71 F10
Berriwillock: Vict., Austl. 71 E10
Berrouaghia: Algeria 35 H18
Berry: N.S.W., Australia 71 J10
Berry: Prov., France 34 H13
Berry Canal: France 37 H9
Berry Head: cape, Devon, England 24 P19
Berry Is.: Bahamas 91 N13
Barrynarbor: Devon, Eng. 24 N17
Berryville: Ark., U.S.A. 90 E7
Berryville: Va., U.S.A. 89 N6
Berseba: SW. Africa 74 B2
Bertam: Malaya, Malaysia 65 c11
Berthierville: Que., Canada 89 P2
BERTOUA: Est., Cameroun 81 G4
Bertraghboy Bay: Galway, Repub. of Ireland 31 B13
Bertrandville: La., U.S.A. 90 Ins.
Bertrix: Belgium 44 L6
Beru: i., Gilbert Is. 67 P2
Berville: France 36 F6
Berwick: La., U.S.A. 90 F11
Berwick, North: Lothian, Scotland 29 O7
Berwick: Pa., U.S.A. 89 N5
Berwick upon Tweed: Northumb., England 26 S8
Berwyn: Ill., U.S.A. 88 H5
Berwyn Mtns.: Gwynedd/Clwyd, Wales 27 P14
Berytus: Phoenician and Roman city at Beirut, Lebanon 56 D5
Bès: riv., France 37 J11
Besalampy: Malagasy Rep. 73 N13
Besbes: Algeria 38 K18
BESANÇON: Doubs, France 40 M8
Besar: i., Indonesia 80 A1
Besar: riv., France 37 J9
Beshahr: Iran 55 H7
Beshkent: Uzbek., U.S.S.R. 51 L7
Besikama: Timor, Indonesia 65 G8
Beşiri: Turkey 57 G3
Beskéré: Chad 79 J6
Beskids, East: mtns., Czech./Poland 43 R12
Beskids, West: mtns., Czech./Poland 43 Q12
Besni: Turkey 56 E3
Bessan: France 37 J12
Bessarabia: geog. reg., Moldavia, U.S.S.R. 43 U13
Bessarabka: Moldavia, U.S.S.R. 39 V13
Bessarabskiy: Kazakh., U.S.S.R. 50 J5
Besse: France 36 F8
Bessebrook: Armagh, N. Irel. 30 J11
Bessèges: France 37 K11
Bessemer: Ala., U.S.A. 91 H9
Bessemer: Mich., U.S.A. 88 F2
Bessines: France 37 G9
Besthorpe: Notts., England 27 U13
Betanzos: Spain 35 B15
Betaré Oya: Cameroun 81 G3
Betchworth: Surrey, Eng. 25 V17
Beth: riv., Morocco 80 K8
Bethal: & Dist., Trans., S. Africa 75 H3
Bethanie: O.F.S., S. Africa 75 F4
Bethanie: & Dist., SW. Afr. 74 B3
Bethany: Okla., U.S.A. 90 C8
Bethany: O.F.S., S. Africa 75 F4
Bethel: Alaska, U.S.A. 84 c5
Bethel: city of ancient Israel in hills about 11 miles N. of Jerusalem 55 b3
Bethesda: Gwynedd, Wales 27 N13
Bethesda Road: S. Africa 75 F5
Bethlehem: Jordan 55 b3
Bethlehem: & Dist., O.F.S., S. Africa 75 H4
Bethlehem: Pa., U.S.A. 89 O5
Bethsaida Julias: Herodian city on N. end of Lake Tiberias 55 b2
Beth-shan: city of ancient Israel (later Scythopolis) near Beisan, Israel 55 b2
Beth-shemesh: city of ancient Israel about 18 miles W. by S. of Jerusalem, Israel 55 a3
Bethulie: & Dist., O.F.S., S. Africa 75 F5
Béthune: France 36 H5
Betioky: Malagasy Rep. 73 N14
Betong: Sarawak, Malaysia 65 E6
Betong: Thailand 65 b11
Betoota: Queens., Australia 69 G5
Bet-pak-dala Steppe: plain, Kazakh., U.S.S.R. 51 M5
Betrieb: SW. Africa 74 A3
Betroka: Malagasy Rep. 73 O14
Betsiamites: Que., Canada 89 R1
Bettles: Alaska, U.S.A. 84 d4
Bettola: Italy 40 P11
Bettws-y-coed: Gwynedd, Wales 27 O13
Bettyhill: Highland, Scotland 28 N2
Bettystown: Meath, Repub. of Ireland 30 J12
Betul: Madhya Pradesh, India 58 N10
Betwa: riv., India 59 N9
Betzdorf: W. Germany 44 N5
Beulah: Vict., Australia 71 E10
Beuvron: riv., France 36 G8
Beuzec: France 36 A7
Beveland, North & South: is., Netherlands 44 J4
Bevensen: W. Germany 45 Q2
Beverley: W. Australia 68 B6
Beverley: Alta., Canada 92 E2

Beverly: Humberside, England 27 V12
Beverly: Mass., U.S.A. 89 Q4
Beverwijk: Netherlands 44 K3
Bewcastle: Cumbria, England 26 Q9
Bewdley: Hereford & Worcester, England 24 R15
Bexhill: E. Sussex, England 25 W18
Bexley: Gt. Ldn., Eng. 25 W17
Beya: U.S.S.R. 51 Q4
Beyazit: Turkey 57 J2
Beyçayiri: Turkey (Dardanelles. Inset) 20 Ins.
Beykoz: Turkey (Bosphorus. Inset) 20 Ins.
BEYLA: & Reg., Guinea 80 C3
Beylan: Turkey 56 E3
Beylerbey: Turkey (Bosporus. Inset) 20 Ins.
Bey Mtns.: Turkey 56 B3
Beypazari: Turkey 57 H6
Beyşehir: & lake, Turkey 56 B3
Beytüşebap: Turkey 57 H3
Bezdan: Yugoslavia 39 Q14
Bezdružice: Czechoslovakia 45 S6
Bezerros: Brazil 94 K5
Bezhetsk: U.S.S.R. 50 D3
Bezhitsa: U.S.S.R. 50 D4
Béziers: France 37 J12
Bezwada: see Vijayawada 58 O11
Bhachau: Gujarat, India 58 M10
Bhagalpur: Bihar, India 59 P9
Bhamo: Burma 59 R10
Bhamragarh: Madhya Pradesh, India 58 O11
Bhandara: Maharashtra, India 58 N10
Bhanpura: Madhya Pradesh, India 58 N10
Bharatpur: Rajasthan, India 58 N9
Bharuch (Broach): Gujarat, India 58 M10
Bharatpur: Madhya Pradesh, India 58 O10
Bhatgaon: Nepal 52 P9
Bhatinda: Punjab, India 58 N8
Bhatkal: Karnataka, India 58 M12
Bhaunagar: Gujarat, India 58 M10
Bhawanipatna: Orissa, India 59 O11
Bhilwara: Rajasthan, India 58 M9
Bhima: riv., India 58 N11
Bhind: Madhya Pradesh, India 58 N9
Bhir: Maharashtra, India 58 N11
Bhiwani: Haryana, India 58 N9
BHOPAL: Mad. Prad., Ind. 58 N10
Bhubaneswar: Orissa, India 59 P10
Bhuj: Gujarat, India 58 L10
Bhusawal: Maharashtra, India 58 N10

Bhutan: Kingdom, 59 Q9
Cap.: Thimphu
Admin. cap.: Paro
Area: 19,305 sq. miles (50,000 sq. km.)
Pop.: 854,000 (1971 E)

Bia: riv., Ghana 80 D3
Bia Mtns.: Zaire 77 C4
Biafra, Bight of: see Bonny, Bight of
Biak: Mauritania 80 A1
Biak: i., Schouten Is., West Irian, Indonesia 61 M12
Biakundi: Ethiopia 54 E12
Biafa: Poland 43 Q12
Biafogard: Poland 45 V1
Biafowieza: Poland 43 S10
BIAŁYSTOK: & Prov., Poland 43 S10
Biancavilla: Italy 40 O10
Biandrate: Italy 40 O10
Biaora: Madhya Pradesh, India 58 N10
Biaro: i., Sangihe Is. Indon. 65 H6
Biarritz: France 37 D12
Bias: France 37 D11
Biasca: Switzerland 40 O9
Bibanga: Zaire 76 B4
Bibb City: Ga., U.S.A. 91 J9
Bibbiena: Italy 41 R12
Biberach: W. Germany 40 P7
Bibert: W. Germany 45 Q6
Bibești: Romania 39 S14
Bibracte: Roman name of Gallic fort at Mt. Beuvray 12 miles W. of Autun, Fr. 36 K9
Bibury: Glos., England 25 S16
Bicaz: Romania 43 U13
Bicester: Oxon., England 25 T16
Bicker: Lincs., England 27 V14
Bickleigh: Devon, England 25 V17
Bicknell: Ind., U.S.A. 88 H6
Biciske: Hungary 43 Q13
Bida: Nigeria 81 F3
Bidache: France 37 D12
Bidanaga: Sudan 76 C1
Bidar: Karnataka, India 58 N11
Biddeford: Maine, U.S.A. 89 Q4
Biddulph: Staffs., England 27 R13
Bidean Nam Bian: mtn., Highland, Scotland 29 L6
Bideford: Devon, England 24 N17
Bideford (Barnstaple) Bay: Devon, England 24 N17
Bidford: War., England 25 S15
Bidi: well, Sudan 54 C11
Bido: Equatorial Guinea 81 G4
Bié: Prov., Angola (cap. Silva Porto) 77 A5
Bié Plateau: Angola 73 H12
Bieber: W. Germany 44 O5
Biebrza: riv., Poland 43 S10
Biedenkopf: W. Germany 44 O5
Biel: & lake, Switzerland 40 N8
Bielefeld: W. Germany 44 O3
Biella: Italy 40 O10
Bielsko Biała: Poland 43 Q12
Bielsk Podlaski: Poland 43 S10
Bien Hoa: Vietnam 64 D4
Bienne, Lake: Que., Can. 85 m6
Bierbank: Queens., Austl. 70 F6
Bière: Switzerland 40 M9
Bierley, East: W. Yorks., Eng. 27 S12
Bierné: France 36 E8
Biesenthal: E. Germany 45 T3
Biesiespoort: S. Africa 74 E5
Bietigheim: W. Germany 40 P7
Bietterans: France 40 L9
Bièvres: France 36 H7
Biga: Turkey 39 U16
Bigadic: Turkey 39 V17
Big Bay: city, Mich., U.S.A. 88 H2
Big Bell: W. Australia 68 B5
Big Belt Mtns.: Mont., U.S.A. 92 E3
Big Bend Nat. Park: Tex., U.S.A. 93 G7
Big Black: riv., Miss., U.S.A. 90 G9
Big Cypress Swamp: Fla., U.S.A. 91 L12
Big Delta: Alaska, U.S.A. 84 E5
Big Eau Pleine Reservoir: Wis., U.S.A. 88 F3
Big Falls: city, Minn., U.S.A. 88 E1
Bigfork: Minn., U.S.A. 88 E2

Big Fork: riv., Minn., U.S.A. 88 E1
Bigga: N.S.W., Australia 71 H10
Biggar: Strath., Scotland 29 O8
Biggar: Sask., Canada 92 F2
Biggeluobal: Norway 46 S2
Biggenden: Queens., Austl. 70 K5
Biggleswade: Beds., England 25 V15
Big Horn: riv., U.S.A. 92 F3
Bighorn Mtns.: Wyo., U.S.A. 92 F4
Big Koniuji: i., Alaska, U.S.A. 84 D6
Bignona: Senegal 80 A2
Big Rapids: Mich., U.S.A. 88 J4
Big River: town, Sask., Can. 92 F2
Big Sable Point: cape, Mich., U.S.A. 88 H3
Big Sioux: riv., Iowa/S. Dak., U.S.A. 92 H4
Big Smoky Valley: Nev., U.S.A. 93 D5
Big Snowy Mount: Mont., U.S.A. 92 F3
Big Spring: Tex., U.S.A. 93 G6
Big Stone Gap: Va., U.S.A. 88 K3
Bigtimber: Mont., U.S.A. 92 F3
Big Trout Lake: Ont., Can. 92 K2
Big Valley: Alta., Canada 92 E2
Big Wood Cay: is., Bahamas 91 N13
Bihać: Yugoslavia 41 V11
Bihar: & State, India (cap. of State Patna) 59 P9
Biharamulo: Tanzania 76 D3
Bihen: Somalia 79 R18
Bihen: waterhole, Somalia 79 R17
Bihor Mtns.: Romania 43 S13
Bijapur: Karnataka, India 58 N11
Bijar: Iran 57 K4
Bijauri: Nepal 58 O9
Bijawar: Madhya Pradesh, India 58 N10
Bijeljina: Yugoslavia 39 Q14
Bijelo Polje: Yugoslavia 39 Q15
Bijistan: Iran 55 J8
Bijni: Assam, India 59 Q9
Bijnor: Uttar Pradesh, India 58 W9
Bikaner: Rajasthan, India 58 M9
Bikié: Congo 81 G5
Bikin: riv., U.S.S.R. 63 Y5
Bikita: Rhodesia 77 D7
Bilanga: Upper Volta 80 D2
Bilaspur: Madhya Pradesh, India 58 O10
Bilatu: Celebes 65 G6
Bilauk Taung Range: Burma/Thailand 59 R12
BILBAO: Vizcaya, Spain 35 E15
Bilbeis: Egypt 56 B6
Bilbilis: Roman town at Calatayud, Spain 35 F16
Bilboa: Carlow, Repub. of Ireland 31 G14
Bildeston: Suff., England 25 X15
Bile Karpaty: mtns., Czech. 43 P12
Bilen: springs, Ethiopia 78 N8
Bilgas: Egypt 56 B6
Bilgoraj: Poland 43 S11
Bili: Zaire 76 C2
Bili: riv., Zaire 76 B2
Bilimba: U.S.S.R. 50 J3
Bilin: Burma 59 R11
Bilir: U.S.S.R. 49 P4
Bilisht: Albania 39 R16
Billericay: Essex, England 25 W16
Billeroy: N.S.W., Australia 71 H8
Billesdon: Leics., England 27 U14
Billiatt Wildlife Reserve: S. Australia 71 D10
Billinge: Gt. Man., England 27 Q12
Billingborough: Lincs., Eng. 27 V14
Billingham: Cleve., Eng. 26 T10
Billinghay: Lincs., England 27 V13
Billings: Mont., U.S.A. 92 F3
Billingshurst: W. Sussex, Eng. 25 V17
Billiton: see Belitung
Billom Olliergues: France 37 J10
Billy: Antrim, N. Ireland 30 J9
Bilma: Niger 78 G6
Biloela: Queens., Australia 70 J5
Biloxi: Miss., U.S.A. 90 G10
Bilpamorea Saltpan: Queens., Australia 69 G5
Bilqas: Egypt 56 B6
Bilsen: Belgium 44 L5
Bilston: W. Mid., England 27 R14
Bilta: Norway 46 R2
BILTINE: & Pref., Chad 79 J7
Bilton: War., England 25 T15
Biltukau Range: Thailand 64 B4
Bimberèke: Benin 81 E2
Bimberi, Mount: N.S.W., Australia 71 H10
Bimbila: Ghana 80 E3
Bimbo: Ombella-M'Poko, Cen. Afr. Rep. 76 A2
Bimini Is.: Bahamas 91 M13
Bimlipatam: Andhra Pradesh, India 59 O11
Bina: Madhya Pradesh, India 58 N10
Binalong: N.S.W., Australia 71 H10
Binatang: Sarawak, Malaysia 65 E6
Binbrook: Lincs., England 27 V13
Binche: Belgium 44 K5
Binchester: see Vinovium
Binda: N.S.W., Australia 71 H10
Binder: Chad 81 G3
Bindle: Queens., Australia 70 H6
Bindura: Rhodesia 77 D6
Binefar: Spain 35 G16
Binegar: Som., England 24 Q17
Binfield: Berks., England 25 U17
Bingara: N.S.W., Australia 71 J8
Bingen: W. Germany 44 N6
Bingerville: Ivory Coast 80 D3
Bingham: Maine, U.S.A. 89 R3
Bingham: Notts., England 27 U14
Bingham Canyon: city, Utah, U.S.A. 93 E4
Binghamstown (An Geata Mo'r): Mayo, Repub. of Ireland 30 A11
Binghamton: N.Y., U.S.A. 89 O4
Bingi: Zaire 76 C3
Bingley: W. Yorks., England 27 S12
BINGÖL (Çapakçur): & Prov., & mtns., Bingöl, Turkey 57 G2
Bingsjö: Sweden 47 O6
Binham: Norf., England 25 X14
Binjai: Sumatra 65 B6
Binnaway: N.S.W., Australia 71 H8
Binnein Mor: mtn., Highland, Scotland 29 M6
Binongko: i., Tukangbesi Is., Indonesia 65 G8
Bint: Iran 55 J9
Bintang: i., Riouw Arch., Indonesia 65 d13
Bintauna: Celebes 65 G6
Bintree: Norf., England 25 X14
Bintuhan: Sumatra 65 C7
Bintulu: Sarawak, Malaysia 65 E6
Binz: Rügen, E. Germany 45 T1
BINZERT (Bizerta) & Governorate, Tunisia 38 L18

Bio-Bio: riv., Chile 96 A4
Biograd: Yugoslavia 41 V12
Biot, Le: France 40 M9
Bippen: W. Germany 44 N3
Bir, Cape: Djibouti 79 Q17
Bira: Celebes 65 G8
Bira: U.S.S.R. 63 Y5
Bir 'Ali: Yemen P.D.R. 55 G12
BIRAO: Vakaga, Cen. Afr. Rep. 79 J7
Biratnagar: Nepal 59 P9
Bir Bala: Iran 55 J9
Bircham, Great: Norf., Eng. 25 X14
Birchington: Kent, England 25 Y17
Birchip: Vict., Australia 71 E10
Birch Mtns.: Alta., Canada 92 E1
Bir Derua: W. Sahara 78 B4
Bir Dibis: Egypt 54 C10
Bird I.: Australia 69 K4
Bird I. (Aves): (Ven.), Leeward Is. 87 b3
Birdoswald: Cumbria, England 26 Q10
Bird Rocks: i., Magdalen Is., Canada 89 V2
Birdsville: Queens., Austl. 69 F5
Birdum: N. Territ., Austl. 68 E3
Birdwood: S. Australia 71 C10
Birecik: Turkey 56 E3
Bir el Duweidar: well, Egypt (Suez Canal. Inset) 32 Ins.
Bir el Ksaib: Mali 78 C5
Bir en Natrun: well, Sudan 54 C11
Bireuen: Sumatra 65 B5
Bir Fadhil: well, Sau. Arab. 55 G10
Birganj: Bihar, India 59 O9
Birgi: Turkey 39 V17
Bir Guenduz: W. Sahara 78 A5
Bir Habbas: W. Sahara 78 B4
Bir Hakeim: well, Libya 32 G5
Bir Hibeita: well, Egypt (Suez Canal. Inset) 32 Ins.
Bir Hooker: Egypt 56 B6
Bir Igueni: Mauritania 78 B5
Bir Jafnan: well, Saudi Arabia 55 H11
Birjand: Iran 55 J8
Birk: Saudi Arabia 54 F11
Birka: Saudi Arabia 54 F10
Birkat Hamad: well, Saudi Arabia/Iraq 57 H6
Birkat 'Ashshar: Sau. Arab. 54 F9
Birkelane: Senegal 80 A2
Birkenfeld: W. Germany 44 N6
Birkenhead: Mers., England 27 P12
Birkfeld: Austria 41 V3
Birkirkara: Malta 32 Ins.
Bir Mahadat: well, Egypt (Suez Canal. Inset) 32 Ins.
Bir Milani: Sudan 54 C11
Birmingham: Ala., U.S.A. 91 H9
Birmingham: W. Mid., Eng. 25 S15
Bir Misâha: well, Egypt 54 C10
Birmitrapur: Orissa, India 59 O10
Bir Muhafir: well, Syria 56 F4
Bir Nagid: well, Egypt (Suez Canal. Inset) 32 Ins.
Bir Nakheila: well, Egypt 54 D10
Birnam: Tayside, Scotland 29 O6
Bir Natrun: Sudan 54 C11
Birni: Dahomey 81 E2
Birnin Gwari: Nigeria 81 F2
Birnin Kebbi: Nigeria 81 E2
Birnin n'Konni: Niger 81 F2
Birniwa: Nigeria 81 G2
BIROBIDZHAN: Jewish Auton. Reg., U.S.S.R. 63 Y5
Birogou Mtns.: Gabon 81 G5
Bir Oum Greine: Mauritania 78 B4
Bir Ounane: Mali 78 D5
Birr (Parsonstown): Offaly, Repub. of Ireland 31 F13
Bir-Rabalou: Algeria 35 H18
Birregurra: Vict., Australia 71 E12
Birrie: riv., N.S.W., Austl. 71 G7
Bir Rouin: W. Sahara 78 B4
Birs: riv., Switzerland 40 N8
Birsay: Mainland, Orkney Is. 28 Ins.
Birsk: U.S.S.R. 50 J3
Birstall: Leics., England 27 T14
Birstall: W. Yorks., England 27 S12
Bir Terfawi: well, Egypt 54 C10
Birthday: Trans., S. Africa 75 J1
Birtley: Northumb., England 26 R9
Birtley: Tyne and Wear, England 26 S10
Birur: Karnataka, India 58 N12
Birzebbugia: Malta 32 Ins.
Birzhai: Lithuania, U.S.S.R. 47 T8
Bir Zreigat: Mauritania 78 C5
Bisalpur: Uttar Pradesh, India 58 N9
Bisbal, La: Spain 35 H16
Bisbee: Ariz., U.S.A. 93 F6
Biscarosse: France 37 D11
Biscarosse et de Parentis, Étang de: lag., France 37 D11
Biscarosse-Plage: France 37 D11
Biscay, Bay of: Atlantic O. 34 D14
Biscayne Bay: Fla., U.S.A. 91 L13
Bischheim: France 40 N7
Bischofsheim: W. Germany 45 Q5
Bischofshofen: Austria 41 T3
Bischofswerda: E. Germany 45 U4
Bischofszell: Switzerland 40 P8
Bischwiller: France 40 N7
Biscoe Is.: Antarctica 9 70S 70W
Biscotasing: Ont., Canada 88 K2
Bisha: wadi & geog. reg., Saudi Arabia 54 F10
Bishampton: Hereford & Worcester, England 24 R15
Bisheh: Iran 57 L5
Bishia: Ethiopia 54 E11
Bishop: Calif., U.S.A. 93 D5
Bishop Auckland: Durham, England 26 S10
Bishop Monkton: North Yorkshire, England 27 T11
Bishop's Cannings: Wilts., England 24 S17
Bishop's Castle: Salop, Eng. 24 Q15
Bishop's Caundle: Dorset, England 24 R18
Bishop's Cleeve: Glos., Eng. 24 R16
Bishops Falls: Newf., Can. 85 v2
Bishop's Lydeard: Som., England 24 P17
Bishop's Nympton: Devon, England 24 O18
Bishop's Stortford: Herts., England 25 W16
Bishop's Tachbrook: War., England 25 S15
Bishop's Tawton: Devon, England 24 N17
Bishopsteignton: Devon, England 24 O18
Bishopstoke: Hants., Eng. 25 T18
Bishopston: W. Glam., Wales 24 N16
Bishop Sutton: Avon, Eng. 24 Q17
Bishop's Waltham: Hants., England 25 T18
Bishopsworth: Avon, Eng. 24 Q17
Bishopton: Strath., Scotland 29 M8

126 Bishopville—Boreham

Bishopville: S.C., U.S.A. 91 L8
Bisitun: Iran 57 K4
Biskotasi Lake: Ont., Can. 88 L2
Biskra: Algeria 32 D5
Bisley: Surrey, England 25 U17
Bismarck: Mo., U.S.A. 88 F7
BISMARCK: N. Dak., U.S.A. 92 G3
Bismarck, Cape: Greenland 85 S2
Bismarck Arch.: Papua/New Guinea 67 K2
Bismark: E. Germany 45 R3
Bismil: Turkey 57 G3
Bison: S. Dak., U.S.A. 92 G3
Bissagos Arch.: Guinea-Bissau 80 A2
BISSAU: Guinea-Bissau 80 A2
Bissendorf: W. Germany 45 P3
Bissikrima: Guinea 80 B2
Bissoram: Guinea-Bissau 80 A2
Bistrica: (*E. of Trieste*), Yugo. 41 U10
Bistrica: (*W. of Kranj*), Yugo. 41 T9
Bistriţa: Romania 43 T13
Bistriţa: *riv.*, Romania 43 U13
Bitam: Gabon 81 G4
Bitburg: W. Germany 44 M6
Bitche: France 44 N6
Bithynia: ancient name of district of NW. Asiatic Turkey, extending E. to about Ereğli on Black Sea and S. to include middle valley of Sakarya 56 B1
Bitki: U.S.S.R. 51 O4
BITLIS: *& Prov.*, Turkey 57 H2
Bitola (Monastir): Yugo. 39 R16
Bitov: Czechoslovakia 45 V7
Bittadon: Devon, England 24 N17
Bitterfeld: E. Germany 45 S4
Bitterfontein: S. Africa 74 C5
Bitter Lake, Great: Egypt (Suez Canal. *Inset*) 32 *Ins.*
Bitter Lake, Little: Egypt (Suez Canal. *Inset*) 32 *Ins.*
Bitterroot Range: Idaho/Mont., U.S.A. 92 E3
Bittou: Upper Volta 80 D2
Bituriges: Gallic tribe with centre at Bourges, France 36 H8
Biu: Nigeria 81 G2
Biumba: Rwanda 76 D3
Biwa, Lake: Japan 63 e3
Biya: *riv.*, U.S.S.R. 51 P4
Biyadh: *plain*, Saudi Arabia 54 G10
Biyar Tuba: Jordan 56 E6
Biysk: U.S.S.R. 51 P4
Bizana: S. Africa 75 H5
Bize: France 37 H12
Bizerta: *see* Binzert.
Bjärka: Sweden 47 O7
Bjela Lasica: *mtn.*, Yugo. 41 U10
Bjellånes: Norway 46 O3
Bjelovar: Yugoslavia 38 P14
Björbo: Sweden 47 O6
Björkfors: Sweden 46 O4
Björkö: *i.*, Sweden 47 Q7
Björksele: Sweden 46 Q4
Bjørna Fiord: Norway 47 J6
Björneborg (Pori): Finland 47 R6
Bjugn: Norway 46 L5
Bjurholm: Sweden 46 Q5
Bjurträsk: Sweden 46 Q4
Bla: Mali 80 C2
Blaavands Huk: *cape*, Den. 47 K9
Bla Bheinn: *mtn.*, Inner Hebr., Scotland 28 J5
Blaby: Leics., England 27 T14
Blachère, La: France 37 K11
Black: *riv.*, Mo./Ark., U.S.A. 90 F8
Black: *riv.*, N.Y., U.S.A. 89 O4
Black: *riv.*, Wis., U.S.A. 88 F3
Blackadder Water: *riv.*, Borders, Scotland 29 R8
Blackall: Queens., Australia 69 H4
Black Bay: La., U.S.A. 90 *Ins.*
Black Bay: Ont., Canada 88 G1
Blackburn: Gram., Scotland 28 R5
Blackburn: Lancs., England 27 R12
Blackburn: Lothian, Scot. 29 O8
Blackburn Mtn.: Alaska, U.S.A. 84 e5
Blackbushe: *airfield*, Hants., England 25 U17
Black Butte: *mtn.*, N. Dak., U.S.A. 92 G3
Black Combe: *mtn.*, Cumbria, England 26 P11
Blackdown Hills: Devon/Som., England 24 P18
Blackduck: Minn., U.S.A. 88 D2
Black Eagle: Mont., U.S.A. 92 E3
Blackfoot: Idaho, U.S.A. 92 E4
Blackford: Tay., Scotland 29 O7
Black Forest: *mtns.*, W. Germany 40 O7
Black Head: *cape*, Clare, Repub. of Ireland 31 C13
Blackhill: Durham, England 26 S10
Blackhill: S. Africa 75 G6
Black Hills: *mtns.*, S. Dak., U.S.A. 92 G4
Black Isle: *penin.*, Highland, Scotland 28 N4
Black Lake: La., U.S.A. 90 E10
Black Lake: N.Y., U.S.A. 89 O3
Black Lake: *city*, Que., Can. 89 Q2
Blacklunans: Tay., Scot. 29 P6
Black Mesa: *mtn.*, U.S.A. 93 G5
Blackmoor: Corn., England 24 M19
Black Mtns.: Ariz., U.S.A. 93 E5
Black Mtns.: Powys, Wales 24 P16
Blackpool: Lancs., England 27 P12
Blackridge: Lothian, Scot. 29 O8
Black River: *town*, Jamaica 86 *Ins.*
Black River Falls: *city*, Wis., U.S.A. 88 F3
Blackrock: Cork, Repub. of Ireland 31 E16
Blackrock: Dublin, Repub. of Ireland 31 J13
Black Rock: S. Australia 71 C9
Blackrock: *hill*, Lim./Cork, Repub. of Ireland 31 D15
Black Rock Desert: Nev., U.S.A. 92 D4
Black Sea: Europe 50 D6
Blackshear: Ga., U.S.A. 91 K10
Blacksod Bay: Mayo, Repub. of Ireland 30 A11
Blackstairs: *mtns.*, Carlow/Wex., Repub. of Ireland 31 H14
Blackstone: Va., U.S.A. 89 N7
Black Sugarloaf: *mtn.*, N.S.W., Australia 71 J8
Black Umfolozi: *riv.*, Natal, S. Africa 75 J4
Blackville: N.S.W., Austl. 71 J8
Blackville: S.C., U.S.A. 91 L9
Black Volta: *riv.*, Upper Volta 80 D2
Black Warrior: *riv.*, Ala., U.S.A. 91 H9
Blackwater: Queens., Austl. 70 H4
Blackwater: Wex., Repub. of Ireland 31 J15
Blackwater: *riv.*, Cork/Wat., Repub. of Ireland 31 E15
Blackwater: *riv.*, Essex, Eng. 25 X16
Blackwater: *riv.*, Meath/Cavan, Repub. of Ireland 30 H12
Blackwater Coalmine: Queens., Australia 70 H4
Blackwater Reservoir: Highland, Scotland 29 M6
Blackwell: Okla., U.S.A. 90 C2
Blackwood: Strath., Scot. 29 O8
Blackwood: Gwent, Wales 24 P16
Blackwood: *riv.*, W. Austl. 68 B6
Blackwoods: S. Africa 74 E6
Bladgrond: S. Africa 74 C4
Blaenau Ffestiniog: Gwynedd, Wales 27 O14
Blaenau Morgannwg: *mtns.*, West/Mid Glam., Wales 24 O16
Blaenavon: Gwent, Wales 24 P16
Blaergwrach: W. Glam., Wales 24 O16
Blagdon: Avon, England 24 Q17
Blagodarnoye: U.S.S.R. 50 F5
Blagodatnoye: Kazakh., U.S.S.R. 51 M4
Blagoevgrad: Bulg. 39 S15
Blagoslovennoye: U.S.S.R. 63 Y5
Blagoveshchenka: U.S.S.R. 51 N4
Blagoveshchensk: U.S.S.R. 49 o7
Blaina: Gwent, Wales 24 P16
Blair, Mount: Tay., Scot. 29 P6
Blair Athol: Queens., Austl. 70 G4
Blair Atholl: Belize 86 *Ins.*
Blair Atholl: Tay., Scot. 29 O6
Blairgowrie: Tay., Scot. 29 P6
Blairmore: Alta., Canada 92 E3
Blaj: Romania 43 S13
Blakeley: Ga., U.S.A. 91 J10
Blake Point: *cape*, Mich., U.S.A. 88 G1
Blakeney: Glos., England 24 R16
Blakeney: Norf., England 25 Y14
Blakesley: Northants., Eng. 25 T15
Blama: Sierra Leone 80 B3
Blâmont: France 40 M7
Blanc, Cape: Mauritania 78 A5
Blanc, Cape: Tunisia 38 L18
Blanc, Le: France 37 G9
Blanc, Mont: *mtn.*, France 40 M10
Blanca, Sierra: *mtn.*, N. Mex., U.S.A. 93 F6
Blanca Peak: Colo., U.S.A. 93 F5
Blanchetown: S. Australia 71 C10
Blanchland: Northumb., Eng. 26 R10
Blanco: *riv.*, Argentina 96 B2
Blanco, Cape: Balearic Is. 35 H17
Blanco, Cape: Oreg., U.S.A. 92 C4
Blancos, Los: Paraguay 96 C1
Blanc Sablon: Que., Canada 85 u1
Bland: *riv.*, N.S.W., Austl. 71 G10
Blandford Forum: Dorset, England 24 R18
Blanding: Utah, U.S.A. 93 F5
Blanes: Spain 35 H16
Blangkejeren: Sumatra 65 B6
Blangpidie: Sumatra 65 B6
Blangy: France 36 G6
Blânice: *riv.*, Czechoslovakia 45 U6
Blankenberge: Belgium 44 J4
Blankenburg: Magdeburg, E. Germany 45 Q4
Blankenburg: Gera, E. Germany 45 R5
Blanquefort: France 37 E11
Blanquilla: *i.*, Venezuela 94 E1
Blanquillo: Uruguay 96 D3
Blansko: Czechoslovakia 43 P12
Blantyre: Malawi 77 E6
Blantyre: Strath., Scotland 29 N8
Blarney: Cork, Repub. of Ireland 31 D16
Blasket, Great: *i.*, Repub. of Ireland 31 A15
Błaszki: Poland 43 Q11
Blatná: Czechoslovakia 45 T6
Blatnitsa: Bulgaria 39 V15
Blatno: Czechoslovakia 45 T5
Blatobulgium: Roman fort at *Birrens*, 1½ miles ENE. of Ecclefechan, Dumfries & Galloway, Scotland 29 P9
Blaubeuren: W. Germany 40 P7
Blavet Canal: France 36 C8
Blaydon: Tyne & Wear, Eng. 26 S10
Blaye: France 37 E10
Blayney: N.S.W., Australia 71 H9
Bled: Yugoslavia 41 U9
Bleicherode: E. Germany 45 Q4
Blekinge: *Co.*, Sweden (*cap.* Karlskrona) 47 O8
Blencarn: Cumbria, England 26 Q10
Blencogo: Cumbria, England 26 P10
Bléneau: France 36 H8
BLENHEIM: Marlborough, South I., New Zealand 70 P15
Blenheim: battlefield on river Danube about 4 miles above Hochstädt, W. Germany 40 Q7
Blennerville: Kerry, Repub. of Ireland 31 B15
Bléré: France 36 G8
Blesbok: *riv.*, Trans., S. Afr. 74 *NIns.*
Blessington: Wick., Repub. of Ireland 31 H13
Bletchingley: Surrey, Eng. 25 U16
Bletchley: Bucks., England 25 V17
Blickling Hall: Norf., Eng. 25 Y14
Blida: Algeria 35 H18
Blidworth: Notts., England 27 T13
Blind Bay: La., U.S.A. 90 *Ins.*
Blind River: *city*, Ont., Can. 88 K2
Blinman: S. Australia 71 C8
Blisland: Corn., England 24 M18
Blithe: *riv.*, Staffs., England 27 S14
Blitta: Togo 80 E3
Block I.: R.I., U.S.A. 89 Q5
Blockley: Glos., England 25 S15
BLOEMFONTEIN: *& Dist.*, O.F.S., S. Africa 75 G4
Bloemhof: *& Dist.*, Trans., S. Africa 75 F3
BLOIS: Loir-et-Cher, France 36 G8
Blokzijl: Netherlands 44 L3
Blönduós: Iceland 46 c4
Błonie: Poland 43 R10
Bloody Foreland: *cape*, Don., Repub. of Ireland 30 E9
Bloomer: Wis., U.S.A. 88 F3
Bloomfield: Ind., U.S.A. 88 H6
Bloomfield: Iowa, U.S.A. 88 E5
Bloomington: Ill., U.S.A. 88 G5
Bloomington: Ind., U.S.A. 88 H6
Bloomsbury: Queens., Austl. 70 H3
Blora: Java 65 E8
Blossburg: Pa., U.S.A. 89 N5
Blosseville Coast: Greenland 85 R4
Blountstown: Fla., U.S.A. 91 J10
Blousyfer: S. Africa 74 D5
Bloxham: Oxon., England 25 T15
Bludenz: Austria 40 P8
Blue Earth: Minn., U.S.A. 88 D4
Bluefield: W. Va., U.S.A. 88 L7
Bluefields: Jamaica 86 *Ins.*
Bluefields: Nicaragua 87 I15
Blue Hill: *city*, Maine, U.S.A. 89 R3
Blue Island: *city*, Ill., U.S.A. 88 H5
Blue Mount: Ark., U.S.A. 90 D8
Blue Mtns.: N.S.W., Austl. 71 J9
Blue Mtns.: Oreg., U.S.A. 93 D3
Blue Nile: *Prov.*, Sudan (*cap.* Wad Medani) 79 L7
Blue Nile: *riv.*, Ethiopia 79 M7
Blue Ridge: *mtns.*, U.S.A. 88 L7
Blue River: B.C., Canada 92 D2
Blue Stack Mtns. (Croaghgorm Mtns.): Don., Repub. of Ireland 30 E10
Bluff: Alaska, U.S.A. 84 c5
Bluff: *& cape*, South I., N.Z. 71 M18
Bluff: Utah, U.S.A. 93 F5
Bluffton: Ind., U.S.A. 88 J5
Blumenau: Brazil 96 F2
Blumenthal: W. Germany 44 O2
Blundeston: Suff., England 25 Z14
Blunham: Beds., England 25 V15
Bluntisham: Cambs., Eng. 25 W15
Bly: Oreg., U.S.A. 92 C4
Blyde River Nature Reserve: Trans., S. Africa 75 J2
Blyth: Northumb., England 26 S9
Blyth: Notts., England 27 T13
Blyth: S. Australia 71 C9
Blyth: *riv.*, Northumb., Eng. 26 S9
Blyth: *riv.*, Suff., England 25 Z15
Blythburgh: Suff., England 25 Z15
Blythe: Calif., U.S.A. 93 E6
Blytheville: Ark., U.S.A. 88 G8
Bo: Southern, Sierra Leone 80 B3
Bø: Telemark, Norway 47 L7
Bø: Vesterålen, Norway 46 O2
Boac: Philippines 64 G4
Boali: Cen. Afr. Rep. 81 H4
Boa Nova: Brazil 94 J6
Boardmills: Down, N. Irel. 30 K11
Boarhills: Fife, Scotland 29 Q7
Boath: Highland, Scot. 28 N4
Boatman: Queens., Austl. 70 G6
Boat of Garten: High., Scot. 28 O5
Boa Vista: Cape Verde Is. 78 *Ins.*
Boa Vista: Rio Grande do Sul, Brazil 96 E3
BOA VISTA: Roraima, Brazil 94 E3
Boaz: Ala., U.S.A. 91 H8
Boaz I.: Bermuda Is. 87 *Ins.*
Bobadah: N.S.W., Australia 71 G9
Bobangui: Congo 81 H5
Bobbili: Andhra Pradesh, India 59 O11
Bobbio: Italy 40 P11
Bobcaygeon: Ont., Canada 89 M3
BOBIGNY: Seine-St. Denis, France 36 H7
Böbingen: W. Germany 41 Q7
Böblingen: W. Germany 40 P7
BOBO-DIOULASSO: Hauts Bassins, Upper Volta 80 D2
Bobolice: Poland 45 W2
Bobonong: Botswana 77 C7
Bóbr: *riv.*, Poland 45 V4
Bobrka: Ukraine 43 T12
Bobrov: U.S.S.R. 50 F4
Bobruysk: Byelorussia 50 C4
Boca, La: Panama 94 *Ins.*
Bôca do Acre: Brazil 94 D5
Bôca do Tapauá: Brazil 94 E5
Bocaranga: Cen. Afr. Rep. 81 H3
Bocas del Toro: Panama 87 I16
Bocay: Nicaragua 86 L15
Bochnia: Poland 43 R12
Bocholt: W. Germany 44 M4
Bochov: Czechoslovakia 45 T5
Bochum: W. Germany 44 N4
Bockhorn: W. Germany 44 O2
Bocking Churchstreet: Essex, England 25 X16
Böckingen: W. Germany 44 P6
Bocşa-Montanâ: Romania 39 R14
Boda: Cen. Afr. Rep. 81 H4
Böda: Öland, Sweden 47 P8
Bodalla: N.S.W., Australia 71 J11
Bodaybo: U.S.S.R. 49 N6
Boddam: Gram., Scotland 28 S5
Bodelé Depression: Chad 81 H1
Boden: Sweden 46 R4
Boden See (Lake Constance): W. Germany/Switzerland 40 P8
Boderg, Lough: Rosc./Leit., Repub. of Ireland 30 F12
Bodhan: Andhra Pradesh, India 58 N11
Bodiam: E. Sussex, England 25 X17
Bodicote: Oxon., England 26 T15
Bodioki: Zaïre 76 B2
Bodmin: Corn., England 24 M19
Bodmin Moor: Corn., Eng. 24 M18
BODØ: Nordland, Norway 46 O3
Bodotria: Roman name of river Forth, Scotland 29 N7
Bodrog: *riv.*, Hungary 43 R12
Bodrum: Turkey 39 U18
Boembé: Congo 81 H5
Boën: France 37 J10
Boende: Zaïre 76 B3
Boeotia: ancient name of district around *Thivai* (Thebes) at E. end of Sterea, Greece. 39 S17
Boeuf: *riv.*, La., U.S.A. 90 F9
BOFFA: *& Reg.*, Guinea 80 B2
Boga: Zaïre 76 C2
Bogalusa: La., U.S.A. 90 G10
Bogan: *riv.*, N.S.W., Austl. 71 G8
Bogandanga: Zaïre 79 J9
Bogande: Upper Volta 80 D2
Bogan Gate: N.S.W., Austl. 71 G9
Bogangolo: Cen. Afr. Rep. 76 A1
Bogantungan: Queens., Australia 70 G4
Boğazlıyan: Turkey 56 D2
Bogbonga: Zaïre 76 A2
Bogdanov: Byelorussia 43 U9
Bogdarin: U.S.S.R. 49 N7
Bogen: W. Germany 41 S7
Bogenfels: SW. Africa 74 A3
Bogense: Funen, Denmark 47 M9
Boggabilla: N.S.W., Austl. 71 J7
Boggabri: N.S.W., Austl. 71 J8
Boggeragh Mtns.: Cork, Repub. of Ireland 31 D15
Boghadoon: Mayo, Repub. of Ireland 30 C11
Boghar Aled: *well*, Somalia 79 R17
Boghé: Mauritania 80 B1
Boghni: Algeria 35 H18
Bogia: Papua/New Guinea 66 H2
Boğlan: Turkey 57 G2
Bognor Regis: W. Sussex, Eng. 25 U18
Bogo: Philippines 64 G4
Bogogobo: Botswana 74 D3
Bogolyubovo: Kazakh., U.S.S.R. 51 L4
Bogor: Java 65 D8
Bogorodits k: U.S.S.R. 50 E4
Bogorodsk: U.S.S.R. 50 F3
BOGOTÁ: Colombia 94 C3
Bogou: Togo 80 E2
Bogra: Bangladesh 59 P10
Boguchany: U.S.S.R. 51 R3
Bohain: France 36 J6
Bohe: Ethiopia 76 E1
Bohemia: *Territ.*, Czech. 42 O12
Bohemian Forest (Böhmer Wald): *mtns.*, West Germany 45 S6
Boherboy: Cork, Repub. of Ireland 31 C15
Bohermeen: Meath, Repub. of Ireland 30 H12
Bohinj Lake: Yugoslavia 41 T9
Böhmer Wald (Bohemian Forest): *mtns.*, West Germany 45 S6
Boho: Ferm., N. Ireland 30 F11
Bohol: *i. & sea*, Philippines 64 G5
Bohotleh: Somalia 79 R18
Boiestown: N.B., Canada 89 S2
Boigu: Queens., Austl. 69 G1
Boila: Mozambique 77 E6
Bois Blanc: *i.*, Mich., U.S.A. 88 J3
Boisdale: Outer Hebr., Scot. 28 G5
BOISE: Idaho, U.S.A. 92 D4
Boise City: Okla., U.S.A. 93 G5
Boizenburg: E. Germany 45 Q2
Bojador: *cape*, W. Sahara 78 B4
Bojo: *i.*, Sumatra 65 B7
Bojuru: Brazil 96 E3
Bokanda: Ivory Coast 80 D3
Bokan Sukhai: Inner Mongolia, China 62 S6
Bokatola: Zaïre 76 A3
BOKÉ: *& Reg.*, Guinea 80 B2
Bokel: W. Germany 44 O2
Bokhara: S. Africa 74 D3
Bokhara: *riv.*, N.S.W., Austl. 71 G7
Boki: Cameroun 81 G3
Bokna Fiord: Norway 47 J7
Bokonbayevskoye: Kirgiz., U.S.S.R. 51 N6
Bokoro: Chad 81 H2
Bokote: Zaïre 76 B3
Bokpyin: Burma 59 R12
Boksburg: Trans., S. Africa 74 *NIns.*
Boksitogorsk: U.S.S.R. 50 D3
Boku: Papua/New Guinea 69 H1
Bokungu: Zaïre 76 B3
Bokwankusu: Zaïre 76 B3
Bolaang: Celebes 65 G7
Bolaiti: Zaïre 76 B3
Bolama: Guinea-Bissau 80 A2
Bolangir: Orissa, India 59 O10
Bolangum Stn.: Vict., Austl. 71 E11
Bolaños: Mexico 86 j13
Bolan Pass: Baluchistan, Pakistan 58 L9
Bolayir (Bulair): Turkey (Dardanelles. *Inset*) 20 *Ins.*
Bolbec: France 36 F6
Bolbitinon: Greek name of Rosetta arm of Nile, Egypt 56 B6
Bolchary: U.S.S.R. 51 L3
Bolderâja: Latvia, U.S.S.R. 47 T8
Bole: Ghana 80 D3
Bolekhov: Ukraine 43 S12
Bolestawiec: Poland 45 V4
BOLGATANGA: Upper, Ghana 80 D2
Bolgrad: Ukraine 50 C5
Boli: Sudan 76 C1
Boliden: Sweden 46 R4
Bolingbroke, New: Lincs., England 27 V13
Bolingbroke, Old: Lincs., England 27 W13
Bolintin Vale: Romania 39 T14
Bolivar: Argentina 96 C4
Bolivar: Colombia 94 B3
Bolivar: Mo., U.S.A. 88 E7
Bolivar: Tenn., U.S.A. 90 G8
Bolivar, Pico: *mtn.*, Ven. 94 C2

Bolivia: *Republic* 94/5 E7
Cap.: La Paz
Area: 424,162 sq. miles (1,098,580 sq. km.)
Pop.: 5,195,000 (*1972 E*)

Bolkhov: U.S.S.R. 50 E4
Bollène: France 37 K11
Bollington: Ches., England 27 R13
Bollnäs: Sweden 47 P6
Bollon: Queens., Australia 70 G7
Bolmen Lake: Sweden 47 N8
Bolney: W. Sussex, England 25 V18
Bolnisi: Georgia, U.S.S.R. 57 J1
Bolo: S. Africa 75 G6
BOLOGNA: Emilia Romana, Italy 41 R11
Bologoye: U.S.S.R. 50 D3
Bolotnoye: U.S.S.R. 51 O3
Bolotwa: S. Africa 75 H5
Bolsena, Lake: Italy 38 M15
Bolshaya Atnya: U.S.S.R. 50 G3
Bolshaya Belozerka: Ukraine 50 D5
Bolshaya Glushitsa: U.S.S.R. 50 H4
Bolshaya Khobda: *riv.*, U.S.S.R. 50 J4
Bolshaya Lepetikha: Ukraine 50 D5
Bol'sheuki: U.S.S.R. 51 M3
Bol'shevik I: Severnaya Zemla, Arctic O. 49 M2
Bolshoy Anyuy: *riv.*, U.S.S.R. 49 s4
Bol'shoy Begichev I.: U.S.S.R. 49 N3
Bolsover: Derby., England 27 T13
Bolsøy: Norway 46 K5
Bolsward: Netherlands 44 L2
Boltaña: Spain 35 G15
Boltby: N. Yorks., England 26 T11
Bolton: Gt. Man., England 27 R12
Bolton by Bowland: Lancashire, England 27 R12
Bolton le Sands: Lancs., England 26 Q11
Bolton upon Dearne: South Yorkshire, England 27 T12
BOLU: *& Prov.*, Turkey 56 B1
Bolus Head: *cape*, Kerry, Repub. of Ireland 31 A16
Bolvadin: Turkey 56 B2
Bolyuchuan: Sinkiang, China 62 Q6
Bolzano: Italy 41 R9
Boma: Zaïre 81 G6
Bomana: Zaïre 76 A2
Bomba: *& gulf*, Libya 33 G5
Bombala: N.S.W., Australia 71 H11
Bombarral: Portugal 35 B17
BOMBAY: Maharashtra, India 58 M11
Bombay Reef: Paracel Is. 64 E3
Bombo: Uganda 76 D2
Bomboma: Zaïre 76 A2
Bom Conselho: Brazil 94 K5
Bom Jesus: Brazil 96 E2
Bom Jesus da Lapa: Brazil 94 J6
Bom Jesus do Gurgueia: Brazil 94 J5
Bømlo: *i.*, Norway 47 J7
Bomnak: U.S.S.R. 49 o7
Bomokandi: *riv.*, Zaïre 76 C2
Bomporto: Italy 41 R11
Bom Retiro: Brazil 96 F2
Bom Sucesso: Brazil 96 G1
Bomu: *riv.*, Central African Republic/Zaïre 76 B2
Bon, Cape: Tunisia 38 M18
Bonahaven: Inner Hebr., Scotland 29 J8
Bonaigarh: Orissa, India 50 O10
Bonaire: *i.*, (Neth.), Carib. Sea 94 D1
Bonalbo: N.S.W., Australia 71 K7
Bonaparte, Joseph: *Gulf*, Australia 66 E4
Bonarbridge: High., Scot. 28 N4
Bonata: Liberia 80 C3
Bonaventure: Que., Canada 89 T1
Bonaventure I.: Que., Can. 89 T1
Bonavista: *& bay*, Newf., Canada 85 w2
Bonby: Humb., England 27 V12
Bondeno: Italy 41 R11
Bondo: Zaïre 76 B2
Bondoukou: Ivory Coast 80 D3
Bondowoso: Java 65 E8
Bône: *see* Annaba.
Bone, Gulf of: Celebes 65 G7
Bonelohe: Salajar, Indon. 65 G8
Bonerate: *i.*, Indonesia 65 G8
Bo'ness: Central, Scot. 29 O7
Bonfield: Ont., Canada 89 M2
Bonfim: Brazil 94 J6
Bong: *Co.*, Liberia (*co. town* Gbanga) 80 C3
Bongandanga: Zaïre 76 B2
Bongka: Celebes 65 G7
Bongo: Gabon 81 G5
BONGOR: Mayo-Kebbi, Chad 81 H2
Bongos, Massif des: *mtns.*, Central African Republic 76 B1
Bonham: Tex., U.S.A. 90 C9
Bonhill: Strath., Scotland 29 M8
Bonifacio: Corsica 38 L16
Bonifacio, Str. of: Corsica/Sardinia 38 L16
Bonifay: Fla., U.S.A. 91 J10
Bonin Is.: (Ogasawara Arch.) (Jap.), Pacific O. 60 N6
BONN: West Germany 44 N5
Bonnat: France 37 G9
Bonndorf: W. Germany 40 O8
Bonne Bay: Newf., Canada 85 t2
Bonners Ferry: *city*, Idaho, U.S.A. 92 D3
Bonner Springs: Kans., U.S.A. 90 D6
Bonnétable: France 36 F7
Bonne Terre: Mo., U.S.A. 88 F7
Bonneval: France 36 G7
Bonneville: France 40 M9
Bonneville Dam: Wash., U.S.A. 92 C3
Bonneville Salt Flats: Utah, U.S.A. 92 E4
Bonnières: France 36 G6
Bonnie Rock: *town*, W. Australia 68 B6
Bonnievale: S. Africa 76 D6
Bonny: France 36 H8
Bonny: Nigeria 81 F4
Bonny, Bight of: Africa 81 F4
Bonnybridge: Central, Scotland 29 O7
Bonnyrigg: Lothian, Scot. 29 P8
Bonnyville: Alta., Canada 92 E2
Bono: Sardinia 38 L16
Bononia: Roman colony at Bologna, Italy 41 R11
Bonorva: Sardinia 38 L16
Bonshaw: N.S.W., Australia 71 J7
Bontang: Borneo 65 F6
Bonthain: Celebes 65 F8
Bonthe: Sierra Leone 80 B3
Bontoc: Luzon, Philippines 64 G3
Bonvouloir Is.: Papua/New Guinea 69 J2
Bonwapitse: Botswana 75 G1
Booborowie: S. Australia 71 C9
Bookaloo: S. Australia 71 B8
Bookham: Surrey, England 25 V17
Booleroo Centre: S. Austl. 71 C9
Booligal: N.S.W., Australia 71 F9
Boolyglass: Kilk., Repub. of Ireland 31 G15
Boom: Belgium 44 K4
Boomi: N.S.W., Australia 71 H7
Boonah: Queens., Australia 70 K6
Boondandilla: Queens., Australia 70 J6
Boone: Iowa, U.S.A. 88 E4
Boone: N.C., U.S.A. 88 L7
Booneville: Ark., U.S.A. 90 E8
Booneville: Miss., U.S.A. 90 G8
Boonville: Ind., U.S.A. 88 H6
Boonville: Mo., U.S.A. 88 E6
Boonville: N.Y., U.S.A. 89 O4
Boorindal: N.S.W., Austl. 71 G8
Booroorban: N.S.W., Austl. 71 F10
Boorowa: N.S.W., Australia 71 H10
Boort: Vict., Australia 71 E11
Boos: France 36 G6
Boot: Cumbria, England 26 P11
Boothbay Harbor: Maine, U.S.A. 89 R4
Boothia, G. of: N.W.T., Canada 85 L4
Boothia Penin.: N.W.T., Canada 84 k3
Boothville: La., U.S.A. 90 *Ins.*
Bootle: Cumbria, England 26 P11
Bootle: Mers., England 27 P13
Booué: Gabon 81 G5
Booysens Dam: S. Africa 74 D5
Bopolu: Liberia 80 B3
Boppard: W. Germany 44 N5
Boquete, El: Chile 96 B1
Bor: Czechoslovakia 45 S6
Bor: Sudan 76 D1
Bor: Turkey 56 D3
Bor: Yugoslavia 39 S14
Borabora: *i.*, Society Is. 83 e3
Borah Peak: Idaho, U.S.A. 92 E4
Borama: Somalia 79 Q18
Boran: *geog. reg.*, Ethiopia 76 E2
Borås: Sweden 47 N8
Borazjan: Iran 55 H9
Borba: Brazil 94 F4
Borba: Portugal 35 C17
Borca: Romania 43 T13
Borçka: Turkey 57 G1
Borda, Cape: Kangaroo I., S. Australia 71 B10
BORDEAUX: Gironde, Fr. 37 E11
Borden I.: N.W.T., Canada 84 h2
Border: S. Africa 75 F3
Borders: *Reg.*, Scotland (*cap.* Newtown St. Boswells) 29 Q8
Bordertown: S. Australia 71 D11
Bordesholm: W. Germany 45 Q1
Bordheyri: Iceland 46 c4
Bordighera: Italy 40 N12
Bordj A. Guettara: Algeria 78 E4
Bordj Arak: Algeria 78 E4
Bordj Bou Arreridj: Algeria 35 J18
Bordj in Eker: Algeria 78 E5
Bordj Méchéhed Salah: Tunisia 32 E5
Bordj Ouallen: Algeria 78 E5
Bordj Tadjmout: Algeria 78 E4
Bordj Viollette: Algeria 78 D4
Bordø: *i.*, Faeroe Is. (Dan.) 46 h5
Bordon: Hants., England 25 U17
Boré: Mali 80 D1
Boreham: Essex, England 25 X16

Boreray: i., Outer Hebr., Scotland 28 G4
Borg: Iceland 46 c4
Borga: see Porvoo. 47 T6
Borga: Sweden 46 O4
Borgentreich: W. Germany 44 P4
Borger: Tex., U.S.A. 93 G5
Börger: W. Germany 44 N3
Borgerhout: Belgium 44 K4
Borgholm: Öland, Sweden 47 P8
Borgholzhausen: W. Germany 44 O3
Borg Massivet: rsch. stn., Antarctica 9 75S 05W
Borgne, Lake: La., U.S.A. 90 Ins.
Borgo: Tuscany, Italy 40 Q12
Borgo: Trentino-Alto Adige, Italy 41 R9
Borgomanero: Italy 40 O10
Borgo San Dalmazzo: Italy 40 N11
Borgo San Lorenzo: Italy 41 R12
Borgosesia: Italy 40 O10
Borgou: geog. reg., Benin/Nigeria 81 E2
Borgo Val di Taro: Italy 40 P11
Borgue: Dumfries & Galloway, Scotland 29 N10
Borgue: High., Scotland 28 P3
Borislav: Ukraine 43 S12
Borisoglebsk: U.S.S.R. 50 F4
Borisov: Byelorussia 43 V9
Borisovka: Kazakh., U.S.S.R. 51 L6
Borispol': Ukraine 50 D4
Bo River: Sudan 76 C1
Borja: Paraguay 96 D2
Borja: Spain 35 F16
Borjas Blancas: Spain 35 G16
Borken: Hesse, W. Germany 44 P4
Borken: North-Rhine-Westphalia W. Germany 44 M4
Borkou: geog. reg., Chad 78 H6
Borkou-Ennedi-Tibesti: Pref., Chad (cap. Largeau) 79 H6
Borkum: i., E. Frisian Is. 44 M2
Borlänge: Sweden 47 O6
Bormes: France 40 M12
Bormida: riv., Italy 40 O11
Bormio: Italy 40 Q9
Borna: E. Germany 45 S4
Borneo: i., East Indies 65 E6
Bornholm: i., Denmark 47 O9
Bornhöved: W. Germany 45 Q1
Borno: State, Nigeria (cap. Maiduguri) 81 G2
Bornu: geog. reg., Nigeria 81 G2
Borodino: battlefield about 70 miles WSW. of Moscow, U.S.S.R. 48 e6
Boroko: Celebes 65 G6
Borol: riv., Chad 81 H2
Boromo: Upper Volta 80 D2
Boronga s.: Burma 59 Q11
Borongan: Philippines 64 H4
Bororen: Queens., Australia 70 J5
Borotol: U.S.S.R. 51 P3
Boroughbridge: North Yorkshire, England 27 T11
Borouj: El Morocco 80 K8
Borovan: Bulgaria 39 S15
Borovë: Albania 39 R16
Borovichi: U.S.S.R. 50 D3
Borovoye: Kazakh., U.S.S.R. 51 K4
Borovsk: U.S.S.R. 50 E3
Borris: Carlow, Repub. of Ireland 31 H14
Borris in Ossory: Laois, Repub. of Ireland 31 F14
Borrisokane: Tip., Repub. of Ireland 31 E14
Borrisoleigh: Tip., Repub. of Ireland 31 F14
Borroloola: N. Territ., Australia 69 F3
Borrow: riv., Cumbria, Eng. 26 Q11
Borrowdale: Cumbria, Eng. 26 P10
Borşa: Romania 43 T13
Børselv: Norway 46 T1
Borssum: W. Germany 45 Q3
Bort: France 37 H10
Borth: Dyfed, Wales 24 N15
Borve: Barra, Outer Hebr., Scotland 28 G5
Borve: Lewis, Outer Hebr., Scotland 28 J3
Borwick: Lancs., England 26 Q11
Borysthenes: Greek name of river Dnieper 33 J2
Borzhev: Ukraine 43 U12
Borzhomi: Georgia, U.S.S.R. 57 H1
Borzna: Ukraine 50 D4
Borzya: U.S.S.R. 49 n7
Bosa: Sardinia 38 L16
Bosanska Gradiška: Yugo. 38 P14
Bosanska Krupa: Yugoslavia 41 W11
Bosanski Novi: Yugoslavia 38 P14
Bosanski Petrovac: Yugo. 41 W11
Bosaso (Bender Kassim): Migiurtinia, Somalia 79 R17
Boscastle: Corn., England 24 M18
Boscobel: Wis., U.S.A. 88 F4
Bosenge: Zaire 76 B2
Bosherston: Dyfed, Wales 24 M16
Boshof: & Dist., O.F.S., S. Africa 75 F4
Boskovice: Czechoslovakia 43 P12
Bosna: riv., Yugoslavia 39 Q14
Bosnek: Schouten Is., West Irian, Indonesia 61 M12
Bosnia-Hercegovina: Repub., Yugoslavia (cap. Sarajevo) 38 P14
Bosobolo: Zaire 76 B2
Boso Penin.: Japan 63 g3
Bosporus: str., Turkey 20 Ins.
Bosque: France 36 H3
Bosque Bonito: Mexico 93 F6
Bosra (Busra): Syria 56 E5
Bossangoa: Ouham, Cen. Afr. Rep. 81 H3
Bossembélé: Cen. Afr. Rep. 81 H3
Bossier City: La., U.S.A. 90 E9
Bosso: Niger 81 G2
Boston: Kildare, Repub. of Ireland 31 H13
Boston: Lincs., England 27 V14
Boston: Mass., U.S.A. 89 Q4
Boston Mtns.: Ark., U.S.A. 90 E8
Boston Spa: W. Yorks., Eng. 27 T12
Bostra: Roman camp at Busra, Syria 56 E5
Botan: riv., Turkey 57 H3
Botany Bay: N.S.W., Austl. 71 J10
Botevgrad: Bulgaria 39 S15
Bothaville: & Dist., O.F.S., S. Africa 75 G3
Bothel: Cumbria, England 26 P10
Bothnia, G. of: Baltic Sea 46 R5
Bothwell: Strath., Scotland 29 N8
Botley: Hants., England 25 T18
Botoşani: Romania 43 U13
Botou: Upper Volta 81 E2

Botswana: Republic 77 B7
Cap. Gaborone
Area: 222,000 sq. miles (574,980 sq. km.)
Pop. 668,000 (1971 E)

Bottersleegte: S. Africa 74 D5
Bottesford: Leics., England 27 U14
Bottineau: N. Dak., U.S.A. 92 G3
Bottisham: Cambs., Eng. 25 W15
Bottrop: W. Germany 44 M4
Botucatu: Brazil 96 F1
Botwood: Newf., Canada 85 v2
Bouaflé: Ivory Coast 80 C3
Bouaké: Centre, Ivory Coast 80 D3
Bouala: Cen. Afr. Rep. 81 H3
Bouali: Gabon 81 G5
Bou Anane: Morocco 80 L8
Bouar: Nana-Mambéré, Cen. Afr. Rep. 81 H3
Bou Arfa: Morocco 80 L8
Bouaye: France 36 D8
Bouba Ndjidda Nat. Park: Cameroun 81 G3
Boucau: France 37 D12
Bouchegrouf: Algeria 38 K18
Bouches-du-Rhône: Dept., France (cap. Marseilles) 37 K12
Boucle du Baoulé National Park: Mali 80 C2
Bou Denib: Morocco 80 L8
Bou Djébéha: Mali 78 D6
Boudreau, Bay: La., U.S.A. 90 Ins.
Boudry: Switzerland 40 M9
Bougainville: i., Solomon Is. 67 L3
Bougainville Reef: Coral Sea 69 H3
Bougaroun, Cape: Algeria 32 D4
Bougouni: Mali 80 C2
Bougta: Chad 81 H2
Bouguerra: Algeria 35 H18
Bou Guezoul: Algeria 35 H19
Bougy: France 36 H8
Bouillon: Belgium 44 L6
Bouira: Algeria 35 H18
Bou Ismail: Algeria 35 H18
Bouka: Cen. Afr. Rep. 76 A1
Boukombé: Upper Volta 80 E2
Boukta: Chad 81 H2
Boula: Cen. Afr. Rep. 81 H4
Bouladuff: Tip., Repub. of Ireland 31 F14
Boulal: Mali 80 C1
Boulay: France 44 M6
Boulder: Colo., U.S.A. 93 F4
Boulder City: Nev., U.S.A. 93 E5
Boulia: Queens., Australia 69 F4
Boullong: Chad 81 H2
Boulogne: Haute Garonne, France 37 F12
Boulogne: Pas-de-Calais, Fr. 36 G5
Bouloire: France 36 F8
Boulou, Le: France 37 H13
Boulouli: Mali 80 C1
Boultham: Lincs., England 27 U13
Boultoum: Niger 81 G2
Bouly: Mauritania 80 B1
Bou Malem: Morocco 80 K8
Boumba: Niger 81 E2
Boumo: Chad 81 H3
Bouna: Ivory Coast 80 D3
Bouna National Park: Ivory Coast 80 D3
Boundary Peak: Calif., U.S.A. 93 D5
Boundiali: Ivory Coast 80 C3
Bourbon-Lancy: France 37 J9
Bourbon L'Archambault: France 37 J9
Bourbonnais: Prov., France 34 H13
Bourbonne: France 40 L8
Bourboule, La: France 37 H10
Bourbourg: France 36 H5
Bourbre: riv., France 40 L10
Bourbriac: France 36 B7
Bourem: Mali 80 D1
Bourg: Ain, France 40 L9
Bourg: Gironde, France 37 E10
Bourganeuf: France 37 G10
Bourg-Argental: France 37 K10
Bourg-d'Oisans, Le: France 40 M10
Bourges: Cher, France 36 H8
Bourget, Lac du: lake, Fr. 37 L10
Bourg-Lastic: France 37 H10
Bourgneuf: France 36 E8
Bourgneuf, Baie de: bay, Fr. 36 C8
Bourgneuf, Le: France 36 E7
Bourgneuf-en-Retz: France 36 D8
Bourgoin: France 40 L10
Bourg-St.-Andéol: France 37 K11
Bourg-St.-Maurice: France 40 M10
Bourke: N.S.W., Australia 71 F8
Bourmont: France 40 L7
Bourne: Lincs., England 27 V14
Bourne: riv., Wilts., England 25 S17
Bournemouth: Dorset, Eng. 25 S18
Bournezeau: France 37 D9
Bouroum: Upper Volta 80 D2
Bourtanger Moor: Netherlands/ W. Germany 44 M3
Bourton: Dorset, England 24 R17
Bourton: Salop, England 27 Q14
Bourton on the Water: Glos., England 25 S16
Bou Saâda: Algeria 35 J19
Boussac: France 37 H9
Boussens: France 37 F12
Bousso: Chad 81 H2
Boussu: Belgium 44 J5
Boutilimit: Mauritania 78 B6
Boutonne: riv., France 37 E9
Boutte: La., U.S.A. 90 Ins.
Bouvet I.: (Nor.), Southern O. 8 55S 00
Bouxwiller: France 40 N7
Bouza: Niger 81 F2
Bouzonville: France 44 M6
Bovec: Yugoslavia 41 T9
Boves: France 36 H6
Bovey: Minn., U.S.A. 88 E2
Bovey, North: Devon, Eng. 24 O18
Bovey Tracey: Devon, Eng. 24 O18
Bovillae: ancient city of Latium on Via Appia about 12 miles SE. of Rome. 38 N16
Bovington: Dorset, England 24 R18
Bovino: Italy 38 O16
Bow: Devon, England 24 O18
Bow: riv., Alta., Canada 92 E2
Bo-Wadrif: S. Africa 74 D6
Bowden: Bord., Scotland 29 Q8
Bowden: Leics., England 25 U15
Bowen: Queens., Australia 70 H3
Bowen: riv., Queens., Austl. 70 G3
Bowes: Durham, England 26 R10
Bowie: Tex., U.S.A. 90 C9
Bow Island: town, Alta., Canada 92 E3
Bowland, Forest of: dist., Lancashire, England 27 Q12
Bowling Green: Ky., U.S.A. 88 H7
Bowling Green: Mo., U.S.A. 88 F6
Bowling Green: Ohio, U.S.A. 88 K5
Bowling Green: Va., U.S.A. 89 N6
Bowling Green, Cape: Queens., Australia 70 G3
Bowman: N. Dak., U.S.A. 92 G3
Bowman Bay: Canada 85 m4
Bowmans: S. Australia 71 C10
Bowmore: Inner Hebr., Scot. 29 J8
Bowness: Cumbria, England 26 P10

Bowness: Cumbria, Eng. 26 Q11
Bowral: N.S.W., Australia 71 A15
Bowraville: N.S.W., Austl. 71 K8
Bowron Lake Prov. Park: B.C., Canada 92 C2
Box: Wilts., England 24 R17
Boxberg: W. Germany 44 P6
Boxford: Berks., England 25 T17
Boxford: Suff., England 25 X15
Boxley: Kent, England 25 X17
Boxmeer: Netherlands 44 L4
Boxtel: Netherlands 44 L4
Boyabat: Turkey 56 D1
Boyalik: Turkey 39 V16
Boyanup: W. Australia 68 B6
Boydton: Va., U.S.A. 89 M7
Boyenge: Zaire 76 A2
Boyle: & riv., Rosc., Repub. of Ireland 30 E12
Boyne: riv., Queens., Austl. 70 J5
Boyne: riv., Repub. of Irel. 30 J12
Boyne City: Mich., U.S.A. 88 J3
Boyne Valley Junction: Queens., Australia 70 J4
Boyoma Falls: Zaire 76 C2
Boyupbrook: W. Australia 68 B6
Božava: Yugoslavia 41 U11
Bozburun: Turkey 39 V18
Bozburun Dağ: mtn., Turkey 56 B3
Bozcaada: i., Turkey 39 U17
Bozdağ: Turkey 39 V18
Bozdoğan: Turkey 39 V18
Bozeat: Northants., England 25 U15
Bozel: France 40 M10
Bozeman: Mont., U.S.A. 92 E3
Bozkır: Turkey 56 C3
Bozo Penin.: Japan 63 g3
Bozouls: France 37 H11
Bozoum: Ouham-Pendé, Cen. Afr. Rep. 81 H3
Bozöyük: Turkey 56 B2
Bozzolo: Italy 40 Q10
Bra: Italy 40 N11
Braan: riv., Tayside, Scotland 29 O6
Brabant: Prov., Belgium (cap. Brussels) 44 K5
Brabanta: Zaire 76 B3
Brabies: S. Africa 74 C4
Brač: i., Yugoslavia 38 P15
Bracadale: Inner Hebr., Scot. 28 J5
Bracara: Roman town at Braga, Portugal 35 B16
Bracciano: Italy 38 N15
Bracebridge: Ont., Canada 89 M3
Brach: Libya 78 G4
Bracieux: France 36 G8
Bräcke: Sweden 46 O5
Brackettville: Tex., U.S.A. 93 G7
Brackley: Northants., Eng. 25 T15
Bracknell: Berks., England 25 U17
Braco: Tayside, Scotland 29 O7
Brad: Romania 43 S13
Bradano: riv., Italy 38 P16
Bradda Head: cape, I. of Man, United Kingdom 26 M11
Bradenton: Fla., U.S.A. 91 K12
Bradfield: Berks., England 25 T17
Bradfield: Essex, England 25 Y16
Bradfield: S. Yorks., England 27 S13
Bradford: Pa., U.S.A. 89 M5
Bradford: W. Yorks., England 27 S12
Bradford on Avon: Wilts., England 24 R17
Brading: I. of Wight, Eng. 25 T18
Bradley: Ill., U.S.A. 88 H5
Bradninch: Devon, England 24 P18
Bradwell: Derby., England 27 S13
Bradwell, North: Bucks., England 25 U15
Bradwell on Sea: Essex, Eng. 25 X16
Bradworthy: Devon, Eng. 24 N18
Brady: Tex., U.S.A. 90 B10
Brae: riv., Shetland Is. 28 Ins.
Brædstrup: Denmark 47 L9
Braehead: Strath., Scotland 29 O8
Braemar: dist. & castle, Gram., Scotland 28 P5
Braemore: High., Scotland 28 O3
Braeriagh: mtn., Grampian, Highland, Scotland 28 O5
Braeside: W. Australia 68 C4
Braga: Minho, Portugal 35 B16
Bragado: Argentina 96 C14
Bragança: Pará, Brazil 94 H4
Bragança: Portugal 35 C16
Bragança: São Paulo, Brazil 96 F1
Bragor: Outer Hebr., Scot. 28 N3
Brahlstorf: E. Germany 45 Q2
Brahmani: riv., India 59 P10
Brahmaputra: riv., Asia 59 Q9
Braich y Pwll: Gwyn., Wales 27 M14
Braidwood: N.S.W., Austl. 71 H10
Brăila: Romania 39 U14
Brailsford: Derby., England 27 S14
Braine: France 36 J6
Braine l'Alleud: Belgium 44 K5
Brainerd: Minn., U.S.A. 88 D2
Braintree: Essex, England 25 X16
Braithwaite: La., U.S.A. 90 Ins.
Braithwell: S. Yorks., England 27 T13
Brak: riv., Cape Prov., S. Africa 74 E4
Brak: riv., Trans., S. Africa 75 H1
Brake: W. Germany 44 O2
Brakel: W. Germany 44 P4
Brakkies: S. Africa 74 E4
Brakna: Dist., Mauritania (cap. Aleg) 78 B6
Brakpan: Trans., S. Africa 74 Nins.
Bram: France 37 H12
Bramber: W. Sussex, England 25 V18
Bramcote: Notts., England 27 T14
Bramford: Suff., England 25 Y15
Bramhall: Gt. Man., England 27 R13
Bramham: W. Yorks., England 27 T12
Bramhope: W. Yorks., Eng. 27 S12
Bramley: Surrey, England 25 U17
Bramloge: W. Germany 44 O2
Brampton: Cambs., England 25 V15
Brampton: Cumbria, England 26 Q10
Brampton: Ont., Canada 89 M4
Brampton: Suff., England 25 Z15
Brampton Bryan: Hereford & Worcester, Eng. 24 Q15
Bramsche: W. Germany 44 N3
Bramshaw: Hants., England 25 S18
Bran: riv., High., Scot. 28 M4
Branco: riv., Brazil 94 E3
Brande: Denmark 47 L9
Brandenburg: E. Ger. 45 S3
Brander, Pass of: Strathclyde, Scotland 29 L7
Brandesburton: Humb., Eng. 27 V12
Brandfort: & Dist., O.F.S., S. Africa 75 G4
Brando: Corsica 38 L15
Brandon: Durham, England 26 S10
Brandon: Man., Canada 92 H3
Brandon: Queens., Austl. 70 G2
Brandon: Suff., England 25 X15
Brandon: Vt., U.S.A. 89 P4

Brandon Bay: Kerry, Repub. of Ireland 31 A15
Brandon-Judson: S.C., U.S.A. 91 K8
Brandon Mtn.: Kerry, Repub. of Ireland 31 A15
Brandsby: N. Yorks., England 26 T11
Brandvlei: S. Africa 74 D5
Brandys: Czechoslovakia 45 U5
Braniewo: Poland 43 Q9
Brankhorstspruit: Trans., S. Africa 75 H2
Bransby: Queens., Australia 70 E7
Bransk: Poland 43 S10
Branson: Mo., U.S.A. 90 E7
Branston: Lincs., England 27 V13
Brantford: Ont., Canada 88 L4
Branthwaite: Cumbria, Eng. 26 P10
Brantôme: France 37 F10
Branxholme: Vict., Austl. 71 D11
Branxton: Northumb., Eng. 26 R8
Branzi: Italy 40 P9
Bras d'Or Lakes: Cape Breton I., Canada 89 V3
BRASÍLIA: & Fed. Dist., Brazil 94 H7

Brazil: Federal Republic 94/5
Cap. Brasília
Area: 3,286,470 sq. miles (8,511,957 sq. km.)
Pop. 95,408,000 (1971 E)

Braslav: Byelorussia 47 U9
Braşov (Orasul Stalin): Romania 43 T14
Brass: Nigeria 81 F4
Brassac: France 37 H12
Brasschaat: Belgium 44 K4
Brassington: Derby., Eng. 27 S13
Brasstown Bald: mtn., Ga., U.S.A. 91 K8
Brătianu: Romania 39 U14
Bratislava: Západoslovenská, Czechoslovakia 43 P12
Bratsk: U.S.S.R. 49 M6
Brattleboro: Vt., U.S.A. 89 P4
Bratton Clovelly: Devon, England 24 N18
Bratton Fleming: Devon, England 24 O17
Braughing: Herts., England 25 W16
Braunau: Austria 41 T7
Braunau (Broumov): Czech. 45 W5
Braunfels: W. Germany 44 O5
Braunschweig (Brunswick): W. Germany 45 Q3
Braunschweig: Distr., Lower Saxony, West Germany 45 Q4
Braunsekop: mtn., O.F.S., S. Africa 75 Ins.
Braunston: Leics., England 27 U14
Braunstone: Northants., Eng. 25 T15
Braunton: Devon, England 24 N17
Braunzip Kop: mtn., O.F.S. S. Africa 75 Ins.
Brava: Somalia 79 N9
Brava: i., Cape Verde Is. 78 Ins.
Bråviken Bay: Sweden 47 P7
Brawley: Calif., U.S.A. 93 D6
Bray: Berks., England 25 U16
Bray: France 36 J7
Bray: Wick., Repub. of Irel. 31 J13
Braye: Alderney, Chan. Is. 25 Ins.
Bray Head: cape, Kerry, Repub. of Ireland 31 A16
Brazeau: Alta., Canada 92 D2
Brazeau, Mount: Alta., Can. 92 D2

Brazil: Ind., U.S.A. 88 H6
Brazil Basin: S. Atlantic O. 8 15S 30W
Brazil Plateau: Brazil 94 J7
Brazoria: Tex., U.S.A. 90 D11
Brazos: riv., Tex., U.S.A. 90 D11
Brazo Sur: riv., Paraguay 96 D1
Brazzaville: Congo 81 H5
Brčko: Yugoslavia 39 Q14
Brda: riv., Poland 43 Q10
Brdy: geog. reg., Czech. 45 T6
Breadalbane: dist., Tayside, Scotland 29 N6
Breage: Cornwall, England 24 L19
Breaksea Sound: South I., N.Z. 71 L17
Bream: Glos., England 24 Q16
Breamore: Hants., England 25 S18
Brecey: France 36 D7
Brechfa: Dyfed, Wales 24 N16
Brechin: Tay., Scotland 29 Q6
Breckenridge: Colo., U.S.A. 93 F5
Breckenridge: Minn., U.S.A. 92 H3
Breckenridge: Tex., U.S.A. 90 B9
Breckhorn: SW. Africa 74 B4
Breckland: dist., Norf./Suff., England 25 X15
Břeclav: Czechoslovakia 43 P12
Brecon: Powys, Wales 24 P16
Brecon Beacons: mtns., Powys, Wales 24 P16
Brecon Beacons National Park: Powys, Wales 24 O16
Breda: Netherlands 44 K4
Bredasdorp: & Dist., S. Africa 74 D7
Brede: E. Sussex, England 25 X18
Bredenbury: Hereford & Worcester, England 24 Q15
Bredgar: Kent, England 25 X17
Bredon: Hereford & Worcester, England 24 R15
Bredstedt: W. Germany 44 O1
Bredy: U.S.S.R. 51 K4
Bree: Belgium 44 L4
Breede: riv., S. Africa 74 D7
Breedon on the Hill: Leics., England 27 T14
Breekkerrie: S. Africa 74 D5
Brega, El: Libya 33 F5
Bregenz: Vorarlberg, Austr. 40 P8
Bregovo: Bulgaria 39 S14
Bréhal: France 36 D7
Bréhat, Île: i., France 36 C7
Breidhavik: Iceland 46 b4
Breidhi Fjord: Iceland 46 b4
Breil: France 40 N12
Breisach: W. Germany 40 N7
Breitenhees: W. Germany 45 Q3
Bremanger: Norway 46 J6
Bremen: Ga., U.S.A. 91 J9
Bremen: Ind., U.S.A. 88 H5
Bremen: & State, W. Ger. 44 O2
Bremenium: Roman fort ½ mile N. of Rochester, Northumb., England 26 R9
Bremerhaven-Wesermünde: W. Germany 44 O2
Bremerton: Wash., U.S.A. 92 C3
Bremervörde: W. Germany 44 P2
Bremetennacum: Roman fort at Ribchester on river Ribble about 4 miles E. of Grimsargh, Lancs., Eng. 27 Q12
Bremgarten: Switzerland 40 O8
Brendon Hills: Som., Eng. 24 P17

Brenham: Tex., U.S.A. 90 C10
Brenish: Outer Hebr., Scot. 28 G3
Brenner Pass: Austria/Italy 41 R8
Brennhaug: Norway 47 L6
Breno: Italy 40 Q10
Brent: Gt. Ldn., England 25 V16
Brent, South: Devon, Eng. 24 O19
Brenta: riv., Italy 41 S10
Brent Knoll: Som., England 24 Q17
Brentnor, North: Devon, Eng. 24 N18
Brent Pelham: Herts., Eng. 25 W16
Brentwood: Essex, England 25 W16
Brereton: Trans., S. Africa 75 J3
Brescello: Italy 40 Q11
Brescia: Italy 40 Q10
Breselenz: W. Germany 45 R2
Breskens: Netherlands 44 J4
Bresle: riv., France 36 G6
Bressanone: Italy 41 R9
Bressay: i., Shetland Is., Scotland 28 Ins.
Bressuire: France 37 E9
Brest: Byelorussia 43 S10
Brest: France 36 A7
Brețcu: Romania 43 U13
Breteuil: Eure, France 36 F7
Breteuil: Oise, France 36 H6
Breton Island: La., U.S.A. 90 Ins.
Breton Sound: La., U.S.A. 90 Ins.
Bretten: W. Germany 44 O6
Bretteville-sur-Laize: France 36 E6
Bretton Woods: city, N.H., U.S.A. 89 Q3
Breu Branco: Brazil 94 H4
Breves: Brazil 94 G4
Brevik: Norway 47 L7
Brewarrina: N.S.W., Austl. 71 G7
Brewood: Staffs., England 27 R14
Brewster: Ala., U.S.A. 91 H9
Brewton: Ala., U.S.A. 91 H10
Breyell: W. Germany 44 M4
Breyten: Trans., S. Africa 75 H3
Brežice: Yugoslavia 41 V10
Březnice: Czechoslovakia 45 T6
Breznik: Bulgaria 39 S15
Březno: Czechoslovakia 43 Q12
Brezolles: France 36 M12
Bria: Haute Kotto, Central African Rep. 76 B1
Briagolong: Vict., Australia 71 G11
Briançon: Hautes-Alpes, France 40 M11
Briare: France 36 H8
Bribbaree: N.S.W., Austl. 71 G10
Bricherasio: Italy 40 N11
Bri Chualann (Bray): Wick., Repub. of Ireland 31 J13
Brickaville: Malagasy Rep. 73 O13
Bricon: France 36 K7
Bricquebec: France 36 D6
Bride: riv., Cork/Wat., Repub. of Ireland 31 E15
Bride: riv., Cork, Repub. of Ireland 31 D16
Bride: village, I. of Man, United Kingdom 26 N11
Bridestowe: Devon, England 24 N18
Bridge: Kent, England 25 Y17
Bridgend: Don., Repub. of Ireland 30 G9
Bridgend: Inner Hebr., Scot. 29 J8
Bridgend: Mid Glam., Wales 24 O16
Bridgend: Tay., Scotland 29 Q6
Bridge of Allan: Central, Scot. 29 O7
Bridge of Balgie: Tayside, Scotland 29 N6
Bridge of Cally: Tay., Scot. 29 P6
Bridge of Dun: Tay., Scot. 29 Q6
Bridge of Earn: Tay., Scot. 29 P7
Bridge of Gaur: village, Tayside, Scotland 29 N6
Bridge of Orchy: Strathclyde, Scotland 29 N6
Bridge of Weir: Strathclyde, Scotland 29 M8
Bridgeport: Ala., U.S.A. 91 J8
Bridgeport: Calif., U.S.A. 93 D5
Bridgeport: Conn., U.S.A. 89 P5
Bridgeport: Nebr., U.S.A. 92 G4
Bridgeport: Tex., U.S.A. 90 C9
Bridgeport Lake: Tex., U.S.A. 90 C9
Bridger: Mont., U.S.A. 92 F3
Bridgeton: N.J., U.S.A. 89 O6
BRIDGETOWN: Barbados, Windward Is. 87 c4
Bridgetown: N.S., Canada 89 T3
Bridgetown: Staffs., England 27 R14
Bridgetown: W. Australia 68 B6
Bridgetown: Wex., Repub. of Ireland 31 H15
Bridgewater: N.S., Canada 89 T3
Bridgford, East: Notts., England 27 U14
Bridgford, West: Notts., Eng. 27 T14
Bridgman, Cape: Greenland 85 R1
Bridgnorth: Salop, England 27 R14
Bridgwater: & bay, Som., England 24 P17
Bridlington: Humb., Eng. 27 V11
Bridport: Dorset, England 24 Q18
Bridport: Tas., Australia 68 H8
Briec: France 36 B7
Brienne-le-Château: France 36 K7
Brienz, Lake: Switzerland 40 N9
Brierfield: Ala., U.S.A. 91 H9
Brierfield: Lancs., England 27 R12
Brier Island: N.S., Canada 89 S3
Brierley Hill: W. Mid., Eng. 24 R15
Briesen: E. Germany 45 U3
Briey: France 36 L6
Brig: Switzerland 40 N9
Brigantium: Roman town at Bregenz, Austria 40 P8
Brigantius: Roman name of L. Constance 40 P8
Brigetio: Roman camp at O-Szöny on Danube about 10 miles E. of Komárno, Hungary 43 Q13
Brigg: Humb., England 27 V12
Briggsdale: Colo., U.S.A. 93 G4
Brigham: Utah, U.S.A. 92 E4
Brighouse: W. Yorks., England 27 S12
Bright: Vict., Australia 71 G11
Brightlingsea: Essex, Eng. 25 Y16
Brighton: E. Sussex, England 25 V18
Brighton: Ont., Canada 89 M3
Brighton: S. Australia 71 C10
Brighton: Tas., Australia 68 H8
Brighton Downs: Queens., Australia 69 G4
Brightons: Central, Scotland 29 O8
Brightwell: Oxon., England 25 T16
Brignoles: France 40 M12
Brigstock: Northants., Eng. 25 U15
Brihuega: Spain 35 E16
Brill: Bucks., England 25 T16
Brillion: Wis., U.S.A. 88 G3
Brilon: W. Germany 44 O4
Brimpton: Berks., England 25 T17
Brindisi: Italy 38 P16
Brinje: Yugoslavia 41 V10
Brinkburn Priory: Ancient monument, Northumb., England 26 S9
Brinkley: Ark., U.S.A. 90 F8

Brinklow: War., England 25 T15
Brinkum: W. Germany 44 O3
Brinkworth: S. Australia 71 C9
Brinkworth: Wilts., England 24 S16
Brintbodarne: Sweden 47 O6
Brion I.: Magdalen Is., Canada 89 V2
Brioni: i., Yugoslavia 41 T11
Brionne: France 36 F6
Brioude: France 37 J10
Briouze: France 36 E7
BRISBANE: Queens., Austl. 70 K6
Brisco: Cumbria, England 26 Q10
Brisighella: Italy 41 R11
Brissac: France 36 E8
BRISTOL: Avon, England 24 Q17
Bristol: Conn., U.S.A. 89 P5
Bristol: Pa., U.S.A. 89 O5
Bristol: R.I., U.S.A. 89 Q5
Bristol: Tenn., U.S.A. 88 K7
Bristol: Vt., U.S.A. 89 P3
Bristol: Va., U.S.A. 88 K7
Bristol Bay: Alaska, U.S.A. 84 D6
Bristol Chan.: est., England/Wales 24 N17
Bristow: Okla., U.S.A. 90 C8
British Chan.: Franz Josef Land 48 G1
British Columbia: Prov., Canada (cap. Victoria) 92 C2
British Honduras: see Belize.
British Indian Ocean Territory: Colony, 19 O 60E
Britof: Yugoslavia 41 U10
Briton Ferry: W. Glam., Wales 24 O16
Brits: & Dist., Trans., S. Africa 75 G2
Britstown: & Dist., S. Africa 74 E5
Brittany: Prov., France 34 E12
Brittle, Loch: Inner Hebr., Scotland 28 J5
Britton: Okla., U.S.A. 90 C8
Britton: S. Dak., U.S.A. 92 H3
Brive: France 37 G10
Briviesca: Spain 35 E15
Brixellum: Roman city at Brescello, Italy 40 Q11
Brixham: Devon, England 24 O19
Brixia: Roman city at Brescia, Italy 40 Q10
Brixlegg: Austria 41 R8
Brixton: Queens., Australia 69 G4
Brixworth: Northants., Eng. 25 U15
Briziana: Algeria 78 E3
Brize Norton: Oxon., Eng. 25 S16
BRNO (Brünn): Jihomoravský, Czech. 43 P12
Broach: see Bharuch.
Broad: riv., S.C., U.S.A. 91 L8
Broad Arrow: W. Australia 68 C6
Broad Bay: Outer Hebr., Scotland 28 J3
Broad Chalke: Wilts., Eng. 24 S17
Broad Clyst: Devon, Eng. 24 P18
Broadford: Clare, Repub. of Ireland 31 D14
Broadford: Inner Hebr., Scotland 28 K5
Broadford: Lim., Repub. of Ireland 31 D15
Broadford: Vict., Australia 71 F11
Broad Haven: bay, Mayo, Repub. of Ireland 30 B11
Broadhembury: Devon, Eng. 24 P18
Broad Hinton: Wilts., Eng. 25 S17
Broad Law: mtn., Borders, Scotland 29 P8
Broadmere: Queens., Austl. 70 H5
Broadmount: Queens., Austl. 70 J4
Broads, The: Norf., England 25 Y14
Broad Sd.: Queens., Austl. 70 H4
Broadstairs: Kent, England 25 Y17
Broadstone: Dorset, Eng. 24 S18
Broadus: Mont., U.S.A. 92 F3
Broadway: Hereford & Worcester, England 25 S15
Broadwindsor: Dorset, Eng. 24 Q18
Broager: Denmark 44 P1
Brochet: Man., Canada 92 G1
Brochu, Lac: lake, Que., Canada 89 O1
Brocken: mtn., E. Germany 45 Q4
Brockenhurst: Hants., England 25 S18
Brock I.: N.W.T., Canada 84 h2
Brockman, Mount: W. Austl. 68 B4
Brockport: N.Y., U.S.A. 89 N4
Brockton: Mass., U.S.A. 89 Q4
Brockville: Ont., U.S.A. 89 O3
Brockway: Pa., U.S.A. 89 M5
Brocton: N.Y., U.S.A. 89 M4
Brod: (on Riv. Sava), Croatia, Yugoslavia 39 Q14
Brod (E. of Rijeka), Croatia, Yugoslavia 41 U10
Brod: Macedonia, Yugo. 39 R16
Brodarevo: Yugoslavia 39 Q15
Brodce: Czechoslovakia 45 U5
Brodeur Penin.: N.W.T., Canada 85 L3
Brock: I. of Arran, Scot. 29 L8
Brodokalmak: U.S.S.R. 51 K3
Brody: Ukraine 43 T11
Broer Ruys, Cape: Grnld. 85 r3
Brogan: Oreg., U.S.A. 92 D4
Broistedt: W. Germany 45 Q3
Broken Arrow: Okla., U.S.A. 90 D7
Broken Bay: N.S.W., Austl. 71 J9
Broken Bow: Nebr., U.S.A. 92 H4
Broken Bow: Okla., U.S.A. 90 D8
Broken Hill: N.S.W., Austl. 71 D8
Broken Hill: see Kabwe.
Broken Ridge: Indian O. 9 30S 90E
Bromborough: Mers., Eng. 27 Q13
Brome: W. Germany 45 Q3
Bromham: Beds., England 25 U15
Bromley: Gt. Ldn., England 25 W17
Bromley, Great: Suff., Eng. 25 Y16
Brompton: N. Yorks., Eng. 26 T11
Bromptonville: Que., Can. 89 Q3
Bromsgrove: Hereford & Worcester, England 24 R15
Bromwich, West: West Midlands, England 27 R14
Bromyard: Hereford & Worcester, England 24 R15
Brønderslev: Denmark 23 L8
Brong-Ahafo: Reg., Ghana (cap. Sunyani) 80 D3
Broni: Italy 40 P10
Bronkhorstspruit: Trans., S. Africa 75 H2
Bronllys: Powys, Wales 24 P16
Brønnøysund: Norway 46 N4
Brook: I. of Wight, England 25 T18
Brooke: Norf., Eng. 25 Y14
Brookeborough: Ferm., N. Ireland 30 G11
Brooke's Point: town, Palawan, Philippines 64 F5
Brooketon: Brunei 65 F5
Brookfield: Mo., U.S.A. 88 E6
Brookhaven: Miss., U.S.A. 90 F10
Brookings: Oreg., U.S.A. 92 C4

Brookings: S. Dak., U.S.A. 92 H4
Brookland: Kent, England 25 X18
Brooks: Alta., Canada 92 E2
Brooks Range: Alaska, U.S.A. 84 d4
Brooksville: Fla., U.S.A. 91 K11
Brookton: W. Australia 68 B6
Brookville: Ind., U.S.A. 88 J6
Brookville: Pa., U.S.A. 89 M5
Brooloo: Queens., Australia 70 K6
Broom, Loch: High., Scot. 28 L4
Broome: W. Australia 68 C3
Broomhill: Northumb., Eng. 26 S9
Bröns: France 36 C7
Brora: & loch, High., Scot. 28 O3
Broseley: Salop, England 27 R14
Brosna: Kerry, Repub. of Ireland 31 C15
Brosna: riv., Offaly/Tip., Repub. of Ireland 31 F13
Brossac: France 37 E10
Brosteni: Romania 39 S14
Brotas: Brazil 94 J6
Brothers, The: is., Indian O. 79 P7
Brothers, The: is., Red Sea 54 D9
Brotton: Cleve., England 26 U10
Brou: France 36 G7
Brough: Cumbria, England 26 R10
Brough: Humb., England 27 U12
Brough: see Anavio.
Brough Head: cape, Mainland, Orkney Is. 28 Ins.
Broughshane: Antrim, N. Ireland 30 J10
Broughton: Borders, Scot. 29 P8
Broughton: Hants., England 25 S17
Broughton: Lancs., England 27 Q12
Broughton: Northants., Eng. 25 U15
Broughton: Notts., England 27 U14
Broughton: N. Yorks., Eng. 26 T11
Broughton: Que., Canada 89 Q2
Broughton Astley: Leics., England 27 T14
Broughton in Furness: Cumbria, England 26 P11
Broughton Moor: village, Cumbria, England 26 P10
Broughty Ferry: Tay., Scot. 29 Q7
Broumov (Braunau): Czech. 45 W5
Brouwershaven: Neth. 44 J4
Brownfield: Tex., U.S.A. 93 G6
Brownhills: W. Mid., England 27 S14
Browning: Mont., U.S.A. 92 E3
Browns Mills: Cork, Rep. of Ireland 31 E16
Brownstown: Ind., U.S.A. 88 H6
Brown's Town: Jamaica 86 Ins.
Brown's Valley: Minn., U.S.A. 92 H3
Brownsville: Tenn., U.S.A. 90 G8
Brownsville: Tex., U.S.A. 90 C13
Brownsville-Brent-Goulding: Fla., U.S.A. 91 H10
Brownsweg: Surinam 94 F2
Brown Willy: mtn., Corn., Eng. 24 M18
Brownwood: Tex., U.S.A. 90 B10
Browse I.: W. Australia 68 C2
Broye: riv., Switzerland 40 M9
Broxa: N. Yorks., England 26 U11
Broxburn: Lothian, Scot. 29 P8
Broxted: Essex, England 25 W16
Bruay: France 36 H5
Bruce, Mount: W. Australia 68 B4
Bruce Bay: town, South I., New Zealand 70 M16
Bruce Rock: W. Australia 68 B6
Bruceton: Tenn., U.S.A. 88 G7
Bruchsal: W. Germany 45 O6
Brück: E. Germany 45 S3
Bruck: Lower Austria 41 W7
Bruck: Salzburg, Austria 41 S8
Bruck: Styria, Austria 41 V8
Brückl: Austria 41 U9
Brue: riv., Som., England 24 Q17
Bruel: E. Germany 45 R2
Bruff: Lim., Repub. of Irel. 31 D15
BRUGES: W. Flanders, Belgium 44 J4
Brugg: Switzerland 40 O8
Brugge: see Bruges.
Brühl: W. Germany 44 M5
Brukkaros: SW. Africa 74 C2
Brûlon: France 36 E8
Brumado: Brazil 94 J6
Brumath: France 40 N7
Brumby: Humb., England 27 U12
Brundidge: Ga., U.S.A. 91 J10
Bruneau: Idaho, U.S.A. 92 D4
Brunei: Br. protected state 65 E6
Cap.: Bandar Seri Begawan
Area: 2,226 sq. miles (5,765 sq. km.)
Pop.: 136,256 (1971 C)
Brunei: town, Brunei see Bandar Seri Begawan.
Brunei Bay: Sarawak, Malaysia 65 F5
Brunette Downs: N. Territ., Australia 69 F3
Brunflo: Sweden 46 O5
Brunico: Italy 41 R9
Bruni I.: Tas., Australia 68 H8
Brünn: Austria 41 W7
Brünn (Brno): Czech. 45 W6
Brunner: South I., N.Z. 70 N16
Brunov: France 36 H7
Brunsbüttel: W. Germany 44 P2
Brunswick: Ga., U.S.A. 91 L10
Brunswick: Maine, U.S.A. 89 R4
Brunswick: Md., U.S.A. 89 N6
Brunswick: Mo., U.S.A. 88 E6
Brunswick (Braunschweig): W. Germany 45 Q3
Bruny I.: Tas., Australia 68 H8
Bruree: Lim., Repub. of Irel. 31 D15
Brusartsi: Bulgaria 39 S15
Brusasco: Italy 40 O10
Brush I.: La., U.S.A. 90 Ins.
Brusque: Brazil 96 F2
BRUSSELS (Bruxelles): Brabant, Belg. 44 K5
Brussels: S. Africa 75 F3
Bruthen: Vict., Australia 71 G11
Bruton: Som., England 24 R17
Bruttium: Roman name for modern Calabria, Italy 38 P17
Bruxelles: see Brussels.
Bruyères: France 40 M7
Bryan: Ohio, U.S.A. 88 J5
Bryan: Tex., U.S.A. 90 C10
BRYANSK: & Reg., U.S.S.R. 50 D4
Bryansky: U.S.S.R. 50 G6
Bryce Canyon Nat. Park: Utah, U.S.A. 93 E5
Brydekirk: Dumfries & Galloway, Scotland 29 P9
Bryher: i., Scilly Is., Eng. 25 J19
Brymbo: Clwyd, Wales 27 P13
Brynamman: Dyfed, Wales 24 O16
Brynmawr: Gwent, Wales 24 P16
Bryson City: N.C., U.S.A. 91 K8
Brzeg: Poland 43 P11

Brześć Kujawski: Poland 43 Q10
Brzesko: Poland 43 R12
Brzeziny: Poland 43 Q11
Bsherri: Lebanon 56 E4
Bualintur: Inner Hebr., Scot. 28 J5
Bü Anafarta: Turkey (Dardan. Inset) 20 Ins.
Buapinang: Celebes 65 G7
Bua Yai: Thailand 64 C3
Buayan: Philippines 65 H5
Buba: Guinea-Bissau 80 B2
Bubaque: Guinea-Bissau 80 A2
Bubasa: Ethiopia 79 Q18
Bubastis: ancient Egyptian city on E. side of Nile Delta about 3 miles S. of Zagazig, Egypt 56 B6
Bubiyan I.: Persian Gulf 57 L7
Bubry: France 36 B8
Bubulu: Uganda 76 D2
Bubwith: Humb., England 27 U12
Bucak: Turkey 56 B3
Bucaramanga: Colombia 94 C2
Bucas Grande: i., Philippines 64 H5
Buch: E. Germany 45 T3
Buchach: Ukraine 43 T12
Buchan: dist., Gram., Scot. 28 R4
BUCHANAN: Grand Bassa, Liberia 80 B3
Buchanan Lake: Tex., U.S.A. 90 B10
Buchan Ness: Gram., Scot. 28 S5
Buchans: Newf., Canada 85 u2
Buchardo: Argentina 96 C3
BUCHAREST (Bucureşti): Romania 39 U14
Buchau: Austria 41 R8
Büchen: W. Germany 45 Q2
Buchholz: W. Germany 45 P2
Buchloe: W. Germany 41 Q7
Buchlyvie: Central, Scot. 29 N7
Buchs: Switzerland 40 P8
Buchy: France 36 G6
Buciumeni: Romania 39 T14
Buck, The: mtn., Grampian, Scotland 28 Q5
Buckden: Cambs., England 25 V15
Buckden: N. Yorks., England 26 R11
Bückeburg: W. Germany 44 P3
Buckenham, New: Norf., England 25 Y15
Buckeye: Ariz., U.S.A. 93 E6
Buckfastleigh: Devon, Eng. 24 O19
Buckhannon: W. Va., U.S.A. 88 L6
Buckhaven: Fife, Scotland 29 P7
Buckhorn Lake: Ont., Can. 89 M3
Buckhurst Hill: town, Greater London, England 25 W16
Buckie: Gram., Scotland 28 Q4
Buckingham: & Co., England (co. town Aylesbury) 25 U16
Buckingham: Que., Canada 89 O3
Buckingham Bay: Australia 69 F2
Buckland: Herts., England 25 V16
Buckland: Kent, England 25 Y17
Buckland Brewer: Devon, England 24 N18
Buckland St. Mary: Som., England 24 P18
Buckland Tableland: plat., Queens., Australia 70 H5
Buckleboo: S. Australia 69 F6
Bucklebury: Berks., Eng. 25 T17
Bucklesham: Suff., England 25 Y15
Buckley: Clwyd, Wales 27 P13
Bucknall: Lincs., England 27 V13
Bucknell: Salop, England 27 Q15
Bucksburn: Gram., Scotland 28 R5
Bucksport: Maine, U.S.A. 89 R3
Buclo: S. Vietnam 64 D5
Buco Zau: Cabindo, Ang. 81 G5
Buctouche: N.B., Canada 89 T2
BUCUREŞTI (Bucharest): Romania 39 U14
Bucyrus: Ohio, U.S.A. 88 K5
Bud: Norway 46 K5
Budafok: Hungary 43 Q13
Budagido: New Guinea 69 G1
Budai'a: Saudi Arabia 54 F10
BUDAPEST: Hungary 43 Q13
Budaun: Uttar Pradesh, India 58 N9
Budawein: Ethiopia 79 Q18
Bud Bud: Somalia 79 R19
Buddon Ness: cape, Tayside, Scotland 29 Q7
Bude: Corn., England 24 M18
Budënnovka: Kazakh., U.S.S.R. 50 H4
Budënny: Kirgiz., U.S.S.R. 51 M6
Budeşti: (NW. of Piteşti), Romania 39 T14
Budeşti: (SE. of Bucharest), Romania 39 U14
Budjala: Zaïre 76 A2
Budleigh, East: Devon, Eng. 24 P18
Budleigh Salterton: Devon, England 24 P18
Budop: Vietnam 64 D4
Budrio: Italy 41 R11
Budun Tala Steppe: Mongolia 62 U5
BUEA: Sud-Ouest, Cameroun 81 F4
Buëch: riv., France 40 L11
Buena Esperanza: Argentina 96 B3
Buenaventura: Colombia 94 B3
Buenaventura: Mexico 93 F7
Buena Vista: Colo., U.S.A. 93 F5
Buenavista: Mexico 93 F7
Buena Vista: Va., U.S.A. 89 M7
BUENOS AIRES: Argentina 96 D3
Buenos Aires: Prov., Arg. (cap. La Plata) 96 C4
Buenos Aires: Panama 94 Ins.
Buenos Aires, Lago: l., Argentina/Chile 95 C13
Buerat el Hsun: Libya 33 F5
Buffalo: Minn., U.S.A. 88 E3
Buffalo: N.Y., U.S.A. 89 M4
Buffalo: Okla., U.S.A. 90 B7
Buffalo: S.C., U.S.A. 91 L8
Buffalo: S. Dak., U.S.A. 92 G3
Buffalo: Wyo., U.S.A. 92 F4
Buffalo: riv., Natal, S. Afr. 75 J3
Buffalo Lake: Alta., Canada 92 E2
Buffalo Lake: N.W.T., Can. 84 H5
Buff Bay: town, Jamaica 86 Ins.
Buffels: riv., S. Africa 74 B4
Buffels Bay: S. Africa 74 Ins.
Buffelsfontein: S. Africa 75 G5
Buford: Ga., U.S.A. 91 J8
Bug: riv., Pol./U.S.S.R. 43 S10
Bug: riv., U.S.S.R. 50 D5
Buga: Colombia 94 B3
Bug Berde: Ethiopia 79 Q18
Bugbrooke: Northants., England 25 T15
Bugeat: France 37 G10
Bugene: Tanzania 76 D3
Bugi: Papua/New Guinea 69 G1
Bugojno: Yugoslavia 38 P14
Bugondo: Uganda 76 D2
Bugones: Norway 46 V2
Bugsuk: i., Philippines 64 F5
Bugue, Le: France 37 F11
Buguey: Luzon, Philippines 64 G3

Bugul'ma: U.S.S.R. 50 H4
Bugumal: New Irel., Bismarck Arch. 67 K2
Bugun': Kazakh., U.S.S.R. 51 K5
Buguruslan: U.S.S.R. 50 H4
Buhabad: Iran 55 J8
Buhera: Rhodesia 77 D6
Buhl: Idaho, U.S.A. 92 E4
Buhl: Minn., U.S.A. 88 E2
Buhoro Flats: geog. reg., Tanzania 77 D4
Buhtan: riv., Turkey 57 H3
Buhusi: Romania 43 U13
Bui Dam: Ghana 80 D3
Builth Wells: Powys, Wales 24 P15
Buin: Bougainville, Solomon Islands 67 L3
Buin: Chile 96 A3
Buirat: Western Sahara 78 C4
Buitenzorg: see Bogor.
Bujalance: Spain 35 D18
Bujaraloz: Spain 35 F16
Buje: Yugoslavia 41 T10
Bujnurd: Iran 55 J7
BUJUMBURA: Burundi 76 C3
Bük: Hungary 41 W8
Buka: i., Solomon Is. 67 K3
Bukachacha: U.S.S.R. 49 n7
Bukakata: Uganda 76 D3
Bukama: Zaïre 77 C4
Bukan: Iran 57 K3
BUKAVU (Costermansville): Kivu, Zaïre 76 C3
Bukene: Tanzania 76 D3
Bukhara: Uzbek., U.S.S.R. 51 K7
Bukhta Ugol'naya: U.S.S.R. 49 I5
Bukittinggi: Sumatra, Indonesia 65 C7
BUKOBA: West Lake, Tanzania 76 D3
Bukombe: Tanzania 76 D3
Bukowo, Lake: Poland 45 W1
Bukuru: Nigeria 81 F3
Bukwium: Nigeria 81 F2
Bula: Moluccas, Indonesia 61 L12
Bula: Guinea-Bissau 80 A2
Bülach: Switzerland 40 O8
Bulad: Ethiopia 76 E1
Bulagan: Mongolia 49 M8
Bulalacao: Philippines 64 G4
Bulan: Luzon, Philippines 64 G4
Bulancak: Turkey 56 F1
Bulanik: Turkey 57 H2
Bulape: Zaïre 76 B3
BULAWAYO: Matabeland North, Rhodesia 77 C7
Buldan: Turkey 56 A2
Buldana: Maharashtra, India 58 N10
Buldir: i., Aleutians 84 a7
Bulford: Wilts., England 25 S17
Bulgaria: *Republic* 39 T15
Cap.: Sofia (Sofiya)
Area: 42,826 sq. miles (110,927 sq. km.)
Pop.: 8,540,000 (1971 E)
Bulgnéville: France 40 L7
Bulgunnia: S. Australia 68 E6
Bulhar: Somalia 79 Q17
Bullaun: Galway, Repub. of Ireland 31 D13
Bulle: Switzerland 40 N9
Buller: riv., South I., N.Z. 70 O15
Buller, Mount: Vict., Austl. 71 G11
Bullfinch: W. Australia 68 B6
Bulli: N.S.W., Australia 71 J10
Bullwallah: Queens., Austl. 70 G3
Bullmoose Mount: B.C., Canada 92 C1
Bull Mtns.: Mont., U.S.A. 92 F3
Bulloo: riv., Queens., Austl. 70 E7
Bulloo, Lake: Queens., Austl. 71 E7
Bulloo Downs: Queens., Australia 71 E7
Bulls: North I., New Zealand 70 P14
Bull Shoals Res.: Mo., U.S.A. 90 E7
Bulmer: N. Yorks., England 27 U11
Bulnes: Chile 96 A4
Bulo Burti: Somalia 79 R19
Bulphan: Essex, England 25 W16
Bultfontein: O.F.S., S. Africa 75 G4
Bulukumba: Celebes 65 G8⁻
Bulun: U.S.S.R. 49 o3
Bulungu: Bandundu, Zaïre 76 A3
Bulungu: Kasai Occidental, Zaïre 76 B4
Bulupari: New Caledonia 67 N6
Bulwer: Natal, S. Africa 75 H4
Bulyea: Sask., Canada 92 G2
Bumba: Zaïre 76 B2
Bumba: Sierra Leone 80 B3
Bumbeni: Natal, S. Africa 75 K3
Bumbeşti Jiu: Romania 39 S14
Bumbuli: Zaïre 76 B3
Buna: Kenya 76 E2
Buna: Papua/New Guinea 69 H1
Buna: Zaïre 76 A3
Bunab: Iran 57 K3
Bunaiyan: well, Sau. Arab. 55 H10
Bunbeg: Don., Repub. of Ireland 30 E9
Bundaberg: Queens., Austl. 70 K5
Bundarra: N.S.W., Australia 71 J8
Bünde: W. Germany 44 O3
Bundella: N.S.W., Australia 71 H8
Bundi: Rajasthan, India 58 N9
Bundibugyo: Uganda 76 D2
Bundilla: Queens., Australia 70 F6
Bundoran: Don., Repub. of Ireland 30 E11
Bundukia: Sudan 76 D1
Bunessan: Inner Hebr., Scot. 29 J7
Bunga: riv., Nigeria 81 F2
Bungay: Suff., England 25 Y15
Bu Ngem: Libya 33 F5
Bungendore: N.S.W., Austl. 71 H10
Bung Kan: Thailand 64 C3
Bungo Chan.: Kyushu/Shikoku, Japan 63 C4
Bunia: Zaïre 76 D2
Bunic: Yugoslavia 41 V11
Buninyong: Vict., Australia 71 E11
Bunji: Jammu and Kashmir 58 M7
Bunkerville: Nev., U.S.A. 93 E5
Bunkeya: Zaïre 77 C5
Bunkie: La., U.S.A. 90 E10
Bunlahy: Long., Repub. of Ireland 30 F12
Bunloit: High., Scotland 28 N5
Bunmahon: Wat., Repub. of Ireland 31 G15
Bunnahowen: Mayo, Repub. of Ireland 30 B11
Bunnanaddan: Sligo, Repub. of Ireland 30 D11
Bunsuru: riv., Nigeria 81 F2
Buntingford: Herts., Eng. 25 V16

Buntok: Borneo 65 E7
Bununu: Nigeria 81 F2
Bunut: Borneo 65 E6
Bünyan: Turkey 56 D2
Bunyip: Vict., Australia 71 F12
Bunza: Nigeria 81 E2
Buol: Celebes 65 G6
Buôn Ngô: Vietnam 64 D4
Buorkhaya Bay: U.S.S.R. 49 P3
Buqbuq: Egypt 54 C8
Buqla: Oman 55 J10
Bur: Sudan 76 D1
Bur, El: Somalia 79 R19
Bura: Kenya 76 E3
Bura: Mali 80 D2
Buraida: Saudi Arabia 54 F9
Buraimi: U.A.E. 55 J10
Burakin: W. Australia 68 B6
Buraki Rajan: Afghanistan 58 L8
Buram: Sudan 79 R17
Buran: Somalia 79 R17
BURAO: North-East, Somalia 79 R18
Burbage: Leics., England 27 T14
Burbage: Wilts., England 25 S17
Burbank: Calif., U.S.A. 93 D6
Burdalyk: Turkmen., U.S.S.R. 51 K7
Burdekin: riv., Queens., Australia 69 H3
Burden, Mount: B.C., Can. 92 C1
Burdesi: Ethiopia 76 E1
Burdigala: Roman city and port at Bordeaux, France 37 E11
Burdur: Lake: Turkey 56 B3
BURDUR: & Prov., Turkey 56 B3
Burdwan: W. Bengal, India 59 P10
Bure: riv., England 25 Z14
Bureá: Sweden 46 R4
Bureau, Lac: Que., Canada 89 O1
Burei: Ethiopia 76 E1
Büren: Switzerland 40 N8
Büren: W. Germany 44 O4
Bures: Essex, England 25 X16
Bureya: U.S.S.R. 49 o8
Bureya: riv., U.S.S.R. 49 P7
Burford: Oxon., England 25 S16
Burg: Fehmarn, W. Germany 45 R1
Burg: Netherlands 44 K2
Burg: Magdeburg, E. Ger. 45 R3
Burgas: Bulgaria 39 U15
Burg Gavo: Somalia 76 F3
Burgaw: N.C., U.S.A. 91 N8
Burgdorf: Switzerland 40 N8
Burgdorf: W. Germany 45 Q3
Burgebrach: W. Germany 45 Q6
Burg el Arab: Egypt 54 C8
Burgenland: Prov., Austria (cap. Eisenstadt) 41 W8
Burgeo: Newf., Canada 85 u3
Burgersdorp: S. Africa 75 G5
Burgerville Road: S. Africa 75 F5
Burgess Hill: town, West Sussex, England 25 V18
Burgh: Netherlands 44 J4
Burghan: oilfield, Kuwait 57 L7
Burghausen: W. Germany 41 S7
Burghclere: Hants., England 25 T17
Burghead: Gram., Scotland 28 P4
Burghfield: Berks., England 25 T17
Burgh le Marsh: Lincs., Eng. 27 W13
Burgh le Marsh: England 27 W13
Burgley House: Northants., England 27 V14
Burgjoss: W. Germany 44 P5
Burgkunstadt: W. Germany 45 R5
Burglengenfeld: W. Germany 45 S6
Burgo de Osma, El: Spain 35 E16
Burgos: Mexico 90 B13
BURGOS: & Prov., Spain 35 E15
Burgsteinfurt: W. Germany 44 N3
Burgsvik: Gotland, Sweden 47 Q8
Burgundy: Prov., France 34 J13
Burham: Kent, England 25 W17
Burhanıye: Turkey 39 U17
Burhanpur: Madhya Pradesh, India 58 N10
Burhou: i., Chan. Is. 25 Ins.
Burias: i., Philippines 64 G4
Burie: France 37 E10
Burin: Newf., Canada 85 v3
Buriram: Thailand 64 C3
Buriti dos Lopes: Brazil 94 J4
Buriton: Hants., England 25 U18
Burj: Norway, England 27 S11
Burji: Ethiopia 76 E1
Burkburnett: Tex., U.S.A. 90 B8
Burke: riv., Queens., Austl. 69 G4
Burkesville: Ky., U.S.A. 88 J7
Burketown: Queens., Austl. 69 F3
Burkheim: W. Germany 40 N7
Burks Falls: city, Ont., Can. 89 M3
Burlescombe: Devon, Eng. 24 P18
Burley: Hants., England 25 S18
Burley: Idaho, U.S.A. 92 E4
Burley: N. Yorks., England 27 S12
Burli: Kazakh., U.S.S.R. 50 H4
Burlington: Colo., U.S.A. 93 G5
Burlington: Iowa, U.S.A. 88 F5
Burlington: Kans., U.S.A. 90 D6
Burlington: N.C., U.S.A. 89 M7
Burlington: Vt., U.S.A. 89 P3
Burlington: Wis., U.S.A. 88 G4

Burma: *Republic* 59 R10
Cap.: Rangoon
Area: 261,789 sq. miles (678,034 sq. km.)
Pop.: 27,584,000 (1970 E)
Burn: N. Yorks., England 27 T12
Burncourt: Tip., Repub. of Ireland 31 E15
Burneside: Cumbria, Eng. 26 Q11
Burneston: N. Yorks., England 26 S11
Burnet: Tex., U.S.A. 90 B10
Burnett: riv., Queens., Austl. 70 J5
Burnett Heads: Queens., Australia 70 K5
Burnham: Bucks., England 25 U16
Burnham Deepdale: Norf., England 25 X14
Burnham Market: Norf., England 25 X14
Burnham on Crouch: Essex, England 25 X16
Burnham on Sea: Som., England 24 Q17
Burnhaven: Gram., Scotland 28 S5
Burnie: Tas., Australia 68 H8
Burnley: Lancs., England 27 R12
Burnmouth: Borders, Scot. 29 R8
Burnopfield: Durham, Eng. 26 S10
Burns: N.S.W., Australia 71 D9
Burnsall: N. Yorks., England 27 S11
Burnside: Harbour (Bathurst Inlet): N.W.T., Canada 84 J4
Burns Lake: town, B.C., Can. 92 B2
Burnt Creek: settlement, Que., Canada 87 N7

Burntisland: Fife, Scotland **29** P7
Burnum: Roman camp about 15 miles W. of Knin, Yugoslavia **38** P14
Burra: S. Australia **71** C9
Burra, West: i., Shetland Is., Scotland **28** Ins.
Burracoppin: W. Australia **68** B6
Burraga: N.S.W., Australia **71** H9
Burrandilla: Queens., Austl. **70** F6
Burravoe: Yell, Shetland Is. **28** Ins.
Burray: i., Orkney Is., Scot. **28** Q2
Burrel: Albania **39** R16
Burrelton: Tay., Scotland **29** P6
Burren Junction: N.S.W., Australia **71** H8
Burriana: Spain **35** F17
Burrinjuck Reservoir: N.S.W., Australia **71** H10
Burrishoole: Mayo, Repub. of Ireland **30** B12
Burrium: Roman fort at Usk, Gwent, Wales **24** Q16
Burro, Serranias del: mtns., Tex./Mex. **93** G7
Burrow Head: cape, Dumfries & Galloway, Scotland **29** N10
Burrwood: La., U.S.A. **90** Ins.
Burry Port: Dyfed, Wales **24** N16
BURSA: & Prov., Turkey **56** A1
Burscheid: W. Germany **44** N4
Burscough: Lancs., England **27** Q12
Burshtyn: Ukraine **43** T12
Burslem: Staffs., England **27** R13
Burstwick: Humb., England **27** V12
Burta: N.S.W., Australia **71** D9
Burt Lake: Mich., U.S.A. **88** J3
Burton: Ches., England **27** P13
Burton: Cumbria, England **26** Q11
Burton, North: North Yorkshire, England **26** V11
Burton Agnes: Humb., Eng. **27** V11
Burton Bradstock: Dorset, England **24** Q18
Burton Joyce: Notts., Eng. **27** T14
Burton Latimer: Northants., England **25** U15
Burton Lazars: Leics., Eng. **27** U14
Burtonport: Don., Repub. of Ireland **30** E10
Burton upon Stather: Humberside, England **27** U12
Burton upon Trent: Staffs., England **27** S14
Burtundy: N.S.W., Australia **71** E9
Buru: i., Indonesia **65** H7
Burujird: Iran **57** L5
Burullus, Lake: Egypt **56** B6

Burundi: Republic **76** C3
Cap.: Bujumbura
Area: 10,739 sq. miles (27,814 sq. km.)
Pop.: 3,615,000 (1971 E)

Bururi: Burundi **76** C3
Burutai: Nigeria **81** G2
Burutu: Nigeria **81** F3
Burwash: E. Sussex, England **25** W18
Burwash Landing: Yukon, Canada **84** F5
Burwell: Cambs., England **25** W15
Bury: Gt. Man., England **27** R12
Buryat A.S.S.R.: U.S.S.R. (cap. Ulan Ude) **49** m7
Bury St. Edmunds: Suff., England **25** X15
Busaiya: Iraq **57** K6
Busalla: Italy **40** O11
Busanga: i., Philippines **64** G4
Busby: Strath., Scotland **29** N8
Busca: Italy **40** N11
Busembatia: Uganda **76** D2
Bushenyi: Uganda **76** D3
Bushey: Herts., England **25** V16
Bush: riv., Antrim, N. Irel. **30** J9
Bushimaie: riv., Zaire **76** B3
BUSHIRE: & Prov., Iran **55** H9
Bush Lot: Guyana **87** d7
Bushman's: riv., S. Africa **75** G6
Bushmills: Antrim, N. Irel. **30** H9
Bushnell: Ill., U.S.A. **88** F5
Bushruiyeh: Iran **55** J8
Businga: Zaire **76** B2
Busk: Ukraine **43** T12
Buskerud: Co., Norway (cap. Drammen) **47** L6
Buslei: Ethiopia **79** Q18
Busoga: Dist., Uganda (cap. Jinja) **76** D2
Busra (Bosra): Syria **56** E5
Bussa: Nigeria **81** E2
Bussana: Italy **40** O12
Bussang: France **40** M8
Busselton: W. Australia **68** B6
Busseto: Italy **40** O11
Bussière-Poitevine: France **37** F9
Bussum: Netherlands **44** L3
Busto Arsizio: Italy **40** O10
Busuanga: i., Philippines **64** F4
Busu Djanoa: Zaire **76** B2
Busu Gongo: Zaire **76** B2
Busùm: W. Germany **44** O1
Busu Melo: Zaire **76** B2
Busun: Iran **57** L2
Buta: Zaire **76** B2
Buta Ranquil: Argentina **96** B4
Butare: Rwanda **76** C3
Butaritari: i., Gilbert Is. **67** O1
Bute: i. & sound, Scotland **29** L8
Bute, Kyles of: str., Strathclyde, Scotland **29** L8
Butere: Kenya **76** D2
BUTHA-BUTHE: & Dist., Lesotho **75** H4
Buthidaung: Burma **59** Q10
Butiaba: Uganda **76** D2
Butleigh: Som., England **24** Q17
Butler: Ind., U.S.A. **88** J5
Butler: Mo., U.S.A. **90** D6
Butler: Pa., U.S.A. **89** M5
Butlerstown: Cork, Repub. of Ireland **31** D15
Butola: Uganda **76** D2
Butser Hill: Hants., England **25** U18
Butte: Mont., U.S.A. **92** E3
Buttelstedt: E. Germany **45** R4
Buttermere: Cumbria, Eng. **26** P10
Butterwick: Lincs., England **27** W14
Butterwick, West: Lincs., Eng. **27** U12
Butterworth: Malaya, Malaysia **65** b11
Butterworth: see Gcuwa
Buttevant: Cork, Repub. of Ireland **31** D15
Button Bay: Man., Canada **84** k6
Butuan: Mindanao, Phil. **64** H5
Butulu: Liberia **80** C3
Butung: i., Indonesia **65** G7
Butung Passage: str., Indonesia **65** G8
Bützbach: W. Germany **44** O5
Bützow: E. Germany **45** S2
Buxières-les-Mines: France **37** H9
Buxted: E. Sussex, England **25** W18
Buxton: Derby:, England **27** S13
Buxton: Norf., England **25** Y14

Buxy: France **37** K9
Buy: U.S.S.R. **50** F3
Buyaga: U.S.S.R. **49** o6
Buyantaiin Huryee: Mongolia **62** R5
Buyin: Iran **57** M4
Buynaksk: U.S.S.R. **50** G6
Buyo: Ivory Coast **80** C3
Buyükdere: Turkey (Bosporus. Inset) **20** Ins.
Büyükliman: Turkey **56** F1
Buzachi Penin.: Kazakh., U.S.S.R. **50** H6
Buzançais: France **37** G9
Buzancy: France **36** K6
Buzău: & riv., Romania **39** U14
Buzet: Yugoslavia **41** T10
Buzi: riv., Mozambique **77** D6
Buzias: Romania **39** R14
Buznabad: Iran **55** J8
Buzuluk: U.S.S.R. **50** H4
Buzzards Bay: Mass., U.S.A. **89** Q5
Bwana Mkabwa: Zambia **77** C5
By: riv., Sweden **47** N7
Byam Martin, Cape: N.W.T., Canada **85** M3
Byam Martin I.: N.W.T., Canada **84** j2
Byblos (Gebal): Phoenician seaport and Roman city at Jbail, Lebanon **56** D4
BYDGOSZCZ: & Prov., Poland **43** Q11
Byelorussian S.S.R.: U.S.S.R. (cap. Minsk). **50** C4
Byfield: Northants., England **25** T15
Byfleet: Surrey, England **25** V17
Bygdeå: Sweden **46** R4
Bygdeträsk: Sweden **46** R4
Byglandsfjord: Norway **47** K7
Bygstad: Norway **47** J6
Bykhov: Byelorussia **50** D4
Bykle: Norway **47** K7
Bylchau: Clwyd, Wales **27** O13
Bylot: i.: N.W.T., Canada **85** M3
Bymount: Queens., Australia **70** H6
Bynack More: mtn., Highland, Scotland **28** O5
Byng Inlet: city, Ont., Canada **88** L3
Byrd Glacier: Antarctica **9** 85S 155E
Byrd Land: Antarctica **9** 80S 135W
Byrd Station: rsch. stn., Antarctica **9** 85S 120W
Byrka: U.S.S.R. **49** n7
Byrne: Natal, S. Africa **75** J4
Byrock: N.S.W., Australia **71** G8
Byron Bay: town, N.S.W., Australia **71** K7
Byrum: Læsø, Denmark **47** M8
Byske: & riv., Sweden **46** R4
Bystřice: Czechoslovakia **45** W6
Bytantay: riv., U.S.S.R. **49** P4
Bytom: Poland **43** Q11
Bytów: Poland **43** P9
Byzantion: Queens., Austl. **70** G6
Byzantium: Greek city at Istanbul, Turkey **39** V16
Bzema: Libya **79** J5

Ca: riv., Laos/Vietnam **64** C3
Caacupé: Paraguay **96** D2
Caaguazú: Paraguay **96** D2
Caapucú: Paraguay **96** D2
Caazapá: Paraguay **96** D2
Cabaia: Angola **77** B4
Cabalian: Philippines **64** H4
Caballeria, C. de: cape, Balearic Is. **35** J16
Caballo Dam: N. Mex., U.S.A. **93** F6
Cabana: Peru **94** B5
Cabanatuan: Luzon, Phil. **64** G3
Cabano: Que., Canada **89** R2
Cabawin: Queens., Australia **70** J6
Cabeza del Buey: Spain **35** D17
Cabezas: Bolivia **94** E7
Cabildo: Chile **96** A3
Cabimas: Venezuela **94** C1
Cabinda: & Prov., Angola **81** G6
Cabinet Mtns.: Idaho/Mont., U.S.A. **92** D3
Cabo Delgado: Dist., Mozambique (cap. Porto Amélia) **77** E5
Cabo Frio: Brazil **96** G1
Cabo Juby: W. Sahara **78** B4
Cabonga Reservoir: Que., Canada **89** N2
Cabool: Mo., U.S.A. **88** E7
Caboolture: Queens., Austl. **70** K6
Caborca: Mexico **93** E6
Caborra Bassa Dam: Mozambique **77** D6
Cabot: Ark., U.S.A. **90** E8
Cabot Strait: Canada **85** O8
Cabourg: France **36** E6
Cabrach: Gram., Scotland **28** P5
Cabrera: i., Balearic Is. (Spain) **35** H17
Cabriel: riv., Spain **35** F17
Cabrière, La: mtns., France **40** M12
Cabrobó: Brazil **94** K5
Caburan: Philippines **65** H5
Cabusa: i., Mergui Arch., Burma **59** R12
Caçador: Brazil **96** E2
Čačak: Yugoslavia **39** R15
Caçapava: Brazil **96** E3
Cacequi: Brazil **96** E2
Cáceres: Brazil **94** F7
Cáceres: Colombia **94** B2
CÁCERES: & Prov., Spain **35** C17
Cachalot: B.C., Canada **92** B3
Cachari: Argentina **96** D4
Cacheu: Guinea-Bissau **80** A2
Cachi: Argentina **96** B2
Cachi, Nevado de: mtn., Argentina **96** B1
Cachimo: Angola **76** B4
Cachinal: Chile **96** B1
Cachiyuyo: Chile **96** A2
Cachoeira: Bahia, Brazil **94** K6
Cachoeira: Rio Grande do Sul, Brazil **96** E3
Cachoeiro: Brazil **95** J8
Cachuela Esperanza: Bolivia **94** D6
Cacine: Guinea-Bissau **80** B2
Cacolo: Angola **77** A5
Caconda: Angola **73** H12
Cadbury, North: Som., Eng. **24** Q17
Cadca: Czechoslovakia **43** Q12
Cadder: fort on Antonine Wall about 4 miles S. of Lennoxtown, Central, Scot. **29** N8
Caddo Lake: Tex./La., U.S.A. **90** D9
Cader Idris: mtn., Gwynedd, Wales **27** O14
Cadillac: France **37** E11
Cadillac: Mich., U.S.A. **88** J3
Cadiz: Calif., U.S.A. **93** D6
Cadiz: Ky., U.S.A. **88** H7
Cadiz: Ohio, U.S.A. **88** L5
Cadiz: Philippines **64** G4
CÁDIZ: & Prov., Spain **35** C18
Cadiz, G. of: Spain **35** C18

Cadnam: Hants., England **25** S18
Cadoxton: S. Glam., Wales **24** P17
CAEN: Calvados, France **36** E6
Caeo: Dyfed, Wales **24** O15
Cære: ancient town of S. Etruria about 5 miles from coast WNW. of Rome. **38** N16
Caergwrle: Clwyd, Wales **27** P13
Caerhûn: Gwynedd, Wales **27** O13
Caerleon: Gwent, Wales **24** Q16
CAERNARVON: Gwyn., Wales **27** N13
Caernarvon Bay: Wales **27** M13
Caerphilly: Mid Glam., Wales **24** P16
Caersws: Powys, Wales **27** P14
Caersws: site of Roman fort, Powys, Wales **27** P14
Caerwys: Clwyd, Wales **27** P13
Caesaraugusta: Roman town at Saragossa, Spain **35** F16
Caesarea: site of Roman city on coast S. of Zikhron Ya'aqov, Israel **55** a2
Caesarea: Roman town at Cherchel, Algeria **35** H18
Cæsarea Philippi (Baniyas): site of temple erected by Herod the Great to Caesar Augustus **51** b1
Caesarobriga: Roman town at Talavera de la Reina, Spain **35** D17
Caetité: Brazil **94** J6
Cafayate: Argentina **96** B2
Cafima: Angola **73** H13
Cafour: Tunisia **38** L18
Cagayan: Mindanao, Phil. **64** G5
Cagayan: riv., Luzon, Phil. **64** G3
Cagayan Sulu: i., Phil. **64** F5
Cagayan Is.: Philippines **64** G5
Cagli: Italy **41** S12
CAGLIARI: & gulf, Sardinia **38** L17
Cagnes: France **40** N12
Caguán: riv., Colombia **94** C3
Caguas: Puerto Rico **87** N14
Caha Mtns.: Kerry/Cork, Repub. of Ireland **31** B16
Caheragh: Cork, Repub. of Ireland **31** C16
Caherconlish: Lim., Repub. of Ireland **31** E14
Caherdaniel: Kerry, Repub. of Ireland **31** A16
Caher I.: Repub. of Ireland **30** A12
Cahir: Tip., Repub. of Irel. **31** F15
Cahirsiveen: Kerry, Repub. of Ireland **31** A16
Cahore Point: cape, Wex., Repub. of Ireland **31** J14
CAHORS: Lot, France **37** G11
Caianda: Angola **77** B5
Caiapónia: Brazil **94** G7
Caicara: Venezuela **94** D2
Caicó: Brazil **94** K5
Caicos Is.: (Br.) W. Indies **87** m13
Caicos Passage: Bahamas **87** m13
Caicus: river flowing S. of Bergama (Pergamum) into Çandarli G., Turkey **39** V16
Cailloma: Peru **94** C7
Caimito: riv., Panama **94** Ins.
Cairn Bannoch: Grampian/ Tayside, Scotland **28** P6
Cairndow: Strath., Scotland **29** M7
Cairn Gorm: mtn., Grampian/ Highland, Scotland **28** O5
Cairngorm Mtns.: Grampian/ Highland, Scotland **28** O5
Cairnharrow: mtn., Dumfries & Galloway, Scotland **29** N10
Cairnryan: Dumfries & Galloway, Scotland **29** L10
Cairns: Queens., Australia **69** H3
Cairnsmore: mtn., Dumfries & Galloway, Scotland **29** N9
Cairn Toul: mtn., Grampian, Scotland **28** O5
CAIRO (El Qahira): Egypt **56** B6
Cairo: Ga., U.S.A. **91** J10
Cairo: Ill., U.S.A. **88** G7
Cairo: Italy **40** O11
Caister on Sea: Norf., Eng. **25** Z14
Caistor: Lincs., England **27** V13
Caiundo: Angola **73** H13
Caiwarro: Queens., Austl. **71** F7
Cajamarca: Peru **94** B5
Cajamarquilla: Peru **94** B5
Cajarc: France **37** G11
Cajuru: Brazil **96** F1
Çakit: riv., Turkey **56** D3
Cakovec: Yugoslavia **41** W9
Cala: S. Africa **75** G5
Cala: Spain **35** C18
Cala, Point: cape, Formentera, Balearic Is. **35** G17
Calabar: Bolívar, Colombia **94** C1
Calamar: Vaupés, Colombia **94** C3
Calamian Group: is., Phil. **64** F4
Calamocha: Spain **35** F16
Calana: Chile **96** B1
Calamajue, Sierra de: mtns., Mexico **93** E7

Calder, West: Lothian, Scotland **29** O8
Caldera: Chile **96** A2
Calder Bridge: Cumbria, Eng. **26** P11
Caldercruix: Strath., Scot. **29** O8
Calderville: Queens., Austl. **70** G5
Çaldiran: Turkey **57** H2
Caldwell: Idaho, U.S.A. **92** D4
Caldwell: Kans., U.S.A. **90** C7
Caldwell: Tex., U.S.A. **90** C10
Caldy I.: Wales **24** M16
Caledon: & Dist., S. Africa **74** C7
Caledon: Tyr., N. Ireland **30** H11
Caledon: riv., S. Africa **75** G5
Caledonia: Minn., U.S.A. **88** F4
Caledonia: Ont., Canada **89** M4
Caledonian Canal: Scotland **28** M5
Calera: Chile **96** A3
Calestano: Italy **40** O11
Caleta Coloso: Chile **96** A1
Calexico: Calif., U.S.A. **93** D6
Calf, The: mtn., Cumbria, England **26** Q11
Calf of Man: i., I. of Man, United Kingdom **26** M11
Calgary: Alta., Canada **92** E2
Calgary: Inner Hebr., Scot. **29** J6
Calhoun: Mo., U.S.A. **90** E6
Calhoun Falls: S.C., U.S.A. **91** K8
Cali: Colombia **94** B3
Calico Rock: Ark., U.S.A. **88** E7
Calicut (Kozhikode): India **58** N12
Caliente: Nev., U.S.A. **93** E5
California: Mo., U.S.A. **88** E6
California: State, U.S.A. (cap. Sacramento) **93** C5
California, G. of: Mexico **93** E7
California, Lower: State, Mexico (cap. Mexicali) **93** E7
California Bay: U.S.A. **90** Ins.
California Point: cape, La., U.S.A. **90** Ins.
Călimăneşti: Romania **43** T14
Calimere, Point: cape, India **58** N12
Călineşti: Romania **39** T14
Calingasta: Argentina **96** B3
Calion: Ark., U.S.A. **90** E9
Calistoga: Calif., U.S.A. **93** C5
Calitzdorp: S. Africa **74** D6
Calivo: Philippines **64** G4
Callabonna: S. Australia **69** G5
Callac: France **36** B3
Callaeci: ancient Spanish tribe of Galicia, Spain **35** B15
Callan: Kilk., Repub. of Ireland **31** G14
Callan: riv., Armagh, N. Irel. **30** H11
Callander: Ont., Canada **89** M2
Callander: Central, Scotland **29** N7
Callanish: Outer Hebr., Scot. **28** H3
Callao: Peru **94** B6
Calle, La: Algeria **38** L18
Calleva Atrebatum: Romano-British town at Silchester, Hants., England **25** T17
Callide: Queens., Australia **70** J5
Callington: Corn., England **24** N18
Calliope: Queens., Australia **70** J4
Callosa de Ensarria: Spain **35** F17
Callow: Mayo, Repub. of Ireland **30** C12
Calmont: Brazil **96** E2
Calne: Wilts., England **24** R17
Caloosahatchee: riv., Fla., U.S.A. **91** L12
Calpe: Roman name of Gibraltar **35** D18
Calstock: Corn., England **24** N19
Caltagirone: Sicily **38** O18
Caltanissetta: Sicily **38** O18
Caluire-et-Cuire: France **37** K10
Calulo: Angola **73** G12
Calunda: Angola **77** B5
Calvados: Dept., France (cap. Caen) **36** E6
Calvert: Tex., U.S.A. **90** C10
Calvert I.: B.C., Canada **92** B2
Calverton: Notts., England **27** T13
Calvi: Corsica **38** L15
Calvinia: & Dist., S. Africa **74** C5
Calvisson: France **37** K12
Calw: W. Germany **40** O7
Calymnos: see Kálimnos.
Cam: riv., Cambs., England **25** V15
Camabatela: Angola **73** H11
Camacupa: Angola **73** H12
Camagüey: Cuba **87** M13
Camaiore: Italy **40** Q12
Camamu: Brazil **94** K6
Camaquã: & riv., Brazil **96** E3
Camargo: Bolivia **94** D8
Camargo: Mexico **93** F7
Camarina: Greek city on coast about due west of Scicli, Sicily **38** O18
Camarinal Point: cape, Spain (Gib. Inset) **32** Ins.
Camaron: Panama **94** Ins.
Camarones: Argentina **95** D12
Camarones: Mexico **93** H8
Camas: Wash., U.S.A. **92** C3
Camastianavaig: Inner Hebr., Scotland **28** J5
Camatambo: Angola **81** H6
Cambados: Spain **35** B15
Cambay: & gulf, Gujarat, India **58** M10
Camberley: Surrey, England **25** U17
Cambo: France **37** D12

Cambodia (Kampuchea): Republic **64** C4
Cap.: Phnom Penh
Area: 70,000 sq. miles (181,300 sq. km.)
Pop.: 6,701,000 (1969 E)

Cambois: Northumb., Eng. **26** S9
Camboon: Queens., Austl. **70** J5
Camborne: Corn., England **24** L19
Cambrai: France **36** J5
Cambremer: France **36** F6
Cambria: Calif., U.S.A. **93** C5
Cambrian Mtns.: Wales **24** O15
CAMBRIDGE: & Co., England **25** W15
Cambridge: Mass., U.S.A. **89** Q4
Cambridge: Md., U.S.A. **89** N6
Cambridge: Minn., U.S.A. **88** E3
Cambridge: North I., N.Z. **70** P13
Cambridge: Ohio, U.S.A. **88** L5
Cambridge: S. Africa **75** G6
Cambridge Bay: settlement, N.W.T., Canada **84** j4
Cambridge Springs: city, Pa., U.S.A. **88** L5
Cambronde: France **37** J10
Cambulo: Angola **76** B4
Camburg: E. Germany **45** R4
Cambuslang: Strath., Scot. **29** N8
Camden: Ark., U.S.A. **90** E9
Camden: Gt. Ldn., England **25** V16
Camden: Maine, U.S.A. **89** R3
Camden: N.J., U.S.A. **89** O6

Camden: N.S.W., Australia **71** J10
Camden: N.Y., U.S.A. **89** O4
Camden: S.C., U.S.A. **91** L8
Camden: Tex., U.S.A. **90** D10
Camden Bay: Alaska, U.S.A. **84** e3
Cameia: Angola **77** B5
Camel: riv., Corn., England **24** M18
Camelford: Corn., England **24** M18
Camelon: fort on Antonine Wall about 1 mile W. of Falkirk, Central, Scot. **29** O8
Cameret-sur-Mer: France **36** A7
Camerino: Italy **38** N15
Cameron: Tex., U.S.A. **90** C10
Cameron Highlands: Malaya, Malaysia **65** b11
Camerota: Italy **38** O16

Cameroun: Republic **81** G3
Cap.: Yaoundé
Area: 183,568 sq. miles (475,441 sq. km.)
Pop.: 5,836,000 (1970 E)

Cameroun Mount: Cameroun **81** F4
Cametá: Brazil **94** H4
Camfer: S. Africa **74** E6
Camiguin: i., Luzon, Phil. **64** G3
Camiguin: i., Mindanao, Phil. **64** G5
Camilla: Ga., U.S.A. **91** J10
Caminada Bay: La., U.S.A. **90** Ins.
Caminada Pass: La., U.S.A. **90** Ins.
Caminha: Portugal **35** B16
Camiri: Bolivia **94** E8
Camlaren: N.W.T., Canada **84** h5
Camlibel Mtns.: Turkey **56** E2
Camlough: Armagh, N. Irel. **30** J11
Cammack: Ark., U.S.A. **90** E8
Camocim: Brazil **94** J4
Camoge: riv., Lim., Repub. of Ireland **31** D14
Camolin: Wex., Repub. of Ireland **31** J14
Camon: Senegal **80** B2
Camooweal: Queens., Austl. **69** F3
Camotes Is.: Philippines **64** G4
Camp: Kerry, Repub. of Ireland **31** B15
Campana: Argentina **96** D3
Campania: Reg., Italy [cap. Napoli (Naples)] **38** O16
Campana I.: Chile **95** B13
Campbell: Mo., U.S.A. **88** F7
Campbell: S. Africa **74** E4
Campbell, Mount: Yukon, Canada **84** F5
Campbellpur: Punjab, Pakistan **58** M8
Campbell River: town, B.C., Canada **92** B2
Campbellsport: Wis., U.S.A. **88** G4
Campbellsville: Ky., U.S.A. **88** J7
Campbellton: N.B., Canada **89** R2
Campbelltown: High., Scot. **28** N4
Campbelltown: N.S.W., Australia **71** J10
Campbell Town: Tas., Austl. **68** H8
Campbeltown: Strath., Scot. **29** K9
Campeche: & bay, Mexico **86** k14
Campénéac: France **36** C7
Campeni: Romania **43** S13
Camperdown: Vict., Australia **71** E12
Camperdown: & Dist., Natal, S. Africa **75** J4
Campillos: Spain **35** D18
Câmpina: Romania **39** T14
Campina Grande: Brazil **94** K5
Campinas: Brazil **96** F1
Campo: Cameroun **81** F4
Campo: Mozambique **77** E6
Campo Alto: Brazil **96** E2
Campobasso: Italy **38** O16
Campo Belo: Brazil **96** F1
Campo del Cielo: Argentina **96** C2
Campo Formio: village about 4 miles SW. of Udine, Italy **41** T9
Campo Formoso: Brazil **94** J6
Campo Gallo: Argentina **96** C2
Campo Grande: Brazil **94** G8
Campo Largo: Brazil **94** J6
Campo Maior: Brazil **94** J4
Campo Maior: Portugal **35** C17
Campona: Mozambique **77** E5
Camporgiano: Italy **40** Q11
Campos: Brazil **96** G1
Campos: plains, Brazil **94** J6
Campos: plains, Brazil **95** G9
Camposampiero: Italy **41** R10
Campos Novos: Brazil **96** E2
Camp Point: city, Ill., U.S.A. **88** F5
Camps Bay: S. Africa **74** Ins.
Campsey Ash: Suff., Eng. **25** Y15
Campsie Fells: Central, Scot. **29** N7
Campti: La., U.S.A. **90** E10
Câmpulung: Romania **43** T14
Câmpulung Moldovenesc: Romania **43** T13
Cam Quelifá: Guinea-Bissau **80** B2
Camrose: Alta., Canada **92** E2
Camrose: Dyfed, Wales **24** L16
Camulodunum: British, later Roman, town at Colchester, Essex, England **25** X16
Camusteel: High., Scot. **28** K5
Çan: Turkey **39** U16
Cana: city of ancient Israel about 9 miles N. of Nazareth, Israel **55** b2
Canaan: ancient name for area now occupied by Israel and Lebanon **56** D5
Cana Brava: Brazil **94** J5

Canada: Dominion **84/5**
Cap.: Ottawa
Area: 3,851,809 sq. miles (9,976,185 sq. km.)
Pop.: 21,569,000 (1972 C)

Cañada de Gomez: Arg. **96** C3
Cañada Honda: Argentina **96** B3
Canadian: Tex., U.S.A. **90** A8
Canadian: riv., U.S.A. **93** G5
ÇANAKKALE: & Prov., Turkey **39** U16
Canale: Italy **40** N11
Canalejas: Argentina **96** B4
Canal Zone: (U.S.A.), Panama **94** Ins.
Canandaigua: N.Y., U.S.A. **89** N4
Cananea: Mexico **93** E6
Cananéia: Brazil **96** F1
Canary Basin: N. Atlantic Ocean **8** 30N 25W
Canary Is.: (Spain), Atlantic O. **78** A4
Canastota: N.Y., U.S.A. **89** O4
Canatlán: Mexico **93** G8
Canaveral, Cape: Fla., U.S.A. **91** L11
Cañaveras: Spain **35** E16
Canavieiras: Brazil **94** K7
Canbelego: N.S.W., Austl. **71** G8

130 Canberra—Castledawson

CANBERRA: Capital Territ., Australia **71** H10
Canby: Minn., U.S.A. **92** H4
Cancale: France **36** D7
Canchas: Chile **96** A2
Canchungo: Guinea-Bissau **80** A2
Cancon: France **37** F11
Çandarli Gulf: Turkey **39** U17
Candas: France **36** H5
Candé: France **36** D8
Candela: Mexico **93** G7
Candelaria: Philippines **64** F3
Candelo: N.S.W., Australia **71** H11
Candia (Iraklion): Crete **39** T19
Cândido de Abreu: Brazil **96** E1
Candiota: Brazil **96** E3
Candle: Alaska, U.S.A. **84** c4
Cando: N. Dak., U.S.A. **92** H3
Candon: Luzon, Philippines **64** G3
Canea (Khania): Crete **39** T19
Canela: Brazil **96** E2
Canelo, El: Mexico **93** G8
Canelones: Uruguay **96** D3
Canet, Étang de: *lag.*, France **37** J13
Cañete: Chile **96** A4
Cañete: Spain **35** F16
Canewdon: Essex, England **25** X16
Caney: Kans., U.S.A. **90** D7
Canfranc: Spain **37** E13
Cangamba: Angola **77** A5
Cangumbe: Angola **77** A5
Canguçu: Brazil **96** E3
Canha: Portugal **35** B17
Caniçado: Mozambique **75** K2
Canicatti: Sicily **38** N18
Canik Mtns.: Turkey **56** E1
Canindé: Brazil **94** K4
Canipan: Palawan, Phil. **64** F5
Canisteo: N.Y., U.S.A. **89** N4
Canisy: France **36** D6
ÇANKIRI: *& Prov.*, Turkey **56** C1
Canna: *i.*, Inner Hebr., Scot. **28** H5
Canna, Sound of: Canna/Rhum, Inner Hebr., Scotland **28** J5
Cannae: Roman battlefield on hill 6 miles SW. from mouth of river Ofanto, Italy **38** O16
Cannanore: Tamil Nadu, India **58** N12
Cannelton: Ind., U.S.A. **88** H7
Cannes: France **40** N12
Cannet, Le: France **40** N12
Cannich: *& glen*, Highland, Scotland **28** M5
Canninefates: ancient German tribe of Holland, Netherlands **44** K3
Cannington: Som., England **24** P17
Canning Town: W. Bengal, India **59** P10
Cannobio: Italy **40** O9
Cannock: Staffs., England **27** R14
Cannock Chase: *dist.*, Eng. **27** S14
Cannonball: *riv.*, N. Dak., U.S.A. **92** G3
Cannouan: *i.*, Grenadines, Windward Is. **87** c4
Canoas: *riv.*, Brazil **96** E2
Canoinhas: Brazil **96** E2
Canonbie: Dumfries & Galloway, Scotland **29** Q9
Canon City: Colo., U.S.A. **93** F5
Canopus: Graeco-Roman city at Abu Qîr, Egypt **56** B6
Canora: Sask., Canada **92** G2
Canosa di Puglia: Italy **38** P16
Canossa: castle (579 m.) on slopes of Apennines 12 miles SW. of Reggio nell' Emilia, Italy **40** Q11
Canowindra: N.S.W., Austl. **71** H9
Canso: *& cape*, N.S., Canada **89** V3
Cantabrian Mtns.: Spain **35** D15
Cantagalo: Brazil **96** G1
Cantal: *Dept.*, France (*cap.* Aurillac) **37** H10
Cantallóps: Spain **37** H13
Cantanhede: Portugal **35** B16
Cantantal: Argentina **96** B3
Canterbury: Kent, England **25** Y17
Canterbury: *Dist. & plains*, South I., N.Z. (*cap.* Christchurch) **70** N16
Canterbury Bight: South I., New Zealand **70** O17
Can Tho: Vietnam **64** D4
Cantin, Cape: Morocco **80** K8
Canton: Ga., U.S.A. **91** J8
Canton: Ill., U.S.A. **88** F5
CANTON (Kwangchow): Kwangtung, China **62** U10
Canton: Miss., U.S.A. **90** F9
Canton: Mo., U.S.A. **88** F5
Canton: N.C., U.S.A. **91** K8
Canton: N.Y., U.S.A. **89** O3
Canton: Ohio, U.S.A. **88** L5
Canton: S. Dak., U.S.A. **92** H4
Canton Reservoir: Okla., U.S.A. **90** B7
Cantú: Italy **40** P10
Canudos: Brazil **94** F5
Canungra: Queens., Austl. **70** K6
Canusium: Graeco-Roman city on right bank of Ofanto about 12 miles from its mouth, Italy **38** P16
Canutama: Brazil **94** E5
Canvey I.: Essex, England **25** X16
Cany-Barville: France **36** F6
Canyon: Tex., U.S.A. **93** G6
Canyon City: Oreg., U.S.A. **92** D4
Canyon de Chelly Nat. Mon.: Ariz., U.S.A. **93** F5
Canyonlands Nat. Park: Utah, U.S.A. **93** E5
Canzar: Angola **76** B4
Cao Bang: Vietnam **64** D2
Caolisport, Loch: Strathclyde, Scotland **29** K8
Caol Mor: *str.*, Inner Hebr., Scotland **28** J5
Caórle: Italy **41** S10
ÇAPAKÇUR (Bingöl): Bingöl, Turkey **57** G2
Cap à l'Aigle: Que., Canada **89** O2
Capanaparo: *riv.*, Venezuela **94** D2
Capanema: Brazil **94** H4
Capão Bonito: Brazil **96** F1
Capátarida: Venezuela **94** C1
Capbreton: France **37** D12
Cap d'Ambre: *cape*, Malagasy Rep. **73** O12
Cape: *riv.*, Queens., Austl. **70** G3
Cape Barren I.: Tas., Austl. **68** H8
Cape Basin: S. Atlantic Ocean **8** 40S 05E
Cape Breton Highlands Nat. Park: Cape Breton I., Canada **89** V2
Cape Breton I.: Canada **89** V2
Cape Charles: *city*, Va., U.S.A. **89** O7
CAPE COAST: *town*, Central, Ghana **80** D3
Cape Cod: *& bay*, Mass., U.S.A. **89** Q5
Cape Dorset: N.W.T., Can. **85** M5
Cape Fear: *riv.*, N.C., U.S.A. **91** M8
Cape Girardeau: *city*, Mo., U.S.A. **88** G7
Capel: Surrey, England **25** V17
Capel Curig: Gwyn., Wales **27** O13
Capella: Queens., Australia **70** H4
Capelle, La: France **36** J6
Capelongo: Angola **73** H12
Cape May: N.J., U.S.A. **89** O6
Capena: city of SE. *Etruria* 20 miles N. of Rome. **38** N15
Capenda Camulemba: Ang. **77** A4
Cape North: Cape Breton I., Canada **89** V2
Cape of Good Hope: S. Afr. **74** C7
Cape of Good Hope Nature Reserve: C.P., S. Africa **74** *Ins.*
Cape Point: S. Africa **74** *Ins.*
Cape Province: S. Africa (*cap.* Cape Town) **75** F5
Cape Rise: S. Atlantic Ocean **8** 45S 20E
Capernaum (Tell Hum): city of ancient *Israel* at NW. corner of Lake Tiberias **55** b2
Cape Tormentine: *town*, N.B., Canada **89** U2
CAPE TOWN: Cape of Good Hope, S. Africa **74** *Ins.*
Cape Verde Basin: N. Atlantic Ocean **8** 20N 30W
Cape Verde Is.: Atlantic Ocean (*cap.* Praia) **78** *Ins.*
Cape Vincent: *city*, N.Y., U.S.A. **89** N3
Cape York Penin.: Queens., Australia **69** G2
Cap Haïtien: Haiti **87** m14
Capheaton: Northumb., Eng. **26** S9
Capiatá: Paraguay **96** D2
Capim: *& riv.*, Brazil **94** H4
Capital Territory: Australia (*cap.* Canberra) **70** H10
Capitán Arturo Prat: *rsch. stn.*, Antarctica **9** 65S 60W
Capitán François: Fr. Gu. **94** G3
Capitán Pastene: Chile **96** A4
Capitán Solari: Argentina **96** D2
Capitol Reef Nat. Mon.: Utah, U.S.A. **93** E5
Capiz: Philippines **64** G4
Capodistria: *see* Koper. **41** T10
Capoompeta: *mtn.*, N.S.W., Australia **71** K7
Caporetto: battlefield about 8 miles SE. of Zaga near Italian border of NW. Yugoslavia **41** T9
Cappadocia: ancient name of district N. of *Cilicia* (q.v.) between rivers Kizil and Euphrates, Turkey **56** D2
Cappagh White: Tip., Repub. of Ireland **31** E14
Cappamore: Lim., Repub. of Ireland **31** E14
Cappoquin: Wat., Repub. of Ireland **31** F15
Capraia: *i.*, Italy **38** L15
Capreol: Ont., Canada **88** L2
Caprera: *i.*, Sardinia **38** L16
Capri: *i.*, Italy **38** O16
Capricorn Group: Austl. **70** K4
Caprino: Italy **41** Q10
Caprivi Strip: *geog. reg.*, SW. Africa **77** B6
Captain's Flat: N.S.W., Australia **71** H10
Captieux: France **37** E11
Capua: Italy **38** O16
Caputh: Tay., Scotland **29** P6
Caquetá: *riv.*, Colombia **94** C4
Caracal: Romania **39** T14
CARACAS: Venezuela **94** D1
Caractonium: Roman name of Catterick, N. Yorks., Eng. **26** S11
Caraga: Mindanao, Phil. **64** H5
Caragh Lough: Kerry, Repub. of Ireland **31** B15
Caraguatatuba: Brazil **96** F1
Caraguatay: Paraguay **96** D2
Carahue: Chile **96** A4
Cara I.: Scotland **29** K8
Carajás, Serra dos: *mtns.*, Brazil **94** G5
Caralps: Spain **37** H13
Caraman: France **37** G12
Caransebeş: Romania **39** S14
Carapeguá: Paraguay **96** D2
Caraquet: N.B., Canada **89** T2
Caráquez, Bahia de: Ecuador **94** A4
Caratasca Lagoon: Hond. **87** I14
Caratinga: Brazil **94** J7
Carauari: Brazil **94** D4
Caraúbas: Brazil **94** K5
Caravaca: Spain **35** F17
Caravelas: Brazil **94** K7
Carázinho: Brazil **96** E2
Carballino: Spain **35** B15
Carballo: Spain **35** B15
Carberry Hill: battlefield on hill to NE. of Dalkeith, Lothian, Scotland **29** P8
Carbó: Mexico **93** E7
Carbon, Cape: Algeria **35** J18
Carbonara, Cape: Sardinia **38** L17
Carbon-Blanc: France **37** E11
Carbondale: Ill., U.S.A. **88** G7
Carbondale: Pa., U.S.A. **89** O5
Carbonear: Newf., Canada **85** w3
Carbon Hill: *city.*, Ala., U.S.A. **91** H9
Carbonia: Sardinia **38** L17
Carbonne: France **37** G12
Carbost: North Skye, Inner Hebr., Scotland **28** J5
Carbost: South Skye, Inner Hebr., Scotland **28** J5
Carbury: Kild., Repub. of Ireland **31** H13
Carcans: France **37** D10
CARCASSONNE: Aude, France **37** H12
Carcès: France **40** M12
Carchemish: site of Syrian city on Euphrates near Birecik, Syria **56** E3
Carcoar: N.S.W., Australia **71** H9
Carcross: Yukon, Canada **84** f5
Cardamun: *i.*, Laccadive Is. **58** M12
Cárdenas: Cuba **87** I13
Cardia: Greek city on N. side of isthmus at easterly end of Gallipoli Penin., Turkey **39** U16
CARDIFF: S. Glam., Wales (*co. town*, Mid. Glam. & S. Glam.) **24** P17
Cardigan: Dyfed, Wales **24** M15
Cardigan Bay: Wales **24** N14
Cardington: Salop, England **27** Q14
Cardoville: Trans., S. Africa **74** M *Ins.*
Cardston: Alta., Canada **92** E3
Cardwell: Queens., Australia **69** H3
Carei: Romania **43** S13
Carenero: Venezuela **94** D1
Carentan: France **36** D6
Careston: Tayside, Scotland **29** Q6
Carevo Selo: Yugoslavia **39** S16
Carey, Lake: W. Australia **68** C5
Careysburg: Liberia **80** B3
Cargados Carajos Is.: (Mauritius), Indian Ocean **19** 10S 50E
Cargan: Antrim, N. Ireland **30** J10
Cargill: Tayside, Scotland **29** P6
Carhué: Argentina **96** C4
Carhaix: France **36** B7
Carham: Northumb., Eng. **26** R8
Caria: Greek name of area bounded approximately by rivers *Maeander* (Menderes) and *Indus* (Dalaman), SW. Turkey **39** U18
Cariati: Italy **38** P17
Caribbean Sea: W. Indies **87** M14
Cariboo Mtns.: B.C., Can. **92** C2
Caribou: Maine, U.S.A. **89** R2
Caribou I.: Ont., Canada **88** J2
Caribou Mtns.: Alta., Can. **84** H6
Carichic: Mexico **93** F7
Carignan: France **36** L6
Carignano: Italy **40** N11
Carillo Puerto: Mexico **86** L14
Carinda: N.S.W., Australia **71** G8
Carinde: Mozambique **77** D6
Cariñena: Spain **35** F16
Carinhanha: Brazil **94** J6
Carini: Sicily **38** N17
Carinthia: *Prov.*, Austria (*cap.* Klagenfurt) **41** T9
Caripito: Venezuela **94** E1
Carisbrooke: I. of Wight, England **25** T18
Cariús: Brazil **94** K5
Cark: Cumbria, England **26** Q11
Carlanstown: Meath, Repub. of Ireland **30** H12
Carleman: SW. Africa **74** A1
Carlet: Spain **35** F17
Carleton: Que., Canada **89** S1
Carleton, Mount: N.B., Can. **89** S2
Carleton Place: Ont., Can. **89** N3
Carletonville: Trans., S. Africa **74L** *Ins.*
Carlin: Nev., U.S.A. **92** D4
Carlingford: *& lough*, Louth, Repub. of Ireland **30** J11
Carlinville: Ill., U.S.A. **88** G6
Carlisle: Ark., U.S.A. **90** F8
CARLISLE: Cumbria, England **26** Q10
Carlisle: Pa., U.S.A. **89** N5
Carlitte, Pic: *mtn.*, France **37** G13
Carlops: Borders, Scotland **29** P8
Carlos Casares: Argentina **96** C4
Carlota, La: Argentina **96** C3
CARLOW: *& Co.*, Repub. of Ireland **31** H14
Carloway: Outer Hebr., Scot. **28** H3
Carlsbad: N. Mex., U.S.A. **93** G6
Carlsbad Caverns Nat. Park: N. Mex., U.S.A. **93** G6
Carlsberg Ridge: Indian Ocean **9** 05N 60E
Carlton: Minn., U.S.A. **88** E2
Carlton: Notts., England **27** T13
Carlton: N. Yorks., England **27** T12
Çarlton: S. Africa **75** F5
Carluke: Strath., Scotland **29** O8
Carlyle: Ill., U.S.A. **88** G6
Carlyle: Sask., Canada **92** G3
Carmacks: Yukon, Canada **84** F5
Carmagnola: Italy **40** N11
Carmania: Graeco-Roman name of area N. of mouth of Persian Gulf, Iran **55** J9
Carmanville: Newf., Canada **85** V2
CARMARTHEN: Dyfed, Wales **24** N16
Carmarthen: *bay*, Wales **24** N16
Carmaux: France **37** H11
Carmel: mtn. S. of Haifa, Israel **56** D5
Carmelo: Uruguay **96** D3
Carmen: Colombia **94** B2
Carmen: Mexico **86** k14
Carmen: Uruguay **96** D3
Carmen: *i.*, Mexico **93** E7
Carmen: *riv.*, Chile **96** A2
Carmen Alto: Chile **96** B1
Carmen del Parana: Paraguay **96** D2
Carmen de Patagonas: Arg. **95** E12
Carmensa: Argentina **96** B4
Carmi: Ill., U.S.A. **88** G6
Carmila: Queens., Australia **70** H3
Carmona: Spain **35** D18
CARMONA: Uige, Angola **73** H11
Carmyllie: Tay., Scotland **29** Q6
Carn: Lon., N. Ireland **30** H10
Carna: Galway, Repub. of Ireland **31** B13
Carna: *i.*, High., Scotland **29** K6
Carnaby: Humb., England **27** V11
Carnac: France **36** B8
Carnarvon: W. Australia **68** A4
Carnarvon: *& Dist.*, S. Africa **74** E5
Carnarvon Gorge National Park: Queens., Australia **70** H5
Carnarvon Range: Queens., Australia **70** H5
Carnarvon Range: W. Austl. **68** C5
Carnatic: *geog. reg.*, India **58** N12
Carn Ban: *mtn.*, High., Scot. **28** N5
Carnbee: Fife, Scotland **29** Q7
Carncastle: Antrim, N. Irel. **30** K10
Carndonagh: Don., Repub. of Ireland **30** G9
Carnduff: Sask., Canada **92** G3
Carnedd Dafydd: *mtn.*, Gwynedd, Wales **27** O13
Carnedd Llywelyn: *mtn.*, Gwynedd, Wales **27** O13
Carnegie: Okla., U.S.A. **90** B8
Carnegie: W. Australia **68** C5
Carnegie, Lake: W. Austl. **68** C5
Carnegie Ridge: S. Pacific Ocean **7** 05S 90W
Carn Eige: *mtn.*, W. Highlands, Scotland **28** L5
Carnero Point: *cape*, Spain (Gib. *Inset*) **32** *Ins.*
Carnew: Wick., Repub. of Ireland **31** J14
Carney: Sligo, Repub. of Ireland **30** D11
Carnforth: Lancs., England **26** Q11
Carnic Alps: Austria/Italy **41** S9
Car Nicobar: *i.*, Nicobar Is. **59** Q13
Carnlough: Antrim, N. Irel. **30** K10
Carn Mairg: *mtn.*, Tayside, Scotland **29** N6
Carn More: *mtn.*, Grampian, Scotland **28** P5
Carn na Caim: *mtn.*, Highland, Scotland **28** N6
Carno: Powys, Wales **27** O14
Carnock: Fife, Scotland **29** O7
Carnot: Central African Rep. **81** H4
Carnoustie: Tayside, Scot. **29** Q6
Carnsore Point: *cape*, Wex., Repub. of Ireland **31** J15
Carnuntum: Roman camp at Petronell, Lower Austria **31** W7
Carnutes: Gallic tribe with centres at Chartres and Orleans, France **36** G7
Carnwath: Strath., Scotland **29** O8
Caro: Alaska, U.S.A. **84** E4
Caro: Mich., U.S.A. **88** K4
Carolina: Brazil **94** H5
Carolina: *& Dist.*, Trans., S. Africa **75** J3
Carolina, La: Spain **35** E17
Caroline Islands: (U.S.A.), N. Pacific Ocean **7** 05N 145E
Caroline I.: (Br.), Pacific O. **83** e2
Caroni: *riv.*, Venezuela **94** E2
Carora: Venezuela **94** C1
Carpathian Mtns.: Europe **43** S12
Carpathos: *see* Karpáthos.
Carpentaria, G. of: Austl. **69** F2
Carpentras: France **37** L11
Carpetani: ancient Spanish tribe of upper Tagus valley **35** E16
Carpi: Italy **41** Q11
Carpolac (Morea): Vict., Australia **71** D11
Carquefou: France **36** D8
Carqueiranne: France **40** M12
Carra, Lough: Mayo, Repub. of Ireland **30** C12
Carrabelle: Fla., U.S.A. **91** J11
Carracastle: Mayo, Repub. of Ireland **30** D12
Carradale: Strath., Scotland **29** L8
Carragh: Kild., Repub. of Ireland **31** H13
Carran: Clare, Repub. of Ireland **31** C13
Carrauntuohil: *mtn.*, Kerry, Repub. of Ireland **31** B15
Carrara: Italy **40** Q11
Carraroe: Galway, Repub. of Ireland **31** B13
Carrathool: N.S.W., Austl. **71** F10
Carrbridge: High., Scotland **28** O5
Carrhae: ancient town of N. *Mesopotamia* at Haran, Turkey **56** F3
Carriacou: *i.*, Windward Is. **87** c4
Carrick: Strath., Scotland **29** M7
Carrick: *dist.*, Strath., Scot. **29** M9
Carrick: Don., Repub. of Ireland **30** D10
Carrick: Wex., Repub. of Ireland **31** H15
Carrickart: Don., Repub. of Ireland **30** F9
Carrickbeg: Wat., Repub. of Ireland **31** G15
Carrickfergus: Antrim, N. Ireland **30** K10
Carrickmacross: Monaghan, Repub. of Ireland **30** H12
Carrickmore: Tyr., N. Irel. **30** G10
CARRICK ON SHANNON: Leit., Repub. of Ireland **30** E12
Carrick-on-Suir: Tip., Repub. of Ireland **31** G15
Carrieton: S. Australia **71** C9
Carrigaholt: Clare, Repub. of Ireland **31** B14
Carrigaline: Cork, Repub. of Ireland **31** E16
Carrigallen: Leit., Repub. of Ireland **30** F12
Carrigans: Don., Repub. of Ireland **30** G10
Carrigkerry: Lim., Repub. of Ireland **31** C15
Carrignavar: Cork, Repub. of Ireland **31** E16
Carrigtohill: Cork, Repub. of Ireland **31** E16
Carrilobo: Argentina **96** C3
Carrington: N. Dak., U.S.A. **92** H3
Carrión de los Condes: Sp. **35** D15
Carrizal Bajo: Chile **96** A2
Carrizalillo: Chile **96** A2
Carrizo Springs: Tex., U.S.A. **90** B14
Carrizozo: N. Mex., U.S.A. **93** F9
Carroll: Iowa, U.S.A. **92** J6
Carrollton: Ga., U.S.A. **91** J6
Carrollton: Ill., U.S.A. **88** F6
Carrollton: Ky., U.S.A. **88** J6
Carrollton: Mo., U.S.A. **88** E6
Carron: *riv.*, Central, Scot. **29** N7
Carron: *riv.*, Highland, Scotland **28** N4
Carron, Loch: Highland, Scotland **28** K5
Carron, Strath: *val.*, Highland, Scotland **28** M4
Carronbridge: Dumfries & Galloway, Scotland **29** O9
Carrot: *riv.*, Sask., Canada **92** G2
Carrouges: France **36** E7
Carrowdore: Down, N. Irel. **30** K10
Carrowmore: Sligo, Repub. of Ireland **30** D11
Carrowmore, Lough: Mayo, Repub. of Ireland **30** B11
Carrshield: Northumb., Eng. **26** R10
Carşamba: *& riv.*, Turkey **56** E1
Carseoli: Roman colony in territory of *Aequi* about 30 miles ENE. of Rome. **38** N15
CARSON CITY: Nev., U.S.A. **93** D5
Carsphairn: Dumfries & Galloway, Scotland **29** N9
Carstairs: Alta., Canada **92** E2
Carstairs: Strath., Scotland **29** O8
Cartagena: Chile **96** A3
Cartagena: Colombia **94** B1
Cartagena: Spain **35** F18
Cartago: Colombia **94** B3
Cartago: Costa Rica **87** I15
Cartaxo: Portugal **35** B17
Cartaya: Spain **35** C18
Carteia: Roman colony between Algeciras and Gibraltar, Spain **35** D18
Carter Cays: Bahamas **91** N12
Carteret: France **36** D6
Carter Fell: *mtn.*, Eng./Scot. **29** Q9
Cartersville: Ga., U.S.A. **91** J8
Carterton: North I., N.Z. **70** P17
Carthage: Ark., U.S.A. **90** E8
Carthage: Ill., U.S.A. **88** F5
Carthage: Miss., U.S.A. **90** G9
Carthage: Mo., U.S.A. **90** D7
Carthage: N.C., U.S.A. **91** M8
Carthage: N.Y., U.S.A. **89** O4
Carthage: Tenn., U.S.A. **88** J7
Carthage: Tex., U.S.A. **90** D9
Carthage: ancient city on G. of Tunis near La Marsa **38** M18
Carthago Nova: Roman town at Cartagena, Spain **35** F18
Carthorpe: N. Yorks., Eng. **26** S11
Cartier I.: *see* Ashmore & Cartier Is.
Cartmel: Cumbria, England **26** Q11
Cartwright: Newf., Canada **84** O7
Caruaru: Brazil **94** K5
Carumbo: Angola **76** B4
Carúpano: Venezuela **94** E1
Carutapera: Brazil **94** H4
Caruthersville: Mo., U.S.A. **88** G7
Carvin: France **36** H5
Caryapundy Swamp: Queens./N.S.W., Austl. **71** E7
Casablanca: Chile **96** A3
CASABLANCA (El Dar el Beida): *& Pref.*, Morocco **80** K8
Casa Branca: Brazil **96** F1
Casale Monferrato: Italy **40** O10
Casalmaggiore: Italy **40** Q11
Casamance: *Reg.*, *& riv.*, Senegal (*cap.* Ziguinchor) **80** A2
Casamozza: Corsica **38** L15
Casa Nova: Brazil **94** J5
Casarsa della Delizia: Italy **41** S10
Casarza: Italy **40** P11
Casas Grandes: Mexico **93** F6
Casas Ibañez: Spain **35** F17
Cascade Point: *cape*, South I., New Zealand **70** M17
Cascade Range: Oreg./Wash., U.S.A. **92** C3
Cascais: Portugal **35** B17
Cascavel: Brazil **94** K4
Cascina: Italy **40** Q12
Caselle: Italy **40** N10
Caseros: Argentina **96** D3
Caserta: Italy **38** O16
Casey: *rsch. stn.*, Antarctica **9** 70S 110E
Casey: Ill., U.S.A. **88** H6
Cashel: Tip., Repub. of Irel. **31** F14
Cashmere: Queens., Austl. **70** H6
Cashmere: Wash., U.S.A. **92** C3
Casiguran: Luzon, Phil. **64** G3
Casilda: Argentina **96** C3
Casina: Italy **40** Q11
Casino: N.S.W., Australia **71** K7
Casiquiare: *riv.*, Venezuela **94** D3
Čáslav: Czechoslovakia **45** V6
Casma: Peru **94** B5
Caso: Spain **35** D15
Caso Nova: Brazil **94** J5
Casola: Italy **41** R11
CasCaspe: Spain **35** F16
Casper: Wyo., U.S.A. **92** F4
Caspian Sea: Central Asia **50** H6
Casquet Banks: Channel Is. (Br.) **25** *Ins.*
Casquets: *rocks*, Channel Is. (Br.) **25** *Ins.*
Cass: W. Va., U.S.A. **89** M6
Cassagnes: France **37** H11
Cassai: Angola **77** B5
Cassamba: Angola **77** B5
Cass City: Mich., U.S.A. **88** K4
Cassel: France **36** H5
Casselton: N. Dak., U.S.A. **92** H3
Casse Tete: *i.*, La., U.S.A. **90** *Ins.*
Cassine: Italy **40** O11
Cassinga: Angola **73** H13
Cassino: Italy **38** N16
Cassis: France **40** L12
Cass Lake: *& city*, Minn., U.S.A. **88** D2
Cassos: *see* Kásos.
Cassville: Mo., U.S.A. **90** E7
Castabala Hieropolis: ancient Cicilian, later Graeco-Roman, town on N. bank of river loop SE. of town of Maraş, Turkey **56** E3
Castagneto: Italy **38** M15
Castagnole: Italy **40** O11
Castanhal: Brazil **94** H4
Castaño: Argentina **96** B3
Castel Benito: Libya **32** E5
Casteldelfino: Italy **40** N11
Castel di Sangro: Italy **38** O16
Castelfiorentino: Italy **41** Q12
Castelfranco dell' Emilia: Italy **41** R11
Castelfranco Veneto: Italy **41** R10
Casteljaloux: France **37** F11
Castellammare: Italy **38** O16
Castellammare: Sicily **38** N17
Castellamonte: Italy **40** N10
Castellane: France **40** M12
Castellazzo: Italy **40** O11
Castell Collen: site of Roman fort about 1½ miles NW. of Llandrindod Wells, Wales **24** P15
Castelli: Buenos Aires, Arg. **96** D4
Castelli: Chaco, Argentina **96** C2
Castellic, Pointe du: *cape*, Fr. **36** C8
Castellón: *Prov.*, Spain (*cap.* Castellón de la Plana) **35** F16
CASTELLÓN DE LA PLANA: Castellón, Spain **35** F17
Castellos: Rhodes, Dodec. **39** U18
Castellote: Spain **35** F16
Castelmoron: France **37** F11
Castelnau: Gironde, France **37** E10
Castelnau: Lot, France **37** G11
Castelnaudary: France **37** G12
Castelnau-Rivière-Basse: Fr. **37** E12
Castelnovo ne' Monti: Italy **40** Q11
Castelnuovo: Italy **40** Q11
Castelnuovo Scriva: Italy **40** O11
CASTELO BRANCO: Beira Baixa, Portugal **35** C17
Castelo de Vide: Portugal **35** C17
Castelrotto: Italy **41** R9
Castel San Giovanni: Italy **40** P10
Castel San Pietro: Italy **41** R11
Castelsarrasin: France **37** G11
Casteltermini: Sicily **38** N18
Castelvetrano: Sicily **38** N18
Castéra-Verduzan: France **37** F12
Casterton: Vict., Australia **71** D11
Castets: France **37** D12
Castex: Argentina **96** C4
Castiglioncello: Italy **40** Q12
Castiglione: Emilia Romagna, Italy **41** R11
Castiglione: Lombardy, It. **40** P10
Castiglione delle Stiviere: It. **40** Q10
Castilla: Chile **96** B1
Castillon: Ariège, France **37** G13
Castillon: Gironde, France **37** E11
Castillonnès: France **37** F11
Castillos: Uruguay **96** E3
Castle Acre: Norf., England **25** X14
CASTLEBAR: Mayo, Repub. of Ireland **30** C12
Castlebay: Outer Hebr., Scotland **28** G6
Castlebellingham: Louth, Repub. of Ireland **30** J12
Castleblakeney: Galway, Repub. of Ireland **31** E13
Castleblaney: Monaghan, Repub. of Ireland **30** H11
Castle Bolton: North Yorkshire, England **26** S11
Castlebridge: Wex., Repub. of Ireland **31** J15
Castle Bytham: Lincs., Eng. **27** U14
Castle Carrock: Cumbria, England **26** Q10
Castle Cary: Som., England **24** Q17
Castlecary: fort on *Antonine Wall* about 4 miles E. of Kilsyth, Strath., Scotland **29** N8
Castlecaulfield: Tyr., N. Irel. **30** H10
Castlecomer: Kilk., Repub. of Ireland **31** G14
Castleconnell: Lim., Repub. of Ireland **31** D14
Castlecor: Cork, Repub. of Ireland **31** D15
Castledawson: Lon., N. Irel. **30** H10

Castlederg—Chapel St. Leonards 131

Castlederg: Tyr., N. Ireland **30** F10
Castledermot: Kild., Repub. of Ireland **31** H14
Castle Donington: Leics., England **27** T14
Castle Douglas: Dumfries & Galloway, Scotland **29** O10
Castle Eden: Durham, Eng. **26** T10
Castlefinn: Don., Repub. of Ireland **30** F10
Castleford: W. Yorks., Eng. **27** T12
Castlegregory: Kerry, Repub. of Ireland **31** A15
Castlehill: Mayo, Repub. of Ireland **30** B12
Castleisland: Kerry, Repub. of Ireland **31** C15
Castlelyons: Cork, Repub. of Ireland **31** E15
Castlemaine: Kerry, Repub. of Ireland **31** B15
Castlemaine: Vict., Austl. **71** F11
Castlemartin: Dyfed, Wales **24** L16
Castlemartyr: Cork, Repub. of Ireland **31** E16
Castlemorton: Hereford & Worcester, England **24** R15
Castle of Mey: High., Scot. **28** P2
Castleplunket: Rosc., Repub. of Ireland **30** E12
Castle Point: North I., N.Z. **70** Q15
Castlepollard: Westmeath, Repub. of Ireland **30** G12
Castlerea: Rosc., Repub. of Ireland **30** E12
Castlereagh: *riv.*, N.S.W., Australia **71** H8
Castle Rock: *city,* Colo., U.S.A. **93** G5
Castlerock: Lon., N. Ireland **30** H9
Castleshane: Monaghan, Repub. of Ireland **30** H11
Castleshaw: site of Roman fort about 2½ miles SW. of Marsden, W. Yorks., Eng. **27** S12
Castleside: Durham, Eng. **26** S10
Castleton: Derby., England **27** S13
Castletown: Cork, Repub. of Ireland **31** D16
Castletown: I. of Man, United Kingdom **26** M11
Castletown: High., Scotland **28** P2
Castletown: Laois, Repub. of Ireland **31** G14
Castletown: Westmeath, Repub. of Ireland **30** G13
Castletown Berehaven: Cork, Repub. of Ireland **31** B16
Castletownroche: Cork, Repub. of Ireland **31** E15
Castletownshend: Cork, Repub. of Ireland **31** C16
Castlewellan: Down, N. Ireland **30** K11
Caston: Norf., England **25** X14
Castra Aeni: Roman fort at Innsbruck, Austria **40** R8
Castra Batava: Roman fort at Passau (border of Germany and Upper Austria) **40** T7
Castres: France **37** H12
Castricum: Netherlands **44** K3
Castries: France **37** J12
CASTRIES: St. Lucia, Windward Is. **87** c4
Castro: Brazil **96** E1
Castro: Chile **95** C12
Castro Alves: Brazil **94** K6
Castro del Rio: Spain **35** D18
Castrogeriz: Spain **35** D15
Castropol: Spain **35** C15
Castro Urdiales: Spain **35** E15
Castro Verde: Portugal **35** B18
Castrovillari: Italy **38** P17
Castuera: Spain **35** D17
Castulo: Roman town about 4 miles ESE. of Linares, Spain **35** E17
Casula: Mozambique **77** D6
Casummit Lake: *town,* Ont., Canada **92** J2
Çat: Turkey **57** G2
Cat: *i.*, Miss., U.S.A. **90** G10
Catacamas: Honduras **86** L15
Catacaos: Peru **94** A5
Catahoula Lake: La., U.S.A. **90** E10
Catalão: Brazil **94** H7
Çatalca: Turkey **39** V16
Catalina: Chile **96** B2
Catalonia: *old prov.*, Spain **35** G16
CATAMARCA: & *Prov.*, Arg. **96** B2
Catanduanes: *i.*, Philippines **64** G4
Catanduva: Brazil **95** H8
Catania: & *gulf,* Sicily **38** O18
CATANZARO: Calabria, Italy **38** P17
Cataouatche, Lake: La., U.S.A. **90** *Ins.*
Catarman: Philippines **64** G4
Catastrophe, Cape: S. Austl. **71** A10
Catavi: Bolivia **94** D7
Catawba: *riv.*, S.C., U.S.A. **91** L8
Catbalogan: Philippines **64** G4
Cat Cays: *is.*, Bahamas **91** M13
Catcott: Som., England **24** Q17
Cateel: Mindanao, Phil. **64** H5
Cateau, Le: France **36** J5
Caterham: Surrey, England **25** V17
Catelet, Le: France **36** J6
Catete: Angola **73** G11
Catfield: Norf., England **25** Z14
Cathcart: N.S.W., Australia **71** H11
Cathcart: & *Dist.*, S. Africa **75** G6
Cathedral Mount: Tex., U.S.A. **93** G6
Cat I.: Bahamas **87** M13
Catival: Panama **94** *Ins.*
Cat Lake: *town,* Ont., Can. **92** J2
Catlettsburg: Ky., U.S.A. **88** K6
Cat Mts.: *see* Koscie Mts.
Catoche, Cape: Mexico **86** L13
Cato I.: Australia **69** K4
Caton: Lancs., England **27** Q11
Catorce: Mexico **86** j13
Catota: Angola **73** H12
Catria: *mtn.*, Italy **41** S12
Catriló: Argentina **96** C4
Catrimâni: Brazil **94** E3
Catrine: Strath., Scotland **29** N8
Catsfield: E. Sussex, England **25** W18
Catskill: N.Y., U.S.A. **89** P4
Catskill Mtns.: N.Y., U.S.A. **89** O4
Cattaro (Kotor): Yugoslavia **39** Q15
Catterall: Lancs., England **27** Q12
Catterick: N. Yorks., England **26** S11
Catterick Camp: N. Yorkshire, England **26** S11
Catterline: Gram., Scotland **28** R6
Cattolica: Italy **41** S12
Catúa: Argentina **96** B1
Catuane: Mozambique **75** K3
Catur: Mozambique **77** E5
Catus: France **37** G11
Catwick Is.: Vietnam **64** D4
Cauayan: Philippines **64** G5
Caucaia: Brazil **94** K4
Caucasia: Colombia **94** B2
Caucasus Mtns.: U.S.S.R. **50** F6
Caudry: France **36** J5
Cauit Point: *cape,* Mindanao, Philippines **64** H5
Caulkerbush: Dumfries & Galloway, Scotland **29** O10
Caulnes: France **36** C7
Caumont: France **36** E6
Caunes: France **37** H12
Caungula: Angola **77** A4
Caunus: Greek city, with outlet to the sea in ancient times, at *Dalian,* S. of Lake Köyceğiz, Turkey **39** V18
Cauquenes: Chile **96** A4
Caura: *riv.*, Venezuela **94** E2
Causapscal: Que., Canada **89** S1
Causeway: Kerry, Repub. of Ireland **31** B15
Causeway Head: *village,* Antrim, N. Ireland **30** H9
Caussade: France **37** G11
Cauterets: France **37** E13
Cautiva, La: Argentina **96** C6
Cauvery: *riv.*, India **58** N12
Cauville: France **36** F6
Cava: *i.*, Orkney Is., Scot. **28** P2
Cávado: *riv.*, Portugal **35** B16
Cavaillon: France **37** L12
Cavalerie, La: France **37** J11
Cavalese: Italy **41** R9
Cavalier: N. Dak., U.S.A. **92** H3
Cavallermaggiore: Italy **40** N11
Cavally: *riv.*, Ivory Coast/Liberia **80** C3
CAVAN: & *Co.*, Repub. of Ireland **30** G12
Cavarzere: Italy **41** S10
Cave, North & South: *villages,* Humb., England **27** U12
Caversham: Berks., England **25** U17
Caverswall: Staffs., England **27** R14
Caves, The: Queens., Austl. **70** J4
Caviana I.: Brazil **94** H3
Cavite: Luzon, Philippines **64** G4
Çavuşçu, Lake: Turkey **56** B2
Cawarral: Queens., Austl. **70** J4
Cawdor: High., Scotland **28** O4
Cawnpore (Kanpur): Uttar Pradesh, India **58** O9
Cawood: N. Yorks., England **27** T12
Cawston: Norf., England **25** Y14
Caxias: Maranhão, Brazil **94** J4
Caxias: Rio Grande do Sul, Brazil **96** E2
Caxito: Angola **73** G11
Çay: Turkey **56** B2
Cayambe: & *volc.*, Ecuador **94** B3
Cayce: S.C., U.S.A. **91** L9
CAYENNE: Fr. Guiana **94** G3
Cayes, Les: Haiti **87** m14
Cayeux: France **36** G5
Caylar, Le: France **37** J12
Caylus: France **37** G11
Cayman Brac: *i.* (Br.), W. Indies (*cap. of is.* Georgetown) **87** M14
Cayman, Grand: *i.* (Br.), W. Indies **87** I14
Cayman, Little: *i.* (Br.), W. Indies **87** I14
Cayman Trench: Caribbean Sea **8** 15N 85W
Cayo: Belize **86** *Ins.*
Cayo Grande: *i.*, Venezuela **94** D1
Cayrols: France **37** H11
Cayster: *riv.*, now called *Little Menderes* flowing through Akincilar into Aegean N. of Kuşadasi, Turkey **39** U17
Caythorpe: Lincs., England **27** U13
Caythorpe: Notts., England **27** U14
Cayton: N. Yorks., England **26** V11
Cayuga Lake: N.Y., U.S.A. **89** N4
Cazage: Angola **77** B5
Cazalla de la Sierra: Spain **35** D18
Cazaubon: France **37** E12
Cazaux: France **37** D11
Cazaux et de Sanguinet, Étang de: *lag.*, France **37** D11
Cazenovia: N.Y., U.S.A. **89** O4
Cazères: France **37** G12
Cazes-Mondenard: France **37** G11
Çazin: Yugoslavia **41** V11
Čazma: Yugoslavia **41** W10
Cazombo: Angola **77** B5
Cea: *riv.*, Spain **35** D15
Ceanannus Mór (Kells): Meath, Repub. of Ireland **30** H12
Ceará: *see* Fortaleza
Ceará: *State,* Brazil (*cap.* Fortaleza) **94** K5
Ceará Mirim: Brazil **94** K5
Cebeciköy: Turkey (Bosporus. *Inset*) **20** *Ins.*
Cebollar: Argentina **96** B2
Cebreros: Spain **35** D16
Cebu: & *i.*, Philippines **64** G4
Ceccano: Italy **38** N16
Cecil Plains: *town,* Queens., Australia **70** J6
Cecilstown: Cork, Repub. of Ireland **31** D15
Cecina: Italy **38** M15
Cecir de Mer: *i.*, Vietnam **64** D4
Ceclavin: Spain **35** C17
Cecryphalea: island to W. of *Aegina,* in Saronic G., Greece **39** S18
Cedar: *riv.*, U.S.A. **88** F5
Cedarburg: Wis., U.S.A. **88** H4
Cedar City: Utah, U.S.A. **93** E5
Cedar Falls: *city,* Iowa, U.S.A. **88** E4
Cedar Key: *i.*, Fla., U.S.A. **91** K11
Cedar Lake: Man., Canada **92** G2
Cedarmont: Trans., S. Afr. **75** H3
Cedar Point: *cape,* Ohio, U.S.A. **88** K5
Cedar Rapids: *city,* Iowa, U.S.A. **88** F5
Cedartown: Ga., U.S.A. **91** J8
Cedarville: S. Africa **75** H5
Cedeira: Spain **35** B15
Cedros: *i.*, Mexico **93** D7
Ceduna: S. Australia **68** E6
Cefalú: Sicily **38** O17
Cegana: Spain **37** C13
Ceggia: Italy **41** S10
Cegléd: Hungary **43** Q13
Cehegín: Spain **35** F17
Çekerek: *riv.*, Turkey **56** D2
Celano: Italy **38** N15
Celanova: Spain **35** C15
Celaya: Mexico **86** j13
Celbridge: Kild., Repub. of Ireland **31** H13
Célé: *riv.*, France **37** G11
Celebes: *i.*, & *Prov.*, Indonesia (*cap.* Makasar) **65** G7
Celebes Sea: Indonesia **65** G6
Celeia: Roman town of *Noricum* at Celje, Yugoslavia **41** V9
Celina: Ohio, U.S.A. **88** J5
Celje: Yugoslavia **41** V9
Celldömölk: Hungary **43** P13
Celle: W. Germany **45** Q3
Celtiberi: ancient Spanish tribe of Upper Douro valley and Sa. de Guadarrama **35** E16
Celtic Sea: British Isles **23** D9
Çemişgeszek: Turkey **56** F2
Cemmaes: Powys, Wales **27** O14
Cenabum: Roman name of Gallic centre at Orléans, France **36** G8
Cenchreae: ancient port of Corinth on Saronic G. **39** S18
Ceno: *riv.*, Italy **40** P11
Center: Tex., U.S.A. **90** D10
Centerville: Iowa, U.S.A. **88** E5
Cento: Italy **41** R11
Central: *Dist.*, Botswana (*cap.* Serowe) **75** G1
Central: *Reg.*, Ghana (*cap.* Cape Coast) **80** D3
Central: *Reg.*, Kenya (*cap.* Nyeri) **76** E3
Central: *Reg.*, Scotland (*cap.* Stirling) **29** N7
Central: *Prov.*, Zambia (*cap.* Kabwe) **77** C5

Central African Republic **78/9** H8
Cap.: Bangui
Area: 241,313 sq. miles (625,001 sq. km.)
Pop.: 1,637,000 (*1971 E*)

Central Auckland: *Dist.*, N.I., New Zealand (*cap.* Auckland) **70** P13
Central, Cordillera: Col. **94** B3
Central, Massif: *mtns.*, Fr. **37** —
Central City: Ky., U.S.A. **88** H7
Central City: Nebr., U.S.A. **92** H4
Central Falls: *city,* R.I., U.S.A. **89** Q5
Centralia: Ill., U.S.A. **88** G6
Centralia: Mo., U.S.A. **88** E6
Centralia: Wash., U.S.A. **92** C3
Central Indian Ridge: Indian Ocean **9** 20S 65E
Central Pacific Basin: N. Pacific Ocean **7** 05N 18O
Central Siberian Plat.: U.S.S.R. **49** M5
Centre: *Dept.*, Benin (*cap.* Abomey) **81** E3
Centre: *Dept.*, Ivory Coast (*cap.* Bouaké) **80** C3
Centre: *Dept.*, Upper Volta (*cap.* Ouagadougou) **80** D2
Centre Canal: France **37** K9
Centre-Est: *Dept.*, Upper Volta (*cap.* Tenkodogo) **80** D2
Centre-Nord: *Dept.*, Upper Volta (*cap.* Kaya) **80** D2
Centre-Ouest: *Dept.*, Ivory Coast (*cap.* Daloa) **80** C3
Centre-Ouest: *Dept.*, Upper Volta (*cap.* Koudougou) **80** D2
Centre-Sud: *Reg.* Cameroun (*cap.* Yaoundé) **81** G4
Centreville: Iowa, U.S.A. **88** E5
Centreville: Md., U.S.A. **89** N6
Centreville: N.B., Canada **89** S2
Centro, El: Calif., U.S.A. **93** D6
Centumcellae: ancient city and port at Civitavecchia, Italy **38** M15
Cephalonia (Kefallinia): *i.*, Ionian Is. (Greece) **39** R17
Cephisia: village of central *Attica* about 8 miles W. of Marathon **39** S17
Cephissus: river of *Attica* flowing into bay of *Phalerum* E. of Piraeus **39** S18
Ceram: *i.* & *sea,* Indonesia **61** K12
Ceratodus: Queens., Austl. **70** J5
Cerbère: France **37** J13
Cerčanny: Czechoslovakia **45** U6
Cercy-la-Tour: France **37** J9
Cerdon: France **36** H8
Cère: *riv.*, France **37** H11
Cereales: Argentina **96** C4
Cérences: France **36** D7
Ceres: Argentina **96** C2
Ceres: Fife, Scotland **29** Q7
Ceres: & *Dist.*, S. Africa **74** C6
Céret: France **37** H13
Cerignola: Italy **38** O16
Cerigo (Kíthira): *i.*, Greece **39** S18
Çerikli: Turkey **56** D2
Cérilly: France **37** H9
Cerisiers: France **36** J7
Cerizay: France **37** E9
Çerkeş: Turkey **56** C1
Cerknica: Yugoslavia **41** U10
Çermik: Turkey **56** F2
Cernavoda: Romania **39** V14
Cernay: France **40** N8
Cerne Abbas: Dorset, Eng. **24** R18
Cerney, North: Glos., Eng. **24** S16
Černovice: Czechoslovakia **45** U6
Cerralvo: Mexico **90** B12
Cerralvo: *i.*, Mexico **93** F8
Cerrig-y-Drudion: Clwyd, Wales **27** O13
Cerrillos, Los: Argentina **96** B3
Cerritos: Mexico **86** j13
Cerro Azul: Brazil **96** F1
Cerro Azul: Peru **94** B6
Cerro Blanco: Argentina **95** D13
Cerro Chato: Uruguay **96** D3
Cerro de Pasco: Peru **94** B6
Cerro Manantiales: Chile **95** D14
Cerro Negro: Chile **96** B1
Certaldo: Italy **41** R12
Cervati, Monte: *mtn.*, Italy **38** O16
Cervera: Spain **35** G16
Cervera del Río Alhama: Spain **35** F15
Cervera de Pisuerga: Spain **35** D15
Cervia: Italy **41** S11
Cervignano: Italy **41** T10
Cervione: Corsica **38** L15
Çervizlik: Turkey **56** F1
Cervo: *riv.*, Italy **40** O10
Cerv Řečice: Czechoslovakia **45** V6
Cesana: Italy **40** M11
Cesena: Italy **41** S11
Cesenatico: Italy **41** S11
Česká Kamenice: Czech. **45** U5
Česká Lípa: Czechoslovakia **45** U5
Česká Třebova: Czech. **45** W6
ČESKÉ BUDĚJOVICE: Jihočeský, Czech. **45** U7
Český Brod: Czechoslovakia **45** U5
Český Krumlov: Czech. **41** U7
Český Les Šumava: *see* Šumava
Český Těšyn: Czech. **43** Q12
Cesme: Turkey **39** U17
Cess Cestos: *riv.*, Liberia **80** C3
Cessnock: N.S.W., Australia **71** J9
Cetatea: Romania **39** S14
Cetinje: Yugoslavia **39** Q15
Cetinkaya: Turkey **56** E2
Cetraro: Italy **38** O17
Ceuta: (Sp.) Morocco **80** K7
Ceuta: *bay,* Morocco (Gib. *Inset*) **32** *Ins.*
Ceva: Italy **40** O11
Cévennes: *mtns.*, France **37** J11
Cevio: Switzerland **40** O9
Cevizlik: Turkey **56** F1
Ceyhan: Turkey **56** D3
Ceyhan: *riv.*, Turkey **56** E3
Ceylânpinar: Turkey **57** G3
Ceylon: *see* **Sri Lanka**
Cézallier, Monts: *mtns.*, Fr. **37** H10
Cèze: *riv.*, France **37** K11
Chaa-Khol': U.S.S.R. **51** Q4

Chad: *Republic* **78/9** H6
Cap.: N'Djamena (Fort Lamy)
Area: 495,752 sq. miles (1,283,998 sq. km.)
Pop.: 3,800,000 (*1971 E*)

Chabanais: France **37** F10
Chabeuil: France **37** L11
Chablis: France **36** J8
Chabubrum: *mtn.*, China **62** R8
Chacabuco: Argentina **96** C3
Chacala: Mexico **93** F8
Chacance: Chile **96** B1
Chachani, Nevado de: *mtn.*, Peru **94** C7
Chachapoyas: Peru **94** B5
Chacharramendi: Argentina **96** B4
Chachoengsao: Thailand **64** C4
Chachran: Punjab, Pak. **58** M9
Chaco: *Prov.*, Argentina (*cap.* Resistencia) **96** C2
Chaco Austral: *prairie,* Arg. **96** C2
Chaco Boreal: *prairie,* Par. **96** C1
Chaco Canyon Nat. Mon.: N. Mex., U.S.A. **93** F5
Chaco Central: *prairie,* Arg./Paraguay **96** C1
Chad (Tchad), Lake: Cameroun/Chad **81** G2
Chadan: U.S.S.R. **51** Q4
Chaddesden: Derby., Eng. **27** T14
Chaddesley Corbett: Hereford & Worcester, England **24** R15
Chadlington: Oxon., Eng. **25** S16
Chadobets: U.S.S.R. **51** R3
Chadron: Nebr., U.S.A. **92** G4
Chadwick: Mo., U.S.A. **88** E7
Chaerhsen: Inner Mongolia, China **63** W5
Chaeronea: Greek city of *Boeotia* about 25 miles NW. of *Thivai* (Thebes) **39** S17
Chafe: Nigeria **81** F2
Chaffee: Mo., U.S.A. **88** G7
Chagai: & *hills,* Baluchistan, Pakistan **58** K9
Chagford: Devon, England **24** O18
Chagny: France **37** K9
Chagoda: U.S.S.R. **50** E3
Chagos Archipelago: (Br. Indian Ocean Territ.), Indian Ocean **19** 00S 70E
Chagos-Laccadive Plateau: Indian Ocean **9** 05S 70E
Chagres: *riv.*, Panama **94** *Ins.*
Chahaerhyui Chung Chi: Inner Mongolia, China **62** U6
Chahar Burjak: Afghanistan **58** K8
Chahbar: Iran **55** K9
Chah-i-Ab: Afghanistan **51** L7
Chahsikang: Tibet, China **58** N8
Chaibasa: Bihar, India **59** P10
Chailey: E. Sussex, England **25** V18
Chailland: France **36** E7
Chaillé-les-Marais: France **37** D9
Chainat: Thailand **64** C3
Chain Fracture Zone: S. Atlantic Ocean **8** 05S 20W
Chairn Bhain, Loch a': Highland, Scotland **28** L3
Chaise-Dieu, La: France **37** J10
Chakar: Sinkiang, China **51** O7
Chakari: Rhodesia **77** C6
Chak Chak: Sudan **76** C1
Chake Chake: Tanzania **76** E4
Chakrata: Uttar Pradesh, India **58** N8
Chakwal: Punjab, Pak. **58** M8
Chalabre: France **37** H13
Chalainoerh: Inner Mongolia, China **62** V5
Chalais: France **37** F10
Chalan Chulan: Iran **57** L5
Chalaping: Chinghai, China **62** R8
Chaláua: Mozambique **77** E6
Chalcedon: Greek city on E. side of Bosporus opposite İstanbul, Turkey **39** V16
Chalcis (Khalkis): Euboea, Greece **39** S17
Chalcis: Graeco-Roman city to E. of river Litani about 20 miles S. of Zahle, Lebanon **56** D5
Chale: I. of Wight, England **25** T18
Chaleur, Baie de: *bay,* N.B./Que., Canada **89** T2
Chalfont St. Giles: Bucks., England **26** U16
Chalford: Glos., England **24** R16
Chalgrove: Oxon., England **25** T16
Chaling: Hunan, China **62** U9
Chaling Hu: *lake,* China **62** R8
Cha Ling Phra: Thailand **64** C5
Chalin Hu: *lake,* Tibet, China **59** P8
Chalki: *see* Khálkia.
Chalk River: Ont., Canada **89** N2
Challacombe: Devon, Eng. **24** O17
Challans: France **36** D9
Challapata: Bolivia **94** D7
Challenger Fracture Zone: S. Pacific Ocean **7** 35S 100W
Challenger Mtns.: Canada **85** I1
Challerange: France **36** K6
Challis: Idaho, U.S.A. **92** E4
Chalmette: La., U.S.A. **90** *Ins.*
Chalna: Bangladesh **59** P10
CHÂLONS-SUR-MARNE: Marne, France **36** K7
Châlon-sur-Saône: France **37** K9
Chalun: Tibet, China **59** O8
Châlus: France **37** F10
Chalus: Iran **55** H7
Chalutechi: Inner Mongolia, China **63** W6
Cham: W. Germany **45** S6
Cham: Switzerland **40** O8
Chama: N. Mex., U.S.A. **93** F5
Chamai: Thailand **64** B5
Chaman: Baluchistan, Pak. **58** L8
Chamangonge: Angola **77** B5
Chamba: Himachal Pradesh, India **58** N8
Chamba: Tanzania **77** E5
Chambal: *riv.*, India **58** N9
Chamberlain: S. Dak., U.S.A. **92** H4
Chamberlain Lake: Maine, U.S.A. **89** R2
Chambersburg: Pa., U.S.A. **89** N6
CHAMBÉRY: Savoie, France **40** L10
Chambezi: Copperbelt, Zambia **77** C5
Chambezi: & *riv.*, N. Prov., Zambia **77** D5
Chambley: France **36** L6
Chambon: France **37** H9
Chambon-Feugerolles, Le: France **37** K10
Chambord: Que., Canada **89** P1
Chamborêt-Meuquet: France **37** G10
Chamboulive: France **37** G10
Chambre, La: France **40** M10
Chamdo (Changtu): Tibet, China **62** R8
Chamical (Gobernacion Gordillo): Argentina **96** B3
Chamo: Ethiopia **76** E1
Chamonix: France **40** M10
Champagnac: France **37** H10
Champagne: Yukon, Canada **84** F5
Champagne: *Prov.*, France **34** J12
Champagne Pouilleuse: *geog. reg.*, France **36** K7
Champagney: France **40** M8
Champagnole: France **40** L9
Champaign: Ill., U.S.A. **88** G5
Champassak: Laos **64** D4
Champerico: Guatemala **86** k15
Champéry: Switzerland **40** M9
Champigné: France **36** E8
Champion: Alta., Canada **92** E2
Champlain, Lake: N.Y., U.S.A. **89** P3
Champlitte: France **40** L8
Champotón: Mexico **86** k14
Champtocé: France **36** E8
Chamrajnagar: Karnataka, India **58** N12
Chamusca: Portugal **35** B17
Chana: Thailand **65** b10
Chañar: Argentina **96** B3
Chañaral: (*Atacama*), Chile **96** A2
Chañaral: (*Coquimbo*), Chile **96** A2
Chañarcillo: Chile **96** A2
Chança: *riv.*, Spain/Portugal **35** C18
Chan-chiang (Fort Bayard): Kwangtung, China **62** U10
Chanco: Chile **96** A4
Chandeleur, Is.: La., U.S.A. **90** *Ins.*
Chandeleur Sd.: La., U.S.A. **90** *Ins.*
Chandernagore: W. Bengal, India **59** P10
CHANDIGARH *Union Terr.*, (*cap.* of Haryana & Punjab), India **58** N8
Chandler: Okla., U.S.A. **90** C8
Chandler: Que., Canada **89** T1
Chandlers Ford: Hants., Eng. **25** T18
Chandpur: Bangladesh **59** Q10
Chandrapur: Maharashtra, India **58** N11
Chanf: Iran **55** K9
Chang: *i.*, Thailand **64** C4
Ch'ang-an (Sian): Shensi, China **62** T8
Changane: *riv.*, Mozambique **77** D7
Changara: Mozambique **77** D6
Changchih: Shansi, China **62** U7
Changchow: Fukien, China **62** V10
Changchuan (St. John's I.): Kwangtung, China **62** U10
CHANGCHUN (Hsinking): Kirin, China **63** X6
Changé: France **36** F8
Changhsien: Kansu, China **62** S8
Changi: Malay, Malaysia **65** d13
Changi: Shantung, China **62** V7
Changjin: N. Korea **63** X6
Changjin Reservoir: N. Korea **63** X6
Changkat Jong: Malaya, Malaysia **65** b12
Changki: Sinkiang, China **51** P6
Changki: *riv.*, China **62** T9
Changkiakow (Kalgan): Hopeh, China **62** U6
Changli: Hopeh, China **62** V7
Changling: Kirin, China **63** W6
Changma: Kansu, China **62** R7
Changning: Hunan, China **62** U9
Changning: Yunnan, China **62** R10
Changpai: China **63** X6
Changpeh: Hopeh, China **62** U6
Changping: Peking Municipality, China **62** V6
Changpu: Fukien, China **62** V10
CHANGSHA: Hunan, China **62** U9
Changshan: Chekiang, China **62** V9
Changshu: Kiangsu, China **63** W8
Changsing: *i.*, Liaoning, China **63** W7
Changsong: S. Korea **63** X7
Chang Tang: *geog. reg.*, China **59** P8
Changteh: Hunan, China **62** U9
Changting (Tingchow): Fukien, China **62** V9
Changtu: Liaoning, China **63** W6
Changtu (Chamdo): Tibet, China **62** R8
Changwu: Liaoning, China **63** W6
Changyang: Liaoning, China **62** U8
Changyeh: Kansu, China **63** S7
Changyon: N. Korea **63** X7
Chanhu-Daro: city of ancient Indus civilization, N. of Tando Adam, Sind, Pak. **58** L9
Channel: Newf., Canada **85** t3
Channel Is.: (Br.), English Chan. **25** *Ins.*
Channing: Tex., U.S.A. **93** G5
Chantada: Spain **35** C15
Chanthaburi: Thailand **33** C15
Chantilly: France **36** H6
Chantonnay: France **37** D9
Chanute: Kans., U.S.A. **90** D7
Chany: U.S.S.R. **51** N3
Chany, Lake: U.S.S.R. **51** N4
Chaoan (Chaochow): Kwangtung, China **62** V10
Chaocheng: Shantung, China **62** V7
Chaochow: Heilungkiang, China **63** X5
Chaochow (Chaoan), Kwangtung, China **62** V10
Chaokioh: Szechwan, China **62** S9
Chaokuang: Heilungkiang, China **63** X5
Chaoping: Kwangsi Chuang, China **62** U10
Chaotung: Heilungkiang, China **63** X5
Chaotung: Yunnan, China **62** S9
Chaource: France **36** K7
Chaoyang: Kwangtung, China **62** V10
Chaoyang: Liaoning, China **63** W6
Chaoyangchen: *see* Huinan.
Chaoyangwan: Inner Mongolia, China **62** V6
Chapandinha: Brazil **94** J4
Chapala, Lake: Mexico **86** j13
Chaparral: Colombia **94** B3
Chapayevsk: U.S.S.R. **50** G4
Chapecó: Brazil **96** E2
Chapel, North: W. Sussex, England **25** U17
Chapel en le Frith: Derby., England **27** S13
Chapel Hill: *city,* N.C., U.S.A. **91** M8
Chapelle-D'Angillon, La: France **36** H8
Chapelle-la-Reine, La: Fr. **36** H7
Chapel St. Leonards: Lincs., England **27** W13

For Abbreviations see list on p.113. Italic type, e.g. *Ephesus,* refers to historical names not on maps. Capital letters, e.g. MADRID, show capitals of countries; small capital letters, e.g. CADIZ, show capitals of provinces, etc. General notes p.116.

Chapelton: Jamaica 86 *Ins.*
Chapelton: Strath., Scot. 29 N8
Chapeltown: Antrim, N. Irel. 30 J10
Chapeltown: Down, N. Irel. 30 K11
Chapeltown: Gram., Scot. 28 P5
Chapeltown: Kerry, Repub. of Ireland 31 B15
Chapleau: Ont., Canada 88 K2
Chaplino: U.S.S.R. 49 u5
Chapman's Bay: S. Africa 74 *Ins.*
Chapoma: U.S.S.R. 48 e4
Chapra: Bihar, India 59 O9
Chapultepec: rocky hill SW. of Mexico City. Site of Aztec fortifications, Mex. 86 K14
Chapus, Le: France 37 D10
Char: Mauritania 78 B5
Charadai: Argentina 96 D2
Charagua: Bolivia 94 E7
Charaña: Bolivia 94 D7
Charata: Argentina 96 C2
Charax Spasinu: ancient Persian port at Khurramshahr, Iran (probably on coast in ancient times) 57 L6
Charcas: Mexico 86 j13
Charchan: *riv.,* Sinkiang, China 51 P7
Chard: Som., England 24 Q18
Chardara: Kazakh., U.S.S.R. 51 L6
Chardon: Ohio, U.S.A. 88 L5
Chardzhou: Turkmen., U.S.S.R. 51 K7
Charente: *Dept.,* France (*cap.* Angoulême) 37 F10
Charente: *riv.,* France 37 E10
Charente-Maritime: *Dept.,* France (*cap.* La Rochelle) 37 E10
Charenton: France 37 H9
Charkhyanka: U.S.S.R. 50 E4
Chari: *riv.,* Chad 81 H2
Chari-Baguirmi: *Pref.,* Chad (*cap.* N'Djamena) 81 H2
CHARIKAR: Parwan, Afghanistan 55 L7
Charing: Kent, England 25 X17
Charité, La: France 36 J8
Chariton: Iowa, U.S.A. 88 E5
Chariton: *riv.,* Mo., U.S.A. 88 E5
Charity Guyana 87 d7
Charlbury: Oxon., England 25 T16
Charlecote: War., England 25 S15
Charleroi: Belgium 44 K5
Charles: Devon, England 24 O17
Charles, Cape: Va., U.S.A. 89 O7
Charles City: Iowa, U.S.A. 88 E4
Charles Sd.: South I., N.Z. 70 L17
Charleston: Ark., U.S.A. 90 D8
Charleston: Ill., U.S.A. 88 G6
Charleston: Miss., U.S.A. 90 F8
Charleston: Mo., U.S.A. 88 G7
Charleston: S.C., U.S.A. 91 M9
CHARLESTON: W. Va., U.S.A. 88 L6
Charleston, South: W. Va., U.S.A. 88 L6
Charleston Peak: Nev., U.S.A. 93 D5
Charlestown: Corn., Eng. 24 M19
Charlestown: Mayo, Repub. of Ireland 30 D12
Charlestown: Natal, S. Afr. 75 H3
Charlestown: Leeward Is. 87 b2
Charles Town: W. Va., U.S.A. 89 N6
Charlestown of Aberlour: Grampian, Scotland 28 P5
Charlesville: Zaire 76 B4
Charleville (Rathluirc): Cork, Repub. of Ireland 31 D15
Charleville: France 36 K6
Charleville: Queens., Austl. 70 G6
Charlevoix: Mich., U.S.A. 88 J3
Charlieu: France 37 K9
Charlotte: Mich., U.S.A. 88 J4
Charlotte: N.C., U.S.A. 91 L8
Charlotte Harbor: *inlet,* Fla., U.S.A. 91 K12
Charlottenberg: Sweden 47 N7
Charlottenburg: Surinam 94 G2
Charlottesville: Va., U.S.A. 89 M6
CHARLOTTETOWN: P.E.I., Canada 89 U2
Charlotte Waters: N. Territ., Australia 68 E5
Charlton: Vict., Australia 71 E11
Charlton, South: Northumb., England 24 S16
Charlwood: S. Africa 75 F6
Charlwood: Surrey, England 25 V17
Charly: France 36 J7
Charmes: France 40 M7
Charmouth: Dorset, Eng. 24 Q18
Charnwood Forest: *dist.,* Leics., England 27 T14
Charny: France 36 J8
Charolais, Monts du: *hills,* France 37 K9
Charolles: France 37 K9
Chârost: France 36 H9
Charouine: Algeria 80 L9
Chars: France 36 G6
Charskiy: Kazakh., U.S.S.R. 51 O5
Charters Towers: Queens., Australia 69 H4
Chartham: Kent, England 25 Y17
Chartre, La: France 36 F8
CHARTRES: Eure-et-Loir, Fr. 36 G7
Charwelton: Northants., England 25 T15
Charyshskoye: U.S.S.R. 51 O4
Chascomús: Argentina 96 D4
Chase City: Va., U.S.A. 89 M7
Chasel'ka: U.S.S.R. 48 K5
Chasetown: Staffs., England 27 S14
Chaska: Minn., U.S.A. 88 E3
Chassenuil: France 37 F10
Chassengue: Angola 77 A5
Chata: Tibet, China 58 N8
Chataigneraie, La: France 37 E9
Chatanika: Alaska, U.S.A. 84 E4
Chatburn: Lancs., England 27 R12
Château, Pointe du: *cape,* Fr. 36 B7
Châteaubriant: France 36 D8
Château-Chinon: France 36 J8
Château d'Oex: Switzerland 40 N9
Château-d-Oléron, Le: Île d'Oléron, France 37 D10
Château-du-Loir: France 36 F8
Châteaudun: France 36 G7
Châteaugiron: France 36 D7
Château-Gontier: France 36 E8
Château-Landon: France 36 H7
Château-la-Vallière: France 36 F8
Châteaulin: France 36 A7
Châteaumeillant: France 37 H9
Châteauneuf: Cher, France 37 H9
Châteauneuf: Eure-et-Loir, France 36 G7
Châteauneuf: Haute-Vienne, France's 37 G10
Châteauneuf: Ille-et-Vilaine, France 36 D7
Châteauneuf-du-Faou: Fr. 36 B7

Châteauneuf-sur-Charente: France 37 E10
Châteauneuf-sur-Loire: Fr. 36 H8
Châteauneuf-sur-Sarthe: Fr. 36 E8
Châteaurenard: France 36 H8
Château-Renault: France 36 F8
CHÂTEAUROUX: Indre, Fr. 37 G9
Château-Salins: France 40 M7
Château-Thierry: France 36 J6
Châteauvillain: France 36 K7
Châtelard: France 40 M11
Châtelard, Le: France 40 M10
Châteldon: France 37 J10
Châtelet: Belgium 44 K5
Châtel-Guyon: France 37 J10
Châtelaillon: France 37 D9
Châtellerault: France 37 F9
Châtenois: France 40 L7
Chatfield: Minn., U.S.A. 88 E4
Chatham: Kent, England 25 X17
Chatham: La., U.S.A. 90 E9
Chatham: Mass., U.S.A. 89 R5
Chatham: N.B., Canada 89 T2
Chatham: N.Y., U.S.A. 89 P4
Chatham: Ont., Canada 88 K4
Chatham: Va., U.S.A. 89 M7
Chatham Is.: New Zealand 67 O10
Chatham Rise: S. Pacific Ocean 7 45S 175E
Châtillon: France 40 L11
Châtillon: Italy 40 N10
Châtillon-Coligny: France 36 H8
Châtillon-en-Bazois: Fr. 36 J8
Châtillon-sur-Chalaronne: France 40 L9
Châtillon-sur-Indre: France 36 G9
Châtillon-sur-Marne: France 36 J6
Châtillon-sur-Seine: France 36 K8
Châtillon-sur-Sèvre: France 36 E9
Chatoumu: Tibet, China 59 O9
Chatra: Bihar, India 59 O10
Chatrapur: Orissa, India 59 O11
Châtre, La: France 37 G9
Chattahoochee: & *riv.,* Fla., U.S.A. 91 J10
Chattanooga: Tenn., U.S.A. 91 J8
Chatteris: Cambs., England 25 W15
Chatti: ancient German tribe of Hesse and upper valley of river Weser, W. Ger. 44 P5
Chatton: Northumb., Eng. 26 S8
Chaturat: Thailand 26 C3
Chau: Ethiopia 76 E1
Chauci: ancient tribe of N. German coast between rivers Ems and Elbe 44 N2
Chaudes-Aigues: France 37 H11
Chaudière: *riv.,* Que., Can. 89 Q2
Chauffailles: France 37 K9
Chauk: Burma 59 Q10
Chaulnes: France 36 H6
CHAUMONT: Haute-Marne, France 36 L7
Chaumont-en-Vexin: France 36 G6
Chauny: France 36 J6
Chaun Bay: U.S.S.R. 49 s4
Chaussin: France 40 L9
Chausy: Byelorussia 50 D4
Chautara: Nepal 59 P9
Chautauqua Lake: N.Y., U.S.A. 89 M4
Chauvigny: France 37 F9
Chaux-de-Fonds, La: Switz. 40 M8
Chavanges: France 36 K7
Chaves: Brazil 94 H4
Chaves: Portugal 35 C16
Chavuma: Zambia 77 B5
Chawang: Thailand 64 B5
Chawaopo: Chinghai, China 62 R7
Chawleigh: Devon, Eng. 24 O18
Chayu: Tibet, China 62 R9
Chazelles: France 37 K10
Chazón: Argentina 96 C3
Cheadle: Gt. Man., Eng. 27 R13
Cheadle: Staffs., England 27 S14
Cheaha Mount: Ala., U.S.A. 91 I9
Cheb: Czechoslovakia 45 S5
CHEBOKSARY: Chuvash, U.S.S.R. 50 G3
Cheboygan: Mich., U.S.A. 88 J3
Chechaouen: Morocco 35 D19
Checheno-Ingush A.S.S.Repub. U.S.S.R. (*cap.* Groznyy) 50 G6
Chech Erg: *desert,* Algeria 78 D4
Checotah: Okla., U.S.A. 90 D8
Chedabucto Bay: N.S., Canada 89 V3
Cheddar: Som., England 24 Q17
Cheddleton: Staffs., Eng. 27 R13
Cheduba: & *i.,* Burma 59 Q11
Chedworth: Glos., England 24 S16
Cheepie: Queens., Austl. 70 F6
Chef-Boutonne: France 37 E9
Chef Menteur: La., U.S.A. 90 *Ins.*
Chega Jangeh: Iran 57 K5
Chegitun: U.S.S.R. 84 b4
Cheikria: *well,* Algeria 78 C4
Cheju: Quelpart I., S. Korea 63 X8
Cheju (Quelpart) I.: S. Korea 63 X8
Cheju Str.: S. Korea 63 X8
Chekiang: *Prov.,* China (*cap.* Hangchow) 62 V9
Chekmagushi: U.S.S.R. 50 H3
Chekunda: U.S.S.R. 49 P7
Chelan: Wash., U.S.A. 92 D3
Chelan, Lake: Wash., U.S.A. 92 C3
Cheleken I.: U.S.S.R. 50 H7
Chelford: Ches., England 27 R13
Chelforó: Argentina 96 B4
Cheli: Yunnan, China 62 S10
Chéliff: *riv.,* Algeria 35 G18
Chelkar: (Aktyubinsk), Kazakh., U.S.S.R. 50 J5
Chelkar (W. Kazakh.), Kazakh., U.S.S.R. 50 H4
Chelkar-Tengiz, Lake: Kazakh., U.S.S.R. 51 K5
Chelkiozero: U.S.S.R. 46 W5
Chellala: Algeria 35 H19
Chellaston: Derby., England 27 T14
Chelles: France 36 H7
Chefm: Poland 43 S11
Chefmno: Poland 43 Q10
Chelmorton: Derby., Eng. 27 S13
CHELMSFORD: Essex, England 25 W16
Chelmsza: Poland 43 Q10
Chelsea: Okla., U.S.A. 90 D7
Chelsea: Vict., Australia 71 F12
Cheltenham: Glos., England 24 R16
Chelva: Spain 35 F17
CHELYABINSK: & *Reg.,* U.S.S.R. 51 K3
Chelyuskin, Cape: U.S.S.R. 49 m2
Chemazé: France 36 E8
Chemba: Mozambique 77 D6
Chemchemal: Iraq 57 J4
Chemdal'sk: U.S.S.R. 49 M6
Chemillé: France 36 E8
Chemin des Dames: battlefield S. of Laon, France 36 J6
Chemiré: France 36 E7

Chemnitz: *see* Karl-Marx-Stadt.
Chemung: *riv.,* N.Y./Pa., U.S.A. 89 N4
Chenab: *riv.,* Pakistan/India 58 M8
Chenachane: Algeria 78 D4
Chenchwasze: Singkiang, China 51 P5
Chengalpattu: Tamil Nadu, India 58 O12
Chengan: Kweichow, China 62 T9
CHENG CHOW: Honan, China 62 U8
Chengfeng: Kweichow, China 62 T9
Chengho: Fukien, China 62 V9
Chengkang (Yungkang): Yunnan, China 62 R10
Chengkiang: Yunnan, China 62 S9
Chengkow: Szechwan, China 62 T8
Chengku: Shensi, China 62 T8
Chengpu: Hunan, China 62 U9
Chengshan, Cape: Shantung, China 63 W7
Chengteh (Jehol): Hopeh, China 62 V6
Chengting: Hopeh, China 62 U7
CHENGTU (Hwayang): Szechwan, China 62 S8
Chenhsien: Hunan, China 62 U9
Chenhsiung: Yunnan, China 62 S9
Chenning: Kweichow, China 62 T9
Chenping: Honan, China 62 U8
Chenping: Shensi, China 62 T8
Chentung: Heilungkiang, China 63 Y5
Chentung: Kirin, China 63 W5
Chenyuan: Kweichow, China 62 T9
Chenyuan: Yunnan, China 62 S10
Chéomkhsan: Cambodia 64 C4
Cheongkong: Hainan, China 62 T11
Chep: Khmer Rep. 64 D4
Chepes: Argentina 96 B3
Chepstow: Gwent, Wales 24 Q16
Cheptsa: *riv.,* U.S.S.R. 50 H3
Chequamegon Bay: Wis., U.S.A. 88 F2
Cher: *Dept.,* France (*cap.* Bourges) 36 H8
Cher: *riv.,* France 36 G8
Cheraw: S.C., U.S.A. 91 M8
Cherbourg: France 36 D6
Cherchel: Algeria 35 H18
Cherdakly: U.S.S.R. 50 G4
Cherdoyak: Kazakh., U.S.S.R. 51 O5
Cherdyn: U.S.S.R. 50 J2
Cheremkhovo: U.S.S.R. 49 M7
Cherepanovo: U.S.S.R. 51 O4
Cherepovets: U.S.S.R. 50 E3
Cherhill: Wilts., England 24 S17
Cheribon: *see* Tjirebon.
Cheriktey: U.S.S.R. 49 P5
Chérisy: France 36 G7
Cheriton: Hants., England 25 T17
Cheriton: Kent, England 25 Y17
Cheriton Bishop: Devon, England 24 O18
Cheriton Fitzpaine: Devon, England 24 O18
Cherkassy: Ukraine 50 D5
CHERKESSK: Karacheyevo-Cherkessk, U.S.S.R. 50 F6
Cherlak: U.S.S.R. 51 M4
Cherlakskiy: U.S.S.R. 51 M4
Chermoz: U.S.S.R. 50 J3
Chermëvo: U.S.S.R. 47 V7
Chernigivka: U.S.S.R. 73 Y6
Chernigov: Ukraine 50 D4
Chernogorsk: U.S.S.R. 51 Q4
Chernaya: U.S.S.R. 48 k3
Chernushka: U.S.S.R. 50 J3
Chernyakhov: Ukraine 43 V11
Chernyakhovsk (Insterburg): U.S.S.R. 47 R9
Chernyanka: U.S.S.R. 50 E4
Cherny Irtysh: *riv.,* U.S.S.R. 51 P5
Cherny Ostrov: Ukraine 43 U12
Chernyy Yar: U.S.S.R. 50 G5
Cherokee: Iowa, U.S.A. 92 H4
Cherokee: Kans., U.S.A. 90 D7
Cherokee: Okla., U.S.A. 90 D7
Cherokees, Lake o' the: Okla., U.S.A. 90 D7
Cherquenco: Chile 96 A4
Cherrabun: W. Australia 68 D3
Cherrapunji: Meghalaya, India 59 Q9
Cherry Burton: Humb., Eng. 27 V12
Cherry Creek: Nev., U.S.A. 93 E5
Cherryfield: Maine, U.S.A. 89 S3
Cherry I. (Anuda): Pacific O. 67 N4
Cherryvale: Kans., U.S.A. 90 D7
Cherskaya: U.S.S.R. 47 V8
Cherskiy Range: U.S.S.R. 49 Q4
Chersonesus: Greek name of Gallipoli penin., Turkey 39 U16
Chersonesus Taurica: Greek name of Crimean penin., U.S.S.R. 33 J2
Chertkovo: U.S.S.R. 50 F5
Chertsey: Surrey, England 25 U17
Cherusci: ancient German tribe of middle valley of river Weser, W. Germany 44 P4
Cherven': Byelorussia 43 V10
Chervonoarmeysk: Ukraine 43 T11
Chervyanka: U.S.S.R. 51 R3
Cherwell: *riv.,* Oxon./Northants., England 25 T16
Chesaning: Mich., U.S.A. 88 J4
Chesapeake: Va., U.S.A. 89 N7
Chesapeake Bay: U.S.A. 89 N6
Chesham: Bucks., England 25 U16
Cheshire: *Co.,* Eng. (*co. town* Chester) 27 Q13
Cheshunt: Herts., England 25 V16
Chesil Beach: Dorset, Eng. 24 Q18
Chesley: Ont., Canada 88 L3
Chesley Hay: Staffs., Eng. 27 R14
Chesne, Le: France 36 K6
Chessu: Inner Mongolia, China 62 U6
CHESTER: Ches., England 27 Q13
Chester: Mont., U.S.A. 92 E3
Chester: N.S., Canada 89 T3
Chester: Pa., U.S.A. 89 O6
Chester: S.C., U.S.A. 91 L8
Chester: Va., U.S.A. 89 N7
Chesterfield: Derby., Eng. 27 T13
Chesterfield Is.: (Fr.), Coral Sea 67 L5
Chesterholm: *see* Vindolanda.
Chesterford: Essex, England 25 W15
Chester le Street: Durham, England 26 S10
Chesters: Bord., Scotland 29 R9
Chesters: *see under* Cilurnum.
Chesterton: Cambs., Eng. 25 W15
Chesterton: Queens., Austl. 70 G5
Chestertown: Md., U.S.A. 89 N6
Chesuncook Lake: Maine, U.S.A. 89 R2
Chetaibi: Algeria 32 D4
Chetamale: Andaman Is. 59 Q12
Chetek: Wis., U.S.A. 88 F3
Chetlat: *i.,* Laccadive Is. 58 M12

Chetopa: Kans., U.S.A. 90 D7
Chevagnes: France 37 J9
Cheveley: Cambs., England 25 W15
Chevington, East & West: Northumb., England 26 S9
Cheviot, The: *mtn.,* Northumb., England 26 R9
Cheviot Hills, The: England/ Scotland 26 R9
Chèvre, Cap de la: *cape,* Fr. 36 A7
Chevreuse: France 36 H7
Chewelah: Wash., U.S.A. 92 D3
Chew Magna: Avon, Eng. 24 Q17
Chewton Mendip: Som., England 24 Q17
CHEYENNE: Wyo., U.S.A. 92 G4
Cheyenne: *riv.,* S. Dak./Wyo., U.S.A. 92 G4
Cheylard, Le: France 37 K11
Chèze, La: France 36 C7
Chhatarpur: Madhya Pradesh, India 58 N10
Chhindwara: Madhya Pradesh, India 58 N10
Chhlong: Cambodia 64 D4
Chi: *riv.,* Thailand 64 C3
Chiacha: Tibet, China 59 Q9
Chiali: Tibet, China 59 Q8
Chiampo: Italy 41 R10
Chiang Dao: Thailand 64 B3
Chiang Khan: Thailand 64 C3
Chiang Mai: Thailand 64 B3
Chiang Rai: Thailand 64 B3
Chiangtso: Yunnan, China 62 R9
Chiangtzu (Gyangtse): Tibet, China 59 Q9
Chiari: Italy 40 P10
Chiababaw: Mozambique 77 D7
Chibi: Rhodesia 77 D7
Chibia: Angola 73 G13
Chibuto: Mozambique 75 K2
Chibwe: Zambia 77 C5
Chicago: Ill., U.S.A. 88 H5
Chicago Heights: Ill., U.S.A. 88 H5
Chical-Có: Argentina 96 B4
Chicamaua Res.: & *dam,* Tenn., U.S.A. 91 J8
Chicaoa: *riv.,* Angola 76 B4
Chicagof I.: Alaska, U.S.A. 84 F6
Chichaoua: Morocco 80 K8
Chichén-Itzá: principal city of the Mayas. Its ruins lie in the jungles of eastern Yucatan, Mexico 86 L13
CHICHESTER: W. Sussex, Eng. 25 U18
Chichi: *i.,* Bonin Is. 60 N6
Chichiaching: Sinkiang, China 62 Q6
Chichibu: Japan 63 f3
Chichihwengkuerh: Sinkiang, China 51 N7
Chichmo: Sinkiang, China 51 P7
Chickasawhay: *riv.,* Miss., U.S.A. 90 G10
Chickasha: Okla., U.S.A. 90 C8
Chiclana: Spain 35 C18
Chiclayo: Peru 94 B5
Chico: Calif., U.S.A. 93 C5
Chico: *riv.,* Argentina 95 D12
Chicoana: Argentina 96 B2
Chicoma Peak: N. Mex., U.S.A. 93 F5
Chicopee: Mass., U.S.A. 89 P4
Chicot, Lake: Ark., U.S.A. 90 F9
Chicoutimi: Que., Canada 89 Q1
Chicualacuala: Mozambique 75 J1
Chicundo: Trans., S. Africa 75 J1
Chidambaram: Tamil Nadu, India 58 N12
Chiddingfold: Surrey, Eng. 25 U17
Chideock: Dorset, England 24 Q18
Chief Toin: Sudan 76 C1
Chiembba: Vietnam 64 D2
Chiem See: *lake,* W. Germany 41 S8
Chienchou: Hunan, China 62 T9
Chiengi: Zambia 77 C4
Chiengsen: Thailand 64 C2
Chienti: *riv.,* Italy 38 N15
Chieri: Italy 40 N10
Chiese: *riv.,* Italy 40 Q10
Chieti: Italy 30 O15
Chieveley: Berks., England 25 T17
Chifokoloki: Zambia 77 B5
Chifumpa: Zambia 77 C5
Chignecto Bay: N.S., Can. 89 T3
Chignik: Alaska, U.S.A. 84 D6
Chiguaioco: Chile 96 A3
Chigubo: Mozambique 77 D7
Chigwell: Gt. London, England 25 W16
Chihcheng: Hopeh, China 62 V6
Chihchin: Kweichow, China 59 T9
Chihfeng: Inner Mongolia, China 62 V6
Chihkiang (Yuanchow): Hunan, China 62 T9
Chihkiang: Kansu, China 62 R6
Chihli (Po Hai), G. of: China 62 V7
Chihpuchang Hu: *lake,* Tibet, China 59 Q8
Chihsien: Honan, China 62 U7
CHIHUAHUA: & *State,* Mexico 93 F7
Chihuichupa: Mexico 93 F7
Chiili: Kazakh., U.S.S.R. 51 L6
Chikalda: Maharashtra, India 58 N10
Chikaskia: *riv.,* Kans., U.S.A. 90 B7
Chiki: Anhwei, China 62 V8
Chikkai: Kwangtung, China 62 U10
Chiknagalur: Karnataka, India 58 N12
Chikuma: *riv.,* Japan 63 f2
Chikumbi: Zambia 77 C6
Chikura: Japan 63 f3
Chikutokaku: Taiwan 63 W10
Chikwawa: Malawi 77 D6
Chilas: Jammu & Kashmir 58 M7
Chilaw: Sri Lanka 58 N13
Chilca: Peru 94 B6
Chilcotin: *riv.,* B.C., Canada 92 C2
Childers: Queens., Austl. 70 K5
Childress: Tex., U.S.A. 90 A4
Childs Ercall: Salop, Eng. 27 R14

Chilham: Kent, England 25 X17
Chilia Veche: Romania 39 V14
Chilik: Kazakh., U.S.S.R. 51 N6
Chilimanzi: Rhodesia 77 D6
Chilin: *see* Kirin.
Chilin Hu: *lake,* Tibet, China 59 P8
Chilivani: Sardinia 38 L16
Chilka, Lake: Orissa, India 59 P11
Chillagoe: Queens., Austl. 69 G3
Chillán: Chile 96 A4
Chillesford: Suff., England 25 Y15
Chillicothe: Ill., U.S.A. 88 G5
Chillicothe: Mo., U.S.A. 88 E6
Chillicothe: Ohio, U.S.A. 88 K6
Chilling: Vict., Australia 71 E10
Chillingham: Northumb., England 26 S8
Chillingollah: Vict., Austl. 71 E10
Chilliwack: B.C., Canada 92 C3
Chilly: Idaho, U.S.A. 92 E4
Chiloe I.: Chile 95 C12
Chilonga: Zambia 77 D5
Chilpancingo: Mexico 86 K14
Chilsworthy: Devon, Eng. 24 N18
Chiltern: Vict., Australia 71 G11
Chiltern Hills: England 25 U16
Chiltington, West: W. Sussex, England 25 V18
Chilton: Wis., U.S.A. 88 G3
Chilton Buildings: *town,* Durham, England 26 S10
Chiluage: Angola 77 B4
Chilung: Tibet, China 59 P9
Chilwa, Lake: Malawi 77 E6
Chimay: Belgium 44 K5
Chimbay: Uzbek., U.S.S.R. 50 J6
Chimborazo: *volc.,* Ecuador 94 B4
Chimbote: Peru 94 B5
Chimji: Malawi 77 D5
CHIMKENT: South Kazakh., U.S.S.R. 51 L6
Chin: *State,* Burma (*cap.* Falam) 59 Q10
Chin: *riv.,* China 62 U7

China: *Republic* 19
Cap.: Peking (Peiping)
Area: 3,691,502 sq. miles (9,560,990 sq. km.)
Pop.: 772,676,000 (1971 E)

China: Mexico 90 B13
Chinandega: Nicaragua 86 L15
China Sea, East: Japan/China 63 X9
China Sea, South: SE Asia 64 E4
Chinati Peak: Tex., U.S.A. 93 G7
Chinavane: Mozambique 75 K2
Chincha Alta: Peru 94 B6
Chinchaichen: Anhwei, China 62 V8
Chin-chi-Khodzi: Sinkiang, China 51 O6
Chinchilla: Queens., Austl. 70 J6
Chinchilla: Spain 35 F17
Chinchón: Spain 35 E16
Chinchou: Kwangsi Chuang, China 62 T10
Chinchoua: Gabon 81 F5
Chinchow: Liaoning, China 63 W7
Chinchow (Chinhsien): Liaoning, China 63 W6
Chincoteague: Va., U.S.A. 89 O7
Chincoteague Bay: Md., U.S.A. 89 O6
Chindamani: Mongolia 62 R5
Chinde: Mozambique 77 E6
Chindio: Mozambique 77 E6
Chindwin: *riv.,* Burma 59 Q10
Chingan: Heilungkiang, China 63 X5
Chinghai (Tsinghai): *Prov.,* China (*cap.* Hsining) 62 R7
Chingho: Sinkiang, China 51 O6
Chingling: Kweichow, China 62 T9
Chingnambun: Burma 59 R9
Chingombe: Zambia 77 C5
Chingovo: *riv.,* Mozambique 75 K1
Chingtao: Kirin, China 63 X6
Chingtechen: Kiangsi, China 62 V9
Chinguetti: Mauritania 78 B5
Chingyü: Kirin, China 63 X6
CHINGYUAN: *see* Paoting.
Chinhae: S. Korea 63 X7
Chinhai: Chekiang, China 63 W9
Chinhsien: *see* Chinchow.
Chiniot: Punjab, Pak. 58 M8
Chinipas: Mexico 93 F7
Chinju: S. Korea 63 X8
Chinju: S. Korea 63 X7
Chinkiang: Kiangsu, China 62 V8
Chinko: *riv.,* Cen. Afr. Rep. 76 B1
Chinnampo: N. Korea 63 X7
Chinnor: Oxon., England 25 U16
Chinobampo: Mexico 93 F7
Chinon: France 36 F8
Chinook: Mont., U.S.A. 92 F3
Chins: *tribe,* Burma 59 Q10
Chinsali: Zambia 77 D5
Chintai: Inner Mongolia, China 62 U6
Chinteche: Malawi 77 D5
Chinwangtao: Hopeh, China 62 V7
Chiny: Belgium 44 L6
Chióco: Mozambique 77 D6
Chioggia: Italy 41 S10
Chios: Greece 39 U17
Chios: *i.,* Greece 39 U17
CHIPATA: Eastern, Zambia 77 D5
Chipembe: Zambia 77 C5
Chipera: Mozambique 77 D6
Chipili: Zambia 77 C5
Chipinga: Rhodesia 77 D7
Chipley: Fla., U.S.A. 91 J10
Chiplun: Maharashtra, India 58 M11
Chipman: N.B., Canada 89 T2
Chipogolo: Tanzania 76 E4
Chipoka: Malawi 77 D6
Chipongwe: Zambia 77 C6
Chippenham: Cambs., Eng. 25 W15
Chippenham: Wilts., Eng. 24 R17
Chippewa: *riv.,* Wis., U.S.A. 88 F3
Chippewa Falls: *city,* Wis., U.S.A. 88 F3
Chipping: Lancs., England 27 Q12
Chipping Campden: Glos., England 25 S15
Chipping Norton: Oxon., England 25 S16
Chipping Ongar: Essex, Eng. 25 W16
Chipping Sodbury: Avon, England 24 R16
Chiputneticook Lakes: N.B., Canada 89 S3
Chique Chique: Brazil 94 J6
Chiquimula: Guatemala 86 L15
Chiquinquiró: Colombia 94 C2
Chiquita, Lake: Argentina 96 C3
Chiradzulu: Malawi 77 E6
Chiramba: Mozambique 77 D6
Chirang: Bhutan 59 Q9
Chiras: Afghanistan 58 L7
Chirbury: Salop, England 27 P14
Chiredzi: Rhodesia 77 D7

Chiricahua Pk.: Ariz., U.S.A. 93 F6
Chirikof: *i.*, Alaska, U.S.A. 84 D6
Chirinda: U.S.S.R. 49 M4
Chiriqui, G. of: Panama 87 I16
Chirk: Clwyd, Wales 27 P14
Chirmiri: Madhya Pradesh, India 58 O10
Chirnside: Borders, Scot. 29 R8
Chiromo: Malawi 77 E6
Chirpan: Bulgaria 39 T15
Chirripó Grande: *mtn.*, Costa Rica 87 I16
Chirundu: Zambia 77 C6
Chiry: France 36 H6
Chisalala: Zambia 77 C5
Chisamba: Zambia 77 C5
Chishill, Gt.: Cambs., Eng. 25 W15
Chisholm: Minn., U.S.A. 88 E2
Chişinău Criş: Romania 43 R13
Chisledon: Wilts., England 25 S16
Chistopol': U.S.S.R. 50 H3
CHITA: & *Reg.*, U.S.S.R. 49 N7
Chitado: Angola 73 G13
Chi-T'ai: Sinkiang, China 51 P6
Chitimba: Malawi 77 D5
Chitipa: Malawi 77 D4
Chitokoloki: Zambia 77 B5
Chitradurga: Karnataka, India 58 N12
Chitral: North West Frontier Province, Pakistan 58 M7
Chitré: Panama 87 I16
Chittagong: Bangladesh 59 Q10
Chittaurgarh: Rajasthan, India 58 M10
Chitterne: Wilts., England 24 R17
Chittoor: Andhra Pradesh, India 58 N12
Chitumba: Malawi 77 D5
Chitung: Kiangsu, China 63 W8
Chiumbe: *riv.*, Angola 77 B4
Chiume: Angola 77 B6
Chiumec: Czechoslovakia 45 V5
Chiunanao: Kwangtung, China 62 V10
Chiure: Mozambique 77 E5
Chiusa: Italy 41 M9
Chiusi: Italy 38 M15
Chiuta: Mozambique 77 D6
Chiuta, Lake: Malawi 77 E5
Chiuyunumo: Yunnan, China 62 R9
Chiva: Spain 35 F17
Chivasso: Italy 40 N10
Chivilcoy: Argentina 96 C3
Chiwefwe: Zambia 77 C5
Chizha 2-aya: Kazakh., U.S.S.R. 50 G4
CHKALOV (Orenburg): & *Reg.*, U.S.S.R. 50 J4
Chkalovsk: U.S.S.R. 50 F3
Chloride: Ariz., U.S.A. 93 E5
Chlumec: Czechoslovakia 45 V5
Chno Dearg: *mtns.*, Highland, Scotland 29 M6
Choapa: *riv.*, Chile 96 A3
Choarta: Iraq 57 J4
Chobe: *Dist.*, Botswana (*cap.* Kasane) 77 B6
Chobham: Surrey, England 25 U17
Chocen: Czechoslovakia 45 W5
Chocolate Mtns.: Calif., U.S.A. 93 D6
Choctawhatchee: *bay & riv.*, Fla., U.S.A. 91 H10
Chodov: Czechoslovakia 45 S5
Chodzież: Poland 43 P10
Choele Choel: Argentina 95 D1
Chohsien: Hopeh, China 62 V7
Chiobalsan (Bayan Tumen): Mongolia 62 U5
Choire, Loch: Highland, Scotland 28 N3
Choiseul: *i.*, Solomon Is. 67 L3
Choisy: France 36 H7
Chojamachi: Japan 63 g3
Chojna: Poland 45 U3
Chojnice: Poland 43 P10
Chojnów: Poland 45 V4
Choke Mtns.: Ethiopia 79 M7
Cholana: SW. Africa 77 B6
Cholderton: Wilts., England 25 S17
Cholet: France 36 E8
Chollerton: Northumb., Eng. 26 R9
Cholo: Malawi 77 E6
Cholsey: Oxon., England 25 T16
Choma: Zambia 77 C6
Chomoi: Vietnam 64 D4
Chomo Lhari: *mtn.*, Bhutan 59 P9
Chomutov: Czechoslovakia 45 T5
Chonan: S. Korea 63 X7
Chondwe: Zambia 77 C5
Chone: Ecuador 94 A4
Chongjin: N. Korea 63 X6
Chongkal: Cambodia 64 C4
Chong Kara Jol: China 51 N6
Chonju: S. Korea 63 X7
Chonnabot: Thailand 64 C3
Chonos Arch.: *is.*, Chile 95 C12
Chopwell: Tyne and Wear, England 26 S10
Chorazin: city of ancient *Israel* about 1½ miles N. of *Capernaum* near NW. corner of Lake Tiberias 55 b2
Chorges: France 40 M11
Chorley: Lancs., England 27 Q12
Chorleywood: Herts., Eng. 25 U16
Chorregon: Queens., Austl. 69 G4
Chorrera, La: Panama 87 J16 *Ins.*
Chorro, El: Argentina 96 C1
Chortkov: Ukraine 43 T12
Chorzów: Poland 43 Q11
Chosan: N. Korea 63 X6
Choshi: Japan 63 g3
Choshien: Hopeh, China 62 V7
Chos Malal: Argentina 96 A4
Choszczno: Poland 45 V2
Choteau: Mont., U.S.A. 92 E3
Chotětov: Czechoslovakia 45 U5
Chott Djerid: *salt lake*, Tunisia 32 D5
Chott Ech Chergui: *salt lake*, Algeria 32 C5
Chott El Hodna: *salt lake*, Algeria 32 C4
Chott Melrir: *salt lake*, Alg. 32 D5
Choucheng: Yunnan, China 62 S9
Choya: Argentina 96 C2
Chrissiemeer: Trans., S. Afr. 75 J3
CHRISTCHURCH: Canterbury, South I., N.Z. 70 O16
Christchurch: Dorset, Eng. 25 S18
Christian, Cape: N.W.T., Canada 85 N3
Christiana: former name of Oslo, Norway 47 M7
Christiana: & *Dist.*, Trans., S. Africa 75 F3
Christiansburg: Va., U.S.A. 88 L7
Christianshaab: Greenland 85 o4
Christian Sound: Alaska, U.S.A. 84 I6
Christiansted: Santa Cruz, Lesser Antilles 87 a2

Christleton: Ches., England 27 Q13
Christmas: *riv.*, W. Australia 68 D3
Christmas Creek: *town*, W. Australia 68 D3
Christmas I.: (Austl.), Indian O. (*cap.* Flying Fish Cove) 65 D9
Christmas I.: (Br.), Line Is., Pacific Ocean 7 00 160W
Christmas Ridge: N. Pacific Ocean 7 05N 165W
Christow: Devon, England 24 O18
Chrudim: Czechoslovakia 45 V6
Chryston: Strath., Scotland 29 N8
Chrzanów: Poland 43 Q11
Chu: & *riv.*, Kazakh., U.S.S.R. 51 M6
Chuanchou: Kwangsi Chuang, China 62 U9
Chuanchow (Tsinkiang): Fukien, China 62 V10
Chubartau: Kazakh., U.S.S.R. 51 N5
Chub Cay: *is.*, Bahamas 91 M13
Chubut: *riv.*, Argentina 95 D12
Chubut: *Prov.*, Argentina (*cap.* Rawson) 95 D12
Chucheng: Shantung, China 62 V7
Chuching: Tibet, China 62 R8
Chuchirto: Sinkiang, China 51 O6
Chuchow (Lishui): Chekiang, China 62 V9
Chucul: Argentina 96 C3
Chucuma: Argentina 96 B3
Chud, Lake (Lake Peipus): U.S.S.R. 47 U7
Chudleigh: Devon, England 24 O18
Chudnov: Ukraine 43 V11
Chudovo: U.S.S.R. 50 D3
Chugach Mtns.: Alaska, U.S.A. 84 E5
Chugoku Mtns.: Japan 63 c3
Chuguyev: Ukraine 50 E5
Chugwater: Wyo., U.S.A. 92 G4
Chuhsien: Anhwei, China 62 V8
Chuhsien: Chekiang, China 62 V9
Chuhsien: Shantung, China 62 V7
Chuhuichupa: Mexico 93 F7
Chui: Brazil 96 E3
Chuka: Kenya 76 E3
Chukai: Malaya, Malaysia 65 c11
Chukchi Sea: U.S.S.R./U.S.A. 49 s3
Chukhloma: U.S.S.R. 50 F3
Chuki: Chekiang, China 63 W9
Chuking (Kutsing): Yunnan, China 62 S9
Chukotsk Range: U.S.S.R. 49 t4
Chukudu Kraal: Botswana 77 B7
Chulbar: Iran 57 L5
Chulkovo: U.S.S.R. 48 k5
Chulmleigh: Devon, Eng. 24 O18
Chulo: Chile 96 A2
Chulucanas: Peru 94 A5
Chulym: U.S.S.R. 51 O3
Chulym: *riv.*, U.S.S.R. 51 P3
Chumar: *riv.*, China 59 Q7
Chumbicha: Argentina 96 B2
Chumdo: Tibet, China 62 R8
Chumphon: (*Isth. of Kra*), Thailand 64 B4
Chumphon: (*NE. of Mak Khaeng*), Thailand 64 C3
Chumuare: Mozambique 77 D5
Chuna: *riv.*, U.S.S.R. 51 R3
Chunchon: S. Korea 63 X7
Chungan: Fukien, China 62 V9
Chunghsien: Szechwan, China 62 T8
Chungju: S. Korea 63 X7
Chungking: Szechwan, China 62 T9
Chungning: Ninghsia Hui, China 62 T7
Chungshan: Kwangsi Chuang, China 62 U9
Chungsiang: Hupeh, China 62 U8
Chungsun: Kwangtung, China 62 U10
Chungtien: Yunnan, China 62 R9
Chungtso (Taiping): Kwangsi Chuang, China 62 T10
Chunoyar: U.S.S.R. 51 R3
Chunya: Tanzania 77 D4
Chunya: *riv.*, U.S.S.R. 49 I5
Chuquibambilla: Peru 94 C6
Chuquicamata: Chile 96 B1
CHUR: Graubünden, Switz. 40 P9
Church: Lancs., England 27 R12
Church Broughton: Derby., England 27 S14
Churchdown: Glos., Eng. 24 R16
Church Eaton: Staffs., Eng. 27 R14
Church Fenton: N. Yorks., England 27 T12
Churchill: Avon, England 24 Q17
Churchill: Don., Repub. of Ireland 30 F10
Churchill: Ferm., N. Ireland 30 F11
Churchill: Man., Canada 84 k6
Churchill: Oxon., England 25 S16
Churchill: *riv.*, Man./Sask., Canada 92 G1
Churchill: *riv.*, Newfoundland, Canada 84 K6
Churchill Falls: Newfoundland, Canada 85 n7
Churchill Lake: Sask., Can. 92 F1
Church Lench: Hereford & Worcester, England 24 S15
Church Minshull: Ches., England 27 Q13
Church Point: *town*, La., U.S.A. 90 E10
Church Pulverbatch: Salop, England 27 Q14
Church Stretton: Salop, England 27 Q14
Churchtown: Cork, Repub. of Ireland 31 D15
Church Town: Cumbria, England 26 Q11
Churchtown: Lim., Repub. of Ireland 31 C15
Churchtown: Lon., N Irel. 30 H10
Churchtown: (*Carnsore Point*), Wex., Repub. of Ireland 31 H15
Churchtown: (*Hook Head*), Wex., Repub. of Ireland 31 J15
Churton: Ches., England 27 Q13
Churu: Rajasthan, India 58 N9
Churysh: *riv.*, U.S.S.R. 51 O4
Chushan: Hupeh, China 62 U8
Chushan: *i. & arch.*, China 63 W8
Chusovoy: U.S.S.R. 50 J3
Chuvash A.S.S.R.: U.S.S.R. (*cap.* Cheboksary) 50 G3
Chuwassu: Tibet, China 62 R9
Chuyen: Inner Mongolia, China 62 S6
Chwangho: Liaoning, China 63 W7
Cibotus: see *Apamea*.
Cibyra: Phrygian, later Graeco-Roman city about 20 miles SSW. of Acıpayam, Turkey 56 A3
Çiçekdaği: Turkey 56 D2
Cicero: Ill., U.S.A. 88 H5
Cicero Dantás: Brazil 94 K6
Cicilian Gates: *pass*, Turkey 56 D3
Cide: Turkey 56 C1
Cidlina: *riv.*, Czechoslovakia 45 V5

Cidones: Spain 35 E16
Ciechanów: Poland 43 R10
Ciechocinek: Poland 43 Q10
Ciego de Avila: Cuba 87 M13
Ciénaga: Colombia 94 C1
Cienfuegos: Cuba 87 I13
Cierp: France 37 F13
Cieszyn: Poland 43 Q12
Cieza: Spain 35 F17
Çiftlik (Kelkit): Turkey 56 F1
Çiftalan: Turkey (Bosporus. *Inset*) 20 *Ins.*
Cigliano: Italy 40 O10
Cijulung: Java 65 D8
Cilacap: Java 65 D8
Cilcennin: Dyfed, Wales 24 N15
Çıldır: & *lake*, Turkey 57 H1
Cilgerran: Dyfed, Wales 24 M15
Cilibia: Romania 39 U14
Cilicia: ancient name of district in Southern Turkey, between *Lycaonia* and the sea and between Taurus Mts. and Iskenderon Gulf 56 C3
Cilician Gates: *pass*, Turkey 57 J3
Cilo Daği: *mtn.*, Turkey 57 J3
Cilurnum: fort of Hadrian's Wall just W. of crossing of river North Tyne at *Chesters*, and 1 mile NW. of Wall, Northumb., Eng. 26 R6
Cilycwm: Dyfed, Wales 24 O15
Cima Dodici: *mtn.*, Italy 41 R10
Cimalmotto: Switzerland 40 O9
Cima Presanella: *mtn.*, Italy 41 Q9
Cimarron: *riv.*, U.S.A. 90 B7
Cincinnati: Ohio, U.S.A. 88 J6
Cinderford: Glos., England 24 R16
Çine: Turkey 39 V18
Ciney: Belgium 44 L5
Cingoli: Italy 41 T12
Cioara: Romania 39 U14
Ciotat, La: France 40 L12
Circeo, Cape: Italy 38 N16
Circesium: Roman fort at confluence of Euphrates and Khabur near Bassira, Syria 57 G4
Circle: Alaska, U.S.A. 84 e4
Circle: Mont., U.S.A. 92 F3
Circleville: Ohio, U.S.A. 88 K6
Cirebon: Java 65 D8
Cirencester: Glos., England 24 S16
Cirene: Libya 33 G5
Cirie: Italy 40 N10
Ciro: Italy 38 P17
Ciron: *riv.*, France 37 E11
Cirta: Roman city at Constantine, Algeria 32 D4
Cisalpine Gaul (Gallia Cisalpina): ancient name of N. Italy comprising (approximately) the regions of Piedmont, Liguria, Lombardy, Venetia, and Emilia Romagna 40 —
Cisaŕský Les: *mtns.*, Czech. 45 S5
Cisco: Tex., U.S.A. 90 B9
Cisleithania: old name for the Austrian portion of Austria-Hungary N. and W. of *Transleithania* including W. Czechoslovakia, Galicia, Northern Bukovina, and Slovenia. Name is derived from Leitha river 33 F2
Cissbury: site of ancient British settlement in downs about 4 miles N. of Worthing, W. Sussex, England 25 V18
Citadella: Italy 41 R10
Cithaeron: *mtn.* of SE. *Boeotia* on frontier with *Attica* about 10 miles S. of Thebes 39 S17
Citium: Phoenician, later Graeco-Roman, city at Larnaca, Cyprus 56 C4
Citlaltepetl: *volc.*, Mexico 86 K14
Citrusdal: S. Africa 74 C6
Citta della Pieve: Italy 38 N15
Città di Castello: Italy 41 S12
Cittanova: Italy 38 P17
Cittanova: *see* Novi Grad.
Ciudad Bolivar: Venezuela 94 E2
Ciudad Chetumal: Mexico (Honduras. *Inset*) 86 *Ins.*
Ciudad de las Casas: Mexico 86 k14
Ciudad de Gómez: Argentina 96 C3
Ciudad Dosente: Spain 35 E15
Ciudadela: Balearic Is. 35 H17
Ciudad Guerrero: Mexico 93 F7
Ciudad Guzmán: Mexico 86 j14
Ciudad Juaréz: Mexico 93 F6
Ciudad Madero: Mexico 86 K13
Ciudad Mante: Mexico 86 K13
Ciudad Mier: Mexico 90 B12
Ciudad Obregón: Mexico 93 F7
CIUDAD REAL: & *Prov.*, Sp. 35 E17
Ciudad Rodrigo: Spain 35 C16
CIUDAD VICTORIA: Tamaulipas, Mexico 86 K13
Cividale del Friuli: Italy 41 T9
Civita Castellana: Italy 38 N15
Civitavecchia: Italy 38 M15
Civray: France 37 F14
Çivril: Turkey 56 A2
Cizre: Turkey 57 H3
Clachan: Strath., Scotland 29 K8
Clachan of Campsie: Strathclyde, Scotland 29 N8
Clachan of Glendaruel: Strathclyde, Scotland 29 L7
Clach Leathad: *mtn.*, Strathclyde, Scotland 29 M6
Clacton on Sea: Essex, Eng. 25 Y16
Cladach: *dist.*, Outer Hebr., Scotland 28 H3
Cladich: Strath., Scotland 29 L7
Clain: *riv.*, France 37 F9
Claire, Lake: Alta., Canada 84 h6
Clairton: Pa., U.S.A. 89 M5
Clairvaux: France 40 L9
Clamecy: France 36 J8
Clane: Kild., Repub. of Irel. 31 H13
Clanfield: Oxon., England 25 S16
Clanoventa: Roman name of Ravenglass, Cumbria, Eng. 26 P11
Clanton: Ala., U.S.A. 91 H9
Clanwilliam: & *Dist.*, S. Afr. 74 C6
Clara: Offaly, Repub. of Irel. 31 F13
Clara: *riv.*, Panama 94 *Ins.*
Claraville: Queens., Austl. 69 G3
Clare: *Co.*, Repub. of Ireland (*cap.* Ennis) 31 C14
Clare: Mich., U.S.A. 88 J4
Clare: S. Australia 71 C9
Clare: Suff., England 25 X15
Clare: *riv.*, Galway, Repub. of Ireland 31 D13
Clarecastle: Clare, Repub. of Ireland 31 D14
Claregalway: Galway, Repub. of Ireland 31 D13
Clare I.: Repub. of Ireland 30 A12
Clareland: Jamaica 86 *Ins.*
Claremont: N. Africa 74 C6
Claremore: Okla., U.S.A. 90 D7

Claremorris: Mayo, Repub. of Ireland 30 C12
Clarence: *riv.*, N.S.W., Austl. 71 K7
Clarence I.: Chile 95 C14
Clarendon: Ark., U.S.A. 90 F8
Clarendon: Tex., U.S.A. 90 A8
Clarenville: Newf., Canada 85 V2
Claresholm: Alta., Canada 92 E2
Clarinbridge: Galway, Repub. of Ireland 31 D13
Clarinda: Iowa, U.S.A. 92 H4
Clarion: Iowa, U.S.A. 88 E4
Clarion: Pa., U.S.A. 89 M5
Clarion Fracture Zone: N. Pacific Ocean 7 15N 135W
Clark: S. Dak., U.S.A. 92 H4
Clarkdale: Ariz., U.S.A. 93 E6
Clarke City: Que., Canada 84 N7
Clarke Range: Queens., Australia 70 G3
Clarke River: Queens., Australia 69 H3
Clarkes Harbour: *city*, N.S., Canada 89 R4
Clark Fork: *riv.*, Mont., U.S.A. 92 D3
Clark Point: *cape*, Ont., Canada 88 L3
Clarks: La., U.S.A. 90 E9
Clarksburg: W. Va., U.S.A. 88 L6
Clarksdale: Miss., U.S.A. 90 F8
Clarkson: S. Africa 75 F7
Clarkston: Wash., U.S.A. 92 D3
Clarksville: Ark., U.S.A. 90 E8
Clarksville: Tenn., U.S.A. 88 H7
Clarksville: Tex., U.S.A. 90 D9
Claro: *riv.*, Brazil 94 G7
Clashmore: High., Scot. 28 N4
Clashmore: Wat., Repub. of Ireland 31 F15
Clashnessie: High., Scot. 28 L3
Clatteingshaws Loch: Dumfries & Galloway, Scotland 29 N9
Claudiopolis: Graeco-Roman city at Bolu, Turkey 56 B1
Claudy: Lon., N. Ireland 30 G10
Claughton: Lancs., England 27 Q11
Clausentum: Roman port at Bitterne about ⅓ mile E. of river Itchen at Southampton, Hants., England 25 T18
Clausthal: W. Germany 44 Q4
Claveria: Luzon, Phil. 64 G3
Clavering I.: Greenland 85 r3
Claverley: Salop, England 27 R14
Claverton: Queens., Austl. 70 F6
Clave Souilly: France 36 H7
Claxby: Lincs., England 27 V13
Claxton: Ga., U.S.A. 91 L9
Clay Center: Kans., U.S.A. 93 H5
Clay Cross: Derby., Eng. 27 T13
Claydon: Suff., England 25 Y15
Clayette, La: France 37 K9
Clay Head: *cape*, I. of Man, United Kingdom 26 N11
Claypole: Lincs., England 27 U13
Clayton: Ala., U.S.A. 91 J10
Clayton: Ga., U.S.A. 91 K8
Clayton: N.Y., U.S.A. 89 N3
Clayton: N.C., U.S.A. 91 M8
Clayton: Okla., U.S.A. 90 D8
Clayton: W. Yorks., England 27 S12
Clayton le Moors: Lancs., England 27 R12
Clazomenae: Greek city in inlet on S. shore of ismir Gulf N. of Urla, Turkey 39 U17
Cleadale: Inner Hebr., Scotland 28 J6
Clear Cape: Clear I., Repub. of Ireland 31 B17
Clearfield: Pa., U.S.A. 89 M5
Clearfield: Utah, U.S.A. 92 E4
Clear I.: Repub. of Ireland 31 C17
Clear Lake: *city*, Iowa, U.S.A. 88 E4
Clearwater: *city*, Fla., U.S.A. 91 K12
Clearwater: *riv.*, Alta., Can. 92 F1
Clearwater Lake: Que., Can. 85 m6
Clearwater Mtns.: Idaho, U.S.A. 92 D3
Clearwater Station: B.C., Canada 92 C2
Clearwell: Glos., England 24 Q16
Cleator Moor: *town*, Cumbria, England 26 O10
Cleburne: Tex., U.S.A. 90 C9
Cleckheaton: W. Yorks., Eng. 27 S12
Cleddau, Eastern: *riv.*, Dyfed, Wales 24 M16
Cleder: France 36 A7
Clee Hills: Salop, England 24 Q15
Cle Elum: Wash., U.S.A. 92 C3
Cleethorpes: Humb., England 27 V12
Cleeve, Old: Som., England 24 P17
Clefmont: France 40 L7
Cleggan: Galway, Repub. of Ireland 30 A12
Cléguérec: France 36 B7
Clehonger: Hereford & Worcester, England 24 Q15
Clejani: Romania 39 T14
Clelles: France 40 L11
Clenchwarton: Norf., England 25 X14
Clent: Hereford & Worcester, England 24 R15
Cleobury Mortimer: Salop, England 21 R15
Cleonae: Greek city of N. *Argolis* 8 miles SW. of Corinth 39 S18
Clerehan: Tip. Repub. of Ireland 31 F15
Clères: France 36 G6
Clerke Reef: W. Australia 68 B3
Clermont: France 36 H6
Clermont: Queens., Austl. 70 G4
Clermont-en-Argonne: Fr. 36 L6
CLERMONT-FERRAND: Puy de Dôme, France 37 J10
Clermont-l'Hérault: France 37 J12
Clerval: France 40 M8
Cléry: France 36 G8
Cles: Italy 41 R9
Cleve: *see* Kleve.
Cleve: S. Australia 71 B9
Clevedon: Avon, England 24 Q17
Cleveland: Miss., U.S.A. 90 F9
Cleveland: Ohio, U.S.A. 88 L5
Cleveland: Okla., U.S.A. 90 C7
Cleveland: Queens., Austl. 70 K6
Cleveland: Tenn., U.S.A. 91 J8
Cleveland: Tex., U.S.A. 90 D10
Cleveland: *Co.*, England (*co. town* Teesside) 26 T10
Cleveland: *dist.*, Cleveland/N. Yorks., England 26 U10
Cleveland Hills: Cleveland/N. Yorks., Eng. 26 T11
Clevelândia: Brazil 96 E2
Clew Bay: Mayo, Repub. of Ireland 30 B12
Clewer: Trans., S. Africa 75 H2
Clifden: Galway, Repub. of Ireland 30 A13
Cliffe: Kent, England 25 W17
Cliffony: Sligo, Repub. of Ireland 30 E11

Clifford: Hereford & Worcester, England 24 P15
Clifford: Queens., Austl. 70 H6
Clifford: S. Africa 75 G5
Clifton: Avon, England 24 Q17
Clifton: Cumbria, England 26 Q10
Clifton: Queens., Australia 70 J6
Clifton: S. Africa 74 *Ins.*
Clifton: Tex., U.S.A. 90 C10
Clifton, Great: Cumbria, England 26 P10
Clifton, South: Notts., Eng. 27 U13
Clifton upon Teme: Hereford & Worcester, England 24 R15
Climax: Sask., Canada 92 F3
Clinch: *riv.*, Va./Tenn., U.S.A. 88 K7
Clinch Mtns.: Va./Tenn., U.S.A. 88 K7
Clingmans Dome: *mtn.*, N.C., U.S.A. 91 K8
Clinton: Ark., U.S.A. 90 E8
Clinton: B.C., Canada 92 C2
Clinton: Ill., U.S.A. 88 G5
Clinton: Ind., U.S.A. 88 H6
Clinton: Iowa, U.S.A. 88 F5
Clinton: Ky., U.S.A. 88 G7
Clinton: Mo., U.S.A. 90 E6
Clinton: N.C., U.S.A. 91 M8
Clinton: Okla., U.S.A. 90 B8
Clinton: Ont., Canada 88 L4
Clinton: S.C., U.S.A. 91 L8
Clinton: South I., N.Z. 71 M8
Clinton: Tenn., U.S.A. 88 J7
Clinton-Colden Lake: N.W.T., Canada 84 J5
Clintonville: Wis., U.S.A. 88 G3
Clio: Mich., U.S.A. 88 K4
Clipperton Fracture Zone: N. Pacific Ocean 7 05N 130W
Clipston: Northants., Eng. 25 U15
Clipstone: Notts., England 27 T13
Clisham: *mtn.*, Outer Hebr., Scotland 28 H4
Clisson: France 36 D8
Clitheroe: Lancs., England 27 R12
Clive: Salop, England 27 Q14
Clocolan: O.F.S., S. Africa 75 G4
Clodomira: Argentina 96 C2
Clogh: Antrim, N. Ireland 30 J10
Clogh: Kilk., Repub. of Ireland 31 G14
Cloghan: Offaly, Repub. of Ireland 31 F13
Cloghane: Kerry, Repub. of Ireland 31 A15
Clogheen: Tip., Repub. of Ireland 31 F15
Clogher: Mayo, Repub. of Ireland 30 C12
Clogher: Tyr., N. Ireland 30 G11
Clogher Head: *cape*, Louth, Repub. of Ireland 30 J12
Cloghjordan: Tip., Repub. of Ireland 31 E14
Clohamon: Wex., Repub. of Ireland 31 H14
Clonakenny: Tip., Repub. of Ireland 31 F14
Clonakilty: Cork, Repub. of Ireland 31 D16
Clonard: Meath, Repub. of Ireland 30 G13
Clonaslee: Laois, Repub. of Ireland 31 F13
Clonbulloge: Offaly, Repub. of Ireland 31 G13
Clonbur: Galway, Repub. of Ireland 30 C12
Cloncurry: Queens., Austl. 69 G4
Cloncurry: *riv.*, Queens., Australia 69 G3
Clondalkin: Dublin, Repub. of Ireland 31 J13
Clonea (*NE. of Dungarvan*), Wat., Repub. of Ireland 31 F15.
Clonea (*W. of Portlaw*), Wat., Repub. of Ireland 31 G15
Clonee: Meath, Repub. of Ireland 31 J13
Clonegall: Carlow, Repub. of Ireland 31 H14
Clones: Monaghan, Repub. of Ireland 30 G11
Clonfert: Galway, Repub. of Ireland 31 E13
Clonmacnoise: Offaly, Republic of Ireland 31 F13
Clonmany: Don., Repub. of Ireland 30 G9
CLONMEL: S. Rid., Tip., Repub. of Ireland 31 F15
Clonmellon: Westmeath, Repub. of Ireland 30 G12
Clonmore: Wick., Repub. of Ireland 31 H14
Clonmult: Cork, Repub. of Ireland 31 E16
Clonoulty: Tip., Repub. of Ireland 31 F14
Clonroche: Wex., Repub. of Ireland 31 H15
Clontarf: Dublin, Repub. of Ireland 31 J13
Clontibret: Monaghan, Republic of Ireland 30 H11
Clonygowan: Offaly, Repub. of Ireland 31 G13
Cloone: Leit., Repub. of Irel. 30 F12
Cloonfad: Rosc., Repub. of Ireland 30 D12
Cloonlara: Clare, Repub. of Ireland 31 D14
Clophill: Beds., England 25 V15
Cloppenburg: W. Germany 44 O3
Cloquet: Minn., U.S.A. 88 E2
Clorinda: Paraguay 96 D2
Closeburn: Dumfries & Galloway, Scotland 29 O9
Clota: Roman name of river Clyde, Scotland 29 O8
Cloud Peak: *mtn.*, Wyo., U.S.A. 92 F4
Clough: Down, N. Ireland 30 K11
Cloughton: N. Yorks., Eng. 26 V11
Clovelly: Devon, England 24 N18
Clovenfords: Borders, Scot. 29 Q8
Clovis: Calif., U.S.A. 93 D6
Clovis: N. Mex., U.S.A. 93 G6
Cloyes: France 36 G8
Cloyne: Cork, Repub. of Ireland 31 E16
Cluanie, Loch: High., Scot. 28 L5
Cluj: Romania 43 S13
Clumber: Notts., England 27 T13
Clun: & *riv.*, Salop, England 24 P15
Clunes: Vict., Australia 71 E11
Clunia: Roman town about 7 miles ENE. of Aranda de Duero, Spain 35 E16
Clunie: Tayside, Scotland 29 P6
Cluny: France 37 K9
Cluny: Queens., Australia 69 F4
Cluses: France 40 M9

134 Clusium—Corfu

Clusium: Roman name of Etruscan and later city at Chiusi, Italy 38 M15
Clusone: Italy 40 P10
Clutha: *riv.*, South I., N.Z. 71 M17
Clwyd: *Co.*, Wales (*co. town* Mold) 27 P13
Clwyd: *riv. & val.*, Clwyd, Wales 27 P13
Clwydian Range: Clwyd, Wales 27 P13
Clydach: Powys, Wales 24 P16
Clydach: Gwent, Wales 24 P16
Clydach: W. Glam., Wales 24 O16
Clyde: N.Y., U.S.A. 89 N4
Clyde: N.W.T., Canada 85 N3
Clyde: Queens., Australia 71 E7
Clyde: South I., N.Z. 70 M17
Clyde: *riv.*, Strath., Scotland 29 O8
Clyde, Firth of: Scotland 29 M8
Clydebank: Strath., Scot. 29 N8
Clydesdale: O.F.S., S. Afr. 75 G3
Clydesdale: *val.*, Strathclyde, Scotland 29 O8
Clynnogfawr: Gwynedd, Wales 27 N13
Cnidus: Greek city at end of peninsula S. of G. of Kerme, Turkey 39 U18
Cnossus: ancient Minoan city about 3 miles from N. coast near Candia, Crete 39 T19
Coachford: Cork, Repub. of Ireland 31 D16
Coagh: Tyr., N. Ireland 30 H10
Coahuila: *State*, Mexico (*cap.* Saltillo) 93 G7
Coakleytown: Bahamas 91 N13
Coal Aston: Derby., Eng. 27 T13
Coalcomán: Mexico 86 j14
Coalgate: Okla., U.S.A. 90 C8
Coal Hill: *city*, Ark., U.S.A. 90 E8
Coalinga: Calif., U.S.A. 93 C5
Coalisland: Tyr., N. Irel. 30 H10
Coalport: Salop, England 27 R14
Coalspur: Alta., Canada 92 D2
Coalville: Leics., England 27 T14
Coari: Brazil 94 E4
Coast: *Reg.*, Kenya (*cap.* Mombasa) 76 E3
Coast: *Reg.*, Tanzania (*cap.* Dar es Salaam) 76 E4
Coast Mtns.: B.C., Canada 84 f6
Coast Ranges: U.S.A. 92 C4
Coatbridge: Strath., Scot. 29 N8
Coates: Cambs., England 25 V14
Coates, North: Lincs., Eng. 27 W13
Coatesville: Pa., U.S.A. 89 O6
Coatham: Cleve., England 26 T10
Coaticook: Que., Canada 89 Q3
Coats I.: N.W.T., Canada 85 I5
Coats Land: Antarctica 9 80S 30W
Coatzacoalcos (Puerto México): Mexico 86 k14
Cobadin: Romania 39 V14
Cobalt: Ont., Canada 89 M2
Cobán: Guatemala 86 k14
Cobar: N.S.W., Australia 71 F8
Cobargo: N.S.W., Australia 71 H11
Cobber Pedy: S. Australia 68 E5
Cobbinshaw: Lothian, Scot. 29 O8
Cobden: Vict., Australia 71 E12
Cobequid Mtns.: N.S., Canada 89 U3
Cobh (Queenstown): Cork, Repub. of Ireland 31 E16
Cobham: Kent, England 25 W17
Cobham: Surrey, England 25 V17
Cobija: Bolivia 94 D6
Cobleskill: N.Y., U.S.A. 89 O4
Cobourg: Ont., Canada 89 M4
Cobourg Penin.: N. Territ., Australia 68 E2
Cobram: Vict., Australia 71 F10
Cobre: Nev., U.S.A. 92 E4
Coburg: W. Germany 45 Q5
Coca: Ecuador 94 B4
Cocamá: Peru 94 C6
Cocanada (Kakinada): Tamil Nadu, India 58 O11
Cochabamba: Bolivia 94 D7
Cochem: W. Germany 44 N5
Cochin & Travancore: (now in Kerala, *State*), India 58 N13
Cochin-China: (now absorbed in S. Vietnam).
Cochran: Ga., U.S.A. 91 K9
Cochrane: Ont., Canada 88 L1
Cochrane: Alta., Canada 84 E5
Cochrane, Cerro: *mtn.*, Arg./Chile 95 C13
Cochrane, Lake: Chile 95 C13
Cock Bridge: Gram., Scot. 28 P5
Cockburn: S. Australia 71 D9
Cockburn I.: Ont., Canada 88 K3
Cockburnspath: Borders, Scotland 29 R8
Cockenzie: Lothian, Scot. 29 Q8
Cockerham: Lancs., Eng. 27 Q12
Cockermouth: Cumbria, England 26 P10
Cockfield: Durham, Eng. 26 S10
Cockfield: Suff., England 25 X15
Cocking: W. Sussex, England 25 U18
Cock of Arran: *cape*, Strathclyde, Scotland 29 L8
Coco, Great & Little: *is.*, Andaman Is. 59 Q12
Cocoa: Fla., U.S.A. 91 L11
Coco Beach: Gabon 81 F4
Coco Channel: Indian O. 59 Q12
Cocos: Brazil 94 J6
Cocos Basin: Indian Ocean 9 05S 90E
Cocos (Keeling) Is.: (Austl.), Indian O. (*cap.* West Island) 9 15S 95E
Cocuy, Sierra Nevada de: *mtns.*, Colombia 94 C2
Cod, Cape: Mass., U.S.A. 89 R5
Codajás: Brazil 94 E4
Coddenham: Suff., England 25 Y15
Codfish I.: New Zealand 71 L18
Codford: Wilts., England 24 R17
Codigoro: Italy 41 S11
Codlea: Romania 39 T14
Codó: Brazil 94 J4
Codogno: Italy 40 P10
Codrington: Barbuda, Leeward Is. 87 c2
Codriopo: Italy 41 S10
Codroy: Newf., Canada 85 t3
Codsall: Staffs., England 27 R14
Cod's Head: *cape*, Cork, Repub. of Ireland 31 A16
Cody: Wyo., U.S.A. 92 F4
Coedpoeth: Clwyd, Wales 27 P13
Coelbren: site of Roman fort about 2 miles NE. of Seven Sisters, Wales 24 O16
Coelesyria: Greek name of ancient Persian satrapy covering approximate area of modern Syria 56 E4
Coelesyria: Greek name of districts of Syria round Damascus and in valleys between Lebanon and Anti Lebanon 56 E5
Coelesyria: province of later Roman Empire in N. Syria and Hatay, Turkey 56 E3
Coen: Queens., Australia 69 G2
Coenbult: SW. Africa 74 C3
Coetivy: *i.*, (Br. Indian Ocean Territ.), Indian Ocean 19 00 50E
Coeur d'Alene: Idaho, U.S.A. 92 D3
Coffeyville: Kans., U.S.A. 90 D7
Coffins Bay Penin.: S. Australia 71 A10
Coff's Harbour: N.S.W., Australia 71 K8
Cofimvaba: S. Africa 75 G5
Cogealac: Romania 39 V14
Coggeshall: Essex, Eng. 25 X16
Cognac: France 37 E10
Cogne: Italy 40 N10
Cogolin: France 40 M12
Cogolludo: Spain 35 E16
Coguno: Mozambique 77 D7
Cohoes: N.Y., U.S.A. 89 P4
Cohuna: Vict., Australia 71 F10
Coiba I.: Panama 94 A2
Coimbatore: Tamil Nadu, India 58 N12
COIMBRA: Beira Litoral, Portugal 35 B16
Coin: Spain 35 D18
Cojede: *riv.*, Venezuela 94 D2
Cojutepeque: El Salvador 86 L15
Coker, East: Som., England 24 Q18
Colac: Vict., Australia 71 E12
Colatina: Brazil 94 J7
Colbeck, Cape: Antarctica 9 80S 160W
Colbinabbin: Vict., Austl. 71 F11
Colbinstown: Wick., Repub. of Ireland 31 H13
Colbitz: E. Germany 45 R3
Colbún: Chile 96 A4
Colby: Kans., U.S.A. 93 G5
Colchester: Essex, England 25 X16
Colchester: S. Africa 75 F6
Colchis: Greek name of region. S. of Caucasus mtns. at E. end of Black Sea 48 F9
Cold Ash: Berks., England 25 T17
Coldbackie: Highland, Scot. 28 N2
Cold Fell: *mtn.*, Cumbria, England 26 Q10
Coldingham: Borders, Scot. 29 R8
Colditz: E. Germany 45 S4
Cold Kirby: N. Yorks., Eng. 26 T11
Cold Lake: *town & lake*, Alberta, Canada 92 F2
Cold Lake: *town*, Man., Canada 92 G1
Cold Spring: *city*, Minn., U.S.A. 88 D3
Coldstream: Borders, Scot. 29 R8
Coldwater: Kans., U.S.A. 90 B7
Coldwater: Mich., U.S.A. 88 J5
Coldwater: *riv.*, Miss., U.S.A. 90 F8
Coleford: Glos., England 24 Q16
Coleford: Natal, S. Africa 76 H4
Coleman: Tex., U.S.A. 90 B10
Coleman: *riv.*, Queens., Australia 69 G2
Colenso: Natal, S. Africa 75 H4
Coleraine: Lon., N. Ireland 30 H9
Coleraine: Vict., Australia 71 D11
Coleridge, Lake: South I., New Zealand 70 N16
Colesberg: *& Dist.*, S. Afr. 75 F5
Coleshill: War., England 25 S15
Colfax: Iowa, U.S.A. 88 E5
Colfax: La., U.S.A. 90 E10
Colfax: Wash., U.S.A. 92 D3
Colico: Italy 40 P9
Colieu: Vietnam 64 D3
Coligny: Trans., S. Africa 75 G3
Colima: Mexico 86 j14
Colinas: Brazil 94 J5
Colinsburgh: Fife, Scot. 29 Q7
Colinton: Lothian, Scot. 29 P8
Coll: *i.*, Inner Hebr., Scot. 29 H6
Collace: Tayside, Scotland 29 P7
Collafirth: Shetland Is. 28 *Ins.*
Collaguasi: Chile 94 D8
Collarenebri: N.S.W., Austl. 71 H7
Collaria: ancient Latin city on left bank of *Anio* about 10 miles. E. of Rome. 38 N16
Collecchio: Italy 40 Q11
Colle di Val d'Elsa: Italy 41 R12
College: Alaska, U.S.A. 84 E5
College Park: Ga., U.S.A. 91 J9
College Station: Tex., U.S.A. 90 C10
Colle Salvetti: Italy 40 Q12
Collie: N.S.W., Australia 71 H8
Collie: W. Australia 68 B6
Collierville: Tenn., U.S.A. 90 G8
Collingbourne Kingston: Wilts., England 25 S17
Collingham: W. Yorks., Eng. 27 T12
Collingham, North & South: Notts., England 27 U13
Collingwood: Ont., Canada 88 L3
Collingwood: South I., N.Z. 70 O15
Collinsville: Ill., U.S.A. 88 G6
Collinsville: Okla., U.S.A. 90 D7
Collinsville: Queens., Austl. 70 G3
Collo: Algeria 32 D4
Collon: Louth, Repub. of Ireland 30 J12
Collonges: France 40 L9
Collooney: Sligo, Repub. of Ireland 30 E11
COLMAR: Haut-Rhin, France 40 N7
Colmars: France 40 M11
Colmenar de Oreja: Spain 35 E16
Colmenar: Viejo: Spain 35 E16
Colmonell: Strath., Scotland 29 M9
Colne: Lancs., England 27 R12
Colne: *riv.*, Essex, England 25 X16
Colne: *riv.*, Herts., Eng. 23 L9
Colne Point: Essex, Eng. 25 Y16
Cologna Veneta: Italy 41 R10
Cologne (Köln): W. Germany 44 M5
Colombe: Cameroun 81 G3
Colombey-les-Belles: Fr. 40 L7

Colombia: *Republic* 94 C3
Cap.: Bogotá
Area: 455,355 sq. miles (1,179,369 sq. km.)
Pop.: 21,772,000 (*1971 E*)

COLOMBO: Sri Lanka 58 N13
Colomiers: France 37 G12
Colón: Buenos Aires: Arg. 96 C3
Colón: Cuba 87 I13
Colón: Entre Rios, Arg. 96 D3
Colón: Panama 94 *Ins.*
Colonia: Uruguay 96 D3
Colonia Agrippinensis: Roman camp (later colony) at Cologne, W. Germany 44 M5
Colonia Catriel: Argentina 96 B4
Colonia Elisa: Argentina 96 D2
Colonia las Heras: Arg. 95 D13
Colonial Nat. Historical Park: Va., U.S.A. 89 N7
Colonia Sarmiento: Arg. 95 D13
Colonsay: *i.*, Inner Hebr., Scotland 29 J7
Colophon: Greek city on Turkish mainland, north of Greek island of Sámos 39 U18
Colorado: *riv.*, Argentina 96 C4
Colorado: *riv.*, Tex., U.S.A. 93 G6
Colorado: *riv.*, U.S.A. 93 E6
Colorado: *State*, U.S.A. (*cap.* Denver) 93 F5
Colorado City: Tex., U.S.A. 93 G6
Colorado Desert: Calif., U.S.A. 93 D6
Colorado Plat.: Ariz., U.S.A. 93 E5
Colorado River Aqueduct: Ariz., U.S.A. 93 E6
Colorados, Los: Argentina 96 B2
Colorado Springs: *city*, Colo., U.S.A. 93 G5
Colossae: early Christian stronghold of *Phrygia*, Asia Minor, whose people were addressed in St. Paul's epistle to Colossians, ruins 15 miles E. of Denizli, Turkey 56 A3
Colquechaca: Bolivia 94 D7
Colquitt: Ga., U.S.A. 91 J10
Colsterworth: Lincs., Eng. 27 U14
Coltishall: Norf., England 25 Y14
Colton: Staffs., England 27 S14
Columbia: Ky., U.S.A. 88 J7
Columbia: Miss., U.S.A. 90 G10
Columbia: Mo., U.S.A. 88 E6
Columbia: N.C., U.S.A. 91 N8
Columbia: Pa., U.S.A. 89 N5
COLUMBIA: S.C., U.S.A. 91 L8
Columbia: Tenn., U.S.A. 91 H8
Columbia: *riv.*, U.S.A. 92 C3
Columbia, Cape: N.W.T., Canada 85 m1
Columbia, Dist. of: U.S.A. (*cap.* Washington) 89 N6
Columbia, Mount: B.C./Alta., Canada 92 D2
Columbia Falls: *city*, Mont., U.S.A. 92 E3
Columbus: Ga., U.S.A. 91 J9
Columbus: Ind., U.S.A. 88 J6
Columbus: Iowa, U.S.A. 88 F5
Columbus: Kans., U.S.A. 90 D7
Columbus: Miss., U.S.A. 90 G9
Columbus: Mont., U.S.A. 92 F3
Columbus: Nebr., U.S.A. 92 H4
COLUMBUS: Ohio, U.S.A. 88 K6
Columbus: Tex., U.S.A. 90 C11
Columbus: Wis., U.S.A. 88 G4
Colville: North I., N.Z. 70 P13
Colville: Wash., U.S.A. 92 D3
Colville: *riv.*, Alaska, U.S.A. 84 D4
Colville Lake: N.W.T., Can. 84 G4
Colville Range: North I., New Zealand 70 P13
Colwall: Hereford & Worcester, England 24 R15
Colwich: Staffs., England 27 S14
Colwyn: Clwyd, Wales 27 O13
Colwyn Bay: *town*, Clwyd, Wales 27 O13
Colyton: Devon, England 24 P18
Comacchio: Italy 41 S11
Comacchio, Lake: Italy 41 S11
Comana: Romania 39 U14
Comana: Cappadocian city, later Roman colony, at W. foot of mtn. about 3 miles NE. of Saimbeyli, Turkey 56 E2
Comana: city of ancient *Pontus* across river and about 20 miles NE. of town of Tokat, Turkey 56 E1
Comanche: Tex., U.S.A. 90 B10
Combarbala: Chile 96 A3
Combeaufontaine: France 40 L8
Combe Martin: Devon, Eng. 24 O17
Comber: Down, N. Ireland 30 K10
Comberton: Cambs., Eng. 25 W15
Combles: France 36 H6
Combourg: France 36 D7
Comboussougou: Upper Volta 80 D2
Comboyne: N.S.W., Austl. 71 K8
Combronde: France 37 J10
Comeragh Mtns.: Wat., Repub. of Ireland 31 F15
Comet: Queens., Australia 70 H4
Comet: *riv.*, Queens., Austl. 70 H5
Comet Downs: Queens., Australia 70 H4
Comilla: Bangladesh 59 Q10
Cominequiers: France 37 D9
Comines: Belgium 44 H5
Comino: *i.*, Malta 32 *Ins.*
Comino, Cape: Sardinia 38 L16
Comitán: Mexico 86 k14
Commagene: ancient name of district between *Cappadocia* and Syria, in Euphrates valley around Samsat, Turkey 56 F3
Commentry: France 37 H9
Commerce: Ga., U.S.A. 91 K8
Commerce: Tex., U.S.A. 90 D9
Commercy: France 40 L7
Committee Bay: N.W.T., Canada 85 L4
Commodore Bay: *town*, New Britain, Bismarck Arch. 67 K3
Commondale: *village*, N. Yorks., England 26 U11
Communism, Mt.: Tadzhik., U.S.S.R. 51 M7
Como: Italy 40 P10
Como: *riv.*, Gabon 81 G4
Como, Lake: Italy 40 P9
Comodoro Rivadavia: Argentina 95 D13
Comoé: *riv.*, Ivory Coast 80 D3
Comondú: Mexico 93 E7
Comongin: Queens., Austl. 70 F6
Comorin, Cape: Tamil Nadu, India 58 N13

Comoro Is.: Indian O. (*cap.* Moroni) 19 10S 40E

Compiègne: France 36 H6
Compostela: Mexico 86 j13
Compreignac: France 37 G10
Compton: Calif., U.S.A. 93 D6
Compton Downs: N.S.W., Australia 71 G8
Compton Wynyates: War., England 25 S15
Comrie: Tayside, Scotland 29 O7
Cona: Italy 41 S10
CONAKRY: Guinea 80 B3
Concarneau: France 36 B8
Conceição do Araguaia: Brazil 94 H5
Concepción: (*Santa Cruz Prov.*), Bolivia 94 E7
Concepción: (*Tarija Prov.*), Bolivia 95 E8
Concepción: Chile 96 A4
Concepción: Cordoba, Arg. 96 C3
Concepción: Corrientes, Arg. 96 D2
Concepción: Misiones, Arg. 96 D2
Concepción: Mexico 86 j13
Concepción: Panama 86 I16
Concepción: Paraguay 96 D1
Concepción del Oro: Mexico 93 G8
Concepción del Uruguay: Argentina 96 D3
Conception Bay: SW. Africa 74 A1
Conchas Dam: N. Mex., U.S.A. 93 G5
Conchas Reservoir: N. Mex., U.S.A. 93 G5
Conches: France 36 F7
Conchi: Chile 95 D8
Conchos: *riv.*, Mexico 93 F7
Concord: N.C., U.S.A. 91 L8
CONCORD: N.H., U.S.A. 89 Q4
Concordia: Argentina 96 D3
Concórdia: Brazil 96 E2
Concordia: Kans., U.S.A. 93 H5
Concordia: Mexico 86 J13
Concordia: S. Africa 74 B4
Concrete: Wash., U.S.A. 92 C3
Condamine: *& riv.*, Queens., Australia 70 J6
Condat: France 37 H10
Condé-en-Brie: France 36 J6
Condé-sur-Huisne: France 36 F7
Condé-sur-Noireau: France 36 E7
Condeúba: Brazil 94 J6
Condobolin: N.S.W., Austl. 71 G9
Condom: France 37 F12
Condon: Oreg., U.S.A. 92 C3
Condore, Poulo: *is.*, S. Vietnam 64 D5
Conecuh: *riv.*, Ala., U.S.A. 91 H10
Conegliano: Italy 41 S10
Conero, Monte: *mtn.*, Italy 41 T12
Conflans: Moselle, France 36 L6
Conflans: Seine et Oise, Fr. 36 H6
Conflict Group: *is.*, New Guinea 69 J2
Confluentes: Roman road-station at Koblenz, W. Ger. 44 N5
Confolens: France 37 F9
Confuso: *riv.*, Paraguay 96 D1
Cong: Mayo, Repub. of Irel. 30 C12
Congleton: Ches., England 27 R13

Congo: *Republic* 81 H5
Cap.: Brazzaville
Area: 132,046 sq. miles (341,999 sq. km.)
Pop.: 958,000 (*1971 E*)

Congo (Kinshasa) *see* **Zaïre**
Congo (Zaïre): *riv.*, Africa 73 H10
Coningsby: Lincs., England 27 V13
Conisbrough: S. Yorks., Eng. 27 T13
Coniston: Cumb., Eng. 26 P11
Conistone: N. Yorks., Eng. 27 R11
Conklin: Alta., Canada 92 E1
Conlie: France 36 E7
Conn, Lough: Mayo, Repub. of Ireland 30 C11
Conna: Cork, Repub. of Ireland 31 E15
Connacht: *Prov.*, Repub. of Ireland 30 D12
Connah's Quay: Clwyd, Wales 27 P13
Conneaut: Ohio, U.S.A. 88 L5
Connecticut: *riv.*, U.S.A. 89 P4
Connecticut: *State*, U.S.A. (*cap.* Hartford) 89 P5
Connel: Strath., Scotland 29 L7
Connell: Wash., U.S.A. 92 D3
Connellsville: Pa., U.S.A. 89 M5
Connemara: Queens., Austl. 69 G4
Connemara: *dist.*, Galway, Repub. of Ireland 30 B13
Connerré: France 36 F7
Connersville: Ind., U.S.A. 88 J6
Conon: *riv.*, Highland, Scotland 28 M4
Conon, Strath: *val.*, Highland, Scotland 28 M4
Cononbridge: Highland, Scotland 28 N4
Conques: Aude, France 37 H12
Conques: Aveyron, France 37 H11
Conquet, Le: France 36 A7
Conrad: Mont., U.S.A. 92 E3
Conroe: Tex., U.S.A. 90 D10
Consandolo: Italy 41 R11
Conseju: Belize 86 *Ins.*
Conselheiro Lafaiete: Brazil 95 J8
Conselice: Italy 41 R11
Consett: Durham, England 26 S10
Constance, Lake (Boden See): W. Ger./Switz. 40 P8
Constância das Baetas: Braz. 94 E5
Constanța: Romania 39 V14
Constantiaberg: *mtn.*, S. Afr. 74 *Ins.*
Constantia Nek: *pass*, S. Afr. 74 *Ins.*
Constantina: Spain 35 D18
CONSTANTINE: *& Dept.*, Alg. 32 D4
Constantine: Corn., Eng. 24 L19
Constantinople: western name for Turkish Istanbul 39 V16
Constitución: Argentina 96 C3
Constitución: Chile 96 A4
Consuegra: Spain 35 E17
Contai: W. Bengal, India 59 P10
Contamana: Peru 94 C5
Contendas: Brazil 94 J6
Contin: High., Scot. 28 M4
Contres: France 36 G8
Contrexéville: France 40 L7
Contwoyto Lake: N.W.T., Canada 84 J4
Conty: France 36 H6
Convoy: Don., Repub. of Ireland 30 F10
Conway: Ark., U.S.A. 90 E8
Conway: Gwynedd, Wales 27 O13
Conway: N.H., U.S.A. 89 Q4
Conway: Queens., Australia 70 H3
Conway: S. Africa 75 F5
Conway: S.C., U.S.A. 91 M9
Conway: *bay & riv.*, Gwynedd, Wales 27 O13
Conway, C.: Queens., Austl. 69 H4
Conway Range National Park: Queens., Australia 70 H3
Conway Reef: Pacific O. 67 P6
Conz: *see* Konz.
Cooch Behar: *see* Koch Bihar
Cook: S. Australia 68 E6
Cook, Cape: B.C., Canada 92 B2
Cook, Mount: South I., N.Z. 70 N16
Cookbury: Devon, England 24 N18
Cookeville: Tenn., U.S.A. 88 J7
Cookham: Berks., England 25 U16
Cookhouse: S. Africa 75 F6
Cookhouse Tunnel: C.P., S. Africa 75 F6
Cook Inlet: Alaska, U.S.A. 84 d5
Cook Is.: Pacific O. (*cap.* Avarua) 70 *Ins.*
Cook's Harbour: Newf., Canada 85 v1
Cookshire: Que., Canada 89 Q3
Cookstown: Tyr., N. Ireland 30 H10
Cook Str.: New Zealand 70 P15
Cooktown: Queens., Austl. 69 H3
Coolabah: N.S.W., Austl. 71 G8
Cooladdi: Queens., Austl. 70 F6
Coolah: N.S.W., Australia 71 H8
Coolamon: N.S.W., Austl. 71 G10
Coolaney: Sligo, Repub. of Ireland 30 D11
Coolangatta: Queens., Austl. 70 K7
Coolboy: Wick., Repub. of Ireland 31 J14
Coolderry: Offaly, Repub. of Ireland 31 F13
Coole: Meath, Repub. of Ireland 30 H13
Coole: Westmeath, Repub. of Ireland 30 G12
Cooleemee: N.C., U.S.A. 91 L8
Coolgardie: W. Australia 68 C6
Coolidge: Ariz., U.S.A. 93 E6
Coolidge Dam: Ariz., U.S.A. 93 E6
Coolrain: Laois, Repub. of Ireland 31 F14
Coolum: Queens., Austl. 70 K6
Cooma: N.S.W., Australia 71 H11
Coomacarrea: *mtn.*, Kerry, Repub. of Ireland 31 A16
Coombe Bissett: Wilts., Eng. 25 S17
Coomera: Queens., Austl. 70 K6
Coonabarabran: N.S.W., Australia 71 H8
Coonalpyn: S. Australia 71 C10
Coonamble: N.S.W., Austl. 71 H8
Coondambo: S. Australia 69 F6
Coondapoor: Karnataka, India 58 M12
Coongoola: Queens., Australia 70 F6
Cooper: Tex., U.S.A. 90 D9
Cooper's Creek (Barcoo): *riv.*, S. Australia 69 F5
Cooper's I.: Bermudas 87 *Ins.*
Cooperstown: N. Dak., U.S.A. 92 H3
Cooperstown: N.Y., U.S.A. 89 O4
Coorabulka: Queens., Austl. 69 G4
Cooraclare: Clare, Repub. of Ireland 31 C14
Coorada: Queens., Austl. 70 H5
Coorg: *State* (now absorbed in Karnataka, *State*), India 58 N12
Coorong, The: *inlet*, S. Austl. 71 C11
Coorow: W. Australia 68 B5
Cooroy: Queens., Australia 70 K6
Coosa: *riv.*, Ala./Ga., U.S.A. 91 J8
Coos Bay: *city*, Oreg., U.S.A. 92 C4
Cootamundra: N.S.W., Australia 71 H10
Cootehill: Cavan, Repub. of Ireland 30 G11
Cooyar: Queens., Australia 70 J6
Copacabana: Argentina 96 B2
Copacabana: Peru 94 D7
Copais: lake NW. of Thivai (*Thebes*), Greece 39 S17
Copeland I.: N. Ireland 30 K10
Copelina, La: Argentina 96 B4
COPENHAGEN (København): Zealand, Denmark 47 N9
Copetonas: Argentina 96 C4
Copiapó: Chile 96 A2
Copinsay: *i.*, Orkney Is., Scotland 28 Q2
Copley: S. Australia 71 C8
Copparo: Italy 41 R11
Copperbelt: *Prov.*, Zambia (*cap.* Ndola) 77 C5
Copper Center: Alaska, U.S.A. 84 E5
Copper Cliff: Ont., Canada 88 L2
Copperfield: Queens., Austl. 70 G4
Coppermine: *& riv.*, N.W.T., Canada 84 H4
Coppermine Point: *cape*, Ont., Canada 88 J2
Copper Queen: Rhodesia 77 C6
Copplestone: Devon, Eng. 24 O18
Copthorne: Surrey, Eng. 25 V17
Coptos: ancient Egyptian city and Roman camp on right bank of Nile about 10 miles S. of Qena, Egypt 54 D9
Coquet: *riv.*, Northumb., England 26 S9
Coquet Dale: *val.*, Northumb., England 26 S9
Coquilhatville: *see* Mbandaka.
Coquille, La: France 37 F10
Coquimbana: Chile 96 A2
Coquimbo: Chile 96 A2
Coquy, Sierra Nevada de: *mtn.*, Colombia 94 C2
Cora: ancient Latin city about 28 miles SE. of Rome. 38 N16
Corabia: Romania 39 T15
Coracora: Peru 94 C7
Cora Divh: *i.*, Laccadive Is. 58 M12
Coraki: N.S.W., Australia 71 K7
Coral Gables: Fla., U.S.A. 91 L13
Coral Harbour: Canada 85 I5
Coral Rapids: *town*, Ont., Canada 85 I7
Coral Sea: Australia 69 J2
Corangamite, Lake: Vict., Australia 71 E12
Corato: Italy 38 P16
Corbeil: France 36 H7
Corbelin: France 40 L10
Corbett Inlet: Canada 85 k5
Corbières: *mtns.*, France 37 H13
Corbigny: France 36 J8
Corbin: Ky., U.S.A. 88 J7
Corbridge: Northumb., Eng. 26 R10
Corby: Lincs., England 27 U14
Corby: Northants., England 25 U15
CORCAIGH (Cork): Cork, Repub. of Ireland 31 E16
Corcovado, G. of: Chile 95 C12
Corcubión: Spain 35 B15
Corcyra: Latinized form of Greek name of island Corfu (Kérkira), Ionian Is. 39 Q17
Corcyra nigra: Roman name for island and Greek city of Korčula (off Yugoslav coast) 38 P15
Cordal: Kerry, Repub. of Ireland 31 C15
Cordele: Ga., U.S.A. 91 K10
Cordell: Okla., U.S.A. 90 B8
Cordero, C.: *town*, Arg. 96 B4
Cordes: France 37 G11
Cordillera Central: *range*, Colombia 94 B3
Cordillera Occidental: *range*, Colombia 94 B3
Cordillera Oriental: *range*, Colombia 94 C3
Cordillo Downs: S. Austl. 69 G5
CÓRDOBA: *& Prov.*, Arg. 96 C3
Córdoba: Durango, Mexico 93 G7
Córdoba: Vera Cruz, Mex. 86 K14
CÓRDOBA: *& Prov.*, Spain 35 D18
Córdoba, Sierras de: *mtns.*, Argentina 96 C3
Cordova: Alaska, U.S.A. 84 E5
Córdova: Peru 94 C6
Corfe: Som., England 24 P18
Corfe Castle: *town*, Dorset, England 24 R18
Corfield: Queens., Austl. 69 G4
Corfinium: Roman town 7 miles N. of Sulmona, It. 38 N15
Corfu: Corfu, Ionian Is. 39 Q17

For Abbreviations see list on p.113. Italic type, e.g. *Ephesus*, refers to historical names not on maps. Capital letters, e.g. MADRID, show capitals of countries; small capital letters, e.g. CADIZ, show capitals of provinces, etc. General notes p.116.

Corfu—Cumberland 135

Corfu (Kérkira): *i.*, Ionian Is. (Greece) **39** Q17
Corgarff: Gram., Scotland **28** P5
Coria: Spain **35** C16
Coricudgy: *mtn.*, N.S.W., Australia **71** J9
Corigliano Calabro: Italy **38** P17
Corinda: Queens., Austl. **69** F3
Coringa Islets: Australia **69** J3
Corinium Dobunorum: Roman town at Cirencester, Glos., England **24** S16
Corinth (Kórinthos): Greece **39** S18
Corinth: Miss., U.S.A. **90** G8
Corinth: N.Y., U.S.A. **89** P4
Corinth, G. of: Greece **39** S17
Corinto: Brazil **94** J7
Corisco: *i.*, Eq. Guinea **81** F4
CORK (Corcaigh): *& Co.*, Repub. of Ireland **31** E16
Cork: *Co.*, Repub. of Irel. [*cap.* Cork (Corcaigh)] **31** D16
Cork Harbour: *est.*, Cork, Repub. of Ireland **31** E16
Corlay: France **36** B7
Corley: War., England **25** S15
Corlough: Cavan, Repub. of Ireland **30** F11
Çorlu: Turkey **39** U16
Cormakiti, Cape: Cyprus **56** C4
Cormeilles: France **36** F6
Cormicy: France **36** J6
Cormons: Italy **41** T10
Cormorant: Man., Canada **92** G2
Cornelia: Ga., U.S.A. **91** K8
Cornelia: O.F.S., S. Africa **75** H3
Cornell: Wis., U.S.A. **88** F3
Corner Brook: Newf., Can. **85** t2
Corney: Cumbria, England **26** P11
Cornforth: Durham, Eng. **26** S10
Cornhill: Gram., Scotland **28** Q4
Cornhill on Tweed: Northumb., England **26** R8
Corniglio: Italy **40** Q11
Corning: Ark., U.S.A. **88** F7
Corning: N.Y., U.S.A. **89** N4
Cornish Flat: N.H., U.S.A. **89** P4
Cornishtown: Bahamas **91** N12
Cornwall: Ont., Canada **89** O3
Cornwall: *Co.*, England (*co. town* Truro) **24** M19
Cornwall: *Prov.*, Jamaica **86** *Ins.*
Cornwallis I.: N.W.T., Can. **84** K3
Coro: Venezuela **94** D1
Coroatá: Brazil **94** J4
Corocoro: Bolivia **94** D7
Corofin: Clare, Repub. of Ireland **31** C14
Corofin: Galway, Repub. of Ireland **31** D13
Coroico: Bolivia **94** D7
Coromandel: North I., N.Z. **70** P13
Coromandel Coast: India **58** O12
Coron: Philippines **64** G4
Corona: N. Mex., U.S.A. **93** F6
Coronado: Calif., U.S.A. **93** D6
Coronado Bay: Costa Rica **86** I16
Coronados: *i.*, Mexico **93** D6
Coronation: Alta., Canada **92** E2
Coronation Gulf: N.W.T., Canada **84** h4
Coronel: Chile **96** A4
Coronel Bogado: Paraguay **96** D2
Coronel Brandsen: Arg. **96** D4
Coronel Dorrego: Argentina **96** C4
Coronel Oviedo: Paraguay **96** D2
Coronel Pringles: Argentina **96** C4
Coronel Suárez: Argentina **96** C4
Coronel Vidal: Argentina **96** D4
Coronie: Surinam **84** F2
Çorovodë: Albania **39** R16
Corowa: N.S.W., Australia **71** G11
Corozal: Belize **86** *Ins.*
Corozal: Panama **94** *Ins.*
Corps: France **40** L11
Corpus Christi: Tex., U.S.A. **90** C12
Corpus Christi Bay: Tex., U.S.A. **90** C12
Corpus Christi, Lake: Tex., U.S.A. **90** C11
Corque: Bolivia **94** D7
Corral: Chile **95** C11
Corral: Mexico **93** F7
Corrales: Uruguay **96** D3
Corrane: Mozambique **77** E6
Corranny: Ferm., N. Ireland **30** G11
Corraun Penin.: Mayo, Repub. of Ireland **30** B12
Corregidor: *i.*, Luzon, Phil. **64** G4
Correntina: Brazil **94** J6
Corrèze: *Dept.*, France (*cap.* Tulle) **37** G10
Corrib, Lough: Galway, Repub. of Ireland **31** C13
Corrie: I. of Arran, Scot. **29** L8
Corrie Common: Dumfries & Galloway, Scotland **29** P9
CORRIENTES: *& Prov.*, Arg. **96** D2
Corrientes: *riv.*, Argentina **96** D3
Corrientes, Cape: Colombia **94** B2
Corrientes, Cape: Mexico **86** J13
Corrigan: Tex., U.S.A. **90** D10
Corrigin: W. Australia **68** B6
Corringham: Lincs., Eng. **27** U13
Corry: Pa., U.S.A. **89** M5
Corryong: Vict., Australia **71** G11
Corry Mtn.: Leit., Repub. of Ireland **30** E11
Corryvreckan, G. of: Jura/Scarba, Scotland **29** K7
Corse, Cap: *cape*, Corsica **38** L15
Corse Hill: Strath., Scot. **29** N8
Corserine: *mtn.*, Dumfries & Galloway, Scotland **29** N9
Corsewall Point: *cape*, Dumfries & Galloway, Scotland **29** L9
Corsham: Wilts., England **24** R17
Corsica: *i. & Dept.*, France (*cap.* Ajaccio) **38** L16
Corsicana: Tex., U.S.A. **90** C9
Corsock: Dumfries & Galloway, Scotland **29** O9
Corston: Wilts., England **24** R16
Cortachy: Tay., Scotland **29** Q6
Cort Adelaer, Cape: Grnld. **85** p5
Corte: Corsica **38** L15
Cortellazzo: Italy **41** S10
Cortemilia: Italy **40** O11
Corteolona: Italy **40** P10
Cortez: Colo., U.S.A. **93** F5
Cortina d'Ampezzo: Italy **41** S9
Cortland: N.Y., U.S.A. **89** N4
Cortona: Italy **38** M15
Coruche: Portugal **35** B17
Çoruh: *riv. & mtns.*, Turkey **57** G1
ÇORUM: *& Prov.*, Turkey **56** D1
Corumbá: Brazil **94** H7
Corunna: S. Australia **71** B9
Corunna: Spain *see* La Coruña.
Corvallis: Oreg., U.S.A. **92** C4
Corvo: *i.*, Azores **78** *Ins.*
Corwen: Clwyd, Wales **27** P14
Corwin: Alaska, U.S.A. **84** C4
Corydon: Iowa, U.S.A. **88** E5
Corydon: Ind., U.S.A. **88** H6
Cos (Kos): *& i.*, Dodec. (Gr.) **39** U18
Coseley: W. Mid., England **27** R14
Cosenza: Italy **38** P17
Cosham: Hants., England **25** T18
Cosheston: Dyfed, Wales **24** M16
Coshocton: Ohio, U.S.A. **88** L5
Cosne: France **36** H8
Cosne d'Allier: France **37** H9
Cosquín: Argentina **96** C3
Cossé-le-Vivien: France **36** E8
Cossonay: Switzerland **40** M9
Costa Blanca: *coast*, Spain **35** H16
Costa Brava: *coast*, Spain **35** F17
Costa de la Luz: *coast*, Spain **35** E18
Costa del Sol: *coast*, Spain **35** D18

Costa Rica: *Republic* **86/7** I16
Cap.: San José
Area: 19,653 sq. miles (50,901 sq. km.)
Pop.: 1,786,000 (*1971 E*)

Costelloe: Galway, Repub. of Ireland **31** B13
Costermansville: *see* Bukavu.
Costeşti: Romania **39** T14
Costigliole: Italy **40** N11
Coswig: E. Germany **45** S4
Cotabato: Mindanao, Phil. **64** G5
Cotacachi: *mtn.*, Ecuador **94** B3
Cotagaita: Bolivia **94** D8
Coteau, Le: France **37** K9
Côteaux du Perche: *hills*, Fr. **36** F7
Côte d'Azur: *coast*, France **34** K15
Côte-d'Or: *Dept. & geog. reg.*, France (*cap.* Dijon) **36** K8
Cotehill: Cumbria, England **26** Q10
Cotentin: *geog. reg.*, France **36** D6
Côte-St.-André, La: France **40** L10
Côtes de Moselle: *hills*, Fr. **44** M6
Côtes-du-Nord: *Dept.*, Fr. (*cap.* St. Brieuc) **36** B7
Cotgrave: Notts., England **27** T14
Cotherstone: Durham, Eng. **26** S10
COTONOU: Sud, Benin **81** E3
Cotopaxi: *mtn.*, Ecuador **94** B4
Cotswold Hills: Glos., Eng. **24** R16
Cottage Grove: *city*, Oreg., U.S.A. **92** C4
COTTBUS: *& Dist.*, E. Germany **45** U4
Cottenham: Cambs., Eng. **25** W15
Cotter: Ark., U.S.A. **88** E7
Cottered: Herts., England **25** V16
Cottesmore: Leics., Eng. **27** U14
Cottian Alps: France/Italy **40** N11
Cottica: Surinam **94** G3
Cottingham: Humb., Eng. **27** V12
Cotton Plant: Ark., U.S.A. **90** F8
Cotton Valley: *city*, La., U.S.A. **90** E9
Cotulla: Tex., U.S.A. **90** B11
Couarde, La: Île de Ré, Fr. **37** D9
Coubre, Pointe de la: *cape*, France **37** D10
Coucy-le-Château: France **36** J6
Couhé: France **37** F9
Couiza: France **37** H13
Coulmiers: France **36** G8
Coulommiers: France **36** J7
Coulon: *riv.*, France **37** L12
Coulonge: *riv.*, Que., Can. **89** N2
Coulonges: France **37** E9
Council: Alaska, U.S.A. **84** c5
Council: Idaho, U.S.A. **92** D4
Council Bluffs: Iowa, U.S.A. **92** H4
Council Grove: Kans., U.S.A. **90** C6
Coundon: Durham, Eng. **26** S10
Countesthorpe: Leics., Eng. **27** T14
Coupar Angus: Tay., Scot. **29** P6
Courantyne: *riv.*, Guyana **87** e8
Courcelles: France **44** M6
Courçon: France **37** E9
Courmayeur: Italy **40** M10
Couronne, La: France **37** F10
Courpière: France **37** J10
Coursan: France **37** J12
Courseulles: France **36** E6
Courson: France **36** J8
Courtaçon: France **36** J7
Courtalain: France **36** G7
Courtelary: Switzerland **40** N8
Courtenay: B.C., Canada **92** B3
Courthézon: France **37** K11
Courtmacsherry: *& bay*, Cork, Repub. of Ireland **31** D16
Courtown Harbour: *village*, Wex., Repub. of Ireland **31** J14
Courtrai: *see* Kortrijk.
Courville: France **36** G7
Coushatta: La., U.S.A. **90** E9
Coussey: France **40** L7
Coutances: France **36** D6
Couterne: France **36** E7
Coutras: France **37** E10
Couvin: Belgium **44** K5
Covadonga: Spain **35** D15
Covane: Mozambique **77** D7
Cove: Grampian, Scotland **28** R5
Cove: Hants., England **25** U17
Covelo: Calif., U.S.A. **92** C5
Coventry: W. Mid., England **25** S15
Covilhã: Portugal **35** C16
Covington: Ga., U.S.A. **91** K9
Covington: Ind., U.S.A. **88** H5
Covington: Ky., U.S.A. **88** J6
Covington: La., U.S.A. **90** F10
Covington: Strath., Scot. **29** O8
Covington: Tenn., U.S.A. **90** G8
Cowal: *dist.*, Strath., Scot. **29** L7
Cowal, Lake: N.S.W., Austl. **71** G9
Cowan, Lake: W. Australia **68** C6
Cowansville: Que., Canada **89** P3
Cowarie: S. Australia **69** F5
Cowary: N.S.W., Australia **71** E9
Cowbit: Lincs., England **27** V14
Cowbridge: S. Glam., Wales **24** P17
Cowdenbeath: Fife, Scot. **29** P7
Cowdray: W. Sussex, England **25** U18
Cowell: S. Australia **71** B9
Cowes: I. of Wight, England **25** T18
Cowes: Vict., Australia **71** F12
Coweta: Okla., U.S.A. **90** D8
Cowfold: W. Sussex, England **25** V18
Cowley: Alta., Canada **92** E3
Cowley: Oxon., England **25** T16
Cowley: Queens., Australia **70** F6
Cowley: Wyo., U.S.A. **92** F4
Cowling: N. Yorks., England **27** R12
Cowra: N.S.W., Australia **71** H9
Cowshill: Durham, England **26** R10
Coxhoe: Durham, England **26** S10
Coxilha Grande: *mtns.*, Braz. **96** E2
Coxim: Brazil **94** G7
Cox's Bazar: Bangladesh **59** Q10
Coxwold: N. Yorks., England **26** T11
Coyame: Mexico **93** F7
Coylton: Strath., Scotland **29** N9
Coyuca: Mexico **86** j14
Cozes: France **37** E10
Cozumel I.: Mexico **86** L13
Crab I. (Vieques): (U.S.A.), Lesser Antilles **87** a1
Cracow (Kraków): *& Prov.*, Poland **43** Q11
Cracow: Queens., Australia **70** J5
Cradley: Hereford & Worcester, England **24** R15
Cradock: *& Dist.*, S. Africa **75** F6
Craig: Colo., U.S.A. **93** F4
Craig Harbour: N.W.T., Canada **85** I2
Craigellachie: Gram., Scot. **28** P5
Craighall: Trans., S. Africa **74** *NIns.*
Craighouse: Inner Hebr., Scotland **29** K8
Craigielands: Dumfries & Galloway, Scot. **29** P9
Craignure: Inner Hebr., Scot. **29** K7
Crail: Fife, Scotland **29** Q7
Crailing: Bord., Scotland **29** R8
Crailsheim: W. Germany **45** Q6
Craiova: Romania **39** S14
Cramlington: Northumb., England **26** S9
Cramond: Lothian, Scot. **29** P8
Crampel: Cen. Afr. Rep. **76** A1
Cranberry Lake: N.Y., U.S.A. **89** O3
Cranberry Portage: Man., Can. **92** G2
Cranborne: Dorset, England **24** S18
Cranborne Chase: *dist.*, Dorset/Wilts., England **24** R18
Cranbrook: B.C., Canada **92** D3
Cranbrook: Kent, England **25** X17
Cranbrook: W. Australia **68** B6
Crandon: Wis., U.S.A. **88** G3
Crane: Tex., U.S.A. **93** G6
Cranfield: Beds., England **25** U15
Cranham: Glos., England **24** R16
Cranleigh: Surrey, England **25** V17
Crannon: Greek city in hills about 20 miles SW. of Larisa, Greece **39** S17
Cranshaws: Borders, Scot. **29** R8
Cranswick: Humb., England **27** V12
Cranwell: Lincs., England **27** V13
Craon: France **36** E8
Craponne: France **37** J10
Crask Inn: High., Scotland **28** M3
Craster: Northumb., Eng. **26** S9
Crater Lake: Oreg., U.S.A. **92** C4
Crater Lake Nat. Park: Oreg., U.S.A. **92** C4
Crateús: Brazil **94** J5
Crathie: Gram., Scotland **28** P5
Crathis: river flowing into SW. corner of G. of Taranto, Italy **38** P17
Crathorne: N. Yorks., Eng. **26** T11
Crati: *riv.*, Italy **38** P17
Cratloe: Clare, Repub. of Ireland **31** D14
Crato: Brazil **94** K5
Craughwell: Galway, Repub. of Ireland **31** D13
Craven: Queens., Australia **70** G4
Craven: *dist.*, N. Yorks., Eng. **27** R12
Craven Arms: Salop, Eng. **24** Q15
Cravo: Colombia **94** C2
Crawford: Nebr., U.S.A. **92** G4
Crawford: Strath., Scotland **29** O9
Crawfordsburn: Down, N. Ireland **30** K10
Crawfordsville: Ind., U.S.A. **88** H5
Crawick: Dumfries & Galloway, Scotland **29** O9
Crawley: Hants., England **25** T17
Crawley: W. Sussex, England **25** V17
Crawley, North: Bucks., England **25** U15
Crawshay Booth: Lancs., England **27** R12
Crazy Mtns.: Mont., U.S.A. **92** E3
Creagan: Strath., Scotland **29** L6
Creag Meagaidh: *mtn.*, Highland, Scotland **28** M6
Creagorry: Outer Hebr., Scotland **28** G5
Creake, South: Norf., Eng. **25** X14
Crécy: France **36** J6
Crécy-en-Brie: France **36** H7
Crécy-en-Ponthieu: France **36** G5
Credenhill: Hereford & Worcester, England **24** Q15
Crediton: Devon, England **24** O18
Cree: *riv.*, Dumfries & Galloway, Scot. **29** M9
Cree Lake: Sask., Canada **92** F1
Creeslough: Don., Repub. of Ireland **30** F9
Creetown: Dumfries & Galloway, Scotland **29** N10
Creggan: Tyr., N. Ireland **30** G10
Creggs: Galway, Repub. of Ireland **30** E12
Creighton: Natal, S. Africa **75** H5
Creighton: Nebr., U.S.A. **92** H4
Creil: France **36** H6
Crema: Italy **40** P10
Crémieu: France **40** L10
Cremona: Italy **40** Q10
Créon: France **37** E11
Crépy-en-Valois: France **36** H6
Creran, Loch: Strath., Scot. **29** L6
Cres: *& i.*, Yugoslavia **41** U11
Crescent: Okla., U.S.A. **90** C8
Crescent City: Calif., U.S.A. **92** C4
Crescent Group: *is.*, Paracel Is. **64** E3
Crescent Lake: Fla., U.S.A. **91** L11
Crescent Lake Migratory Bird Refuge: Nebr., U.S.A. **92** G4
Cresco: Iowa, U.S.A. **88** E4
Crespino: Italy **41** R11
Crespo: Argentina **96** C3
Cressage: Salop, England **27** Q14
Cresswell: Northumb., Eng. **26** S9
Cressy: Vict., Australia **71** E12
Crest: France **37** L11
Creston: B.C., Canada **92** D3
Creston: Iowa, U.S.A. **92** J4
Crestview: Fla., U.S.A. **91** H10
Creswell: Derby., England **27** T13
Creswick: Vict., Australia **71** E11
Crete (Kriti): *i.* (Grc.), Medit. Sea **39** T19
Crete, Sea of: S. Europe **39** T19
CRÉTEIL: Val-de-Marne, France **36** H7
Creus, Cape: Spain **35** H15
Creuse: *riv.*, France **37** G9
Creuse: *Dept.*, France (*cap.* Guéret) **37** H9
Creusot, Le: France **37** K9
Creussen: W. Germany **45** R6
Creuzburg: E. Germany **45** Q4
Crèvecœur: France **36** F6
Crevillente: Spain **35** F17
Crewe: Ches., England **27** R13
Crewe: Va., U.S.A. **89** M7
Crewkerne: Som., England **24** Q18
Crianlarich: Central, Scot. **29** M7
Cribyn: Dyfed, Wales **24** N15
Criccieth: Gwynedd, Wales **27** N14
Crich: Derby., England **27** T13
Criciúma: Brazil **96** F2
Crick: Northants., England **25** T15
Crickadarn: Powys, Wales **24** P15
Crickhowell: Powys, Wales **24** P16
Cricklade: Wilts., England **25** S16
Crieff: Tayside, Scotland **29** O7
Criel: France **36** G5
Criffell: *mtn.*, Dumfries & Galloway, Scot. **29** O10
Crikvenica: Yugoslavia **41** U10
Crimea: *Reg. & penin.*, Ukraine (*cap.* Simferopol') **50** D5
Crimmitschau: E. Germany **45** S5
Crimond: Gram., Scotland **28** S4
Crimplesham: Norf., Eng. **25** W14
Crinan: Strath., Scotland **29** K7
Crindle: Lon., N. Ireland **30** H9
Crinkill: Offaly, Repub. of Ireland **31** F13
Crisa: variant ancient Greek name of *Cirrha* (q.v.) **39** S17
Crişana-Maram: *Prov.*, Rom. **43** S13
Crisfield: Md., U.S.A. **89** O7
Cristalina: Brazil **94** H7
Cristóbal: Panama **94** *Ins.*
Cristóbal Colón, Pico: *mtn.*, Colombia **94** C1
Crivitz: E. Germany **45** R2
Crna Gora: *see* Montenegro.
Crnomelj: Yugoslavia **41** V10
Croagh: Don., Repub. of Ireland **30** E10
Croagh: Lim., Repub. of Ireland **31** D14
Croaghgorm Mtns. (Blue Stack Mtns.): Don., Repub. of Ireland **30** E10
Croagh Patrick: *mtn.*, Mayo, Repub. of Ireland **30** B12
Croatia: *Repub.*, Yugoslavia (*cap.* Zagreb) **38** P14
Crocketford: Dumfries & Galloway, Scot. **29** O9
Crockett: Tex., U.S.A. **90** D10
Crockham Hill: *village*, Kent, England **25** W17
Crocodile: *riv.*, Trans., S. Africa **75** J2
Crocodile (Limpopo): *riv.*, Trans., S. Africa **75** G1
Crodo: Italy **40** O9
Croft: N. Yorks., England **26** S11
Croick: High., Scot. **28** M4
Croisette, Cap: *cape*, France **37** L12
Croisic, Le: France **36** C8
Croisilles: France **36** H5
Croixille, La: France **36** D7
Croker I.: Australia **68** E2
Cromarty: *& firth*, Highland, Scotland **28** N4
Cromdale: High., Scotland **28** O5
Cromdale, Hills of: Grampian/Highland, Scotland **28** P5
Cromer: Norf., England **25** Y14
Cromford: Derby., England **27** S13
Cromwell: South I., N.Z. **70** M17
Cronin Mount: B.C., Can. **92** B2
Cronnel: O.F.S., S. Africa **75** *Ins.*
Cronulla: N.S.W., Australia **71** J10
Crook: Durham, England **26** S10
Crooked I.: Bahamas **87** m13
Crookston: Minn., U.S.A. **92** H3
Crookstown: Cork, Repub. of Ireland **31** D16
Crookwell: N.S.W., Austl. **71** H10
Croom: Lim., Repub. of Ireland **31** D14
Croppa Creek: *town*, N.S.W., Australia **71** J7
Cropredy: Oxon., England **25** T15
Cropton: N. Yorks., Eng. **26** U11
Crosby: I. of Man, United Kingdom **26** M11
Crosby: Mers., England **27** P13
Crosby: Minn., U.S.A. **88** E2
Crosby: N. Dak., U.S.A. **92** G3
Crosby Ravensworth: Cumbria, England **26** Q10
Cross: Clare, Repub. of Irel. **31** B14
Cross: Mayo, Repub. of Irel. **30** C12
Cross: *riv.*, Nigeria **81** F3
Crossakeel: Meath, Repub. of Ireland **30** G12
Cross Barry: Cork, Repub. of Ireland **31** D16
Crossbost: Outer Hebr., Scotland **28** J3
Cross City: Fla., U.S.A. **91** K11
Crossdoney: Cavan, Repub. of Ireland **30** G12
Crossett: Ark., U.S.A. **90** F9
Crossfell: *mtn.*, Cumbria, England **26** R10
Crossfield: Alta., Canada **92** E2
Crossford: Strath., Scot. **29** O8
Crossgar: Down, N. Ireland **30** K11
Cross Hands: Dyfed, Wales **24** N16
Crosshaven: Cork, Repub. of Ireland **31** E16
Crosshill: Strath., Scotland **29** M9
Cross Keys: Gwent, Wales **24** P16
Crosskeys: Kild., Repub. of Ireland **31** G13
Cross Lake: Man., Canada **92** H2
Crossmaglen: Armagh, N. Ireland **30** H11
Crossmichael: Dumfries & Galloway, Scotland **29** O10
Crossmolina: Mayo, Repub. of Ireland **39** C11
Cross Plains: *city*, Tex., U.S.A. **90** B9
Cross River: *State*, Nigeria (*cap.* Calabar) **81** F3
Crossville: Tenn., U.S.A. **91** J8
Croston: Lancs., England **27** Q12
Crotone: Italy **38** P17
Crotoy, Le: France **36** G5
Crouch: *riv.*, Essex, England **25** X16
Crowborough: E. Sussex, England **25** W17
Crowcombe: Som., England **24** P17
Crowell: Tex., U.S.A. **90** B7
Crowes: Vict., Australia **71** E12
Crowland: Lincs., England **27** V14
Crowle: Humb., England **27** U12
Crowley: La., U.S.A. **90** E10
Crown Point: Ind., U.S.A. **88** H5
Crown Prince Christian Land: Greenland **85** r1
Crow's Nest: Queens., Austl. **70** K6
Crowsnest Pass: B.C./Alta., Canada **92** E3
Crowthorne: Berks., Eng. **25** U17
Croxton: Norf., England **25** X15
Croxton Kerrial: Leics., Eng. **27** U14
Croydon: Gt. Ldn., England **25** V17
Croydon: Queens., Australia **69** G3
Croydon: South I., N.Z. **71** M18
Crozet Basin: Indian Ocean **9** 40S 60E
Crozet Is.: (Fr.), Indian Ocean **9** 50S 50E
Crozon: France **36** A7
Crudgington: Salop, Eng. **27** Q14
Crudwell: Wilts., England **24** R16
Crumlin: Antrim, N. Ireland **30** J10
Crusheen: Clare, Repub. of Ireland **31** D14
Cruz, La: Argentina **96** D2
Cruz Alta: Argentina **96** C3
Cruz Alta: Brazil **96** E2
Cruz del Eje: Argentina **96** C3
Cruzeiro: Brazil **96** G1
Cruzeiro do Sul: Brazil **94** C5
Cruz Grande: Chile **96** A2
Crymmych Arms: Dyfed, Wales **24** M16
Crynant: W. Glam., Wales **24** O16
Cryon: N.S.W., Australia **71** H7
Crystal Brook: *town*, S. Austl. **71** C9
Crystal City: Tex., U.S.A. **90** B11
Crystal Falls: *city*, Mich., U.S.A. **88** G2
Crystal Mtns.: Gabon **81** G4
Crystal Springs: *city*, Miss., U.S.A. **90** F10
Csongrád: Hungary **43** R13
Csorna: Hungary **43** P13
Csurgó: Hungary **43** P13
Ctesiphon: site of former capital of Sassanid (Persian) Empire, Iraq **57** J5
Cuaig: Highland, Scot. **28** K4
Cuanavale: *riv.*, Angola **77** A6
Cuando: Angola **77** B6
Cuando: *riv.*, Angola **77** B5
Cuando-Cubango: *Prov.*, Angola (*cap.* Serpa Pinto) **77** A6
Cuangar: Angola **77** A6
Cuango: *& riv.*, Angola **81** H6
Cuanza Norte: *Prov.*, Angola (*cap.* Salazar) **73** H11
Cuanza Sul: *Prov.*, Angola (*cap.* Novo Redondo) **73** H12
Cuarto: *riv.*, Argentina **96** C3
Cuatro Ciénegas de Carranza: Mexico **93** G7
Cuarto de Febrero: Arg. **96** C3

Cuba: *Republic* **87** M13
Cap.: Havana
Area: 44,218 sq. miles (114,525 sq. km.)
Pop.: 8,657,000 (*1971 E*)

Cuba: N.Y., U.S.A. **89** M4
Cuba: Portugal **35** C17
Cubango: *riv.*, Angola **77** A6
Cubbington: War., England **25** S15
Cubert: Corn., England **24** L19
Çubuk: Turkey **56** C1
Cuchi: Angola **73** H12
Cuchillo Có: Argentina **96** C4
Cuckfield: W. Sussex, Eng. **25** V17
Cucuí: Brazil **94** D3
Cucuta: Colombia **94** C2
Cudahy: Wis., U.S.A. **88** H4
Cudal: N.S.W., Australia **71** H9
Cuddalore: Tamil Nadu, India **58** N12
Cuddapah: Andhra Pradesh, India **58** N12
Cudgewa: Vict., Australia **71** G11
Cudworth: Sask., Canada **92** F2
Cudworth: S. Yorks., England **27** T12
Cue: W. Australia **68** B5
Cuéllar: Spain **35** D16
Cuenca: Ecuador **94** B4
CUENCA: *& Prov.*, Spain **35** E16
Cuero: Tex., U.S.A. **90** C11
Cuers: France **40** M12
Cueva, La: Mexico **93** F7
Cuevas: Spain **35** F18
Cuevo: Bolivia **94** E8
Cugir: Romania **39** S14
CUIABÁ: Mato Grosso, Brazil **94** F7
Cuiabá: *riv.*, Brazil **94** F7
Cuicuina: Nicaragua **86** I15
Cuil: High., Scotland **29** L6
Cuilcagh: *mtn.*, N. Ireland/Repub. of Ireland **30** F11
Cuillin Hills: *mtns.*, Inner Hebr., Scotland **28** J5
Cuilo: *riv.*, Angola **76** A4
Cuiseaux: France **40** L9
Cuisery: France **40** L9
Cuito: *riv.*, Angola **77** B6
Cuito Cuanavale: Angola **77** A6
Culan: France **37** H9
Culbertson: Mont., U.S.A. **92** G3
Culbokie: High., Scot. **28** N4
Culcabock: High., Scotland **28** N5
Culcairn: N.S.W., Australia **71** G10
Culdaff: Don., Repub. of Ireland **30** G9
Culebra: (P.R.), Lesser Antilles **87** a1
Culebra (Gaillard) Cut: Panama Canal **94** *Ins.*
Culgaith: Cumbria, Eng. **26** Q10
Culgoa: Vict., Australia **71** E10
Culgoa: *riv.*, Queens., Austl. **71** G7
Culham: Oxon., England **25** T16
CULIACÁN: Sinaloa, Mexico **93** F8
Culion: *i.*, Calamian Group, Philippines **64** F4
Cullahill: Laois, Repub. of Ireland **31** G14
Cúllar de Baza: Spain **35** E18
Culleen's: Sligo, Repub. of Ireland **30** D11
Cullen: Cork, Repub. of Irel. **31** C15
Cullen: Gram., Scotland **28** Q4
Cullen: Tip., Repub. of Irel. **31** E14
Cullera: Spain **35** F17
Cullercoats: Tyne & Wear, England **26** T9
Cullin, Lough: Mayo, Repub. of Ireland **30** C12
Cullinan: Trans., S. Africa **75** H2
Cullion: Tyr., N. Ireland **30** G10
Culloden Muir: battlefield about 6 miles E. of Inverness, Scotland **28** N5
Cullompton: Devon, England **24** P18
Cullybackey: Antrim, N. Ireland **30** J10
Cullyhanna: Armagh, N. Irel. **30** H11
Culmington: Salop, England **24** Q15
Culmor: *mtn.*, Highland, Scotland **28** L3
Culmstock: Devon, England **24** P18
Culoz: France **40** L10
Culpeper: Va., U.S.A. **89** N6
Culross: Fife, Scotland **29** O7
Cultowa: N.S.W., Australia **71** F8
Culvain: *mtn.*, Highland, Scot. **28** L6
Culverden: South I., N.Z. **70** O16
Culworth: Northants., Eng. **25** T15
Cumae: Greek and Roman city on Campania coast about 12 miles W. of Naples, Italy **38** O16
Cumae: Greek city on S. coast of Çandarli G. about 3 miles SSW. of Aliağa, Turkey **39** U17
Cumali: Turkey (Dardan. *Inset*) **20** *Ins.*
Cumaná: Venezuela **94** E1
Cumberland: Md., U.S.A. **89** M6
Cumberland: Wis., U.S.A. **88** E3
Cumberland: *i.*, Ga., U.S.A. **91** L10
Cumberland: *penin. & sound*, N.W.T., Canada **85** N4
Cumberland: *riv.*, U.S.A. **88** J7

For Abbreviations see list on p.113. Italic type, e.g. *Ephesus*, refers to historical names not on maps. Capital letters, e.g. MADRID, show capitals of countries; small capital letters, e.g. CADIZ, show capitals of provinces, etc. General notes p.116.

136 Cumberland Gap—De Leon

Cumberland Gap: pass, Ky./Tenn., U.S.A. 88 K7
Cumberland House: Sask., Canada 92 G2
Cumberland Is.: Queens., Australia 70 H3
Cumberland, Lake: Ky., U.S.A. 91 J7
Cumberland Lake: Sask., Canada 92 G2
Cumberland Mtns.: Ky./Tenn., U.S.A. 88 K7
Cumberland Plat.: U.S.A. 91 J8
Cumbernauld: Strathclyde, Scotland 29 O8
Cumborah: N.S.W., Austl. 71 G7
Cumbrae, Great: i., Strathclyde, Scotland 29 M8
Cumbrae, Little: i., Strathclyde, Scotland 29 M8
Cumbres de Monterrey Nat. Park: Mexico 93 G7
Cumbria: Co., England (co. town Carlisle) 26 Q10
Cumbrian Mtns.: Cumbria, England 26 P11
Cumbum: Andhra Pradesh, India 58 N11
Cumiana: Italy 40 N11
Cuminestown: Gram., Scot. 28 R4
Cummertrees: Dumfries & Galloway, Scotland 29 P10
Cummins: S. Australia 71 A10
Cumnock: Strath., Scotland 29 N9
Cumnock: N.S.W., Austl. 71 H9
Cumnor: Oxon., England 25 T16
Çumra: Turkey 56 C3
Cumrew: Cumbria, England 26 Q10
Cumwhitton: Cumbria, Eng. 26 Q10
Cunani: Brazil 94 G3
Cuñapirú: Uruguay 96 D3
Cunaxa: ancient battlefield N. of Babylon, Iraq 57 J5
Cunderdin: W. Australia 68 B6
Cunene: Prov., Angola 73 H13
Cuneo: Italy 40 N11
Cunjamba: Angola 77 B6
Cunnamulla: Queens., Austl. 70 F7
Cunninghame: dist., Strathclyde, Scotland 29 M8
Cuorgne: Italy 40 N10
CUPAR: Fife, Scotland 29 P7
Ćuprija: Yugoslavia 39 R15
Curaçao: i., (Neth.), Carib. Sea. 94 D1
Curacautín: Chile 96 A4
Curacó: riv., Argentina 96 B4
Curanilahue: Chile 96 A4
Cure: riv., France 36 J8
Curepto: Chile 96 A4
Cures: ancient Sabine city near right bank of Tiber about 22 miles NNE. of Rome. 38 N15
Curiapo: Venezuela 94 E2
Curicó: Chile 96 A3
CURITIBA: Paraná, Brazil 96 F2
Curitibanos: Brazil 96 E2
Curlew Is.: La., U.S.A. (Mississippi Delta. Inset) 90 Ins.
Curlewis: N.S.W., Australia 71 J8
Curmi (Qormi): Malta 32 Ins.
Curnamona: S. Australia 71 C8
Curragh, The: dist., Kild., Repub. of Ireland 31 H13
Currais Novos: Brazil 94 K5
Curralinho: Brazil 94 H4
Curramulka: S. Australia 71 B10
Currane, Lough: Kerry, Repub. of Ireland 31 A16
Currans: Kerry, Repub. of Ireland 31 B15
Currawilla: Queens., Australia 69 G5
Current: riv., U.S.A. 88 F7
Currie: King I., Tas., Austl. 68 G7
Currie: Lothian, Scotland 29 P8
Currituck: N.C., U.S.A. 89 N7
Currituck Sound: N.C., U.S.A. 89 O7
Curry: Sligo, Repub. of Ireland 30 D11
Curryglass: Cork, Repub. of Ireland 31 B16
Curry, North: Som., England 24 Q17
Curry Rivel: Som., England 24 Q17
Curtea de Argeş: Romania 39 T14
Curtis I.: Kermadec Is., Pacific O. 67 Q8
Curtis I.: Queens., Australia 70 J4
Curtis: chan. & cape, Queens., Australia 70 J4
Curuá: Brazil 94 G3
Curuá: riv., Brazil 94 G5
Curuçá: Brazil 94 H4
Curuguaty: Paraguay 96 D1
Cururupu: Brazil 94 J4
Curuzú Cuatiá: Argentina 96 D2
Curvelo: Brazil 94 J7
Cusco: Peru 94 C6
Cushendall: Antrim, N. Ireland 30 J9
Cushendun: Antrim, N. Ireland 30 J9
Cushing: Okla., U.S.A. 90 C8
Cusihuiriachic: Mexico 93 F7
Cusna, Monte: Italy 40 Q11
Cusset: France 37 J9
Custer: S. Dak., U.S.A. 92 G4
Cutara: riv., U.S.S.R. 51 R3
Cut Bank: Mont., U.S.A. 92 E3
Cuthbert: Ga., U.S.A., 91 J10
Cut Off: La., U.S.A. 90 Ins.
Cutra, Lough: Galway, Repub. of Ireland 31 D13
Cuttack: Orissa, India 59 P10
Cuxhaven: W. Germany 44 O2
Cuyahoga Falls: city, Ohio, U.S.A. 88 L5
Cuyk: Netherlands 44 L4
Cuyo: & Is., Philippines 64 G4
Cuyo, El: Mexico 86 L13
Cuyuni: riv., Guyana 87 d7
Cwm: Gwent, Wales 24 P16
Cwmbran: Gwent, Wales 24 P16
Cwmcarn: Gwent, Wales 24 P16
Cybistra: ancient Hittite, later Graeco-Roman, town at Ereğli, Turkey 56 D3
Cyclades (Kiklàdhes): is., Greece 39 T18
Cygnet: Tas., Australia 68 H8
Cynoscephalus: range of hills W. of Velestinon and S. of Lárisa, Greece 39 S17
Cynossema: Greek name of promontory on E. side of Gallipoli penin. extending into Dardanelles opposite town of Çanakkale, Turkey 39 U16
Cynthiana: Ky., U.S.A. 88 J6
Cynuria: mountainous district NE. from Spárti, Greece 39 S18
Cynwyd: Clwyd, Wales 27 P14
Cynwyl Elfed: Dyfed, Wales 24 N16
Cypress Hills: Sask., Canada 92 F3

Cyprus: Republic 56 C4
Cap.: Nicosia (Levkósia)
Area: 3,572 sq. miles (9,251 sq. km.)
Pop.: 659,000 (1972 E)

Cyrenaica: Dist., Libya 33 G5
Cyrrhus: Greek city and Roman camp about 10 miles W. of Kilis on borders of Turkey and Syria 56 E3
Cyzicus: Greek city at W. side of base of peninsula Kapi Dağ, Turkey (possibly an island in early times) 39 U16
Czaplinek: Poland 45 W2
Czarnków: Poland 3 P10

Czechoslovakia: Republic 42/3
Cap.: Prague (Praha)
Area: 49,371 sq. miles (127,871 sq. km.)
Pop.: 14,500,000 (1971 E)

Czegléd: Hungary 43 Q13
Czeremcha: Poland 43 S10
Częstochowa: Poland 43 Q11

Daaden: W. Germany 44 N5
Daan Viljoen Game Park: SW. Africa 74 B1
Dabaga: Tanzania 76 E4
Dabakala: Ivory Coast 80 D3
Dabaro: well, Somalia 79 R18
Dabat: Ethiopia 54 E12
Dabeiba: Colombia 94 B2
Dabie: Poland 45 U2
DABOLA: & Reg., Guinea 80 B2
Daboya: Ghana 80 D3
Dąbrowa: Poland 43 R11
Dabwali: Punjab, India 58 M9
DACCA: Bangladesh 59 Q10
Dachau: W. Germany 41 R7
Dachstein: mtn., Austria 41 T8
Dacia: kingdom, later Roman province, N. of middle Danube 43
Dačice: Czechoslovakia 45 V6
Dacre: Cumbria, England 26 Q10
Dacre: N. Yorks., England 27 S11
Dadanawa: Guyana 87 d9
Daday: Turkey 56 C1
Dade City: Fla., U.S.A. 91 K11
Dadeville: Ala., U.S.A. 91 J9
Dadu: Sind, Pakistan 58 L9
Dædalus Reef: Red Sea 54 E10
Daet: Luzon, Philippines 64 G4
Dafina: Saudi Arabia 54 F10
Dafi: Saudi Arabia 54 E10
Daflas: tribe, Arunachal Pradesh, India 59 Q9
Daga: Sudan 79 L8
Dagahbur: Ethiopia 79 Q18
Dagajie: Ethiopia 76 F1
Dagali: Norway 47 L6
Dagana: Senegal 80 A1
Dağardi: Turkey 56 A2
Dagebüll: W. Germany 44 O1
Dagestan A.S.S. Repub: U.S.S.R. (cap. Makhachkala) 50 G6
Daghghara: Iraq 57 J5
Daglösen: Sweden 47 O7
Dagupan: Luzon, Phil. 64 G3
Dahamsha: tribal area, Iraq 57 H6
Dahana: Afghanistan 58 L7
Dahanu: Maharashtra, India 58 M10
Dahlak Arch.: Red Sea 54 F11
Dahlem: W. Germany 44 M5
Dahlen: E. Germany 45 T4
Dahme: Cottbus, E. Germany 45 T4
Dahme: Schleswig-Holstein, W. Germany 45 R1
Dahna: desert, Saudi Arabia 55 G10
Dahne: riv., E. Germany 45 T4

Dahomey: see **Benin**

Daigo: Japan 63 g2
Dailekh: Nepal 58 O9
Dailly, New: Strath., Scot. 29 M9
Daimiel: Spain 35 E17
Dairen: see Lü-ta.
Dairut: Egypt 54 D9
Daiyur: Iran 55 H9
Dajarra: Queens., Australia 69 F4
Dakaka: sand reg., Saudi Arabia 55 H11
Dakala: Niger 81 E2
DAKAR: & Reg., Senegal 80 A2
Dakawa: Tanzania 76 E4
Dakaye: Upper Volta 80 D2
Dakhla: Western Sahara 78 A5
Dakhla Oasis: Egypt 54 C9
Dakina: Saudi Arabia 54 G10
Dakingari: Nigeria 81 E2
Dakovica: Yugoslavia 39 R15
Dakovo: Yugoslavia 39 Q14
Dakto: Vietnam 64 D4
Dakwa: Zaire 76 C2
Dal: riv., Sweden 47 P6
Dala: Angola 77 B5
DALABA: & Reg., Guinea 80 B2
Dalai Nor: lake, Inner Mongolia, China 62 V6
Dalaman: & riv., Turkey 56 A3
Dalan Dzadagad: Mongolia 62 S6
Dalat: Vietnam 64 D4
Dalay Sayn Shanda: see Sain Shanda.
Dalbandin: Baluchistan, Pak. 58 K9
Dalbeattie: Dumfries & Galloway, Scotland 29 O10
Dalbo Lake: Sweden 47 N7
Dalby: I. of Man, United Kingdom 26 M11
Dalby: Queens., Australia 70 J6
Dalby, Great: Leics., Eng. 27 U14
Dalcour: La., U.S.A. 90 Ins.
Dalcross: airfield, Highland, Scotland 28 N4
Dale: Norway 47 J6
Dale End: village, N. Yorks., England 26 U11
Dale Hollow Dam: Tenn., U.S.A. 88 J7
Dale Hollow Reservoir: Tenn., U.S.A. 88 J7
Dalen: Netherlands 44 M3
Daleside: Trans., S. Africa 74 N Ins.
Dalfors: Sweden 47 O6
Dalgety: N.S.W., Australia 71 H11
Dalhart: Tex., U.S.A. 93 G5
Dalhousie: Himachal Pradesh, India 58 N8
Dalhousie: N.B., Canada 89 S1
Dalhousie Cape: N.W.T., Canada 84 f3
Daliburgh: Outer Hebr., Scotland 28 G5
Dalkeith: Lothian, Scot. 29 P8
Dalkey: Dublin, Repub. of Ireland 31 J13
Dallarnil: Queens., Austl. 70 K5
Dallas: Ga., U.S.A. 91 J9
Dallas: Grampian, Scotland 28 P4
Dallas: Oreg., U.S.A. 92 C4
Dallas: & lake, Tex., U.S.A. 90 C9
Dalleagles: Strath., Scotland 29 N9
Dalles, The: Oreg., U.S.A. 92 C3
Dallington: E. Sussex, Eng. 25 W18
Dalma: i., Persian Gulf 55 H10
Dalmally: Strath., Scotland 29 M7
Dalmatia: geog. reg., Yugo. 38 P15
Dalmatovo: U.S.S.R. 51 K3
Dalmellington: Strathclyde, Scotland 29 N9
Dalmeny: Lothian, Scotland 29 P3
Dalnegorsk: U.S.S.R. 63 Z6
Dalnerečensk: U.S.S.R. 63 Y5
Dal'niy (Dairen): China 63 W7
DALOA: Centre-Ouest, Ivory Coast 80 C3
Dalqan: Saudi Arabia 54 G10
Dalriada: kingdom of the Scots on SW. coast of Scotland which united with the Picts in the ninth century. Combined territories formed the greater part of Scotland 22 D9
Dalry: Dumfries & Galloway, Scotland 29 N9
Dalry: Strath., Scotland 29 M8
Dalrymple: Strath., Scot. 29 M9
Dalserf: Strath., Scotland 29 O8
Dalston: Cumbria, England 26 Q10
Dalswinton: Dumfries & Galloway, Scotland 29 O9
Dalton: Ga., U.S.A. 91 J8
Dalton: Natal, S. Africa 75 J4
Dalton: N. Yorks., England 27 U12
Dalton, Cape: Greenland 85 r4
Daltonganj: Bihar, India 59 O10
Dalton in Furness: Cumbria England 26 P11
Dalupiri: i., Philippines 64 G3
Dalvik: Iceland 46 d4
Dalwallinu: W. Australia 68 B6
Dalwhinnie: High., Scotland 28 N6
Daly: riv., N. Territ., Austl. 68 E2
Daly River Reserve: N. Territ., Australia 68 D2
Daly Waters: N. Territ., Australia 68 E3
Dam: Surinam 94 F3
Damagaram: geog. reg., Niger 81 F2
Damanhûr: Egypt 56 B6
Damantan: Senegal 80 B2
Daman: India [cap. (with Goa and Diu) Panjim] 58 M10
Damara: Cen. Afr. Rep. 76 A1
Damar Is.: Indonesia 61 K13
Damascus: Va., U.S.A. 88 L7
DAMASCUS: & Prov., Syria 56 E5
Damaturu: Nigeria 81 G2
Damba: Angola 81 H6
Damba: Szechwan, China 62 S8
Dambacha: Ethiopia 79 M7
Damberta: Nigeria 81 F2
Dâmbovnic: riv., Romania 39 T14
Dambulla: Sri Lanka 58 O13
Damerham: Hants., Eng. 25 S18
Damghan: Iran 55 H7
Damh, Loch: Highland, Scotland 28 K5
Damietta: Egypt 56 B6
Dammam: Saudi Arabia 55 H9
Dammartin: France 36 H6
Dammastock: mtn., Switz. 40 O9
Damme: W. Germany 44 O3
Damodar: riv., India 59 P10
Damoh: Madhya Pradesh, India 58 N10
Damot (Domo): Ethiopia 79 R18
Damous: Algeria 35 G18
Damqut: Yemen P.D.R. 55 H11
Dampier: W. Australia 68 B4
Dampier Land: geog. reg., W. Australia 68 C3
Damrao: Chad 81 H2
Damslaagte: S. Africa 74 D6
Damville: France 36 G7
Damvillers: France 36 L6
Dan: city of ancient Israel about 3 miles WNW. of Baniyas, Syria 55 b1
Dan: Israelite tribe which inhabited (1) Sea Coast S. of Jaffa. (2) Region of L. Hula, Palestine 55 Ins.
Dana: i., Indonesia 65 G9
Danai: Sumatra 65 C6
Danakil: geog. reg., Ethiopia 79 N7
Danané: Ivory Coast 80 C3
Da Nang: Vietnam 64 D3
Danao: Philippines 64 G4
Danbury: Conn., U.S.A. 89 P5
Danbury: Essex, England 25 X16
Dandenong: Vict., Australia 71 F11
Dandougou: Upper Volta 80 D2
Danforth: Maine, U.S.A. 89 S3
Dang Mts.: Ivory Coast 80 C3
Danga: Sudan 79 L8
Danga: Cen. Afr. Rep. 76 B1
Dange: France 36 F9
Danger Point: S. Africa 74 C7
Dangila: Ethiopia 79 M7
Dangouadougou: Upper Volta 80 D2
Danguno: Nigeria 81 F2
Dani: Upper Volta 80 D2
Dania: Fla., U.S.A. 91 L12
Daniel's Hope: S. Africa 74 D5
Danielskuil: S. Africa 74 E4
Danilov: U.S.S.R. 50 F3
Danilov Grad: Yugoslavia 39 Q15
Danilovka: Kazakh., U.S.S.R. 51 M4
Danilovka: Volgograd U.S.S.R. 50 F4
Dankama: Nigeria 81 F2
Dankhar: Himachal Pradesh, India 58 N8
Danmarks Fiord: Greenland 85 r1
Dannemora: N.Y., U.S.A. 89 P3
Dannenberg: W. Germany 45 R2
Dannevirke: North I., N.Z. 70 Q15
Dannhauser: Natal, S. Africa 75 J4
Dansalan: Mindanao, Phil. 64 G5
Dansville: N.Y., U.S.A. 89 N4
Dante (Hafun): Somalia 79 S17
Dante: Va., U.S.A. 88 K7
Danube: riv., Europe 33 G3
Danube Delta National Park: Romania 39 V14
Danum: Roman name of Doncaster, S. Yorks., Eng. 27 T12
Danville: Ill., U.S.A. 88 H5
Danville: Ky., U.S.A. 88 J7
Danville: Que., Canada 89 P3
Danville: Va., U.S.A. 89 M7
Danzig, Gulf of: Baltic Sea 43 Q9
Danzig: see Gdańsk.
Daon: France 36 E8
Daoulas: France 36 A7
Daoura: riv., Algeria 80 L8
Dapa: Philippines 64 H5
Dapchi: Nigeria 81 G2
Daphnae: Graeco-Roman fort about 8 miles W. of El Qantara, Egypt 56 C6
Dapitan: Mindanao, Phil. 64 G5
Darab: Iran 55 H9
Darabani: Romania 43 U12
Darap: Borneo 65 E7
Darasun: U.S.S.R. 49 n7
Daraw: Egypt 54 D10
Darazo: Nigeria 81 G2
Darb: Saudi Arabia 54 F11
Darband: Iran 57 L5
Darbhanga: Bihar, India 59 P9
Darby: Mont., U.S.A. 92 E3
Dardanelles: str., Turkey 20 Ins.
Dareel: Queens., Australia 71 H7
Darende: Turkey 56 E2
Darenth: Kent, England 25 W17
DAR ES SALAAM: Coast, Tanzania 76 E4
Darfield: S. Yorks., England 27 T12
Darfo: Italy 40 Q10
Darfur, Northern: Prov., Sudan (cap. El Fasher 79 J6
Darfur, Southern: Prov., Sudan (cap. Nyala) 79 J7
Dargaville: North I., N.Z. 70 O12
Dargo: Vict., Australia 71 G11
Dargol: Upper Volta 80 E2
Dar Hamra: Saudi Arabia 54 E9
Darien: Panama 94 Ins.
Darién, Gulf of: Colombia 94 B2
Darjeeling: W. Bengal, India 59 P9
Darke Peak: town, S. Austl. 71 B9
Darkhain: Iran 57 L6
Darkton: Swaziland 75 J3
Darlaston: W. Mid., England 27 R14
Darling: S. Africa 74 C6
Darling: riv., N.S.W., Austl. 71 F8
Darling Downs: grassland, Queens., Australia 70 H6
Darling Penin.: N.W.T., Can. 85 M1
Darling Range: mtns., W. Australia 68 B6
Darlington: Durham, Eng. 26 S10
Darlington: S.C., U.S.A. 91 M8
Darlington: Wis., U.S.A. 88 F4
Darlington Point: town, N.S.W., Australia 71 G10
Darłowo: Poland 45 W1
Darmstadt: W. Germany 44 O6
Darmstadt: Dist., Hesse, West Germany 44 O5
Darney: France 40 M7
Darnley, Cape: Antarctica 9 70S 65E
Darnley Bay: N.W.T., Can. 84 g4
Daroca: Spain 35 F16
Daror: Ethiopia 79 Q18
Darowen: Powys, Wales 27 O14
Darregueira: Argentina 96 C4
Darreh Gaz: Iran 55 J7
Darror: watercourse, Somalia 79 S17
Darss: penin., E. Germany 45 S1
Darsser Ort: cape, E. Germany 45 S1
Dart: riv., Devon, England 24 O19
Dartford: Kent, England 25 W17
Dartmoor: Devon, England 24 O18
Dartmoor National Park: Devon, England 24 O18
Dartmouth: Devon, Eng. 24 O19
Dartmouth: N.S., Canada 89 U3
Daru: New Guinea 69 G1
Daruvar: Yugoslavia 38 P14
Darvaza: Turkmen., U.S.S.R. 50 J6
Darvel: Strathclyde, Scotland 29 N8
Darvel Bay: Sabah, Malaysia 65 F6
Darwen: Lancs., England 27 R12
Darwendale: Rhodesia 77 D6
DARWIN: N. Territ., Austl. 68 E2
Darya Khan: Punjab, Pakistan 58 M8
Darya-yi-Namak: lake, Iran 55 H8
Das: i., Persian Gulf 55 H9
Da'sal: Oman 55 J10
Dascylium: Phrygian and Persian capital on SE. shore of Lake Manyas, to N. of town Manyas, Tur. 39 U16
Dashato: riv., Ethiopia 79 Q18
Dashoba: Inner Mongolia, China 62 S6
Dasht: riv., Baluchistan, Pakistan 58 K9
Dashtiari: Iran 55 K9
Dasht-i-Kavir: desert, Iran 55 H8
Dasht-i-Lut: desert, Iran 55 J8
Daspalla: Orissa, India 59 O10
Dassa Zoume: Benin 81 E3
Dassen I.: S. Africa 74 C6
Datça: Turkey 39 U18
Datchet: Berks., England 25 U17
Datia: Madhya Pradesh, India 58 N9
Datuk, Cape: Sarawak, Malaysia 65 D6
Datumakuta: Borneo 65 F6
Daugavpils: Latvia, U.S.S.R. 47 U9
Dauha: see Doha.
Daulatabad: Afghanistan 51 K7
Daulatabad: Iran 55 J9
Daulatabad (Malayer): Iran 57 L4
Daulat Yar: Afghanistan 58 L8
Daun: W. Germany 44 M5
D'Aunay Bay: Greenland 85 r4
Dauphin: & lake, Man., Canada 92 H2
Dauphin: i., Ala., U.S.A. 90 G10
Dauphiné: Prov., France 34 J14
Daur: Iraq 57 H4
Daura: Nigeria 81 F2
Davangere: Karnataka, India 58 N12
Davant: La., U.S.A. 90 Ins.
Davao: & gulf, Mindanao, Philippines 65 H5
Davar Panah: Iran 55 K9
Davel: Trans., S Africa 75 H3
Davenham: Ches., England 27 Q13
Davenport: Iowa, U.S.A. 88 F5
Davenport: Wash., U.S.A. 92 D3
Davenport Downs: Queens., Australia 69 G4
Daventry: Northants., Eng. 25 T15
David: Panama 87 I 16
David-Gorodok: Byelorussia 43 U10
Davidson: Sask., Canada 92 F2
Davignab: SW. Africa 74 C3
Davington: Dumfries & Galloway, Scotland 29 P9
Davis: rsch. stn., Antarctica 9 70S 75E
Davis: Calif., U.S.A. 93 C5
Davis Dam: Ariz., U.S.A. 93 E5
Davis Str.: Grnld./Can. 85 O4
Davos: Switzerland 40 P9
Davyhurst: W. Australia 68 C6
Dawa: riv., Ethiopia 76 F2
Dawa Aleh: Ethiopia 79 Q18
Dawasir: wadi, Saudi Arabia 54 F10
Dawes Range: Queensland, Australia 69 J4
Dawley: Salop, England 27 R14
Dawlish: Devon, England 24 P18
Dawna Range: Burma/Thai. 59 R11
Dawson: Ga., U.S.A. 91 J10
Dawson: N. Mex., U.S.A. 93 G5
Dawson: Okla., U.S.A. 90 D7
Dawson: Yukon, Canada 84 F5
Dawson: riv., Queens., Austl. 70 H5
Dawson Creek: town, B.C., Canada 92 C1
Dawson Springs: city, Ky., U.S.A. 88 H7
Dax: France 37 D12
Dayboro: Queens., Austl. 70 K6
Dayle: Czechoslovakia 45 U6
Daylesford: Vict., Austl. 71 F11
Dayton: Ohio, U.S.A. 88 J6
Dayton: Tenn., U.S.A. 91 J8
Dayton: Wash., U.S.A. 92 D3
Daytona Beach: city, Fla., U.S.A. 91 L11
Dé: Mali 80 D2
De Aar: & Dist., S. Africa 75 F5
Dead Sea: Israel/Jordan 55 b3
Deadwood: S. Dak., U.S.A. 92 G4
Deal: Kent, England 25 Y17
Dealesville: O.F.S., S. Africa 75 F4
Dean: riv., B.C., Canada 92 B2
Dean, East & West: W. Sussex, England 24 U18
Dean, Forest of: Glos., England 24 Q16
Deán Funes: Argentina 96 C3
Dearborn: Mich., U.S.A. 88 K4
Dearham: Cumbria, Eng. 26 P10
Dearn, Strath: val., Highland, Scotland 28 N5
Dease Lake: town, B.C., Canada 84 f6
Dease Str.: N.W.T., Canada 84 J4
Death Valley: Calif., U.S.A. 93 D5
Death Valley Nat. Mon.: Calif., U.S.A. 93 D5
Deauville: France 36 F6
Debar: Yugoslavia 39 R16
Deben: riv., Suff., England 25 Y15
Debenham: Suff., England 25 Y15
De Beque: Colo., U.S.A. 93 F5
Debica: Poland 43 R11
De Bilt: Netherlands 44 L3
Deblin: Poland 43 R11
Debno: Poland 45 U3
DEBRA MARKOS: Goljam, Ethiopia 79 M7
Debra Tabor: Ethiopia 79 M7
Debrecen: Hungary 43 R13
Decatur: Ala., U.S.A. 91 H8
Decatur: Ga., U.S.A. 91 J9
Decatur: Ill., U.S.A. 88 G6
Decatur: Ind., U.S.A. 88 J5
Decatur: Mich., U.S.A. 88 J4
Decatur: Tex., U.S.A. 90 C9
Decazeville: France 37 H11
Deccan: geog. reg., India 58 N11
Decelea: Greek village of N. Central Attica
Děčín: Czechoslovakia 45 U5
Decize: France 37 J9
Decorah: Iowa, U.S.A. 88 F4
Deda: Romania 43 T13
Dedaye: Burma 59 R11
Deddington: Oxon., Eng. 25 T16
Dedeagach (Alexandroupolis): Greece 39 T16
Dedelow: E. Germany 45 T2
Dedham: Essex, England 25 X16
Dédi: Ivory Coast 80 D3
De Doorns: S. Africa 74 C6
DÉDOUGOU: Volta Noire, Upper Volta 80 D2
Dedza: Malawi 77 D5
Dee: riv., Dumfries & Galloway, Scotland 29 O10
Dee: riv., England/Wales 27 P13
Dee: riv., Grampian, Scot. 28 R5
Dee: riv., Louth/Meath, Repub. of Ireland 30 J12
Deel: riv., Lim., Repub. of Ireland 31 D15
Deeping Gate: Northants., England 27 V14
Deeping St. Nicholas: Lincs., England 25 V14
Deepwater: Ala., U.S.A. 90 E6
Deepwater: N.S.W., Austl. 71 J7
Deer: i., Alaska, U.S.A. 84 c7
Deer, New & Old: Grampian, Scotland 28 R4
Deerfield Beach: Fla., U.S.A. 91 L12
Deering: Alaska, U.S.A. 84 c4
Deer Isle: Maine, U.S.A. 89 R3
Deerlake: Newf., Canada 85 u2
Deer Lodge Mtns.: Mont., U.S.A. 92 E3
Deer Park: city, Wash., U.S.A. 92 D3
Deer River: city., Minn., U.S.A. 88 E2
Deesa: Gujarat, India 58 M10
Deeside: val., Gram., Scot. 28 Q5
Defferrari: Argentina 96 D4
Defiance: Ohio, U.S.A. 88 J5
De Funiak Springs: city, Fla., U.S.A. 91 H10
Degeberga: Sweden 47 O9
Degema: Nigeria 81 F4
Degeendorf: W. Germany 41 S7
De Grey: riv., W. Australia 68 B4
Dehra Dun: Uttar Pradesh, India 58 N8
Deh Salm: Iran 55 J8
Deim Zubeir: Sudan 76 C1
Deiniolen: Gwyn., Wales 27 N13
Deira: kingdom of Saxon England in Yorkshire Wolds 27 U11
Deir el Balah: Egypt 55 a3
DEIR EZ ZOR: & Prov., Syria 57 G4
Deir Hafir: Syria 56 E3
Dej: Romania 43 S13
Deje: Sweden 47 N7
Dekala: Nigeria 81 E2
De Kalb: Ill., U.S.A. 88 G5
Dekani: Yugoslavia 41 T10
Dekese: Zaire 76 B3
De Keur: S. Africa 74 C6
Dekhanabad: Uzbek., U.S.S.R. 51 L7
De Klerk: S. Africa 74 E5
Dékoa: Cen. Afr. Rep. 76 A1
De Kol: S. Africa 75 G6
Delabole: Corn., England 24 M18
Delacroix: La., U.S.A. 90 Ins.
Delagoa Bay: see Lourenço Marques Bay 75 K2
Delamere: N. Territ., Austl. 68 E3
De Land: Fla., U.S.A. 91 L11
Delano Peak: Utah, U.S.A. 93 E5
Delareyville: S. Africa 75 F3
Delavan: Wis., U.S.A. 88 G4
Delaware: Ohio, U.S.A. 88 K5
Delaware: riv., U.S.A. 89 O5
Delaware: State, U.S.A. (cap. Dover) 89 O6
Delaware Bay: Del., U.S.A. 89 O6
Delaware Water Gap: city, Pa., U.S.A. 89 O5
Delbrück: W. Germany 44 O4
Delčevo: Yugoslavia 39 S16
Delden: Netherlands 44 M3
Delegate: N.S.W., Australia 71 H11
Deleitosa: Spain 35 D17
Delémont: Switzerland 40 N8
De Leon: Tex., U.S.A. 90 B9

For Abbreviations see list on p.113. Italic type, e.g. Ephesus, refers to historical names not on maps. Capital letters, e.g. MADRID, show capitals of countries; small capital letters, e.g. CADIZ, show capitals of provinces, etc. General notes p.116.

Delft—Domfront 137

Delft: Netherlands **44** K3
Delft: *i.*, Palk Strait, India **58** N13
Delfzijl: Netherlands **44** M2
Delgado, Cape: Mozam. **77** F5
Delgany: Wick., R. of Irel. **31** J13
Delgo: Sudan **54** D10
DELHI: & *Union Terr.*, India **58** N9
Delhi: La., U.S.A. **90** F9
Delhi: N.Y., U.S.A. **89** O4
Delice: *riv.*, Turkey **56** D2
Delimara Point: *cape*, Malta **32** *Ins.*
Delitzsch: E. Germany **45** S4
Delium: ancient temple and battlefield on north coast of *Attica*
Dell: Outer Hebr., Scotland **28** J3
Dellach: Austria **41** T9
Dell Rapids: *city*, S. Dak., U.S.A. **92** H4
Dellys: Algeria **35** H18
Delmas: Trans., S. Africa **75** H3
Delmenhorst: W. Germany **44** O2
Delminium: Roman camp at *Gardun* about 10 miles E. of Split, W. Yugoslavia **38** P15
Delmore: Trans., S. Africa **74** N *Ins.*
Delnice: Yugoslavia **41** U10
Del Norte: Colo., U.S.A. **93** F5
De Long Fiord: Greenland **85** P1
De Long Mtns.: Alaska, U.S.A. **84** c4
Deloraine: Tas., Australia **68** H8
Delos: small island at SW. corner of island Mikonos, Aegean Sea **39** T18
Delphi: Ind., U.S.A. **88** H5
Delphi: ancient Greek shrine on lower S. slopes of Parnassos overlooking G. of Corinth, Greece **39** S17
Delphos: Ohio, U.S.A. **88** J5
Delray Beach: *city*, Fla., U.S.A. **91** L12
Del Rio: Tex., U.S.A. **93** G7
Delta Colo., U.S.A. **93** F5
Delta: Utah, U.S.A. **93** E5
Delta Downs: Queens., Austl. **69** G3
Delungra: N.S.W., Australia **71** J7
Delve: W. Germany **44** P1
Del Verme Falls: Ethiopia **76** F1
Delvin: Westmeath, Repub. of Ireland **30** G12
Delvinákion: Greece **39** R17
Delvine: Albania **39** R17
Delyatin: Ukraine **43** T12
Dema: *riv.*, U.S.S.R. **50** J4
Demarcation Point: *cape*, Alaska, U.S.A. **84** e4
Demavend: *mtn.*, Iran **55** H7
Demba: Zaïre **76** B4
Dembia: Zaïre **76** C2
Demerara: *Co. & riv.*, Guyana **87** d8
Demetrias: ancient Greek city at Vólos, Thessaly, Greece **39** S17
Deming: N. Mex., U.S.A. **93** F6
Demirci: Turkey **56** A2
Demirciköy: Turkey **56** A2
Demirköy: Turkey **39** U16
Demmin: E. Germany **45** T2
Demnat: Morocco **80** K8
Demonte: Italy **40** N11
Demopolis: Ala., U.S.A. **91** H9
Demyansk: U.S.S.R. **50** D3
Demyanskoye: U.S.S.R. **51** L3
Denain: France **36** J5
Denau: Uzbek., U.S.S.R. **51** L7
Denbigh: Clwyd, Wales **27** P13
Denby Dale: *town*, S. Yorks., England **27** S12
Denchin: Tibet, China **62** R8
Denchin Gompa: Tibet, China **62** R8
Dendang: Billiton, Indon. **65** D7
Dendermonde: Belgium **44** K4
Dendre: *riv.*, Belgium **44** K5
Denekamp: Netherlands **44** N3
Denfina: Mali **80** C2
Dengdeng: Cameroun **81** G3
Dengshol: Sudan **76** D1
Denham Range: Queens., Australia **70** G3
Denham Sound: W. Austl. **68** A5
Denham Springs: La., U.S.A. **90** F10
Den Helder: Netherlands **44** K3
Denholm: Bord., Scotland **29** Q9
Denholm: Sask., Canada **92** F2
Denia: Spain **35** G17
Deniliquin: N.S.W., Austl. **71** F10
Denison: Iowa, U.S.A. **92** H4
Denison: Texas, U.S.A. **90** C9
DENIZLI: & *Prov.*, Turkey **56** A3
Denman: N.S.W., Australia **71** J9

Denmark: *Kingdom* **47** L9
Cap.: Copenhagen
Area: 16,615 sq. miles
(43,033 sq. km.)
Pop.: 4,963,000 (*1971 E*)

Denmark: S.C., U.S.A. **91** L9
Denmark: W. Australia **68** B6
Denmark Str.: Greenland **85** R4
Dennington: Suff., England **25** Y15
Dennis Head: *cape*, N. Ronaldsay, Orkney Is. **28** *Ins.*
Denniston: South I., N.Z. **70** N15
Denny: Central, Scotland **29** O7
Denpasar: Bali, Indonesia **65** F8
Denstone: Staffs., England **27** S14
Dent: Cumbria, England **26** R11
Dent Blanche: *mtn.*, Switz. **40** N9
Denton: Gt. Man., England **27** R13
Denton: Lincs., England **27** U14
Denton: Md., U.S.A. **89** O6
Denton: Tex., U.S.A. **90** C9
D'Entrecasteaux Is.: New Guinea **69** J1
D'Entrecasteaux Reef: Loyalty Is. **67** M5
DENVER: Colo., U.S.A. **93** G5
Denver: Trans., S. Africa **74** N *Ins.*
Déo: *riv.*, Cameroun **81** G3
Deogarh: Orissa, India **59** O10
Deogarh: Rajasthan, India **58** M9
Deoghar: Bihar, India **59** P10
Deolali: Maharashtra, India **58** M11
Deoli: Rajasthan, India **58** N9
De Pere: Wis., U.S.A. **88** G3
Depot Harbour: Ont., Can. **88** L3
De Queen: Ark., U.S.A. **90** D8
De Quincy: La., U.S.A. **90** E10
Der: *watercourse*, Somalia **79** R18
DERA'A: & *Prov.*, Syria **56** E5
Dera Ghazi Khan: Punjab, Pakistan **58** M8
Deraheib: Sudan **54** E10
Dera Ismail Khan: NW. Front. Prov., Pakistan **58** M8
Derazhnya: Ukraine **43** U12
Derbe: town of *Lycaonia* near Çumra, Turkey **56** C3
Derbent: U.S.S.R. **50** G6
Derbisaka: Cen. Afr. Rep. **76** B1
Derby: Conn., U.S.A. **89** P5
Derby: Derby., England **27** T14
Derby: W. Australia **68** C3
Derbyshire: *Co.*, England (*co. town* Matlock) **27** S13
Dere, El-: Somalia **79** R18
Derecske: Hungary **43** R13
Dereham, East: Norf., Eng. **25** X14
Dereseki: Turkey (Bosporus *Inset*) **20** *Ins.*
Derevyansk: U.S.S.R. **50** H2
Derg: Libya **78** G3
Derg: *riv.*, Tyr., N. Ireland **30** F10
Derg, Lough: Don., Repub. of Ireland **30** F10
Derg, Lough: Repub. of Irel. **31** E14
Dergachi: U.S.S.R. **50** G4
De Ridder: La., U.S.A. **90** E10
Derik: Turkey **57** G3
Dermbach: E. Germany **45** Q5
Dermott: Ark., U.S.A. **90** F9
DERNA: & *Prov.*, Libya **33** G5
Derniere, Ile: La., U.S.A. **90** F11
Déroute, Passage de la: *channel*, Channel Is./Fr. **25** *Ins.*
Derravaragh, Lough: Westmeath, Repub. of Ireland **30** G12
Derre: Mozambique **77** E6
Derrinallum: Vict., Australia **71** E11
Derry: N.H., U.S.A. **89** Q4
Derrybrien: Galway, Repub. of Ireland **31** D13
Derrygonnelly: Ferm., N. Irel. **30** F11
Derrylin: Ferm., N. Ireland **30** F11
Derrynasaggart Mtns.: Kerry/Cork, Repub. of Ireland **31** C16
Derryveagh Mtns.: Don., Repub. of Ireland **30** E10
Dersingham: Norf., England **25** X14
Dertona: Roman colony at Tortona, Italy **40** O11
Dertosa: Roman town at Tortosa, Spain **35** G16
Derudeb: Sudan **54** E11
De Rust: S. Africa **74** E6
Dervaig: Inner Hebr., Scot. **29** J6
Derventa: Yugoslavia **38** P14
Dervock: Antrim, N. Ireland **30** J9
Derwent: *riv.*, Cumbria, Eng. **26** P10
Derwent: *riv.*, Derby., Eng. **27** S13
Derwent: *riv.*, Durham/Northumb., England **26** S10
Derwent: *riv.*, Humberside/N. Yorks., Eng. **27** U12
Derwent: *riv.*, Tas., Austl. **68** H8
Derwent Water: *lake*, Cumbria, England **26** P10
Derzhavinsk: Kazakh., U.S.S.R. **51** L4
Desaguadero: *riv.*, Argentina **96** B3
Des Arc: Ark., U.S.A. **90** F8
Desborough: Northants., England **25** U15
Deschaillons: Que., Canada **89** P2
Deschambault Lake: Sask., Canada **92** G2
Deschutes: *riv.*, Oreg., U.S.A. **92** C4
Deseada: Chile **96** B1
Desenzano: Italy **40** Q10
Deseronto: Ont., Canada **89** N3
Desertas: *i.*, Madeira **78** A3
Desert Center: Calif., U.S.A. **93** D6
Desford: Leics., England **27** T14
Désirade: *i.*, (Fr.), Leeward Is. **87** c2
De Smet: S. Dak., U.S.A. **92** H4
DES MOINES: Iowa, U.S.A. **88** E5
Des Moines: N. Mex., U.S.A. **93** G5
Des Moines: *riv.*, U.S.A. **92** J4
Des Moines, West: *riv.*, Iowa, U.S.A. **88** E4
Desna: *riv.*, U.S.S.R. **50** D4
Desolation I.: Chile **95** C14
Desordem, Serra da: *mtns.*, Brazil **94** H4
De Soto: Mo., U.S.A. **88** F6
Despatch: S. Africa **75** F6
Des Quinze, Lac: *lake*, Que., Canada **89** M2
Dessaguadero: *riv.*, Arg. **96** B3
Dessau: E. Germany **45** S4
DESSYE: Welo, Ethiopia **79** M7
Desvres: France **36** G5
Deta: Romania **39** R14
Detmold: W. Germany **44** O4
Detmold: *Dist.*, North-Rhine-Westphalia, West Germany **44** O4
Detour, Point: *cape*, Mich., U.S.A. **88** H3
Detroit: Mich., U.S.A. **88** K4
Detroit Lakes: *city*, Minn., U.S.A. **92** H3
Dett: Rhodesia **77** C6
Dettenhausen: W. Germany **40** P7
Dettingen: battlefield about 10 miles NW. of Aschaffenburg, W. Germany **44** P5
Deung: *riv.*, Indo-China **64** D4
Deurne: Netherlands **44** L4
Deutsche Pretzier: E. Ger. **45** R3
Deutschlandsberg: Austria **41** V9
Deux Frères, Les: Vietnam **64** D5
Deux-Sèvres: *Dept.*, France (*cap.* Niort) **37** E9
Deva: Romania **39** S14
Deva: Spain **35** E15
Deva: Roman camp at Chester, England **27** Q13
Develi: Turkey **56** D2
Deventer: Netherlands **44** M3
Deveron: *riv.*, Grampian, Scotland **28** Q4
Devgarh: Maharashtra, India **58** M11
Devilsbit: *hill*, Tip, Repub. of Ireland **31** F14
Devil's Bridge: Dyfed, Wales **24** O15
Devil's Lake: *city & lake*, N. Dak., U.S.A. **92** H3
Devin: Bulgaria **39** T16
Devine: Tex., U.S.A. **90** B11
Devizes: Wilts., England **24** S17
Devoll: *riv.*, Albania **39** R16
Devoluy: *mtns.*, France **40** L11
Devon: Trans., S. Africa **75** H3
Devon: *Co.*, England (*co. town* Exeter) **24** O18
Devondale: S. Africa **75** F3
Devon I.: N.W.T., Canada **85** L2
Devonport: Devon, England **24** N19
Devonport: North I., N.Z. **70** P13
Devonport: Tas., Australia **68** H8
Devoran: Cornwall, England **24** L19
Devrek: Turkey **56** B1
Devrez: *riv.*, Turkey **56** C1
Dewas: Madhya Pradesh, India **58** N10
Dewetsdorp: & *Dist.*, O.F.S., S. Africa **75** G4
Dewey: Okla., U.S.A. **90** D7
De Witt: Ark., U.S.A. **90** F8
De Witt: Iowa, U.S.A. **88** F5
Dewsbury: W. Yorks., Eng. **27** S12
Dexter: Maine, U.S.A. **89** R3
Deyrou: Turkmen., U.S.S.R. **51** K7
Dezh Shahpur: Iran **57** K4
Dhaba': Saudi Arabia **54** E9
Dhabalil: *wadi*, Sau. Arab./Oman **55** G11
Dhafara: *geog. reg.*, Saudi Arabia **55** H10
Dhafir: Asir, Saudi Arabia **54** F11
Dhafir: *tribal area*, Iraq **57** J6
Dhahaban: Saudi Arabia **54** E10
Dhahiriya: Jordan **55** a3
Dhahran: Asir, Saudi Arabia **54** F11
Dhahran: Hasa, Saudi Arabia **55** H9
Dhamar: Yemen **54** F12
Dhamtari: Mad., Prad., Ind. **58** O10
Dhana: *desert*, Saudi Arabia **55** G10
Dhanbad: Bihar, India **59** P10
Dhangarhi: Nepal **58** O9
Dhankuta: Nepal **59** P9
Dhanushkodi: Tamil Nadu, India **58** N13
Dhar: Madhya Pradesh, India **58** N10
Dharmjaygarh: Madhya Pradesh, India **59** O10
Dharmsala: Himaçhal Pradesh, India **58** N8
Dharwar: Karnataka, India **58** N11
Dhasan: *riv.*, India **58** N10
Dhaufir: Saudi Arabia **55** H10
Dhaulagiri: *mtn.*, Nepal **59** O9
Dheskati: Greece **39** R17
Dhidhimótikhon: Greece **39** U16
Dholpur: Rajasthan, India **58** N9
Dhomokós: Greece **39** S17
Dhond: Maharashtra, India **58** M11
Dhoraji: Gujarat, India **58** M10
Dhubri: Assam, India **59** P9
Dhufar: *geog. reg.*, Òman **55** H11
Dhuizon: France **36** G8
Dhulia: Maharashtra, India **58** M10
Dhuran: Yemen **54** F12
Diabaig: High., Scot. **28** K4
Diablo Range: *mtns.*, Calif., U.S.A. **93** C5
Diafarabé: Mali **80** D2
Diago: Mali **80** C2
Diaha: Morocco **78** B4
Diala: Mali **80** C2
Dialakoro: Mali **80** C2
Dialoubé: Senegal **80** B1
Diamante: Argentina **96** C3
Diamantina: Brazil **94** J7
Diamantina: *riv.*, Queens., Australia **69** G4
Diamantina Fracture Zone: Indian Ocean **9** 40S 100E
Diamantino: Brazil **94** F6
Diamantura Lakes: *town*, Queens., Australia **69** G4
Diamond: La., U.S.A. **90** *Ins.*
Diamond Harbour: W. Bengal, India **59** P10
Diamond Islets: Australia **69** J3
Diamond Mtns: Nev., U.S.A. **93** D4
Diamondville: Wyo., U.S.A. **92** E4
Diano Marina: Italy **40** O12
Dianópolis: Brazil **94** H6
Diapaga: Upper Volta **81** E2
Diatz Point: SW. Africa **74** A3
Dibaya: Zaïre **76** B4
Dibba: U.A.E. **55** J9
Dibbis: Sudan **79** J7
Dibdiba: *geog. reg.*, Iraq/Kuwait **57** K7
Dibega: Iraq **57** H4
Dibete: Botswana **77** C7
Diboll: Tex., U.S.A. **90** D10
Dibouangui: Gabon **81** G5
Dibrugarh: Assam, India **59** Q9
Dickinson: N. Dak., U.S.A. **92** G3
Dickleburgh: Norf., Eng. **25** Y15
Dickson: Tenn., U.S.A. **88** H7
Dicle (Tigris): *riv.*, Turkey **57** G3
Dicomano: Italy **41** R12
Dicte: ancient Greek name of mtn. N. of Áno Viánnos in E. Crete **39** T19
Didcot: Oxon., England **25** T16
Didia: Tanzânia **76** D3
Didmarton: Glos., England **24** R16
Didsbury: Alta., Canada **92** E2
Die: France **40** L11
Diébougou: Upper Volta **80** D2
Dieburg: W. Germany **44** O6
Diego Garcia: *i.* (Br. Indian Ocean Territ.), Indian Ocean **19** 0S 70E
DIEGO SUAREZ (Antsirane): & *Prov.*, Malagasy Rep. **73** O12
Diégoum: *well*, Mauritania **80** B1
Diekirch: Luxembourg **44** M6
Diemel: *riv.*, W. Germany **44** O4
Diênbiênphu: Vietnam **64** C2
Diên Khánh: Vietnam **64** D4
Diepenau: W. Germany **44** O3
Diepholz: W. Germany **44** O3
Dieppe: France **36** G6
Diep River: S. Africa **74** *Ins.*
Dierks: Ark., U.S.A. **90** D8
Diessen: W. Germany **41** R8
Diessenhofen: Switzerland **40** O8
Diest: Belgium **44** L4
Dieulefit: France **40** L11
Dielouard: France **40** M7
Dieuze: France **40** M7
Diez: W. Germany **44** O5
Dif: Kenya **76** F2
DIFFA: & *Dept.*, Niger **81** G1
Difuma: Zaïre **76** C3
Digboi: Assam, India **59** R9
Digby: Lincs., England **27** V13
Digby: N.S., Canada **89** T3
Diggs, Point: Mexico **93** E6
Dighton: Kans., U.S.A. **90** A6
DIGNE: Alpes-de-Haute-Provence, France **40** M11
Digny: France **36** G7
Digoel: *riv.*, West Irian, Indonesia **61** N13
Digoin: France **37** K9
Digor: Turkey **57** H1
Dihang: *riv.*, Arunachal Pradesh, India **59** Q9
DIJON: Côtes d'Or, France **36** L8
Dikili: Turkey **39** U17
Dikkil: Djibouti **79** Q17
Dikwa: Nigeria **81** G2
Dilam: Saudi Arabia **54** G10
Dili: Zaïre **76** C2
Díli: Timor, Indonesia **65** H8
Dilingat: Egypt **56** B6
Di Linh: Vietnam **64** D4
Dilizhan: Armenia, U.S.S.R. **57** J1
Dillenburg: W. Germany **44** O5
Dilli Abbas: Iraq **57** J4
Dilling: Sudan **79** K7
Dillingen: W. Germany **40** Q7
Dillingham: Alaska, U.S.A. **84** D6
Dillon: Mont., U.S.A. **92** E3
Dillon: S.C., U.S.A. **91** M8
Dilman: Iran **57** L3
Dilolo: Zaïre **77** B5
Dilpar: Sinkiang, China **51** P6
Dilwar: Iran **57** L5
Dilwyn: Hereford & Worcester, England **24** Q15
Dimapur: Assam, India **59** O9
Dimaro: Italy **41** Q9
Dimarsang: Chinghai, China **59** Q8
Dimbelenge: Zaïre **76** B4
Dimbokro: Ivory Coast **80** D3
Dimboola: Vict., Australia **71** E11
Dimitrovgrad: Bulgaria **39** T15
Dimitrovgrad: Yugoslavia **39** S15
Dimitrovo: Bulgaria **39** S15
Dinagat: & *i.*, Philippines **64** H4
Dinajpur: Bangladesh **59** P9
Dinan: France **36** C7
Dinant: Belgium **44** K5
Dinapore: Bihar, India **59** O9
Dinar: Turkey **56** B2
Dinard: France **36** C7
Dinaric Alps: Yugoslavia **38** P14
Dinas Head: *cape*, Dyfed, Wales **24** M15
Dinas Mawddwy: Gwynedd, Wales **27** O14
Dinas Powis: S. Glam., Wales **24** P17
Dinder: Sudan **54** D12
Dinder National Park: Ethiopia **79** M7
Dindigul: Tamil Nadu, India **58** N12
Dinga: Zaïre **81** H6
Dingelstadt: E. Germany **45** Q4
Dingle: & *bay*, Kerry, Repub. of Ireland **31** A15
Dingle Penin.: Kerry, Repub. of Ireland **31** A15
Dingo: Queens., Australia **70** H4
Dingras: Luzon, Philippines **64** G3
DINGUIRAYE: & *Reg.*, Guinea **80** B2
Dingwall: High., Scot. **28** N4
Dinh, Cape: Vietnam **64** D4
Dinkelsbühl: W. Germany **45** Q6
Dinlap: Vietnam **64** D2
Dinnet: Gram., Scotland **28** Q5
Dinnington: S. Yorks., Eng. **27** T13
Dinokwe: Botswana **77** C7
Dinosaur Nat. Mon.: Utah/Colo., U.S.A. **93** F4
Dinslaken: W. Germany **44** M4
Dinton: Wilts., England **24** S17
Dinuba: Calif., U.S.A. **93** D5
Dioka: Mali **80** B2
Dioliba: *riv.*, Guinea **80** B2
Diomede Is. (U.S.A. & U.S.S.R.), Bering Strait **84** C4
Diongoï: Mali **80** C2
Dionisia: Argentina **96** D4
Dionísio Cerqueira: Brazil **96** E2
Diorbivol: Senegal **80** B1
Dioulabaya: Guinea **80** B2
Diouloulou: Senegal **80** A2
Dioundou: Niger **81** E2
Dioungani: Mali **80** D2
Dioura: Mali **80** C2
DIOURBEL: & *Reg.*, Senegal **80** A2
Dippoldiswalde: E. Germany **45** T5
Diptford: Devon, England **24** O19
Dipton: Durham, England **26** S10
Dir: NW. Frontier Province, Pakistan **58** M7
Dira: *well*, Niger **81** G1
Dire: Mali **80** D1
Diredawa: Ethiopia **79** Q18
Dirico: Angola **77** B6
Dirishebira: Ethiopia **76** F1
Dirk Hartog I.: W. Australia **68** A5
Dirleton: Lothian, Scot. **29** Q7
Dirranbandi: Queens., Austl. **71** H7
Dirri: *well*, Somalia **79** R19
Disappointment Is.: (Fr.), Pacific O. **83** g2
Disappointment, Lake: W. Australia **68** C4
Discovery Bank: Indon. **65** D7
Discovery Bay: Jamaica **86** *Ins.*
Discovery Reef: Paracel Is. **64** E3
Discovery Reefs: S. China Sea **64** E4
Disentis/Mustèr: Switzerland **40** O9
Dishforth: N. Yorks., Eng. **26** T11
Disko: *i.*, Greenland **85** o4
Diskofjord: Greenland **85** o4
Disna: Byelorussia **47** V9
Disna: *riv.*, Byelorussia **47** U9
Disraeli: Que., Canada **89** Q3
Diss: Norf., England **25** Y15
Distaghil: *mtn.*, Jammu & Kashmir **58** N7
Distington: Cumbria, Eng. **26** O10
Disuq: Egypt **56** B6
Ditam: Cameroun **81** G3
Ditchling: E. Sussex, Eng. **25** V18
Ditinn: Guinea **80** B2
Ditsinane: Botswana **77** C7
Ditton Priors: Salop, Eng. **27** Q14
Diu: & *Union Territory*, India [*cap.* (*with Goa and Daman*) Panaji] **58** M10
Dium: Greek city on S. side of Athos peninsula, probably towards W. end, Greece **39** T16
Divenié: Congo **81** G5
Divichi: Azerbaydzhan, U.S.S.R. **57** L1
Divilacan Bay: Luzon, Phil. **64** G3
Divis: *hill*, Antrim, N. Irel. **30** J10
Diviso, El: Colombia **94** B3
Divo: Ivory Coast **80** C3
Divodurum: Roman name of Gallic centre at Metz, Fr. **44** M6
Divriği: Turkey **56** F2
Diwaniya: Iraq **57** J6
Diwen Darreh: Iran **57** K4
Dixfield: Maine, U.S.A. **89** Q3
Dixmude: Belgium **44** H4
Dixon: Ill., U.S.A. **88** G5
Dixon: Mont., U.S.A. **92** E3
Dixon Entrance: *sound*, B.C., Canada **84** f7
Diyadin: Turkey **57** H2
Diyala: *Prov.*, Iraq (*cap.* Baquba) **57** J5
Diyala: *riv.*, Iraq **57** J4
DIYARBAKIR: & *Prov.*, Tur. **57** G3
Diz: *riv.*, Iran **57** L5
Dize: Turkey **57** J3
Dizeh: Azerbaijan-e Bakhtari, Iran **57** J3
Dizeh: Gilan, Iran **57** L3
Dizful: Iran **57** L5
Dja: *riv.*, Cameroun **81** G4
Djado: & *plat.*, Niger **78** G5
*Djailolo: Moluccas, Indon. **61** K11
*DJAKARTA: Java, Indonesia **65** D8
Djamba: Cameroun **81** G3
Djambala: Congo **81** G5
Djambani: Congo **81** G5
*Djambuair Point: Sumatra **65** B5
Djanet' Algeria **88** F5
*Djatiberang: Java **65** D8
*Djatinegara: Java **65** D8
Dyaya Peak: West Irian, Indonesia **61** M12
*Djaya Pura: West Irian, Indonesia **61** N12
Djedeida: Tunisia **38** L18
Djelfa: Algeria **32** C5
Djem, El: Tunisia **32** E4
Djéma: Cen. Afr. Rep. **76** C1
*Djemadja: *i.*, Anambas Is., Indonesia **65** D6
*Djember: Java **65** E8
*Djeneponto: Celebes **65** F8
Djenien bou Rezg: Algeria **80** L8
Djenné: Mali **80** D2
*Djenu: Borneo **65** D7
Djerba: & *i.*, Tunisia **32** E5
Djibo: Upper Volta **80** D2

Djibouti: Republic **79** *Ins.*
Cap.: Djibouti
Area: 8,996 sq. miles
(23,299 sq. km.)
Pop.: 97,000 (*1971 E*)

Djidjelli: Algeria **35** J18
Djiring: Vietnam **64** D4
Djoléré: Cameroun **81** G3
Djolu: Zaïre **76** B2
Djouah: *riv.*, Congo/Gabon **81** G4
Djougou: Benin **81** E3
Djoum: Cameroun **81** G4
Djugu: Zaïre **76** D2
Djuma: Zaïre **76** A3
Djupivogur: Iceland **46** f4
Djurdjevac: Yugoslavia **38** P13
Djursholm: Sweden **47** Q7
Dmitriyev: U.S.S.R. **50** E4
Dmitriyevskoye: U.S.S.R. **50** F5
Dmitrov: U.S.S.R. **50** E3
Dneprodzerzhinsk: Ukraine **50** D5
Dnepropetrovsk: Ukraine **50** D5
Dnieper: *riv.*, U.S.S.R. **50** D5
Dnieper Plain: Ukraine **50** D4
Dnieper Plat.: Ukraine **50** D5
Dniester: *riv.*, U.S.S.R. **33** H2
Dno: U.S.S.R. **50** D3
Doagh: Antrim, N. Ireland **30** J10
Doaghbeg: Don., Repub. of Ireland **30** F9
Doangdoangan Is.: Indon. **65** F8
Doaro: Papua, New Guinea **69** G1
DOBA: Logone Oriental, Chad **81** H3
Dobané: Cen. Afr. Rep. **76** B1
Dobbiaco: Italy **41** S9
Dobbyn: Queens., Australia **69** F3
Dobele: Latvia, U.S.S.R. **47** S8
Döbeln: E. Germany **45** T4
Doberai Penin.: West Irian, Indonesia **61** L12
Doberan: E. Germany **45** R1
Dobiegniew: Poland **45** V3
Doblas: Argentina **96** C4
Dobo: Aroe Is., Indonesia **61** L13
Doboj: Yugoslavia **39** Q14
Dobřany: Czechoslovakia **45** T6
Dobre Miasto: Poland **43** R10
Dobri: Hungary **41** W9
Dobřis: Czechoslovakia **45** U6
Dobromil': Ukraine **43** S12
Dobrush: Byelorussia **50** D4
Dobrzyń: Poland **43** Q10
Docking: Norf., England **25** X14
Doclea: Roman town about 5 miles N. of Titograd, Yugoslavia **39** Q15
Dockyard: Bermuda Is. **87** *Ins.*
Doctor González: Mexico **93** H7
Doda Betta: *mtn.*, Tamil Nadu, India **58** N12
Doda, Lac: *lake*, Que., Can. **89** O1
Doddington: Cambs., Eng. **25** W15
Doddington: Kent, England **25** X17
Doddington: Northumb., England **26** R8
Dodecanese (Sporades): *is.*, Greece (*cap.* Rhodes) **39** U18
Dodekaschoinos: Graeco-Roman name of area between 1st and 2nd Cataracts, Egypt **54** D10
Dodge Center: Minn., U.S.A. **88** E3
Dodge City: Kans., U.S.A. **90** A7
Dodgeville: Wis., U.S.A. **88** F4
Dodleston: Ches., England **27** Q13
Dodman Point: Corn., Eng. **24** M19
Dodo: Cameroun **81** G3
Dodolo: Ethiopia **76** E1
DODOMA: & *Reg.*, Tanzania **76** E4
Dodona: ancient Greek shrine in mtns. E. of Konispol, Greece **39** R17
Doesburg: Netherlands **44** M3
Doetinchem: Netherlands **44** M4
Dog Creek: *town*, B.C., Can. **92** C2
Doggar Bank: North Sea **22** N6
Dog Lake: Ont., Canada **88** G1
Dog Lake: Ont., Canada **88** J1
Dogondoutchi: Niger **81** E2
Doğukaraağaç: Turkey **56** B2
DOHA: Qatar **55** H9
Dohuk: & *Prov.*, Iraq **57** H3
Doi Luang: *range*, Laos **64** C3
Dojran: Yugoslavia **39** S16
Doka: Sudan **54** E12
Dokka: & *riv.*, Norway **47** M6
Dokkas: Sweden **46** R3
Dokkum: Netherlands **44** M2
Dokshitsy: Byelorussia **47** U9
Dol: France **36** D7
Dolak I.: West Irian, Indonesia **61** M13
Dolbeau: Que., Canada **89** P1
Dolbenmaen: Gwyn., Wales **27** N14
Dôle: France **40** L8
Dolenji Logatec: Yugo. **41** U10
Dolgellau: Gwyn., Wales **27** O14
Dolina: Ukraine **43** T12
Dolinsk: U.S.S.R. **63** ZZ5
Dolinskaya: Ukraine **50** D5
Dolisic: *see* Loubomo
Dollar: Central, Scotland **29** O7
Dollar Law: *mtn.*, Borders, Scotland **29** P8
Dolle: E. Germany **45** R3
Dolní Dvořiště: Czech. **41** U7
Dolní Kounice: Czech. **45** W6
Dolní Kubin: Czech. **43** Q12
Dolo: Ethiopia **76** F2
Dolomites: *mtns.*, Italy **41** R9
Doloon (Sergelen): Mongolia **62** T5
Dolores: Argentina **96** D4
Dolores: & *riv.*, Colo., U.S.A. **93** F5
Dolores: Guatemala **86** L14
Dolores: Mexico **93** F7
Dolores: Spain **35** F17
Dolores: Uruguay **96** D3
Dolphin & Union Str.: N.W.T., Canada **84** H4
Dolphinton: Strath., Scot. **29** P8
Dölsach: Austria **41** S9
Dolton: Devon, England **24** N18
Dolwyddelan: Gwyn., Wales **27** O13
Dolzhanskaya: U.S.S.R. **50** E5
Dom: *mtn.*, Switzerland **40** N9
Doma: Nigeria **81** F3
Domadere: Somalia **76** F2
Domaniç: Turkey **56** A2
Domažlice: Czechoslovakia **45** S6
Dombås: Norway **47** L5
Dombasle: France **36** M7
Dombe Grande: Angola **73** G12
Dómbóvár: Hungary **43** Q13
Dombrád: Hungary **43** R12
Domburg: Netherlands **44** J4
Domel: *i.*, Mergui Arch., Burma **59** R12
Domène: France **40** L10
Domfront: France **36** E7

* Dj in Indonesian names has now been replaced by J.

For Abbreviations see list on p.113. Italic type, e.g. *Ephesus*, refers to historical names not on maps. Capital letters, e.g. MADRID, show capitals of countries; small capital letters, e.g. CADIZ, show capitals of provinces, etc. General notes p.116.

138 Dominica—Durocortorum

Dominica: *Br. associated state* 87 c3
Cap.: Roseau
Area: 290 sq. miles (751 sq. km.)
Pop.: 72,000 (*1971 E*)

Dominican Republic 87 m14
Cap.: Santo Domingo
Area: 18,704 sq. miles (48,443 sq. km.)
Pop.: 4,188,000 (*1971 E*)

Dominion City: Man., Can. 92 H3
Dömitz: E. Germany 45 R2
Domme: France 37 G11
Dommitzsch: E. Germany 45 S4
Domo (Damot): Ethiopia 79 R18
Domodossola: Italy 40 O9
Dom Pedrito: Brazil 96 E3
Dompierre-sur-Besbre: Fr. 37 J9
Domsjö: Sweden 46 Q5
Domuyo: *mtn.*, Argentina 96 A4
Domvraina: Greece 39 S17
Domžale: Yugoslavia 41 U9
Don: *riv.*, Gram., Scotland 28 R5
Don: *riv.*, S. Yorks., England 27 U12
Don: *riv.*, U.S.S.R. 50 F5
Donabate: Dublin, Repub. of Ireland 30 J13
Donagh: Ferm., N. Ireland 30 G11
Donaghadee: Down, N. Irel. 30 K10
Donaghmore: Down, N. Irel. 30 J11
Donaghmore: Laois, Repub. of Ireland 31 F14
Donaghmore: Tyr., N. Irel. 30 H10
Donaghmoyne: Monaghan, Repub. of Ireland 30 H11
Donald: Vict., Australia 71 E11
Donaldsonville: La., U.S.A. 90 F10
Donald Station: B.C., Can. 92 D2
Donalsonville: Ga., U.S.A. 91 J10
Donard: Wick., Repub. of Ireland 31 H13
Donau (Danube): *riv.*, W. Ger./Austria 42 N12
Donaueschingen: W. Germany 40 O8
Donauwörth: W. Germany 41 Q7
Donawitz: Austria 41 V8
Don Benito: Spain 35 D17
Doncaster: S. Yorks., England 27 T12
Dondo: Angola 73 G11
Dondo: Mozambique 77 D6
Dondra Head: *cape.*, Sri Lanka 58 O13
Donegal: *& bay*, Don., Repub. of Ireland 30 E10
Donegal: *Co.*, Repub. of Ireland (*co. town* Lifford) 30 F10
Doneraile: Cork, Repub. of Ireland 31 D15
Donets: *riv.*, U.S.S.R. 50 E5
Donetsk: Ukraine 50 E5
Donfar: Ethiopia 79 R18
Donfar, El: Somalia 79 R17
Donga: *& riv.*, Nigeria 81 G3
Dongara: W. Australia 68 A5
Dongba: Tibet, China 59 O9
Donges: France 36 C8
Donggala: Celebes 65 F7
Dong Hoi: Vietnam 64 D3
Donglik: China 53 N4
Dongo: Zaire 76 A2
DONGOLA: Northern, Sudan 54 D11
Dongou: Congo 81 H4
Dongphu: Vietnam 64 D3
Doñihue: Chile 96 A3
Donington: Lincs., England 27 V14
Donington: Salop, England 27 R14
Donington on Bain: Lincs., England 27 V13
Doniphan: Mo., U.S.A. 88 F7
Donja Lendava: Yugo. 41 W9
Donja-Stubica: Yugoslavia 41 V10
Donji Milanovac: Yugo. 39 S14
Donji Vakuf: Yugoslavia 38 P14
Donjon, Le: France 37 J9
Donko: Nigeria 81 F2
Don Martin, Lake: Mexico 93 G7
Dønna: *i.*, Norway 46 N3
Donnaz: Italy 40 N10
Donnelly: Alta., Canada 92 D1
Donner Pass: Calif., U.S.A. 93 C5
Donnington: Salop, Eng. 27 R14
Donnybrook: Natal, S. Afr. 75 H4
Donnybrook: Queens., Australia 70 G6
Donnybrook: W. Australia 68 B6
Donohill: Tip., Repub. of Ireland 31 E14
Donors Hills: *town*, Queens., Australia 69 G3
Donoughmore: Cork, Repub. of Ireland 31 D16
Donzenac: France 37 G10
Donzy: France 36 J8
Dooagh: Achill I., Repub. of Ireland 30 A12
Doocharry: Don., Repub. of Ireland 30 E10
Dooega: Achill I., Repub. of Ireland 30 A12
Doogort: Achill I., Repub. of Ireland 30 A11
Dookie: Vict., Australia 71 F11
Doon: Lim., Repub. of Irel. 31 E14
Doon: *riv.*, Strath., Scot. 29 N9
Doon, Loch: Strath./Dumf. & Gall., Scotland 29 N9
Doonaha: Clare, Repub. of Ireland 31 B14
Doondi: Queens., Australia 70 H7
Doonerak: *mtn.*, Alaska, U.S.A. 84 d4
Door Point: *cape*, La., U.S.A. 90 *Ins.*
Dopokoy: U.S.S.R. 50 E4
Dor: city on coast of ancient *Israel* at *et-Tantūrah* about 10 miles N. of Caesarea 55 a2
Dora, Lake: W. Australia 68 C4
Dora Baltea: *riv.*, Italy 40 N10
Dorada, La: Colombia 94 C2
Dorah Pass: Pak./Afghan. 55 M7
Dora Riparia: *riv.*, Italy 40 N10
Dorat, Le: France 37 G9
DORCHESTER: Dorset, Eng. 24 R18
Dorchester: Oxon., England 25 T16
Dordabis: SW. Africa 77 A7
Dordogne: *Dept.*, France (*cap.* Perigueux) 37 F11
Dordogne: *riv.*, France 37 E11
Dordrecht: Netherlands 44 K4
Dordrecht: S. Africa 75 G5
Dore: S. Yorks., England 27 S13
Dore: *riv.*, France 37 J10
Dore, Mont: *mtn.*, France 37 H10
Doré Lake: Sask., Canada 92 F2
Dorenni: Ethiopia 76 E1
Dores: Highland, Scotland 28 N5
Dores de Camaqua: Brazil 96 E3
Dôres do Indaiá: Brazil 94 H7
Dorfen: W. Germany 41 S7
Dorfmark: W. Germany 45 P3
Dorganata: Turkmen., U.S.S.R. 51 K6
Dori: Ethiopia 76 E1
DORI: Sahel, Upper Volta 80 E2
Doring: *riv.*, Cape Prov., S. Africa 74 C5
Doring: *riv.*, O.F.S., S. Afr. 75 *Ins.*
Doringdraai: S. Africa 74 E6
Doringkop: Trans., S. Afr. 75 H2
Doris: small district midway between Parnassos and the western end of the Gulf of Euboea 39 S17
Dorisvale: N. Territ., Austl. 68 E2
Dorking: Surrey, England 25 V17
Dormans: France 36 J6
Dornakal: Andhra Pradesh, India 58 O11
Dornbirn: Austria 40 P8
Dornburg: E. Germany 45 R4
Dornie: Highland, Scot. 28 L5
Dornoch: *& firth*, Highland, Scotland 28 N4
Dornock: Dumfries & Galloway, Scotland 29 P10
Dornum: W. Germany 44 N2
Dorohoi: Romania 43 U13
Dorohusk: Poland 43 S11
Doromo: Zaire 76 C2
Dorotea: Sweden 46 P4
Dorre I.: W. Australia 68 A5
Dorrigo: N.S.W., Australia 71 K8
Dorset: *Co.*, England (*co. town* Dorchester) 24 R18
Dorset Downs, North & South: *hills*, Dorset, Eng. 24 R18
Dortsen: W. Germany 44 M4
Dorstone: Hereford & Worcester, England 24 Q15
Dortmund: W. Germany 44 N4
Dortmund-Ems Canal: W. Germany 44 N3
Dörtyol: Turkey 56 E3
Dorum: W. Germany 44 O2
Doruma: Zaire 76 C2
Dosso: *& Dept.*, Niger 81 E2
Dossor: Kazakh., U.S.S.R. 50 H5
Dothan: Ala., U.S.A. 91 J10
Dötlingen: W. Germany 44 O3
Douai: France 36 J5
Douako: Guinea 80 B3
DOUALA: Littoral, Cameroun 81 F4
Douarnenez: *& bay*, France 36 A7
Doubala: Mali 80 C2
Double Mountain Fork: *riv.*, Tex., U.S.A. 90 A9
Doubs: *Dept.*, France (*cap.* Besançon) 40 M8
Doubs: *riv.*, France 40 L8
Doubtful Sound: South I., New Zealand 71 L17
Doudeville: France 36 F6
Doudou Mtns.: Gabon 81 G5
Doué: Ivory Coast 80 C3
Douékoué: Ivory Coast 80 C3
Douentza: Mali 80 D2
Douglas: Ariz., U.S.A. 93 F6
Douglas: Cork, Repub. of Ireland 31 E16
Douglas: Ga., U.S.A. 91 K10
DOUGLAS: I. of Man, U.K. 26 N11
Douglas: Strath., Scotland 29 O8
Douglas: S. Africa 74 E4
Douglas: Wyo., U.S.A. 92 F4
Douglasville: Ga., U.S.A. 91 J9
Douglas Water: *village*, Strathclyde, Scotland 29 O8
Douirat: Tunisia 32 E5
Doulevant-le-Château: Fr. 36 K7
Doullens: France 36 H5
Doulus Head: *cape*, Kerry, Repub. of Ireland 31 A16
Doumakaba: Cen. Afr. Rep. 76 B1
Doumé: Cameroun 81 G4
Douna: Mali 80 C2
Dounby: Mainland, Orkney Is. 28 P2
Doune: Central, Scotland 29 N7
Doune: Highland, Scot. 28 M4
Dounsou: Upper Volta 80 E2
Doupovské Hory: *mtns.*, Czechoslovakia 45 T5
Dourados: Brazil 95 G8
Dourdan: France 36 H7
Dourgne: France 37 H12
Douro: *Prov. & riv.*, Port. (*cap. of Prov.* Oporto) 35 B16
Douvres: France 36 E6
Douvres, Roches: *is.*, English Channel 36 C6
Dove: *riv.*, Derby./Staffs., England 27 S14
Dove Bay: Greenland 85 S2
DOVER: Del., U.S.A. 89 O6
Dover: Kent, England 25 Y17
Dover: N.H., U.S.A. 89 Q4
Dover: N.J., U.S.A. 89 O5
Dover: O.F.S., S. Africa 75 G3
Dover, Str. of: Eng./Fr. 25 Y18
Dover-Foxcroft: Maine, U.S.A. 89 R3
Doveridge: Derby., England 27 S14
Dovey: *riv.*, Gwynedd/Powys, Wales 27 O14
Dovje: Yugoslavia 41 T9
Dovrefjell: *mtns.*, Norway 46 L5
Dowa: Malawi 77 D5
Dowagiac: Mich., U.S.A. 88 H5
Dowally: Tayside, Scotland 29 O6
Dowerin: W. Australia 68 B6
Dowlais: Mid Glam., Wales 24 P16
Dow Lake: Botswana 77 B7
Down: *Co.*, N. Ireland (*co. town* Downpatrick) 30 J11
Downham: Cambs., England 25 W15
Downham: Lancs., England 27 R12
Downham Market: Norf., England 25 W14
Downhill: Lon., N. Ireland 30 H9
DOWNPATRICK: Down, N. Ireland 30 K11
Downpatrick Head: *cape*, Mayo, Repub. of Ireland 30 C11
Downton: Wilts., England 25 S18
Dowra: Leit., Repub. of Irel. 30 E11
Dow Sar: Iran 57 L4
Dra: *watercourse*, Morocco 80 K9
Dra, Hamada of: *plat.*, Alg. 80 K9
Drac: *riv.*, France 40 M11
Drachten: Netherlands 44 M2
Drăgănești: Romania 39 T14
Drăgășani: Romania 39 T14
Draghoender: S. Africa 74 E4
DRAGUIGNAN: Var, France 40 M12
Drakensberg: *range*, S. Afr. 75 H5
Drake Passage: Southern Ocean 9 60S 60W
Drake Peak: Oreg., U.S.A. 92 C4
Dráma: Greece 39 T16
DRAMMEN: Buskerud, Nor. 47 M7
Drangadra: Gujarat, India 58 M10
Drangan: Tip., Repub. of Ireland 31 F14
Drangiana: ancient Greek name of district in E. Iran and W. Afghanistan N. of Helmand valley 55 K8
Dranse: E. Germany 45 S2
Dransfeld: W. Germany 45 P4
Draperstown: Lon., N. Irel. 30 H10
Drau (Dráva): *riv.*, Austria 41 S9
Dráva: *riv.*, Yugo./Hung. 39 Q14
Dravograd: Yugoslavia 41 V9
Drawsko: Poland 45 V2
Drawsko, Lake: Poland 45 W2
Drax: N. Yorks., England 27 U12
Draycott: Derby., England 27 T14
Draycott: Som., England 24 Q17
Draycott in the Moors: Staffs., England 27 R14
Drazen: Czechoslovakia 45 T6
Dre (Yangtze): *riv.*, China 59 Q8
Drebkau: E. Germany 45 U4
Drechu Rabdun: Chinghai, China 62 R8
Dreghorn: Strath., Scotland 29 M8
Drem: Lothian, Scotland 29 Q7
Drenovo: Bulgaria 39 T15
Drenthe: *Prov.*, Netherlands (*cap.* Assen) 44 M3
Drepanon, Cape: Greece 39 T17
DRESDEN: *& Dist.*, E. Ger. 45 T4
Dreux: France 36 G7
Drevsjø: Norway 47 N6
Drewe: Miss., U.S.A. 90 F9
Drewitz: E. Germany 45 S3
Dreżnik: Yugoslavia 41 V11
Drigg: Cumbria, England 26 P11
Drimnin: Strath., Scotland 29 K6
Drimoleague: Cork, Repub. of Ireland 31 C16
Drin: *riv.*, Alb./Yugo. 39 R15
Drina: *riv.*, Yugoslavia 39 Q14
Drinagh: Cork, Repub. of Ireland 31 C16
Drin Gulf: Albania 39 Q16
Dripsey: Cork, Repub. of Ireland 31 D16
Drisiyeh: Iran 57 L6
Drissa: Byelorussia 47 U9
Drniš: Yugoslavia 38 P15
Drobetae: Roman station on river Danube at Turnu-Severin, Romania 39 S14
Droëputs: S. Africa 74 D5
Drogheda: Louth, Repub. of Ireland 30 J12
Drogichin: Byelorussia 43 T10
Drogobych: Ukraine 43 S12
Droichead Nuadh (Newbridge): Kild., Repub. of Ireland 31 H13
Droitwich: Hereford & Worcester, England 24 R15
Drom: Tip., Repub. of Irel. 31 F14
Dromahair: Leit., Repub. of Ireland 30 E11
Dromara: Down, N. Ireland 30 J11
Dromcolliher: Lim., Repub. of Ireland 31 D15
Drôme: *Dept. & riv.*, France (*cap.* Valence-sur-Rhône) 37 L11
Dromin: Louth, Repub. of Ireland 30 J12
Dromina: Cork, Repub. of Ireland 31 D15
Dromiskin: Louth, Repub. of Ireland 30 J12
Dromod: Leit., Repub. of Ireland 30 F12
Dromore: Down, N. Ireland 30 J11
Dromore: Sligo, Repub. of Ireland 30 D11
Dromore: Tyr., N. Ireland 30 G10
Dronero: Italy 40 N11
Dronfield: Derby., England 27 T13
Dronley: Tayside, Scotland 29 P6
Dronne: *riv.*, France 37 F10
Droogegrond: S. Africa 74 D4
Drosendorf: Austria 41 V7
Drosh: N.W. Front. Prov., Pak. 58 M7
Droué: France 36 G7
Drouin: Vict., Australia 71 F12
Drozhzhanoye: U.S.S.R. 50 G4
Druentia: Roman name of river Durance, France 40 K12
Drug: Madhya Pradesh, India 58 O10
Druid: Clwyd, Wales 27 P14
Drum: Monaghan, Repub. of Ireland 30 G11
Drumbeg: High., Scotland 28 L3
Drumburgh: Cumbria, Eng. 26 P10
Drumcliff: Sligo, Repub. of Ireland 30 D11
Drumclog: Strath., Scot. 29 N8
Drumcondra: Meath, Repub. of Ireland 30 H12
Drumcree: Westmeath, Repub. of Ireland 30 G12
Drumelzier: Borders, Scot. 29 P8
Drumfearn: Inner Hebr., Scotland 28 K5
Drumgask: High., Scotland 28 N5
Drumheller: Alta., Canada 92 E2
Drumkeerin: Leit., Repub. of Ireland 30 E11
Drumlish: Long., Repub. of Ireland 30 F12
Drumlithie: Gram., Scot. 28 R6
Drummond I.: Mich., U.S.A. 88 K3
Drummondville: Que., Can. 89 P3
Drummore: Dumfries & Galloway, Scotland 29 M10
Drumnadrochit: High., Scot. 28 N5
Drumnin: High., Scot. 29 K6
Drumone: Meath, Repub. of Ireland 30 G12
Drumquin: Tyr., N. Ireland 30 G10
Drumright: Okla., U.S.A. 90 C8
Drumshanbo: Leit., Repub. of Ireland 30 E11
Drumsna: Leit., Repub. of Ireland 30 F12
Drumsurn: Lon., N. Ireland 30 H10
Drvar: Yugoslavia 41 W11
Drwęca: *riv.*, Poland 43 Q10
Drybrook: Glos., England 24 Q16
Drygarn Fawr: *mtn.*, Powys, Wales 24 O15
Dry Harts: *riv.*, S. Africa 75 F3
Drymen: Central, Scotland 29 N7
Dry Mills: Mayo, Repub. of Ireland 30 D12
Drysdale: *riv.*, W. Australia 68 D3
Dry Tortugas: *is.*, Fla., U.S.A. 87 e13
Dschang: Cameroun 81 G3
Duagh: Kerry, Repub. of Ireland 31 C15
Duaringa: Queens., Austl. 70 H4
Duart Point: *cape*, Strathclyde, Scotland 29 K7
Duba: Czechoslovakia 45 U5
Dubai: U.A.E. 55 J9
Dubawnt: *riv. & lake*, N.W.T., Canada 84 j5
Dubbo: N.S.W., Australia 71 H9
Düben: E. Germany 45 S4
Dubh Artach: *rock*, Inner Hebr., Scotland 29 H7
Dublin: Ga., U.S.A. 91 K9
DUBLIN (Baile Atha Cliath): & Co., Repub. of Irel. 31 J13
Dublin: Tex., U.S.A. 90 B9
Dublin Bay: Dublin, Repub. of Ireland 31 J13
Dubna: U.S.S.R. 50 E4
Dubno: Ukraine 43 T11
Du Bois: Pa., U.S.A. 89 M5
Dubrae: Roman name of Dover, Kent, England 25 Y17
DUBRÉKA: *& Reg.*, Guinea 80 B3
Dubrovitsa: Ukraine 43 U11
Dubrovnik (Ragusa): Yugo. 39 Q15
Dubuque: Iowa, U.S.A. 88 F4
Duchcov: Czechoslovakia 45 T5
Duchesne: Utah, U.S.A. 93 E4
Duchess: Queens., Austl. 69 F4
Ducie I.: (Br.), S. Pacific Ocean 7 25S 125W
Duck: *riv.*, Tenn., U.S.A. 91 H8
Duck Lake: *town*, Sask., Canada 92 F2
Duck Mtn.: Man., Canada 92 G2
Duclair: France 36 F6
Duddo: Northumb., Eng. 26 R8
Duddon: *riv.*, Cumbria, Eng. 26 P11
Duddon Sands: *est.*, Cumbria, England 26 P11
Dudelange: Luxembourg 44 M6
Duderstadt: W. Germany 45 Q4
Dudhi: Uttar Pradesh, India 59 O10
Dudinka: U.S.S.R. 48 k4
Dudley: W. Mid., England 27 R14
Dudo: *well*, Somalia 79 S18
Dudub: Ethiopia 79 R18
Duffel: Belgium 44 K4
Duffield: Derby., England 27 T14
Duff Is. (Br.), Pacific O. 67 N3
Dufftown: Gram., Scotland 28 P5
Duffus: Gram., Scotland 28 P4
Dufton: Cumbria, England 26 R10
Dugi Otok: *i.*, Yugoslavia 41 V12
Dugo Selo: Yugoslavia 41 W10
Duhak: Iran 55 J8
Duich, Loch: High., Scot. 28 L5
Duida, Cerro: *mtn.*, Ven. 94 D3
Duin Dui: New Hebrides 67 N5
Duineveld: SW. Africa 74 B1
Duino: Italy 41 T10
Duirinish: *dist.*, I. of Skye, Inner Hebr., Scotland 28 H5
Duirinish: High., Scot. 28 K5
Duisburg-Hamborn: W. Ger. 44 M4
Dukana: Kenya 76 E2
Duke of Gloucester Is.: Tuamotu Arch. 83 g4
Dukestown: Gwent, Wales 24 P16
Duk Fadiat: Sudan 76 D1
Duk Faiwil: Sudan 76 D1
Dukhan: Qatar 55 H9
Dukhani: Ethiopia 76 E1
Dukhovshchina: U.S.S.R. 50 D3
Dukinfield: Gt. Man., Eng. 27 R13
Dukla: Poland 43 R12
Dukszty: Lithuania, U.S.S.R. 47 U9
Duku: Nigeria 81 G2
Dula: Zaire 76 B2
Dulaim: *tribal area*, Iraq 57 H4
Dulbydilla: Queens., Austl. 70 G6
Dulce: *riv.*, Argentina 96 C2
Duleek: Meath, Repub. of Ireland 30 J12
Dulgalakh: *riv.*, U.S.S.R. 49 P4
Dŭlgopol: Bulgaria 39 U15
Dull: Tayside, Scotland 29 O6
Dullabchorra: Assam, India 59 Q10
Dullingham: Cambs., Eng. 25 W15
Dullstroom: Trans., S. Afr. 75 J2
Dülmen: W. Germany 44 N4
Dulnainbridge: High., Scot. 28 O5
Dulovo: Bulgaria 39 U15
Duluth: Minn., U.S.A. 88 E2
Dulverton: Som., England 24 O17
Duma: Botswana 77 B6
Duma: Syria 56 E5
Dumaran: *& i.*, Philippines 64 F4
Dumarao: Philippines 64 G4
Dumaring: Borneo 65 F6
Dumas: Ark., U.S.A. 90 F9
Dumata: Ethiopia 79 Q18
Dumbarton: Strath., Scot. 29 M8
Dumboa: Nigeria 81 G2
Dumbrăveni: Romania 43 T13
DUMFRIES: Dumf. & Gall., Scotland 29 O9
Dumfries and Galloway: *Reg.*, Scotland (*cap.* Dumfries) 29 O9
Dumka: Bihar, India 59 P10
Dumlupinar: Turkey 56 B2
Dümmer See: *lake*, W. Ger. 44 O3
Dumoine, Lac: *lake*, Que., Canada 89 N2
Dumont d'Urville: *rsch. stn.*, Antarctica 9 70S 140E
Dun: Cher, France 37 H9
Dun: Meuse, France 36 L6
Dunaff Head: *cape*, Don., Repub. of Ireland 30 F9
Dunaföldvár: Hungary 43 Q13
Dunan: I. of Skye, Inner Hebr., Scotland 28 K5
Dunany Point: *cape*, Louth, Repub. of Ireland 30 J12
Dunarea (Danube): *riv.*, Bulgaria/Romania 39 U15
Dunav (Danube): *riv.*, Yugo. 39 R14
Dunay: U.S.S.R. 63 Y6
Dunayevtsy: Ukraine 43 U12
Dunback: South I., N.Z. 70 N17
Dunbar: Lothian, Scot. 29 Q7
Dunbar: Queens., Australia 69 G3
Dunbeath: High., Scotland 28 P3
Dunblane: Central, Scot. 29 O7
Dunblane: Sask., Canada 92 F2
Dunboyne: Meath, Repub. of Ireland 30 J13
Duncan: B.C., Canada 92 C3
Duncan: Okla., U.S.A. 90 C8
Duncan Passage: Andaman Is. 59 Q12
Duncan's: Jamaica 86 *Ins.*
Duncansby Head: *cape*, Highland, Scotland 28 P2
Dunchurch: War., Eng. 25 T15
Duncormick: Wex., Repub. of Ireland 31 H15
Duncow: Dumf. & Gall., Scot. 29 O9
DUNDALK (Dun Dealgan): Louth, Repub. of Ireland 30 J12
Dundalk Bay: Louth, Repub. of Ireland 30 J12
Dundas: Greenland 85 N2
Dundas: Ont., Canada 89 M4
Dundas: Tas., Australia 68 H8
Dundas, Lake: W. Australia 68 C6
Dundas Str.: Australia 68 E2
DUN DEALGAN (Dundalk): Louth, Repub. of Ireland 30 J12
DUNDEE: Tayside, Scotland 29 Q7
Dundee: *& Dist.*, Natal, S. Africa 75 J4
Dundonald: Down, N. Irel. 30 K10
Dundoo: Queens., Australia 70 F6
Dundrennan: Dumfries & Galloway, Scotland 29 O10
Dundrum: *& bay*, Down, N. Ireland 30 K11
Dundrum: Dublin, Repub. of Ireland 31 J13
Dundrum: Tip., Repub. of Ireland 31 E14
DUNEDIN: Otago, South I., New Zealand 71 N17
Dunedoo: N.S.W., Austl. 71 H9
Dunfanaghy: Don., Repub. of Ireland 30 F9
Dunfermline: Fife, Scotland 29 P7
Dungannon: Tyr., N. Irel. 30 H10
Dungapur: Rajasthan, India 58 M10
Dungarvan: Kilk., Repub. of Ireland 31 G14
Dungarvan: *& harbour*, Wat., Repub. of Ireland 31 F15
Dungas: Niger 81 F2
Dungavel Hill: Strathclyde, Scotland 29 N8
Dungeness: *cape*, Kent, Eng. 25 X18
Dungiven: Lon., N. Ireland 30 H10
Dunglow: Don., Repub. of Ireland 30 E10
Dungog: N.S.W., Australia 71 J9
Dungourney: Cork, Repub. of Ireland 31 E16
Dungowan: N.S.W., Austl. 71 J8
Dungu: Zaire 76 C2
Dunham, Little: Norf., Eng. 25 X14
Dunholme: Lincs., England 27 V13
Dunipace: Central, Scotland 29 O7
Dunkassa: Benin 81 E2
Dunkeld: Tayside, Scotland 29 O6
Dunkellin: *riv.*, Galway, Repub. of Ireland 31 D13
Dunkerque (Dunkirk): Fr. 36 H4
Dunkerrin: Offaly, Repub. of Ireland 31 F14
Dunkery Beacon: *hill*, Som., England 24 O17
Dunkineely: Don., Repub. of Ireland 30 E10
Dunkirk (Dunkerque): Fr. 36 H4
Dunkirk: Ind., U.S.A. 88 J5
Dunkirk: N.Y., U.S.A. 89 M4
Dunkur: Ethiopia 79 M7
Dunkwa: Ghana 80 D3
Dún Laoghaire (Kingstown): Dublin, Repub. of Ireland 31 J13
Dunlavin: Wick., Repub. of Ireland 31 H13
Dunleer: Louth, Repub. of Ireland 30 J12
Dun-le-Palleteau: France 37 G9
Dunlop: Strath., Scotland 29 M8
Dunloy: Antrim, N. Ireland 30 J9
Dunmanus: Cork, Repub. of Ireland 31 B16
Dunmanway: Cork, Repub. of Ireland 31 C16
Dunmarra: N. Territ., Austl. 68 E3
Dunmore: Galway, Repub. of Ireland 30 D12
Dunmore: Pa., U.S.A. 89 O5
Dunmore East: Wat., Repub. of Ireland 31 H15
Dunmore Town: Bahamas 91 N13
Dunmow, Great: Essex, Eng. 25 W16
Dunmurry: Antrim, N. Irel. 30 J10
Dunn: N.C., U.S.A. 91 M8
Dunnamanagh: Tyr., N. Irel. 30 G10
Dunnellon: Fla., U.S.A. 91 K11
Dunnet: *& head*, High., Scot. 28 P2
Dunning: Tayside, Scotland 29 O7
Dunnington: N. Yorks., Eng. 27 U12
Dunnottar: Trans., S. Africa 74 N*Ins.*
Dunolly: Vict., Australia 71 E11
Dunoon: Strath., Scotland 29 M8
Dunqul: *well*, Egypt 54 D10
Dunragit: Dumfries & Galloway, Scotland 29 M10
Duns: Borders, Scotland 29 R8
Dunscore: Dumfries & Galloway, Scotland 29 O9
Dunsford: Devon, England 24 O18
Dunshaughlin: Meath, Repub. of Ireland 30 H12
Dunsmuir: Calif., U.S.A. 92 C4
Dunstable: Beds., England 25 U16
Dunster: Som., England 24 P17
Dun's Tew: Oxon., England 25 T16
Dunston: Lincs., England 27 V13
Dunston: Staffs., England 27 R14
Dunsyre: Strath., Scotland 29 P8
Dunton Bassett: Leics., Eng. 27 T14
Duntroon: A.C.T., Austl. 71 H10
Duntroon: South I., N.Z. 70 N17
Dunvegan: *& loch*, I. of Skye, Inner Hebr., Scotland 28 H5
Dunvegan Head: *cape*, Inner Hebr., Scotland 28 H4
Dunwich: Suff., England 25 Z15
Duongdong: Vietnam 64 C4
Duparquet: Que., Canada 89 M1
Duperre Is.: Natuna Is., Indonesia 65 D6
Dupree: S. Dak., U.S.A. 92 G3
Duquesne: Pa., U.S.A. 89 M5
Du Quoin: Ill., U.S.A. 88 G6
Dura: Jordan 55 b3
Durack Range: W. Australia 68 D3
Durack: *riv.*, W. Australia 68 D3
Dura-Europus: Graeco-Roman city at Salahiya, E. Syria 57 G4
Durak: Iran 57 L5
Durak: Turkey 39 V17
Durance: *riv.*, France 40 L12
Durand: Wis., U.S.A. 88 F3
Durango: Colo., U.S.A. 93 F5
DURANGO: *& State*, Mexico 86 j13
Durango: Spain 35 E15
Durant: Miss., U.S.A. 90 G9
Durant: Okla., U.S.A. 90 C8
Durazno: Uruguay 96 D3
Durazzo (Durrës): Albania 39 Q16
Durban: France 37 H13
Durban: Natal, S. Africa 75 J4
Durbanville: S. Africa 74 C6
Durbe: Latvia, U.S.S.R. 47 R8
Durbuy: Belgium 44 L5
Düren: W. Germany 44 M5
Durge Nor: *lake*, Mongolia 49 L8
DURHAM: *& Co.*, England 26 S10
Durham: N.C., U.S.A. 91 M8
Durham: Ont., Canada 88 L3
Durham Downs: Queens., Australia 69 G5
Durian Tipus: Malaya, Malaysia 65 c12
Durius: Roman name of river Douro, Spain and Portugal 35 B16
Durlach: W. Germany 40 O7
Durma: Saudi Arabia 54 G10
Durmitor: *mtn.*, Yugoslavia 39 Q15
Durness: Highland, Scotland 28 M2
Dürnkrut: Austria 41 W7
Durnovaria: Romano-British town at Dorchester, Dorset, England 24 R18
Durobrivae: Roman settlement at Castor about 4 miles W. of Peterborough, Cambs., England 27 V14
Durobrivae: Romano-British town at Rochester, Kent, England 25 W17
Durocortorum: Roman name of Gallic centre at Reims, France 36 K6

Durong—El Fashn 139

Durong: Queens., Austl. **70** J5
Durostorum: Roman camp on river Danube at Silistra, Ruse, Bulgaria **39** U14
Durovernum Cantiacorum: Romano-British town at Canterbury, Kent, Eng. **25** Y17
Durrës (Durazzo): Albania **39** Q16
Durrie: Queens., Australia **69** G5
Durrington: Wilts., England **25** S17
Durrohrsdorf: E. Germany **45** T4
Durrow: Laois, Repub. of Ireland **31** G14
Durrow: Offaly, Repub. of Ireland **31** F13
Durrus: Cork, Repub. of Ireland **31** B16
Dursey: *i. & cape*, Repub. of Ireland **31** A16
Dur Sharrukin: palace of Assyrian kings at *Khorsabad* few miles N. of Mosul, Iraq **57** H3
Dursley: Glos., England **24** R16
Dursunbey: Turkey **56** A2
Durtal: France **36** E8
Duru: *tribal area*, Sau. Arab. **55** J10
Durud: Iran **57** L5
D'Urville, Cape: W. Irian, Indonesia **66** G2
D'Urville I.: New Zealand **70** O15
Durwuljin: Inner Mongolia, China **62** S6
Dush: Egypt **54** D10
DUSHANBE: Tadzhik., U.S.S.R. **51** L7
Dusheti: Georgia, U.S.S.R. **50** F6
Dusky Sound: South I., N.Z. **71** L17
DÜSSELDORF: *& Dist.*, North Rhine-Westphalia, W. Germany **44** M4
Dutch Harbor: Aleutians **84** C7
Duvan: U.S.S.R. **50** J3
Duwadami: Saudi Arabia **54** F10
Duwum, Ustan (2nd Prov.): Iran **55** H7
Duxford: Cambs., England **25** W15
Duzce: Turkey **56** B1
Duzdab (Zahidan): Iran **55** K9
Duzza: Ethiopia **76** E1
Dve-Mogili: Bulgaria **39** T15
Dverberg: Vesterålen, Nor. **46** O2
Dvina, West: *riv.*, U.S.S.R. **47** T8
Dvor: Yugoslavia **41** W10
Dvorets: U.S.S.R. **51** R3
Dvůr Králové: Czech. **45** V5
Dwaal: S. Africa **75** F5
Dwarka: Gujarat, India **58** L10
Dwight: Ill., U.S.A. **88** G5
Dwingfontein: S. Africa **75** F6
Dwyka: S. Africa **74** D6
Dyasonsklip: S. Africa **74** D4
Dyat'kovo: U.S.S.R. **50** D4
Dyatlovo: Byelorussia **43** T10
Dyce: *& airfield*, Grampian, Scotland **28** R5
Dyer Cape: N.W.T., Canada **85** n4
Dyer Bay: N.W.T., Canada **84** g2
Dyerem: *riv.*, Cameroun **81** G3
Dyersburg: Tenn., U.S.A. **88** G7
Dyersville: Iowa, U.S.A. **88** F4
Dyfed: *Co.*, Wales (*co. town* Carmarthen) **24** N15
Dyje (Thaya): *riv.*, Czech. **45** W7
Dyke: Grampian, Scotland **28** O4
Dylife: Powys, Wales **27** O14
Dymchurch: Kent, England **25** X17
Dymer: Ukraine **50** D4
Dymock: Glos., England **24** R16
Dyrrachium: later Greek and Roman name of *Epidamnus*, city at Durrës, Albania **39** Q16
Dysart: Fife, Scotland **29** P7
Dyserth: Clwyd, Wales **27** P13
Dysseldorp: S. Africa **74** E6
Dza (Mekong): *riv.*, China **62** R8
Dzabhan: *riv.*, Mongolia **62** R5
Dzamin Ude: Mongolia **62** U6
Dzau Dzhikau (Ordzhonikidze): U.S.S.R. **50** F6
Džban: *geog. reg.*, Czechoslovakia **45** T5
Dzerzhinsk: Byelorussia **47** U10
Dzerzhinsk: U.S.S.R. **50** F3
Dzezdiy: Kazakh., U.S.S.R. **51** L5
Dzezkazgan: Kazakh., U.S.S.R. **51** L5
Dzhala-Abad: Kirgiz., U.S.S.R. **51** M6
Dzhalilabad: Azerbaydzhan, U.S.S.R. **57** L2
Dzhalinda: U.S.S.R. **49** O7
Dzhaman Sor, Lake: Kazakh., U.S.S.R. **50** H5
Dzhambeyty: Kazakh., U.S.S.R. **50** H4
DZHAMBUL: *& Reg.*, Kazakh., U.S.S.R. **51** M6
Dzhankoy: U.S.S.R. **50** D5
Dzhansugurov: Kazakh., U.S.S.R. **51** N5
Dzhardhan: U.S.S.R. **49** O4
Dzhebel: Turkmen, U.S.S.R. **50** H7
Dzhebrail: Azerbaydzhan, U.S.S.R. **57** K2
Dzherba: U.S.S.R. **49** n5
Dzhetygara: Kazakh., U.S.S.R. **51** K4
Dzhirgatal': Tadzhik., U.S.S.R. **51** M7
Dzhizak: Uzbek., U.S.S.R. **51** L6
Dzhul'fa: Nakhichevan, Azerbaydzhan, U.S.S.R. **57** J2
Dzhusaly: Kazakh., U.S.S.R. **51** K5
Dzialdowo: Poland **43** R10
Dzierżoniów: Poland **43** P11
Dzioua: Algeria **32** D5
Dziwnów: Poland **45** U1
Dzokang: Tibet, China **62** R9
Dzungaria: *geog. reg.*, Sinkiang, China **51** P6

Eads: Colo., U.S.A. **93** G5
Eagle: Alaska, U.S.A. **84** e5
Eagle Grove: Iowa, U.S.A. **88** E4
Eaglehawk: Vict., Australia **71** F11
Eagle Lake: Maine, U.S.A. **89** R2
Eagle Lake: *city*, Tex., U.S.A. **90** C11
Eagle Pass: Tex., U.S.A. **93** G7
Eagle Peak: N. Mex., U.S.A. **93** F6
Eagle River: *city*, Wis., U.S.A. **88** G3
Eaglesfield: Dumfries & Galloway, Scotland **29** P9
Eaglesham: Strath., Scotland **29** N8
Eakring: Notts., England **27** U13
Ealing: Gt. Ldn., England **25** V16
Earby: Lancs., England **27** R12
Eardisley: Hereford & Worcester, England **24** Q15
Earle: Ark., U.S.A. **90** F8
Earlestown: Mers., England **27** Q13
Earls Barton: Northants., England **25** U15
Earls Colne: Essex, England **25** X16
Earlsferry: Fife, Scotland **29** Q7
Earl Shilton: Leics., England **27** T14
Earl Soham: Suff., England **25** Y15
Earlston: Borders, Scotland **29** Q8
Earl Stonham: Suff., Eng. **25** Y15
Earn: *riv.*, Tayside, Scotland **29** O7
Earn, Loch: Tay., Scotland **29** N7
Earn, Strath.: *val.*, Tayside, Scotland **29** O7
Earsdon: Northumb., Eng. **26** T9
Easebourne: W. Sussex, Eng. **25** U17
Easington: Durham, Eng. **26** T10
Easington: Humb., England **27** W12
Easingwold: N. Yorks., Eng. **27** T11
Eask, Lough: Don., Repub. of Ireland **30** E10
Easky: Sligo, Repub. of Irel. **30** D11
Easley: S.C., U.S.A. **91** K8
East: *Dist.*, Botswana **75** G2
East Aberthaw: S. Glam., Wales **24** P17
East Allington: Devon, Eng. **24** O19
East Anglia: *geog. reg.*, Norf./Suff., England **25** X15
East Angus: Que., Canada **89** Q3
East Barkwith: Lincs., Eng. **27** V13
East Bay: La., U.S.A. **90** *Ins.*
East Bergholt: Suff., Eng. **25** Y16
EAST BERLIN: East Germany **45** T3
East Beskids: *mtns.*, Czech./Poland **43** R12
East Bierley: W. Yorks., Eng. **27** S12
Eastbourne: E. Sussex, Eng. **25** W18
Eastbourne: North I., N.Z. **70** P15
East Bridgeford: Notts., Eng. **27** U14
East Budleigh: Devon, Eng. **24** P18
East Cape: North I., N.Z. **70** R13
East Caroline Basin: N. Pacific Ocean **7** 0 145E
East Chevington: Northumb., England **26** S9
East Chicago: Ind., U.S.A. **88** H5
East China Sea: Japan/China **63** X9
Eastchurch: Kent, England **25** X17
East Coast: *Dist.*, N.I., New Zealand (*cap.* Gisborne) **70** Q14
East Coker: Som., England **24** Q18
East Cowes: I. of Wight, England **25** T18
Eastdean: E. Sussex, England **25** W18
East Dean: W. Sussex, Eng. **25** U18
East Dereham: Norf., Eng. **25** X14
East End: Sask., Canada **92** F3
Easter I.: (Chile), S. Pacific Ocean **7** 30S 110W
Easter Island Fracture Zone: S. Pacific Ocean **7** 30S 105W
Eastern: *Dist.*, Uganda **76** D2
Eastern: *Prov.*, Sierra Leone (*cap.* Kenema) **80** B3
Eastern: *Prov.*, Zambia (*cap.* Chipata) **77** D5
Eastern: *Reg.*, Ghana (*cap.* Koforidua) **80** D3
Eastern: *Reg.*, Kenya (*cap.* Embu) **76** E2
Eastern Cleddau: *riv.*, Dyfed, Wales **24** M16
Eastern Fields: *reef*, Austl. **69** H2
Eastern Ghats: *hills*, India **58** N11
Eastern Sayan: *mtns.*, U.S.S.R. **49** l7
Eastern Sierra Madre: *range*, Mexico **86** K13
Easter Ross: *geog. reg.*, Highland, Scotland **28** M4
East Falkland: *i.*, Falkland Is. (Br.) **95** F14
East Flanders: *Prov.*, Belg. (*cap.* Ghent) **44** J4
East Fork (White Riv.): *riv.*, Ind., U.S.A. **88** H6
East Frisian Is.: W. Germany **44** N2

East Germany: *Republic* **45** S3
Cap.: East Berlin
Area: 40,646 sq. miles (105,273 sq. km.)
Pop.: 15,962,000 (*1971 E*)

East Grinstead: W. Sussex, England **25** V17
East Haddon: Northants., England **25** T15
East Halton: Humb., England **27** V12
Eastham: Mers., England **27** Q13
East Harling: Norf., England **25** X15
East Hoathly: East Sussex, Eng. **25** W18
East Ilsley: Berks., England **25** T16
East Island: Magdalen Is., Canada **89** V2
East Jordan: Mich., U.S.A. **88** J3
East Kazakhstan: *Reg.*, Kazakhstan, U.S.S.R. (*cap.* Ust' Kamenogorsk) **51** O5
East Kilbride: Strath., Scot. **29** N8
East Kirus: S.W. Africa **74** C3
East Knoyle: Wilts., Eng. **24** R17
Eastland: Tex., U.S.A. **90** B9
East Lansing: Mich., U.S.A. **88** J4
Eastleach: Glos., England **25** S16
East Leake: Notts., England **27** T14
Eastleigh: Hants., England **25** T18
Eastleigh: Trans., S. Africa **75** G3
East Linton: Lothian, Scot. **29** Q8
East Liverpool: Ohio, U.S.A. **88** L5
East Loch Roag: I. of Lewis, Outer Hebr., Scotland **28** H3
East Loch Tarbert: Outer Hebr., Scotland **28** H4
East London: *& Dist.*, S. Africa **75** G6
East Looe: Corn., England **24** N19
Eastmain: Que., Canada **85** M7
Eastmain: *riv.*, Canada **85** m7
Eastman: Ga., U.S.A. **91** K9
East Mariana Basin: N. Pacific Ocean **7** 10N 150E
East Markham: Notts., Eng. **27** U13
East Norton: Leics., Eng. **27** U14
East Nunukan: *i.*, Borneo **65** F6
Eastoft: Humb., England **27** U12
Easton: Dorset, England **24** R18
Easton: Md., U.S.A. **89** N6
Easton: Pa., U.S.A. **89** O5
Easton: Suff., England **25** Y15
Easton, Great: Leics., Eng. **27** U14
East Pacific Basin: N. Pacific Ocean **7** 15N 155W
East Pacific Ridge: S. Pacific Ocean **7** 25S 110W
East Point: Ga., U.S.A. **91** J9
East Point: *cape*, Anticosti I., Canada **89** V1
East Point: *cape*, P.E.I., Can. **89** V2
Eastport: Maine, U.S.A. **89** S3
East Prairie: Mo., U.S.A. **88** G7
East Putford: Devon, Eng. **24** N18
East Quantoxhead: Som., England **24** P17
East Retford: Notts., Eng. **27** U13
Eastriggs: Dumfries & Galloway, Scotland **29** P10
Eastrington: Humb., Eng. **27** U12
East Rudham: Norf., Eng. **25** X14
Eastry: Kent, England **25** Y17
East St. Louis: Ill., U.S.A. **88** F6
East Scotia Basin: Southern Ocean **8** 60S 35W
East Siberian Sea: U.S.S.R. **49** S3
East Sussex: *Co.*, England (*co. town* Lewes) **25** W17
East Tavaputs Plat: Utah, U.S.A. **93** F5
East Timbalier I.: La., U.S.A. **90** *Ins.*
Eastville: Lincs., England **27** W13
Eastville: Va., U.S.A. **89** O7
Eastwell: Leics., England **27** U14
East Wemyss: Fife, Scotland **29** P7
East Winch: Norf., England **25** X14
East Witton: N. Yorks., England **26** S11
Eastwood: Notts., England **27** T13
East Worlington: Devon, England **24** O18
Eaton: Ches., England **27** Q13
Eaton: Ohio, U.S.A. **88** J6
Eaton Bray: Beds., England **25** U16
Eaton Rapids: *city*, Mich., U.S.A. **88** J4
Eaton Socon: Beds., England **25** V15
Eatonville: Wash., U.S.A. **92** C3
Eau Claire: Wis., U.S.A. **88** F3
Eauripik: *i.*, Caroline Is. **61** N10
Eauripik Ridge: N. Pacific Ocean **7** 0 140E
Eaux-Bonnes, Les: France **37** E13
Eauze: France **37** F12
Eaval: *hill*, Outer Hebr., Scotland **28** G4
Ebal: Biblical name of mtn. NE. of Nablus (*Shechem*), Jordan **55** b2
Ebberston: N. Yorks., England **26** U11
Ebbw Vale: Gwent, Wales **24** P16
Ebchester: Durham, England **26** S10
Ebeleben: E. Germany **45** Q4
Ebeneerde: S.W. Africa **74** B2
Ebenfurth: Austria **41** W8
Ebensee: Austria **41** T8
Eberbach: W. Germany **44** P6
Eber, Lake: Turkey **56** B2
Ebern: E. Germany **45** Q5
Ebersbach: East Germany **45** U4
Ebersberg: W. Germany **41** R7
Eberswalde: E. Germany **45** T3
Ebineyon: Eq. Guinea **81** G4
Ebingen: W. Germany **40** P7
Ebolova: Cameroun **81** G4
Ebony: S.W. Africa **74** A1
Ebora: Roman town at Evora, Portugal **35** C17
Eboracum, see *Eburacum*
Ebrach: W. Germany **45** Q6
Ebreichsdorf: Austria **41** W8
Ebro: *riv.*, Spain **35** F16
Ebrodunum: Roman town at Yverdon, Switzerland **40** M9
Ebsana: Ethiopia **76** F1
Ebstorf: W. Germany **45** Q2
Eburacum: Roman camp and city at York, England **27** T12
Eburones: Gallic tribe in area of Limburg, Belgium **44** L4
Ebusus: Roman name of island of Iviza (Balearics) **35** G17
Ecbatana: cap. of the Median Empire, now Hamadan, Iran **57** L4
Ecclefechan: Dumfries & Galloway, Scotland **29** P9
Eccles: Gt. Man., England **27** R13
Eccles: Norf., England **25** X15
Ecclesfield: S. Yorks., England **27** T13
Eccleshall: Staffs., England **27** R14
Eccleston: Ches., England **27** Q13
Eccleston: Lancs., England **27** Q12
Eccleston, Great: Lancs., England **27** Q12
Eceabat: Turkey (Dardan. *Inset*) **20** *Ins.*
Echallens: Switzerland **40** M9
Echizen, Cape: Japan **63** d3
Echmiadzin: Armenia, U.S.S.R. **57** J1
Echoing: *riv.*, Man., Canada **92** J1
Echt: Grampian, Scotland **28** R5
Echternach: Luxembourg **44** M6
Echuca: Vict., Australia **71** F11
Ecija: Spain **35** D18
Eck, Loch: Strath., Scotland **29** M7
Eckernförde: W. Germany **45** P1
Eckernförder Bay: W. Germany **45** Q1
Eckford: Borders, Scotland **29** R8
Eckington: Derby., England **27** T13
Eckington: Hereford & Worcester, England **24** R15
E. C. Manning Prov. Park: B.C., Canada **92** C3
Ecommog: France **36** F8
Ecouen: France **36** H6

Ecuador: *Republic* **94** B4
Cap.: Quito
Area.: 105,685 sq. miles (273,724 sq. km.)
Pop.: 6,508,000 (*1972 E*)

Ecueillé: France **36** G8
Edale: Derby., England **27** S13
Edam: Netherlands **44** L3
Eday: *i.*, Orkney Is., Scot **28** *Ins.*
Edd: Ethiopia **79** Q17
Ed Dab'a: Egypt **54** C8
Ed-Dacar: *well*, Libya **79** J4
ED DAMAR: Nile, Sudan **54** D11
Ed Debba: Sudan **54** D11
Edderton: High., Scot. **28** N4
Ed Dirr *see* El Dirr.
Eddleston: Borders, Scot. **29** P8
Eddrachillis Bay: Highland, Scotland **28** L3
ED DUEIM: White Nile, Sudan **54** D12
Eddystone Rocks: England **24** N19
Eddyville: Ky., U.S.A. **88** G7
Ede: Netherlands **44** L3
Ede: Nigeria **81** E3
Edea: Cameroun **81** G4
Edefors: Sweden **46** R3
Eden: Antrim, N. Ireland **30** K10
Eden: N.S.W., Australia **71** H11
Eden: Tex., U.S.A. **90** B10
Eden: *riv.*, Cumbria, England **26** Q10
Edenbridge: Kent, England **25** W17
Edenburg: *& Dist.*, O.F.S., S. Africa **75** F4
Edendale: South I., N.Z. **71** M18
Edenderry: Offaly, Repub. of Ireland **31** G13
Edenfield: Lancs., England **27** R12
Edenhope: Vict., Australia **71** D11
Edenkoben: W. Germany **44** O6
Edenside: *val.*, Cumbria, England **26** Q10
Edenton: N.C., U.S.A. **89** N7
Edenvale: Trans., S. Africa **74** N *Ins.*
Edenville: O.F.S., S. Africa **75** G3
Edeowie: S. Australia **71** C8
Eder: *riv.*, W. Germany **44** O4
Edern: Gwynedd, Wales **27** M14
Ederny: Ferm., N. Ireland **30** F10
Edessa: Graeco-Roman city at Urfa, Turkey **56** F3
Edgartown: Mass., U.S.A. **89** Q5
Edgefield: S.C., U.S.A. **91** L9
Edgehill: battlefield on ridge SE of Kineton, War., England **25** T15
Edge I.: Spitsbergen **48** D2
Edgemont: S. Dak., U.S.A. **92** G4
Edgerton: Wis., U.S.A. **88** G4
Edgeside: Lancs., England **27** R12
Edgeworthstown: Long., Repub. of Ireland **30** F12
Edgmond: Salop, England **27** R14
Edhessa: Greece **39** S16
Edievale: South I., N.Z. **71** M17
Edina: Liberia **80** B3
Edina: Mo., U.S.A. **88** E5
Edinbain: Inner Hebr., Scot. **28** J5
Edinburg: Tex., U.S.A. **90** B12
EDINBURGH: Lothian, Scotland **29** P8
Edington: Wilts., England **24** R17
EDIRNE (Adrianople): Edirne Prov., Turkey **39** U16
Edirne: *Prov.*, Turkey [*cap.* Edirne (Adrianople)] **39** U16
Edithburg: S. Australia **71** B10
Edith Cavell, Mount: Alta., Canada **92** D2
Edlingham: Northumb., Eng. **26** S9
Edmond: Okla., U.S.A. **90** C8
Edmondsley: Durham, Eng. **26** S10
EDMONTON: Alta., Canada **92** E2
Edmundston: N.B., Canada **89** R2
Edna: Texas, U.S.A. **90** C11
Ednam: Borders, Scotland **29** R8
Edolo: Italy **40** Q9
Edom: *geog. reg.*, Jordan **56** D6
Edom: name for ancient nation and region SW. of Dead Sea, Israel **56** D6
Edremit: *& Gulf*, Turkey **39** U17
Edrengiyn Nuruu: *range*, Mongolia **62** R6
Edri: Libya **78** G4
Edrom: Borders, Scotland **29** R8
Edsbyn: Sweden **47** O6
Edson: Alta., Canada **92** D2
Edward Lake: Uganda/Zaïre **76** C3
Edward, Mt.: Antarctica **9** 80S 70W
Edwards Plat: Tex., U.S.A. **93** G6
Edwardsville: Ill., U.S.A. **88** G6
Edwechterdamm: W. Germany **44** N2
Edwinstowe: Notts., England **27** T13
Edzell: Tayside, Scotland **29** Q6
Eekloo: Belgium **44** J4
Eendekuil: S. Africa **74** C6
Efate: *i.*, New Hebrides **67** N5
Eferding: Austria **41** U7
Effingham: Ill., U.S.A. **88** G6
Efsus: Turkey **56** E2
Egadi Is.: Sicily **38** N18
Eganville: Ont., Canada **89** N3
Egbe: Nigeria **81** F3
Egedesminde: Greenland **85** o4
Egegik: Alaska, U.S.A. **84** D6
Eg-khaya: U.S.S.R. **49** P4
Egeln: E. Germany **45** R4
Eger: Hungary **43** R13
Eger (Ohře): *riv.*, Czech. **45** T5
Egersund: Norway **47** J7
Egerton, Mount: W. Austl. **68** B4
Eggenfelden: W. Germany **41** S7
Eggleston: Durham, Eng. **26** S10
Egham: Surrey, England **25** U17
Eğil: Turkey **57** G2
Egletons: France **37** H10
Eglingham: Northumb., England **26** S9
Eglinton I.: N.W.T. Canada **84** H2
Egliseneuve-d'Entraigues: France **37** H10
Eglish: Tyr., N. Ireland **30** H11
Egloshayle: Corn., England **24** M18
Egloskerry: Corn., England **24** N18
Eglwyswrw: Dyfed, Wales **24** M15
Egmond Aan Zee: Netherlands **44** K3
Egmont, Cape: North I., New Zealand **70** O14
Egmont, Mount: North I., New Zealand **70** P14
Egremont: Cumbria, Eng. **26** O11
Eğridir: *& lake*, Turkey **56** B3
Egton: N. Yorks., England **26** U11
Egum: *i.*, New Guinea **69** J1
Eguzon: France **37** G9

Egypt: *Republic* **54** C9
Cap.: Cairo (El Qâhira)
Area: 386,872 sq. miles (1,001,998 sq. km.)
Pop.: 34,839,000 (*1972 E*)

Ehen: *riv.*, Cumbria, England **26** O11
Ehime: *Pref.*, Japan (*cap.* Matsuyama) **63** c4
Ehingen: W. Germany **40** P7
Ehra: W. Germany **45** Q3
Ehrwald: Austria **41** Q8
Eiao: *i.*, Marquesas Is. **83** g1
Eichstätt: W. Germany **41** R7
Eidfjord: Norway **47** K6
Eidsborg: Norway **47** L7
Eidsbugarden: Norway **47** L6
Eidsvold: Queens., Australia **70** J5
Eidsvoll: Norway **47** M6
Eifel: *mtns.*, W. Germany **44** M5
Eigg: *i.*, Inner Hebr., Scot. **28** J6
Eigg, Sound of: Inner Hebr., Scotland **28** J6
Eight Degree Chan: Indian Ocean **58** M13
Eighty Mile Beach: W. Austl. **68** C3
Eik: Somalia **79** R18
Eikefjord: (*part of* Flora), Norway **47** J6
Eiken: Norway **47** K7
Eikenhof: Trans., S. Afr. **74** M*Ins.*
Eil: Somalia **79** R18
Eil, Loch: Scotland **29** L6
Eil Chillako: Ethiopia **76** F2
Eildon, Lake: *res.*, Vict., Austl. **71** G11
Eilean Mor: *i.*, Outer Hebr., Scotland **28** G3
Eilean Trodday: *i.*, Inner Hebr., Scotland **29** J4
Eileen, Lake: N.W.T., Can. **84** J5
Eilenburg: E. Germany **45** S4
Eilsleben: E. Germany **45** R3
Einasleigh: *& riv.*, Queens., Australia **69** G3
Einbeck: W. Germany **45** P4
Eindhoven: Netherlands **44** L4
Eindpaal: SW. Africa **73** H15
Einich: *mtn.*, Scotland **28** O5
Einsiedeln: Switzerland **40** O8
Einville: France **40** M7
Eion: Greek city on E. side of mouth of Struma river, Greece **39** S16
Eire: *see under* **Ireland.**
Eirunepé: Brazil **94** D5
Eiseb: *riv.*, S.W. Africa **77** A7
Eisenach: E. Germany **45** Q5
Eisenburg: E. Germany **45** R5
Eisenerz: Austria **41** U8
Eisenhüttenstadt: Frankfurt, East Germany **45** U3
Eisenkappel: Austria **41** U9
EISENSTADT: Burgenland, Austria **41** W8
Eisfeld: E. Germany **45** Q5
Eisleben: E. Germany **45** R4
Eitorf: W. Germany **44** N5
Ejea de los Caballeros: Spain **35** F15
Ejeda: Malagasy Rep. **73** N14
Ejura: Ghana **80** D3
Ejutla de Crespo: Mexico **86** K14
Ekenäs: *see* Tammisaari.
Ekeren: Belgium **44** K4
Eket: Nigeria **81** F4
Eketahuna: North I., N.Z. **70** P15
Ekohla: Malawi **77** D5
Ekombe: Zaïre **76** B2
Ekron: city of ancient *Philistia* about 4 miles SSE. of Yibna, Israel **55** a3
Eksjö: Sweden **47** O8
Ekwendeni: Malawi **77** D5
Ekybastuz-Ugol': Kazakh., U.S.S.R. **51** N4
El Aaiun: Western Sahara **78** B4
El Aarida: Lebanon **56** D4
Elaeus: Greek city near C. Helles at tip of Gallipoli penin., Turkey **39** U16
El Afweina: Somalia **79** R17
El Agheila: Libya **33** F5
Elai: Somalia **79** R18
El 'Aiyat: Egypt **56** B7
El 'Al: Syria **55** b2
El 'Alamein: Egypt **54** C8
El Alamo: Mexico **93** D6
Elam: Iran **57** K5
Elam: ancient kingdom and people E. of Lower Tigris in and to S. of Lorestan, Iran **57** L5
El 'Âmirîya: Egypt **56** A6
El Amria: Algeria **35** F19
Elands: *riv.*, Trans., S. Afr. **75** G2
Elandsvlei: S. Africa **74** C6
El Aouinet: Algeria **38** K19
El Aricha: Algeria **80** L8
El 'Arish: *& wadi*, Egypt **56** C6
Elasa: city of ancient *Israel* about 10 miles NNE. of Jerusalem **55** b3
EL ASNAM (Orléansville): *& Dept.*, Algeria **35** G18
Elassón: Greece **39** S17
Elatea: Greek city of N. *Phocis* between Amfiklia and Levadhia **39** S17
El 'Auja: Egypt **56** D6
Elayu: Somalia **79** R17
Elâzığ: *& Prov.*, Turkey (*cap.* Elâzığ) **56** F2
Elba: Ala., U.S.A. **91** H10
Elba: *i.*, Italy **38** M15
El Bab: Syria **56** E3
El Ballâh: Egypt (Suez Canal *Inset*) **32** *Ins.*
El Banco: Colombia **94** C2
El Barco de Avila: Spain **35** D16
Elbasan: Albania **39** R16
El Baúl: Venezuela **94** D2
El Bawiti: Egypt **54** C9
El Bayadh: Algeria **78** E3
Elbe: *riv.*, W. & E. Ger./Czech. **44** P2
Elbert, Mount: Colo., U.S.A. **93** F5
Elberton: Ga., U.S.A. **91** K8
Elbeuf: France **36** G6
Elbistan: Turkey **56** E2
Elbląg: Poland **43** Q9
El Boquete: Chile **96** B1
El Borouj: Morocco **80** K8
Elbow: Sask., Canada **92** F2
El Brega: Libya **33** F5
Elbrus: *mtn.*, Georgia, U.S.S.R. **50** F6
Elbsandstein Gebirge: *mtns.*, E. Germany **45** T5
El Buitz: Morocco (Gib., *Inset*) **32** *Ins.*
El Bur: Somalia **79** R19
Elburg: Netherlands **44** L3
El Burgo de Osma: Spain **35** E16
Elburz Mtns: Iran **55** H7
El Calafate: Argentina **95** C14
El Campo: Tex., U.S.A. **90** C11
El Canelo: Mexico **93** G8
El Centro: Calif., U.S.A. **93** D6
Elche: Spain **35** F17
El Chorro: Argentina **96** C1
El Cobre: Mexico **93** G7
El Cuyo: Mexico **86** L13
Eldama Ravine: Kenya **76** E2
EL DAR EL BEIDA (Casablanca): *& Pref.*, Morocco **80** K8
Eldena: E. Germany **45** R2
El Dirr: Egypt **79** L5
El Diviso: Colombia **94** B3
El Djem: Tunisia **32** E4
El Djezair (Algiers): Algeria **35** H18
Eldon: Iowa, U.S.A. **88** E5
Eldon: Mo., U.S.A. **88** E6
El Donfar: Somalia **79** R17
Eldora: Iowa, U.S.A. **88** E4
Eldorado: Argentina **96** E2
El Dorado: Ark., U.S.A. **90** E9
Eldorado: Brazil **96** F1
Eldorado: Ill., U.S.A. **88** G7
El Dorado: Kans., U.S.A. **90** C7
Eldorado: Mexico **93** F8
Eldorado Springs: Mo., U.S.A. **90** D7
Eldoret: Kenya **76** E2
Electra: Tex., U.S.A. **90** B8
Electric Peak: Mont., U.S.A. **92** E3
Elegeia: ancient city of Armenia on upper Euphrates about 40 miles W. of Erzurum, Turkey **57** G2
Elekmonar: U.S.S.R. **51** P4
Elena: Bulgaria **39** T15
Elephant: *riv.*, SW. Africa **74** C2
Elephant Butte Dam: N. Mex., U.S.A. **93** F6
Elephantine: Egyptian city site at *Philae*, nr. Aswan, Egypt **54** D10
Elerch: Dyfed, Wales **24** O15
El Ergh: Libya **79** J4
El Escorial: Spain **35** D16
El Eulma: Algeria **35** J18
Eleusis: Greek village of W. *Attica* at head of Saronic G. **39** S17
Eleutherea: fort of W. *Attica* on frontier with *Boeotia* 10 miles S. of Thebes **39** S17
Eleuthera I.:Bahamas **91** N13
Elevsis: Greece **39** S17
El Faiyum: Egypt **56** B7
EL FASHER: Northern Dafur, Sudan **79** K7
El Fashn: Egypt **54** D9

For Abbreviations see list on p.113. Italic type, e.g. *Ephesus*, refers to historical names not on maps. Capital letters; e.g. MADRID, show capitals of countries; small capital letters, e.g. CADIZ, show capitals of provinces, etc. General notes p.116.

140 El Ferrol—Estrada, La

El Ferrol: Spain 35 B15
El Fogaha: Libya 78 H4
Elford: Staffs., England 27 S14
El Fud: Ethiopia 79 Q18
El Fuerte: Mexico 93 F7
Elgå: Norway 47 M5
El Gatrun: Libya 78 H5
El Geddahia: Libya 33 F5
El Geili: Sudan 54 D11
Elgena: Ethiopia 54 E11
El Geneina: Sudan 79 J7
El Geteina: Sudan 54 D12
El Gezira: Libya 79 J4
Elgin: Grampian, Scotland 28 P4
Elgin: Ill., U.S.A. 88 G4
Elgin: Oreg., U.S.A. 92 D3
Elgin: Tex., U.S.A. 90 C10
Elgol: I. of Skye, Inner Hebr., Scotland 28 J5
El Golea: Algeria 78 E3
Elgon, Mount: Uganda 76 D2
El Goran: Ethiopia 79 Q18
El Gubba: Libya 33 G5
El'gyay: U.S.S.R. 49 n5
Elham: Kent, England 25 Y17
El Hamdaniya: Syria 56 E4
El Hamra Hamada: plat., Libya 32 E5
El Hamurre: Somalia 79 R18
El Harasc: well, Libya 79 J4
El Hasi: Libya 78 G4
El Hasiheisa: Sudan 54 D12
El Hassam: Niger 81 F2
El Hathob: riv., Tunisia 38 L19
El Houbrat: Algeria 78 E3
El Huecú: Argentina 96 A4
El Hur: Somalia 79 R19
Elida: N. Mex., U.S.A. 93 G6
Elie: Fife, Scotland 29 Q7
Elila: & riv., Zaire 76 C3
Elim: S. Africa 74 C7
Eliott's Pike: mtn., Northumb., England 26 Q9
Elis: ancient district with centre of same name near Amalias, Greece 39 R18
Elisabethville see Lubumbashi
Elisenvaara: Karelia, U.S.S.R. 47 V6
ELISTA: Kalmyk, U.S.S.R. 50 F5
Elizabeth: La., U.S.A. 90 E10
Elizabeth: N.J., U.S.A. 89 O5
Elizabeth Cape: Maine, U.S.A. 89 Q4
Elizabeth City: N.C., U.S.A. 89 N7
Elizabeth Point: cape, S.W. Africa 74 A3
Elizabeth Reef: Tasman Sea 67 L7
Elizabethton: Tenn., U.S.A. 88 K7
Elizabethtown: Ky., U.S.A. 88 J7
Elizondo: Spain 37 D12
EL JADIDA: & Prov., Morocco 80 K8
El Jaralito: Mexico 93 G7
El Jof: Libya 79 J5
Ełk: Poland 43 S10
El Kab: Egypt (Suez Canal) Inset) 32 Ins.
El Kala: Algeria 38 L18
El Kantara: Algeria 32 D4
El Kantara, East and West see El Qantara 32 Ins.
El Karre: Ethiopia 79 Q18
Elk City: Okla., U.S.A. 90 B8
EL KEF: & Governorate, Tunisia 38 L18
Elkedra: N. Territ., Austl. 69 F4
El Kelaa: Morocco 80 K8
Elkenhof: Trans., S. Africa 74M Ins.
Elkesley: Notts., England 27 U13
El Khandaq: Sudan 54 D11
El Kharga: Egypt 54 D9
Elkhart: Ind., U.S.A. 88 J5
Elkhorn: riv., Nebr., U.S.A. 92 H4
Elkhovo: Bulgaria 39 U15
Elkin: N.C., U.S.A. 88 L7
Elkins: W. Va., U.S.A. 89 M6
Elk Lake: town, Ont., Can. 88 L2
Elkland: Pa., U.S.A. 89 N5
Elko: Nev., U.S.A. 92 D4
El Krachem: Algeria 35 H19
Elk River: Minn., U.S.A. 88 E3
El Kseur: Algeria 35 J18
Elkton: Ky., U.S.A. 88 H7
Elkton: Md., U.S.A. 89 O6
El Kûbri: Egypt (Suez Canal Inset) 32 Ins.
El Ladhiqiya (Latakia): Syria 56 D4
Elland: W. Yorks., England 27 S12
Ellef Ringnes I.: N.W.T., Canada 84 j2
Ellen: riv., Cumbria, Eng. 26 P10
Ellendale: N. Dak., U.S.A. 92 H3
Ellensburg: Wash., U.S.A. 92 C3
Ellenville: N.Y., U.S.A. 89 O5
Ellerton: Trans., S. Africa 75 J1
Ellesmere: Salop, England 27 Q14
Ellesmere I.: N.W.T., Can. 85 l2
Ellesmere Port: Ches., Eng. 27 Q13
Ellice Is.: see Tuvalu
Ellingen: W. Germany 45 Q6
Ellingham: Norf., England 25 Y15
Ellingham: Northumb., Eng. 26 S8
Elliot: & Dist., S. Africa 75 G5
Elliotdale: see Xhora
Ellis: Kans., U.S.A. 90 B6
Elliston: S. Australia 68 E6
Ellisville: Miss., U.S.A. 90 G10
El Llano: Mexico 93 E6
Ellon: Grampian, Scotland 28 R5
Ellora: Maharashtra, India 58 N10
Ellore (Eluru): Tamil Nadu, Ind. 58 O11
Elloughton: Humb., England 27 U12
Ellrich: W. Germany 45 Q4
Ellsworth: Kans., U.S.A. 90 B6
Ellsworth: Wis., U.S.A. 88 E3
Ellsworth Land: Antarctica 9 80S 85W
Ellwangen: W. Germany 40 Q7
Ellwood City: Pa., U.S.A. 88 L5
Elm: W. Germany 44 P2
Elma: Wash., U.S.A. 92 C3
Elmacik Daği: mtn., Turkey 56 B1
Elma Daği: mtn., Turkey 56 C2
El Madiq: Egypt 54 D10
El Mafaza: Sudan 54 D12
El Mahsama: Egypt (Suez Canal Inset) 32 Ins.
Elmalı: Turkey 56 A3
El Mansûra: Egypt 56 B6
El Manzala: Egypt (Suez Canal Inset) 32 Ins.
El Marj: Libya 33 G5
El Marsa: Tunisia 38 M18
El Matariya: Egypt 56 C6
Elmdon: airfield, War., Eng. 25 S15
El Meghaier: Algeria 32 D5
El Mekili: Libya 33 G5
Elmham, North: Norf., Eng. 25 X14
El Mina: Lebanon 56 D4
El Minya: Egypt 54 D9
Elmira: N.Y., U.S.A. 89 N4
Elmira: P.E.I., Canada 89 U2
Elmore: Vict., Australia 71 F11
El Mrayer: Mauritania 78 C5
El Mreiti: Mauritania 78 C5
Elmshorn: W. Germany 44 P2
Elmsted: Kent, England 25 Y17
Elmswell: Suff., England 25 X15
Elmtree: Trans., S. Africa 75 H3
El Muglad: Sudan 79 K7
Elmwood: Rhodesia 77 D6
EL OBEID: Northern Kordofan, Sudan 54 D12
Elobey: i., Eq. Guinea 81 F4
Eloff: Trans., S. Africa 74 O Ins.
Eloi Bay: La., U.S.A. 90 Ins.
El Odre: Argentina 96 B4
Elortondo: Argentina 96 C3
El Oued: Algeria 32 D5
Elouera: N.S.W., Australia 71 F8
El Ousseukh: Algeria 32 C5
El Palmar: Venezuela 87 c7
El Palmito: Mexico 93 G7
El Paso: Ill., U.S.A. 88 G5
El Paso: Tex., U.S.A. 93 F6
El Peñon: Argentina 96 B2
Elphin: Rosc., Repub. of Ireland 30 E12
Elphin: Highland, Scotland 28 L3
Elphinstone: i., Burma 59 R12
El Pintado: Argentina 96 C1
El Portal: Calif., U.S.A. 93 D5
El Porvenir: Mexico 93 F6
El Progreso: Guatemala 86 k14
El Puente del Arzobispo: Sp. 35 D17
El Qâhira (Cairo): Egypt 56 B6
El Qantara, East: Egypt (Suez Canal Inset) 32 Ins.
El Qantara, West: Egypt (Suez Canal Inset) 32 Ins.
El Qasr: Egypt 54 C9
El Real: Panama 94 B2
El Reno: Okla., U.S.A. 90 C8
Elroy: Wis., U.S.A. 88 F4
El Salado: Mexico 93 G8
El Salto: Mexico 86 J13

El Salvador: Republic 86 L15
Cap.: San Salvador
Area: 8,260 sq. miles (21,393 sq. km.)
Pop.: 3,549,260 (1971 C)

Elsberry: Mo., U.S.A. 88 F6
Elsburg: Trans., S. Africa 74 N Ins.
Elsdon: Northumb., England 26 R9
Elsdorf: W. Germany 44 P2
Elsey: N. Territ., Australia 68 E2
Elsfleth: W. Germany 44 O2
El Shallûfa: Egypt (Suez Canal Inset) 32 Ins.
Elsham: Humb., England 27 V12
El Shatt: Egypt (Suez Canal Inset) 32 Ins.
Elsinore: Calif., U.S.A. 93 D6
Elsinore: Utah, U.S.A. 93 E5
Elsrickle: Strath., Scotland 29 P8
Elst: Netherlands 44 L4
Elstead: Surrey, England 25 U17
Elster: riv., E. Germany 45 S4
Elsterwerda: E. Germany 45 T4
Elston: Notts., England 27 U13
Elstree: Herts., England 25 V16
Elswick: Lancs., England 27 Q12
Elsworth: Cambs., England 25 V15
Eltanin Fracture Zone: S. Pacific Ocean 7 45S 160W
Eltham: North I., N.Z. 70 P14
El Tigre: Venezuela 94 E2
Eltisley: Cambs., England 25 V15
Eltmann: W. Germany 45 Q6
Elton: Derby., England 27 S13
Elton: Cambs., England 25 V14
El'ton: U.S.S.R. 50 G5
El Tránsito: Chile 96 A2
El Trébol: Argentina 96 C3
El Triunfo: Mexico 93 E8
Eluru: Andhra Pradesh, India 58 O11
Elvanfoot: Strath., Scotland 29 O9
Elvas: Portugal 35 C17
Elveden: Suff., England 25 X15
Elven: France 36 C8
Elverum: Norway 47 M6
El Vigia: Venezuela 94 C2
Elvington: N. Yorks., England 27 U12
Elvins: Mo., U.S.A. 88 F7
El Volcán: Chile 96 A3
El Wak: Kenya 76 F2
El Walej, Shaib: wadi, Iraq 56 F5
El Wasta: Egypt 54 D9
El Wigh el Kebir: Libya 78 H5
Elwood: Ind., U.S.A. 88 J5
Elworth: Ches., England 27 R13
Elwy: riv., Clwyd, Wales 27 O13
Ely: Cambs., England 25 W15
Ely: Minn., U.S.A. 88 F2
Ely: Nev., U.S.A. 93 E5
Ely: S. Glam., Wales 24 P17
Ely, Isle of: reg. Cambs., England 25 W14
Elyria: Ohio, U.S.A. 88 K5
Elz: riv., W. Germany 40 N7
El Zape: Mexico 93 F7
Elze: W. Germany 45 P3
Ema: riv., Estonia, U.S.S.R. 47 U7
Emba: & riv., Kazakh., U.S.S.R. 50 J5
Embarcación: Argentina 96 C1
Emberton: Bucks., England 25 U15
Embira: riv., Brazil 94 C5
Embleton: Northumb., Eng. 26 S9
Embo: Highland, Scotland 28 N4
Embrun: France 40 M11
Embsay: N. Yorks., England 27 S12
EMBU: Eastern, Kenya 76 E3
Emden: W. Germany 44 N2
Emerald: Queens., Australia 70 H4
Emerald: i., N.W.T., Can. 84 h2
Emerita: Roman colony at Mérida, Spain 35 C17
Emerson: Man., Canada 92 H3
Emet: Turkey 56 A2
Emfeni: Malawi 77 D5
Emfouchiki: Congo 81 H5
Emi Koussi: mtn., Chad 78 H6
Emil'chino: Ukraine 43 U11
Emilia Romagna: Reg., Italy (cap. Bologna) 41 Q11
Emincik: Turkey 56 B1
Emine, Cape: Bulgaria 39 U15
Emirau: i., Bismarck Arch. 66 J2
Emirdağ: & mtn., Turkey 56 B2
Emly: Tip., Repub. of Irel. 31 E15
Emmaboda: Sweden 47 O8
Emmahaven: Sumatra 65 C7
Emmaste: Estonia, U.S.S.R. 47 S7
Emmaus: village of ancient Palestine about 13 miles WNW. of Jerusalem 55 b2
Emmaville: N.S.W., Austl. 71 J7
Emme: riv., Switzerland 40 N9
Emmen: Netherlands 44 M3
Emmendingen: W. Germany 40 N7
Emmerich: W. Germany 44 M4
Emmet: Queens., Australia 69 G4
Emmetsburg: Iowa, U.S.A. 92 J4
Emmett: Idaho, U.S.A. 92 D4
Emneth: Norf., England 25 W14
Emo: Ont., Canada 88 E1
Emona: Roman camp and colony at Ljubljana, Yugo. 41 U9
Emory Peak: Tex., U.S.A. 93 G7
Empangeni: Natal, S. Africa 75 J4
Empedrado: Argentina 96 D2
Emperor Seamounts: N. Pacific Ocean 7 40N 165E
Empingham: Leics., England 27 U14
Empire: La., U.S.A. 90 Ins.
Empoli: Italy 41 Q12
Emporia: Kans., U.S.A. 90 C6
Emporia: Va., U.S.A. 89 N7
Emporium: Pa., U.S.A. 89 M5
Ems: riv., W. Germany 44 N3
Ems Channel, West: str., Netherlands/West Germany 44 M2
Emseleni: Natal, S. Africa 75 K3
Ems-Jade Canal: W. Germany 44 N2
Emsworth: W. Sussex, England 25 U18
Emu Park: Queens., Austl. 70 J4
Emyvale: Monaghan, Repub. of Ireland 30 H11
Enard Bay: High., Scot. 28 L3
Encantada, Cerro de la: mtn., Mexico 93 D6
Encantadas, Serra: mtns., Brazil 96 E3
Encarnación: Paraguay 96 D2
Enchi: Ghana 80 D3
Encinillas: Mexico 93 F7
Encontrados: Venezuela 94 C2
Encounter Bay: Australia 71 C10
Encruzilhada: Brazil 96 E3
Enda: Ethiopia 54 E12
Endau: Malaya, Malaysia 65 c12
Ende: Flores, Indonesia 65 G8
Enderby: Leics., England 27 T14
Enderby Land: Antarctica 9 70S 50E
Enderlin: N. Dak., U.S.A. 92 H3
Endicott: N.Y., U.S.A. 89 N4
Endicott: Trans., S. Africa 74 O Ins.
Endicott Mtns.: Alaska, U.S.A. 84 d4
Endorf: W. Germany 41 S8
Energia: Argentina 96 D4
Enes: Norway 47 K6
Enez: Turkey 39 U16
Enfidaville: Tunisia 38 M18
Enfield: Gt. Ldn., England 25 V16
Enfield: N.C., U.S.A. 89 N7
Engaño, Cape: Luzon, Phil. 64 G3
Engaru: Japan 63 ZZ6
Engcobo: S. Africa 75 H5
Engelberg: Switzerland 40 O9
Engelhard: N.C., U.S.A. 91 O8
Engel's: U.S.S.R. 50 G4
Engen: W. Germany 40 O8
Enggano: i., Sumatra 65 C8
England: Ark., U.S.A. 90 F8

England: United Kingdom (cap. London) 20 —

Englehart: Ont., Canada 89 M2
English Bazar: W. Bengal, India 59 P9
English Chan.: Eng./Fr. 24 R19
English River: Ont., Canada 88 F1
Enguera: Spain 35 F17
Enid: Okla., U.S.A. 90 C7
Enis: Trans., S. Africa 75 J1
Enkeldoorn: Rhodesia 77 D6
Enkhuizen: Netherlands 44 L3
Enköping: Sweden 47 P7
Enmylin: U.S.S.R. 49 U4
Enna: Sicily 38 O18
En Nahud: Sudan 54 C12
Ennedi: geog. reg., Chad 79 J6
Ennei Domar: watercourse, Chad 78 H6
Ennell, Lough: Westmeath, Repub. of Ireland 30 G13
Ennerdale: Natal, S. Africa 75 H4
Enngonia: N.S.W., Austl. 71 F7
ENNIS: Clare, Repub. of Irel. 31 D14
Ennis: Texas, U.S.A. 90 C9
Enniscorthy: Wex., Repub. of Ireland 31 H14
Enniskean: Cork, Repub. of Ireland 31 D16
Enniskerry: Wick., Repub. of Ireland 31 J13
ENNISKILLEN: Ferm., N. Irel. 30 F11
Ennistymon: Clare, Repub. of Ireland 31 C14
En Nofilia: Libya 33 F5
Enns: Austria 41 U7
Enns: riv., Austria 41 U8
Ennstal: valley, Austria 41 U8
Eno: Finland 46 W5
Enontekio: Finland 46 S2
Enrick: riv., High., Scotland 28 M5
Ensay: i., Outer Hebr., Scotland 28 G4
Enschede: Netherlands 44 M3
Ensenada: Mexico 93 D6
Enshih (Shihnan): Hupeh, China 62 T8
Enshu Gulf: Japan 63 e3
Ensisheim: France 40 N8
Enstone: Oxon., England 25 T16
Enta: Tibet, China 62 R8
Entebbe: Uganda 76 D2
Enteng (Yungting): Fukien, China 62 V10
Enterkinfoot: Dumfries & Galloway, Scotland 29 O9
Enterprise: Ala., U.S.A. 91 J10
Enterprise: Oreg., U.S.A. 92 D3
Entlebuch: Switzerland 40 O9
Entonjaneni: Dist., Natal, S. Africa 75 J4
Entrains: France 36 J8
Entrecasteaux Is., d': New Guinea 69 J1
Entrecasteaux Reefs, d': Loyalty Is. 67 M5
Entre Rios: Mozambique 77 E5
Entre Rios: Prov., Argentina (cap. Parana) 96 D3
Entrevaux: France 40 M12
Entry I.: Magdalen Is., Can. 89 V2
Entwistle: Alta., Canada 92 E2
ENUGU: Anambra, Nigeria 81 F3
Enurmin: U.S.S.R. 49 u4
Envermeu: France 36 G6
Enyelle: Congo 76 A2
Enz: riv., W. Germany 40 O7
Enza: riv., Italy 40 Q11
Enzan: Japan 63 f3
Eoropie: I. of Lewis, Outer Hebr., Scotland 28 J2
Eouo: Congo 81 G5
Epanomi: Greece 39 S16
Epe: Netherlands 44 L3
Epe: Nigeria 81 E3
Epena: Congo 81 H4
Epernay: France 36 J6
Epernon: France 36 G7
Ephesus: Greek city (originally on coast) on river N. of Kuşadasi, Turkey 39 U18
Ephraim: Israelite tribe which lived in hills S. of Nablus, Jordan 55 b2
Ephrata: Wash., U.S.A. 92 D3
Epi: i., New Hebrides 67 N5
Epidamnus: Greek city at Durrës (Durazzo), Albania 39 Q16
Epidaurus: Greek city about centre of E. coast of Argolis, 25 miles SE. of Corinth 39 S18
Epila: Spain 35 F16
Epinac: France 36 K9
ÉPINAL: Vosges, France 40 M7
Epiphanie: l': Que., Canada 89 P3
Epire: Guyana 87 e8
Epirus: Reg., Greece 39 R17
Episkopi: Cyprus 56 C4
Eporedia: Roman colony at Ivrea, Italy 40 N10
Epping: & forest, Greater London Essex, England 25 W16
Eppleby: N. Yorks., England 26 S10
Epsom: Surrey, England 25 V17
Epuisay: France 36 F8
Epukiro: S.W. Africa 77 A7
Epu-Pel: Argentina 96 C4
Epworth: Humb., England 27 U12
Equateur: Prov., Zaire (cap. Mbandaka) 76 B2
Equatoria: Prov., Sudan (cap. Juba) 76 D2

Equatorial Guinea: Republic 81 F4
Cap.: Malabo (Santa Isabel)
Area: 10,832 sq. miles (28,055 sq. km.)
Pop.: 289,000 (1971 E)

Equeurdreville: France 36 D6
Eran: Palawan, Philippines 64 F5
Eranga: Zaire 76 A3
Erbaa: Turkey 56 E1
Erbach: W. Germany 44 P6
Erbendorf: W. Germany 45 S6
Erbes: mtn., W. Germany 44 N6
ERBIL: & Prov., Iraq 57 J3
Erçek, Lake: Turkey 57 H2
Erciş: Turkey 57 H2
Erciyas: mtn., Turkey 56 D2
Erdek: & gulf, Turkey 39 U16
Erdeni Dzuu: Mong. 62 S5
Erdëtski: Yugoslavia 41 W10
Erding: W. Germany 41 R7
Erdington: W. Mid., Eng. 27 S14
Erdre: riv., France 36 D8
Erech: Sumerian city site at Warka, E. of Samawa, Iraq 57 J6
Erechim: Brazil 95 G9
Erebus, Mt.: Antarctica 90 80S 165E
Ereğli: Konya, Turkey 56 D3
Ereğli: Zonguldak, Turkey 56 B1
Erego: Mozambique 77 E6
Erenköy: Turkey (Bosporus Inset) 20 Ins.
Erentsab: Mongolia 49 n8
Eretria: city of Euboea on coast opposite mainland about 12 miles SE of Chalcis 39 S17
Eretum: ancient Sabine city to E. of Tiber about 15 miles NE. of Rome 38 N15
Erfde: W. Germany 44 P1
Erfoud: Morocco 80 L8
Erft: riv., W. Germany 44 M5
ERFURT: & Dist., E. Germany 45 R5
Ergani: Turkey 56 F2
Ergeninadeni: Turkey 56 F2
Ergene: riv., Turkey 39 U16
Ergh, El: Libya 79 J4
Ergig: riv., Chad 81 H2
Ergoldsbach: W. Germany 41 S7
Ergué-Armel: France 36 A8
Ergu Khara: range, Inner Mongolia, China 62 S6
Erhkung: Sinkiang, China 62 Q6
Erhlien: Inner Mongolia, China 62 U6
Erhsui: Taiwan 63 W10
Erhyuan: Yunnan, China 62 R9
Eriboll: & loch, Scotland 28 M3
Erice: Sicily 38 N17
Ericht, Loch: Highland/Tayside, Scotland 29 N6
Erick: Okla., U.S.A. 90 B8
Eridu: Sumerian city site at Abu Shahrain, SW. of Nasiriya, Iraq 57 K6
Erie: Kans., U.S.A. 90 D7
Erie: Pa., U.S.A. 88 L4
Erie, Lake: Canada/U.S.A. 88 L4
Erieux: riv., France 37 K11
Erigavo: Somalia 79 R17
Erimo, Cape: Japan 63 ZZ6
Eriskay: i., Outer Hebr., Scotland 28 G5
Eriswell: Suff., England 25 X15
Eritrea: Prov., Ethiopia (cap. Asmara) 79 M6
ERIVAN (Yerevan): Armenia, U.S.S.R. 57 J1
Erkelenz: W. Germany 44 M4
Erlach: Switzerland 40 N8
Erlangen: E. Germany 45 R6
Erldunda: N. Territ., Austl. 68 E5
Erlestoke: Wilts., England 24 R17
Ermelo: Netherlands 44 L3
Ermelo: & Dist., Trans., S. Africa 75 J3
Ermenek: Turkey 56 C3
Ermington: Devon, Eng. 24 O19
Ermoupolis (Siros): Cyclades (Grc.) 39 T18
Ernakulam: Kerala, India 58 N12
Erne: riv., Repub. of Irel./N. Irel. 30 E11
Erne, Lough: Ferm., N. Irel. 30 F11
Ernée: France 36 E7
Ernstbrunn: Austria 41 W7
Erode: Tamil Nadu, India 58 N12
Eromanga: Queens., Austl. 69 G5
Erromanga: i., New Hebrides 67 N5
Erota: Ethiopia 54 E11
Erpingham: Norf., England 25 Y14
Erquy: France 36 C7
Erradale, North: Highland, Scotland 28 K4
Er Rahad: Sudan 54 D12
Er-Renk: Sudan 79 L7
Errer: riv., Ethiopia 79 Q18
Errick, Strath: val., Highland Scotland 28 N5
Er-Rif: geog. reg., Morocco 80 L7
Erriff: riv., Mayo, Repub. of Ireland 30 B12
Errigal: mtn., Don., Repub. of Ireland 30 E9
Erris Head: cape, Mayo, Repub. of Ireland 30 A11
Errogie: Highland, Scotland 28 N5
Errol: Tayside, Scotland 29 P7
Errol Island: La., U.S.A. 90 Ins.
Erseke: Albania 39 R16
Erstein: France 40 N7
Erstfeld: Switzerland 40 O9
Erudina: S. Australia 71 C8
Eruh: Turkey 57 H3
Erval: Brazil 96 E3
Ervik: Norway 46 J5
Ervy: France 36 J7
Erwald: Austria 41 Q8
Erxleben: E. Germany 45 R3
Erythrae: Greek city in W. bay of promontory which faces Chios, Turkey 39 U17
Eryx: mtn. and Sicel Settlement E. of Trapani, NW. Sicily 38 N18
Erz Gebirge: mtns., East Germany 45 S5
ERZINCAN: & Prov., Turkey 56 F2
ERZURUM: & Prov., Turkey 57 G2
Esa-Ala: D'Entrecasteaux Is. 69 J1
Esashi: N. Hokkaido, Japan 63 ZZ6
Esashi: S. Hokkaido, Japan 63 ZZ6
Esbjærg: Denmark 47 L9
Escala, La: Spain 35 H15
Escalante: Utah, U.S.A. 93 E5
Escalon: Mexico 93 G7
Escalona: Spain 35 D16
Escanaba: Mich., U.S.A. 88 H3
Escaut: riv., see Scheldt
Eschede: W. Germany 45 Q3
Escholzmatt: Switzerland 40 N9
Esch-sur-Alzette: Lux. 44 L6
Eschwege: W. Germany 45 Q4
Eschweiler: W. Germany 44 M5
Escobal: Panama 94 Ins.
Escondido: Calif., U.S.A. 93 D6
Escorial, El: Spain 35 D16
Escoumains, Les: Que., Can. 89 R1
Escource: France 37 D11
Escrick: N. Yorkshire, England 27 T12
Escuintla: Guatemala 86 k15
Escuintla: Mexico 86 k14
Escuminac, Point: cape, N.B., Canada 89 T2
Esdraelon: alternative Biblical name of valley of Jezreel 55 b2
Eséka: Cameroun 78 G9
Eşen: Turkey 56 A3
Esens: W. Germany 44 N2
Esha Ness: cape, Mainland, Shetland Is. 28 Ins.
Eshek: i., Lake Urmia, Iran 57 J3
Esher: Surrey, England 25 V17
Eshowe: & Dist., Natal, S. Africa 75 J4
ESH SHAM (Damascus): Syria 56 E5
Esh Shiweref: Libya 32 E6
Esino: riv., Italy 41 T12
Esk: Queens., Australia 70 K6
Esk: riv., Cumbria, England 26 P11
Esk: riv., Lothian, Scotland 29 P8
Esk: riv., Scotland/England 29 Q9
Esk: riv., N. Yorks., England 26 U11
Esk, North & South: riv., Gram./Tay., Scotland 29 Q6
Eskbank: Lothian, Scotland 29 P8
Eskdale: val., Dumfries & Galloway, Scotland 29 P9
Eskdale Green: Cumbria, England 26 P11
Eskifjordhur: Iceland 46 g4
Eskilstuna: Sweden 47 P7
Eskimo Lakes: N.W.T., Can. 84 f4
Eskimo Point: N.W.T., Can. 84 k5
ESKIŞEHIR: & Prov., Turkey 56 B2
Esla: riv., Spain 35 D16
Eslov: Sweden 47 N9
Eşme: Turkey 56 A2
Esmeralda: Queens., Austl. 69 G3
Esmeralda: Venezuela 94 D3
Esmeraldas: Ecuador 94 B3
Esnagi Lake: Ont., Canada 88 J1
Esnein: Egypt (Suez Canal Inset) 32 Ins.
Espalion: France 37 H11
Espanola: Ont., Canada 88 L2
Espe: Kazakh., U.S.S.R. 51 M6
Esperance: W. Australia 68 C6
Esperançe Rock, l': Kermadec Is., Pacific O. 67 Q8
Esperanza: rsch. stn., Antarctica 9 65S 60W
Esperanza: Argentina 96 C3
Esperanzas, Las: Mexico 93 G7
Espichel, Cape: Portugal 35 B17
Espiguette, Pointe de l': cape, France 37 K12
Espinasses: France 40 M11
Espinhaço, Serra do: mtns., Brazil 94 J7
Espinho: Portugal 35 B16
Espinosa: Spain 35 E15
Espinouse, Monts de l': mtns., France 37 H12
Espirito Santo: State, Brazil (cap. Vitoria) 94 J7
Espiritu Santo: i., Mexico 93 E8
Espiritu Santo: i., New Hebr. 67 N5
Espiritu Santo Bay: Mexico 86 L14
Espungabera: Mozambique 77 D7
Esquel: Argentina 95 C12
Es Saff: Egypt 56 B7
Es Sâlhiya: Egypt (Suez Canal Inset) 32 Ins.
Es Sarfaia: oasis, Libya 78 H5
Essarts, Les: France 37 D9
Esschen: Belgium 44 K4
Essen: Lower Saxony, W. Ger. 44 N3
Essen: North Rhine-Westphalia, W. Ger. 44 N4
Essequibo: Co & riv., Guyana 87 d7
Essex: Co., England (co. town Chelmsford) 25 W16
Essexville: Mich., U.S.A. 88 K4
Esslingen: W. Germany 40 P7
Essone: Gabon 81 G4
Essonne: Dept., France (cap. Évry) 36 H7
Essonne: riv., France 36 H7
Essou: Congo 81 H5
Essoyes: France 36 K7
Est: Dept., Ivory Coast (cap. Abengourou) 80 D3
Est: Dept., Upper Volta (cap. Fada-N'Gourma) 80 E2
Est: Reg., Cameroun (cap. Bertoua) 81 G4
Estaca de Bares, Pta.: cape, Spain 35 C15
Estacado, Llano: plain, N. Mex./Tex., U.S.A. 93 G6
Estagel: France 37 H13
Estância: Brazil 94 K6
Estancia: N. Mex., U.S.A. 93 F6
Estats, Pic d': mtn., Pyrénées 37 G13
Estavayer: Switzerland 40 M9
Estcourt: & Dist., Natal, S. Africa 75 H4
Este: town about 5 miles W. of Monselice, Italy 41 R10
Esterias, Cape: Gabon 78 F9
Estella: Spain 35 E15
Estepa: Spain 35 D18
Estepona: Spain 35 D18
Esternay: France 36 J7
Estevan: Sask., Canada 92 G3
Estherville: Iowa, U.S.A. 92 J4
Estissac: France 36 J7
Eston: Natal, S. Africa 75 J4
Eston: Sask., Canada 92 F2
Eston: Cleveland, England 26 T10
Estonian S.S. Repub.: U.S.S.R. (cap. Tallinn) 47 T7
Estrada, La: Spain 35 B15

For Abbreviations see list on p.113. Italic type, e.g. Ephesus, refers to historical names not on maps. Capital letters, e.g. MADRID, show capitals of countries; small capital letters, e.g. CADIZ, show capitals of provinces, etc. General notes p.116.

Estrées-St.-Denis—Fimi 141

Estrées-St.-Denis: France 36 H6
Estreito: Brazil 96 E3
Estrêla: Brazil 96 E2
Estremadura: Prov., Port., [cap. Lisbôa (Lisbon)] 35 B17
Estremadura: Old Prov., Sp. 35 C17
Estremoz: Portugal 35 C17
Estrondo, Serra do: mtns., Brazil 94 H5
Estuaire: Reg., Gabon (cap. Libreville) 81 G4
Esztergom: Hungary 43 Q13
Etables: France 36 C7
Etah: Greenland 85 m2
Etah: Uttar Pradesh, India 58 N9
Etain: France 36 L6
Étampes: France 36 H7
Étang: France 37 K9
Étaples: France 36 G5
Etawah: Uttar Pradesh, India 58 N9
Etel: France 36 B8
Eten: Peru 94 B5

Ethiopia: Empire 79 M8
Cap.: Addis Ababa
Area: 457,142 sq. miles (1,183,998 sq. km.)
Pop.: 25,248,000 (1971 E)

Etive, Loch: Strath., Scot. 29 L7
Etna: volc., Sicily 38 O18
Etoile: Zaire 77 C5
Etoiles, Chaîne de l': hills, France 40 L12
Etolin Str.: Alaska, U.S.A. 84 C5
Eton: Berkshire, England 25 U17
Eton: Queens., Australia 70 H3
Etorofu (Iturup): i., Kuril Is. 63 YY6
Etosha Game Park: SW. Africa 73 G13
Etosha Pan: salt lake, SW. Afr. 73 H13
Etoumbi: Congo 78 G9
Etowah: Tenn., U.S.A. 91 J8
Etrépagny: France 36 G6
Etretat: France 36 F6
Etsin: riv., China 62 S6
Ettelbrück: Luxembourg 44 M6
Et Tih Plat.: Egypt 56 D7
El Tina: Egypt (Suez Canal Inset) 32 Ins.
Ettington: War., England 25 S15
Ettlingen: W. Germany 40 O7
Ettrick: & forest, Borders, Scotland 29 P9
Etusimola: Finland 47 V6
Etwall: Derby., England 27 S14
Eu: France 36 G5
Eua: i., Tonga 67 R6
Euabalong: N.S.W., Austl. 71 G9
Euboea (Evvoia): i., Greece 39 S17
Euboea, Gulf of: Greece 39 S17
Eucla: W. Australia 68 D6
Eucumbene, L.: N.S.W., Australia 71 H11
Eudaemon: see Arabia Felix.
Eudora: Ark., U.S.A. 90 F9
Eudunda: S. Australia 71 C10
Eufaula: Ala., U.S.A. 91 J10
Eufaula: Okla., U.S.A. 90 D8
Eufaula Res.: Okla., U.S.A. 90 D8
Eugendorf: Austria 41 T8
Eugene: Oreg., U.S.A. 92 C4
Eugenia, Point: cape, Mexico 93 D7
Euglo: N.S.W., Australia 71 G9
Eugowra: N.S.W., Austl. 71 H9
Eulo: Queens., Australia 70 F7
Eumundi: Queens., Austl. 70 K6
Eumungerie: N.S.W., Austl. 71 H8
Eungella National Park: Queens., Australia 70 H3
Eunice: La., U.S.A. 90 E10
Eupen: Belgium 44 M5
Euphrates: riv., Iraq/Turkey 57 K6
Eura: Finland 47 S6
Eure: Dept., France (cap. Evreux) 36 F6
Eure: riv., France 36 G6
Eure-et-Loir: Dept., France (cap. Chartres) 36 G7
Eureka: Calif., U.S.A. 92 C4
Eureka: Kans., U.S.A. 90 C7
Eureka: Nev., U.S.A. 93 D5
Eureka: S. Dak., U.S.A. 92 H3
Eureka Springs: city, Ark., U.S.A. 90 E7
Euriowie: N.S.W., Australia 71 D8
Euripus: ancient name of strait between Chalcis (Euboea, Greece) and mainland 39 S17
Euroa: Vict., Australia 71 F11
Eurombah: Queens., Austl. 70 H5
Europa I.: (Fr.), Indian O. 77 F7
Europoort: Netherlands 42 J11
Eurotas: river flowing past Spárti into G. of Lakonia, Greece 39 S18
Eurymedon: Greek name of river Kopra flowing S. into Mediterranean past Serik, Turkey 56 B3
Euskirchen: W. Germany 44 M5
Eustis: Fla., U.S.A. 91 L11
Euston: N.S.W., Australia 71 E10
Eutaw: Ala., U.S.A. 91 H9
Eutin: W. Germany 45 Q1
Eutsuk Lake: B.C., Canada 92 B2
Euxton: Lancs., England 27 Q12
Evale: Angola 73 H13
Evans, Cape: N.W.T., Can. 85 I1
Evans Head: town, N.S.W., Australia 71 K7
Evanston: Ill., U.S.A. 88 H4
Evanston: Wyo., U.S.A. 92 E4
Evansville: Ind., U.S.A. 88 H6
Evansville: Wis., U.S.A. 88 G4
Evanton: High., Scot. 28 N4
Evart: Mich., U.S.A. 88 J4
Evaton: Trans., S. Africa 74 M Ins.
Evaux: France 37 H9
Eveleth: Minn., U.S.A. 88 E2
Evenley: Northants., Eng. 25 T15
Everard, Cape: Vict., Austl. 71 H11
Everard, Lake: S. Australia 69 F6
Evercreech: Som., England 24 R17
Everest: mtn., Himalayas 59 P9
Everett: Wash., U.S.A. 92 C3
Evergem: Belgium 44 J4
Everglades: Fla., U.S.A. 91 L13
Everglades, The: swamp, Fla., U.S.A. 91 L12
Everglades Nat. Park: Fla., U.S.A. 91 L12
Evershot: Dorset, England 24 Q18
Everton: Notts., England 27 U13
Evesham: & vat., Hereford & Worcester, England 24 S15
Evian: France 40 M9
Evijärvi: Finland 46 S5
Evje: Norway 47 K7
Evora: Portugal 35 C17
Evran: France 36 D7
Evreşe: Turkey (Dardan. Inset) 20 Ins.
EVREUX: Eure, France 36 G6
Evron: France 36 E7
EVRY: Essonne, France 36 H7
Evvoia: see Euboea.
Ewa: Hawaiian Is. 83 b2
Ewab (Kai) Is.: Indonesia 61 L13
Ewe, Loch: High., Scot. 28 K4
Ewell: Surrey, England 25 V17
Ewhurst: Surrey, England 25 V17
Ewyas Harold: Hereford & Worcester, England 24 Q16
Exaltación: Bolivia 94 D6
Exbourne: Devon, Eng. 24 N18
Exbury: Hants., England 25 T18
Excel: Alta., Canada 92 E2
Excelsior: O.F.S., S. Africa 75 G4
Excideuil: France 37 G10
Exe: riv., Devon/Som., Eng. 24 P18
EXETER: Devon, England 24 O18
Exeter: Ont., Canada 88 L4
Exford: Som., England 24 O17
Exminster: Devon, England 24 P18
Exmoor: Som./Devon, Eng. 24 O17
Exmoor National Park: Devon/Som., England 24 O17
Exmouth: Devon, England 24 P18
Exmouth: W. Australia 68 A4
Exmouth Gulf: W. Austl. 68 A4
Exning: Suff., England 25 W15
Expedition Range: Queens., Australia 70 H5
Exton: Som., England 24 O17
Exuma Is.: Bahamas 87 H13
Eyadeyon: Gabon 81 G5
Eyam: Derby., England 27 S13
Eyasi, Lake: Tanzania 76 D3
Eye: Cambs., England 25 V14
Eye: Suff., England 25 Y15
Eyemouth: Borders, Scot. 29 R8
Eye Penin.: I. of Lewis, Outer Hebr., Scotland 28 J3
Eyeries: Cork, Repub. of Irel. 31 B16
Eygues: riv., France 37 K11
Eygurande: France 37 H10
Eyjafjallajökull: mtn., Ice. 46 d5
Eylau: battlefield at Ilawka on frontier of Kaliningrad, U.S.S.R., and Mazuria, Poland 43 R9
Eymet: France 37 F11
Eymoutiers: France 37 G10
Eynsham: Oxon., England 25 T16
Eyre: W. Australia 68 D6
Eyre: riv., Queens., Australia 69 F4
Eyre, Lake: S. Australia 69 F5
Eyrecourt: Galway, Repub. of Ireland 31 E13
Eyre Mtns.: South I., N.Z. 70 M17
Eyre's Penin.: S. Australia 71 A9
Eysden: Belgium 44 L5
Eystrup: W. Germany 44 P3
Eythorne: Kent, England 25 Y17
Ezine: Turkey 39 U17
Ez Zuetina: Libya 33 G5

Faaborg: Funen, Denmark 47 M9
Faaita: i., Tuamotu Arch. 83 f3
Faba, Glen: val., I. of Man, England 26 M11
Fabala: Guinea 80 C3
Fabens: Tex., U.S.A. 93 F6
Fabrateria nova: Roman colony on right bank of Trerus about 50 miles SE. of Rome 38 N16
Fabrateria vetus: ancient Latin city at Ceccano, Latium, Italy 38 N16
Fachi: Niger 78 G6
Facinas: Spain (Gib. Inset) 32 Ins.
Facture: France 37 E11
Facundo: Argentina 95 D13
Fada: Chad 79 J6
FADA-N'GOURMA: Est, Upper Volta 80 E2
Fadd: Hungary 43 Q13
Faddeyevskiy I.: U.S.S.R. 49 Q2
Fadyadougou: Ivory Coast 80 C3
Faemund Lake: Norway 47 M5
Faenza: Italy 41 R11
Faeroe Is.: (Dan.), N. Atlantic O. (cap. Thorshavn) 46 Ins.
Fafa: Mali 80 E1
Fafa: riv., Cen. Afr. Rep. 76 A1
Fafen: riv., Ethiopia 79 Q18
Făgăraș: Romania 39 T14
Fagerhult: Sweden 47 O8
Fagernes: Norway 47 L6
Fagersta: Sweden 47 O7
Fāget: Romania 39 S14
Faguibine, Lake: Mali 80 D1
Fahan: Don., Repub. of Ireland 30 G9
Fahchow: Kwangtung, China 62 U10
Fahrej (Iranshahr): Iran 55 K9
Faid: Saudi Arabia 54 F9
Faido: Switzerland 40 O9
Faiki: Nigeria 81 F2
Failaka: i., Persian Gulf 57 L7
Failsworth: Gt. Man., Eng. 27 R12
Fairbanks: Alaska, U.S.A. 84 E5
Fairbourne: Gwynedd, Wales 27 N14
Fairburn: N. Yorks., England 27 T12
Fairbury: Ill., U.S.A. 88 G5
Fairbury: Nebr., U.S.A. 93 H4
Fairfax: Minn., U.S.A. 88 D3
Fairfax: Okla., U.S.A. 90 C7
Fairfield: Ala., U.S.A. 91 H9
Fairfield: Derby., England 27 S13
Fairfield: Ill., U.S.A. 88 G6
Fairfield: Iowa, U.S.A. 88 F5
Fairfield: Maine, U.S.A. 89 R3
Fairfield: Queens., Australia 70 H5
Fairford: Glos., England 25 S16
Fair Haven: Vt., U.S.A. 89 O4
Fair Head (Benmore Head): cape, Antrim, N. Ireland 30 J9
Fairhope: Ala., U.S.A. 91 H10
Fair Isle: i., Shetland Is., Scotland 28 Ins.
Fairlie: Strathclyde, Scotland 29 M8
Fairlie: South I., N.Z. 70 N17
Fairlight: E. Sussex, England 25 X18
Fairmont: Minn., U.S.A. 88 D4
Fairmont: N.C., U.S.A. 91 M8
Fairmont: W. Va., U.S.A. 88 L6
Fairport: N.Y., U.S.A. 89 N4
Fairway Reef: New Caledonia 67 M6
Fairweather: mtn. & cape, Alaska, U.S.A. 84 F6
Fais: i., Caroline Is. 61 N10
Faisaliya: Iraq 57 J6
Faish Khabur: Iraq 57 H3
Faith: S. Dak., U.S.A. 92 G4
FAIZABAD: Badakhshan, Afghanistan 55 M7
Faizabad (Fyzabad): India 58 C9
Faizabad: Iran 55 J8
Fajr: wadi, Saudi Arabia 54 E9
Fakaofo: i., Tokelau Is. 70 Ins.
Fakarava: i., Tuamotu Arch. 83 f3
Fakenham: Norf., England 25 X14
Fakfak: W. Irian, Indonesia 61 L12
Fakiya: Bulgaria 39 U15
Fakse: Zealand, Denmark 47 N9
Faktoriya: U.S.S.R. 49 m3
Faktoriya Amo: U.S.S.R. 49 M5
Faku: Liaoning, China 63 W6
Fal: riv., Corn., England 24 M19
Fala: Lothian, Scotland 29 Q8
Falaba: Sierra Leone 80 B3
Falaise: France 36 E7
FALAM: Chin, Burma 59 Q10
Falama: Guinea 80 C2
Falcarragh: Don., Repub. of Ireland 30 E9
Fălciu: Romania 39 V13
Falcon Res.: Tex., U.S.A. 90 B12
Falcone, Cape of: Sardinia 38 L16
Falesht: Moldavia, U.S.S.R. 43 U13
Falfield: Avon, England 24 R16
Falkenberg: Sweden 47 N8
Falkenham: Suff., England 25 Y15
Falkenstein: Bavaria, W. Ger. 45 S6
Falkenstein: Saxony, E. Ger. 45 S5
Falkirk: Central, Scotland 29 O7
Falkland: Fife, Scotland 29 P7
Falkland Is.: (Br.), Atlantic O. (cap. Stanley) 95 F14
Falkland Plateau: S. Atlantic Ocean 8 55S 55W
Falknov: Czechoslovakia 45 S5
Falköping: Sweden 47 N7
Fallon: Nev., U.S.A. 93 D5
Fallou: Mali 80 C2
Fall River: city, Mass., U.S.A. 89 Q5
Falls City: Nebr., U.S.A. 93 H4
Falluja: Iraq 57 H5
Falmer: E. Sussex 25 V18
Falmouth: Antigua, Leeward Is. 87 c2
Falmouth: Jamaica 86 Ins.
Falmouth: Ky., U.S.A. 88 J6
Falmouth: Mass., U.S.A. 89 Q5
Falmouth: & bay, Corn., England 24 L19
False Bay: S. Africa 74 C7
False Divi Point: cape, India 58 O11
False Obi: i., Vietnam 64 C5
False Point: cape, India 59 P10
Falset: Spain 35 G16
Falster: i., Denmark 47 N9
Falsterbo: Sweden 47 N9
Falstone: Northumb., Eng. 26 R9
Falterona, Monte: mtn., Italy 41 R12
Fălticeni: Romania 43 U13
FALUN: Kopparberg, Swed. 47 O6
Famagusta: Cyprus 56 C4
Famaka: Sudan 79 L7
Famatina: Argentina 96 B2
Famatina, Cordillera de: range, Argentina 96 B2
Family Lake: Man., Canada 92 H2
Fanad Head: cape, Don., Repub. of Ireland 30 F9
Fanâra: Egypt (Suez Canal Inset) 32 Ins.
Fanárion: Greece 39 R17
Fanchang: Anhwei, China 62 V8
Fane: riv., Louth/Monaghan, Repub. of Ireland 30 J12
Fangahina: i., Tuamotu Arch. 83 g3
Fangak: Sudan 79 L8
Fangataufa: i., Tuamotu Arch. 83 h4
Fangcheng: Heilungkiang, China 63 X5
Fangcheng: Honan, China 62 U8
Fangcheng: Kwangsi Chuang, China 62 T10
Fangtsun: Kweichow, China 62 T9
Fannich, Loch: Highland, Scotland 28 M4
Fanning I.: N. Pacific Ocean 7 0 160W
Fano: Italy 41 T12
Fanø: i., Denmark 47 L9
Fanuch: Iran 55 J9
Fanuda: Saudi Arabia 54 F9
Fao: Iraq 57 L7
Faouët, Le: France 36 B7
Fâqûs: Egypt 56 B6
Fara: i., Orkney Is., Scot. 28 P2
Faradje: Zaire 76 C2
Farafangana: Malagasy Rep. 73 O14
Farafra Oasis: Egypt 54 C9
FARAH: & Prov. & riv., Afghanistan 55 K8
Faraid Head: cape, Highland, Scotland 28 M2
Faraja: well, Saudi Arabia 55 H10
Farallon de Medinilla: i., Mariana Is. 61 O8
Farallon de Pajaros: Mariana Is. 60 O7
Faramin: Mor. (Gib. Inset) 32 Ins.
FARANAH: & Reg., Guinea 80 B2
Faras: Egypt 54 D10
Farasan Is.: Red Sea 54 F11
Faraway, Mt.: Antarctica 9 80S 30W
Farcet: Cambs., England 25 V14
Fare, Hill of: Gram., Scot. 28 Q5
Fareham: Hants, England 25 T18
Farewell: Alaska, U.S.A. 84 d5
Farewell Cape: Greenland 85 p6
Farewell, Cape: South I., New Zealand 70 O15
Fargo: N. Dak., U.S.A. 92 H3
Faribault: Minn., U.S.A. 88 E3
Faridkot: Punjab, India 58 M8
Faridpur: Bangladesh 59 P10
Farim: Guinea-Bissau 80 A2
Farina: S. Australia 69 F6
Faringdon: Oxon., England 25 S16
Farington: Lancs., England 27 Q12
Farkašd: Czechoslovakia 43 P12
Farkovo: U.S.S.R. 48 k4
Farkwa: Tanzania 76 E4
Farlam: Cumbria, England 26 Q10
Farleigh: Queens., Austl. 70 H3
Farmersville: Texas, U.S.A. 90 C9
Farmington: Maine, U.S.A. 89 Q3
Farmington: Mo., U.S.A. 88 F7
Farmington: N.H., U.S.A. 89 Q4
Farmington: N. Mex., U.S.A. 93 F5
Far Moor: village, Lancs., England 27 Q12
Farmville: Va., U.S.A. 89 M7
Farnborough: Hants, Eng. 25 U17
Farndale East: N. Yorks., England 26 U11
Farndon: Ches., England 27 Q13
Farndon: Notts., England 27 U13
Farne Is.: England 26 S8
Farnell: Tayside, Scotland 29 Q6
Farnham: Que., Canada 89 P3
Farnham: Surrey, England 25 U17
Farnham, Mount: B.C., Can. 92 D2
Farnham Royal: Bucks., England 25 U16
Farnhill: N. Yorks., England 27 R12
Farningham: Kent, England 25 W17
Farnsfield: Notts., England 27 T13
Farnworth: Gt. Man., Eng. 27 R12
FARO: Algarve, Portugal 35 C18
Faro: Brazil 94 F4
Faro: riv., Cameroun 81 G3
Fårön: i., Sweden 47 Q8
Farr: Highland, Scotland 28 N2
Farranfore: Kerry, Repub. of Ireland 31 B15
Farrar, Strath: val., Highland, Scotland 28 M5
Farringdon: Hants., England 25 U17
Farrukhabad: Uttar Pradesh, India 58 W9
Fars: Prov. & geog. reg., Iran (cap. Shiraz) 55 H9
Farsley: W. Yorks., England 27 S12
Farsund: Norway 47 K7
Fartura, Serra da: mtns., Brazil 96 E2
Farur: i., Persian Gulf 55 H9
Farwell: Tex., U.S.A. 93 G6
Faryab: Prov., Afghanistan (cap. Maimana) 55 K7
Fasana Chan.: str., Yugo. 41 T11
Fasano: Italy 38 P16
Fasher, El: Darfur, Sudan 79 K7
Fashn, El: Egypt 54 D9
Fastnet Rock: Repub. of Ireland 31 B17
Fastov: Ukraine 50 C4
Fataka (Mitre I.): Pacific O. 67 O4
Fatala: riv., Guinea 80 B2
Fatehpur: Rajasthan, India 58 N9
Fatehpur: Uttar Pradesh, India 58 O9
Fateşti: Romania 39 U14
Fatezh: U.S.S.R. 50 E4
Father Lake: Que., Canada 89 O1
Fatick: Senegal 80 A2
Fatih: Turkey (Bosporus Inset) 20 Ins.
Fatsa: Turkey 56 E1
Fatu Hiva: i., Marquesas Is. 83 h2
Fatu Huku: i., Marquesas Is. 83 h1
Faucilles, Les Monts: mtns., France 40 L7
Faughan: riv., N. Ireland 30 G10
Fauldhouse: Lothian, Scot. 29 O8
Faulquemont: France 44 M6
Fauresmith: & Dist., O.F.S., S. Africa 75 F4
Fauske: Norway 46 O3
Fauville: France 36 F6
Faverges: France 40 M10
Faverolles: Seine-et-Oise, France 36 G7
Faversham: Kent, England 25 X17
Fawa: Nigeria 81 F2
Fawley: Berks., England 25 T16
Fawley: Hants., England 25 T18
Faxa Bay: Iceland 46 b4
Faxe: riv., Sweden 46 P5
Faya: see Largeau.
Fayal: i., Azores 78 Ins.
Fayence: France 40 M12
Fayette: Ala., U.S.A. 91 H9
Fayetteville: Ark., U.S.A. 90 D7
Fayetteville: N.C., U.S.A. 91 M8
Fâyid: Egypt (Suez Canal Inset) 32 Ins.
Fays-Billot: France 40 L8
Fazeley: Staffs., England 27 S14
Fazilka: Punjab, India 58 M8
F'Dérik: Mauritania 78 B5
Feakle: Clare, Repub. of Ireland 31 D14
Feale: riv., Kerry/Lim., Repub. of Ireland 31 C15
Fear, Cape: N.C., U.S.A. 91 N9
Fearby: N. Yorks., England 26 S11
Fearn, Hill of: village, Highland, Scotland 28 O4
Featherston: North I., N.Z. 70 P15
Fécamp: France 36 F6
Feckenham: Hereford and Worcester, England 24 S15
Fedaan: tribal area, Iraq 57 G4
Fedamore: Lim., Repub. of Ireland 31 D14
Federación: Argentina 96 D3
Federal Capital Territory: Nigeria 81 F3
Federovka: U.S.S.R. 50 J4
Feeagh, Lough: Mayo, Repub. of Ireland 30 B12
Feenagh: Lim., Repub. of Ireland 31 D15
Feeny: Lon., N. Ireland 30 G10
Feetham: N. Yorks., England 26 R11
Fehérgyarmat: Hungary 43 S13
Fehmarn: i., W. Germany 45 R1
Fehrbellin: E. Germany 45 S3
Feihsien: Shantung, China 62 V7
Feijó: Brazil 94 C5
Feilding: North I., N.Z. 70 P15
Feira: Zambia 77 D6
Feira de Santana: Brazil 94 K6
Feistritz: Austria 41 U9
Feke: Turkey 56 D3
Felanitz: Maj., Balearic Is. 35 H17
Felchow: E. Germany 45 U2
Feldkirch: Austria 40 P8
Feldkirchen: Austria 41 U9
Feliciano: riv., Argentina 96 D3
Felindre: Powys, Wales 24 P15
Felixstowe: Suff., England 25 Y16
Felletin: France 37 H10
Félou Falls: Mali 80 B2
Felsted: Essex, England 25 W16
Felton: Northumb., Eng. 26 S9
Felton, West: Salop, Eng. 27 Q14
Feltre: Italy 41 R9
Feltwell: Norf., England 25 X15
Femer Belt: str., Denmark/W. Germany 47 M9
Femunmarka National Park: Norway 46 M5
Femund Lake: Norway 47 M5
Fen: riv., China 62 U7
Fenagh: Leit., Repub. of Ireland 30 F11
Fenelon Falls: city, Ont., Canada 89 M3
Fénérive: Malagasy Rep. 73 O13
Fenestrelle: Italy 40 N10
Fengchen: Inner Mongolia, China 62 U6
Fengcheng: Kiangsi, China 62 V9
Fengcheng: Liaoning, China 63 W6
Fengching: Yunnan, China 62 R10
Fenghsien: Shensi, China 62 V8
Fengshien: Shensi, China 62 T8
Fenghwa: Chekiang, China 63 W9
Fengkieh: Szechwan, China 62 T8
Fengshan: Heilungkiang, China 63 X5
Fengsiang: Shensi, China 62 T8
Fengtai: Anhwei, China 62 V8
Fengyang: Anhwei, China 62 V8
Feni Is.: Bismarck Arch. 67 K2
Fennagh: Carlow, Repub. of Ireland 31 H14
Fenny: Bangladesh 59 Q10
Fenny Stratford: Bucks., England 25 U16
Fenouillèdes: mtns., France 37 H13
Fens, The: dist., England 25 W15
Fens Fiord: Norway 47 J6
Fenton: Mich., U.S.A. 88 K4
Fenton: Staffs., England 27 R14
Fenwick: Strath., Scotland 29 N8
Fenyang: Shansi, China 62 U7
Feock: Corn., England 24 L19
Feolin Ferry: Jura, Inner Hebr., Scotland 29 J8
Fer, Point Au: cape, La., U.S.A. 90 F11
Ferbane: Offaly, Repub. of Ireland 31 F13
Ferdan: see Firdan.
Ferdinand: Bulgaria 39 S15
Ferdinandshof: E. Germany 45 T2
Fère, La: France 36 J6
Fère-Champenoise: France 36 J7
Fère-en-Tardenois: France 36 J6
Ferentinum: ancient Hernican city on Via Latina about 40 miles SSE. of Rome 38 N16
Ferfer: Somalia 79 R18
Fergana: Uzbek., U.S.S.R. 51 M6
Fergana Range: Kirgiz., U.S.S.R. 51 M6
Fergus: riv., Clare, Repub. of Ireland 31 D14
Fergus Falls: city, Minn., U.S.A. 92 H3
Fergusson I.: New Guinea 69 J1
Feriana: Tunisia 32 D5
Ferkane: Algeria 32 D5
Ferlach: Austria 41 U9
Ferleiten: Austria 41 S8
Ferlo: riv., Senegal 80 B1
Ferlo Desert: Senegal 80 B2
Fermanagh: Co., N. Ireland (co. town Enniskillen) 30 F11
Fermo: Italy 38 N15
Fermoy: Cork, Repub. of Ireland 31 E15
Fern: Tayside, Scotland 29 Q6
Fernandina: Fla., U.S.A. 91 L10
Fernando de Noronha: i. & Terr., Brazil (cap. Vila dos Remédios) 94 L4
Fernando Póo (Macias Nguema Biyogo): i., Equatorial Guinea, G. of Guinea (cap. Malabo) 81 F4
Fernan Vaz: Gabon 81 F5
Fernhurst: W. Sussex, Eng. 25 U17
Fernie: B.C., Canada 92 D3
Ferns: Wex., Repub. of Irel. 31 H14
Férrai: Greece 39 U16
Ferrara: Italy 41 R11
Ferrato, Cape: Sardinia 38 L17
Ferreira do Zêzere: Port. 35 B17
Ferret, Cap: cape, France 37 D11
Ferrette: France 40 N8
Ferriby, North: N. Yorks., England 27 V12
Ferriday: La., U.S.A. 90 F10
Ferriere: Italy 40 P11
Ferring: W. Sussex, England 25 V18
Ferrol, El: Spain 35 B15
Ferryhill: Durham, England 26 S10
Ferryland: Newf., Canada 85 w3
Ferryside: Dyfed, Wales 24 N16
Ferryville: Tunisia 38 L18
Ferté-Bernard, La: France 36 F7
Ferté-Fresnel, La: France 36 F7
Ferté-Gaucher, La: France 36 J7
Ferté-Macé, La: France 36 E7
Ferté-St.-Aubin, La: France 36 G8
Ferté-sous-Jouarre, La: Fr. 36 J7
Ferté-Vidame, La: France 36 F7
Fertöszentmiklós: Hungary 41 W8
Fès (Fez): & Prov., Morocco 80 L8
Feshi: Zaire 76 A4
Festus: Mo., U.S.A. 88 F6
Feteşti: Romania 39 U14
Fethard: Tip., Repub. of Ireland 31 F15
Fethard: Wex., Repub. of Ireland 31 H15
Fethiye: Turkey 56 A3
Fetlar: i., Shetland Is., Scot. 28 Ins.
Fetterangus: Gram., Scot. 28 R4
Fettercairn: Gram., Scotland 28 Q6
Feuchtwangen: W. Germany 45 Q6
Feuillie, La: France 36 G6
Feuquières: France 36 G5
Feurs: France 37 K10
Fevzipaşa: Turkey 56 E3
Fez see Fès.
Ffestiniog: Gwynedd, Wales 27 O14
Fforest Fawr: mtns., Powys, Wales 24 O16
Fiambala: Argentina 96 B2
FIANARANTSOA: & Prov., Malagasy Rep. 73 O14
Fianga: Chad 81 H3
Fiaray: i., Outer Hebr., Scotland 28 G5
Fich: Ethiopia 79 Q18
Fichtel Gebirge: mtns., W. Germany 45 S5
Ficksburg: & Dist., O.F.S., S. Africa 75 G4
Fiddown: Kilk., Repub. of Ireland 31 G15
Fidenae: ancient Sabine or Latin city near left bank of Tiber 7 miles N. of Rome 38 N16
Fidenza: Italy 40 Q11
Fieberbrunn: Austria 41 S8
Fier: Albania 39 Q16
Fieries: Kerry, Repub. of Ireland 31 B15
Fiery Cross Reef: China Sea 64 E5
Fiesole: Italy 41 R12
Fife: Reg., Scotland (cap. Cupar) 29 P7
Fife Ness: cape, Fife, Scot. 29 Q7
Figalo, Cape: Algeria 35 F19
Figeac: France 37 H11
Figline: Italy 41 R12
Figtree: Rhodesia 77 C7
Figueira da Foz: Portugal 35 B16
Figueira de Castelo Rodrigo: Portugal 35 C16
Figueras: Spain 35 H15
Figuig: Morocco 80 L8

Fiji: Dominion 67 P5
Cap.: Suva
Area: 7,055 sq. miles (18,272 sq. km.)
Pop.: 541,000 (1972 E)

Fika: Nigeria 81 G2
Filabusi: Rhodesia 77 C7
Filakovo: Czechoslovakia 43 Q12
Filchner Ice Shelf: Antarctica 9 80S 40W
Filey: N. Yorks., England 26 V11
Filiaşi: Romania 39 S14
Filiates: Greece 39 R17
Filiatra: Greece 39 R18
Filicudi: i., Lipari Is. (It.) 38 O17
Filingué: Niger 81 E2
Filipstad: Sweden 47 O7
Filisur: Switzerland 40 P9
Filkins: Oxon., England 25 S16
Fillongley: War., England 25 S15
Fils: riv., W. Germany 40 P7
Filton: Avon, England 24 Q16
Filyos: riv., Turkey 56 C1
Fimi: riv., Zaire 81 H5

For Abbreviations see list on p.113 Italic type, e.g. Ephesus, refers to historical names not on maps. Capital letters, e.g. MADRID, show capitals of countries; small capital letters, e.g. CADIZ, show capitals of provinces, etc. General notes p.116.

Finale: Italy 41 R11
Finale Marina: Italy 40 O11
Finchingfield: Essex, Eng. 25 W16
Findhorn: Gram., Scotland 28 O4
Findhorn: riv. Scotland 28 O5
Findlay: Ohio, U.S.A. 88 K5
Findochty: Gram., Scotland 28 Q4
Findon: W. Sussex, England 24 V18
Finedon: Northants., Eng. 25 U15
Fines: Norway 46 M5
Fingal: Tas., Australia 68 H8
Finglas: Dublin, Repub. of Ireland 31 J13
Fingoè: Mozambique 77 D6
Finguila: Nigeria 81 E2
Finike: Turkey 56 B3
Finistère: Dept., France
  (cap. Quimper) 36 A7
Finisterre, Cape: Spain 35 B15
Finke: N. Territ, Australia 68 E5
Finke: riv., S. Australia 69 F5

Finland: Republic 46/7 U5
  Cap.: Helsinki
  Area: 130,119 sq. miles
  (337,008 sq. km.)
  Pop.: 4,653,000 (1972 E)

Finland, G. of: Fin./U.S.S.R. 47 T7
Finlay Forks: B.C., Canada 92 C1
Finlay: riv., Canada 84 G6
Finley: N.S.W., Australia 71 F10
Finn: riv., Repub. of Irel. 30 F10
Finnea: Westmeath, Repub. of Ireland 30 G12
Finnegan: Alta., Canada 92 E2
Finningley: S. Yorks., Eng. 27 U13
Finnmark: Co., Norway
  (cap. Vadso) 46 T1
Finnskog: Norway 47 N6
Finowfurt: E. Germany 45 T3
Finschhafen: Papua/New Guinea 66 J3
Finspång: Sweden 47 O7
Finsteraarhorn: mtn., Switz. 40 N9
Finsterwalde: E. Germany 45 T4
Finstown: Orkney Is. 28 P2
Fintona: Tyr., N. Ireland 30 G11
Fintown: Don., Repub. of Ireland 30 E10
Fintry: Central, Scotland 29 N7
Finuge: Kerry, Repub. of Ireland 31 B15
Finvoy: Antrim, N. Ireland 30 H9
Fionn Loch: High., Scot. 28 L4
Fionnphort: I. of Mull, Scot. 29 J7
Fiordland: geog. reg., South I., New Zealand 71 L17
Fiordland National Park:
  New Zealand 70 L17
Fiorenzuola d'Arda: Italy 40 P11
Fiq: Syria 55 b2
Firat (Euphrates): riv., Tur. 56 F3
Firdân: Egypt (Suez Inset) 32 Ins.
Firdaus: Iran 55 J8
Fireh, Shaib: wadi, Iraq 57 J6
FIRENZE (Florence): Tuscany,
  Italy 41 R12
Firenzuola: Italy 41 R11
Firghia: Guinea 80 B2
Firkessèdougou: Ivory Coast 80 C3
Firle, West: E. Sussex, Eng. 25 W18
Firmat: Argentina 96 C3
Firminy: France 37 K10
Firozpur: Punjab, India 58 M8
Firuzabad: Iran 55 H9
Firuzkuh: Iran 55 H7
Fischbach Alps: Austria 41 V8
Fish Bay: S. Africa 74 E7
Fisheries, The: S. Africa 74 D7
Fisher Str.: N.W.T., Can. 85 I5
Fishguard: Dyfed, Wales 24 M16
Fish Hoek: S. Africa 74 Ins.
Fishlake: S. Yorks., England 27 T12
Fish River Canyon Nature Reserve:
  SW. Africa 74 B3
Fishwater: S. Africa 74 C5
Fiskars: Finland 47 S6
Fiskenaesset: Greenland 85 o5
Fismes: France 36 J6
Fitchburg: Mass., U.S.A. 89 Q4
Fitful Head: Shetland Is. 28 Ins.
Fittleworth: W. Sussex, England 25 U18
Fitzgerald: Alta., Canada 84 h6
Fitzgerald: Ga., U.S.A. 91 K10
Fitzgerald: Tas., Australia 68 H8
Fitzpatrick: Que., Canada 89 P2
Fitz Roy: Argentina 95 D13
Fitzroy: riv., Queens., Austl. 70 J4
Fitzroy, Cerro: mtn., S. Am. 95 C13
Fitzroy Crossing: W. Austl. 68 D3
Fitzwilliam I.: Ont., Canada 88 L3
Fiume (Rijeka): Yugoslavia 41 U10
Fiume, G. of: Yugoslavia 41 U10
Fivemiletown: Tyr., N. Irel. 30 G11
Fives Lille: Argentina 96 C1
Fivizzano: Italy 40 Q11
Fizi: Zaire 76 C3
Fizuli: Azerbaydzhan, U.S.S.R. 57 K2

Fjaera: Norway 47 K7
Fjaerland: Norway 47 K6
Fjällbacka: Sweden 47 M7
Fjerritslev: Denmark 47 L6
Flå: Norway 47 L6
Fladdabister: Shetland Is. 28 Ins.
Fladdachuain: i., Scotland 28 J4
Fladungen: W. Germany 45 Q5
Flaga: Iceland 46 d5
Flagstaff: Ariz., U.S.A. 93 E5
Flagstaff: see Siphaqeni
Flakstadøy: i., Lofoten Is.
  (Norway) 46 N2
Flå Lake: Sweden 46 O4
Flåm: Norway 47 K6
Flamanrieu: riv., Wis., U.S.A. 88 F3
Flamborough: Humb., Eng. 27 V11
Flamborough Head: cape,
  Humberside, England 27 V11
Flamenco: Chile 96 A2
Flanders East: Prov., Belg.
  (cap. Ghent) 44 J4
Flanders, West: Prov., Belg.
  (cap. Bruges) 44 H4
Flandreau: S. Dak., U.S.A. 92 H4
Flanigan: Nev., U.S.A. 92 C4
Flannan Is.: Outer Heb., Scotland 28 G3
Flasher: N. Dak., U.S.A. 92 G3
Flat: Alaska, U.S.A. 84 D5
Flåtadal: Norway 46 N4
Flateyri: Iceland 46 b3
Flathead L.: Mont., U.S.A. 92 E3
Flathead Mts.: Mont., U.S.A. 92 E3
Flatmark: Norway 46 M5
Flat River: city, Mo., U.S.A. 88 F7
Flatrock Lake: Man., Can. 92 G1
Flattery, C.: Wash., U.S.A. 92 C3
Flattery, C.: Queens., Austl. 69 H2
Flaxton: N. Dak., U.S.A. 92 G3
Flechas, Cerro: mtn., Mexico 93 F7
Flèche, La: France 36 E8

Fleet: Hants., England 25 U17
Fleet, Strath: valley, Highland,
  Scotland 28 N4
Fleetwood: Lancs., England 27 P12
Flekkfjord: Norway 47 K7
Fleming: Ky., U.S.A. 88 K7
Flemingsburg: Ky., U.S.A. 88 K6
Flen: Sweden 47 P7
Flensburg: W. Germany 44 P1
Flers: France 36 E7
Flesko Cape: Celebes 65 G6
Fleurance: France 37 F12
Fleur de Lys: Newf., Canada 85 u1
Fleurier: Switzerland 40 M9
Fleury: Eure, France 36 G6
Fleury: Meuse, France 36 L6
Fleury-les-Aubrais: France 36 G8
Fleuve: Reg., Senegal (cap. St. Louis) 80 B1
Flevoland, East: geog. reg.,
  IJsselmeer, Netherlands 44 L3
Flevoland, South: geog. reg.,
  IJsselmeer, Netherlands 44 L3
Fliedon: W. Germany 44 P5
Fliess: Austria 41 Q8
Flimby: Cumbria, England 26 O10
Flims: Switzerland 40 P9
Flinders: riv., Queens., Austl. 69 G4
Flinders I.: Queens., Austl. 69 G2
Flinders I.: Tas., Australia 68 H7
Flinders Passage: Great Barrier
  Reef, Australia 70 H2
Flinders Range: S. Austl. 71 C8
Flinders Reefs: Coral Sea 70 H1
Flin Flon: Man., Canada 92 G2
Flint: Clwyd, Wales 27 P13
Flint: Mich., U.S.A. 88 K4
Flint: riv., Ga., U.S.A. 91 J10
Flint Hills: Kans., U.S.A. 90 C7
Flint I.: Pacific O. 83 e2
Flinton: Queens., Australia 70 H6
Flisa: Norway 47 N6
Flitcham: Norf., England 25 X14
Flitwick: Beds., England 25 V16
Flixborough: Humb., Eng. 27 U12
Flixton: Suff., England 25 Y15
Flodday, North: i., Scot. 28 G6
Flodday, South: i., Scot. 28 G6
Flodden: battlefield about 1 mile S.
  of Branxton, Northumberland,
  England 26 R8
Flood Range: Antarctica 9 80S 140W
Flora: Ill., U.S.A. 88 G6
Flora: Ind., U.S.A. 88 H5
Flora: Norway 47 J6
Florac: France 37 J11
Florala: Ala., U.S.A. 91 H10
Florence: Ala., U.S.A. 91 H8
Florence: Kans., U.S.A. 90 C6
Florence: S.C., U.S.A. 91 M8
FLORENCE (Firenze): Tuscany,
  Italy 41 R12
Florencia: Argentina 96 D2
Florencia: Colombia 94 B3
Florenville: Belgium 44 L6
Flores: Guatemala
  (Honduras Inset) 86 Ins.
Flores: i., Azores 78 Ins.
Flores: i. & sea: Indonesia 65 G8
Floreshty: Moldavia, U.S.S.R. 43 V13
Floresville: Tex., U.S.A. 90 B11
Forno di Zoldo: Italy 41 S9
Fornovo di Taro: Italy 40 Q11
Forres: Gram., Scotland 28 O4
Forrest: Vict., Australia 71 E12
Forrest: W. Australia 68 D6
Forrest City: Ark., U.S.A. 90 F8
Forrest River Mission: W. Australia 68 D3
Forró: Hungary 43 R12
Forsand: Norway 47 K7
Forsayth: Queens., Austl. 69 G3
Forsbrook: Staffs., England 27 R14
Forsinard: High., Scotland 28 O3
Forssa: Finland 47 S6
Forssa: Sweden 47 P6
Forst: E. Germany 45 U4
Forsyth: Ga., U.S.A. 91 K9
Forsyth: Mont., U.S.A. 92 F3
Fort Abbas: Punjab, Pakistan 58 M9
Fort Albany: Ont., Canada 85 I7
FORTALEZA (Ceará): Ceará,
  Brazil 94 K4
Fortaleza Santa Teresa: Uruguay 96 E3
Fort Amador: Panama 94 Ins.
FORT ARCHAMBAULT: see SARH.
Fort Atkinson: Wis., U.S.A. 88 G4
Fort Augustus: High., Scot. 28 M5
Fort Bayard: see Chan-chiang.
Fort Beaufort: & Dist., S. Africa 75 G6
Fort Bell: Bermudas 87 Ins.
Fort Benton: Mont., U.S.A. 92 E3
Fort Bragg: Calif., U.S.A. 93 C5
Fort Brown: S. Africa 75 G6
Fort Burger: Trans., S. Afr. 75 J2
Fort Cappuzo: Libya 33 H5
Fort Carnot (Ban Houei Sai): Laos 64 C2
Fort Chimo: Que., Canada 84 N6
Fort Chipewyan: Alta., Canada 84 h6
Fort Collins: Colo., U.S.A. 93 F4
Fort Collinson: N.W.T., Canada 84 H3
Fort Coulonge: Que., Can. 89 N3
Fort Crampel: Central African Empire 81 J7
Fort-Dauphin: Malagasy Rep. 73 O14
FORT-DE-FRANCE: Martinique,
  Windward Is. 87 c3
Fort Dodge: Iowa, U.S.A. 88 D4
Forteau Bay: town, Newf.,
  Canada 85 u1
Fort Edward: N.Y., U.S.A. 89 P4
Fort Edward: Trans., S. Afr. 75 H1
Forter: Tayside, Scotland 29 P6
Forte Roçadas: Angola 73 H13
Fortescue: riv., W. Austl. 68 B4
Fortevoit: Tay., Scotland 29 O7
Fort Fairfield: Maine, U.S.A. 89 S2
Fort Frances: Ont., Canada 88 E1
Fort Franklin: N.W.T., Can. 84 g4
Fort Frazer: B.C., Canada 92 C2
Fort George: High., Scotland 28 N4
Fort George: & riv., Que., Canada 85 M7
Fort Gibson: Okla., U.S.A. 90 D8
Fort Good Hope: N.W.T., Canada 84 G4
Fort Grahame: B.C., Can. 92 C1
Fort Grey: N.S.W., Austl. 71 D7
Forth: Strath, Scotland 29 O8
Forth: riv., Scotland 29 N7
Forth, Firth of: Scotland 29 Q7
Fort Hall: see Muranga
Fort Hall: Idaho, U.S.A. 92 D4
Fort Hertz: see Putao
Fortín Avalos Sánchez: Paraguay 96 C1
Fortín Boquerón: Paraguay 96 C1
Fortingall: Tay., Scotland 29 N6
Fortín Gral Diaz: Paraguay 96 C1
Fortín Lavalle: Argentina 96 C2
Fortín Olmos: Argentina 96 C2
Fortín: río: Argentina 96 B4
Fort Jameson: see Chipata.
Fort Johnston: see Mangoche
Fort Kent: Maine, U.S.A. 89 R2
Fort Knox: Ky., U.S.A. 88 J7
Fort Lallemand: Algeria 78 F3
Fort Lamy: see N'Djamena
Fort Laperrine: Algeria 78 F5

Fort Lauderdale: Fla., U.S.A. 91 L12
Fort Liard: N.W.T., Canada 84 g5
Fort Loudon Dam: Tenn., U.S.A. 91 J8
Fort Mackay: Alta., Canada 92 E1
Fort Macleod: Alta., Canada 92 E3
Fort Macmahon: Algeria 78 E4
Fort McMurray: Alta., Can. 92 E1
Fort Macpherson: N.W.T., Canada 84 f4
Fort Madison: Iowa, U.S.A. 88 F5
Fort Maguire: Malawi 77 D5
Fort Meade: Fla., U.S.A. 91 L12
Fort Miribel: Algeria 78 E4
Fort Morgan: Colo., U.S.A. 93 G4
Fort Munro: Punjab, Pakistan 58 L9
Fort Myers: Fla., U.S.A. 91 L12
Fort Nelson: B.C., Canada 84 g6
Fort Norman: N.W.T., Can. 84 G5
Fortore: riv., Italy 38 O16
Fort Payne: Ala., U.S.A. 91 J8
Fort Peck: & reservoir, & dam,
  Mont., U.S.A. 92 F3
Fort Pierce: Fla., U.S.A. 91 L12
Fort Portal: Uganda 76 D2
Fort Providence: N.W.T., Canada 84 h5
Fort Rae: N.W.T., Canada 84 H5
Fort Resolution: N.W.T., Canada 84 h5
Fort Riley: Kans., U.S.A. 90 C6
Fort Rixon: Rhodesia 77 C7
FORT ROUSSET: see OWANDO
Fort Rupert: Que., Canada 85 M7
Fort Saint: Tunisia 78 F3
Fort St. John: B.C., Canada 92 C1
Fort Sandeman: Baluchistan,
  Pakistan 58 L8
Fort Saskatchewan: Alta., Canada 92 E2
Fort Scott: Kans., U.S.A. 90 D7
Fort Selkirk: Yukon, Canada 84 F5
Fort Severn: Ont., Canada 85 L6
Fort Shevchenko: Kazakh.,
  U.S.S.R. 50 H6
Fort Sibut: see Sibut.
Fort Sill: Okla., U.S.A. 90 B8
Fort Simpson: N.W.T., Can. 84 g5
Fort Smith: Ark., U.S.A. 90 D8
Fort Smith: N.W.T., Canada 84 h5
Fort Stedman: Burma 59 R10
Fort Stockton: Tex., U.S.A. 93 G6
Fort Sumner: N. Mex., U.S.A. 93 G6
Fort Supply Reservoir: Okla.,
  U.S.A. 90 B7
Fort Thomas: Ky., U.S.A. 88 J6
Fort Tregear: Mizoram, India 59 Q10
Fortuna: Calif., U.S.A. 92 C4
Fortune Bay: Newf., Canada 85 v3
Fortuneswell: Dorset, Eng. 24 R18
Fort Valley: city, Ga., U.S.A. 91 K9
Fort Vermilion: Alta., Can. 84 H6
FORT VICTORIA: Victoria, Rhodesia 77 D7
Fort Wayne: Ind., U.S.A. 88 J5
Fort William: High., Scot. 29 L6
Fort William: Ont., Canada 88 G1
Fort Worth: Tex., U.S.A. 90 C9
Fortymile: Yukon, Canada 84 e5
Fort Yukon: Alaska, U.S.A. 84 E4
Forum Appii: Roman station about
  40 miles SE. of Rome. 38 N16
Forum Clodii: Roman town NW. of
  Rome. 38 N15
Fos, Golfe de: gulf, France 37 K12
Fosdyke: Lincs., England 27 V14
Foshan: Kwangtung, China 62 U10
Fosheim Penin.: N.W.T., Canada 85 I2
Foss: Tayside, Scotland 29 O6
Fossano: Italy 40 N11
Fossil Bluff: rsch. stn., Antarctica 9 75S 70W
Fossil Downs: W. Austl. 68 D3
Fossombrone: Italy 41 S12
Foster: Vict., Australia 71 G12
Foster Bay: Greenland 85 r3
Foster Lakes: Sask., Canada 92 G1
Fostoria: Ohio, U.S.A. 88 K5
Fotheringhay: Northants., England 25 V14
Fouesnant: France 36 A8
Fougères: France 36 D7
Fouju: i., Shetland Is., Scot. 28 Ins.
Foul Bay: Egypt 54 E10
Foulksmills: Wex., Repub. of Ireland 31 H15
Foulness: i. & cape, Eng. 25 X16
Foul Point: cape, Sri Lanka 58 O13
Foulridge: Lancs., England 27 R12
Foulsham: Norf., England 25 Y14
Foulwind, Cape: South I., New
  Zealand 70 N15
Foumban: Cameroun 81 G3
Foum Zguid: Morocco 80 K8
Foundiougne: Senegal 80 A2
Fountainhall: Bord., Scot. 29 Q8
Fountains Abbey: N. Yorks.,
  England 27 S11
Fouras: France 37 D10
Fourchambault: France 36 J8
Fouriesburg: O.F.S., S. Afr. 75 H4
Fourmies: France 36 K5
Four Mountains, Is. of the:
  Aleutians 84 C6
Fouroumbala: Central African
  Republic 76 B2
Fours: France 37 J9
Fouta Djalon: mtns., Guinea 80 B2
Foveaux Str.: N.Z. 71 M18
Foveran: Gram., Scotland 28 R5
Fowey: Corn., England 24 M19
Fowey: riv., Corn., England 24 M18
Fowler: Colo., U.S.A. 93 G5
Fowler: Ind., U.S.A. 88 H5
Fowler's Bay: town, S. Austl. 68 E6
Fowling: Szechwan, China 62 T9
Fowlis Wester: Tay., Scot. 29 O7
Fowning: Kiangsu, China 63 V8
Fowping: Honan, China 62 U7
Fowyang: Anhwei, China 62 V8
Foxdale: I. of Man, U.K. 26 M11
Foxe Basin: N.W.T., Can. 85 M4
Foxe Penin.: & chan., N.W.T.,
  Canada 85 M5
Foxford: Mayo, Repub. of Ireland 30 C12
Fox Is.: Mich., U.S.A. 88 J3
Fox Is.: Aleutians 84 C7
Foxton: North I., N.Z. 70 P15
Fox Valley: town, Sask., Canada 92 F2
Foyers: Highland, Scotland 28 N5

Foyle: riv., Lon., N. Ireland 30 G10
Foyle, Lough: N. Ireland/Repub.
  of Ireland 30 G9
Foynes: Lim., Repub. of Ireland 31 C14
Foz do Iguaçu: Brazil 96 E2
Foz do Jordão: Brazil 94 C5
Foz do Riozinho: Brazil 94 C5
Fozuzo: Peru 94 B5
Fraga: Spain 35 G16
Fraize: France 40 N7
Frameries: Belgium 44 J5
Framlingham: Suff., Eng. 25 Y15
Framsden: Suff., England 25 Y15
Franca: São Paulo, Brazil 94 H8
França: Bahia, Brazil 94 J6
Francavilla Fontana: Italy 38 P16

France: Republic 36/7
  Cap.: Paris
  Area: 212,973 sq. miles
  (551,600 sq. km.)
  Pop.: 51,720,000 (1972 E)

France, Île de: Greenland 85 S2
Frances: S. Australia 71 D11
Frances Lake Post: Yukon, Canada 84 G5
FRANCEVILLE: Haut-Ogooué, Gabon 81 G5
Franche Comté: Prov., Fr. 34 K13
Francis Case, Lake: Nebr./S. Dak.,
  U.S.A. 92 H4
FRANCISTOWN: North East, Botswana 77 C7
François Lake: B.C., Can. 92 B2
Franconia: early medieval duchy in
  the Main River valley,
  W. Germany 44 O5
Franconian Jura: mtns., W. Germany 45 R6
Franeker: Netherlands 44 L2
Frangy: France 40 L9
Frankenau: W. Germany 44 O4
Frankenberg: W. Germany 44 O4
Frankenmarkt: Austria 41 T8
Frankenthal: W. Germany 44 O6
Frankenwald: mtns., W. Ger. 45 R5
Frankfield: Jamaica 86 Ins.
Frankford (Kilcormac): Offaly,
  Repub. of Ireland 31 F13
Frankfort: Ind., U.S.A. 88 H5
FRANKFORT: Ky., U.S.A. 88 J6
Frankfort: Mich., U.S.A. 88 H3
Frankfort & Dist., O.F.S., S. Africa 75 H3
Frankfurt-am-Main: W. Ger. 44 O5
FRANKFURT-AN-DER-ODER: & Dist.,
  E. Germany 45 U3
Fränkische Saale: riv., W. Germany 45 P5
Fränkische Schweiz: geog. reg.,
  W. Germany 45 R6
Franklin: Ind., U.S.A. 88 H6
Franklin: Ky., U.S.A. 88 H7
Franklin: La., U.S.A. 90 F11
Franklin: N.H., U.S.A. 89 Q4
Franklin: N.J., U.S.A. 89 P5
Franklin: N.Y., U.S.A. 91 K8
Franklin: Ohio, U.S.A. 88 J6
Franklin: Pa., U.S.A. 89 M5
Franklin: S. Africa 75 H5
Franklin: Tenn., U.S.A. 91 H8
Franklin: Va., U.S.A. 89 N7
Franklin: Dist., N.W.T., Canada 85 L3
Franklin Bay: N.W.T., Can. 84 G4
Franklin Str.: N.W.T., Can. 84 K3
Franklinton: La., U.S.A. 90 F10
Franklinville: N.Y., U.S.A. 89 N4
Frankston: Vict., Austl. 71 F12
Franschoek: S. Africa 74 C6
Franske Is.: Greenland 85 S2
Frant: E. Sussex, England 25 W17
Frantasou: Chad 81 H2
Franz: Ont., Canada 88 J1
Franzburg: E. Germany 45 S1
Franzfontein: S. W. Africa 73 H14
Franz Josef Land: is., (U.S.S.R.),
  Arctic O. 48 G1
Frasca, Cape: Sardinia 38 L17
Frascati: Italy 38 N16
Frasdorf: W. Germany 41 S8
Fraser: riv., B.C., Canada 92 C2
Fraserburg: & Dist., S. Afr. 74 D5
Fraserburgh: Gram., Scot. 28 R4
Fraserburg Road: S. Africa 74 E6
Fraser (Great Sandy) I.: Queens.,
  Australia 70 K5
Fraser's Hill: Malaya, Malaysia 65 b12
Frasne: France 40 M9
Frastanz: Austria 40 P8
FRAUENFELD: Thurgau,
  Switzerland 40 O8
Fray Bentos: Uruguay 96 D3
Frechen: W. Germany 44 M5
Freckleton: Lancs., England 27 Q12
Fredericia: Denmark 47 L9
Frederick: Md., U.S.A. 89 N6
Frederick: Okla., U.S.A. 90 B8
Frederick Reef: Australia 69 J4
Fredericksburg: Tex., U.S.A. 90 B10
Fredericksburg: Va., U.S.A. 89 N6
FREDERICTON: N.B., Canada 89 S3
Fredericktown: Mo., U.S.A. 88 F7
Frederikshaab: Greenland 85 P5
Frederikshavn: Denmark 47 M8
Frederikssund: Zealand, Denmark 47 N9
Frederiksstad: Trans., S. Afr. 75 G3
Fredonia: Ariz., U.S.A. 93 E5
Fredonia: Kans., U.S.A. 90 D7
Fredrika: Sweden 46 O4
Fredriksberg: Sweden 47 O6
Fredrikstad: Norway 47 M7
Freeland: Pa., U.S.A. 89 O5
Freeling: S. Australia 71 C10
Freemason Is.: La., U.S.A. 90 Ins.
Freemount: Cork, Repub. of Ireland 31 D15
Freeport: Ill., U.S.A. 88 G4
Freeport: Maine, U.S.A. 89 Q4
Freeport: New York, U.S.A. 89 P5
Freeport: Tex., U.S.A. 90 D11
Freeport: The Bahamas 91 M12
Freer: Tex., U.S.A. 90 B12
FREETOWN: Sierra Leone 80 B3
Fregellae: ancient Latin city on Via
  Latina and river Liris (Garigliano)
  about 50 miles SE. of Rome.
  38 N16
Fregenae: Roman city near coast
  about 10 miles NNW. of Ostia.
  38 N16
Fregenal de la Sierra: Spain 35 C17
Fréhel, Cap: cape, France 36 C7
Freiberg: E. Germany 45 T5
Freiburg: Lower Saxony, W. Ger.
  44 P2
Freiburg im Breisgau: W. Germany 40 N8
Freienwalde: E. Germany 45 U3
Freijido: Spain 35 C15

Freising—Geba 143

Freising: W. Germany **41** R7
Freistadt: Austria **41** U7
Freital: E. Germany **45** T5
Freixo: Portugal **35** C16
Fréjus: France **40** M12
Fremantle: W. Australia **68** B6
Fremont: Mich., U.S.A. **88** J4
Fremont: Nebr., U.S.A. **92** H4
Fremont: Ohio, U.S.A. **88** K5

French Guiana: *Fr. overseas dept.* **94** G3
Cap.: Cayenne
Area: 35,135 sq. miles (91,000 sq. km.)
Pop.: 51,000 (*1970 E*)

Frenchpark: Rosc., Repub. of Ireland **30** E12
Frenda: Algeria **35** G19
Freshford: Kilk., Repub. of Ireland **31** G14
Freshwater: I. of Wight, Eng. **25** S18
Fesko: Ivory Coast **80** C3
Fresnay-sur-Sarthe: Fr. **36** F7
Fresnes-en-Woevre: France **36** L6
Fresnillo: Mexico **86** j13
Fresno: Calif., U.S.A. **93** D5
Fresnoy-Folny: France **36** G6
Fressingfield: Suff., England **25** Y15
Freswick: High., Scotland **28** P2
Fretzdorf: E. Germany **45** S2
Freu, Cape: Maj., Balearic Is. **35** H17
Freuchie: Fife, Scotland **29** P7
Freuchie, Loch: Tay., Scot. **29** O6
Freudenberg: W. Germany **44** N5
Freudenstadt: W. Germany **40** O7
Frevent: France **36** H5
Freyenstein: E. Germany **45** S2
Frias: Argentina **96** B2
Frias: Spain **35** E15
FRIBOURG: *& Canton*, Switz. **40** N9
Frickingen: W. Germany **40** P8
Friday Bridge: Cambs., Eng. **25** W14
Fridaythorpe: Humb., Eng. **27** U11
Friedberg: Austria **41** W8
Friedberg: W. Germany **44** O5
Friedburg: Austria **41** T7
Friedland: E. Germany **45** T2
Friedland: battlefield on river (*Alle*) about 25 miles SE. of Kaliningrad, U.S.S.R. **43** R9
Friedrichshafen: W. Germany **40** P8
Friedrichskoog: W. Germany **44** O1
Friedrichstadt: W. Germany **44** P1
Friedrichswalde: E. Germany **45** T2
Friendly Is.: *see* Tonga
Fries: Va., U.S.A. **88** L7
Friesach: Austria **41** U9
Friesack: W. Germany **45** S3
Friesland: *Prov.*, Netherlands (*cap.* Leeuwarden) **44** L2
Friesoythe: W. Germany **44** N2
Frihetsli: Norway **46** Q2
Frijoles: Panama **94** *Ins.*
Frijoles: *riv.*, Panama **94** *Ins.*
Frimley: Surrey, England **25** U17
Frinton on Sea: Essex, Eng. **25** Y16
Frio: *riv.*, Tex., U.S.A. **90** B11
Friockheim: Tayside, Scot. **29** Q6
Frisches Haff: *lag.*, Poland **47** Q9
Frisian Is., East: W. Germany **44** N2
Frisian Is., North: W. Ger. **44** O1
Frisian Is., West: Neth. **44** K2
Friskney: Lincs., England **27** W13
Friston: Suff., England **25** Z15
Fritzlar: W. Germany **44** P4
Friuli-Venezia Giulia: *Reg.*, Italy (*cap.* Trieste) **41** S9
Frizington: Cumb., Eng. **26** P10
Frobisher Bay: *& bay*, N.W.T., Canada **85** N5
Frobisher Lake: Sask., Can. **92** F1
Frodingham, North: N. Yorks., England **27** V12
Frodsham: Ches., England **27** Q13
Fro Havet: Norway **46** L5
Froissy: France **36** H6
Frolovo: U.S.S.R. **50** F5
Fromberg: Mont., U.S.A. **93** F3
Frome: Som., England **24** R17
Frome: *riv.*, Dorset, Eng. **24** Q18
Frome, Lake: S. Australia **71** C8
Frome Downs: S. Australia **71** C8
Fronteira: Portugal **35** C17
Frontenac: Kans., U.S.A. **90** D7
Frontenay-Rohan: France **37** E9
Fronteras: Mexico **93** F6
Frontignan: France **37** J12
Front Range: Colo., U.S.A. **93** F5
Front Royal: Va., U.S.A. **89** M6
Frosinone: Italy **38** N16
Frostburg: Md., U.S.A. **89** M6
Frosterley: Durham, Eng. **26** S10
Frostproof: Fla., U.S.A. **91** L12
Frovi: Sweden **47** O7
Frøya: *i.*, Norway **46** L5
Frozen Str.: N.W.T., Canada **85** I 4
Fruges: France **36** H5
Fruita: *riv.*, Colo., U.S.A. **93** F5
Frumuşica: Romania **43** U13
FRUNZE: Kirgizia, U.S.S.R. **51** M6
Frusino: ancient Hernican city on *Via Latina* about 45 miles SE. of Rome **38** N16
Frutigen: Switzerland **40** N9
Frydek: Czechoslovakia **43** Q12
Frydlant: Czechoslovakia **45** V5
Fryvaldov: Czechoslovakia **43** P11
Fu: *riv.*, China **62** V9
Fucecchio: Italy **41** Q12
Fuchin: Heilungkiang, China **63** Y5
Fuchow: Kiangsi, China **62** V9
Fuchow: Liaoning, China **63** W7
Fuchu: Japan **63** c3
Fuchwan: Kwangsi Chuang, China **62** U10
Fucinus: lake 1½ miles E. of *Avezzano* and about 40 miles E. of Rome **38** N15
Fud, El: Ethiopia **79** Q18
Fuday: *i.*, Outer Hebr., Scot. **28** G5
Fuengirola: Spain **35** D18
Fuente de Cantos: Spain **35** C17
Fuente del Arco: Spain **35** D17
Fuenteovejuna: Spain **35** D17
Fuentesauco: Spain **35** D16
Fuentes de Oñoro: Spain **35** C16
Fuerte: *riv.*, Mexico **93** F7
Fuerte, El: Mexico **93** F7
Fuerteventura: *i.*, Canary Is. **78** B4
Fuerty: Rosc., Repub. of Ireland **30** E12
Fuga: *i.*, Philippines **64** G3
Fuglø: *i.*, Faeroe Is. (Dan.) **46** h5
Fuhai: Sinkiang, China **51** P5
Fuhsien: Shensi, China **62** T7
Fuiay: *i.*, Outer Hebr., Scot. **28** G5
Fuji: *mtn. & riv.*, Japan **63** f3
Fujiomiya: Japan **63** f3
Fujisawa: Japan **63** f3
Fuka: Egypt **54** C8
Fukae: *i.*, Goto Is., Japan **63** X8
Fukawa: Japan **63** b3
Fukien: *Prov.*, China (*cap.* Foochow) **62** V9
Fukuchiyama: Japan **63** d3
FUKUI: *& Pref.*, Japan **63** e2
FUKUOKA: *& Pref.*, Japan **63** b4
Fukura: Japan **63** d3
FUKUSHIMA: *& Pref.*, Japan **63** g2
Fukushima: Hokkaido, Japan **63** ZZ6
Fukushima: Nagano, Japan **63** e3
Fukuyama: Hokkaido, Jap. **63** ZZ6
Fukuyama: Honshu, Japan **63** c3
Fulacunda: Guinea-Bissau **80** A2
Fulanga: *i.*, Fiji Is. **67** Q5
Fulbourn: Cambs., England **25** W15
Fulda: *& riv.*, W. Germany **44** P5
Fuli: *well*, Somalia **79** R18
Fullarton: Strath., Scotland **29** M8
Fulnek: Czechoslovakia **43** P12
Fulo: Hainan, China **62** T11
Fulpmes: Austria **41** R8
Fulstow: Lincs., England **27** W13
Fulton: Ill., U.S.A. **88** F5
Fulton: Ky., U.S.A. **88** G7
Fulton: Miss., U.S.A. **90** G8
Fulton: Mo., U.S.A. **88** F6
Fulton: N.Y., U.S.A. **89** N4
Fulton, South: Tenn., U.S.A. **88** G7
Fulwood: Lancs., England **27** Q12
Fulwood: S. Yorks., England **27** S13
Fumel: France **37** F11
Fumen: Iran **57** L3
Funabashi: Japan **63** f3
Funafuti: *i.*, **Tuvalu 67 P3**
Funakawaminato: Japan **63** Z7
Funan Cuba: Ethiopia **76** E2
Funasdalen: Sweden **46** N5
Funatsu: Japan **63** e2
FUNCHAL: Madeira **78** A3
Fundão: Portugal **35** C16
Fundikh: Turkey (Dardan. *Inset*) **20** *Ins.*
Fundy, Bay of: Canada **89** T3
Funen: *i.*, Denmark **47** M9
Fungshun: Kwangtung, China **62** V10
Funhaluro: Mozambique **77** D7
Funing (Siapo): Fukien, China **63** W9
Funing: Yunnan, China **62** T10
Funtua: Nigeria **81** F2
Furancungo: Mozambique **77** D5
Furano: Japan **63** ZZ6
Furbero: Mexico **86** K13
Furg: Iran **55** J9
Furka Pass: Switzerland **40** O9
Furmanovo: (*W. Kazakh.*), Kazakh., U.S.S.R. **50** G5
Furmanovo: (*Dzhambul*), Kazakh., U.S.S.R. **51** M6
Furnace: Strath., Scotland **29** L7
Furneaux Group: *is.*, Tas., Australia **68** H8
Furnes: *see* Veurne
Furness Fells: *mtns.*, Cumbria, England **26** P11
Furstenau: W. Germany **44** N3
Furstenberg: Hesse, W. Germany **45** O4
Furstenberg: Potsdam, E. Ger. **45** T2
Furstenfeld: Austria **41** W8
Furstenfeldbruck: W. Ger. **41** R7
Furstenwalde: E. Germany **45** U3
Furth: Oberpfalz, W. Ger. **45** S6
Furth: Mittelfranken, W. Ger. **45** Q6
Furtwangen: W. Germany **40** O7
Furudal: Sweden **47** O6
Fusch: Austria **41** S8
Fuse: Japan **63** d3
Fusea: Romania **39** T14
Fushih (Yenan): Shensi, China **62** T7
Fushimi: Japan **63** d3
Fushun: Liaoning, China **63** W6
Fusin: Liaoning, China **63** W6
Fusio: Switzerland **40** O9
Fussen: W. Germany **41** Q8
Fusung: Kirin, China **63** X6
Futamata: Japan **63** e3
Futing: Fukien, China **63** W9
Futsing: Fukien, China **62** V9
Futuna: *i.*, Fr. [*cap.* (with Wallis) Mata Utu] Pacific O. **67** Q4
Fuveau: France **40** L12
Fuyang: Chekiang, China **62** V8
Fuyu: Heilungkiang, China **63** W5
Fuyu: Kirin, China **63** W5
Fuyuan: Heilungkiang, China **63** Y5
Fuynan: Yunnan, China **62** S9
Fuzesabony: Hungary **43** R13
Fužine: Yugoslavia **41** U10
Fylde: *dist.*, Lancs., England **27** Q12
Fylingdales: N. Yorks., Eng. **26** U11
Fyn: *see* Funen
Fyne, Loch: Strath., Scot. **29** L7
Fyres Lake: Norway **47** K7
Fyvie: Grampian, Scotland **28** R5
Fyzabad: Uttar Pradesh, India **58** O9

Gaase Land: Greenland **85** R3
Gabana: Ethiopia **76** F1
Gabarus Bay: Cape Breton I., Canada **89** V3
Gabas: *riv.*, France **37** E12
Gabeh: *riv.*, Iran **57** K4
Gabela: Angola **73** G12
Gaberones: *see* Gaborone
Gabes: *& gulf*, Tunisia **32** E5
Gabgaba: *wadi*, Sudan **54** D10
Gabii: ancient Latin city about 12 miles E. of Rome **38** N16
Gąbin: Poland **43** Q10

Gabon: *Republic* **81** G5
Cap.: Libreville
Area: 102,317 sq. miles (265,001 sq. km.)
Pop.: 500,000 (*1970 E*)

GABORONE (Gaberones): Botswana **75** F2
Gaborone Dam: Botswana **75** F2
Gabredare: Ethiopia **79** Q18
Gabrovo: Bulgaria **39** T15
Gabu: Zaire **76** C2
Gace: France **36** F7
Gacilly, La: France **36** C8
Gacko: Yugoslavia **39** Q15
Gad: Israelite tribe which inhabited region around Salt, Jordan **55** b3
Gadag: Karnataka, India **58** N11
Gadames: Libya **78** F3
Gadara: Hellenistic city at Umm Qeis, Jordan **55** b2
Gaddede: Sweden **46** O4
Gaddoule: Niger **81** G2
Gadebusch: E. Germany **45** R2
Gadein: Sudan **76** C1
Gades: ancient town and port at Cadiz, Spain **35** C18
Gadra: Sind, Pakistan **58** M9
Gadsden: Ala., U.S.A. **91** J8
Gadsden: Ariz., U.S.A. **93** E6
Gadyach: Ukraine **50** D4
Gael Hamkes Bay: Grnld. **85** r3
Găeşti: Romania **39** T14
Gaeta: Italy **38** N16
Gaffney: S.C., U.S.A. **91** L8
Gafsa: Tunisia **32** D5
Gagare: *riv.*, Nigeria **81** F2
Gagarin: U.S.S.R. **50** E3
Gagnoa: Ivory Coast **80** C3
Gagnon: Que., Canada **85** N7
Gago Coutinho: Angola **77** B5
Gagry: Georgia, U.S.S.R. **50** F6
Gail: *riv.*, Austria **41** T9
Gaildorf: W. Germany **40** P7
Gaillac: France **37** G12
Gaillard (Culebra) Cut: Panama Canal **94** *Ins.*
Gainesville: Fla., U.S.A. **91** K11
Gainesville: Ga., U.S.A. **91** K8
Gainesville: Tex., U.S.A. **90** C9
Gainford: Durham, England **26** S10
Gainsborough: Lincs., Eng. **27** U13
Gairdner, Lake: S. Australia **69** F6
Gair Loch: High., Scot. **28** K4
Gairloch: High., Scot. **28** K4
Gairlochy: High., Scotland **28** M6
Gairsay: *i.*, Orkney Is., Scot. **28** P2
Gakarusa: *mtn.*, S. Africa **74** E3
Gakem: Nigeria **81** F3
Galadi: Ethiopia **79** R18
Galana: *riv.*, Kenya **76** E3
Galangale: Somalia **76** F3
Galapagos Is.: (Ecuador), Pacific Ocean **83** O 90W
Galapagos Fracture Zone: S. Pacific Ocean **7** 05S 110W
Galashiels: Bord., Scotland **29** Q8
Galaţi: Romania **39** V14
Galatia: district conquered by Celts in central Asiatic Turkey with centre at Ankara **56** C2
Galatina: Italy **39** Q16
Galax: Va., U.S.A. **88** L7
Galay: Guinea **80** C3
Galbally: Lim., Repub. of Ireland **31** E15
Galbraith: Queens., Austl. **69** G3
Galdhøpiggen: *mtn.*, Nor. **47** K6
Gale: Mali **80** C2
Galeana: Mexico **93** F6
Galeata: Italy **41** R12
Galena: Alaska, U.S.A. **84** D5
Galena: Ill., U.S.A. **88** F4
Galena: Kans., U.S.A. **90** D7
Galena Park: *city*, Tex., U.S.A. **90** D11
Galeota Point: *cape*, Trinidad **87** c5
Galesburg: Ill., U.S.A. **88** F5
Galesville: Wis., U.S.A. **88** F3
Galeta I.: Panama **94** *Ins.*
Galeton: Pa., U.S.A. **89** N5
Galey: *riv.*, Kerry, Repub. of Ireland **31** C15
Galgate: Lancs., England **27** Q12
Galhak: Sudan **79** L7
Galich: U.S.S.R. **50** F3
Galicia: *old Prov.*, Spain **35** C15
Galicia: *geog. reg.*, Poland **43** R12
Galilee: northern district of ancient *Judaea* in New Testament period, lying W. of the Jordan, SW. of L. Hula, and NE. of vale of *Jezreel* **55** b2
Galilee, Sea of: Biblical name of Lake Tiberias (see also *Gennesaret*) **55** b2
Galilee, L.: Queens., Austl. **69** H4
Galion: Ohio, U.S.A. **88** K5
Galište: Yugoslavia **39** R16
Galita Is.: Tunisia **38** L18
GALKAYU: Mudugh, Somalia **79** R18
Gallabat: Sudan **54** E12
Gallan Head: *cape*, I. of Lewis, Outer Hebr., Scot. **28** G3
Gallarate: Italy **40** O10
Gallatin: Tenn., U.S.A. **88** H7
Galle: Sri Lanka **58** O13
Gallego: Mexico **93** F7
Gallego: *riv.*, Spain **35** F16
Gellagos: *riv.*, Argentina **95** C14
Galley Head: *cape*, Cork, Repub. of Ireland **31** D16
Galliate: Italy **40** O10
Gallina Mtns.: N. Mex., U.S.A. **93** F6
Gallinas, Cape: Colombia **94** C1
Gallipoli: Italy **39** Q16
Gallipoli (Gelibolu): Turkey (Dardan. *Inset*) **20** *Ins.*
Gallipoli Penin.: Turkey (Dardan. *Inset*) **20** *Ins.*
Gallipolis: Ohio, U.S.A. **88** K6
Gallivare: Sweden **46** R3
Gallneukirchen: Austria **41** U7
Gallo: Sweden **46** O5
Galloway: *dist.*, Dumfries & Galloway, Scotland **29** N10
Galloway, Mull of: *cape*, Dumf. & Gall., Scotland **29** M10
Galloway, New: Dumfries & Galloway, Scotland **29** N9
Gallup: N. Mex., U.S.A. **93** F5
Gallya-Aral: Uzbek., U.S.S.R. **51** L7
Galong: N.S.W., Australia **71** H10
Gal Oya: Sri Lanka **58** O13
Galston: Strath., Scotland **29** N8
Gal Tardo: *well*, Somalia **79** R19
Galtee Mtns.: Lim./Tip., Repub. of Ireland **31** E15
Galtymore: *mtn.*, Lim./Tip., Repub. of Ireland **31** E15
Galur: Java **65** E8
Galva: Ill., U.S.A. **88** F5
Galveston: Tex., U.S.A. **90** D11
Galveston Bay: Tex., U.S.A. **90** D11
Galvez: Argentina **96** C3
GALWAY: *& Co.*, Repub. of Ireland **31** C13
Galway Bay: Repub. of Irel. **31** C13
Gamaches: France **36** G6
Gamarra: Colombia **94** C2
Gambaga: Ghana **80** D2
Gambang: Malaya, Malaysia **65** c12
Gambela Post: Ethiopia **76** D1
Gambell: St. Lawrence I., Bering Sea **84** b5
Gambia: *riv.*, The Gambia **80** A2

Gambia, The: *Republic* **80** A2
Cap.: Banjul (Bathurst)
Area: 4,003 sq. miles (10,368 sq. km.)
Pop.: 375,000 (*1971 E*)

Gambie: *riv.*, Senegal **80** B2
Gambier Is.: Tuamotu Arch. **83** h4
Gamblesby: Cumb., Eng. **26** Q10
Gamboa: Panama **94** *Ins.*
Gamboa, South: Panama **94** *Ins.*
Gamboma: Congo **81** H5
Gambos (Ghivemba): Angola **73** G13
Gamboula: Cen. Afr. Rep. **81** H4
Gamka: *riv.*, S. Africa **74** D6
Gamleby: Sweden **47** P8
Gamlingay: Cambs., Eng. **25** V15
Gamoep: S. Africa **74** C4
Ga-Mopedi: S. Africa **74** E3
Gamou: Niger **81** F2
Gamtoos: S. Africa **75** F6
Gamvik: Norway **46** V1
Gan: France **37** E12
Ganado: Ariz., U.S.A. **93** F5
Ganale Dorya: *riv.*, Ethiopia **76** E1
Ganane: Somalia **79** N9
Gananoque: Ont., Canada **89** N3
Ganaweh: Iran **55** H9
Gand: *see* Ghent
Gandak: *riv.*, India **59** O9
Gandava: Baluchistan, Pakistan **58** L9
Gander: Newf., Canada **85** V2
Gandersheim: W. Germany **45** Q4
Gandesa: Spain **35** G16
Gandia: Spain **35** F17
Gandis: Borneo **65** E7
Ganga: *mtn.*, Cameroun **81** G3
Ganga: *riv.*, *see* Ganges
Ganganagar: Rajasthan, India **58** M9
Gangapur: Rajasthan, India **58** N9
Gangara: Niger **81** F2
Gangaw: Burma **59** Q10
Ganges: France **37** J12
Ganges: *riv.*, India/Bangladesh **59** P10
Gan Goriama Mtns.: Cameroun **81** G3
Gangra: ancient Paphlagonian city at Çankiri, Turkey **56** A3
GANGTOK: Sikkim **59** P9
Gani: Halmahera, Moluccas **61** K12
Ganiadje: Cameroun **81** G3
Ganjam: Orissa, India **59** O11
Ganmain: N.S.W., Austl. **71** G10
Gannat: France **37** J9
Gannett Peak: Wyo., U.S.A. **92** E4
Ganongga: *i.*, Solomon Is. **67** L3
Gans Baai: S. Africa **74** C7
Ganton: N. Yorks., England **26** V11
Gantsevichi: Byelorussia **43** U10
Ganyesa: S. Africa **75** F3
GAO: *& Reg.*, Mali **80** D1
GAOUA: Sud-Ouest, Upper Volta 80 D2
GAOUAL: *& Reg.*, Guinea **80** B2
Gap: Hautes-Alpes, France **40** M11
Gara, Lough: Sligo, Repub. of Ireland **30** E12
Garad: Somalia **79** R18
Garah: N.S.W., Australia **71** H7
Gara Hitrino: Bulgaria **39** U15
Garamantes: ancient Berber tribe in desert south of Tripolitania **32** E6
Garamba National Park: Zaire **76** C2
Garanhuns: Brazil **94** K5
Garantah: Sumbawa, Indonesia **65** F8
Garba Tula: Kenya **76** E2
Garber: Okla., U.S.A. **90** C7
Garboldisham: Norf., Eng. **25** X15
Garcia de Sola, Embalse de: *res.*, Spain **35** D17
Gard: *Dept. & riv.*, France (*cap.* Nîmes) **37** K12
Garda: Italy **41** Q10
Garda, Lake of: Italy **40** Q10
Gardanne: France **40** L12
Gardelegen: E. Germany **45** R3
Garden: Mich., U.S.A. **88** H3
Garden City: Kans., U.S.A. **90** A7
Garden Island Bay: La., U.S.A. **90** *Ins.*
Gardenstown: Gram., Scot. **28** R4
GARDEZ: Paktia, Afghanistan **55** L8
Gardiner: Maine, U.S.A. **89** R3
Gardiner: Mont., U.S.A. **92** E3
Gardiner: Ont., Canada **88** L1
Gardiner: Oreg., U.S.A. **92** C4
Garding: W. Germany **44** O1
Gardner: Mass., U.S.A. **89** Q4
Gardner I.: Phoenix Islands **7** 05S 175W
Gardo: Somalia **79** R18
Gårdsjo: Sweden **47** O7
Gare Loch: Strath., Scot. **29** M7
Garelochhead: Strath., Scotland **29** M7
Gareloi: *i.*, Aleutians **84** B7
Garessio: Italy **40** O11
Garff: *dist.*, I. of Man, U.K. **26** N11
Garforth: W. Yorks., England **27** T12
Gargalianoi: Greece **39** R18
Gargano, Cape: Italy **38** P16
Gargantua, Cape: Ont., Can. **88** J2
Gargellen: Austria **40** P9
Gargett: Queens., Australia **70** H3
Gargnano: Italy **40** Q10
Gargrave: N. Yorks., England **27** R12
GARIAN: Al Jabal al-Gharbi, Libya **78** G3
Garib: S.W. Africa **74** B1
Garibaldi Prov. Park: B.C., Canada **92** C2
Garies: S. Africa **74** B5
Gariganus Nature Reserve: SW. Africa **74** C3
Garinais: S.W. Africa **74** C3
Garini: Oman **55** J10
Garioch: *dist.*, Gram., Scot. **28** R5
Garisa: Somalia **79** Q17
GARISSA: North Eastern, Kenya **76** E3
Garland: Tex., U.S.A. **90** C9
Garliestown: Dumfries & Galloway, Scotland **29** N10
Garlin: France **37** E12
Garlstorf: W. Germany **45** Q2
Garmi: Iran **57** L2
Garmisch: W. Germany **41** R8
Garmouth: Gram., Scot. **28** P4
Garmsar: Iran **55** H7
Garnache, La: France **36** D9
Garnett: Kans., U.S.A. **90** D6
Garnish: Newf., Canada **85** v3
Garoe: Somalia **79** R18
Garo Hills: Meghalaya, India **59** Q9
Garonne: *riv.*, France **37** E11
GAROUA: Nord, Cameroun **81** G3
Garoua: Niger **81** G2
Garrabost: I. of Lewis, Outer Hebr., Scotland **28** J3
Garrane: Cork, Repub. of Ireland **31** C16
Garraway: Liberia **80** C4
Garrel: W. Germany **44** O3
Garrigill: Cumbria, England **26** R10
Garrigues: *geog. reg.*, Fr. **37** J12
Garrison: Ferm., N. Ireland **30** E11
Garrison: N. Dak., U.S.A. **92** G3
Garristown: Dublin, Repub. of Ireland **30** J12
Garroch Head: *cape*, Strathclyde, Scotland **29** L8
Garron Point: *cape*, Antrim, N. Ireland **30** K9
Garrovillas: Spain **35** C17
Garruchos: Brazil **96** D2
Garry: *loch & glen*, Tayside, Scotland **29** N6
Garry: *riv.*, Tay., Scotland **29** O6
Garry, Lake: N.W.T., Can. **84** K4
Garry, Loch: High., Scot. **28** M5
Garrynahine: I. of Lewis, Outer Hebr., Scotland **28** H3
Garsen: Kenya **76** F3
Garsington: Oxon., England **25** T16
Garstang: Lancs., England **27** Q12
Gartan, Lough: Don., Repub. of Ireland **30** F10
Gartempe: *riv.*, France **37** G9
Gartmore: Tay., Scotland **29** N7
Gartocharn: Strath., Scot. **29** M7
Gartok: *see* Kaerh
Garub: S.W. Africa **74** B3
Garuk: Iran **55** J9
Garut: Java **65** D8
Garvagh: Lon., N. Ireland **30** H10
Garvald: Lothian, Scot. **29** Q8
Garve: High., Scot. **28** M4
Garvellachs: *is.*, Scotland **29** K7
Garwang Post: Sudan **76** D1
Garwitz: E. Germany **45** R2
Garwolin: Poland **43** R11
Gary: Ind., U.S.A. **88** H5
Garz: Rugen, E. Germany **45** T1
Garza: Argentina **96** C2
Garzon: Colombia **94** B3
Gasan-Kuli: Turkmen, U.S.S.R. **50** H7
Gasconade: *riv.*, Mo., U.S.A. **88** E7
Gascony: *Prov.*, France **34** F15
Gascoyne: *riv.*, W. Australia **68** B5
Gascoyne Junction: W. Australia **68** B5
Gash: *riv.*, Ethiopia/Sudan **54** E11
Gashaka: Nigeria **81** G3
Gasherbrum: *mtn.*, Jammu & Kashmir/China **58** N7
Gashun: Chinghai, China **62** R7
Gashun Tsaka: Chinghai, China **62** Q7
Gasmata: New Britain, Bismarck Arch. **67** K3
Gaspar Str.: Indonesia **65** D7
Gaspe: Que., Canada **89** T1
Gaspe Penin.: *& cape*, Que., Canada **89** T1
Gaspesian Prov. Park: Que., Can. **89** T1
Gassaway: W. Va., U.S.A. **88** L6
Gasselsdorf: Austria **41** V9
Gasselte: Netherlands **44** M3
Gassino: Italy **40** N10
Gassol: Nigeria **81** G3
Gaston, Lake: N.C./Va., U.S.A. **91** N7
Gastonia: N.C., U.S.A. **91** L8
Gastre: Argentina **95** D12
Gat: Libya **78** G4
Gata, Cape: Cyprus **56** C4
Gata, C. de: *cape*, Spain **35** E18
Gata, Sierra de: *mtns.*, Spain **35** C16
Gataia: Romania **39** R14
Gatanga: Sudan **76** C1
Gatcha: Loyalty Is. **67** N6
Gatchina: U.S.S.R. **47** W7
Gate City: Va., U.S.A. **88** K7
Gatehouse of Fleet: Dumfries & Galloway, Scotland **29** N10
Gatelo: Ethiopia **76** E1
Gateshead: Tyne & Wear, England **26** S10
Gatesville: Tex., U.S.A. **90** C10
Gath: Philistine city E. of Gaza **55** a3
Gathersnow Hill: Strathclyde/Borders, Scotland **29** O8
Gatico: Chile **96** A1
Gâtine, Hauteurs de: *hills*, France **37** E9
Gatineau: *riv.*, Que., Canada **89** O2
Gatlinburg: Tenn., U.S.A. **91** K8
Gatooma: Rhodesia **77** C6
Gatrun, El: Libya **78** H5
Gatton: Queens., Australia **70** K6
Gatun: *& riv.*, Panama **94** *Ins.*
Gatuncillo: *& riv.*, Panama **94** *Ins.*
Gatun Dam: Panama **94** *Ins.*
Gatun Lake: Panama **94** *Ins.*
Gatwick: *airfield*, W. Sussex, England **25** V17
Gatyana: Transkei, S. Africa **75** H6
Gau: Somalia **79** R17
Gaucin: Spain **35** D18
Gaud-i-Zirreh: *lake*, Afghan. **58** K9
Gauer Lake: Man., Canada **92** H1
Gaugamela: ancient battlefield on plain about 40 miles W. of Erbil, Iraq **57** J3
Gauhati: Assam, India **59** Q9
Gaulanitis: ancient Greek name of district E. and NE. of L. Tiberias, Syria **56** D5
Gaunersdorf: Austria **41** W7
Guardak: Turkmen., U.S.S.R. **51** L7
Gauri Sankar: *mtn.*, Himalayas **59** P9
Gauthiot Falls: Chad **81** G3
Gavarnie: France **37** E13
Gavdhos: *i.*, Greece **39** T19
Gave-de-Pau: *riv.*, France **37** E12
Gave d'Oloron: *riv.*, France **37** E12
Gavião: Portugal **35** C17
Gavkhaneh, Lake: Iran **55** H8
GAVLE: *& bay*, Gavleborg, Sweden **47** P6
Gavleborg: *Co.*, Sweden (*cap.* Gavle) **47** O6
Gavray: France **36** D7
Gavriel: Ethiopia **54** E12
Gawachab: S.W. Africa **74** B3
Gaweinstal: Austria **41** W7
Gawler: S. Australia **71** C10
Gawsworth: Ches., England **27** R13
Gaya: Bihar, India **59** P10
Gaya: Niger **81** E2
Gaya: Nigeria **81** F2
Gayaza: Uganda **76** D3
Gaylord: Mich., U.S.A. **88** J3
Gayndah: Queens., Austl. **70** J5
Gayny: U.S.S.R. **50** H2
Gayton: Norf., England **25** X14
Gayvoron: Ukraine **50** C5
Gaza: Cen. Afr. Rep. **81** H4
Gaza: Egypt **55** a3
Gaza: *Dist.*, **Mozambique (cap. Xai-Xai) 77 D7**
Gazi: Kenya **76** E3
GAZIANTEP: *& Prov.*, Turkey **56** E3
Gazik: Iran **55** K8
Gazipasa: Turkey **56** C3
Gazzaniga: Italy **40** P10
GBANGA: Bong, Liberia **80** C3
Gboko: Nigeria **81** F3
Gcuwa: Transkei, S. Africa **75** H6
GDANSK (Danzig): *& Prov.*, Poland **43** Q9
Gdov: U.S.S.R. **47** U7
Gdyel: Algeria **35** F19
Gdynia: Poland **43** Q9
Geary: Okla., U.S.A. **90** B8
Geashill: Offaly, Repub. of Ireland **31** G13
Geaune: France **37** E12
Geba: *riv.*, Guinea-Bissau **80** B2

For Abbreviations see list on p.113. Italic type, e.g. *Ephesus*: refers to historical names not on maps. Capital letters, e.g. MADRID, show capitals of countries; small capital letters, e.g. CADIZ, show capitals of provinces, etc. General notes p.116

144 Gebal—Goldendale

Gebal: see Byblos.
Gebe: i., W. Irian, Indonesia 61 K12
Gebeit: Sudan 54 E10
Gebel Iweibid: Egypt (Suez Canal Inset) 32 Ins.
Gebesee: E. Germany 45 Q4
Gebile: Somalia 79 Q18
Gebo: Wyo., U.S.A. 92 F4
Gebze: Turkey 56 A1
Gedaref: Sudan 54 E12
Geddahia, El: Libya 33 F5
Geddington: Northants., England 25 U15
Gedinne: Belgium 44 K6
Gedintailor: Inner Hebr., Scotland 28 J5
Gediz: Turkey 56 A2
Gediz: riv., Turkey 39 V17
Gedney Drove End: Lincs., England 25 W14
Gedney Hill: Lincs., England 25 V14
Gedongbatin: Sumatra 65 C7
Gedrosia: ancient Greek name of region (Baluchistan) along N. coast of Indian O. in Makran, Iran and Pakistan 55 K9
Gedser: Falster, Denmark 47 M9
Geduld: Trans., S. Africa 74 N Ins.
Geel: Belgium 44 K4
Geelong: Vict., Australia 71 F12
Geerardsbergen: Belgium 44 J5
Geeveston: Tas., Australia 68 H8
Geidam: Nigeria 81 G2
Geili, El: Sudan 54 D11
Geilo: Norway 47 L6
Geinab: riv., S.W. Africa 74 C4
Geisa: E. Germany 45 P5
Geisenfeld: W. Germany 41 R7
Geisingen: W. Germany 40 O8
Geislingen: W. Germany 40 P7
Geita: Tanzania 76 D3
Gela: Sicily 38 O18
Gelam: i., Borneo 65 E7
Gelenbe: Turkey 39 U17
Gelderland: Prov., Neth. (cap. Arnhem) 44 L3
Geldern: W. Germany 44 M4
Geldrop: Netherlands 44 L4
Gelib: Somalia 76 F2
Gelibolu (Gallipoli): Turkey (Dardan. Inset) 20 Ins.
Gelindere: Turkey 56 C3
Gelinsor: Somalia 79 R18
Gelling: W. Germany 45 P1
Gellygaer: site of Roman fort about 7 miles NNW. of Caerphilly, Wales 24 P16
Gelnhausen: W. Germany 44 P5
Gelsenkirchen: W. Germany 44 N4
Gelston: Dumfries & Galloway, Scotland 28 O10
Geluk: S. Africa 75 F3
Geluks Kraal: Trans., S. Africa 75 H2
Gemas: Malaya, Malaysia 65 c12
Gembloux: Belgium 44 K5
Gembrook: Vict., Austl. 71 F11
Gemeiza: Sudan 76 D1
Gemena: Zaire 76 A2
Gemert: Netherlands 44 L4
Gemlik: & Gulf, Turkey 56 A1
Gemona: Italy 41 T9
Gemozac: France 37 E10
Gemsa: Egypt 54 D9
Gemu Gefa: Prov., Ethiopia (cap. Arba Minch) 79 M8
Gemünd: W. Germany 44 M5
Gemünden: W. Germany 44 P5
Gemunden: Hesse, W. Ger. 44 O5
Genappe: Belgium 36 K5
Genç: Turkey 57 G2
Genck: Belgium 36 L5
Gende (Gongola): riv., Nig. 81 G2
Gendringen: Netherlands 44 M4
Geneina, El: Sudan 79 J7
General Acha: Argentina 96 C4
General Alvarado (Miramar): Argentina 96 D4
General Alvear: Buenos Aires, Argentina 96 C4
General Alvear: Mendoza, Argentina 96 B3
General Arenales: Argentina 96 C3
General Artigas: Paraguay 96 D2
General Belgrano: rsch. stn., Antarctica 9 80S 40W
General Belgrano: Arg. 96 D4
General Bernardo O'Higgins: rsch. stn., Antarctica 9 65S 60W
General Capdevila: Arg. 96 C2
General Cepeda: Mexico 93 G7
General Conesa: Argentina 95 E12
General Guido: Argentina 96 D4
Generalissimul Suvarov: Romania 39 U14
General José de San Martin: Argentina 96 D2
General la Madrid: Arg. 96 C4
General Lavalle: Argentina 96 D4
General Madariaga: Arg. 96 D4
General Mitre: Córdoba, Argentina 96 C3
General Paz: Buenos Aires, Argentina 96 D4
General Paz: Corrientes, Argentina 96 D2
General Pico: Argentina 96 C4
General Pinedo: Argentina 96 C2
General Pinto: Argentina 96 C3
General Roca: Argentina 96 B4
Generalski Stol: Yugoslavia 41 V10
General Trias: Mexico 93 F7
General Viamonte: Arg. 96 C4
General Villegas: Arg. 96 C4
Genesee: Idaho, U.S.A. 92 D3
Genesee: riv., U.S.A. 89 M4
Geneseo: Ill., U.S.A. 88 F5
Geneva: N.Y., U.S.A. 89 N4
Geneva: Ohio, U.S.A. 88 L5
GENEVA (Genève): Geneva Canton, Switzerland 40 M9
Geneva, Lake of (Lac Léman): Switz./France 40 M9
Gengenbach: West Germany 40 O7
Genichesk: Ukraine 50 D5
Genil: riv., Spain 35 D18
Genillé: France 36 G8
Génissiat Dam: France 40 L9
Genk: Belgium 44 L5
Gennes: Maine-et-Loire, Fr. 36 E8
Gennes: Mayenne, France 36 E8
Gennesaret: N.T. name of Lake Tiberias, between Syria, Jordan, and Israel 55 b2
GENOA (Genova): Liguria, Italy 40 O11
Genoa: Nebr., U.S.A. 92 H4
Genoa: Vict., Austl. 71 H11
Genoa, Gulf of: Italy 40 O12
Genteng, Cape: Java 65 D8
Genthin: E. Germany 45 S3
Gentioux: France 37 H10
Geographical Society I.: Greenland 85 r3
Geokchay: Azerbaydzhan, U.S.S.R. 57 K1
Geok-Tepe: Turkmen., U.S.S.R. 50 J7
George: & Dist., S. Africa 74 E6
George: riv., Canada 85 N6
George, Lake: Fla., U.S.A. 91 L11
George, Lake: N.S.W., Australia 71 H10
George, Lake: N.Y., U.S.A. 89 P4
George Bay: N.S., Canada 89 V3
Georgeham: Devon, Eng. 24 N17
George Lake: Uganda 76 D3
George Land: Franz Josef Land 48 F1
George Sound: South I., N.Z. 70 M17
George VI Sound: Antarctica 9 75S 70W
Georgetown: Del., U.S.A. 89 O6
GEORGETOWN: Guyana 87 d7
Georgetown: Ill., U.S.A. 88 H6
Georgetown: Ohio, U.S.A. 88 K6
GEORGE TOWN: Malaysia see Pinang.
Georgetown: P.E.I., Canada 89 U2
Georgetown: Queens., Austl. 69 G3
Georgetown: St. Vincent, Windward Is. 87 c4
Georgetown: S.C., U.S.A. 91 M9
Georgetown: Tas., Austl. 68 H8
Georgetown: Tex., U.S.A. 90 C10
George West: Tex., U.S.A. 90 B11
Georgia: State, U.S.A. (cap. Atlanta) 91 K9
Georgia, Str. of: B.C., Can. 92 C3
Georgiana: Ala., U.S.A. 91 H10
Georgian Bay: Ont., Can. 88 L3
Georgian S.S. Repub.: U.S.S.R. (cap. Tbilisi) 50 F6
Georgida: S. Africa 74 E6
Georgina: riv., Queens., Australia 69 F4
Georgiu-Dezh: U.S.S.R. 50 E4
Georgiyevka: Kazakh., U.S.S.R. 51 M6
Georgsdorf: W. Germany 44 N3
Ger: France 37 E12
GERA: & Dist., E. Germany 45 S5
Geral de Goiás, Serra: range, Brazil 94 H6
Geraldine: South I., N.Z. 70 N17
Geraldton: W. Australia 68 A5
Geranea: ancient name of mtns. W. of Megara, Greece. 39 S17
Gerar: early city of the Philistines, S. of Gaza, Egypt 55 a3
Gérardmer: France 40 M7
Gerasa: Graeco-Roman city on site of more ancient city at Jerash, Jordan 55 b2
Gerbéviller: France 40 M7
Gerbstedt: E. Germany 45 R4
Gercuş: Turkey 57 G3
Gerdine, Mount: Alaska, U.S.A. 84 d5
Gerede: & riv., Turkey 56 C1
Gérgal: Spain 35 E18
Gergovia: Roman name of Gallic fort about 5 miles S. of Clermont-Ferrand, France 37 J10
Gering: Nebr., U.S.A. 92 G4
Gerizim: Biblical name of mtn. W. of Nablus (Shechem) Israel 55 b2
Gerlach: Nev., U.S.A. 92 D4
Gerlogubi: Ethiopia 79 R18
Germania: Argentina 96 C3
Germania Land: Greenland 85 r2
Germany: see East Germany and West Germany.
Germiston: Trans., S. Africa 74 N Ins.
Gernsheim: W. Germany 44 O6
Gerolstein: W. Germany 44 M5
Gerolzhofen: W. Germany 45 Q6
Geron: Ethiopia 79 R18
GERONA: & Prov., Spain 35 H16
Gerrans: Corn., England 24 M19
Gerrards Cross: Bucks., England 25 U16
Gerrer: riv., Ethiopia 79 Q18
Gers: Dept. & riv., France (cap. Auch) 37 F12
Gersfeld: W. Germany 45 P5
Gersoppa: Karnataka, India 58 M12
Gerze: Turkey 56 D1
Gseke: W. Germany 44 O4
Gesoriacum: Roman name of port at Boulogne, France 36 G5
Getafe: Spain 35 E16
Gettorf: W. Germany 45 P1
Gettysburg: Pa., U.S.A. 89 N6
Gettysburg: S. Dak., U.S.A. 92 H3
Geurie: N.S.W., Australia 71 H9
Gevaş: Turkey 57 H2
Gevelsburg: W. Germany 44 N4
Gevgelija: Yugoslavia 39 S16
Gevry-Chambertin: France 36 K8
Gex: France 40 M9
Geyik Dağ: mtn., Turkey 56 C3
Geyo: Ethiopia 76 E1
Geysdorp: Trans., S. Africa 75 F3
Geyser Bank: i., Malagasy Rep. 73 O12
Geysir: Iceland 46 c4
Geyve: Turkey 56 B1
Gezer: city of ancient Israel about 7 miles S. of Lydda, Israel 55 a3
Ghadaf: wadi, Iraq 57 H5
Ghaghara: riv., see Gogra.
Ghaidha: Yemen P.D.R. 55 H11
Ghail: Saudi Arabia 54 G10

Ghana: Republic 81 D3
Cap.: Accra
Area: 92,100 sq. miles (238,539 sq. km.)
Pop.: 8,858,000 (1971 E)

Ghandava: Baluchistan, Pakistan 58 L9
Ghanim: sand reg., Saudi Arabia 55 H11
GHANZI: & Dist., Botswana 77 B7
Ghardaia: Algeria 78 E3
Ghardimaou: Tunisia 38 L18
Ghat: Saudi Arabia 54 G9
Ghazaouet: Algeria 35 F19
Ghazian: Iran 57 L3
Ghazipur: Uttar Prad., Ind. 59 O9
GHAZNI: & Prov., Afghanistan 55 L8
Ghazzala: Saudi Arabia 54 F9
Ghedi: Italy 40 Q10
Ghemines: Libya 33 G5
GHENT: East Flanders, Belgium 44 J4
Gheorgheni: Romania 43 T13
Gherbi: i., Kerkenna Is. 32 E5
Gherla: Romania 43 S13
Gheruen, Mount: Somalia 79 S17
Ghilarza: Sardinia 38 L16
Ghimeş: Romania 43 U13
Ghisonaccia: Corsica 38 L15
Ghitha: Iraq 57 J6
Ghivemba (Gambos): Ang. 73 G13
Ghizao: Afghanistan 58 C8
Ghoho: well, Somalia 79 R18
Ghor: prov., Afghanistan 55 K8
Ghorband: Afghanistan 58 L7
Ghriss: Algeria 35 G19
Ghurian: Afghanistan 58 K8
GIAMAME: Lower Juba, Somalia 79 N9
Giangthanh: Vietnam 64 C4
Giannutri: i., Italy 38 M15
Giant's Causeway: Antrim, N. Ireland 30 H9
Giarre: Sicily 38 O18
Giat: France 37 H10
Gibara: Cuba 87 M13
Gibb River: town, W. Austl. 68 D3
Gibbs Fracture Zone: N. Atlantic Ocean 8 50N 40W
Gibeah: city of ancient Israel about 7 miles N. of Jerusalem 55 b3
Gibeon: & Dist., S.W. Africa 74 B2
Gibeon: city of ancient Israel about 7 miles NNW. of Jerusalem 55 b3

Gibraltar: Br. colony 32 Ins.
Cap.: Gibraltar
Area: 2 sq. miles (5 sq. km.)
Pop.: 27,000 (1971 E)

Gibraltar, Str. of: Europe/Africa 32 Ins.
Gibsland: La., U.S.A. 90 E9
Gibson City: Ill., U.S.A. 88 G5
Gibson Desert: W. Australia 68 D4
Gibsons: B.C., Canada 92 C3
Giddings: Tex., U.S.A. 90 C10
Gidole: Ethiopia 79 M8
Gien: France 36 H8
Giens, Golfe de: gulf, France 40 L12
Gier: riv., France 37 K10
Giessen: W. Germany 44 O5
Gieten: Netherlands 44 M3
Giethoorn: Netherlands 44 M3
Gifford: Lothian, Scot. 29 Q8
Gifhorn: W. Germany 45 Q3
GIFU: & Pref., Japan 63 e3
Giganta, Sierra de la: Mexico 93 E7
Gigante: Panama 94 Ins.
Gigena: Argentina 96 C3
Giggleswick: N. Yorks., Eng. 27 R11
Gigha: i. & sound, Scotland 29 K8
Gighay: i., Scotland 28 G5
Giglio: i., Italy 38 M15
Gignac: France 37 J12
Gignod: Italy 40 N10
Gijón: Spain 35 D15
Gila: riv., U.S.A. 93 E6
Gilan: Prov., Iran (cap. Resht) 57 L3
Gilberdyke: Humb., England 27 U12
Gilbert: riv., Queens., Austl. 69 G3
Gilbert, Mount: B.C., Can. 92 C2
Gilbert Is.: (Br.), Pacific O. [cap. (with Ellice Is.) Tarawa] 67 P2
Gilbert River: town, Queens., Australia 69 G3
Gilboa: O.T. name of mtn. NE. of Jenin and W. of Beisan, Israel 55 b2
Gilcrux: Cumbria, England 26 P10
Gilé: Mozambique 77 E6
Gilead: Old Testament traditional district name, Jordan 55 b2
Gilf Kebir Plat.: Egypt 54 C10
Gilford: Down, N. Ireland 30 J11
Gilgal: city of ancient Israel at Qalqiliya, Jordan 55 a2
Gilgandra: N.S.W., Austl. 71 H8
Gilgil: Kenya 76 E3
GILGIT: & Agency, Jammu & Kashmir 58 M7
Gilgunnia: N.S.W., Austl. 71 G9
Gill, Lough: Repub. of Irel. 30 E11
Gillam: Man., Canada 92 J1
Gillamoor: N. Yorks., Eng. 26 U11
Gillen, Lake: W. Australia 68 D5
Gilles, Lake: S. Australia 71 B9
Gillespie: Ill., U.S.A. 88 G6
Gillette: Wyo., U.S.A. 92 F4
Gilley: France 40 M8
Gillhov: Sweden 46 O5
Gilling: N. Yorks., England 26 S11
Gillingham: Dorset, Eng. 24 R17
Gillingham: Kent, England 25 X17
Gilman: Ill., U.S.A. 88 H5
Gilmer: Tex., U.S.A. 90 D9
Gilroy: Calif., U.S.A. 93 C5
Gilsland: Cumbria, England 26 Q10
Gilston, New: Fife, Scot. 29 Q7
Gilwern: Gwent, Wales 24 P16
Gimal'skoye Lake: Karelia, U.S.S.R. 46 W5
Gimli: Man., Canada 92 H2
Gimone: riv., France 37 F12
Gimont: France 37 F12
Gineifa: Egypt 56 C6
Gineifa: Egypt (Suez Canal Inset) 32 Ins.
Gineifa, Gebel: hills, Egypt (Suez Canal Inset) 32 Ins.
Gin Gin: Queens., Australia 70 J5
Gin Gin: W. Australia 68 B6
Gingoog: Mindanao, Phil. 64 H5
Gingst: Rügen, E. Germany 45 T1
Ginguni: Zaire 73 H11
Ginir: Ethiopia 76 F1
Ginosa: Italy 38 P16
Ginzo: Spain 35 C15
Gio I.: Vietnam 64 D3
Gioher: Somalia 79 R19
Gioja del Colle: Italy 38 P16
Gippsland: geog. reg., Vict., Australia 71 G11
Giran (Ilan): Taiwan 63 W10
Girard: Kans., U.S.A. 90 D7
Girard: Pa., U.S.A. 88 L4
GIRESUN: & Prov., Turkey 56 F1
Girgarre: Vict., Australia 71 F11
Giridih: Bihar, India 59 P10
Girilambone: N.S.W., Austl. 71 G8
Girishk: Afghanistan 58 K8
Giromagny: France 40 M8
Gironde: Dept., France (cap. Bordeaux) 37 E11
Gironde: est., France 37 E10
Gironville: France 40 L7
Girton: Cambs., England 25 W15
Giru: Queens., Australia 70 G2
Girvan: Strath., Scotland 29 M9
GISBORNE: East Coast, North I., N.Z. 70 R14
Gisburn: Lancs., England 27 R12
Gischala: city of ancient Israel about 8 miles NW. of Safad, Israel 55 b1
Gislaved: Sweden 47 N8
Gisors: France 36 G6
Giulianova: Italy 38 N15
Giurgiu: Romania 39 T15
Givet: France 36 K5
Givors: France 37 K10
Givry: France 37 K9
Givry-en-Argonne: France 36 K7
Giza: Egypt 56 B6
Gizhduvan: Uzbek., U.S.S.R. 51 K6
Gizhiga: U.S.S.R. 49 S5
Gizhiga Bay: U.S.S.R. 49 r5
Gizil: riv., Iran 57 L3
Giżycko: Poland 43 R9
Gjerstad: Norway 47 L7
Gjirokaster: Albania 39 R16
Gjøvik: Norway 47 M6
Glace Bay: Cape Breton I., Canada 89 V2
Glacier Bay Nat. Mon.: Alaska, U.S.A. 84 F6
Glacier Creek: Yukon, Can. 84 e5
Glacier Peak: Wash., U.S.A. 92 C[illegible]
Glackbea: High., Scotland 28 N5
Gladbeck: W. Germany 44 M4
Gladchau: E. Germany 45 S5
Gladestry: Powys, Wales 24 P15
Gladewater: Tex., U.S.A. 90 D9
Gladstone: Mich., U.S.A. 88 H3
Gladstone: Queens., Austl. 70 J4
Gladstone: S. Australia 71 C9
Gladstone: Tas., Australia 68 H8
Gladstone: W. Australia 68 A5
Gladwin: Mich., U.S.A. 88 J4
Glafs Fiord: lake, Sweden 47 N7
Glåma: riv., Norway 47 M7
Glamis: Tayside, Scotland 29 P6
Galmoč: Yugoslavia 38 P14
Glamorgan, Vale of: val., S. Glam. Gwent, Wales 24 P16
Glan: Philippines 65 H5
Glan: riv., W. Germany 44 N6
Glan: Dyfed, Wales 24 O16
Glanaruddery Mtns.: Kerry, Repub. of Ireland 31 C15
Glandore: Cork, Repub. of Ireland 31 C16
Glanmire: Cork, Repub. of Ireland 31 E16
Glantane: Cork, Repub. of Ireland 31 D15
Glanton: Northumb., Eng. 26 S9
Glanworth: Cork, Repub. of Ireland 31 E15
GLARUS: & Canton, Switz. 40 P8
Glasbury: Powys, Wales 24 P15
Gasgow: Ky., U.S.A. 88 J7
GLASGOW: Strath., Scotland 29 N8
Glasgow: Mo., U.S.A. 88 D6
Glasgow: Mont., U.S.A. 92 F3
Glaslough: Monaghan, Repub. of Ireland 30 H11
Glas Maol: mtn., Grampian Highlands, Scotland 28 P6
Glass, Loch: High., Scot. 28 M4
Glassan: Westmeath, Repub. of Ireland 30 F13
Glasserton: Dumfries & Galloway, Scotland 29 N10
Glassford: Strath., Scotland 29 N8
Glasson: Lancs., England 27 Q12
Glass, Strath: valley, Highland, Scotland 28 M5
Glastonbury: Som., Eng. 24 Q17
Glatton: Cambs., England 25 V15
Glauchau: E. Germany 45 S5
Glazov: U.S.S.R. 50 H3
Gfda: riv., Poland 43 P10
Gleichenberg: Austria 41 V9
Glein Alps: Austria 41 V8
Gleisdorf: Austria 41 V8
Glemsford: Suff., England 25 X15
Glen: riv., Lincs., England 27 V14
Glenade: Leit., Repub. of Ireland 30 E11
Glenarm: Antrim, N. Irel. 30 K10
Glenavy: Antrim, N. Irel. 30 J10
Glenavy: South I., N.Z. 70 N17
Glenbarr: Strath., Scotland 29 K8
Glenbeigh: Kerry, Repub. of Ireland 31 B15
Glenboig: Strathclyde, Scotland 29 N8
Glenborrodale: High., Scot. 29 K6
Glenbuck: Strath., Scotland 29 O8
Glencairn: S. Africa 74 Ins.
Glencar: Kerry, Repub. of Ireland 31 B16
Glencarse: Tayside, Scotland 29 P7
Glencoe: val., High., Scot. 29 L6
Glencoe: Minn., U.S.A. 88 D3
Glencoe: Natal, S. Africa 75 J4
Glencoe: S. Australia 71 D11
Glencolumbkille: Don., Repub. of Ireland 30 D10
Glencoul, Loch: High., Scot. 28 M3
Glencraig: Fife, Scotland 29 P7
Glendale: Ariz., U.S.A. 93 E6
Glendale: Calif., U.S.A. 93 D6
Glendalough: Wick., Repub. of Ireland 31 J13
Glendevon: Tayside, Scot. 29 O7
Glendhu, Loch: High., Scot. 28 M3
Glendive: Mont., U.S.A. 92 G3
Gleneagles: Tay., Scotland 29 O7
Glenealy: Wick., Repub. of Ireland 31 J14
Gleneely: Don., Repub. of Ireland 30 G9
Glenelg: Highland, Scotland 28 K5
Glenelg: S. Australia 71 C10
Glenelg: riv., Vict., Austl. 71 D11
Glenfaba: I. of Man, United Kingdom 26 M11
Glenfarg: Tayside, Scotland 29 P7
Glenfinnan: High., Scotland 28 L6
Glengariff: Cork, Repub. of Ireland 31 B16
Glengarnock: Strath., Scot. 29 M8
Glen Grey: Dist., S. Africa 75 G5
Glengyle: Queens., Austl. 69 F5
Glenhope: South I., N.Z. 70 O15
Glen Innes: N.S.W., Austl. 71 J7
Glenisland: Mayo, Repub. of Ireland 30 C12
Glenkens, The: dist., Dumfries & Galloway, Scotland 29 N9
Glenlivet: Gram., Scotland 28 P5
Glenluce: Dumfries & Galloway, Scotland 29 M10
Glen Lyon: S. Africa 74 E4
Glenmora: La., U.S.A. 90 E10
Glenmore: Kilk., Repub. of Ireland 31 G15
Glen More National Park: Highland, Scotland 28 O5
Glenmorgan: Queens., Austl. 70 H6
Glennamaddy: Galway, Repub. of Ireland 30 D12
Glenns Ferry: Idaho, U.S.A. 92 D4
Glenreagh: N.S.W., Austl. 71 K8
Glenrock: Wyo., U.S.A. 92 F4
Glenrothes: Fife, Scotland 29 P7
Glenroy: Trans., S. Africa 74 N Ins.
Glenroy: W. Australia 68 D3
Glens Falls: N.Y., U.S.A. 89 P4
Glenside: Natal, S. Africa 75 J4
Glentham: Lincs., England 27 V13
Glenthompson: Vict., Austl. 71 E11
Glenties: Don., Repub. of Ireland 30 E10
Glentrool Forest Park: Strathclyde, Scotland 29 M9
Glenville: Cork, Repub. of Ireland 31 E15
Glenwhilly: Dumfries & Galloway, Scotland 29 M10
Glenwood: Hawaiian Is. 83 d3
Glenwood Springs: city, Colo., U.S.A. 93 F5
Gleouraich: mtn., High., Scot. 28 L5
Gleschendorf: W. Germany 45 Q1
Glevum: Roman town at Gloucester, England 24 R16
Glin: Lim., Repub. of Irel. 31 C14
Glina: Yugoslavia 41 W10
Glina: riv., Yugoslavia 41 V10
Glittertind: mtn., Norway 47 L6
Gliwice: Poland 43 Q11
Globe: Ariz., U.S.A. 93 E6
Glogau (Glogow): Poland 45 W4
Gloggnitz: Austria 41 V8
Glogów (Glogau): Poland 45 W4
Glommersträsk: Sweden 46 Q4
Glorenza: Italy 40 Q9
Gloria: La., U.S.A. 90 Ins.
Glória do Goitá: Brazil 94 K5
Glorieuses Is.: Malagasy Rep. 73 O12
Glos-la-Ferrière: France 36 F7
Glossop: Derby., England 27 S13
GLOUCESTER: & Co., England 24 R16
Gloucester: Mass., U.S.A. 89 Q4
Gloucester: N.S.W., Austl. 71 J8
Gloucester, Cape: New Britain, Bismarck Arch. 66 J3
Gloucester, Vale of: England 24 R16
Gloup Ness: cape, Shetland Is., Scotland 28 Ins.
Gloversville: N.Y., U.S.A. 89 O4
Glowen: E. Germany 45 S3
Glubczyce: Poland 43 P11
Glubokoye: Kazakh., U.S.S.R. 51 O4
Glubokoe: Byelorussia 50 C3
Glückstadt: W. Germany 44 P2
Glukhov: Ukraine 50 D4
Glusk: Byelorussia 43 V10
Glyder Fawr: mtn., Gwynedd, Wales 27 N13
Glyncorrwg: W. Glam., Wales 24 O16
Glynde: E. Sussex, England 25 W18
Glyn Dyfrdwy: Clwyd, Wales 27 P14
Glyngøre: Denmark 23 L8
Glynn: Antrim, N. Ireland 30 K10
Glynn: Carlow, Repub. of Irel. 31 H14
Glynn: Wex., Repub. of Irel. 31 H15
Glyn Neath: W. Glam., Wales 24 O16
Glyntawe: Powys, Wales 24 O16
Gmünd: Carinthia, Austria 41 T9
Gmund: W. Germany 40 P7
Gmünd: Lower Austria 41 U7
Gmunden: Austria 41 T8
Gnali: mtn., Guinea 80 C3
Gnalta: N.S.W., Australia 71 E8
Gnarrenburg: W. Germany 44 P2
Gneevgullia: Kerry, Repub. of Ireland 31 C15
Gnesta: Sweden 47 P7
Gnezjan: Iran 57 L3
Gniezno: Poland 43 P10
Gnivan': Ukraine 43 V12
Gnjilane: Yugoslavia 39 R15
Gnoien: E. Germany 45 S2
Gnosall: Staffs., England 27 R14
Gnowangerup: W. Australia 68 B6
Goalpara: Assam, India 59 Q9
Goaso: Ghana 80 D3
Goat Fell: mtn., I. of Arran, Scotland 29 L8
Goathland: N. Yorks., Eng. 26 U11
GOBA: Bale, Ethiopia 76 F1
Goba: (Boran), Ethiopia 76 E2
Goba: Mozambique 75 K3
GOBABIS: & Dist., SW. Africa 77 A7
Gobi: desert, Mongolia 62 T6
Gobo: Japan 63 d4
Gobowen: Salop, England 27 P14
Goch: W. Germany 44 M4
Gocham: Arunachal Pradesh, India 59 Q9
Gochas: S.W. Africa 74 C2
Gochas: SW. Africa 77 A7
Gôcong: Vietnam 64 D4
Godalming: Surrey, England 25 U17
Godavari: riv., India 58 O11
Godda: Bihar, India 59 P10
God Dere: Ethiopia 79 Q18
Godech: Bulgaria 39 S15
Goderich: Ont., Canada 88 L4
Goderville: France 36 F6
Godhavn: Greenland 85 o4
Godhan Nayrhan Uula: Mongolia 62 R5
Godhra: Gujarat, India 58 M10
Godisso Kurro: Ethiopia 76 F1
Godmanchester: Cambridgeshire, England 25 V15
Godollo: Hungary 43 Q13
Godovik: Yugoslavia 41 U10
Gods: riv., Man., Canada 92 J1
Godshill: I. of Wight, Eng. 25 T18
Gods Lake: Man., Canada 92 J2
God's Mercy, Bay of: Can. 85 L5
Godstone: Surrey, England 25 V17
GODTHAAB: Greenland 85 o5
Godwane River: town, Trans., S. Africa 75 J2
Goedgegun: Swaziland 75 J3
Goeland, Lac au: Que., Can. 89 N1
Goeree: i., Netherlands 44 J4
Goes: Netherlands 44 J4
Gogland: i., Estonia, U.S.S.R. 47 U6
Gog Magog Hills: Eng. 25 W15
Gogra (Ghaghara): riv., India 59 O9
Gogrial: Sudan 76 C1
Goiana: Brazil 94 L5
GOIÂNIA: Goiás, Brazil 94 H7
Goiás: & State, Brazil (cap. Goiânia) 94 G7
Goil, Loch: Strath., Scotland 29 M7
Gojome: Japan 63 ZZ7
Gok: riv. (Black Sea), Tur. 56 D1
Gok: riv. (Seyhan Riv.), Tur. 56 E3
Gok: riv., Içel, Turkey 56 C3
Gokçay: riv., Turkey 56 C3
Göksun: Turkey 56 E2
Gokteik: Burma 59 R10
Gokwe: Rhodesia 77 C6
Gol: Norway 47 L6
Golaghat: Assam, India 59 Q9
Gola I.: Repub. of Ireland 30 E9
Golcar: W. Yorks., England 27 S12
Golconda: Ill., U.S.A. 88 G7
Golčuv Jenikov: Czech. 45 V6
Goldap: Poland 43 S9
Gold Beach: city, Oreg., U.S.A. 92 C4
Goldberg: E. Germany 45 S2
Gold Bridge: B.C., Canada 92 C2
Goldcliff: Gwent, Wales 24 Q16
Golden: B.C., Canada 92 D2
Golden: Colo., U.S.A. 93 F5
Golden: Tip., Rep. of Irel. 31 F14
Golden Bay: South I., N.Z. 70 O15
Goldendale: Wash., U.S.A. 92 C3

For Abbreviations see list on p.113. Italic type, e.g. Ephesus, refers to historical names not on maps. Capital letters, e.g. MADRID, show capitals of countries, small capital letters, e.g. CADIZ, show capitals of provinces, etc. General notes p.116.

Golden Hinde—Gredos 145

Golden Hinde: mtn., B.C., Canada 92 B3
Golden Lake: Ont., Canada 89 N3
Golden Meadow: La., U.S.A. 90 Ins.
Golden Ridge: W. Australia 68 C6
Golden Vale: Repub. of Irel. 31 E14
Gold Hill: city, Oreg., U.S.A. 92 C4
Gold Hill: city, Utah, U.S.A. 93 E4
Goldkronach: W. Germany 45 R5
Goldpines: Ont., Canada 92 J2
Goldsand Lake: Man., Can. 92 G1
Goldsboro: N.C., U.S.A. 91 N8
Goldsworthy: W. Australia 68 B4
Goldstream: S. Africa 74 E6
Goldthwaite: Tex., U.S.A. 90 B10
Göle: Turkey 57 H1
Goléa, El: Algeria 78 E3
Goleen: Cork, Repub. of Ireland 31 B17
Golem Iskr: riv., Bulgaria 39 S15
Goleniów: Poland 45 U2
Goljam: Prov., Ethiopia (cap. Debra Markos) 79 M7
Gölköy: Turkey 56 E1
Gollel: Trans., S. Africa 75 J3
Golling: Austria 41 T8
Gölmarmara: Turkey 39 U17
Golmo: Chinghai, China 62 Q7
Golondrina: Argentina 96 C2
Golovin: Alaska, U.S.A. 84 c5
Golpayegan: Iran 55 H8
Gölpazarı: Turkey 56 B1
Golspie: Highland, Scotland 28 O4
Golssen: E. Germany 45 T4
Golufa: Ethiopia 76 F1
Golungo Alto: Angola 73 G11
Golzow: E. Germany 45 S3
Gomagoi: Italy 40 Q9
Gombad-e Kavus: Iran 50 J7
Gombe: Nigeria 81 G2
Gombe Falls: Zaïre 81 G6
Gombelo: Tanzania 76 E3
Gomel': Byelorussia 50 D4
Gomera: i., Canary Is. 78 A4
Gometra: i., Inner Hebr., Scotland 29 J7
Gomez Palacio: Mexico 93 G7
Gomo Selung: Tibet, China 59 P8
Gona: New Guinea 69 H1
Gonaives: Haiti 87 m14
Gona-Re-Zhou Game Reserve: Rhodesia 77 D7
Gonave I.: Haiti 87 m14
Goncelin: France 40 L10
Gonda: Uttar Pradesh, India 58 O9
GONDAR: Begemdir & Simen, Ethiopia 79 M7
Gondia: Maharashtra, India 58 O10
Gondola: Mozambique 77 D6
Gondrecourt: France 40 L7
Gönen: Turkey 39 U16
Gonerby, Great: Lincs., Eng. 27 U14
Gonesse: France 36 H7
Gonfaron: France 40 M12
Gongola (Gende): riv., Nig. 81 G2
Gongola: State, Nigeria (cap. Yola) 81 G3
Gongolgon: N.S.W., Austl. 71 G8
Gonja: Tanzania 76 E3
Gonsé: Upper Volta 80 D2
Gonzaga: Italy 41 Q11
Gonzales: Tex., U.S.A. 90 C11
González, J.V.: Argentina 96 C1
González Chaves: Argentina 96 C4
Goodenough I.: New Guinea 69 J1
Gooderstone: Norf., Eng. 25 X14
Good Hope, Cape of: S. Afr. 74 C7
Goodhouse: S. Africa 74 C4
Gooding: Idaho, U.S.A. 92 E4
Goodland: Kans., U.S.A. 93 G5
Goodman: Wis., U.S.A. 88 G3
Goodna: Queens., Australia 70 K6
Goodooga: N.S.W., Austl. 71 G7
Goodwell: Okla., U.S.A. 93 G5
Goodwick: Dyfed, Wales 24 M16
Goodwin Sands: England 25 Y17
Goodwood: Queens., Austl. 69 G4
Goole: Humb., England 27 U12
Gooloogong: N.S.W., Austl. 71 H9
Goomalling: W. Australia 68 B6
Goomally: Queens., Austl. 70 H5
Goombalia: N.S.W., Austl. 71 F7
Goombungee: Queens., Austl. 70 J6
Goomburra: Queens., Austl. 70 K7
Goomeri: Queens., Austl. 70 K6
Goondiwindi: Queens., Australia 71 J7
Goondoola: Queens., Austl. 70 H7
Goondoon: Queens., Austl. 70 K5
Goondublui: N.S.W., Austl. 71 H7
Goongarrie: W. Australia 68 C6
Goonyella: Queens., Australia 70 H3
Goor: Netherlands 44 M3
Goose Bay: Newf., Canada 85 n7
Goose Lake: Calif., U.S.A. 92 C4
Goosnargh: Lancs., England 27 Q12
Goostrey: Ches., England 27 R13
Göppingen: W. Germany 40 P7
Goquao: Vietnam 64 D5
Gor: Spain 35 E18
Góra: Poland 45 W4
Gora Chen: mtn., U.S.S.R. 49 Q4
Gorakhpur: Uttar Pradesh, India 59 O9
Goran, El: Ethiopia 79 Q18
Goranba: Queens., Austl. 70 J6
Gorda Rise: N. Pacific Ocean 7 40N 130W
Gördes: Turkey 56 A2
Gordium: Phrygian city at confluence of rivers Sakarya and Porsuk, NW. of Polatlı, Turkey 56 B2
Gordon: Borders, Scotland 29 Q8
Gordon: Nebr., U.S.A. 92 G4
Gordon: S. Australia 71 C9
Gordon: riv., Tas., Australia 68 H8
Gordon Downs: W. Austl. 68 D3
Gordonia: Dist., S. Africa 74 D3
Gordonsville: Va., U.S.A. 89 M6
GORE: Ilubaber, Ethiopia 76 E1
Goré: Chad 81 H3
Gore: South I., N.Z. 71 M18
Gore Bay: city, Ont., Can. 88 K3
Goreda: W. Irian, Indonesia 61 M12
Görele: Turkey 56 F1
Goresbridge: Kilk., Repub. of Ireland 31 H14
Gorey: Jersey, Chan. Is. 25 Ins.
Gorey: Wex., Repub of Irel. 31 J14
Gorgol: Dist., Mauritania (cap. Kaédi) 80 B1
Gorgona: i., Italy 38 L15
Gorgorum: Nigeria 81 G2
Gorham: N.H., U.S.A. 89 Q3
Gori: Ethiopia 76 E1
Gori: Georgia, U.S.S.R. 57 J1
Goring: Oxon., England 25 T16
Goring by Sea: W. Sussex, England 25 V18
Goris: Armenia, U.S.S.R. 57 K2
Gorizia: Italy 41 T10
Gorjanci Range: Yugoslavia 41 V10
GOR'KIY: & Reg., U.S.S.R. 50 F3
GOR'KIY: Reg., U.S.S.R. 50 F3
Gor'kovskoye: U.S.S.R. 51 M3
Gorkum: Netherlands 44 L4
Gorleston: Norf., England 25 Z14
Gorlice: Poland 43 R12
Görlitz: E. Germany 45 U4
Gorlovka: Ukraine 50 E5
Gormanston: Tas., Austl. 68 H8
Gormanstown: Meath, Repub. of Ireland 30 J12
Gorna Orekhovitsa: Bulgaria 39 T15
Gorni Mstislavl': Byelorussia 50 D4
Gornji Kosinj: Yugoslavia 41 V11
Gorno Altay: Auton. Reg., U.S.S.R. (cap. Gorno-Altaysk) 51 P4
GORNO-ALTAYSK: Gorno Altay, U.S.S.R. 51 P4
Gorno-Badakhshan: Auton. Reg., Tadzhik, U.S.S.R. (cap. Khorog) 51 M7
Gorno-Slinkino: U.S.S.R. 51 L3
Gorodenka: Ukraine 43 T12
Gorodnitsa: Ukraine 43 U11
Gorodno: Byelorussia 43 U11
Gorodnya: Ukraine 50 D4
Gorodok: Minsk, Byelorussia 43 U9
Gorodok: Ukraine 43 S12
Gorodok: U.S.S.R. 49 M7
Gorodok: Vitebsk, Byelorussia 50 C3
Gorong Is.: Indonesia 61 L12
Gorontalo: Celebes 65 G6
Gorrahei: Ethiopia 79 Q18
Gorron: France 36 E7
Gorseinon: W. Glam., Wales 24 N16
Gort: Galway, Repub. of Irel. 31 D13
Gortatlea: Kerry, Repub. of Ireland 31 B15
Gorteen: Sligo, Repub. of Ireland 30 D12
Gortin: Tyr., N. Ireland 30 G10
Gortnahoo: Tip., Repub. of Ireland 31 F14
Gorumna I.: Repub. of Irel. 31 B13
Goryn: riv., Ukraine 43 U11
Gorzów Wielkopolski: Pol. 45 V3
Gosainthan: mtn., Tibet, China 59 P9
Gosberton: Lincs., England 27 V14
Göschenen: Switzerland 40 O9
Gosford: N.S.W., Australia 71 J9
Gosforth: Cumb., England 26 P11
Gosforth: Tyne & Wear, England 26 S9
Goshcha: Ukraine 43 U11
Goslar: W. Germany 45 Q4
Gospić: Yugoslavia 41 V11
Gosport: Hants., England 25 T18
Gossen: i., Norway 46 K5
Gossinga: Sudan 76 C1
Gostivar: Yugoslavia 39 R16
Gostyń: Poznan, Poland 43 P11
Gostyń: Koszalin, Pol. 45 V1
Gostynin: Poland 43 Q10
Götaland: dist., Sweden 47 O8
GÖTEBORG: Göteborg och Bohus, Sweden 47 M8
Göteborg och Bohus: Co., Sweden (cap. Göteborg) 47 M7
Gotha: E. Germany 45 Q5
Gothernburg: Nebr., U.S.A. 93 G4
Gotherington: Glos., Eng. 24 R16
Gotland: i., Sweden (cap. Visby) 47 Q8
Goto Is.: Japan 63 X8
Gotska Sandön: i., Sweden 47 Q7
Gotsu: Japan 63 c3
Göttingen: W. Germany 45 P4
Gott Peak: B.C., Canada 92 C2
Gottwaldov (Zlín): Czech. 43 P12
Gouarec: France 36 B7
Goubéré: Cen. Afr. Rep. 76 C1
Gouda: Netherlands 44 K3
Gouda: S. Africa 74 C6
Goudhurst: Kent, England 25 W17
Goudoumaria: Niger 81 G2
Gough I.: S. Atlantic Ocean 8 40S 10W
Gouina Falls: Mali 80 B2
Gouin Reservoir: & dam, Que., Canada 89 O1
Goulburn: N.S.W., Austl. 71 H10
Goulburn: riv., Vict., Austl. 71 F11
Goulceby: Lincs., England 27 V13
Gouldsboro: Maine, U.S.A. 89 R3
Goulette, La: Tunisia 38 M18
Goulimine: Morocco 80 J9
Goulmina: Morocco 80 L8
Gouménissa: Greece 39 S16
Goundam: Mali 80 D1
Gouraya: Algeria 35 G18
Gourdon: France 37 G11
Gourdon: Gram., Scotland 28 R6
Gouré: Niger 81 G2
Gourin: France 36 B7
Gouritz: riv., S. Africa 74 D7
Gourma: geog. reg., Mali 80 D1
Gournay: France 36 G6
Gouro: Chad 78 H6
Gourock: Strath., Scotland 29 M8
Gourock Range: N.S.W., Australia 71 H10
Gourrama: Morocco 80 L8
Goursélik: Niger 81 G2
Gouveneur: N.Y., U.S.A. 89 O3
Gouzon: France 37 H9
Govenlock: Sask., Canada 92 F3
Governador Valadarez: Braz. 94 J7
Gowanda: N.Y., U.S.A. 89 M4
Gowan Range: Queens., Australia 69 G4
Gowder's Lagoon: town, S. Australia 69 F3
Gower: penin., W. Glam., Wales 24 N16
Gowerton: W. Glam., Wales 24 N16
Gowganda: Ont., Canada 88 L2
Gowna, Lough: Long., Repub. of Ireland 30 F12
Gowran: Kilk., Repub. of Ireland 31 G14
Gowrie, Carse of: dist., Tayside, Scotland 29 P7
Goxhill: Humb., England 27 V12
Goya: Argentina 96 D2
Goyder, Lake: Queens., Australia 69 G5
Göynük: Turkey 56 B1
Goz Beïda: Chad 79 J7
Gozo: i., Malta 32 Ins.
Goz Regeb: Sudan 54 E11
Gozzano: Italy 40 O10
Graaf-Reinet: & Dist., S. Africa 75 F6
Grabo: Ivory Coast 80 C4
Grabouw: S. Africa 74 C7
Grabtsovy: U.S.S.R. 51 N3
Gračac: Yugoslavia 41 V11
Gračanica: Yugoslavia 39 Q14
Graçay: France 36 G8
Grace, Lake: W. Australia 68 B6
Gracefield: Que., Canada 89 N2
Graceville: Fla., U.S.A. 91 J10
Gracias á Dios, C.: Nic. 87 I 15
Graciosa: i., Azores 78 Ins.
Gradačac: Yugoslavia 39 Q14
Gradacmali: Yugoslavia 41 W10
Gradaús, Serra dos: Braz. 94 G5
Gradets: Bulgaria 39 U15
Gradisca: Italy 41 T10
Gradizhsk: Ukraine 50 D5
Grado: Italy 41 T10
Graemsay: i., Orkney Is., Scotland 28 P2
Grafenau: W. Germany 41 T7
Gräfenberg: W. Germany 45 R6
Gräfenhainichen: E. Ger. 45 S4
Grafenschlag: Austria 41 V7
Gräfenthal: E. Germany 45 R5
Grafenwöhr: W. Germany 45 R6
Grafton: N.S.W., Australia 71 K7
Grafton: N. Dak., U.S.A. 92 H3
Grafton: W. Va., U.S.A. 89 M6
Grafton: N. Yorks., England 27 T11
Graham: N.C., U.S.A. 89 M7
Graham: Ont., Canada 88 F1
Graham: Tex., U.S.A. 90 B9
Graham, Mount: Ariz., U.S.A. 93 E6
Graham Bell I.: Franz Josef Land 48 H1
Graham I.: B.C., Canada 84 f7
Graham Land: Antarctica 9 70S 65W
Graham Moore, Cape: N.W.T., Canada 85 M3
Grahamstown: S. Africa 75 G6
Grahovo: Yugoslavia 41 T9
Graian Alps: France/Italy 40 N10
Graiba: Tunisia 32 E5
Graiguenamanagh: Kilk., Repub. of Ireland 31 H14
Grain: Kent, England 25 X17
Grain Coast: Liberia 80 B3
Grajagan: Java 65 E8
Grajaú: Brazil 94 H5
Grajaú: riv., Brazil 94 H4
Grajewo: Poland 43 S10
Gramat: France 37 G11
Grameros: Argentina 96 B2
Grampian: Reg., Scotland (cap. Aberdeen) 28 Q5
Grampian Highlands: mtns.,Scotland 29 N6
Grampians: mtns., Vict., Australia 71 E11
Grampound: Corn., England 24 M19
Gramsbergen: Netherlands 44 M3
Gramzow: E. Germany 45 U2
Granada: Nicaragua 86 L15
Granada: Queens., Australia 69 G4
GRANADA: & Prov., Spain 35 E18
Granados: Mexico 93 F7
Granard: Long., Repub. of Ireland 30 F12
Granby: Mo., U.S.A. 90 D7
Granby: Que., Canada 89 P3
Gran Canaria: i., Canary Is. 78 A4
Gran Chaco: geog. reg., S. America 96 C1
Grand: i., Mich., U.S.A. 88 H2
Grand: riv., Mich., U.S.A. 88 J4
Grand: riv., Mo., U.S.A. 90 D6
Grand: riv., Ont., Canada 88 L4
Grand: riv., S. Dak., U.S.A. 92 G3
Grand, Cape Le: W. Austl. 68 C6
Grand Bahama: i., Bahamas 91 M12
Grand Banks: Newf., Can. 85 v3
Grand Bassa: Co., Liberia (co. town Buchanan) 80 C3
Grand Bassam: Ivory Coast 80 D3
Grand Bay: La., U.S.A. 90 Ins.
Grand Bourg: Marie Galante, Leeward Is. 87 c3
Grand Bourg, Le: France 37 G9
Grand Brière: marsh, France 36 C8
Grandcamp-les-Bains: Fr. 36 D6
Grand Canal: Repub. of Irel. 31 G13
Grand Canyon: Ariz., U.S.A. 93 E5
Grand Canyon: city, Ariz., U.S.A. 93 E5
Grand Canyon Nat. Mon.: Ariz., U.S.A. 93 E5
Grand Canyon Nat. Park: Ariz., U.S.A. 93 E5
Grand Cape Mount: Co., Liberia (co. town Robertsport) 80 B3
Grand Cayman: i., (Br.) W. Indies 87 I 14
Grand Cays: i., Bahamas 91 M12
Grand Cess: Liberia 80 C4
Grandchamp: France 36 C8
Grand Combin: mtn., Switz. 40 N10
Grand Coulee: & dam, Wash., U.S.A. 92 D3
Grande: riv., Brazil 94 H7
Grande: riv., Nicaragua 86 I 15
Grande (Rio Grande): riv., U.S.A./Mexico 86 j12
Grande Prairie: town, Alta., Canada 92 D1
Grandes Bergeronnes: Quebec, Canada 89 R1
Grande Valley: Que., Can. 89 T1
Grand Falls: town, N.B., Canada 89 S2
Grand Falls: town, Newf., Canada 85 v2
Grand Forks: B.C., Canada 92 D3
Grand Forks: city, N. Dak., U.S.A. 92 H3
Grand Gedeh: Co., Liberia (co. town Tchien) 80 C3
Grand Haven: Mich., U.S.A. 88 H4
Grand Island: La., U.S.A. 90 Ins.
Grand Island: city, Nebr., U.S.A. 93 H4
Grand Isle: & city, La., U.S.A. 90 Ins
Grand Junction: Colo., U.S.A. 93 F5
Grand Lahou: Ivory Coast 80 C3
Grand Lake: N.B., Canada 89 T2
Grand Lake: La., U.S.A. 90 F11
Grand Lake: La., U.S.A. 90 Ins.
Grand Lake: Maine, U.S.A. 89 S3
Grand Lake: Newf., Canada 85 u2
Grand Ledge: city, Mich., U.S.A. 88 J4
Grand Lieu, Lac de: lake, Fr. 36 D8
Grand-Lucé, Le: France 36 F8
Grand Manan I.: N.B., Can. 89 S3
Grand Marais: Mich., U.S.A. 88 J2
Grand Marais: Minn., U.S.A. 88 F2
Grand' Mère: Que., Canada 89 P2
Grand Narrows: city, Cape Breton I., Canada 89 V3
Grândola: Portugal 35 B17
Grand Popo: Benin 81 E3
Grand Portage: Minn., U.S.A. 88 G2
Grand Prairie: city, Tex., U.S.A. 90 C9
Grand-Pressigny, Le: France 36 F9
Grand Rapids: city, Mich., U.S.A. 88 J4
Grand Rapids: city, Minn., U.S.A. 88 E2
Grand Saline: Tex., U.S.A. 90 D9
Grand Terre Is.: La., U.S.A. 90 Ins.
Grand Teton: mtn., Wyo., U.S.A. 92 E4
Grand Traverse Bay: Mich., U.S.A. 88 J3
Grandtully: Tay., Scotland 29 O6
Grand Vallée: Que., Canada 89 T1
Grandvilliers: France 36 G6
Grane: Norway 46 N4
Granet, Lac: Que., Canada 89 N2
Graney, Lough: Clare, Repub. of Ireland 31 D14
Grange: Cumbria, England 26 P10
Grange: Cumbria, England 26 Q11
Grange: Sligo, Repub. of Ireland 30 D11
Grange Bay, La: town, W. Australia 68 C3
Grangemouth: Central, Scotland 29 O7
Granger: Tex., U.S.A. 90 C10
Granger: Wyo., U.S.A. 92 E4
Grangetown: Cleve., Eng. 26 T10
Grangeville: Idaho, U.S.A. 92 D3
Granicus: river flowing N. into Sea of Marmara with outlet near Karabiga, Turkey 39 U16
Granite City: Ill., U.S.A. 88 F6
Granite Falls: city, Minn., U.S.A. 92 H4
Granite Peak: mtn., Mont., U.S.A. 92 F3
Granites, The: N. Territ., Australia 68 E4
Graniteville: S.C., U.S.A. 91 L9
Granitola, Cape: Sicily 38 N18
Granja: Brazil 94 J4
Grankulla: Finland 47 T6
Gränna: Sweden 47 O7
Granön: Sweden 46 Q4
Gran Paradiso: mtn., Italy 40 N10
Gran Sabana, La: plat., Ven. 94 E2
Gransden, Great: Cambs., England 25 V15
Gransee: E. Germany 45 T2
Grant: Nebr., U.S.A. 93 G4
Grant, Mount: (S. of Walker Lake), Nev., U.S.A. 93 D5
Grant, Mount: (N. of Shoshone Mtns.), Nev., U.S.A. 93 D5
Grantham: Lincs., England 27 U14
Granton: Lothian, Scot. 29 P8
Grantown on Spey: Highland, Scotland 28 O5
Grant Range: mtns., Nev., U.S.A. 93 D5
Grants Pass: city, Oreg., U.S.A. 92 C4
Grantsburg: Wis., U.S.A. 88 E3
Grantshouse: Borders, Scot. 29 R8
Grantsville: Utah, U.S.A. 93 E4
Granville: France 36 D7
Granville: N.Y., U.S.A. 89 P4
Granville: Tyr., N. Ireland 30 H11
Granville Lake: Man., Can. 92 G1
Granvin: Norway 47 K6
Grão Mogol: Brazil 94 J7
Grappenhall: Ches., Eng. 27 Q13
Gras, Lac de: N.W.T., Can. 84 h5
Grasdorf: W. Germany 45 Q3
Graskop: Trans., S. Africa 75 J2
Grasmere: Trans., S. Africa 74 MIns.
Grasmere: Cumbria, Eng. 26 P11
Gräsö: i., Sweden 47 Q6
Grasplatz: SW. Africa 74 A3
Grasse: France 40 M12
Grassington: N. Yorks., Eng. 27 S11
Grass Patch: W. Australia 68 C6
Grass River Prov. Park: Man., Canada 92 G2
Grass Valley: Calif., U.S.A. 93 C5
Grassy Butte: N. Dak., U.S.A. 92 G3
Grassy Park: town, C.P., S. Africa 74 Ins.
Grateley: Hants., England 25 S17
Grates Cove: Newf., Canada 85 w2
Grau, Le: France 37 K12
Graubünden: Canton, Switz. (cap. Chur) 40 P9
Graulhet: France 37 G12
Graus: Spain 35 G15
Gravarne: Sweden 47 M7
Grave: Netherlands 44 L4
Grave, Pte de: cape, France 37 B10
Gravedona: Italy 40 P9
Gravelbourg: Sask., Canada 92 F3
Gravelines: France 36 H5
Gravenhage: see 's-Gravenhage.
Gravenhurst: Ont., Canada 89 M3
Graver: Outer Hebr., Scot. 28 J3
Gravesend: Kent, England 25 W17
Gravesend: N.S.W., Austl. 71 J7
Gravette: Ark., U.S.A. 90 D7
Grawin: N.S.W., Australia 71 G7
Gray: France 40 L8
Grayling: Mich., U.S.A. 88 J3
Grayrigg: Cumbria, Eng. 26 Q11
Grayson: Ky., U.S.A. 88 K6
Grays Peak: mtn., Colo., U.S.A. 93 F5
Grays Thurrock: Essex, Eng. 25 W17
Grayville: Ill., U.S.A. 88 G6
GRAZ: Styria, Austria 41 V8
Grazalema: Spain 35 D18
Grdelica: Yugoslavia 39 S15
Greasborough: S. Yorks., England 27 T13
Greasby: Mers., England 27 P13
Great Abaco I.: Bahamas 91 N12
Great Altcar: Lancs., Eng. 27 P12
Great Anyuy: riv., U.S.S.R. 49 s4
Great Asby: Cumbria, Eng. 26 R10
Great Australian Bight 68 D6
Great Badminton: Avon, England 24 R16
Great Bardfield: Essex, Eng. 25 W16
Great Barford: Beds., Eng. 25 V15
Great Barrier I.: N.Z. 70 P13
Great Barrier Reef: Austl. 69 H3
Great Barrington: Mass., U.S.A. 89 P4
Great Basin: Nev., U.S.A. 93 D5
Great Bear Lake: N.W.T., Canada 84 g4
Great Bedwyn: Wilts., Eng. 25 S17
Great Belt: str., Denmark 47 M9
Great Bend: Kans., U.S.A. 90 B6
Great Bernera: i., Outer Hebr., Scotland 28 H3
Great Bircham: Norf., Eng. 25 X14
Great Bitter Lake: Egypt (Suez Canal Inset) 32 Ins.
Great Blasket: i., Repub. of Ireland 31 A15
Great Britain: see United Kingdom of Great Britain & Northern Ireland.
Great Bromley: Essex, Eng. 25 Y16
Great Bushman Land: geog. reg., S. Africa 74 C4
Great Chishill: Cambs., Eng. 25 W15
Great Clifton: Cumb., Eng. 26 P10
Great Coco: i., Andaman Is. 59 Q12
Great Cumbrae: i., Bute., Scotland 29 M8
Great Dalby: Leics., England 27 U14
Great Dividing Range: Austl. 69 H4
Great Driffield: Humb., Eng. 27 V12
Great Dunmow: Essex, Eng. 25 W16
Greater London: Metropolitan Co., England 25 V16
Greater Manchester: Metropolitan Co., England (co. town Manchester) 27 R13
Great Eastern Erg: desert, Algeria 78 F3
Great Easton: Leics., Eng. 27 U14
Great Eccleston: Lancs., England 27 Q12
Great Exhibition Bay: North I., New Zealand 70 O12
Great Exuma: i., Bahamas 87 M13
Great Fall: Demarara Riv., Guyana 87 d8
Great Falls: city, Mont., U.S.A. 92 E3
Great Falls: city, S.C., U.S.A. 91 L8
Great Fish: riv., S. Africa 74 D5
Great Fish: riv., S. Africa 75 G6
Great Fish: riv., S.W. Africa 74 B3
Great Ganz Mtn.: S.W. Afr. 74 B1
Great Gidding: Cambs., Eng. 25 V15
Great Gonerby: Lincs., Eng. 27 U14
Great Gransden: Cambridgeshire England 25 V15
Great Guana Cay: is. Bahamas 91 N12
Greatham: Cleveland, Eng. 26 T10
Great Hanish I.: Red Sea 79 Q17
Great Harbour Cay: is., Bahamas 91 N13
Great Harwood: Lancs., Eng. 27 R12
Great Himalaya Range: India 58 O9
Great Inagua: i., Bahamas 87 m13
Great Indian Desert (Thar Desert): India 58 M9
Great Karas Mtns.: S.W. Afr. 74 C3
Great Karroo Plat.: S. Afr. 74 E6
Great Keppel I.: Queens., Australia 70 J4
Great Khingan: range, Inner Mongolia, China 63 W5
Great Letaba: riv., Trans., S. Africa 75 J1
Great Limber: Lincs., Eng. 27 V12
Great Livermere: Suff., Eng. 25 X15
Great Longstone: Derby., England 27 S13
Great Malvern: Hereford & Worcester, England 24 R15
Great Massingham: Norf., England 25 X14
Great Milton: Oxon., Eng. 25 T16
Great Missenden: Bucks., England 25 U16
Great Nama Land: geog. reg., S.W. Africa 74 B2
Great Natuna: i., Indonesia 65 D6
Great Nicobar: i., Nicobar Is. 59 Q13
Great Oakley: Northants., England 25 U15
Great Oakley: Essex, Eng. 25 Y16
Great Offley: Herts., Eng. 25 V16
Great Ormes Head: cape, Gwynedd Wales 27 O13
Great Paternoster Point: S. Africa 74 B6
Great Ponton: Lincs., Eng. 27 U14
Great Rissington: Glos., England 25 S16
Great Rowsley: Derby., England 27 S13
Great Ruaha: riv., Tanzania 76 E4
Great Russel: str., Chan. Is. 25 Ins.
Great Ryburgh: Norf., Eng. 25 X14
Great St. Bernard Pass: Switzerland/Italy 40 N10
Great Sale Cay: i., The Bahamas 91 M12
Great Salkeld: Cumb., Eng. 26 Q10
Great Salt Lake: Utah, U.S.A. 92 E4
Great Salt Lake Desert: Utah, U.S.A. 93 E4
Great Salt Plain Reservoir: Okla., U.S.A. 90 B7
Great Sampford: Essex, England 25 W16
Great Sand Dunes Nat. Mon.: Colo., U.S.A. 93 F5
Great Sand Hills: Sask., Can. 92 F2
Great Sandy Desert: W. Australia 68 C4
Great Sandy (Fraser) I.: Queens., Australia 70 K5
Great Sitkin: i., Aleutians 84 B7
Great Slave Lake: N.W.T., Canada 84 h5
Great Smeaton: N. Yorks., Eng. 26 T11
Great Smoky Mtns. Nat. Park: N.C., U.S.A. 91 K8
Great Staughton: Cambridgeshire, England 25 V15
Great Stirrup Cay: is., Bahamas 91 M13
Great Stour: riv., Kent, England 25 X17
Great Strickland: Cumbria, England 26 Q10
Great Tenasserim: riv., Burma/Thailand 59 R12
Great Tew: Oxon., England 25 T16
Great Thurlow: Suff., Eng. 25 W15
Great Torrington: Devon, England 24 N18
Great Totham: Essex, Eng. 25 X16
Great Victoria Desert: W./S. Australia 68 D5
Great Wakering: Essex, Eng. 25 X16
Great Wall: China 62 T7
Great Waltham: Essex, Eng. 25 W16
Great Western Erg: desert, Algeria 80 L9
Great Whale: riv., Que., Canada 85 M6
Great Whittington: Northumb., England 26 S9
Great Wilbraham: Cambs., England 25 W15
Great Wishford: Wilts., England 25 S17
Great Witley: Hereford & Worcester, England 24 R15
Great Yarmouth: Norf., England 25 Z14
Great Yeldham: Essex, Eng. 25 X15
Grebbestad: Sweden 47 M7
Greco, Cape: Cyprus 56 D4
Grede: Yugoslavia 41 V10
Greding: W. Germany 45 R6
Gredos, Sierra de: range, Spain 35 D16

For Abbreviations see list on p.113. Italic type, e.g. Ephesus, refers to historical names not on maps. Capital letters, e.g. MADRID, show capitals of countries; small capital letters, e.g. CADIZ, show capitals of provinces, etc. General notes p.116.

Greece: *Republic* **39** R17
Cap. Athens
Area: 50,547 sq. miles
(130,917 sq. km.)
Pop. 8,768,648 *(1971 C)*

Greeley: Colo., U.S.A. **93** G4
Greely Fiord: N.W.T., Can. **85** M1
Green, The: Cumbria, Eng. **26** P11
Green: *riv.*, Ky., U.S.A. **88** H7
Green: *riv.*, Utah/Wyo., U.S.A. **93** F5
Green Bay: Wis./Mich., U.S.A. **88** H3
Green Bay: *city*, Wis., U.S.A. **88** H3
Greenbrier: *riv.*, W. Va., U.S.A. **88** L6
Greencastle: Don., Repub. of Ireland **30** H9
Greencastle: Ind., U.S.A. **88** H6
Green Cove Springs: *city*, Fla., U.S.A. **91** L11
Greeneville: Tenn., U.S.A. **88** K7
Greenfield: Ind., U.S.A. **88** J6
Greenfield: Mass., U.S.A. **89** P4
Greenfield: Mo., U.S.A. **90** E7
Greenfield: Tenn., U.S.A. **88** G7
Green Is.: Bismarck Arch. **67** K2
Green Island: *town*, Jamaica **86** Ins.
Green Lake: *town*, Sask., Canada **92** F2
Greenland: *i.* (Dan.), Arctic O. *(cap.* Godthaab) **85** P3
Greenland Sea: Arctic O. **85** S2
Greenlaw: Borders, Scot. **29** R8
Greenloaning: Tay., Scot. **29** O7
Greenly I.: S. Australia **68** E6
Green Mtns.: Vt., U.S.A. **89** P3
Greenock: Strath., Scotland **29** M8
Greenodd: Cumbria, England **26** P11
Grenore: Louth, Repub. of Ireland **30** J11
Greenore Point: *cape*, Wex., Repub. of Ireland **31** J15
Greenough: *riv.*, W. Austl. **68** B5
Greenport: N.Y., U.S.A. **89** P5
Green River: Wyo., U.S.A. **92** F4
Greensboro: Ala., U.S.A. **91** H9
Greensboro: Ga., U.S.A. **91** K9
Greensboro: N.C., U.S.A. **89** M7
Greensburg: Ind., U.S.A. **88** J6
Greensburg: Kans., U.S.A. **90** B7
Greensburg: Pa., U.S.A. **89** M5
Greenstone Point: *cape*, Highland, Scotland **28** K4
Greenville: Ala., U.S.A. **91** H10
Greenville: Ill., U.S.A. **88** G6
Greenville: Ky., U.S.A. **88** H7
GREENVILLE: Sinoe, Liberia **80** C4
Greenville: Maine, U.S.A. **89** R3
Greenville: Mich., U.S.A. **88** J4
Greenville: Miss., U.S.A. **90** F9
Greenville: N.C., U.S.A. **89** N8
Greenville: Ohio, U.S.A. **88** J5
Greenville: Pa., U.S.A. **88** L5
Greenville: S.C., U.S.A. **91** K8
Greenville: Tex., U.S.A. **90** C9
Greenwich: Gt. Ldn., Eng. **25** V17
Greenwood: Ind., U.S.A. **88** H6
Greenwood: Miss., U.S.A. **90** F9
Greenwood: S.C., U.S.A. **91** K8
Greer: S.C., U.S.A. **91** K8
Greetham: Leics., England **27** U14
Greetland: W. Yorks., England **27** S12
Greetsiel: W. Germany **44** N2
Greggton: Tex., U.S.A. **90** D9
Gregory: S. Dak., U.S.A. **92** H4
Gregory: *riv.*, Queens., Austl. **69** F3
Gregory Downs: Queens., Australia **69** F3
Greifenburg: Austria **41** T9
Greifswald: E. Germany **45** T1
Greifswalder Bodden: *bay*, E. Germany **45** T1
Grein: Austria **41** U7
Greiner Wald: *mtns.*, Austria **41** U7
Greiz: E. Germany **45** S5
Grenaa: Denmark **47** M8
Grenada: Miss., U.S.A. **90** G9

Grenada: *Independent State* **87** C4
Cap. St. George's
Area 133 sq. miles (344 sq. km.)
Pop. 96,000 *(1971 E)*

Grenade: Haute-Garonne, France **37** G12
Grenade: Landes, France **37** E12
Grenadines: *is.*, Windward Is. **87** c4
Grenagh: Cork, Repub. of Ireland **31** D15
Grenay: France **36** H5
Grenfell: N.S.W., Australia **71** H9
GRENOBLE: Isère, France **40** L10
Grenville: Windward Is. **87** c4
Gréoux: France **40** L12
Gresford: Clwyd, Wales **27** Q13
Gresik: Java **65** E8
Gresso: Switzerland **40** O9
Gressoney: Italy **40** N10
Greta: N.S.W., Australia **71** J9
Greta: *riv.*, N. Yorks., England **26** Q11
Gretna: Dumfries & Galloway, Scotland **29** P10
Gretna: La., U.S.A. **90** Ins.
Gretna Green: Dumfries & Galloway, Scotland **29** P9
Gretton: Northants., Eng. **27** U14
Greussen: E. Germany **45** Q4
Greve: Italy **41** R12
Grevena: Greece **39** R16
Grevenbroich: W. Germany **44** M4
Grevesmühlen: E. Germany **45** R2
Greyabbey: Down, N. Irel. **30** K10
Greybull: Wyo., U.S.A. **92** F4
Greyhound Is.: Indonesia **65** C7
Grey Is.: Newf., Canada **85** v1
Greylingstad: Trans., S. Afr. **75** H3
GREYMOUTH: Westland, South I., New Zealand **70** N16
Grey Range: Queens., Austl. **70** E6
Greysouthen: Cumbria, Eng. **26** P10
Greystoke: Cumbria, Eng. **26** Q10
Greystone: S. Africa **75** F6
Greystones: Wick., Repub. of Ireland **31** J13
Greyton: S. Africa **74** C7
Greytown: Natal, S. Africa **75** J4
Greytown (San Juan del Norte): Nicaragua **87** I15
Greytown: North I., N.Z. **70** P15
Gribingui: *riv.*, Cen. Afr. Rep. **76** A1
Grieben: E. Germany **45** R3
Grieskirchen: Austria **41** T7
Griffen: Austria **41** U9
Griffin: Ga., U.S.A. **91** J9
Griffith: N.S.W., Australia **71** G10
Griffithstown: Gwent, Wales **24** P16
Grigno: Italy **41** R9
Grignols: France **37** E11
Grigny: France **37** K10
Gripskerk: Netherlands **44** M2
Grik: Malaya, Malaysia **65** b11
Grimari: Cen. Afr. Rep. **76** B1
Grimaud: France **40** M12

Grimma: E. Germany **45** S4
Grimmen: E. Germany **45** T1
Grimoldby: Lincs., England **27** W13
Grimsargh: Lancs., England **27** Q12
Grimsay: *i.*, Outer Hebr., Scotland **28** G5
Grimsby: Humb., England **27** V12
Grimsby: Ont., Canada **89** M4
Grimsel Pass: Switzerland **40** O9
Grims Ey: *i.*, Iceland **46** e3
Grimshaw: Alta., Canada **92** D1
Grimstadhir: Iceland **46** e4
Grimstad: Norway **47** L7
Grimston: Norf., England **25** X14
Grindavik: Iceland **46** b5
Grindelwald: Switzerland **40** O9
Grindon: Northumb., Eng. **26** R8
Grindsted: Denmark **47** L9
Grindstone Island: *town*, Magdalen Is., Canada **89** V2
Gringley on the Hill: Notts., England **27** U13
Grinnell: Iowa, U.S.A. **88** E5
Grinnell Penin.: N.W.T., Canada **84** k2
Grinzens: Austria **41** R8
Griqualand East: *geog. reg.*, S. Africa **75** H5
Griqualand West: *geog. reg.*, S. Africa **74** E4
Griquatown: S. Africa **74** E4
Gris Nez, Cap: *cape*, France **36** G5
Grisolles: France **37** G12
Gristhorpe: N. Yorks., Eng. **26** V11
Gritley: Mainland, Ork. Is. **28** Ins.
Grjotli: Norway **46** K5
Grmeč Range: Yugoslavia **41** W11
Grobelno: Yugoslavia **41** V9
Gröbming: Austria **41** T8
Grodekovo: U.S.S.R. **63** Y6
Grodno: Byelorussia **43** S10
Grodzisk: Poland **45** W3
Groenlo: Netherlands **44** M3
Groenwater: *riv.*, S. Africa **74** E4
Groesbeck: Tex., U.S.A. **90** C10
Groesbeek: Netherlands **44** L4
Grogport: Strath., Scotland **29** L8
Groix, Île de: *i.*, France **36** B8
Grombalia: Tunisia **38** M18
Grömitz: W. Germany **45** Q1
Gronant: Clwyd, Wales **27** P13
Gronau: W. Germany **44** N3
Grondola: Italy **40** P11
Grong: Norway **46** N4
Groningen: E. Germany **45** R4
GRONINGEN: & *Prov.*, Neth. **44** M2
Groomsport: Down, N. Irel. **30** K10
Groot Berg: *riv.*, S. Africa **74** C6
Groot Constantia: *house*, S. Africa **74** Ins.
Grootdoring: S. Africa **74** E4
Grootdrink: S. Africa **74** D4
Groote: *riv.*, S. Africa **74** D6
Groote: *riv.*, S. Africa **74** E6
Groote Eylandt: Australia **69** F2
Groote Laagte: *riv.*, S.W. Africa **77** B7
Grootefehn: W. Germany **44** N2
Grossenbrode: W. Germany **45** R1
Grossenhain: E. Germany **45** T4
Grossenkneten: W. Germany **44** O3
Grosser Klutz Hoved: *bay*, E. Germany **45** R1
Grosser Plöner See: *lake*, W. Germany **45** Q1
Grosser Reken: W. Germany **44** N4
Grosseto: Italy **38** M15
Grossevichi: U.S.S.R. **63** Z5
Gross Gerau: W. Germany **44** O6
Gross Gerungs: Austria **41** U7
Gross Glockner: *mtn.*, Austr. **41** S8
Gros Perdou: Austria **41** U7
Gross Raming: Austria **41** U8
Gross Schonebeck: E. Ger. **45** T3
Gross Siegharts: Austria **41** V7
Gross Umstadt: W. Germany **44** O6
Gross Venediger: *mtn.*, Austr. **41** S8
Gross Waabs: W. Germany **45** Q1
Grosuplje: Yugoslavia **41** U10
Groton: N.Y., U.S.A. **89** N4
Groton: S. Dak., U.S.A. **92** H3
Grouard: Alta., Canada **92** D1
Groundhog: *riv.*, Ont., Can. **88** K1
Grouse Creek: *city*, Utah, U.S.A. **92** E4
Grouw: Netherlands **44** L2
Grove: Oxon., England **25** T16
Grove: Okla., U.S.A. **90** D7
Grovely Ridge: Wilts., Eng. **24** R17
Groveton: N.H., U.S.A. **89** Q3
GROZNYY: Checheno-Ingush, U.S.S.R. **50** G6
Gruda: Yugoslavia **39** Q15
Grudziadz: Poland **43** Q10
Grue: Norway **47** N6
Gruinard Bay: High., Scot. **28** K4
Gruinart: & *loch*, Inner Hebr., Scotland **29** J8
Gruissan: France **37** J12
Grünau: Austria **41** T8
Grünau: S.W. Africa **74** C3
Grünberg: W. Germany **44** O5
Grundisburgh: Suff., Eng. **25** Y15
Grundorner: S.W. Africa **74** B2
Grundy: Va., U.S.A. **88** K7
Grundy Center: Iowa, U.S.A. **88** E4
Grungedal: Norway **47** K7
Grunow: E. Germany **45** U3
Grunstadt: W. Germany **44** O6
Gruyeres: Switzerland **40** N9
Gruža: Yugoslavia **39** R15
Gryazi: U.S.S.R. **50** F4
Gryazovets: U.S.S.R. **50** F3
Grycksmyra: Sweden **47** O6
Gryfice: Poland **45** V2
Gryfino: Poland **45** U2
Gryke: Albania **39** Q16
Gstaad: Switzerland **40** N9
Guachipas: Argentina **96** B2
Guadalajara: Mexico **86** j13
GUADALAJARA: & *Prov.*, Sp. **35** E16
Guadalaviar: *riv.*, Spain **35** F17
Guadalcanal: Spain **35** D17
Guadalcanal: *i.*, Solomon Is. **67** L3

Guadelete: *riv.*, Spain **35** D18
Guadalimar: *riv.*, Spain **35** E17
Guadalope: *riv.*, Spain **35** F16
Guadalquivir: *riv.*, Spain **35** D18
Guadalupe: Spain **35** D17
Guadalupe: *i.*, Mexico **93** D7
Guadalupe: *riv.*, Tex., U.S.A. **90** C11
Guadalupe de los Reyes: Mexico **93** F8
Guadalupe Peak: *mtn.*, Tex., U.S.A. **93** G6
Guadarrama: Spain **35** D16
Guadarrama, Sierra de: *range*, Spain **35** E16

Guadeloupe: *Fr. overseas dept.* **87** c2
Cap. Basse Terre
Area: 686 sq. miles
(1,770 sq. km.)
Pop. 332,000 *(1971 E)*

Guadiana: *riv.* Sp./Port. **35** C17
Guadix: Spain **35** E18
Guafo, G. of: Chile **95** C12
Guainia: *riv.*, Colombia **94** D3
Guaira, La: Venezuela **94** D1
Guaira Falls (Sete Quedes): Brazil **96** E1
Guaitecas I.: Chile **95** C12
Guajará-Mirim: Brazil **94** D6
Gualañe: Chile **96** A3
Gualeguay: & *riv.*, Arg. **96** D3
Gualeguaychú: Argentina **96** D3
Guam: *i.* (U.S.A.), Mariana Is. *(cap.* Agaña) **61** N9
Guamini: Argentina **96** C4
Guampita, La: Argentina **96** C2
Gua Musang: Malaya, Malaysia **65** c11
Guanabara: Brazil **94** C6
Guanabara: *State*, Brazil *(cap.* Rio de Janeiro) **96** G1
Guanacevi: Mexico **93** F7
Guanajuato: Mexico **86** j13
Guanambi: Brazil **94** J6
Guanare: Venezuela **94** D2
Guanare: *riv.*, Venezuela **94** D2
Guandacol: Argentina **96** B2
Guane: Cuba **86** I3
Guantánamo: Cuba **87** M13
Guapi: Colombia **94** B3
Guaporé: Brazil **96** E2
Guaporé: *State*, Brazil **94** E6
Guaporé: *riv.*, Brazil **94** E6
Guaqui: Bolivia **94** D7
Guara: *riv.*, Nigeria **81** F3
Guarabira: Brazil **94** K5
Guaragi: Brazil **96** E2
Guaranda: Ecuador **94** B4
Guarapari: Brazil **95** J8
Guarapuava: Brazil **96** E2
Guaraqueçaba: Brazil **96** F2
Guaratingueta: Brazil **96** F1
Guaratuba: Brazil **96** F2
Guarayos, Llanos de: *plain*, Bolivia **94** E7
Guarda: Portugal **35** C16
Guardafui, Cape: Somalia **79** S17
Guardia, La: Argentina **96** B2
Guardia, La: Pontevedra, Sp. **35** B16
Guasdualito: Venezuela **94** C2
Guasipati: Venezuela **94** E2
Guastalla: Italy **40** Q11

Guatemala: *Republic* **86** K14
Cap. Guatemala
Area 42,042 sq. miles
(108,889 sq. km.)
Pop. 5,348,000 *(1971 E)*

GUATEMALA: Guatemala **86** k15
Guatimozin: Argentina **96** C3
Guatrache: Argentina **96** C4
Guaviare: *riv.*, Colombia **94** C3
Guaxupé: Brazil **96** F1
Guayaquil: Ecuador **94** B4
Guayama: Puerto Rico **87** N14
Guaymas: Mexico **93** E7
Guazapares: Mexico **93** F7
Gubakha: U.S.S.R. **50** J3
Guban: *geog. reg.*, Somalia **79** Q17
Gubba, El: Libya **33** G5
Gubbi: *riv.*, Nigeria **81** F2
Gubbio: Italy **41** S12
Guberovo: U.S.S.R. **63** Y5
Gubin: Poland **45** U4
Gubio: Nigeria **81** G2
Gudermes: U.S.S.R. **50** G6
Gudebwiler: France **40** N8
Gueguen, Lac: Que., Canada **89** N1
GUEKEDOU: & *Reg.*, Guinea **80** B3
Guelma: Algeria **32** D4
Guelph: Ont., Canada **88** L4
Guen.ar: Algeria **32** D5
Guémené: France **36** B7
Guémene: France **36** B7
Güémes: Argentina **96** B1
Guéné: Benin **81** E2
Guer: France **36** C8
Guera: *Pref.*, Chad *(cap.* Mongo) **81** H3
Guerande: France **36** C8
Guerche, La: France **36** D8
Guerche-sur-l'Aubois, La: France **36** H9
Guercif: Morocco **80** L8
GUERET: Creuse, France **37** G9
Guerigny: France **36** J8
Guernica: Spain **35** E15
Guernsey: Wyo., U.S.A. **92** G4
Guernsey: *i.*, Chan. Is. (Br.) *(cap.* St. Peter Port) **25** Ins.
Guerra, Pic du: *mtn.*, Chad **81** H2
Guerrero: Mexico **93** G7
Gueugnon: France **37** K9
Gueydan: La., U.S.A. **90** E10
Guezenti: Chad **78** H5
Gufudalur: Iceland **46** b4
Gughe: *mtn.*, Ethiopia **76** E1
Guguan: *i.*, Mariana Is. **61** O8
Guiana Basin: N. Atlantic Ocean **8** 10N 55W
Guiana Highlands: S.A. **94** F3
Guichen: France **36** D8
Guidel: France **36** B8
Guider: Cameroun **81** G3
Guidimaka: *Dist.*, Mauritania *(cap.* Selibaby) **80** B1
Guiers, Lac de: Senegal **80** A1
Guiglo: Ivory Coast **80** C3
Guija: & *Dist.*, Mozambique **75** K2
Guilberville: France **36** E7
Guilden Sutton: Ches., England **27** Q13
Guildford: Surrey, England **25** U17
Guilford: Maine, U.S.A. **89** R3
Guillaumes: France **40** M11
Guillestre: France **40** M11
Guilvinec: France **36** A8
Guimarães: Portugal **35** B16
Guimaras: *i.*, Philippines **64** G4
Guindulman: Philippines **64** G5

Guinea: *Republic* **80** B2
Cap. Conakry
Area 94,925 sq. miles
(245,856 sq. km.)
Pop. 4,010,000 *(1971 E)*

Guinea Basin: N. Atlantic Basin **8** 0 10W

Guinea-Bissau: *Republic* **80** B2
Cap. Bissau
Area 13,948 sq. miles
(36,125 sq. km.)
Pop. 563,000 *(1971 E)*

Guinea Fracture Zone: N. Atlantic Ocean **8** 05N 40W
Guinea, G. of: Africa **78** E9
Guines: Cuba **87** I13
Guines: France **36** G5
Guingamp: France **36** B7
Guipuzcoa: *Prov.*, Spain *(cap.* San Sebastian) **35** E15
Guir: Mali **78** D6
Guir: *riv.*, *de plat.*, Morocco/Algeria **80** L8
Guira de Melena: Cuba **87** I13
Guiratinga: Brazil **94** G7
Guiria: Venezuela **87** b5
Guisanborough: Fr. Guiana **94** G3
Guisborough: Cleve., England **26** T10
Guiscard: France **36** J7
Guiscriff: France **36** B7
Guise: France **36** J6
Guiseley: W. Yorks., England **27** S12
Guita Koulouba: Central African Republic **76** B1
Guiuan: Philippines **64** H4
Gujarat: *State*, India *(cap.* Ahmadabad) **58** L10
Gujranwala: Punjab, Pakistan **58** M8
Gujrat: Punjab, Pak. **58** M8
Guk: Iran **55** J9
Gulbarga: Karnataka, India **58** N11
Gulbene: Latvia, U.S.S.R. **47** U8
Gul'cha: Kirgiz., U.S.S.R. **51** M6
Gulen: Norway **47** J6
Gulgir: Iran **57** L6
Gulgong: N.S.W., Australia **71** H9
Gulkana: Alaska, U.S.A. **84** E5
Gullane: Lothian, Scotland **29** Q7
Gullfoss: *waterfall*, Iceland **46** d4
Gull Lake: *town*, Sask., Canada **92** F2
Gulluk: Turkey **39** U18
Gulmarg: Jammu & Kashmir **58** M8
Gulmar: Turkey **56** C3
Gulram: Afghanistan **58** K7
Gulsehir: Turkey **56** D2
Gulta: Ethiopia **76** E1
Gulu: Uganda **76** D2
Gulwe: Tanzania **76** E4
Guma (Pishan): Sinkiang, China **51** N7
Gumbardo: Queens., Austl. **70** F6
Gumel: Nigeria **81** F2
Gumma: *Pref.*, Japan *(cap.* Maebashi) **63** f2
Gummersbach: W. Germany **44** N4
Gummi: Nigeria **81** F2
Gumti (Gomati): *riv.*, India **58** O9
GUMUŞANE: & *Prov.*, Turkey **56** F1
Gumushacikoy: Turkey **56** D1
Gumuskoy: Turkey (Bosporus *inset*) **20** Ins.
Guna: Madhya Pradesh, India **58** N10
Gunalda: Queens., Austl. **70** K5
Gunbar: N.S.W., Australia **71** F10
Gunchu: Japan **63** c4
Gundagai: N.S.W., Austl. **71** H10
Gundelsheim: W. Germany **44** P6
Gunderbooka: N.S.W., Australia **71** F8
Gundlupet: Queens., Austl. **70** K5
Gundogmus: Turkey **56** C3
Guney: Turkey **56** A2
Gungu: Zaire **76** A4
Gunnarn: Sweden **46** P4
Gunnedah: N.S.W., Austl. **71** J8
Gunnewin: Queens., Austl. **70** H5
Gunning: N.S.W., Austl. **71** H10
Gunnislake: Corn., England **24** N18
Gunnison: & *riv.*, Colo., U.S.A. **93** F5
Gunnison: Utah, U.S.A. **93** E5
Gunongsugi: Sumatra **65** D7
Gunsburg: W. Germany **40** Q7
Guntakal: Andhra Pradesh, India **58** N11
Guntersdorf: Austria **41** W7
Guntersville: Ala., U.S.A. **91** H8
Guntur: Andhra Pradesh, India **58** O11
Gunungsitoli: Nias, Sumatra **65** B6
Gunupur: Orissa, India **59** O11
Gunzenhausen: W. Germany **45** Q6
Gura Humorului: Romania **43** T13
Gurais: Jammu & Kashmir **58** M8
Gurdaspur: Punjab, India **58** N8
Gurdon: Ark., U.S.A. **90** E9
Gureci: Turkey (Dardan. *inset*) **20** Ins.
Gurgan: Iran **55** H7
Gurgan: *riv.*, Iran **55** J7
Gurgaon: Haryana, India **58** N9
Gurkha: Nepal **59** O9
Gurpinar: Turkey **57** H2
Gurralarda: Ethiopia **76** E1
Gurskøy: *i.*, Norway **46** J5
Gurun: Turkey **56** E2
Gurupa: Brazil **94** G4
Gurupi: *riv.*, Brazil **94** H4
GUR'YEV: & *Reg.*, Kazakh., U.S.S.R. **50** H5
Gusau: Nigeria **81** F2
Gusev: U.S.S.R. **47** S9
Gusinje: Yugoslavia **39** Q15
Guspini: Sardinia **38** L17
Gussing: Austria **41** W8
Gustav Holm, Cape: Grnld. **85** q4
Gustavus: Alaska, U.S.A. **84** F6
Gusten: E. Germany **45** R4
Gustrow: E. Germany **45** S2
Gusyatin Solobkovtsy: Ukraine **43** U12
Guta: Czechoslovakia **43** P13
Gutara: *riv.*, U.S.S.R. **51** R3
Gutenstein: Austria **41** V8
Gutersloh: W. Germany **44** O4
Guthalungra: Queens., Australia **70** G2
Guthrie: Tayside, Scotland **29** Q6
Guthrie: Ky., U.S.A. **88** H7
Guthrie: Okla., U.S.A. **90** C8
Gutu: Rhodesia **77** D6
Guweira: Jordan **56** D7

Guyana: *Republic* **87** Ins.
Cap. Georgetown
Area 83,000 sq. miles
(214,970 sq. km.)
Pop. 736,000 *(1971 E)*

Guyandot: *riv.*, W. Va., U.S.A. **88** K6

Guyenne: *Prov.*, France **34** G14
Guyra: N.S.W., Australia **71** J8
Guysborough: N.S., Canada **89** V3
Guzar: Uzbek., U.S.S.R. **51** L7
Guzmán: & *lake*, Mexico **93** F6
Gwa: Burma **59** Q11
Gwaai: Rhodesia **77** C6
Gwabegar: N.S.W., Austl. **71** H8
Gwadar (Oman): Baluchistan, Pakistan **58** K9
Gwadar West Bay: Baluchistan, Pakistan **58** K9
Gwalchmai: Gwynedd, Wales **27** N13
Gwalior: Madhya Pradesh, India **58** N9
Gwanda: Rhodesia **77** C7
Gwandu: Nigeria **81** E2
Gwane: Zaire **76** C2
Gwaram: Nigeria **81** F2
Gwatar: Iran **55** K9
Gweebarra: *riv.* & *bay*, Don., Repub. of Ireland **30** E10
Gweedore: Don., Repub. of Ireland **30** E9
Gweesalia: Mayo, Repub. of Ireland **30** B11
GWELO: Midlands, Rhodesia **77** C6
Gwenddwr: Powys, Wales **24** P15
Gwennap: Corn., England **24** L19
Gwent: *Co.*, Wales *(co. town* Newport) **24** Q16
Gwese: Zaire **76** B2
Gwinn: Mich., U.S.A. **88** H2
Gwona: Nigeria **81** G3
Gwydir: *riv.*, N.S.W., Austl. **71** H7
Gwynedd: *Co.*, Wales *(co. town* Caernarvon) **27** O14
Gwytherin: Clwyd, Wales **27** O13
Gyala: Tibet, China **59** Q9
Gyangtse: *see* Chiangtzu.
Gyda: *penin.* & *gulf*, U.S.S.R. **48** j3
Gydan (Kolyma) Range: U.S.S.R. **49** r5
Gydayamo: U.S.S.R. **48** j3
Gylcen: Cork, Repub. of Ireland **31** E16
Gyljen: Sweden **46** S3
Gympie: Queens., Australia **70** K6
Gynym: U.S.S.R. **49** o6
Gyongyos: Hungary **43** Q13
Györ: Hungary **43** P13
Gypsumville: Man., Canada **92** H2
Gyuetsevo: Bulgaria **39** S15
Gyula: Hungary **43** R13

Haag: Austria **41** T7
Haag: W. Germany **41** S7
Haag Markt: Austria **41** U7
Haalenberg: S.W. Africa **74** A3
Haapai Group: *is.*, Tonga **67** R6
Haapamäki: Finland **46** T5
HAARLEM: North Holland, Netherlands **44** K3
Haarlemmermeer: Neth. **44** K3
Haarstrang: *hills*, W. Ger. **44** O4
Haast: South Is., N.Z. **70** M16
Haataja: Finland **46** V3
Hab: *riv.*, Baluchistan/Sind, Pakistan **58** L9
Habarut: *well*, Saudi Arabia **55** H11
Habas, Las: Spain (Gib. *Inset*) **32** Ins.
Habaswein: Kenya **76** E2
Habay La Neuve: Belgium **44** L6
Habbaniya: & *lake*, Iraq **57** H5
Habiganj: Bangladesh **59** Q10
Habitancum: Roman fort about 2 miles NNW. of Ridsdale, Northumb., Eng. **26** R9
Haboro: Japan **63** ZZ6
Hacha: *well*, Chad **81** H1
Hachenburg: W. Germany **44** N5
Hachijo: *i.*, Nanpo Is., Pacific O. **63** f4
Hachiman: Japan **63** e3
Hachinohe: Japan **63** ZZ6
Hachioji: Japan **63** f3
Hacht: Belgium **44** K5
Hacibektas: Turkey **56** D2
Hacigelen: Turkey (Dardan. *Inset*) **20** Ins.
Hackensack: N.J., U.S.A. **89** O5
Hacketstown: Carlow, Repub. of Ireland **31** H14
Hackney: Gt. Ldn., England **25** V16
Hadama: Ethiopia **76** E1
Haddar: Saudi Arabia **54** G10
Haddenham: Bucks., Eng. **25** U16
Haddenham: Cambs., Eng. **25** W15
Haddington: Lothian, Scotland **29** Q8
Haddon, East & West: Northants., England **25** T15
Haded Plain: Somalia **79** R17
Hadejia: Nigeria **81** G2
Hadejia: *riv.*, Nigeria **81** F2
Hademarschen: W. Germany **44** P1
Haden: Queens., Austl. **70** J6
Hadera: Israel **55** a2
Haderslev: Denmark **47** L9
Hadhal: Mongolia **49** M7
Hadhauda: *oasis*, Sau. Arab. **56** F6
Hadhramaut: *geog. reg.*, Yemen P.D.R. **55** G11
Hadida: *meteorite craters*, Saudi Arabia **55** H10
Hadim: Turkey **56** C3
Haditha: Iraq **57** H4
Haditha: *well*, Jordan/Saudi Arabia **56** E6
Hadiya: Saudi Arabia **54** E9
Hadjadj: Algeria **35** G18
Hadjout: Algeria **35** H18
Hadleigh: Essex, England **25** X16
Hadleigh: Suff., England **25** X15
Hadley: Salop, England **27** R14
Hadlow: Kent, England **25** W17
Hadnall: Salop, England **27** Q14
Hadrian's Wall: Northumb./Cumbria, England **26** R9
Hadrumetum: Punic and Roman city at Sousse, Tunisia **38** M19
Haegeland: Norway **47** K7
Haeju: N. Korea **63** X7
Haemus: Roman name for Balkan mtns., Bulgaria **39** T15
Haenam: S. Korea **63** X8
Hafar al Batin: *pump. station*, Saudi Arabia **54** G9
Haffa: Syria **56** E2
Hafik: Turkey **56** E2
Haflong: Assam, India **59** Q9
Hafnarfjördhur: Iceland **46** c4
Haft Kel: Iran **57** L6
Hafun: *i.* (Dante): Somalia **79** S17
Hag 'Abdulla: Sudan **54** D12
Hagedis: *i.*, Indonesia **65** G8
Hageland: *geog. reg.*, Belg. **44** K5
Hagen: W. Germany **44** N4
Hagenow: E. Germany **45** R2

Hagerman—Hawaiian Ridge 147

Hagerman: N. Mex., U.S.A. 93 G6
Hagerstown: Md., U.S.A. 89 N6
Hagersville: Ont., Canada 88 L4
Hagetmau: France 37 E12
Hagfors: Sweden 47 N6
Häggsjövik: Sweden 46 O5
Hagi: Iceland 46 b4
Hagi: Japan 63 b3
Hagiang: Vietnam 64 C2
Hagley: Hereford & Worcester, England 24 R15
Hagondange: France 44 M6
Hague, Cap de la: *cape*, Fr. 36 D6
HAGUE, THE ('s-Gravenhage): Netherlands 44 K3
Haguenau: France 40 N7
Hagworthingham: Lincs., England 27 W14
Haha: *i.*, Bonin Is. 60 N6
Hahn: W. Germany 44 N5
Haib: S.W. Africa 74 C4
Haibak: Afghanistan 58 L7
Haicheng: Liaoning, China 63 W6
Haichow (Tunghai): Kiangsu, China 62 V8
Haiderabad: Iran 57 J3
Haiding: Austria 41 T7
Haiduong: Vietnam 64 D2
Haifa: Israel 55 a2
Haikang: Kwangtung, China 62 U10
Haiki: Japan 63 a4
Haikow: Hainan, China 62 U10
Haiku: Hawaiian Is. 83 c2
Hail: Saudi Arabia 54 F9
Hailar (Hulun): Inner Mongolia, China 62 V5
Haile: Cumbria, England 26 P11
Hailey: Idaho, U.S.A. 92 E4
Haileybury: Ont., Canada 89 M2
Hailsham: E. Sussex, Eng. 25 W18
Hailun: Heilungkiang, China 63 X5
Hailuoto (Karlo): & *i.*, Finland 46 T4
Haimen: Chekiang, China 63 W9
Haimen: Kiangsu, China 63 W8
Hainan: *i. & str.*, China 62 T11
Hainaut: *Prov.*, Belgium (*cap.* Mons) 44 J5
Haines City: Fla., U.S.A. 91 L11
Hainfeld: Austria 41 V7
Hainichen: E. Germany 45 T5
Haining: Chekiang, China 63 W8
Hainleite: *hills*, E. Germany 45 Q4
Haiphong: Vietnam 64 D2
Hais: Yemen 54 F12
Haitan: *i.*, Fukien, China 62 V9

Haiti: *Republic* 87 m14
Cap.: Port-au-Prince
Area: 10,714 sq. miles (27,749 sq. km.)
Pop.: 5,100,000 (*1972 E*)

Haiya: Sudan 54 E11
Haiyang: Shantung, China 63 W7
Haiyaniya: *well*, Sau. Arab. 54 F9
Haiyuan: Ninghsia Hui, China 62 T7
Hajara: *geog. reg.*, Saudi Arabia 57 H7
Hajar Banga: Sudan 79 J7
Hajdúböszörmény: Hungary 43 R13
Hajdunánás: Hungary 43 R13
Hajiabad: Iran 55 H8
Hajiki, Cape: Japan 63 f1
Hajjar Tsaka: Chinghai, China 62 Q7
Hajnówka: Poland 43 S10
Haka: Burma 59 Q10
Hakalau: Hawaiian Is. 83 d3
Hakalwoo: N. Korea 63 X6
Håkantorp: Sweden 47 N7
Hakâri: *Prov.*, Turkey (*cap.* Cölemerik) 57 H3
Hakodate: Japan 63 ZZ6
Hakonola: Inner Mongolia, China 63 W5
Halachó: Mexico 86 k13
Hala Hu: *lake*, China 62 R7
Halaib: Sudan 54 E10
Halasu: Inner Mongolia, China 63 W5
Halba: Lebanon 56 E4
Halberstadt: E. Germany 45 R4
Halberton: Devon, England 24 P18
Halchow (Tunghai): Kiangsu, China 62 V8
Halden: Norway 47 M7
Hale: Gt. Man., England 27 R13
Hale: Cheshire, England 27 Q13
Haleakala: *mtn.*, Hawaiian Is. 83 c2
Haleb (Aleppo): Syria 56 E3
Hale Center: Tex., U.S.A. 93 G6
Halesowen: W. Mid., Eng. 24 R15
Halesworth: Suff., England 25 Y15
Haleyville: Ala., U.S.A. 91 H8
Halfain: *wadi*, Oman 55 J10
Half-Moon Bay: *town*, Stewart I., New Zealand 71 M18
Halhul: Jordan 55 b3
Haliartus: Greek city of *Boeotia* S. of L. *Copais*, 12 miles ENE. of Thebes 39 S17
Haliburton: Ont., Canada 89 M3
Halicarnassus: Greek city at Bodrum, Turkey 39 U18
Halidon Hill: battlefield about 2½ miles NW. of Berwick upon Tweed, Northumb., England 26 R8
Halieis: ancient Greek settlement on SW. promontory of peninsula running E. from Argos, Greece 39 S18
HALIFAX: N.S., Canada 89 U3
Halifax: Queens., Austl. 69 H3
Halifax: W. Yorks., England 27 S12
Halin: Somalia 79 R18
Haliri: *riv.*, Iran 55 J9
Halkin Mt.: Clwyd, Wales 27 P13
Halkirk: High., Scotland 28 P2
Hall: Austria 41 R8
Hall: W. Germany 44 P6
Halladale: *riv.*, High., Scot. 28 O3
Hallam, West: Derby., Eng. 27 T14
Halland: *Co.*, Sweden (*cap.* Halmstad) 47 N8
Hallaniya: *i.*, Kuria Muria Is. 55 J11
Hallaton: Leics., England 27 U14
Halle: Belgium 44 K5
HALLE: & *Dist.*, E. Germany 45 R4
Hällefors: Sweden 47 O7
Hallein: Austria 41 T8
Hallenberg: W. Germany 44 O4
Hallet, Cape: Antarctica 9 75S 170E
Hallettsville: Tex., U.S.A. 90 C11
Halley Bay: *rsch. stn.*, Antarctica 9 80S 30W
Hallin: Inner Hebr., Scot. 28 H4
Hallingdal: *riv.*, Norway 47 L6
Hallington: Northumb., Eng. 26 R9
Hall I.: (U.S.A.), Bering Sea 84 b5
Hall I.: Franz Josef Land 48 g1
Hall Land: Greenland 85 O1
Hällnäs: Sweden 46 Q4
Hallock: Minn., U.S.A. 92 H3
Hallowell: Maine, U.S.A. 89 R3
Halls: Tenn., U.S.A. 90 G8
Hallstahammar: Sweden 47 P7
Hallsberg: Sweden 47 O7
Hall's Creek: *town*, W. Austl. 68 D3
Hallstavik: Sweden 47 Q6
Halluin: France 36 J5
Hallviken: Sweden 46 O5
Hallworthy: Corn., England 24 M18
Halmahera: *i.*, Moluccas, Indonesia 61 K11
HALMSTAD: Halland, Swed. 47 N8
Halohsin: *riv.*, Inner Mongolia, China 62 V5
Halq el Oued: Tunisia 38 M18
Halsa: Norway 46 L5
Hälsingborg: Sweden 47 N8
Halstead: Essex, England 25 X16
Halstead: Kans., U.S.A. 90 C7
Halstock: Dorset, England 24 Q18
Haltern: W. Germany 44 N4
Halton: Ches., England 27 Q13
Halton, East: Lincs., Eng. 27 V12
Halton Gill: N. Yorks., Eng. 26 R11
Haltwhistle: Northumb., England 26 R10
Halul: *i.*, Persian Gulf 55 H9
Halunarshan: Inner Mongolia, China 62 V5
Halvergate: Norf., England 25 Z14
Halwell: Devon, England 24 O19
Halwill: Devon, England 24 N18
Halys: Greek and Roman name of river Kızıl, Tur. 56 D1
Ham: Shetland Is. 28 *Ins.*
Ham: France 36 J6
Ham: Chad 78 H7
HAMA: & *Prov.*, Syria 56 E4
Hamad (Syrian Desert): SW. Asia 56 F5
Hamada: Japan 63 c3
HAMADAN: & *Governorate*, Iran 57 L4
Hamada of Dra: *geog. reg.*, Algeria 80 K9
Hamada of Guir: *geog. reg.*, Morocco/Algeria 80 L8
Hamam: Saudi Arabia 54 G10
Hamama: Israel 55 a3
Hamamatsu: Japan 63 e3
Hamanskraal: Trans., S. Afr. 75 H2
HAMAR: Hedmark, Norway 47 M6
Hamar: Saudi Arabia 54 G10
Hamasaka: Japan 63 d3
Hambantota: Sri Lanka 58 O13
Hamber Prov. Park: B.C., Canada 92 D2
Hambleden: Bucks., Eng. 25 U16
Hambledon: Hants., England 25 T18
Hambleton: Lancs., England 27 Q12
Hambleton Hills: N. Yorks., England 26 T11
Hambridge Wildlife Reserve: S. Australia, Australia 71 A9
Hamburg: Ark., U.S.A. 90 F9
HAMBURG: & *State*, W. Germany 45 Q2
Hamburg: Pa., U.S.A. 89 O5
Hamburg: N.Y., U.S.A. 89 M4
Hamburg: S. Africa 75 G6
Hamdaniya, El: Syria 56 E4
Hamdh: *wadi*, Saudi Arabia 54 E9
Hamdha: Saudi Arabia 54 F11
Häme: *Prov.*, Finland (*cap.* Hämeenlinna) 47 T6
HÄMEENLINNA: Häme, Fin. 47 T6
Hamelin Pool: W. Austl. 68 A5
Hameln: W. Germany 44 P3
Hamersley Range: W. Austl. 68 B4
Hamhung: N. Korea 63 X7
Hami (Qomul): Sinkiang, China 62 Q6
Hamidiye: Turkey (Dardan. *Inset*) 20 *Ins.*
HAMILTON: Bermuda 87 *Ins.*
Hamilton: Strath., Scotland 29 N8
Hamilton: Mont., U.S.A. 92 E3
Hamilton: N.Y., U.S.A. 89 O4
HAMILTON: South Auckland – Bay of Plenty, North I., N.Z. 70 P13
Hamilton: Ohio, U.S.A. 88 J6
Hamilton: Ont., Canada 89 M4
Hamilton: Tex., U.S.A. 90 B10
Hamilton: Vict., Australia 71 E11
Hamilton: *riv.*, Queens., Australia 69 G4
Hamilton Cove (Ste. Anne de Portneuf): Que., Can. 89 R1
Hamilton, Lake: Ark., U.S.A. 90 E8
Hamilton Downs: N. Territ., Australia 68 E4
Hamilton Inlet: Newf., Can. 85 O7
Hamina: Finland 47 U6
Hamiota: Man., Canada 92 G2
Hamir: *wadi*, Saudi Arabia 57 G6
Hamirpur: Uttar Pradesh, India 58 O9
Hamlet: N.C., U.S.A. 91 M8
Hamley Bridge: S. Austl. 71 C10
Hamlin: Tex., U.S.A. 90 A9
Hamm: W. Germany 44 N4
Hammam: Syria 56 F4
Hammam Bou Hadjar: Alg. 35 F19
Hammamet: & *gulf*, Tunisia 38 M18
Hammanskraal: Trans., S. Africa 75 H2
Hammar: Iraq 57 K6
Hamme: Belguim 44 K4
Hammelburg: W. Germany 45 P5
Hammerfest: Norway 46 S1
Hammersmith: Gt. Ldn., England 25 V17
Hamminkeln: W. Germany 44 M4
Hammond: Ind., U.S.A. 88 H5
Hammond: La., U.S.A. 90 F10
Hammond: S. Australia 71 C9
Hampden: South I., N.Z. 70 N17
Hampshire: *Co.*, England (*co. town* Winchester) 25 T17
Hampshire Downs: Eng. 25 T17
Hampstead Norris: Berks., England 25 T17
Hampton: Ark., U.S.A. 90 E9
Hampton: Iowa, U.S.A. 88 E4
Hampton: N.B., Canada 89 T3
Hampton in Arden: W. Mid., England 25 S15
Hamra: Saudi Arabia 54 E10
Hams, South: *dist.*, Devon, England 27 T14
Hamsterley: Durham, Eng. 26 S10
Ham Street: Kent, England 25 X17
Hamun-i-Helmand: *lake*, Afghanistan/Iran 55 K8
Hamun-i-Jaz Murian: *lake*, Iran 55 J9
Hamun-i-Lora: *lake*, Pak. 58 K9
Han: Ghana 80 D2
Han: *riv.*, Hupeh/Shensi, China 62 U8
Han: riv., Kwangtung, China 62 V10
Hanak: Saudi Arabia 54 E9
Hanakiya: Saudi Arabia 54 F10
Hanam Plat: S.W. Africa 74 B2
Hanang: *mtn.*, Tanzania 76 E3
Hanau: W. Germany 44 O5
Hanbury: Hereford and Worcester, England 24 R15
Hancheng: Shensi, China 62 U7
Hanchung (Nancheng): Shensi, China 62 T8
Hancock: Mich., U.S.A. 88 G2
Handa: Japan 63 e3
Handa: Somalia 79 S17
Handa I.: High., Scotland 28 L3
Handeni: Tanzania 76 E4
Handforth: Ches., England 27 R13
Handley: Dorset, England 24 R18
Handöl: Sweden 46 N5
Hane: Japan 63 c3
HANGCHOW: Chekiang, China 63 W8
Hanghei: Somalia 79 R17
Hangö (Hanko): & *fiord*, Finland 47 S7
Haniya: *hills*, Iraq 57 K7
Hankey: S. Africa 75 F6
Hankow (*part of* Wuhan): Hupeh, China 62 U8
Hanko (Hangö): & *fiord*, Finland 47 S7
Hankpinar: Turkey 57 G3
Hanley: Staffs., England 27 R13
Hanmer, Clwyd, Wales 27 Q14
Hann, Mount: W. Austl. 68 D3
Hanna: Alta., Canada 92 E2
Hanna: Wyo., U.S.A. 92 F4
Hanney: Oxon., England 25 T16
Hannibal: Mo., U.S.A. 88 F6
Hannington: Hants., Eng. 25 T17
Hanö Bay: Sweden 47 O9
HANOI: Vietnam 64 D2
HANOVER: Lower Saxony, W. Germany 44 P3
Hannover: *Dist.*, Lower Saxony, West Germany 44 O3
Hanover: Ont., Canada 88 L3
Hanover: Pa., U.S.A. 89 N6
Hanover: & *Dist.*, S. Africa 75 F5
Hanover I.: Chile 95 C14
Hanover Road: S. Africa 75 F5
Han Pijesak: Yugoslavia 39 Q14
Hansen: Idaho, U.S.A. 92 E4
Hansi: Haryana, India 58 N9
Hantams: *riv.*, S. Africa 74 C5
Hantsport: N.S., Canada 89 T3
Hantsun: Hopeh, China 62 V7
Hanumangarh: Rajasthan, India 58 M9
Hanun: Oman 55 H11
Hanyang (*part of* Wuhan): Hupeh, China 62 U8
Hanyin: Shensi, China 62 T8
Hanyuan: Szechwan, China 62 S9
Hao: *i.*, Tuamotu Arch. 83 g3
Haogoundou, Lake: Mali 80 D1
Haparanda: Sweden 46 T4
Hapeville: Ga., U.S.A. 91 J9
Happisburgh: Norf., Eng. 25 Z14
Haqal: Saudi Arabia 56 D7
Haradh: Saudi Arabia 55 G10
Haraiba: Saudi Arabia 54 E9
Haraiki: *i.*, Tuamotu Arch. 83 g3
Haraja: Saudi Arabia 54 F11
Haram Dagh: *mtn.*, Iran 57 K3
Haramosh: *mtn.*, Jammu & Kashmir 58 M7
Haran: Turkey 56 F3
Harappa: ruins of city of ancient Indus civilization, Montgomery dist. Punjab, Pakistan 58 M8
Harar: *Prov.*, Eth. 79 Q18
Harardera: Somalia 79 R19
Harardiget: Ethiopia 79 Q18
Hararekh: Morocco (Gib. *Inset*) 32 *Ins.*
Hara Usu Nor: *lake*, Mong. 51 Q5
Harb: *tribal area*, Sau. Arab. 54 F10
Harberton: Devon, Eng. 24 O19
HARBIN (Pinkiang): Heilungkiang, China 63 X5
Harbor Beach: *city*, Mich., U.S.A. 88 K4
Harbor Springs: *city*, Mich., U.S.A. 88 J3
Harbottle: Northumb. Eng. 26 R9
Harbour Breton: Newf., Canada 85 v3
Harbour Grace: Newf., Canada 85 w3
Harburg: W. Germany 41 Q7
Harburg-Wilhelmsburg: W. Ger. 45 P2
Harbury: War., England 25 T15
Harby: Leics., England 27 U14
Harby: Notts., England 27 U13
Harcourt: N.B., Canada 89 T2
Harda: Madhya Pradesh, India 58 N10
Hardanger Fiord: Norway 47 K6
Hardangervidda: Norway 47 K6
Hardenberg: Netherlands 44 M3
Haderwijk: Netherlands 44 L3
Hardin: Mont., U.S.A. 92 F3
Harding: Natal, S. Africa 75 H5
Hardingstone: Northants., Eng. 25 U15
Hardisty: Alta., Canada 92 E2
Hardoi: Uttar Pradesh, Ind. 58 O9
Hardwick: Ga., U.S.A. 91 K9
Hardy: Algeria 35 G19
Hardy: Ark., U.S.A. 88 F7
Hare Bay: Newf., Canada 85 v1
Hareidlandet: *i.*, Norway 46 J5
Harewood: W. Yorks., Eng. 27 S12
Harfleur: France 36 F6
Harga: Cen. Afr. Rep. 76 B1
HARGEISA: North-West, Somalia 79 Q18
Hargrave: Suff., England 25 X15
Hari *riv.*, Afghanistan 58 K8
Hari: *riv.*, Sumatra 65 C7
Harim: Syria 56 E3
Harima Gulf: Japan 63 d3
Haringey: Gt. Ldn., England 25 V16
Hariq: Saudi Arabia 54 G10
Haris: S.W. Africa 74 B1
Harlan: *city*, Ky., U.S.A. 88 K7
Hârlău: Romania 43 U13
Harlech: Gwynedd, Wales 27 N14
Harlem: Mont., U.S.A. 92 F3
Harleston: Norf., England 25 Y15
Harlestone: Northants., Eng. 25 U15
Harling, East: Norf., Eng. 25 X15
Harlingen: Netherlands 44 L2
Harlingen: Tex., U.S.A. 90 C12
Harlosh: I. of Skye, Inner Hebr., Scotland 28 H5
Harlow: Essex, England 25 W16
Harlowton: Mont., U.S.A. 92 F3
Harmånger: Sweden 47 P6
Harnai: Baluchistan, Pak. 58 L8
Harney Basin: Oreg., U.S.A. 92 D4
Harney Lake: Oreg., U.S.A. 92 D4
Harney Peak: S. Dak., U.S.A. 92 G4
HÄRNÖSAND: Västernorrland, Sweden 46 P5
Haro: Spain 35 E15
Haroldswick: Shetland Is. 28 *Ins.*
Harome: N. Yorks., England 26 T11
Haros: *riv.*, Mexico 93 F7
Harpenden: Herts., England 25 V16
Harper: Kans., U.S.A. 90 B7
HARPER: Maryland, Liberia 80 C4
Harper Springs: N. Territ., Australia 68 E4
Harper Town: Northumb., England 26 Q10
Harpley: Norf., England 25 X14
Harport, Loch: Inner Hebr., Scotland 28 J5
Harptree, West: Som., Eng. 24 Q17
Harrawa: Ethiopia 79 Q18
Harray, Loch of: Mainland, Orkney Is. 28 P2
Harricanaw: *riv.*, Ont./Que., Canada 85 M7
Harrietfield: Tayside, Scot. 29 O7
Harrietsham: Kent, England 25 X17
Harriman: Tenn., U.S.A. 91 J8
Harrington: Cumbria, Eng. 26 O10
Harrington Harbour: Que., Canada 85 t1
Harringworth: Northants., England 27 U14
Harris: *dist.*, Outer Hebr., Scotland 28 H4
Harris, Lake: Fla., U.S.A. 91 K11
Harris, Sound of: Outer Hebr., Scotland 28 G4
Harrisburg: Ark., U.S.A. 88 F8
Harrisburg: Ill., U.S.A. 88 G7
Harrisburg: Oreg., U.S.A. 92 C4
HARRISBURG: Pa., U.S.A. 89 N5
Harrismith: & *Dist.*, O.F.S., S. Africa 75 H4
Harrison: Ark., U.S.A. 88 E7
Harrison: Mich., U.S.A. 88 J3
Harrison, Cape: Newf., Can. 84 O7
Harrison Bay: Alaska, U.S.A. 84 d3
Harrisonburg: Va., U.S.A. 89 M6
Harrisonville: Mo., U.S.A. 90 D6
Harriston: Ont., Canada 88 L4
Harrisville: Mich., U.S.A. 88 K3
Harrisville: Queens., Austl. 70 K6
Harrodsburg: Ky., U.S.A. 88 J7
Harrogate: N. Yorks., Eng. 27 S12
Harrold: Beds., England 25 U15
Harrow: Gt. Ldn., England 25 V16
Harrowden: Northants., England 25 U15
Harsefeld: W. Germany 44 P2
Harsin: Iran 57 K4
Harşit: *riv.*, Turkey 56 F1
Hârşova: Romania 39 U14
Harsprånget: Sweden 46 Q3
Harstad: Vesterålen, Norway 46 P2
Hart: Mich., U.S.A. 88 H4
Hartbees: *riv.*, S. Africa 74 D4
Hartbees Dam: Trans., S. Africa 75 G2
Hartbeesfontein: Trans., S. Africa 75 G3
Hartbeeskuil: S. Africa 74 E6
Hartberg: Austria 41 V8
Hartest: Suff., England 25 X15
Hartfield: E. Sussex, England 25 W17
HARTFORD: Conn., U.S.A. 89 P5
Hartford: Ala., U.S.A. 91 J10
Hartford: Cambs., England 25 V15
Hartford: Ky., U.S.A. 88 H7
Hartford: Mich., U.S.A. 88 H4
Hartford: Wis., U.S.A. 88 G4
Hartford City: Ind., U.S.A. 88 J5
Harthill: Strath., Scotland 29 O8
Hartington: Derby., Eng. 27 S13
Harti Warre: Ethiopia 76 F1
Hartland: Devon, England 24 N18
Hartland: N.B., Canada 89 S2
Hartland Point: *cape*, Devon, England 24 M17
Hartlebury: Hereford & Worcester, England 24 R15
Hartlepool: Cleveland, Eng. 26 T10
Hartley: Northumb., Eng. 26 T9
Hartley: Rhodesia 77 D6
Hartley Wintney: Hants., England 25 U17
Hartola: Finland 47 U6
Hartpury: Glos., England 24 R16
Harts: *riv.*, Trans., S. Africa 75 F3
Hartselle: Ala., U.S.A. 91 H8
Hartshill: War., England 27 S14
Hartshorne: Okla., U.S.A. 90 D8
Hartsville: S.C., U.S.A. 91 L8
Hartsville: Tenn., U.S.A. 88 H7
Hartwell: Ga., U.S.A. 91 K8
Hartwell: Northants., Eng. 25 U15
Harvard: Ill., U.S.A. 88 G4
Harvey: Ill., U.S.A. 88 H5
Harvey: La., U.S.A. 90 *Ins.*
Harvey: N. Dak., U.S.A. 92 H3
Harvey: W. Australia 68 B6
Harvington: Hereford & Worcester, England 24 S15
Harwell: Oxfordshire, England 25 T16
Harwich: Essex, England 25 Y16
Harwood, Gt.: Lancs., Eng. 27 R12
Haryana: *State*, India (*cap.* Chandigarh) 58 N9
Harz: *mtns.*, E./W. Ger. 45 Q4
Harzand: Iran 57 J2
Harzburg: W. Germany 45 Q4
Harzgerode: E. Germany 45 R4
Hasa: *geog. reg.*, Sau. Arab. 55 G9
Hasankale: Turkey 57 G2
Hasankeyf: Turkey 57 G3
Hasantu: Inner Mongolia, China 62 T6
Hase: *riv.*, W. Germany 44 N3
Haselünne: W. Germany 44 N3
Hashimiya: Iraq 57 J5
Hashimoto: Japan 63 d3
Hasi, El: Libya 78 G4
Hasi Aruiles: Western Sahara 78 B5
Hasi Dumus: Western Sahara 78 B5
Hasiheisa, El: Sudan 54 D12
Haskeir I.: Outer Hebr., Scotland 28 G4
Haskell: Okla., U.S.A. 90 D8
Haskell: Tex., U.S.A. 90 B9
Haslach: W. Germany 40 O7
Haslemere: Surrey, England 25 U17
Haslingden: Lancs., Eng. 27 R12
Hasparren: France 37 D12
Hassa: Turkey 56 E3
Hassam, El: Niger 81 F2
Hassan: Karnataka, India 58 N12
Hassana: Morocco (Gib. *Inset*) 32 *Ins.*
Hassela: Sweden 47 P5
Hasselfelde: E. Germany 45 Q4
HASSELT: Limbourg, Belg. 44 L5
Hasselt: Netherlands 44 M3
HASSETCHE: & *Prov.*, Syria 57 G3
Hassfurt: W. Germany 45 Q5
Hassi el Krenig: Algeria 78 E4
Hassi in Sokki: Algeria 78 E4
Hassi Inifel: Algeria 78 E4
Hassi Mana: *well*, Algeria 80 L9
Hassi Sougued: Algeria 78 F4
Hassi Touareg: Algeria 78 F3
Hässleholm: Sweden 47 N8
Haste Dam: Calif., U.S.A. 92 C4
Hästholmen: Sweden 47 O7
Hastings: Mich., U.S.A. 88 J4
Hastings: Nebr., U.S.A. 93 H4
Hastings: North I., N.Z. 70 Q14
Hastings: Ont., Canada 89 N3
Hastings: E. Sussex, England 25 X18
Hastings: Wis., U.S.A. 88 E3
Hastings Range: N.S.W., Australia 71 J8
Hästveda: Sweden 47 N8
Hasvik: Norway 46 S1
Haswaia: Yemen P.D.R. 55 H11
Hatay: *Prov.*, Turkey [*cap.* Antakya (Antioch)] 56 E3
Hatch Beauchamp: Som., England 24 Q18
Hatches Creek: *town*, N. Territ., Australia 69 F4
Hatchie: *riv.*, Tenn., U.S.A. 90 G8
Haţeg: Romania 39 S14
Hatfield: Herts., England 25 V16
Hatfield: N.S.W., Australia 71 E9
Hatfield: S. Yorks., England 27 U12
Hatfield Broad Oak: Essex, England 25 W16
Hatfield Peverel: Essex, Eng. 25 X16
Hatherleigh: Devon, Eng. 24 N18
Hathern: Leics., England 27 T14
Hatherop: Glos., England 25 S16
Hathersage: Derby., Eng. 27 S13
Hathob, El: *riv.*, Tunisia 38 L19
Hathras: Uttar Pradesh, India 58 N9
Ha Tien: Vietnam 64 C4
Hatinh: Vietnam 64 D3
Hatra: Parthian city, later Roman fort about 50 miles W. of Qaiyara, Iraq 57 H3
Hatsamas: SW. Africa 74 B1
Hatson: *airfield*, Mainland, Orkney Is. 28 Q2
Hattah: Vict., Australia 71 E10
Hattah Lakes National Park: Vict., Australia 71 E10
Hattem: Netherlands 44 M3
Hatteras, Cape: N.C., U.S.A. 91 O8
Hattiesburg: Miss., U.S.A. 90 G10
Hattfjelldal: Norway 46 N4
Hatton: Grampian, Scotland 28 S5
Hatutu: *i.*, Marquesas Is. 83 g1
Hatvan: Hungary 43 Q13
Hat Yai: Thailand 65 b10
Hâu Bôn: Vietnam 64 D4
Haubourdin: France 36 H5
Haud: *geog. reg.*, Ethiopia 79 R18
Hauersæter: Norway 47 M6
Hauf: Yemen P.D.R. 55 H11
Haugesund: Norway 47 J7
Haugh of Urr: Dumfries & Galloway, Scotland 29 O10
Haughley: Suff., England 25 X15
Haughton: Staffs., England 27 R14
Hauki Lake: Finland 46 V5
Haukipudas: Finland 46 T4
Haukivuori: Finland 47 U6
Haura: Yemen P.D.R. 79 R17
Hauraki Gulf: North I., N.Z. 70 P13
Haur al Hammar: *lake*, Iraq 57 K6
Hauran: *wadi*, Iraq 57 G5
Hauran: Volcanic plateau N. of line between L. Tiberias and Dera'a, Damascus, Syria 56 E5
Haur as Suwaiqiya: *swamp*, Iraq 57 K5
Haur Dalmaj: *swamp*, Iraq 57 J5
Hauroko, Lake: South I., New Zealand 71 L18
Haur Sanniya: *swamp*, Iraq 57 K5
Haus: Austria 41 T8
Hauta: Hadhramaut, Yemen P.D.R. 55 G11
Hauta (Hilla): Saudi Arabia 54 G10
Hautefort: France 37 G10
Haute-Garonne: *Dept.*, Fr. (*cap.* Toulouse) 37 G12
Haute-Kotto: *Pref.*, Cen. Afr. Rep. (*cap.* Bria) 76 B1
Haute-Loire: *Dept.*, France (*cap.* Le Puy) 37 J10
Haute-Marne: *Dept.*, Fr. (*cap.* Chaumont) 36 L8
Hautes-Alpes: *Dept.*, France (*cap.* Briançon) 40 M11
Haute Sangha: *Pref.*, Central African Rep. (*cap.* Berberati) 81 H4
Haute-Saône: *Dept.*, France (*cap.* Vesoul) 40 M8
Haute-Savoie: *Dept.*, France (*cap.* Annecy) 40 M10
Hautes Fagnes: *mtns.*, Belg. 44 L6
Hautes-Pyrenees: *Dept.*, France (*cap.* Tarbes) 37 F12
Haute-Vienne: *Dept.*, France (*cap.* Limoges) 37 G10
Hauteville: France 40 L10
Haut'M'Bomou: *Pref.*, Cen. Afr. Rep. (*cap.* Obo) 76 C1
Hautmont: France 36 J5
Haut-Ogooué: *Reg.*, Gabon (*cap.* Franceville) 81 G5
Haut-Rhin: *Dept.*, France (*cap.* Colmar) 40 N8
Hauts-Bassins: *Dept.*, Upper Volta (*cap.* Bobo-Dioulasso) 80 D2
Haut-Zaïre: *Prov.*, Zaïre (*cap.* Kisangani) 76 C2
Hauzien: Ethiopia 54 E12
HAVANA: Cuba 87 I13
Havana: Ill., U.S.A. 88 F5
Havant: Hants., England 25 U18
Havasu Lake: Ariz., U.S.A. 93 E6
Havel: *riv.*, E. Germany 45 S3
Havelberg: E. Germany 45 S3
Havelland: *geog. reg.*, W. Ger. 42 N10
Havelock: Ont., Canada 89 N3
Havelock: South I., N.Z. 70 O15
Havelock North: North I., New Zealand 70 Q14
Haven, South: Mich., U.S.A. 88 H4
Haverfordwest: Dyfed, Wales 24 M16
Haverhill: Mass., U.S.A. 89 Q4
Haverhill: Suff., England 25 W15
Haveri: Karnataka, India 58 N12
Haverigg: Cumbria, Eng. 26 P11
Havering: Gt. Ldn., England 25 W16
Haverstraw: N.Y., U.S.A. 89 P5
Havlíčkův Brod: Czechoslovakia 45 V6
Havre: Mont., U.S.A. 92 F3
Havre, Le: France 36 F6
Havre Aubert: Magdalen Is., Canada 89 V2
Havre de Grace: Md., U.S.A. 89 N6
Havza: Turkey 56 D1
Hawaii: *is. & State*, U.S.A. 83 d3
Hawaii: *riv.*, Nigeria 81 G2
Hawaii: *State*, U.S.A. (*cap.* Honolulu) 83 *Ins.*
Hawaiian Ridge: N. Pacific Ocean 7 20N 170W

For Abbreviations see list on p.113. Italic type, e.g. *Ephesus*, refers to historical names not on maps. Capital letters, e.g. MADRID, show capitals of countries; small capital letters, e.g. CADIZ, show capitals of provinces, etc. General notes p.116.

Hawarden: Clwyd, Wales 27 P13
Hawarden: Iowa, U.S.A. 92 H4
Hawea, Lake: South I., N.Z. 70 M17
Hawera: North I., N.Z. 70 P14
Hawes: N. Yorks., England 26 R11
Hawes Bank: Inner Hebr.,
    Scotland 29 H6
Hawes Water: lake, Cumbria,
    England 26 Q10
Hawi: Hawaiian Is. 83 d2
Hawick: Borders, Scotland 29 Q9
Hawizeh: Iran 57 L6
Hawk Channel: Fla., U.S.A. 91 L13
Hawke, Cape: N.S.W., Austl. 71 K9
Hawke Bay: North I., New Zealand
    70 Q14
Hawker: S. Australia 71 C8
Hawkes Bay: Dist., N. I., New
    Zealand (cap. Napier) 70 Q14
Hawkesbury: Ont., Canada 89 O3
Hawkhurst: Kent, England 25 X17
Hawkinge: Kent, England 25 Y17
Hawkinsville: Ga., U.S.A. 91 K9
Hawkshead: Cumbria, Eng. 26 P11
Hawkwood: Queens., Austl. 70 J5
Haworth: W. Yorks., England 27 S12
Hawston: S. Africa 74 C7
Hawthorne: Nev., U.S.A. 93 D5
Haxby: N. Yorks., England 27 T11
Haxey: Humb., England 27 U13
Haxtun: Colo., U.S.A. 93 G4
Hay: Powys, Wales 24 P15
Hay: N.S.W., Australia 71 F10
Hay: Dist., S. Africa 74 E4
Hay: riv., Canada 84 H6
Hayange: France 44 M6
Haycock: Alaska, U.S.A. 84 c4
Hayden: Ariz., U.S.A. 93 E6
Haydon Bridge: Northumb.,
    England 26 R10
Haye Descartes, La: France 36 F9
Haye, La: Iceland 46 d5
Haye-du-Puits, La: France 36 D6
Haye-Pesnel, La: France 36 D7
Hayes: (near Uxbridge), Greater
    London, England 25 V16
Hayes, Mount: mtn., Alaska,
    U.S.A. 84 E5
Hayes: riv., Canada 92 J1
Hayfield: Derby., England 27 S13
Hayle: Corn., England 25 L19
Hayling, South: Hants., Eng. 24 U18
Hayling I.: Hants., England 25 U18
Haymarau: Turkey 56 C2
Haynes: Beds., England 25 V15
Haynesville: La., U.S.A. 90 E9
Hay Point: Queens., Australia
    70 H3
Hayrabolu: Turkey 39 U16
Hay River: N.W.T., Can. 84 H5
Hays: Kans., U.S.A. 90 B6
Hays: Mont., U.S.A. 92 F3
Hayti: Mo., U.S.A. 88 G7
Hayton: Cumbria, England 26 Q10
Hayward: Wis., U.S.A. 88 F2
Haywards Heath: W. Sussex,
    England 25 V18
Hazar, Lake: Turkey 56 F2
Hazarajat: geog. reg., Afghanistan
    58 L8
Hazard: Ky., U.S.A. 88 K7
Hazaribagh: Bihar, India 59 P10
Hazebrouck: France 36 H5
Hazel Grove: Gt. Man., Eng. 27 R13
Hazelton: B.C., Canada 92 B1
Hazen Str.: N.W.T., Can. 84 h2
Hazim: well, Jordan 56 E6
Hazimi: wadi, Iraq 57 G5
Hazleh 'st: Ga., U.S.A. 91 K10
Hazlehu 'x: Miss., U.S.A. 90 F10
Hazleton: Pa., U.S.A. 89 O5
Hazor: city of ancient Israel in mtns.
    SW. of L. Hula, near border
    of Israel and Syria 55 b1
Hazrat Iran: Afghanistan 51 L7
Hazur: SW. Africa 74 C3
Heacham: Norf., England 25 W14
Headcorn: Kent, England 25 X17
Headek: Czechoslovakia 47 W7
Headford: Galway, Repub. of
    Ireland 31 C13
Headington: Oxon., Eng. 25 T16
Headland: Ga., U.S.A. 91 J10
Headley: Hants., England 25 U17
Head of Passes: La., U.S.A. 90 Ins.
Headsburg: Calif., U.S.A. 93 C5
Healdton: Okla., U.S.A. 90 C8
Healesville: Vict., Austl. 71 F11
Heanor: Derby., England 27 T13
Heard I.: (Austl.), Indian Ocean
    9 55S 70E
Hearne: Tex., U.S.A. 90 C10
Hearst: Ont., Canada 88 K1
Heart: riv., N. Dak., U.S.A. 92 G3
Hearts Content: Newf., Canada
    85 w3
Heathcote: Vict., Australia 71 F11
Heathfield: Devon, England 24 O18
Heathfield: S. Africa 74 Ins.
Heathfield: E. Sussex, England 25 W18
Heavener: Okla., U.S.A. 90 D8
Hebburn: Tyne & Wear, England
    26 S10
Hebden Bridge: W. Yorks.,
    England 27 R12
Hebel: Queens., Australia 71 G7
Heber: Utah, U.S.A. 93 E4
Heber Springs: city, Ark., U.S.A.
    90 E8
Hebrides, Sea of the: Inner/Outer
    Hebr., Scotland 28 G6
Hebrides (Western Isles): is.,
    Scotland 29 G6
HEBRON: Al Khalil, Jordan
    55 b3
Hebron: Newf., Canada 84 n6
Hebron: Nebr., U.S.A. 93 H4
Hebron: N. Dak., U.S.A. 92 G3
Hebronville: Tex., U.S.A. 90 B12
Hebrus: Greek name for river
    Maritsa 39 U16
Heby: Sweden 47 P7
Hecate Str.: B.C., Canada 84 f7
Hechingen: W. Germany 40 O7
Hecho: Spain 37 E13
Heckington: Lincs., England 27 V14
Hector: Minn., U.S.A. 88 D3
Hedaru: Tanzania 76 E3
Hede: Sweden 46 N5
Hedemora: Sweden 47 P6
Hedesunda: Sweden 47 P6
Hedgehope: South I., N.Z. 71 M18
Hedingly: Queens., Austl. 69 F4
Hedley: B.C., Canada 92 C3
Hedmark: Co., Norway (cap.
    Hamar) 47 M6
Hednesford: Staffs., England 27 R14
Hedon: Humb., England 27 V12
Heede: W. Germany 44 N3
Heek: W. Germany 44 N3
Heemstede: Netherlands 44 K3
Heerenveen: Netherlands 44 L3
Heerlen: Netherlands 44 L5
Heflin: Ala., U.S.A. 91 J9
Hegyeshalom: Hungary 41 X8
Heho: Burma 59 R10

Heiban: Sudan 79 L7
Heide: W. Germany 44 P1
Heide: SW. Africa 74 B1
Heidelberg: W. Germany 44 O6
Heidelberg: S. Africa 74 D7
Heidelberg: Trans., S. Africa 74 N.Ins.
Heidelberg: Dist., Trans., S. Africa
    75 H3
Heidenfeld: W. Germany 44 P6
Heidenheim: W. Germany 40 Q7
Heidenreichstein: Austria 41 V7
Heigamkhab: S.W. Africa 74 A1
Heighington: Durham, Eng. 26 S10
Heighington: Lincs., Eng. 27 V13
Heigun: i., Japan 63 c4
Heiho: Tibet, China 59 Q8
Heilbron: & Dist., O.F.S., S. Africa
    75 G3
Heilbronn: W. Germany 44 P6
Heiligenblut: Austria 41 S8
Heiligendamm: E. Germany 45 R1
Heiligenhafen: E. Germany 45 Q1
Heiligenstadt: E. Germany 45 Q4
Heilungkiang: Prov., China [cap.
    Harbin (Pinkiang)] 63 X5
Heimsheim: W. Germany 40 O7
Heinersdorf: E. Germany 45 U3
Heinola: Finland 47 U6
Heinsburg: Alta., Canada 92 E2
Heinsburg: W. Germany 44 M4
Heinze Basin: bay, Burma 59 R12
Heis: Somalia 79 R17
Heishan: Liaoning, China 63 W6
Heishui: Inner Mongolia,
    China 62 V6
Heisker (Monarch) Is.: Outer Hebr.,
    Scotland 28 G4
Heist: Belgium 44 J4
Hejaz: see Hijaz.
Hekimhan: Turkey 56 E2
Hekla: mtn., Iceland 46 d5
Hekura: i., Japan 63 Z7
Hel: Poland 43 Q9
Helags Mtns.: Sweden 46 N5
Heldburg: E. Germany 45 Q5
Helder, den: Netherlands 44 K3
Heldrungen: E. Germany 45 R4
Helen's, Point aux: cape. La.,
    U.S.A. 90 Ins.
HELENA: Ark., U.S.A. 90 F8
HELENA: Mont., U.S.A. 92 E3
Helen Mine: Ont., Canada 88 J1
Helen Reef: Pacific O. 61 L11
Helensburgh: Strath., Scot. 29 M7
Helen Springs: N. Territ., Australia
    68 E3
Helensville: North I., N.Z. 70 P13
Helgafell: Iceland 46 b4
Helgheim: Norway 47 K6
Helicon: ancient name of mtn.
    SSW. of Lake Copais and 20
    miles SW. of Thivai, Grc.
    39 S17
Heligoland: i., W. Germany 44 N1
Heligoland Bight: bay, W. Ger. 44 N1
Heliopolis: Graeco-Roman town
    about 7 miles NNE. of Cairo,
    Egypt 56 B6
Heliopolis: see On
Helles Cape: Turkey (Dardan.
    Inset) 20 Ins.
Hellevoetsluis: Netherlands 44 K4
Hellifield: N. Yorks., England 27 R11
Helligskogen: Norway 46 R2
Hellin: Spain 35 F17
Hellingly: E. Sussex, England 25 W18
Hellisay: i., Outer Hebr., Scotland
    28 G5
Hellmonsödt: Austria 41 U7
Hellville: Malagasy Rep. 73 O12
Hellwege: W. Germany 44 P2
Helmand: Prov. & riv., Afghanistan
    55 K8
Helmarshausen: W. Germany 44 P4
Helmdon: Northants., England
    25 T15
Helmond: Netherlands 44 L4
Helmsdale: & riv., Highland,
    Scotland 28 O3
Helmsley: N. Yorks., England 26 T11
Helmstedt: W. Germany 45 R3
Helperby: N. Yorks., England 27 T11
Helpmekaar: & Dist., Natal,
    S. Africa 75 J4
Helpringham: Lincs., Eng. 27 V14
Helpston: Cambs., England 25 V14
Helsby: Ches., England 27 Q13
Helsingor: Zealand, Den. 47 N8
HELSINKI: (Helsingfors): Finland
    47 T6
Helston: Corn., England 25 L19
Helstorf: W. Germany 44 P3
Helvecia: Argentina 96 C3
Helvellyn: mtn., Cumbria,
    England 26 P10
Helvetii: Gallic tribe of NW.
    Switzerland 40 N8
Helvick Head: cape. Wat., Repub.
    of Ireland 31 F15
Helwân: Egypt 56 B7
Hemau: W. Germany 45 R6
Hemel Hempstead: Herts., England
    25 V16
Hemingbrough: N. Yorks.,
    England 27 U12
Hemingby: Lincs., England 27 V13
Hemne: Norway 46 L5
Hemnesberget: Norway 46 N3
Hempnall: Norf., England 25 Y15
Hempstead: Essex, England 25 W15
Hempstead: N.Y., U.S.A. 89 P5
Hempstead: Tex., U.S.A. 90 C10
Hemse: Gotland, Sweden 47 Q8
Hemslingen: W. Germany 44 P2
Hemswell: Lincs., England 27 U13
Hemsworth: W. Yorks., Eng. 27 T12
Hemyock: Devon, England 24 P18
Henares: riv., Spain 35 E16
Henbury: N. Territ., Austl. 68 E4
Hendaye: France 37 D12
Hendek: Turkey 56 B1
Henderson: Ky., U.S.A. 88 H7
Henderson: Nev., U.S.A. 93 D5
Henderson: N.C., U.S.A. 89 M7
Henderson: Tenn., U.S.A. 90 G8
Henderson: Tex., U.S.A. 90 D9
Hendersonville: N.C., U.S.A. 91 K8
Hendrik Vervoerd Dam: O.F.S./
    C.P., South Africa 75 F5
Hendrina: Trans., S. Africa 75 H3
Hendy: Dyfed, Wales 24 N16
Henfield: W. Sussex, England 25 V18
Heng-ch'un: Taiwan 63 W10
Hengelo: Overijssel, Neth. 44 M3
Hengersberg: W. Germany 41 T7
Henghsien: Kwangsi Chuang, China
    62 T10
Hengoed: Mid. Glam., Wales 24 P16
Hengoed: Salop, England 27 P14
Hengshan: Hunan, China 62 U9
Hengshan: Shensi, China 62 T7
Hengyang: Hunan, China 62 U9
Henin: France 36 H5
Henley Harbour: Newf., Can. 85 v1
Henley in Arden: War., England 25 S15
Henley-on-Klip: Trans., S. Africa
    74 N Ins.

Henley on Thames: Oxon.,
    England 25 U16
Henlopen, Cape: Del., U.S.A. 89 O6
Henlow: Beds., England 25 V15
Hennebont: France 36 B8
Hennenman: O.F.S., S. Afr. 75 Ins.
Hennessey: Okla., U.S.A. 90 C7
Hennock: Devon, England 24 O18
Henrichemont: France 36 H8
Henrietta: Tex., U.S.A. 90 B9
Henrietta Maria, Cape: Ont.,
    Canada 85 I6
HENRIQUE DE CARVALHO: Luanda,
    Angola 77 B4
Henry, Cape: Va., U.S.A. 89 O7
Henryetta: Okla., U.S.A. 90 D8
Henry Kater Penin.: Canada 85 N4
Henshaw: Northumb., Eng. 26 R10
Hensingham: Cumbria, Eng. 26 O10
Henstridge: Som., England 24 R18
Hentey: Dist., Mongolia 62 U5
Henty: N.S.W., Australia 71 G10
Henwick: Hereford & Worcester,
    England 24 R15
Henzada: Burma 59 R11
Heppner: Oreg., U.S.A. 92 D3
Hepworth: N. Yorks., Eng. 27 S12
Heraclea: Greek city at Ereğli,
    Turkey 33 J3
Heraclea: Greek and Roman city on
    G. of Taranto about 20
    miles SW. of Metaponto,
    Italy 38 P16
Heras, Las: Argentina 96 B3
Herat: & Prov., Afghanistan
    55 K8
Herau: Iran 57 L3
Hérault: Dept. & riv., France (cap.
    Montpellier) 37 J12
Herbault: France 36 G8
Herbert: Dist., S. Africa 75 F4
Herbert, Mount: W. Austl. 68 D3
Herberton: Queens., Austl. 69 H3
Herbertsdale: S. Africa 74 D6
Herbertstown: Lim., Repub. of
    Ireland 31 E14
Herbes, Point aux: cape. La.,
    U.S.A. 90 Ins.
Herbiers, Les: France 36 D9
Herbignac: France 36 C8
Herborn: W. Germany 44 O5
Herbrandston: Dyfed, Wales 24 L16
Herchmer: Man., Canada 92 J1
Herceg Novi: Yugoslavia 39 Q15
Hercegovina: see Bosnia-
    Hercegovina
Herculaneum: Roman city overlooking
    sea on hill to W. of Mount
    Vesuvius, Italy 38 O16
Hereford and Worcester: Co.,
    England (co. town Worcester)
    24 Q15
Hereford: Hereford & Worcester,
    England 24 Q15
Hereford: Tex., U.S.A. 93 G6
Herefoss: Norway 47 L7
Hereheretue: i., Tuamotu Arch.
    83 g3
Heremakono: Guinea 80 B3
Herencia: Spain 35 E17
Herenthals: Belgium 44 K4
Herford: W. Germany 44 O3
Héricourt: France 40 M8
Heringen: E. Germany 45 Q4
Herington: Kans., U.S.A. 90 C6
Heriot: Borders, Scotland 29 Q8
HERISAU: Appenzell, Switz. 40 P8
Herkimer: N.Y., U.S.A. 89 O4
Herm: i., Channel Is. (Br.) 25 Ins.
Hermagor: Austria 41 T9
Herma Ness: Shetland Is. 28 Ins
Hermann: Mo., U.S.A. 88 F6
Hermannsburg: N. Territ., Australia
    68 E4
Hermannstadt: see Sibiu
Hermansville: Mich., U.S.A. 88 H3
Hermanus: S. Africa 74 C7
Hermenault, l': France 37 E9
Herment: France 37 H10
Hermidale: N.S.W., Austl. 71 G8
Hermil: Lebanon 56 E4
Hermina, Trans.: S. Africa 74 MIns.
Hermione: Greek city on mainland
    opposite Idhra, Greece 39 S18
Hermiston: Oreg., U.S.A. 92 D3
Hermit Is.: Papua New Guinea
    66 J2
Hermon: S. Africa 74 C6
Hermon, Mount: Lebanon 56 D5
HERMOSILLO: Sonora, Mex. 93 E7
Hermsdorf: see Sobieszow
Hermunduri: ancient German
    tribe which inhabited Bavaria N.
    of river Danube 42 M12
Hermus: Greek name of river Gediz,
    Turkey 39 U17
Hernandarias: Argentina 96 D3
Hernandarias: Paraguay 96 E2
Hernando: Miss., U.S.A. 90 G8
Herne: W. Germany 44 N4
Herne Bay: town, Kent, England
    25 Y17
Hernhill: Kent, England 25 X17
Hernici: ancient tribe to SE. of Rome
    38 N16
Herning: Denmark 47 L8
Herrenalb: W. Germany 40 O7
Herrera del Duque: Spain 35 D17
Herrera de Pisuerga: Spain 35 D15
Herreras, Los: Mexico 90 B13
Herrard: Hants., England 25 T17
Herrick: Tas., Australia 68 H4
Herrin: Ill., U.S.A. 88 G7
Herrington: Tyne & Wear, England
    26 T10
Herrljunga: Sweden 47 N7
Herry: France 36 H8
Hersbruck: W. Germany 45 R6
Herschel: & Dist., S. Afr. 75 G5
Herschel: & i., Yukon, Canada
    84 F4
Herseaux: Belgium 44 J5
Hersfeld: W. Germany 44 P5
Hersin: France 36 H5
Herstal: Belgium 44 L5
Herstmonceux: E. Sussex, England
    25 W18
HERTFORD: N.C., U.S.A. 89 N7
HERTFORD: & Co., England 25 V16
Hertzogville: O.F.S. & Afr. 75 F4
Hervas: Spain 35 D16
Herve: Belgium 44 L5
Hervey Bay: Queens., Australia
    70 K5
Hervey Is.: Cook Is. 70 Ins.
Herxheim: W. Germany 44 O6
Herzberg: Cottbus, E. Germany
    45 T4
Herzfelde: E. Germany 45 T3
Herzliya: Israel 55 a2
Herzogenbuchsee: Switzerland
    40 N8
Hesdigneul: France 36 G5
Hesdin: France 36 H5

Heshbon: city of ancient Israel
    about 5 miles S. of Na'ur, Jordan
    55 b3
Heslerton, West: N. Yorks., England
    26 U11
Hesse: State, W. Germany (cap.
    Wiesbaden) 44 O5
Hessen: E. Germany 45 Q3
Hessen: Prov., see Hesse.
Hessisch Oldendorf: W. Ger. 44 P3
Hessle: Humb., England 27 V12
Hesso: S. Australia 71 B9
Hest Bank: Lancs., England 27 Q11
Heswall: Mers., England 27 P13
Heteniemi: Finland 46 V4
Hethe: Oxon., England 25 T16
Hethersett: Norf., England 25 Y14
Hethersgill: Cumbria, England 26 Q10
Hettinger: N. Dak., U.S.A. 92 G3
Hetton, South: Durham, Eng. 26 T10
Hetton le Hole: Tyne & Wear,
    England 26 T10
Hettstedt: E. Germany 45 R4
Heumis, Les: Algeria 35 G18
Heuningskloof: S. Africa 75 F4
Hève, Cap de la: cape. Fr. 36 F6
Hevenk: Turkey 56 F3
Heversham: Cumbria, Eng. 26 Q11
Heves: Hungary 43 R13
Hevik: Iran 57 L2
Hewelsfield: Glos., England 24 Q16
Hexham: Northumb., Eng. 26 R10
Heybridge: Essex, England 25 X16
Heyfield: Vict., Australia 71 G11
Heyford, Lower: Oxon., Eng. 25 T16
Heysham: Lancs., England 27 Q11
Heyst-op-den-Berg: Belgium 44 K4
Heytesbury: Wilts., England 24 R17
Heywood: Gt. Man., Eng. 27 R12
Heywood: Vict., Australia 71 D12
Hiaking: Kweichow, China 62 T9
Hialeah: Fla., U.S.A. 91 L13
Hibaldstow: Humb., Eng. 27 U12
Hibbing: Minn., U.S.A. 88 E2
Hibernia Reef: Indian O. 65 G9
Hickling: Notts., England 27 U14
Hickory: N.C., U.S.A. 91 L8
Hick's Bay: town, North I., New
    Zealand 70 R13
Hicksville: Ohio, U.S.A. 88 J5
Hico: Tex., U.S.A. 90 B9
Hida: Japan 63 b4
Hidalgo: Mexico 93 H8
Hidalgo del Parral: Mexico 93 F7
Hida Mtns.: Japan 63 e2
Hiddensee: i., E. Germany 45 T1
Hieflau: Austria 41 U8
Hierro: i., Canary Is. 78 A4
Hietaniemi: Sweden 46 S3
Higashine: Japan 63 f2
Higgins Lake: Mich., U.S.A. 88 J3
Higginsville: Mo., U.S.A. 90 E6
Higham: Kent, England 25 W17
Higham Ferrers: Northants.,
    England 25 U15
Higham on the Hill: Leics., England
    27 T14
Highampton: Devon, Eng. 24 N18
High Atlas: range, Morocco 80 K8
High Bentham: N. Yorks., England
    26 Q11
High Bickington: Devon, England
    24 O18
High Bray: Devon, England 24 O17
Highbridge: Som., England 24 Q17
Highclere: Hants., England 25 T17
High Desert: Oreg., U.S.A. 92 C4
Highflats: Natal, S. Africa 75 J5
High Halden: Kent, Eng. 25 X17
High Ham: Som., England 24 Q17
High Hesket: Cumbria, England 26 Q10
Highland Park: city, Ill., U.S.A.
    88 H4
Highley: Salop, England 24 R15
Highmore: S. Dak., U.S.A. 92 H4
High Plateaux: Algeria 80 L8
High Point: city, N.C., U.S.A.
    91 M8
High Prairie: town, Alta., Canada
    92 D1
High River: town, Alta., Can. 92 E2
Highrock Lake: Man., Can. 92 G1
High Roding: Essex, Eng. 25 W16
High Springs: city, Fla., U.S.A.
    91 K11
High Street: mtn., Cumbria, England
    26 Q11
Hightae: Dumfries & Galloway,
    Scotland 29 P9
High Tatry National Park:
    Czechoslovakia/Poland 43 Q12
Hightown: Mers., England 27 P12
High Willhays: mtn., Devon, England
    24 N18
Highworth: Wilts., England 25 S16
High Wycombe: Bucks., England
    25 U16
Higuer, Cap: cape. Spain 37 D12
Hiiumaa I.: Estonia, U.S.S.R. 50 B3
Hijar: Spain 35 F16
Hijaz: geog. reg., Saudi Arabia
    54 E7
Hikone: Japan 63 e3
Hikueru: i., Tuamotu Arch. 83 g3
Hikurangi: North I., N.Z. 70 P12
Hilborough: Norf., England 25 X14
Hilchenbach: W. Germany 44 O5
Hildavale: Botswana 75 F2
Hildburghausen: E. Germany 45 Q5
Hildenborough: Kent, Eng. 25 W17
Hildesheim: W. Germany 45 P3
Hildesheim: Dist., Lower Saxony
    West Germany 45 Q4
Hilgay: Norf., England 25 W14
Hill: Avon, England 24 Q16
Hilla: Saudi Arabia 54 G10
Hilla: Iraq 57 J5
Hillared: Sweden 47 N8
Hill Bank: Belize 86 Ins.
Hillcrest: Natal, S. Africa 75 J4
Hillebyn: Sweden 47 P6
Hillegom: Netherlands 44 K3
Hillerød: Zealand, Denmark 47 N9
Hillingdon: Gt. Ldn., England
    25 V16
Hillman: Mich., U.S.A. 88 K3
Hillsboro: Ill., U.S.A. 88 G6
Hillsboro: Kans., U.S.A. 90 C6
Hillsboro: N. Dak., U.S.A. 92 H3
Hillsboro: Ohio, U.S.A. 88 K6
Hillsboro: Oreg., U.S.A. 92 C3
Hillsboro: Tex., U.S.A. 90 C9
Hillsborough: Down, N. Irel. 30 J11
Hillsdale: Mich., U.S.A. 88 J5
Hillside: W. Australia 68 B4
Hillston: N.S.W., Austl. 71 F9
Hillstreet: Rosc., Reput. of Ireland
    30 F12
Hillswick: Mainland, Shetland Is.
    28 Ins.
Hilltown: Down, N. Ireland 30 J11
Hillwood: Zambia 77 B5

Hilmarton: Wilts., England 24 S17
Hilo: Hawaiian Is. 83 d3
Hilpoltstein: W. Germany 45 R6
Hilsbach: W. Germany 44 O6
Hilton: Cumbria, England 26 R10
Hilvan: Turkey 56 F3
Hilversum: Netherlands 44 L3
Hilwa: Saudi Arabia 54 F11
Himachal Pradesh: Union
    Territory, India (cap. Simla)
    58 W8
Himalaya Mtns.: India 58 O9
Himanka: Finland 46 S4
Himare: Albania 39 Q16
Hime: i., Japan 63 b4
Hime: riv., Japan 63 e2
Himeji: Japan 63 d3
Himera: Greek city about 10 miles
    E. of Termini, Sicily 38 N18
Himeville: & Dist., Natal, S. Africa
    75 H4
Himi: Japan 63 e2
Hinako Is.: Sumatra 65 B6
Hinatuan: Mindanao, Phil. 64 H5
Hinchinbrook I.: Queens., Australia
    69 H3
Hinckley: Leics., England 27 T14
Hinckley: Minn., U.S.A. 88 E3
Hincks Murlong & Nicholls Wildlife
    Reserve: S. Australia 71 B9
Hindås: Sweden 47 N8
Hindeloopen: Netherlands 44 L3
Hinderwell: Cleve., Eng. 26 U10
Hindhead: Surrey, England 25 U17
Hindjan: Iran 57 L6
Hindiya: & barrage, Iraq 57 J5
Hindley: Gt. Man., England 27 Q12
Hindmarsh, Lake: Vict., Australia
    71 D11
Hindon: Wilts., England 24 R17
Hindubagh: Baluchistan, Pakistan
    58 L8
Hindu Kush: range, Afghan. 58 L8
Hindupur: Andhra Pradesh, India
    58 N11
Hines Creek: town, Alta., Canada
    92 D1
Hingan (Ankang): Shensi, China
    62 T8
Hinganghat: Maharashtra, India
    58 N10
Hingcheng: Liaoning, China
    63 W6
Hingham: Norf., England 25 X14
Hinghsien: Shansi, China 62 U7
Hingi: Kweichow, China 62 T9
Hingol: riv., Baluchistan, Pakistan
    58 L9
Hingoli: Maharashtra, India 58 N11
Hingwa (Putien): Fukien, China
    62 V9
Hinis: Turkey 57 G2
Hinnoy: i., Vesterålen, Nor. 46 O2
Hinoemata: Japan 63 f2
Hinojosa del Duque: Spain
    35 D17
Hinomi Point: cape. Japan 63 c3
Hinoura: Japan 63 a4
Hinstock: Salop, England 27 R14
Hintlesham: Suff., England 25 Y15
Hinton: W. Va., U.S.A. 88 L7
Hinton, Little: Wilts., Eng. 25 S16
Hippo Diarrhytus: Punic and Roman
    city at Bizerta, Tunisia 38 L18
Hippo Regius: ancient port, later
    Roman town, near Annaba,
    Algeria 38 K18
Hippos: Hellenistic city on Lake
    Tiberias, Israel, due W. of
    Fiq, Syria 55 b2
Hirado: i., Japan 63 a4
Hiraiso: Japan 63 g2
Hiran: Reg., Somalia (cap.
    Belet Uen) 79 R19
Hiratsuka: Japan 63 f3
Hirawi: Iran 57 K4
Hirgiz Nor: lake, Mongolia
    49 L8
Hiriz: Iran 57 K2
Hirnant: Powys, Wales 27 P14
Hiraoka: Japan 63 e3
Hirosaki: Japan 63 ZZ6
Hiro: Japan 63 c3
Hiroo: Japan 63 ZZ6
Hirose: Japan 63 b3
HIROSHIMA: & Pref., Japan 63 c3
Hirschau: W. Germany 45 R6
Hirschberg: W. Germany 45 R5
Hirson: France 36 K6
Hirtshals: Denmark 47 L8
Hiruharama: North I., N.Z. 70 P14
Hirwaun: Mid. Glam., Wales
    24 O16
Hisar: Turkey (Bosporus. Inset)
    20 Ins.
Hisaronu: Turkey 56 B1
Hisb, Shaib: wadi, Iraq 57 H6
Hispalis: Roman town at Seville,
    Spain 35 D18
Hispaniola: i., West Indies 87 m14
Hissar: Punjab, India 58 N9
Histon: Cambs., England 25 W15
Hit: Iraq 57 H5
Hita: Japan 63 b4
Hitachi: Japan 63 g2
Hitcham: Suff., England 25 X15
Hitchin: Herts., England 25 V16
Hitoyoshi: Japan 63 b4
Hitra: i., Norway 46 L5
Hitzacker: W. Germany 45 R2
Hiva Oa: i., Marquesas Is. 83 b1
Hiwasa: Japan 63 d4
Hizan: Turkey 57 H2
Hjalmaren: lake, Sweden 47 O7
Hjardharholt: Iceland 46 c4
Hjo: Sweden 47 N7
Hjørring: Denmark 47 L8
Hlabisa: & Dist., Natal, S. Africa
    75 J4
Hlatikulu: Swaziland 75 J3
Hlinsko: Czechoslovakia 45 V6
Hlobane: Natal, S. Africa 75 J3
Hlohovec: Czechoslovakia 43 P12
Hluhluwe Game Reserve: Natal,
    S. Africa 75 J4
Hluleka: S. Africa 75 H5
Hluti: Swaziland 75 J3
Ho: Volta, Ghana 80 E3
Hoa Binh: Vietnam 64 D2
Hoachanas: S.W. Africa 74 C1
Hoai Nhon: Vietnam 64 D4
Hoathly, East: E. Sussex, England
    25 W18
Hoathly, West: E. Sussex, England
    25 V17
Hobart: Ind., U.S.A. 88 H5
HOBART: Tas., Australia 68 H4
Hobbs: N. Mex., U.S.A. 93 G6
Hobkirk: Bord., Scotland 29 Q9
Hoboken: Belgium 44 K4
Hoboken: N.J., U.S.A. 89 O5
Hobro: Denmark 47 L8
Hochatown: Okla., U.S.A. 90 D8
Hochgolling: mtn., Austria 41 T8

Hochih—Hurd, Cape 149

Hochih: Kwangsi Chuang, China 62 T10
Ho Chi Minh City (Saigon): Vietnam 64 D4
Hoching: Sinkiang, China 51 P6
Hoch Moor: W. Germany 44 N2
Hochschober: *mtn.*, Austria 41 S9
Hochschwab: *mtns.*, Austria 41 V8
Hochst: W. Germany 44 O5
Hochstadt: W. Germany 40 Q7
Hochstadt: W. Germany 45 Q6
Hochwan: Szechwan, China 62 T8
Hockenheim: W. Germany 44 O6
Hockham: Norf., England 25 X15
Hockina: S. Australia 71 C8
Hockley: Essex, England 25 X16
Hockliffe: Beds., England 25 U16
Hoddesdon: Herts., Eng. 25 V16
Hodeida: Yemen 54 F12
Hodge: La., U.S.A. 90 E9
Hodgenville: Ky., U.S.A. 88 J7
Hodgson: Man., Canada 92 H2
Hodgson: Queens., Austl. 70 H6
Hodh Occidental: *Dist.*, Mauritania (*cap.* Aïoune el Atrous) 78 B6
Hodh Oriental: *Dist.*, Mauritania (*cap.* Néma) 78 C6
Hodmezövásarhely: Hung. 43 R13
Hodnet: Salop, England 27 Q14
Hodonin: Czechoslovakia 43 P12
Hoedjies Bay: *town*, S. Afr. 74 B6
Hoeksche Waard: *i.*, Neth. 44 K4
Hoek van Holland (Hook of Holland): Netherlands 44 K4
Hof: W. Germany 45 R5
HOFEI: Anhwei, China 62 V8
Hofgastein: Austria 41 T8
Hofgeismar: W. Germany 44 P4
Hofheim: W. Germany 45 Q5
Hofmeyr: S. Africa 75 F5
Hofn: Iceland 46 f4
Hofors: Sweden 47 P6
Hofrat en Nahas: Sudan 79 J8
Hofsjökull: *ice cap*, Iceland 46 d4
Hofu: Japan 63 b3
Hofuf (Hufhuf): Sau. Arab. 55 G9
Höganäs: Sweden 47 N8
Hogansville: Ga., U.S.A. 91 J9
Hogback Mount: Mont., U.S.A. 92 E4
Hoggar: *geog. reg.*, Algeria 78 E5
Hogoro: Tanzania 76 E4
Hogs Back: *ridge*, Surrey, England 25 U17
Hogsthorpe: Lincs., Eng. 27 W13
Hohenau: Austria 41 W7
Hohenems: Austria 40 P8
Hohenhameln: W. Germany 45 Q3
Hohenkirchen: W. Germany 44 N2
Hohenstein: E. Germany 45 S5
Hohenwald: Tenn., U.S.A. 91 H8
Hohenwestedt: W. Germany 44 P1
Hohenzethen: W. Germany 45 Q2
Hohe Rhön: *mtns.*, W. Ger. 45 P5
Hohe Tauern: *mtns.*, Austria 41 S8
Hohewarte: S.W. Africa 74 B1
Hohne: W. Germany 45 Q3
Hohneck: *mtn.*, France 40 M7
Hohsien: Anhwei, China 62 V8
Hohsien: Kwangsi Chuang, China 62 U10
Hohwacht: Germany 45 Q1
Hoifung: Kwangtung, China 62 V10
Hoima: Uganda 76 D2
Hoixuan: Vietnam 64 D2
Hojo: Japan 63 c4
Hokhuvud: Sweden 47 Q6
Hokiang: Szcechwan, China 62 T9
Hokiang: *Prov.* (*now absorbed in* Heilungkiang), China
Hokien: Hopeh, China 62 V7
Hokitika: South I., N.Z. 70 N16
Hokkaido: *i.*, Japan 63 ZZ6
Hokodta: Japan 63 g2
Hokow: Yunnan, China 62 S10
Hoku: Shansi, China 62 U7
Hokumon: Taiwan 63 W10
Holar: Iceland 46 d4
Holbæk: Zealand, Denmark 47 M9
Holbeach: Lincs., England 25 W14
Holbrook: Ariz., U.S.A. 93 E6
Holbrook: N.S.W., Austl. 71 G10
Holbrook: Suff., England 25 Y16
Holcombe Rogus: Devon, England 24 P18
Holden: Mo., U.S.A. 90 E6
Holdenville: Okla., U.S.A. 90 C8
Holderness: *penin.*, Humberside, England 27 V12
Holdredge: Nebr., U.S.A. 93 H4
Holfontein: O.F.S., S. Afr. 75 *Ins.*
Holguin: Cuba 87 M13
Holice: Czechoslovakia 45 V5
Holinkoerh: Inner Mongolia, China 62 U6
Holitun: Inner Mongolia, China 63 W5
Holjes: Sweden 47 N6
Holland: *see* Netherlands.
Holland: Mich., U.S.A. 88 H4
Hollandbush: Strath., Scot. 29 O8
Hollandale: Miss., U.S.A. 90 F9
Holland Bay: Jamaica 86 *Ins.*
Hollenstedt: W. Germany 44 P2
Hollesley: Suff., England 25 Y15
Hollfeld: W. Germany 45 R6
Hollick-Kenyon Plateau: Antarctica 9 85S 95W
Hollingworth: Greater Manchester, England 27 S13
Hollis: Okla., U.S.A. 90 B8
Hollister: Calif., U.S.A. 93 C5
Hollymount: Mayo, Repub. of Ireland 30 C12
Holly Springs: *city*, Miss., U.S.A. 90 G8
Hollywood: Fla., U.S.A. 91 L12
Hollywood: Wick., Repub. of Ireland 31 H13
Holmavik: Iceland 46 c4
Holme: Cambs., England 25 V15
Holme next the Sea: Norf., England 25 X14
Holmes Chapel: Ches., Eng. 27 R13
Holmesdale: *val.*, Surrey, England 25 V17
Holmes Reef: Australia 69 H3
Holmestrand: Norway 47 M7
Holme upon Spalding Moor: Humb., England 27 U12
Holmfirth: W. Yorks., Eng. 27 S12
Holmfors: Sweden 46 Q4
Holm Lake: Sweden 47 O5
Holms Land: Greenland 85 S1
Holm Sound: Orkney Is., Scotland 28 Q2
Holmsund: Sweden 46 R5
Holmträsk: Sweden 46 R3
Holmwood: Surrey, Eng. 25 V17
Holo: Hainan, China 62 U11
Holoog: S.W. Africa 74 B3
Holopaw: Fla., U.S.A. 91 L11
Holroyd: *riv.*, Queens., Australia 69 G2
Holsatia: S.W. Africa 74 A2
Holstebro: Denmark 47 L8
Holsteinborg: Greenland 85 o4
Holston: *riv.*, U.S.A. 88 K7
Holsworthy: Devon, Eng. 24 N18
Holt: Clwyd, Wales 27 Q13
Holt: Norf., England 25 Y14
Holtby: N. Yorks., England 27 U12
Holten: Netherlands 44 M3
Holton: Suff., England 25 Z15
Holton le Clay: Lincs., Eng. 27 V13
Holung: Kirin, China 63 X6
Holwick: Durham, England 26 R10
Holy Cross: Alaska, U.S.A. 84 D5
Holycross: Tip., Repub. of Ireland 31 F14
Holyhead: Gwynedd, Wales 27 M13
Holy I. (Lindisfarne): Northumb., England 26 S8
Holy I.: Strath., Scotland 29 L8
Holyoke: Colo., U.S.A. 93 G4
Holyoke: Mass., U.S.A. 89 P4
Holyport: Berks., England 25 U17
Holystone: Northumb., Eng. 26 R9
Holytown: Strath., Scot. 29 O8
Holywell: Clwyd, Wales 27 P13
Holywood: Down, N. Irel. 30 K10
Holywood: Dumfries & Galloway, Scotland 29 O9
Holzkirchen: W. Germany 41 R8
Holzminden: W. Germany 44 P4
Homa: Kenya 76 D3
Homalin: Burma 59 Q10
Homberg: W. Germany 44 P5
Hombori: Mali 80 D1
Homburg: Hesse, W. Ger. 44 O5
Homburg: Saarland, W. Ger. 44 N6
Home Bay: N.W.T., Canada 85 N4
Home Hill: *town*, Queens., Australia 70 G2
Homeplace: La., U.S.A. 90 *Ins.*
Homer: Alaska, U.S.A. 84 d6
Homer: La., U.S.A. 90 E9
Homerville: Ga., U.S.A. 91 K10
Homestead: Fla., U.S.A. 91 L13
Homewood: Ala., U.S.A. 91 H9
Hominy: Okla., U.S.A. 90 C7
Hommelvik: Norway 46 M5
HOMS: & *Prov.*, Libya 78 G3
HOMS: & *Prov.*, Syria 56 E4
Homs: *riv.*, S.W. Africa 74 C4
Hon: Libya 33 F6
Honan: *Prov.*, China (*cap.* Chengchow) 62 U8
Honaz Dağ: *mtn.*, Turkey 56 A3
Honchong: Vietnam 64 C4
Honda: Colombia 94 C2
Honda Bay: Palawan, Phil. 64 F5
Hondefontein: S. Africa 74 D6
Hondeklip Bay: *town*, S. Afr. 74 B5
Hondewater: S. Africa 74 D6
Hondo: Mexico 93 G7
Hondo: N. Mex., U.S.A. 93 F6
Hondo: Tex., U.S.A. 90 B11
Honschoote: Belgium 36 H5
Honduras, G. of: Belize 86 *Ins.*

Honduras: *Republic* 86 L14
Cap.: Tegucigalpa
Area: 43,277 sq. miles (112,087 sq. km.)
Pop.: 2,582,000 (*1970 E*)

Honea Path: S.C., U.S.A. 91 K8
Honesdale: Pa., U.S.A. 89 O5
Honey Grove: Tex., U.S.A. 90 D9
Honfleur: France 36 F6

Hong Kong: *Br. colony* 62 U10
Cap.: Victoria
Area: 398 sq. miles (1,031 sq. km.)
Pop.: 4,045,000 (*1971 E*)

Hongo: Japan 63 e3
Hongsa: Laos 64 C2
Hongsong: S. Korea 63 X7
Hongu: Japan 63 d4
HONIARA: Solomon Is. 67 L3
Honing: Norf., England 25 Y14
Honingham: Norf., Eng. 25 Y14
Honington: Lincs., Eng. 27 U14
Honiton: Devon, England 24 P18
Honjo: Japan 63 ZZ7
Honkajoki: Finland 47 S6
Honley: W. Yorks., England 27 S12
Hon Lon: *i.*, Vietnam 64 D4
Honnef: W. Germany 44 N5
HONOLULU: Hawaiian Is. 83 c2
Honquan: Vietnam 64 D4
Honshu: *i.*, Japan 63 Z7
Hoo: Kent, England 25 X17
Hood, Mount: Oreg., U.S.A. 92 C3
Hood River: Oreg., U.S.A. 92 C3
Hooge: *i.*, W. Germany 44 O1
Hoogeveen: Netherlands 44 M3
Hoogezand: Netherlands 44 M2
Hook: Hants., England 25 U17
Hookena: Hawaiian Is. 83 d3
Hooker: Okla., U.S.A. 90 A7
Hook Head: *cape*, Wex., Repub. of Ireland 31 H15
Hook I.: Queens., Austl. 70 H3
Hook Norton: Oxon., Eng. 25 T16
Hook of Holland (Hoek van Holland): Netherlands 44 K4
Hook Point: *cape*, Queens., Australia 70 K5
Hoonah: Alaska, U.S.A. 84 F6
Hooper, Cape: N.W.T., Canada 85 N4
Hoopeston: Ill., U.S.A. 88 H5
Hoopstad: & *Dist.*, O.F.S., S. Africa 75 F3
Hoorn: Netherlands 44 L3
Hoosick Falls: *town*, N.Y., U.S.A. 89 P4
Hoover Dam: Nev., U.S.A. 93 E5
Hopa: Turkey 57 G1
Hope: Alaska, U.S.A. 84 E5
Hope: Ark., U.S.A. 90 E9
Hope: B.C., Canada 92 C3
Hope: Clwyd, Wales 27 P13
Hope: Ind., U.S.A. 88 J6
Hope: N. Dak., U.S.A. 92 H3
Hope, Loch: High., Scot. 28 M3
Hope, Point: *cape*, Alaska, U.S.A. 84 C4
Hopedale: Newf., Canada 85 n6
Hopefield: S. Africa 74 C6
Hopeh: *Prov.*, China (*cap.* Shihkiachwang) 62 V7
Hope I.: Spitsbergen 48 d2
Hopeman: Gram., Scot. 28 P4
Hope Point: *cape*, Burma 59 R11
Hopes Advance, Cape: Que., Canada 85 N5
Hopetoun: Vict., Australia 71 E10
Hopetoun: W. Australia 68 C6
Hope Town: Bahamas 91 N12
Hopetown: & *Dist.*, S. Afr. 75 F4
Hope under Dinmore: Hereford & Worcester, England 24 Q15
Hopewell: Va., U.S.A. 89 N7
Hopewell Cape: *city*, N.B., Canada 89 T3
Hôpital-du-Gros-Bois, l': France 40 M8
Hopkins: *riv.*, Vict., Austl. 71 E11
Hopkins, Lake: W. Austl. 68 D4
Hopkinsville: Ky., U.S.A. 88 H7
Hopo: Kwangtung, China 62 V10
Hoppo: Kwangsi Chuang, China 62 T10
Hopton: Suff., England 25 Z14
Hoquiam: Wash., U.S.A. 92 C3
Hora Svatého: Czech. 45 T5
Horaždovice: Czech. 45 T6
Horb: W. Germany 40 O7
Horbranz: Austria 40 P8
Horcajo: Spain 35 E17
Horcasitas: Mexico 93 E7
Hordaland: *Co.*, Norway (*cap.* Bergen) 47 K6
Horde: W. Germany 44 N4
Horden: Durham, England 26 T10
Hordio: Somalia 79 S17
Horgen: Switzerland 40 O8
Hori: Japan 63 b3
Hořice: Czechoslovakia 45 V5
Horin (Feng-lui): Taiwan 63 W10
Horley: Surrey, England 25 V17
Hormigas: Mexico 93 F7
Hormuz, Str. of: Sau. Arab./Iran 55 J9
Horn: Austria 41 V7
Horn: *i.*, Miss., U.S.A. 90 G10
Horn, Cape: Chile 95 D15
Hornån: *lake*, Sweden 46 P3
Hornberg: W. Germany 40 O7
Horncastle: Lincs., England 27 V13
Horndean: Hants., England 25 T18
Horneburg: W. Germany 44 P2
Hornefors: Sweden 46 Q5
Hornell: N.Y., U.S.A. 89 N4
Hornepayne: Ont., Canada 88 J1
Hornerkirchen: W. Germany 45 P2
Horn Head: *cape*, Don., Repub. of Ireland 30 E9
Horni Cerekev: Czech. 45 V6
Horningsham: Wilts., Eng. 24 R17
Horn Is.: Pacific O. 67 Q4
Horni Vltavice: Czech. 41 T7
Hornkranz: S.W. Africa 74 B1
Hornsby: N.S.W., Austl. 71 J9
Hornsea: Humb., England 27 V12
Hornsjo: Sweden 46 Q5
Hořovice: Czechoslovakia 45 T6
Horqueta: Paraguay 96 D1
Horr, North & South: Kenya 76 E2
Horrabridge: Devon, Eng. 24 N18
Horse Cave: *city*, Ky., U.S.A. 88 J7
Horseheads: N.Y., U.S.A. 89 N4
Horse House: N. Yorks., Eng. 26 S11
Horse Mount: N. Mex., U.S.A. 93 F6
Horsens: Denmark 47 L9
Horsey: Norf., England 25 Z14
Horsford: Norf., England 25 Y14
Horsforth: W. Yorks., Eng. 27 S12
Horsham: W. Sussex, England 25 V17
Horsham: Vict., Australia 71 E11
Horsington: Lincs., England 27 V13
Horsington: Som., England 24 R17
Horsmonden: Kent, England 25 W17
Horspath: Oxon., England 25 T16
Horst: Poland 45 V1
Horsted Keynes: W. Sussex, England 25 V17
HORTA: Faial I., Azores, Portugal 78 *Ins.*
Horten: Norway 47 M7
Hortlax: Sweden 46 R4
Horton: *riv.*, N.W.T., Canada 84 g1
Horton in Ribblesdale: N. Yorks., England 26 R11
Horup: W. Germany 44 P1
Horvik: Sweden 47 O8
Horwich: Gt. Man., England 27 Q12
Horwood Lake: Ont., Can. 88 K1
Horyo: Taiwan 63 W10
Hoşap: Turkey 57 H2
Hoseyniyeh-ye Khoda Dad: Iran 57 L5
Hoshangabad: Madhya Pradesh, India 58 N10
Hoshiarpur: Punjab, India 58 N8
Hoshihtolokai: Sinkiang, China 51 P5
Hososhima: Japan 63 b4
Hospet: Karnataka, India 58 N11
Hospital: Lim., Repub. of Ireland 31 E15
Hospitalet, l': France 37 G13
Hossa: Finland 46 V4
Hosseina: Ethiopia 76 E1
Hoste I.: Chile 94 D15
Hostens: France 37 E11
Hostoun: Czechoslovakia 45 S6
Hosur: Tamil Nadu, India 58 N12
Hotaka: Japan 63 e2
Hotchkiss: Colo., U.S.A. 93 F5
Hotei (Putai): Taiwan 63 W10
Hotham, Mount: Vict., Austl. 71 G11
Hotien (Khotan): & *riv.*, Sinkiang, China 51 O7
Hoting: Sweden 46 P4
Hotseh: Shantung, China 62 V7
Hot Springs: Alaska, U.S.A. 84 d5
Hot Springs: Ark., U.S.A. 90 E8
Hot Springs: S. Dak., U.S.A. 92 G4
Hot Springs: Va., U.S.A. 89 M7
Hot Springs Nat. Park: Ark., U.S.A. 90 E8
Hottah, Lake: N.W.T., Can. 84 H5
Hottentot Bay: S.W. Africa 74 A3
Hotazel: C.P., S. Africa 74 E3
Hou: *riv.*, Laos 64 C2
Houat, Ile: *i.*, France 36 C8
Houbrat, El: Algeria 78 E3
Houdan: France 36 G7
Houeilles: France 37 F11
Houffalize: Belgium 44 L5
Houghton: Cumbria, Eng. 26 Q10
Houghton: Mich., U.S.A. 88 G2
Houghton Lake: Mich., U.S.A. 88 J3
Houghton le Spring: Tyne & Wear, England 26 T10
Houghton St. Giles: Norf., England 25 X14
Houhoek: S. Africa 74 C7
Houlton: Maine, U.S.A. 89 S2
Houma: La., U.S.A. 90 F11
Houmoed: S. Africa 74 C4
Houndé: Upper Volta 80 D2
Hounslow: Gt. Ldn., Eng. 25 V17
Hourn, Loch: Highland, Scot. 28 K5
Hourtin: France 37 D10
Hourtin, Etang d': *lag.*, Fr. 37 D10
Housatonic: *riv.*, Conn., U.S.A. 89 P5
Houston: Miss., U.S.A. 90 G9
Houston: Tex., U.S.A. 90 D11
Hout Bay: & *bay*, S. Africa 74 *Ins.*
Houtkraal: S. Africa 75 F5
Houtman (Abrolhos): *is.*, W. Australia 68 A5
Houwater: S. Africa 74 E5
Hovd: Mongolia 60 C2
Hove: E. Sussex, England 25 V18
Hovgaards I.: Greenland 85 S2
Hovingham: N. Yorks., Eng. 26 U11
Howar: *wadi*, Sudan 79 J6
Howard: Kans., U.S.A. 90 C7
Howard: Queens., Austl. 70 K5
Howden: Humb., England 27 U12
Howe, Cape: N.S.W., Austl. 71 H11
Howe of the Mearns: Grampian, Scotland 28 Q6
Howell: Mich., U.S.A. 88 K4
Howick: Natal, S. Africa 75 J4
Howick Group: *is.*, Queens., Australia 69 G2
Howmore: Outer Hebr., Scotland 28 G5
Hownam: Bord., Scotland 29 R9
Howrah: W. Bengal, India 59 P10
Howth: & *head*, Dublin, Repub. of Ireland 31 J13
Hoxie: Ark., U.S.A. 88 F7
Hoxne: Suff., England 25 Y15
Höxter: W. Germany 44 P4
Hoy: *i.*, Orkney Is., Scotland 28 P2
Hoyerswerda: E. Germany 45 U4
Hoylake: Mers., England 27 P13
Hoyland: S. Yorks., England 27 T13
Hoyos: Spain 35 C16
Hoyo Strait: Japan 63 b4
Hoy Sound: Orkney Is. 28 P2
Hoyun: Kwangtung, China 62 U10
Hozat: Turkey 56 F2
Hrádek: Czechoslovakia 41 W7
HRADEC KRÁLOVÉ: Východočeský, Czech. 45 V5
Hranice: Czechoslovakia 43 P12
Hrochuv Tynec: Czech. 45 V6
Hron: *riv.*, Czechoslovakia 43 Q12
Hrotovice: Czechoslovakia 45 W6
Hrubieszów: Poland 43 S11
Hrušovany: Czechoslovakia 41 W7
Hrvatska: *see* Croatia.
Hsenwi: Burma 59 R10
Hsiangchou: Kwangsi Chuang, China 62 T10
Hsiang Jihte: Chinghai, China 62 R7
Hsiaochin: Szechwan, China 62 S8
Hsichang (Ningyuan): Szechwan, China 62 S9
Hsiehkaerh: Tibet, China 59 P9
Hsiehtungmen: Tibet, China 59 P9
Hsifeng: Kweichow, China 62 T9
Hsihaochitewangfu: Inner Mongolia, China 62 V6
Hsilipuko: Tibet, China 59 O8
Hsilung: Kwangsi Chuang, China 62 T10
Hsinchiu: Liaoning, China 62 V6
Hsinchu (Sinchiku): Taiwan 63 W10
Hsingan: *Prov.* (*now absorbed in* Inner Mongolia), China.
Hsin-hai-lien (Tung-hai): Kiangsu, China 62 V8
Hsinhsing: Kwangtung, China 62 U10
Hsinhui *see* Kongmoon.
Hsining (Sining): Chinghai (Tsinghai), China 62 S7
Hsinking (Changchun): Kirin, China 63 X6
Hsinkoerh: Sinkiang, China 53 N3
Hsinlung: Tibet, China 62 S8
Hsinping: Yunnan, China 62 S10
Hsipaw: Burma 59 R10
Hsuanwei: Yunnan, China 62 S9
Hsuchang: Honan, China 62 U8
Hsüehka: Tibet, China 59 Q8
Htawgaw: Burma 59 R9
Huachinera: Mexico 93 F6
Huacho: Peru 94 B6
Huaco: Argentina 96 B3
Huahine: *i.*, Society Is. 83 e3
Huahsien: Honan, China 62 U7
Huai Sai: Thailand 64 C5
Huallaga: *riv.*, Peru 94 B5
Hualpai Peak: *mtn.*, Ariz., U.S.A. 93 E5
HUAMBO: & *Prov.*, Angola 73 H12
Huancabamba: Peru 94 B5
Huancané: Peru 94 D7
Huancavelica: Peru 94 B6
Huancayo: Peru 94 B6
Huanchaca: Bolivia 94 D8
Huanchiang: Kwangsi Chuang, China 62 T10
Huangping: Kweichow, China 62 T9
Huanguelen: Argentina 96 C4
Huanta: Peru 94 C6
Huánuco: Peru 94 B5
Huaping: Yunnan, China 62 S9
Huaral: Peru 94 B6
Huarás: Peru 94 B5
Huari: Bolivia 94 D7
Huarmey: Peru 94 B6
Huascaran, Mt.: Peru 94 B5
Huasco: Chile 96 A2
Huaylas: Peru 94 B5
Huayuan: Hunan, China 62 T9
Hubbard: Tex., U.S.A. 90 C10
Hubbard Lake: Mich., U.S.A. 88 K3
Huben: Austria 41 S9
Hubli: Karnataka, India 58 N11
Huchang: N. Korea 63 X6
Huchu: Chinghai, China 62 S7
Hucklow: Derby., England 27 S13
Hucknall Torkard: Notts., England 27 T13
Huddersfield: W. Yorks., Eng. 27 S12
Hude: W. Germany 44 O2
Hudiksvall: Sweden 47 P6
Hudson: Mich., U.S.A. 88 J5
Hudson: N.Y., U.S.A. 89 P4
Hudson: Ont., Canada 92 J2
Hudson: Wis., U.S.A. 88 E3
Hudson: Wyo., U.S.A. 92 F4
Hudson: *riv.*, N.Y., U.S.A. 89 P4
Hudson Bay: N.W.T., Canada 85 L5
Hudson Bay: *town*, Sask., Canada 92 G2
Hudson Hope: B.C., Can. 92 C1
Hudson Land: Greenland 85 r3
Hudson Str.: N.W.T., Canada 85 m5
Hudun: Somalia 79 R18
Huê: Vietnam 64 D3
Huecu, El: Argentina 96 A4
Huedin: Romania 43 S13
Huelgoat: France 36 B7
HUELVA: & *Prov.*, Spain 35 C18
Huércal Overa: Spain 35 F18
HUESCA: & *Prov.*, Spain 35 F15
Huescar: Spain 35 E18
Huetamo: Mexico 86 j14
Huete: Spain 35 E16
Hufhuf (Hofuf): Sau. Arab. 55 G9
Huggate: Humb., England 27 U12
Hugginstown: Kilk., Repub. of Ireland 31 G15
Hughenden: Queens., Austl. 69 G4
Hughes: Alaska, U.S.A. 84 d4
Hughes: Ark., U.S.A. 90 F8
Hugh Town: Scilly Is. 25 J19
Hugo: Okla., U.S.A. 90 D8
HUHEHOT (Kweisui): Inner Mongolia, China 62 U6
Huiarau Ra.: North I., N.Z. 70 Q14
Huib Plat.: S.W. Africa 74 B3
Huichon: N. Korea 63 X6
Huila: *Prov.*, Angola (*cap.* Sá de Bandeira) 73 H13
Huila, Nevado del: *mtn.*, Col. 94 B3
Huinan: Kirin, China 63 X6
Huinca Renanco: Argentina 96 C3
Huish Champflower: Som., England 24 P17
Huisne: *riv.*, France 36 F7
Huitse (Tungchwan): Yunnan, China 62 S9
Hukow: Kiangsi, China 62 V9
Hukuntsi: Botswana 77 B7
Hula, Lake: Israel 55 b1
Hulaifa: Saudi Arabia 54 F9
Hulan: Heilungkiang, China 63 X5
Hulin: Heilungkiang, China 63 Y5
Hulkko: U.S.S.R. 46 W2
Hull: Que., Canada 89 O3
Hull: Humb., England, *see* Kingston upon Hull.
Hull: *riv.*, Humb., England 27 V12
Hullavington: Wilts., Eng. 24 R16
Hulme End: Staffs., England 27 S13
Hulst: Netherlands 44 K4
Hultsfred: Sweden 47 O8
Hulun (Hailar): Inner Mongolia, China 62 V5
Hulun Chih: *lake*, Inner Mongolia, China 62 V5
Hulup: *riv.*, S.W. Africa 74 B2
Humacao: Puerto Rico 87 a1
Humahuaca: Argentina 96 B1
Humaidan: *well*, Sau. Arab. 55 H10
Humaitá: Brazil 94 E5
Humaitá: Paraguay 96 D2
Humansdorp: & *Dist.*, S. Afr. 75 F7
Humansville: Mo., U.S.A. 90 E7
Humaya: *riv.*, Mexico 93 F7
Humbécourt: France 36 K7
Humber: *est.*, Humb., Eng. 27 U12
Humber, Mouth of the: *est.*, Humb., England 27 W12
Humbermouth: Newf., Can. 85 u2
Humberside: *Co.*, England (*co. town* Kingston upon Hull) 27 U12
Humboldt: Iowa, U.S.A. 88 D4
Humboldt: Kans., U.S.A. 90 D7
Humboldt: Sask., Canada 92 F2
Humboldt: Tenn., U.S.A. 90 G8
Humboldt: *riv.*, Nev., U.S.A. 92 D4
Humboldt Glac.: Greenland 85 n2
Hume (Murray): *riv.*, Vict./N.S.W., Australia 71 F10
Humeburn: Queens., Austl. 70 F6
Hume, Lake: *res.*, Vict./N.S.W., Australia 71 G10
Humfeld: W. Germany 44 P3
Humphrey: Ark., U.S.A. 90 F8
Humphreys Pk.: Ariz., U.S.A. 93 E5
Humpolec: Czechoslovakia 45 V6
Humppila: Finland 47 S6
Humsanes: Morocco (Gib. *Inset*) 32 *Ins.*
Humshaugh: Northumb., England 26 R9
Húna Bay: Iceland 46 c4
Hunan: *Prov.*, China (*cap.* Changsha) 62 U9
Hunchun: Kirin, China 63 Y6
Hundalee: South I., N.Z. 70 O16
Hundleton: Dyfed, Wales 24 M16
Hundon: Suff., England 25 X15
Hundred Mile House: B.C., Canada 92 C2
Hunfeld: W. Germany 45 P5

Hungary: *Republic* 43 Q13
Cap.: Budapest
Area: 35,919 sq. miles (93,030 sq. km.)
Pop.: 10,395,000 (*1972 E*)

Hungen: W. Germany 44 O5
Hungerford: Berks., Eng. 25 S17
Hungerford: Queens., Austl. 71 F7
Hunghwaliangtzu: Inner Mongolia, China 63 W5
Hungshui: *riv.*, China 62 T10
Hungtze, Lake: China 62 V8
Huni Valley: *town*, Ghana 80 D3
Hunker: Yukon, Canada 84 F5
Hunmanby: N. Yorks., Eng. 26 V11
Hunnebostrand: Sweden 47 M7
Hunsrück: *mtns.*, W. Germany 44 N6
Hunstanton, New: Norf., England 25 W14
Hunte: *riv.*, W. Germany 44 O3
Hunter: *riv.*, N.S.W., Austl. 71 J9
Hunter I.: B.C., Canada 92 B2
Hunter I.: Ont., Canada 88 F1
Hunter I.: Pacific O. 67 O6
Hunter I.: Tas., Australia 68 G8
Hunter Range: N.S.W., Australia 71 J9
Hunter's Quay: Strath., Scot. 29 M8
Hunterville: North I., N.Z. 70 P14
Huntingburg: Ind., U.S.A. 88 H6
Huntingdon: Cambs., England 25 V15
Huntingdon: Pa., U.S.A. 89 M5
Huntingdon: Que., Canada 89 O3
Huntingdon: Tenn., U.S.A. 88 G7
Hunting I.: S.C., U.S.A. 91 L9
Huntington: Ind., U.S.A. 88 J5
Huntington: N. Yorks., Eng. 27 T12
Huntington: Oreg., U.S.A. 92 D4
Huntington: Staffs., Eng. 27 R14
Huntington: Utah, U.S.A. 93 E5
Huntington: W. Va., U.S.A. 88 K6
Huntley: Glos., England 24 R16
Huntly: Grampian, Scotland 28 Q5
Huntly: North I., N.Z. 70 P13
Hunton: N. Yorks., England 26 S11
Huntsham: Devon, England 24 P18
Huntspill: Som., England 24 Q17
Huntsville: Ala., U.S.A. 91 H8
Huntsville: Mo., U.S.A. 88 E6
Huntsville: Ont., Canada 89 M3
Huntsville: Tex., U.S.A. 90 D10
Hunyani: *riv.*, Rhodesia 77 D6
Hunyani Range: Rhodesia 77 D6
Hunyuan: Shansi, China 62 U7
Huon Penin: Papua/New Guinea 66 J3
Hupeh: *Prov.*, China (*cap.* Wuchang) 62 U8
Huqaf: *geog. reg.*, Oman 55 J10
Huraidha: Yemen P.D.R. 55 G11
Huraimala: Saudi Arabia 54 G9
Hurd, Cape: Ont., Canada 88 L3

For Abbreviations see list on p.113. Italic type, e.g. *Ephesus*, refers to historical names not on maps. Capital letters, e.g. MADRID, show capitals of countries; small capital letters, e.g. CADIZ, show capitals of provinces, etc. General notes p.116.

150 Hur, El—Ionian Sea

Hur, El: Somalia **79** R19
Hurghada: Egypt **54** D9
Huriel: France **37** H9
Hurler's Cross: Clare, Repub. of Ireland **31** D14
Hurn: *airfield*, Dorset, Eng. **25** S18
Huron: S. Dak., U.S.A. **92** H4
Huron, Lake: Can./U.S.A. **88** K3
Hurricane: Utah, U.S.A. **93** E5
Hursley: Hants., England **25** T17
Hurstbourne Priors: Hants., England **25** T17
Hurstbourne Tarrant: Hants., England **25** T17
Hurstbridge: Vict., Austl. **71** F11
Hurstpierpoint: W. Sussex, Eng. **25** V18
Hurtado: *riv.*, Chile **96** A3
Hurunui: *riv.*, South I., N.Z. **70** O16
Husås: Sweden **46** N5
Husavik: Iceland **46** e3
Husbands Bosworth: Leics., England **25** T15
Huşi: Romania **39** V13
Huskisson: N.S.W., Austl. **71** J10
Huskvarna: Sweden **47** O8
Husn: Jordan **55** b2
Husthwaite: N. Yorks., Eng. **26** T11
Hustopeče: Czechoslovakia **41** W7
Husum: W. Germany **44** P1
Hutanopan: Sumatra **65** B6
Hutchinson: Kans., U.S.A. **90** C6
Hutchinson: Minn., U.S.A. **88** D3
Hutchinson Junction: S. Afr. **74** E5
Huto: *riv.*, China **62** U7
Hutou: Heilungkiang, China **63** Y5
Huttig: Ark., U.S.A. **90** E9
Huttoft: Lincs., England **27** W13
Hutton: Borders., Scotland **29** R8
Huttwil: Switzerland **40** N8
Huy: Belgium **44** L5
Huyton: Mers., England **27** Q13
Hval Sound: Greenland **85** m2
Hvammur: Iceland **46** d4
Hvar: *i.*, Yugoslavia **38** P15
Hveravellir: Iceland **46** d4
Hwai: *riv.*, China **62** U8
Hwaian: Hopeh, China **62** U6
Hwaian: Kiangsu, China **62** V8
Hwailai: Hopeh, China **62** V6
Hwaining (Anking): Anhwei, China **62** V8
Hwaiyang: Honan, China **62** U8
Hwaiyin (Tsingkiang): Kiangsu, China **62** V8
Hwaiyuan: Anhwei, China **62** V8
Hwalung: Chinghai, China **62** S7
Hwang: *riv.*, China **62** V7
Hwanghsien: Hunan, China **62** T9
Hwanghsien: Shantung, China **63** W7
Hwangmei: Hupeh, China **62** V8
Hwangyuan (Tangar): Chinghai, China **62** S7
Hwanjen: Liaoning, China **63** X6
Hwaping: Ninghsia Hui, China **62** T7
HWAYANG (Chengtu): Szechwan, China **62** S8
Hwei: *riv.*, China **62** R7
Hweianpao: Ninghsia Hui, China **62** T7
Hweichang: Kiangsi, China **62** V9
Hweilai: Kwangtung, China **62** V10
Hweimin: Shantung, China **62** V7
Hweinan: Kirin, China **63** X6
Hweitung: Hunan, China **62** T9
Hwohsien: Shansi, China **62** U7
Hwoshan: Anhwei, China **62** V8
Hyargas Nor: *lake*, Mongolia **60** C2
Hyde: Gt. Man., England **27** R13
Hyden: W. Australia **68** B6
Hyde Park: Guyana **87** d7
Hyder: Alaska, U.S.A. **84** f6
HYBERABAD: Andhra Pradesh, India *former cap. of* Hyderabad **58** N11
Hyderabad: *State* (now absorbed in Andhra, Maharashtra & Karnataka, *States*), India.
Hyderabad: Sind., Pakistan **58** L9
Hyenville: France **36** D7
Hyères: France **40** M12
Hyères, Iles de: *is.*, France **40** M12
Hyllestad: Norway **47** J6
Hyltebruk: Sweden **47** N8
Hyndman Peak: *mtn.*, Idaho, U.S.A. **92** E4
Hyogo: *Pref.*, Japan (*cap.* Kobe) **63** d3
Hypanis: Greek name of river Bug reaching sea at Nikolayev, U.S.S.R. **33** J2
Hyrcania: Graeco-Roman name of area S. of Caspian Sea, Iran **55** H7
Hyrcanian Sea: ancient Greek name of Caspian Sea **55** H6
Hyrra Banda: Cen. Afr. Rep. **76** B1
Hyrum: Utah, U.S.A. **92** E4
Hyrynsalmi: Finland **46** V4
Hythe: Alta., Canada **92** D1
Hythe: Hants., England **25** T18
Hythe: Kent, England **25** Y17
Hyvinkää: Finland **47** T6

Iader: Roman town at Zadar, W. Yugoslavia **41** V11
Ialomita: *riv.*, Romania **39** U14
Ian: Heilungkiang, China **63** X5
Iarconnaught: *dist.*, Galway, Repub. of Ireland **31** C13
Iaşi: Romania **43** U13
Iasus: Greek city about 5 miles N. of Gulluk at head of gulf of Mandalya, Turkey **39** U18
Iazyges: Sarmatian tribe which in Roman imperial times lived between rivers Danube and Tisza, E. Hungary **43** R13
Iba: Luzon, Philippines **64** G3
IBADAN: Oyo, Nigeria 81 E3
Ibagué: Colombia **94** B3
Ibaiti: Brazil **96** E1
Ibar: *riv.*, Yugoslavia **39** R15
Ibaraki: *Pref.*, Japan (*cap.* Mito) **63** g2
Ibarra: Ecuador **94** B3
Ibb: Yemen **54** F12
Ibba (Tonj): *riv.*, Sudan **76** C1
Ibbenburen: W. Germany **44** N3
Ibembo: Zaire **76** B2
Ibengo: *riv.*, Congo **81** H4
Iberis: Roman name of river Ebro, Spain **35** G16
Ibeto: Nigeria **81** F2
Ibi: Nigeria **81** F3
Ibia: Brazil **94** H7
Ibicui: & *riv.*, Brazil **96** D2
Ibicuy: Argentina **96** D3
Ibigawa: Japan **63** e3
Ibipetuba: Brazil **94** J6
Ibitinga: Brazil **96** F1
Ibiza: Iviza, Balearic Is. **35** G17
Ibiza (Iviza): *i.*, Balearic Islands **35** G17
Ibo: Mozambique **77** F5
'Ibri: Oman **55** J10
Ibstock: Leics., England **27** T14
Iburg: W. Germany **44** O3
Ica: Peru **94** B6
Içana: Brazil **94** D3
Icaño: Argentina **96** C2
İÇEL: *see* Mersin.
Icel: *Prov.*, Turkey [*cap.* Mersin (Icel)] **56** C3

Iceland: *Republic* **46** *Ins.*
Cap.: Reykjavik
Area: 39,702 sq. miles (102,828 sq. km.)
Pop.: 206,000 (*1971 E*)

Icha: U.S.S.R. **49** r6
Ichang: Hupeh, China **62** U8
Icheng: Hupeh, China **62** U8
Ichenhausen: W. Germany **40** Q7
Ichikawa: Japan **63** f3
Ichinomiya: Aichi, Japan **63** e3
Ichinomiya: Ishikawa, Japan **63** e2
Ichinoseki: Japan **63** ZZ7
Ichnya: Ukraine **50** D4
Icht: Morocco **80** K9
Ichun: Kiangsi, China **62** U9
Ichun: Shensi, China **62** T7
Ichwan: Honan, China **62** U8
Icklesham: E. Sussex, Eng. **25** X18
Ickleton: Cambs., England **25** W15
Icklingham: Suff., England **25** X15
Icó: Brazil **94** K5
Iconium: ancient town of Lycaonia, later Roman colony, at Konya, Turkey **56** C3
Ida: Japan **63** b4
Ida: mtn. (2456m.) in centre of Crete **39** T19
Ida: chain of mtns. N. of head of Edremit Gulf, Turkey **39** U17
Idabel: Okla, U.S.A. **90** D9
Ida Grove: Iowa, U.S.A. **92** H4
Idah: Nigeria **81** F3
Idaho: *State*, U.S.A. (*cap.* Boise) **92** D3
Idaho City: Idaho, U.S.A. **92** D4
Idaho Falls: *city*, Idaho, U.S.A. **92** E4
Idaho Springs: Colo., U.S.A. **93** F5
Idalia: Trans., S. Africa **75** J3
Idar: Gujarat, India **58** M10
Idar: W. Germany **44** N6
'Idd el Ghanam: Sudan **79** J7
Iddesleigh: Devon, England **24** N18
Iddidole: Ethiopia **79** Q18
Ide: Devon, England **24** O18
Ideford: Devon, England **24** O18
Idehan: *geog. reg.*, Libya **78** G4
Idélimen: *well*, Mali **81** E1
Idenburg: *riv.*, New Guinea **61** M12
Idfu: Egypt **54** D9
Idhra: *i.*, Greece **39** S18
Idi: Sumatra **65** B6
Idil: Turkey **57** G3
Idiofa: Zaire **76** A4
Idirtu: Chinghai, China **62** R7
Idkerberg: Sweden **47** O6
Idku, Lake: Egypt **56** B6
Idle: W. Yorks., England **27** S12
Idle: *riv.*, Notts., England **27** U13
IDLIB: & *Prov.*, Syria **56** E4
Ido: *well*, Niger **81** G2
Idomene: Greek city at NE. end of G. of Amvrakia, Greece **39** R17
Idre: Sweden **47** N6
Idrija: Yugoslavia **41** U9
Idrinskoye: U.S.S.R. **51** Q4
Idro, Lake: Italy **40** Q10
Idstein: W. Germany **44** O5
Idumaea: Edomite kingdom of N.T. period south of *Judaea* in Negeb, Israel **56** D6
Idutywa: S. Africa **75** H6
Idzhevan: Armenia, U.S.S.R. **57** J1
Iefren: Libya **32** E5
Ieper (Ypres): Belgium **36** H5
Ierápetra: Crete **39** T19
Ierissós: Greece **39** S16
Ierzu: Sardinia **38** L17
Iesi: Italy **41** T12
Iesolo: Italy **41** S10
Iet: Somalia **79** Q19
Ifakara: Tanzania **76** E4
Ife: Nigeria **81** E3
Iferouane: Niger **78** F6
Iffendic: France **36** C7
Iffley: Queens., Australia **69** G3
Ifni: Morocco **80** J9
Ifon: Nigeria **81** F3
Igalula: Tanzania **76** D4
Iganga: Uganda **76** D2
Igarka: U.S.S.R. **48** k4
Igatimi: Paraguay **96** D1
Igbetti: Nigeria **81** E3
Igbo Ora: Nigeria **81** E3
Iğdir: Turkey **57** J2
Iggesund: Sweden **47** P6
Ightham: Kent, England **25** W17
Iglesia: Argentina **96** B3
Iglesias: Sardinia **38** L17
Igli: Algeria **80** L8
Igloole: Ethiopia **79** Q18
Igloolik: N.W.T., Canada **85** l 4
Igma: *oasis*, Algeria **80** K9
Ignace: Ont., Canada **92** J3
Igneada: Turkey **39** U16
Igneada, Cape: Turkey **39** V16
Igoumenitsa: Greece **39** R17
Iguaçú, Foz do: Brazil **96** E2
Iguaçú: *riv.* & *Nat. Park*, Brazil **96** E2
Iguaçú Falls: Brazil **96** E2
Iguala: Mexico **86** K14
Igualada: Spain **35** G16
Iguapé: Brazil **96** F1
Iguatu: Brazil **94** K5
Iguéla: Gabon **81** F5
Iguidi Erg: *desert*, Algeria **78** C4
Igula: Tanzania **76** D4
Iharhar: *watercourse*, Algeria **78** F4
Ihavandiffulu Atoll: Maldive Is. **58** M13
Ih Bogd Uul: *mtn.*, Mongolia **62** S6
Ihosy: Malagasy Rep. **73** O14
Ii: Finland **46** T4
Iida: Japan **63** e3
Iijo: *riv.*, Finland **46** U4
Ii Lake: Finland **46** V2
Iisalmi: Finland **46** U5
Ijebu Ode: Nigeria **81** E3
Ijmuiden: Netherlands **44** K3
Ijssel: *riv.*, Netherlands **44** M3
Ijsselmeer (Zuider Zee): *lag.*, Netherlands **44** L3
Ijui: & *riv.*, Brazil **96** E2
Ijuin: Japan **63** b5
Ijzendijke: Netherlands **44** J4
Ik: *riv.*, U.S.S.R. **50** H4
Ikaalinen: Finland **47** S6
Ikali: Zaire **76** B3
Ikamiut: Greenland **85** o4
Ikaria (Nikaria): *i.*, Greece **39** U18
Ikeda: Hokkaido, Japan **63** ZZ6
Ikeda: Osaka, Japan **63** d3
Ikeda: Tokushima, Japan **63** c3
Ikela: Zaire **76** B3
Ikelemba: Congo **81** H4
Ikelemba: *riv.*, Zaire **76** A2
Iken: Suff., England **25** Z15
Ikerasak: Greenland **85** o3
Ikerre: Nigeria **81** F3
Ikhtiman: Bulgaria **39** S15
Iki: *i.*, Japan **63** a4
Iki Strait: Japan **63** a4
Ikitsuki: Japan **63** a4
Ikom: Nigeria **81** F3
Ikoma: Tanzania **76** D3
Ikoo: Kenya **76** E3
Ikot Ekpene: Nigeria **81** F3
Ikoto: Sudan **76** D2
Ikryanoye: U.S.S.R. **50** G5
Iksa: *riv.*, U.S.S.R. **51** O3
Ikuchi Hu: *lake*, Tibet, China **59** P8
Ikungi: Tanzania **76** D4
Ikungu: Tanzania **76** D4
Ikuno: Japan **63** d3
Ikyâd: Egypt (Suez Canal *Inset*) **32** *Ins.*
Ilafok: Algeria **78** E5
Ilagan: Luzon, Philippines **64** G3
Ilaha: Heilungkiang, China **63** X5
Ilam: Nepal **59** P9
Ilam: *Governorate*, Iran (*cap.* Abdanan) **57** K5
Ilan: Heilungkiang, China **63** X5
Ilanskiy: U.S.S.R. **51** R3
Ilanz: Switzerland **40** P9
Ilaro: Nigeria **81** E3
Ilava: Czechoslovakia **43** Q12
Ilave: Peru **94** D7
Iława: Poland **43** Q10
Ilawka: U.S.S.R. **47** R9
Ilchester: Som., England **24** Q18
Ilderton: Northumb., Eng. **26** S9
Ile à la Crosse, Lake: Sask., Canada **92** F1
Ileanda: Romania **43** S13
Ilebo: Zaire **76** B3
Île-Bouchard, l': France **35** F8
Île-de-France: *Prov.*, France **34** H12
Île-d'Elle, l': France **37** E9
Ilek: *riv.*, U.S.S.R. **50** J4
Ilen: *riv.*, Cork, Repub. of Ireland **31** C16
Ilerda: Roman town and battlefield at Lérida, Spain **35** G16
Ilergetes: ancient tribe of district around Lérida, Sp. **35** G16
Île-Rousse: Corsica **38** L15
Ilford: Man., Canada **92** H1
Ilfracombe: Devon, England **24** N17
Ilgaz: & *mtns.*, Turkey **56** C1
Ilgin: Turkey **56** B2
Ilhabela: Brazil **96** F1
Ilhavo: Portugal **35** B16
Ilheus: Brazil **94** K6
Ili: Kazakh., U.S.S.R. **51** N6
Ili: *riv.*, U.S.S.R. China **51** N6
Ilia: Romania **39** S14
Iliamna: & *lake*, Alaska, U.S.A. **84** D6
Iliç: Turkey **56** F2
Il'ich: Uzbek., U.S.S.R. **51** L6
Il'ichovsk: Azerbaydzhan, U.S.S.R. **57** J2
Iligan: Mindanao, Phil. **64** G5
Ilikotu: Inner Mongolia, China **63** W5
Ilin: Philippines **64** G4
Il'intsy: Ukraine **50** C5
Iliodhromia (Alón): *i.*, N. Sporades, Greece **39** S17
Ilium: *see* Troy.
Illizi: Algeria **78** F4
Ilkeston: Derby., England **27** T14
Ilkley: W. Yorks., England **27** S12
Illampu: *mtn.*, Bolivia **94** D7
Illana Bay: Mindanao, Phil. **64** G5
Illapel: Chile **96** A3
Ille-et-Vilaine: *Dept.*, France (*cap.* Rennes) **36** D7
Illela: Niger **81** F2
Iller: *riv.*, W. Germany **40** Q7
Illertissen: W. Germany **40** Q7
Illescas: Spain **35** E16
Illescas: Uruguay **96** D3
Illettes, Bay de: La., U.S.A. **90** *Ins.*
Illiers: France **36** G7
Illimani: *mtn.*, Bolivia **94** D7
Illinois: *riv.*, Ill., U.S.A. **88** F6
Illinois: *State*, U.S.A. (*cap.* Springfield) **88** G5
Illnau: Switzerland **40** O8
Illo: Nigeria **81** E2
Illogan: Corn., England **24** L19
Ilm: *riv.*, E. Germany **45** R5
Ilmajoki: Finland **46** S5
Il'men', Lake: U.S.S.R. **50** D3
Ilmenau: E. Germany **45** Q5
Ilmenau: *riv.*, W. Germany **45** Q2
Ilmington: War., England **25** S15
Ilminster: Som., England **24** Q18
Ilo: Peru **94** C7
Iloilo: Philippines **64** G4
Ilomantsi: Finland **46** W5
Ilomba: Tanzania **76** D4
ILORIN: Kwara, Nigeria **81** E3
Ilovik: *i.*, Yugoslavia **41** U11
Ilovlya: U.S.S.R. **50** F5
Ilsenburg: E. Germany **45** Q4
Ilshofen: W. Germany **45** P6
Ilsington: Devon, England **24** O18
Ilsley, East & West: Berks., England **25** T16
Ilubabor: *Prov.*, Ethiopia (*cap.* Gore) **79** L8
Iluka: N.S.W., Australia **71** K7
Ilula: Tanzania **76** D3
Ilva: Roman name of island of Elba **38** M15
Ilwaco: Wash., U.S.A. **92** C3
Ilwaki: Wetar, Indonesia **65** H8
Ilyek: U.S.S.R. **50** H4
Iizuka: Japan **63** b4
Imabari: Japan **63** c3
Imala: Mozambique **77** E5
Imamzadeh Abbas: Iran **57** K5
Imandra, Lake: U.S.S.R. **46** X3
Imari: Japan **63** a4
Imatra: Finland **47** V6
Imbaimadai: Guyana **87** c8
Imber: Wilts., England **24** R17
Imbituba: Brazil **96** F2
Imbituva: Brazil **96** E2
Imboden: Ark., U.S.A. **88** F7
Imbros: *see* Imroz.
Imeni Kirova: U.S.S.R. **51** N6
Iméno: Gabon **81** G5
Imi: Ethiopia **76** F1
Imi N'Tanout: Morocco **80** K8
Imishli: Azerbaydzhan, U.S.S.R. **57** L2
Immarna: S. Australia **63** E6
Immenhausen: W. Germany **44** P4
Immenstadt: W. Germany **40** Q8
Immingham: Humb., Eng. **27** V12
Imola: Italy **41** R11
Imotski: Yugoslavia **38** P15
Imperatriz: Brazil **94** H5
Imperia: Italy **40** O12
Imperial: Nebr., U.S.A. **93** G4
Imperial Dam: Ariz., U.S.A. **93** E6
Imperial Valley: Calif., U.S.A. **93** D6
Imperieuse Reef: W. Austl. **68** B3
IMPFONDO: Likouala, Congo **81** H4
IMPHAL: Manipur, India **59** Q10
Imphy: France **37** J9
Impio Finland **46** U4
Impruneta: Italy **41** R12
Imrali: & *i.*, Turkey **39** V16
Imroz (Imbros): & *i.*, Turkey **39** T16
Imshash: *well*, Saudi Arabia **56** F6
Imst: Austria **41** Q8
Imuris: Mexico **93** E6
Imvani: S. Africa **75** G6
Ina: *riv.*, Poland **45** U2
Inamba: *i.*, Japan **63** f4
In Amguel: Algeria **78** F5
Inanda: *Dist.*, Natal, S. Afr. **75** J4
Inangahua Junction: South I., New Zealand **70** N15
Iñapari: Peru **94** D6
Inari: Finland **46** U2
Inari, Lake: Finland **46** U2
Inawashiro, Lake: Japan **63** g2
Inca: Majorca, Balearic Is. **35** H17
Incacamachi: *mtn.*, Chile **94** D7
Inca de Oro: Chile **96** B2
Incahuasi: *mtn.*, Argentina/Chile **96** B2
İnce, Cape: Turkey **56** D1
İncekum, Cape: Turkey **56** C3
Incesu: Turkey **56** D2
Inch: Kerry, Repub. of Irel. **31** B15
Inch: Wex., Repub. of Irel. **31** J14
Inchard, Loch: High., Scot. **28** L3
Inchbare: Tayside, Scotland **29** Q6
Inchcape Rock (Bell Rock): Scotland **29** R7
Inchigeelagh: Cork, Repub. of Ireland **31** C16
Inchike: *riv.*, Sinkiang, China **51** P6
Inch I.: Donegal, Repub. of Ireland **30** F9
Inchiri: *Dist.*, Mauritania (*cap.* Akjoujt) **78** A5
Inchkeith: *i.*, Firth of Forth, Scotland **29** P9
Inchmarnock: *i.*, Strathclyde, Scotland **29** L8
Inchnadamph: High., Scot. **28** M3
Inchon: S. Korea **63** X7
Inchture: Tayside, Scotland **29** P7
Inchtuthill: site of Roman camp on left bank of river Tay about 2 miles W. of Cargill, Tayside, Scotland **29** P6
Incomati: *riv.*, Mozambique **75** K2
Indaal, Loch: Inner Hebr., Scotland **29** J8
I-n-Dagouber: *well*, Mali **78** D5
Indal: & *riv.*, Sweden **46** P5
Indaw: Burma **59** R10
Inde: Mexico **93** F7
Independence: Calif., U.S.A. **93** D5
Independence: Iowa, U.S.A. **88** F4
Independence: Kans., U.S.A. **90** D7
Independence: La., U.S.A. **90** F10
Independence: Mo., U.S.A. **90** D6
Independence Fiord: Grnld. **85** R1
Independence Mtns.: Nev., U.S.A. **92** D4
Independencia: Argentina **96** B3
Inderacha: Ethiopia **76** E1
Inderagiri: *riv.*, Sumatra **65** C7
Inderborskiy: Kazakh., U.S.S.R. **50** H5

India: *Republic* **58/9**
Cap.: New Delhi
Area: 1,229,919 sq. miles (3,185,490 sq. km.)
Pop.: 547,367,926 (*1971 C*)
N.B. The area & population figures include the Indian-held part of Jammu & Kashmir.

Indiana: *State*, U.S.A. (*cap.* Indianapolis) **88** H6
INDIANAPOLIS: Ind., U.S.A. **88** H6
Indian Ocean **9**
Indian Head: Sask., Canada **92** G2
Indian Lake: N.Y., U.S.A. **89** O4
Indianola: Iowa, U.S.A. **88** E5
Indianola: Miss., U.S.A. **90** F9
Indiga: U.S.S.R. **48** f4
Indigirka: *riv.*, U.S.S.R. **49** q3
Indispensable Reefs: Coral Sea **67** M4

Indonesia: *Republic* **61** J12
Cap.: **Jakarta**
Area: **742,600 sq. miles (1,923,334 sq. km.)**
Pop.: **119,846,499 (*1971 C*)**

Indore: Madhya Prad., Ind. **58** N10
Indramayu: Java 65 D8
Indre: *riv.* & *Dept.*, France (*cap.* Châteauroux) **36** G9
Indre-et-Loire: *Dept.*, France (*cap.* Tours) **36** F8
Indre Fræna: Norway **46** K5
Indus: *riv.*, Pakistan/India **58** L9
Indwe: S. Africa **75** G5
Ine: Japan **63** d3
Inebolu: Turkey **56** C1
I-n-Edek: Niger **78** F6
Inegol: Turkey **56** A1
Ineu: Romania **43** R13
Inevi: Turkey **56** C2
Infantes: Spain **35** E17
I-n-Gall: Niger **81** F1
Ingatestone: Essex, England **25** W16
Ingende: Zaire **76** A3
Ingeniero Luiggi: Argentina **96** C4
Ingersoll: Ont., Canada **88** L4
Ingham: Queens., Australia **69** H3
Ingham: Suff., England **25** X15
Ingleborough: *mtn.*, N. Yorks., England **26** R11
Inglefield Land: Greenland **85** N2
Ingleside: Tex., U.S.A. **90** C12
Ingleton: N. Yorks., England **26** R11
Inglewood: Calif., U.S.A. **93** D6
Inglewood: North I., N.Z. **70** P14
Inglewood: Queens., Austl. **71** J7
Inglewood: Vict., Australia **71** E11
Inglewood Forest: *dist.*, Cumbria, England **26** Q10
Ingoldsby: Lincs., England **27** V14
Ingolfs Fiord: Greenland **85** S1
Ingolstadt: W. Germany **41** R7
Ingonish: N.S., Canada **89** V2
Ingram: Northumb., Eng. **26** S9
I-n-Guezzam: Algeria **78** F6
Inhacoro: Mozambique **77** D6
INHAMBANE: & *Dist.*, Mozambique **77** E7
Inhambane Bay: Mozam. **77** E7
Inhambane Dismur Game Reserve: Mozambique **75** K2
Inhambupe: Brazil **94** K6
Inhaminga: Mozambique **77** D6
Inharrime: Mozambique **77** E7
Ining: Sinkiang, China **51** O6
Inirida: *riv.*, Colombia **94** D3
Inishark: *i.*, Repub. of Ireland **30** A12
Inishbofin: *i.*, Repub. of Irel. **30** A12
Inishbofin: *i.*, Repub. of Irel. **30** E9
Inishcrone: Sligo, Repub. of Ireland **30** C11
Inisheer: *i.*, Aran Is., Repub. of Ireland **31** B13
Inishkea: *is.*, Repub of Irel. **30** A11
Inishkeen: Monaghan, Repub. of Ireland **30** H11
Inishmaan: *i.*, Aran Is., Repub. of Ireland **31** B13
Inishmore: *i.*, Aran Is., Repub. of Ireland **31** B13
Inishmurray: *i.*, Repub. of Ireland **30** D11
Inishowen Head: *cape*, Don., Repub. of Ireland **30** H9
Inishowen Penin.: Don., Repub. of Ireland **30** G9
Inishshark: *i.*, Repub. of Ireland **30** A12
Inishtrahull: *i.*, Repub. of Ireland **30** G9
Inishturk: *i.*, Repub. of Irel. **30** A12
Inistioge: Kilk., Repub. of Ireland **31** G15
Injune: Queens., Australia **70** H5
Inkberrow: Hereford & Worcester, England **24** S15
Inkerman: *(SE of Townsville)*. Queens., Australia **70** G2
Inkerman: *(G of Carpentaria)*. Queens., Austl. **69** G3
Inkisi: *riv.*, Zaire/Angola **81** H6
Inland Sea: Japan **63** c3
Inn: *riv.*, Austria **41** T7
Innamincka: S. Australia **69** G5
Innellan: Strath., Scotland **29** M8
Inner Hebrides: *is.*, Scotland **29** H7
Innerleithen: Borders., Scot. **29** P8
Inner Mongolia: *Aut. Reg.*, China [*cap.* Huhehot (Kweisui)] **62** U6
Inner Sound: Inner Hebr./ Scotland **28** K5
Innerwick: Lothian, Scot. **29** R8
Innfield: Meath, Repub. of Ireland **31** H13
Inning: W. Germany **41** R7
Innisfail: Queens., Australia **69** H3
INNSBRUCK: Tyrol, Austria **41** R8
Inntal: *valley* Austria **41** R8
Inny: *riv.*, Kerry, Repub. of Ireland **31** A16
Inny: *riv.*, Long./Westmeath, Repub. of Ireland **30** G12
Ino: Japan **63** c4
Inongo: Zaire **76** A3
Inonü: Turkey **56** B2
Inoucdjouac (Port Harrison): Que., Canada **85** M6
Inowrocław: Poland **43** Q10
Insch: Grampian, Scotland **28** Q5
Insein: Burma **59** R11
Inset: Norway **46** M5
Insh: Highland, Scotland **28** O5
Inshar: Nigeria **81** F3
Inskip: Lancs., England **27** Q12
Insterburg (Chernyakhovsk): U.S.S.R. **47** R9
Instow: Devon, England **24** N17
I-n-Tadreft: Niger **78** F6
Intae: Borneo **65** F7
Intepe: Turkey (Dardan. *Inset*) **20** *Ins.*
Interamna: Roman city at Terni, Italy **38** N15
Interamna: Roman city about 5 miles S. of Cassino, Italy **38** N16
Interamnia: Roman city at Teramo, Italy **38** N15
Interlaken: Switzerland **40** N9
International Falls: *city*, Minn., U.S.A. **88** E1
Interview: *i.*, Andaman Is. **59** Q12
Intiyaco: Argentina **96** C2
Intorsura: Buzăului, Rom. **39** U14
Introbio: Italy **40** P10
Intu: Borneo **65** F7
Inubo, Cape: Japan **63** g3
Inukai: Japan **63** b4
Inuvik: N.W.T., Canada **84** f4
Inver: Don., Repub. of Irel. **30** E10
Inver: Highland, Scotland **28** O4
Inver Alligin: High., Scot. **28** K4
Inverallochy: Grampian, Scot. **28** S4
Inveran: Highland, Scotland **28** N4
Inveraray: Strath., Scot. **29** L7
Inverarity: Tay., Scotland **29** Q6
Inverbervie: Gram., Scot. **28** R6
INVERCARGILL: Southland, New Zealand **71** M18
Inverdruie: High., Scotland **28** O5
Inverell: N.S.W., Australia **71** J7
Inverey: Gram., Scotland **28** O6
Invergarry: Highland, Scotland **28** M5
Invergordon: High., Scot. **28** N4
Inverharity: Tayside, Scot. **29** P6
Inverinate: High., Scot. **28** L5
Inverkeilor: Tay., Scotland **29** Q6
Inverkeithing: Fife, Scot. **29** P7
Inverkeithny: Gram., Scot. **28** Q4
Inverkip: Strath., Scotland **29** M8
Inverkirkaig: High., Scot. **28** L3
Invermoriston: High., Scot. **28** M5
Inverness: Cape Breton I., Canada **89** V2
INVERNESS: High., Scotland **28** N5
Invershin, Highland, Scotland **28** N4
Inverurie: Gram., Scotland **28** R5
Inverway: N. Territ., Austl. **68** D3
Investigator Gp.: S. Austl. **68** E6
Investigator Shoal: S. China Sea **64** E5
Investigator Str.: S. Australia **71** B10
Inya: U.S.S.R. **51** P4
Inyanga: Rhodesia **77** D6
Inyonga: Tanzania **76** D4
Inyo Range: Calif., U.S.A. **93** D5
Inzia: *riv.*, Zaire **81** H5
Ioánnina (Yannina): Grc. **39** R17
Iola: Kans., U.S.A. **90** D7
Iolotan: Turkmen., U.S.S.R. **51** K7
Ioma: New Guinea **69** H1
Iona: *i.*, Inner Hebr., Scot. **29** J7
Ion Corvin: Romania **39** U14
Ionia: Mich., U.S.A. **88** J4
Ionian Is.: Greece **39** R17
Ionian Sea: S. Europe **39** Q17

For Abbreviations see list on p.113. Italic type, e.g. *Ephesus*, refers to historical names not on maps. Capital letters, e.g. MADRID, show capitals of countries; small capital letters, e.g. CADIZ, show capitals of provinces, etc. General notes p.116.

Ionicești: Romania 39 T14
Iora: *riv.*, U.S.S.R. 57 K1
Ios: *i.*, Cyclades (Grc.) 39 T18
Iouavoulendé: Gabon 81 G4
Iovkovo: Bulgaria 39 V15
Iowa: *State*, U.S.A. *(cap.* Des Moines) 88 E4
Iowa: *riv.*, U.S.A. 88 E5
Iowa City: Iowa, U.S.A. 88 F5
Iowa Falls: *city*, Iowa, U.S.A. 88 E4
Iowa Park: Tex., U.S.A. 90 B9
Ipameri: Brazil 94 H7
Ipehum: Brazil 96 D1
Iphigenia Bay: Alaska, U.S.A. 84 f6
Ipiales: Colombia 94 B3
Ipin: Szechwan, China 62 S9
Ipiranga: Brazil 96 E1
Ipiros: *see* Epirus
Ipoa, Lake: Paraguay 96 D2
IPOH: Perak, Malaya, Malaysia 65 b11
Ippener: W. Germany 44 O3
Ipplepen: Devon, England 24 O19
Ippy: Cen. Afr. Rep. 76 B1
Ipsala: Turkey 39 U16
Ipstones: Staffs., England 27 S13
Ipswich: Queens., Australia 70 K6
IPSWICH: Suff., England 25 Y15
Ipu: Brazil 94 J4
Ipu: Sumatra 65 C7
Ipusukulu: Zambia 77 D5
Iquique: Chile 94 C8
Iquitos: Peru 94 C4
Iraconbo: Fr. Guiana 94 G2
Irafshan: Iran 55 K9
Irago Strait: Japan 63 e3
Iráklion (Candia): Crete 39 T19
Irak Pass: Afghanistan 55 L8

Iran: *Empire* 55 H8
Cap.: Tehran
Area: 636,363 sq. miles
1,648,180 sq. km.)
Pop.: 30,284,000 (1972 E)

Iran Mtns: Borneo 65 E7
Iranshahr (Fahrej): Iran 55 K9
Irapa: Venezuela 94 E1
Irapuato: Mexico 86 j13

Iraq: *Republic* 57 H5
Cap.: Baghdad
Area: 167,567 sq. miles
(433,999 sq. km.)
Pop.: 9,750,000 (1971 E)

Irará: Brazil 94 K6
Irazu: *volc.*, Costa Rica 86 I15
Irbeyskoye: U.S.S.R. 51 R3
IRBID: & *Dist.*, Jordan 55 b2
Irbit: U.S.S.R. 51 K3
Irchester: Northants., Eng. 25 U15
Ireby: Cumbria, England 26 P10

Ireland: *Republic* 30/1
Cap.: Dublin
Area: 26,600 sq. miles
(68,894 sq. km.)
Pop.: 2,978,248 (1971 C)

Ireland I.: Bermudas 87 Ins.
Iréna: Chad 76 A1
Irene: Trans., S. Africa 75 H2
Ireng: *riv.*, Braz./Guyana 87 d8
Iren Tala Steppe: Inner Mongolia, China 62 U6
Irgiz: Kazakh., U.S.S.R. 51 K5
Irgiz: *riv.*, Kazakh., U.S.S.R. 51 K5
Iri: S. Korea 63 X7
Irian, West: *Prov.*, Indonesia *(cap.* Jayapura) 61 M12
Irigoyen: Argentina 96 C3
IRINGA: & *Reg.*, Tanzania 76 E4
Iriomote: *i.*, (Jap.), China Sea 63 W10
Iriona: Honduras 86 L14
Irish Sea: Br. Isles 27 N12
Irituia: Brazil 94 H4
IRKUTSK: & *Reg.*, U.S.S.R. 49 M7
Irlam: Gt. Man., England 27 R13
Irmak: Turkey 56 C2
Iro, Cape: Japan 63 f3
Iroise: *bay*, France 36 A7
Iron Acton: Avon, England 24 R16
Iron Baron: S. Australia 71 B9
Iron Bridge: Salop, England 27 R14
Iron Gate: *defile*, Romania/ Yugoslavia 39 S14
Iron Knob: S. Australia 71 B9
Iron Monarch: S. Australia 71 B9
Iron Mountain: *city*, Mich., U.S.A. 88 G3
Iron River: *city*, Mich., U.S.A. 88 G2
Ironton: Mo., U.S.A. 88 F7
Ironton: Ohio, U.S.A. 88 K6
Ironwood: Mich., U.S.A. 88 F2
Iroquois Falls: *city*, Ont., Canada 88 L1
Irqa: Yemen P.D.R. 54 G12
Irrawaddy: *riv.*, Burma 59 R11
Irrawaddy: *State*, Burma *(cap.* Bassein) 59 Q11
Irt: *riv.*, Cumbria, England 26 P11
Irthing: *riv.*, Cumbria, England 26 Q10
Irthlingborough: Northants., England 25 U15
Irtysh: *riv.*, U.S.S.R. 51 L3
Irtyshsk: Kazakh., U.S.S.R. 51 N4
Irumu: Zaire 76 C2
Irun: Spain 37 D12
Irurzun: Spain 37 D13
Iruya: Argentina 96 B1
Irvine: Alta., Canada 92 E3
Irvine: Strath., Scotland 29 M8
Irvine: Ky., U.S.A. 88 K7
Irvinestown: Ferm., N. Irel. 30 F11
Irymple: Vict., Australia 71 E10
Isaacs: *riv.*, Queens., Austl. 70 H4
Isaba: Spain 37 E13
Isabelle, Point: *cape*, Mich., U.S.A. 88 H2
Isaccea: Romania 39 V14
Isachsen, Cape: N.W.T., Canada 84 J2
Isfjördhur: Iceland 46 b3
Isahaya: Japan 63 b4
Işalnita: Romania 39 S14
Isangi: Zaire 76 B2
Isar: *riv.*, W. Germany 41 S7
Isara: Roman name of river Isère, France 40 L10
Isarco: *riv.*, Italy 41 R9
Isca Dumnoniorum: Romano-British town at Exeter, Devon, England 24 O18
Isca Silurum: Roman camp at Caerleon, Gwent, Wales 24 Q16
Ischia: *i.*, Italy 38 N16
Ischl: Austria 41 T8
Isdell: *riv.*, W. Australia 68 D3
Isdud: Israel 55 a3
Ise: Japan 63 e3
Ise Bay: Japan 63 e3

Iseke: Tanzania 76 E4
Iseo: & *lake*, Italy 40 Q10
Isère: *riv.* & *Dept.*, France *(cap.* Grenoble) 40 L10
Iserlohn: W. Germany 44 N4
Isernia: Italy 38 O16
Isesaki: Japan 63 f2
Iset': *riv.*, U.S.S.R. 51 L3
Iseyin: Nigeria 81 E3
ISFAHÁN: & *Prov.*, Iran 55 H8
ISHA BAIDOA: Upper Juba, Somalia 79 N9
Ishan: Kwangsi Chuang, China 62 T10
Ishigaki: *i.* (Jap.), China Sea 63 W10
Ishikawa: *Pref.*, Japan *(cap.* Kanazawa) 63 e2
Ishiki: Japan 63 e3
Ishim: U.S.S.R. 51 L3
Ishim: *riv.*, U.S.S.R. 57 L3
Ishimbay: U.S.S.R. 50 J4
Ishinomaki: Japan 63 ZZ7
Ishioka: Japan 63 g2
Ishkashim: Afghanistan 51 M7
Ishliq: Iran 57 K3
Ishpeming: Mich., U.S.A. 88 H2
Isigny: France 36 D6
Işik Daği: *mtn.*, Turkey 56 C1
Isil'-Kul: U.S.S.R. 51 M3
Isiolo: Eastern, Kenya 76 E2
Isipingo: Natal, S. Africa 75 J4
Isipofu: Natal, S. Africa 75 J5
Isiro: Zaire 76 C2
Isis: Queens., Australia 70 K5
Isisford: Queens., Australia 69 G4
Iskelikòy (Karataş): Turkey 56 D4
Iskenderon: & *Gulf*, Turkey 56 E3
Iskilip: Turkey 56 D1
Isla: *riv.*, Tayside, Scotland 29 P6
Isla Cabellos: Uruguay 96 D3
Islâhiye: Turkey 56 E3
ISLAMABAD: Punjab, Pakistan 58 M8
Island Falls: *city*, Maine, U.S.A. 89 R2
Island Falls: *city*, Ont., Can. 88 L1
Island Lagoon: S. Australia 71 B8
Island Lake: Man., Canada 92 J2
Island Pond: *city*, Vt., U.S.A. 89 Q3
Islands, Bay of: Newf., Can. 85 t2
Islands, Bay of: North I., New Zealand 70 P12
Islay: *i. & sound*, Inner Hebr., Scotland 29 J8
Isle: *riv.*, France 37 F10
Isle Adam, I': France 36 H6
Isle au Pitre: La., U.S.A. 90 Ins.
Isle-de-Noé, I': France 37 F12
Iseham: Cambs., England 25 W15
Isle-Jourdain, I': Vienne, Fr., 37 F9
Isle-Jourdain, I': Gers., Fr. 37 G12
Isle of Whithorn: *village*, Dumfries & Galloway, Scotland 29 N10
Isle of Wight: *i.* & *Co.*, England *(co. town* Newport) 25 T18
Isle-sur-la-Sorgue, I': Fr. 37 L12
Isle-sur-le-Doubs, I': France 40 M8
Isle-sur-Serein, I': France 36 K8
Isle Verte: *town*, Que., Can. 89 R1
Islington: Gt. Ldn., England 25 V16
Islip: Oxon., England 25 T16
Islivig: Outer Hebr., Scot. 28 G3
Islon: Chile 96 A2
Ismail: U.S.S.R. 39 V14
Ismailia: Egypt (Suez Canal *Inset*) 32 Ins.
Ismaning: W. Germany 41 R7
Isna: Egypt 54 D9
Isny: W. Germany 40 Q8
Isojoki: Finland 47 R5
Isoka: Zambia 77 D5
Isola d'Scala: Italy 41 R10
Isolato: Italy 40 P9
Isonzo: *riv.*, Italy 41 T9
Ispagnac: France 37 J11
ISPARTA: & *Prov.*, Turkey 56 B3
Isperikh: Bulgaria 39 U15
Ispir: Turkey 57 G1

Israel: *Republic* 56 D6
Cap.: Tel Aviv - Jaffa
Area: 7,992 sq. miles
(20,699 sq. km.)
Pop.: 3,105,000 (1972 E)

Issachar: Israelite tribe which lived N. and W. of Beisan, Israel 55 b2
Issambres, Pointe des: *cape*, France 40 M12
Issano: Guyana 87 d8
Issia: Ivory Coast 80 C3
Issigeac: France 37 F11
Issineru: Guyana 87 c7
Issoire: France 37 J10
Issoudon: France 36 G9
Issus: Tanzania 76 D4
Is-sur-Tille: France 40 L8
Issus: plain and city on coast immediately NW. of pass leading SE. to Iskenderon, Turkey 56 E3
Issyk: Kazakh., U.S.S.R. 51 N6
Issyk-Kul': *lake*, Kirgiz., U.S.S.R. 51 N6
Issy-L'Evêque: France 37 J9
Ist: *i.*, Yugoslavia 41 U11
Istabulat: Iraq 57 H4
ISTANBUL: Istanbul Prov., Turkey (Bosporus *Inset*) 20 Ins.
istanbul: *Prov.*, Turkey *(cap* istanbul) 39 V16
Isthmia: Greece 39 S18
Istiaia (Xirokhóri): Euboea, Greece 39 S17
Istokpogo, Lake: Fla., U.S.A. 91 L12
Istra: *penin.*, Yugoslavia 41 T10
Istranca: Italy 41 S10
Istranca: Turkey 39 V16
Istranca Mtns: Turkey 39 U16
Istres: France 37 K12
Istrus: Greek city on island south of southernmost Danube mouth, Romania 39 V14
Isudan: New Guinea 69 J2
Isurium: Roman town at Aldborough 1 mile E. of Boroughbridge, N. Yorkshire, England 27 T11
Ita: Paraguay 96 D2
Itabaiainha: Brazil 94 K6
Itaberaba: Brazil 94 J6
Itabira: Brazil 94 J7
Itabuna: Brazil 94 K6
Itacoatiara: Brazil 94 F4
Itaeté: Brazil 94 J6
Itaituba: Brazil 94 F4
Itajaí: Brazil 96 F2
Itajubá: Brazil 96 F1
Itaka: Tanzania 77 D4

Itala: Somalia 79 R19
Italica: Roman town at Santiponce about 8 miles N. of Sevilla, Spain 35 D18

Italy: *Republic* 38
Cap.: Rome (Roma)
Area: 116,303 sq. miles
(301,225 sq. km.)
Pop.: 53,770,331 (1971 C)

Itambé: Brazil 94 J7
Itanhaém: Brazil 96 F1
Itapaci: Brazil 94 H6
Itapecuru: *riv.*, Brazil 94 J5
Itapecuru-Mirim: Brazil 94 J4
Itaperuna: Brazil 96 G1
Itapetininga: Brazil 96 F1
Itapeva: Brazil 96 F1
Itapipoca: Brazil 94 K4
Itapira: Brazil 94 K6
Itapiranga: Brazil 94 F4
Itapocu: Brazil 96 F2
Itaporanga: Brazil 96 F1
Itapuá: Brazil 96 E3
Itaqui: Brazil 96 D2
Itararé: Brazil 96 F1
Itarsi: Madhya Pradesh, India 58 N10
Itasca: Tex., U.S.A. 90 C9
Itatinga: Brazil 96 F1
Itbayat: *i.*, Philippines 64 G2
Itchen: & *riv.*, Hants., Eng. 25 T17
Itende: Tanzania 76 D4
Ithaca (Itháki): & *i.*, Ionian Is. (Grc.) 39 R17
Ithaca: N.Y., U.S.A. 89 N4
Itháki (Ithaca): & *i.*, Ionian Is. (Grc.) 39 R17
Itigi: Tanzania 76 D4
Itimbiri: *riv.*, Zaire 76 B2
Itivdleq: Greenland 85 o4
Itsukaichi: Japan 63 c3
Itta Bena: Miss., U.S.A. 90 F9
Ittiri: Sardinia 38 L16
Itu: Brazil 96 F1
Itu: Nigeria 81 F3
Ituiutaba: Brazil 94 H7
Itula: Zaire 76 C3
Itumbiara: Brazil 94 H7
Ituna: Roman name of river Solway, Scotland 26 O10
Itung: Kirin, China 63 X6
Ituraea: ancient Arab kingdom, including mounts Lebanon, Anti Lebanon, and Hermon, Lebanon and W. Syria 56 E5
Iturbe: Argentina 96 B1
Ituri: *riv.*, Zaire 76 C2
Iturup (Etorofu): *i.*, Kuril Is. 63 YY6
Ituxy: *riv.*, Brazil 94 D5
Ityai el Bárud: Egypt 56 B6
Itzawisis: S.W. Africa 74 C3
Itzehoe: W. Germany 44 P2
Itzer: Morocco 80 L8
Iudrio: *riv.*, Italy 41 T9
Iuka: Miss., U.S.A. 90 G8
Iuluti: Mozambique 77 E6
Iva: S.C., U.S.A. 91 K6
Ivai: *riv.*, Brazil 96 E1
Ivailovgrad: Bulgaria 39 U16
Ivalo: & *riv.*, Finland 46 U2
Ivanec: Yugoslavia 41 W9
Ivanić Grad: Yugoslavia 41 W10
Ivangrad: Yugoslavia 39 Q15
Ivanhoe: N.S.W., Australia 71 F9
Ivanjica: Yugoslavia 39 R15
Ivankovo: Ukraine 43 V11
Ivano-Frankovsk: Ukraine 43 T12
Ivanovo: Byelorussia 43 T10
IVANOVO: & *Reg.*, U.S.S.R. 50 F3
Ivanteyevka: U.S.S.R. 50 G4
Ivantsevichi: Byelorussia 43 T10
Ivdel': U.S.S.R. 51 K2
Iver: Bucks., England 25 U16
Ivigtut: Greenland 85 P5
Ivindo: *riv.*, Gabon 81 G4
Iviza (Ibiza): *i.*, Balearic Is. (Sp.) 35 G17
Ivrea: Italy 40 N10
Ivrindi: Turkey 39 U17
Ivry: France 36 G7
Ivybridge: Devon, England 24 O19
Ivychurch: Kent, England 25 X17
Iv'ye: Byelorussia 43 T10
Iwade: Kent, England 25 X17
Iwaki: Japan 63 g2
Iwakuni: Japan 63 c3
Iwanai: Japan 63 ZZ6
Iwanuma: Japan 63 g1
Iwataki: Japan 63 d3
Iweibid Station: Egypt (Suez Canal *Inset*) 32 Ins.
Iwerne Minster: Dorset, England 24 R18
Iwo: Nigeria 81 E3
Iwo Jima (Naka): *i.*, Kazan. Is. 60 N7
Iwon: N. Korea 63 X6
Iwu: Chekiang, China 63 W9
Iwu: Sinkiang, China 62 Q6
Ixopo: & *Dist.*, Natal, S. Africa 75 J5
Ixtaccihuatl: *volc.*, Mexico 86 K14
Ixtepec: Mexico 86 K14
Ixtlán del Rio: Mexico 86 j13
Ixworth: Suff., England 25 X15
Iya: Japan 63 c3
Iyo Gulf: Japan 63 c4
Iž: *i.*, Yugoslavia 41 V11
Izabal, Lake: Guatemala (Belize. *Inset*) 86 Ins.
Izberbash: U.S.S.R. 50 G6
Izegem: Belgium 44 J5
Izeh: Iran 57 L6
IZHEVSK: Udmurt A.S.S. Repub., U.S.S.R. 50 H3
Izhma: U.S.S.R. 48 G4
Izinzac: France 36 B8
Izmail: Ukraine 39 V14
İZMIR: & *Prov.*, Turkey 39 U17
Izmir Gulf: Turkey 39 U17
İZMIT: Kocaeli, Turkey 56 A1
Izmit Gulf: Turkey 39 V16
Iznallos: Spain 35 E18
Iznik: & *lake*, Turkey 56 A1
Izola: Yugoslavia 41 T10
Izu: Syria 56 E5
Izu Is.: Japan 63 f3
Izumi: Japan 63 b4
Izu Penin.: Japan 63 f3
Izvestiy Tsik Is.: U.S.S.R. 48 K2
Izvestkovy: Kazakh., U.S.S.R. 51 N4
Izvilinka: U.S.S.R. 63 Y6
Izyaslav: Ukraine 43 U11
Izyum: Ukraine 50 E5
'Izz: Oman 55 J10

Jabal: *see note under Jebel.*
Jabal Abyadh: *mtn.*, Saudi Arabia 54 F9
Jabal Akhdar: *mtn.*, Oman 55 J10
Jabal Anaiza: *mtn.*, Iraq 56 F5
Jabal Faya: *mtn.*, United Arab Emirates 55 J9
Jabal Hafit: *mtn.*, Oman 55 J10
Jabal Hamra: *mtn.*, Saudi Arabia 54 E10
Jabal Ja'alan: *mtn.*, Oman 55 J10
Jabal Kaur: *mtn.*, Oman 55 J10
Jabalon: *riv.*, Spain 35 E17
Jabalpur *see* Jubbulpore
Jabal Shammar: *geog. reg.*, Saudi Arabia 54 F9
Jabal Shefa: *hills*, Saudi Arabia 54 E9
Jabal Sinjar: *range*, Iraq 57 G3
Jabal Tuwaiq: *range*, Saudi Arabia 54 G10
Jabbok: ancient name of tributary to left bank of river Jordan with confluence 17 miles NNE. of Jericho, Jordan 55 b2
Jabesh-Gilead: city of ancient Israel about 8 miles W. of Ajlun, Jordan 55 b2
Jablanac: Yugoslavia 41 U11
Jablanac, Cape: Cres., Yugo. 41 U10
Jablonec: Czechoslovakia 45 V5
Jablonné: Czechoslovakia 45 W5
Jablunkov: Czechoslovakia 43 Q12
Jaboatão: Brazil 94 K5
Jabonga: Mindanao, Phil. 64 H5
Jabrin: Oman 55 J10
Jabrin: Saudi Arabia 55 G10
Jabukovac: Yugoslavia 39 S14
Jaca: Spain 35 F15
Jacareí: Brazil 96 F1
Jacarèzinho: Brazil 96 F1
Jáchal: Argentina 96 B3
Jáchymov: Czechoslovakia 45 S5
Jacksboro: Tex., U.S.A. 90 B9
Jackson: Ala., U.S.A. 91 H10
Jackson: Calif., U.S.A. 93 C5
Jackson: Ga., U.S.A. 91 K9
Jackson: Ky., U.S.A. 88 K7
JACKSON: Miss., U.S.A. 90 F9
Jackson: Mich., U.S.A. 88 J4
Jackson: Mo., U.S.A. 88 G7
Jackson: Ohio, U.S.A. 88 K6
Jackson: Queens., Australia 70 H6
Jackson: Tenn., U.S.A. 88 H7
Jackson: Wyo., U.S.A. 92 E4
Jacksonville: Ala., U.S.A. 91 J9
Jacksonville: Ark., U.S.A. 90 E8
Jacksonville: Fla., U.S.A. 91 L10
Jacksonville: Ill., U.S.A. 88 F6
Jacksonville: N.C., U.S.A. 91 N8
Jacksonville: Tex., U.S.A. 90 D10
Jacksonville Beach: *city*, Fla., U.S.A. 91 L10
Jacmel: Haiti 87 m14
Jacobabad: Sind, Pakistan 58 L9
Jacobecua: Mozambique 77 D7
Jacobina: Brazil 94 J6
Jacobsdal: & *Dist.*, O.F.S., S. Africa 75 F4
Jacobstow: Corn., England 24 M18
Jacques Cartier: Que., Can. 89 P3
Jacques Cartier, Mt.: Can. 89 T1
Jacquet River: N.B., Canada 89 S2
Jacuí: *riv.*, Brazil 96 E2
Jade Bay: W. Germany 44 O2
JAEN: & *Prov.*, Spain 35 E18
Jafarabad: Iran 57 L4
Jaffa: Israel, *see* Tel Aviv-Jaffa.
Jaffa, Cape: S. Australia 71 C11
Jaffna: Ceylon 58 O13
Jafr: Jordan 56 E6
Jafura: *desert*, Saudi Arabia 55 H10
Jagdalpur: Madhya Pradesh, India 58 O11
Jagersfontein: O.F.S., S. Afr. 75 F4
Jagfontein: Trans., S. Africa 74 M Ins.
Jaghaur: *riv.*, China 62 R7
Jagst: *riv.*, W. Germany 44 P6
Jagtial: Andhra Pradesh, India 58 N11
Jaguarão: Brazil 96 E3
Jaguari: Brazil 96 E2
Jaguariaíva: Brazil 96 F1
Jaguaruna: Brazil 96 F2
Jague: Argentina 96 B2
Jaime Prats: Argentina 96 B3
JAIPUR: Rajasthan, India 58 N9
Jais: Uttar Pradesh, India 58 O9
Jaisalmer: Rajasthan, India 58 M9
Jajarm: Iran 55 J7
Jajce: Yugoslavia 38 P14
Jajpur: Orissa, India 59 P10
Jakalswater: S.W. Africa 74 A1
Jakarta: *see* Djakarta
Jakhal: Haryana, India 58 N9
Jäkkvik: Sweden 46 P3
Jakobshavn: Greenland 85 o4
Jakobstadt: *see* Pietarsaari
Jal: N. Mex., U.S.A. 93 G6
Jalajil: Saudi Arabia 54 G9
JALALABAD: *see* Jalal-Kut
Jal al Batin: *escarp.*, Iraq 57 J7
Jalal-Kut: Nangahar: Afghan. 58 M8
Jalapa: Mexico 86 K14
Jalapa: Nicaragua 86 L15
Jaleswar: Nepal 59 P9
Jalgaon: Maharashtra, India 58 N10
Jalingo: Nigeria 81 G3
Jalkot: NW. Front. Prov., Pakistan 58 M7
Jalna: Maharashtra, India 58 N11
Jalogir: Iran 57 K5
Jalón: *riv.*, Spain 35 F16
Jalo Oasis: Libya 79 J4
Jalor: Rajasthan, India 58 M9
Jalpaiguri: W. Bengal, India 59 P9
Jalq: Iran 55 K9
Jama: Tunisia 38 L18

Jamaica: *Commonwealth* 86 Ins.
Cap.: Kingston
Area: 4,411 sq. miles
(11,424 sq. km.)
Pop.: 1,897,000 (1971 E)

Jamaike: Surinam 94 G3
Jamalpur: Bangladesh 59 P10
Jaman Tau: *mtn.*, Kirgiz., U.S.S.R. 51 M6
Jamberoo: N.S.W., Austl. 71 J10
Jambin: Queens., Australia 70 J5

James: *riv.*, S. Dak., U.S.A. 92 H4
James: *riv.*, Va., U.S.A. 89 M7
James Bay: Canada 85 I 7
Jameson Land: Greenland 85 r3
Jameson Park: Trans., S. Afr. 74 N Ins.
Jamesport: Mo., U.S.A. 88 E6
James Ross Str.: N.W.T., Canada 84 K3
Jamestown: Leit., Repub. of Ireland 30 E12
Jamestown: N.Y., U.S.A. 89 M4
Jamestown: N. Dak., U.S.A. 92 H3
Jamestown: S. Africa 75 G5
Jamestown: S. Australia 71 C9
Jamestown: Tenn., U.S.A. 88 J7
Jamiltepec: Mexico 86 K14
Jamkhandi: Karnataka, India 58 N11
Jamkhed: Maharashtra, India 58 N11
JAMMU: *winter cap.* of Indian-held territory, Jammu & Kashmir, 58 M8
Jammu & Kashmir: *State*, sovereignty disputed between India & Pakistan [*cap.* of Indian-held territory: Srinagar (summer); Jammu (winter); cap of Pakistan-held territory Muzaffarabad) 58 N8
Jamnagar: *see* Navanagar
Jamnia: Hellenistic city at Yibna, Israel 55 a3
Jamno, Lake: Poland 45 W1
Jämsä: Finland 47 T6
Jamshedpur: Bihar, India 59 P10
Jamtland: Co., Sweden *(cap.* Ostersund) 46 O5
Janara: Kuwait 57 K7
Janda, Lake: Spain (Gib. *Inset*) 32 Ins.
Jandaq: Iran 55 H8
Jandowae: Queens., Austl. 70 J6
Janesville: Wis., U.S.A. 88 G4
Janettown: Highland., Scot. 28 P3
Jani-Khel: Afghanistan 58 L8
Jan Mayen I.: (Nor.), Arc. O. 8 70N 10W
Jánoshalma: Hungary 43 Q13
Janovice: Czechoslovakia 45 T6
Janów Lubelski: Poland 43 S11
Janów Podlaski: Poland 43 S10
Jansenville: & *Dist.*, S. Afr. 75 F6
Janteinmiao: Inner Mongolia, China 62 V5
Januária: Brazil 94 J7
Janville: France 36 G7
Janzé: France 36 D8
Jaochow (Poyang): Kiangsi, China 62 V9
Jaoho: Heilungkiang, China 63 Y5
Jaora: Madhya Pradesh, India 58 N10

Japan: *Empire* 63 Z7
Cap.: Tokyo
Area: 143,574 sq. miles
(371,857 sq. km.)
Pop.: 105,529,000 (1972 E)

Japan, Sea of: Asia 63 Y7
Japan Trench: N. Pacific Ocean 7 30N 140E
Japonesa, La: Argentina 96 B4
Japurá: *riv.*, Brazil 94 D4
Jarabub: Libya 33 G6
Jaraga: Queens., Australia 70 G3
Jaraguá: Goiás, Brazil 94 H7
Jaraguá: Sta. Catarina, Braz. 96 F2
Jaraito, El: Mexico 93 G7
Jaramillo: Argentina 95 D13
Jarandilla: Spain 35 D16
Jardines de la Reina: *is.*, Cuba 87 M13
Jargeau: France 36 G8
Jari: *riv.*, Brazil 94 G3
Jaria Jhanjail: Bangladesh 59 Q9
Jarmen: E. Germany 45 T2
Jarnac: France 37 E10
Jarny: France 36 L6
Jarocin: Poland 43 P11
Jaromeř: Czechoslovakia 45 V5
Jarosław: Poland 43 S11
Jarrahi: *riv.*, Iran 57 L6
Jarrow: Tyne & Wear, Eng. 26 T10
Jarú: Brazil 94 E6
Järva-Jaani: Estonia, U.S.S.R. 47 T7
Järvenpää: Finland 46 V2
Jasin: Malaya, Malaysia 65 c12
Jask: Iran 55 J9
Jasfo: Poland 43 R12
Jason Is.: Falkland Is. 95 E14
Jasonville: Ind., U.S.A. 88 H6
Jasper: Ala., U.S.A. 91 H9
Jasper: & *nat. park*, Alta., Can. 92 D2
Jasper: Fla., U.S.A. 91 K10
Jasper: Ind., U.S.A. 88 H6
Jasper: La., U.S.A. 90 E10
Jasper: Mo., U.S.A. 90 D7
Jasper: Tex., U.S.A. 90 E10
Jassan: Iraq 57 J5
Jastrebarsko: Yugoslavia 41 V10
Jastrowie: Poland 43 P10
Jászárokszállás: Hungary 43 Q13
Jászberény: Hungary 43 Q13
Jászladany: Hungary 43 R13
Jatai: Brazil 94 G7
Jath: Maharashtra, India 58 N11
Jativa: Spain 35 F17
Jatobal: Brazil 94 H4
Jat Poti: Afghanistan 58 L8
Jatznick: E. Germany 45 T2
Jaud: Yemen P.D.R. 55 G12
Jauf: Yemen 54 F11
Jauhari: Yemen P.D.R. 55 H11
Jauja: Peru 94 B6
Jaulnay: France 37 F9
Jaunpiebalga: Latvia 47 U8
Jaunpur: Uttar Prad. Ind. 59 O9
Jaunsaras: Spain 37 D13
Java: *i.*, Indonesia 65 D8
Java Head: *cape*, Java 65 D8
Java Head National Park: Java 65 D8
Java Sea: Indonesia 65 E7
Java Trench: Indian Ocean 9 10S 105E
Javron: France 36 E7
Jawan: Iraq 57 G3
Jawor: Poland 45 W4
Jazir: Oman 55 J11
Jazira, Al: *geog. reg.*, Iraq 57 H4
Jbail: Lebanon 56 D4
J.B. Arruābarrena (San Jaime): Argentina 96 D3
Jeanerette: La., U.S.A. 90 F11
Jebba: Nigeria 81 E3
Jebbul: & *lake*, Syria 56 E4
Jebel: Arabic for 'mountain' (for mountain names in Saudi Arabia and Iraq see under Jabal).
Jebel Arkenu: Libya 54 B10
Jebel Asoteriba: *mtn.*, Sudan 54 E10
Jebel Babein: Libya/Egypt 54 C10

152 Jebelein—Kameldoorn

Jebelein: Sudan **54** D12
Jebel esh Sharqi (Anti Lebanon): *mtns.*, Lebanon/Syria **56** D5
Jebel Hamata: *mtn.*, Egypt **54** E10
Jebel Hamoyet: *mtn.*, Sudan/Ethiopia **54**/E11
Jebel Haraza: *mtn.*, Sudan **54** D11
Jebel Katherina (Mt. Sinai): *mtn.*, Egypt **54** D9
Jebel Liban: *mtns.*, Lebanon **56** D5
Jebel Oda: *mtn.*, Sudan **54** E10
Jebel 'Uweinat: *mtn.*, Libya/Egypt **54** C10
Jebene: Djibouti 79 Q17
Jeble: Syria **56** D4
Jedabia: Lybia **33** G5
Jedburgh: Bord., Scotland **29** Q9
Jedi: *watercourse*, Algeria **78** E3
Jedrzejów: Poland **43** R11
Jeetze: *riv.*, E./W. Germany **45** R2
Jefferson: Gal., U.S.A. **91** K8
Jefferson: Iowa, U.S.A. **92** J4
Jefferson: Tex., U.S.A. **90** D9
Jefferson: Wis., U.S.A. **88** G4
Jefferson: *riv.*, Mont., U.S.A. **92** E3
Jefferson, Mt.: U.S.A. **92** C4
JEFFERSON CITY: Mo., U.S.A. **88** E6
Jefferson City: Tenn., U.S.A. **88** K7
Jeffersonville: Ind., U.S.A. **88** J6
Jeffreston: Dyfed, Wales **24** M16
Jeffreys Bay: *town*, S. Africa **75** F7
Jega: Nigeria **81** E2
Jehol: Hopeh, China **62** V6
Jehol: *Prov.* (now absorbed in Liaoning, Hopeh and Inner Mongolia), China
Jėkabpils: Latvia, U.S.S.R. **47** T8
Jekyll: *i.*, Ga., U.S.A. **91** L10
Jelebu (Kuala Klawang): Malaya, Malaysia **65** c12
Jelenia Góra: Poland **45** V5
Jelib: Somalia **79** N9
Jellicoe: Ont., Canada **85** L8
Jemappes: Belgium **44** J5
Jembongan: *i.*, Sabah, Malaysia **65** F5
Jemimaville: High., Scot. **28** N4
Jemnice: Czechoslovakia **45** V6
Jena: E. Germany **45** R5
Jenbach: Austria **41** R8
JENDOUBA: & *Governorate*, Tunisia **38** L18
Jenin: Jordan **55** b2
Jenkins: Ky., U.S.A. **88** K7
Jenks: Okla., U.S.A. **90** D7
Jennings: La., U.S.A. **90** E10
Jenolan Caves: N.S.W., Australia **71** J9
Jensen: Utah, U.S.A. **93** F4
Jeparit: Vict., Australia **71** E11
Jeppo: Finland **46** S5
Jequié: Brazil **94** J6
Jequitinhonha: & *riv.*, Brazil **94** J7
Jerablus: Syria **56** F3
Jerantut: Malaya, Malaysia **65** c12
Jerash: Jordan **55** b2
Jérémie: Haiti **87** m14
Jerez de la Frontera: Spain **35** C18
Jerez de los Caballeros: Sp. **35** C17
Jericho: Jordan **55** b3
Jericho: Queens., Australia **69** H4
Jericho: Trans., S. Africa **75** G2
Jerichow: E. Germany **45** S3
Jerilderie: N.S.W., Australia **71** F10
Jersey: *i.*, Channel Is. (Br.), (*cap.* St. Helier) **25** *Ins.*
Jersey City: N.J., U.S.A. **89** O5
Jersey Shore: *city*, Pa., U.S.A. **89** N5
Jerseyville: Ill., U.S.A. **88** F6
Jerúmenha: Brazil **94** J5
JERUSALEM: Israel/Jordan (*cap.* of Al Quds District of Jordan) **55** b3
Jervis Bay: N.S.W., Austl. **71** J10
Jersenice: Slovenia, Yugo. **41** U9
Jessains: France **36** K7
Jesselton: *see* Kota Kinabalu.
Jessen: E. Germany **45** S4
Jessore: Bangladesh **59** P10
Jesup: Ga., U.S.A. **91** L10
Jesús Carranza: Mexico **86** K14
Jesús Maria: Argentina **96** C3
Jethou: *i.*, Chan. Is. **25** *Ins.*
Jetpur: Gujarat, India **58** M10
Jeumont: France **36** K5
Jevenstedt: W. Germany **44** P1
Jever: W. Germany **44** N2
Jevnaker: Norway **47** M6
Jewish Auton. Reg.: U.S.S.R. (*cap.* Birobidzhan) **63** Y5
Jezerane: Yugoslavia **41** V10
Jezreel: Biblical name of valley NNW. of Jenin and E. of Afula, Israel **55** b2
Jhabua: Madhya Pradesh, India **58** M10
Jhalawar: Rajasthan, India **58** N10
Jhang Maghiana: Punjab, Pakistan **58** M8
Jhansi: Uttar Pradesh, India **58** N9
Jhelum: Punjab, Pakistan **58** M8
Jhelum: *riv.*, Pakistan/India **58** M8
Jhunjhunu: Rajasthan, India **58** N9
Jiado: Libya **32** E5
Jibhalanta (Uliastay): Mongolia **62** R5
Jibila: Tangier (Gib. *Inset)* **32** *Ins.*
Jibou: Romania **43** S13
Jičin: Czechoslovakia **45** V5
Jidali: *watercourse*, Somalia **79** R17
Jidda: Ethiopia **79** M8
Jidda: Saudi Arabia **54** E10
Jiddat Harasis: *plain*, Oman **55** J11
Jihchao: Shantung, China **62** V7
Jihkatse (Shigatse): Tibet, China **59** P9
Jihlava: Czechoslovakia **45** V6
Jihlava: *riv.*, Czechoslovakia **45** W6
Jihočesky: *Reg.*, Czechoslovakia (*cap.* České Budějovice) **45** U6
Jihomoravsky: *Reg.*, Czechoslovakia (*cap.* Brno) **45** V6
Jihtu: Tibet, China **58** N8
Jijiga: Ethiopia **79** Q18
Jilei: Somalia **79** R19
Jilemnice: Czechoslovakia **45** V5
Jilida: *plain*, Saudi Arabia **54** G11
Jimasa: Sinkiang, China **51** P6
Jiménez: Mexico **93** G7
JIMMA: Kėfa, Ethiopia **79** M8
Jindabyne: N.S.W., Austl. **71** H11
Jindřichův Hradec: Czech. **45** V6
JINJA: Busoga, Uganda **76** D2
Jisr Esh Shughur: Syria **56** E4
Jitin: *mtn.*, Kirgiz., U.S.S.R. **51** N6
Jitra: Malaya, Malaysia **65** b10
Jiu: *riv.*, Romania **39** S14
Jiza: Jordan **55** b3
Jizera: *riv.*, Czechoslovakia **45** U5
Jizerskė Hory: *mtns.*, Czech. **45** V5
Jizl: *wadi*, Saudi Arabia **54** E9
Joaçaba: Brazil **96** E2
Joachimsthal: E. Germany **45** T3
Joadja Creek: *town*, N.S.W., Australia **71** J10
Joal: Senegal **80** A2
JOÃO PESSOA: Paraiba, Brazil **94** L5
João Pinheiro: Brazil **94** H7
Joapemi: Brazil **96** D1
Joaquin Valley: Calif., U.S.A. **93** C5
Jochberg: Austria **41** S8
Jochiang: Sinkiang, China **48** K10
Jocoli: Argentina **96** B3
Jodhpur: Rajasthan, India **58** M9
Jodoigne: Belgium **44** K5
JOENSUU: Pohjois-Karjala, Finland **46** V5
Jof, El: Libya **79** J5
Jofane: Mozambique **77** D7
Jofra Oasis: Libya **78** H4
Jogboi: Ghana **80** D3
Joge: Japan **63** c3
Joggins: N.S., Canada **89** T3
Jogindarnagar: Himachal Pradesh, India **58** N8
Jogjakarta: *see* **Yogyakarta**
Johana: Japan **63** e2
Johannesburg: Trans., S. Afr. **74** *Ins.*
Johann-Georgenstadt: E. Ger. **45** S5
John Day: & *riv.*, Oreg., U.S.A. **92** D4
John H. Kerr Res.: N.C./Va., U.S.A. **91** M7
John o' Groats: High., Scot. **28** P2
Johnshaven: Gram., Scotland **29** R6
Johnsonburg: Pa., U.S.A. **89** M5
Johnson City: Tenn., U.S.A. **88** K7
Johnson Peak: *mtn.*, Mexico **93** E7
Johnston: Dyfed, Wales **24** M16
Johnston City: Ill., U.S.A. **88** G7
Johnstone: Strath., Scotland **29** M8
Johnstone Lake: Sask., Canada **92** F2
Johnston Falls: *see* Mambiliama Falls
Johnston I.: (U.S.A.), N. Pacific Ocean **7** 15N 170W
Johnston Lake: W. Australia **68** C6
Johnstown: Kild., Repub. of Ireland **31** H13
Johnstown: Kilk., Repub. of Ireland **31** F14
Johnstown: Pa., U.S.A. **89** M5
John's Town: Dyfed, Wales **24** N16
Johore: *riv.*, Malaya, Malaysia **65** c13
Johore: *State*, Malaysia (*cap.* Johore Bahru) **65** c12
JOHORE BAHRU: Johore, Malaya, Malaysia **65** c13
Joigny: France **36** J8
Joinville: Brazil **96** F2
Joinville: France **36** L7
Joinville I.: Antarctica **9** 65S 60W
Jokar: Iran **57** L4
Jokkmokk: Sweden **46** Q3
Joliet: Ill., U.S.A. **88** G5
Joliette: Que., Canada **89** P2
Jolo: & *i.*, Sulu Arch., Phil. **65** G5
Jomo: Tanzania **76** D3
Jones, Cape: Que., Canada **85** M7
Jonesboro: Ark., U.S.A. **90** F8
Jonesboro: Ill., U.S.A. **88** G7
Jonesboro: La., U.S.A. **90** E9
Jonesborough: Armagh, N. Ireland **30** J11
Jones Sound: N.W.T., Can. **85** L2
Jonesville: La., U.S.A. **90** F10
Jongka: Tibet, China **59** P9
Jonglei: Sudan **76** D1
Jonkergrab: S.W. Africa **74** B1
JÖNKÖPING: & *Co.*, Sweden **47** O8
Jonquière: Que., Canada **89** Q1
Jonzac: France **37** E10
Joplin: Mo., U.S.A. **90** D7
Joppa: ancient name of Jaffa, Israel **55** a2
Jordan: Mont., U.S.A. **92** F3
Jordan: *riv.*, Israel/Jordan **56** D5

Jordan: *Kingdom* **54** E8
Cap. Amman
Area: 37,297 sq. miles (96,599 sq. km.)
Pop.: 2,418,000 (*1972 E*)

Jordan, East: Mich., U.S.A. **88** J3
Jordan Dam: Ala., U.S.A. **91** H9
Jordan Valley: *city*, Oreg., U.S.A. **92** D4
Jorhat: Assam, India **59** Q9
Jorm: Sweden **46** O4
Jörn: Sweden **46** R4
Jos: Plateau, Nigeria **81** F3
José Baille y Ordoñez: Uruguay **96** D3
José de San Martin: Argentina **95** C12
José Maria Blanco: Argentina **96** C4
Jose Pañganiban: Luzon, Philippines **64** G4
Joseph: Oreg., U.S.A. **92** D3
Joseph, Lake: Ont., Canada **89** M3
Joseph Bonaparte Gulf: W. Australia **68** D2
Joshimath: Uttar Pradesh, India **58** N8
Joshua Tree Nat. Mon.: Calif., U.S.A. **93** D6
Jos Plateau: Nigeria **81** F2
Jossa: W. Germany **44** P5
Josselin: France **36** C8
Jostadals Breen: *mtns.*, Nor. **47** K6
Jotapata: fortress of Herodian period about 10 miles N. of Nazareth, Israel **55** b2
Jotunheimen: *mtns.*, Norway **47** L6
Joubertina: S. Africa **74** E6
Joubertskroon: Trans., S. Africa **75** H1
Joué-lès-Tours: France **36** F8
Joué-sur-Erdre: France **36** D8
Jourdanton: Tex., U.S.A. **90** B11
Joutsa: Finland **47** U6
Jouy: France **36** G7
Jovita: Argentina **96** C3
Jowzjan: *Prov.*, Afghanistan (*cap.* Shibarghan) **55** L7
Joya: La., Mexico **93** F7
Joyce's Country: *dist.*, Galway, Repub. of Ireland **30** B12
Joyeuse: France **37** K11
Juan Aldama: Mexico **93** G8
Juan de Fuca, Str. of: Canada/U.S.A. **92** C3
Juan E. Barra: Argentina **96** C4
Juan Fernández Is.: Chile, Pacific O. **95** A10
Juani I: Tanzania **76** E4
Juárez: Argentina **96** D4
Juárez, Sierra de: *range*, Lower Calif., Mexico **93** D6
Juaso: Ghana **80** D3
Juàzeiro: Brazil **94** J5
Juàzeiro do Norte: Brazil **94** K5
JUBA: Equatoria, Sudan **76** D2
Juba: *riv.*, Somalia **76** F2
Jubail: Saudi Arabia **55** G9
Jubbulpore (Jabalpur): Madhya Pradesh, India **58** N10
Jübek: W. Germany **44** P1
Júcar: *riv.*, Spain **35** F17
Júcaro: Cuba **87** M13
Juchitán: Mexico **86** K14
Judaea: New Testament district name, *Palestine* **55** a3
Judah: Israelite tribe which inhabited hills around Hebron, Jordan **55** b3
Judaidat 'Ar'ar: *well*, Iraq/Saudi Arabia **57** G6
Judenburg: Austria **41** U8
Judith Point: R.I., U.S.A. **89** Q5
Judsonia: Ark., U.S.A. **90** F8
Jugjur Range: U.S.S.R. **49** p6
Jugon: France **36** C7
Juilly: France **36** H6
Juimand (Jumin): Iran **55** J8
Juist: *i.*, E. Frisian Is., W. Ger. **44** M2
Juiz de Fora: Brazil **96** G1
JUJUY: & *Prov.*, Argentina **96** B1
Jukao: Kiangsu, China **63** W8
Juktan: *riv.*, Sweden **46** P4
Julaca: Bolivia **94** D8
Julesburg: Colo., U.S.A. **93** G4
Julia Creek: Queens., Austl. **69** G4
Julian Alps: Italy/Yugoslavia **41** T9
Juliana Peak: W. Irian, Indonesia **66** H2
Julianehaab: Greenland **85** P5
Julianstown: Meath, Repub. of Ireland **30** J12
Jülich: W. Germany **44** M5
Julier Pass: Switzerland **40** P9
Julimes: Mexico **93** F7
Júlio de Castilhos: Brazil **96** E2
Julio, 9 de: Argentina **95** E11
Jullundur: Punjab, India **58** N8
Jumaima: *well*, Iraq/Arabia **57** H7
Jum'at al Qa'ara: *geog. reg.*, Iraq **57** G5
Jumbo: Somalia **76** F3
Jumet: Belgium **44** K5
Jumilla: Spain **35** F17
Jumin (Juimand): Iran **55** J8
Jumla: Nepal **58** O9
Jumna: *riv.*, *see* Yamuna.
Junaitha: Saudi Arabia **54** F9
Junan: Honan, China **62** U8
Junction: Tex., U.S.A. **90** B10
Junction City: Ark., U.S.A. **90** E9
Junction City: Kans., U.S.A. **90** C6
Junction City: Oreg., U.S.A. **92** C4
Junction Hill: *town*, Queens., Australia **70** H5
Jundiai: Brazil **96** F1
JUNEAU: Alaska, U.S.A. **84** f6
Juneau: Wis., U.S.A. **88** G4
Junee: N.S.W., Australia **71** G10
Jungfrau: *mtn.*, Switzerland **40** N9
Jungkiang: Kweichow, China **62** T9
Juniata: *riv.*, Pa., U.S.A. **89** N5
Junin: Buenos Aires, Arg. **96** C3
Junin: Mendoza, Argentina **96** B3
Juniya: Lebanon **56** D5
Junosuando: Sweden **46** S3
Juntura: Oreg., U.S.A. **92** D4
Junuba: *tribal area*, Oman **56** J10
Juo Lake: Finland **46** V5
Juquiá: Brazil **96** F1
Jura: *i.* & *sound*, Scotland **29** K8
Jura: *Dept.*, France (*cap.* Lons-le-Saunier) **40** L9
Jura, Paps of: *mtns.*, Scot. **29** J8
Jurado: Colombia **94** B2
Jura Mtns.: France/Switz. **40** M9
Jurby: Isle of Man, U.K. **26** M11
Jurf Darawish: Jordan **56** D6
Juries, Los: Argentina **96** C2
Juring: Sierra Leone **80** B3
Jurm: Afghanistan **51** M7
Juruá: *riv.*, Brazil **94** D5
Juruena: & *riv.*, Brazil **94** F6
Juruti: Brazil **94** F4
Jussey: France **40** L8
Justo Daract: Argentina **96** B3
Juterbog: E. Germany **45** T4
Juticalpa: Honduras **86** L15
Jutland: *penin.*, Denmark **47** L8
Juuka: Finland **46** V5
Juva: Finland **46** U6
Juvigny: France **36** D7
Juvisy: France **36** H7
Juwain: Afghanistan **58** K8
Juwara: Oman **55** J11
Juwun: Iran **55** H9
Juzennecourt: France **36** K7
Jyekundo (Yushu): Chinghai, China **62** R8
Jylland: *see* Jutland.
JYVÄSKYLÄ: Keski-Suomi, Finland **46** T5

K2 (Godwin-Austen): *mtn.*, China/Jammu & Kashmir **58** N7
Ka: *riv.*, Nigeria **81** F2
Kaabong: Uganda **76** D2
Kaaing Veld: *plain*, S. Afr. **74** E5
Kaakhka: Turkmen., U.S.S.R. **50** J7
Kaal'mer-Sede: U.S.S.R. **48** j4
Kaamanen: Finland **46** U2
Kaapmuiden: Trans., S. Afr. **75** J2
Kaap Plat.: S. Africa **75** F4
Kaaps: S.W. Africa **74** B1
Kaaresuvanto: Finland **46** S2
Kabaena: *i.*, Celebes **65** G8
Kabaish: Iraq **57** K6
Kabala: Sierra Leone **80** B3
Kabale: Uganda **76** C3
Kabalo: Zaïre **76** C4
Kabambale: Zaïre **76** C3
Kabanga: Zambia **77** C6
Kabardino A.S.S. Repub.: U.S.S.R. (*cap.* Nal'chik) **50** F6
Kabare: Zaïre **76** C3
Kabarnet: Kenya **76** E2
Kabasalan: Mindanao, Phil. **64** G5
Kabba: Nigeria **81** F3
Kabba: *riv.*, Sierra Leone **80** B3
Kabcha Gompa: Chingai, China **62** R8
Kabe: *well*, Niger **81** G2
Kabele, Lake: Zaïre **77** C4
Kabelega Falls: Uganda **76** D2
Kabelvåg: Norway **46** O2
Kaberamaido: Uganda **76** D2
Kabgaye: Rwanda **76** C3
Kabilcevaz: Turkey **57** G2
Kabinakagami Lake: & *riv.*, Ont., Canada **88** J1
Kabin Buri: Thailand **64** C4
Kabinda: Zaïre **76** B4
Kabinu: Borneo **65** F6
Kabir Kuh: *range*, Iran **57** K5
Kabo: Central African Rep. **81** H3
Kabondo Dianda: Zaïre **77** C4
Kabongo: Zaïre **76** C4
Kabonpo: *riv.*, Zambia **77** B5
Kaboudia, Cape: Tunisia **32** E4
Kabud Gonbad: Iran **55** J7
Kabugao: Luzon, Phil. **64** G3
KABUL: & *Prov.*, Afghanistan **58** L8
Kabul: *riv.*, Pak./Afghan. **58** M8
Kabula: Uganda **76** D3
Kabumbulu: Zaïre **76** C4
Kabunda: Zaïre **77** C5
Kabutarahang: Iran **57** L4
KABWE: Central Zambia **77** C5
Kabwe, Lake: Zaïre **77** C4
Kačanik: Yugoslavia **39** R15
Kacha: U.S.S.R. **48** g4
Kacheliba: Kenya **76** E2
Kachia: Nigeria **81** F3
Kachin: *State*, Burma (*cap.* Myitkyina) **59** R9
Kachins: *tribe*, Burma **59** R9
Kachkim Ozero: U.S.S.R. **46** W2
Kachug: U.S.S.R. **49** m7
Kaco: North I., N.Z. **70** O12
Kacoonda: S. Australia **71** C10
Kaczanów: Poland **45** V4
Kaczawa: *riv.*, Poland **45** W4
Kade: Ghana **80** D3
Kadei: *riv.*, Cameroun/Central African Republic **81** G4
Kadesh: ancient city on upper *Orontes* near south bank of Lake Homs, Syria **56** E4
Kadhimain: Iraq **57** J5
Kadina: S. Australia **71** B9
Kadınhai: Turkey **56** C2
Kadiri: Andhra Pradesh, India **58** N12
Kadirli: Turkey **56** E3
Kadjema: Cen. Afr. Rep. **76** C1
KADUGLI: Southern Kordofan, Sudan 79 K7
Kadur: Karnataka, India **58** N12
KADUNA: & *riv.*, Kaduna, Nigeria 81 F2
KAÉDI: Gorgol, Mauritania **80** B1
Kaeo: North I., N.Z. **70** O12
Kaerh (Gartok): Tibet, China **58** O8
Kaerhkunsha: Tibet, China **58** N8
Kaesong: S. Korea **63** X7
Kaetalovka: Kazakh., U.S.S.R. **50** G5
Kafa: *geog. reg.*, Ethiopia **76** E1
Kafai: *i.*, Persian Gulf **55** H10
Kafakumba: Zaïre **77** B4
Kafan: Armenia, U.S.S.R. **57** K2
Kafanchan: Nigeria **81** F3
Kaffir: *riv.*, O.F.S., S. Africa **75** G4
Kafia Kingi: Sudan **79** J8
Kafiristan: *geog. reg.*, Afghanistan **58** M7
Kafr esh Sheikh: Egypt **56** B6
Kafr ez Zaiyat: Egypt **56** B6
Kafue: & *riv.*, Zambia **77** C6
Kafue Hook: Zambia **77** C5
Kafue National Park: Zambia **77** C6
Kafulwe: Zambia **77** C4
Kagadi: Uganda **76** D2
Kagarko: Nigeria **81** F3
Kagawa: *Pref.*, Japan (*cap.* Takamatsu) **63** d3
Kagera: *riv.*, Tanzania **76** D3
Kagi (Chia'i): Taiwan **63** W10
Kağizman: Turkey **57** H1
Kagnar: Senegal **80** B1
KAGOSHIMA: & *Pref.*, Japan **63** b5
Kagul: Moldavia, U.S.S.R. **39** V14
Kahalan: *riv.*, Borneo **65** E7
Kahama: Tanzania **76** D3
Kahan: Baluchistan, Pak. **58** L9
Kahana: Hawaiian Is. **83** c2
Kaharan: Iran **57** L3
Kahe: Tanzania **76** E3
Kahemba: Zaïre **76** A4
Kahla: E. Germany **45** R5
Kahoka: Mo., U.S.A. **88** F5
Kahoolawe: *i.*, Hawaiian Is. **83** c2
Kahriz: Iran **55** K8
Kahsing: Chekiang, China **63** W8
Kaiama: Nigeria **81** E3
Kaiapoi: South I., N.Z. **70** O16
Kaibo: Upper Volta **80** D2
Kaieteur Falls: Guyana **87** d8
Kaifeng: Honan, China **62** U8
Kaihsien: Szechwan, China **62** T8
Kaihu: North I., N.Z. **70** O12
Kaihwa (Wenshan): Yunnan, China **62** S10
Kai (Ewab) Is.: Indonesia **61** L13
Kaikiang: Szechwan, China **62** T6
Kaikohe: North I., N.Z. **70** O12
Kaikoura: & *range*, South I., New Zealand **70** O16
Kailas: *range*, Tibet, China **58** O8
Kailu: Inner Mongolia, China **63** W6
Kailua: Hawaiian Is. **83** c3
Kaimana: W. Irian, Indon. **61** L12
Kaimanawa Mtns.: North I., New Zealand **70** P14
Kaimes: Strathclyde, Scotland **29** N8
Kainan: Honshu, Japan **63** d3
Kaiping: Liaoning, China **63** W6
Kaipong Is.: Kwangtung, China **62** U10
Kairiioenpirtti: Finland **46** V3
Kairiru: *i.*, Papua New Guinea **66** H2
KAIROUAN: & *Governorate* Tunisia **38** M19
Kairuku: Papua/New Guinea **69** H1
Kaiserlautern: W. Germany **44** N6
Kaiserstuhl: Switzerland **40** O8
Kaitaia: North I., N.Z. **70** O12
Kaitangata: South I., N.Z. **71** M18
Kaitu Ho: *riv.*, Sinkiang, China **51** O6
Kaitum Lake: Sweden **46** O3
Kaitung: Kirin, China **63** W6
Kaiwaka: North I., N.Z. **70** P13
Kaiwi Chan.: Hawaiian Is. **83** c2
Kaiyuan: Liaoning, China **63** W6
Kaiyuan: Yunnan, China **62** S10
Kaizuka: Japan **63** d3
Kajaani: Finland **46** U4
Kaja Apu: Enganno Is., Sumatra **65** C8
Kajabbi: Queens., Australia **69** F4
Kajakai Dam: Afghanistan **55** L8
Kajang: Malaya, Malaysia **65** b12
Kajiado: Kenya **76** E3
Kajok: Sudan **76** C1
Kajuadi: *i.*, Indonesia **65** G8
Kaka: Sudan **79** L7
Kaka: Cen. Afr. Rep. **76** C1
Kakada: *well*, Chad **81** H1
Kakamas: S. Africa **74** D4
KAKAMEGA: Western, Kenya **76** D2
Kakamoeka: Congo **81** G5
Kakata: Liberia **80** B3
Kake: Japan **63** c3
Kakeya: Japan **63** c3
Kakhovka: Ukraine **50** D5
Kaninada (Cocanada): Andhra Pradesh, India **58** O11
Kakogawa: Japan **63** d3
Kakpin: Ivory Coast **80** D3
Kakuma: Kenya **76** D2
Kalaa Djerda: Tunisia **38** L19
Kalabahi: Alor, Indonesia **65** G8
Kalabáka: Greece **39** R17
Kalabo: Zambia **77** B5
Kalabsha: Egypt **54** D10
Kalach: U.S.S.R. **50** F5
Kalachinsk: U.S.S.R. **51** M3
Kaladan: *riv.*, Burma/India **59** Q10
Kalahari Desert: Botswana **77** B7
Kalahari Game Reserve: S. Africa **74** D3
Kalahari Gemsbok Nat. Park: S. Africa **74** D2
Kalajoki: Finland **46** S4
Kalakamati: Botswana **77** C7
Kalakashih: *riv.*, Sinkiang, China **58** N7
Kalaki: Uganda **76** D2
Kalam: Ethiopia **76** E2
Kalámai (Kalamata): Greece **39** S18
Kalamazoo: & *riv.*, Mich., U.S.A. **88** J4
Kalamita Bay: U.S.S.R. **50** D6
Kalamoti: Chios, Greece **39** U17
Kalannie: W. Australia **68** B6
Kalao: *i.*, Indonesia **65** G8
Kalaotoa: *i.*, Indonesia **65** G8
Kalat: Baluchistan, Pakistan **58** L9
KALAT-I-GHILZAI: Zabul, Afghanistan **55** L8
Kalaupapa: Hawaiian Is. **83** c2
Kalávrita: Greece **39** S17
Kalba: U.A.E. **55** J10
Kalbar: Queens., Australia **70** K6
Kalbe: W. Germany **45** R3
Kale: Antalya, Turkey **56** B3
Kale: Bingöl, Turkey **57** G2
Kalecik: Turkey **56** C1
Kaledupa: *i.*, Tukanbesi Is., Indonesia **65** G8
Kalegauk: *i.*, Burma **59** R11
Kalehe: Zaïre **76** C3
Kalembe Lembe: Zaïre **76** C3
Kalemi: Zaïre **76** C4
Kalemyo: Burma **59** Q10
Kalene: Zambia **77** B5
Kalevala: Karelia, U.S.S.R. **46** W4
Kalewa: Burma **59** Q10
Kálfafell: Iceland **46** e5
Kálfafellsstadhur: Iceland **46** f4
Kálfshamarsvik: Iceland **46** c3
Kalgan (Changkiakow): Hopeh, China **62** U6
Kalgoorlie: W. Australia **68** C6
Kaliakra, Cape: Bulgaria **39** V15
Kalianda: Sumatra **65** D8
Kalimantan: Indonesia **65** E7
Kálimnos: *i.*, Dodec. (Grc.) **39** U18
Kalimpong: W. Bengal, India **59** P9
KALININ: & *Reg.*, U.S.S.R. **50** E3
KALININGRAD (Königsberg): & *Reg.*, U.S.S.R. **47** R9
Kalininsk: U.S.S.R. **50** F4
Kalinovichi: Byelorussia **43** V10
Kalinova: Ukraine **43** V12
Kalispell: Mont., U.S.A. **92** E3
Kalisz: Poznan, Poland **43** Q11
Kalisz: Koszalin, Pol. **45** V2
Kaliua: Tanzania **76** D4
Kalix: *riv.*, Sweden **46** S3
Kalixfors: Sweden **46** R3
Kalka: Punjab, India **58** N8
Kalkan: Turkey **56** A3
Kalkaska: Mich., U.S.A. **88** J3
Kalk Bay: S. Africa **74** *Ins.*
Kalkfontein: Botswana **77** B7
Kalkfontein Dam: O.F.S., S. Africa **75** F4
Kalk Plat: S.W. Africa **74** C2
Kalkpoort: S. Africa **74** D3
Kalkrand: S.W. Africa **74** B2
Kalksluit: S. Africa **74** D4
Kalkum: Guyana **87** e8
Kalkvlakte: O.F.S., S. Africa **75** *Ins.*
Kallafo: Ethiopia **79** Q18
Kallavesi: *lake*, Finland **46** U5
Kallis: Somalia **79** R18
Kallista: Tas., Australia **68** H8
Kall Lake: Sweden **46** N5
Kalloni: Lesbos, Greece **39** U17
Kalmalo: Nigeria **81** F2
KALMAR: & *Co.*, Sweden **47** P8
Kalmar Sound: Sweden **47** P8
Kalmyk A.S.S. Rep.: U.S.S.R. (*cap.* Elista) **50** E5
Kalmykovo: Kazakh., U.S.S.R. **50** H5
Kalo: New Guinea **69** H2
Kalofer: Bulgaria **39** T15
Kalomo: Zambia **77** C6
Kalong: Nigeria **81** F3
Kalonga: Zaïre **77** C5
Kalongana: Karakelong Is., Indonesia **65** H6
Kalozhno, Lake: U.S.S.R. **46** W3
Kalpeni: *i.*, Laccadive Is. **58** M12
Kalpi: Uttar Pradesh, India **58** N9
Kals: Austria **41** S8
Kaltag: Alaska, U.S.A. **84** D5
Kaltungo: Nigeria **81** G3
KALUGA: & *Reg.*, U.S.S.R. **50** E4
Kalundborg: Zealand, Den. **47** M9
Kalush: Ukraine **43** T12
Kalut: Iran **55** J7
Kalutara: Sri Lanka **58** O13
Kalvariya: Lithuania, U.S.S.R. **47** S9
Kalyazin: U.S.S.R. **50** E3
Kalzhat: Kazakh., U.S.S.R. **51** O6
Kam: *riv.*, S.W. Africa **74** B1
Kama: Zaïre **76** C3
Kama: *riv.*, U.S.S.R. **50** H3
Kamaing: Burma **59** R9
Kamaishi: Japan **63** ZZ7
Kamakabra: Guyana **87** d8
Kamakura: Japan **63** f3
Kamakusa: Guyana **87** d8
Kamakwi: Sierra Leone **80** B3
Kamalo: Hawaiian Is. **83** c2
Kamalu: Sierra Leone **80** B3
Kamaniola: Zaïre **76** C3
Kamapanda: Zambia **77** B5
Kamaran Is.: (Yemen P.D.R.), Red Sea **54** F11
Kamarod: Baluchistan, Pakistan **58** K9
Kamassa: Cameroun **81** G3
Kambara: *i.*, Fiji Is. **67** Q5
Kambata: *geog. reg.*, Eth. **76** E1
Kambélé: Ivory Coast **80** D3
Kamberg: W. Germany **44** O5
Kambole: Zambia **77** D4
Kamchatka: *penin.* & *bay*, U.S.S.R. **49** S6
Kamchatka: *riv.*, U.S.S.R. **49** r6
Kamden: S. Africa **74** E3
Kame I: Lake Victoria **76** D3
Kameldoorn: *riv.*, S.W. Afr. **74** B4

For Abbreviations see list on p.113. Italic type, e.g. *Ephesus*, refers to historical names not on maps. Capital letters, e.g. MADRID, show capitals of countries; small capital letters, e.g. CADIZ, show capitals of provinces, etc. General notes p.116.

Kamen--Keiskammahoek 153

Kamen: U.S.S.R. **51** O4
Kamen: W. Germany **44** N4
Kamenets: Byelorussia **43** S10
Kamenets-Podol'skiy: Ukraine **43** U12
Kamenice: (*NE. of Jihlava*), Czechoslovakia **45** V6
Kamenice: (*SW. of Jihlava*), Czechoslovakia **45** V6
Kamenjak, Cape: Yugo. **41** T11
Kamenka: U.S.S.R. **50** F5
Kamen'-Kashirskiy: Ukraine **43** T11
Kamenka-Strumilova: Ukraine **43** T11
Kamennogorsk: U.S.S.R. **47** V6
Kamennoye, Lake: Karelian A.S.S. Repub., U.S.S.R. **46** W4
Kamensk: U.S.S.R. **50** F5
Kamenskoye: U.S.S.R. **49** S5
Kamensk Uralskiy: U.S.S.R. **51** K3
Kamenz: E. Germany **45** U4
Kames: Strath., Scotland **29** L8
Kamet: *mtn.*, India **58** N8
Kameyama: Japan **63** e3
Kamienna Gora: Poland **45** W5
Kamien Pomorski: Poland **45** U2
Kamieskroon: S. Africa **74** B5
Kamigori: Japan **63** d3
Kamina: Zaire **77** C4
Kaministikwia: Ont., Can. **88** G1
Kamkeut: Laos **64** C3
Kamlin: Sudan **54** D11
Kamloops: B.C., Canada **92** C2
Kamnik: Yugoslavia **41** U9
Kamo: Japan **63** f2
Kamo: North I., N.Z. **70** P12
Kamouraska: Que., Canada **89** R2
Kampa: Bangka, Indonesia **65** D7
KAMPALA: Uganda **76** D2
Kampar: *riv.*, Sumatra **65** C6
Kampen: Netherlands **44** L3
Kamphaeng Phet: Thailand **64** B3
Kampolombo, Lake: Zambia **77** C5
Kampong Raja: Malaya, Malaysia **65** c11
Kampot: Cambodia 64 C4
Kampong Saom: Cambodia 64 C4
Kamptee: Maharashtra, India **58** N10
Kampti: Upper Volta **80** D2
Kampuchea: *see* **Cambodia**
Kamsack: Sask., Canada **92** G2
Kamsuma: Somalia **76** F2
Kamuela: Hawaiian Is. **83** d2
Kamukova: U.S.S.R. **49** q4
Kamuli: Uganda **76** D2
Kamyshin: U.S.S.R. **50** G4
Kamyshlov: U.S.S.R. **51** K3
Kamyzyak: U.S.S.R. **50** G5
Kan: Burma **59** Q10
Kan: *riv.*, China **62** V9
Kanaaupscow: *riv.*, Canada **85** M7
Kanab: Utah, U.S.A. **93** E5
Kanaga: *i.*, Aleutians **84** B7
Kanagawa: *Pref.*, Japan (*cap.* Yokohama) **63** f3
Kanal: Yugoslavia **41** T9
Kanalla: Nicobar Is. **57** Q13
KANANGA: Kasai Occidental, Zaire **76** B4
Kanash: U.S.S.R. **50** G3
Kanastraion, Cape: Greece **39** S17
Kanatak: Alaska, U.S.A. **84** D6
Kanawha: *riv.*, W. Va., U.S.A. **88** L6
Kanaya: Japan **63** f3
KANAZAWA: Ishikawa, Japan **63** e2
Kanbalu: Burma **59** R10
Kanchalon: U.S.S.R. **49** t4
Kanchanaburi: Thailand **64** B4
Kanchindu: Zambia **77** C6
Kanchipuram: Tamil Nadu, India **58** N12
Kanchow: Kiangsi, China **62** U9
Kanchuan: Shensi, China **62** T7
Kanchuerhmiao: Inner Mongolia, China **62** V5
KANDAHAR: *& Prov.*, Afghanistan **55** L8
Kanda Kanda: Zaire **76** B4
Kandakovo: U.S.S.R. **49** R4
Kandala: Somalia **79** R17
Kandalaksha: U.S.S.R. **46** X3
Kandalaksha, G. of: Karelian A.S.S. Rep., U.S.S.R. **48** E4
Kandale: Zaire **76** A4
Kandanga: Queens., Austl. **70** K6
Kandangan: Borneo **65** F7
Kandaniyemi: Karelian A.S.S. Rep., U.S.S.R. **46** W4
Kandanos: Crete **39** S19
Kandavu: *i.*, Fiji Is. **67** P5
Kandefwe: Zaire **76** C4
Kandel: W. Germany **44** O6
Kandi: Benin 81 E2
Kandira: Turkey **56** B1
Kandla: Gujarat, India **58** M10
Kandos: N.S.W., Australia **71** H9
Kandreho: Malagasy Rep. **73** O13
Kandukur: Andhra Pradesh, India **58** N11
Kanduna: *riv.*, Nigeria **81** F3
Kandy: Sri Lanka **58** O13
Kane: Pa., U.S.A. **89** M5
Kane Basin: Greenland/Can. **85** m2
Kanem: Hainan, China **62** T11
Kanem: *geog. reg.*, Chad **81** H2
Kanem: *Pref.*, Chad (*cap.* Mao) **81** H1
Kanevskaya: U.S.S.R. **50** E5
Kaneyama: Japan **63** g2
Kanfanar: Yugoslavia **41** T10
Kangal: Turkey **56** E2
Kangâmiut: Greenland **85** o4
KANGAR: Perlis, Malaya, Malaysia **65** b10
Kangaroo I.: S. Australia **71** B10
Kangaruma: Guyana **87** d8
Kangasala: Finland **47** T6
Kangâtsiao: Greenland **85** o4
Kangavar: Iran **57** K4
Kangchenjunga: *mtn.*, Nepal **59** P9
Kangean: *i. & Is.*, Indon. **65** F8
Kangetet: Kenya **76** E2
Kanggye: N. Korea **63** X6
Kanghsien (Paimakwan): Kansu, China **62** T8
Kangkung: Sumatra **65** C7
Kangnung: S. Korea **63** X7
Kangpa: Tibet, China **59** P9
Kangpao: Hopeh, China **62** U6
Kangping: Liaoning, China **63** W6
Kangting (Tatsienlu): Szechwan, China **62** S8
Kangtissu: *mtn.*, Tibet, China **58** O8
Kaniapiskau, Lake: Que., Canada **84** N7
Kaniet: *i.*, Papua/New Guinea **66** J2
Kanin, Cape: U.S.S.R. **48** F4
Kaniva: Vict., Australia **71** D11
Kanjut: *mtn.*, Jammu & Kashmir **58** N7
Kankakee: *& riv.*, Ill., U.S.A. **88** H5
KANKAN: *& Reg.*, Guinea **80** C2
Kanker: Madhya Pradesh, India **58** O10
Kankiya: Nigeria **81** F2
Kanlica: Turkey (Bosporus, *Inset*) **20** *Ins.*
Kannapolis: N.C., U.S.A. **91** L8
Kannauj: Uttar Pradesh, India **58** N9
Kannus: Finland **46** S5
KANO: *& State*, Nigeria **81** F2
Kanowit: Sarawak, Malaysia **65** E6
Kanpur (Cawnpore), Uttar Pradesh, India **58** O9
Kanrach: Baluchistan, Pakistan **58** L9
Kansanshi: Zambia **77** C5
Kansas: *riv.*, Kans., U.S.A. **93** H5
Kansas: *State*, U.S.A. (*cap.* Topeka) **93** H5
Kansas City: Kans., U.S.A. **90** D6
Kansas City: Mo., U.S.A. **90** D6
Kansk: U.S.S.R. **51** R3
Kansu: *Prov.*, China [*cap.* Lanchow (Kaolan)] **62** S7
Kant: Kirgiz., U.S.S.R. **51** N6
Kantara: *see* El Qantara
Kantchari: Upper Volta **81** E2
Kantishna: Alaska, U.S.A. **84** d5
Kanto Mtns.: Japan **63** f2
Kantoutou: Guinea **80** B2
Kantse: Tibet, China **62** S8
Kantulong: Burma **59** R11
Kanturk: Cork, Repub. of Ireland **31** D15
Kanuku Mtns.: Guyana **87** d9
Kanuma: Japan **63** f2
Kanus: S.W. Africa **74** C3
Kanyato: Tanzania **76** D3
KANYE: Ngwaketse, Botswana **75** F2
Kanzenze: Zaire **77** C5
Kaoan: Kiangsi, China **62** V9
Kaobang: Vietnam 64 D2
Kaochow: Kwangtung, China **62** U10
Kao Doi: Vietnam 64 D3
Kaohsiung (Takao): Taiwan **63** W10
KAOLACK: Sine-Saloum, Senegal **80** A2
Kaolan (Lanchow): Kansu, China **62** S7
Kaomi: Shantung, China **62** V7
Kaoura Debbe: Niger **81** E2
Kaoyu Lake: China **62** V8
Kapaa: Hawaiian Is. **83** b1
Kapanga: Bandundu, Zaire **81** H6
Kapanga: Shaba, Zaire **76** B4
Kapatu: Zambia **77** D4
KAPCHORWA: Sebei, Uganda **76** D2
Kapela Mtns.: Yugoslavia **41** V11
Kapanguria: Kenya **76** E2
Kapfenberg: Austria **41** V8
Kapidaği: *penin.*, Turkey **39** U16
Kapii Mposhi: Zambia **77** C5
Kapit: Sarawak, Malaysia **65** E6
Kapiti I.: New Zealand **70** P15
Kaplan: La., U.S.A. **90** E10
Kaplice: Czechoslovakia **41** U7
Kapoe: Thailand **64** B5
Kapoeta: Sudan **76** D2
Kapoho: Hawaiian Is. **83** d3
Kapongolo: Zaire **76** C4
Kapos: *riv.*, Hungary **43** Q13
Kaposvár: Hungary **43** P13
Kappeln: W. Germany **45** P1
Kapsabet: Kenya **76** E2
Kapsan: N. Korea **63** X6
Kapsukas: Lithuania, U.S.S.R. **43** S9
Kapteinskraal: S. Africa **74** C5
Kapuas: *riv.*, Borneo (*South*) **65** E7
Kapuas: *riv.*, Borneo (*West*) **65** E6
Kapunda: S. Australia **71** C10
Kapurthala: Punjab, India **58** N8
Kapuskasing: *& riv.*, Ont., Canada **88** K1
Kaputir: Kenya **76** E2
Kapuvar: Hungary **43** P13
Kara: U.S.S.R. **48** h4
Kara: *riv.*, Turkey **56** F2
Karababa Dagh: *mtn.*, Turkey **56** E2
Karabash: U.S.S.R. **51** K3
Karabiga: Turkey **39** U16
Kara-Bogaz-Gol: *& bay*, Turkmen., U.S.S.R. **50** H6
Karabük: Turkey **56** C1
Karacabey: Turkey **39** V16
Karacasu: Turkey **56** A3
Karachayevo-cherkess Auton. Reg.: U.S.S.R. (*cap.* Cherkessk) **50** F6
Karachayevsk: Georgia, U.S.S.R. **50** F6
Karachev: U.S.S.R. **50** E4
KARACHI: Sind, Pakistan **58** L10
Karad: Maharashtra, India **58** M11
Karadağ: Turkey (Dardan. *Inset*) **20** *Ins.*
Kara Dağ: *mtn.*, Turkey **56** C3
Karaga: Ghana **80** D3
Karaga: U.S.S.R. **49** S6
KARAGANDA: *& Reg.*, Kazakh., U.S.S.R. **51** M5
Karaginskiy: I.: U.S.S.R. **49** s6
Karaisalı: Turkey **56** D3
Karaj: Iran **55** H7
KARAK: *& Dist.*, Jordan **56** D6
Karak: Tibet, China **58** N8
Kara-Kala: Turkmen., U.S.S.R. **50** J7
Kara-Kalpak A.S.S. Repub.. Uzbek S.S. Repub., U.S.S.R. (*cap.* Nukus) **50** J6
Karakas: Kazakh., U.S.S.R. **51** O5
Karakash: *riv.*, Sinkiang, China **51** N7
Karakelong Is.: Indonesia **65** H6
Karakhoto: *ruins*, Inner Mongolia, China **62** S6
Karakitang: *I.*, Sangihe Is., Indonesia **65** H6
Karakoram: *range & pass*, Jammu & Kashmir/China **58** N7
Karakoro: *riv.*, Mali/Mauritania **80** B1
Karakorum: capital of Genghiz Khan's empire. Its ruins lie on river Orthon, W. of Urga, Mongolia **62** T5
KARAKÖSE: Ağri, Turkey **57** H2
Kara-Kul': Tadzhik., U.S.S.R. **51** M7
Karakul': Uzbek., U.S.S.R. **51** K7
Kara Kum: *desert*, Turkmen., U.S.S.R. **51** K7
Karakuwise: S.W. Africa **77** A6
Karala: Estonia, U.S.S.R. **47** R7
Karaman: Turkey **56** C3
Karambu: Borneo **65** F7
Karamea Bight: South I., New Zealand **70** N15
Karamoja: *Dist.*, Uganda (*cap.* Moroto) **76** D2
Karamursel: Turkey **56** A1
Karamyshevo: U.S.S.R. **47** V8
Karangana: Mali **80** C2
Karangasem: Bali, Indon. **65** F8
Karapniar: Turkey **56** C3
Karasay: Kazakh., U.S.S.R. **51** K5
Karasburg: S.W. Africa **74** C4
Kara Sea: U.S.S.R. **48** H3
Karashagan: Kazakh., U.S.S.R. **51** N5
Kara-Shahr (Yenki): Sinkiang, China **51** P6
Karasjok: Norway **46** T2
Karasu: Turkey **56** B1
Karasuk: U.S.S.R. **51** N4
Karasuyama: Japan **63** g2
Karata: Ethiopia **79** M7
Karataş (Iskeliköy): Turkey **56** D3
Karatong: Sudan **76** D1
Kara-Tau: *range*, Kazakh., U.S.S.R. **51** L6
Karats Lake: Sweden **46** Q3
Karatsu: Japan **63** a4
Karaul: U.S.S.R. **48** K3
Karavostasi: Cyprus **56** C4
Karawanken Mtns.: Austria/Yugoslavia **41** U9
KARBALA: *& Prov.*, Iraq **57** J5
Karcag: Hungary **43** R13
Kardelievo: Yugoslavia **39** P15
Kardhitsa: Greece **39** R17
Kareima: Sudan **54** D11
Karelian A.S.S. Republic: U.S.S.R. (*cap.* Petrozavodsk) **46** W4
Karema: Tanzania **76** D4
Karé Mtns.: Cen. Afr. Rep. **81** H3
Karenko (Hua-lien): Taiwan **63** W10
Karet: *geog. reg.*, Mauritania **78** C5
Karganrud, Iran **57** L3
Kargasok: U.S.S.R. **51** O3
Kargat: U.S.S.R. **51** O3
Kargı: Turkey **56** D1
Kargil: Jammu & Kashmir **58** N8
Kargopol': U.S.S.R. **50** E2
Karhi Lake: Finland **47** S6
Kari: Nigeria **81** G2
Kariba Lake: *and dam*, Rhodesia/Zambia **77** C6
KARIBIB: *& dist.*, S.W. Africa **74** A1
Kariega: S. Africa **75** F6
Karigasniemi: Finland **46** T2
Karikal: India **58** N12
Karimata: Karimata Arch., Indonesia **65** D7
Karimata: *str. & arch.*, Indonesia **65** D7
Karimganj: Bangladesh **59** Q10
Karimnagar: Andhra Pradesh, India **58** N11
Karimun: *i.*, Riau Arch., Indonesia **65** c13
Karimundjowo Is.: Indon. **65** E8
Karin: Miguirtinia, Somalia **79** R17
Karin: North-East, Somalia **79** R17
Karind: Iran **57** K4
Karis: Finland **47** S6
Karisimbi: *mtn.*, Zaire **76** C3
Karistos: Euboea, Greece **39** T17
Karkabat: Ethiopia **54** E11
Karkar: *i.*, New Guinea **66** J2
Karkaralinsk: Kazakh., U.S.S.R. **51** N5
Karkheh: *riv.*, Iran **57** L6
Karkinitskiy Bay: U.S.S.R. **50** D5
Karkkila: Finland **47** T6
Karkoj: Sudan **54** D12
KARL-MARX-STADT: *& Dist.*, East Germany **45** S5
Karlo (Hailuoto): *& i.*, Fin. **46** T4
Karlobag: Yugoslavia **41** V11
Karlovac: Yugoslavia **41** V10
Karlovo: Bulgaria **39** T15
Karlovy Vary (Karlsbad): Czechoslovakia **45** S5
Karlsbad (Karlovy Vary): Czechoslovakia **45** S5
Karlsborg: Sweden **47** O7
Karlsburg: German name of Alba-Iulia, Romania **43** S13
Karlshamn: Sweden **47** O8
Karlskoga: Sweden **47** O7
KARLSKRONA: Blekinge, Sweden **47** O8
Karlsruhe: W. Germany **44** O6
KARLSTAD: Värmland, Sweden **47** N7
Karlstadt: W. Germany **45** P6
Karluk: Alaska, U.S.A. **84** d6
Karma: Niger **81** E2
Karmaskaly: U.S.S.R. **50** J4
Karmøy: *i.*, Norway **47** J7
Karnak: site of excavations on right bank of Nile about 3 miles N. of Luxor, Egypt **54** D9
Karnal: Haryana, India **58** N9
Karnataka: *State*, India (*cap.* Bangalore) **58** N12
Karniów: Poland **43** P11
Karnobat: Bulgaria **39** U15
Karnes City: Tex., U.S.A. **90** C11
Karnten: *see* Carinthia
Karonga: Malawi **77** D4
Karor: Palau Is. **61** L10
Karosa: Celebes **65** F7
Karossa, Cape: Sumba, Indonesia **65** F8
Karota: Sudan **54** E11
Karow: E. Germany **45** S2
Karpathos: *i.*, Dodec. (Grc.) **39** U19
Karpathos Str., Rhodes/Karpathos **39** U19
Karpenision: Greece **39** R17
Karpinsk: U.S.S.R. **50** J3
Karragullen: W. Australia **68** B6
Karratha: W. Australia **68** B4
Karre, El: Ethiopia **79** Q18
Karreeberge: *range*, S. Africa **74** E5
Karridale: W. Australia **68** B6
Karroo, Great: *plat.*, S. Afr. **74** E6
Karroo, Little: *plat.*, S. Afr. **74** D6
KARS: *& Prov.*, Turkey **57** H1
Karsakpay: Kazakh., U.S.S.R. **51** L5
Kärsämäki: Finland **46** T5
Kārsava: Latvia, U.S.S.R. **47** U8
Karshi: Uzbek., U.S.S.R. **51** L7
Karstula: Finland **46** T5
Kartal: Turkey **56** A1
Kartaly: U.S.S.R. **51** K4
Kartun: U.S.S.R. **63** Y5
Karub: S.W. Africa **74** A1
Karuizawa: Japan **63** f2
Karumba: Queens., Austl. **69** G3
Karumwa: Tanzania **76** D3
Karun: *riv.*, Iran **57** L6
Karungie: W. Australia **68** D3
Karungu: Kenya **76** D3
Karup: Denmark **47** L8
Karur: Tamil Nadu, India **58** N12
Karvia: Finland **47** S5
Karwar: Karnataka, India **58** M12
Kasache: Malawi **77** D5
Kasai: *riv.*, Zaire **76** A3
Kasai Occidental: *Prov.*, Zaire (*cap.* Kananga) **76** B4
Kasai Oriental: *Prov.*, Zaire (*cap.* Mbuji-Mayi) **76** B3
KASAMA: Northern, Zambia **77** D5
Kasan-Asma: Sinkiang, China **51** O6
Kasanga: Tanzania **76** D4
Kasangulu: Zaire **81** H5
Kasanka Game Reserve: Zambia **77** D5
Kasba Lake: N.W.T., Canada **84** j5
Kasba Tadla: Morocco **80** K8
Kasbek: *mtn.*, Georgia, U.S.S.R. **50** F6
Kasekow: E. Germany **45** U2
Kasempa: Zambia **77** C5
Kasenga: Zaire **77** C5
Kasenyi: Zaire **76** D2
Kashan: Iran **55** H8
Kashgar (Sufu): Sinkiang, China **51** N7
Kashima: Fukushima, Japan **63** g2
Kashima: Ibarak, Japan **63** g3
Kashin: U.S.S.R. **50** E3
Kashira: U.S.S.R. **50** E4
Kashitu: Zambia **77** C5
Kashiwazaki: Japan **63** f2
Kashka: *riv.*, Uzbek., U.S.S.R. **51** L7
Kashmar: Iran **55** J7
Kashmir, & Jammu: *State claimed by both* India and Pakistan (*cap.* Srinagar) **58** N8
Kashmor: Sind, Pakistan **58** L9
Kasho: *i.*, Taiwan **63** W10
Kashum Hu: *lake*, Tibet, China **59** P8
Kasigao: Kenya **76** E3
Kasimbila: Nigeria **81** F3
Kasimov: U.S.S.R. **50** F3
Kasindi: Zaire **76** C2
Kaskaskia: *riv.*, Ill., U.S.A. **88** G6
Kaskinen: Finland **46** R5
Kaskong: Cambodia 64 C4
Kasli: U.S.S.R. **51** K3
Kaslo: B.C., Canada **92** D3
Kasoma: Zambia **77** C5
Kasongo: Zaire **76** C3
Kasongo Lunda: Zaire **81** H6
Kásos: *i.*, Dodec., (Grc.) **39** U19
Kásos Strait: Crete/Kásos **39** U19
Kašperské Hory: Yugoslavia **41** T6
Kaspi: Georgia, U.S.S.R. **57** J1
Kaspiyskiy: U.S.S.R. **50** G5
Kassaba: Chad **81** H2
KASSALA: *& Prov.*, Sudan **54** E11
Kassan: Uzbek., U.S.S.R. **51** L7
Kassándra: *penin.*, Greece **39** S17
Kassansay: Uzbek., U.S.S.R. **51** M6
Kassel: W. Germany **44** P4
Kassel: *Dist.*, Hesse, West Germany **44** P4
Kasserine: Tunisia **32** D4
Kasson: Minn., U.S.A. **88** E3
KASTAMONU: *& Prov.*, Tur. **56** C1
Kastav: Yugoslavia **41** U10
Kastel: W. Germany **44** O5
Kastellaun: W. Germany **44** N5
Kastélli: Crete **39** S19
Kastéllion: Crete **39** T19
Kastellos: Rhodes **39** U18
Kastoria: *& lake*, Greece **39** R16
Kastornoye: U.S.S.R. **50** E4
Kástron: Lemnos, Greece **39** T17
Kasubuchi: Japan **63** c3
Kasulu: Tanzania **76** D3
Kasungan: Borneo **65** E7
Kasungu: Malawi **77** D5
Kasupi: Malawi **77** E6
Kasur: Punjab, Pakistan **58** M8
Kataba: Zambia **77** C6
Katada: Japan **63** d3
Katagum: Nigeria **81** G2
Katahdin, Mount Maine, U.S.A. **89** R3
Katakai: Japan **63** g3
Katako Kombe: Zaire **76** B3
Katakolon: Greece **39** R18
Katakwa: Nigeria **81** F3
Katakwi: Uganda **76** D2
Katalla: Alaska, U.S.A. **84** e5
Katamatite: Vict., Australia **71** F11
Katanga: *reg.*, Zaire **76** B4
Katangli: U.S.S.R. **49** Q7
Katanino: Zambia **77** C5
Katanning: W. Australia **68** B6
Katarnian Ghat: Uttar Pradesh, India **58** O9
Katav-Ivanovsk: U.S.S.R. **50** J4
Katawaz Urgun: *prov.*, Afghanistan (*cap.* Urgun) **55** L8
Katcha: Nigeria **81** F3
Katchall: *i.*, Nicobar Is. **59** Q13
Kate: Tanzania **76** D4
Katende: Zaire **76** B4
Katerini: Greece **39** S16
Katesbridge: Down, N. Irel. **30** J11
Katha: Burma **59** R10
Katherine: *& riv.*, N. Territ., Australia **68** E2
Kathiawar: *penin.*, Gujarat, India **58** M10
Kathu: S. Africa **74** E3
Katiet: Mentawai Is., Indon. **65** B7
Katihar: Bihar, India **59** P9
Katiola: Ivory Coast **80** C3
Katiu: *i.*, Tuamotu Arch. **83** g3
Katkop: S. Africa **75** H5
Katmai Mount: Alaska, U.S.A. **84** D6
Katmai Nat. Park: Alaska, U.S.A. **84** d6
KATMANDU: Nepal **59** P9
Kato (Chiatung): Taiwan **63** W10
Katon Karagay: U.S.S.R. **51** P5
Katoomba: N.S.W., Austl. **71** J9
Kato Stavros: Greece **39** S16
KATOWICE: *& Prov.*, Poland **43** Q11
Katrineholm: Sweden **47** P7
Katrine, Loch: Central, Scot. **29** M7
Katshi: Zaire **76** C4
Katsina: Nigeria **81** F2
Katsina: *riv.*, Nigeria **81** G3
Katsina Ala: Nigeria **81** F3
Katsuyama: Japan **63** c3
Katta-Kurgan: Uzbek., U.S.S.R. **51** L7
Kattarp: Sweden **47** N8
Kattegat: *str.*, Den./Sweden **47** M8
Katun': *riv.*, U.S.S.R. **51** P5
Katupa: Sumbawa, Indon. **65** F8
Katwijk aan Zee: Neth. **44** K3
Katyshka: U.S.S.R. **51** L3
Kauai: *i. & chan.*, Hawaiian Is. **83** b1
Kaub: W. Germany **44** N5
Kauehi: *i.*, Tuamotu Arch. **83** f3
Kaufbeuren: W. Germany **40** Q8
Kaufman: Tex., U.S.A. **90** C9
Kaugama: Nigeria **81** F2
Kauhajoki: Finland **46** S5
Kauhava: Finland **46** S5
Kaukauna: Wis., U.S.A. **88** G3
Kaukauveld Plain: S.W. Afr. **77** B6
Kaukonen: Finland **46** T3
Kaukura: *i.*, Tuamotu Arch. **83** f3
Kaula: Hawaiian Is. **83** a2
Kaulakahi Chan.: Hawaiian Is. **83** a1
Kauliranta: Finland **46** S3
Kaunan: Heilungkiang, China **63** W5
Kaunas: Lithuania, U.S.S.R. **47** S9
Kaura Namoda: Nigeria **81** F2
Kauro: Nigeria **81** F2
Kautokeino: Norway **46** S2
Kavacha: U.S.S.R. **49** T5
Kavadarci: Yugoslavia **39** S16
Kavajë: Albania **39** Q16
Kavak: Turkey (Dardan. *Inset*) **20** *Ins.*
Kavali: Andhra Pradesh, India **58** O12
Kavála: Greece **39** T16
Kavandeh: *riv.*, Iran **55** H7
Kavar: Iran **55** H9
Kavaratti: *i.*, Laccadive Is. **58** M12
Kavarna: Bulgaria **39** V15
Kavieng: New Irel., Bismarck Arch. **67** K2
Kavir-i-Namak: *desert*, Iran **55** J8
Kawagoe: Japan **63** f3
Kawaguchi: Niigata, Japan **63** f2
Kawaguchi: Saitama, Japan **63** f3
Kawajiri Point: *cape*, Japan **63** b3
Kawakawa: North I., N.Z. **70** P12
Kawambwa: Zambia **77** C4
Kawardha: Madhya Pradesh, India **58** O10
Kawasaki: Japan **63** f3
Kawhia: North I., N.Z. **70** P14
Kawkareik: Burma **59** R11
Kawthule: *State*, Burma (*cap.* Pa-an) **59** R11
KAYA: Centre-Nord, Upper Volta 80 D2
Kaya: Japan **63** d3
Kayah: *State*, Burma (*cap.* Loikaw) **59** R11
Kayambi: Zambia **77** D4
Kayangel Is.: (U.S.A.), Pacific O. **61** L10
Kaydale: Trans., S. Africa **74** N/*ns.*
KAYES: *& Reg.*, Mali **80** B2
Kayly: U.S.S.R. **51** M3
Kaynary: Moldavia, U.S.S.R. **39** V13
KAYSERI: *& Prov.*, Turkey **56** D2
Kayuagung: Sumatra **65** C7
Kazachye: U.S.S.R. **49** p3
Kazakh: Azerbaydzhan, U.S.S.R. **57** J1
Kazakh: *uplands*, U.S.S.R. **51** K5
Kazakhstan S.S. Repub.: U.S.S.R. (*cap.* Alma-Ata) **51** K5
Kazalinsk: Kazakh., U.S.S.R. **51** K5
KAZAN': Tatar., U.S.S.R. **50** G3
Kazan: *riv.*, Canada **84** K5
Kazandzhik: Turkmen., U.S.S.R. **50** J7
Kazan Is.: (Jap.), Pacific O. **60** N7
Kazanlŭk: Bulgaria **39** T15
Kazatin: Ukraine **43** V12
Kazaure: Nigeria **81** F2
Kazbek: *mtn.*, Georgia, U.S.S.R. **50** F6
Kazerun: Iran **55** H9
Kazhim: U.S.S.R. **50** H2
Kazi Magomed: Azerbaydzhan, U.S.S.R. **57** L1
Kazungula: Zambia **77** C6
Kazym: *riv.*, U.S.S.R. **51** L2
Kazyr: *riv.*, U.S.S.R. **51** Q4
Kdyně Nova: Czech. **45** T6
Kéa: *& i.*, Cyclades, Greece **39** T18
Keaau: Hawaiian Is. **83** d3
Keadby: Humb., England **27** U12
Keadew: Rosc., Repub. of Ireland **30** E11
Keady: Armagh, N. Ireland **30** H11
Kealkill: Cork, Repub. of Ireland **31** C16
Keana: Nigeria **81** F3
Kearney: Nebr., U.S.A. **93** H4
Kearney: Ont., Canada **89** M3
Kearsney: Natal, S. Africa **75** J4
Kearvaig: Highland, Scotland **28** M2
Keauhau: Hawaiian Is. **83** d3
Keban: Turkey **56** F2
Kebatu: *i.*, Indonesia **65** D7
Kebbi: *riv.*, Nigeria **81** E2
Kebezen: U.S.S.R. **51** P4
Kebili: Tunisia **32** D5
Kebkabiya: Sudan **79** J7
Kebnekaise: *mtn.*, Sweden **46** Q3
Kebumen: Java **65** D8
Kecha: Ethiopia **76** E1
Keçiborlu: Turkey **56** B3
Kecskemét: Hungary **43** Q13
Kedabek: Azerbaydzhan, U.S.S.R. **57** J1
Kedah: *State*, Malaya, Malaysia (*cap.* Alor Setar) **65** b11
Kediri: Java **65** E8
Kedoua: *well*, Chad **81** H1
Kédougou: Senegal **80** B2
Kedvavom: U.S.S.R. **50** H2
Keel: Achill I., Repub. of Ireland **30** A12
Keelby: Lincs., England **27** V12
Keele Peak: Yukon, Canada **84** f5
Keeling (Cocos) Is.: (Austl), Indian O. (*cap.* West Island) **9** 15S 95E
Keelung (Kirun): Taiwan **63** W9
Keen, Mount: *mtn.*, Gram./Tayside, Scotland **28** Q6
Keenagh: Long., Repub. of Ireland **30** F12
Keene: N.H., U.S.A. **89** P4
Keeper Hill: Tip., Repub. of Ireland **31** E14
Keeseville: N.Y., U.S.A. **89** P3
Keetmanshoop: *& Dist.*, S.W. Africa **74** C3
Keewatin: Minn., U.S.A. **88** E2
Keewatin: *Dist.*, N.W.T., Canada **84** K5
Keewong: N.S.W., Austl. **71** F9
Kēfa: *Prov.*, Ethiopia (*cap.* Jimma) **79** M8
Kefallinia: *see* Cephalonia.
Kefamenanu: Timor, Indon. **65** G8
Keffi: Nigeria **81** F3
Keflavik: Iceland **46** b4
Kegali: U.S.S.R. **49** S5
Kegen: Kazakh., U.S.S.R. **51** N6
Kegueur Terbi: *mtn.*, Chad **78** H5
Kegworth: Leics., England **27** T14
Keheili: Sudan **54** D11
Kehl: W. Germany **40** P7
Kehsi Mansam: Burma **59** R10
Kei: *riv.*, S. Africa **75** G6
Keig: Grampian, Scotland **28** Q5
Keighley: W. Yorks., England **27** S12
Keila: Estonia, U.S.S.R. **47** T7
Keimoes: S. Africa **74** D4
Kei Mouth: *town*, S. Africa **75** H6
Kei Road: S. Africa **75** G6
Keiskammahoek: S. Africa **75** G6

154 Keiss—Killiecrankie

Keiss: Highland, Scotland **28** P2
Keitele: Finland **46** U5
Keitele Lake: Finland **46** T5
Keith: Grampian, Scotland **28** Q4
Keith: S. Australia **71** D11
Kekaha: Hawaiian Is. **83** b2
Kekvidze: U.S.S.R. **50** F4
Kelaa, El: Morocco **80** K8
Kelak: Uganda **76** D2
Kelang: Malaya, Malaysia **65** b12
Kelantan: *riv.*, Malaya, Malaysia **65** b11
Kelantan: *State*, Malaya, Malaysia (*cap.* Kota Bharu) **65** c11
Kelbra: E. Germany **45** R4
Keld: N. Yorks., England **26** R11
Kelham: Notts., England **27** U13
Kelheim: W. Germany **41** R7
Kelibia: Tunisia **38** M18
Kelidonya, Cape: Turkey **56** B3
Kelkit (Çiftlik): Turkey **56** F1
Kelkit: *riv.*, Turkey **56** F1
Kellett, Cape: N.W.T., Can. **84** G3
Kellmunz: W. Germany **40** Q7
Kellog: U.S.S.R. **51** P2
Kellogg: Idaho, U.S.A. **92** D3
Kelloselkä: Finland **46** V3
Kells: Antrim, N. Ireland **30** J10
Kells: Kilk., Repub. of Ireland **31** G14
Kells (Ceanannus Mór): Meath, Repub. of Ireland **30** H12
Kells, Rhinns of: *hills*, Dumf. & Gall., Scotland **29** N9
Kelme: Lithuania, U.S.S.R. **47** S9
Kélo: Chad **81** H3
Kelontekemä: Finland **46** T3
Kelowna: B.C., Canada **92** D3
Kelsall: Ches., England **27** Q13
Kelsey, North: Lincs., England **27** V13
Kelso: Natal, S. Africa **75** J5
Kelso: Borders, Scotland **29** R8
Kelso: Wash., U.S.A. **92** C3
Keltneyburn: Tay., Scot. **29** N6
Kelty: Fife, Scotland **29** P7
Kelvedon: Essex, England **25** X16
Kelvedon Hatch: Essex, England **25** W16
Kelvington: Sask., Canada **92** G2
Kem: Karelian A.S.S. Repub., U.S.S.R. **48** E4
Kema: Celebes **65** H6
Ké Macina: Mali **80** C2
Kemah: Turkey **56** F2
Kemaliye: Turkey **56** F2
Kemasik: Malaya, Malaysia **65** c11
Kemberg: E. Germany **45** S4
Kemble: Glos., England **24** R16
Kemboma: Gabon **81** G4
Kemerburgaz: Turkey (Bosporus. *Inset*) **20** *Ins.*
KEMEROVO: *& Reg.*, U.S.S.R. **51** P3
Kemi: Finland **46** T4
Kemi: *riv.*, Finland **46** T3
Kemijärvi: Finland **46** U3
Kemi Lake: Finland **46** U3
Kemmerer: Wyo., U.S.A. **92** E4
Kemnath: W. Germany **45** R6
Kemnay: Gram., Scotland **28** R5
Kémo-Gribingui: *Pref.*, Cen. Afr. Rep. (*cap.* Sibut) **76** A1
Kemp, Lake: Tex., U.S.A. **90** B9
Kempele: Finland **46** T4
Kempsey: N.S.W., Austl. **71** K8
Kempsey: Hereford & Worcester, England **24** R15
Kempston: Beds., England **25** V15
Kempten: W. Germany **40** Q8
Kempt Lake: Que., Canada **89** O2
Kempton Park: Trans., S. Africa **74** N*Ins.*
Ken: *riv.*, Dumf. & Gall., Scotland **29** N9
Ken, Loch: Dumfries & Galloway, Scotland **29** N9
Kenadsa: Algeria **80** L8
Kenai: *& penin.*, Alaska, U.S.A. **84** d5
Kenamuke Swamp: *marsh*, Sudan **76** D1
Kendal: Java **65** E8
Kendal: Cumbria, England **26** Q11
Kendal: Trans., S. Africa **75** H3
Kendall: N.S.W., Australia **71** K8
Kendallville: Ind., U.S.A. **88** J5
Kendari: Celebes **65** G7
Kendawangan: Borneo **65** E7
Kendrapara: Orissa, India **59** P10
Kendrew: S. Africa **75** F6
Kenedy: Tex., U.S.A. **90** C11
Kenegha Drift: S. Africa **75** H5
KENEMA: Eastern, Sierra Leone **80** B3
Kenga: *riv.*, U.S.S.R. **51** O3
Kenge: Zaire **81** H5
Kengtawng: Burma **59** R10
Kengtung: Burma **59** R10
Kenhardt: *& Dist.*, S. Africa **74** D4
Keni: Benin **81** E3
KENITRA: *& Prov.*, Morocco **80** K8
Kenilworth: S. Africa **74** *Ins.*
Kenilworth: War., England **25** S15
Kenimekh: Uzbek., U.S.S.R. **51** L6
Keningau: Sabah, Malaysia **65** F5
Kenly: N.C., U.S.A. **91** M8
Kenmare: Kerry, Repub. of Ireland **31** B16
Kenmare: N. Dak., U.S.A. **92** G3
Kenmare River: *est.*, Kerry, Repub. of Ireland **31** A16
Kenmore: N.S.W., Austl. **71** H10
Kenmore: Tayside, Scotland **29** O6
Kenn: Avon, England **24** Q17
Kennebec: *riv.*, Maine, U.S.A. **89** R3
Kennebunk: Maine, U.S.A. **89** Q4
Kennedy, Cape: *see* Canaveral, Cape.
Kenner: La., U.S.A. **90** *Ins.*
Kennet: *riv.*, Berks./Wilts., England **25** T17
Kennet, Vale of: England **23** K9
Kennett: Mo., U.S.A. **88** F7
Kennewick: Wash., U.S.A. **92** D3
Kennicott: Alaska, U.S.A. **84** e5
Kenninghall: Norf., Eng. **25** X15
Kennington: Kent, England **25** X17
Kenn Reef: Australia **69** K4
Kenogami: Que., Canada **89** Q1
Keno Hill: *settlement*, Yukon, Canada **84** F5
Kenora: Ont., Canada **92** J3
Kenosha: Wis., U.S.A. **88** H4
Kenova: W. Va., U.S.A. **88** K6
Kensaleyre: I. of Skye, Inner Hebr., Scotland **28** J5
Kensington: P.E.I., Canada **89** U2
Kensington & Chelsea: Gt. Ldn., England **25** V17
Kent: Ohio, U.S.A. **88** L5
Kent: *Co. & val.*, England (*co. town* Maidstone) **25** X17
Kent: *riv.*, Cumbria, Eng. **26** Q11
Kentallen: High., Scotland **29** L6
Kentani: S. Africa **75** H6
Kentford: Suff., England **25** X15
Kentisbury: Devon, England **24** O17
Kentland: Ind., U.S.A. **88** H5
Kentmere: Cumbria, Eng. **26** Q11
Kenton: Devon, England **24** P18
Kenton: Ohio, U.S.A. **88** K5
Kent Penin.: N.W.T., Can. **84** J4
Kentucky: *riv.*, Ky., U.S.A. **88** J6
Kentucky: *State*, U.S.A. (*cap.* Frankfort) **88** H7
Kentucky Dam: Ky., U.S.A. **88** G7
Kentucky L.: Ky./Tenn., U.S.A. **90** G7
Kentville: N.S., Canada **89** T3
Kentwood: La., U.S.A. **90** F10

Kenya: *Republic* **76** E2
Cap.: Nairobi
Area: 224,960 sq. miles (582,646 sq. km.)
Pop.: 12,067,000 (*1971 E*)

Kenya, Mount: Kenya **76** E3
Kenyon: Minn., U.S.A. **88** E3
Kenza: *riv.*, U.S.S.R. **51** O3
Kenzingen: W. Germany **40** N7
Keokuk: Iowa, U.S.A. **88** F5
Keonjhargarh: Orissa, India **59** P10
Kep: Cambodia **64** C4
Kepno: Poland **43** P11
Keppel Bay: Queens., Austl. **70** J4
Kerak: *& geog. reg.*, Jordan **56** D6
Kerala: *State*, India (*cap.* Trivandrum) **58** N13
Kerama: *i.*, Ryukyu Is. **63** X9
Kerang: Vict., Australia **71** E10
Kurava: Finland **47** T6
Kerch: *& str.*, U.S.S.R. **50** E5
Kerchemya: U.S.S.R. **50** H2
Kerema: New Guinea **69** H1
Keren: Ethiopia **54** E11
Kerguelen Is.: (Fr.), Indian Ocean **9** 50S 65E
Kerguelen Plateau: Southern Ocean **9** 55S 70E
Kericho: Kenya **76** E3
Kerikeri: North I., N.Z. **70** O12
Kerintji: *mtn.*, Sumatra **65** C7
Keriya (Yutien): *& riv.*, Sinkiang, China **51** O7
Kerkenna Is.: Tunisia **32** E5
Kerki: Turkmen., U.S.S.R. **51** L7
Kérkira (Corfu): *i.*, Ionian Is. (Grc.) **39** Q17
Kerma: Sudan **54** D11
Kermadec Is. (N.Z.): Pacific Ocean **67** Q8
Kermadec Trench: S. Pacific Ocean **7** 35S 180
KERMAN: *& Prov.*, Iran **55** J8
KERMANSHAH: Kermanshahan/Iran **57** K4
Kermanshahan: *Prov.*, Iran (*cap.* Kermanshah) **57** K4
Kerme, G. of: Turkey **39** U18
Kernersville: N.C., U.S.A. **88** L7
Kerns: Switzerland **40** O9
KÉROUANÉ: *& Reg.*, Guinea **80** C3
Kérouané, Mount: *mtn.*, Guinea **80** C3
Kerpe, Cape: Turkey **56** B1
Kerre: Ethiopia **76** E1
Kerrera: *i.*, Scotland **29** K7
Kerribree: N.S.W., Austl. **71** F7
Kerripi: Sudan **76** D2
Kerrobert: Sask., Canada **92** F2
Kerrville: Tex., U.S.A. **90** B10
Kerry: Powys, Wales **24** P15
Kerry: *Co.*, Repub. of Irel. (*cap.* Tralee) **31** B15
Kerry Head: *cape*, Repub. of Ireland **31** B15
Kersey: Suff., England **25** X15
Kerulen: *riv.*, Mong. **62** U5
Kerzaz: Algeria **80** L9
Keşan: Turkey **39** U16
Kese: Zaire **76** A3
Kesennuma: Japan **63** ZZ7
Kesh: Ferm., N. Ireland **30** F10
Kesh: Sligo, Repub. of Ireland **30** E11
Keshcarrigan: Leit., Repub. of Ireland **30** F11
Keshwar: Iran **57** L5
Keskin: Turkey **56** C2
Keski-Suomi: *Prov.*, Finland (*cap.* Jyväskylä) **46** T5
Kessingland: Suff., England **25** Z15
Kessock: High., Scot. **28** N4
Kestel, Lake: Turkey **56** B3
Kestell: O.F.S., S. Africa **75** H4
Kesten'ga: Karelian A.S.S. Repub., U.S.S.R. **46** W4
Kesuma: Botswana **77** C6
Keswick: Cumbria, England **26** P10
Keszthely: Hungary **43** P13
Ket': *riv.*, U.S.S.R. **51** O3
Keta: Ghana **80** E3
Ketapang: Borneo **65** D7
Ketchikan: Alaska, U.S.A. **84** f6
Kete Krachi: Ghana **80** D3
Ketley: Salop, England **27** R14
Ketrzyn: Poland **43** R9
Kettering: Northants., England **25** U15
Kettle River Range: *mtns.*, Wash., U.S.A. **92** D3
Kettlewell: N. Yorks., England **26** R11
Ketton: Leics., England **27** U14
Keuka Lake: N.Y., U.S.A. **89** N4
Keushki: U.S.S.R. **51** L2
Kevelaer: W. Germany **44** M4
Kewagama Lake: Que., Can. **89** M1
Kewanee: Ill., U.S.A. **88** G5
Kewaunee: Wis., U.S.A. **88** H3
Keweenaw Bay: *& penin.*, Mich., U.S.A. **88** G2
Kexborough: S. Yorks., Eng. **27** S12
Key, Lough: Rosc., Repub. of Ireland **30** E11
Key Harbour: Ont., Canada **88** L3
Keyingham: Humb., Eng. **27** V12
Keynsham: Avon, England **24** R17
Keyser: W. Va., U.S.A. **89** M6
Key West: Fla., U.S.A. **91** L13
Keyworth: Notts., England **27** T14
Kezhma: U.S.S.R. **49** M6
Kežmarok: Czechoslovakia **43** R12
Kgalagadi: *Dist.*, Botswana (*cap.* Tshabong) **74** D2
Kgatleng: *Dist.*, Botswana (*cap.* Mochudi) **75** G2
Kgokgole: *riv.*, S. Africa **74** E3
Khaapsalu: Estonia, U.S.S.R. **47** S7
Khaba: Saudi Arabia **55** H10
KHABAROVSK: *& Territ.*, U.S.S.R. **49** p8
Khabb: Yemen **54** G11
Khabur: *riv.*, Iraq **57** H3
Khabur: *riv.*, Syria **57** G4
Khaburah: Oman **55** J10
Khachmas: Azerbaydzhan, U.S.S.R. **50** G6
Khadkhal: Mongolia **49** M7
Khadia: Algeria **35** G18
Khaf: Iran **55** K8
Khafs: Saudi Arabia **54** G10
Khafus: U.A.E. **55** H10
Khaibar: Asir, Saudi Arabia **54** F11
Khaibar: Hijaz, Sau. Arab. **54** E9
Khairpur: Sind, Pakistan **58** L9
Khakass: *Auton. Reg.*, U.S.S.R. (*cap.* Abakan) **51** Q4
Khakhea: Botswana **77** B7
Khalafabad: Iran **57** L6
Khalkuta: U.S.S.R. **50** G5
Khálki: *i.*, Dodec. (Grc.) **39** U18
Khalkis (Chalcis): Greece **39** S17
Khalturin: U.S.S.R. **50** G3
Khaluf: Oman **55** J10
Khalung: Tibet, China **59** Q8
Khamgaon: Maharashtra, India **58** N10
Khamis Mushait: Sau. Arab. **54** F11
Khammam: Andhra Pradesh, India **58** O11
Khamthongnoi: Laos **64** D3
Khan: *& riv.*, S.W. Africa **74** A1
Khanabad: Afghanistan **51** L7
Khanaqin: Iraq **57** J4
Khan Baghdadi: Iraq **57** H5
Khan Bani Sa'ad: Iraq **57** J5
Khandak: Sudan **76** D1
Khandaq, El: Sudan **54** D11
Khand Pass: Pak./Afghan. **55** L8
Khandwa: Madhya Pradesh, India **58** N10
Khan Esh Shamat: Syria **56** E5
Khangans: S.W. Africa **74** A1
Khan Hammad: Iraq **57** J5
Khania (Canea): Crete **39** T19
Khanka, Lake: U.S.S.R. **63** Y6
Khanlar: Azerbaydzhan, U.S.S.R. **57** K1
Khanpur: Punjab, Pak. **58** M9
Khan Ruhba: Iraq **57** J6
Khan Tengri: *mtn.*, Sinkiang, China **51** O6
Khanty-Mansiysk: U.S.S.R. **51** L2
Khanu: Iran **55** J9
Khan Yunis: Egypt **55** a3
Khan Zur: Iraq **57** J4
Khapalu: Jammu & Kashmir **58** N7
Khapcheranga: U.S.S.R. **49** N8
Khar: *i.*, Persian Gulf **55** H9
Khara Usu Nor: *see* Hara Usu Nor
Kharagpur: W. Bengal, India **59** P10
Kharan Kalat: Baluchistan, Pakistan **58** L9
Kharaulakh: U.S.S.R. **49** o3
Kharfa: Saudi Arabia **54** G10
Kharg: *i.*, Persian Gulf **55** H9
Kharga, El: Egypt **54** D9
Kharga Oasis: Egypt **54** D9
Khar'kov: Ukraine **50** E5
Kharlovka: U.S.S.R. **48** e4
Kharm: Iraq **57** J6
Kharmanli: Bulgaria **39** T16
KHARTOUM: *& Prov.*, Sudan **54** D11
Khasab: Oman **55** J9
Khasavyurt: U.S.S.R. **50** G6
Khash: *& riv.*, Afghanistan **58** K8
Khashuri: Georgia, U.S.S.R. **57** H1
Khasi Hills: Meghalaya, India **59** O9
Khaskovo: Bulgaria **39** T16
Khasm el Girba: Sudan **54** E12
Khatanga: U.S.S.R. **49** M3
Khatanga: *riv.*, U.S.S.R. **49** M3
Khattushash: Hittite capital; site at Boğaz Keui S. of Sungurlu, Turkey **56** D1
Khatyrchi: Uzbek., U.S.S.R. **51** L6
Khau Lau: Thailand **65** b11
Khaur Dhuwaihin: *bay*, United Arab Emirates **55** H10
Khaur Saif: Saudi Arabia **55** H10
Khaur 'Udaid: *bay*, U.A.E./Qatar **55** H10
Khazail: *tribal area*, Iraq **57** J5
Khazarasp: Uzbek., U.S.S.R. **51** K6
Khemchik: *riv.*, U.S.S.R. **51** Q4
Khemis Mil: Algeria **35** H18
Khemisset: Morocco **80** K8
Khemmarat: Thailand **64** D3
Khenchela: Algeria **32** D4
Khenifra: Morocco **80** K8
Kherson: Ukraine **50** D5
Kheta: *riv.*, U.S.S.R. **49** l3
Khetinsiring: Chinghai, China **59** Q8
Khevkhen'yarvi: U.S.S.R. **46** V2
Khidhr: Iraq **57** J6
Khilchipur: Madhya Pradesh, India **58** N10
Khilok: U.S.S.R. **49** N7
Khin: Saudi Arabia **55** G10
Khingan, Little: *range*, Heilungkiang, China **63** X5
Khios: *see* Chios.
Khitola: U.S.S.R. **47** V6
Khiuma (Hiiumaa): *i.*, Estonia, U.S.S.R. **47** S7
Khiva: Uzbek., U.S.S.R. **51** K6
Khmel'nik: Ukraine **43** U12
Khmel'nitskiy: Ukraine **43** U12
Khoal: *well*, Chad **81** H2
Khobso Gol Nor: *lake*, Mongolia **60** E1
Khodorov: Ukraine **43** T12
Khodzheyli: Uzbek., U.S.S.R. **50** J6
Khogali: Sudan **76** C1
Khoi: Iran **57** J2
Khokhlovo: U.S.S.R. **51** M3
Khok Kloi: Thailand **64** B5
Kholm: Afghanistan **55** L7
Kholm: U.S.S.R. **50** D3
Kholmsk: U.S.S.R. **63** ZZ5
Khône: Laos **64** D4
Khong: *i.*, Cambodia **64** C4
Khongokurt: U.S.S.R. **51** K2
Khon Kaen: Thailand **64** C3
Khonu: U.S.S.R. **49** Q4
Khoper: *riv.*, U.S.S.R. **50** F4
Khora Sfakion: Crete **39** T19
Khorinsk: U.S.S.R. **49** m7
KHOROG: Gorno-Badakhshan, Tadzhik., U.S.S.R. **51** M7
Khotan (Hotien): *& riv.*, Sinkiang, China **51** N7
Khotan: *riv.*, Sinkiang, China **51** O7
Khotin: Ukraine **43** U12
KHOURIBGA: *& Prov.*, Morocco **80** K8
Khrisoupolis: Greece **39** T16
Khrom-Tau: Kazakh., U.S.S.R. **50** J4
Khuan Mao: Thailand **64** B5
Khudeira: Sudan **54** C11
Khufaifiya: Saudi Arabia **54** F10
Khulna: Bangladesh **59** P10
Khulo: Georgia, U.S.S.R. **57** H1
Khumain: Iran **57** M5
Khur: (Dasht-i-Kavir), Iran **55** J8
Khur: (*near Birjand*), Iran **55** J8
Khurasan: *geog. reg.*, Iran **55** J8
Khurda: Orissa, India **59** P10
Khurja: Uttar Pradesh, India **58** N9
Khurma: Saudi Arabia **54** F10
Khurr: *wadi*, Iraq/Sau. Arab. **57** H6
KHURRAMABAD: Lurestan, Iran **57** L5
Khurramdarreh: Iran **57** L3
Khurramshahr: Iran **57** L6
Khurunaq: Iran **55** H8
Khust: Ukraine **43** S12
Khuzdar: Baluchistan, Pakistan **58** L9
Khvalynsk: U.S.S.R. **50** G4
Khvoina: Bulgaria **39** T16
Khyber Pass: Pakistan **58** M8
Khyzy: Azerbaydzhan, U.S.S.R. **57** L1
Kiahsien: Shensi, China **62** U7
Kialineq: Greenland **85** q4
Kialing: *riv.*, China **62** T8
Kialuwa: Szechwan, China **62** S8
Kiama: N.S.W., Australia **71** J10
Kiambi: Zaire **76** C4
Kiamboni: Somalia **76** F3
Kiambu: Kenya **76** E3
Kiamichi: *riv.*, Okla., U.S.A. **90** D8
Kiamusze: Heilungkiang, China 63 Y5
Kian: Kiangsi, China **62** V9
Kiana: Alaska, U.S.A. **84** c4
Kiang: Szechwan, China **62** S9
Kiangan: Luzon, Phil. **64** G3
Kiangan: Szechwan, China **62** T9
Kiangcheng: Yunnan, China **62** S10
Kiangling (Kingchow): Hupeh, China **62** U8
Kiangpeh: Szechwan, China **62** T9
Kiangsi: *Prov.*, China (*cap.* Nanchang) **62** V9
Kiangsu: *Prov.*, China (*cap.* Nanking) **62** V8
Kiangti: Yunnan, China **62** S9
Kiangtsing: Szechwan, China **62** T9
Kiangtu: Kiangsu, China **62** V8
Kianta: Finland **46** V4
Kianta Lake: Finland **46** V4
Kiaoho: Kirin, China **63** X6
Kiaohsien: Shantung, China **62** V7
Kiaokia: Szechwan, China **62** S9
Kiating (Loshan): Szechwan, China **62** S9
Kiayukwan: Kansu, China **62** R7
Kibali: *riv.*, Zaire **76** C2
Kibambi: Zaire **61** H6
Kibanga Port: Uganda **76** D2
Kibau: Tanzania **77** E4
Kibaya: Tanzania **76** E4
Kiberashi: Tanzania **76** E4
Kiberege: Tanzania **76** E4
Kibi: Ghana **80** D3
Kibiti: Tanzania **76** E4
Kibombo: Zaire **76** C3
Kibondo: Tanzania **76** D3
Kibungu: Rwanda **76** D3
Kibworth Harcourt: Leics., England **27** U14
Kičevo: Yugoslavia **39** R16
Kichiga: U.S.S.R. **49** S6
Kichun: Hupeh, China **62** V8
Kicking Horse Pass: B.C./Alta., Canada **92** D2
Kidal: Mali **78** E6
Kidami: Ethiopia **76** E1
Kidan: *geog. reg.*, Sau. Arab. **55** H10
Kidatu: Tanzania **76** E4
Kidderminster: Hereford & Worcester, England **24** R15
Kidd's Beach: S. Africa **75** G6
Kidete: Tanzania **76** E4
Kidira: Senegal **80** B2
Kidlington: Oxon., England **25** T16
Kidsgrove: Staffs., England **27** R13
Kidston: Queens., Australia **69** G3
Kidugallo: Tanzania **76** E4
Kidwelly: Dyfed, Wales **24** N16
KIEL: Schleswig-Holstein, W. Germany **45** Q1
Kiel: Wis., U.S.A. **88** G4
Kiel Bay: W. Germany **42** M9
Kiel Canal: W. Germany **45** P1
KIELCE: *& Prov.*, Poland **43** R11
Kieler Förde: *est.*, W. Germany **45** Q1
Kienberg: Austria **41** V8
Kienchwan: Yunnan, China **62** R9
Kienhsi: Kweichow, China **62** T9
Kienkiang: Szechwan, China **62** T9
Kienko: Szechwan, China **62** T8
Kienli: Hupeh, China **62** U9
Kienning: Fukien, China **62** V9
Kienow: Fukien, China **62** V9
Kienshui: Yunnan, China **62** S10
Kienteh: Chekiang, China **62** V9
Kienyang: Hunan, China **62** T9
Kienyang: Szechwan, China **62** S8
Kiernki: Poland **46** T3
Kieta: Bougainville, Solomon Is. **67** L3
KIEV: Ukraine **50** D4
Kiewietskuil: S. Africa **74** E6
KIFFA: Assaba, Mauritania **80** B1
Kifl: Iraq **57** J5
Kifri: Iraq **57** J4
KIGALI: Rwanda **76** D3
Kiği: Turkey **57** G2
Kigille: Sudan **76** D1
KIGOMA: *& Reg.*, Tanzania **76** C3
Kihoe (Nkana): Zambia **77** C5
Kihurio: Tanzania **76** E3
Kii Mtns.: Japan **63** d4
Kii Strait: Japan **63** d4
Kijabe: Kenya **76** E3
Kikai: Amami Is., Ryukyu Is. **63** Y9
Kikale: Tanzania **76** E4
Kikinda: Yugoslavia **39** R14
Kiklades (Cyclades): *is.*, Grc. **39** T18
Kikombo: Tanzania **76** E4
Kikori: Papua/New Guinea **66** H3
Kikwit: Zaire **76** A4
Kil: Sweden **47** N7
Kilafors: Sweden **47** P6
Kilauea: Hawaiian Is. **83** b1
Kilauea: *volc.*, Hawaiian Is. **83** d3
Kilbaha: Clare, Repub. of Ireland **31** B14
Kilbarchan: Strath., Scotland **29** M8
Kilbeggan: Westmeath, Repub. of Ireland **31** F13
Kilbeheny: Lim., Repub. of Ireland **31** E15
Kilberry: Kild., Repub. of Ireland **31** G13
Kilberry: Meath, Repub. of Ireland **30** H12
Kilberry: Strath., Scotland **29** K8
Kilbirnie: Strath., Scotland **29** M8
Kilbrannan Sound: I. of Arran/Strath., Scotland **29** L8
Kilbride: Strath., Scotland **29** L7
Kilbride: Outer Heb., Scot. **28** G5
Kilbride (*NE of Blessington*), Wick., Repub. of Irel. **31** J13
Kilbride: (*S. of Wicklow*), Wick., Repub. of Ireland **31** J14
Kilbride, East: Strath., Scot. **29** N8
Kilbride, West: Strath., Scot. **29** M8
Kilbrittain: Cork., Repub. of Ireland **31** D16
Kilbuck Mtns.: Alaska, U.S.A. **84** D5
Kilcar: Don., Repub. of Irel. **30** D10
Kilchiaran: Inner Hebr., Scotland **29** J8
Kilchoan: High., Scotland **29** J6
Kilchoman: Inner Hebr., Scotland **29** J8
Kilchreest: Galway, Repub. of Ireland **31** D13
Kilchrenan: Strath., Scot. **29** L7
Kilchu: N. Korea **63** X6
Kilclief: Down, N. Ireland **30** K11
Kilcock: Kild., Repub. of Ireland **31** H13
Kilcolgan: Galway, Repub. of Ireland **31** D13
Kilconly: Galway, Repub. of Ireland **30** D12
Kilconly: Kerry, Repub. of Ireland **31** B14
Kilconnell: Galway, Repub. of Ireland **31** E13
Kilcoole: Wick., Repub. of Ireland **31** J13
Kilcormac (Frankford): Offaly, Repub. of Ireland **31** F13
Kilcorney: Cork, Repub. of Ireland **31** D15
Kilcotty: Wex., Repub. of Ireland **31** J15
Kilcoy: Queens., Australia **70** K6
Kilcreggan: Strath., Scot. **29** M8
Kilcrohane: Cork, Repub. of Ireland **31** B16
Kilcullen: Kild., Repub. of Ireland **31** H13
Kilcummin: Queens., Austl. **70** G4
Kildalkey: Meath, Repub. of Ireland **30** H12
Kildare: *& Co.*, Repub. of Ireland (*co. town* Naas) **31** H13
Kildimo: Lim., Repub. of Ireland **31** D14
Kil'din: *& i.*, U.S.S.R. **46** Y2
Kildonan: Rhodesia **77** D6
Kildonan: High., Scotland **28** O3
Kildonan: Strath., Scotland **29** L9
Kildorrery: Cork, Repub. of Ireland **31** E15
Kildrummy: Gram., Scotland **28** Q5
Kilembe: Zaire **76** A4
Kilfeakle: Tip., Repub. of Ireland **31** E15
Kilfenora: Clare, Repub. of Ireland **31** C14
Kilfinan: Strath., Scotland **29** L8
Kilfinnane: Lim., Repub. of Ireland **31** E15
Kilflynn: Kerry, Repub. of Ireland **31** B15
Kilgarvan: Kerry, Repub. of Ireland **31** C16
Kilglass: Sligo, Repub. of Ireland **30** C11
Kilgobnet: Kerry, Repub. of Ireland **31** B15
Kilgore: Tex., U.S.A. **90** D9
Kilham: Northumb., Eng. **26** R8
Kilham: Humb., England **27** V11
Kilian Qurghan: Sinkiang, China **51** N7
Kilifi: Kenya **76** E3
Kilik Pass: China/Jammu & Kashmir **58** M7
Kilimanjaro: *Reg. & mtn.*, Tanzania (*cap.* Moshi) **76** E3
Kilimatindi: Tanzania **76** D4
Kilinailau Is.: Solomon Is. **67** L2
Kilindini: Kenya **76** E3
Kilindoni: Tanzania **76** E4
Kilingi-Nymme: Estonia, U.S.S.R. **47** T7
Kilis: Turkey **56** E3
Kiliya: Ukraine **39** V14
Kilkea: Kild., Repub. of Ireland **31** H14
Kilkee: Clare, Repub. of Ireland **31** B14
Kilkeel: Down, N. Ireland **30** J11
Kilkelly: Mayo, Repub. of Ireland **30** D12
KILKENNY: *& Co.*, Repub. of Ireland **31** G14
Kilkerran: Strath., Scotland **29** K9
Kilkerrin: Galway, Repub. of Ireland **30** D12
Kilkhampton: Corn., Eng. **24** N18
Kilkieran: *& bay*, Galway, Repub. of Ireland **31** B13
Kilkis: Greece **39** S16
Kilkishen: Clare, Repub. of Ireland **31** D14
Kilkivan: Queens., Austl. **70** K6
Kill: Kild., Repub. of Ireland **31** H13
Kill: Wat., Repub. of Irel. **31** G15
Killadeas: Ferm., N. Ireland **30** F11
Killadysert: Clare., Repub. of Ireland **31** C14
Killala: *& bay*, Mayo, Repub. of Ireland **30** C11
Killaloe: Clare, Repub. of Ireland **31** E14
Killaloe Station: Ont., Can. **89** N3
Killamarsh: Derby., Eng. **27** T13
Killane: Wex., Repub. of Ireland **31** H14
Killarney: Kerry, Repub. of Ireland **31** C15
Killarney: Man., Canada **92** H3
Killarney: Queens., Austl. **71** K7
Killarney Prov. Park: Ont., Canada **88** L2
Killary Harbour: Mayo/Galway, Repub. of Ireland **30** B12
Ķilla Saifulla: *see* Qila Saifulla
Killashandra: Cavan, Repub. of Ireland **30** F11
Killashee: Long., Repub. of Ireland **30** F12
Killavullen: Cork, Repub. of Ireland **31** D15
Killead: Antrim, N. Ireland **30** J10
Killeagh: Cork, Repub. of Ireland **31** F16
Killean: Strath., Scotland **29** K8
Killeany: Aran Is., Repub. of Ireland **31** B13
Killearn: Central, Scotland **29** N7
Killegray: *i.*, Outer Hebrides, Scotland **28** G4
Killeigh: Offaly, Repub. of Ireland **31** G13
Killena: Wex., Repub. of Ireland **31** J14
Killenaule: Tip., Repub. of Ireland **31** F14
Killeter: Tyr., N. Ireland **30** F10
Killiecrankie, Pass of: Tayside, Scotland **29** O6

For Abbreviations see list on p.113. Italic type, e.g. *Ephesus*, refers to historical names not on maps. Capital letters, e.g. MADRID, show capitals of countries; small capital letters, e.g. CADIZ, show capitals of provinces, etc. General notes p.116.

Killilan—Knapdale 155

Killilan: High., Scotland 28 L5
Killimer: Clare, Repub. of Ireland 31 C14
Killimor: Galway, Repub. of Ireland 31 E13
Killin: Central, Scotland 29 N7
Killinaboy: Clare, Repub. of Ireland 31 C14
Killiney: Dublin, Repub. of Ireland 31 J13
Killingworth: Tyne & Wear, England 26 S9
Killini: Greece 39 R18
Killinick: Wex., Repub. of Ireland 31 J15
Killinkere: Cavan, Repub. of Ireland 30 G12
Killogeary: Mayo, Repub. of Ireland 30 C11
Killorglin: Kerry, Repub. of Ireland 31 B15
Killough: Down, N. Ireland 30 K11
Killucan: Westmeath, Repub. of Ireland 30 G12
Killwinning: Strath., Scot. 29 M8
Killybegs: Don., Repub. of Ireland 30 E10
Killygordon: Don., Repub. of Ireland 30 F10
Killylea: Armagh, N. Irel. 30 H11
Killyleagh: Down, N. Irel. 30 K11
Kilmacolm: Strath., Scot. 29 M8
Kilmacow: Kilk., Repub. of Ireland 31 G15
Kilmacrenan: Don., Repub. of Ireland 30 F9
Kilmacthomas: Wat., Repub. of Ireland 31 G15
Kilmaganny: Kilk., Repub. of Ireland 31 G15
Kilmaine: Mayo, Repub. of Ireland 30 C12
Kilmallock: Lim., Repub. of Ireland 31 D15
Kilmaluag: I. of Skye, Inner Hebr., Scotland 28 J4
Kilmanagh: Kilk., Repub. of Ireland 31 G14
Kilmany: Fife, Scotland 29 Q7
Kilmarnock: Strath., Scot. 29 N8
Kilmartin: Strath., Scotland 29 L7
Kilmaurs: Strath., Scotland 29 M8
Kilmeadan: Wat., Repub. of Ireland 31 G15
Kilmeedy: Lim., Repub. of Ireland 31 D15
Kilmelford: Strath., Scot. 29 L7
Kilmessan: Meath, Repub. of Ireland 30 H12
Kilmichael: Cork, Repub. of Ireland 31 C16
Kilmichael Glassary: Strathclyde, Scotland 29 L7
Kilmihil: Clare, Repub. of Ireland 31 C14
Kilmore: Strath., Scotland 29 L7
Kilmore: Armagh, N. Irel. 30 H11
Kilmore: Down, N. Ireland 30 K11
Kilmore: Vict., Australia 71 F11
Kilmore: Wex., Repub. of Ireland 31 H15
Kilmore Quay: Wex., Repub. of Ireland 31 H15
Kilmory: High., Scotland 29 K6
Kilmory: Strath., Scotland 23 L9
Kilmory: Inner Hebr., Scot. 28 J5
Kilmovee: Mayo, Repub. of Ireland 30 D12
Kilmuir: High., Scot. 28 N4
Kilmun: Strath., Scotland 29 M8
Kilmurry: Clare, Repub. of Ireland 31 D14
Kilnaleck: Cavan, Repub. of Ireland 30 G12
Kilnamona: Clare, Repub. of Ireland 31 C14
Kilninian: I. of Mull, Inner Hebr., Scotland 29 J6
Kilninver: Strath., Scotland 29 K7
Kilnsea: Humb., England 27 W12
Kilo: Zaïre 76 D2
Kilombero: riv., Tanzania 76 E4
Kilosa: Tanzania 76 E4
Kilpis Lake: Finland 46 R2
Kilrea: Lon., N. Ireland 30 H10
Kilreekill: Galway, Repub. of Ireland 31 E13
Kilrenny: Fife, Scotland 29 Q7
Kilronan: Aran Is., Repub. of Ireland 31 B13
Kilrush: Clare, Repub. of Ireland 31 C14
Kilsaran: Louth, Repub. of Ireland 30 J12
Kilsby: Northants., England 25 T15
Kilshanny: Clare, Repub. of Ireland 31 C14
Kilsheelan: Tip., Repub. of Ireland 31 F15
Kilskeer: Meath, Repub. of Ireland 30 H12
Kilsyth: Strath., Scotland 29 N8
Kiltamagh: Mayo, Repub. of Ireland 30 D12
Kiltartan: Galway, Repub. of Ireland 31 D13
Kiltegan: Wick., Repub. of Ireland 31 H14
Kiltormer: Galway, Repub. of Ireland 31 E13
Kiltulagh: Galway, Repub. of Ireland 31 D13
Kiltyclogher: Leit., Repub. of Ireland 30 E11
Kilvaxter: Inner Hebr., Scotland 28 J4
Kilwa: Zambia 77 C4
Kilwa Kisiwani: Tanzania 77 E4
Kilwa Kivinje: Tanzania 77 E4
Kilworth: & mtns., Cork, Repub. of Ireland 31 E15
Kilyos: Turkey (Bosporus Inset) 20 Ins.
Kim: Tadzhik., U.S.S.R. 51 M6
Kimamba: Tanzania 76 E4
Kimambi: Tanzania 77 E4
Kimba: S. Australia 71 B9
Kimball: Nebr., U.S.A. 92 G4
Kimberley: B.C., Canada 92 D3
Kimberley: Norf., England 25 Y14
Kimberley: Notts., England 27 T14
Kimberley: & Dist., S. Africa 75 F4
Kimberley: geog. reg., W. Australia 68 D3
Kimbolton: Cambs., England 25 V15
Kimboto: Congo 81 G5
Kimen: Anhwei, China 62 V9
Kimi: Cameroun 81 G3
Kimi: Euboea, Greece 39 T17
Kimito: i., Finland 47 S6
Kimkang (Tsingmai): Hainan, China 62 T11
Kimolos: i., Cyclades (Grc.) 39 T18
Kimpanzou: Congo 81 G5
Kimpese: Zaïre 81 G6
Kimpton: Hants., England 25 S17
Kimpton: Herts., England 25 V16
Kimry: U.S.S.R. 50 E3
Kinabalu: mtn., Sabah, Malaysia 65 F5
Kinbrace: High., Scotland 28 O3
Kincardine: Fife, Scotland 29 O7
Kincardine: Ont., Canada 88 L3
Kincardine: High., Scot. 28 N4
Kincardine O'Neil: Grampian, Scotland 28 Q5
Kinchwan: Kirin, China 63 X6
Kincraig: Highland, Scotland 28 O5
Kinda: Zaïre 77 C4
Kinder: La., U.S.A. 90 E10
Kinder Scout: mtn., Derby., England 27 S13
Kindersley: Sask., Canada 92 F2
KINDIA: & Reg., Guinea 80 B2
Kindu: Zaïre 76 C3
Kinel': U.S.S.R. 50 H4
Kinel'-Cherkasy: U.S.S.R. 50 H4
Kineshma: U.S.S.R. 50 F3
Kineton: War., England 25 T15
Kinfauns: Tay., Scotland 29 P7
King: i., Mergui Arch., Burma 59 R12
King: riv., China 62 T8
Kingairloch: dist., Highland, Scotland 29 K6
Kingaroy: Queens., Austl. 70 J6
Kingarth: Strath., Scotland 29 L8
Kingcheng: Heilungkiang, China 63 X5
Kingchow (Kiangling): Hupeh, China 62 U8
King Christian I.: N.W.T., Canada 84 j2
King Christian IX Land: Greenland 85 Q4
King Christian X Land: Greenland 85 R3
Kingchwan: Kansu, China 62 T7
Kingcome Inlet: town, B.C., Canada 92 B2
Kingerban: Iraq 57 J4
King Frederik VI Coast: Greenland 85 p5
King Frederik VIII Land: Greenland 85 R2
King George Mt.: B.C./Alta., Canada 92 E2
Kinghan, Great: mtns., Inner Mongolia, China 63 W5
Kinghan, Little: mtns., Heilungkiang, China 63 X5
Kinghorn: Fife, Scotland 29 P7
Kingisepp: U.S.S.R. 47 V7
Kingissepp: Estonia, U.S.S.R. 47 S7
King I.: B.C., Canada 92 B2
King I.: Tas., Australia 68 G7
King Karl Land: is., Spits. 48 d2
Kingku: Yunnan, China 62 S10
King Lake National Park: Vict., Australia 71 F11
King Leopold Ranges: W. Australia 68 D3
Kingman: Kans., U.S.A. 90 B7
Kingmen: Hupeh, China 62 U8
Kingoonya: S. Australia 69 F6
King Oscars Fiord: Grnld. 85 r3
Kingsand: Corn., England 24 N19
Kingsbarns: Fife, Scotland 29 Q7
Kingsbridge: Devon, Eng. 24 O19
Kings Bromley: Staffs., Eng. 27 S14
Kingsbury Episcopi: Som., England 24 Q18
Kings Canyon Nat. Park: Calif., U.S.A. 93 D5
King's Caple: Hereford & Worcester, England 24 Q16
Kingsclere: Hants., England 25 T17
Kingscote: S. Africa 75 H5
Kingscote: S. Australia 71 B10
Kingscourt: Cavan, Repub. of Ireland 30 H12
Kingsing: Heilungkiang, China 63 W5
Kingskerswell: Devon, Eng. 24 O19
Kingkettle: Fife, Scotland 29 P7
Kingsland: Hereford & Worcester, England 24 Q15
King's Langley: Herts., Eng. 25 V16
Kingsley: Ches., England 27 Q13
Kingsley: Hants., England 25 U17
Kingsley: Natal, S. Africa 75 J3
Kingsley: Staffs., England 27 S13
Kingsley Dam: Nebr., U.S.A. 92 G4
King's Lynn: Norf., England 25 W14
Kingsmill Group: is., Gilbert Is. 67 P2
Kings Mountain: city, N.C., U.S.A. 91 L8
Kingsnorth: Kent, England 25 X17
King's Norton: W. Mid., Eng. 24 S15
King's Nympton: Devon, England 24 O18
King Sound: W. Australia 68 C3
Kings Peak: Utah, U.S.A. 93 E4
Kings Point: Newf., Canada 85 u2
Kingsport: Tenn., U.S.A. 88 K7
King's Somborne: Hants., England 25 T17
King's Sutton: Northants., England 25 T15
Kingsteignton: Devon, Eng. 24 O18
Kingston: Devon, England 24 O19
Kingston: Gram., Scotland 28 P4
Kingston: Gt. Ldn., England 25 V17
KINGSTON: Jamaica 86 Ins.
Kingston: N.Y., U.S.A. 89 O5
Kingston: Ont., Canada 89 N3
Kingston: Pa., U.S.A. 89 O5
Kingston: S. Australia 71 C11
Kingston: South I., N.Z. 70 M17
Kingston Bagpuize: Oxon., England 25 T16
Kingstone: Hereford & Worcester, England 24 Q15
Kingston upon Hull: Humberside, England 27 V12
Kingstown (Dun Laoghaire): Dublin, Repub. of Ireland 31 J13
KINGSTOWN: St. Vincent, Windward Is. 87 c4
Kingstree: S.C., U.S.A. 91 M9
Kingsville: Tex., U.S.A. 90 C12
Kingswear: Devon, England 24 O19
Kingswood: Avon, England 24 R17
Kingswood: Trans., S. Afr. 75 F3
Kingtai: Kansu, China 62 S7
Kington: Hereford & Worcester, England 24 P15
Kingtung: Yunnan, China 62 S10
Kingussie: High., Scotland 28 N5
King William I.: N.W.T., Canada 84 K4
King William Land: Grnld. 85 r2
Kingwilliamstown: Cork, Repub. of Ireland 31 C15
King William's Town: & Dist., S. Africa 75 G6
Kingwood: W. Va., U.S.A. 89 M6
Kingyang: Kansu, China 62 T7
Kingyuan: Chekiang, China 62 V9
Kinhwa: Chekiang, China 62 V9
Kiniama: Zaïre 77 C5
Kinkala: Congo 81 G5
Kinki: Ninghsia Hui, China 62 T7
Kin Kin: Queens., Austl. 70 K6
Kinloch: Inner Hebr., Scot. 28 J5
Kinlochbervie: High., Scot. 28 L3
Kinlocheil: Strath., Scot. 29 L6
Kinlochewe: High., Scot. 28 L4
Kinlochleven: High., Scot. 29 M6
Kinloch Rannoch: Tayside, Scotland 29 N6
Kinloss: Gram., Scotland 28 O4
Kinlough: Leit., Repub. of Ireland 30 E11
Kinn: Iceland 46 e3
Kinnairds Head: Gram., Scot. 28 S4
Kinneff: Gram., Scotland 28 R6
Kinnegad: Westmeath, Repub. of Ireland 30 G13
Kinnesswood: Tay., Scot. 29 P7
Kinnitty: Offaly, Repub. of Ireland 31 F13
Kinnula: Finland 46 T5
Kino: riv., Japan 63 d3
Kinomoto: Mie, Japan 63 e4
Kinomoto: Shiga, Japan 63 e3
Kinoni: Uganda 76 D3
Kinross: Tayside, Scotland 29 P7
Kinsale: Cork, Repub. of Ireland 31 D16
Kinsale Harbour: Cork, Repub. of Ireland 31 E16
Kinsarvik: Norway 47 K6
Kinsha (Yangtze): riv., China 62 S9
KINSHASA: Zaïre 81 H5
Kinsiang: Shantung, China 62 V8
Kinsley: Kans., U.S.A. 90 B7
Kinston: N.C., U.S.A. 91 N8
Kinta: Kansu, China 62 R6
Kintail: dist., High., Scotland 28 L5
Kintampo: Ghana 80 D3
Kintap: Borneo 65 F7
Kintbury: Berks., England 25 T17
Kintinku: Tanzania 76 E4
Kintore: Gram., Scotland 28 R5
Kintra: Inner Hebr., Scot. 29 J8
Kintyre: penin., Strathclyde, Scotland 29 K8
Kintyre, Mull of: cape, Strathclyde, Scotland 29 K9
Kinu: Burma 59 R10
Kinuso: Alta., Canada 92 D1
Kinvarra: Galway, Repub. of Ireland 31 D13
Kinyangiri: Tanzania 76 D3
Kinzig: riv., W. Germany 40 O7
Kiolen Mtns: Norway Sweden 46 O3
Kiomboi: Tanzania 76 D3
Kioshan: Honan, China 62 U8
Kiowa: Kans., U.S.A. 90 B7
Kiowezi: Kenya 76 E3
Kiparissia: & gulf, Greece 39 R18
Kipawa, Lake: Que., Canada 89 M2
Kipembawe: Tanzania 76 D4
Kipfenberg: W. Germany 41 R7
Kipili: Tanzania 76 D4
Kipilingu: Zaïre 77 C5
Kipini: Kenya 76 F3
Kippax: W. Yorks., England 27 T12
Kippen: Central, Scotland 29 N7
Kippure: mtn., Wick., Dublin, Repub. of Ireland 31 J13
Kipushi: Zaïre 77 C5
Kipushia: Kasai Oriental, Zaïre 76 C4
Kipushia: Shaba, Zaïre 77 C5
Kira Kira: Solomon Is. 67 M4
Kiraz: Turkey 39 V17
Kirazli: Turkey (Dardan Inset) 20 Ins.
Kirby Moorside: N. Yorks., England 26 U11
Kirby, West: Ches., England 27 P13
Kirby Muxloe: Leics., Eng. 27 T14
Kirchberg: W. Germany 44 N6
Kirchberg: Styria, Austria 41 V9
Kirchberg: Tirol, Austria 41 S8
Kirchdorf: Austria 41 U8
Kirch Grubenhagen: E. Ger. 45 S2
Kirchhain: Cottbus, E. Germany 45 T4
Kirchhain: Hesse, W. Ger. 44 O5
Kirchheim: W. Germany 40 P7
Kirchhundem: W. Germany 44 O4
Kircubbin: Down, N. Irel. 30 K11
Kirensk: U.S.S.R. 49 m6
Kirganik: U.S.S.R. 49 r7
Kirgiz S.S. Repub.: U.S.S.R. (cap. Frunze) 51 M6
Kirgiz-Miyaki: U.S.S.R. 50 H4
Kiri: Zaïre 76 A3
Kiri: Mali 80 D2
Kırıkhan: Turkey 56 E3
Kırıkkale: Turkey 56 C2
Kirillov: U.S.S.R. 50 E3
Kirin (Chilin): Kirin, China 63 X6
Kirin: Prov. China [cap. Changchun (Hsinking)] 63 X6
Kirit: Somalia 79 R18
Kiriwina: i., New Guinea 69 J1
Kirkabister: Shetland Is. 28 Ins.
Kirkağaç: Turkey 39 U17
Kirkbampton: Cumbria, Eng. 26 P10
Kirkbean: Dumfries & Galloway, Scotland 29 O10
Kirkbride: Cumbria, Eng. 26 P10
Kirkbuddo: Tay., Scotland 29 Q6
Kirkby: Mers., England 27 Q13
Kirkby, South: W. Yorks., England 27 T12
Kirkby in Ashfield: Notts., England 27 T13
Kirkby Lonsdale: Cumbria, England 26 Q11
Kirkby Malham: N. Yorks., England 27 R11
Kirkby Mallory: Leics., Eng. 27 T14
Kirkby Malzeard: N. Yorks., England 26 S11
Kirkby Stephen: Cumbria, England 26 R11
Kirkby Thore: Cumbria, England 26 Q10
Kirkcaldy: Fife, Scotland 29 P7
Kirkcambeck: Cumb., Eng. 26 Q9
Kirkcolm: Dumfries & Galloway, Scotland 29 L10
Kirkconnel: Dumfries & Galloway, Scotland 20 O9
Kirkcowan: Dumfries & Galloway, Scotland 29 M10
Kircudbright: Dumfries & Galloway, Scotland 29 N10
Kirkee: Maharashtra, India 58 M11
Kirkenes: Norway 46 W2
Kirkgunzeon: Dumfries & Galloway, Scotland 29 O10
Kirkham: Lancs., England 27 Q12
Kirkham: N. Yorks., England 27 U11
Kirkhill of Kennethmont: Grampian, Scotland 28 Q5
Kirkibost I.: Outer Hebr., Scotland 28 G4
Kirkinner: Dumfries & Galloway, Scotland 29 N10
Kirkintilloch: Strath., Scot. 29 N8
Kirk Ireton: Derby., Eng. 27 S13
Kirkiston Range: South I., New Zealand 70 N17
Kirkjubæjarklaustur: Iceland 46 d5
Kirkjubær: Iceland 46 f4
Kirkland: Dumfries & Galloway, Scotland 20 O9
Kirkland Lake: city, Ont., Canada 88 L1
Kirk Langley: Derby., Eng. 27 S14
KIRKLARELI: & Prov., Tur. 39 U16
Kirkliston: Lothian, Scotland 29 P8
Kirkliston Range: South I., New Zealand 70 N17
Kirkmaiden: Dumfries & Galloway, Scotland 29 M10
Kirkmichael: I. of Man, U.K. 26 M11
Kirkmichael: Tay., Scotland 29 P6
Kirk of Mochrum: Dumfries & Galloway, Scotland 29 M10
Kirkoswald: Strath., Scot. 29 M9
Kirkoswald: Cumbria, Eng. 26 Q10
Kirkpatrick: Dumfries & Galloway, Scotland 29 P9
Kirkpatrick Durham: Dumfries & Galloway, Scotland 29 O9
Kirkstead: Lincs., England 27 V13
Kirksville: Mo., U.S.A. 88 E5
Kirkton of Durris: Grampian, Scotland 28 R5
Kirkton of Glenbuchat: Grampian, Scotland 28 P5
Kirkton of Glenisla: Tayside, Scotland 29 P6
Kirkton of Kingoldrum: Tayside, Scotland 29 P6
Kirkton of Menmuir: Tayside, Scotland 29 Q6
Kirktown of Alvah: Grampian, Scotland 28 Q4
Kirktown of Auchterless: Grampian, Scotland 28 R5
Kirktown of Clatt: Grampian, Scotland 28 Q5
Kirktown of Deskford: Grampian, Scotland 28 Q4
Kirktown of Slains: Grampian, Scotland 28 S5
Kirkuk: Iraq 57 J4
KIRKWALL: Mainland, Orkney Is. 28 Q2
Kirkwhelpington: Northumb., England 26 R9
Kirkwood: S. Africa 75 F6
Kirman: see Kerman.
Kirmasti: riv., Turkey 56 A2
Kirmir: riv., Turkey 56 C1
Kirn: W. Germany 44 N6
KIROV: & Reg., U.S.S.R. 50 G3
Kirovabad: Azerbaydzhan, U.S.S.R. 57 K1
Kirovakan: Armenia, U.S.S.R. 57 J1
Kirovgrad: U.S.S.R. 51 K3
Kirov Is.: U.S.S.R. 48 k2
Kirovo: Kirgiz., U.S.S.R. 51 M6
Kirovograd: Ukraine 50 D5
Kirovsk: Turkmen., U.S.S.R. 51 K7
Kirovsk: U.S.S.R. 48 E4
Kirovskiy: Astrakhan, U.S.S.R. 50 G5
Kirovskiy: Kazakh., U.S.S.R. 51 N6
Kirovskiy: U.S.S.R. 63 Y5
Kirovskoye: Kirgiz., U.S.S.R. 51 M6
Kirriemuir: Tay., Scotland 29 P6
Kirs: U.S.S.R. 50 H3
Kirsanov: U.S.S.R. 50 F4
KIRŞEHIR: & Prov., Turkey 56 D2
Kirtachi: Niger 81 E2
Kirte (Krithia): Turkey (Dardan. Inset) 20 Ins.
Kirtlington: Oxon., England 25 T16
Kirtomy: High., Scotland 28 N2
Kirton: Lincs., England 27 V14
Kirton in Lindsey: Humberside, England 27 U13
Kirun (Keelung): Taiwan, 63 W9
Kiruna: Sweden 46 R3
Kirundu: Zaïre 76 C3
Kirurumo: Tanzania 76 D4
Kirus, West: S.W. Africa 74 C3
Kirus, East: S.W. Africa 74 C3
Kirwee: South I., N.Z. 70 O16
Kiryu: Japan 63 f2
Kisa: Japan 63 c3
Kisaki: Tanzania 76 E4
Kisandji: Zaïre 76 A4
KISANGANI: Haut-Zaïre, Zaïre 76 C2
Kisangire: Tanzania 76 E4
Kisar: i., Indonesia 65 H8
Kisengwa: Zaïre 76 C4
Kisenyi: Rwanda 76 C3
Kish: Sumerian city site at Tall al-Uhēmir, N. of Hilla, Iraq 57 J5
Kishangarh: Rajasthan, India 58 M9
Kishi: Nigeria 81 E3
KISHINEV: Moldavia, U.S.S.R. 50 C5
Kishiwada: Japan 63 d3
Kishm: Afghanistan 51 L7
Kishon: biblical name of river rising near Megiddo and flowing NW. to sea at Haifa, Israel 55 a2
Kishorganj: Bangladesh 59 Q10
Kishtwar: Jammu & Kashmir 58 N8
Kisii: Kenya 76 D3
Kisiju: Tanzania 76 E4
Kisikli: Turkey (Bosporus Inset) 20 Ins.
Kisiwani: Tanzania 76 E3
Kiska: i., Aleutians 84 a7
Kiskorös: Hungary 43 Q13
Kiskunfelegyháza: Hungary 43 Q13
Kiskunhalas: Hungary 43 Q13
Kiskunmajsa: Hungary 43 Q13
Kislingbury: Northants., England 25 U15
Kislovodsk: U.S.S.R. 50 F6
Kismayu: Somalia 76 F3
Kiso: riv., Japan 63 e3
Kiso Mtns.: Japan 63 e3
Kisseraing: i., Mergui Arch., Burma 59 R12
KISSIDOUGOU: & Reg., Guinea 80 B3
Kissimmee: Fla., U.S.A. 91 L11
Kissimmee: riv., Fla., U.S.A. 91 L12
Kissimmee, Lake: Fla., U.S.A. 91 L12
Kissinger: B.C., Canada 92 C3
Kississing: lake, Man., Canada 92 G1
Kistna (Krishna): riv., India 58 N11
Kistrand: Norway 46 T1
Kisujszállás: Hungary 43 R13
Kisuki: Japan 63 c3
KISUMU: Nyanza, Kenya 76 D3
Kisvárda: Hungary 43 S12
Kiswere: Tanzania 77 E4
Kita: Mali 80 C2
Kita: i. (Jap.), Philippine Sea 60 L6
Kita Iwo: i., Kazan Is. 60 H6
Kitakata: Japan 63 f2
Kitakyushu: Japan 63 b4
Kitale: Kenya 76 E2
Kitangari: Tanzania 77 E5
Kit Carson: Colo., U.S.A. 93 G5
Kitchener: Ont., Canada 88 L4
Kitega: Burundi 76 C3
Kitete: Tanzania 76 E4
Kitgum: Uganda 76 D2
Kithira: Greece 39 S18
Kithira (Cerigo): i., Greece 39 S18
Kithirai Str.: Crete/Andikithera 39 S19
Kithnos (Thermia): i., Grc. 39 T18
Kitimat: B.C., Canada 92 B2
Kitoma: Uganda 76 D2
Kitsuki: Japan 63 b4
Kittanning: Pa., U.S.A. 89 M5
Kittilä: Finland 46 T3
Kitty Hawk: N.C., U.S.A. 89 O7
Kitui: Kenya 76 E3
Kitunda: Tanzania 76 D4
Kitwe: Zambia 77 C5
Kitzbühel: Austria 41 S8
Kitzbühel Alps: Austria 41 S8
Kitzingen: W. Germany 45 Q6
Kiucheng: Yunnan, China 62 R10
Kiuchuan (Suchow): Kansu, China 62 R7
Kiukiang: Kiangsi, China 62 V9
Kiunglai: Szechwan, China 62 S8
Kiungshan: China 62 U11
Kiupeh: Yunnan, China 62 S10
Kiuruvesi: Finland 46 U5
Kivak: U.S.S.R. 49 u5
Kivalina: Alaska, U.S.A. 84 c4
Kivi Lake: Finland 46 T5
Kivitoo: N.W.T., Canada 85 n4
Kivu: Prov., Zaïre (cap. Bukavu) 76 C3
Kivu Lake: Rwanda/Zaïre 76 C3
Kiwalik: Alaska, U.S.A. 84 c4
Kiya, U.S.S.R. 48 F4
Kiya: riv., U.S.S.R. 51 P3
Kiyakty: Kazakh., U.S.S.R. 51 L5
Kiyang: Hunan, China 62 U9
Kiyeng-Yuryakh: U.S.S.R. 49 P5
Kiyevka: Kazakh., U.S.S.R. 51 M4
Kiyma: Kazakh., U.S.S.R. 51 L4
Kizel: U.S.S.R. 50 J3
Kızıl: riv., Turkey 56 D1
Kızılcahamam: Turkey 56 C1
Kizil'skoye: U.S.S.R. 50 J4
Kiziltepe (Koçhisar): Turkey 57 G3
Kiziltoprak: Turkey (Bosporus Inset) 20 Ins.
Kizlyar: U.S.S.R. 50 G6
Kizu: Japan 63 d3
Kizyl-Arvat: Turkmen., U.S.S.R. 50 J7
Kizyl-Atrek: Turkmen., U.S.S.R. 50 H7
Kjelvik: Norway 46 U1
Kjerringøy: Norway 46 O3
Klaarstroom: S. Africa 74 E6
Kladanj: Yugoslavia 39 Q14
Kladno: Czechoslovakia 45 U5
Kladovo: Yugoslavia 39 S14
Kladow: E. Germany 45 T3
Kladuša: Yugoslavia 41 V10
KLAGENFURT: Carinthia, Austria 41 U9
Klaipeda (Memel): Lithuania, U.S.S.R. 47 R9
Klamath: riv., Calif./Oreg., U.S.A. 92 C4
Klamath Falls: city, Oreg., U.S.A. 92 C4
Klamath Mtns.: Calif., U.S.A. 92 C4
Klanjec: Yugoslavia 41 V9
Klar: riv., Sweden/Norway 47 N6
Klar (Trysil): riv., Norway 47 M6
Klašterec: Czechoslovakia 45 T5
Klatovy: Czechoslovakia 45 T6
Klaus: Austria 41 U8
Klausenburg: German name of Romanian town Cluj 39 S13
Klauszewo: Poland 45 W2
Klawer: S. Africa 74 C5
Kle: Mali 80 C2
Klein: Austria 41 V9
Kleinbegin: S. Africa 74 D4
Kleinenberg: W. Germany 44 O4
Kleinkaras: S.W. Africa 74 C3
Kleinmond: S. Africa 74 C7
Kleinpoort: S. Africa 75 F6
Klein Reifling: Austria 41 U8
Kleinriet: riv., S. Africa 74 D5
Klepp: Norway 47 J7
Klerksdorp: & Dist., Trans., S. Africa 75 G3
Klerkskraal: Trans., S. Afr. 75 G3
Kleve: W. Germany 44 M4
Klinaklini: riv., B.C., Can. 92 B2
Kling: Mindanao, Phil. 65 G5
Klinghardt Mtns.: S.W. Africa 74 A3
Klintsy: U.S.S.R. 50 D4
Klip: riv., Cape Prov., S. Africa 75 H3
Klip: riv., Natal, S. Africa 75 H4
Klip: riv., Trans., S. Africa 74 M Ins.
Klipdam: S.W. Africa 74 C3
Klipgat: S. Africa 75 F6
Klipkrans: S. Africa 74 E6
Klippan: O.F.S., S. Africa 75 G3
Klippan: Sweden 47 N8
Klipplaat: S. Africa 75 F6
Kliprivier: Trans., S. Africa 74 N Ins.
Klipspruit: O.F.S., S. Africa 75 G3
Kliuč: Yugoslavia 38 P14
Kłobucko: Poland 43 Q11
Kłodawa: Poland 43 Q10
Kłodzko: Poland 43 P11
Klondike: small stream entering river Yukon at Dawson. Since 1897 has given its name to the entire goldfields of this area, Yukon, Canada 84 F5
Klong: riv., Thailand 64 B4
Klos: Albania 39 R16
Klosterneuburg: Austria 41 W7
Klosters: Switzerland 40 P9
Kloster Zinna: E. Germany 45 T3
Klotze: E. Germany 45 R3
Klouto: Togo 80 E3
Klovsjö: Sweden 46 O5
Kluane: Yukon, Canada 84 F5
Kluang: Malaya, Malaysia 65 c12
Kluczbork: Poland 43 Q11
Klyuchi: Altai, U.S.S.R. 51 N4
Klyuchi: U.S.S.R. 49 S6
Knapdaar: S. Africa 75 G5
Knapdale: dist., Strathclyde, Scotland 29 K8

For Abbreviations see list on p.113. Italic type, e.g. *Ephesus*, refers to historical names not on maps. Capital letters, e.g. MADRID, show capitals of countries; small capital letters, e.g. CADIZ, show capitals of provinces, etc. General notes p.116.

Knapton: Norf., England 25 Y14
Knaresborough: N. Yorks.,
England 27 T11
Knayton: N. Yorks., Eng. 26 T11
Knebworth: Herts., Eng. 25 V16
Knee Lake: Man., Canada 92 J1
Kneesall: Notts., England 27 U13
Knezha: Bulgaria 39 T15
Knighton: Powys, Wales 24 P15
Knightstown: Kerry, Repub.
of Ireland 31 A16
Knin: Yugoslavia 38 P14
Knittelfeld: Austria 41 U8
Kniveton: Derby., England 27 S13
Knjaževac: Yugoslavia 39 S15
Knock: Grampian, Scotland 28 Q4
Knock: Clare, Repub. of
Ireland 31 C14
Knock: I. of Lewis, Outer
Hebr., Scotland 28 J3
Knock: Mayo, Repub. of
Ireland 30 D12
Knockaderry: Lim., Repub.
of Ireland 31 D15
Knockadoon Head: cape,
Cork, Repub. of Ireland 31 F16
Knockando: Gram., Scot. 28 P5
Knockanteagal: Outer Hebr.,
Scotland 28 G5
Knockboy: mtn., Cork/Kerry,
Repub. of Ireland 31 C16
Knockbridge: Louth, Repub.
of Ireland 30 J12
Knockcroghery: Rosc., Repub.
of Ireland 30 E12
Knockholt: Kent, England 25 W17
Knockin: Salop, England 27 P14
Knocklayd: hill, Antrim,
N. Ireland 30 J9
Knocklong: Lim., Repub. of
Ireland 31 E15
Knockmahon: Wat., Repub.
of Ireland 31 G15
Knockmealdown Mtns.: Tip./Wat.,
Repub. of Ireland 31 F15
Knocknagashel: Kerry, Repub.
of Ireland 31 C15
Knocknagree: Cork, Repub.
of Ireland 31 C15
Knockraha: Cork, Repub. of
Ireland 31 E16
Knocktopher: Kilk., Repub.
of Ireland 31 G15
Knokke: Belgium 44 J4
Knottingley: W. Yorks., Eng. 27 T12
Knowle: W. Midlands, England
25 S15
Knowstone: Devon, England 24 O18
Knox: Ind., U.S.A. 88 H5
Knoxville: Iowa, U.S.A. 88 E5
Knoxville: Tenn., U.S.A. 88 K7
Knoydart: dist., High., Scot 28 K5
Knoyle, East: Wilts., Eng. 24 R17
Knucklas: Powys, Wales 24 P15
Knud Rasmussens Land:
Greenland 85 R4
Knutsford: Ches., England 27 R13
Knyazhaya Guba: U.S.S.R. 46 X3
Knysna: & Dist., S. Africa 74 E7
Koa: riv., S. Africa 74 C4
Koba: Bangka, Indonesia 65 D7
Koba: Chad 81 H2
Kobarid: Yugoslavia 41 T9
Kobayashi: Japan 63 b5
Kobdo: riv., Mongolia 51 Q5
KOBE: Hyogo, Japan 63 d3
København: see Copenhagen.
Koblenz: W. Germany 44 N5
Koblenz: Dist., Rhineland-Palatinate,
West Germany 44 N5
Kobo: see Tekossu.
Kobrin: Byelorussia 43 T10
Kobroör: i., Aru Is., Indon. 61 L13
Kobuchizawa: Japan 63 f3
Kobuk: riv., Alaska, U.S.A. 84 D4
Kobuleti: Georgia, U.S.S.R. 57 G1
Koca: riv., Turkey 56 A3
Kocaçeşme: Turkey (Dardan.
Inset) 20 Ins.
Kocaeli: Prov., Turkey
(cap. Izmit) 56 B1
Kočani: Yugoslavia 39 S16
Koceljeva: Yugoslavia 39 Q14
Kočevje: Yugoslavia 41 U10
Ko Chan: i., Thailand 64 B5
Koch Bihar: W. Bengal, India
59 P9
Kochel: W. Germany 41 R8
Kochenevo: U.S.S.R. 51 O3
Kocher: riv., W. Germany 44 P6
KOCHI: & Pref., Japan 63 c5
Koçhisar: Ankara, Turkey 56 C2
Koçhisar: Mardin, Turkey
see Kiziltepe.
Kochki: U.S.S.R. 51 O4
Kochkorka: Kirgiz., U.S.S.R. 51 N6
Kochumdek: U.S.S.R. 49 L5
Kocie Mtns.: Poland 45 V4
Kocksoord: Trans., S. Africa 74 M Ins.
Kodaikanal: Tamil Nadu,
India 58 N12
Kodiak: & i., Alaska, U.S.A. 84 d6
Kodinar: Gujarat, India 58 M10
Kodok: Sudan 79 L8
Koedoesrand: geog reg.,
S. Africa 75 G1
Koegas: S. Africa 74 E4
Koegrabie: S. Africa 74 D4
Koekenaap: S. Africa 74 C5
Koes: S.W. Africa 74 C2
Koesfeld: W. Germany 44 N4
Koevorden: Netherlands 44 M3
Koffiefontein: O.F.S., S. Africa
75 F4
Kofiau: i., W. Irian, Indon. 61 K12
Koflach: Austria 41 V8
KOFORIDUA: Eastern, Ghana 80 D3
KOFU: Yamanashi, Japan 63 f3
Koga: Japan 63 f2
Kogan: Queens., Australia 70 J6
Køge: Zealand, Denmark 47 N9
Koggiung: Alaska, U.S.A. 84 D6
Kogoni: Mali 80 C2
Kogushi: Japan 63 b3
Kohat: N.W. Front. Prov.,
Pak. 58 M8
KOHIMA: Nagaland, India 59 Q9
Kohsan: Afghanistan 58 K8
Kohukohu: North I., N.Z. 70 O12
Koichab: riv., S.W. Africa 74 A3
Koide: Japan 63 f2
Koimekeah: Nicobar Is. 59 Q13
Koin: i., Lake Urmia, Iran 57 J3
Koi Sanjaq: Iraq 57 J3
Koitere Lake: Finland 46 W5
Kojrro: Japan 63 c3
Kojonup: W. Australia 68 B6
Kokand: Uzbek., U.S.S.R. 51 M6
Kokas: W. Irian, Indonesia 61 L12
Kokawa: Japan 63 d3
KOKCHETAV: & Reg.,
Kazakh., U.S.S.R. 51 L4
Kokemäen: riv., Finland 47 R6
Kokemäki: Finland 47 S6
Kokerboom: S.W. Africa 74 C4

Kokhtla-Yarve: Estonia,
U.S.S.R. 47 U7
Koki: Senegal 80 A1
Kokiu: Yunnan, China 62 S10
Kokkola: Finland 46 S5
Koko: Nigeria 81 E2
Kokoda: New Guinea 69 H1
Kokomo: Ind., U.S.A. 88 H5
Koko Nor (Tsing Hai): lake,
China 62 S7
Kokon Selka: lake, Finland 47 V6
Kokopo: New Britain, Bismarck
Arch. 67 K2
Kokoro: Benin 81 E3
Koko Shili: range, Tibet,
China 59 P7
Kokoshili: Chingai, China 62 Q7
Kokpekty: Kazakh., U.S.S.R. 51 O5
Koksan: N. Korea 63 X7
Koksoak: riv., Canada 85 N6
Kokstad: S. Africa 75 H5
Kokterek: Kazakh., U.S.S.R. 51 N5
Kola: U.S.S.R. 46 X2
Kolaka: Celebes 65 G7
Kolan: Shansi, China 62 U7
Kola Penin.: U.S.S.R. 48 e4
Kolar: Karnataka, India 58 N12
Kolari: Finland 46 T5
Kolarovgrad: Bulgaria 39 U15
Kolåsen: Sweden 46 N5
Kolayat: Rajasthan, India 58 M9
Kolbano: Timor, Indonesia 65 G8
Kolbio: Kenya 76 F3
Kol'chugino: U.S.S.R. 50 E3
Kolda: Senegal 80 B2
Kolding: Denmark 47 L9
Kole: Haute Zaire, Zaire 76 C2
Kole: Kasai Oriental, Zaire
76 B3
Kolente: riv., Sierra Leone/
Guinea 80 B3
Kolga Gulf: Estonia,
U.S.S.R. 47 T7
Kolguyev I.: U.S.S.R. 48 f4
Kolhapur: Maharashtra, India 58 M11
Kolima Lake: Finland 46 T5
Kolin: Czechoslovakia 45 V5
Kolka: Latvia, U.S.S.R. 47 S8
Kolkas, Cape: Latvia, U.S.S.R. 47 S8
Kolki: Ukraine 43 T11
Kolkhozabad: Tadzhik., U.S.S.R. 51 L7
Kolleda: E. Germany 45 R4
Kollum: Netherlands 44 M2
Kolmanskop: S.W. Africa 74 A3
Kolm-Saigurn: Austria 41 S8
Köln (Cologne): W. Germany 44 M5
Köln: Dist., North Rhine-Westphalia,
West Germany 44 N5
Kolno: Poland 43 R10
Kolo: Tanzania 76 E3
Koloban: Senegal 80 A2
Kolobrzeg: Poland 45 V1
Kologriv: U.S.S.R. 50 F3
Kolokani: Mali 80 C2
Kolombangara: i., Solomon
Is. 67 L3
Kolomna: U.S.S.R. 50 E3
Kolomyya: Ukraine 43 T12
Kolonodale: Celebes 65 G7
Kolossia: Kenya 76 E2
Kolozero, Lake: U.S.S.R. 46 X2
Kolpashevo: U.S.S.R. 51 O3
Kolpino: U.S.S.R. 47 W7
Koluk: Turkey 56 F3
Kolulli: Ethiopia 54 F12
Kolvik: Norway 46 T1
Kolwezi: Zaire 77 C5
Kolyma: riv., U.S.S.R. 49 r4
Kolyma Bay: U.S.S.R. 49 S3
Kolyma Plain: U.S.S.R. 49 R4
Kolyma (Gydan) Range:
U.S.S.R. 49 r5
Kolyuchin, G. of: U.S.S.R. 49 Q4
Kolyvan': Altai, U.S.S.R. 51 O4
Kolyvan': Novosibirsk,
U.S.S.R. 51 O3
Koma: Japan 63 ZZ7
Komadugu Gana: riv., Nig. 81 G2
Komadugu Yobe: riv., Nig. 81 G2
Komaggas: S. Africa 74 B4
Komai: Tibet, China 62 R9
Komandor I.: U.S.S.R. 49 s6
Komarno: Czechoslovakia 43 Q13
Komarom: Hungary 43 Q13
Komas Highland: S.W. Africa 74 B1
Komati: riv., Swaziland 75 J3
Komatipoort: Trans., S. Africa 75 J2
Komatom: Ethiopia 76 D1
Komatsu: Japan 63 e2
Komba: Zaire 76 B2
Kombone: Cameroun 81 F4
Komboti: Greece 39 R17
Komgha: & Dist., S. Africa 75 G6
Kommetjie: S. Africa 74 Ins.
Kommunar: U.S.S.R. 51 R4
Kommunarsk: Ukraine 50 E5
Komodo: i., Indonesia 65 F8
Komoro: Japan 63 f2
Komotini: Greece 39 T16
Kompongcham: Cambodia 64 D4
Kompongkleang: Cambodia 64 C4
Kompongsom: & bay, Cambodia 64
C4
Kompongspeu: Cambodia 64 C4
Komrat: Moldavia, U.S.S.R. 39 V13
Komsomolabad: Tadzhik.,
U.S.S.R. 51 M7
Komsomolets Bay: Kazakh.,
U.S.S.R. 50 H5
Komsomolets I.: Severnaya
Zemlya, Arctic O. 49 I1
Komsomol'sk: U.S.S.R. 49 p7
Kon: riv., U.S.S.R. 51 L5
Konarha: Prov., Afghanistan 55 M7
Konawa: Okla., U.S.A. 90 C8
Konda: riv., U.S.S.R. 51 L3
Kondinin: W. Australia 68 B6
Kondoa: Tanzania 76 E3
Kondopoga: U.S.S.R. 50 D2
Kondor Is.: Vietnam 64 D5
Konduyak: U.S.S.R. 51 Q3
Koné: New Caledonia 67 M6
Kong: Ivory Coast 80 D3
Kongettit: Sudan 76 D1
Kongkemul: mtn., Borneo 65 F6
Kongmoon (Hsinhui),
Kwangtung, China 62 U10
Kongolo: Zaire 76 C4
Kongor: Sudan 76 D1
Kongorong: S. Australia
71 D11
Konsberg: Norway 47 L7
Kongsmoen: Norway 46 N4
Kongsvinger: Norway 47 N6
Kongsvoll-Hjerkinn-Snøhetta National
Park: Norway 46 L5
Kongwa: Tanzania 76 E4
Koniakori: Mali 80 B2
Königgratz: German name for
town of Hradec Kralové,
Czechoslovakia 42 O11

KÖNIGSBERG (Kaliningrad):
Kaliningrad Reg., U.S.S.R. 47 R9
Königsbrück: E. Germany 45 T4
Königssee: lake, W. Germany 41 S8
Königshofen: W. Germany 45 Q5
Königslutter: W. Germany 45 Q3
Königstein: W. Germany 45 U5
Königswiesen: Austria 41 U7
Königs-Wusterhausen: E. Ger. 45 T3
Konin: Poland 43 Q10
Konispol: Albania 39 R17
Konitsa: Greece 39 R16
Konjic: Yugoslavia 38 P15
Konjice: Yugoslavia 41 V9
Konkiep: riv., S.W. Africa 74 B3
Konkoure: riv., Guinea 80 B2
Konnern: E. Germany 45 R4
Konom Dzong: Tibet, China 59 Q9
Konongo: Ghana 80 D3
Konosha: U.S.S.R. 50 F2
Konosu: Japan 63 f2
Konotop: Ukraine 50 D4
Konpougou: Upper Volta 81 E2
Konskie: Poland 43 R11
Konstantinovka: Ukraine 50 E5
Konstantynow: Poland 43 Q11
Konstanz: W. Germany 40 P8
Kontagora: Nigeria 81 F2
Kontcha: Cameroun 81 G3
Kontiomaki: Finland 46 V4
Konttajarvi: Finland 46 T5
Kontum: Vietnam 64 D4
KONYA: & Prov., Turkey 56 C3
Konz: W. Germany 44 M6
Konza: Kenya 76 E3
Kookabookra: N.S.W.,
Australia 71 K8
Koolatah: Queens., Austl. 69 G3
Koomooloo: S. Australia 71 C9
Koondrook: Vict., Austl. 71 F10
Koopmansfontein: S. Africa 75 F4
Koorakee: N.S.W., Austl. 71 E10
Koorawatha: N.S.W., Austl. 71 H10
Koorda: W. Australia 68 B6
Koori: Japan 63 g2
Kootenay: riv., U.S.A./Can. 92 D3
Kootjieskolk: S. Africa 74 D5
Koo-wee-rup: Vict., Austl. 71 F12
Kopaonik: mtns., Yugoslavia 39 R15
Kopasker: Iceland 46 e3
Kopatkevichi: Byelorussia 43 V10
Kopcivnica: Yugoslavia 38 P13
Koper (Capodistria): Yugoslavia
41 T10
Kopervik: Norway 47 J7
Kopet Dagh: range, Iran/
U.S.S.R. 55 J7
Kopidlno: Czechoslovakia 45 V5
Koping: Sinkiang, China 51 N6
Köping: Sweden 47 O7
Kop Mtns.: Turkey 56 F1
Koppang: Norway 47 M6
Kopparberg: Sweden 47 O7
Kopparberg: Co., Sweden
(cap. Falun) 47 O6
Koppies: O.F.S., S. Africa 75 G3
Köprü: riv., Turkey 56 B3
Kopychinsty: Ukraine 43 T12
Kora (Kura): riv., Turkey 57 H1
Koraka Cape: Turkey 39 U17
Korana: riv., Yugoslavia 41 V10
Koranna Land: geog. reg.,
S. Africa 74 D4
Koraput: Orissa, India 59 O11
Korbach: W. Germany 44 O4
Korçe (Koritsa): Albania 39 R16
Korčula: i., Yugoslavia 38 P15
Kordofan, Northern: Prov. Sudan (cap.
El Obeid) 79 K7
Kordofan, Southern: Prov., Sudan
(cap. Kadugli) 79 K7
Korea: see North Korea and
South Korea.
Korea, G. of: Yellow Sea 63 W7
Korea Strait: Japan/S. Korea 63 X8
Korenica: Yugoslavia 41 V11
Korets: Ukraine 43 U11
KORHOGO: Nord, Ivory Coast 80 C3
Koriabo: Guyana 87 d7
Kori Creek: inlet, Gujarat,
India 58 L10
Koringplaas: S. Africa 74 D6
Korinthos (Corinth): Greece 39 S18
Koritsa (Korçe): Albania 39 R16
Koriyama: Japan 63 g2
Korkino: U.S.S.R. 51 K4
Korkudeli: Turkey 56 B3
Kröliki: U.S.S.R. 51 O2
Kormend: Hungary 41 W8
Kornat: i., Yugoslavia 41 V12
Korneshty-Tryg: Moldavia,
U.S.S.R. 43 U13
Korneuburg: Austria 41 W7
Kornsjø: Norway 47 M7
Koro: Ivory Coast 80 C3
Koro: i. & sea, Fiji Is. 67 P5
Korodougou: Mali 80 C2
Koroglu: mtn., Turkey 56 B1
Korogwe: Tanzania 76 E4
Koroit: Vict., Australia 71 E12
Koromo: Japan 63 e3
Korong-vale: Vict., Austl. 71 E11
Koroni: Greece 39 R18
Koropi: Greece 39 R18
Koror: Babelthuap, Papua Is. 61 L10
Korosten: Ukraine 43 V11
Korostyshev: Ukraine 43 V11
Koro Toro: Chad 81 H1
Korpilombolo: Sweden 46 S3
Korpiselka: Finland 46 W5
Korsakov: U.S.S.R. 63 ZZ5
Korsnäs: Finland 46 R5
Korsnes: Norway 46 P2
Korsør: Zealand, Denmark 47 M9
Kortgene: Netherlands 44 J4
Korti: Sudan 54 D11
Kortrijk: Belgium 44 J5
Korumburra: Vict., Austl. 71 F12
Koryak Range: U.S.S.R. 49 T5
Kos (Cos): & i., Dodec.
(Grc.) 39 U18
Koschagyl: Kazakh.,
U.S.S.R. 50 H5
Koscian: Poland 43 P9
Koscierzyna: Poland 43 P9
Kosciusko: Miss., U.S.A. 90 G9
Kosciusko, Mount: N.S.W.,
Australia 71 H11
Kosciusko State Park: N.S.W.,
Australia 71 H10
Kosenow: E. Germany 45 T2
Kosha: Ethiopia 76 E1
Kosh-Agach: U.S.S.R. 51 P4
Koshan: Heilungkiang, China 63 X5
Koshiki Group: is., Japan 63 a5
Koshki: U.S.S.R. 50 H4
Koshun (Hengchun):
Taiwan 63 W10
Kosi: riv., Nepal/India 59 P9
Kosi Lake: Natal, S. Afr. 75 K3

KOŠICE: Vychodoslovenská,
Czechoslovakia 43 R12
Kosikha: U.S.S.R. 51 O4
Kosiv: S.W. Africa 74 B2
Koskats: Sweden 46 R3
Koski: Finland 47 S6
Kosov: Ukraine 43 T12
Kosovska Mitrovica: Yugo. 39 R15
Kossa: Ethiopia 76 E1
Kossovo: valley to W. of
Priština, Yugoslavia 39 R15
Kostajnica: Yugoslavia 41 W10
Kostamo: Finland 46 U3
Kostanjevica: Yugoslavia 41 V10
Kostelec: (SE. of Prague),
Czechoslovakia 45 U6
Kostelec: (SW of Jihlava),
Czechoslovakia 45 V6
Kostelec: (E. of Pardubice),
Czechoslovakia 45 U6
Koster: Trans., S. Africa 75 G2
Kosti: Sudan 54 D12
Kostomuksha: Karelian
A.S.S. Rep., U.S.S.R. 46 W4
Koston Lake: Finland 46 V4
Kostopol': Ukraine 43 U11
KOSTROMA: & Reg., U.S.S.R. 50 F3
Kostrzyn Odrzanski: Poland 45 U3
KOSZALIN: & Prov., Poland 43 P9
Koszeg: Hungary 41 W8
Kota Agung: Sumatra 65 C8
Kotabaru: Borneo 65 F7
Kotabaru: Sumatra 65 C7
KOTA BHARU: Kelantan,
Malaya, Malaysia 65 c10
Kotabumi: Sumatra 65 C7
Kotadaik: Lingga Arch.,
Indonesia 65 C7
Kotah: Rajasthan, India 58 N9
KOTA KINABALU: Sabah, Malaysia 65 F5
Kota Kota: Malawi, 77 D5
Kotala: Finland 46 V3
Kotamobaju: Celebes 65 G6
Kota Tinggi: Malaya,
Malaysia 65 c13
Kotchek: Syria 57 H3
Kotel: Bulgaria 39 U15
Kotel'nich: U.S.S.R. 50 G3
Kotel'nikovo: U.S.S.R. 50 F5
Kotel'nny I.: New Siberian
Is., U.S.S.R. 49 p2
Kotenko: U.S.S.R. 49 q3
Köthen: E. Germany 45 R4
Kotka: Kymi, Finland 47 U6
Kotlas: U.S.S.R. 50 G2
Kotlik: Alaska, U.S.A. 84 c5
Koto: i., Taiwan 63 W10
Kotonira: Japan 63 c3
Kotonkoro: Nigeria 81 F2
Kotor (Cattaro): Yugo. 39 Q15
Kotor Varoš: Yugoslavia 38 P14
Kotovsk: Ukraine 50 C5
Kotovskoye: U.S.S.R. 39 V13
Kotri: Sind, Pakistan 58 L9
Kottayam: Kerala, India 58 N13
Kotto: riv., Cen. Afr. Rep. 76 B2
Kotzebue: Alaska, U.S.A. 84 c4
Kotzesrus: S. Africa 74 B5
Kouango: Cen. Afr. Rep. 76 B1
Kouba Kalta: well, Chad 81 H1
KOUDOUGOU: Centre-Ouest, Upper
Volta 80 D2
Kouga: riv., S. Africa 75 F6
Kouilou: riv., Congo 81 G5
Kouki: Cen. Afr. Rep. 81 H3
Koukourou: riv., Central
African Republic 76 B1
Koukraal: O.F.S., S. Africa 75 G5
KOULA-MOUTOU: Ogooue-Lolo,
Gabon 81 G5
Kouikoro: Mali 80 C2
Kouloua: Chad 81 G2
Koumala: Queens., Austl. 70 H3
Koumbia: Guinea 80 B2
Koumra: Chad 81 H3
KOUNDARA: & Reg., Senegal 80 B2
Kounde: Cen. Afr. Rep. 81 G3
Kounov: Czechoslovakia 45 T5
Kounradskiy: Kazakh.,
U.S.S.R. 51 N5
Kountze: Tex., U.S.A. 90 D10
Koup: S. Africa 74 D6
Koupela: Upper Volta 80 D2
Kouremale: Mali 80 C2
Kourou: Fr. Guiana 94 G2
Kourouba: Mali 80 C2
KOUROUSSA: & Reg., Guinea 80 C2
Koussa Arma: Niger 81 G1
Koussanar: Senegal 80 B2
Koutiala: Mali 80 C2
KOUVOLA: Kymi, Finland 47 U6
Kouyou: riv., Congo 81 H5
Kovdozero, Lake: U.S.S.R. 46 W3
Kovel': Ukraine 43 T11
Kovic Bay: Que., Canada 85 M5
Kovin: U.S.S.R. 49 e6
Kovrov: U.S.S.R. 50 F3
Kowloon: Hong Kong 62 U10
Kowon: N. Korea 63 X7
Kowpangtze: Liaoning,
China 63 W6
Koya: Japan 63 d3
Köysegiz: Turkey 39 V18
Koyukuk: riv., Alaska,
U.S.A. 84 D4
Koyulhisar: Turkey 56 E1
Kozan: Turkey 56 D3
Kozani: Greece 39 R16
Kozdere: riv., Turkey 56 C3
Kozhikode: see Calicut.
Kozhva: U.S.S.R. 48 g4
Kozienice: Poland 43 R11
Kozina: Yugoslavia 41 T10
Kozle: Poland 43 Q11
Kozlov, Cape: U.S.S.R. 49 S7
Kozlovshchina: Byelorussia 43 T10
Kozluk: Yugoslavia 39 Q14
Koz'modem'yansk: U.S.S.R. 50 G3
Kozu: i., Japan 63 f3
Kożuchow: Poland 45 V4
Kpandu: Ghana 80 D3
Kra, Isthmus of: Thailand 64 B5
Kraai: riv., S. Africa 75 G5
Kraankuil: S. Africa 75 F4
Kraanvoel: S. Africa 74 E4
Krabbendijke: Netherlands 44 K4
Krabi: Thailand 64 B6
Kracheh: Cambodia 64 D4
Kragerø: Norway 47 L7
Kraggas River: S. Africa 74 D6
Kragujevac: Yugoslavia 39 R14
Krakatau: i. & volc., Indon. 65 D8
Krakatau National Park: Indonesia
65 D8
Krak des Chevaliers: castle,
Syria 56 E4
Krakor: Cambodia 64 C4
Kraków: see Cracow.
Krakower See: lake, E. Ger. 45 S2
Kraljevo: Yugoslavia
39 R15
Kralovice: Západočeský,
Czechoslovakia 45 T6
Kralovice: Středočeský,
Czechoslovakia 45 V6
Kralupy: Czechoslovakia 45 U5

Kramatorsk: Ukraine 50 E5
Kramfors: Sweden 46 P5
Krampen: Sweden 47 O7
Krampenes: Norway 46 W1
Krange: Sweden 46 P5
Krania: Greece 39 R17
Kranj: Yugoslavia 41 U9
Kranskop: & Dist., Natal,
S. Africa 75 J4
Krapina: Yugoslavia 41 V9
Krapivinskiy: U.S.S.R. 51 P4
Krasilov: Ukraine 43 U12
Krasino: U.S.S.R. 48 G3
Kraskino: U.S.S.R. 63 Y6
Kraslava: Latvia, U.S.S.R. 47 U9
Kraslice: Czechoslovakia 45 S5
Krasnaya Gorka: U.S.S.R. 50 J3
Krasnaya Polyana: U.S.S.R. 50 F5
Krasnik: Poland 43 S11
Krasnoarmeysk: U.S.S.R. 50 G4
KRASNODAR: & Territ.,
U.S.S.R. 50 E5
Krasnogorodsk: U.S.S.R. 47 V8
Krasnograd: Ukraine 50 E5
Krasnoslobodsk: Mordov.,
U.S.S.R. 50 F4
Krasnoslobodsk: Volgograd,
U.S.S.R. 50 F5
Krasnoturansk: U.S.S.R. 51 Q4
Krasnoufimsk: U.S.S.R. 50 J3
Krasnoural'sk: U.S.S.R. 51 K3
Krasnovarardeysk: U.S.S.R. 50 D3
Krasnovishersk: U.S.S.R. 50 J2
Krasnovodsk: Turkmen.,
U.S.S.R. 50 H6
KRASNOYARSK: & Territ.,
U.S.S.R. 51 Q3
Krasnozersk: U.S.S.R. 51 N4
Krasnoznamenskiy: Kazakh.,
U.S.S.R. 51 L4
Krasnystaw: Poland 43 S11
Krasnyye Baki: U.S.S.R. 50 G3
Krasnyy Kholm: U.S.S.R. 50 H4
Krasnyy Kut: U.S.S.R. 50 G4
Krasnyy Sulin: U.S.S.R. 50 F5
Krasnyy Yar: U.S.S.R. 50 G5
Kraulshavn: Greenland 85 O3
Krawang: Java 65 D8
Krdzhali: Bulgaria 39 T16
Krefeld: W. Germany 44 M4
Kremenchug: Ukraine 50 D5
Kremenets: Ukraine 43 T11
Kremmen: E. Germany 45 T3
Krems: Austria 41 V7
Krest Bay: U.S.S.R. 49 U4
Kresty: Krasnoyarsk Territ.,
U.S.S.R. 49 M3
Kretinga: Lithuania,
U.S.S.R. 47 R9
Kreuzburg (Creuzburg):
E. Germany 45 Q4
Kreuznach: W. Germany 44 N6
Kribi: Cameroun 81 F4
Krimml: Austria 41 S8
Krioneri: Greece 39 R17
Krios, Cape: Crete 33 G4
Krishnagar: W. Bengal, India 59 P10
KRISTIANSAND: Vest Agder,
Norway 47 K7
KRISTIANSTAD: & Co., Swed. 47 O8
Kristiansund: Norway 46 K5
Kristiinankaupunki: Finland 47 R5
Kristinehamn: Sweden 47 O7
Kristinestad: see Kristiinan-
kaupunki.
Krithia (Kirte): Turkey
(Dardan. Inset). 20 Ins.
Kriti (Crete): i., (Grc.),
Medit. Sea (cap. Canea) 39 T19
Kritovo: U.S.S.R. 51 P3
Krivi Put: Yugoslavia 41 U10
Krivoy Rog: Ukraine 50 D5
Križanov: Czechoslovakia 45 W6
Križevci: Yugoslavia 41 W9
Krk: & i., Yugoslavia 41 U10
Krkonoše National Park: Czech.
42 O11
Krmeli: Yugoslavia 41 V10
Krnjak: Yugoslavia 41 V10
Krnov: Czechoslovakia 43 P11
Krobia: Poland 45 W4
Krøderen: Norway 47 L6
Krohstorf: W. Germany 41 S7
Kroměříž: Czechoslovakia 43 P12
Kromme: riv., S. Africa 74 C5
Krom River: S. Africa 74 E5
Kronach: W. Germany 45 R5
Kronoberg: Co., Sweden
(cap. Växjö) 47 O8
Kronoby: Finland 46 S5
Kronotskiy Bay: U.S.S.R. 49 S7
Kronshtadt: U.S.S.R. 47 V7
Kroonstad: & Dist., O.F.S.,
S. Africa 75 G3
Kröpelin: E. Germany 45 R1
Kropotkin: U.S.S.R. 50 F5
Krosno: Poland 43 R12
Krosno Odrzanski: Poland 45 V3
Krotoszyn: Poland 43 P11
Krško: Yugoslavia 41 V10
Kru Coast: geog. reg., Lib. 80 C3
Kruger Nat. Park: Trans.,
S. Africa 73 L12
Krugersdorp: Trans. S. Afr.
74 Mins.
Krugersdorp: Dist., Trans., S. Africa
75 G2
Krui: Sumatra 65 C8
Kruis: S. Africa 74 C6
Kruje: Albania 39 Q16
Krumbach: W. Germany 40 Q7
Krumovgrad: Bulgaria 39 T16
Krung Thep: see Bangkok.
Krupnik: Bulgaria 39 S16
Kruševac: Yugoslavia 39 R15
Kruševo: Yugoslavia 39 R16
Krustpils: Latvia, U.S.S.R. 47 T8
Krutikha: U.S.S.R. 51 O4
Krutinka: U.S.S.R. 51 M3
Krylbo: Sweden 47 P6
Krzepice: Poland 43 Q11
Krzywin: Poland 45 W4
Krzyż: Poland 45 W3
Ksabi: Algeria 80 L9
Ksar: Morocco 80 L8
Ksar El Boukhari: Algeria 35 H19
Ksar-el-Kebir: Morocco 80 K7
KSAR ES-SOUK: & Prov.,
Morocco 80 L8
Kseur, El: Algeria 35 J18
Ksour: Tunisia 38 L19
Ktima: Cyprus 56 C4
Kuah: Langkawi Is., Malaya,
Malaysia 65 a10
Kuala: Sumatra 65 B6
Kuala Brang: Malaya,
Malaysia 65 c11
Kuala Dungun: Malaya,
Malaysia 65 c11
Kuala Kangsar: Malaya,
Malaysia 65 b11
Kualakapuas: Borneo 65 E7
Kuala Klawang (Jelebu):
Malaya, Malaysia 65 c12

Kuala Krai—La Grange 157

Kuala Krai: Malaya, Malaysia 65 c11
Kuala Kubu Bahru: Malaya, Malaysia 65 b12
Kualakurun: Borneo 65 E7
Kualalangsa: Sumatra 65 B6
Kualan Shan: *mtn.*, Tibet, China 59 Q9
Kuala Lipis: Pahang, Malaya, Malaysia 65 c11
KUALA LUMPUR: Malaya, Malaysia 65 b12
Kuala Marang: Malaya, Malaysia 65 c11
Kuala Nerang: Malaya, Malaysia 65 b10
Kualapembuang: Borneo 65 E7
Kuala Pilah, Malaya, Malaysia 65 c12
Kuala Selangor: Malaya, Malaysia 65 b12
KUALA TRENGGANU: Trengganu, Malaya, Malaysia 65 c11
Kualatungkal: Sumatra 65 C7
Kuamut: Sabah, Malaysia 65 F5
Kuan: Hopeh, China 62 V7
Kuandang: Celebes 65 G6
Kuanghua: Hupeh, China 62 U8
Kuânit: Greenland 85 P5
Kuan Mao: Thailand 64 B5
KUANTAN: Pahang, Malaya, Malaysia 65 c12
Kuarao: Vietnam 64 C3
Kub: S.W. Africa 74 B2
Kuba: Azerbaydzhan, U.S.S.R. 50 G6
Kuba: Japan 63 c3
Kubaisa: Iraq 57 H5
Kubakawa: Japan 63 c4
Kuban: *riv.*, U.S.S.R. 50 E5
Kubarah: Oman 55 J10
Kubas: S.W. Africa 74 A1
Kubenskoye, Lake: U.S.S.R. 50 E3
Kuberle: U.S.S.R. 50 F5
Kuboos: S. Africa 74 B4
Kubrat: Bulgaria 39 U15
Kubri, El: Egypt (Suez Canal *Inset*) 32 *Ins.*
Kubumesaäi: Borneo 65 F6
Kučevo: Yugoslavia 39 R14
Kucha: Sinkiang, China 51 O6
Kucheng: Hupeh, China 62 U8
Kuch-i-Isfahan: Iran 57 L3
KUCHING: Sarawak, Malaysia 65 E6
Kuchinotsu: Japan 63 b4
Kuçulsköy: Turkey (Bosporus *Inset*) 20 *Ins.*
Kudamaguba: U.S.S.R. 46 X5
Kudan: Nigeria 81 F2
Kudaru: Nigeria 78 F7
Kudat: Sabah, Malaysia 64 F5
Kudus: Java 65 E8
Kudymkar: U.S.S.R. 50 H3
Kueitun: *riv.*, Sinkiang, China 51 O6
Kuerh: Sinkiang, China 51 O5
Kufa: Iraq 57 J5
Kufra Oasis: Libya 79 J5
Kufstein: Austria 41 S8
Kuga: Japan 63 c3
Kugaly: Kazakh., U.S.S.R. 51 N6
Kugas: Afghanistan 51 M7
Kugul'ta: U.S.S.R. 50 F5
Kuhaifiya: Saudi Arabia 54 F9
Kuhbach: W. Germany 41 R7
Kuh-i-Alwand: *mtn.*, Iran 57 L4
Kuh-i-Bazkush: *range*, Iran 57 K3
Kuh-i-Dasht: Iran 57 K5
Kuh-i-Malik-Siah: *mtn.*, Iran/Afghanistan 55 K9
Kuhin: Iran 57 L3
Kuh-i-Savalan: *mtn.*, Iran 57 K2
Kuh-i-Taftan: Iran 55 K9
Kuh-i-Taftan: *mtn.*, Iran 58 K9
Kuhmo: Finland 46 V4
Kuhnsdorf: Austria 41 U9
Kuh Rud: *range*, Iran 55 H8
Kuh Sultan Ahmad: *mtn.*, Iran 57 K4
Kuibis: S.W. Africa 74 B3
Kuinre: Netherlands 44 L3
Kui Nua: Thailand 64 B4
Kuis: S.W. Africa 74 B2
Kuiseb: *riv.*, S.W. Africa 74 A1
Kuisha (Yangtze): *riv.*, China 62 R8
Kuivaniemi: Finland 46 T4
Kuji: Japan 63 ZZ6
Kuk: *mtn.*, Yugoslavia 41 V11
Kuka Drift: S. Africa 75 H5
Kukawa: Nigeria 81 G2
Kuke: Botswana 77 B7
Kukes: Albania 39 R15
Kuki: Yunnan, China 62 S10
Kukmor: U.S.S.R. 50 H3
Kukong (Shaokuan): Kwangtung, China 62 U10
Kukup: Malaya, Malaysia 65 c13
Kula: Bulgaria 39 S15
Kula: Turkey 56 A2
Kula: Yugoslavia 39 Q14
Kulaly: *i.*, Caspian Sea 50 H6
Kulamantata: *mtn.*, Tibet, China 58 O8
Kulanaoti: Sinkiang, China 51 N7
Kulang: Kansu, China 62 S7
Kulay: U.S.S.R. 51 N3
Kuldiga: Latvia, U.S.S.R. 47 R8
Kulen Vakuf: Yugoslavia 41 W11
Kulgera: N. Territ., Austl. 68 E5
Kul'ja: *see* Ining
Kulim: Malaya, Malaysia 65 b11
Kulin: W. Australia 68 B6
Kullaa: Finland 47 S6
Kulmbach: W. Germany 45 R5
Kulossu: Tibet, China 59 O8
Kulpawa: *riv.*, Ghana 80 D2
Kul'tbaza: U.S.S.R. 51 K2
Kulumadau: Murua I., Papua/New Guinea 69 J1
Kulunamuchi: Tibet, China 59 Q9
Kulunchi: Inner Mongolia, China 63 W6
Kulunda Steppe: *plain*, Kazakh., U.S.S.R. 51 N4
Kulundinskoye, Lake: U.S.S.R. 51 O4
Kulwin: Vict., Australia 71 E10
Kulyab: Tadzhik., U.S.S.R. 51 L7
Kuma: *riv.*, U.S.S.R. 50 G6
Kumagaya: Japan 63 f2
Kumai: Borneo 65 E7
Kumai Bay: Borneo 65 E7
Kumait: Iraq 57 K5
Kumaka: Guyana 87 d8
KUMAMOTO: & *Pref.*, Japan 63 b4
Kumano Gulf: Japan 63 c4
Kumanovo: Yugoslavia 39 R15
Kumara: South I., N.Z. 70 N16
KUMASI: Ashanti, Ghana 80 D3
Kumba: Cameroun 81 F4
Kumbakonam: Tamil Nadu, India 58 N12
Kumbarilla: Queens., Austl. 70 J6
Kumbo: Upper Volta 80 D2
Kumbo: Cameroun 81 G3
Kumchon: N. Korea 63 X7
Kume: *i.*, Ryukyu Is. 63 X9
Kumi: Uganda 76 D2
Kumizan: Iran 57 L4
Kumla: Sweden 47 O7
Kummerower See: *lake*, E. Germany 45 S2
Kumonda: U.S.S.R. 51 R2
Kumrabi: Sierra Leone 80 B3
Kums: S.W. Africa 74 C4
Kumshe: Nigeria 81 G2
Kumta: Karnataka, India 58 M12
Kunar: *riv.*, Pakistan/Afghanistan 58 M8
Kunashir: *i.*, Kuril Is. 63 YY6
Kunda: Estonia, U.S.S.R. 47 U7
Kundar: Iran 57 L5
Kundelungu Mtns.: Zaire 77 C4
Kunduz: *Prov.*, Afghanistan 55 L7
KUNEITRA: & *Prov.*, Syria 56 D5
Kunene: *riv.*, Angola 73 G13
Kungal: Sweden 47 N8
Kungchissu Ho: *riv.*, Sinkiang, China 51 O6
Kungchuling: Kirin, China 63 W6
Kungho: Chinghai, China 62 S7
Kungka: Tibet, China 59 Q9
Kungka Shan: *mtn.*, Szechwan, China 62 S9
Kung Liu: Sinkiang, China 51 O6
Kungrad: Uzbek., U.S.S.R. 50 J6
Kungsbacka: Sweden 47 N8
Kungshan: Tibet, China 62 R9
Kungson: Vietnam 64 D4
Kungsor: Sweden 47 P7
Kungur: U.S.S.R. 50 J3
Kungur: *mtn.*, Sinkiang, China 51 N7
Kungurri: Queens., Austl. 70 H3
Kungutas: Tanzania 76 D4
Kungveld Plain: S.W. Africa 77 A6
Kunhsien: Hupeh, China 62 U8
Kunlong: Burma 59 R10
Kunlun Mtns.: China 51 O7
KUNMING (Yunnan): Yunnan, China 62 S9
Kunrau: E. Germany 45 R3
Kunsan: S. Korea 63 X7
Kunszentmiklós: Hungary 43 Q13
Kuntaur: The Gambia 80 B2
Kuntilla: Egypt 56 D6
Kuntsevo: U.S.S.R. 50 E3
Kuntu: Inner Mongolia, China 63 W6
Kununurra: W. Australia 68 D3
Kunzelsau: W. Germany 44 P6
Kuolayarvi: Karelia, U.S.S.R. 46 V3
KUOPIO: & *Prov.*, Finland 46 U5
Kuosku: Finland 46 V3
Kupa: *riv.*, Yugoslavia 41 V10
Kupang: W. Timor, Indon. 65 G9
Kupino: U.S.S.R. 51 N4
Kupishkis: Lithuania, U.S.S.R. 47 T9
Kupyansk: Ukraine 50 E5
Kur: *riv.*, Iran 55 H8
Kura: *riv.*, U.S.S.R. 57 K1
Kuragino: U.S.S.R. 51 Q4
Kurakh: U.S.S.R. 50 G6
Kuran: *riv.*, Iran 57 L6
Kurashiki: Japan 63 c3
Kurba: *i.*, Yugoslavia 41 V12
Kurdistan: *geog. reg.*, Turkey/Iran 57 H3
Kurdestan: *Prov.*, Iran (*cap.* Sanadaj) 57 H3
Kure: Horishima, Japan 63 c3
Kure: Kochi, Japan 63 c4
Küre: Turkey 56 C1
Kureyka: U.S.S.R. 48 k4
Kurgal'-Dzhino: Kazakh., U.S.S.R. 51 M4
KURGAN: & *Reg.*, U.S.S.R. 51 L3
Kurgan-Tyube: Tadzhik., U.S.S.R. 51 L7
Kuria: *i.*, Gilbert Is. 67 O1
Kuria Muria Is.: & *bay*, Oman 55 J11
Kurikka: Finland 46 S5
Kuril Is.: (U.S.S.R.), NE. Asia 49 R8
Kuril Ridge: Sea of Okhotsk 7 45N 145E
Kuril'sk: Etorofu, Kuril Is. 63 YY5
Kuril Trench: N. Pacific Ocean 7 45N 150E
Kurin, Cape: Azerbaydzhan, U.S.S.R. 57 L2
Kuring Kuru: S.W. Africa 77 A6
Kurino: Japan 63 b5
Kûrivody: Czechoslovakia 45 U5
Kurmuk: Sudan 79 L7
Kurnool: Andhra Pradesh, India 58 N11
Kuroiso: Japan 63 g2
Kurow: South I., N.Z. 70 N17
Kurri-Kurri: N.S.W., Austl. 71 J9
Kursavka: U.S.S.R. 50 F6
KURSK: & Reg., U.S.S.R. 50 E4
Kurskiy Zaliv: *lag.*, U.S.S.R. 47 R9
Kurskoye: Kazakh., U.S.S.R. 51 L4
Kuršumlija: Yugoslavia 39 R15
Kurtamysh: U.S.S.R. 51 K4
Kurtoğlu, Cape: Turkey 39 V18
Kuru: *riv.*, Sudan 76 C1
Kuruman: & *Dist.*, S. Afr. 74 E3
Kuruman: *riv.*, S. Africa 74 D3
Kurume: Japan 63 b4
Kurunegala: Sri Lanka 58 O13
Kurupukari: Guyana 87 d8
Kurusku: Egypt 54 D10
Kusa: U.S.S.R. 50 J3
Kusadak: Yugoslavia 39 R14
Kuşadasi: Turkey 39 U18
Kusagaki Is.: Japan 63 X8
Kusango Swamp: *marsh*, Zambia 77 C5
Kusatsu: Japan 63 f2
Kusel: W. Germany 44 N6
Kushan: Liaoning, China 63 W7
Kushantze: Kirin, China 63 X6
Kushchinskaya: U.S.S.R. 50 E5
Kushih: Honan, China 62 V8
Kushikino: Japan 63 b5
Kushimoto: Japan 63 d4
Kushiro: Japan 63 ZZ6
Kushk: Afghanistan 58 K8
Kushka: Turkmen., U.S.S.R. 51 K7
Kushnarenkovo: U.S.S.R. 50 J4
Kushui: Sinkiang, China 62 Q6
Kushva: U.S.S.R. 50 J3
Kusiyara: *riv.*, Bangladesh 59 Q10
Kuskokwim: *riv.*, Alaska, U.S.A. 84 D5
Kuskokwim Bay: Alaska, U.S.A. 84 c6
Kusnacht: Switzerland 40 O8
KUSTANAY: & *Reg.*, Kazakh., U.S.S.R. 51 K4
Kusten Canal: W. Germany 44 N2
Kut: *i.*, Thailand 64 C4
Kuta: Nigeria 81 F3
Kut Abdullah: Iran 57 L6
Kutacane: Sumatra 65 B6
KUTAHYA: & *Prov.*, Turkey 56 B2
Kutaisi: Georgia, U.S.S.R. 50 F6
Kut al Hai: Iraq 57 K5
Kutch: *reg.*, Gujarat, India 58 M10
Kutch, Gulf of: Gujarat, India 58 L10
Kutch, Rann of: *marsh*, Gujarat, India 58 L10
Kutchan: Japan 63 ZZ6
Kutkashen: Azerbaydzhan, U.S.S.R. 57 K1
Kutná Horá: Czechoslovakia 45 V6
Kutno: Poland 43 Q10
Kutsing (Chuking): Yunnan, China 62 S9
Kutu: Zaire 76 A3
Kutum: Sudan 79 J7
Kuty: Czechoslovakia 41 X7
Kützberg: W. Germany 45 Q5
Kuuli-Mayak: Turkmen., U.S.S.R. 50 H6
Kuusamo: Finland 46 V4
Kuusjärvi: Finland 46 V5
Kuvandyk: U.S.S.R. 50 J4
Kuvshinovo: U.S.S.R. 50 D3

Kuwait: *Sheikhdom* 54 G9
Cap.: Kuwait
Area: 7,780 sq. miles (20,150 sq. km.)
Pop. 914,000 (*1972 E*)

Kuwana: Japan 63 e3
Kuwo: Shansi, China 62 U7
Kuyang: Inner Mongolia, China 62 U6
KUYBYSHEV: & *Reg.*, U.S.S.R. 50 H4
Kuybyshev: Novosibirsk, U.S.S.R. 51 N3
Kuyeh: Shantung, China 62 V7
Kuyto, Lake: Karelian A.S.S. Rep., U.S.S.R. 46 W4
Kuyuan: Hopeh, China 62 V6
Kuyuan: Ninghsia Hui, China 62 T7
Kuyumba: U.S.S.R. 49 l5
Kuyuwinni: *riv.*, Guyana 87 d9
Kuzino: U.S.S.R. 50 J3
Kuznetsk: U.S.S.R. 50 G4
Kuznetsovo: Primorsk, U.S.S.R. 63 Z5
Kuznetsovo: Sverdlovsk, U.S.S.R. 51 K3
Kvaløy, North: *i.*, Norway 46 Q1
Kvaløy, South: *i.*, Norway 46 Q2
Kvalsund: Norway 46 S1
Kvarkeno: U.S.S.R. 50 J4
Kvarner: Yugoslavia 38 O14
Kvarnerić: *str.*, Yugoslavia 41 U11
Kvikkjokk: Sweden 46 P3
Kvikne: Norway 46 M5
Kvilda: Czechoslovakia 45 T6
Kwa: *riv.*, Zaire 81 H5
Kwaatsi Flat: *plain*, Botswana 77 B7
Kwabhaca: Transkei, S. Africa 75 H5
Kwaggafontein: S. Africa 74 E5
Kwaggashoek: O.F.S., S. Africa 75 F4
Kwakoegron: Surinam 94 F3
Kwala: Nigeria 81 F3
Kwale: Kenya 76 E3
Kwa-Mbonambi: Natal, S. Africa 75 K4
Kwamouth: Zaire 81 H5
Kwa Mtoro: Tanzania 76 E4
Kwando: *riv.*, Angola/Zambia 77 B6
Kwangan: Szechwan, China 62 T8
Kwangchang: Kiangsi, China 62 V9
Kwangchow: *see* Canton
Kwangchowan: *i.*, China 62 U10
Kwanghan: Szechwan, China 62 S8
Kwangju: S. Korea 63 X7
Kwangnan: Yunnan, China 62 T10
Kwango: *riv.*, Zaire 81 H5
Kwangshui: Hupeh, China 62 U8
Kwangshun: Kweichow, China 62 T9
Kwangsi Chuang: *Auton. Reg.*, China [*cap.* Nanning (Yungning)] 62 T10
Kwangtung: *Prov.*, China (*cap.* Canton) 62 U10
Kwanhaiwei: Chekiang, China 63 W8
Kwanhsien: Szechwan, China 62 S8
Kwania, Lake: Uganda 76 D2
Kwanho: Yunnan, China 62 S10
Kwantung Penin.: Liaoning, China 63 W7
Kwara: *state*, Nigeria (*cap.* Ilorin) 81 E3
Kweichih: Anhwei, China 62 V8
Kweichow: *Prov.*, China [*cap.* Kweiyang (Kweichu)] 62 T9
KWEICHU (Kweiyang): Kweichow, China 62 T9
Kweihsien: Kwangsi Chuang, China 62 T10
Kweiki: Kiangsi, China 62 V9
Kweilin: Kwangsi Chuang, China 62 U9
Kweiping (Sunchow): Kwangsi Chuang, China 62 U10
KWEISUI (Huhehot): Inner Mongolia, China 62 U6
Kweiteh: Chinghai, China 62 S7
Kweitung: Hunan, China 62 U9
Kweiyang: Hunan, China 62 U9
KWEIYANG (Kweichu): Kweichow, China 62 T9
Kweneng: *Dist.*, Botswana (*cap.* Molepolole) 77 B7
Kwenge: *riv.*, Zaire 76 A4
Kwidzyn: Poland 43 Q10
Kwilu: *riv.*, Zaire 76 A3
Kwinana: W. Australia 68 B6
Kwinhagak: Alaska, U.S.A. 84 c6
Kwisa: *riv.*, Poland 45 V4
Kwoka: *mtn.*, W. Irian, Indonesia 66 F2
Kwokiatun: Hopeh, China 62 V6
Kwollu: Ethiopia 76 E1
Kwongning: Kwangtung, China 62 U10
Kwongoma: Nigeria 81 F2
Kyabram: Vict., Australia 71 F11
Kyaikto: Burma 59 R11
Kyaka: Tanzania 76 D3
Kyakhta: U.S.S.R. 49 m7
Kyangin: Burma 59 R11
Kyango: Sudan 76 C1
Kyardla: Estonia, U.S.S.R. 47 S7
Kyaukkyi: Burma 59 R11
Kyaukpyu: Burma 59 Q11
Kyaukse: Burma 59 R10
Kyauktaw: Burma 59 Q10
Kyaunggon: Burma 59 R11
Kyeikdon: Burma 59 R11
Kyeintali: Burma 59 Q11
Kyelang: Himachal Pradesh, India 58 N8
Kyeri: Uganda 76 D2
Kyle: *dist.*, Strath., Scot. 29 N8
Kyleakin: I. of Skye, Inner Hebr., Scotland 25 K5
Kyle of Lochalsh: *village*, Highland, Scotland 28 K5
Kyllburg: W. Germany 44 M5
Kymi: *Prov.*, Finland (*cap.* Kouvola) 47 U6
Kyneton: Vict., Australia 71 F11
Kyoga, Lake: Uganda 76 D2
Kyoga Point: *cape*, Japan 63 d3
Kyogle: N.S.W., Australia 71 K7
Kyomipo: N. Korea 63 X7
Kyongju: S. Korea 63 X7
Kyongsong (Seoul): S. Korea 63 X7
Kyonkadun: Burma 59 R11
KYOTO: & *Pref.*, Japan 63 d3
Kyra: U.S.S.R. 49 N8
Kyrenia: Cyprus 56 C4
Kyritz: E. Germany 45 S3
Kyrkslätt: Uusimaa, Finland 47 T6
Kyrön: *riv.*, Finland 46 S5
Kyshtym: U.S.S.R. 51 K3
Kysperk: Czechoslovakia 45 W5
Kysuké Nové Mesto: Czech. 43 Q12
Kysyl-Balykta: U.S.S.R. 49 q4
Kytalyktakh: U.S.S.R. 49 P4
Kytlym: U.S.S.R. 50 J3
Kytmanovo: U.S.S.R. 51 P4
Kytyl: U.S.S.R. 49 o5
Kyungyaung: Burma 59 R11
Kyurdamir: Azerbaydzhan, U.S.S.R. 57 L1
Kyushu: *i.*, Japan 63 b4
Kyushu Mtns.: Japan 63 b4
Kyushu Palau Ridge: Philippine Sea 7 15N 135E
Kyustendil: Bulgaria 39 S15
Kywong: N.S.W., Australia 71 G10
Kyyjärvi: Finland 46 T5
Kyzas: U.S.S.R. 51 P4
KYZYL: Tuva, U.S.S.R. 51 Q4
Kyzyl-Kiya: Kirgiz., U.S.S.R. 51 M6
Kyzyl-Kum: *desert*, Uzbek., U.S.S.R. 51 K6
Kyzl-Kyya: Kazakh., U.S.S.R. 51 N5
Kyzyl-Mazhalik: U.S.S.R. 51 Q4
KYZYL-ORDA: & *Reg.*, Kazakh., U.S.S.R. 51 L6
Kyzyl-Rabot: Tadzhik., U.S.S.R. 51 M7
Kyzylzhar: (*Artyubinsk*), Kazakh., 39 U18
Kyzylzhar: (*W. Kazakh.*), Kazakh., U.S.S.R. 50 H5
Kzyl-Tu: Kazakh., U.S.S.R. 51 M4

Laa: Austria 41 W7
Laage: E. Germany 45 S2
La Aguera: W. Sahara 78 A5
La Albuera: Spain 35 C17
La Argentina: Argentina 95 C14
La Asturiana: Argentina 96 B4
La Asunción: Venezuela 94 E1
Labala: Lomblen, Indon. 65 G8
La Banda: Argentina 96 C2
La Bañeza: Spain 35 D15
Labang: Sarawak, Malaysia 65 E6
La Barca: Mexico 86 j13
La Barre-de-Monts: France 36 C9
Labasheeda: Clare, Repub. of Ireland 31 C14
La Bassee: France 36 H5
La Bastide: France 37 E11
La Bastide-de-Serou: France 37 G12
La Baule: France 36 C8
Labayen: Spain 37 D12
La Bazoche-Gouet: France 36 F7
LABÉ: & *Reg.*, Guinea 80 B2
Labe (Elbe): *riv.*, Czech. 45 U5
La Belle: Mo., U.S.A. 88 F5
Labelle: Que., Canada 89 O2
Labenne: France 37 D12
Labiau: *see* Polessk
Labicum: ancient Latin city about 13 miles SE. of Rome 38 N16
Labin: Yugoslavia 41 U10
Labinskaya: U.S.S.R. 50 F6
Labis: Malaya, Malaysia 65 c12
La Bisbal: Spain 35 H16
La Blachère: France 37 K11
La Boca: Panama 94 *Ins.*
Laborde: Argentina 96 C3
La Bosse: France 36 G6
Labota: Celebes 65 G7
Labouheyre: France 37 E11
Laboulaye: Argentina 96 C3
La Bourboule: France 37 H10
Labrador: Newf., Canada 85 n7
Labrador Basin: N. Atlantic Ocean 8 55N 55W
Labraunda: Greek city of *Caria* about 10 miles N. of Mylasa, Turkey 39 U18
Lábrea: Brazil 94 E5
Labrède: France 37 E11
Labrit: France 37 E11
Labroye: France 36 H5
Labuan I.: Sabah, Malaysia 65 F5
Labuha: Moluccas, Indon. 61 K12
Labuhan: Java 65 D8
Labuhanbajo: Flores, Indon. 65 F8
Labuhanbilik: Sumatra 65 C6
Labuk Bay: Sabah, Malaysia 65 F5
Labutta: Burma 59 Q11
La Cabrière: *mtns.*, France 40 M12
Lac à la Truite: *lake*, Que., Can. 89 N2
La Calle: Algeria 38 L18
Lacanau, Etang de: *lag.*, Fr. 37 D11
Lacanau-Medoc: France 37 D11
Lacanau-Océan: France 37 D10
La Capelle: France 36 J6
Lacapelle-Marival: France 37 G11
La Carlota: Argentina 96 C3
La Carolina: Spain 35 E17
Lacaune: France 37 H12
Lacaune, Monts de: *mtns.*, France 37 H12
La Cautiva: Argentina 96 C6
La Cavalerie: France 37 J11
Lacaze, J.: Uruguay 96 D3
Lac Bouchette: Que., Canada 89 P1
Laccadive Is.: Lakshadweep, India 58 M12
Laccadive Sea: Indian O. 58 M12
Lac du Bonnet: *town*, Man., Canada 92 H2
Lac du Flambeau: Wis., U.S.A. 88 G3
Laceby: Humb., England 27 V12
Lacerdonia: Mozambique 77 E6
Lac Etchemin: *town*, Que., Canada 89 Q2
Lac Frontière: *city*, Que., Canada 89 Q2
Lacha, Lake: U.S.S.R. 50 E2
La Chaise-Dieu: France 37 J10
La Chambre: France 40 M10
La Chapelle-D'Angillon: Fr. 36 H8
La Chapelle-la-Reine: Fr. 36 H7
La Charité: France 36 J8
La Chartre: Sarthe, France 36 F8
La Châtre: Indre, France 37 G9
la Châtaigneraie: France 37 E9
La Chaux-de-Fonds: Switz. 40 M8
La Chèze: France 36 C7
Lachiassu: Chinghai, China 62 S8
Lachin: Azerbaydzhan, U.S.S.R. 57 K2
Lachish: Judean city, site at *Tell Duwair*, 6 miles S. of Beit Jibrin, Israel 55 a3
Lachlan: *riv.*, N.S.W., Austl. 71 F10
La Chorrera: Panama 94 *Ins.*
La Ciotat: France 40 L12
Lack: Ferm., N. Ireland 30 F10
Lackan: Wick., Repub. of Ireland 31 J13
Lackawanna: N.Y., U.S.A. 89 M4
Lacken Res.: Wick., Repub. of Ireland 31 H13
Lac la Biche: *town*, Alta., Canada 92 E2
Lac la Ronge: Sask., Canada *see* La Ronge
Lac la Ronge Prov. Park: Sask., Canada 92 G1
La Clayette: France 37 K9
La Cocha: Argentina 96 B2
Lacock: Wilts., England 24 R17
Lacombe: Alta., Canada 92 E2
Laconi: Sardinia 38 L17
Laconia: N.H., U.S.A. 89 Q4
La Copelina: Argentina 96 B4
La Coquille: France 37 F10
LA CORUÑA (Corunna): & *Prov.*, Spain 35 B15
La Côte-St.-André: France 40 L10
La Couarde: Île de Ré, France 37 D9
La Couronne: France 37 F10
La Courtine: France 37 H10
Lacovia: Jamaica 86 *Ins.*
La Croixille: France 36 D7
La Crosse: Kans., U.S.A. 90 B6
La Crosse: Wis., U.S.A. 88 F4
La Cruz: Argentina 96 D2
Lactodurum: Roman name of Towcester, Northants., England 27 U15
La Cueva: Mexico 93 F7
La Cygne: Kans., U.S.A. 90 D6
Ladakh Range: Jammu and Kashmir 58 N8
Ladder Hills: Scotland 28 P5
Ladd Reef: S. China Sea 64 E5
Ladenburg: W. Germany 44 O6
Ladgasht: Baluchistan, Pakistan 58 K9
Ladhar Bheinn: *mtn.*, Highland, Scotland 28 K5
Ladhiqiya, El (Latakia): Syr. 56 D4
Ladignac: France 37 G10
Lâdik: Turkey 56 D1
Ladismith: & *Dist.*, S. Afr. 74 D6
Ladnun: Rajasthan, India 58 M9
Ladock: Cornwall, England 24 M19
Ladoga: & *lake*, U.S.S.R. 50 D2
La Dorada: Colombia 94 C2
Ladrone Is. (Wanshan): Kwangtung, China 62 U10
Ladybank: Fife, Scotland 29 P7
Ladybrand: & *Dist.*, O.F.S., S. Africa 75 G4
Lady Elliot I.: Queensland, Australia 70 K5
Lady Evelyn Lake: Ont., Canada 88 L2
Lady Frere: S. Africa 75 G5
Lady Grey: S. Africa 75 G5
Ladysmith: B.C., Canada 92 C3
Ladysmith: & *Dist.*, Natal, S. Africa 75 H4
Ladysmith: Wis., U.S.A. 88 F3
Lae: Papua/New Guinea 66 J3
La Escala: Spain 35 H15
Læsø: *i.*, Denmark 47 M8
La Estrada: Spain 35 B15
Lævvajåk: Norway 46 U2
Lafayette: Ala., U.S.A. 91 J9
Lafayette: Colo., U.S.A. 93 F5
La Fayette: Ga., U.S.A. 91 J8
Lafayette: Ind., U.S.A. 88 H5
Lafayette: La., U.S.A. 90 E10
Lafayette, West: Ind., U.S.A. 88 H5
La Fère: France 36 J6
La Ferté-Bernard: France 36 F7
La Ferté-Fresnel: France 36 F7
La Ferté-Gaucher: France 36 J7
La Ferté-Macé: France 36 E7
La Ferté-St.-Aubin: France 36 G8
La Ferté-sous-Jouarre: Fr. 36 J7
La Ferté-Vidame: France 36 F7
La Feuillie: France 36 G6
Lafia: Nigeria 81 F3
Lafiagi: Nigeria 81 F3
Lafitte Village: La., U.S.A. 90 *Ins.*
La Flèche: France 36 E8
La Florencia: Argentina 96 C1
Lafnitz: *riv.*, Austria 41 W8
La Follette: Tenn., U.S.A. 88 J7
Lafrançaise: France 37 G11
Laful: Nicobar Is. 59 Q13
La Gacilly: France 36 C8
Lagan: *riv.*, Down/Antrim, N. Ireland 30 K10
La Garnache: France 36 D9
Lagarto: Brazil 94 K6
Lagarto, Serra Do: *mtns.*, Brazil 96 E1
Lage: W. Germany 44 O4
Lågen: *riv.*, Buskerud, Nor. 47 L7
Lågen: *riv.*, Opland, Norway 47 L6
Lagernoye Camp: Novaya Zemlya, U.S.S.R. 48 G3
Lagg: Jura, Inner Hebr., Scotland 29 K8
Laggan: Highland, Scotland 28 N5
Laggan, Loch: High., Scot. 28 M6
Laghey: Don., Repub. of Ireland 30 E10
Laghman: *prov.*, Afghanistan 55 M7
Laghouat: Algeria 78 E3
Lagich: Azerbaydzhan, U.S.S.R. 57 L1
Lagnieu: France 40 L10
Lagny: France 36 H7
Lagoa Vermelha: Brazil 96 E2
Lagonegro: Italy 38 O16
Lagonoy, Gulf: Philippines 64 G4
Lagos: Chile 95 C11
LAGOS: Nigeria 81 E3
Lagos: Portugal 35 B18
Lagos de Moreno: Mexico 86 j13
Lagosta (Lastovo): *i.*, Yugo. 38 P15
Lagow: Poland 45 V3
La Grande: Oreg., U.S.A. 92 D3
La Grange: Ga., U.S.A. 91 J9
Lagrange: Ind., U.S.A. 88 J5
Lagrange: Wyo., U.S.A. 92 G4
La Grange: W. Australia 68 C3

158 La Gran Sabana—Lavernock

La Gran Sabana: Venez. **94** E2
Lagrasse: France **37** H12
La Guaira: Venezuela **94** D1
La Guampita: Argentina **96** C2
Laguardia: Alava, Spain **35** E15
La Guardia: Argentina **96** B2
La Guardia: Pontevedra, Sp. **35** B16
La Guerche: France **36** D8
La Guerche-sur-L'Aubois: France **36** H9
Laguiole: France **37** H11
Laguna: Brazil **96** F2
Laguna-Paiva: Argentina **96** C3
Lagundo: Italy **41** R9
Lagunillas: Bolivia **94** E7
Lagunillas: Venezuela **94** C1
Laha: Heilungkiang, China **63** W5
Lahad Datu: Sabah, Malaysia **65** F5
Lahaina: Hawaiian Is. **83** c2
Lahardane: Mayo, Repub. of Ireland **30** C11
Lahat: Sumatra **65** C7
Lahave: *riv.*, N.S., Canada **89** T3
La Haye Descartes: France **36** F9
La Haye-du-Puits: France **36** D6
La Haye-Pesnel: France **36** D7
Lahewa: Nias, Indonesia **65** B6
Lahijan: Iran **57** M3
Lahinch: Clare, Repub. of Ireland **31** C14
Lahj: Yemen P.D.R. **54** F12
Lähn (Wlen): Poland **45** V4
Lahn: *riv.*, W. Germany **44** O5
Lahnstein: W. Germany **44** N5
Laholm: *& bay*, Sweden **47** N8
LAHORE: Punjab, Pakistan **58** M8
Lahr: W. Germany **40** N7
Lahri: Baluchistan, Pakistan **58** L9
Lahti: Finland **47** T6
La Hutte: France **36** F7
Lai: (De Behagle), Tandjilé, Chad **81** H3
Laibach: German name of Yugoslav town Ljubljana, Yugoslavia **41** V9
Lai Chau: Vietnam **64** C2
Laich o' Moray: *dist.*, Grampian, Scotland **28** O4
Laidley: Queens., Australia **70** K6
Laidon, Loch: Strathclyde/Tayside, Scotland **29** M6
Laigle: France **36** F7
Laignes: France **36** K8
L'Aiguillon: France **37** D9
Laihka: Burma **59** R10
Laila: Saudi Arabia **54** G10
Laindon: Essex, England **25** W16
Laingsburg: *& Dist.*, S. Afr. **74** D6
Lainio (Råsto): *riv.*, Sweden **46** S3
Lairg: Highland, Scotland **28** N3
Lais: Sumatra **65** C7
Laisamis: Kenya **76** E2
Laissac: France **37** H11
Laisvall: Sweden **46** P3
Laitia: Finland **47** R6
Laives: Italy **41** R9
Laiwui: Moluccas, Indon. **61** K12
Laiyang: Shantung, China **63** W7
Laiyuan: Hopeh, China **62** U7
La Japonesa: Argentina **96** B4
Lajas, Las: Argentina **96** A4
Lajas, Las: Panama **94** *Ins.*
Lajeado: Brazil **96** E2
Lajes: Brazil **96** E2
Lajo: Ethiopia **76** E1
La Joya: Mexico **93** F7
La Junta: Colo., U.S.A. **93** G5
Lak: Iran **57** L4
Lak Bor: *riv.*, Kenya **76** F2
Lak Dera: *riv.*, Kenya **76** E2
Lake Arthur: La., U.S.A. **90** E10
Lake Boga: Vict., Australia **71** E10
Lake Cargelligo: N.S.W., Australia **71** G9
Lake Charles: La., U.S.A. **90** E10
Lake City: Fla., U.S.A. **91** K10
Lake City: Minn., U.S.A. **88** E3
Lake City: S.C., U.S.A. **91** M9
Lake District: *geog. reg.*, Cumbria, England **26** P11
Lake District Nat. Park: Cumbria, England **26** P11
Lake Geneva: Wis., U.S.A. **88** G4
Lake Grace: W. Australia **68** B6
Lake Harbour: N.W.T., Can. **85** N5
Lakeland: Fla., U.S.A. **91** L11
Lakeland: Ga., U.S.A. **91** K10
Lake Louise: Alta., Canada **92** D2
Lake Manyara National Park: Tanzania **76** E3
Lakemba: *i.*, Fiji Is. **67** Q5
Lake Mead Nat. Rec. Area: Ariz., U.S.A. **93** E5
Lake Mills: Iowa, U.S.A. **88** E4
Lake Nash: N. Territ., Austl. **69** F4
Lakenheath: Suffolk, Eng. **25** X15
Lake Placid: N.Y., U.S.A. **89** P3
Lake Providence: La., U.S.A. **90** F9
Lakes Entrance: Victoria, Australia **71** H11
Lakeside: S. Africa **74** *Ins.*
Lake Stewart: N.S.W., Austl. **71** D7
Lake Superior Prov. Park: Ont., Canada **88** J2
Lakeview: Oreg., U.S.A. **92** C4
Lake Village: Ark., U.S.A. **90** F9
Lake Wales: Fla., U.S.A. **91** L12
Lakewood: Ohio, U.S.A. **88** L5
Lake Worth: Fla., U.S.A. **91** L12
Lakhdaria: Algeria **35** H18
Lakhdenpokh'ya: Karelian A.S.S. Rep., U.S.S.R. **47** W6
Lakhimpur: Uttar Pradesh, India **58** 09
Lakhimpur North: Assam, India **59** Q9
Lakhpat: Gujarat, India **58** L10
Laki Marwat: NW. Front. Prov., Pakistan **58** M8
Lakin: Burma **59** R9
Lakki: N.W. Front. Prov., Pak. **58** M8
Lakonia, Gulf of: Greece **39** S18
Lakorichoke: Sudan **76** D1
Lakota: Ivory Coast **80** C3
Lakota: N. Dak., U.S.A. **92** H3
Lakse Fiord: Norway **46** U1
Lala Bazar: Assam, India **59** Q10
Lala Musa: Punjab, Pak. **58** M8
Lalapaşa: Turkey **39** U16
La Lara: Gabon **81** G4
Lalaua: Mozambique **77** E5
Lalendorf: E. Germany **45** S2
Laleston: Mid Glam., Wales **24** O16
Lali: Iran **57** L5
La Libertad: Guatemala **86** k14
La Ligua: Chile **96** A3
Lalin: Spain **35** B15
Lalinde: France **37** F11
La Linea: Spain (Gib. *Inset*) **32** *Ins.*
Lalishan: *mtn.*, Tibet, China **58** O8
Lalitpur: Uttar Pradesh, India **58** N10
La Loche, Lac: *lake.*, Sask., Canada **92** F1
La Loupe: France **36** G7
La Louvière: Belgium **44** K5
Laluque: France **37** E12
Lam: Vietnam **64** D2
La Machine: France **37** J9
Lamag: Sabah, Malaysia **65** F5
Lamaing: Burma **59** R11
La Malbaie (Murray Bay): Que., Canada **89** Q2
Lamalou: France **37** J12
Lamar: Colo., U.S.A. **93** G5
Lamar: Mo., U.S.A. **90** D7
La Maroma: Argentina **96** B4
Lamarque: Tex., U.S.A. **90** D11
La Martre, Lac: N.W.T., Canada **84** H5
Lamastre: France **37** K11
Lambach: Austria **41** T7
Lambaesis: Roman camp S. of Batna mtn. and about 60 miles NNE. of Biskra, Algeria **32** D4
Lamballe: France **36** C7
LAMBARÉNÉ: Moyen-Ogooué, Gabon **81** G5
Lambasa: Vanua Levu, Fiji Is. **67** P5
Lambayeque: Peru **94** B5
Lambay I.: Repub. of Irel. **30** K13
Lambeg: Antrim, Northern Ireland **30** J10
Lamberhurst: Kent, Eng. **25** W17
Lambert Glacier: Antarctica **9** 75S 65E
Lambert's Bay: *town*, S. Afr. **74** C6
Lamberts Land: Greenland **85** r2
Lambesc: France **40** L12
Lambeth: Gt. Ldn., England **25** V17
Lambia: Greece **39** R18
Lambourn: Berks., England **25** S16
Lambro: *riv.*, Italy **40** P10
Lamb's Head: *cape*, Kerry, Repub. of Ireland **31** A16
Lambton: Que., Canada **89** Q3
Lambton, Cape: N.W.T., Canada **84** g3
Lamdesar: Tanimbar Is., Indonesia **61** L13
Lamé: Chad **81** G3
Lamego: Portugal **35** C16
Lamenu: New Hebrides **67** N5
La Merced: Argentina **96** B2
Lameroo: S. Australia **71** D10
Lamerton: Devon, England **24** N18
Lamesa: Tex., U.S.A. **93** G6
Lamia: Greece **39** S17
Lamington: Queens., Austl. **70** K7
Lamington: Strath., Scot. **29** O8
Lamitan: Philippines **65** G5
Lamlash: Strath., Scotland **29** L8
Lammermuir: *dist.*, Borders, Scotland **29** R8
Lammermuir Hills: Lothian/Borders, Scotland **29** Q8
Lamo Hu: *lake*, Tibet, China **59** Q8
Lamon Bay: Philippines **64** G4
Lamone: *riv.*, Italy **41** R11
La Mothe: France **37** E9
La Mothe-Achard: France **37** D9
La Motte, Lac: *lake*, Que., Canada **89** M1
Lamotte-Beuvron: France **36** H8
La Motte-du-Caire: France **40** M11
La Motte-Servolex: France **40** L10
La Moure: N. Dak., U.S.A. **92** H3
Lampa: Peru **94** C7
Lampang: Thailand **64** B3
Lampasas: Tex., U.S.A. **90** B10
Lampazos: Mexico **93** G7
Lampedusa: *i.*, Italy **32** E4
Lampertheim: W. Germany **44** O6
Lampeter: Dyfed, Wales **24** N15
Lamphun: Thailand **64** B3
Lampione: *i.*, Italy **32** E4
Lam Pao Reservoir: Thailand **64** C3
Lampsacus: Greek city at Lapseki, Turkey **39** U16
Lamu: Burma **59** Q11
Lamu: Kenya **76** F3
La Mure: Isère, France **40** L11
Lamure: Rhône, France **37** K9
Lana: Italy **41** R9
Lanai: *i.*, Hawaiian Is. **83** c2
Lanai City: Hawaiian Is. **83** c2
Lanak Pass: China/Jammu & Kashmir **58** N8
Lanao, Lake: Mindanao, Philippines **64** G5
Lanark: Strath., Scotland **29** O8
Lancashire: *Co. & plain*, Eng. (*co. town* Preston) **27** Q12
Lancaster: Ky., U.S.A. **88** J7
Lancaster: Lancs., England **27** Q11
Lancaster: Ohio, U.S.A. **88** K6
Lancaster: Pa., U.S.A. **89** N5
Lancaster: S.C., U.S.A. **91** L8
Lancaster: Wis., U.S.A. **88** F4
Lancaster Reef: Austral Is. **83** f5
Lancaster Sound: N.W.T., Canada **85** L3
Lancefield: Vict., Australia **71** F11
Lanchester: Durham, England **26** S10
LANCHOW (Kaolan): Kansu, China **62** S7
Lanciano: Italy **38** O15
Lancing: W. Sussex, England **25** V18
Łańcut: Poland **43** S11
Lândana: Cabinda, Angola **81** G6
Landau: Bavaria, W. Ger. **41** S7
Landau: Rhineland Palatinate, W. Ger. **44** O6
Landeck: Austria **40** Q8
Lander: Wyo., U.S.A. **92** F4
Landerneau: France **36** A7
Landeryd: Sweden **47** N8
Landes: *Dept.*, France (*cap.* Mont-de-Marsan) **37** E12
Landes, Les: *geog. reg.*, Fr. **37** D11
Landi Muhammed Amin Khan: Afghanistan **58** K8
Landivisiau: France **36** A7
Landivy: France **36** D7
Landsberg: Bavaria, W. Ger. **41** Q7
Landsberg: Halle, E. Germany **45** S4
Landsborough: Queens., Australia **70** K6
Land's End: *cape & airfield*, Corn., England **25** K19
Land's End: *cape*, N.W.T., Canada **84** g2
Landshut: W. Germany **41** S7
Landskrona: Sweden **47** N9
Lands Lokk: N.W.T., Can. **84** k1
Landstuhl: W. Germany **44** N6
Landu: *i.*, Indonesia **65** G9
Lane End: Bucks., England **25** U16
Lanercost Priory: *ancient monument*, Cumbria, Eng. **26** Q10
Lanesboro: Minn., U.S.A. **88** F4
Lanesborough: Long., Repub. of Ireland **30** F12
Lanett: Ala., U.S.A. **91** J9
La Neuveville: Switzerland **44** N8
Langadhás: Greece **39** S16
Langana, Lake: Ethiopia **76** E1
Langap: Borneo **65** F6
Langarud: Iran **57** M3
Langasiko: Tanzania **76** D4
Langavat, Loch: Outer Hebr., Scotland **28** H3
Langberg: *range*, (Griqualand West), S. Africa **74** E4
Langberge: *range*, S. Africa **74** C5
Langchung (Paoning): Szechwan, China **62** T8
Langdales: Cumbria, Eng. **26** P11
Langdon: N. Dak., U.S.A. **92** H3
Langeac: France **37** J10
Langeais: France **36** F8
Langebaan: S. Africa **74** C6
Langebaanweg: S. Afr. **75** C6
Langeberg: *range*, S. Africa **74** D6
Langen: Hesse, W. Germany **44** O6
Langenburg: W. Germany **45** P6
Langenes: Vesterålen, Norway **46** O2
Längenfeld: Austria **41** Q8
Langensalza: E. Germany **45** Q4
Langenthal: Switzerland **40** N8
Langenzenn: W. Germany **45** Q6
Langeoog: *i.*, E. Frisian Is. **44** N2
Langesund: Norway **47** L7
Långfiordbotn: Norway **46** V2
Långflon: Sweden **47** N6
Langford: Beds., England **25** V15
Langford Budville: Som., England **24** P18
Langförden: W. Germany **44** O3
Langham: Leics., England **27** U14
Langhirano: Italy **40** Q11
Langholm: Dumfries & Galloway, Scotland **29** P9
Lang Jökull: *ice cap*, Iceland **46** c4
Langkatzu: Tibet, China **59** Q9
Langkawi Is.: Malaya, Malaysia **65** a10
Langki: Anhwei, China **62** V8
Langlaagte: Trans., S. Afr. **74** *M Ins.*
Langley: Essex, England **25** W16
Langlo: *riv.*, Queens., Austl. **70** F5
Langlo Downs: Queens., Australia **70** F5
Langogne: France **37** J11
Langold: N. Yorks., England **27** T13
Langon: France **37** E11
Langonnet: France **36** B7
Langøy: *i.*, Vesterålen, Norway **46** O2
Langport: Som., England **24** Q17
Langreo: Spain **35** D15
Langres: France **36** L8
Langres, Plat. de: *plat.*, Fr. **36** K8
Langsa: Sumatra **65** B6
Långsele: Västerbotten, Sweden **46** O4
Långsele: Västernorrland, Sweden **46** P5
Langsett: S. Yorks., England **27** S13
Langson: Vietnam **64** D2
Lang Suan: Thailand **64** B5
Langthwaite: N. Yorks., Eng. **26** S11
Langtoft: Lincs., England **25** V14
Långträsk: Sweden **46** R4
Languedoc: *Prov.*, France **34** H15
Languidic: France **36** B8
Langwarden: W. Germany **44** O2
Langwathby: Cumbria, Eng. **26** Q10
Langwell, West: Highland, Scotland **28** N3
Langwith, Nether: Notts., England **27** T13
Lanhsien: Shansi, China **62** U7
Lanigan: Sask., Canada **92** F2
Lanin, Volc.: Chile **95** C11
Lannemezan: France **37** F12
Lannilis: France **36** A7
Lannion: France **36** B7
La Nouvelle: France **37** J12
Lanping: Yunnan, China **62** R9
Lanreath: Corn., England **24** M19
Lans, Montagnes de: *mtns.*, France **40** L11
Lansdale: Pa., U.S.A. **89** O5
Lansdowne: Uttar Pradesh, India **58** N9
L'Anse: Mich., U.S.A. **88** G2
Lansi: Heilungkiang, China **63** X5
Lansing: Iowa, U.S.A. **88** F4
LANSING: Mich., U.S.A. **88** J4
Lansing, East: Mich., U.S.A. **88** J4
Lanslebourg: France **40** M10
Lantewa: Nigeria **81** G2
Lanton: Borders, Scotland **29** Q9
Lantosque: France **40** N12
Lantsang (Mekong): *riv.*, China **62** S10
Lanusei: Sardinia **38** L17
Lanuvium: ancient city of *Latium* in hills about 18 miles SE. of Rome **38** N16
Lanuza: Mindanao, Phil. **64** H5
Lanvéoc: France **36** A7
Lanvollon: France **36** C7
Lanz: E. Germany **45** R2
Lanzarote: *i.*, Canary Is. **78** B4
Lanzo: Italy **40** N10
Laoag: Luzon, Philippines **64** G3
Laoang: Philippines **64** H4
Laobao: Laos **64** D3
Lao Cai: Vietnam **64** C2
Laodicea ad Lycum: Graeco-Roman city at town of Denizli, Turkey **39** V18
Laoho: *riv.*, Inner Mongolia, China **63** W6
Laois: *Co.*, Repub. of Ireland [*cap.* Port Laoise (Maryborough)] **31** G14
Laokai: Yunnan, China **62** R9
LAON: Aisne, France **36** J6
Laona: Wis., U.S.A. **88** G3
Laora: Celebes **65** G7
La Orilla: Mexico **86** j14
La Oroya: Peru **94** B6

Laos: *Kingdom* **64** C3
Cap.: Vientiane
Area: 91,428 sq. miles (236,799 sq. km.)
Pop.: 3,106,000 (*1972 E*)

Laotowkow: Kirin, China **63** X6
Lapa: Brazil **96** F2
Lapalisse: France **37** J9
La Pallice: France **37** D9
La Palma: Panama **94** B2
La Palma: Spain **35** C18
La Palma: *i.*, Canary Is. **78** A4
La Pampa: *Prov.*, Argentina (*cap.* Santa Rosa) **96** B4
La Panne: Belgium **36** H4
Lapar: U.S.S.R. **49** O3
LA PAZ: Bolivia **94** D7
La Paz: Entre Rios, Argentina **96** D3
LA PAZ: Lower Calif. (S. Territ.), Mexico **93** E8
La Paz: Mendoza, Argentina **96** B3
Lapeer: Mich., U.S.A. **88** K4
La Pelada: Argentina **96** C3
La Pérouse (Soya) Str., Sakhalin/Japan **63** ZZ5
Lapford: Devon, England **24** O18
Lapinlahti: Finland **46** U5
Lapland: *geog. reg.*, N. Scandinavia **46** T2
LA PLATA: Buenos Aires, Argentina **96** D3
La Plata: Md., U.S.A. **89** N6
La Pobla de Lillet: Spain **35** G15
La Popa: Mexico **93** G7
La Porte: Ind., U.S.A. **88** H5
Laporte: Pa., U.S.A. **89** N5
La Porte City: Iowa, U.S.A. **88** E4
Lapoutroye: France **40** N7
Lappa Lake: Finland **46** S5
Lappeenranta: Finland **47** V6
Lappi: Finland **46** T4
Lappi: *Prov.* (*cap.* Rovahiemi) **46** U3
Lappträsk: Finland **47** U6
Lappträsk: Sweden **46** S3
Lâpseki: Turkey (Dardan. *Inset*) **20** *Ins.*
Laptev Sea: U.S.S.R. **49** O2
Laptev Str.: U.S.S.R. **49** Q3
Lapua: Finland **46** S5
Lapuan: *riv.*, Finland **46** S5
La Puebla: Spain **35** D17
Lapuepie: France **37** G11
La Purisima: Mexico **93** E7
Lapushna: Ukraine **43** T12
Laqiya Arba'in: *well*, Sudan **54** C10
La Quiaca: Argentina **95** D8
L'AQUILA: Abruzzi Molise, Italy **38** N15
Lar: Iran **55** H9
Lara, La: Gabon **81** G4
Larache: Morocco **80** K7
Laracor: Meath, Repub. of Ireland **30** H12
Laragh: Wick., Repub. of Irel. **31** J13
La Rambla: Spain **35** D18
Laramie: Wyo., U.S.A. **92** F4
Laramie Peak: Wyo., U.S.A. **92** F4
Laramie Range: Wyo., U.S.A. **92** F4
Laragne: France **40** L11
Larantuka: Flores, Indon. **65** G8
L'Arba: Algeria **35** H18
L'Arbresle: France **37** K10
Lärbro: Gotland, Sweden **47** Q8
Larche: Alpes de Haute Provence, Fr. **40** M11
Larche: Corrèze, France **37** G10
Larde: Mozambique **77** E6
Lardier, Cap: *cape*, France **40** M12
Laredo: Spain **35** E15
Laredo: Tex., U.S.A. **90** B12
La Reine: Que., Canada **89** M1
Laren: Netherlands **44** L3
La Réole: France **37** E11
LARGEAU (Faya): Borku-Ennedi-Tibesti, Chad **78** H6
Largentière: France **37** K11
L'Argentières: France **40** M11
Largs: Strath., Scotland **29** M8
Lariang: Celebes **65** F7
Larijan: Iran **57** K2
Larimore: N. Dak., U.S.A. **92** H3
Larino: Italy **38** O16
LA RIOJA: *& Prov.*, Argentina **96** B2
La Rioja: Chile **96** B1
Lárisa: Greece **39** S17
Laristan: *geog. reg.*, Iran **55** H9
Larius: Roman name of L. Como, Italy **40** P9
Lark: *riv.*, Suff., England **25** X15
Larkana: Sind, Pakistan **58** L9
Larkhall: Strath., Scotland **29** O8
Lark Harbour: Newf., Can. **85** t2
Larkhill: Wilts., England **25** S17
Larnaca: Cyprus **56** C4
Larne: Antrim, N. Ireland **30** K10
Larned: Kans., U.S.A. **90** B6
La Robla: Spain **35** D15
La Roca: Spain **35** C17
Laroche: Belgium **44** L5
La Roche: France **40** M9
La Roche-Bernard: France **36** C8
La Roche-Chalais: France **37** F10
La Rochefoucauld: France **37** F10
LA ROCHELLE: Charente-Maritime, France **37** D9
LA ROCHE-SUR-YON: Vendée, France **37** D9
La Roda: Spain **35** E17
La Romana: Dominican Rep. **87** N14
La Ronge: Sask., Canada **92** G1
Laroquebrou: France **37** H11
Laroque-Timbaut: France **37** F11
Läroro: Gotland, Sweden **47** Q8
Larose: La., U.S.A. **90** *Ins.*
Larrau: France **37** E12
Larsa: Sumerian city, site at *Senkereh*, E. of Samawa, Iraq **57** J6
La Rubia: Argentina **96** C3
Larsen Ice Shelf: Antarctica **9** 70S 65W
Laruns: France **37** E13
Larvik: Norway **47** M7
Laryak: U.S.S.R. **51** O2
Larzac, Causse du: *plat.*, Fr. **37** H12
Lasa: Italy **40** Q9
La Sábana: Argentina **96** D2
La Sagra: *mtn.*, Spain **35** E18
Lasalle: France **37** J11
La Salle: Ill., U.S.A. **88** G5
La Salvetat: France **37** H12
Las Animas: Chile **96** A2
Las Animas: Colo., U.S.A. **93** G5
Las Anod: Somalia **79** R18
Las Avispas: Argentina **96** C2
Las Cabras: Chile **96** A3
Las Cascades: Panama **94** *Ins.*
Lascano: Uruguay **96** E3
Las Catitas: Argentina **96** B3
Las Cejas: Argentina **96** C2
La Scie: Newf., Canada **85** v2
Las Cruces: N. Mex., U.S.A. **93** F6
Las Dureh: Somalia **79** R17
La Selle-en-Luitré: France **36** D7
La Seña: Argentina **96** B3
La Serena: Chile **96** A2
Las Esperanzas: Mexico **93** G7
La Seyne-sur-Mer: France **40** L12
Las Flores: Argentina **96** D4
Lash: Afghanistan **58** K8
Las Habas: Spain (Gib. *Inset*) **32** *Ins.*
Lasham: Hants., England **25** T17
Las Heras: Argentina **96** B3
Lashio: Burma **59** R10
Lashkar: Madhya Pradesh, India **58** N9
Las Khoreh: Somalia **79** R17
Laško: Yugoslavia **41** V9
Las Lajas: Argentina **96** A4
Las Lajas: Panama **94** *Ins.*
Las Lomitas: Argentina **96** C1
Las Marismas: *marsh*, Spain **35** C18
Las Mesteñas: Mexico **93** G7
Lasolo Bay: Celebes **65** G7
La Souterraine: France **37** G9
Las Palmas: Argentina **96** D2
LAS PALMAS: *& Prov.*, Canary Is. **78** A4
Las Palomas: Spain (Gib. *Inset*) **32** *Ins.*
Las Perlas: Nicaragua **87** I15
La Spezia: Italy **40** P11
Las Piedras: Uruguay **96** D3
Las Piedras: Venezuela **87** m15
Las Pipinas: Argentina **96** D4
Las Plumas: Argentina **95** D12
Las Rosas: Argentina **96** C3
Lassan: E. Germany **45** T2
Lassay: France **36** E7
Lassen Peak: Calif., U.S.A. **92** C4
Lassen Volcanic Nat. Park: Calif., U.S.A. **92** C4
L'Assomption: Que., Can. **89** P3
Lasswade: Lothian, Scotland **29** P8
Las Tablas: Panama **87** I16
Lastingham: N. Yorks., Eng. **26** U11
Last Mountain Lake: Sask., Canada **92** F2
Lastourville: Gabon **81** G5
Lastovo (Lagosta): *i.*, Yugo. **38** P15
Lastra: Italy **41** R12
Las Tres Virgenes: *mtn.*, Mexico **93** E7
Lastrup: W. Germany **44** N3
La Suze: France **36** F8
Las Varillas: Argentina **96** C3
Las Vegas: Nev., U.S.A. **93** D5
Las Vegas: N. Mex., U.S.A. **93** F5
Las Yungas: *mtns.*, Bolivia **94** D7
Latacunga: Ecuador **94** B4
La Tagua: Colombia **94** C3
LATAKIA: *& Prov.*, Syria **56** D4
La Tamba: Guinea **80** B2
Latchingdon: Essex, Eng. **25** X16
La Teste de Buch: France **37** D11
Lathen: W. Germany **44** N3
Latheron: Highland, Scotland **28** P3
Lathus: France **37** F9
Latina: Italy **38** N16
Latisana: Italy **41** T10
Latium: *Reg.*, Italy [*cap.* Rome (Roma)] **38** N15
La Tortuga: *i.*, Venezuela **94** D1
Latouche: Alaska, U.S.A. **84** E5
La Tour-du-Pin: France **40** L10
La Tranche: France **37** D9
La Tremblade: France **37** D10
La Trimouille: France **37** G9
Latrobe: Pa., U.S.A. **89** M5
Latrobe: Tas., Australia **68** H8
Latse: Tibet, China **59** O8
Latrun: Jordan **55** a3
La Tuque: Que., Canada **89** P2
Latur: Maharashtra, India **58** N11
Latvian S.S. Repub.: U.S.S.R. (*cap.* Riga) **47** S8
Lau: Nigeria **81** G3
Laucha: E. Germany **45** R4
Lauchheim: W. Germany **40** Q7
Lauda: W. Germany **44** P6
Laudal: Norway **47** K7
Lauder: Borders, Scotland **29** Q8
Lauderdale: *val.*, Borders, Scotland **29** Q8
Laudona: Latvia, U.S.S.R. **47** U8
Lauenburg: W. Germany **45** Q2
Lauf: W. Germany **45** R6
Laufen: W. Germany **41** S8
Laufen: Switzerland **40** N8
Laufenburg: Switzerland **40** O8
Laugharne: Dyfed, Wales **24** N16
Laughlin Is.: New Guinea **69** J1
Laughlin Peak: N. Mex., U.S.A. **93** G5
Laughton: E. Sussex, England **25** W18
Langsett: S. Yorks., Eng. **27** S13
Lau Group: *is.*, Fiji Is. **67** Q5
Launceston: Corn., England **24** N18
Launceston: Tas., Austl. **68** H8
Laune: *riv.*, Kerry, Repub. of Ireland **31** B15
La Unión: Chile **95** C12
La Unión: Mexico **86** j14
La Unión: El Salvador **86** L15
Launois: France **36** K6
Laupheim: W. Germany **40** P7
Laura: Queens., Australia **69** G3
Laura: S. Australia **71** C9
Lauragh: Kerry, Repub. of Ireland **31** B16
Laurel: Md., U.S.A. **89** N6
Laurel: Miss., U.S.A. **90** G10
Laurel: Mont., U.S.A. **92** F3
Laurencekirk: Grampian, Scot. **28** R6
Laurencetown: Galway, Repub. of Ireland **31** E13
Laurens: S.C., U.S.A. **91** K8
Laurentides Provincial Park: Que., Canada **85** m8
Laurentum: ancient city of *Latium* near coast about 8 miles S.E. of Ostia **38** N16
Lauria: Italy **38** O16
Lauriacum: Roman fort at confluence of Danube and Enns, Austria **41** U7
Laurière: France **37** G9
Laurieston: Dumfries & Galloway, Scotland **29** N10
Laurieston: Central, Scotland **29** O8
Laurinburg: N.C., U.S.A. **91** M8
Lauritsala: Finland **47** V6
Laurium: Mich., U.S.A. **88** G2
Lauro: *mtn.*, Sicily **38** O18
Lauro Müller: Brazil **96** F2
LAUSANNE: Vaud, Switz. **40** M9
Lausick: E. Germany **45** S4
Laut: *i.*, Borneo **65** F7
Lautaro: Chile **96** A4
Lauterbach: W. Germany **44** P5
Lauterbourg: France **40** O7
Lauterbrunnen: Switz. **40** N9
Lauterecken: W. Germany **44** N6
Lauterhofen: W. Germany **45** R6
Lautoka: Viti Levu, Fiji Is. **67** P5
Lautrec: France **37** H12
Lauzerte: France **37** G11
Lauzès: France **37** G11
Lauzet, Le: France **40** M11
Lauzon: Que., Canada **89** Q2
Lava Beds Nat. Mon.: Calif., U.S.A. **92** C4
Lava Hot Springs: *city*, Idaho, U.S.A. **92** E4
LAVAL: Mayenne, France **36** E7
Lavalle: Argentina **96** B3
Lavangen: Norway **46** P2
Lavant: W. Sussex, England **25** U18
Lavant: *riv.*, Austria **41** U9
Lavar: Iran **55** H9
Lavardac: France **37** F11
Lavatrae: Roman name of Bowes, Durham, England **26** R10
Lavaur: France **37** G12
Lavaveix: France **37** G12
La Vega: Dominican Rep. **87** m14
Lavelanet: France **37** G13
Lavendon: Bucks., England **25** U15
Lavenham: Suff., England **25** X15
Laveno: Italy **40** O10
La Verendrye Prov. Park: Que., Canada **89** N2
La Vernarède: France **37** J11
Lavernock: S. Glam., Wales **24** P17

For Abbreviations see list on p.113. Italic type, e.g. *Ephesus*, refers to historical names not on maps. Capital letters, e.g. MADRID, show capitals of countries; small capital letters, e.g. CADIZ, show capitals of provinces, etc. General notes p.116.

Laversburg: Trans., S. Afr. **74** Olns.
Laverton: W. Australia **68** C5
La Veuve: France **36** K6
Lavik: Norway **47** J6
Lavinium: ancient city of *Latium* about 3 miles from coast SSW. of Rome **38** N16
Lavis: Italy **41** R9
Lavit: France **37** F12
Lavongai: *i.*, Bismarck Arch. **67** K2
Lavonia: Ga., U.S.A. **91** K8
Lavoulte-sur-Rhône: Fr. **37** K11
Lavras: Ceará, Brazil **94** K5
Lavras: Minas Gerais, Braz. **96** G1
Lavras: Rio Grande do Sul, Brazil **96** R14
Lavrojærg: Denmark **47** L8
Lávrion: Greece **39** T18
Law: Strath., Scotland **29** O8
Lawagan: New Ireland **67** K2
Lawers: Tayside, Scotland **29** N6
Lawgi: Queens., Australia **70** J5
Lawksawk: Burma **59** R10
Lawlers: W. Australia **68** C5
Lawley: Trans., S. Africa **74** Mns.
Lawn Hill: *town*, Queens., Australia **69** F3
Lawra: Ghana **80** D2
Lawrence: Kans., U.S.A. **90** D6
Lawrence: Mass., U.S.A. **89** Q4
Lawrence: South I., N.Z. **71** M17
Lawrenceburg: Ky., U.S.A. **88** J6
Lawrenceburg: Tenn., U.S.A. **91** H8
Lawrencetown: Down, N. Irel. **30** J11
Lawrencetown: N.S., Can. **89** T3
Lawrenceville: Ga., U.S.A. **91** K9
Lawrenceville: Ill., U.S.A. **88** H6
Lawrenceville: Va., U.S.A. **89** N7
Lawshall: Suff., England **25** X15
Lawton: Okla., U.S.A. **90** B8
Lawn: *mtn.*, Java **65** E8
Laxå: Sweden **47** O4
Laxay: Outer Hebr., Scot. **28** H3
Laxey: I. of Man, U.K. **26** N11
Laxfield: Suff., England **25** Y15
Laxford, Loch: High., Scot. **28** L3
Laxsjö: Sweden **46** O5
Laxton: Humb., England **27** U12
Laxton: Notts., England **27** U13
Lay: *riv.*, France **37** D9
Layer de la Haye: Essex, Eng. **25** X16
Layon: *riv.*, France **36** E8
Layrac: France **37** F11
L'Ayrolle, Etang de: *lag.*, Fr. **37** J12
Laytonville: Calif., U.S.A. **92** C5
Laytown: Meath, Repub. of Ireland **30** J12
Lazarevac: Yugoslavia **39** R14
Lazdijay: Lithuania, U.S.S.R. **43** S9
Lazio: *see* Latium.
Lazonby: Cumbria., Eng. **26** Q10
Lea: Hereford & Worcester, England **24** R16
Lea: *riv.*, England **25** V16
Lead: S. Dak., U.S.A. **92** G4
Leadburn: Lothian, Scot. **29** P8
Leadenham: Lincs., England **27** U13
Leaden Roding: Essex, Eng. **25** W16
Leader: Sask., Canada **92** F2
Leadhills: Strath., Scotland **29** O9
Leaf: *riv.*, Canada **85** m6
Leaf: *riv.*, Miss., U.S.A. **90** G5
Leaf, Lake: Que., Canada **85** m6
Leafield: Oxon., England **25** S16
Leake, East: Notts., Eng. **27** T14
Leake, Old: Lincs., England **27** W13
Lealholm: N. Yorks., Eng. **26** U11
Lealt: Inner Hebr., Scotland **28** J4
Leamington: Ont., Canada **88** K4
Leamington: War., England **25** S15
Leane, Lough: Kerry, Repub. of Ireland **31** B15
Leannan: *riv.*, Don., Repub. of Ireland **30** F9
Leap: Cork, Repub. of Irel. **31** C16
Learmount: Lon., N. Irel. **30** G10
Leatherhead: Surrey, Eng. **25** V17
Leavenworth: Kans., U.S.A. **93** H5
Leavenworth: Wash., U.S.A. **92** C3
Leba: Poland **43** P9
Lebadea: Saarland, W. Ger. **44** M6
Lebadea: Greek city of *Boeotia*, about 25 miles NW. of Thebes, Greece **39** S17
Lebak: Mindanao, Phil. **65** G5

Lebanon: *Republic* **56** D5
Cap.: Beirut
Area: 4,015 sq. miles (10,399 sq. km.)
Pop.: 2,873,000 *(1971 E)*

Lebanon: Ind., U.S.A. **88** H5
Lebanon: Mo., U.S.A. **88** E7
Lebanon: N.H., U.S.A. **89** P4
Lebanon: Ohio, U.S.A. **88** J6
Lebanon: Oreg., U.S.A. **92** C4
Lebanon: Pa., U.S.A. **89** N5
Lebanon: Tenn., U.S.A. **88** H7
Le Barp: France **37** E11
Le Beausset: France **40** L12
Lebedyan': U.S.S.R. **50** E4
Lebesby: Norway **46** U1
Le Biot: France **40** M9
Le Blanc: France **37** G9
Lebo: Zaire **76** B2
Lebombo Mtns.: Mozambique/ S. Africa **75** K2
Lębork: Poland **43** P9
Le Boulou: France **37** H13
Le Bourg-d'Oisans: France **40** M10
Le Bourgneuf: France **36** E7
Lebrija: Spain **35** C18
Lebu: Chile **96** A4
Le Bugue: France **37** F11
Lebus: E. Germany **45** U3
Lebyazh'ye: U.S.S.R. **51** L3
Le Cannet: France **40** N12
Le Cateau: France **36** J5
Le Catelet: France **36** J6
Le Caylar: France **37** J12
Lecce: Italy **39** Q16
Lecco: Italy **40** P10
Lech: *riv.*, W. Ger./Austria **41** Q8
Le Chable: Switzerland **40** N9
Lechaeum: ancient port of Corinth due N. of city on G. of Corinth, Greece **39** S17
Le Chambon-Fuegerolles: France **37** K10
Le Chapus: France **37** D10
Le Château-D'Oléron: Île d'Oléron, France **37** D10
Le Châtelard: France **40** M10
Le Châtelet: Ardennes, Fr. **36** K6
Lechbruck: W. Germany **41** Q8
Le Chesne: France **36** K6
Le Cheylard: France **37** K11
Lechhausen: W. Germany **41** Q7
Lechlade: Glos., England **25** S16
Lechtal: *val.*, Austria **41** Q8
Leck: W. Germany **44** O1
Leckmelm: High., Scot. **28** L4
Lecompte: La., U.S.A. **90** E10
Le Conquet: France **36** A7

Le Coteau: France **37** K9
Le Creusot: France **37** K9
Le Croisic: France **36** C8
Le Crotoy: France **36** G5
Lectoure: France **37** F12
Lęczna: Poland **43** S11
Lęczyca: Poland **43** Q10
Ledaig: Strath., Scotland **29** L7
Ledbury: Hereford & Worcester, England **24** R15
Ledeberg: Belgium **44** J4
Ledeč: Czechoslovakia **45** V6
Lederata: Roman station about 10 miles S. of Bela Crkva (on Yugoslav/Romanian border) **39** R14
Ledesma: Argentina **96** C1
Ledesma: Spain **35** D16
Lédi: Ivory Coast **80** D3
Lédignan: France **37** K12
Ledo: Arunachal Pradesh, India **59** R9
Le Donjon: France **37** J9
Le Dorat: France **37** G9
Lee: *riv.*, Cork, Repub. of Ireland **31** D16
Leech Lake: Minn., U.S.A. **88** D2
Leeds: Ala., U.S.A. **91** H9
Leeds: W. Yorks., England **27** S12
Leek: Staffs., England **27** R13
Leeming: N. Yorks., England **26** S11
Leenaun: Galway, Repub. of Ireland **30** B12
Leer: W. Germany **44** N2
Leerdam: Netherlands **44** L4
Lees: Gt. Man., England **27** R12
Leesburg: Fla., U.S.A. **91** L11
Leesburg: W. Va., U.S.A. **89** N6
Leese: W. Germany **44** P3
Lees Summit: *city*, Mo., U.S.A. **90** D6
Leesville: La., U.S.A. **90** E10
Leeton: N.S.W., Australia **71** G10
Leeudoringstad: S. Africa **75** G3
Leeudrif: Trans., S. Africa **74** Mlns.
LEEUWARDEN: Friesland, Netherlands **44** L2
Leeward Is.: W. Indies **87** b2
Le Faouët: France **36** B7
Lefini: *riv.*, Congo **81** G5
Lefka: Cyprus **56** C4
Lefroy, Lake: W. Australia **68** C6
Legaspi: Luzon, Phil. **64** G4
Legbourne: Lincs., England **27** W13
Legden: W. Germany **44** N3
Lege: France **36** D9
Legerwood: Borders, Scot. **29** Q8
Leghorn (Livorno): Italy **38** M15
Legnago: Italy **41** R10
Legnano: Italy **40** O10
Legnica: Poland **45** W4
Legraa: Algeria **78** C4
Le Grand, Cape: W. Austl. **68** C6
Le Grand Bourg: France **37** G9
Le Grand-Lucé: France **36** F8
Le Grand-Pressigny: France **36** F9
Le Grau: France **37** K12
Le Gros-Dagnon: France **37** G9
Léguevin: France **37** G12
Leh: Jammu & Kashmir **58** N8
Le Havre: France **36** F6
Lehi: Utah, U.S.A. **93** E4
Lehighton: Pa., U.S.A. **89** O5
Lehinch: E. Germany **45** S3
Lehrberg: W. Germany **45** Q6
Lehrte: W. Germany **45** P3
Lehututu: Botswana **77** E7
Leiah: Punjab, Pakistan **58** M8
Leibnitz: Austria **41** V9
Leichhardt Range: Queens., Australia **69** G3
Leiden: Netherlands **44** K3
Leigh: Dorset, England **24** Q18
Leigh: Glos., England **24** R16
Leigh: Gt. Man., England **27** Q13
Leigh: Kent, England **25** W17
Leigh: North I., N.Z. **70** P13
Leigh, North: Oxon., Eng. **25** T16
Leigh Creek: *town*, S. Austl. **71** C8
Leighlinbridge: Carlow, Repub. of Ireland **31** H14
Leighterton: Glos., England **24** R16
Leighton Buzzard: Beds., England **25** U16
LEIKANGER: Sogn og Fjordane, Norway **47** K6
Leine: *riv.*, W. Germany **45** P3
Leinster: *Prov.*, Repub. of Ireland **31** G13
Leinster, Mount: *mtn.*, Carlow/Wex., Repub. of Ireland **31** H14
Leintwardine: Hereford & Worcester, Eng. **24** Q15
Leipoldtville: S. Africa **74** C6
LEIPZIG: & *Dist.*, E. Germany **45** S4
Leiranger: Norway **46** O3
Leiria: Portugal **35** B17
Leirvik: Norway **47** J7
Leiston: Suff., England **25** Z15
Leitchfield: Ky., U.S.A. **88** H7
Leitha: *riv.*, Austria **41** W8
Leith Hill: Surrey, England **25** V17
Leitholm: Borders, Scot. **29** R8
Leitrim: Leit., Repub. of Ireland **30** E12
Leitrim: *Co.*, Repub. of Ireland (*cap.* Carrick on Shannon) **30** E11
Leiwuchi: Tibet, China **62** R8
Leix: *see* Laois.
Leixlip: Kild., Repub. of Irel. **31** H13
Leiyang: Hunan, China **62** V9
Leiza: Spain **37** D12
Lek: *riv.*, Netherlands **44** L4
Leka: Norway **46** M4
Lekei: Gabon **81** G5
Lekhainá: Greece **39** R18
Leksand: Sweden **47** O6
Leksula: Buru, Indonesia **65** H7
Leksvik: Norway **46** M5
Lelantus: ancient name of river of Euboea between Chalcis & Nea Psara, Greece **39** S17
Le Lauzet: France **40** M11
Lel'chitsy: Byelorussia **43** V11
Le Lion-d'Angers: France **36** E8
Le Locle: Switzerland **40** M8
La Madonie: *mtn.*, Sicily **38** O18
Lema Is.: Kwangtung, China **62** U10
Léman, Lac (Lake of Geneva): Switzerland/Fr. **40** M9
Lemanis: Roman shore-fort at Lympne, about 2 miles W. of Hythe, Kent, Eng. **25** Y17
Lemannus: Roman name of L. of Geneva **40** M9
Le MANS: Sarthe, France **36** F7

Le Mars: Iowa, U.S.A. **92** H4
Le Mayet-de-Montagne: Fr. **37** J9
Lembach: France **41** N6
Lembeye: France **37** E12
Leme Gulf: Yugoslavia **41** T10
Le Merlerault: France **36** F7
Lemförde: W. Germany **44** O3
Lemgo: W. Germany **44** P3
Lemhi Range: *mtns.*, Idaho, U.S.A. **92** E4
Lemmenjoen National Park: Finland **46** T2
Lemmer: Netherlands **44** L3
Lemmon: S. Dak., U.S.A. **92** G3
Lemmon Mount: Ariz., U.S.A. **93** E6
Lemnos (Límnos): *i.*, Greece **39** T17
Le Monastier: France **37** J11
Le Mont-Dore: France **37** H10
Lemukutan: *i.*, Indonesia **65** D6
Le Muy: France **40** M12
Lemvig: Denmark **47** L8
Lena: *riv.*, U.S.S.R. **49** O4
Lenakel: New Hebrides **67** N5
Lendalfoot: Strath., Scot. **29** M9
Lendelin: France **36** D6
Lene, Lough: Westmeath, Repub. of Ireland **30** G12
Lengerich: North-Rhine-Westphalia, W. Germany **44** N3
Lenggries: W. Germany **41** R8
Lengoue: *riv.*, Congo **81** H4
Lenham: Kent, England **25** X17
Leninabad: Tadzhik., U.S.S.R. **51** L6
Leninakan: Armenia., U.S.S.R. **57** H1
LENINGRAD: & *Reg.*, U.S.S.R. **50** D3
Leninogorsk: Kazakh., U.S.S.R. **51** M7
Lenin Peak: *mtn.*, Tadzhik., U.S.S.R. **51** M7
Leninsk: U.S.S.R. **50** G5
Leninsk: Uzbek., U.S.S.R. **51** M6
Leninskiy: U.S.S.R. **49** N6
Leninsk-Kuznetskiy: U.S.S.R. **51** P4
Leninskoye: Kazakh., U.S.S.R. **51** L6
Leninskoye: U.S.S.R. **63** Y5
Lenk: Switzerland **40** N9
Lenkoran': Azerbaydzhan, U.S.S.R. **57** L2
Lenne: *riv.*, W. Germany **44** N4
Lennox Hills: Central, Scot. **29** N7
Lennoxton: Strath., Scot. **29** N8
Lennoxville: Que., Canada **89** Q3
Lenoir: N.C., U.S.A. **91** L8
Lenoir City: Tenn., U.S.A. **91** J8
Lens: France **36** H5
Lensahn: W. Germany **45** Q1
Lentiira: Finland **46** V4
Lentini: Sicily **38** O18
Lentua Lake: Finland **46** V4
Lenvik: Norway **46** Q2
Lenya: Burma **59** R12
Lenzie: Strath., China **29** N8
Leo: Upper Volta **80** D2
Leoben: Austria **41** V8
Leochel Cushnie: Grampian, Scotland **28** Q5
Leominster: Hereford & Worcester, England **24** Q15
Leominster: Mass., U.S.A. **89** Q4
León: France **37** D12
León: Iowa, U.S.A. **88** E5
León: Mexico **86** j13
León: Nicaragua **86** L15
LEÓN: & *Prov.* (*old* & *new*), Spain **35** D15
Leon: *riv.*, Tex., U.S.A. **90** B10
Leona Point: *cape*, Morocco (Gib. Insel) **32** Ins.
Leonardtown: Md., U.S.A. **89** N6
Leonardville: S.W. Africa **77** A7
Leongatha: Vict., Australia **71** G12
Leonidhion: Greece **39** S18
Leonora: W. Australia **68** C5
Leonstein: Austria **41** U8
Leontes: ancient name of Litani river, Lebanon **56** D5
Leontini: Greek city at *Lentini* about 20 miles S. of Catania, Sicily **38** O18
Leo Pargial: *mtn.*, China/India **58** N8
Leopold Down: W. Austl. **68** D3
Leopold II Lake (Mai Ndombe): Zaire **76** A3
Leopoldshagen: E. Germany **45** T2
Léopoldville: *see* Kinshasa.
Leoville: Sask., Canada **92** F2
Leovo: Moldavia, U.S.S.R. **43** V13
Le-Palais: Belle Île, France **36** B8
Lepanto: Ark., U.S.A. **88** F8
Lepanto: Italian name of Greek port Návpaktos and adjacent strait **39** R17
Lepar: *i.*, Indonesia **65** D7
Le Péage: France **37** K10
Lepel': Byelorussia **50** C4
Le Pellerin: France **36** D8
Le Petit Quevilly: France **36** G6
Lephepe: Botswana **77** C7
Lepini Mtns.: Italy **38** N16
L'Epiphanie: Que., Canada **89** P3
Le Poire-sur-Vie: France **37** D9
Lepontine Alps: Switzerland/ Italy **40** O9
Le Port-de-Piles: France **36** F9
Lepreum: Greek city of Peloponnese near S. end of coastal plain about due W. of Megalopolis, Greece **39** R18
Lepsinsk: Kazakh., U.S.S.R. **51** O5
Lepsy: Kazakh., U.S.S.R. **51** N5
Leptis Magna: Punic and Roman city on N. African coast about 60 miles E. of Tripoli **38** K19
Leptis (Minor): Roman town on S. of G. of Hammamet about 15 miles SE. of Sousse, Tunisia **38** M19
Le Puy: Haute-Loire, Fr. **37** J10
Lercara Friddi: Sicily **38** N18
Lère: *riv.*, Cameroun/Chad **81** G3
LERIBE: & *Dist.*, Lesotho **75** H4
Lerici: Italy **40** P11
LÉRIDA: & *Prov.*, Spain **35** G16
Lerik: Azerbaydzhan, U.S.S.R. **57** L2
Lerma: Spain **35** E15
Léros: *i.*, Dodecanese (Grc.) **39** U18
Leroy: N.Y., U.S.A. **89** N4
Lerrig: Kerry, Repub. of Irel. **31** B15
Le Russey: France **40** M8
LERWICK: Mainland, Shetland Is. **28** Ins.
Lery, Lake: La., U.S.A. **90** Ins.
Lesaca: Spain **37** D12
Les Baronnies: *mtns.*, Fr. **40** L11
Lesbos (Lésvos): *i.*, Greece **39** U17

Lesbury: Northumb., Eng. **26** S9
Lescar: France **37** E12
Les Cayes: Haiti **87** m14
Lesce: Yugoslavia **41** V11
Les Deux Frères: Vietnam **64** D5
Les Eaux-Bonnes: France **37** E13
Leseru: Kenya **76** E2
Les Escoumins: Que., Can. **89** R1
Les Essarts: France **37** D9
Les Herbiers: France **36** D9
Les Heumis: Algeria **35** G18
Lesjaskog: Norway **46** L5
Leskovac: Yugoslavia **39** R15
Leskovik: Albania **39** R16
Les Landes: *geog. reg.*, Fr. **37** D11
Leslie: Fife, Scotland **29** P7
Leslie: Trans., S. Afr. **75** H3
Lesmahagow: Strath., Scot. **29** O8
Les Mées: France **40** L11
Lesmont: France **36** K7
Lesna: Poland **45** V4
Lesneven: France **36** A7
Les Monts Faucilles: Fr. **40** L7
Lesnoy: U.S.S.R. **48** E4

Lesotho: *Kingdom* **75** H4
Cap.: Maseru
Area: 11,716 sq. miles (30,344 sq. km.)
Pop.: 952,000 *(1972 E)*

Lesozavodsk: U.S.S.R. **63** Y5
Lesparre: France **37** E10
L'Esperance Rock: Pac. O. **67** Q8
Les Pieux: France **36** D6
Les Riceys: France **36** K8
Les Sables-D'Olonne: Fr. **37** D9
Les Saintes Maries: France **37** K12
Les Salins: France **40** M12
Lessay: France **36** D6
Lesse: *riv.*, Belgium **44** K5
Les Sept Îles: France **36** B7
Lesser Antilles: *is.*, W. Indies **87** N14
Lesser Slave Lake: Alta., Canada **92** E1
Lesser Sunda Is.: Indonesia **66** D3
Lessines: Belgium **44** J5
Lestijärvi: Finland **46** T5
Les Trois Evêchés: *mtn.*, Fr. **40** M11
Le Sueur: Minn., U.S.A. **88** E3
Les Vans: France **37** K11
Lésvos: *see* Lesbos.
Leswalt: Dumfries & Galloway, Scotland **29** L10
Leszno: Poland **45** W4
Letaba: & *Dist.*, Trans., S. Afr. **75** J1
Letchworth: Herts., Eng. **25** V16
Le Teil: France **37** K11
Letham: Tayside, Scotland **29** Q6
Lethbridge: Alta., Canada **92** E3
Le Theil: France **36** F7
Lethem: Guyana **87** d9
Le Thillot: France **40** M8
Letiahau: *riv.*, Botswana **77** B7
Letichev: Ukraine **43** U12
Leticia: Colombia **94** C4
Letjiesbos: S. Africa **74** E6
Le Touquet: France **36** G5
Letpadan: Burma **59** R11
Le Tréport: France **36** G5
Letschin: E. Germany **45** U3
Letskraal: S. Africa **75** F6
Lette: N.S.W., Australia **71** E10
Letterfrack: Galway, Repub. of Ireland **30** B12
Letterkenny: Don., Repub. of Ireland **30** F10
Lettermore I.: Repub. of Irel. **31** B13
Letterston: Dyfed, Wales **24** M16
Letur: Spain **35** E17
Leucate: France **37** J13
Leucate, Cap: *cape*, France **37** J13
Leucate, Etang de: *lag.*, Fr. **37** J13
Leuchars: Fife, Scotland **29** Q7
Leuctra: ancient Greek village where the Thebans destroyed the Spartans 371 B.C., near Thívai, Grc. **39** S17
Leuk: Switzerland **40** N9
Leuke Kome: Graeco-Roman port on E. coast of Red Sea just S. of Wajh, Sau. Arab. **54** E9
Leukerbad: Switzerland **40** N9
Leura: Queens., Australia **70** H4
Leurbost: Outer Hebr., Scotland **28** J3
Leushi: U.S.S.R. **51** L3
Leutkirch: W. Germany **40** Q8
Leutwein: S.W. Africa **74** B1
Leuven: Belgium **44** K5
Leuze: Belgium **44** J5
Leuze: Belgium **44** J5
Levádhia: Greece **39** S17
Le Val-d'Ajol: France **40** M8
Levanger: Norway **46** M5
Levanto: Italy **40** P11
Leven: Fife, Scotland **29** Q7
Leven: Humb., England **27** V12
Leven, Loch: High., Scot. **29** L6
Leven Loch: Tay., Scot. **29** P7
Levens: Cumbria, England **26** Q11
Leveque, Cape: W. Austl. **68** C3
Leverburgh: Outer Hebr., Scotland **28** G4
Le Verdon: France **37** D10
Leverkusen: W. Germany **44** M4
Leverton: Notts., England **27** U13
Levet: France **37** H9
Levice: Czechoslovakia **43** Q12
Levico: Italy **41** R9
Levier: France **40** M8
Le Vigan: France **37** J12
Levin: North I., N.Z. **70** P15
Lévis: Que., Canada **89** Q2
Levisa Fork: *riv.*, Ky., U.S.A. **88** K7
Levkás: Ionian Is. (Grc.) **39** R17
Levkás (San Maura): *i.*, Ionian Is. (Grc.) **39** R17
Levkosia (Nicosia): Cyprus **56** C4
Levoča: Czechoslovakia **43** R12
Levroux: France **36** G9
Levskigrad: Bulgaria **39** T15
Levy: Ark., U.S.A. **90** E8
Lewannick: Corn., England **24** N18
Lewes: Del., U.S.A. **89** O6
Lewes: East Sussex, Eng. **25** W18
Lewis, Butt of: *cape*, Outer Hebr., Scotland **28** J2
Lewis, Isle of: Outer Hebr., Scotland **28** H3
Lewisburg: Tenn., U.S.A. **91** H8
Lewisburg: W. Va., U.S.A. **88** L7
Lewsham: Gt. Ldn., England
Lewis Range: Mont., U.S.A. **92** E3
Lewisporte: Newf., Canada **85** v2
Lewiston: High., Scotland **28** N5
Lewiston: Idaho, U.S.A. **92** D3
Lewiston: Maine, U.S.A. **89** Q3
Lewiston: Utah, U.S.A. **92** E4
Lewistown: Ill., U.S.A. **88** F5
Lewistown: Mont., U.S.A. **92** F3
Lewistown: Pa., U.S.A. **89** N5
Lexden: Essex, England **25** X16

Lexfield: Suff., England **25** Y15
Lexington: Ky., U.S.A. **88** J6
Lexington: Mass., U.S.A. **89** Q4
Lexington: Miss., U.S.A. **90** F9
Lexington: Mo., U.S.A. **90** E6
Lexington: N.C., U.S.A. **93** H4
Lexington: N.C., U.S.A. **91** L8
Lexington: Tenn., U.S.A. **90** G8
Leyburn: N. Yorks., England **26** S11
Leyburn: Queens., Australia **70** J7
Leydsdorp: Trans., S. Africa **75** J1
Leyland: Lancs., England **27** Q12
Leyre: *riv.*, France **37** E11
Leysdown: Kent, England **25** X17
Leyte: *i.* & *gulf*, Philippines **64** G4
Lez: *riv.*, France **40** L11
Leżajsk: Poland **43** S11
Lézardrieux: France **36** B7
Lezay: France **37** F9
Lezhë: Albania **39** Q16
Lézignan: France **37** H12
Leznaya: Byelorussia **43** T10
Lezoux: France **37** J10
L'gov: U.S.S.R. **50** E4
Lhakhang Dzong: Tibet, China **59** Q9
Lhanbryd: Gram., Scotland **28** P4
LHASA: Tibet, China **59** Q9
Lhatse: Tibet, China **59** P9
L'Hermenault: France **37** E9
Lhobu Dzong: Tibet, China **59** Q9
Lho Dzong (Lolung): Tibet, China **62** R8
Lhokseumawe: Sumatra **65** B5
Lhoksukon: Sumatra **65** B5
L'Hôpital-du-Gros-Bois: Fr. **40** M8
L'Hospitalet: France **37** G13
Li (Litang): *riv.*, Tibet, China **62** S9
Lia: Cen. Afr. Rep. **81** H3
Liancourt: France **36** H6
Liancourt Rocks (Take Shima): Sea of Japan **63** Y7
Liandambia: Zambia **77** D5
Lianga: Mindanao, Phil. **64** H5
Liangping: Szechwan, China **62** T8
Liangcheng: Inner Mongolia, China **62** U6
Liangchow (Wuwei): Kansu, China **62** S7
Liant, Cape: Thailand **64** C4
Liao: *riv.*, Liaoning, China **63** w6
Liaocheng: Shantung, China **62** V7
Liaochung: Liaoning, China **63** W6
Liaoning: *Prov.*: China [*cap.* Shenyang (Mukden)] **63** W6
Liaotun: Sinkiang, China **62** Q6
Liaotung Bay: China **63** W6
Liaoyang: Liaoning, China **63** W6
Liaoyuan: Liaoning, China **63** W6
Liard: *riv.*, Canada **84** g5
Liart: France **36** K6
Liat: *i.*, Indonesia **65** D7
Libano: Colombia **94** B3
Libberton: Strath., Scotland **29** O8
Libby: Mont., U.S.A. **92** D3
Libebe: S.W. Africa **77** B6
Libenge: Zaire **81** H4
Liberal: Kans., U.S.A. **90** A7
Liberal: Mo., U.S.A. **90** D6
Liberec: Czechoslovakia **45** V5

Liberia: *Republic* **80** B3
Cap.: Monrovia
Area: 43,000 sq. miles (111,370 sq. km.)
Pop.: 1,571,000 *(1971 E)*

Liberia: Costa Rica **86** L15
Libertad: Mexico **93** E7
Libertad, La: Guatamala **86** k14
Liberty: Mo., U.S.A. **90** D6
Liberty: N.Y., U.S.A. **89** O5
Liberty: S.C., U.S.A. **91** K8
Liberty: Tex., U.S.A. **90** D10
Libknekhta: Ukraine **50** D5
Libochovice: Czechoslovakia **45** U5
Libode: S. Africa **75** H5
Libos: France **37** F11
Libourne: France **37** E11
Libramont: Belgium **44** L6
LIBREVILLE: Gabon **81** F4

Libya: *Republic* **78** 9
Caps.: Tripoli & Benghazi
Area: 679,536 sq. miles (1,759,998 sq. km.)
Pop.: 2,035,000 *(1971 E)*

Libyan Desert: Libya/Egypt **79** J4
Libyan Plat.: Egypt **54** C8
Lincanten: Chile **96** A4
Licata: Sicily **38** N18
Lice: Turkey **57** G2
Lich: W. Germany **44** O5
Lichfield: Staffs., England **27** S14
Lichhoithuong: Vietnam **64** D5
LICHINGA: Niassa, Mozambique **77** E5
Lichtenau: Baden Württemberg, Germany **40** P7
Lichtenau: Hesse, W. Germany **44** P4
Lichtenau: North Rhine-Westphalia, W. Germany **44** O4
Lichtenburg: & *Dist.*, Trans., S. Africa **75** G3
Lichtenfels: W. Germany **45** R5
Lichuan: Inner Mongolia, China **63** W5
Lichwan: Kiangsi, China **62** U9
Licking: *riv.*, Ky., U.S.A. **88** K6
Liconi: Gabon **81** G5
Licungo: *riv.*, Mozambique **77** E6
Lida: Byelorussia **43** T10
Liddel Water: *riv.*, Borders, Scotland **29** Q9
Liddesdale: *val.*, Borders, Scot. **29** Q9
Lidgerwood: N. Dak., U.S.A. **92** H3
Lidhult: Sweden **47** N8
Lidice: small village W. of Prague whose inhabitants were put to death by the Germans in the Second World War, Czech. **45** U5
Lidköping: Sweden **47** N7
Lido: Venice, Italy **41** S10
Lido di Roma: Italy **38** M16
Liebenwalde: E. Germany **45** T3
Liebenwerda: E. Germany **45** T4
Lieberose: E. Germany **45** U4
Lieboch: Austria **41** V9

Liechtenstein: *Principality* **40** P8
Cap.: Vaduz
Area: 61 sq. miles (158 sq. km.)
Pop.: 21,350 *(1970 C)*

LIÈGE: & *Prov.*, Belgium **44** L5
Lieksa: Finland **46** V5
Lienhwa: Kiangsi, China **62** U9
Lienhwang: Fukien, China **62** V9
Lienz: Tyrol, Austria **41** S9
Liepāja: Latvia, U.S.S.R. **47** R8
Lier: Belgium **44** K4
Lierhcha: Chinghai, China **62** S7

160 Liestal—Lodja

LIESTAL: Basel, Switzerland 40 N8
Lieurey: France 36 F6
Liévin: France 36 H5
Lièvre, du: riv., Que., Canada 89 O2
Liezen: Austria 41 U8
Liffey: riv., Repub. of Ireland 31 J13
LIFFORD: Don., Repub. of Ireland 30 G10
Liffré: France 36 D7
Liffiya: well, Sau. Arab./Iraq 57 H6
Lifton: Devon, England 24 N18
Lifu: i., Loyalty Is. 67 N6
Liganga: Tanzania 77 E5
Ligardes: France 37 F11
Lightfoot, Lake: W. Austl. 68 C5
Lightning Ridge: N.S.W., Australia 71 G7
Lignac: France 37 G9
Lignano: Italy 41 T10
Ligné: France 36 D8
Lignières: France 37 H9
Ligny: Belgium 44 K5
Ligny-en-Barrois: France 36 L7
Ligny-le-Châtel: France 36 J8
Ligny-le-Ribault: France 36 G8
Ligonha: riv., Mozambique 77 E6
Ligonier: Ind., U.S.A. 88 J5
Ligowola: Mozambique 77 E5
Ligua, La: Chile 96 A3
Ligueil: France 36 F8
Liguria: Reg., Italy [cap. Genoa (Genova)] 40 O11
Ligurian Alps: Italy 40 O11
Ligurian Appennines: mtns., Italy 40 P11
Ligurian Sea: S. Europe 38 L15
Lihir: i., Bismarck Arch. 67 K2
Lihou Reef: Coral Sea 67 K5
Lihsien: Hunan, China 62 U9
Lihsien: Kansu, China 62 T8
Lihue: Hawaiian Is. 83 b2
Liikanen: Finland 46 V3
Likasi: Zaïre 77 C5
Likhoslavl': U.S.S.R. 50 E3
Likhula: Estonia, U.S.S.R. 47 T7
Likiang: Yunnan, China 62 S9
Likma: Madhya Pradesh, India 58 O10
Likouala: riv., Congo 81 H4
Likouala Aux Herbes: riv., Congo 81 H4
Lilayi: Zambia 77 C6
L'Île-Bouchard: France 36 F8
L'Île-d'Elle: France 37 E9
Lilienfeld: Austria 41 V8
Liling: Hunan, China 62 U9
LILLE: Nord, France 36 J5
Lillebonne: France 36 F6
LILLEHAMMER: Opland, Nor. 47 M6
Lillers: France 36 H5
Lillesand: Norway 47 L7
Lilleshall: Salop, England 27 R14
LILLESTRØM: Akershus, Norway 47 M7
Lillhärdal: Sweden 47 O6
Lilliesleaf: Bord., Scotland 29 Q8
Lillo: Spain 35 E17
Lillooet: B.C., Canada 92 C2
LILONGWE: Malawi 77 D5
Lilo Viejo: Argentina 96 C2
Lilybaeum: Greek, Carthaginian, and Roman city at Marsala, W. Sicily 38 N18
Lilydale: Vict., Australia 71 F11
Lima: Ohio, U.S.A. 88 J5
Lima: Paraguay 96 D1
LIMA: Peru 94 B6
Limache: Chile 96 A3
Lima Duarte: Brazil 96 G1
Limagne: geog. reg., France 37 J10
Liman: U.S.S.R. 50 G5
Limanowa: Poland 43 R12
Limassol: Cyprus 56 C4
Limavady: Lon., N. Irel. 30 H9
Limay: riv., Argentina 95 D11
Limay Mahuida: Argentina 96 B4
Limbang: Sarawak, Malaysia 65 E6
Limbazhi: Latvia, U.S.S.R. 47 T8
Limbe: Malawi 77 E6
Limber, Great: Lincs., England 27 V12
Limbunya: N. Territ., Austl. 68 D3
Limburg: W. Germany 44 O5
Limburg: Prov., Belgium (cap. Hasselt) 44 L4
Limburg: Prov., Netherlands (cap. Maastricht) 44 L4
Limchow: see Hoppo, Kwangsi Chuang, China.
Limedsforsen: Sweden 47 N6
Limeira: Brazil 96 E2
Limenária: Thasos, Greece 39 T16
LIMERICK: & Co., Repub. of Ireland 31 D14
Limerick Junction: Tip., Repub. of Ireland 31 E14
Lim Fiord: Denmark 47 L8
Limia: riv., Spain/Portugal 35 C15
Limiera: Brazil 96 F1
Liminka: Finland 46 T4
Limko: Hainan, China 62 T11
Limmared: Sweden 47 N8
Limmen Bight: Australia 69 F2
Limni: Euboea, Greece 39 S17
Limnos (Lemnos): i., Greece 39 T17
Limoeiro: Brazil 94 K5
LIMOGES: Haute-Vienne, Fr. 37 G10
Limogne: France 37 G11
Limon: Colo., U.S.A. 93 G5
Limon Bay: Panama 94 Ins.
Limone: Italy 40 N11
Limours: France 36 H7
Limousin: Prov., France 34 G14
Limoux: France 37 H12
Limpopo: riv., Africa 75 K1
Lina: Saudi Arabia 54 F9
Linapacan: i., Philippines 64 F4
Linards: France 37 G10
Linares: Chile 96 A4
Linares: Mexico 93 H8
Linares: Spain 35 E17
Linaro, Cape: Italy 38 M15
Lincoln: Argentina 96 C3
Lincoln: Ark., U.S.A. 90 D8
Lincoln: Ill., U.S.A. 88 G5
Lincoln: Kans., U.S.A. 90 B6
LINCOLN: Lincs., England 27 U13
Lincoln: Maine, U.S.A. 89 R3
LINCOLN: Nebr., U.S.A. 93 H4
Lincoln: N.H., U.S.A. 89 Q3
Lincoln Heath: Lincs., Eng. 27 U13
Lincoln I.: Paracel Is. 64 E3
Lincoln Marsh: Lincs., Eng. 27 W13
Lincoln Sea: Grnld./Can. 85 O1
Lincolnshire: Co., England (co. town Lincoln) 27 V13
Lincolnshire Wolds: hills, England 27 V13
Lincolnton: N.C., U.S.A. 91 L8
Lincoln Wildlife Reserve: S. Australia 71 A10
Lindale: Cumbria, England 26 Q11
Lindale: Ga., U.S.A. 91 J8
Lindau: Bavaria, W. Germany 40 P8
Lindau: Magdeburg, E. Germany 45 S3
Linde: riv., U.S.S.R. 49 O4
Linden: Tex., U.S.A. 90 D9
Linden: Guyana 87 d7
Lindenberg: Frankfurt, E. Germany 45 U3
Lindenberg: Potsdam, E. Germany 45 S2
Lindenfels: W. Germany 44 O6
Lindequesdrif: S. Africa 75 G3
Lindesberg: Sweden 47 O7
Lindfield: W. Sussex, England 25 V17
Lindholm: W. Germany 44 O1
LINDI: & Reg., Tanzania 77 E4
Lindi: riv., Zaïre 76 C2
Lindisfarne (Holy I.): Eng. 26 S8
Lindley: & Dist., O.F.S., S. Africa 75 G3
Lindley: W. Yorks., England 27 S12
Lindos: Rhodes, Dodec. 39 V18
Lindsay: Mont., U.S.A. 92 F3
Lindsay: Okla., U.S.A. 90 C8
Lindsay: Ont., Canada 89 M3
Lindsborg: Kans., U.S.A. 90 C6
Lindum: Roman camp and city at Lincoln, England 27 U13
Line Islands: (Br.), Pacific Ocean 7 00 160W
Linea, La: Spain (Gib. Inset) 32 Ins.
Linfen: Shansi, China 62 U7
Ling: Kwangtung, China 62 U9
Lingayen: & gulf, Luzon, Philippines 64 G3
Lingchwan: Kwangsi Chuang, China 62 U9
Lingeh: Iran 55 H9
Lingen: W. Germany 44 N3
Lingen: Here. & Worcs., England 24 Q15
Lingfield: Surrey, England 25 V17
Lingga: i. & arch., Indon. 65 C7
Linghed: Sweden 47 O6
Linghsien: Hunan, China 62 U9
Lingig: Mindanao, Phil. 64 H5
Lingling: Hunan, China 62 U9
Lingones: Gallic tribe with centre at Langres, France 36 L8
Lingpi: Anhwei, China 62 V8
Lingshui: Hainan, China 62 T11
Linguère: Senegal 80 A1
Lingwu: Ninghsia Hui, China 62 T7
Lingyuan: Liaoning, China 62 V6
Lingyun (Szecheng): Kwangsi Chuang, China 62 T10
Linhai (Taichow): Chekiang, China 63 W9
Linhares: Brazil 94 J7
Linho: Inner Mongolia, China 62 T6
Linhsien: Honan, China 62 U7
Linhsien: Kwangtung, China 62 U10
Lini: Shantung, China 62 V7
Linju: Honan, China 62 U8
Linkiang: Kirin, China 63 X6
LINKÖPING: Östergötland, Sweden 47 O7
Linkow: Heilungkiang, China 63 Y5
Linlithgow: Lothian, Scot. 29 O8
Linn: Mo., U.S.A. 88 F6
Liney Head: cape, Dyfed, Wales 24 L16
Linnhe, Loch: Highland/Strathclyde, Scotland 29 L16
Linosa: i., Italy 32 E4
Linping: Kwangtung, China 62 U10
Lins: Brazil 95 H8
Linshan: Kwangtung, China 62 U10
Linshui: Szechwan, China 62 T8
Linsi: Inner Mongolia, China 62 V6
Linslade: Bucks., England 25 U16
Linstead: Jamaica 86 Ins.
Lintan: Kansu, China 62 S8
Lintao: Kansu, China 62 S7
Linthal: Switzerland 40 P9
Lintien: Heilungkiang, China 63 W5
Linton: Borders, Scotland 29 R8
Linton: Cambs., England 25 W15
Linton: Ind., U.S.A. 88 H6
Linton: N. Dak., U.S.A. 92 G3
Linton: N. Yorks., England 27 S11
Linton: Vict., Australia 71 E11
Linton, East: Lothian, Scot. 29 Q8
Linton, West: Borders, Scot. 29 P8
Lintsang: Yunnan, China 62 S10
Lintseh: Kansu, China 62 S7
Linwu: Hunan, China 62 U9
Linxe: France 37 D12
Linyu: Hopeh, China 62 V6
LINZ: Upper Austria Prov., Austria 41 U7
Lion-d'Angers, Le: France 36 E8
Lionel: Outer Hebr., Scot. 28 J3
Lions, G. of: France 35 J15
Lions Head: mtn., S. Africa 74 Ins.
Lions River: Dist., Natal, S. Africa 75 J4
Lipa: Czechoslovakia 45 U5
Lipa: Yugoslavia 41 W11
Lipari: i., Lipari Is. (It.) 38 O17
Lipari Is.: Italy 38 O17
LIPETSK: & Reg., U.S.S.R. 50 E4
Liphook: Hants., England 25 U17
Lipiany: Poland 45 U2
Liping: Kweichow, China 62 T9
Lipkany: Moldavia, U.S.S.R. 43 U12
Lipno: Poland 43 Q10
Lipova: Romania 43 R13
Lippe: riv., W. Germany 44 O4
Lippstadt: W. Germany 44 O4
Lipsói: i., Dodecanese (Grc.) 39 U18
Lira: Uganda 76 D2
Liranga: Congo 81 H5
Lircay: Peru 94 C6
Liri: riv., Italy 38 N16
Liria: Sudan 76 D2
Liria: Spain 35 F17
Lisacul: Rosc., Repub. of Irel. 30 D12
Lisala: Zaïre 76 B2
Lisany: Czechoslovakia 45 T5
Lisbellaw: Ferm., N. Ireland 30 F11
Lisbon: N. Dak., U.S.A. 92 H3
LISBON (Lisboa): Portugal 35 B17
Lisburn: Antrim, N. Ireland 30 J10
Lisburne, Cape: Alaska, U.S.A. 84 C4
Liscannor: & bay, Clare, Repub. of Ireland 31 C14
Liscarroll: Cork, Repub. of Ireland 31 D15
Lisycasey: Clare, Repub. of Ireland 31 C14
Liscomb: N.S., Canada 89 U3
Lisdoonvarna: Clare, Repub. of Ireland 31 C13
Lishih: Shansi, China 62 U7
Lishuchen: Heilungkiang, China 63 Y5
Lishui (Chuchow): Chekiang, China 62 V9
Li Siang: riv., Kwangsi Chuang, China 62 T10
Lisianski: i., Hawaiian Islands 7 25N 175W
Lisieux: France 36 F6
Liskeard: Corn., England 24 N19
Lisko: Poland 43 S12
L'Isle Adam: France 36 H6
L'Isle-de-Noë: France 37 F12
L'Isle-Jourdain: Gers, Fr. 37 G12
L'Isle-Jourdain: Vienne, Fr. 37 F9
L'Isle-sur-la-Sorgue: France 37 L12
L'Isle-sur-le-Doubs: France 40 M8
L'Isle-sur-Serein: France 36 K8
Lisle-sur-Tarn: France 37 G12
Lismore: N.S.W., Australia 71 K7
Lismore: Vict., Australia 71 E11
Lismore: Wat., Republic of Ireland 31 F15
Lismore I.: Scotland 29 K6
Lisnaskea: Ferm., N. Ireland 30 G11
Lisno, Lake: Byelorussia 47 V8
Lišov: Czechoslovakia 45 U6
Liss: Hants., England 25 U17
Lissar: Iran 57 L3
Lisselton: Kerry, Repub. of Ireland 31 B15
Lissielo: Congo 81 H5
Lister Fiord: Norway 47 K7
Listopadovka: U.S.S.R. 50 F4
Listowel: Kerry, Repub. of Ireland 31 C15
Listowel: Ont., Canada 88 L4
Lit: France 37 D11
Litang: Tibet, China 62 S9
Litang (Li): riv., Tibet, China 62 S9
Litani: riv., Lebanon 56 D5
Litcham: Norf., England 25 X14
Litchfield: Hants., England 25 T17
Litchfield: Ill., U.S.A. 88 G6
Litchfield: Minn., U.S.A. 88 D3
Lith: Saudi Arabia 55 F10
Lithgow: N.S.W., Australia 71 J9
Lithuanian S.S. Repub.: U.S.S.R. (cap. Vil'nyus) 47 S9
Litija: Yugoslavia 41 U9
Litin: Ukraine 43 V12
Litoměřice: Czechoslovakia 45 U5
Litomyšl: Czechoslovakia 45 W6
Litschau: Austria 41 V7
Litsing: Shantung, China 62 V7
Little: riv., Okla., U.S.A. 90 D8
Little Abaco I.: Bahamas 91 N12
Little Abitibi: riv., Ont., Canada 88 L1
Little Andaman: i., Ind. O. 59 Q12
Little Anyuy: riv., U.S.S.R. 49 s4
Little Atlas: range, Algeria 35 H18
Little Barrier I.: N.Z. 70 P13
Little Bay: city, Bahamas 91 N13
Little Belt: str., Denmark 47 L9
Little Belt Mtns.: Mont., U.S.A. 92 E3
Little Berkhamsted: Herts., England 25 V16
Little Bitter Lake: Egypt (Suez Canal Inset) 32 Ins.
Littleborough: Gt. Man., Eng. 27 R12
Little Brosna: riv., Offaly/Tip., Repub. of Ireland 31 F13
Little Bushman Land: geog. reg., S. Africa 74 C4
Little Cayman: i., (Jam.), W. Indies 87 114
Little Coco: i., Andaman Is. 59 Q12
Little Colorado: riv., Ariz., U.S.A. 93 F6
Little Cumbrae: i., Strathclyde, Scotland 29 M8
Little Current: city, Ont., Canada 88 L3
Little Dunham: Norf., Eng. 25 X14
Little Falls: city, Minn., U.S.A. 88 D3
Little Falls: city, N.Y., U.S.A. 89 O4
Littleferry: High., Scotland 28 N4
Littlefield: Tex., U.S.A. 93 G6
Littlehampton: W. Sussex, Eng., 25 U18
Little Hinton: Wilts., Eng. 25 S16
Little Kanawha: riv., W. Va., U.S.A. 88 L6
Little Karroo: plat., S. Afr. 74 D6
Little Khingan Mts.: Heilungkiang, China 63 X5
Little Lake: La., U.S.A. 90 Ins.
Little Laut Is.: Indonesia 65 F7
Little Loch Broom: Highland, Scotland 28 L4
Little Makin I.: Gilbert Is. 67 O1
Littlemill: High., Scotland 28 O4
Little Minch, The: chan., Outer Hebr./Inner Hebr., Scotland 28 H4
Little Missouri: riv., U.S.A. 92 G3
Little Nicobar: i., Nicobar Is. 59 Q13
Little Ouse: riv., England 25 W15
Littleport: Cambs., England 25 W15
Little Red: riv., Ark., U.S.A. 88 D8
Little River: town, South I., New Zealand 70 O16
LITTLE ROCK: city, Ark., U.S.A. 90 E8
Little Sable Point: cape, Mich., U.S.A. 88 H4
Little St. Bernard Pass: France/Italy 40 M10
Little Sitkin: i., Aleutians 84 a7
Little Smokey: riv., Alta., Canada 92 D2
Little Steeping: Lincs., Eng. 27 W13
Littlestone on Sea: Kent, England 25 X18
Little Sutton: Ches., England 37 Q13
Little Tanaga: i., Aleutians 84 B7
Littleton: N.H., U.S.A. 89 Q3
Littleton: Tip., Repub. of Ireland 31 F14
Little Wabash: riv., Ill., U.S.A. 88 G6
Little Walsingham: Norf., England 25 X14
Little Witley: Hereford & Worcester, England 24 R15
Little Zab: riv., Iraq 57 H4
Litton: Derby., England 27 S13
Littoral: Reg., Cameroun (cap. Douala) 81 G4
Littry: France 36 E6
Litunde: Mozambique 77 E5
Liuan: Anhwei, China 62 V8
Liuchow: Kwangsi Chuang, China 62 T10
Liucura: Chile 96 A4
Liuho: Kirin, China 63 X6
Liunghai: Hainan, China 62 U11
Liupa: Shensi, China 62 T8
Liupo: Mozambique 77 F6
Liuwa: Zambia 77 B5
Liuwa Plain: Zambia 77 B5
Liuyang: Hunan, China 62 U9
Livāni: Latvia, U.S.S.R. 47 U8
Livarot: France 36 F6
Livengood: Alaska, U.S.A. 84 E4
Live Oak: Fla., U.S.A. 91 K10
Livermere, Great: Suff., Eng. 25 X15
Livermore: Ky., U.S.A. 88 H7
Livermore, Mt.: Tex., U.S.A. 93 G6
Livermore Falls: city, Maine, U.S.A. 89 Q3
Livernon: France 37 G11
LIVERPOOL: Mers., England 27 Q13
Liverpool: N.S.W. Austl. 71 J9
Liverpool: N.S., Canada 89 T3
Liverpool, East: Ohio, U.S.A. 88 L5
Liverpool Bay: Eng./Wales 27 P13
Liverpool Bay: N.W.T., Can. 84 f3
Liverpool Land: Greenland 85 r3
Liverpool Range: & plain, N.S.W., Australia 71 J8
Livingston: Guatemala (Honduras Inset) 86 Ins.
Livingston: Mont., U.S.A. 92 E3
Livingston: Tenn., U.S.A. 88 J7
Livingston: Tex., U.S.A. 90 D10
Livingstone: see Maramba.
Livingstone Memorial: Zambia 77 D5
Livingstonia: Malawi 77 D5
Livno: Yugoslavia 38 P15
Livny: U.S.S.R. 50 E4
Livo: riv., Finland 46 U4
Livorno: Piedmont, Italy 40 O10
Livorno (Leghorn): Tuscany, Italy 38 M15
Livradois, Massif du: mtns., France 37 J10
Livramento: Brazil 96 D3
Livron: France 57 K11
Livry: France 36 H7
Liwa: geog. reg., Sau. Arab. 55 H10
Liwale: Tanzania 77 E4
Liwonde: Malawi 77 E6
Lixnaw: Kerry, Repub. of Ireland 31 B15
Lixoúrion: Cephalonia, Grc. 39 R17
Lizard: & penin., Corn., Eng. 25 L19
Lizard Point: cape, Corn., England 25 L19
Lizy-sur-Ourcq: France 36 J6
Lizzola: Italy 40 Q9
Lizzie Weber: reef, S. China Sea 64 E5
Ljubinje: Yugoslavia 39 Q15
LJUBLJANA: Slovenia, Yugoslavia 41 U9
Ljubuški: Yugoslavia 38 P15
Ljurgarn: Gotland, Sweden 47 Q8
Ljungan: riv., Sweden 47 P5
Ljungby: Sweden 47 N8
Ljusdal: Sweden 47 P6
Ljusnan: riv., Sweden 47 O6
Ljutomer: Yugoslavia 41 W9
Llanaelhaearn: Gwyn., Wales 27 N14
Llanafan: Dyfed, Wales 24 O15
Llanafanfechan: Powys, Wales 24 O15
Llanallgo: Gwynedd, Wales 27 N13
Llanarmon: Clwyd, Wales 27 P13
Llanarth: Dyfed, Wales 24 N15
Llanarthney: Dyfed, Wales 24 N16
Llanbadarn-Fawr: Dyfed, Wales 24 N15
Llabadarn Fynydd: Powys, Wales 24 P15
Llanbedr-gôch: Gwynedd, Wales 27 N13
Llanbedrog: Gwynedd, Wales 27 N14
Llanberis: Gwynedd, Wales 27 N13
Llanbister: Powys, Wales 24 P15
Llanblethian: S. Glam., Wales 24 P17
Llanboidy: Dyfed, Wales 24 M16
Llancanelo, Salina: salt pan, Argentina 96 B4
Llandaff: S. Glam., Wales 24 P17
Llanddarog: Dyfed, Wales 24 N16
Llandderfel: Gwynedd, Wales 27 O14
Llanddewi Brefi: Dyfed, Wales 24 O15
Llanddewi Rhydderch: Gwent, Wales 24 Q16
Llanddewi Ystradenny: Powys, Wales 24 P15
Llandefeilog: Dyfed, Wales 24 N16
Llandilo: Dyfed, Wales 24 O16
Llandinam: Powys, Wales 24 P15
Llandovery: Dyfed, Wales 24 O16
Llandrillo: Clwyd, Wales 27 P14
LLANDRINDOD WELLS: Powys, Wales 24 P15
Llandudno: Gwynedd, Wales 27 O13
Llandudno: S. Africa 74 Ins.
Llandwrog: Gwynedd, Wales 27 N13
Llandybie: Dyfed, Wales 24 O16
Llandysilio: Powys, Wales 27 P14
Llandyssil: Powys, Wales 27 P14
Llandyssul: Dyfed, Wales 24 N15
Llanegryn: Gwynedd, Wales 27 N14
Llanelidan: Clwyd, Wales 27 P13
Llanelli: Dyfed, Wales 24 N16
Llanelltyd: Gwynedd, Wales 27 O14
Llanenddwyn: Powys, Wales 27 N14
Llanengan: Gwynedd, Wales 27 M14
Llanerchymedd: Gwynedd, Wales 27 N13
Llanerfyl: Powys, Wales 27 P14
Llanes: Spain 35 D15
Llanfachraeth: Gwynedd, Wales 27 M13
Llanfaelog: Gwynedd, Wales 27 N13
Llanfaethlu: Gwynedd, Wales 27 M13
Llanfair-ar-y-bryn: Dyfed, Wales 24 O15
Llanfair Caereinion: Powys, Wales 27 P14
Llanfairfechan: Gwyn., Wales 27 O13
Llanfair Talhaiarn: Clwyd, Wales 27 O13
Llanfechain: Powys, Wales 27 P14
Llanfechell: Gwynedd, Wales 27 N13
Llanfihangel Glyn Myfyr: Clwyd, Wales 27 O13
Llanfihangel-nant-bran: Powys, Wales 24 O16
Llanfihangel yng Ngwynfa: Powys, Wales 27 P14
Llanfihangel Ystrad: Dyfed, Wales 24 N15
Llanfillo: Powys, Wales 24 P16
Llanfyllin: Powys, Wales 27 P14
Llanfynydd: Dyfed, Wales 24 N16
Llanfyrnach: Dyfed, Wales 24 M16
Llangadfan: Powys, Wales 27 P14
Llangadog: Dyfed, Wales 24 O16
Llangathen: Dyfed, Wales 24 N16
Llangattock: Powys, Wales 24 P16
Llangefni: Gwynedd, Wales 27 N13
Llangendeirne: Dyfed, Wales 24 N16
Llangernyw: Clwyd, Wales 27 O13
Llangian: Gwynedd, Wales 27 M14
Llangibby: Gwent, Wales 24 Q16
Llanglydwen: Dyfed, Wales 24 M16
Llangollen: & val., Clwyd, Wales 27 P14
Llangorse: Powys, Wales 24 P16
Llangower: Gwynedd, Wales 27 O14
Llangranog: Dyfed, Wales 24 N15
Llangurig: Powys, Wales 24 O15
Llangwm: Clwyd, Wales 27 O14
Llangwm: Dyfed, Wales 24 M16
Llangybi: Dyfed, Wales 24 N15
Llangybi: Gwent, Wales 24 Q16
Llangybi: Gwynedd, Wales 27 N14
Llangynidr: Powys, Wales 24 P16
Llangynog: Powys, Wales 27 P14
Llanharan: Mid. Glam., Wales 24 P16
Llanharry: S. Glam., Wales 24 P16
Llanhilleth: Gwent, Wales 24 P16
Llanidloes: Powys, Wales 24 O15
Llanilar: Dyfed, Wales 24 N15
Llanllwchaern: Dyfed, Wales 24 N15
Llanllyfni: Gwynedd, Wales 27 N13
Llanmadoc: W. Glam., Wales 24 N16
Llanmorlais: W. Glam., Wales 24 N16
Llannefydd: Clwyd, Wales 27 O13
Llannon: Dyfed, Wales 24 N16
Llano: Tex., U.S.A. 90 B10
Llano: riv., Tex., U.S.A. 90 B10
Llano, El: Mexico 93 E6
Llano Estacado: plain, N. Mex./Tex., U.S.A. 93 G6
Llanon: Dyfed, Wales 24 N15
Llanos de Mojos: plain, Bolivia 94 E7
Llanos de Urgel: Spain 35 G16
Llanpumsaint: Dyfed, Wales 24 N16
Llanrhaeadr: Clwyd, Wales 27 P13
Llanrhaeadr-ym-mochnant: Powys, Wales 27 P14
Llanrhidian: W. Glam., Wales 24 N16
Llanrian: Dyfed, Wales 24 L16
Llanrug: Gwynedd, Wales 27 N13
Llanrwst: Clwyd, Wales 27 O13
Llansannan: Clwyd, Wales 27 O13
Llansantffraid Glyn Ceiriog: Clwyd, Wales 27 P14
Llansawel: Dyfed, Wales 24 N15
Llansilin: Clwyd, Wales 27 P14
Llanstephan: Dyfed, Wales 24 N16
Llantilio Crossenny: Gwent, Wales 24 Q16
Llantrisant: Mid. Glam., Wales 24 P16
Llantwit Major: S. Glam., Wales 24 P17
Llanuwchllyn: Gwyn., Wales 27 O14
Llanwddyn: Powys, Wales 27 P14
Llanwinio: Dyfed, Wales 24 M16
Llanwnda: Gwynedd, Wales 27 N13
Llanwnen: Dyfed, Wales 24 N15
Llanwrthwl: Powys, Wales 24 O15
Llanwrtyd Wells: Powys, Wales 24 O15
Llanybyther: Dyfed, Wales 24 N15
Llanycefn: Dyfed, Wales 24 M16
Llanychaer: Dyfed, Wales 24 M16
Llanymawddwy: Gwynedd, Wales 27 O14
Llata: Peru 94 B5
Llavorsi: Spain 37 G13
Llay: Clwyd, Wales 27 Q13
Llerena: Spain 35 C17
Lleyn: penin., Gwyn., Wales 24 M14
Llico: Chile 96 A3
Llivia: Spain 37 G13
Lloydminster: Alta., Can. 92 E2
Lloyd Shoals Res.: Ga., U.S.A. 91 K9
Lluchmayor: Majorca, Balearic Is. 35 H17
Llullaillaco: volc., Arg./Chile 96 B1
Llysworney: S. Glam., Wales 24 O17
Lo: riv., China 62 T7
Loa: riv., Chile 96 B1
Loai Ta: reef, S. China Sea 64 E4
Loange: riv., Zaïre 76 A4
Loango: Congo 81 G5
Loanhead: Lothian, Scot. 29 P8
Loano: Italy 40 O11
Lobatse: Botswana 75 F2
Löbau: E. Germany 45 U4
Lobaye: Pref. & riv., Cen. Afr. Rep. (cap. M'Baiki) 81 H4
Lobenstein: E. Germany 45 R5
Loberia: Buenos Aires, Arg. 96 D4
Loberia: Chibut, Argentina 95 E12
Łobez: Poland 45 V2
Lobinstown: Meath, Repub. of Ireland 30 H12
Lobito: Angola 73 G12
Loboko: Congo 81 H5
Lobos: Argentina 96 D4
Lobos: i., Mexico 93 E7
Locarno: Switzerland 40 O9
Locha: Tibet, China 59 Q9
Lochaber: dist., High., Scot. 28 M6
Lochailort: High., Scotland 28 K6
Lochaline: High., Scotland 29 K6
Lochboisdale: Outer Hebr., Scotland 28 G5
Lochbuie: Inner Hebr., Scot. 29 K7
Lochcarron: High., Scot. 28 K5
Lochdon Head: Inner Hebr., Scotland 29 K7
Loche, Lac La: lake, Sask., Canada 92 F1
Lochearnhead: Central, Scotland 29 N7
Lochem: Netherlands 44 M3
Locheng: Hainan, China 62 U11
Loches: France 36 G8
Lochgelly: Fife, Scotland 29 P7
Lochgilphead: Strath., Scot. 29 L7
Lochgoilhead: Strath., Scot. 29 M7
Lochiel: S. Australia 71 C9
Lochinver: High., Scotland 28 L3
Lochmaben: Dumfries & Galloway, Scotland 29 P9
Lochmaddy: Outer Hebr., Scotland 28 G4
Lochanagar: N.S.W., Austl. 71 E9
Lochnagar: mtn., Grampian, Scotland 28 P6
Lochore: Fife, Scotland 29 P7
Lochranza: I. of Arran, Scot. 29 L8
Lochwinnoch: Strath., Scot. 29 M8
Lochy, Loch: High., Scotland 28 M6
Lock: S. Australia 71 A9
Lockerbie: Dumfries & Galloway, Scotland 29 P9
Lockesburg: Ark., U.S.A. 90 D9
Lockhart: N.S.W., Austl. 71 G10
Lockhart: S.C., U.S.A. 91 L8
Lockhart: Tex., U.S.A. 90 C11
Lock Haven: Pa., U.S.A. 89 N5
Lockington: Humb., Eng. 27 V12
Löcknitz: E. Germany 45 U2
Lockport: Ill., U.S.A. 88 G5
Lockport: N.Y., U.S.A. 89 M4
Lockton: N. Yorks., England 26 U11
Locle, Le: Switzerland 40 M8
Locmaria: Belle Île, France 36 B8
Locminé: France 36 C8
Locri: Italy 38 P17
Locri Epizephrii: Greek coastal city about 2 miles S. of Gerace Marina, Italy 38 P17
Locris, Opuntia or Epicnemidia: ancient Greek district on S. coast of Gulfs of Malis and Euboea around Atalándi, Greece 39 S17
Locris Ozolis: ancient Greek district in country along G. of Corinth, N. of Návpaktos, Greece 39 S17
Lod (Lydda): Israel 55 a3
Loddiswell: Devon, Eng. 24 O19
Loddon: Norf., England 25 Y14
Loddon: riv., Vict., Austl. 71 E11
Lodève: France 37 J12
Lodeynoye Pole: U.S.S.R. 50 D2
Lodhran: Punjab, Pakistan 58 M9
Lodi: Calif., U.S.A. 93 C5
Lodi: Italy 40 P10
Lodi: Wis., U.S.A. 88 G4
Lødingen: Vesterålen, Nor. 46 O2
Lodja: Zaïre 76 B3

Lods: France 40 M8
Lodwar: Kenya 76 E2
ŁÓDŹ: & Prov., Poland 43 Q11
Loei: Thailand 64 C3
Loeriesfontein: S. Africa 74 C5
Lofer: Austria 41 S8
Loffa: Co., Liberia (co. town Voinjama) 80 C3
Loffa: riv., Liberia 80 B3
Lofoten Is.: Norway 46 N2
Lofthouse: N. Yorks., Eng. 26 S11
Loftus: Cleve., England 26 U10
Logan: Mont., U.S.A. 92 E3
Logan: N. Mex., U.S.A. 93 G5
Logan: Ohio, U.S.A. 88 K6
Logan: Utah, U.S.A. 92 E4
Logan: W. Va., U.S.A. 88 L7
Logan: riv., Queens., Austl. 70 G4
Logan, Mount: Yukon, Can. 84 e5
Logansport: Ind., U.S.A. 88 H5
Logansport: La., U.S.A. 90 E10
Logar: prov., Afghanistan 55 L8
Lögde: riv., Sweden 46 Q4
Loghill: Lim., Repub. of Ireland 31 C14
Login: Dyfed, Wales 24 M16
Logo: Sudan 76 D2
Logone: riv., Chad 81 H3
Logone Occidental: Pref., Chad (cap. Moundou) 81 H3
Logone Oriental: Pref., Chad (cap. Doba) 81 H3
Logoysk: Byelorussia 43 U9
LOGROÑO: & Prov., Spain 35 E15
Logrosan: Spain 35 D17
Løgstør: Denmark 47 L8
Loharu: Haryana, India 58 N9
Lohatlha: S. Africa 74 E4
Lohiniva: Finland 46 T3
Lohja: Finland 47 T6
Lohjan Lake: Finland 47 S6
Lohmen: E. Germany 45 S2
Lohne: W. Germany 44 O3
Lohr: W. Germany 44 P6
Loiano: Italy 41 R11
L'Oie: France 37 D9
LOIKAW: Kayah, Burma 59 R11
Loimaa: Finland 47 S6
Loing: riv., France 36 H7
Loir: riv., France 36 E8
Loire: Dept., France (cap. St. Etienne) 37 J10
Loire: riv., France 36 D8
Loire-Atlantique: Dept., Fr. (cap. Nantes) 36 D8
Loire Lateral Canal: France 37 J9
Loiret: Dept., France (cap. Orléans) 36 H8
Loir-et-Cher: Dept., France (cap. Blois) 36 G8
Loiron: France 36 E7
Loisach: riv., W. Germany 41 R8
Loitz: E. Germany 45 T2
Loiwing: Yunnan, China 62 R10
Loja: Ecuador 94 B4
Loja: Spain 35 D18
Loka: Sudan 76 D2
Lokandu: Zaire 76 C3
Lokbatu: Borneo 65 F7
Lokchang: Kwangtung, China 62 U9
Lokeren: Belgium 44 J4
Lokichoggio: Kenya 76 D2
Lokitaung: Kenya 76 E2
Lokka: Finland 46 U3
Løkken: Denmark 47 L8
Løkken: Norway 46 L5
Loko: Nigeria 81 F3
Lokoja: Nigeria 81 F3
Lokolo: riv., Zaire 76 B3
Lokoro: riv., Zaire 76 B3
Lokot': Altai, U.S.S.R. 51 O4
Lokot': Bryansk, U.S.S.R. 50 D4
Loks Lands: N.W.T., Canada 85 n5
Lokwabe: Botswana 77 B7
Lola: Guinea 80 C3
Lolimi: Sudan 76 D2
Loliondo: Tanzania 76 E3
Lolland: i., Denmark 47 M9
Lolo: riv., Gabon 81 G5
Loloda: Moluccas, Indon. 61 K11
Lolodorf: Cameroun 81 G4
Lolowau: Nias, Indonesia 65 B6
Lolta Plains: Kenya 76 E3
Lolung (Lho Dzong): Tibet, China 62 R8
Lom: Bulgaria 39 S15
Lom: riv., Cameroun 81 G3
Lomami: riv., Zaire 76 B3
Loma Mtns.: Sierra Leone 80 B3
Lomas: Peru 94 C7
Lombardia: see Lombardy.
Lombardy: Reg. & plain, It. [cap. Milan (Milano)] 40 P10
Lombez: France 37 F12
Lomblen: i., Indonesia 65 G8
Lombok: i., & str., Indon. 65 F8
LOMÉ: Togo 81 E3
Lomela: & riv., Zaire 76 B3
Lomie: Cameroun 81 G4
Lomitas, Las: Argentina 96 C1
Lommatzsch: E. Germany 45 T4
Lommel: Belgium 44 L4
Lomond, Loch: Central/Strathclyde, Scotland 29 M7
Lomond Hills: Fife, Scot. 29 P7
Lomonosov: U.S.S.R. 47 V7
Lomonosovo: U.S.S.R. 50 D3
Lomonosovskiy: Kazakh., U.S.S.R. 51 L4
Lomphat: Cambodia 64 D4
Lompoc: Calif., U.S.A. 93 C6
Lom Sak: Thailand 64 C3
Łomża: Poland 43 S10
Lonate: Italy 40 O10
Loncoche: Chile 95 C11
Loncopué: Argentina 96 A4
Londiani: Kenya 76 E3
Londinières: France 36 G6
LONDON: Gt. Ldn., U.K. 25 V16
London: Ky., U.S.A. 88 J7
London: Ohio, U.S.A. 88 K6
London: Ont., Canada 88 L4
London, East: & Dist., S. Afr. 75 G6
London Airport: Greater London, England 25 V17
London Colney: Herts., Eng. 25 V16
LONDONDERRY: & Co., N. Ireland 30 G10
London Reefs: S. China Sea 64 E5
Londrina: Brazil 96 E1
Long, Loch: Strathclyde, Scotland 29 M7
Longa: Angola 77 A5
Longarone: Italy 41 S9
Long Ashton: Avon, Eng. 24 Q17
Longaya: Sarawak, Malaysia 65 E6
Long Bay: S.C., U.S.A. 90 Ins.
Long Beach: Calif., U.S.A. 93 D6
Longbeleh: Borneo 65 F6
Long Bennington: Lincs., England 27 U14
Long Buckby: Northants., England 25 T15
Long Burton: Dorset, Eng. 24 R18
Long Crendon: Bucks., Eng. 25 T16
Longdon: Hereford & Worcester, England 24 R15
Long Eaton: Derby., Eng. 27 T14
LONGFORD: & Co., Repub. of Ireland 30 F12
Longford: Offaly, Repub. of Ireland 31 F13
Longford: Tas., Australia 68 H8
Longformacus: Borders, Scotland 29 R8
Longframlington: Northumb., England 26 S9
Longhorsley: Northumb., England 26 S9
Longhoughton: Northumb., England 26 S9
Longido: Tanzania 76 E3
Longiram: Borneo 65 F6
Long I.: Bahamas 87 m13
Long I.: Chesterfield Is. 67 L6
Long I.: & sound, N.Y., U.S.A. 89 P5
Long I.: Papua/New Guinea 66 J3
Long I.: N.S., Canada 89 S3
Long I.: Queens., Australia 70 H4
Long Itchington: War., Eng. 25 T15
Longlac: Ont., Canada 85 L8
Long Lake: N.Y., U.S.A. 89 O3
Long Lake: Ont., Canada 88 H1
Longlama: Sarawak, Malaysia 65 E6
Longleat: house, Wilts., Eng. 24 R17
Longmanhill: Gram., Scot. 28 R4
Long Melford: Suff., Eng. 25 X15
Longmont: Colo., U.S.A. 93 F4
Long Mtn.: Salop, England 27 P14
Long Mynd: Salop, Eng. 27 Q14
Longnawan: Borneo 65 E6
Longniddry: Lothian, Scot. 29 Q8
Longnor: Staffs., England 27 S13
Longny: France 36 F7
Longotoma: Chile 96 A3
Long Pine: Nebr., U.S.A. 92 H4
Long Point: cape, Ont., Can. 88 L4
Long Prairie: city, Minn., U.S.A. 88 D3
Longpré: France 36 G5
Long Preston: N. Yorks., Eng. 27 R11
Long Range Mtns.: Newf., Canada 85 u1
Longreach: Queens., Austl. 69 G4
Longridge: Lancs., England 27 Q12
Longsdon: Staffs., England 27 R13
Longsegah: Borneo 65 F6
Longside: Grampian, Scotland 28 S4
Longs Peak: Colo., U.S.A. 93 F4
Long Stanton: Cambs., Eng. 25 W15
Longstone, Great: Derby., England 27 S13
Long Stratton: Norf., Eng. 25 Y15
Long Sutton: Lincs., Eng. 25 W14
Long Sutton: Som., Eng. 24 Q17
Longton: Lancs., Eng. 27 Q12
Longton: Staffs., England 27 R14
Longtown: Cumbria, England 26 Q9
Longtown: Hereford & Worcester, England 24 Q16
Longué: France 36 E8
Longueville: France 36 G6
Longuyon: France 36 L6
Longview: Alta., Canada 92 E2
Longview: Tex., U.S.A. 90 K6
Longview: Wash., U.S.A. 92 C3
Longwood: Meath, Repub. of Ireland 30 H13
Longwy: France 36 L6
Longxuyên: Vietnam 64 D4
LONGYEARBYEN: Spitzbergen 48 c2
Loning: Honan, China 62 U8
Löningen: W. Germany 44 N3
Lonoke: Ark., U.S.A. 90 F8
Lønsdal: Norway 46 O3
LONS-LE-SAUNIER: Jura, Fr. 40 L9
Lontulla: Ethiopia 76 F1
Looc: Philippines 64 G4
Looe, East & West: Corn., England 24 N19
Lookout, Cape: N.C., U.S.A. 91 N8
Lookout, Cape: Ont., Can. 85 16
Lookout Mount: N. Mex., U.S.A. 93 F5
Loolmalasin: mtn., Tanzania 76 E3
Loongana: W. Australia 68 D6
Loop Head: cape, Clare, Repub. of Ireland 31 B14
Loose: Kent, England 25 X17
Lopez, Cape: Gabon 81 F5
Lopham, North: Norf., England 25 X15
Loping: Yunnan, China 62 S9
Lop Nor: see Lopu Po.
Loppa: Norway 46 R1
Lopphavet: bay, Norway 46 R1
Loppington: Salop, Eng. 27 Q14
Loptyuga: U.S.S.R. 50 G2
Lopu: Sinkiang, China 51 O7
Lopu Po (Lop Nor): lake, Sinkiang, China 53 O3
Lora del Rio: Spain 35 D18
Lorain: Ohio, U.S.A. 88 K5
Loralai: Baluchistan, Pakistan 58 L8
Lorca: Spain 35 F18
Lord Howe Atoll (Otong Java Is.): Solomon Is. 67 L3
Lord Howe I.: (Austl.), Tasman Sea 67 L8
Lord Howe Rise: S. Pacific Ocean 7 35S 160E
Lordsburg: N. Mex., U.S.A. 93 F6
Lorena: Brazil 96 F1
Lorengau: Admiralty Is. 66 J2
Lorenzago: Italy 41 S9
Loreo: Italy 41 S10
Loreto: Brazil 94 H5
Loreto: Italy 41 T12
Loreto: Mexico 93 E7
Lorgues: France 40 M12
Lorica: Colombia 94 B2
Lorient: France 36 B8
Loriol: France 37 K11
Lormes: France 36 J8
Lorne: Vict., Australia 71 E12
Lorne: dist. Strath., Scot. 29 L7
Lorne, Firth of: Scotland 29 K7
Lornel, Pointe de: France 36 G5
Lörrach: W. Germany 40 N8
Lorraine: Queens., Austl. 69 F3
Lorraine: Prov., France 34 J12
Lorrez-le-Bocage: France 36 H7
Lorrha: Tip., Repub. of Irel. 31 E13
Lorris: France 36 H8
Lorugumu: Kenya 76 E2
Loruth Post: Sudan 76 E2
Los Alamos: N. Mex., U.S.A. 93 F5
Los Aldamas: Mexico 90 B12
Los Andes: Chile 96 A3
Los Angeles: Calif., U.S.A. 93 D6
Los Angeles: Chile 96 A4
Losarcos: Spain 37 C13
Los Banos: Calif., U.S.A. 93 C5
Los Barrios: Spain (Gib. Inset) 32 Ins.
Los Blancos: Paraguay 96 C1
Los Cerrillos: Argentina 96 B3
Los Colorados: Argentina 96 B2
Loshan: Honan, China 62 U8
Loshan (Kiating): Szechwan, China 62 S9
Los Herreras: Mexico 90 B13
Lošinj: & i., Yugoslavia 41 U11
Los Juries: Argentina 96 C2
Loskop Dam: Trans., S. Afr. 75 H2
Los Mochis: Mexico 93 F7
Loso Lava: New Hebrides 67 N4
Los Patos: riv., Argentina 96 B3
Los Patos Lake: Brazil 96 E3
Los Pezos: Chile 96 A2
Los Roques Is.: Venezuela 94 D1
Los Santos de Maimona: Spain 35 C17
Los Sauces: Chile 96 A4
Lossiemouth: Gram., Scot. 28 P4
Los Teques: Venezuela 94 D1
Los Tigres: Argentina 96 C2
Lost River Range: Idaho, U.S.A. 92 E4
Lostwithiel: Corn., England 24 M19
Losuia: Trobriand Is., New Guinea 69 J1
Los Vientos: Chile 96 B1
Los Vilos: Chile 96 A3
Lot: Dept. & riv., France (cap. Cahors) 37 G11
Lota: Chile 96 A4
Lota: U.S.S.R. 46 W2
Lotagipi Swamp: marsh, Sudan/Kenya 76 D2
Lotbinière: Que., Canada 89 Q2
Lot-et-Garonne: Dept., Fr. (cap. Agen) 37 F11
Lothair: Trans., S. Africa 75 J3
Lothian: Reg., Scotland (cap. Edinburgh) 29 P8
Loting: Kwangtung, China 62 U10
Loto: Zaire 76 B3
Lotsani: riv., Botswana 75 G1
Lotta: riv., U.S.S.R. 46 V2
Lotu: Chinghai, China 62 S7
Loubomo: Congo 81 G5
Loudéac: France 36 C7
Loudima: Congo 81 G5
Loudon: Tenn., U.S.A. 91 J8
Loudun: France 36 F8
Loue: riv., France 40 L8
Louga: Senegal 80 A1
Louge: riv., France 37 G12
Loughborough: Leics., Eng. 27 T14
Loughbrickland: Down, N. Ireland 30 J11
Lougheed: Alta., Canada 92 E2
Lougheed I.: N.W.T., Can. 84 j2
Loughgall: Armagh, N. Irel. 30 H11
Loughglinn: Rosc., Repub. of Ireland 30 D12
Loughmoe: Tip., Repub. of Ireland 31 F14
Loughor: W. Glam., Wales 24 N16
Loughor: riv., Wales 24 O16
Loughrea: Galway, Repub. of Ireland 31 D13
Loughros More Bay: Don., Repub. of Ireland 30 D10
Loughton: Essex, England 25 W16
Louhans: France 37 L9
Louisa: Ky., U.S.A. 88 K6
Louisa Reef: S. China Sea 65 E5
Louisburg: Cape Breton I., Canada 89 V3
Louisburg: N.C., U.S.A. 89 M7
Louisburg: Mayo, Repub. of Ireland 30 B12
Louiseville: Que., Canada 89 P2
Louisiade Arch.: New Guin. 69 J2
Louisiana: Mo., U.S.A. 88 F6
Louisiana: State, U.S.A. (cap. Baton Rouge) 90 E10
Louis Trichardt: Trans., S. Africa 75 H1
Louisville: Ga., U.S.A. 91 K9
Louisville: Ky., U.S.A. 88 J6
Louisville: Miss., U.S.A. 90 G9
Louisville: Nebr., U.S.A. 92 H4
Loukoléla: Congo 81 H5
Loulay: France 37 E9
Loulé: Portugal 35 B18
Louny: Czechoslovakia 45 T5
Loup City: Nebr., U.S.A. 92 H4
Loupe, La: France 36 G7
Lourdes: France 37 E12
Lourenço Marques Bay (Delagoa Bay): Mozambique 75 K3
Lourenço Marques: see Maputo
Lourinhã: Portugal 35 B17
Lourmel: Algeria 35 E19
Louth: Lincs., England 27 V13
Louth: Louth, Repub. of Ireland 30 H12
Louth: N.S.W., Australia 71 F8
Louth: Co., Repub. of Irel. (cap. Dundalk) 30 J12
Loutra Aidhipsou: Euboea, Greece 39 S17
Loutre, Pass a: La., U.S.A. 90 Ins.
Louvain: see Leuven.
Louvière, La: Belgium 44 K5
Louviers: France 36 G6
Louvigné: France 36 D7
Louwsburg: Natal, S. Afr. 75 J3
Lövånger: Sweden 46 R4
Lovat: O.F.S., S. Africa 75 G3
Lövberga: Sweden 46 O5
Lovech: Bulgaria 39 T15
Loveland: Colo., U.S.A. 93 F4
Lovell: Wyo., U.S.A. 92 F4
Lovere: Italy 40 Q10
Loves Creek: town, N. Territ., Australia 68 E4
Loviisa: Finland 47 U6
Lovinac: Yugoslavia 41 V11
Lovington: N. Mex., U.S.A. 93 G6
Lövnäs: Sweden 47 N6
Lövnäsvallen: Sweden 47 N6
Lövö: Hungary 41 W8
Lövoa: Angola 77 B5
Lovoi: riv., Zaire 76 C4
Lovosice: Czechoslovakia 45 U5
Lövsta: Sweden 47 P6
Lövua: Angola 76 B4
Lowa: & riv., Zaire 76 C3
Low (Tuamotu) Arch.: (Fr.), Pacific O. 83 g3
Low Desert: Oreg., U.S.A. 92 C4
Lowdham: Notts., England 25 U13
Lowell: Ariz., U.S.A. 93 F6
Lowell: Mass., U.S.A. 89 Q4
Löwenberg: E. Germany 45 T3
Lower Arrow Lake: B.C., Canada 92 D3
Lower Austria: Prov., Austr. [cap. Vienna (Wien)] 41 V7
Lower Beeding: W. Sussex, England 25 V17
Lower Bentham: N. Yorks., England 26 Q11
Lower California (Baja California): (N. & S. Territs.), Mexico (cap. of N. Territ. Mexicali; of S. Territ. La Paz) 93 E7
Lower Heyford: Oxon., Eng. 25 T16
Lower Hutt: North I., N.Z. 70 P15
Lower Lake: Calif., U.S.A. 92 C4
Lower Post: B.C., Canada 84 G6
Lower Red Lake: Minn., U.S.A. 88 D2
Lower Sabie: Trans., S. Afr. 75 J2
Lower Saxony: State, W. Germany, (cap. Hanover) 44 N2
Lower Slaughter: Glos., Eng. 25 S16
Lower Tugela: Dist., S. Afr. 74 J4
Lower Tunguska: riv., U.S.S.R. 49 m5
Lowestoft: Suff., England 25 Z15
Loweswater: Cumbria, Eng. 26 P10
Low Fell: town, Tyne & Wear, England 26 S10
Lowick: Northumb., Eng. 26 S8
Łowicz: Poland 43 Q10
Lowmead: Queens., Austl. 70 J5
Low Moor: town, W. Yorks., England 27 S12
Lowood: Queens., Australia 70 K6
Lowther: riv., Cumbria, Eng. 26 Q10
Lowther Castle: Cumbria, England 26 Q10
Lowther Hills: Strath./Dumf. & Gall., Scotland 29 O9
Lowville: N.Y., U.S.A. 89 O4
Loxton: S. Africa 74 E5
Loxton: S. Australia 71 D10
Loyal, Loch: High., Scot. 28 N3
Loyalty Is: (Fr.), Pacific O. 67 N6
Loyang: Honan, China 62 U8
Loyang: Kwangsi Chuang, China 62 T10
Loyar, Cape: Borneo 65 F7
Loyev: Ukraine 50 D4
Loyez: U.S.S.R. 48 H4
Loyuan: Fukien, China 62 V9
Lož: Yugoslavia 41 U10
Lozère: Dept., France (cap. Mende) 37 J11
Lteto: Zambia 77 C5
Lua: riv., Zaire 76 A2
Luabo: Mozambique 77 E6
Luachimo: riv., Angola 77 B4
Lualaba (Congo): riv., Zaire 76 C3
Luama: riv., Zaire 76 C3
Luampa: Zambia 77 B6
Luan: Mindanao, Phil. 65 G5
LUANDA: & Prov., Angola 73 G11
Luangprabang: Laos 64 C3
Luangue: riv., Angola 77 A4
Luanguinga: riv., Angola 77 B5
Luangwa: riv., Zambia 77 D5
Luangwa Game Reserve: Zambia 77 D5
Luanshya: Zambia 77 C5
Luanpula: Prov., Zambia (cap. Mansa) 77 C5
Luapula: riv., Zambia/Zaire 77 C5
Luarca: Spain 35 C15
Luashi: Zaire 77 B5
Luati: Angola 77 B5
Lubaczów: Poland 43 S11
Lubalo: Angola 77 A4
Lubań: Poland 45 V4
Lubana Lake: Latvia, U.S.S.R. 47 U8
Lubang Is.: Philippines 64 G4
LUBANGO: Huíla, Angola 73 G12
Lubartów: Poland 43 S11
Lubawa: Poland 43 Q10
Lübbecke: W. Germany 44 O3
Lübben: E. Germany 45 T4
Lübbenau: E. Germany 45 T4
Lubbock: Tex., U.S.A. 93 G6
Lübeck: W. Germany 45 Q2
Lubeck: Vict., Australia 71 E11
Lübeck Bay: E./W. Germany 45 Q1
Lubefu: & riv., Zaire 76 B3
Lüben: E. Germany 45 R3
Lubenec: Czechoslovakia 45 T5
Lubenham: Leics., England 25 U15
Lubéron, Montagne du: mtns., France 40 L12
Lubi: riv., Zaire 76 B4
Lubilash: riv., Zaire 77 B4
Lubin: Poland 45 W4
LUBLIN: & Prov., Poland 43 S11
Lubliniec: Poland 43 Q11
Lubmin: E. Germany 45 T1
Lubnaig, Loch: Central, Scotland 29 N7
Lubny: Ukraine 50 D4
Lubombo: Zambia 77 C6
Lubosalma: Karelian A.S.S. Rep., U.S.S.R. 46 W5
Lubraniec: Poland 43 Q10
Lubsko (Sommerfeld): Poland 45 U4
Lübtheen: E. Germany 45 R2
Lubuagan: Luzon, Phil. 64 G3
Lubudi; Kasai – Occidental, Zaire 76 B4
Lubudi: Shaba, Zaire 77 C4
Lubudi: riv., Zaire 77 C4
Lubuklinggau: Sumatra 65 C7
Lubukpakam: Sumatra 65 B6
Lubuksikaping: Sumatra 65 C6
LUBUMBASHI: Shaba, Zaire 77 C5
Lubutu: Zaire 76 C3
Lubwy: Ukraine 50 D4
Lübz: E. Germany 45 S2
Luc, Le: France 40 M12
Lucala: Angola 73 H11
Lucan: Dublin, Repub. of Ireland 31 J13
Lucano: Angola 77 B5
Lucas Chan.: Ont., Canada 88 L3
Lucca: Italy 40 Q12
Luccombe: Som., England 24 O17
Luce: Yugoslavia 41 U9
Luce: riv., Dumfries & Galloway, Scotland 29 M10
Luce, New: Dumfries & Galloway, Scotland 29 M10
Lucea: Jamaica 86 Ins.
Luce Bay: Dumfries & Galloway, Scotland 29 M10
Lucena: Castellón, Spain 35 F16
Lucena: Córdoba, Spain 35 D18
Lucena: Luzon, Philippines 64 G4
Lučenec: Czechoslovakia 43 Q12
Lucera: Italy 38 O16
LUCERNE (Luzern): Luzern, Switzerland 40 O8
Lucerne, Lake: Switzerland 40 O8
Luceville: Que., Canada 89 R1
Luché: France 36 F8
Luchico: riv., Angola 76 A4
Luchou: Szechwan, China 62 T9
Luchow (Hofei): Anhwei, China 62 V8
Lüchow: W. Germany 45 R3
Luchwan: Kwangsi Chuang, China 62 U10
Lucin: Utah, U.S.A. 92 E4
Lucipara Is.: Indonesia 61 K13
Luckau: E. Germany 45 T4
Luckenwalde: E. Germany 45 T3
Lucker: Northumb., Eng. 26 S8
Luckhoff: O.F.S., S. Africa 75 F4
LUCKNOW: Uttar Pradesh, India 58 O9
Lucma: Peru 94 B5
Luçon: France 37 D9
Lucus Augusti: Roman town at Lugo, Spain 35 C15
Lucusse: Angola 77 B5
Ludborough: Lincs., Eng. 27 V13
Ludbreg: Yugoslavia 41 W9
Lude, Le: France 36 F8
Lüdenscheid: W. Germany 44 N4
Lüderitz: E. Germany 45 R3
Lüderitz: & Dist., S.W. Africa 74 A3
Lüderitz Bay: S.W. Africa 74 A3
Ludford: Lincs., England 27 V13
Ludgershall: Bucks., Eng. 25 T16
Ludgershall: Wilts., England 25 S17
Ludgvan: Corn., England 25 L19
Ludham: Norf., England 25 Z14
Ludhiana: Punjab, India 58 N8
Lüdinghausen: W. Germany 44 N4
Ludington: Mich., U.S.A. 88 H4
Ludlow: Calif., U.S.A. 93 D6
Ludlow: Salop, England 24 Q15
Ludlow: Vt., U.S.A. 89 P4
Ludvika: Sweden 47 O6
Ludwigsburg: W. Germany 40 P7
Ludwigshafen: W. Germany 44 O6
Ludwigslust: E. Germany 45 R2
Ludza: Latvia, U.S.S.R. 47 U8
Luebo: Zaire 76 B4
Lueki: Zaire 76 C3
Luembe: riv., Angola 77 B4
Luena: riv., Angola/Zambia 77 B5
Luepa: Venezuela 94 E2
Lufeng: Kwangtung, China 62 V10
Lufeng: Yunnan, China 62 S9
Luffenham, North: Leicestershire, England 27 U14
Lufira: riv., Zaire 77 C4
Lufkin: Tex., U.S.A. 90 D10
Luga: U.S.S.R. 50 C3
Luga: riv., U.S.S.R. 47 V7
Lugagnano: Italy 40 P11
Lugano: Switzerland 40 O9
Luganville: New Hebrides 67 N5
Lugar: Strath., Scotland 29 N9
Lugards Falls: Kenya 76 E3
Lugdunensis: Roman province in France and W. Switzerland lying between Aquitania and Belgica 40 L9
Lugdunum: Roman colony lying on right bank of river Rhône at Lyons, Fr. 37 K10
Lugenda: riv., Mozambique 77 E5
Lugg: riv., Hereford & Worcester, England 24 Q15
Luginy: Ukraine 43 V11
Lugnaquilla: mtn., Wick., Repub. of Ireland 31 J14
Lugny: France 37 K9
Lugo: Italy 41 R11
LUGO: & Prov., Spain 35 C15
Lugoj: Romania 39 R14
Lugskaya Gulf: U.S.S.R. 47 V7
Lugulu: riv., Zaire 76 C3
Luguvallium: Roman name of Carlisle, Cumbria, Eng. 26 Q10
Luhaiya: Yemen 54 F11
Luhanyando: Tanzania 77 E4
Luhit: riv., Arunachal Pradesh, India 59 R9
Luho: Kiangsu, China 62 V8
Luhsi: Yunnan, China 62 S10
Luia: Angola 77 B4
Lula: riv., Mozambique 77 D6
Luiana: & riv., Angola 77 B6
Luichart, Loch: High., Scot. 28 M4
Luichow Penin.: Kwangtung, China 62 U10
Luik: see Liège.
Luime: Angola 73 H12
Luing: i., Scotland 29 K7
Luipaardsvlei: Trans., S. Africa 74 M Ins.
Luiro: riv., Finland 46 U3
Luisa: Zaire 76 B4
Luishia: Zaire 77 C5
Luján: Argentina 96 D3
Lukafu: Zaire 77 C5
Lukanga Swamp: marsh, Zambia 77 C5
Lukenie: riv., Zaire 76 B3
Lukk: Libya 33 G5
Lukluk: Sudan 76 D1
Lukmanier Pass: Switz. 40 O9
Lukolela: Zaire 81 H5
Lukoléla: Cen. Afr. Rep. 81 H5
Lukona: Zambia 77 B6
Lukovit: Bulgaria 39 T15
Luków: Poland 43 S11
Lukoyansk: U.S.S.R. 50 F3
Luksefjeld: Norway 47 L7
Lukuga: riv., Zaire 76 C4
Lukula: Zaire 73 G11
Lule: riv., Sweden 46 R3
LULEÅ: Norrbotten, Sweden 46 S4
Lüleburgaz: Turkey 39 U16
Luling: Hopeh, China 62 V7
Luling: La., U.S.A. 90 Ins.
Luling: Tex., U.S.A. 90 C11
Lullaka: riv., Zaire 76 B3
Lulonga: & riv., Zaire 76 A2
Lulua: riv., Zaire 76 B4
Luluabourg: see Kananga.
Lulworth, West: Dorset, England 24 R18
Lumai: Angola 77 B5
Lumajang: Java 65 E8
Lumaling: Tibet, China 59 Q9
Lumbala: Angola 77 B5
Lumberton: Miss., U.S.A. 90 G10
Lumberton: N.C., U.S.A. 91 M8
Lumbier: Spain 37 D13
Lumbis: Borneo 65 F6
Lumbres: France 36 H5
Lumding: Assam, India 59 Q9
Lumphanan: Gram., Scot. 28 Q5
Lumpkin: Ga., U.S.A. 91 J9
Lumsden: Gram., Scotland 28 Q5
Lumsden: South I., N.Z. 71 M17
Lumu: Celebes 65 F7
Lumut: Malaya, Malaysia 65 b11
Lun: Yugoslavia 41 U11
Lunan Bay: Tay., Scot. 29 R6
Lunavada: Gujarat, India 58 M10
Luncarty: Tay., Scotland 29 P7
Lund: Sweden 47 N9
Lund: Humberside, England 27 U12
Lunda: Prov., Angola (cap. Henrique de Carvalho) 77 B5
Lundazi: Zambia 77 D5
Lundi: riv., Rhodesia 77 D7
Lundie: Tayside, Scotland 29 P6
Lundin Mill: Fife, Scot. 29 Q7
Lundu: Sarawak, Malaysia 65 D6
Lundy I.: England 24 M17
Lune: riv., Cumbria/Lancs., England 26 Q11

For Abbreviations see list on p.113. Italic type, e.g. Ephesus, refers to historical names not on maps. Capital letters, e.g. MADRID, show capitals of countries; small capital letters, e.g. CADIZ, show capitals of provinces, etc. General notes p.116.

Lüneberg: Dist., Lower Saxony, West Germany 45 Q3
Lüneburg: W. Germany 45 Q2
Luneburg: Trans., S. Afr. 75 J3
Lüneburg Heath: W. Ger. 45 P2
Lunel: France 37 K12
Lünen: W. Germany 44 N4
Lunenburg: N.S., Canada 89 T3
Lunenburg: Va., U.S.A. 91 M7
Luneville: France 44 M7
Lunga: i., Scotland 29 K7
Lunga: i., Treshnish Is., Scot. 29 J7
Lungan: Kwangsi Chuang, China 62 T10
Lungan (Pingwu): Szechwan, China 62 S8
Lungchen: Heilungkiang, China 63 X5
Lungchow: Kwangsi Chuang, China 62 T10
Lungern: Switzerland 40 O9
Lunghsien: Shensi, China 62 T8
Lunghwa: Hopeh, China 62 V6
Lungkiang (Tsitsihar): Heilungkiang, China 63 W5
Lungkukang: Szechwan, China 62 S8
Lungleh: Mizoram, India 59 Q10
Lungling: Yunnan, China 62 R10
Lungmatoko: Tibet, China 58 O8
Lungming: Kwangsi Chuang, China 62 T10
Lungmoon: Kwangtung, China 62 U10
Lungnan: Kiangsi, China 62 U10
Lungshan: Hunan, China 62 T9
Lungsheng: Kwangsi Chuang, China 62 T9
Lungsi: Kansu, China 62 S8
Lungue Bungo: riv., Angola 77 B5
Lungyen: Fukien, China 62 V9
Luni: Rajasthan, India 58 M9
Luni: riv., India 58 M9
Luninets: Byelorussia 43 U10
Lunskiip: Trans., S. Africa 75 H2
Lunwaniche: Kansu, China 62 S8
Lunyuk: Sumbawa, Indon. 65 F8
Lunz: Austria 41 V8
Luofu: (SW. of L. Edward) Zaire 76 C3
Luofu: (W. of L. Edward) Zaire 76 C3
Luozi: Zaire 81 G5
Lupa Market: Tanzania 77 D4
Lupani: Rhodesia 77 C6
Lupeni: Romania 39 S14
Lupiri: Angola 77 A5
Lupiro: Tanzania 76 E4
Łupków: Poland 43 S12
Lupon: Philippines 65 H5
Luqa: Malta 32 Ins.
Luque: Paraguay 96 D2
Luray: Va., U.S.A. 89 M6
Lurcy-Lévy: France 37 H9
Lure: France 40 M8
Lurestan: Governorate, Iran (cap. Khurramabad) 57 L5
Lurgain, Loch: High., Scot. 28 L3
Lurgan: Armagh, N. Irel. 30 J11
Luribay: Bolivia 94 D7
Lúrio: Mozambique 77 F5
Lurio: riv., Mozambique 77 E5
Luristan: geog. reg., Iran 57 L5
Lusaka: Zaire 76 C4
LUSAKA: Zambia 77 C6
Lusambo: Zaire 76 B3
Lusancay Is.: New Guinea 69 J1
Lusenga Plain: Zaire 77 C4
Lushai Hills: Mizoram, India 59 Q10
Lushih: Honan, China 62 U8
Lushnjë: Albania 39 Q16
Lushoto: Tanzania 76 E3
Lusi: Yunnan, China 62 R10
Lusignan: France 37 F9
Lusigny: France 36 K7
Lusikisiki: S. Africa 75 H5
Lusitania: Roman province comprising Portugal and parts of W. Spain 35 C16
Lusk: Dublin, Repub. of Irel. 30 J12
Lusk: Wyo., U.S.A. 92 G4
Luso: Moxico, Angola 77 A5
Luss: Strath., Scotland 29 M7
Lussac-les-Châteaux: Fr. 37 F9
Lussvale: Queens., Austl. 70 G6
Lü-ta: Liaoning, China 63 W7
Lutago: Italy 41 R9
Lutai: Hopeh, China 62 V7
Lutcher: La., U.S.A. 90 F10
Lutembo: Angola 77 B5
Lutetia: Roman name of Gallic centre on island at Paris, France 36 H7
Luthermuir: Gram., Scot. 29 Q6
Luthrie: Fife, Scotland 29 P7
Lutihe: Botswana 77 B7
Lütjenburg: W. Germany 45 Q1
Lutnes: Norway 47 N6
Lutoba: Zambia 77 B5
Luton: Beds., England 25 V16
Lutsk: Ukraine 43 T11
Lütter: W. Germany 45 P5
Lutterworth: Leics., Eng. 25 T15
Lutton: Northants., Eng. 25 V15
Lützelflüh: Switzerland 40 N8
Lützen: E. Germany 45 S4
Luusua: Finland 46 U3
Luverne: Ala., U.S.A. 91 H10
Luvia: Finland 47 R6
Luvua: riv., Zaire 76 C4
Luwegu: riv., Tanzania 77 E4
Luwingu: Zambia 77 D5
Luwuk: Celebes 65 G7

Luxembourg: Grand Duchy 44 M6
Cap.: Luxembourg
Area: 999 sq. miles (2,587 sq. km.)
Pop: 345,000 (1971 E)

LUXEMBOURG: Lux. 44 M6
Luxembourg: Prov., Belgium (cap. Arlon) 44 L5
Luxeuil: France 40 M8
Luxey: France 37 E11
Luxor: Egypt 54 D9
Luxulyan: Corn., England 24 M19
Luz: Brazil 94 H7
Luz: France 37 E13
Luza: riv., U.S.S.R. 50 G2
Luzarches: France 36 H6
LUZERN (Lucerne): Switz. 40 O8
Luzern: Canton, Switzerland (cap. Luzern) 40 O8
Luziânia: Brazil 94 H7
Luzilândia: Brazil 94 J4
Łužnice: riv., Czech. 45 U6
Luzon: i., Philippines 64 G3
Luzon Str.: Philippines 64 G2
Luzy: France 37 J9
L'vov: Ukraine 43 S12
Lwanping: Hopeh, China 62 V6
Lwowek: Poland 45 V4
Lyady: U.S.S.R. 47 V7
Lyakhov Is.: U.S.S.R. 49 Q3
Lyakhovtsy: Ukraine 43 U11

Lyallpur: Punjab, Pak. 58 M8
Lyaskeya: Karelian A.S.S. Rep., U.S.S.R. 47 W6
Lybster: High., Scotland 28 P3
Lycaonia: ancient name of district of southern Turkey with centre at Konya 56 C3
Lychen: E. Germany 45 T2
Lychnidus: Greek name of Ohrid Lake, border of Albania and Yugoslavia 39 R16
Lycia: ancient name of district of southern Turkey between Caria and Pamphylia 56 A3
Lyckele: Sweden 46 Q4
Lydd: Kent, England 25 X18
Lydda: see Lod.
Lydenburg: & Dist., Trans., S. Africa 75 J2
Lydford: Devon, England 24 N18
Lydia: ancient name of district of western Turkey between Mysia and Caria (Lydian Kingdom at greatest extent included all W. Turkey to river Kizil) 56 A2
Lydney: Glos., England 24 Q16
Lye: W. Mid., England 24 R15
L'yeksa Lake: Karelian A.S.S. Rep., U.S.S.R. 46 W5
L'yintsy: Ukraine 50 C5
Lyme Bay: Dorset/Devon, England 24 Q18
Lyme Regis: Dorset, England 24 Q18
Lyminge: Kent, England 25 Y17
Lymington: Hants., England 25 S18
Lymm: Ches., England 27 R13
Lympne: airfield, Kent, England 25 Y17
Lympne: see Lemanis.
Lympstone: Devon, England 24 P18
Lynchat: High., Scotland 28 N5
Lynchburg: Va., U.S.A. 89 M7
Lynd: riv., Queens., Austl. 69 G3
Lynden: Wash., U.S.A. 92 C3
Lyndhurst: Hants., England 25 S18
Lyndhurst: S. Australia 69 F6
Lyndonville: Vt., U.S.A. 89 P3
Lyne: riv., Cumbria, England 26 Q9
Lyneham: Wilts., England 24 S17
Lyngdal: Norway 47 K7
Lynher: riv., Corn., England 24 N19
Lynmouth: Northumb., Eng. 26 S9
Lynn: Mass., U.S.A. 89 Q4
Lynn Lake: town, Man., Can. 92 G1
Lynsted: Kent, England 25 X17
Lynton: Devon, England 24 O17
LYON: Rhône, France 37 K10
Lyon: riv., Tay., Scotland 29 N6
Lyon, Glen: Tay., Scot. 29 N6
Lyonnais: Prov., France 34 H14
Lyons: see Lyon, France.
Lyons: Ga., U.S.A. 91 K9
Lyons: Kans., U.S.A. 90 B6
Lyons: N.Y., U.S.A. 89 N4
Lyons: riv., W. Australia 68 B4
Lyonshall: Hereford & Worcester, England 24 Q15
Lyra Reef: Bismarck Arch., 67 K2
Lys: riv., Belgium 44 J5
Lysá: Czechoslovakia 45 U5
Lysekil: Sweden 47 M7
Lyshovo: U.S.S.R. 50 F3
Lyss: Switzerland 40 N8
Lystra: ancient town of Lycaonia, later Roman colony about midway between Konya and L. Sugla, Turkey 56 C3
Lys'va: U.S.S.R. 50 J3
Lysvik: Sweden 47 N6
Lytchett Matravers: Dorset, England 24 R18
Lytchett Minster: Dorset, England 24 R18
Lytham: Lancs., England 27 Q12
Lyttelton: South I., N.Z. 70 O16
Lytton: B.C., Canada 92 C2
Lyuban': Byelorussia 43 V10
Lyubar: Ukraine 43 U12
Lyubcha: Byelorussia 43 U10
Lyubeshov: Ukraine 43 T11
Lyubitovo: U.S.S.R. 63 Y5
Lyuboml': Ukraine 43 T11
Lyudinovo: U.S.S.R. 50 D4

Ma: i., Thailand 64 C4
Ma (Hwang): riv., China 62 R8
Ma: riv., Laos/Vietnam 64 C2
Ma'ad: Jordan 55 b2
Maam: Galway, Repub. of Irel. 30 B12
Maam Cross: Galway, Repub. of Ireland 31 B13
Maamturk Mtns.: Galway, Repub. of Ireland 30 B12
MA'AN: & Dist., Jordan 56 D6
Maaninka: Finland 46 V3
Ma'aniya: well, Iraq/Saudi Arabia 57 H6
Ma'arat en Nu'man: Syria 56 E4
Maaruig: Outer Hebr., Scot. 28 H4
Maas: Don., Repub. of Irel. 30 E10
Maas: Somalia 79 R19
Maas (Meuse): riv., Neth. 44 L4
Maasbree: Netherlands 44 M4
Maaseik: Belgium 44 L4
Maasin: Philippines 64 G4
Ma'asir: well, Saudi Arabia 58 F6
MAASTRICHT: Limburg, Netherlands 44 L5
Mabaruma: Guyana 87 d6
Mabein: Burma 59 R10
Mablethorpe: Lincs., Eng. 27 W13
Mabose: Mozambique 75 K1
Mabote: Mozambique 77 D7
Mabou: Cape Breton I., Can. 89 V2
Mabres, Pta.: cape, Minorca, Balearic Is., 35 J17
Mabrous: Niger 78 G5
Mabuki: Tanzania 76 D3
Mabula: S. Africa 75 F2
Mabumbu: Zambia 77 B6
McAdam: N.B., Can. 89 S3
Macaé: Brazil 96 G1
Macaene: Mozambique 75 K2
Macaiba: Brazil 94 K5
McAlester: Okla., U.S.A. 90 D8
Macalister: Queens., Austl. 70 J6
McAlister: mtn., N.S.W. Australia 71 H10
McAllen: Tex., U.S.A. 90 B12
MacAlpine, La.: N.W.T., Can. 84 j4
Macamic: Que., Canada 89 M1
Macanda: Mozambique 75 K2

Macao: Port. overseas prov. 62 U10
Cap.: Macao
Area: 6 sq. miles (16 sq. km.)
Pop.: 321,000 (1971 E)

MACAPÁ: Amapá, Brazil 94 G3
Macará: Ecuador 94 B4
Macarani: Brazil 94 J7

Macarthur: Vict., Australia 71 D12
Macas: Ecuador 94 B4
Macau: Brazil 94 K5
Macauba: Brazil 94 G6
Macaúbas: Brazil 94 J6
Macauley I.: Kermadec Is., Pacific O. 67 Q8
McBride: B.C., Canada 92 C2
McCall: Idaho, U.S.A. 92 D4
McCamey: Tex., U.S.A. 93 G6
McCammon: Idaho, U.S.A. 92 E4
MacCarthy: The Gambia 80 B2
McCaysville: Ga., U.S.A. 91 J8
Macclesfield: Ches., Eng. 27 R13
M'Clintock Chan.: N.W.T., Canada 84 j3
McCloud: Calif., U.S.A. 92 C4
Maddalena: i., Sardinia 38 L16
M'Clure Str.: N.W.T., Can. 84 H3
McColl: S.C., U.S.A. 91 M8
McComb: Miss., U.S.A. 90 F10
McCook: Nebr., U.S.A. 93 G4
McCormick: S.C., U.S.A. 91 K9
McCrory: Ark., U.S.A. 90 F8
McDermitt: Nev., U.S.A. 92 D4
McDonald: Lake: W. Austl. 68 D4
Macdonald Peak: Mont., U.S.A. 92 E3
Macdonnell Ranges: N. Territ., Australia 68 E4
McDonoughville: La., U.S.A. 90 Ins.
Macdougall, Lake: N.W.T., Canada 84 K4
MacDowell Lake: Ont., Can. 92 J2
Macduff: Grampian, Scotland 28 R4
Macedonia: Reg., Greece 39 S16
Macedonia: Repub., Yugo. (cap. Skopje) 39 R16
MACEIÓ: Alagoas, Brazil 94 K5
McElhany: Mo., U.S.A. 90 D7
MACENTA: & Reg., Guinea 80 C3
Macerata: Italy 38 N15
Macfarlane, Lake: S. Austl. 71 B8
McGehee: Ark., U.S.A. 90 F9
McGill: Nev., U.S.A. 92 E5
Macgillycuddy's Reeks: mtns., Kerry, Repub. of Irel. 31 B16
McGrath: Alaska, U.S.A. 84 D5
McGregor: Minn., U.S.A. 88 E2
McGregor: S. Africa 74 C6
McGregor: Tex., U.S.A. 90 C9
McGuire, Mt.: Idaho, U.S.A. 92 E2
Macha: Zambia 77 C6
Machado: Brazil 96 F1
Machadodorp: Trans., S. Afr. 75 J2
Machaerus: Herodian city about 9 miles WSW. of Libb, Jordan 55 b3
Machakos: Kenya 76 E3
Machala: Ecuador 94 B4
Machanga: Mozambique 77 D7
Machans, The: dist., Outer Hebr., Scotland 28 G5
Machar: Sudan 76 D1
Machars, The: dist., Dumfries & Galloway, Scotland 29 M10
Machaze: Mozambique 77 D7
Machecoul: France 36 D9
Macheke: Rhodesia 77 D6
Macherla: Andhra Pradesh, India 58 N11
Machias: Maine, U.S.A. 89 S3
Machichaco, Cape: Spain 35 E15
Machida: Japan 63 f3
Machilipatnam: Andhra Pradesh, India 58 O11
Machine, La: France 37 J9
Machioneal: Jamaica 86 Ins.
Machrihanish: Strath., Scot. 29 K9
Machuan (Tamchok): riv., Tibet, China 59 P9
Machu Picchu: Peru 94 C6
Machynlleth: Powys, Wales 27 O14
Macia: Mozambique 75 K2
Macias Nguema Biyogo (Fernando Poo): i., Equatorial Guinea (cap. Malabo) 81 F4
Macina: geog. reg., Mali 80 D2
Macinaggio: Corsica 38 L15
McIntosh: S. Dak., U.S.A. 92 G3
McIntyre: riv., Queens./N.S.W., Australia 71 H7
Mackay: Idaho, U.S.A. 92 E4
Mackay: Queens., Austl. 70 H3
Mackay, Cape: N.W.T., Can. 84 H3
Mackay, Lake: W. Austl. 68 D4
McKeesport: Pa., U.S.A. 89 M5
Mackenna: Argentina 96 C3
Mackenzie: see Linden (Guyana)
McKenzie: Tenn., U.S.A. 88 G7
Mackenzie: riv., N.W.T., Canada 84 h5
Mackenzie: riv., Canada 84 g5
Mackenzie: riv., Queens., Australia 70 H4
Mackenzie Bay: Canada 84 F4
Mackenzie King I.: N.W.T., Canada 84 h2
Mackenzie Mtns.: Canada 84 f5
Mackies: Ont., Canada 88 J3
Mackinac: is., Mich., U.S.A. 88 J3
Mackinac, Str. of: Mich., U.S.A. 88 J3
Mackinaw City: Mich., U.S.A. 88 J3
McKinley: Queens., Austl. 69 G4
McKinley, Mt.: Alaska, U.S.A. 84 d5
McKinley Bay: N.W.T., Can. 84 f3
McKinley Park Station: Alaska, U.S.A. 84 E5
McKinney: Tex., U.S.A. 90 C9
Mackinnon Road: town, Kenya 76 E3
McKittrick: Calif., U.S.A. 93 D5
Macksville: N.S.W., Austl. 71 K8
Maclean: N.S.W., Austl. 71 K7
McLeansboro: Ill., U.S.A. 88 G6
Maclear: & Dist., S. Africa 75 H5
Macleay: riv., N.S.W., Austl. 71 K8
McLennan: Alta., Canada 92 D1
Macleod: see Fort Macleod.
McLeod, Lake: lag., W. Australia 68 A4
Macmillan: riv., Canada 84 f5
McMinnville: Tenn., U.S.A. 89 J8
McMurdo: rsch. stn., Antarctica 9 80S 165E
McMurdo Sound: Antarctica 9 80S 165E
McNary: Ariz., U.S.A. 93 F6
McNary Dam: Oreg., U.S.A. 92 D3
Macnean, Lough: N. Irel./Repub. of Ireland 30 F11
Macomb: Ill., U.S.A. 88 F5
Macomer: Sardinia 38 L16
Macomia: Mozambique 77 F5
Macon: Ga., U.S.A. 91 K9
Macon: Mo., U.S.A. 88 E6
MÂCON: Saône-et-Loire, Fr. 37 K9
Macondo: Angola 77 B5
Macossa: Mozambique 77 D6
Macovane: Mozambique 77 E7
McPherson: Kans., U.S.A. 90 C6
Macquarie: riv., N.S.W., Australia 71 G8
McRae: Ga., U.S.A. 91 K9
Macroom: Cork, Repub. of Ireland 31 D16
Macugnaga: Italy 40 N10

Macusani: Peru 94 C6
Macuze: Mozambique 77 E6
Madaba: Jordan 56 O6
Madaba: Tanzania 77 E4
Madagascar: see Malagasy Republic.
Madagascar Basin: Indian Ocean 9 30S 50E
Madagascar Ridge: Indian Ocean 9 35S 40E
Madain Salih: Sau. Arab. 54 E9
Madama: Niger 78 G5
Madame I.: N.S., Canada 89 V3
Madang: Papua/New Guinea 66 J3
Madaoua: Niger 81 F2
Madawaska: riv., Ont., Can. 89 N3
Madaya: Burma 59 R10
Maddalena: i., Sardinia 38 L16
Madden Dam: village & lake, Panama 94 Ins.
Madderty: Tayside, Scot. 29 O7
Made: Netherlands 44 K4
Madeira: i. (Port.), Atlantic O. (cap. Funchal) 78 A3
Madeira: riv., Brazil 94 E5
Madeley: Salop, England 27 R14
Madeley: Staffs., England 27 R14
Madeline: i., Wis., U.S.A. 88 F2
Maden: Turkey 56 F2
Madera: Calif., U.S.A. 93 C5
Madera: Mexico 93 F7
Madhya Pradesh: State, India (cap. Bhopal) 58 O10
Madial: Sudan 76 D2
Madibogo: S. Africa 75 F3
Madill: Okla., U.S.A. 90 C8
Madimba: Zaire 81 H5
Madina: Iraq 57 K6
Madina: Iraq 57 K6
Madinat El: Egypt 54 D10
Madison: Fla., U.S.A. 91 K10
Madison: Ga., U.S.A. 91 K9
Madison: Ind., U.S.A. 88 J6
Madison: Maine, U.S.A. 89 R3
Madison: N.C., U.S.A. 89 M7
Madison: S. Dak., U.S.A. 92 H4
MADISON: Wis., U.S.A. 88 G4
Madisonville: Ky., U.S.A. 88 H7
Madisonville: Tex., U.S.A. 90 D10
Madiun: Java 65 E8
Madjori: Upper Volta 80 E2
Madona: Latvia, U.S.S.R. 47 U8
Madonie, Le: mtns., Sicily 38 O18
Madraka, Cape: Oman 55 J11
MADRAS: Tamil Nadu, India 58 O12
Madre, Laguna: lag., U.S.A./Mexico 90 C12
Madre de Dios: riv., Bolivia 94 D6
Madre de Dios I.: Chile 95 B14
MADRID: & Prov., Spain 35 E16
Madridejos: Spain 35 E17
Madron: Corn., England 25 K19
Madronal: Panama 94 Ins.
Madura: Tamil Nadu, India 58 N13
Madurai: i., Indonesia (cap. Pamekasan) 65 E8
Madytus: Greek city on NW. side of Dardanelles, probably about 5 miles SW of Sestos, Turkey 39 U16
Maeander: Greek name of river Menderes, Turkey 39 V18
MAEBASHI: Gumma, Japan 63 f2
Mae Hong Son: Thailand 64 B3
Mae la Luang: Thailand 64 B3
Maël-Carhaix: France 36 B7
Maelström: strait S. of Moskenesøy, noted for its whirlpool and dangerous current, Lofoten Is., Nor. 46 N3
Maenclochog: Dyfed, Wales 24 M16
Maengsan: N. Korea 63 X7
Mae Ramat: Thailand 64 B3
Mae Sariang: Thailand 64 B3
Maesteg: W. Glam., Wales 24 O16
Maestra: Italy 41 S10
Maevatanana: Malagasy Rep. 73 O13
Maewo (Aurora): i., New Hebrides 67 N5
Mafa: Nigeria 81 G2
Mafeking: C.P., S. Africa 75 F2
Mafeteng: & Dist., Lesotho 75 G4
Maffra: Vict., Australia 71 G11
Mafia I.: Tanzania 76 E4
Mafra: Brazil 96 F2
Mafra: Portugal 35 B17
Mafraq: Jordan 56 E5
Mafube: S. Africa 75 H5
Magadan: U.S.S.R. 49 R6
Magadi: Kenya 76 E3
Magadi, Lake: Kenya 76 E3
Maga'la: Saudi Arabia 54 G9
Magalakwena: riv., Trans., S. Africa 77 C7
Magaliesburg: Trans., S. Afr. 75 G2
Magalo: Ethiopia 76 F1
Maganga: Zaire 76 C2
Magangue: Colombia 94 C2
Magaria: Niger 81 F2
Magarinos: Argentina 96 C1
Magatain: Yemen P.D.R. 79 R17
Magazine Mt.: Ark., U.S.A. 90 E8
Magburaka: Sierra Leone 80 B3
Magdala: Ethiopia 79 M7
Magdala: E. Germany 45 R5
Magdala: Hellenistic city on W. coast of Lake Tiberias, probably about 4 miles NW. of Tiberias, Israel 55 b2
Magdalena: Argentina 96 D4
Magdalena: Bolivia 94 E6
Magdalena: N. Mex., U.S.A. 93 F6
Magdalena: i., Mexico 93 E8
Magdalena: riv., Mexico 93 E6
Magdalena, Llano de la: Mexico 93 E8
Magdalena: i. (Que), Canada 89 V2
MAGDEBURG: & Dist., E. Germany 45 R3
Magee I.: penin., Antrim, N. Ireland 30 K10
Magelang: Java 65 E8
Magellan, Str. of: Chile 95 C14
Magenta: Italy 40 O10
Magenta: N.S.W., Austl. 71 E9
Magerøy: i., Norway 46 U1
Magescq: France 37 D12
Maggiore, Lake: It./Switz. 40 O10
Maghaghah: riv., Egypt 54 D10
Maghera: Lon., N. Ireland 30 H10
Magherafelt: Lon., N. Irel. 30 H10
Maghery: Armagh, N. Irel. 30 H10
Maghnia: Algeria 35 F19
Maghull: Mers., England 27 Q12
Magilligan: Lon., N. Irel. 30 H9
Magnesia ad Maeandrum: Greek city north of southward bend of Menderes river E. of Söke, Turkey 39 U18
Magnesia ad Sipylum: Greek city south of river Gediz at Manisa, Turkey 39 U17
Magnetic I.: Queens., Austl. 70 G2
Magnetic Pole, North: 85 k3
Magnitogorsk: U.S.S.R. 50 j4
Magnolia: Ark., U.S.A. 90 E9

Magnolia: La., U.S.A. 90 Ins.
Magnolia: Miss., U.S.A. 90 F10
Magny: France 36 G6
Mago: Roman name of town at Mahón, Minorca 35 J17
Magog: Que., Canada 89 P3
Magon Bushmen: tribal area, Botswana 77 B7
Magor: Gwent, Wales 24 Q16
Magoye: Zambia 77 C6
Magpie: riv., Ont., Canada 88 J1
Magrath: Alta., Canada 92 E3
Magude: Mozam. 75 K2
Maguey, Cerro: Mexico 86 J13
Maguire's Bridge: Ferm., N. Ireland 30 G11
Magumeri: Nigeria 81 G2
Magwe: Burma 59 Q10
Magwe: State, Burma (cap. Yenangyaung) 59 Q11
Magyaróvár: Hungary 43 P13
Maha: Kweichow, China 62 T9
Mahabaleshwar: Maharashtra, India 58 M11
Maha Chai: Thailand 64 C4
Mahaddei Wen: Somalia 79 R19
Mahagi: Zaire 76 D2
Mahaicony: Guyana 87 e7
Mahail: Saudi Arabia 54 F11
Mahakam: riv., Borneo 65 F6
Mahakam Delta: Borneo 65 F7
Mahalapye: Botswana 75 G1
Mahalla el Kubra: Egypt 56 B6
Mahamba: Swaziland 75 J3
Mahanadi: riv., India 59 O10
Mahanje: Tanzania 77 E4
Mahanoro: Malagasy Rep. 73 O13
Maharashtra: State, India (cap. Bombay) 58 M11
Mahaxay: Laos 64 D3
Mahbubnagar: Andhra Pradesh, India 58 N11
Mahd Dhahab: gold mine, Saudi Arabia 54 F10
Mahdia: Tunisia 38 M19
Mahé: India 58 N12
Mahenge: Tanzania 77 E4
Mahesana: Gujarat, India 58 M10
Mahia Penin.: North I., N.Z. 70 Q14
Mahlabatini: Natal, S. Afr. 75 J4
Mahlberg: W. Germany 44 N7
Mahmudiya: Iraq 57 J5
Mahndorf: W. Germany 44 P2
Mahnomen: Minn., U.S.A. 92 H3
Mahoba: Uttar Pradesh, India 58 N9
Mahón: Minorca, Balearic Is. 35 J17
Mahone Bay: city, N.S., Can. 89 T3
Mahoonagh: Lim., Repub. of Ireland 31 D15
Mahoua: Chad 81 H2
Mahra: tribe, Yemen P.D.R. 55 H11
Mahsama, El: Egypt (Suez Canal Inset) 32 A11
Mahuta: Tanzania 77 E5
Mahuva: Gujarat, India 58 M10
Maiana: i., Gilbert Is. 67 O1
Maibang: Alor, Indonesia 65 G8
Maiche: France 40 M8
Maidan: Afghanistan 58 L8
Maidan: Iraq 57 J4
Maidan-i-Naftun: Iran 57 L6
Maiden Bradley: Wilts., Eng. 24 R17
Maidenhead: Berks., Eng. 25 U16
Maiden Newton: Dorset, England 24 Q18
Maidens: Strath., Scotland 29 M9
Maidens: rocks, N. Ireland 30 K10
Maidi: Yemen 54 F11
MAIDSTONE: Kent, England 25 X17
MAIDUGURI: Borno, Nigeria 81 G2
Maigue: riv., Lim., Repub. of Ireland 31 D14
Mailag: Mindanao, Phil. 64 H5
Mailani: Uttar Pradesh, India 58 O9
Mailly: France 36 K7
MAIMANA: Faryab, Afghanistan 55 K7
Mai Munene: Zaire 76 B4
Main: riv., Antrim, N. Irel. 30 J10
Main: riv., W. Germany 44 P6
Ma'in (Minaea): ancient kingdom in S. Arabia; cap. Qarnaw, between Najran and Jauf, Yemen 54 F11
Main Barrier Range, N.S.W., Australia 71 D8
Main-Danube Canal: W. Ger. 45 Q6
Mai Ndombe (Leopold II Lake): lake, Zaire 76 A3
Maine: Prov., France 34 F12
Maine: State, U.S.A. (cap. Augusta) 89 R3
Maine, Gulf of: U.S.A. 89 R4
Maine-et-Loire: Dept., Fr. (cap. Angers) 36 E8
Maine Soroa: Niger 81 G2
Maingkwan: Burma 59 R9
Main I.: Bermuda Is. 87 Ins.
Mainland: i., Orkney Is., Scotland 28 Ins.
Mainland: i., Shetland Is., Scotland 28 Ins.
Main Pass: La., U.S.A. 90 Ins.
Mainpuri: Uttar Pradesh, India 58 N9
Mainsriddle: Dumfries & Galloway, Scotland 29 O10
Maintenon: France 36 G7
Maintirano: Malagasy Rep. 73 N13
MAINZ: Rhineland-Palatinate, W. Germany 44 O6
Maio: i., Cape Verde Is. 78 Ins.
Maipo: volc., Chile 96 B3
Maipo: Argentina 96 D4
Maipures: Colombia 94 D2
Maira: riv., Italy 40 N11
Maisach: W. Germany 41 R7
Maiskhal: i., Bangladesh 59 Q10
Maison Carrée: Algeria 35 H18
Mait: & i., Somalia 79 R17
Maitencillo: Chile 96 A3
Maitland: N.S.W., Austl. 71 J9
Maitland: C.P., S. Africa 74 Ins.
Maitland: S. Australia 71 B9
Maitland, Lake: W. Austl. 68 C5
Maizuru: Japan 63 d3
Maja: i., Borneo 65 D7
Majdaha: & cape, Yemen P.D.R. 55 G12
Majene: Celebes 65 F7
Maji: Ethiopia 76 E1
Majidabad: Iran 57 L3
Majma'a: Saudi Arabia 54 G9
Majorca: Vict., Australia 71 E11
Majorca (Mallorca): i., (Sp.) Balearic Is. (cap. Palma) 35 H17
MAJUNGA: & Prov., Malagasy Rep. 73 O13
Maka: Senegal 80 B2
Makah: Rhodesia 77 D6
MAKALE: Tigre, Ethiopia 79 M7
Makalehi: i., Sangihe Is., Indonesia 65 H6
Makamik: see Macamic.

Makanchi—Marcus I. 163

Makanchi: Kazakh., U.S.S.R. 51 O5
Makari: Cameroun 81 G2
Makarikari Salt Pan: *see* Makgadikgadi Salt Pan
Makarska: Yugoslavia 38 P15
Makar'yev: U.S.S.R. 50 F3
MAKASAR: *see* UJUNG PANDANG
Makat: Kazakh., U.S.S.R. 50 H5
Makatéa: *i.*, Tuamotu Arch. 83 f3
Makedhonia: (Greece), *see* Macedonia.
Makemo: *i.*, Tuamotu Arch. 83 g3
MAKENI: Northern, Sierra Leone 80 B3
Makerere: Uganda 76 D2
Makeyevka: Ukraine 50 E5
Makgadikgadi Salt Pan: Botswana 77 C7
MAKHACHKALA: Daghestan, U.S.S.R. 50 G6
Makhai: Chinghai, China 62 Q7
Makharadze: Georgia, U.S.S.R. 57 H1
Makhmur: Iraq 57 H4
Makhowe: Natal, S. Africa 75 K3
Makhsar: Iran 57 L6
Maki: Japan 63 f2
Makim, Little I.: Gilbert Is. 67 O1
Makindu: Kenya 76 E3
Makin Is.: Gilbert Is. 67 O1
Mak Khaeng (Udon Thani): Thailand 64 C3
Makkinga: Netherlands 44 M3
Makkum: Netherlands 44 L2
Makó: Hungary 43 R13
MAKOKOU: Ogooué-Ivindo, Gabon 81 G4
Makokskraal: Trans., S. Afr. 75 G3
Makoli: Zambia 77 C6
Makoua: Congo 81 H4
Makounda: Cen. Afr. Rep. 81 H3
Maków: Poland 43 Q12
Makram: Saudi Arabia 54 E10
Makran: *geog. reg.*, Pak./Iran 55 K9
Maksimkin Yar: U.S.S.R. 51 P3
Maksotag: Iran 55 K9
Maksutlu: Turkey 39 U16
Maktar: Tunisia 38 L19
Maku: Iran 57 J2
Makumbako: Tanzania 77 D4
Makumbi: Zaire 76 B4
Makunguwira: Tanzania 77 E5
Makurazaki: Japan 63 Y8
MAKURDI: Benue, Nigeria 81 F3
Makushino: U.S.S.R. 51 L3
Ma Kut: Thailand 64 C4
Makuyuni: Tanzania 76 E3
Makwan: Yunnan, China 62 S10
Makwassie: Trans., S. Afr. 75 F3
Makwiro: Rhodesia 77 D6
Mal: Mauritania 78 B6
Malå: Sweden 66 Q4
Malabang: Mindanao, Phil. 64 G5
Malabar Coast: India 58 N12
Malabata, Point: *cape*, Tangier (Gib. *Inset*) 32 *Ins.*
MALABO: (Santa Isabel): Equatorial Guinea 81 F4
Malabu: Nigeria 81 G3
MALACCA: & *state*, Malaya, Malaysia 65 c12
Malacca, Str. of: Malaya/Sum. 65 c13
Malacky: Czechoslovakia 41 X7
Malad City: Idaho, U.S.A. 92 E4
Málaga: Colombia 94 C2
MÁLAGA: & *Prov.*, Spain 35 D18
Malagarasi: & *riv.*, Tanzania 76 D4
Malagas: S. Africa 74 D7
Malagasy Fracture Zone: Indian Ocean 9 45S 40E

Malagasy Republic 73 *Ins.*
Cap.: Tananarive
Area: 230,035 sq. miles (595,791 sq. km.)
Pop.: 6,750,000 (*1970 E*)

Malah: *well*, Saudi Arabia 54 F11
Malaha: Yemen 54 G11
Malahide: Dublin, Repub. of Ireland 30 J13
Malaita: *i.*, Solomon Is. 67 M3
Malak: Saudi Arabia 54 F10
MALAKAL: Upper Nile, Sudan 79 L8
Malakand: NW. Front. Prov., Pakistan 58 M8
Malakoff: Algeria 35 G18
Malakoff: Tex., U.S.A. 90 D9
Malakwal: Punjab, Pak. 58 M8
Malalbergo: Italy 41 R11
Malampaya Sound: Palawan, Philippines 64 F4
Malang: Java 65 E8
Malangwa: Nepal 59 P9
MALANJE: & *Prov.*, Angola 73 H11
Malans: Switzerland 40 P9
Malanville: Benin 81 E2
Mälar, Lake: Sweden 47 P7
Malagüé: Argentina 96 B4
Malartic: Que., Canada 89 M1
Malaspina: Argentina 95 D12
Malatayur: Borneo 65 E7
Malåträsk: Sweden 46 Q4
MALATYA: & *Prov.*, Turkey 56 F2
Malatya Mtns.: Turkey 56 F2
Malaucène: France 40 L11
Malaunay: France 36 G6
Malawali: *i.*, Sabah, Malaysia 64 F5

Malawi: *Republic* 77 D5
Cap.: Lilongwe
Area: 45,747 sq. miles (118,485 sq. km.)
Pop.: 4,666,000 (*1972 E*)

Malawi (Nyasa), Lake: East Africa 77 D5
Malaya: U.S.S.R. 49 R4
Malaya: *penin.*, Asia 65 c12
Malaya Anyuy: *riv.*, U.S.S.R. 49 s4
Malaya Vishera: U.S.S.R. 50 D3
Malaybalay: Mindanao, Phil. 64 H5
Malayer (Daulatabad): Iran 57 L4
Malay Reef: Australia 69 H3

Malaysia: *Federal Constitutional Monarchy* 65
Cap.: Kuala Lumpur
Area: 128,328 sq. miles (332,370 sq. km.)
Pop.: 10,674,000 (*1971 E*)

Malâzgirt: Turkey 57 H2
Malbaie, La (Murray Bay): Que., Canada 89 Q2
Malbon: Queens., Australia 69 G4
Malbork: Poland 43 Q9
Malbrán: Argentina 96 C2
Malcesine: Italy 41 Q10
Malchin: E. Germany 45 S2
Malchow: E. Germany 45 S2
Malcolm: W. Australia 68 C5
Malda: W. Bengal, India 59 P9
Maldegem: Belgium 44 J4
Malden: Mass., U.S.A. 89 Q4
Malden: Mo., U.S.A. 88 G7
Malden I.: S. Pacific Ocean 7 05S 155W

Maldives: *Republic* 52 K10
Cap.: Malé
Area: 115 sq. miles (298 sq. km.)
Pop.: 110,000 (*1971 E*)

Maldon: Essex, England 25 X16
Maldon: Vict., Australia 71 F11
Maldonado: Uruguay 96 E3
Male: Italy 41 Q9
MALÉ: Maldives Rep. 52 K11
Mâle, Lac du: Que., Can. 89 O1
Maléa, Cape: Greece 39 S18
Malegaon: Maharashtra, India 58 M10
Malé Karpaty: *mtns.*, Czech. 43 P12
Malekula: *i.*, New Hebrides 67 N5
Malela: Zaire 76 C3
Malelane: Trans., S. Africa 75 J2
Malembé: Congo 81 G5
Malème: Senegal 80 A2
Malenge: S. Africa 75 H5
Malente: W. Germany 45 Q1
Maleny: Queens., Austl. 70 K6
Maler Kotla: Punjab, India 58 N8
Malesherbes: France 36 H7
Malestroit: France 36 C8
Malgobek: U.S.S.R. 50 F6
Malha: *water hole*, Sudan 79 K6
Malham: N. Yorks., England 27 R11

Mali: *Republic* 78 C7
Cap.: Bamako
Area: 464,873 sq. miles (1,204,021 sq. km.)
Pop.: 5,257,000 (*1972 E*)

MALI: & *Reg.*, Guinea 80 B2
Mali: *riv.*, Burma 59 R9
Malicorne: France 36 E8
Malik: Celebes 65 G7
Malik Kandi: Iran 57 K3
Malili: Celebes 65 G7
Målilla: Sweden 47 O8
Malimba: Cameroun 81 F4
Malimba Mtns.: Zaire 76 C4
Malin: Don., Repub. of Irel. 30 G9
Malin: Ukraine 43 V11
Malinau: Borneo 65 F6
Malindi: Kenya 76 F3
Malinec: Czechoslovakia 43 Q12
Malines: *see* Mechelen.
Malingping: Java 65 D8
Malin Head: *cape*, Don., Repub. of Ireland 30 G9
Malinmore: Don., Repub. of Ireland 30 D10
Malinska: Yugoslavia 41 U10
Malinyi: Tanzania 77 E4
Malis, G. of: ancient name of gulf E. of Lamia and W. of N. Euboea, Greece 39 S17
Malita: Mindanao, Phil. 65 H5
Maliwun: Burma 59 R12
Malka Dube: Ethiopia 79 Q18
Malkapur: Maharashtra, India 58 N10
Malkara: Turkey 39 U16
Malkinia: Poland 43 S10
Malko Trnovo: Bulgaria 39 U16
Mallacoota: Vict., Austl. 71 H11
Mallaig: High., Scotland 28 K5
Mallam Moussa: *well*, Chad 81 G2
Mallaranny: Mayo, Repub. of Ireland 30 B12
Mallawi: Egypt 54 D9
Malles: Italy 40 Q9
Malling, West: Kent, Eng. 25 W17
Malloch, Cape: N.W.T., Canada 84 h2
Mallorca (Majorca): *i.* (Sp.) Balearic Is. (*cap.* Palma) 35 H17
Mallow: Cork, Repub. of Ireland 31 D15
Mallwyd: Gwynedd, Wales 27 O14
Malmberget: Sweden 46 R3
Malmédy: Belgium 44 M5
Malmesbury: & *Dist.*, C.P., S. Africa 74 C6
Malmesbury: Wilts., Eng. 24 R16
Malmesbury, Vale of: Wilts., England 24 R17
MALMÖ: Malmöhus, Sweden 47 N9
Malmöhus: *Co.*, Sweden (*cap.* Malmö) 47 N9
Malmyzh: U.S.S.R. 50 H3
Maloja Pass: Switzerland 40 P9
Malokaragiyevka: U.S.S.R. 51 N3
Malolos: Luzon, Phil. 64 G4
Malombe, Lake: Malawi 77 E5
Malone: N.Y., U.S.A. 89 O3
Malonga: Zaire 77 B5
Malorita: Byelorussia 43 T11
Malpas: Ches., England 27 Q13
Malpas: Gwent, Wales 24 Q16
Malpelo I.: Colombia 94 A3
Malpeque Bay: P.E.I., Can. 89 U2
Malplaquet: *site of battlefield*, France 36 J5
Målselv: Norway 46 Q2

Malta: *Republic* 32 *Ins.*
Cap.: Valletta
Area: 122 sq. miles (316 sq. km.)
Pop.: 319,000 (*1972 E*)

Malta: Mont., U.S.A. 92 F3
Maltahöhe: & *Dist.*, S.W. Afr. 74 B2
Maltby: S. Yorks., England 27 T13
Malton: N. Yorks., England 26 U11
Maluku: *see* Moluccas.
Malung: Sweden 47 N6
Maluso: Philippines 65 G5
Maluti Mtns: Lesotho 75 H4
Malvaglia: Switzerland 40 O9
Malvan: Maharashtra, India 58 M11
Malvern: Ark., U.S.A. 90 E8
Malvern, Great: Hereford & Worcester, England 24 R15
Malvern, West: Hereford & Worcester, England 24 R15
Malvern Hills: Hereford & Worcester, England 24 R15
Malvernia: Mozambique 77 D7
Malvern Link: Hereford & Worcester, England 24 R15
Malvern Wells: Hereford & Worcester, England 24 R15
Mal'viaymen: Karelian A.S.S. Rep., U.S.S.R. 46 W4
Mama: U.S.S.R. 49 N6
Mamaku: North I., N.Z. 70 Q14
Maman: Sudan 54 E11
Mamanguape: Brazil 94 K5
Mamasa: Celebes 65 F7
Mamba: Japan 63 f2
Mambasa: Zaire 76 C2
Mamberamo: *riv.*, New Guinea 61 M12
Mambéré: *riv.*, Central African Rep. 81 H4
Mambili: *riv.*, Congo 81 H4
Mambiliama Falls: Zaire 75 C5
Mambirima: Zaire 77 C5
Mamble: Hereford & Worcester, England 24 R15
Mambrui: Kenya 76 F3
Mamehak: Borneo 65 F6
Mamers: France 36 F7
Mamfe: Cameroun 81 F3
Mamihara: Japan 63 b4
Mammoth Cave Nat. Park: Ky., U.S.A. 88 J7
Mamontovo: U.S.S.R. 51 O4
Mamore: *riv.*, Bolivia 94 E7
Mamore Forest: High., Scot. 29 L6
MAMOU: & *Reg.*, Guinea 80 B2
Mamou: La., U.S.A. 90 E10
Mampong: Ghana 80 D3
Mamre: C.P., S. Africa 74 C6
Mamre: city of ancient *Israel* near Halhul, Jordan 55 b3
Mamuju: Celebes 65 F7
Mamura: Saudi Arabia 55 H11
MAN: Ouest, Ivory Coast 80 C3
Man, Isle of: U.K. (*cap.* Douglas) 26 M11
Mana: Fr. Guiana 94 G2
Mana: Sumatra 65 C7
Mana: *riv.*, Ethiopia 76 F2
Mana: *riv.*, U.S.S.R. 51 Q3
Manaar: & *gulf*, Sri Lanka 58 N13
Manacapurú: Brazil 94 E4
Manaccan: Corn., England 25 L19
Manacor: Maj., Balearic Is. 35 H17
MANADO: & *Prov.*, Celebes 65 G6
MANAGUA: Nicaragua 86 L15
Manah: Oman 55 J10
Manahil: *tribal area*, Saudi Arabia 55 H11
Manaia: North I., N.Z. 70 P14
Manakara: Malagasy Rep. 73 O14
Manakha: Yemen 54 F11
Manakwari: W. Irian, Indonesia 61 L12
Manam: *i.*, New Guinea 66 J2
MANAMA: Bahrain I. 55 H9
Mananara: Malagasy Rep. 73 O13
Mananjary: Malagasy Rep. 73 O14
Manankoro: Mali 80 C2
Manantenina: Malagasy Rep. 73 O14
Mana Pass: Tibet, China 58 N8
Manaos: *see* Manaus.
Manapouri: South I., N.Z. 71 L17
Manara: N.S.W., Australia 71 E9
Manas: *riv.*, India/Bhutan 59 Q9
Manasa: Madhya Pradesh, India 58 N10
Manasarowar, Lake: Tibet, China 58 O8
Manasir: *tribal area*, Saudi Arabia 55 H10
Manass: & *riv.*, Sinkiang, China 51 P6
Manassas: Va., U.S.A. 89 N6
Manasseh: Israelite tribe which inhabited hills N. of Nablus and those of Ajlun, Jordan 55 o2
Manatee: Fla., U.S.A. 91 K12
Manaton: Devon, England 24 O18
Manatuto: Port. Timor 65 H8
MANAUS (Manaos): Amazonas, Brazil 94 E4
Manavgat: Turkey 56 B3
Manay: Mindanao, Phil. 64 H5
Manâyif Oasis, El: Egypt (Suez Canal *Inset*) 32 *Ins.*
Mancelona: Mich., U.S.A. 88 J3
Mancha Real: Spain 35 E18
Manche: *Dept.*, France (*cap.* St. Lô) 36 D6
Manchester: Conn., U.S.A. 89 P5
Manchester: Ga., U.S.A. 91 J9
MANCHESTER: Gt. Man., Eng. 27 R13
Manchester: Iowa, U.S.A. 88 F4
Manchester: Ky., U.S.A. 88 K7
Manchester: N.H., U.S.A. 89 Q4
Manchester: Tenn., U.S.A. 91 H8
Manchichi: Malawi 77 D5
Manchioneal: Jamaica 86 *Ins.*
Manchouli: Inner Mongolia, China 62 V5
Manchuria: *geog. reg.*, China 63 X5
Manciano: Italy 38 M15
Máncora: Peru 94 A4
Mancos: Colo., U.S.A. 93 F5
Mand: *riv.*, Iran 55 H9
Manda: Sumatra 65 D8
Manda: Tanzania 77 D5
Mandaguari: Brazil 96 E1
Mandal: Norway 47 K7
MANDALAY: & *State.*, Burma 59 R10
Mandali: Iraq 57 J5
Mandalya Gulf: Turkey 39 U18
Mandaoua Gadaoule: Niger 81 G2
Mandara Mtns.: Nigeria 81 G2
Mandasor: Madhya Pradesh, India 58 N10
Mandeka: S.W. Africa 77 B6
Mandelieu: France 40 M12
Mandello: Italy 40 O10
Mandera: Kenya 76 F2
Mandeville: Jamaica 86 *Ins.*
Mandi: Himachal Pradesh, India 58 N8
Mandi Angin: *mtn.*, Malaya, Malaysia 65 c11
Mandie: Mozambique 77 D6
Mandimba: Mozambique 77 E5
Mandjafa: Chad 81 H2
Mandla: Madhya Pradesh, India 58 O10
Mandoúdhion: Euboea, Grc. 39 S17
Mandritsara: Malagasy Rep. 73 O13
Mandurah: W. Australia 68 B6
Mandurama: N.S.W., Austl. 71 H9
Manduria: Italy 38 P16
Mandvi: Gujarat, India 58 L10
Mané: Upper Volta 80 D2
Manea: Cambs., England 25 W15
Mâneciu Ungureni: Rom. 39 T14
Manfalut: Egypt 54 D9
Manfred: N.S.W., Australia 71 E9
Manfredonia: Italy 38 O16
Manfredonia, G. of: Italy 38 P16
Manga: *geog. reg.*, Niger/Chad 81 G2
Mangache: Malawi 77 E5
Mangai: Zaire 76 A3
Mangaia: *i.*, Cook Is. 70 *Ins.*
Mangalia: Romania 39 V15
Mangallala: *riv.*, Queens., Australia 70 G6
Mangalore: Karnataka, India 58 M12
Mangalore: Queens., Austl. 70 G6
Manganitis: Ikaria, Greece 39 U18
Mangaweka: North I., N.Z. 70 P14
Mangawhai: North I., N.Z. 70 P13
Mange: Sierra Leone 80 B3
Mangenda: Zambia 77 C5
Mangerton Mtn.: Kerry, Repub. of Ireland 31 C16
Manggar: Billiton, Indon. 65 D7
Mangit: Uzbek., U.S.S.R. 51 K6
Mangkalihat, Cape: Borneo 65 F6
Manglutan: Andaman Is. 59 Q12
Mangole: *i.*, Sula Is., Indon. 65 H7
Mangonui: North I., N.Z. 70 O12
Mangoupa: Cen. Afr. Rep. 76 B1
Mangrol: Gujarat, India 58 M10
Mangrove Cay: *is.* Bahamas 91 N13
Mangsang: Sumatra 65 C7
Mangubu: Zaire 76 C3
Mangueigne: Chad 79 J7
Mangum: Okla., U.S.A. 90 B8
Mangyshlak: *penin.*, Kazakh., U.S.S.R. 50 H6
Manhao: Yunnan, China 62 S10
Manhattan: Kans., U.S.A. 93 H5
Manhattan: Nev., U.S.A. 93 D5
Manhica: Inhambane, Mozambique 77 E7
Manhica: Maputo, Mozam. 75 K2
Maniago: Italy 41 S9
Maniamba: Mozambique 77 D5
Manica: Mozambique 77 D6
Manica and Sofala: *Dist.*, Mozambique (*cap.* Beira) 77 D6
Manicaland: *Prov.*, Rhodesia (*cap.* Umtali) 77 D6
Manicoré: Brazil 94 E5
Manifa: Saudi Arabia 55 G9
Manifold, Cape: Queens., Australia 70 J4
Manihi: *i.*, Tuamotu Arch. 83 f2
Manila: Luzon, Phil. 64 G4
Manildra: N.S.W., Austl. 71 H9
Manilla: N.S.W., Australia 71 J8
Maninian: Ivory Coast 80 C2
Manipur: *Union Territ.* & *riv.*, India (*cap.* Imphal) 59 Q10
MANISA: & *Prov.*, Turkey 39 U17
Manistee: Mich., U.S.A. 88 H3
Manistee: *riv.*, Mich., U.S.A. 88 J3
Manistique: Mich., U.S.A. 88 H3
Manistique Lake: Mich., U.S.A. 88 J2
Manitoba: *Prov.*, Canada (*cap.* Winnipeg) 84 k6
Manitoba, Lake: Man., Can. 92 H2
Manitor Range: Nev., U.S.A. 93 D5
Manitou: *i.*, Mich., U.S.A. 88 H3
Manitou Is.: Mich., U.S.A. 88 H3
Manitou Lakes: Ont., Can. 92 J3
Manitoulin: *i.*, Ont., Canada 88 K3
Manitou Springs: Colo., U.S.A. 93 G5
Manitouwadge: Ont., Can. 88 J1
Manitowoc: Wis., U.S.A. 88 H3
Maniwaki: Que., Canada 89 O2
Manizales: Colombia 94 B2
Manja: Malagasy Rep. 73 N14
Manjacase: Mozambique 77 D7
Manjil: Iran 57 L3
Manjimup: W. Australia 68 B6
Manjra: *riv.*, Maharashtra, India 58 N11
Mank: Austria 41 V7
Mankaiana: Swaziland 75 J3
Mankato: Minn., U.S.A. 88 E3
Mankhali: *well*, Sau. Arab. 54 G11
Mankono: Ivory Coast 80 C3
Mankoya: Zambia 77 B5
Mankulam: Sri Lanka 58 O13
Manlleu: Spain 35 H15
Manly: Iowa, U.S.A. 88 E4
Manly: N.S.W., Australia 71 J9
Manma: Nepal 58 O9
Manmad: Maharashtra, India 58 M10
Mannahill: S. Australia 71 D9
Mannargudi: Tamil Nadu, India 58 N12
Mannheim: W. Germany 44 O6
Manning: Hainan, China 62 U11
Manning: S.C., U.S.A. 91 L9
Manning, Cape: N.W.T., Canada 84 g2
Mannington: W. Va., U.S.A. 88 L6
Manningtree: Essex, Eng. 25 Y16
Mannum: S. Australia 71 C10
Mano: Sierra Leone 80 B3
Mano: *riv.*, Liberia 80 B3
Manokwari: W. Irian, Indonesia 61 L12
Manombo: Malagasy Rep. 73 N14
Manono: Zaire 76 C4
Manorbier: Dyfed, Wales 24 M16
Manorcunningham: Don., Repub. of Ireland 30 F10
Manor Hamilton: Leit., Repub. of Ireland 30 E11
Manosque: France 40 L12
Manresa: Spain 35 G16
MANSA: Luapula, Zambia 77 C5
Mansel I.: Canada 85 l5
Manselkä: *ridge*, Finland 46 V3
Mansell Lacy: Hereford & Worcester, England 24 Q15
Mansfeld: E. Germany 45 R4
Mansfield: La., U.S.A. 90 E9
Mansfield: Mo., U.S.A. 90 E7
Mansfield: Notts., England 27 T13
Mansfield: Ohio, U.S.A. 88 K5
Mansfield: Pa., U.S.A. 89 N5
Mansfield: Vict., Australia 71 G11
Mansfield Woodhouse: Notts., England 27 T13
Mansi: Burma 59 R10
Mansilla de las Mulas: Sp. 35 D15
Mansle: France 37 F10
Mansoura: Algeria 35 J18
Mansura, El: Egypt 56 B6
Manta: Ecuador 94 A4
Mantare: Tanzania 76 D3
Mantas: Niger 81 E1
Mantekamu Hu: *lake*, Tibet, China 59 P8
Manteo: N.C., U.S.A. 91 O8
Mantes-Gassicourt: France 36 G7
Manthelan: France 36 F8
Manti: Utah, U.S.A. 93 E5
Mantilla: Argentina 96 D2
Mantiqueira, Serra da: *mtn.*, Brazil 96 G1
Manton: Mich., U.S.A. 88 J3
Manton: Leics., England 27 U14
Mantova (Mantua): Italy 41 Q10
Mantsinsari: *i.*, L. Ladoga, U.S.S.R. 47 W6
Mänttä: Finland 47 T5
Mantua (Mantova): Italy 41 Q10
Mantuan Downs: Queens., Australia 70 G5
Manturovo: U.S.S.R. 50 F3
Mäntyharju: Finland 47 U6
Mäntyluoto: Finland 47 R6
Manu: Peru 94 C6
Manu: *i.*, Society Is. 83 e3
Manua: *i.*, Samoa Is. 70 *Ins.*
Manuan, Lac: Que., Can. 89 O2
Manuden: Essex, England 25 W16
Manuel Benavides: Mexico 93 G7
Manuhangi: *i.*, Tuamotu Arch. 83 g3
Manui: *i.*, Celebes 65 G7
Manulla: & *riv.*, Mayo, Repub. of Ireland 30 C12
Manus: *i.*, Admiralty Is. 66 J2
Manwakh: *well*, Saudi Arabia 55 G11
Many: La., U.S.A. 90 E10
Manyang: Sudan 76 C1
Manyara, Lake: Tanzania 76 E3
Manyas: Turkey 39 U16
Manyberries: Alta., Canada 92 E3
Manyin: Yunnan, China 62 R10
Manyoni: Tanzania 76 D4
Many Peaks: *town*, Queens., Australia 70 J5
Manzai: NW. Front. Prov., Pakistan 58 M8
Manzala, El: Egypt (Suez Canal *Inset*) 32 *Ins.*
Manzala, Lake: Egypt (Suez Canal *Inset*) 32 *Ins.*
Manzanares: Spain 35 E17
Manzanillo: Cuba 87 M13
Manzanillo: Mexico 86 j14
Manzanillo Point: *cape*, Panama 94 B2
Manzano Peak: N. Mex., U.S.A. 93 F6
Manzat: France 37 H10
Manzini: Swaziland 75 J3
Manzinkert: Byzantine city and battlefield between Euphrates and Lake Van, Turkey 57 H2
MAO: Kanem, Chad 81 H2
Maomu (Tingsin): Kansu, China 62 R6
Mapai: Mozambique 75 J1
Mapanza: Zambia 77 C6
Maphumulo: & *Dist.*, Natal, S. Africa 75 J4
Mapia (St. David) Is.: W. Irian, Indonesia 61 L11
Mapien: Szechwan, China 62 S9
Mapimi: Mexico 93 G7
Mapimi, Bolsón de: Mexico 93 G7
Mapinhane: Mozambique 77 D7
Mapiri: Bolivia 94 D7
Maple Creek: *town*, Sask., Canada 92 F3
Mapuera: *riv.*, Brazil 94 F4
Mapulanguene: Moz. 75 K2
Mapumulo: & *Dist.*, Natal, S. Africa 75 J4
MAPUTO: & *Dist.*, Mozambique 75 K2
Maputo Elephant Reserve: Mozambique 75 K3
Maqainama: *wells*, Saudi Arabia 55 G10
Maqaishat: *i.*, Persian Gulf 55 H10
Ma'qil: Iraq 57 K6
Maqna: Saudi Arabia 54 D9
Maquelo do Zombo: Angola 81 H6
Maquinchao: Argentina 95 D12
Maquoketa: Iowa, U.S.A. 88 F4
Maqwa: *oil field*, Kuwait 57 L7
Mar: *dist.*, Gram., Scotland 28 Q5
Mar, Serra Do: *mtns.*, Braz. 96 F2
Mara: Arunachal Pradesh, India 59 Q9
Mara: *Reg.*, Tanzania (*cap.* Musoma) 76 D3
Mara: Trans., S. Africa 75 H1
Mara: *riv.*, Tanzania 76 D3
Marabá: Brazil 94 H5
Maraba: Yemen 54 F12
Maracaibo: Venezuela 94 C1
Maracaibo, Lake: Ven. 94 C2
Maracá I.: Brazil 94 G3
Maracassumé: Brazil 94 H4
Maracay: Venezuela 94 D1
Marada: Libya 33 F6
MARADI: *Dept.,& riv.*, Niger 81 F2
Maragheh: Iran 57 K3
Marah: Saudi Arabia 54 G9
Marahadiassa: Ivory Coast 80 C3
Maraisburg: Trans., S. Afr. 74 *Mins.*
Maraisburg: *Dist.*, S. Africa 75 F5
Marajó I. of: Brazil 94 H4
Marakei: *i.*, Gilbert Is. 67 O1
Maralal: Kenya 76 E2
Marali: Cen. Afr. Rep. 76 A1
Maram: Manipur, India 59 Q9
MARAMBA (Livingstone): Southern, Zambia 77 C6
Maran: Malaya, Malaysia 65 c12
Marand: Iran 57 J2
Marandellas: Rhodesia 77 D6
Maranello: Italy 41 Q11
Marang: Sumatra 65 C8
Maranguape: Brazil 94 K4
Maranhão: *State*, Brazil (*cap.* São Luís) 94 J4
Maranoa: *riv.*, Australia 70 H6
Marañon: *riv.*, Peru 94 B4
Marans: France 37 E9
Marapanim: Brazil 94 H4
MARAS: & *Prov.*, Turkey 56 E3
Maraş: *mtns.*, Turkey 56 E3
Mărășești: Romania 39 U14
Marathon: Fla., U.S.A. 91 L13
Marathon: Greece 39 S17
Marathon: Ont., Canada 88 H1
Maratua: *i.*, Borneo 65 F6
Maravehtepe: Iran 55 J7
Marayes: Argentina 96 B3
Marazion: Corn., England 25 L19
Marbat: Oman 55 H11
Marbella: Spain 35 D18
Marble Bar: W. Australia 68 B4
Marble Hall: Trans., S. Afr. 75 H2
Marble Plot: S.W. Africa 74 A2
Marburg: Queens., Austl. 70 K6
Marburg: W. Germany 44 O5
Marceline: Mo., U.S.A. 88 E6
Marcelino: Brazil 94 D3
Marcelino (Santa Fé): Brazil 94 D4
Marcelino Ramos: Brazil 96 E2
Marcelona: Mich., U.S.A. 88 J3
Marcenat: France 37 H10
March: I. of Ely, Cambs., England 25 W14
Marchand: Morocco 80 K8
Marche: Belgium 44 L5
Marche: *Prov.*, France 34 G13
Marche: *geog. reg.*, France 37 G9
Marchegg: Austria 41 W7
Marcheprime: France 37 E11
Marches, The: *Reg.*, Italy (*cap.* Ancona) 38 N15
Marchienne: Belgium 44 K5
Marchiennes: France 36 J5
Marchington: Staffs., Eng. 27 S14
Marchwiel: Clwyd, Wales 27 Q13
Marchwood: Hants., Eng. 25 T18
Marcigny: France 37 K9
Marcillac: France 37 H11
Marcillat: France 37 H9
Marcilly-le-Hayer: France 36 J7
Marck: France 36 G5
Marckolsheim: France 40 N7
Marcomanni: ancient German tribe which in Imperial times lived in Bohemia, Czechoslovakia 42 O12
Marcos Juárez: Argentina 96 C3
Marcus Baker, Mt.: Alaska, U.S.A. 84 E5
Marcus I.: N. Pacific Ocean 7 20N 155E

For Abbreviations see list on p.113. Italic type, e.g. *Ephesus*, refers to historical names not on maps. Capital letters, e.g. MADRID, show capitals of countries; small capital letters, e.g. CADIZ, show capitals of provinces, etc. General notes p.116.

164 Marcus Necker Rise—Mazar-i-Sharif

Marcus Necker Rise: N. Pacific Ocean **7** 15N 165E
Marcy, Mount: N.Y., U.S.A. **89** P3
Mardakert: Azerbaydzhan, U.S.S.R. **57** K1
Mardan: NW. Front. Prov., Pakistan **58** M8
Mar del Plata: Argentina **96** D4
Marden: Kent, England **25** W17
Mardie: W. Australia **68** B4
MARDIN: *& Prov.*, Turkey **57** G3
Maré: *i.*, Loyalty Is. **67** N6
Mareb: *riv.*, Ethiopia **54** E12
Marechal Deodoro: Brazil **94** K5
Maree, Loch: High., Scot. **28** L4
Mareeba: Queens., Austl. **69** H3
Mareetsani: C.P., S. Africa **75** F3
Mareham le Fen: Lincs., England **27** V13
Marek: Bulgaria **39** S15
Marek: Celebes **61** J12
Maréna: Mali **80** C2
Marenberg (Radlje ob Dravi): Yugoslavia **41** V9
Marengo: Iowa, U.S.A. **88** E5
Marengo: battlefield about 5 miles ESE. of Alessandria, Italy **40** O11
Marennes: France **37** D10
Maresfield: E. Sussex, Eng. **25** W17
Mareuil: Dordogne, France **37** F10
Mareuil: Oise, France **36** J6
Mareuil: Vendée, France **37** D9
Marfa: Tex., U.S.A. **93** G6
Mar Forest: Gram., Scotland **28** O5
Margable: Ethiopia **79** Q17
Margam: W. Glam., Wales **24** O16
Margão: Goa, India **58** M11
Margaree Harbour : *city*, Cape Breton I., Canada **89** V2
Margaret River: *town*, W. Australia **68** D3
Margaret Bay: *town*, B.C., Canada **92** B2
Margarita I.: Venezuela **94** E1
Margaritovo: U.S.S.R. **63** Y6
Margate: Kent, England **25** Y17
Margate: Natal, S. Africa **75** J5
Margaux: France **37** E10
Margeride, Monts de la: *mtns.*, France **37** J11
Margherita: *see* Giamame.
Marghita: Romania **43** S13
Margidunum: Roman fort at Castle Hill about 1 mile NNW. of Bingham, Notts., England **27** U14
Margone: Italy **40** N10
Marham: Norf., England **25** X14
Marhamchurch: Corn., Eng. **24** M18
Marhoum: Algeria **80** L8
Mari: Sumerian and Semitic city at *Tell el-Hariri* on Euphrates near mouth of Khabur, Syria **57** G4
Mariana Is.: N. Pacific Ocean [*cap.* (with other Pacific Ocean Trust Terr.) Saipan] **8** 15N 145E
Mariana Ridge: N. Pacific Ocean **7** 15N 145E
Mariana Trench: N. Pacific Ocean **7** 15N 145E
Mari A.S.S. Repub.: U.S.S.R., (*cap.* Yoshkar-Ola) **50** G3
María Elena: Chile **96** B1
Maria Is.: Austral Is. **83** e4
Marianao: Cuba **87** e13
Marian Downs: Queens., Australia **69** F4
Marianna: Ark., U.S.A. **90** F8
Marianna: Fla., U.S.A. **91** J10
Mariánské Lázně (Marienbad): Czechoslovakia **45** S6
Marias: *riv.*, Mont., U.S.A. **92** E3
Maria Van Diemen: *cape*, North I., New Zealand **70** O12
Mariazell: Austria **41** V8
Marib: Yemen **54** G11
Maribor: Yugoslavia **41** V9
Marico: *Dist.*, Trans., S. Afr. **75** G2
Marico: *riv.*, S. Africa **75** G2
Maricourt (Wakenham): Newfoundland, Canada **85** m5
Maridi: Sudan **76** C2
Maridi: *riv.*, Sudan **76** C1
Marie Galante: *i.*, (Fr.), Leeward Is. **87** c3
MARIEHAMN: Åland Is., Fin. **47** R6
Mariembourg: Belgium **44** K5
Marienbad (Mariánské Lázně): Czechoslovakia **45** S6
Marienberg: E. Germany **45** T5
Mariental: S.W. Africa **74** B2
MARIESTAD: Skaraborg, Sweden **47** N7
Marietta: Ga., U.S.A. **91** J9
Marietta: Ohio, U.S.A. **88** L6
Marietta: Okla., U.S.A. **90** C9
Marigny: France **36** D6
Mariinsk: U.S.S.R. **51** P3
Marikana: Trans., S. Africa **75** G2
Marilia: Brazil **95** H8
Marimba: Angola **73** H11
Marina di Ravenna: Italy **41** S11
Mar'ina Gorka: Byelorussia **43** V10
Marinduque: *i.*, Philippines **64** G4
Marine City: Mich., U.S.A. **88** K4
Marines: France **36** G6
Marinette: Wis., U.S.A. **88** H3
Maringa: Brazil **96** E1
Maringue: Mozambique **77** D6
Maringues: France **37** J10
Marini: Argentina **96** C3
Marion: Ala., U.S.A. **91** H9
Marion: Ill., U.S.A. **88** G7
Marion: Ind., U.S.A. **88** J5
Marion: Iowa, U.S.A. **88** F4
Marion: Kans., U.S.A. **90** C6
Marion: Ky., U.S.A. **88** G7
Marion: Ohio, U.S.A. **88** K5
Marion: S.C., U.S.A. **91** M8
Marion: Va., U.S.A. **88** L7
Marion: Wis., U.S.A. **88** G3
Marion Lake: S.C., U.S.A. **91** L9
Marion Reef: Coral Sea **70** K2
Mariposas: Chile **96** A4
Marisa: Celebes **65** G6
Marismas, Las: *marsh*, Spain **35** C18
Marissa: Ill., U.S.A. **88** G6
Marisus: Roman name of river Mures, Romania and E. Hungary **39** R13
Maritime Alps: France **40** M11
Maritsa: Bulgaria **39** T15
Maritsa: *riv.*, Bulg./Grc./Turkey **39** U16
Mariveg: Outer Hebr., Scot. **28** J3
Marjan: Afghanistan **58** L8
Marjayun: Lebanon **56** D5
Mark: Som., England **24** Q17
Marka-Kol': *lake*, Kazakh., U.S.S.R. **51** P5
Markala: Mali **80** C2
Markaryd: Sweden **47** N8
Markdale: Ont., Canada **88** L3
Markdorf: W. Germany **40** P8
Marked Tree: *city*, Ark., U.S.A. **90** F8
Market Bosworth: Leics., England **27** T14
Market Deeping: Lincs., England **25** V14
Market Drayton: Salop, England **27** R14
Market Harborough: Leics., England **25** U15
Markethill: Armagh, N. Irel. **30** H11
Market Lavington: Wilts., England **24** S17
Market Rasen: Lincs., Eng. **27** V13
Market Weighton: Humberside, England **27** U12
Markha: *& riv.*, U.S.S.R. **49** n5
Markham Mt.: Antarctica **9** 85S 160E
Markinch: Fife, Scotland **29** P7
Markovo: U.S.S.R. **49** T5
Markranstädt: E. Germany **45** S4
Marks: Miss., U.S.A. **90** F8
Marks Tey: Essex, England **25** X16
Marksville: La., U.S.A. **90** E10
Marktbreit: W. Germany **45** Q6
Markt Oberdorf: W. Germany **40** Q8
Marktredwitz: W. Germany **45** S6
Markt Schwaben: W. Ger. **41** R7
Markyate: Herts., England **25** V16
Marlborough: Queens., Australia **70** H4
Marlborough: Wilts., Eng. **25** S17
Marlborough: *Dist.*, South I., N.Z. (*cap.* Blenheim) **70** O15
Marlborough Downs: *hills*, Wilts., England **25** S17
Marle: France **36** J6
Marles: France **36** H5
Marlin: Tex., U.S.A. **90** C10
Marlinton: W. Va., U.S.A. **88** L6
Marlo: Vict., Australia **71** H11
Marloes: Dyfed, Wales **24** L16
Marlow: Bucks., England **25** U16
Marlow: E. Germany **45** S1
Marlow: Okla., U.S.A. **90** C8
Marls, The: *is.*, Bahamas **91** N12
Marmagão: Goa, India **58** M11
Marmande: France **37** F11
Marmara: *i.*, Turkey **39** U16
Marmara, Sea of: Turkey **39** V16
Marmaraereglisi: Turkey **39** U16
Marmaris: Turkey **39** V18
Marmath: N. Dak., U.S.A. **92** G3
Marmette, Lac: Que., Can. **89** O1
Marmion Lake: Ont., Can. **88** F1
Marmit: *riv.*, Turkey **57** H2
Marmolada, Monte: *mtn.*, Italy **41** R9
Marmora: Ont., Canada **89** N3
Marnay: France **40** L8
Marne: W. Germany **44** P2
Marne: *Dept. & riv.*, France (*cap.* Châlons-sur-Marne) **36** K7
Marnitz: E. Germany **45** R2
Marnoo: Vict., Australia **71** E12
Maroa: Venezuela **94** D3
Maroantsetra: Malagasy Rep. **73** O13
Marokau: *i.*, Tuamotu Arch. **83** g3
Maroma, La: Argentina **96** B4
Maromandia: Malagasy Rep. **73** O12
Maromme: France **36** G6
Maroni (Marowijne): *riv.*, Fr. Guiana/Surinam **94** G3
Marónia: Greece **39** T16
Maronne: *riv.*, France **37** H10
Maroona: Vict., Australia **71** E11
Maros: Celebes **65** F8
Maroua: Cameroun **81** G2
Marovoay: Malagasy Rep. **73** O13
Marowijne (Maroni): *riv.*, Surinam/Fr. Guiana **94** G3
Marple: Gt. Man., England **27** R13
Marquard: O.F.S., S. Africa **75** G4
Marquesas Is.: (Fr.) Pac. O. **83** h1
Marquesas Keys: *is.*, Fla., U.S.A. **91** K13
Marquette: Mich., U.S.A. **88** H2
Marquise: France **36** G5
Marradi: Italy **41** R11
MARRAKESH: *& Prov.*, Morocco **80** K8
Marra Mts.: Sudan **79** J7
Marrawah: Tas., Australia **68** G8
Marree: S. Australia **69** F5
Marrick: N. Yorks., England **26** S11
Marromeu: Mozambique **77** E6
Marroqui Point: *Cape*, Spain (Gib. *Inset*) **32** *Ins.*
Marrupa: Mozambique **77** E5
Marsa Ben Mehidi: Algeria **35** E19
Marsa, La: Tunisia **38** M18
Marsabit: Kenya **76** E2
Marsabit National Reserve: Kenya **76** E2
Marsac: France **37** J10
Marsala: O.F.S., S. Africa **75** H3
Marsala: Sicily **38** N18
Marsberg: W. Germany **44** O4
Marsden: N.S.W., Australia **71** G9
Marsden: W. Yorks., England **27** S12
MARSEILLE (Marseilles): Bouches-du-Rhône, Fr. **37** L12
Marseille-en-Beauvaisis: Fr. **36** G6
MARSEILLES (Marseille): Bouches-du-Rhône, Fr. **37** L12
Marseilles: Ill., U.S.A. **88** G5
Marsh: Vict., Australia **71** F11
Marsh: *i.*, La., U.S.A. **90** F11
Marsh, The: Lincs., England **25** W14
Marshall: Alaska, U.S.A. **84** c5
Marshall: Ark., U.S.A. **90** E8
Marshall: Ill., U.S.A. **88** H6
Marshall: Liberia **80** B3
Marshall: Minn., U.S.A. **92** H4
Marshall: Mo., U.S.A. **88** E6
Marshall: N.C., U.S.A. **91** K8
Marshall: Tex., U.S.A. **90** D9
Marshall Bennett Is.: New Guinea **69** J1
Marshall Is.: N. Pacific Ocean [*cap.* (*with other Pacific O. Trust Terr.*) Saipan] **7** 05 167E
Marshalltown: Iowa, U.S.A. **88** E4
Marsh Baldon: Oxon., Eng. **25** T16
Marsh Chapel: Lincs., Eng. **27** W13
Marshfield: Avon, England **24** R17
Marshfield: Mo., U.S.A. **88** E7
Marshfield: Wis., U.S.A. **88** F3
Marsh Gibbon: Bucks., Eng. **25** T16
Marsh Harbour: Bahamas **91** N12
Mars Hill: Maine, U.S.A. **89** S2
Marsi: ancient tribe of central Italy in mtns. due E. of Rome, Italy **38** N16
Marske: Cleve., England **26** T10
Mars-la-Tour: France **36** L6
Marson: France **36** K7
Marston: Ches., England **27** Q13
Marston Magna: Som., Eng. **24** Q18
Marston Moor: battlefield about 1 mile NE. of Tockwith, N. Yorks., England **27** T12
Marstrand: Sweden **47** M8
Mart: Tex., U.S.A. **90** C10
Martaban: *& gulf*, Burma **59** R11
Martapura: Borneo **65** E7
Martapura: Sumatra **65** C7
Marte: Nigeria **81** G2
Martel: France **37** G11
Martelange: Belgium **36** L6
Martfeld: W. Germany **44** P3
Martham: Norf., England **25** Z14
Martha's Vineyard: *i.*, Mass., U.S.A. **89** Q5
Martigné-Briand: France **36** E8
Martigné-Ferchaud: France **36** D8
Martigny: Switzerland **40** N9
Martigues: France **37** L12
Martin: Hants., England **24** S18
Martin: Lincs., England **27** V13
Martin: S. Dak., U.S.A. **92** G4
Martin: Tenn., U.S.A. **88** G7
Martina Franca: Italy **38** P16
Martinboro: North I., New Zealand **70** P15
Martinhoe: Devon, England **24** O17

Martinique: *Fr. overseas dept.* **87** c3
Cap.: Fort-de-France
Area: 431 sq. miles (1,116 sq. km.)
Pop.: 341,000 (*1971 E*)

Martin I.: La., U.S.A. **90** *Ins.*
Martin Lake: Ala., U.S.A. **91** H9
Martinsberg: Austria **41** V7
Martinsburg: W. Va., U.S.A. **89** N6
Martins Ferry: Ohio, U.S.A. **88** L5
Martinstown: Lim., Repub. of Ireland **31** E15
Martinsville: Ind., U.S.A. **88** H6
Martinsville: Va., U.S.A. **89** M7
Martin Vaz: *i.* (Braz.), S. Atlantic Ocean **8** 25S 30W
Martlesham: Suff., England **25** Y15
Martletwy: Dyfed, Wales **24** M16
Martley: Hereford & Worcester, England **24** R15
Martock: Som., England **24** Q18
Marton: Lincs., England **27** U13
Marton: North I., N.Z. **70** P15
Marton: Cleve., England **26** T10
Martos: Spain **35** E18
Martre, Lac La: N.W.T., Canada **84** H5
Martuni: Armenia, U.S.S.R. **57** J1
Martynovka: U.S.S.R. **50** F5
Marudi: Guyana **87** d9
Marudi: Sarawak, Malaysia **65** E6
Maruf: Afghanistan **58** L8
Marugame: Japan **63** Y8
Marum: Netherlands **44** M2
Marungu Mtns., Zaïre **76** C4
Marutea, North: *i.*, Tuamotu Arch. **83** g3
Marvas: Iran **55** H8
Marvejols: France **37** J11
Marvine, Mount: Utah, U.S.A. **93** E5
Marwick Head: Mainland, Orkney Is. **28** P1
Marwood: Devon, England **24** N17
Mary (Merv): Turkmen., U.S.S.R. **51** K7
Mar'yama: Estonia, U.S.S.R. **47** T7
MARYBOROUGH (Port Laoise): Laois, Repub. of Ireland **31** G13
Maryborough: Queens., Australia **70** K5
Maryborough: Vict., Austl. **71** E11
Maryburgh: High., Scotl. **28** N4
Maryculter: Gram., Scotland **28** R5
Marydale: C.P., S. Africa **74** E4
Mar'yevka: Kazakh., U.S.S.R. **51** L4
Marykirk: Gram., Scotland **29** Q6
Maryland: *Co.*, Liberia (*co. town* Harper) **80** C4
Maryland: Rhodesia **77** D6
Maryland: *State*, U.S.A. (*cap.* Annapolis) **89** N6
Maryport: Cumbria, England **26** O10
Marystown: Newf., Canada **85** v3
Marysvale: Utah, U.S.A. **93** E5
Marysville: Kans., U.S.A. **93** H5
Marysville: N.B., Canada **89** S3
Marysville: Ohio, U.S.A. **88** K5
Maryvale: N.S.W., Austl. **71** H9
Maryvale: Queens., Austl. **70** K7
Maryville: Mo., U.S.A. **93** J4
Maryville: Tenn., U.S.A. **91** K8
Mas'abi: *i.*, Saudi Arabia **54** E9
Masada: fortress of Maccabean and Herodian periods on W. coast of Dead Sea about 20 miles ESE. of Yalta, Israel **55** b3
Masai Mara Game Reserve: Kenya **76** E3
Masai Steppe: Tanzania **76** E3
Masaka: Uganda **76** D3
Masally: Azerbaydzhan, U.S.S.R. **57** L2
Masamba: Celebes **65** G7
Masan: S. Korea **63** X7
Masango: C.P., S. Africa **75** G5
Masasi: Tanzania **77** E5
Masbate: *& i.*, Philippines **64** G4
Mascara: Algeria **35** G19
Mascarene Basin: Indian Ocean **9** 15S 50E
Mascoutah: Ill., U.S.A. **88** G6
Maseme: Botswana **77** C6
Masequa: Trans., S. Africa **75** H1
MASERU: *& Dist.*, Lesotho **75** G4
Mashaba: Rhodesia **77** D7
Mashaki: Afghanistan **58** L8
Masham: N. Yorks., England **26** S11
Masherbrum: *mtn.*, Jammu & Kashmir **58** N7
Mashegu: Nigeria **81** F2
Mashike: Japan **63** ZZ6
Mashombo: Tanzania **77** D4
Mashonaland North: *Prov.*, Rhodesia (*cap.* Sinoia) **77** D6
Mashonaland South: *Prov.*, Rhodesia (*cap.* Salisbury) **77** D6
Mashowing: *riv.*, S. Africa **74** E3
Mashrufa: Saudi Arabia **54** F11
Mashtagi: Azerbaydzhan, U.S.S.R. **57** M1
Masi-Manimba: Zaïre **81** H5
Masibi: Angola **77** B5
Masila: *wadi*, Hadhramaut, Yemen P.D.R. **55** H11
Masindi: Uganda **76** D2
Masindi Port: Uganda **76** D2
Masira: *i. & gulf*, Oman **55** J10
Masisea: Peru **94** C5
Masisi: Zaïre **76** C3
Masjid-i-Sulaiman: Iran **57** L6
Mask, Lough: Mayo, Repub. of Ireland **30** C12
Mask Hutan: Iran **55** J9
Maslyanino: U.S.S.R. **51** O4
Masoala, Cape: Malagasy Rep. **73** O13
Mason: Mich., U.S.A. **88** J4
Mason: Tex., U.S.A. **90** B10
Mason, Lake: W. Australia **68** B5
Mason City: Ill., U.S.A. **88** G5
Mason City: Iowa, U.S.A. **88** E4
Måsøy: Norway **46** T1
Massa: (*S. of Siena*), Tuscany, Italy **38** M15
Massa: (*near Carrara*), Tuscany, Italy **40** Q11
Massachusetts: *State*, U.S.A. (*cap.* Boston) **89** P4
Massachusetts Bay: Mass. U.S.A. **89** Q4
Massagetae: ancient tribe of lower Oxus valley in Uzbek. and NE. Turkmen., U.S.S.R. **55** K6
Massaguet: Chad **81** H2
Massakori: Chad **81** H2
Massa Lombarda: Italy **41** R11
Massangena: Mozambique **77** D7
Massapê: Brazil **94** J4
Massawa: Ethiopia **54** E11
Massay: France **36** H8
Massena: N.Y., U.S.A. **89** O3
Massénya: Chad **81** H2
Massérac: France **36** D8
Massering: Botswana **77** B7
Massett: B.C., Canada **84** f7
Masseube: France **37** F12
Massey: Ont., Canada **88** K2
Massiac: France **37** J10
Massif Central: *mtns.*, France **37** —
Massilia: ancient city and port at Marseilles, France **37** L12
Massillon: Ohio, U.S.A. **88** L5
Massinga: Mozambique **77** E7
Mastakh: U.S.S.R. **49** O5
Mastergeehy: Kerry, Repub. of Ireland **31** A16
Masterton: North I., N.Z. **70** P15
Mastuj: Jammu & Kashmir **58** M7
Mastung: Baluchistan, Pakistan **58** L9
Mastura: Saudi Arabia **54** E10
Masugnsbyn: Sweden **46** S3
Masuku: Zambia **77** C6
Masuleh: Iran **57** L3
Masyaf: Syria **56** E4
Maszewo: Szczecin, Poland **45** V2
Maszewo: Zielona Góra, Poland **45** U3
Mata Amarilla: Argentina **95** C13
Matabahan: Borneo **65** E7
Matabeleland North: *Prov.*, Rhodesia (*cap.* Bulawayo) **77** C6
Matabeleland South: *Prov.*, Rhodesia (*cap.* Shabani) **77** C7
Mataboor: W. Irian, Indon. **61** M12
MATADI: Bas Zaïre, Zaïre, **81** G6
Matador: Tex., U.S.A. **93** G6
Matagalpa: Nicaragua **86** L15
Matagorda Bay: Tex., U.S.A. **90** C11
Mataiva: *i.*, Tuamotu Arch. **83** f2
Matak: *i.*, Anambas Is., Indonesia **65** D6
Matakana I.: North I., N.Z. **70** Q13
Mataki: *well*, Oman **55** H11
Matale: Sri Lanka **58** O13
Matam: Senegal **80** B1
Matamata: North I., N.Z. **70** P13
Matamoros: Campeche, Mexico **86** k14
Matamoros: Tamaulipas, Mexico **90** C13
Matandu: *riv.*, Tanzania **77** E4
Matane: Que., Canada **89** S1
Matang: Malaya, Malaysia **65** b11
Matanuska: Alaska, U.S.A. **84** E5
Matanzas: Cuba **87** I13
Matapan (Tainaron), Cape: Greece **39** S18
Matapédia: Que., Canada **89** S2
Matapozuelos: Spain **35** D16
Matará: Argentina **96** C2
Matara: Sri Lanka **58** O13
Mataram: Lombok, Indon. **65** F8
Mataranka: N. Territ., Austl. **68** E2
Matariya, El: Egypt **56** C6
Matarka: Morocco **80** L8
Mataró: Spain **35** H16
Matatiele: S. Africa **75** H5
Mataura: South I., N.Z. **71** M18
Mataura: *riv.*, South I., N.Z. **71** M17
Matay: Kazakh., U.S.S.R. **51** N5
Matchi-Manitou, Lake: Qué., Canada **89** N2
Matehuala: Mexico **86** j13
Mateka Falls: Congo/Zaïre **81** G5
Mateke Hills: Rhodesia **77** D7
Matemo I.: Mozambique **77** F5
Matera: Italy **38** P16
Matese Mtns.: Italy **38** O16
Mátészalka: Hungary **43** S13
Matetsi: Rhodesia **77** C6
Mateur: Tunisia **38** L18
Matfen: Northumb., Eng. **26** S9
Matha: France **37** E10
Mathews: Va., U.S.A. **89** N7
Mathieu, Point de: France **34** D12
Mathis: Tex., U.S.A. **90** C11
Mathry: Dyfed, Wales **24** L16
Mathura: *see* Muttra.
Mati: Mindanao, Phil. **65** H5
Matiakouali: Upper Volta **80** E2
Matibane: Mozambique **77** F5
Matignon: France **36** C7
Matinicus: *i.*, Maine, U.S.A. **89** R4
Matitan: Kweichow, China **62** T9
Matjiesfontein: C.P., S. Africa **74** D6
Matlabas: *& riv.*, Trans., S. Africa **75** G2
MATLOCK: Derby., England **27** S13
Matlock Bank: Derby., Eng. **27** S13
Matlock Bath: Derby., Eng. **27** S13
Matmata: Tunisia **32** D5
Mato: Zaïre **76** B4
Matochkin Shar Str.: Novaya Zemlya, U.S.S.R. **48** g3
Mato Grosso: *State*, Brazil (*cap.* Cuiabá) **94** F6
Mato Grosso: *ruin*, Brazil **94** F7
Mato Grosso, Plat. of: Brazil **94** G7
Matonchi: Zambia **77** B5
Matopo Hills: Rhodesia **77** C7
Matopos: Rhodesia **77** C7
Matrah: Oman **55** J10
Matrei: Austria **41** R8
Matrei-in-Osttirol: Austria **41** S8
Matrûh: Egypt **54** C8
MATSUE: Shimane, Japan **63** c3
Matsumoto: Honshu, Japan **63** e2
Matsuo: Japan **63** e3
MATSUYAMA: Ehime, Japan **63** c4
Matsuzaka: Japan **63** e3
Mattagami: *riv.*, Ont., Can. **88** L1
Mattagami Lake: Ont., Can. **88** L2
Mattamuskeet, Lake: N.C., U.S.A. **91** N8
Mattawa: Ont., Canada **89** M2
Mattawamkeag: Maine, U.S.A. **89** R3
Matterdale: Cumbria, Eng. **26** Q10
Matterhorn: *mtn.*, Switz./It. **40** N10
Matthew I.: Pacific O. **67** O6
Mattoon: Ill., U.S.A. **88** G6
Mattsmyra: Sweden **47** O6
Matua: Borneo **65** E7
Matuku: *i.*, Fiji Is. **67** P5
Matun: Afghanistan **58** L8
Maturín: Venezuela **94** E2
Maúa: Mozambique **77** E5
Maubara: Timor, Indon. **65** H8
Maubeuge: France **36** J5
Maubin: Burma **59** R11
Maubourguet: France **37** F12
Mauchline: Strath., Scotland **29** N8
Maud: Grampian, Scotland **28** R4
Maud: Okla., U.S.A. **90** C8
Maude: N.S.W., Australia **71** F10
Mauerkirchen: Austria **41** T7
Maués: Brazil **94** F4
Maug: *i.*, Mariana Is. **60** O7
Maughold Head: *cape*, I. of Man, United Kingdom **26** N11
Mauguio: France **37** K12
Maui: *i.*, Hawaiian Is. **83** c2
Mauke: *i.*, Cook Is. **70** *Ins.*
Maulbronn: W. Germany **40** O7
Maule: France **36** G7
Maule: *riv.*, Chile **96** A4
Mauléon: France **37** E12
Maumee: Ohio, U.S.A. **88** K5
Maumee: *riv.*, U.S.A. **88** J5
Maumere: Flores, Indon. **65** G8
MAUN: Ngamiland, Botswana **77** B7
Maun: *i.*, Yugoslavia **41** U11
Mauna Kea: *volc.*, Hawaiian Is. **83** d3
Mauna Loa: *volc.*, Hawaiian Is. **83** d3
Maung: Cambodia **64** C4
Maunoir Lake: N.W.T., Can. **84** g4
Maupiti: Society Is. **83** e3
Maure: France **36** D8
Maurepas, Lake: La., U.S.A. **90** F10

Mauritania: *Republic* **78** C5
Cap.: Nouakchott
Area: 419,229 sq. miles (1,085,803 sq. km.)
Pop.: 1,200,000 (*1971 E*)

Mauretania Caesariensis: Roman province of N. Africa between *Mauretania Tingitana* and *Numidia*, Algeria **32** C4
Mauretania Tingitana: the most westerly Roman province of N. Africa **32** A5
Mauriac: France **37** H10

Mauritius: *Republic* **9** 25S 55E
Cap.: Port Louis
Area: 787 sq. miles (2,038 sq. km.)
Pop.: 847,000 (*1971 E*)

Mauron: France **36** C7
Maurs: France **37** H11
Mauston: Wis., U.S.A. **88** F4
Mauterndorf: Austria **41** T8
Mauthausen: Austria **41** U7
Mauvezin: France **37** F12
Mauzé: France **37** E9
Mavila: Mozambique **77** D6
Mavinga: Angola **77** B6
Mawai: Malaya, Malaysia **65** d13
Mawang Shan: *mtn.*, Tibet, China **58** O8
Mawarena: Bougainville, Solomon Is. **67** L3
Mawasangka: Celebes **65** G8
Mawbray: Cumbria, England **26** P10
Mawchi: Burma **59** R11
Mawgan: Corn., England **25** L19
Mawit: Iraq **57** J4
Mawiya: Yemen **54** F12
Mawkmai: Burma **59** R10
Mawlaik: Burma **59** Q10
Mawson: *rsch. stn.*, Antarctica **9** 70S 60E
Mawuga: Tanzania **76** D4
Max: N. Dak., U.S.A. **92** G3
Maxaila: Mozambique **77** D7
Maxesibeni: Transkei, S. Africa **75** H5
Maxixe: Mozambique **77** E7
Maxmo: Finland **46** S5
Maxwelton: Queens., Austl. **69** G4
Maxwelltown: Dumfries & Galloway, Scotland **29** O9
May, Isle of: Scotland **29** Q7
Maya: *riv.*, U.S.S.R. **49** p6
Mayaguana: *i.*, Bahamas **87** m13
Mayagüez: Puerto Rico **87** N14
Mayama: Congo **81** G5
Maya Mtns.: Belize **86** *Ins.*
Mayapán: old capital of Mayas. Its ruins exist S. of Mérida, Yucatán, Mex. **86** L13
Mayar: *mtn.*, Tay., Scotland **28** P6
Maybole: Strath., Scotland **29** M9
Mayen: W. Germany **44** N5
Mayenne: *& riv.*, France **36** E7
Mayenne: *Dept.*, France (*cap.* Laval) **36** E7
Mayet: France **36** F8
Mayet-de-Montagne, Le: Fr. **37** J9
Mayfield: Ky., U.S.A. **88** G7
Mayfield: E. Sussex, England **25** W17
Maykain: Kazakh., U.S.S.R. **51** N4
MAYKOP: Adygei, U.S.S.R. **50** F6
Maymyo: Burma **59** R10
Mayna-Pyl'gin: U.S.S.R. **49** t5
Maynooth: Kild., Repub. of Ireland **31** H13
Maynooth: Ont., Canada **89** N3
Mayo: *& Co.*, Repub. of Irel. (*cap. of co.* Castlebar) **30** C12
Mayo: *riv.*, Mexico **93** F7
Mayo Bay: Philippines **65** H5
Mayo Faran: Nigeria **81** G3
Mayo-Kebbi: *Pref.*, Chad (*cap.* Bongor) **81** H3
Mayo Landing: Yukon, Can. **84** F5
Mayom: Sudan **76** D1
Mayor I.: New Zealand **70** Q13
Mayoumba: Gabon **81** G5
May Pen: Jamaica **86** *Ins.*
Mayrán, Lago de: Mexico **93** G7
Mayrhofen: Austria **41** R8
Maysan: *Prov.*, Iraq **57** K6
Mayskiy: U.S.S.R. **49** P7
Maysville: Ky., U.S.A. **88** K6
Maytown: Queens., Austl. **69** G3
Mayu: *i.*, Indonesia **65** H6
Mayville: N. Dak., U.S.A. **92** H3
Mayville: Wis., U.S.A. **88** G4
Maywood: Ill., U.S.A. **88** H5
Maza: Argentina **96** C4
Mazabuka: Zambia **77** C6
Mazagão: Brazil **94** G4
Mazamet: France **37** H12
Mazán: Argentina **96** B2
Mazara del Vallo: Sicily **38** N18
MAZAR-I-SHARIF: Balkh, Afghan. **51** L7

For Abbreviations see list on p.113. Italic type, e.g. *Ephesus*, refers to historical names not on maps. Capital letters, e.g. MADRID, show capitals of countries; small capital letters, e.g. CADIZ, show capitals of provinces, etc. General notes p.116.

Mazarrón: Spain 35 F18
Mazatan: Mexico 93 E7
Mazatlán: Mexico 86 J13
Mazgirt: Turkey 56 F2
Mazheikyay: Lithuania, U.S.S.R.
    47 S8
Mazirb: Latvia, U.S.S.R. 47 S8
Mazlumlar: Turkey 56 A2
Mazoe: Rhodesia 77 D6
Mazowsze: geog. reg., Pol. 43 R10
Mazrub: well, Sudan 54 C12
Mazuria: geog. reg., Poland 43 R10
MBABANE: Swaziland 75 J3
Mbahiakro: Ivory Coast 80 D3
M'BAIKI: Lobaye, Cen. Afr. Rep.
    81 H4
Mbala: Cen. Afr. Rep. 76 B1
Mbala: Zambia 77 D4
Mbale: Uganda 76 D2
M'Balmayo: Cameroun 81 G4
Mbam: riv., Cameroun 81 G3
MBANDAKA: Equateur, Zaire
    73 H10
Mbanga: Cameroun 81 F4
Mbanza Ngungu: Zaire 81 G6
Mbarara: Uganda 76 D3
Mbari: Sudan 76 C1
M'Bari & riv., Central African
    Republic 76 B1
Mbemkumu: riv., Tanzania 77 E4
Mbengga: i., Fiji Is. 67 P5
M'Bère: riv., Cameroun/Chad 81 H3
MBEYA: & Reg., Tanzania 77 D4
Mbia: Sudan 76 C1
M'Bigou: Gabon 81 G5
Mboamaji: Tanzania 76 E4
Mbogo: Tanzania 76 D4
Mboi: Zaire 76 B4
M'Bomou: Pref., Cen. Afr. Rep.
    (cap. Bangassou) 76 B1
M'Bomou: riv., Zaire/Central African
    Republic 76 B2
Mboul: Senegal 80 B2
M'Bour: Senegal 80 A2
Mbout: Mauritania 80 B1
M'Bres: Cen. Afr. Rep. 76 A1
Mbugani: Tanzania 76 D4
MBUJI-MAYI: Kasai Oriental,
    Zaire 76 B3
Mbulu: Tanzania 76 E3
Mbuma: Zaire 76 B2
Mburga: Tanzania 77 E5
Mburucuyá: Argentina 96 D2
Mbuyuni: Tanzania 76 E4
Mchinja: Tanzania 77 E4
Mchinji: Malawi 77 D5
Mchungu: Tanzania 76 E4
Mdandu: Tanzania 77 D4
Mdina (Notabile): Malta 32 Ins.
Mead, Lake: Nev., U.S.A. 92 E5
Meade: Kans., U.S.A. 90 A7
Meadie, Loch: High., Scot. 28 M3
Meadow Lake: town, Sask., Canada
    92 F2
Meadow Lake Prov. Park:
    Sask., Canada 92 F2
Meadow Valley Wash: riv., Nev.,
    U.S.A. 93 E5
Meadville: Pa., U.S.A. 88 L5
Meaford: Ont., Canada 88 L3
Mealasta I.: Outer Hebr., Scotland
    28 G3
Mealhada: Portugal 35 B16
Meandarra: Queens., Austl. 70 H6
Meander River: town, Alta.,
    Canada 84 H6
Meare: Som., England 24 Q17
Meares, Cape: Oreg., U.S.A. 92 C3
Mearns: Strath., Scotland 29 N8
Mearns, Howe of the: dist., Grampian,
    Scotland 28 Q6
Mears Ashby: Northants., England
    25 U15
Measham: Leics., England 27 T14
Meath: Co., Repub. of Irel. (cap.
    Navan) 30 H12
Meaux: France 36 H7
Mecanhelas: Mozambique 77 E6
Mecca: Saudi Arabia 54 E10
Mechanicsburg: Pa., U.S.A. 89 N5
Mechanicsville: Md., U.S.A. 89 N6
Mechanicville: N.Y., U.S.A. 89 P4
Mechelen: Belgium 44 K4
Méchéria: Algeria 80 L8
Mechetinskaya: U.S.S.R. 50 F5
Mechroha: Algeria 38 K18
Mecidiye: Turkey 56 B1
Mecitozu: Turkey 56 D1
Mecklenburg Bay: E. Germany
    45 R1
Meconta: Mozambique 77 E6
Mecufi: Mozambique 77 F5
Mecula: Mozambique 77 E5
Medak: Andhra Pradesh, India
    58 N11
Medak: Yugoslavia 41 V11
Medan: Sumatra, Indon. 65 B6
Médano: Mexico 93 E7
Médanos: Argentina 96 C4
Medanosa Point: cape, Arg. 95 D13
Medbourne: Leics., England 27 U14
MÉDÉA: & Dept., Algeria 35 H18
Medellín: Colombia 94 B3
Medemblik: Netherlands 44 L3
Médenine: Tunisia 32 E5
Méderdra: Mauritania 80 A1
Medetsiz: mtn., Turkey 56 D3
Medford: Mass., U.S.A. 89 Q4
Medford: Okla., U.S.A. 90 C7
Medford: Oreg., U.S.A. 92 C4
Medford: Wis., U.S.A. 88 F3
Medgidia: Romania 39 V14
Medi: Sudan 76 D1
Media: see Adiabene.
Medias: Romania 43 T13
Medical Lake: city, Wash., U.S.A.
    92 D3
Medicine Bow: Wyo., U.S.A. 92 F4
Medicine Bow Peak: Wyo., U.S.A.
    92 F4
Medicine Hat: Alta., Canada 92 E3
Medicine Lodge: Kans., U.S.A.
    90 B7
Medina: Saudi Arabia 54 E10
Medina: N.Y., U.S.A. 89 M4
Medina: riv., Tex., U.S.A. 90 B11
Medinaceli: Spain 35 E16
Medina del Campo: Spain 35 D16
Medina de Rioseco: Spain 35 D16
Medina Sidonia: Spain 35 D18
Medinat-ash-Sha'b: Yemen P.D.R.
    79 Q17
Mediolanum: Roman city at Milan,
    Italy 40 P9
Mediomatrici: Gallic tribe with
    centre at Metz, Fr. 44 M6
Mediterranean Sea 32-3
Medje: Zaire 76 C2
Medjerda: riv., Tunisia/Algeria
    38 L18
Medjez el Bab: Tunisia 38 L18
Mednogorsk: U.S.S.R. 50 J4
Médoc: geog. reg., France 37 E10
Medstead: Hants., England 25 T17
Medulin: Yugoslavia 41 T11

Medumurje: geog. reg., Yugoslavia
    41 W9
Medvednica: mtn., Yugo. 41 V10
Medvezh'yegorsk: U.S.S.R. 48 E5
Medvezh'yi Is.: E. Siberian Sea
    49 S3
Medvide: Yugoslavia 41 V11
Medway: riv., Kent/E. Sussex,
    England 25 W17
Medyn: U.S.S.R. 50 E4
Medzhibozh: Ukraine 43 U12
Meekatharra: W. Australia 68 B5
Meeker: Colo., U.S.A. 93 F4
Meelin: Cork, Repub. of Irel. 31 C15
Meerane: E. Germany 45 S5
Meersburg: W. Germany 40 P8
Meerut: Uttar Pradesh, India 58 N9
Mées, Les: France 40 L11
Meester Cornelis: see Jatinegara
Meeteetse: Wyo., U.S.A. 92 F4
Mega: Ethiopia 76 E2
Mega: i., Mentawai Is., Indonesia
    65 C7
Megalópolis: Greece 39 S18
Meganom, Cape: U.S.S.R. 50 E6
Megantic: Que., Canada 89 Q3
Mégara: Greece 39 S17
Megara Hyblaea: Greek city near
    Augusta, Sicily 38 O18
Meghalaya: State, India (cap.
    Shillong) 59 Q9
Megiddo: city of ancient Israel
    about 18 miles SE. of Haifa,
    Israel 55 a2
Mégiscane, Lac: Que., Can. 89 O1
Megri: Armenia, U.S.S.R. 57 K4
Mehabad (Saujbulagh): Iran 57 J3
Mehetia: i., Society Is. 83 f3
Mehrevan: Iran 57 K2
Meia Meia: Tanzania 76 E4
Meifod: Powys, Wales 27 P14
Meig: riv., High., Scot. 28 M4
Meiganga: Cameroun 81 G3
Meighen I.: N.W.T., Canada 84 K1
Meigle: Tay., Scotland 29 P6
Meihsien: Kwangtung, China 62 V10
Meiktila: Burma 59 R10
Meilen: Switzerland 40 O8
Meiningen: E. Germany 45 Q5
Meirheath: Staffs., England 27 R14
Meiringen: Switzerland 40 O9
Meishan: Szechwan, China 62 S8
Meissen: E. Germany 45 T4
Meitan: Kweichow, China 62 T9
Mejillones: Chile 96 A1
Mekambo: Gabon 81 G4
Mekhé: Senegal 80 A1
Mekhtar: Baluchistan, Pak.
    58 L8
Mekili, El: Libya 33 G5
Mekleta: U.S.S.R. 50 G5
MEKNÈS: & Prov., Morocco 80 K8
Meko: Nigeria 81 E3
Mekong: riv., S.E. Asia 64 D4
Mekra: riv., W. Africa 81 E2
Mekrou: riv., West Africa 81 E2
Melalap: Sabah, Malaysia 65 F5
Melambes: Crete 39 T19
Melanesia: geog. reg., Pacific
    Ocean 7 —
Melbourne: Cambs., England 25 W15
Melbourne: Derby., Eng. 27 T14
Melbourne: Fla., U.S.A. 91 L11
Melbourne: Humb., Eng. 27 U12
MELBOURNE: Vict., Austl. 71 F11
Melcham: N. Yorks., Eng. 27 S12
Melchor Ocampo: Mexico 93 G8
Meldola: Italy 41 S11
Meldon: Northumb., Eng. 26 S9
Meldorf: W. Germany 44 P1
Meldreth: Cambs., England 25 W15
Mele, Cape: Italy 40 O12
Meleden: Somalia 79 R17
Melegnano: Italy 40 P10
Melekess: U.S.S.R. 50 G4
Melendiz Mtns.: Turkey 56 D2
Melenki: U.S.S.R. 50 F3
Meleuz: U.S.S.R. 50 J4
Melfi: Chad 81 H2
Melfi: Italy 38 O16
Melfort: Sask., Canada 92 G2
Melgaço: Brazil 94 G4
Melhus: Norway 46 M5
Meliden: Clwyd, Wales 27 P13
Meligalá: Greece 39 R18
Melilla: (Sp.), Morocco 35 E19
Melimoyu, Monte: mtn., Chile
    95 C12
Melinda Downs: Queens., Australia
    69 G3
Melipilla: Chile 96 A3
Mélisey: France 40 M8
Melita: Man., Canada 92 G3
Melita: Roman name of island
    of Malta 38 O19
Melitene: Roman camp and city at
    Malatya, Turkey 56 F2
Melito: Italy 38 O18
Melitopol': Ukraine 50 E5
Melk: Austria 41 V7
Melksham: Wilts., England 24 R17
Mellansel: Sweden 46 Q5
Melle: France 37 E9
Melle: W. Germany 44 O3
Mellègue: riv., Tunisia/Alg. 38 L18
Mellen: Wis., U.S.A. 88 F2
Mellerud: Sweden 47 N7
Mellid: Spain 35 B15
Mellieha: Malta 32 Ins.
Melling: Lancs., England 26 Q11
Mellis: Suff., England 25 Y15
Mellish Reef: Coral Sea 67 L5
Mellit: Sudan 79 K7
Mellon Charles: Highland,
    Scotland 28 K4
Mellrichstadt: W. Germany 45 Q5
Melmerby: Cumbria, Eng. 26 Q10
Melmerby: N. Yorks., Eng. 26 T11
Melmoth: Natal, S. Africa 75 J4
Melness: High., Scotland 28 N2
Melnik: Bulgaria 39 S16
Mělnik: Czechoslovakia 45 U5
Melo: Argentina 96 C3
Melo: Uruguay 96 D3
Meloco: Mozambique 77 E5
Mololo: Sumba, Indon. 65 G8
Melrose: Borders, Scotland 29 Q8
Melrose: Minn., U.S.A. 88 D3
Melrose: N. Mex., U.S.A. 93 G6
Melrose: S. Australia 71 C9
Melsenheim: W. Germany 44 N6
Melsetter: Rhodesia 77 D6
Melsonby: N. Yorks., England 26 S11
Melsungen: W. Germany 44 P4
Meltaus: Finland 46 T3
Meltham: W. Yorks., England 27 S12
Melton: Suff., England 25 Y15
Melton Constable: Norf., England
    25 Y14
Melton Mowbray: Leics., England
    27 U14
Meluan: Sarawak, Malaysia 65 E6
Meluco: Mozambique 77 E5

Meluge: Mozambique 77 F5
MELUN: Seine-et-Marne, Fr. 36 H7
Melut: Sudan 79 L7
Melvaig: High., Scot. 28 K4
Melvich: High., Scotland 28 O2
Melville: La., U.S.A. 90 F10
Melville: Sask., Canada 92 G2
Melville, Cape: Queens., Australia
    69 G2
Melville, Lake: Newf., Can. 85 O7
Melville Bay: Greenland 85 n2
Melville I.: Australia 68 E2
Melville I.: N.W.T., Canada 84 h2
Melville Penin.: N.W.T., Canada
    85 l4
Melville Sound: Canada 84 J3
Melvin, Lough: Leit., Repub. of
    Ireland 30 E11
Memba: Mozambique 77 F5
Membij: Syria 56 F3
Memboro: Sumba, Indon. 65 F8
Memel (Klaipeda): Lithuania,
    U.S.S.R. 47 R9
Memel: O.F.S., S. Africa 75 H3
Memmingen: W. Germany 40 Q8
Mempakan: Sabah, Malaysia 65 F5
Mempakul: Sabah, Malaysia 65 F5
Mempawah: Borneo 65 D6
Memphis: Mo., U.S.A. 88 E5
Memphis: Tenn., U.S.A. 91 H8
Memphis: Tex., U.S.A. 90 A8
Memphis (Noph): ancient Egyptian
    city on left bank of Nile about
    10 miles S. of Cairo, Egypt 56 B7
Memphremagog, Lake: Que.,
    Canada 89 P3
Memsie: Gram., Scotland 28 R4
Mena: Ark., U.S.A. 90 D8
Menai Bridge: town, Gwynedd,
    Wales 27 N13
Menai Str.: Gwyn., Wales 27 N13
Ménaka: Mali 81 E1
Menanga: Sula Is., Indon. 65 G7
Menard: Tex., U.S.A. 90 B10
Menasha: Wis., U.S.A. 88 G3
Mendanau: i., Indonesia 65 D7
Mendawai: riv., Borneo 65 E7
MENDE: Lozère, France 37 J11
Mende: Greek city near SW.
    promontory of Kassándra
    peninsula, Greece 39 S16
Mendebo Mtns.: Ethiopia 76 E1
Menderes: riv., Turkey 39 V18
Mendesion: Greek name of Nile
    mouth emerging in centre of
    Lake Manzala 56 B6
Mendif: Cameroun 81 G2
Mendip Hills: Som., Eng. 24 Q17
Mendlesham: Suff., Engl. 25 Y15
Mendocino, C.: Calif., U.S.A 86 g9
Mendocino Fracture Zone:
    N. Pacific Ocean 7 40N 145W
Mendong Gompa: Tibet, China
    59 P8
Mendota: Ill., U.S.A. 88 G5
MENDOZA: & Prov., Arg. 96 B3
Mendoza: Panama 94 Ins.
Mène: Congo 76 H9
Ménéac: France 36 C7
Menemen: Turkey 39 U17
Meneville: Algeria 35 H18
Menesjoensuu: Finland 46 U2
Menfi: Sicily 38 N18
Mengcheng: Anhwei, China 72 V8
Mengen: W. Germany 40 P7
Mengeringhausen: W. Ger. 44 O4
Menggala: Sumatra 65 D7
Mengha: Yunnan, China 62 S10
Mengma: Yunnan, China 62 R10
Mengpeng: Yunnan, China 62 R10
Mengshan: Kwangsi Chuang, China
    62 U10
Mengting: (near Burmese Frontier),
    Yunnan, China 62 R10
Mengting: (near Vietnam Frontier),
    Yunnan, China 62 S10
Mengtsz: Yunnan, China 62 S10
Mengwang: Yunnan, China 62 S10
Mengyin: Shantung, China 62 V7
Menheniot: Cornwall, England
    24 N19
Ménigoute: France 37 E9
Menin: Belgium 44 J5
Menindee: & lake, N.S.W.,
    Australia 71 E9
Meningie: S. Australia 71 C10
Menizla: Morocco (Gib. Inset)
    32 Ins.
Menkatab: Malaya, Malaysia 65 c12
Menlough: (near Galway), Galway,
    Repub. of Irel. 31 C13
Menlough: (W. of Castleblakeney),
    Galway, Repub. of Ireland 31 D13
Mennetou-sur-Cher: France 36 G8
Menomimee: & riv., Mich., U.S.A.
    88 H3
Menomonie: Wis., U.S.A. 88 F3
Menorca (Minorca): i., Balearic
    Is. (Sp.) 35 J17
Mens: France 40 L11
Men'shikov, Cape: U.S.S.R.
    48 g3
Menston: W. Yorks., England 27 S12
Mentawai Is.: Indonesia 65 B7
Mentawai Ridge: Indian Ocean
    9 00 95E
Mentekab: Malaya, Malaysia 65 c12
Menton: France 40 N12
Mentz, Lake: S. Africa 75 F6
Menyapa: mtn., Borneo 65 F6
Menze: Tibet, China 58 O8
Menzelinsk: U.S.S.R. 50 H3
Menzies: W. Australia 68 C5
Meole Brace: Salop, Eng. 27 Q14
Meon: riv., Hants., England 25 T18
Meon, West: Hants., England 25 T17
Meonstoke: Hants., England 25 T18
Meopham: Kent, England 25 W17
Meoqui: Mexico 93 F7
Mepal: Cambs., England 25 W15
Meppel: Netherlands 44 M3
Meppen: W. Germany 44 N3
Mer: France 36 G8
Merabéllos, G. of: Crete 39 T19
Merah: Borneo 65 F6
Merala: geog. reg., Mauritania 78 C6
Merak: Java 65 D8
Meramec: riv., Mo., U.S.A. 88 F6
Merauke: W. Irian, Indon. 61 N13
Merano: Italy 41 R9
Merapit: Borneo 65 E7
Merate: Italy 40 P10
MERCA: Benadir, Somalia 79 N9
Mercara: Karnataka, India 58 N12
Mercatino Marecchia: Italy 41 S12
Mercato Saraceno: Italy 41 S12
Merced: Calif., U.S.A. 93 C5
Merced, La: Argentina 96 B2
Mercedario: mtn., Argentina 96 A3
Mercedes: Buenos Aires, Arg. 96 D3
Mercedes: Corrientes, Arg. 96 D2
Mercedes: San Luis, Arg. 96 B3
Mercedes: Tex., U.S.A. 90 C12

Mercedes: Uruguay 96 D3
Merceditas: Chile 96 A2
Mercês: Brazil 96 G1
Merchtem: Belgium 44 K5
Mercia: kingdom of Saxon England
    originating in Trent valley
    and forming 'march' against
    British in west 27 U13
Mercoya: Mali 80 C2
Mercurea: Romania 43 S14
Mercury Is.: N.I., New
    Zealand 70 P13
Merdingnac: France 36 C7
Mere: Wilts., England 24 R17
Méré: Chad 81 H2
Meregh: Somalia 79 R19
Merei: geog. reg., Mauritania
    78 C6
Mererale: Ethiopia 79 Q18
Méréville: France 36 H7
Mérinchal: France 37 H10
Merinda: Queens., Austl. 70 H3
Mering: W. Germany 41 R7
Merino: C.P., S. Africa 75 F6
Merino: Vict., Australia 71 D11
Merir: i., Pacific O. 61 L11
Merke: Kazakh., U.S.S.R. 51 M6
Merkel: Tex., U.S.A. 90 A9
Merkendorf: W. Germany 45 Q6
Merlerault, Le: France 36 F7
Mermaid Reef: W. Austl. 68 B3
Mern Merna: S. Australia 71 C8
Meroe: ancient district between
    Merowe and Atbara 54 D11
Merowe: Sudan 54 D11
Merowe: W. Australia 68 B6
Merredin: W. Australia 68 B6
Merrick: mtn., Dumfries & Galloway,
    Scotland 29 N9
Merrill: Wis., U.S.A. 88 G3
Merrimack: riv., N.H./Mass.,
    U.S.A. 89 Q4
Merriott: Som., England 24 Q18
Merritt: B.C., Canada 92 C2
Merriwa: N.S.W., Austl. 71 J9
Merriwagga: N.S.W., Austl. 71 F9
Merrow: Surrey, England 25 U17
Mersa Fatma: Ethiopia 54 F12
Mersch: Luxembourg 44 M6
Merse: dist., Bord., Scot. 29 R8
Mersea I.: England 25 X16
Merseburg: E. Germany 45 R4
Mersey: riv., England 27 Q13
Merseyside: Metropolitan Co.,
    England (co. town Liverpool)
    27 P13
Mersham: Kent, England 25 X17
MERSIN (İçel): İçel, Turkey
    56 D3
Mersin Bay: Turkey 56 D3
Mersing: Malaya, Malaysia 65 c12
Mērsrags: Latvia, U.S.S.R. 47 S8
Merstham: Surrey, England 25 V17
Merta: Rajasthan, India 58 M9
Merthyr Cynog: Powys, Wales
    24 P15
Merthyr Tydfil: Mid Glamorgan,
    Wales 24 P16
Mertola: Portugal 35 C18
Merton: Devon, England 24 N18
Merton: Gt. Ldn., England 25 V17
Merton: Lincs., England 27 U13
Merton: Vict., Australia 71 F11
Méru: France 36 H6
Meru: Kenya 76 E2
Meru: mtn., Tanzania 76 E3
Meru Game Reserve: Kenya 76 E2
Merv (Mary): Turkmen., U.S.S.R.
    51 K7
Merville: France 36 H5
Merweville: C.P., S. Africa 74 D6
Merzifon: Turkey 56 D1
Merzig: Saarland, W. Germany 44 M6
Mesa: Ariz., U.S.A. 93 E6
Mesabi Range: mtns., Minn.,
    U.S.A. 88 E2
Mesagne: Italy 38 P16
Mésanger: France 36 D8
Mesará Bay: Crete 39 T19
Mesa Verde Nat. Park: Colo.,
    U.S.A. 93 F5
Meschede: W. Germany 44 O4
Meshaw: Devon, England 24 O18
MESHED: Khorāsān, Iran 55 J7
Meshra-er-Req: Sudan 76 C1
Meskene: Syria 56 F3
Meskin: Sudan 76 C1
Meškuičiai: Lithuania, U.S.S.R. 47 S8
Meslay: France 36 E8
Mesmiya: Syria 56 E5
Mesnana: Tangier (Gib. Inset)
    32 Ins.
Mesolóngion: Greece 39 R17
Mesopotamia: geog. reg., Iraq 57 J5
Mésou-Volimais: Zante, Ionian
    Is. (Grc.) 39 R18
Messancy: Belgium 44 L6
Messac: France 36 E7
Messent Wildlife Reserve:
    S. Australia 71 C11
Messina: Sicily 38 O17
Messina: Trans., S. Africa 75 J1
Messina, Str. of: Italy/Sicily 38 O17
Messingen: W. Germany 44 N3
Messingham: Humb., Eng. 27 U12
Messini: & gulf, Greece 39 S18
Messkirch: W. Germany 40 P8
Messo: U.S.S.R. 48 j4
Mesta: riv., Bulgaria/Greece 39 T16
Mesteñas, Las: Mexico 93 G7
Mestre: Italy 41 S10
Mestys Zelzená Ruda:
    Czechoslovakia 41 T6
Mesudiye: Turkey 56 F1
Mesule: mtn., Italy/Austria 41 R9
Meta: riv., Colombia 94 D2
Metabetchouan: see St. Jérôme.
Metairie: La., U.S.A. 91 G10
Metán: Argentina 96 C2
Metangula: Mozambique 77 D5
Metaponto: Italy 38 P16
Metauro: riv., Italy 41 S12
Metellinum: Roman colony between
    Mérida and Villanueva de la
    Serena, Sp. 35 D17
Metengo Balame: Mozam. 77 D5
Metfield: Suff., England 25 Y15

Methana: promontory projecting
    N. due E. of Nauplia 39 S18
Metheringham: Lincs., England
    27 V13
Methil: Fife, Scotland 29 P7
Methlick: Gram., Scotland 28 R5
Methone: Greek city at mouth of
    river Aliakmon, Greece 39 S16
Méthoni: Greece 39 R18
Methuen: Mass., U.S.A. 89 Q4
Methven: South I., N.Z. 70 N16
Methwold: Norf., England 25 X14
Methymna: Greek city at N. end of
    island, Lesbos, Aegean Sea 39 U17
Metileo: Argentina 96 C4
Metlakahtla: B.C., Canada 92 A1
Metlaoui: Tunisia 32 D5
Metlika: Yugoslavia 41 V10
Metnitz: Austria 41 U9
Metolola: Mozambique 77 E6
Metorica: Mozambique 77 E5
Metropolis: Ill., U.S.A. 88 G7
Métsovon: Greece 39 R17
Metter: Ga., U.S.A. 91 K9
Mettur: Tamil Nadu, India 58 N12
Metula: Israel 55 b1
METZ: Moselle, France 44 M6
Metzingen: W. Germany 40 P7
Meu: riv., France 36 D7
Meuban: riv., Cam./Gab. 81 G4
Meucon: France 36 C8
Meulaboh: Sumatra 65 B6
Meulan: France 36 G6
Meureudu: Sumatra 65 B5
Meursault: France 36 K9
Meurthe-et-Moselle: Dept., France
    (cap. Nancy) 40 M7
Meuse: Dept., France (cap. Bar le
    Duc) 36 L6
Meuse (Maas): riv., France/Belgium
    44 L5
Mevagissey: Corn., England 24 M19
Mew I.: N. Ireland 30 K10
Mex: Egypt 56 B6
Mexborough: S. Yorks., England
    27 T13
Mexia: Tex., U.S.A. 90 C10
Mexiana I.: Brazil 94 H3
MEXICALI: Lower Calif. (N. Territ.),
    Mexico 93 D6
Mexican Plat.: Mexico 86 j13

Mexico: Republic 86 j13
    Cap.: Mexico City
    Area: 761,601 sq. miles
    (1,972,547 sq. km.)
    Pop.: 52,641,000 (1972 E)

MEXICO (Mexico City): Mexico
    86 K14
Mexico: Mo., U.S.A. 88 F6
Mexico, G. of: America 86 k13
Meximieux: France 37 L10
Meyadin: Syria 57 G4
Meyenburg: E. Germany 45 S2
Meyersdale: Pa., U.S.A. 89 Mb
Meyerton: Trans., S. Africa 75 H3
Meylieu-Montrond: France 37 K10
Meylltteyn: Gwynedd, Wales 27 M14
Meymac: France 37 H10
Meyronne: Sask., Canada 92 F3
Meyruei's: France 37 J11
Meyssac: France 37 G10
Mezdra: Bulgaria 39 S15
Mèze: France 37 J12
Mezen': U.S.S.R. 48 F4
Mezen: riv., U.S.S.R. 48 f5
Mézenc: mtn., France 37 K11
Mezhdusharsky I.: U.S.S.R. 48 G3
Mezhizchi-Koretskiye: Ukraine
    43 U11
Mézidon: France 36 E6
MÉZIÈRES: Ardennes, France
    36 K6
Mézières: Haute-Vienne, Fr. 37 F9
Mezöberény: Hungary 43 R13
Mezöhegyes: Hungary 43 R13
Mezökövesd: Hungary 43 R13
Mézos: France 37 D11
Mezötúr: Hungary 43 R13
Mezre: Jordan 55 b3
Mezzolombardo: Italy 41 R9
Mfongozi: Natal, S. Africa 75 J4
Mfrica: Tanzania 77 E4
Mgori: Tanzania 76 D3
Mhor, Loch: High., Scotland 28 N5
Mhow: Madhya Pradesh,
    India 58 N10
Mhunze: Tanzania 76 D3
Miagao: Philippines 64 G4
Miah: wadi, Syria 56 F4
Miajadas: Spain 35 D17
Miami: Ariz., U.S.A. 93 E6
Miami: Fla., U.S.A. 91 L13
Miami: Okla., U.S.A. 90 D7
Miami: Rhodesia 77 C6
Miami: riv., Ohio, U.S.A. 88 J5
Miami Beach: city, Fla., U.S.A.
    91 L13
Miandetta: N.S.W., Austl. 71 G8
Miandrivazo: Malagasy Rep. 73 O13
Mianeh: Iran 57 K3
Mianwali: Punjab, Pak. 58 M8
Miarinarivo: Malagasy Rep. 73 O13
Miass: U.S.S.R. 51 K4
Miastko: Poland 43 P9
Mibu: Japan 63 c3
Mica: Trans., S. Africa 75 J2
Micaune: Mozambique 77 E6
Micay: Colombia 94 B3
Michael: dist., I. of Man, U.K. 26 M11
Michaelstow: Corn., Eng. 24 M18
Michaud Point: cape, Cape Breton
    I., Canada 89 V3
Micheh: Shensi, China 62 U7
Micheldever: Hants., Eng. 25 T17
Michelmersh: Hants., Eng. 25 S17
Michelson: mtn., Alaska, U.S.A. 84 e4
Michelstadt: W. Germany 44 P6
Michigan: State, U.S.A. (cap.
    Lansing) 88 J3
Michigan, Lake: U.S.A. 88 H4
Michigan City: Ind., U.S.A. 88 H5
Michikamau, Lake: Newf., Canada
    85 n7
Michipicoten Harbour: Ont.,
    Canada 88 J2
Michipicoten I.: Ont., Can. 88 J2
Michmash: city of ancient Israel
    about 9 miles NNE. of Jerusalem
    55 b3
Michurinsk: U.S.S.R. 50 F4
Mickle Fell: mtn., Durham,
    England 26 R10
Mickleover: Derby., Eng. 27 S15
Mickleton: Durham, Eng. 26 R10
Mickleton: Glos., England 25 S15
Micronesia: geog. reg., Pacific
    Ocean 7 —
Midai: i., Indonesia 65 D6
Midale: Sask., Canada 92 G3
Mid Calder: Lothian, Scot. 29 P8

Middelburg: & *Dist.*, Cape Prov.,
S. Africa **75** F5
Middelburg: & *Dist.*, Trans.,
S. Africa **75** H2
MIDDELBURG: Zeeland, Neth. **44** J4
Middelfart: Funen, Den. **47** L9
Middelpos: S. Africa **74** D5
Middelvlei: Trans., S. Africa **74** M*lns.*
Middelwit: Trans., S. Africa **75** G2
Middle: *dist.*, I. of Man, U.K. **26** N11
Middle Alkali Lake: Calif., U.S.A.
92 C4
Middle Andaman: *i.*, Andaman
Is. **59** Q12
Middle Atlas: *range*, Mor. **80** L8
Middle Barton: Oxon., Eng. **25** T16
Middlebie: Dumfries & Galloway,
Scotland **29** P9
Middle Ground: *i.*, La., U.S.A.
90 *Ins.*
Middleham: N. Yorks., Eng. **26** S11
Middle Loup: *riv.*, Nebr., U.S.A.
92 G4
Middleport: Ohio, U.S.A. **88** K6
Middlesboro: Ky., U.S.A. **88** K7
Middlesbrough: Cleve., Eng. **26** T10
Middlesex: Belize **86** *Ins.*
Middlesex: *Prov.*, Jamaica **86** *Ins.*
Middleton: C.P., S. Africa **75** F6
Middleton: Cork, Repub. of
Ireland **31** E16
Middleton: Cumbria, England
26 Q11
Middleton: Derby., England **27** S13
Middleton: Gt. Man., England **27** R12
Middleton: Northumb., Eng. **26** S8
Middleton: N.S., Canada **89** T3
Middleton: Queens., Austl. **69** G4
Middleton: Suff., England **25** Z15
Middleton: War., England **27** S14
Middleton: W. Sussex, Eng. **25** U18
Middleton in Teesdale: Durham,
England **26** R10
Middleton Reef: Tasman Sea **67** L7
Middleton Tyas: N. Yorks., England
26 S11
Middletown: Armagh, N. Ireland
30 H11
Middletown: Conn., U.S.A. **89** P5
Middletown: Del., U.S.A. **89** O6
Middletown: N.Y., U.S.A. **89** O5
Middletown: Ohio, U.S.A. **88** J6
Middletown: Pa., U.S.A. **89** N5
Middle Wallop: Hants., Eng. **25** S17
Middlewater: C.P., S. Africa **75** F6
Middlewich: Ches., England **27** R13
Midea: Greek village about 8
miles to E. of Argos, Greece
39 S18
Midelt: Morocco **80** L8
Midfield: Mayo, Repub. of
Ireland **30** D12
Mid Glamorgan: *Co.*, Wales (*co.
town* Cardiff) **24** P16
Midhurst: W. Sussex, England **25** U18
Midi Canal: France **37** G12
Mid-Indian Basin: Indian Ocean
9 10S 80E
Mid-Indian Ridge: Indian Ocean
9 30S 70E
Midland: Mich., U.S.A. **88** J4
Midland: Ont., Canada **89** M3
Midland: Tex., U.S.A. **93** G4
Midland Junction: W. Austl. **68** B6
Midlands: *Prov.*, Rhodesia (*cap.
Gwelo*) **77** C6
Midnapore: W. Bengal, India **59** P10
Midocean Ridge: N. Atlantic
Ocean **8** 70N 10W
Midongy-Sud: Malagasy Rep. **73** O14
Midouze: *riv.*, France **37** E12
Midsayap: Mindanao, Phil. **64** G5
Midsomer Norton: Avon,
England **24** R17
Midtown Brae: High., Scot. **28** K4
Midway-Hardwick: *see* Hardwick.
Midway Is.: Hawaiian Islands
7 25N 180
Midway Mtns: B.C., Can. **92** D3
Midwest: Wyo., U.S.A. **92** F4
Midwest City: Okla., U.S.A. **90** C8
Midyat: Turkey **57** G3
Midye: Turkey **39** V16
Mid Yell: Shetland Is. **28** *Ins.*
Mie: Japan **63** b4
Mie: *Pref.*, (*cap.* Tsu) Japan **63** e3
Miécaze: France **37** H11
Miechów: Poland **43** R11
Miedwie, Lake: Poland **45** U2
Międzychód: Poland **45** V3
Międzylesie: Poland **43** P11
Międzyrzec: Poland **43** S11
Międzyrzecz: Poland **45** V3
Miélan: France **37** F12
Mielec: Poland **43** R11
Mienhsien: Shensi, China **62** T8
Mienning: Szechwan, China **62** S9
Mienshan: Szechwan, China **62** S9
Mientuho: Inner Mongolia,
China **63** W5
Mienyang: Hupeh, China **62** U8
Mienyang: Szechwan, China **62** S8
Miercurea Cinc: Romania **43** T13
Mieres: Spain **35** D15
Miesbach: W. Germany **41** R8
Migiurtinia: *Reg.*, Somalia
(*cap.* Bosaso) **79** R18
Migliarino: Italy **41** R11
Mignon: Ala., U.S.A. **91** H9
Miguel Alves: Brazil **94** J4
Mihaliççik: Turkey **56** B2
Mihara: Japan **63** c3
Miho Bay: Japan **63** c3
Mijares: *riv.*, Spain **35** F16
Mikawa: Japan **63** e2
Mikhaylov: U.S.S.R. **50** E4
Mikhaylovka: Altai, U.S.S.R. **51** N4
Mikhaylovka: Primorsk,
U.S.S.R. **63** Y6
Mikhaylovka: Volgograd,
U.S.S.R. **50** F4
Mikhaylovskoye: U.S.S.R. **51** O4
Mikindani: Tanzania **77** F5
MIKKELI: & *Prov.*, Finland **47** U6
Miklibær: Iceland **46** d4
Mikonos: *i.*, Cyclades (Grc.) **39** T18
Mikoyai: Armenia, U.S.S.R. **57** J2
Mikulov: Czechoslovakia **41** W7
Mikumi National Park: Tanzania
76 E4
Mikuni: Japan **63** e2
Mikuni Mtns: Japan **63** f2
Mikura: *i.*, Japan **63** f4
Milaca: Minn., U.S.A. **88** E3
Milagro: Argentina **96** B3
Milagros: Philippines **64** G4
Milam: Uttar Pradesh, India **58** O8
MILAN (Milano): Lombardy,
Italy **40** P10
Milan: Mo., U.S.A. **88** E5
Milan: Tenn., U.S.A. **90** G8
Milang: S. Australia **71** C10
Milange: Mozambique **77** E6
MILANO (Milan): Lombardy,
Italy **40** P10

Milås: Turkey **39** U18
Milazzo: Sicily **38** O17
Milbank: S. Dak., U.S.A. **92** H3
Milborne: Dorset, England **24** R18
Milbourne: Northumb., England
26 S9
Milborne Port: Som., Eng. **24** R18
Milbridge: Maine, U.S.A. **89** S3
Mildenhall: Suff., England **25** X15
Mildura: Vict., Australia **71** E10
Miléai: Greece **39** S17
Miles: Queens., Australia **70** J6
Miles City: Mont., U.S.A. **92** F3
Miletus: Greek city on headland
S. of ancient mouth of river
Maeander (Menderes), Turkey
(site now 5 miles inland) **39** U18
Milevsko: Czechoslovakia **42** O12
Milfield: Northumb., Eng. **26** R8
Milford: Cork, Repub. of
Ireland **31** D15
Milford: Del., U.S.A. **89** O6
Milford: Mass., U.S.A. **89** Q4
Milford: N.H., U.S.A. **89** Q4
Milford: Surrey, England **25** U17
Milford: Utah, U.S.A. **92** E5
Milford Haven: Dyfed,
Wales **24** L16
Milford on Sea: Hants., Eng. **25** S18
Milford Sound: South I.,
New Zealand **70** L9
Milgarra: Queens., Austl. **69** G3
Milha Ashgar: *salt marsh*,
Iraq **57** G4
Miliana: Algeria **35** H18
Miliane: *riv.*, Tunisia **38** M18
Milicín: Czechoslovakia **45** U6
Milicz: Poland **43** P11
Miling: W. Australia **68** B6
Milk: *riv.*, Mont., U.S.A. **92** F3
Milk River: *town*, Alta.,
Canada **92** E3
Millas: France **37** H13
Millau: France **37** J11
Millbrook: Corn., England **24** N19
Millbrook: Ont., Canada **89** M3
Mill City: Oreg., U.S.A. **92** C4
Milledgeville: Ga., U.S.A. **91** K9
Mille Lacs, Lac des: Ont.,
Canada **88** F1
Mille Lacs Lake: Minn.,
U.S.A. **88** E2
Millen: Ga., U.S.A. **91** L9
Miller: S. Dak., U.S.A. **92** H4
Millerovo: U.S.S.R. **50** F5
Miller Peak: Ariz., U.S.A. **93** E6
Millersburg: Ohio, U.S.A. **88** L5
Miller's Point: S. Africa **74** *Ins.*
Milleur Point: Dumfries &
Galloway, Scotland **29** L9
Millford: Don., Rep. of Irel. **30** F9
Millicent: S. Australia **71** D11
Millie: N.S.W., Australia **71** H7
Millinocket: Maine, U.S.A. **89** R3
Millmerran: Queens., Austl. **70** J6
Millom: Cumbria, England **26** P11
Millport: Strath., Scotland **29** M8
Millstatt: Austria **41** T9
Millstream: W. Australia **68** B4
Millstreet: Cork, Repub. of
Ireland **31** C15
Milltown: Cavan, Repub. of
Ireland **30** G11
Milltown: Galway, Repub.
of Ireland **30** D12
Milltown: Kerry, Repub. of
Ireland **31** B15
Milltown Malbay: Clare,
Repub. of Ireland **31** C14
Milltownpass: Westmeath, Repub.
of Ireland **30** G13
Millvale: Trans., S. Africa **75** G2
Millville: N.J., U.S.A. **89** O6
Milly: France **36** H7
Milmerran: Queens., Austl. **69** J5
Milnathort: Tay., Scotland **29** P7
Milne Land: Greenland **85** R3
Milnerton: C.P., S. Africa **74** *Ins.*
Milnet: Ont., Canada **88** L2
Milngavie: Strath., Scotland **29** N8
Milnrow: Gt. Man., England **27** R12
Milnthorpe: Cumbria, Eng. **26** Q11
Milo: Maine, U.S.A. **89** R3
Milo: *riv.*, Guinea **80** C3
Milos: *i.*, Cyclades (Grc.) **39** T18
Milovaig: Inner Hebr., Scot. **28** H5
Milparinka: N.S.W., Austl. **71** D7
Miltenberg: W. Germany **44** P6
Milton: Fla., U.S.A. **91** H10
Milton: N.S.W., Australia **71** J10
Milton: N.S., Canada **89** T3
Milton: Oreg., U.S.A. **92** D3
Milton: Pa., U.S.A. **89** N5
Milton: South I., N.Z. **71** M18
Milton, Great: Oxon., Eng. **25** T16
Milton, New: Hants., Eng. **24** S18
Milton: Sevth: Devon, Eng. **24** O19
Milton Abbas: Dorset, Eng. **24** R18
Milton Abbot: Devon, Eng. **24** N18
Milton Damerel: Devon, England
24 N18
Milton Keynes: Bucks., England **25**
U15
Milton of Clova: Tayside,
Scotland **28** P6
Milton Regis: Kent, England **25** X17
Milumba: Tanzania **76** D4
Milverton: Som., England **24** P17
Milwaukee: Wis., U.S.A. **88** H4
Mimizan: France **37** D11
Mimizan-Plage: France **37** D11
Mimms, South: Greater London,
England **25** V16
Mimoň: Czechoslovakia **45** U5
Mimongo: Gabon **81** G5
Min: *riv.*, Fukien, China **62** V9
Min: *riv.*, Szechwan, China **62** S9
Mina: Nev., U.S.A. **93** D5
Mina, El: Lebanon **56** D4
Mina al Ahmadi: Kuwait **57** L7
Minab: Iran **55** J9
Minaea: *see under* Ma'in.
Minakuchi: Japan **63** e3
Minamata: Japan **63** b4
Minami: *i.*, (Jap.), Philippine
Sea **60** L6
Minami Iwo: *i.*, Kazan Is. **60** N7
Minari: Japan **63** c3
Minas: Uruguay **96** D3
Minas Basin: N.S., Canada **89** T3
Minas-Cué: Paraguay **95** E8
Minas de Riotinto: Spain **35** C18
Minas Gerais: *State*, Brazil (*cap.*
Belo Horizonte) **94** J7
Minas Novas: Brazil **94** J7
Minatitlán: Mexico **86** k14
Minbu: Burma **59** Q10
Minbya: Burma **59** Q10
Minch, North: *chan.*, Outer Hebr.,
Scotland **28** K3
Minch, The Little: *chan.*, Outer
Hebr./Inner Hebr., Scotland **28** H4
Minchinhampton: Glos.,
England **24** R16

Mincio: *riv.*, Italy **41** Q10
Minda: Congo **81** G5
Mindanao: *i. & sea*, Phil. **64** G5
Mindelheim: W. Germany **40** Q7
Minden: W. Germany **44** O3
Minden: La., U.S.A. **90** E9
Minden: Nebr., U.S.A. **93** H4
Minden: Nev., U.S.A. **93** D5
Mindengue: Congo **81** H4
Mindon: Burma **59** Q11
Mindoro: *i & str.*, Phil. **64** G4
Mindouli: Congo **81** G5
Mindszent: Hungary **43** R13
Mine Centre: Ont., Canada **88** E1
Minehead: Som., England **24** P17
Mine Head: Wat., Rep. of
Ireland **31** F16
Mineola: Tex., U.S.A. **90** D9
Minera: Clwyd, Wales **27** P13
Minera: Trans., S. Africa **75** H3
Mineral: Va., U.S.A. **89** N6
Mineral'nye: U.S.S.R. **50** F6
Mineral Point: *city*, Wis.,
U.S.A. **88** F4
Mineral Springs: Ark., U.S.A. **90** E9
Mineral Wells: Tex., U.S.A. **90** B9
Minerva Reefs: Pacific O. **67** Q6
Mineryino Murge: Italy **38** P16
Minety: Wilts., England **24** S16
Minfeng: Sinkiang, China **51** O7
Minga: Zaire **77** C5
Mingan: Que., Canada **85** n7
Mingary: S. Australia **71** D9
Mingchi: Fukien, China **62** V9
Mingechaurskoye Res.: Azerbayd-
zhan, U.S.S.R. **57** K1
Mingela: Queens., Australia **70** G2
Mingenew: W. Australia **68** B5
Mingin: Burma **59** Q10
Minginish: *dist.*, Inner Hebr.,
Scotland **28** J5
Mingio: Tanzania **76** D4
Mingo Junction: Ohio,
U.S.A. **88** L5
Mingoyo: Tanzania **77** E5
Mingshui: Heilungkiang, China **62** X5
Mingshui: Sinkiang, China **62** R6
Mingulay: *i.*, Outer Hebr.,
Scotland **29** G6
Minhla: Burma **59** Q11
Minho: Chinghai, China **62** S7
Minho: *Prov.*, Portugal (*cap.*
Braga) **35** B16
Minho: *riv.*, Spain/Portugal **35** B15
Minhow (Foochow): Fukien,
China **62** V9
Minicoy: *i.*, Laccadive Is. **58** M13
Minintàn: Man., Canada **92** G2
Minkebé: Gabon **81** G4
Min'kino: U.S.S.R. **46** X2
Minlaton: S. Australia **71** B10
Minlo: Kansu, China **62** S7
Minna: Niger, Nigeria **81** F3
Minnaar: Trans., S. Africa **75** H3
Minneapolis: Minn., U.S.A. **88** E3
Minnedosa: Man., Canada **92** H2
Minnesota: *riv.*, Minn., U.S.A. **92** H3
Minnesota: *State*, U.S.A.
(*cap.* St. Paul) **88** D3
Minnigaff: Dumfries & Galloway,
Scotland **29** N10
Minnipa: S. Australia **69** F6
Mino: Japan **63** e3
Minorca (Menorca): *i.*, Balearic
Is., (Sp.) **35** J17
Minot: N. Dak., U.S.A. **92** G3
Minozero: Karelian A.S.S. Rep.,
U.S.S.R. **46** W4
Minquiers, Plat. des: *is.*, Fr. **36** C7
MINSK: Byelorussia **43** U10
Mińsk Mazowiecki: Poland **43** S10
Minstead: Hants., England **25** S18
Minster: I. of Sheppey, Eng. **25** X17
Minsterley: Salop, England **27** Q14
Minto: Borders, Scotland **29** Q9
Minto, Lake: Que., Canada **85** m6
Mintsin: Kansu, China **62** S7
Minturnae: Roman city about 10
miles E. of Formia on road to
Capua, Italy **38** N16
Minuf: Egypt **56** B6
Minusinsk: U.S.S.R. **51** S4
Minya, El: Egypt **56** B6
Minya el Qamh: Egypt **56** B6
Minyar: U.S.S.R. **50** J3
Minyip: Vict., Australia **71** E11
Mio: Mich., U.S.A. **88** J3
Miquelon I.: (Fr.), North America
[*cap.* (with St. Pierre) St. Pierre]
85 s3
Mira: Italy **41** S10
Mira: *wadi*, Saudi Arabia **57** G6
Mira Bay: Cape Breton I.,
Canada **89** V2
Mirador: Brazil **94** J5
Miraflores: Mexico **93** F8
Miraflores: Panama **94** *Ins.*
Miramare (General Alvarado):
Argentina **96** D4
Miramare: Italy **41** T10
Miramas: France **37** L12
Mirambeau: France **37** E10
Miramichi Bay: N.B., Can. **89** T2
Miramont: France **37** F11
Miram Shah: NW. Front. Prov.,
Pakistan **58** M8
Miranda: Brazil **94** F8
Miranda de Ebro: Spain **35** E15
Miranda do Corvo: Portugal **35** B16
Miranda do Douro: Portugal **35** C16
Mirande: France **37** F12
Mirandela: Portugal **35** C16
Mirandola: Italy **41** R11
Mirani: Queens., Australia **70** H3
Mira Pampa: Argentina **96** C4
Mir Bashir: Azer., U.S.S.R. **57** K1
Mirboo: Vict., Australia **71** G12
Mir: *mtn.*, Yugoslavia **41** U10
Mirebeau: Côte d'Or, Fr. **40** L8
Mirebeau: Vienne, Fr. **37** F9
Mirecourt: France **40** M7
Mirepoix: France **37** G12
Mirfa: U.A.E. **55** H10
Mirfield: W. Yorks., England **27** S12
Miri: Sarawak, Malaysia **65** F4
Miriam Vale: Queens., Austl. **70** J5
Mirik, Cape: Mauritania **78** A6
Mirim, Lake: Brazil **96** E3
Miris: *tribe*, Arunachal Pradesh/
Assam, India **59** Q9
Mirjawa: Iran **55** K9
Mirnyy: Yugoslavia **41** V10
Mirny: *rsch. stn.*, Antarctica
9 70S 90E
Miroşi: Romania **39** T14
Mirotice: Czechoslovakia **45** U6
Mirow: E. Germany **45** S2
Mirpur Khas: Sind, Pak. **58** L9
Mirror Landing (Smith): Alta.,
Canada **92** E1
Mirsale: *well*, Somalia **79** R18
Mirtoón Sea: S. Europe **39** S18
Miruro: Mozambique **77** D6
Mirzachul': Uzbek., U.S.S.R.
51 L6

Mirzapur: Uttar Pradesh,
India **59** O9
Misaki: Ehime, Japan **63** c4
Misaki: Kanagawa, Japan **63** f3
Misamis: Mindanao, Phil. **64** G5
Misawa: Japan **63** ZZ6
Miscou I.: N.B., Canada **89** T2
Miscou Point: *cape*, N.B.,
Canada **89** T1
Misenum: ancient town and naval
station about 12 miles WSW.
of Naples, Italy **38** O16
Miserden: Glos., England **24** R16
Misgar: Jammu & Kashmir **58** M7
Misgund: C.P., S. Africa **74** E6
Mishan: Heilungkiang, China
63 Y5
Mishawaka: Ind., U.S.A. **88** H5
Misheguk Mt: N.W.T., Can. **84** c4
Mishima: Japan **63** f3
Mishkin: Iran **57** K2
Mishkino: U.S.S.R. **50** J3
Mishmi Hills: Arunachal Pradesh, India
59 R9
Mishmis: *tribe*, Arunachal Pradesh,
India **59** R9
Misho: Japan **63** c4
Misima: *i.*, Louisiade Arch. **69** J2
Misiones: *Prov.*, Argentina
(*cap.* Posadas) **96** E2
Miski: Sudan **79** J7
Miskin: Oman **55** J10
Miskolc: Hungary **43** R12
Misoöl: *i.*, W. Irian, Indon. **61** L12
Missenden, Great: Bucks.,
England **25** U16
Missinaibi Lake: Ont., Can. **88** K1
Missinata: Mali **80** D1
Mission: Tex., U.S.A. **90** B12
Mission City: B.C., Canada **92** C3
Mississagi: *riv.*, Ont., Can. **88** K2
Mississagi Prov. Park: Ont.,
Canada **88** K2
Mississippi: *riv.*, U.S.A. **86** L10
Mississippi: *State*, U.S.A.
(*cap.* Jackson) **90** G9
Mississippi River Delta: La.,
U.S.A. **90** *Ins.*
Mississippi Sound: Miss., U.S.A.
90 G10
Misson: Notts., England **27** U13
Missoula: Mont., U.S.A. **92** E3
Missour: Morocco **80** L8
Missouri: *riv.*, U.S.A. **86** j8
Missouri: *State*, U.S.A. (*cap.*
Jefferson City) **88** E6
Mistake: *riv.*, Queens., Austl. **70** G4
Mistassibi: *riv.*, Que., Can. **89** P1
Mistassini: & *riv.*, Que., Can. **89** P1
Mistassini: *lake*, Que., Can. **85** m7
Mistlebach: Austria **41** W7
Mistra: medieval foundation on W.
side of river *Eurotas* opposite
Spárti, Greece **39** S18
Mistretta: Sicily **38** O18
Misumi: Japan **63** b4
MISURATA: & *Prov.*, Libya **78** H3
Mitatib: Sudan **54** E11
Mitcheldean: Glos., Eng. **24** R16
Mitchell: Ind., U.S.A. **88** H6
Mitchell: Queens., Austl. **70** G6
Mitchell: S. Dak., U.S.A. **92** H4
Mitchell: *riv.*, Queens., Austl. **69** G3
Mitchell: *riv.*, Vict., Austl. **71** G11
Mitchell, Mount: N.C.,
U.S.A. **91** K8
Mitchell I.: U.S.A. **90** *Ins.*
Mitchell River Mission Station:
Queens., Austl. **69** G3
Mitchelstown: Cork, Repub. of
Ireland **31** E15
Miteda: Mozambique **77** E5
Mitford: Northumb., Eng. **26** S9
Mit Ghamr: Egypt **56** B6
Mitiaro: *i.*, Cook Is. **70** *Ins.*
Mitilini: Lesbos, Greece **39** U17
Mit(o: Ibaraki, Japan **63** g2
Mitre I. (Fataki): Pacific O. **67** O4
Mittagong: N.S.W., Austl. **71** J10
Mitta Mitta: & *riv.*, Vict.,
Australia **71** G11
Mittelfranken: *Dist.*, Bavaria,
West Germany **45** Q6
Mittelland Canal: W. Germany
44 O3
Mittelmark: *geog. reg.*,
E. Germany **42** N10
Mittenwald: W. Germany **41** R8
Mittenwalde: E. Germany **45** T3
Mittersill: Austria **41** S8
Mitterteich: W. Germany **45** S6
Mittweida: W. Germany **45** S5
Mitu: Colombia **94** C3
Mituba Mtns.: Zaire **76** C3
Mitumba Range: Zaire **76** C4
Mitwaba: Zaire **77** C4
Mityana: Uganda **76** D2
Mitzic: Gabon **81** G4
Mixnitz: Austria **41** V8
Miyagi: *Pref.*, Japan (*cap.* Sendai)
63 g1
Miyaji: Japan **63** b4
Miyake: *i.*, Japan **63** f3
Miyako: Japan **63** ZZ7
Miyako: *i.*, Ryukyu Is. **63** X10
Miyakonojo: Japan **63** b5
Miyandasht: Iran **55** J7
Miyanduab: Iran **57** K3
Miyata: Japan **63** b4
Miyauchi: Japan **63** g1
MIYAZAKI: & *Pref.*, Japan
63 b5
Miyoshi: Japan **63** c3
Miysakyula: Estonia,
U.S.S.R. **47** T7
Miyun: Peking Municipality,
China **62** Y6
Mi'zal: Saudi Arabia **54** G10
Mizda: Libya **32** E5
Mizen Head: *cape*, Cork, Repub.
of Ireland **31** B17
Mizen Head: *cape*, Wick.,
Repub. of Ireland **31** J14
Mizil: Romania **39** U14
Mizoch: Ukraine **43** U11
Mizque: Bolivia **94** D7
Mizusawa: Japan **63** ZZ7
Mjällom: Sweden **46** Q5
Mjanji: Uganda **76** D2
Mjölby: Sweden **47** O7
Mjösa: Lake: Norway **47** M6
Mkalama: Tanzania **76** D3
Mkamba: Tanzania **76** E4
Mkoe: Tanzania **77** E4
Mkokotoni: Tanzania **76** E4
Mkushi: Zambia **77** C5
Mkuze: Natal, S. Africa **75** K3
Mkwaya: Tanzania **77** E5
Mlada Boleslav: Czech. **45** U5
Mladá Vožice: Czech. **45** U6
Mladenovac: Yugoslavia **39** R14
Mlanje: Malawi **77** E6
Mława: Poland **43** R10
Mljet: *i.*, Yugoslavia **38** P15
Mnichovo Hradiště: Czech. **45** U5

Mo: Hedmark, Norway **47** M6
Mo: Nordland, Norway **46** O3
Mo.: Telemark, Norway **47** K7
Moa: Tanzania **76** E3
Moa: *i.*, Indonesia **61** K13
Moab: Utah, U.S.A. **93** F5
Moab: region E. of Dead Sea.
O.T. traditional name **55** b3
Moabi: Gabon **81** G5
Moala: *i.*, Fiji Is. **67** P5
Moama: N.S.W., Australia **71** F11
Moamba: Mozambique **75** K2
Moascar: Egypt (Suez Canal
Inset) **32** *Ins.*
Moate: Westmeath, Repub. of
Ireland **31** F13
Moba: Zaire **76** C4
MOBAYE: Basse-kotto, Cen. Afr.
Rep. **76** B2
Mobayi: Zaire **76** B2
Moberly: Mo., U.S.A. **88** E6
Mobile: Ala., U.S.A. **90** G10
Mobile Point: *cape*, Ala.,
U.S.A. **91** H10
Mobridge: S. Dak., U.S.A. **92** G3
Mocajuba: Brazil **94** H4
Moçambique: *see* Mozambique.
MOÇÂMEDES: & *Prov.*, Angola
73 G13
Mocha: Yemen **54** F12
Mocha I.: Chile **96** A4
MOCHUDI: Kgatleng, Botswana
75 G2
Mochukungka: Tibet, China
59 Q9
Mochy: Poland **45** W3
Mocimboa da Praia: Moz. **77** F5
Mocimboa do Rovuma:
Mozambique **77** E5
Möckeln Lake: Sweden **47** O8
Moclips: Wash., U.S.A. **92** C3
Mocoa: Colombia **94** B3
Mococa: Brazil **96** F1
Mocomoco: Bolivia **94** D7
Mocorito: Mexico **93** E7
Moctezuma: Chihuahua,
Mexico **93** F6
Moctezuma: San Luis Potosi,
Mexico **86** j13
Moctezuma: Sonora, Mexico **93** F7
Mocuba: Mozambique **77** E6
Mocuburi: Mozambique **77** E5
Modane: France **40** M10
Modbury: Devon, England **24** O19
Modder: *riv.*, O.F.S., S. Africa
75 F4
Modderbee: Trans., S. Afr. **74** N *Ins.*
Modder East: Trans., S. Africa
74 N *Ins.*
Modelligo: Wat., Repub. of
Ireland **31** F15
Modena: Italy **41** Q11
Modesto: Calif., U.S.A. **93** C5
Mödhrudalur: Iceland **46** f4
Mödhruvellir: Iceland **46** d4
Modica: Sicily **38** O18
Modigliana: Italy **41** R11
Modlin: Poland **43** R10
Mödling: Austria **41** W7
Modowi: W. Irian, Indon. **61** L12
Modřany: Czechoslovakia **45** U5
Modu: *riv.*, Nigeria **81** F3
Moe: Vict., Australia **71** G12
Moeb Bay: S.W. Africa **74** A2
Moebrani: W. Irian, Indon. **61** L12
Moëlan: France **36** B8
Moelfre: Gwynedd, Wales **27** N13
Moena: Italy **41** R9
Moeris: Graeco-Roman name of
El Faiyum, Egypt **54** D9
Moeris, Lake: name of an artificial
lake SW. of Cairo, near Lake
Qarun, Egypt **54** D9
Moesia: Roman province bounded
by Danube, Drina, and the
summit of the Balkan mtns., E.
Yugoslavia and Bulgaria **39** R14
Moeswal: S. Africa **74** E3
Moffat: & *riv.*, Dumfries &
Galloway, Scotland **29** P9
MOGADISCIO (Mogadishu):
Somalia **79** R19
Mogador: Morocco **80** K8
Mogadouro: Portugal **35** C16
Mogar: Ethiopia **79** E1
Mogaung: Burma **59** R9
Moghena: Chad **81** H3
Mogi das Cruzes: Brazil **96** F1
Mogilev: Byelorussia **50** D4
Mogilev-Podol'skiy: Ukraine **43** U12
Mogi Mirim: Brazil **96** F1
Mogincual: Mozambique **77** F6
Mogocha: U.S.S.R. **49** n7
Mogochin: U.S.S.R. **51** O3
Mogok: Burma **59** R10
Mogokori: Somalia **79** R19
Mogol: *riv.*, Trans., S. Africa
75 G1
Mogollon: N. Mex., U.S.A. **93** F6
Mogollon Plat.: Ariz., U.S.A. **93** E6
Moguer: Spain **35** C18
Mogumber: W. Australia **68** B6
Moguntiacum: Roman camp and city
at Mainz, W. Ger. **44** N6
Mogur: Ethiopia **79** F2
Mohács: Hungary **43** Q14
Mohales Hoek: & *Dist.*,
Lesotho **75** G5
Mohall: N. Dak., U.S.A. **92** G3
Mohammadia: Algeria **35** G19
Mohammedia: Morocco **80** K8
Mohavano: Mexico **93** G7
Mohave City: Ariz., U.S.A. **93** E5
Mohawk: N.Y., U.S.A. **89** O4
Mohenjo-Daro: city of ancient
Indus civilisation, 25 miles S. of
Larkana, Sind, Pakistan **58** L9
Moher, Cliffs of: Clare, Repub.
of Ireland **31** C14
Mohill: Leit., Repub. of Irel. **30** F12
Mohoro: Tanzania **76** E4
Moi: Norway **47** K7
Moia: Sudan **76** C1
Moidart: *loch & dist.*, Highland,
Scotland **29** K6
Moimenta da Beira: Port. **35** C16
Mointy: & *riv.*, Kazakh.,
U.S.S.R. **51** M5
Moira: Down, N. Ireland **30** J11
Moira: N.S.W., Australia **71** F11
Moirans: Isère, France **40** L10
Moirans: Jura, France **40** L9
Moisés Ville: Argentina **96** C3
Moisie: Que., Canada **84** N7
Moissac: France **37** G11
Moissala: Chad **81** H3
Moito: Chad **81** H2
Mojave: Calif., U.S.A. **93** D5
Mojave Desert: Calif., U.S.A.
93 D6
Mojo: *i.*, Indonesia **65** F8
Mojokerto: Java **65** E8
Moju: Brazil **94** H4
Mokabe Kasari: Zaire **77** C4

Mokai: North I., N.Z. **70** P14
Mokambo: Zaire **77** C5
Mokau: North I., N.Z. **70** P14
MOKHOTLONG: & *Dist.*, Lesotho **75** H4
Mokine: Tunisia **38** M19
Mokoko: Congo **81** H4
Mokolo: Cameroun **81** G2
Mokpo: S. Korea **63** X8
Mokrousovo: U.S.S.R. **51** L3
Moktar, Al: Niger **81** F2
Mokwa: Nigeria **81** F3
Mol: Belgium **44** L4
Mola di Bari: Italy **38** P16
Molat: *i.*, Yugoslavia **41** U11
MOLD: Clwyd, Wales **27** P13
Moldau (Vltava): *riv.*, Czech. **41** U7
Moldava: Czechoslovakia **43** R12
Moldavian S.S. Repub.: U.S.S.R. (*cap.* Kishinev) **50** C5
MOLDE: & *fiord*, Møre og Romsdal, Norway **46** K5
Moldova-Nouă: Romania **39** R14
Mole: *riv.*, Surrey, England **25** V17
Molen River: S. Africa **74** E4
MOLEPOLOLE: Kweneng, Botswana **75** F2
Molesey: Surrey, England **25** V17
Molfetta: Italy **38** P16
Molières: France **37** G11
Molina: Argentina **96** B3
Molina: Chile **96** B4
Molina: Spain **35** F17
Molina de Aragón: Spain **35** F16
Moline: Ill., U.S.A. **88** F5
Molinos: Argentina **96** B2
Moliro: Zaire **76** D4
Molitawatawoerhtsutzuchihchi: Heilungkiang, China **63** W5
Molko-Igol: U.S.S.R. **51** N2
Molland: Devon, England **24** O17
Mollendo: Peru **94** C7
Mollières-Vidame: France **36** H6
Mölln: W. Germany **45** G2
Mölndal: Sweden **47** N8
Molodechno: Byelorussia **47** U9
Molodenzhnaya: *rsch. stn.*, Antarctica **9** 70S 45E
Molodo: Mali **80** C2
Molokai: *i.*, Hawaiian Is. **83** c2
Molokai Fracture Zone: N. Pacific Ocean **7** 20N 150W
Moloma: *riv.*, U.S.S.R. **50** G3
Molong: N.S.W., Australia **71** H9
Molopo: *riv.*, S. Africa **74** E2
MOLOTOV (Perm): & *Reg.*, U.S.S.R. **50** J3
Molsheim: France **40** N7
Molson Lake: Man., Can. **92** H2
Molteno: & *Dist.*, S. Africa **75** G5
Molton, North: Devon, Eng. **24** O17
Molton, South: Devon, Eng. **24** O17
Moluccas: *is.*, Indonesia **61** K12
Molucca Sea: Indonesia **65** G7
Molumbo: Mozambique **77** E6
Moma: Zaire **76** B3
Moma: Mozambique **77** E6
Moma Mtns.: U.S.S.R. **49** q4
MOMBASA: Coast, Kenya **76** E3
Mombetsu: Japan **63** ZZ6
Mombo: Tanzania **76** E3
Mombongo: Zaire **76** B2
Momence: Ill., U.S.A. **88** H5
Momi: Zaire **76** C3
Mominabad: Maharashtra, India **58** N11
Mommark: Denmark **47** M9
Mompono: Zaire **76** B2
Mompós: Colombia **94** C2
Møn: Denmark **47** N9
Mona: Roman name of Anglesey **27** N13
Mona: *i.*, Puerto Rico **87** N14
Monach, Sound of: Outer Hebr., Scotland **28** G4
Monach (Heisker) Is.: Outer Hebr., Scotland **28** G4

Monaco: *Principality* **40** N12
Cap.: Monaco-Ville
Area: 0.8 sq. miles (2.07 sq. km.)
Pop.: 23,000 (*1971 E*)

Monadhliath Mtns.: Highland, Scotland **28** N5
MONAGHAN: & *Co.*, Repub. of Ireland **30** H11
Monamolin: Wex., Repub. of Ireland **31** J14
Monapo: Mozambique **77** F5
Mona Quimbundo: Angola **77** A4
Monar, Loch: High., Scot. **28** L5
Monarch Mount: B.C., Canada **92** B2
Monashee Mtns.: B.C., Canada **92** D2
Monasterace Marina: Italy **38** P17
Monasterevin: Kild., Repub. of Ireland **31** G13
Monastier, Le: France **37** J11
Monastir: Sardinia **38** L17
Monastir (Bitolj): Yugo. **39** R16
Monavullagh Mtns.: Wat., Repub. of Ireland **31** F15
Monbahus: France **37** F11
Moncalieri: Italy **40** N10
Monção: Portugal **35** B15
Moncay (Monkay): Vietnam **64** D2
Monchegorsk: U.S.S.R. **46** X3
Mönchen Gladbach: W. Ger. **44** M4
Monchiero: Italy **40** N11
Monchique: Portugal **35** B18
Monclova: Mexico **93** G7
Moncontour: Côtes-du-Nord, France **36** C7
Moncontour: Deux-Sèvres, France **36** E9
Moncoutant: France **37** E9
Moncton: N.B., Canada **89** T2
Mondego: *riv. & cape*, Port. **35** B16
Mondjuku: Zaire **76** B3
Mondo: Tanzania **76** E3
Mondolfo: Italy **41** T12
Mondombe: Zaire **76** B3
Mondoñedo: Spain **35** C15
Mondoubleau: France **36** F8
Mondovi: Italy **40** N11
Mondovi: Wis., U.S.A. **88** F3
Mondragone: Italy **38** N16
Mondsee: Austria **41** T8
Moneague: Jamaica **86** *Ins.*
Monemvasia: Greece **39** S18
Moneron: *i.*, (U.S.S.R.), G. of Tartary **63** ZZ5
Monessen: Pa., U.S.A. **89** M5
Monestier: France **40** L11
Monet: Que., Canada **89** O1
Monetnyy: U.S.S.R. **51** K3
Monett: Mo., U.S.A. **90** E7
Moneygall: Offaly, Repub. of Ireland **31** F14
Moneymore: Lon., N. Irel. **30** H10
Moneyneany: Lon., N. Irel. **30** H10

Monfalcone: Italy **41** T10
Monfestino: Italy **41** Q11
Monflanquin: France **37** F11
Monforte: Portugal **35** C17
Monforte: Spain **35** C15
Monga: Zaire **76** B2
Mongala: *riv.*, Zaire **76** A2
Mongalla: Sudan **76** D1
Mongana: Zaire **76** B2
Monger, Lake: W. Australia **68** B5
Monghopung: Burma **59** S10
Monghsat: Burma **59** R10
Monghyr: Bihar, India **59** P9
Mongkung: Burma **59** R10
Mongmit: Burma **59** R10
Mongnai: Burma **59** R10
Mongnawng: Burma **59** R10
Mongnim: Burma **59** R10
Mongo: Guera, Chad **78** H7
Mongo: *riv.*, Sierra Leone **80** B3

Mongolia: *Republic* **60** E2
Cap.: Ulan Bator
Area: 604,247 sq. miles (1,565,000 sq. km.)
Pop.: 1,283,000 (*1971 E*)

Mongonu: Nigeria **81** G2
Mongororo: Chad **79** J7
Mongoumba: Cen. Afr. Rep. **76** A2
Mongpan: Burma **59** R10
Mongpu: Burma **59** R10
Mongton: Burma **59** R10
MONGU: Western, Zambia **77** B6
Monguelfo: Italy **41** S9
Mongyal: Burma **59** R10
Mongyawng: Burma **59** S10
Monheim: W. Germany **41** Q7
Moniaive: Dumfries & Galloway, Scotland **29** O9
Monifieth: Tay., Scotland **29** Q7
Monikie: Tay., Scotland **29** Q6
Monitor Range: Nev., U.S.A. **93** D5
Monivea: Galway, R. of Irel. **31** D13
Monkey Point: *cape*, Nic. **87** I 15
Monkey River: Belize **86** *Ins.*
Monk Fryston: N. Yorks., England **27** T12
Monkland: Hereford & Worcester, England **24** Q15
Monkoto: Zaire **76** B3
Monkseaton: Tyne & Wear, England **26** T9
Monkton: Strath., Scotland **29** M8
Monmouth: Gwent, Wales **24** Q16
Monmouth: Ill., U.S.A. **88** F5
Monnickendam: Netherlands **44** L3
Monnow: *riv.*, England **24** Q16
Mono: *lake*, Calif., U.S.A. **93** D5
Mono: *riv.*, Togo **81** E3
Mono (Treasury) Is.: Solomon Is. **67** L3
Monomoy Point: *cape*, Mass., U.S.A. **89** R5
Monopoli: Italy **38** P16
Monor: Hungary **43** Q13
Monreal del Campo: Spain **35** F16
Monreith: Dumfries & Galloway, Scotland **29** M8
Monroe: Ga., U.S.A. **91** K9
Monroe: La., U.S.A. **90** E9
Monroe: Mich., U.S.A. **88** K5
Monroe: N.C., U.S.A. **91** L8
Monroe: Utah, U.S.A. **93** E5
Monroe: Wis., U.S.A. **88** G4
Monroe City: Mo., U.S.A. **88** F6
Monroeville: Ala., U.S.A. **91** H10
MONROVIA: Liberia **80** B3
MONS: Hainaut, Belgium **44** J5
Monschau: W. Germany **44** M5
Monségur: France **37** F11
Monselice: Italy **41** R10
Monserrate: *i.*, Mexico **93** E7
Monsomshi Lake: Ont., Canada **92** K2
Monsterås: Sweden **47** P8
Mont: France **36** G8
Montabaur: W. Germany **44** N5
Montacute: Som., England **24** Q18
Montagnac: France **37** J12
Montagnana: Italy **41** R10
Montagrier: France **37** F10
Montagu: & *Dist.*, S. Africa **74** D6
Montague: Mich., U.S.A. **88** H4
Montague: *i.*, Alaska, U.S.A. **84** E5
Montaigu: France **36** D9
Montaigut: France **37** G12
Montana: *geog. reg.*, Peru **94** C5
Montana: *State*, U.S.A. (*cap.* Helena) **92** F3
Montanaro: Italy **40** N10
Montánchez: Spain **35** C17
Montargis: France **36** H8
Montauban: Ille-et-Vilaine, France **36** C7
MONTAUBAN: Tarn-et-Garonne, France **37** G11
Montauk Point: *cape*, N.Y., U.S.A. **89** Q5
Montbard: France **36** K8
Montbéliard: France **40** M8
Mont Belvieu: Tex., U.S.A. **90** D11
Montblanch: Spain **35** G16
Montbrison: France **37** K10
Montbron: France **37** F10
Montceau-les-Mines: France **37** K9
Montcenis: France **37** K9
Mont Cenis: France **40** M10
Montcornet: France **36** K6
Montcuq: France **37** G11
MONT-DE-MARSAN: Landes, France **37** E12
Montdidier: France **36** H6
Mont-Dore, Le: France **37** H10
Monte, Pointe de: *cape*, Fr. **36** C9
Monteagudo: Argentina **96** E2
Monte Alegre: Minas Gerais, Brazil **94** H7
Monte Alegre: Pará, Brazil **94** G4
Montebello: Italy **41** R10
Monte Bello Is.: W. Austl. **68** B4
Montebelluno: Italy **41** S10
Monte Carlo: Monaco **40** N12
Monte Caseros: Argentina **96** D3
Montecatini Terme: Italy **41** Q12
Montech: France **37** G12
Monte Comán: Argentina **96** B3
Monte Cristo: *i.*, Italy **38** M15
Montedor: Portugal **35** B16
Montefiascone: Italy **38** N15
Montefrio: Spain **35** D18
Montego Bay: *town*, Jam. **86** *Ins.*
Monteiro: Brazil **94** K5
Montel-de-Gelat: France **37** H10
Montélimar: France **37** K11
Monte Lirio: Panama **94** *Ins.*
Montello: Wis., U.S.A. **88** G4
Montemagno: Italy **40** O11
Montemorelos: Mexico **93** H7
Montendre: France **37** E10
Montenegro: Brazil **96** F2

Montenegro (Amapá): Brazil **94** G3
Montenegro: *Repub.*, Yugoslavia (*cap.* Titograd) **39** Q15
Montepescali: Italy **38** M15
Montepuez: Mozambique **77** E5
Montepulciano: Italy **38** M15
Montereau: France **36** H7
Monterey: Calif., U.S.A. **93** C5
Monterey: Tenn., U.S.A. **88** J7
Monteria: Colombia **94** B2
Monteriggioni: Italy **41** R12
Monteros: Argentina **96** B2
MONTERREY: Nuevo Leon, Mexico **93** G7
Monte San Savino: Italy **41** R12
Monte Sant' Angelo: Italy **38** O16
Monte Santo: Brazil **94** K6
Monte Santu, Cape: Sardinia **38** L16
Montes Claros: Brazil **94** J7
Montese: Italy **41** Q11
Montevarchi: Italy **41** R12
Monte Verde: Angola **73** H11
MONTEVIDEO: Uruguay **96** D3
Montevideo: Minn., U.S.A. **92** H4
Monte Vista: Colo., U.S.A. **93** F5
Montezuma: Ga., U.S.A. **91** J9
Montezuma: Iowa, U.S.A. **88** E5
Montfaucon: Maine-et-Loire, France **36** D8
Montfaucon: Meuse, France **36** L6
Montfort: Eure, France **36** F6
Montfort: Ille-et-Vilaine, Fr. **36** D7
Montfort: Landes, France **37** E12
Montfort-l'Amaury: France **36** G7
MONTGOMERY: Ala., U.S.A. **91** H9
Montgomery: Minn., U.S.A. **88** E3
Montgomery: Powys, Wales **27** P14
Montgomery: W. Va., U.S.A. **88** L6
Montgomery City: Mo., U.S.A. **88** F6
Montguyon: France **37** E10
Monthey: Switzerland **40** M9
Monthureux: France **36** L7
Monti: Sardinia **38** L16
Monticelli D'Ongina: Italy **40** P10
Monticello: Ark., U.S.A. **90** F9
Monticello: Fla., U.S.A. **91** K10
Monticello: Ga., U.S.A. **91** K9
Monticello: Ill., U.S.A. **88** G5
Monticello: Ind., U.S.A. **88** H5
Monticello: Iowa, U.S.A. **88** F4
Monticello: Ky., U.S.A. **88** J7
Monticello: Maine, U.S.A. **89** S2
Monticello: Utah, U.S.A. **93** F5
Montichiari: Italy **40** Q10
Montier-en-Der: France **36** K7
Montiers-sur-Saulx: France **36** L7
Montifiorino: Italy **40** Q11
Montignac: France **37** G10
Montigny-le-Roi: France **40** L8
Montilla: Spain **35** D18
Montivilliers: France **36** F6
Mont Joli: *city*, Que., Can. **89** R1
Mont Laurier: *city*, Que., Canada **89** O2
Montlieu: France **37** E10
Mont Louis: Que., Canada **89** T1
Montluçon: France **37** H9
Montluel: France **37** L10
Montmarault: France **37** H9
Mont Martin: France **36** D7
Montmédy: France **36** L6
Montmélian: France **40** M10
Montmirail: Marne, France **36** J7
Montmirail: Sarthe, France **36** F7
Montmoreau: France **37** F10
Montmorency: Que., Can. **89** Q2
Montmorillon: France **37** F9
Montmort: France **36** J7
Monto: Queens., Australia **70** J5
Montoire: France **36** F8
Montoro: Spain **35** D17
Montpelier: Idaho, U.S.A. **92** E4
MONTPELIER: Vt., U.S.A. **89** R3
MONTPELLIER: Hérault, Fr. **37** J12
Montpézat: France **37** K11
Montpon: France **37** F10
Montréal: France **37** F12
Montréal: Que., Canada **89** P3
Montreal: *riv.*, Ont. (Algoma), Canada **88** J2
Montreal: *riv.*, Ont. (Timiskaming), Canada **88** L2
Montreal Lake: *town & lake*, Sask., Canada **92** F2
Montredon-Labessonnie: Fr. **37** H12
Montréjeau: France **37** F12
Montrésor: France **36** G8
Montreuil: France **36** H5
Montreuil-Bellay: France **36** E8
Montreux: Switzerland **40** M9
Montrevel: France **37** L9
Montrichard: France **36** G8
Montrond: France **37** H9
Montrose: Colo., U.S.A. **93** F5
Montrose: Pa., U.S.A. **89** P5
Montrose: Tayside, Scotland **29** R6
Mont-St.-Michel: France **36** D7
Montsalvy: France **36** H11
Montserrado: *Co.*, Liberia (*co. town* Monrovia) **80** B3

Montserrat: *Br. colony* **87** b2
Cap.: Plymouth
Area: 32 sq. miles (83 sq. km.)
Pop.: 12,300 (*1970 C*)

Mont Tremblant Prov. Park: Que., Canada **89** O2
Mont Valier, Pic de: France **37** G13
Monveda: Zaire **76** B2
Monymusk: Gram., Scotland **28** Q5
Monywa: Burma **59** R10
Monza: Italy **40** P10
Monze: Zambia **77** C6
Monzie: Tayside, Scotland **29** O7
Monzón: Spain **35** G16
Moocalla: S. Australia **71** B8
Mooetong: Celebes **65** G6
Mooi: *riv.*, Natal, S. Africa **75** J4
Mooiplaas: C.P., S. Africa **75** H6
Mooirivier: Natal, S. Afr. **75** H4
Mooncoin: Kilk., Republic of Ireland **31** G15
Moone: Kild., Repub. of Ireland **31** H14
Moongulla: N.S.W., Austl. **71** H7
Moonie: *riv.*, Queens., Austl. **70** H6
Moonta: S. Australia **71** B10
Moora: W. Australia **68** B6
Moorcroft: Wyo., U.S.A. **92** G4
Moordrift: Trans., S. Afr. **75** H2
Moorea: *i.*, Society Is. **83** E3
Moorefield: W. Va., U.S.A. **89** M6
Moorends: S. Yorks., England **27** U12
Moorfoot Hills: Loth., Scot. **29** P8
Moorhead: Minn., U.S.A. **92** H3
Moorhead: Miss., U.S.A. **90** F9
Moorna: N.S.W., Australia **71** E14
Mooroopna: Vict., Austl. **71** F11
Moorreesburg: C.P., S. Africa **74** C6

Moors, The: *dist.*, Dumfries & Galloway, Scotland **29** M10
Moosburg: W. Germany **41** R7
Moosehead Lake: Maine, U.S.A. **89** R3
Moose Jaw: Sask., Canada **92** F2
Moose Lake: Man., Canada **92** G2
Moose Lake: *city*, Minn., U.S.A. **88** E2
Moose Mountain Prov. Park: Sask., Canada **92** G3
Moosomin: Sask., Canada **92** G2
Moosonee: Ont., Canada **85** I7
Mopéa Velha: Mozambique **77** E6
Mopélia: Society Is. **83** e3
Mopipi: Botswana **77** B7
Mopoi: Cen. Afr. Rep. **76** C1
MOPTI: & *Reg.*, Mali **80** D2
Moqatta: Sudan **54** E12
Moquegua: Peru **94** C7
Mora: Cameroun **81** G2
Mora: Minn., U.S.A. **88** E3
Móra: Portugal **35** B17
Mora: Spain **35** E17
Mora: Sweden **47** O6
Mora de Rubielos: Spain **35** F16
Morafenobé: Malagasy Rep. **73** N13
Moramanga: Malagasy Rep. **73** O13
Moran: Wyo., U.S.A. **92** E4
Morane: *i.*, Tuamotu Arch. **83** h4
Morannes: France **36** E8
Morano: Italy **38** P17
Morant Bay: *town*, Jamaica **86** *Ins.*
Morar, Loch: High., Scotland **28** K6
Morar, North: *dist.*, Highland, Scotland **28** K6
Morar, South: *dist.*, Highland, Scotland **28** K6
Moratalla: Spain **35** F17
Moratuwa: Sri Lanka **58** N13
Morava: *riv.*, Czechoslovakia **43** P12
Morava: *riv.*, Yugoslavia **39** R14
Moravia: *geog. reg.*, Czech. **43** P12
Moravská Ostrava: Czech. **43** Q12
Moravské Budějovice: Czech. **45** V6
Morawa: W. Australia **68** B5
Morawhanna: Guyana **87** d6
Moray Firth: Scotland **28** O4
Morbach: W. Germany **44** N6
Morbegno: Italy **40** P9
Morbihan: *Dept.*, France (*cap.* Vannes) **36** C8
Mörbylånga: Sweden **47** P8
Morcenx: France **37** E11
Morchard Bishop: Devon, England **24** O18
Mordelles: France **36** D7
Mordialloc: Vict., Australia **71** F12
Mordon A.S.S. Repub.: U.S.S.R. (*cap.* Saransk) **50** F4
Mordovo: U.S.S.R. **50** F4
Mordvinof, Cape: Aleutians **84** c7
Mordy-Yakha: U.S.S.R. **48** h3
More, Glen: *val.*, High., Scot. **28** M5
More, Loch: High., Scot. **28** N3
More, Loch: High., Scot. **28** M3
Morea (Carpolac): Vict., Australia **71** D11
Morea (Peloponnese): *reg.*, Greece **39** S18
Moreau: *riv.*, S. Dak., U.S.A. **92** G3
Morebath: Devon, England **24** P17
Morebattle: Bord., Scotland **29** R8
Morecambe: Lancs., Eng. **27** Q11
Morecambe Bay: Lancs., England **26** Q11
Morée: France **36** G8
Moree: N.S.W., Australia **71** H7
Morehead: Ky., U.S.A. **88** K6
Morehead City: N.C., U.S.A. **91** N8
Morelia: Mexico **86** j14
Morella: Queens., Australia **69** G4
Morella: Spain **35** F16
Morenci: Ariz., U.S.A. **93** F6
Morenci: Mich., U.S.A. **88** K5
Moreno: Argentina **96** D3
Møre og Romsdal: *Co.*, Norway (*cap.* Molde) **46** K5
Moresby: Cumbria, England **26** O10
Moresby I.: B.C., Canada **84** f7
Moresnet: France **40** L10
Moret: France **36** H7
Moreton: Essex, England **24** W16
Moreton: Mers., England **27** P13
Moreton Bay: Queens., Australia **70** K6
Moretonhampstead: Devon, England **24** O18
Moreton in Marsh: Glos., England **25** S16
Moreton I. & *bay*, Queens., Australia **70** K6
Moreton Pinkney: Northants., England **25** T15
Morez: France **40** M9
Morgan: S. Australia **71** C9
Morgan City: La., U.S.A. **90** F11
Morganfield: Ky., U.S.A. **88** H7
Morgan Harbor: La., U.S.A. **90** *Ins.*
Morgans: W. Australia **68** D5
Morganton: N.C., U.S.A. **91** L8
Morgantown: W. Va., U.S.A. **89** M6
Morganville: Queens., Austl. **70** J5
Morgenzon: Trans., S. Afr. **75** H3
Morges: Switzerland **40** M9
Morgex: Italy **40** N10
Morgny: France **36** G6
Morhange: France **40** M7
Mori: Hokkaido, Japan **63** ZZ6
Mori: Italy **41** Q10
Mori: Oita, Japan **63** b4
Mori: *riv.*, S. Africa **75** J1
Morie, Loch: High., Scotland **28** N4
Morin: *riv.*, China **63** X7
Moringen: W. Germany **45** P4
Morini: Gallic tribe in Pas-de-Calais, France **36** G5
Morioka: Japan **63** ZZ7
Morioka: Mexico **93** F7
Morisset: N.S.W., Australia **71** J9
Moriston, Glen: High., Scot. **28** M5
Morita: Japan **63** e2
Morjärv: Sweden **46** S3
Morkalla: Vict., Australia **71** D10
Morkoka: *riv.*, U.S.S.R. **49** N4
Morlaix: France **36** B7
Morley: W. Yorks., England **27** S12
Morley: Vict., Austl. **71** F12
Mornington I.: Australia **69** F3

Morokweng: S. Africa **74** E3
Moromaho: *i.*, Tukangbesi Is., Indonesia **65** G8
Morombe: Malagasy Rep. **73** N14
Morón: Cuba **87** M13
Morona: *riv.*, Ecuador/Peru **94** B4
Morondava: Malagasy Rep. **73** N14
Morón de la Frontera: Spain **35** D18
Moronii Huryee: Mongolia **49** M8
Morotai: *i.*, Moluccas, Indon. **61** K11
MOROTO: Karamoja, Uganda **76** D2
Moroubas: Cen. Afr. Rep. **76** B1
Morowali: Celebes **65** G7
Morozovali: U.S.S.R. **50** F5
Morpeth: Northumb., England **26** S9
Morphou: Cyprus **56** C4
Morretes: Brazil **96** F2
Morrilton: Ark., U.S.A. **90** E8
Morrinhos: Brazil **94** H7
Morrinsville: North I., N.Z. **70** P13
Morris: Ill., U.S.A. **88** G5
Morris: Man., Canada **92** H3
Morris: Minn., U.S.A. **92** H3
Morris, Mount: U.S.A. **88** K4
Morris Jesup, Cape: Greenland **85** q1
Morrison: Ill., U.S.A. **88** G5
Morrison: W. Glam., Wales **24** O16
Morristown: N.J., U.S.A. **89** O5
Morristown: N.Y., U.S.A. **89** O3
Morristown: Tenn., U.S.A. **88** K7
Morrisville: Vt., U.S.A. **89** P3
Morro Bay: *city*, Calif., U.S.A. **93** C5
Morro do Chapéu: Brazil **94** J6
Morrovalle: Italy **41** T12
Morrumbene: Mozambique **77** E7
Morshansk: U.S.S.R. **50** F4
Mörsil: Sweden **46** N5
Morsott: Algeria **38** L19
Mortagne: Charente-Inférieure, France **37** E10
Mortagne: Orne, France **36** F7
Mortagne-sur-Sèvre: France **36** E9
Mortágua: Portugal **35** B16
Mortain: France **36** E7
Mortara: Italy **40** O10
Morteau: France **40** M8
Morteaux-Couliboeuf: Fr. **36** E7
Morteros: Argentina **96** C3
Mortimer's Cross: Hereford & Worcester, England **24** Q15
Mortlake: Vict., Australia **71** E12
Morton: Lincs., England **27** V14
Morundah: N.S.W., Austl. **71** G10
Moruya: N.S.W., Australia **71** J10
Morvan: *geog. reg.*, France **36** J8
Morven: Queens., Australia **70** G6
Morven: *mtn.*, High., Scot. **28** O3
Morven: *dist.*, High., Scot. **29** K6
Morwell: Vict., Australia **71** G12
Morwenstow: Corn., Eng. **24** M18
Moryn: France **40** M9
Mosal'sk: U.S.S.R. **50** D4
Mosbach: W. Germany **44** P6
Moščenice: Yugoslavia **41** U10
Moscos Is.: Burma **59** R12
Moscow: U.S.S.R. (*cap.*) Idaho, U.S.A. **92** D3
Moscow: Strath., Scotland **29** N8
MOSCOW (Moskva): & *Reg.*, U.S.S.R. **50** E3
Mosedal: Cumbria, England **26** P10
Mosel (Moselle): *riv.*, W. Germany **44** N5
Moselle: *Dept.*, France (*cap.* Metz) **44** M6
Moselle (Mosel): *riv.*, France **44** M6
Moserboden: Austria **41** S8
Moses Lake: Wash., U.S.A. **92** D3
Moses Reef: Austral. Is. **83** e4
Mosgiel: South I., N.Z. **71** N17
Moschchnyy: *i.*, U.S.S.R. **47** U6
MOSHI: Kilimanjaro, Tanzania **76** E3
Moshupa: Botswana **75** F2
Mosi: Tanzania **77** D4
Mosinee: Wis., U.S.A. **88** G3
Mosito: C.P., S. Africa **75** F3
Mosjøen: Norway **46** N4
Moskenesøy: *i.*, Lofoten Is., (Nor.) **46** N3
MOSKVA (Moscow): U.S.S.R. **50** E3
Møs Lake: Norway **47** L7
Mosomane: Botswana **75** G2
Moson: Hungary **41** X8
Mosonmagyaróvár: Hungary **43** P13
Mosonszentjános: Hungary **41** X8
Mosquera: Colombia **94** B3
Mosquito Lagoon: Fla., U.S.A. **91** L11
Mosquitos, G. of: Panama **87** I16
Moss: Clwyd, Wales **27** P13
Moss Østfold: Norway **47** M7
Mossaka: Congo **81** H5
Mossâmedes: Angola **73** G13
Mossbank: Mainland, Shetland Is. **28** *Ins.*
Mossburn: South I., N.Z. **71** M17
Mossel Bay: C.P., S. Africa **74** E7
Mossel Bay: *town & District*, S. Africa **74** E7
Mossendjo: Congo **81** G5
Mossgiel: N.S.W., Australia **71** F9
Mossley: Gt. Man., England **27** R12
Mossman: Queens., Austl. **69** H3
Mossoró: Brazil **94** K5
Moss Point: *city*, Miss., U.S.A. **90** G10
Moss Vale: N.S.W., Austl. **71** J10
Most: Czechoslovakia **45** T5
Mosta: Malta **32** *Ins.*
MOSTAGANEM: & *Reg.*, Algeria **35** G19
Mostar: Yugoslavia **39** P15
Mostardas: Brazil **96** E3
Møsting, Cape: Greenland **85** p5
Mostiska: Ukraine **43** S12
Mosty: Byelorussia **43** T10
Mostyn: Clwyd, Wales **27** P13
Mosul: Iraq **57** H3
Mosulpo: Quelpart I., S. Korea **63** X8
Motaba: *riv.*, Congo **81** H4
Mota del Marqués: Spain **35** D16
Motala: Sweden **47** O7
Motale: *riv.*, Trans., S. Africa **75** J1
Motane: *i.*, Marquesas **83** h1
Motegi: Japan **63** g2
Mothe, La: France **37** E9
Mothe-Achard, La: France **37** D9
Motherwell: Strath., Scotland **29** O8
Moti: Kwangtung, China **62** T10
Motihari: Bihar, India **59** P9
Motilla del Palancar: Spain **35** F17
Motiti I.: North I., N.Z. **70** Q13
Motnik: Yugoslavia **41** U9
Motol': Byelorussia **43** T10
Motomo: Mozambique **77** E6
Motovsky Pogost: U.S.S.R. **46** W2
Motovun: Yugoslavia **41** T10
Motril: Spain **35** E18
Mott: N. Dak., U.S.A. **92** G3
Motta di Livenza: Italy **41** S10
Motte, Lac La: *lake*, Que., Canada **89** M1
Motte-Beuvron, La: France **36** H8
Motte-du-Caire, La: France **40** M4
Motte-Servolex, La: France **40** L10
Mottisfont: Hants., England **25** S17

Motueka: South I., N.Z. 70 O15
Motuhora: see Moutohora.
Motu Iti: i., Marquesas Is. 83 g1
Motu-Iti: i., Society Is. 83 e3
Motul: Mexico 86 L13
Motupe: Peru 94 B5
Motutunga: i., Tuamotu Arch. 83 g3
Motygina: U.S.S.R. 51 Q3
Moudjeria: Mauritania 78 B6
Moudon: Switzerland 40 M9
Moudros (Mudros): Lemnos, Greece 39 T17
MOUILA: N'Gounié, Gabon 81 G5
Mouille Point: cape, S. Africa 74 Inc.
Mouit: Mauritania 78 B5
Mouka: Central African Repub. 76 B1
Moukani: Gabon 81 G5
Moulamein: N.S.W., Austl. 71 F10
Moulapamok: Laos 64 D4
Mould Bay: weather station, N.W.T., Canada 84 H2
Moulin: Tayside, Scotland 29 O6
MOULINS: Allier, France 37 J9
Moulins-Engilbert: France 36 J9
Moulins-la-Marche: France 36 F7
Moulismes: France 37 F9
MOULMEIN: Tenasserim, Burma 59 R11
Moulouya: riv., Morocco 80 L8
Moulton: Ches., England 27 Q13
Moulton: Iowa, U.S.A. 88 E5
Moulton: Lincs., England 25 V14
Moulton: Northants., Eng. 25 U15
Moulton: N. Yorks., England 26 R13
Moultrie: Ga., U.S.A. 91 K10
Moultrie, Lake: S.C., U.S.A. 91 L9
MOUNDOU: Logone Occidental, Chad 81 H3
Moundsville: W. Va., U.S.A. 88 L6
Mountainair: N. Mex., U.S.A. 93 F6
Mountain Ash: Mid Glamorgan, Wales 24 P16
Mountain City: Tenn., U.S.A. 88 L7
Mountain Grove: Mo., U.S.A. 88 E7
Mountain Home: Idaho, U.S.A. 92 D4
Mountain Park: town, Alta., Canada 92 D2
Mountain Pine: Ark., U.S.A. 90 E8
Mountain View: Ark., U.S.A. 90 E8
Mount Airy: N.C., U.S.A. 88 L7
Mount Alfred: Queens., Australia 70 Ff
Mount Aycliff: see Maxesibeni
Mount Ayr: Iowa, U.S.A. 92 J4
Mount Barker: S. Australia 71 C10
Mount Barker: W. Australia 68 B6
Mount Barnett: W. Austl. 68 D3
Mount Bellew: Galway, Repub. of Ireland 30 E13
Mountbolus: Offaly, Repub. of Ireland 31 F13
Mount Buffalo National Park, Vict., Australia 71 G11
Mount Carmel: Ill., U.S.A. 88 H6
Mount Carrol: Ill., U.S.A. 88 G4
Mount Clemens: Mich., U.S.A. 88 K4
Mount Communism: Tadzhik., U.S.S.R. 55 M7
Mount Cook National Park: S.I., New Zealand 70 N16
Mount Coolon: Queens., Australia 70 G3
Mount Currie: Dist., S. Afr. 75 H5
Mount Cuthbert: Queens., Australia 69 F3
Mount Darwin: Rhodesia 77 D6
Mount Desert I.: Maine, U.S.A. 89 R3
Mount Dora: Fla., U.S.A. 91 L11
Mount Doreen: N. Territ., Australia 68 E4
Mount Drysdale: N.S.W., Australia 71 F8
Mount Eba: S. Australia 69 F6
Mount Edwards: Queens., Australia 70 K7
Mountfield: Tyrone, N. Irel. 30 G10
Mount Fletcher: S. Africa 75 H5
Mount Forest: Ont., Canada 88 L4
Mount Frere: see Kwabhaca
Mount Gambier: S. Austl. 71 D11
Mount Garnet: Queens., Australia 69 H3
Mount Harris: Colo., U.S.A. 93 F4
Mount Hawke: Corn., Eng. 24 L19
Mount Hope: N.S.W., Austl. 71 F9
Mount Hope: Panama 94 Ins.
Mount Hope: S. Australia 71 A10
Mount Ida: W. Australia 68 C5
Mount Isa: Queens., Austl. 69 F3
Mount Jewett: Pa., U.S.A. 89 M5
Mount Lofty Range: S. Australia 71 C10
Mount MacConnel: Queens., Australia 70 G3
Mount Magnet: W. Austl. 68 B5
Mountmellick: Laois, Repub. of Ireland 31 G13
Mount Montgomery: Nev., U.S.A. 93 D5
Mount Morgan: Queens., Australia 70 J4
Mount Morris: N.Y., U.S.A. 89 N4
Mount Morris: Queens., Australia 70 F5
Mount Mulligan: Queens., Australia 69 G3
Mountnessing: Essex, Eng. 24 W16
Mount Newman: W. Australia 68 B4
Mount Norris: Armagh, N. Ireland 30 J11
Mount Nugent: Cavan, Repub. of Ireland 30 G12
Mount Olive: N.C., U.S.A. 91 M8
Mount Peake: N. Territ., Australia 68 E5
Mount Perry: Queens., Austl. 70 J5
Mount Pleasant: Iowa, U.S.A. 88 F5
Mount Pleasant: Mich., U.S.A. 88 J4
Mount Pleasant: S. Austl. 71 C10
Mount Pleasant: S.C., U.S.A. 91 M9
Mount Pleasant: Tenn., U.S.A. 91 H8
Mount Pleasant: Tex., U.S.A. 90 D9
Mount Pleasant: Utah, U.S.A. 93 E5
Mount Pulaski: Ill., U.S.A. 88 G5
Mount Rainier Nat. Park: Wash., U.S.A. 92 C3
Mountrath: Laois, Repub. of Ireland 31 G13
Mount's Bay: Corn., Eng. 25 L19
Mountshannon: Clare, Repub. of Ireland 31 E14
Mountsorrel: Leics., Eng. 27 T14
Mount Sterling: Ill., U.S.A. 88 F6
Mount Sterling: Ky., U.S.A. 88 K6
Mount Stewart: C.P., S. Africa 75 F6
Mount Surprise: Queens., Australia 69 G3
Mount Swan: N. Territ., Australia 69 F4
Mount Union: Pa., U.S.A. 89 N5
Mount Vernon: Ala., U.S.A. 90 G10
Mount Vernon: Ill., U.S.A. 88 G6
Mount Vernon: Ind., U.S.A. 88 H7
Mount Vernon: Ky., U.S.A. 88 J7
Mount Vernon: Mo., U.S.A. 90 E7
Mount Vernon: N.Y., U.S.A. 89 P5
Mount Vernon: Ohio, U.S.A. 88 K5

Mount Vernon: Wash., U.S.A. 92 C3
Mount Willoughby: S. Austl. 68 E5
Moura: Brazil 94 E4
Moura: Portugal 35 C17
Mourabilla: N.S.W., Austl. 71 G7
Mourão: Portugal 35 C17
Mourdiah: Mali 80 C2
Mourdi Depression: Chad 79 J6
Mourmelon: France 36 K6
Mourme Mtns.: Down, N. Ireland 30 J11
Mouscron: Belgium 44 J5
Mousehole: Corn., England 25 K19
Moussoro: Chad 81 H2
Moustey: France 37 E11
Mouswald: Dumfries & Galloway, Scotland 29 P9
Moutamba: Congo 81 G5
Mouthe: France 40 M9
Mouthoumet: France 37 H13
Mouti, Mt.: Cameroon 81 G3
Moutier: Switzerland 40 N8
Moutiers: France 40 M10
Moutohora: North I., N.Z. 70 Q14
Mouyondzi: Congo 81 G5
Mouzon: France 36 L6
Movile: Don., Repub. of Irel. 30 G9
Mowbray: C.P., S. Africa 74 Ins.
Mowbullah: mtn., Australia 70 B4
Mowcop: Ches., England 27 R13
Mowping: Shantung, China 63 W7
Mowu: Inner Mongolia, China 62 R6
Moxico: Prov., Angola (cap. Luso) 77 B5
Moy: Tyr., N. Ireland 30 H11
Moy: riv., Mayo/Sligo, Repub. of Ireland 30 C11
Moyale: Kenya 76 E2
Moyamba: Sierra Leone 80 B3
Moyasta: Clare, Repub. of Ireland 31 B14
Moycullen: Galway, Repub. of Ireland 31 C13
Moydow: Long., Repub. of Ireland 30 F12
Moyen-Chari: Pref., Chad (cap. Sarh) 81 H3
Moyeni: Natal, S. Africa 75 J4
Moyen-Ogooué: Reg., Gabon (cap. Lambaréné) 81 G5
Moyeuvre-la-Grande: France 44 M6
Moylgrove: Dyfed, Wales 24 M15
Moynalty: Meath, Repub. of Ireland 30 H12
Moyne: Tip., Repub. of Irel. 31 F14
Moyo: Uganda 76 D2
Moyobamba: Peru 94 B5
Moyowosi: riv., Tanzania 76 D3
Moyrazès: France 37 H11
Moyvore: Westmeath, Repub. of Ireland 30 F12

Mozambique: Republic 73 L13
Cap. Maputo
Area: 303,073 sq. miles (784,959 sq. km.)
Pop.: 8,233,834 (1970 C)

Mozambique: Niassa, Mozambique 77 F6
Mozambique: Dist., Mozambique (cap. Nampula) 77 E5
Mozambique Basin: Indian Ocean 9 35S 35E
Mozambique Fracture Zone: Indian Ocean 9 45S 30E
Mozambique Point: cape, La., U.S.A. 90 Ins.
Mozambique Ridge: Indian Ocean 9 35S 35E
Mozdok: U.S.S.R. 50 F6
Mozhaysk: U.S.S.R. 50 E3
Mozhga: U.S.S.R. 50 H3
Mozirje: Yugoslavia 41 U9
Mozyr: Byelorussia 43 V10
Mozyr': riv., Sarawak, Malaysia 65 E6
Mpanda: Tanzania 76 D4
Mpela: Tanzania 76 D4
Mpendle: & Dist., Natal, S. Africa 75 H4
Mpésoba: Mali 80 C2
Mpigi: Uganda 76 D2
Mpika: Zambia 77 D5
M'Pimbe: Malawi 77 E6
Mpofana: Natal, S. Africa 75 J4
Mporokoso: Zambia 77 D4
M'Pouya: Congo 81 H5
Mpraeso: Ghana 80 D3
Mpui: Tanzania 76 D4
Mpulungu: Zambia 77 D4
Mpuapwa: Tanzania 76 E4
Mqanduli: S. Africa 75 H5
Mrayer, El: Mauritania 78 C5
Mreti, El: Mauritania 78 C5
Mrewa: Rhodesia 77 D6
Msalu: riv., Mozambique 77 E5
Msata: Tanzania 76 E4
Mšeno: Czechoslovakia 45 U5
M'sila: Algeria 35 J19
Msoga: Tanzania 76 D4
Mtakuja: Tanzania 76 D4
Mtama: Tanzania 77 E5
Mtambo: Tanzania 76 E4
Mtera: Tanzania 76 E4
Mtito Andei: Kenya 76 E3
Mtoko: Rhodesia 77 D6
Mtubatuba: Natal, S. Afr. 75 K4
Mtuga: Zambia 77 C5
Mtundo I.: Mozambique 77 F5
Mtunzini: dist., Natal, S. Africa 75 J4
MTWARA: & Reg., Tanzania 77 F5
Mu: riv., Burma 59 R10
Muaguide: Mozambique 77 F5
Mualama: Mozambique 77 E6
Muaná: Brazil 94 H4
Muangai: Angola 77 A5
Muang Hot: Thailand 64 B3
Muang Phayao: Thailand 64 B3
Muang Phen: Thailand 64 C3
Muar (Bandar Maharani): Malaya, Malaysia 65 c12
Muara: Sumatra 65 C7
Muara Aman: Sumatra 65 C7
Muarabeliti: Sumatra 65 C7
Muarabungo: Sumatra 65 C7
Muarajului: Borneo 65 E7
Muarakaman: Borneo 65 F7
Muaralabuh: Sumatra 65 C7
Muaralasan: Borneo 65 F6
Muarapahu: Borneo 65 F7
Muara Siberut: Mentawai Is., Indonesia 65 B7
Muaratembesi: Sumatra 65 C7
Muaratewe: Borneo 65 E7
Muarawahau: Borneo 65 F6
Muatua: Mozambique 77 E6
Mubairik: Saudi Arabia 54 E10
Mubarraz: Saudi Arabia 55 G9
Mubende: Uganda 76 D2
Mubi: Nigeria 81 G2
Mubur: i., Anambas Is., Indonesia 65 D6
Much: W. Germany 44 N5
Muchalls: Gram., Scotland 28 R5
Much Birch: Hereford & Worcester, England 24 Q16

Mücheln: E. Germany 45 R4
Muchelney: Som., England 24 Q17
Much Hadham: Herts., Eng. 25 W16
Much Hoole: Lancs., England 27 Q12
Muchinga Mtns.: Zambia 77 D5
Muchkap: U.S.S.R. 50 F4
Much Wenlock: Salop, England 27 Q14
Mück: i., Inner Hebr., Scot. 28 H5
Muckadilla: Queens., Austl. 70 H6
Muckish: mtn., Don., Repub. of Ireland 30 F9
Muckle Flugga: i., Shetland Is., Scotland 28 Ins.
Muckle Roe: i., Shetland Is., Scotland 28 Ins.
Mucklestone: Staffs., Eng. 27 R14
Mucojo: Mozambique 77 F5
Mucomaze: Mozambique 75 K3
Mucubela: Mozambique 77 E6
Mucur: Turkey 56 D2
Mucuri: Brazil 94 K7
Mucusso: Angola 77 B6
Mudanya: Turkey 56 A1
Muddo Gashi: Kenya 76 E2
Muddus National Park: Sweden 46 R3
Müden: W. Germany 45 Q3
Mudgee: N.S.W., Australia 71 H9
Mudhaibi: Oman 55 J10
Mudhail: well, Oman 55 H11
Mudhnib: Saudi Arabia 54 F9
Mudigere: Karnataka, India 58 N12
Mudros (Moudhros): Lemnos, Greece 39 T17
Mudugh: Reg., Somalia (cap. Galkayu) 79 R18
Muden: Turkey 56 B1
Muecate: Mozambique 77 E5
Mueda: Mozambique 77 E5
Muembe: Mozambique 77 E5
Muff: Don., Repub. of Irel. 30 G9
Mufulira: Zambia 77 C5
Mugeary: Inner Hebr., Scot. 28 J5
Mugeba: Mozambique 77 E6
Mughair Shuaib: Sau. Arab. 54 E9
Mughshin: wadi, Sau. Arab. 55 H11
Muglad, El: Sudan 79 K7
Mugulo: Papua/New Guin. 66 H3
Mugur an Na'am: well, Iraq/ Saudi Arabia 57 G6
MUGLA: & Prov., Turkey 39 V18
Muhaiwir: Iraq 57 G5
Muhammad, Al Bu: tribe, Iraq 57 K6
Muhammad Qol: Sudan 54 E10
Muhari, Shaib: wadi, Iraq 57 J6
Muhembo Drift: geog. reg., Botswana 77 B6
Muheza: Tanzania 76 E4
Muhinga: Burundi 76 D3
Muhinji Chini: Tanzania 77 E4
Mühlberg: E. Germany 45 T4
Mühldorf: W. Germany 41 S7
Mühlhausen: E. Germany 45 Q4
Muhos: Finland 46 U4
Muhu: & i., strait, Estonia, U.S.S.R. 47 S10
Muhutwe: Tanzania 76 D3
Muidumbe: Mozambique 77 E5
Muie: Angola 77 B5
Muine Beag (Bagenalstown): Carlow, Repub. of Ireland 31 H14
Muirdrum: Tay., Scotland 29 Q6
Muirhead: Tay., Scotland 29 P7
Muirkirk: Strath., Scotland 29 N8
Muir of Fowlis: Gram., Scot. 28 Q5
Muir of Ord: High., Scot. 28 N4
Mui Ron, Cape: Vietnam 64 D3
Muiskraal: C.P., S. Africa 74 D6
Muite: Mozambique 77 E5
Muizenberg: C.P., S. Africa 74 Ins.
Mujila Mtns.: Zaire 76 C4
Mujimbeji: Zambia 77 B5
Mujong: riv., Sarawak, Malaysia 65 E6
Mukachevo: Ukraine 43 S12
Mukah: Sarawak, Malaysia 65 E6
Mukalla: Yemen P.D.R. 55 G12
MUKDEN (Shenyang): Liaoning, China 63 W6
Muker: N. Yorks., England 26 R11
Mukhavets: riv., Byelorussia 43 T10
Mukinbudin: Western Australia 68 B6
Muko: i., Bonin Is. 60 N6
Mukomuko: Sumatra 65 C7
Mukono: Uganda 76 D2
Muktui: Mongolia 49 m8
Mukur: Afghanistan 58 L8
Mula: Spain 35 F17
Mulatos: Mexico 93 F7
Mulazzo: Italy 40 P11
Mulben: Grampian, Scotland 28 P4
Mulberry: Ark., U.S.A. 90 D8
Mulberry: Fla., U.S.A. 91 L12
Mulchén: Chile 96 A4
Mulde: riv., E. Germany 45 S4
Muldoanich: i., Outer Hebrides, Scotland 28 G6
Muleba: Tanzania 76 D3
Mulegé: Mexico 93 E7
Mule Peak: N. Mex., U.S.A. 93 F6
Mules: Italy 41 R9
Mulevala: Mozambique 77 E6
Mulga Downs: Queens., Australia 71 G7
Mulga Downs: W. Australia 68 B4
Mulgeldie: Queens., Austl. 70 J5
Mulgrave: N.S., Canada 89 V3
Mulgrave: r., Queens., Australia 69 G2
Mulhacén: mtn., Spain 35 E18
Mülheim: Cologne, W. Ger. 44 N5
Mülheim: Düsseldorf, W. Germany 44 M4
Mulhouse: France 40 N8
Muliama: New Irel., Bismarck Arch. 67 K2
Muling: riv., Heilungkiang, China 63 Y5
Mulingchan: Heilungkiang, China 63 Y6
Mull, I. of: Inner Hebr., Scot. 29 K7
Mull, Sound of: I. of Mull/ Strathclyde, Scotland 29 K6
Mullagh: Cavan, Repub. of Ireland 30 H12
Mullagh: Clare, Repub. of Ireland 31 C14
Mullaghareirk Mtns.: Lim./Cork, Repub. of Ireland 31 C15
Mullaghmore: Sligo, Repub. of Ireland 30 E11
Mullaittivu: Sri Lanka 58 O13
Müller, Mts.: Borneo 65 E6
Müller Range: New Guinea 66 H3
Mullerville: Mayo, Repub. of Ireland 30 A11
Mullewa: W. Australia 68 B5
Mull Head: cape, Papa Westray, Orkney Is. 28 Ins.
Müllheim: W. Germany 40 N8

Mullinahone: Tip., Repub. of Ireland 31 G14
Mullinavat: Kilk., Repub. of Ireland 31 G15
MULLINGAR: Westmeath, Repub. of Ireland 30 G12
Mullins: S.C., U.S.A. 91 M8
Mullins River: Belize 86 Ins.
Mullion: Corn., England 25 L19
Mullumbimby: N.S.W., Australia 71 K7
Mulobezi: Zambia 77 C6
Multai: Madhya Pradesh, India 58 N10
Multan: Punjab, Pakistan 58 M8
Multia: Finland 46 T5
Multyfarnham: Westmeath, Repub. of Ireland 30 G12
Mulungu: Zaire 76 C3
Mulungushi Dam: Zambia 77 C5
Mulupan: Borneo 65 F6
Mulvane: Kans., U.S.A. 90 C7
Mulwala: N.S.W., Austl. 71 G10
Mumai: Zaire 76 B2
Mumap: Afghanistan 58 L8
Mumbles, The: W. Glam., Wales 24 O16
Mumbwa: Zambia 77 C5
Mumias: Kenya 76 D2
Mumra: U.S.S.R. 50 G5
Muna: Botswana 77 C7
Muna: i., Celebes 65 G7
München: W. Germany 45 R5
Müncheberg: E. Germany 45 U3
MÜNCHEN (Munich): Bavaria, W. Germany 41 R7
München-Gladbach (Mönchen-Gladbach): W. Ger. 44 M4
Muncie: Ind., U.S.A. 88 J5
Muncy: Pa., U.S.A. 89 N5
Munda: Roman town and battle-field near Montilla, Spain 35 D18
Munday: Tex., U.S.A. 90 B9
Münden: W. Germany 44 P4
Munderkingen: W. Germany 40 P7
Mundesley: Norf., England 25 Y14
Mundford: Norf., England 25 X14
Mundi Mundi: Solomon Is. 67 L3
Mundiwindi: W. Australia 68 C4
Mundoora: S. Australia 71 C9
Mundubbera: Queens., Australia 70 J5
Mungallala: Queens., Austl. 70 G6
Mungana: Queens., Austl. 69 G3
Mungari: Mozambique 77 D6
Mungar Junction: Queens., Australia 70 K5
Mungbere: Zaire 76 C2
Mungindi: N.S.W., Austl. 71 H7
Munhongo: Angola 77 A5
MUNICH (München): Bavaria, W. Germany 41 R7
Munising: Mich., U.S.A. 88 H2
Munja: W. Australia 68 C3
Munkedal: Sweden 47 M7
Munkelv: Norway 46 V2
Munkflohögen: Sweden 46 O5
Munkfors: Sweden 47 N7
Munlochy: High., Scot. 28 N4
Munnerstadt: W. Germany 45 Q5
Münsingen: Switzerland 40 N9
Munslow: Salop, England 24 Q15
Munster: France 40 N7
Münster: Switzerland 40 O9
Münster: W. Germany 44 N4
Münster: Dist., North Rhine-Westphalia, West Germany 44 N3
Munster: Prov., Ireland 31 B16
Munster: riv., Kilk./Tip., Repub. of Ireland 31 G14
Münstereifel: W. Germany 44 M5
Munster Lager: W. Germany 45 Q3
Münstermaifeld: W. Germany 44 N5
Muntafiq: tribal area, Iraq 57 K6
Muntar: well, Iraq 57 H5
Muntervary Head (Sheep's Head): cape, Cork, Repub. of Ireland 31 B16
Muntok: Bangka, Indonesia 65 D7
Muntu: Zaire 76 A3
Muntur: wadi, Iraq 57 G5
Munyak: Uzbek., U.S.S.R. 50 J6
Munzur Mtns.: Turkey 56 F2
Muobede: Mozambique 77 E6
Muo Lake: Finland 46 V4
Muqam: Iran 55 H9
Muqat: Jordan 56 E4
Mur: France 36 C7
Mur (Mura): riv., Austria 41 V8
Mura: riv., Yugo./Austria 38 P13
Muradabad: Iran 57 K5
Muradiye: Manisa, Turkey 39 U17
Muradiye: Van, Turkey 57 H2
Murakami: Japan 63 f1
Murallón: mtn., Argentina/ Chile 95 C13
Muranga: Kenya 76 E3
Murani: Iran 57 K5
Murashi: U.S.S.R. 50 G3
Murat: France 37 H10
Murat: riv., Turkey 57 H2
Muratli: Turkey 39 U16
Murau: Austria 41 U8
Murchh Khur: Iran 55 H8
Murchison: Vict., Austl. 71 F11
Murchison: riv., W. Austl. 68 B5
Murchison Falls: see Kabelega Falls.
MURCIA: & Prov. Spain 35 F18
Murcia: old Prov., Spain 35 F17
Mur-de-Sologne: France 36 G8
Murdo: S. Dak., U.S.A. 92 G4
Mure, La: France 40 L11
Mureck: Austria 41 V9
Mürefte: Turkey 39 U16
Muren: Mongolia 49 M8
Mures: riv., Romania 43 R13
Muret: France 37 G12
Murfreesboro: Ark., U.S.A. 90 E8
Murfreesboro: Tenn., U.S.A. 91 H8
Murg: W. Germany 40 O7
Murgab: Tadzhik., U.S.S.R. 51 M7
Murgab: riv., Turkmen., U.S.S.R. 51 K7

Murgha: Baluchistan, Pakistan 58 L8
Murgon: Queens., Australia 70 J6
Murgoo: W. Australia 68 B5
Muriaé: Brazil 96 G1
Murias de Paredes: Spain 35 C15
Murieje: Angola 77 B4
Müritz: E. Germany 45 S1
Müritz See: lake, E. Germany 45 S2
Murle: Ethiopia 76 E1
MURMANSK: & Reg., U.S.S.R. 46 X2
Muro, Cap: cape, Corsica 38 L16
Murom: U.S.S.R. 50 F3
Muromtsevo: U.S.S.R. 51 N3
Muron: France 37 E9
Muroran: Japan 63 ZZ6
Muros: Spain 35 B15
Muroto: & cape, Japan 63 d4
Murphy: Idaho, U.S.A. 92 D4
Murphy: N.C., U.S.A. 91 J8
Murphysboro: Ill., U.S.A. 88 G7
Murra Murra: Queens., Australia 70 G7
Murray: Ky., U.S.A. 88 G7
Murray: Utah, U.S.A. 93 E4
Murray: riv., SE. Australia 71 C10
Murray, Lake: S.C., U.S.A. 91 L8
Murray Bay (La Malbaie): Que., Canada 89 Q2
Murray Bridge: S. Australia 71 C10
Murray Fracture Zone: N. Pacific Ocean 7 25N 155W
Murray Harbour: P.E.I., Canada 89 U2
Murraysburg & Dist., C.P., S. Africa 74 E5
Murrayville: Vict., Austl. 71 D10
Mürren: Switzerland 40 N9
Murrhardt: W. Germany 40 P7
Murringo: N.S.W., Austl. 71 H10
Murrintown: Wex., Repub. of Ireland 31 H15
Murrow: Cambs., England 25 W14
Murrumbidgee: riv., N.S.W., Australia 71 F10
Murrumburrah: N.S.W., Australia 71 H10
Murrurundi: N.S.W., Austl. 71 J8
Mursa: Roman colony at Osijek, Yugoslavia 43 Q14
Murshidabad: W. Bengal, India 59 P10
Murska Sobota: Yugoslavia 41 W9
Murten: Switzerland 40 N9
Murtoa: Vict., Australia 71 E11
Murton: Cumbria, England 26 R10
Murton: Durham, England 26 T10
Murua (Woodlark): i., New Guinea 69 J1
Murundu: Brazil 96 G1
Mururoa Is., Tuamotu Arch. 83 h4
Murviel: France 37 J12
Murwara: Madhya Pradesh, India 58 O10
Murweh: Queens., Austl. 70 G6
Murwillumbah: N.S.W., Australia 71 K7
Murzuch: Libya 78 G4
Mürzzuschlag: Austria 41 V8
Mus: Nicobar Is. 59 Q13
Muş: & Prov., Turkey 57 G2
Musadi: Zaire 76 B3
Musaijid: Iraq 57 J6
Musaijid: Saudi Arabia 54 E10
Musairik: wadi, Sau. Arab. 54 F11
Musaiyib: Iraq 57 J5
Musala: i., Sumatra 65 B6
Musan: N. Korea 63 X6
Musashino: Japan 63 f3
Musawa: Nigeria 81 F2
Musbury: Devon, England 24 P18
MUSCAT: Oman 55 J10
Muscat & Oman: see Oman.
Muscatine: Iowa, U.S.A. 88 F5
Musgrave: Queens., Austl. 69 G2
Musgrave Ranges: Austl. 68 E5
Mushairif: U.A.E. 55 H10
Mushie: Rwanda 76 C3
Mushie: Zaire 81 H5
Music Mount: mtn., Ariz., U.S.A. 93 E5
Muskegon: Mich., U.S.A. 88 H4
Muskegon: riv., Mich., U.S.A. 88 H4
Muskegon Heights: city, Mich., U.S.A. 88 H4
Muskingum: riv., Ohio, U.S.A. 88 L6
Muskogee: Okla., U.S.A. 90 D8
Muskoka, Lake: Ont., Can. 89 M3
Muslimiya: Syria 56 E1
Muslyumovo: U.S.S.R. 50 H3
Musmar: Sudan 54 E11
MUSOMA: Mara, Tanzania 76 D3
Mussau: i., Bismarck Arch. 66 J2
Musselburgh: Lothian, Scotland 29 P8
Musselshell: riv., Mont., U.S.A. 92 F3
Mussha Shan: mtn., Sinkiang, China 51 O7
Mussidan: France 37 F10
Mussoorie: Uttar Pradesh, India 58 N8
Mussuma: Angola 77 B5
Mustafa Kemalpaşa: Tur. 39 V16
Mustahil: Ethiopia 79 Q8
Mustang: Nepal 59 O9
Mustique: i., Grenadines, Windward Is 87 c4
Mustla: Estonia, U.S.S.R. 47 T7
Mustvee: Estonia, U.S.S.R. 47 U7
Muswellbrook: N.S.W., Australia 71 J9
Mustyala: Estonia, U.S.S.R. 47 S7
Mut: Egypt 54 C9
Mut: Turkey 56 C3
Muta: Ethiopia 76 E1
Mutair: tribal area, Saudi Arabia 54 G9
Mutambara: Trans., S. Africa 75 J1
Mutambara: Rhodesia 77 D6
Mutanda: Zambia 77 C5
Mutankiang: Heilungkiang, China 63 X6
Mutano: Angola 73 G13
Mutarara: Mozambique 77 E6
Mutha: Kenya 76 E3
Muthanna: Prov., Iraq 57 J6
Muthill: Tayside, Scotland 29 O7
Muthlane: C.P., S. Africa 74 E2
Mutina: Roman colony at Modena, Italy 41 Q11
Mutki: Turkey 57 G2
Mutombo Mukulu: Zaire 76 B4
Mutoray: U.S.S.R. 49 M5
Mutshatsha: Zaire 77 B5
Muttaburra: Queens., Austl. 69 G4
Mutton I.: Repub. of Ireland 31 B14
Muttra: Uttar Pradesh, India 58 N9

Muwaih—Necochea 169

Muwaih: Saudi Arabia **54** F10
Muwaila: Saudi Arabia **54** E9
Muwaiqih: U.A.E. **55** J10
Muxima: Angola **73** G11
Muy, Le: France **40** M12
Muya: Japan **63** d3
Muya: U.S.S.R. **49** n6
Muynak: Uzbek., U.S.S.R. **50** J6
Muyumba: Zaïre **76** C4
Muyun Kum: *desert,* Kazakh., U.S.S.R. **51** M6
MUZAFFARABAD: *cap. of Pakistan held territory, Jammu & Kashmir* **58** M8
Muzaffargarh: Punjab, Pakistan **58** M8
Muzaffarpur: Bihar, India **59** P9
Muz Art Pass: China **51** O6
Muzillac: France **36** C8
Múzquiz: Mexico **93** G7
Muztagh Ata: *mtn.,* China **51** N7
Muztagh Pass: China/Jammu & Kashmir **58** N7
Muzzafarnagar: Uttar Pradesh, India **58** N9
Mvandi: Gabon **81** G4
Mvela: Malawi **77** D5
Mvolo: Sudan **76** D1
M'Vouti: Congo **81** G5
MWANZA: & *Reg.,* Tanzania **76** D3
Mwanza: Zaïre **76** C4
Mwanza: Zambia **77** B6
Mwatate: Kenya **76** E3
Mwaya: Mbeya, Tanzania **77** E4
Mwaya: Morogoro, Tanzania **77** D4
Mweka: Zaïre **76** B3
Mwenga: Zaïre **76** C3
Mwengwa: Zambia **77** C6
Mwenimpanza: Zambia **77** D4
Mwenzo: Zambia **77** D4
Mwera: Tanzania **76** E4
Mweru, Lake: Zaïre **77** C4
Mweru Marsh Game Reserve: Zambia **77** C4
Mwilambwe: Zaïre **76** C4
Mwingi: Kenya **76** E3
Mwinilunga: Zambia **77** B5
Mwomboshi: Zambia **77** C5
Mya: *watercourse,* Algeria **78** E3
Myaungmya: Burma **59** Q11
Mybster: High., Scotland **28** P3
Mycale: mtn. and promontory on mainland opposite Sámos, Turkey **39** U18
Mycenae: ancient city about 7 miles N. of Argos, Grc. **39** S18
Myddle: Salop, England **29** Q14
Mydrim: Dyfed, Wales **24** N16
Mydroilyn: Dyfed, Wales **24** N15
Myingyan: Burma **59** R10
MYITKYINA: Kachin, Burma **59** R9
Myitta: Burma **59** R12
Myjava: Czechoslovakia **43** P12
Mylae: Greek city at Milazzo, NE. Sicily **38** O17
Mylasa: Greek city at Milâs, Turkey **39** U18
Mymensingh: Bangladesh **59** Q10
Mynfontein: C.P., S. Africa **74** E5
Mynydd Du: *mtns.,* Dyfed, Wales **24** O16
Mynydd Eppynt: *mtns.,* Powys, Wales **24** O15
Mynydd Hiraethog: *mtns.,* Clwyd, Wales **27** O13
Mynydd Prescelly: *mtns.,* Dyfed, Wales **24** M16
Myohaung: Burma **59** Q10
Myongophon: N. Korea **63** X6
Myos Hormos: Graeco-Roman port on W. side of G. of Suez opposite Tor, Egypt **54** D9
Myrcinus: Greek name of site in ancient Thrace about 10 miles N. of Amfipolis, Greece **39** S19
Myrdalsjökull: *ice cap,* Iceland **46** d5
Myriandus: Phoenician city at iskenderon, Turkey **56** E3
Myrtle Beach: *city,* S.C., U.S.A. **91** M9
Myrtleford: Vict., Australia **71** G11
Myrtle Grove: La., U.S.A. **90** *Ins.*
Myrtle Point: *city,* Oreg., U.S.A. **92** C4
Myshall: Carlow, Repub. of Ireland **31** H14
Mysia: ancient name of NW. district of Asiatic Turkey, later incorporated in *Bithynia* (q.v.) **39** U17
Myśliborz: Poland **45** U3
Mysore: Karnataka, India **58** N12
Mystic: Iowa, U.S.A. **88** E5
Mytho: Vietnam **64** D4
Myton on Swale: N. Yorks., England **27** T11
Mże: *riv.,* Czechoslovakia **45** S6
Mzimba: Malawi **77** D5

Naab: *riv.,* W. Germany **45** S6
Na'amiya: Iraq **57** J5
Naantali: Finland **47** S6
NAAS: Kild., Rep. of Irel. **31** H13
Näätamo: *riv.,* Fin./Nor. **46** V2
Nababiep: C.P., S. Africa **74** B4
Naband: Iran **55** H9
Nabanes: Trans., S. Africa **75** H2
Nabas: C.P., S. Africa **74** B4
Nabataea: ancient Arab kingdom of Hellenistic and Roman periods in S. Jordan **56** E6
Nabberoo, Lake: W. Austl. **68** C5
Nabburg: W. Germany **45** S6
Naberera: Tanzania **76** E3
Naberi: Sudan **54** D10
Nabesna: Alaska, U.S.A. **84** e5
NABEUL: & *Governorate,* Tunisia **38** M18
Nabk Abu Qasr: *well,* Saudi Arabia **56** F6
NABLUS: & *Dist.,* Jordan **55** b2
Nabomo: Cameroun **81** G3
Naboomspruit: Trans., S. Africa **75** H2
Nabúri: Mozambique **77** E6
Naburn: N. Yorks., England **27** T12
Nacala: Mozambique **77** F5
Nacarôa: Mozambique **77** E5
Nacham: Vietnam **64** D2
Nachingwea: Tanzania **77** E5
Náchod: Czechoslovakia **45** W5
Nackara: S. Australia **71** C9
Nacław: Poland **45** W1
Nacogdoches: Tex., U.S.A. **90** D10
Nacozari: Mexico **93** F6
Nacton: Suff., England **25** Y15
Nacuñán: Argentina **96** B3
Nadadores: Mexico **93** G7
Nădlac: Romania **43** R13
NADOR: & *Prov.,* Morocco **35** E19
Nadur: Gozo, Malta **32** *Ins.*
Nadushita: Moldavia, U.S.S.R. **43** U12
Naerbø: Norway **47** J7
Naerøy: Norway **47** K6
Næstved: Zealand, Den. **47** M9
Nafada: Nigeria **81** G2
Näfels: Switzerland **40** P8
Nafferton: Humb., England **27** V11
Nafka: Ethiopia **54** E11
Naft-i-Shah: Iran **57** J5
Naft Khana: Iraq **57** J4
Nafud: *desert,* Sau. Arab. **54** F9
Nafud Dahi: *desert,* Saudi Arabia **54** F10
Naga: Luzon, Philippines **64** G4
Naga: *i.,* Japan **63** b4
Nagagami, L.: Ont., Can. **88** J1
Nagahama: Japan **63** c4
Naga Hills: Burma **59** R9
Nagai: *i.,* Alaska, U.S.A. **84** c6
Nagaland: *State,* India (*cap.* Kohima) **59** Q9
Nagambie: Vict., Australia **71** F11
NAGANO: & *Pref.,* Japan **63** f2
Nagaoka: Japan **63** f2
Nagapattinam: Tamil Nadu, India **58** N12
Nagar: Punjab, India **58** N8
Nagar Parkar: Sind, Pakistan **58** M10
NAGASAKI: & *Pref.,* Japan **63** a4
Nagashima: Japan **63** e3
Nagaur: Himachal Pradesh, India **58** M9
Nagercoil: Tamil Nadu, India **58** N13
Nag Hammâdi: Egypt **54** D9
Nagi: *i.,* Alaska, U.S.A. **74** c6
Nagishot: Sudan **76** D2
Nagina: Uttar Pradesh, India **58** N9
Nagles Mtns.: Cork, Repub. of Ireland **31** D15
Nago: Okinawa, Ryukyu Is. **63** X9
Nagold: W. Germany **40** O7
Nagoorin: Queens., Austl. **70** J5
Nagorno Karabakh: *Auton. Reg.,* Azerbaydzhan, U.S.S.R. (*cap.* Stepanakert) **57** K2
Nagornyy: U.S.S.R. **49** O6
NAGOYA: Aichi, Japan **63** e3
Nagpur: Maharashtra, India **58** N10
Nagyecsed: Hungary **43** S13
Nagykanizsa: Hungary **43** P13
Nagykáta: Hungary **43** Q13
Nagykőrös: Hungary **43** Q13
NAHA: Okinawa, Ryukyu Is. **63** X9
Nahabuan: Borneo **65** E6
Nahan: Himachal Pradesh, India **58** N8
Nahariya: Israel **55** b1
Nahe: *riv.,* W. Germany **44** N6
Nahiya: Iraq: **57** G4
Nahma: Mich., U.S.A. **88** H3
Nahr el Assi (Orontes): *riv.,* Syria **56** E4
Nahwitti: B.C., Canada **92** B2
Naichi: Chinghai, China **62** Q7
Naifa: *well,* Saudi Arabia **55** H11
Naik: Afghanistan **58** L8
Naikliu: Timor, Indonesia **65** G8
Naila: W. Germany **45** R5
Nailsea: Avon, England **24** Q17
Nailsworth: Glos., England **24** R16
Naimakka: Sweden **46** R2
Nain: Newf., Canada **85** n6
Naini Tal: Uttar Pradesh, India **58** N9
Nairn: High., Scotland **28** O4
Nairn: La., U.S.A. **90** *Ins.*
Nairn: *riv.,* Highland, Scot. **28** O4
Nairn, Strath: *val.,* Highland, Scotland **28** N5
NAIROBI: Kenya **76** E3
Naissus: Roman town at Niš, E. Yugoslavia **39** R15
Naitung: Tibet, China **59** Q9
Naivasha: Kenya **76** E3
Najac: France **37** G11
Najaf: *& Prov.,* Iraq **57** J6
Najd: *geog. reg.,* Sau. Arab. **54** F9
Nájera: Spain **35** E15
Najin: N. Korea **63** Y6
Najma: Iraq **57** H4
Najran: Saudi Arabia **54** F11
Naka: Japan **63** c3
Naka (Iwo Jima): *i.,* Kazan Is. **60** N7
Nakadori: *i.,* Goto Is., Japan **63** X8
Nakama: Japan **63** b4
NAKAMTI: Welēga, Ethiopia **79** M8
Nakamura: Fukushima, Jap. **63** g2
Nakamura: Kochi, Japan **63** c4
Nakasiretoko, Cape: U.S.S.R. **63** ZZ5
Nakasongola: Uganda **76** D2
Nakatsu: Japan **63** b4
Na Keal, Loch: Inner Hebr., Scotland **29** J7
Nakfa: Ethiopia **54** E11
NAKHICHEVAN': *& A.S.S. Republic,* U.S.S.R. **50** G7
Nakhodka: U.S.S.R. **63** Y6
Nakhon Nayok: Thailand **64** C4
Nakhon Phanom: Thailand **64** C3
Nakhon Ratchasima: Thailand **64** C4
Nakhon Sawan: Thailand **64** C3
Nakhon Sri Thammarat: Thailand **64** B5
Nakhtakhe: U.S.S.R. **63** Z5
Nakina: Ont., Canada **85** L7
Näkkälä: Finland **46** S2
Nakło: Poland **43** P10
Naknek: Alaska, U.S.A. **84** D6
Nako: Upper Volta **80** D2
Nakop: S.W. Africa **74** C4
Nakskov: Lolland, Denmark **47** M9
NAKURU: Rift Valley, Kenya **76** E3
Nakusp: B.C., Canada **92** D2
NAL'CHIK: Kabardino, U.S.S.R. **50** F6
Nalgonda: Andhra Pradesh, India **58** N11
Nalimka: U.S.S.R. **51** P3
Nalliers: France **37** D9
Nallihan: Turkey **56** B1
Na'l Shikan: Iran **57** L5
Nalut: Libya **32** E5
Nam: S.W. Africa **74** B2
Namaacha: Mozambique **75** K2
Namacunde: Angola **73** H13
Namah: Borneo **65** F6
Namakorabis: S.W. Africa **74** B1
Namangan: Uzbek., U.S.S.R. **51** M6
Namantombwa: Zambia **77** C6
Namanyere: Tanzania **76** D4
Namapa: Mozambique **77** E5
Namaqualand: *Dist.,* S. Afr. **74** B4
Namaqualand Nature Reserve: C.P., S. Africa **74** C4
Namasagali: Uganda **76** D2
Namatanai: New Ireland, Bismarck Arch. **67** K2
Namatelle: Tanzania **77** E5
Nambala: Zambia **77** C6
Nambona Falls: Zambia **77** B5
Nambour: Queens., Austl. **70** K6
Nambouwalu: Vanua Levu, Fiji Is. **67** P5
Nambucca Heads: N.S.W., Australia **71** K8
Namcha Barwa: *mtn.,* China **59** R9
Namdalseid: Norway **46** M4
Namdinh: Vietnam **64** D2
Náměšt nad Oslava: Czech. **45** W6
Námestovo: Czechoslovakia **43** Q12
Nametil: Mozambique **77** E6
Namib Desert: S.W. Africa **73** G14
Namib Desert Park: **74** A1
Namibia: *see* South West Africa
Namie: Japan **63** g2
Namies: C.P., S. Africa **74** C4
Namiquipa: Mexico **93** F7
Namlea: Buru, Indonesia **65** H7
Namoi: *riv.,* N.S.W., Austl. **71** H8
Nampa: Finland **46** U3
Nampa: Idaho, U.S.A. **92** D4
Nampala: Mali **80** C1
Nampont: France **36** G5
NAMPULA: Mozambique, Mozambique **77** E6
Namru: *geog. reg.,* Tibet, China **59** P8
Namsen: *riv.,* Norway **46** N4
Nams Lake: Norway **46** N4
Namsos: Norway **46** M4
Namtow: Kwangtung, China **62** U10
Namtu: Burma **59** R10
Namu Hu: *lake,* Tibet, China **59** Q8
Namuno: Mozambique **77** E5
NAMUR: & *Prov.,* Belgium **44** K5
Namuruputh: Kenya **76** E2
Namutoni: S.W. Africa **73** H13
Namwala: Zambia **77** C6
Namwera: Malawi **77** E5
Namwon: S. Korea **63** X7
Namysłow: Poland **43** P11
Namyung: Kwangtung, China **62** U9
Nan: & *riv.,* Thailand **64** C3
Nana Barya: *riv.,* Central African Republic **81** H3
Nana Candundo: Angola **77** B5
Nanaimo: B.C., Canada **92** C3
Nanam: N. Korea **63** X6
Nana-Mambére: *Pref.,* Central African Rep. (*cap.* Bouar) **81** H3
Nanan (Tayu): Kiangsi, China **62** V9
Nanango: Queens., Austl. **70** K6
Nananib Plat.: S.W. Africa **74** B2
Nanao: Japan **62** e2
Nanatsu Is.: Japan **63** e2
Nanbu: Japan **63** f3
Nancefield: Trans., S. Afr. **74** M*Ins.*
Nanchang: Hupeh, China **62** U8
NANCHANG: Kiangsi, China **62** V9
Nancheng: Kiangsi, China **62** V9
Nancheng (Hanchung): Shensi, China **62** T8
Nanchung (Shunking): Szechwan, China **62** T8
NANCY: Meurthe-et-Moselle, France **40** M7
Nanda Devi: *mtn.,* Utter Pradesh, India **58** N8
Nanded: Maharashtra, India **58** N11
Nandi: Rhodesia **77** D7
Nandi: Viti Levu, Fiji Is. **67** P5
Nandod: *see* Rajpiple.
Nandyal: Andhra Pradesh, India **58** N11
Nanfeng: Kiangsi, China **62** V9
Nangade: Mozambique **77** E5
Nanga Eboko: Cameroun **81** G4
Nanga Parbat: *mtn.,* Jammu & Kashmir **58** M7
Nangapinoh: Borneo **65** E7
Nangaraun: Borneo **65** E6
Nangarhar: *prov.,* Afghanistan (*cap.* Jalalabad) **55** M8
Nangasai: Borneo **65** E6
Nangatajap: Borneo **65** E7
Nangchen Japo: *mtn.,* China **59** Q8
Nangis: France **36** J7
Nangola: Mali **80** C2
Nangoma: Zambia **77** B6
Nanhua: Yunnan, China **62** S9
Nankang: Kiangsi, China **62** U9
Nankiang: Szechwan, China **62** T8
NANKING: Kiangsu, China **62** V8
Nan Ling: *mtns.,* China **62** U9
Nanmulin: Tibet, China **59** P9
Nannaka: Sweden **46** R2
Nannine: W. Australia **68** B5
NANNING: Kwangsi Chuang, China **62** T10
Nannup: W. Australia **68** B6
Nanortalik: Greenland **85** P5
Nanping (Yenping): Fukien, China **62** V9
Nanpu: Szechwan, China **62** T8
Nansei (Ryukyu) Is.: (Jap.), China Sea **63** X9
Nansens Land: Greenland **85** p1
Nansen Sound: N.W.T., Canada **85** k1
Nan Shan: *range,* China **62** R7
Nanshan: *reef,* S. China Sea **64** F4
Nansio: Tanzania **76** D3
Nantan: Kwangsi Chuang, China **62** T9
NANTERRE: Hauts-de-Seine, France **36** H7
NANTES: Loire-Atlantique, France **36** D8
Nantes-Brest Canal: France **36** D8
Nanteuil-le-Haudouin: Fr. **36** H6
Nanticoke: Pa., U.S.A. **89** N5
Nanton: Alta., Canada **92** E2
Nantua: France **40** L9
Nantucket: Mass., U.S.A. **89** Q5
Nantucket: *i.,* Mass., U.S.A. **89** R5
Nantucket Sound: Mass., U.S.A. **89** Q5
Nantulo: Mozambique **77** E5
Nantung: Kiangsu, China **63** W8
Nantwich: Ches., England **27** Q13
Nantyglo: Gwent, Wales **24** P16
Nanty Glo: Pa., U.S.A. **89** M5
Nan Uamh, Loch: High., Scot. **28** K6
Nanumanga: *i.,* Tuvalu **67** P3
Nanumea: *i.,* Tuvalu **67** P3
Nanya: Queens., Australia **70** G4
Nanyang: Honan, China **62** U8
Nanyuki: Kenya **76** E2
Nanzhila: Zambia **77** C6
Nao, C. de la: *cape,* Spain **35** G17
Naoetsu: Japan **63** f2
Naos I.: Panama **94** *Ins.*
Napa: Calif., U.S.A. **93** C5
Napaku: Borneo **65** F6
Napaleofú: Argentina **96** D4
Napanee: Ont., Canada **89** N3
Napassoq: Greenland **85** o4
Napata: ancient Ethiopian city at Merowe, Sudan **54** D11
Naphtali: Israelite tribe which lived on E. side of *Galilean Hills* around Safad, Israel **55** b2
NAPIER: Hawkes Bay, North I., New Zealand **70** Q14
Napier: C.P., S. Africa **74** C7
Naples: Fla., U.S.A. **91** L12
NAPLES (Napoli): Campania, Italy **38** O16
Napo: Kwangsi Chuang, China **62** T10
Napoca: Roman town at Cluj, Romania **39** S13
Napoleon: N. Dak., U.S.A. **92** H3
Napoleon: Ohio, U.S.A. **88** J5
NAPOLI (Naples): Campania, Italy **38** O16
Napoule, Golfe de la: *gulf,* France **40** N12
Napov: U.S.S.R. **51** O3
Nappanee: Ind., U.S.A. **88** J5
Naqb Ashtar: Jordan **56** D7
Naqra: Saudi Arabia **54** G9
Naqura: Lebanon **55** b1
Nar: *riv.,* Norf., England **25** X14
NARA: & *Pref.,* Japan **63** d3
Nara: Mali **80** C1
Nara: *riv.,* Sind, Pakistan **58** L9
Naracoorte: S. Australia **71** D11
Naradhan: N.S.W., Austl. **71** G9
Narathiwat: & *State,* Thailand **65** b10
Narayanganj: Bangladesh **59** Q10
Narbada: *riv.,* India **58** N10
Narberth: Dyfed, Wales **24** M16
Narbonensis: Roman province bounded by Alps, Cevennes, and the western edge of the Garonne valley, S. France **34** H14
Narbonne: France **37** J12
Narborough: Norf., Eng. **25** X14
Narcondam: *i.,* Andaman Is. **59** Q12
Nare: Argentina **96** C3
Narembeen: W. Australia **68** B6
Nares Land: Greenland **85** p1
Nares Strait: Greenland/Canada **85** m1
Narew: *riv.,* Poland **43** R10
Narib: S.W. Africa **74** B2
Narika: Japan **63** c3
Narin: Afghanistan **58** C7
Narin: Don., Repub. of Irel. **30** E10
Narino (Vila Bittencourt): Brazil **94** D4
Narita: Japan **63** g3
Nariya: *pump. station,* Saudi Arabia **55** G9
Narkaba: Ethiopia **54** E12
Narnaul: Haryana, India **58** N9
Narnia: Roman city on river Nera about 10 miles SW. of Terni, Italy **38** N15
Naroch', Lake: Byelorussia **47** U9
Narodichi: Ukraine **43** V11
Naroegas: C.P., S. Africa **74** D4
Naro-Fominsk: U.S.S.R. **50** E3
Narok: Kenya **76** E3
Naro Moru: Kenya **76** E3
Narona: Roman town 4 miles N. of Metković, SW. Yugoslavia **38** P15
Narooma: N.S.W., Austl. **71** J11
Naroviya: Byelorussia **43** V11
Narrabri: N.S.W., Austl. **71** H8
Narran: *riv.,* N.S.W., Austl. **71** G7
Narrandera: N.S.W., Austl. **71** G10
Narromine: N.S.W., Austl. **71** H9
Narrogin: W. Australia **68** B6
Narrows: Va., U.S.A. **88** L7
Narsimhampur: Madhya Pradesh, India 58 N10
Narsipatnam: Andhra Pradesh, India **59** O11
Narssalik: Greenland **85** P5
Narssaq: Greenland **85** o5
Narubis: S.W. Africa **74** C3
Narugas: C.P., S. Africa **74** C4
Narva: Estonia, U.S.S.R. **47** V7
Narva: *riv. & bay,* Estonia, U.S.S.R. **47** U7
Narvik: Norway **46** P2
Nar'yan-Mar: U.S.S.R. **48** G4
Naryilco: Queens., Austl. **71** D7
Naryn: Kirgiz., U.S.S.R. **51** N6
Naryn: U.S.S.R. **49** I7
Naryn: *riv.,* U.S.S.R. **51** M6
Nasarawa: Nigeria **81** F3
Năsăud: Romania **43** T13
Nasca: Peru **94** C6
Nasca Ridge: S. Pacific Ocean **7** 25S 85W
Naseby: Northants., Eng. **25** U15
Naseby: South I., N.Z. **70** N17
Nash: Bucks., England **25** U15
Nashua: N.H., U.S.A. **89** Q4
Nashville: Ark., U.S.A. **90** E9
Nashville: Ga., U.S.A. **91** K10
Nashville: Ill., U.S.A. **88** G6
NASHVILLE: Tenn., U.S.A. **88** H7
Nashwauk: Minn., U.S.A. **88** E2
Našice: Yugoslavia **39** Q14
Nasielsk: Poland **43** R10
Nasik: Iran **57** J2
Nasik: Maharashtra, India **58** M11
Nasi Lake: Finland **47** S6
Nasir: Sudan **76** D1
Nasirabad: Rajasthan, India **58** M9
Nasiri (Ahwaz): Iran **57** L6
Nasiriya: Iraq **57** L6
Nasrani: *well,* Sau. Arab. **56** E6
Nasratabad (Zabul): Iran **58** K8
Nasratabad: Iran **55** J9
Nass: *riv.,* B.C., Canada **92** B1
Nassau: old duchy of western Germany. Its capital was at Wiesbaden, Hesse, W. Ger. **44** O5
NASSAU: Bahamas **91** N13
Nassau: *riv.,* Queens., Austl. **69** G3
Nassau Mtns.: Indonesia **61** M12
Nasséré: Mauritania **78** A6
Nässjö: Sweden **47** O8
Nastätten: W. Germany **44** N5
Nata: Saudi Arabia **55** G9
NATAL: Rio Grande do Norte, Brazil **94** K5
Natal: Sumatra **65** B6
Natal: *Prov.,* S. Africa (*cap.* Pietermaritzburg) **75** J4
Natal Downs: Queens., Australia **69** H4
Natalspruit: Trans., South Africa **74** N*Ins.*
Natanya: Israel **55** a2
Natashquan: Que., Canada **84** n7
Natchez: Miss., U.S.A. **90** F10
Natchitoches: La., U.S.A. **90** E10
Nathdwara: Rajasthan, India **58** M10
Natimuk: Vict., Australia **71** D11
NATITINGOU: Nord-Ouest, Benin **81** E2
Natividad: Bolivia **94** D6
Natividad: *i.,* Mexico **93** D7
Natividade: Brazil **94** H6
Natkyizin: Burma **59** R12
Nätra: Sweden **46** Q5
Natron, Lake: Tanzania **76** E3
Natrûn, Wadi: *watercourse,* Egypt **56** B6
Natuna Is.: Indonesia **65** D6
Natural Bridge: Va., U.S.A. **89** M7
Naturaliste, Cape: W. Austl. **68** A6
Naucratis: Greek settlement in Egypt E. of Rosetta arm of Nile about 14 miles SE. of Damanhur, Egypt **56** B6
Nauders: Austria **40** Q9
Nauen: E. Germany **45** S3
Naugatuck: Conn., U.S.A. **89** P5
Naukhas: S.W. Africa **74** B1
Naul: Dublin, Repub. of Ireland **30** J12
Naulila: Angola **73** G13
Naulochus: ancient harbour about 10 miles E. of Milazzo, Sicily **38** O17
Naumburg: E. Germany **45** R4
Naunton: Glos., England **25** S16
Nauplia (Návplion): Greece **39** S18
Nauportus: Roman town at *Ober-Laibach* about 12 miles WSW. of Ljubljana, Yugoslavia **41** U10
Na'ur: Jordan **55** b3

Nauru: *Republic* **67** N2
Cap.: Uaboe District
Area: 8 sq. miles (21 sq. km.)
Pop.: 7,000 (*1971 E*)

Nauta: Peru **94** C4
Nautla: Mexico **86** K13
Nautsi: U.S.S.R. **46** V2
Nauzad: Afghanistan **58** K8
Nava: Mexico **93** G7
Nava del Rey: Spain **35** D16
Navahermosa: Spain **35** D17
Navajo Mount: Utah, U.S.A. **93** E5
Navalcarnero: Spain **35** D16
Navalmoral: Spain **35** D17
NAVAN (An Uaimh): Meath, Repub. of Ireland **30** H12
Navanagar (Jamnagar): Gujarat, India **58** M10
Navarino: modern name of bay off Pilos, Greece **39** R18
Navarin: Cape: U.S.S.R. **49** t5
Navarino, Bay of: Greece **39** R18
Navarino I.: Chile **95** D15
Navarra: *Prov. & old Prov.,* Spain (*cap.* Pamplona) **35** F15
Navarre: Vict., Australia **71** E11
Navarre: *Prov.,* France **35** F15
Navarrenx: France **37** E12
Navarro: Argentina **96** D4
Navascués: Spain **37** D13
Navasota: Tex., U.S.A. **90** C10
Navenby: Lincs., England **27** U13
Naver: *riv. & loch,* Highland, Scotland **28** N3
Naves: France **37** G10
Navibandar: Gujarat, India **58** L10
Navojoa: Mexico **93** F7
Návpaktos: Greece **39** R17
Návplion (Nauplia): Greece **39** S18
Navrongo: Ghana **80** D2
Navsari: Gujarat, India **58** M10
Nawabganj: Uttar Pradesh, India **58** O9
Nawabshah: Sind, Pakistan **58** L9
Nawakot: Nepal **59** P9
Náxos: & *i.,* Cyclades (Grc.) **39** T18
Naxos: Greek city about 5 miles S. of Taormina, Sicily **38** O18
Nay: France **37** E12
Nay Band: Iran **55** J8
Nayland: Essex, England **25** X16
Näyrämio: Finland **46** U3
Nazaré: Brazil **94** K6
Nazareth: Israel **55** b2
Nazas: *riv.,* Mexico **93** G7
Naze: Amami, Ryukyu Is. **63** X9
Naze, The: *cape,* Essex, England **25** Y16
Nazeing: Essex, England **25** W16
Nazik, Lake: Turkey **57** H2
Nazilli: Turkey **39** V18
Nâzimiye: Turkey **56** F2
Nazirhat: Bangladesh **59** Q10
Nazwa: Oman **55** J10
Nazyvayevsk: U.S.S.R. **51** M3
Nchanga: Zambia **77** C5
Ncheu: Malawi **77** D5
N'cuto: Cabinda, Angola **81** G5
Ndala: Tanzania **76** D3
Ndali: Benin **81** E3
Ndamba: Gabon **81** G5
N'DJAMENA (Fort Lamy): Chad **81** H2
N'DÉLÉ: Bamingui-Bangoran, Cen. Afr. Rep. **76** B1
Ndendé: Gabon **81** G5
Ndeni: *i.,* Santa Cruz Is., Pacific O. **67** N4
Ndiaien: Senegal **80** B1
Ndikinimeki: Cameroun **81** G4
N'djolé: Gabon **81** G5
NDOLA: Copperbelt, Zambia **77** C5
Ndoli: Sudan **76** C1
Ndumbwe: Tanzania **77** E5
Ndumu Game Reserve: Natal, S. Africa **75** K3
Né: *riv.,* France **37** E10
Nea: *riv.,* Norway **46** M5
Neagh, Lough: N. Ireland **30** J10
Neah Bay: *town,* B.C., Can. **92** C3
Néa Kallikrátia: Greece **39** S16
Neanderthal: valley between Düsseldorf and Wuppertal where skull of prehistoric man was found, W. Ger. **44** M4
Neápolis: Crete **39** T19
Neápolis: Grc. **39** R16
Neápolis: Peloponnese, Greece **39** S18
Néa Psará: Euboea, Greece **39** S17
Near Is.: Aleutians **84** A7
Neath: & *riv.,* W. Glam., Wales **24** O16
Neba: Japan **63** e3
Nebel: N. Frisian Is., W. Ger. **44** O1
Nebeur: Tunisia **38** L18
Nebine: *riv.,* Queens., Austl. **70** G6
Nebit Dag: U.S.S.R. **50** H7
Nebk: Syria **56** E4
Nebljusi: Yugoslavia **41** V11
Nebo: Queens., Australia **70** H3
Nebo: Biblical name of mtn. about 4 miles NW. of Madaba, Jordan **55** b3
Nebraska: *State,* U.S.A. (*cap.* Lincoln) **92** G4
Nebraska City: Nebr., U.S.A. **93** H4
Nebrodi Mtns.: Sicily **38** O18
Necedah: Wis., U.S.A. **88** F3
Nechako: *riv.,* B.C., Canada **92** C2
Neches: *riv.,* Tex., U.S.A. **90** D10
Nechí: & *riv.,* Colombia **94** C2
Neckar: *riv.,* W. Germany 44 P6
Neckarsulm: W. Germany **44** P6
Necochea: **Argentina 96** D4

For Abbreviations see list on p.113. Italic type, e.g. *Ephesus,* refers to historical names not on maps. Capital letters, e.g. MADRID, show capitals of countries; small capital letters, e.g. CADIZ, show capitals of provinces, etc. General notes p.116.

Necton: Norf., England 25 X14
Nederkalix: Sweden 46 S4
Nederland: Tex., U.S.A. 90 E11
Nedroma: Algeria 35 F19
Needham Market: Suff., England 25 Y15
Needle Peak: mtn., South I., New Zealand 71 L17
Needles: Calif., U.S.A. 93 E6
Needles, The: cape, I. of Wight, England 25 S18
Neemuch: Madhya Pradesh, India 58 M10
Neenah: Wis., U.S.A. 88 G3
Neenah: Salop, England 24 Q15
Neepawa: Man., Canada 92 H2
Neermoor: W. Germany 44 N2
Nefta: Tunisia 32 D5
Neftechala: Azerbaydzhan, U.S.S.R. 57 L2
Neftegorsk: U.S.S.R. 50 E6
Nefyn: Gwynedd, Wales 27 M14
Negapatam: Tamil Nadu, India 58 N12
Negara: Bali, Indonesia 65 E8
Negaunee: Mich., U.S.A. 88 H2
Negeb (Negev): geog. reg. Israel 56 D6
Negelpi: Ethiopia 76 E1
Negero: Tanzania 76 E4
Negoiul: mtn., Romania 39 T14
Negomano: Mozambique 77 E5
Negombo: Sri Lanka 58 N13
Negoreloye: Byelorussia 43 U10
Negotin: Yugoslavia 39 S14
Negotino: Yugoslavia 39 S16
Negra Point: cape, Luzon, Philippines 64 G3
Nègrepelisse: France 37 G11
Negri Sembilan: State, Malaya, Malaysia (cap. Seremban) 65 c12
Negro: riv., Argentina 96 B4
Negro: riv., Brazil 94 E4
Negro: riv., Uruguay 96 D3
Negro Bay: Somalia 79 R18
Negros: i., Philippines 64 G5
Negru Vodă: Romania 39 V15
Nehavend: Iran 57 L4
Nehbandan: Iran 55 K8
Nehoiaşu: Romania 39 U14
Neiafu: Tonga 67 R5
Neikiang: Szechwan, China 62 T9
Neillsville: Wis., U.S.A. 88 F3
Neilston: Strath., Scotland 29 N8
Neisse: riv., E. Ger./Poland 45 U4
Neiva: Colombia 94 B3
Nejd (Najd): geog. reg., Saudi Arabia 54 F9
Nekhl: Egypt 56 D7
Neksø: Bornholm, Denmark 47 O9
Nel' Gekhe: riv., U.S.S.R. 49 p4
Nelidovo: U.S.S.R. 50 D3
Neligh: Nebr., U.S.A. 92 H4
Nel'kan: U.S.S.R. 49 p6
Nell, Loch: Strath., Scotland 29 L7
Nellore: Andhra Pradesh, India 58 N12
Nel'ma: U.S.S.R. 63 Z5
Nelson: B.C., Canada 92 D3
Nelson: Lancs., England 27 R12
Nelson: & cape., Vict., Austl. 71 D12
NELSON: & Dist., South I., New Zealand 70 O15
Nelson: riv., Man., Canada 92 J1
Nelson Forks: B.C., Canada 84 g6
Nelson Head: cape, N.W.T., Canada 84 g3
Nelson Lakes National Park: S.I., New Zealand 70 O16
Nelsonville: Ohio, U.S.A. 88 K6
Nelspoort: C.P., S. Africa 74 E6
Nelspruit: Trans., S. Africa 75 J2
NÉMA: Hodh Oriental, Mauritania 80 C1
Neman: & riv., U.S.S.R. 47 S9
Nemausus: Roman city at Nîmes, France 37 K12
Neméa: Greece 39 S18
Německé Jablonné: Czech. 45 U5
Německé Pravno: Czech. 43 Q12
Německý Brod: Czech. 45 V6
Nemirov: Ukraine 43 V12
Nemorensis: lake about 15 miles SE. of Rome. 38 N16
Nemours: France 36 H7
Nemuro: Japan 63 YY6
NENAGH: & riv., N. Riding, Tip., Repub. of Ireland 31 E14
Nenana: Alaska, U.S.A. 84 E5
Nene: riv., England 25 W14
Nengonengo: i., Tuamotu Arch. 83 g3
Nennhausen: E. Germany 45 S3
Neno: Malawi 77 D6
Nenthead: Cumbria, Eng. 26 R10
Neodesha: Kans., U.S.A. 90 D7
Neoga: Ill., U.S.A. 88 G6
Néon Petritsi: Greece 39 S16
Neosho: Mo., U.S.A. 90 D7
Neosho: riv., Kans./Okla., U.S.A. 90 D7
Nepa: U.S.S.R. 49 m6

Nepal: Kingdom 58/9 O9
Cap.: Katmandu
Area: 54,362 sq. miles (140,798 sq. km.)
Pop.: 11,290,000 (1971 C)

Nephi: Utah, U.S.A. 93 E5
Nephin: mtn., Mayo, Repub. of Ireland 30 C11
Nephin Beg Range: Mayo, Repub. of Ireland 30 B11
Nepoko: Zaïre 76 C2
Nepomuk: Czechoslovakia 45 T6
Nera: riv., Italy 38 N15
Nérac: France 37 F11
Nerchinsk: U.S.S.R. 49 n7
Nerchinskiy Zavod: U.S.S.R. 49 n7
Neresheim: W. Germany 40 Q7
Néris: France 37 H9
Nero: La., U.S.A. 90 Ins.
Néronde: France 37 K10
Nérondes: France 36 H9
Nerpio: Spain 35 E17
Nerrima: W. Australia 68 C3
Nervi: Italy 40 P11
Nervii: Gallic tribe in area of Hainault and NW. Belg. 44 K5
Nes: U.S.S.R. 48 F4
Nes: W. Frisian Is., Neth. 44 L2
Nesbyen: Norway 47 L6
Nesebǔr: Bulgaria 39 U15
Neskaupstadhur: Iceland 46 g4
Nesle: France 36 H6
Nesque: riv., France 37 L11
Ness: dist., Outer Hebr., Scotland 28 J3
Ness, Loch: High., Scotland 28 N5
Ness City: Kans., U.S.A. 90 B6
Nesseby: Norway 46 V1
Nesselwang: W. Germany 40 Q8
Nesset: Norway 46 L5

Neston: Ches., England 27 P13
Nestos: riv., Greece 39 T16
Nestus: Greek name of river Mesta (Thrace) 39 T16
Nesvizh: Byelorussia 43 U10
Nes Ziona: Israel 55 a3
Netheravon: Wilts., England 25 S17
Netherby: site of Roman fort about 2 miles NNE. of Longtown (Cumbria), England. 26 Q9
Netherdale: Queens., Austl. 70 H3

Netherlands: Kingdom 44 L3
Cap.: Amsterdam
Seat of Govt.: The Hague
Area: 13,967 sq. miles (36,175 sq. km.)
Pop.: 13,362,000 (1972 E)

Netherlands Antilles: part of the Netherlands realm 87 N15
Cap.: Willemstad
Area: 317 sq. miles (821 sq. km.)
Pop.: 225,000 (1971 E)

Netherlands Guiana: see Surinam.
Nether Langwith: Derby., England 27 T13
Nether Poppleton: N. Yorks., England 27 T12
Nether Stowey: Som., Eng. 24 P17
Netherton: Northumb., Eng. 26 R9
Nether Whitacre: War., Eng. 27 S14
Netherwitton: Northumb., England 26 S9
Nethy Bridge: High., Scotland 28 O5
Netley: Hants., England 25 T18
Netolice: Czechoslovakia 45 U6
Nettancourt: France 36 K7
Nettilling Lake: Canada 85 m4
Nettlebed: Oxon., England 25 T16
Nettleham: Lincs., England 27 V13
Neu: Japan 63 c3
NEUBRANDENBURG: & Dist., E. Germany 45 T2
Neubukow: E. Germany 45 R1
Neuburg: Austria 41 V8
Neuburg: Bavaria, W. Germany 41 R7
Neuburg: Rostock, E. Germany 45 R2
NEUCHÂTEL: & canton, Switzerland 40 M9
Neuchâtel, Lake: Switz. 40 M9
Neudenau: W. Germany 44 P6
Neuenhaus: W. Germany 44 M3
Neuenstein: W. Germany 44 P6
Neuerburg: W. Germany 44 M5
Neufbrisach: France 40 N7
Neufchâteau: Belgium 44 L6
Neufchâteau: France 40 L7
Neufchâtel: France 36 G6
Neufchâtel: France 40 N7
Neufelden: Austria 41 U7
Neufreistett: W. Germany 40 N7
Neugersdorf: East Germany 45 U5
Neuhaus: W. Germany 44 P2
Neuhausen: Baden-Würtemberg, W. Germany 40 P7
Neuhof: S.W. Africa 74 B2
Neuhofen: Austria 41 U7
Neuillé-Pont-Pierre: France 36 F8
Neuilly le Réal: France 37 J9
Neu Isenburg: W. Germany 44 O5
Neukalen: E. Germany 45 S2
Neukirchen: Hesse, W. Ger. 44 P5
Neukirchen: Schleswig-Holstein, W. Germany 44 O1
Neulengbach: Austria 41 V7
Neumarkt: (NE. of Munich), Bavaria, W. Germany 41 S7
Neumarkt: (SE of Nuremberg), Bavaria, W. Germany 45 R6
Neumarkt: Styria, Austria 41 U8
Neumünster: W. Germany 45 P1
Neunkirchen: Austria 41 W8
Neunkirchen: Saarland, W. Germany 44 N6
NEUQUÉN: & Prov., Arg. 96 B4
Neuquén: riv., Argentina 96 B4
Neurara: Chile 96 B1
Neuruppin: E. Germany 45 S3
Neuse: riv., N.C., U.S.A. 91 N8
Neusiedl: Austria 41 W8
Neusiedler Lake: Austria/ Hungary 41 W8
Neuss: W. Germany 44 M4
Neussargues: France 37 H10
Neustadt: (on river Aisch), Bavaria, W. Germany 45 Q6
Neustadt: (on river Danube), Bavaria, W. Germany 41 R7
Neustadt: (on river Saale), Bavaria, W. Germany 45 Q5
Neustadt: Potsdam, E. Germany 45 S3
Neustadt: Lower Saxony, W. Germany 44 P3
Neustadt: Rhineland-Palatinate, W. Germany 44 O6
Neustadt: Schleswig-Holstein, W. Germany 45 Q1
Neustift: Austria 41 R8
Neustrelitz: E. Germany 45 T2
Neuveville: La: Switzerland 40 N8
Neuvic: Corrèze, France 37 H10
Neuvic: Dordogne, France 37 F10
Neuville: Vienne, France 37 F9
Neuville-aux-Bois: France 36 H7
Neuvy: Cher, France 36 H8
Neuvy: Indre, France 37 G9
Neuvy-le-Roi: France 36 F8
Neuwerk: i., W. Germany 44 O2
Neuwied: W. Germany 44 N5
Neva: riv., U.S.S.R. 47 W7
Nevada: Iowa, U.S.A. 88 E4
Nevada: Mo., U.S.A. 90 D7
Nevada: State, U.S.A. (cap. Carson City) 93 D5
Nevada, Cerro: mtn., Arg. 96 B4
Neveklov: Czechoslovakia 45 U6
Nevel': U.S.S.R. 50 C3
Nevel'sk: U.S.S.R. 63 ZZ5
Never: U.S.S.R. 49 O7
NEVERS: Nièvre, France 36 J9
Nevertire: N.S.W., Austl. 71 G8
Neville's Cross: battlefield about 1 mile SW. of Durham, England 26 S10
Nevinnomyskk: U.S.S.R. 50 F6
Nevis: i., see St. Christopher-Nevis-Anguilla.
Nevis, Loch: High., Scotland 28 K6
Nevrokop: Bulgaria 39 S16
NEVŞEHIR: & Prov., Turkey 56 D2
New: riv., Guyana 87 e9
New: riv., U.S.A. 88 L7
New Abbey: Dumfries & Galloway, Scotland 29 O10
New Aberdour: Grampian, Scotland 28 R4
Newala: Tanzania 77 E5
New Albany: Ind., U.S.A. 88 J6
New Alresford: Hants., England 25 T17
New Amsterdam: Guyana 87 e7

New Amsterdam: i., Indian Ocean 9 40S 75E
Newark: Del., U.S.A. 89 O6
Newark: N.J., U.S.A. 89 O5
Newark: Ohio, U.S.A. 88 K5
Newark upon Trent: Notts., England 27 U13
Newaygo: Mich., U.S.A. 88 J4
Newbald: North: N. Yorks., England 27 U12
New Bedford: Mass., U.S.A. 89 Q5
New Bern: N.C., U.S.A. 91 N8
Newbern: Tenn., U.S.A. 88 G7
Newberry: Mich., U.S.A. 88 J2
Newberry: S.C., U.S.A. 91 L8
New Bethesda: C.P., S. Africa 75 F5
Newbiggin by the Sea: Northumb., England 26 S9
Newbigging: Strath., Scot. 29 O8
Newbliss: Monaghan, Repub. of Ireland 30 G11
Newbold: Derby., England 27 T13
New Bolingbroke: Lincs., England 27 V13
Newborough: Cambs., England 25 V14
Newborough: Gwynedd, Wales 27 N13
New Boston: Ohio, U.S.A. 88 K6
New Bradwell: Bucks., Eng. 25 U15
New Braunfels: Tex., U.S.A. 90 B11
Newbridge (Droichead Nuadh): Kild., Repub. of Ireland 31 H13
Newbridge: Gwent, Wales 24 P16
Newbridge: Lim., Repub. of Ireland 31 D14
Newbridge on Wye: Powys, Wales 24 P15
New Brighton: South I., New Zealand 70 O16
New Britain: Conn., U.S.A. 89 P5
New Britain: i., Bismarck Arch. 67 K3
Newbrough: Northumb., England 26 R9
New Brunswick: N.J., U.S.A. 89 O5
New Brunswick: Prov., Can. (cap. Fredericton) 89 S2
New Buckenham: Norf., England 25 Y15
Newburgh: Fife., Scotland 29 P7
Newburgh: Gram., Scotland 28 R5
Newburgh: N.Y., U.S.A. 89 O5
Newburn: Tyne & Wear, England 26 S10
Newbury: Berks., England 25 T17
Newburyport: Mass., U.S.A. 89 Q4
Newby Bridge: Cumbria, Eng. 26 Q11
New Bussa: Nigeria 81 E3
Newbyth: Gram., Scotland 28 R4

New Caledonia: Fr. overseas territ. 67 M6
Cap.: Nouméa
Area: 8,548 sq. miles (22,139 sq. km.)
Pop.: 107,000 (1971 E)

New Caledonia Basin: S. Pacific Ocean 7 30S 165E
New Carlisle: Que., Canada 89 T1
New Castile: old Prov., Spain 35 E17
New Castle: Del., U.S.A. 89 O6
Newcastle: Down, N. Ireland 30 K11
Newcastle: Dublin, Repub. of Ireland 31 J13
New Castle: Ind., U.S.A. 88 J6
Newcastle: Lim., Repub. of Ireland 31 C15
Newcastle: & Dist., Natal, S. Africa 75 H3
Newcastle: N.B., Canada 89 T2
Newcastle: N.S.W., Austl. 71 J9
Newcastle: Ont., Canada 89 M4
New Castle: Pa., U.S.A. 88 L5
Newcastle: Tip., Repub. of Ireland 31 F15
Newcastle: Wick., Repub. of Ireland 31 J13
Newcastle: Wyo., U.S.A. 92 G4
Newcastle Creek: riv., N. Territ., Australia 68 E3
Newcastle Emlyn: Dyfed, Wales 24 N15
Newcastle Mine: town, Alta., Canada 92 E2
Newcastleton: Bord., Scot. 29 Q9
Newcastle under Lyme: Staffs., England 27 R13
NEWCASTLE UPON TYNE: Tyne & Wear, England 26 S10
Newcastle Waters: N. Territ., Australia 68 E3
Newchurch: Dyfed, Wales 24 N16
Newchurch: Powys, Wales 24 P15
Newchwang (Yingkow): Liaoning, China 63 W6
New Cumnock: Strathclyde, Scotland 29 N9
New Dailly: Strath., Scot. 29 M9
New Deer: Gram., Scot. 28 R4
Newdegate: W. Australia 68 B6
NEW DELHI: Delhi, India 58 N9
New Denver: B.C., Canada 92 D2
Newdigate: Surrey, England 25 V17
New England Range: N.S.W., Australia 71 J8
Newenham, Cape: Alaska, U.S.A. 84 c6
Newent: Glos., England 24 R16
New Era: Trans., S. Africa 74 N/Ins.
New Forest: Hants., England 25 S18
Newfoundland: Prov., Can. (cap. St. John's) 85 O8
Newfoundland Basin: N. Atlantic Ocean 8 40N 45W
New Franklin: Mo., U.S.A. 88 E6
New Galloway: Dumfries & Galloway, Scotland 29 N9
New Gatun: Panama 94 Ins.
New Georgia: i., Solomon Is. 67 L3
New Gilston: Fife, Scotland 29 Q7
New Glasgow: N.S., Canada 89 U3
New Guinea: i., E. Indies 66 G2
Newhall: Calif., U.S.A. 93 D6
Newhall: Derby., England 27 S14
Newham: Gt. Ldn., England 25 W16
New Hampshire: State, U.S.A., (cap. Concord) 89 Q4
New Hampton: Iowa, U.S.A. 88 E4
New Hanover: Natal, S. Afr. 75 J4
New Harmony: Ind., U.S.A. 88 H6
New Haven: Conn., U.S.A. 89 P5
Newhaven: E. Sussex, Eng. 25 W18

New Hebrides: Br. & Fr. condominium 67 N5
Cap.: Vila
Area: 5,700 sq. miles (14,763 sq. km.)
Pop.: 84,000 (1971 E)

New Hebrides Trench: S. Pacific Ocean 7 20S 165E
New Holland: Humb., England 27 V12
New Hunstanton: Norf., England 25 W14
New Iberia: La., U.S.A. 90 F10
Newick: E. Sussex, Eng. 25 W18
Newington: Trans., S. Afr. 75 J2
New Inn: Tip., Repub. of Ireland 31 F15
New Ireland: i., Bismarck Arch. 67 K2
New Jersey: State, U.S.A. (cap. Trenton) 89 O5
New Kensington: Pa., U.S.A. 89 M5
Newkirk: Gram., Scotland 28 Q5
Newkirk: Okla., U.S.A. 90 C7
Newlands: C.P., S. Africa 74 Ins.
New Lexington: Ohio, U.S.A. 88 K6
New Limon: Panama 94 Ins.
New Liskeard: Ont., Canada 89 M2
New London: Conn., U.S.A. 89 P5
New London: Wis., U.S.A. 88 G3
New Luce: Dumfries & Galloway, Scotland 29 M10
Newlyn: Corn., England 25 K19
Newlyn East: Corn., England 24 L19
Newmachar: Gram., Scot. 28 R5
New Madrid: Mo., U.S.A. 88 G7
Newmains: Strath., Scot. 29 O8
Newmarket: Cork, Repub. of Ireland 31 D15
Newmarket: Ont., Canada 89 M3
Newmarket: Suff., England 25 W15
Newmarket on Fergus: Clare, Repub. of Ireland 31 D14
New Martinsville: W. Va., U.S.A. 88 L6
New Meadows: Idaho, U.S.A. 92 D4
New Mexico: State, U.S.A. (cap. Santa Fe) 93 F6
Newmill: Borders, Scotland 29 Q9
New Mills: Derby., England 27 R13
Newmills: Don., Republic of Ireland 30 F10
Newmilns: Strath., Scotland 29 N8
New Milton: Hants., Eng. 25 S18
New Mirpur: Jammu & Kashmir 58 M8
Newnan: Ga., U.S.A. 91 J9
Newnes Jcn.: N.S.W., Austl. 71 J9
Newnham: Glos., England 24 R16
New Norfolk: Tas., Austl. 68 H8
New Orleans: La., U.S.A. 90 Ins.
New Philadelphia: Ohio, U.S.A. 88 L5
New Pitsligo: Gram., Scotl 28 R4
NEW PLYMOUTH: Taranaki, North I., N.Z. 70 P14
Newport: Ark., U.S.A. 90 F8
Newport: Dyfed, Wales 24 M15
Newport: Essex, England 25 W16
Newport: Fife, Scotland 29 Q7
NEWPORT: Gwent, Wales 24 Q16
NEWPORT: I. of Wight, Eng. 25 T18
Newport: Ky., U.S.A. 88 J6
Newport: Maine, U.S.A. 89 R3
Newport: Mayo, Repub. of Ireland 30 B12
Newport: N.H., U.S.A. 89 P4
Newport: Oreg., U.S.A. 92 C4
Newport: Que., Canada 89 T1
Newport: R.I., U.S.A. 89 Q5
Newport: Salop, England 27 R14
Newport: Tenn., U.S.A. 91 K8
Newport: Tip., Repub. of Ireland 31 E14
Newport: Vt., U.S.A. 89 P3
Newport: Wash., U.S.A. 92 D3
Newport News: Va., U.S.A. 89 N7
Newport Pagnell: Bucks., England 25 U15
New Prague: Minn., U.S.A. 88 E3
New Providence: i., Bahamas 91 N13
Newquay: Corn., England 24 L19
New Quay: Dyfed, Wales 24 N15
New Radnor: Powys, Wales 24 P15
New Richmond: Que., Can. 89 T1
New Richmond: Wis., U.S.A. 88 E3
New Roads: La., U.S.A. 90 F10
New Romney: Kent, Eng. 25 X18
New Ross: Wex., Repub. of Ireland 31 H15
Newry: & riv., Down, N. Ireland 30 J11
Newry: N. Territ., Australia 68 D3
New Scone: Tay., Scotland 29 P7
New Siberian Is. (Novosibirskiye Ostrova): (U.S.S.R.), Arctic O. 49 Q2
New Smyrna Beach: city, Fla., U.S.A. 91 L11
Newsome Park-Hilton Park: Va., U.S.A. 91 N7
New South Wales: State, Australia (cap. Sydney) 71 G/L8
Newstead: see under Trimontium.
Newton: Ill., U.S.A. 88 G6
Newton: Iowa, U.S.A. 88 E5
Newton: Kans., U.S.A. 90 C6
Newton: Lancs., England 27 R12
Newton: Mass., U.S.A. 88 Q4
Newton: Miss., U.S.A. 88 G9
Newton: N.J., U.S.A. 89 O5
Newton: N.C., U.S.A. 91 L8
Newton: Strath., Scotland 29 N7
Newton Abbot: Devon, Eng. 24 O18
Newton by the Sea: Northumb., England 26 S8
Newton Ferrers: Devon, England 24 N19
Newton Forbes: Long., Repub. of Ireland 30 F12
Newton Grange: Lothian, Scotland 29 P8
Newton-le-Willows: Mers., England 27 Q13
Newtonmore: High., Scot. 28 N5
Newton St. Cyres: Devon, England 24 O18
Newton Stewart: Dumfries & Galloway, Scotland 29 N10
Newton Tony: Wilts., Eng. 25 S17
Newton Tracey: Devon, Eng. 24 N17
Newton upon Ouse: N. Yorks., England 27 T11
Newtown: Bord., Scotland 29 Q8
Newtown: Gt. Man., Eng. 27 Q12
Newtown: Long., Repub. of Ireland 30 F12
Newtown: Powys, Wales 27 P14
Newtownabbey: Antrim, N. Ireland 30 K10
Newtownards: Down, N. Irel. 30 K10
Newtownbarry: Wex., Repub. of Ireland 31 H14
Newtownbreda: Down, N. Ireland 30 K10
Newtown Butler: Ferm., N. Ireland 30 G11
Newtown Cunningham: Don., Repub. of Ireland 30 F10

Newton Gore: Leit., Repub. of Ireland 30 F11
Newtown Hamilton: Armagh, N. Ireland 30 H11
Newtown Mount Kennedy: town, Wick., Repub. of Ireland 31 J13
Newtown St. Boswells: Borders, Scotland 29 Q8
Newtown Sandes: Kerry, Repub. of Ireland 31 C14
Newtown Stewart: Tyr., N. Ireland 30 G10
New Tupton: Derby., Eng. 27 T13
Newtyle: Tayside, Scotland 29 P6
New Ulm: Minn., U.S.A. 88 D3
New Waterford: N.S., Can. 89 V2
New Westminster: B.C., Can. 92 C3
New York: N.Y., U.S.A. 89 P5
New York: State, U.S.A. (cap. Albany) 89 O4

New Zealand: Dominion 70/1 — —
Cap.: Wellington
Area: 103,736 sq. miles (268,676 sq. km.)
Pop.: 2,904,000 (1972 E)

Nexon: France 37 G10
Neya: U.S.S.R. 50 G3
Neyland: Dyfed, Wales 24 M16
Ney-To, Lake: U.S.S.R. 48 J3
Nezhin: Ukraine 50 D4
Nezvěstice: Czechoslovakia 45 T6
Ngabang: Borneo 65 D6
Ngambé: Cameroun 81 G3
Ngambwe Falls: Zambia 77 B6
Ngami, Lake: Botswana 77 B7
Ngamiland: Dist., Botswana (cap. Maun) 77 B6
Ngamiland: geog. reg., Bots. 77 B7
Ngangala: Sudan 76 D2
N'gaoundéré: Cameroun 81 G3
Ngapara: South I., N.Z. 70 N17
Ngara Binsam: Congo 81 G4
Ngaruawahia: North I., N.Z. 70 P13
Ngathainggyaung: Burma 59 R11
Ngau: i., Fiji Is. 67 P5
Ngauruhoe: mtn., North I., New Zealand 70 P14
Ngaunga: Cameroun 81 H4
Ngoko: riv., Cam./Congo 81 H4
N'Gola Plain: Gabon 81 F5
Ngoma: Malawi 77 D5
Ngonye: Kenya 76 E3
Ngonye Falls: Zambia 77 B6
Ngop: Sudan 76 D1
Ngora: Uganda 76 D2
Ngorongoro: Tanzania 76 E3
Ngorongoro Conservation Area: Tanzania 76 E3
Ngosa: Zambia 77 C5
Ngoto: Cen. Afr. Rep. 81 H4
Ngotsche: Dist., Natal, S. Africa 75 J3
N'Gounié: Reg. & riv., Gabon (cap. Mouila) 81 G5
N'Gouri: Chad 81 H2
Ngourou: Cen. Afr. Rep. 79 J8
N'Gourti: Niger 81 G1
Ngozi: Burundi 76 C3
Nggeleni: S. Africa 75 H5
Nguigmi: Niger 81 G2
Ngulu: i., Caroline Is. 61 M10
Nguru: Nigeria 81 G2
Ngurumahija: Tanzania 77 E5
Ngunju, C.: Sumba, Indon. 65 G9
Ngwaketse: Dist., Botswana (cap. Kanye) 75 F2
Ngwavuma: & Dist., Natal, South Africa 75 K3
Ngwenja: Swaziland 75 J3
Nhamacurra: Mozambique 77 E6
Nhamarroe: Mozambique 77 E6
Nhamundá: riv., Brazil 94 F4
Nhatrang: Vietnam 64 D4
Nhill: Vict., Australia 71 D11
Nhommarat: Laos 64 D3
Nhuvera: Brazil 96 D1
Niafounké: Mali 80 D1
Niagané: Mali 80 C2
Niagara Falls: cities, Ont., Can./ N.Y., U.S.A. 89 M4
Niagassola: Guinea 80 C2
NIAMEY: & Dept., Niger 81 E2
Niampak: Karakelong I., Indonesia 65 H6
Nianga: Zaïre 76 B4
Niangara: Zaïre 76 C2
Niangbo: Ivory Coast 80 C3
Niapu: Zaïre 76 C2
Niari: riv., Congo 81 G5
Nias: i., Sumatra 65 B6
Niassa: Dist., Mozambique (cap. Vila Cabral) 77 E6
Nibe: Denmark 47 L8
Nicaea: Graeco-Roman city at İznik, Turkey 39 V16
Nicaj: Albania 39 R15

Nicaragua: Republic 86 L15
Cap.: Managua
Area: 57,143 sq. miles (148,000 sq. km.)
Pop.: 1,911,543 (1971 C)

Nicastro: Italy 38 P17
NICE: Alpes Maritimes, Fr. 40 N12
Niceville: Fla., U.S.A. 91 H10
Nichicun, Lake: Que., Can. 85 m7
Nicholasville: Ky., U.S.A. 88 J7
Nicholson: riv., Queens., Australia 69 F3
Nicholson, West: Rhodesia 77 C7
Nickernich: W. Germany 44 N5
Nicobar Is.: (India), [cap. (with Andaman Is.) Port Blair], Indian O. 59 Q13
Nicola: B.C., Canada 92 C2
Nicolet: Que., Canada 89 P2
Nicolls Town: Bahamas 91 M13
Nicomedia: Greek city at İzmit, Turkey 56 A1
Nicopolis: Roman camp 3 miles E. of Alexandria, Egypt 56 A6
Nicopolis ad Haemum (at Istrum): Roman fort and town about 20 miles W. of Strazhitsa, Bulgaria 39 T15
Nicopolis ad Nestum: Roman colony of uncertain site in upper valley of Nestuo (Mesta), Plovdiv, Bulgaria 39 S15
NICOSIA (Levkosia): Cyprus 56 C4
Nicosia: Sicily 38 O18
Nictau: N.B., Canada 89 S2
Nidd: riv., N. Yorks., Eng. 27 T12
Nidda: W. Germany 44 P5
Nidda: riv., W. Germany 44 O5
Nidzica: Poland 43 R10
Nebüll: W. Germany 44 O1
Nied: riv., France 44 M6
Niederbayern: Dist., Bavaria, West Germany 41 S7
Niederbronn: France 40 N7
Niedere Tauern: mtns., Austria 41 T8
Niedersachsen: see Lower Saxony.
Nieder Stotzingen: W. Germany 40 Q7

Nieder Zerf—Nossebro 171

Nieder Zerf: W. Germany 44 M6
Niekerkshoop: C.P., S. Africa 74 E4
Niellé: Ivory Coast 80 C2
Nielloumolé: *riv.*, Senegal 80 B1
Niemce: Poland 45 W1
Niemegk: E. Germany 45 S3
Niemisel: Sweden 46 S3
Nienburg: W. Germany 44 P3
Nienhagen: W. Germany 45 Q3
Niep: S.W. Africa 74 B2
Niepołomice: Poland 43 R11
Niéré: Chad 79 J7
Nieul-le-Dolent: France 37 D9
Nieuwefontein: S.W. Africa 74 C4
Nieuwhoudtville: C.P., S. Africa 74 C5
Nieuw-Nickerie: Surinam 94 F2
Nieuwpoort: Belgium 36 H4
Nieuwpoort: Netherlands 44 K4
Nieuw Singkil: Sumatra 65 B6
Nieuwveld: *see* Nuweveld.
Nièvre: *Dept.*, France (*cap.* Nevers) 36 J8
Nifisha: Egypt (Suez Canal. *Inset*) 32 *Ins.*
Nigar: Iran 55 J9
NIĞDE: *& Prov.*, Turkey 56 D3
Nigel: Trans., S. Africa 74 N *Ins.*

Niger: *Republic* 78 F6
Cap.: Niamey
Area: 489,206 sq. miles (1,267,004 sq. km.)
Pop.: 4,243,000 (*1972 E*)

Niger: *riv.*, Africa 78 D6
Niger: *State*, Nigeria (*cap.* Minna) 81 F3

Nigeria: *Republic* 81 F3
Cap.: Lagos
Area: 356,699 sq. miles (923,850 sq. km.)
Pop.: 69,524,000 (*1972 E*)

Nigg: Highland, Scot. 28 O4
Nightcaps: South I., N.Z. 71 M17
Night Hawk Lake: Ont., Can. 88 L1
Nightingale I.: Vietnam 64 D2
Nigrita: Greece 39 S16
Nihiru: *i.*, Tuamotu Arch. 83 g3
Nihoa: *i.*, Hawaiian Islands 7 20N 165W
Nii: *i.*, Japan 63 f3
NIIGATA: *& Pref.*, Japan 63 f2
Niihama: Japan 63 c4
Niihau: *i.*, Hawaiian Is. 83 a2
Niitsu: Japan 63 Z7
Nijkerk: Netherlands 44 L3
Nijmegen: Netherlands 44 L4
Nikana (Ikaría): *i.*, Greece 39 U18
Nikel': U.S.S.R. 46 W2
Nikiforos: Greece 39 T16
Nikki: Benin 81 E3
Nikko: Japan 63 f2
Nikolayev: Ukraine 50 D5
Nikolayevsk: U.S.S.R. 49 Q7
Nikolayevskiy: U.S.S.R. 50 G5
Nikolayevskoye: U.S.S.R. 49 N7
Nikolsk: Penza, U.S.S.R. 50 G4
Nikol'sk: Vologda, U.S.S.R. 50 G3
Nikol'skaya: Karelian A.S.S. Repub., U.S.S.R. 46 W3
Nikol'skoye: U.S.S.R. 50 G5
Nikopol: Bulgaria 39 T15
Nikopol': Ukraine 50 D5
Niksar: Turkey 56 E1
Nikshahr: Iran 55 K9
Nikšić: Yugoslavia 39 Q15
Nikunau: *i.*, Gilbert Is. 67 P2
Nilambur: Tamil Nadu, India 58 N12
Nile: *Dist.*, Uganda 76 D2
Nile: *Prov.*, Sudan (*cap.* Ed Damer) 79 L6
Nile: *riv.*, Africa 79 L5
Niles: Mich., U.S.A. 88 H5
Nilgiri Hills: India 58 N12
Nimali: Iran 57 L3
Nimba: *Co.*, Liberia (*co. town* Sanniquellie) 80 C3
Nimba Mtn.: Ivory Coast 80 C3
Nimbin: N.S.W., Australia 71 K7
NIMES: Gard, France 37 K12
Nimmitabel: N.S.W., Austl. 71 H11
Nimran: Saudi Arabia 54 F10
Nimrod Res.: Ark., U.S.A. 90 E8
Nimruz: *Prov.*, Afghanistan (*cap.* Qaleh-i-kang) 55 K8
Nimule: Sudan 76 D2
Nin: Yugoslavia 41 V11
Ninda: Angola 77 B5
Nindigully: Queens., Austl. 70 H7
Nine Degree Chan.: Indian O. 58 M13
Nine Mile Burn: Lothian, Scotland 29 P8
Ninemilehouse: Tip., Repub. of Ireland 31 G15
Ninety East Ridge: Indian Ocean 9 20S 85E
Ninety Mile Beach: Vict., Australia 71 G12
Ninety Six: S.C., U.S.A. 91 K8
Nineveh: Assyrian capital, ruin near Mosul, Iraq 57 H3
Ninfield: E. Sussex, England 25 W18
Ningan: Heilungkiang, China 63 X6
Ningching: Tibet, China 62 R9
Ningerh (Puerh): Yunnan, China 62 S10
Ninghai: Chekiang, China 63 W9
Ninghsia: *see* Yin-ch'uan.
Ninghsia Hui: *Auton. Reg.*, China [*cap.* Yinch'uan (Ninghsia)] 62 T7
Ninghsien: *see* Ningpo.
Ninghsien: Kansu, China 62 T7
Ningi: Nigeria 81 F2
Ningkiang: Shensi, China 62 T8
Ningkwo (Suancheng): Anhwei, China 62 V8
Ninglang: Yunnan, China 62 S9
Ningming: Kwangsi Chuang, China 62 T10
Ningpo (Ninghsien): Chekiang, China 63 W9
Ningshen: Shensi, China 62 T8
Ningsiang: Hunan, China 62 U9
Ningteh: Fukien, China 62 V9
Ningtu: Kiangsi, China 62 V9
Ningwu: Shansi, China 62 U7
Ningyuan (Hsichang): Szechwan, China 62 S9
Ninhhoa: Vietnam 64 D4
Ninigo Is.: Papua/New Guinea 66 H2
Ninove: Belgium 44 K5
Nio: Japan 63 c3
Nioaque: Brazil 94 F8
Niobrara: *riv.*, Nebr., U.S.A. 92 G4
Nioro: Mali 80 C1
Nioro: Senegal 80 A2
NIORT: Deux-Sèvres, France 37 E9
Niout: Mauritania 80 C1
Nipan: Queens., Australia 70 J5
Nipani: Karnataka, India 58 M11
Nipawin: Sask., Canada 92 G2
Nipawin Prov. Park: Sask., Canada 92 G2
Nipigon: Ont., Canada 88 G1
Nipigon, Lake: Ont., Can. 88 G1
Nipigon Bay: Ont., Canada 88 G1
Nipisiguit: *riv.*, N.B., Can. 89 S2
Nipissing, Lake: Ont., Can. 89 M2
Nippur: Sumerian city, site at Nuffar, NW. of Diwaniya, Iraq 57 J5
Niquelândia: Brazil 94 H6
Niquero: Cuba 87 M13
Nir: Iran 57 K2
Niriz: *& lake*, Iran 55 H9
Nirmal: Andhra Pradesh, India 58 N11
Niš: Yugoslavia 39 R15
Nisa: Portugal 35 C17
Nisaea: ancient port of Mégara on Saronic G., Greece 39 S18
Nishapur: Iran 55 J7
Nishiichi: Japan 63 b3
Nishino: *i.*, Bonin Is., Pacific O. 60 N6
Nishinomiya: Japan 63 d3
Nishinoomote: Ōsumi Is., Japan 63 Y8
Nishinotoro, Cape: U.S.S.R. 63 ZZ5
Nishiwaki: Japan 63 d3
Nisibis: Graeco-Roman city at Nusaybin, on borders of Turkey and Syria 57 G3
Nisiros: *i.*, Dodec. (Grc.) 39 U18
Nissan: France 37 J12
Nisui (Erhsui): Taiwan 63 W10
NITERÓI: Rio de Janeiro, Brazil 96 G1
Nith: *riv.*, Strath./Dumf. & Gall., Scotland 29 O9
Nithsdale: *val.*, Dumfries & Galloway, Scotland 29 O9
Niti Pass: India/Tibet, China 58 N8
Nitra: *& riv.*, Czech. 43 Q12
Nittenau: W. Germany 45 S6
Niuafo'ou: *i.*, Pacific O. 67 Q5
Niulakita: Ellice Is., Pac. O. 67 P4
Niut: *mtn.*, Borneo 65 D6
Niutao: *i.*, Tuvalu, Pacific O. 67 P3
Nivala: Finland 46 T5
Nive Downs: *town*, Queens., Australia 70 G5
Nivelles: Belgium 44 K5
Nivernais: *Prov.*, France 34 H13
Nivskiy: U.S.S.R. 46 X3
Nixon: Tex., U.S.A. 90 C11
Niza: Iran 55 J9
Nizamabad: Andhra Pradesh, India 58 N11
Nizhnaya Salda: U.S.S.R. 51 K3
Nizhne-Chirskaya: U.S.S.R. 50 F5
Nizhne-Ilmsk: U.S.S.R. 49 M6
Nizhne-Kamchatsk: U.S.S.R. 49 S6
Nizhne-Kolymsk: U.S.S.R. 49 S4
Nizhne-Kuranakh: U.S.S.R. 49 o6
Nizhne-Savina: U.S.S.R. 51 Q3
Nizhne-Shadrino: U.S.S.R. 51 Q3
Nizhne-Tagil: U.S.S.R. 50 J3
Nizhne-Troitskiy: U.S.S.R. 50 H4
Nizhne-Udinsk: U.S.S.R. 49 I6
Nizhneye Chalmozero, Lake: U.S.S.R. 46 W3
Nizhni: U.S.S.R. 49 M3
Nizhniy Lomov: U.S.S.R. 50 F4
Nizhniy Novgorod: Russian city renamed Gor'kiy (q.v.) in 1932 after the Russian author 50 F3
Nizhniy Sergi: U.S.S.R. 50 J3
Nizina Sandomierska: *geog. reg.*, Poland 43 R11
Nizip: Turkey 56 E3
Njardhvik: Iceland 46 g4
Njombe: Tanzania 77 D4
Njoro: Tanzania 76 E4
Njuonjes: Sweden 46 P3
Njurunda: Sweden 47 P5
Nkala: Zambia 77 C6
Nkambe: Cameroun 81 G3
Nkana (Kihoe): Zambia 77 C5
Nkandla: *& Dist.*, Natal, S. Africa 75 J4
Nkata Bay: *town*, Malawi 77 D5
N'Kongsamba: Cameroun 81 F4
Nkoranza: Ghana 80 D3
Nkwalini: Natal, S. Africa 75 J4
Nmai: *riv.*, Burma 59 R9
No (*Thebes*): Egyptian city, site at *Karnak*, near Luxor, Egypt 54 D9
Noachabeb: S.W. Africa 74 C3
Noailles: France 36 H6
Noakhali: Bangladesh 59 Q10
Noatak: Alaska, U.S.A. 84 c4
Noatak: *riv.*, Alaska, U.S.A. 84 D4
Nobber: Meath, Repub. of Ireland 30 H12
Nobeoka: Japan 63 b4
Nobi: *riv.*, Heilungkiang, China 63 Y5
Noblesville: Ind., U.S.A. 88 J5
Noccundra: Queens., Austl. 70 E6
Noce: *riv.*, Italy 41 Q9
Nocera: Italy 38 O16
Nochten: E. Germany 45 U4
Nocona: Tex., U.S.A. 90 C9
Nocton: Lincs., England 27 V13
Noda: Japan 63 f3
Noeux: France 36 H5
Nogal: *geog. reg.*, Somalia 79 R18
Nogales: Ariz., U.S.A. 93 F6
Nogales: Mexico 93 E6
Nogal Valley: Somalia 79 R18
Nogara: Italy 41 R10
Nogara: *riv.*, Queens., Austl. 70 G5
Nogaro: France 37 E12
Nogata: Japan 63 b4
Nogaysk: Ukraine 50 E5
Nogent-en-Bassigny: France 40 L7
Nogent-le-Roi: France 36 G7
Nogent-le-Rotrou: France 36 F7
Nogent-sur-Seine: France 36 J7
Nogent-sur-Vernisson: Fr. 36 H8
Noginsk: U.S.S.R. 50 E3
Noginskiy: U.S.S.R. 49 L5
Nogoli: Argentina 96 B3
Nogoya: Argentina 96 D3
Nohar: Rajasthan, India 58 M9
Nohaval: Cork, Repub. of Ireland 31 E16
Noheji: Japan 63 ZZ6
Noho: Heilungkiang, China 63 W5
Noire: *riv.*, Vietnam 64 C2
Noirmoutier: Île de Noirmoutier, France 36 C8
Noirmoutier, Île de: *i.*, France 36 C9
Nojima, Cape: Honshu, Japan 63 f3
Nokaning: Botswana 77 B6
Nokia: Finland 47 S6
Nokilalaki: *mtn.*, Celebes 65 G7
Nok Kundi: Baluchistan, Pakistan 58 K9
Nokomis: Ill., U.S.A. 88 G6
Nokomis: Sask., Canada 92 G2
Noksi: U.S.S.R. 49 Q7
Nola: Central African Rep. 81 H4
Nola: Roman (and modern) city of Campania about 20 miles E. of Naples, Italy 38 O16
Nolay: France 36 K9
Noli: Italy 40 O11
Noli: Tanzania 77 E5
Nolinsk: U.S.S.R. 50 G3
Nome: Alaska, U.S.A. 84 C5
Nomentum: ancient Sabine or Latin city about 13 miles NE. of Rome. 38 N15
Noméný: France 40 M7
Nominingue: Que., Canada 89 O2
Nomo, Cape: Japan 63 a4
Nomtsas: S.W. Africa 74 B2
Nonacho, Lake: N.W.T., Canada 84 J5
Nonancourt: France 36 G7
Nonant: France 36 F7
Nondweni: Natal, S. Africa 75 J4
Nong Khai: Thailand 64 C3
Nong Lu: Thailand 64 B3
Nongoma: *& Dist.*, Natal, S. Africa 75 J3
Nonni (Nun): *riv.*, China 63 W5
Nonno: Ethiopia 76 E1
Nonoava: Mexico 93 F7
Nonouti: *i.*, Gilbert Is. 67 O2
Nontron: France 37 F10
Noojee: Vict., Australia 71 G11
Noondera: W. Australia 68 D6
Noondoo: Queens., Austl. 71 H7
Noonkanbah: W. Australia 68 C3
Noordhoek: C.P., S. Africa 74 *Ins.*
Noordwijk Aan Zee: Neth. 44 K3
Noorvik: Alaska, U.S.A. 84 c4
Nootka: B.C., Canada 92 B3
Noph (*Memphis*): Egyptian city site near *Bedrashen*, S. of Giza, Egypt 56 B7
Noqui: Angola 81 G6
Nora: Sweden 47 O7
Noranda: Que., Canada 89 M1
Noranside: Queens., Austl. 69 G4
Norba: ancient Latin city about 30 miles SE. of Rome. 38 N16
Nor Bayazet: Armenia, U.S.S.R. 57 J1
Norborne: Mo., U.S.A. 88 E6
Nord: *Dept.*, France (*cap.* Lille) 36 J5
Nord: *Dept.*, Ivory Coast (*cap.* Korhogo) 80 C3
Nord: *Dept.*, Upper Volta (*cap.* Ouahigouya) 80 D2
Nord: *Reg.*, Cameroun (*cap.* Garoua) 81 G3
Nordbaden: *Dist.*, Baden-Württemberg, West Germany 44 O6
Nord-Bout-du-Bois: France 36 D8
Nordegg: *see* Brazeau.
Norden: Gt. Man., Eng. 27 R12
Norden: W. Germany 44 N2
Nordenham: W. Germany 44 O2
Norderney: *i.*, E. Frisian Is. 44 N2
Norderstapel: W. Germany 44 P1
Nord-Est: *Dept.*, Benin (*cap.* Parakou) 81 E2
Nordeste: Angola 76 B4
Nord Fiord: Norway 46 J6
Nordfold: Norway 46 O3
Nord-Fron: Norway 47 L6
Nordhausen: E. Germany 45 Q4
Nordhorn: W. Germany 44 N3
Nordkinn Penin.: Norway 46 U1
Nordland: *Co.*, Norway (*cap.* Bodø) 46 O3
Nördlingen: W. Germany 40 Q7
Nordmaling: Sweden 46 Q5
Nordmarsch: W. Germany 44 O1
Nord-Ouest: *Dept.*, Benin (*cap.* Natitingou) 81 E2
Nord-Ouest: *Reg.*, Cameroun (*cap.* Bamenda) 81 F3
Nordreisa: Norway 46 R2
Nordstrand: *i.*, N. Frisian Is. 44 O1
Nord Trøndelag: *Co.*, Nor. (*cap.* Steinkjer) 46 N4
Nordvik: U.S.S.R. 49 N3
Nordwalde: W. Germany 44 N3
Nordwürttemberg: *Dist.*, Baden-Württemberg, West Germany 40 P6
Nore: *riv.*, Kilk./Laois, Repub. of Ireland 31 G14
Nore: *sandbank & est.*, England 25 X17
Noreia: pre-Roman city of *Noricum* at or near Neumarkt, Austria 41 U8
Norfolk: Nebr., U.S.A. 92 H4
Norfolk: Va., U.S.A. 89 N7
Norfolk: *Co.*, England (*co. town* Norwich) 25 X14
Norfolk I.: (Austl.), Pacific O. (*cap.* Kingston) 67 N7
Norfork Reservoir: Ark., U.S.A. 88 E7
Norham: Northumb., Eng. 26 R8
Nori: U.S.S.R. 48 J4
Noricum: Roman province lying mainly in Austria, between Danube, Inn, and the Carnic Alps 42 N13
Noril'sk: U.S.S.R. 48 k4
Nor Lake: Norway 47 L7
Norley: Queens., Australia 70 E6
Normal: Ill., U.S.A. 88 G5
Norman: Ark., U.S.A. 90 E8
Norman: Okla., U.S.A. 90 C8
Norman: *riv.*, Queens., Australia 69 G3
Normanby: N. Yorks., Eng. 26 U11
Normanby: *i.*, New Guinea 69 J1
Norman Cay: *is.*, Bahamas 91 N13
Normandie, Collines de: *hills*, France 36 E7
Normandin: Que., Canada 89 P1
Normandy: *Prov.*, France 34 F12
Normans Castle: Bahamas 91 N12
Normanton: Queens., Austl. 69 G3
Normanton: W. Yorks., England 27 T12
Norman Wells: N.W.T., Can. 84 G4
Nornmi: Japan 63 c3
Nornalup: W. Australia 68 B6
Norphpet: Ark., U.S.A. 90 E9
Norquinco: Argentina 95 C12
Norra Bergnäs: Sweden 46 Q3
Norraryd: Sweden 47 O8
Norrbotten: *Co.*, Sweden (*cap.* Luleå) 46 Q3
Norris Reservoir: *& dam*, Tenn., U.S.A. 88 J7
Norristown: Pa., U.S.A. 89 O5
Norrköping: Sweden 47 P7
Norrland: *geog. reg.*, Sweden 46 O4
Norrsundet: Sweden 47 P6
Norrtälje: Sweden 47 Q7
Norseman: W. Australia 68 C6
Norsjö: Sweden 46 Q4
Norske I.: Greenland 85 S2
Nort: France 36 D8
Norte, Ponta Do: *cape*, Braz. 94 K4
Norte, Serra do: *mtns.*, Braz. 94 F6
North Cape: Cape Breton I., Canada 89 V2
North Adams: Mass., U.S.A. 89 P4
NORTHALLERTON: N. Yorks., England 26 T11
Northam: Devon, England 24 N17
Northam: W. Australia 68 B6
North American Basin: N. Atlantic Ocean 8 30N 60W
NORTHAMPTON: *& Co.*, England 25 U15
Northampton: Mass., U.S.A. 89 P4
Northampton: W. Austl. 68 A5
Northampton Uplands: *hills*, Northants./War., England 25 T15
North Andaman: *i.*, Andaman Is. 59 Q12
North Anson: Maine, U.S.A. 89 R3
North Atlantic Ocean 8
North Augusta: S.C., U.S.A. 91 L9
North Battleford: Sask., Can. 92 F2
North Bay: Ont., Canada 89 M2
North Bend: Oreg., U.S.A. 92 C4
North Bend: Nebr., U.S.A. 92 H4
North Berwick: Lothian, Scotland 29 Q7
North Beveland: *i.*, Neth. 44 J4
North Bovey: Devon, Eng. 24 O18
North Brabant: *Prov.*, Neth. (*cap.* 's-Hertogenbosch) 44 L4
North Brentor: Devon, England 24 N18
North Buganda: *Dist.*, Uganda 76 D2
North Burton: Humberside, England 26 V11
North Cadbury: Som., Eng. 24 Q17
North Canadian: *riv.*, U.S.A. 90 B8
North Cape: Norway 46 U1
North Cape: North I., N.Z. 70 O12
North Cape: Spitsbergen 48 c1
North Cape: *town & cape*, Celebes 65 H6
North Caribou Lake: Ont., Canada 92 J2
North Carolina: *State*, U.S.A. (*cap.* Raleigh) 91 M8
North Cave: *village*, Humberside, England 27 U12
North Cerney: Glos., Eng. 24 S16
North Chan.: Ont., Canada 88 K2
North Chan.: Scot./Irel. 29 K9
North Chapel: W. Sussex, England 25 U17
North Chicago: Ill., U.S.A. 88 H4
Northcliffe: W. Australia 68 B6
North Coates: Lincs., Eng. 27 W13
North Crawley: Bucks., Eng. 25 U15
North Curry: Som., Eng. 24 Q17
North Dakota: *State*, U.S.A. (*cap.* Bismarck) 92 G3
North Dalton: Humb., Eng. 27 U12
North Danger: *reef*, S. China Sea 64 E4
North Dorset Downs: *hills*, Dorset, England 24 R18
North Downs: *hills*, Kent, England 25 X17
North Dvina: *riv.*, U.S.S.R. 50 G2
North East: *Dist.*, Botswana (*cap.* Francistown) 77 C7
North-East: *Reg.*, Somalia (*cap.* Burao) 79 R18
North Eastern: *Reg.*, Kenya (*cap.* Garissa) 76 E2
North East Providence Channel: Bahamas 91 N13
North East Land: *i.*, Spitsbergen 48 D2
Northeast Pass: La., U.S.A. 90 *Ins.*
Northeim: W. Germany 45 Q4
North Elmham: Norf., Eng. 25 X14
Northern: *Prov.*, Sierra Leone (*cap.* Makeni) 80 B3
Northern: *Dist.*, **Uganda 76 D2**
Northern: *Prov.*, Sudan (*cap.* Dongola) 79 K6
Northern: *Prov.*, Zambia (*cap.* Kasama) 77 D5
Northern: *Reg.*, Ghana (*cap.* Tamale) 80 D3
Northern Ireland: U.K. (*cap.* Belfast) 30 H10
Northern Sporades: *is.*, Grc. 39 T17
Northern Territory: Austl. (*cap.* Darwin) 68 E3
North Erradale: Highland, Scotland 28 K4
North Esk: *riv.*, Tayside/Grampian, Scotland 29 Q6
North Ferriby: Humb., Eng. 27 V12
Northfield: Minn., U.S.A. 88 E3
Northfield: Vt., U.S.A. 89 P3
Northfield: W. Mid., Eng. 24 S15
North Fiji Basin: S. Pacific Ocean 7 20S 170E
Northfleet: Kent, England 25 W17
North Foreland: *cape*, Kent, England 25 Y17
North Fork (Red Riv.): *riv.*, Tex./Okla., U.S.A. 90 A8
North Frisian Is.: Den./W. Ger. 47 L9
North Frodingham: Humb., England 27 V12
North Hafun Bay: Somalia 79 S17
North Harris: *dist.*, Outer Hebr., Scotland 28 H4
North Hill: *village*, Corn., England 24 N18
North Holland: *Prov.*, Neth. (*cap.* Haarlem) 44 K3
North Horr: Kenya 76 E2
Northiam: E. Sussex, Eng. 25 X18
North Indian Lake: Man., Canada 92 H1
North I.: New Zealand 70 P14
North Is.: La., U.S.A. 90 *Ins.*
North Kazakhstan: *Reg.*, Kazakhstan, U.S.S.R. (*cap.* Petropavlovsk) 51 L4
North Kelsey: Lincs., England 27 V13

North Korea: *Republic* 63 X7
Cap.: Pyongyang
Area: 46,768 sq. miles (121,129 sq. km.)
Pop.: 14,281,000 (*1971 E*)

North Kvalpy: *i.*, Norway 46 Q1
North Land (Severnaya Zemlya): *is.* (U.S.S.R.), Arctic O. 49 I2
Northland: *Dist.*, N.I., New Zealand (*cap.* Whangarei) 70 O12
Northleach: Glos., England 25 S16
Northleigh: Devon, England 24 P18
North Leigh: Oxon., Eng. 25 T16
Northlew: Devon, England 24 N18
North Little Rock: *city*, Ark., U.S.A. 90 E8
North Lopham: Norf., Eng. 25 X15
North Loup: *riv.*, Nebr., U.S.A. 92 H4
North Luconia Shoals: S. China Sea 65 E5
North Luffenham: Leics., England 27 U14
North Magnetic Pole: N.W.T., Canada 84 K2
North Manchester: Ind., U.S.A. 88 J5
North Marutea: *i.*, Tuamotu Arch. 83 g3
North Minch: *chan.*, Outer Hebr., Scotland 28 K3
North Molton: Devon, England 24 O17
North Morar: *dist.*, Highland, Scotland 28 K6
North Natuna Is.: Indonesia 65 D6
North Newbald: Humb., England 27 U12
North Osetia A.S.S. Rep.: U.S.S.R. (*cap.* Ordzhonikidze) 50 F6
North Pacific Ocean 7
North Pagai: *i.*, Mentawai Is., Indonesia 65 C7
North Pass: La., U.S.A. 90 *Ins.*
North Petherton: Som., Eng. 24 P17
North Platte: Nebr., U.S.A. 92 G4
North Platte: *riv.*, U.S.A. 92 G4
North Point: *cape*, Mich., U.S.A. 88 K3
North Point: *cape*, P.E.I., Canada 89 U2
Northport: Ala., U.S.A. 91 H9
North Pretoria: Trans., S. Africa 75 H2
North Reef: Paracel Is. 64 E3
North Rhine-Westphalia: *State*, W. Germany (*cap.* Düsseldorf) 44 O4
North Rona: *i.*, Scotland 28 K2
North Ronaldsay: *i.*, Orkney Is., Scotland 28 *Ins.*
North Saskatchewan: *riv.*, Alta./Sask., Canada 92 E2
North Scarle: Lincs., Eng. 27 U13
North Sea: Europe 26 U8
North Sentinel: *i.*, Andaman Is. 59 Q12
North Shawbost: Outer Hebr., Scotland 28 H3
North Shields: *see* Tynemouth.
North Somercotes: Lincs., England 27 W13
North Sos'va: *riv.*, U.S.S.R. 51 K2
North Sound: Repub. of Ireland 31 B13
North Sound, The: Orkney Is., Scotland 28 *Ins.*
North Stradbroke I.: Queens., Australia 70 K6
North Sunderland: Northumb., England 26 S8
North Sydney: Cape Breton I., Canada 89 V2
North Taranaki Bight: North I., New Zealand 70 P14
North Tawton: Devon, Eng. 24 O18
North Thoresby: Lincs., Eng. 27 V13
North Tolsta: Outer Hebr., Scotland 28 J3
Northton: Outer Hebr., Scot. 28 G4
North Tonawanda: N.Y., U.S.A. 89 M4
North Truchas Peak: New Mexico, U.S.A. 93 F5
North Tyne: *riv.*, Northumb., England 26 R9
North Udde: *cape*, Öland, Sweden 47 P8
North Uist: *i.*, Outer Hebr., Scotland 28 G4
Northumberland: N.H., U.S.A. 89 Q3
Northumberland: *Co.*, Eng. (*co. town* Newcastle) 26 R9
Northumberland Is.: Queens., Australia 70 J3
Northumberland Str.: Can. 89 U2
North Vancouver: B.C., Can. 92 C3
North Vernon: Ind., U.S.A. 88 J6

North Vietnam: *see* **Vietnam**

North Walpole: N.H., U.S.A. 89 P4
North Walsham: Norf., Eng. 25 Y14
North Weald Bassett: Essex 25 W16
North-West: *Reg.*, Somalia (*cap.* Hargeisa) 79 Q18
Northwest Atlantic Basin: N. Atlantic Ocean 8 30N 70W
North West Cape: W. Austl. 68 A4
North-Western: *State*, Nigeria (*cap.* Sokoto) 81 F2
North-Western: *Prov.*, Zambia (*cap.* Solwezi) 77 B5
North West Frontier Prov.: Pakistan (*cap.* Peshawar) 58 M8
Northwest Pacific Basin: N. Pacific Ocean 7 30N 155E
North West Providence Chan.: Bahamas 91 M12
Northwest River: Newf., Can. 85 n7
Northwest Territories: Can. (*cap.* Yellowknife) 84 G4
North Wheatley: Notts., England 27 U13
Northwich: Ches., England 27 Q13
Northwold: Norf., England 25 X14
Northwood: Iowa, U.S.A. 88 E4
Northwood: N. Dak., U.S.A. 92 H3
North Wootton: Norf., Eng. 25 W14
North York Moors: N. Yorks., England 26 U11
North York Moors Nat. Park: N. Yorks., England 26 U11
North Yorkshire: *Co.*, England (*co. town* Northallerton) 26 T11
Norton: Kans., U.S.A. 93 H5
Norton: N. Yorks., Eng. 27 T12
Norton: Powys, Wales 24 P15
Norton: S. Yorks., Eng. 26 U11
Norton: Va., U.S.A. 88 K7
Norton, East: Leics., Eng. 27 U14
Norton St. Philip: Som., England 24 R17
Norton Sound: Alaska, U.S.A. 84 c5
Nortorf: W. Germany 45 P1
Norvegia, Cape: Antarctica 9 75S 15W
Norwalk: Conn., U.S.A. 89 P5
Norwalk: Ohio, U.S.A. 88 K5

Norway: *Kingdom* 46/7
Cap.: Oslo
Area: 125,181 sq. miles (324,219 sq. km.)
Pop.: 3,930,000 (*1972 E*)

Norway: Mich., U.S.A. 88 H3
Norway House: Man., Can. 92 H2
Norwegian Bay: N.W.T., Canada 85 L2
Norwegian Sea: 8 65N 05W
Norwich: Conn., U.S.A. 89 P5
Norwich: N.Y., U.S.A. 89 O4
NORWICH: Norf., England 25 Y14
Norwich: Ont., Canada 88 L4
Norwick: Shetland Is., Scot. 28 *Ins.*
Norwood: Ohio, U.S.A. 88 J6
Noshiro: Japan 63 ZZ6
Noshul': U.S.S.R. 50 G2
Nosovshchina: U.S.S.R. 50 E2
Nossebro: Sweden 47 N7

Nossen: E. Germany 45 T4
Noss Head: *cape*, Highland, Scotland 28 P3
Nossob: S.W. Africa 74 B1
Nossob: *riv.*, S. Africa 74 D2
Nosy Bé: *i.*, Malagasy Rep. 73 O12
Nosy-Varika: Malagasy Rep. 73 O14
Notabile (Mdina): Malta 23 *Ins.*
Noteć: *riv.*, Poland 43 P10
Notikewin: Alta., Canada 92 D1
Notium: ancient Greek port of Colophon (q.v.), Turkey 39 U18
Noto: Sicily 38 O18
Noto: *i.*, Japan 63 e2
Notobe: Japan 63 e2
Notodden: Norway 47 L7
Noto Penin.: Japan 63 e2
Notozero, Lake: U.S.S.R. 46 X3
Notre Dame Bay: Newf., Canada 85 v2
Notre Dame du Nord: Que., Canada 89 M2
Notre Dame Mtns.: Que., Canada 89 S1
NOTTINGHAM: Notts., Eng. 27 T14
Nottingham I.: Canada 85 M5
Nottingham Road: Natal, S. Africa 75 H4
Nottinghamshire: *Co.*, Eng. (*co. town* Nottingham) 27 U13
Nottoway: Va., U.S.A. 91 M7
Notwani: *riv.*, Botswana 75 G2
NOUADHIBOU (Port Étienne): Baie du Lévrier, Mauritania 78 A5
NOUAKCHOTT: Mauritania 78 A6
Nouan-le-Fuzelier: France 36 H8
Nouatia: Togo 80 E3
NOUMÉA: New Caledonia 67 N6
Noupoort: C.P., S. Africa 75 F5
Nouvelle, La: France 37 J12
Nouvelle Anvers: *antiq.*, Zaire 76 A2
Nouvion, Le: France 36 J5
Nouzonville: France 36 K6
Nóva: Hungary 41 W9
Nová Bystřice: Czech. 45 V6
Nova Chaves: Angola 77 B5
Novae: Roman camp on river Danube at Svishchtov, Bulgaria 39 T15
Novaesium: Roman camp at Neuss, on Rhine opposite Düsseldorf, W. Germany 44 M4
Nova Freixo: Mozambique 77 E5
Nova Friburgo: Brazil 96 G1
Nova Gaia: Angola 73 H12
Nova Goa: see Panjim
Nova Granada: Brazil 94 H8
Nova Iguaçu: Brazil 96 G1
Nova Lima: Brazil 94 J8
NOVA LISBOA: *see* HUAMBO
Novalja: Yugoslavia 41 U11
Nova Luzitânia: Moz. 77 D6
Nova Mambone: Moz. 77 E7
Novara: Italy 40 O10
Nova Russas: Brazil 94 J4
Nova Scotia: *Prov.*, Canada (*cap.* Halifax) 89 U3
Nova Scotia Basin: N. Atlantic Ocean 8 35N 60W
Nova Sofala: Mozambique 77 D7
Nova Soure: Brazil 94 K6
Nova Trento: Brazil 96 F2
Nova Varoš: Yugoslavia 39 Q15
Nova Venécia: Brazil 94 J7
Novaya Kazanka: Kazakh., U.S.S.R. 50 G5
Novaya Lyalya: U.S.S.R. 51 K3
Novaya Sibir´ I.: New Siberian Is., U.S.S.R. 49 q2
Novaya Vyzhva: Ukraine 43 T11
Novaya Zemlya: *is.*, U.S.S.R. 48 g3
Nova Zagora: Bulgaria 39 U15
Nové Hrady: Czech. 41 U7
Novelda: Spain 35 F17
Novellara: Italy 41 Q11
Nové Město: Czech. 45 W6
Nové Strašeci: Czech. 45 T5
Nové Zámky: Czech. 43 Q13
NOVGOROD: & *Reg.*, U.S.S.R. 50 D3
Novgorod-Severskiy: Ukraine 50 D4
Novi: Yugoslavia 41 U10
Novi Bečej: Yugoslavia 39 R14
Novi Grad: Yugoslavia, *formerly* Cittanova-Trieste 41 T10
Novi Ligure: Italy 40 O11
Novi Marof: Yugoslavia 41 W9
Noviomagus: Romano-Br. town at Chichester, W. Sussex, England 25 U18
Noviomagus: Roman camp at Nijmegen, Netherlands 44 L4
Novi Pazar: Bulgaria 39 U15
Novi Pazar: Yugoslavia 39 R15
Novi Sad: Yugoslavia 39 Q14
Novoaltaysk: U.S.S.R. 51 O4
Novobogatinskoye: Kazakh., U.S.S.R. 50 H5
Novocherkassk: U.S.S.R. 50 F5
Novograd Volynskiy: Ukraine 43 U11
Novogrudok: Byelorussia 43 T10
Novokazalinsk: Kazakh., U.S.S.R. 51 K5
Novokuznetsk: U.S.S.R. 51 P4
Novolazarevskaya: *rsch. stn.*, Antarctica 9 75S 10E
Novolyubino: U.S.S.R. 51 M3
Novo Mesto: Yugoslavia 41 V10
Novomoskovsk: U.S.S.R. 50 E4
NOVO REDONDO: Cuanza Sul, Angola 73 G12
Novorossiysk: U.S.S.R. 50 E6
Novorzhev: U.S.S.R. 50 C3
Novoseltsi: Bulgaria 39 S15
Novosel´ye: U.S.S.R. 47 V7
NOVOSIBIRSK: & *Reg.*, U.S.S.R. 51 O3
Novosibirskiye Ostrova (New Siberian Is.): (U.S.S.R.), Arctic O. 49 Q2
Novospasskoye: U.S.S.R. 50 G4
Novosukhotino: Kazakh., U.S.S.R. 51 L4
Novo-Ushitsa: Ukraine 43 U12
Novozensk: U.S.S.R. 50 G4
Novozensk: U.S.S.R. 50 G4
Novska: Yugoslavia 38 P14
Nový Bydžov: Czech. 45 U5
Nový Jičín: Czechoslovakia 43 Q12
Novyy Buyan: U.S.S.R. 50 H3
Novyy Oskol: U.S.S.R. 50 E4
Novyy Port: U.S.S.R. 48 J4
Nowa Ruda: Poland 45 W5
Nowa Sól: Poland 45 V4
Nowata: Okla., U.S.A. 90 D7
Nowe Miasto: Poland 43 R11
Nowgong: Assam, India 59 Q9
Nowgong: Madhya Pradesh, India 58 N9
Nowingi: Vict., Australia 71 E10
Nowogard: Poland 45 V2

Nowra: N.S.W., Australia 71 J10
Nowshera: NW. Front. Prov., Pakistan 58 M8
Nowy Sącz: Poland 43 R12
Nowy Targ: Poland 43 Q12
Nowy Tomysl: Poland 45 W3
Noxubee: *riv.*, Miss./Ala., U.S.A. 90 G9
Noya: Spain 35 B15
Noyant: Maine-et-Loire, Fr. 36 F8
Noyelles: France 36 G5
Noyen-sur-Sarthe: France 36 E8
Noyes: France 37 K12
Noyon: France 36 H6
Nozay: France 36 D8
Nqamakwe: S. Afr. 75 G6
Nqutu: & *Dist.*, Natal, S. Africa 75 J4
N´riquinha: Angola 77 B6
Nsanje: Malawi 77 E6
Nsukka: Nigeria 81 F3
Ntabamhlope: Natal, S. Afr. 75 H4
Ntabankulu: & *Dist.*, S. Afr. 75 H5
Ntem: *riv.*, Cameroun 81 G4
N'Tima: Congo 81 G5
Ntola: S. Africa 75 H5
Ntondwe: Zambia 77 C6
Ntumeni: Natal, S. Africa 75 J4
Ntywenka: S. Africa 75 H5
Nu (Salween): *riv.*, China 62 R9
Nuaillé: France 36 E8
Nuanetsi: & *riv.*, Rhodesia 77 D7
Nuas Lake: Finland 46 U4
Nubaran: Iran 57 L4
Nubia: name given to a region of the upper Nile. Formerly part of Ethiopia it now lies in Sudan 79 L6
Nubian Desert: Sudan 54 D10
Nuble: *riv.*, Chile 96 A4
Nuchek: Alaska, U.S.A. 84 E5
Nudo Coropuna: *mtn.*, Peru 94 C7
Nudushan: Iran 55 H8
Nueces: *riv.*, Tex., U.S.A. 90 B11
Nueil: France 36 E9
Nueltin, Lake: N.W.T., Can. 84 K5
Nueva Galia: Argentina 96 B4
Nueva Gerona: Cuba 87 I13
Nueva Imperial: Chile 96 A4
Nueva Palmira: Uruguay 96 D3
Nueva Pompeya: Argentina 96 C1
Nueva Rosita: Mexico 93 G7
Nueve de Julio: Argentina 96 C4
Nuevitas: Cuba 87 M13
Nuevo G.: Argentina 95 E12
Nuevo Juncal: Chile 96 B2
Nuevo Laredo: Mexico 90 B12
Nuevo Leon: *State*, Mexico (*cap.* Monterrey) 93 H7
Nuevo San Juan: Panama 94 *Ins.*
Nûgâtsiaq: Greenland 85 o3
Nûgssuaq: Greenland 85 o3
Nuguria Group: *is.*, Bismarck Arch. 67 K2
Nuhaka: North I., N.Z. 70 O14
Nui: *i.*, Tuvalu, Pacific O. 67 P3
Nuits-St.-Georges: France 36 K8
Nuj: Iran 57 H3
Nukhaib: *well*, Iraq 57 H5
Nukheila: *well*, Sudan 54 C11
NUKUALOFA: Tonga 67 Q6
Nukufetau: Tuvalu, Pac. O. 67 P3
Nuku Hiva: *i.*, Marquesas Is. 83 g1
Nukulaelae: *i.*, Tuvalu, Pacific O. 67 P3
Nukumanu Is.: Solomon Is. 67 L2
Nukunono: *i.*, Tokelau Is. 70 *Ins.*
Nukus: Kara-Kalpak, U.S.S.R. 50 J6
Nukutavake: *i.*, Tuamotu Arch. 83 h3
Nukutipipi: *i.*, Tuamotu Arch. 83 g4
Nulato: Alaska, U.S.A. 84 D5
Nules: Spain 35 F17
Nullagine: W. Australia 68 C4
Nullarbor Plain: W./S. Austl. 68 D6
Numan: Nigeria 81 G3
Numata: Japan 63 f2
Numazu: Japan 63 f3
Numidia: kingdom and later Roman province of N. Africa E. of Mauretania and W. of modern Tunisia 32 D4
Numurkah: Vict., Austl. 71 F11
Nun (Nonni): *riv.*, China 63 W5
Nun Bank: Scotland 28 M2
Nuneaton: War., England 27 T14
Nungan: Kirin, China 63 X6
Nungo: Mozambique 77 E5
Nunivak: *i.*, Alaska, U.S.A. 84 C5
Nunkiang: Heilungkiang, China 63 X5
Nunney: Som., England 24 R17
Nunnington: N. Yorks., Eng. 26 U11
Nunspeet: Netherlands 44 L3
Nunukan, East: Borneo 65 F6
Nuorgam: Finland 46 T2
Nuoro: Sardinia 38 L16
Nuqdis: *well*, Iraq 57 H5
Nurata: Uzbek., U.S.S.R. 51 L6
Nura-Tau: *mtns.*, Uzbek., U.S.S.R. 51 L6
Nurek: Tadzhik., U.S.S.R. 51 L7
Nuremberg (Nürnberg): W. Germany 45 R6
Nurmes: Finland 46 V5
Nürnberg: (Nuremberg): W. Germany 45 R6
Nurney: Carlow, Repub. of Ireland 31 H14
Nurney: Kild., Repub. of Ireland 31 H13
Nurri: Sardinia 38 L17
Nurrootpa: S. Australia 71 C10
Nusaybin: Turkey 57 G3
Nushagak: Alaska, U.S.A. 84 D6
Nushki: Baluchistan, Pakistan 58 L9
Nuso, Cape: Iviza, Balearic Is. 35 G17
Nuthe: *riv.*, E. Germany 45 T3
Nutwood Downs Station: N. Territ., Australia 68 E3
Nuwara Eliya: Sri Lanka 58 O13
Nuwerus: S. Africa 74 C6
Nuweveld Range: S. Africa 74 D6
Nyack: N.Y., U.S.A. 89 P5
Nyahanga: Tanzania 76 D3
Nyahururu: Kenya 76 E2
Nyahwest: Vict., Australia 71 E10
Nyakabindi: Tanzania 76 D3
Nyakisiku: Tanzania 76 E4
Nyakwa: Malawi 77 D5
Nyala: Sudan 79 J7
Nyalam: Tibet, China 59 P9
Ny-Ålesund: Spitsbergen 48 C2
Nyalikungu: Tanzania 76 D3
Nyamandhlovu: Rhodesia 77 C6
Nyambiti: Tanzania 76 D3
Nyamlell: Sudan 79 K8
Nyamtumbo: Tanzania 77 E5
Nyandoma: U.S.S.R. 50 F2
Nyanga: *Reg. & riv.*, Gabon (*cap.* Tchibanga) 81 G5

Nyanguge: Tanzania 76 D3
Nyangwe: Zaïre 76 C3
Nyangwene: Zambia 77 C6
Nyanza: Rwanda 76 C3
Nyanza: *Reg.*, Kenya (*cap.* Kisumu) 76 D3
Nyanza Lac: *town*, Burundi 76 C3
Nyasa (Malawi), Lake: East Africa 77 D5
Nyaunglebin: Burma 59 R11
Nyazepetrovsk: U.S.S.R. 50 J3
Nyborg: Funen, Denmark 47 M9
Nybro: Sweden 47 O8
Nyda: U.S.S.R. 48 J4
Nyeboes Land: Greenland 85 O1
Nyenchen Tanglha: *mtn. & range*, Tibet, China 59 Q8
NYERI: Central, Kenya 76 E3
Nyerol: Sudan 76 D1
Nyíregyháza: Hungary 43 R13
Nyiru: *mtn.*, Kenya 76 E2
Nyiru: *mtn.*, Kenya 76 E3
Nykarleby: Finland 46 S5
Nykøbing: Jutland, Den. 47 L8
Nykøbing: Falster, Den. 47 M9
Nykøbing: Zealand, Den. 47 M9
NYKÖPING: Södermanland, Sweden 47 P7
Nylga: U.S.S.R. 50 H3
Nylstroom: Trans., S. Afr. 75 H2
Nymagee: N.S.W., Austl. 71 G9
Nymburk: Czechoslovakia 45 V5
Nynäshamn: Sweden 47 P7
Nyngan: N.S.W., Austl. 71 G8
Nyon: Switzerland 40 M9
Nyong: *riv.*, Cameroun 81 G4
Nyons: France 37 L11
Nyřany: Czechoslovakia 45 T6
Nysa: Poland 43 P11
Nysa: *riv.*, see Neisse.
Nysa Lużycka: *riv.*, Poland/ East Germany 45 U4
Nyunzu: Zaïre 76 C4
Nyur: Inner Mongolia, China 62 S6
Nyuzen: Japan 63 e2
Nzabé: Central African Rep. 76 B1
Nzébéla: Guinea 80 C3
Nzega: Tanzania 76 D3
N´ZÉRÉKORÉ: & *Reg.*, Guinea 80 C3
Nzi: *riv.*, Ivory Coast 80 D3

O: *i.*, Japan 63 f3
Oa, Mull of: *cape*, Inner Hebr., Scotland 29 J8
Oadby: Leics., England 27 T14
Oahe Reservoir: S. Dak., U.S.A. 92 G3
Oahu: *i.*, Hawaiian Is. 83 c2
Oakbank: S. Australia 71 D9
Oak Creek: *town*, Colo., U.S.A. 93 F4
Oakdale: Calif., U.S.A. 93 C5
Oakdale: La., U.S.A. 90 E10
Oakengates: Salop, England 26 R14
Oakes: N. Dak., U.S.A. 92 H3
Oakey: Queens., Australia 70 J6
Oakford: Devon, England 24 O18
Oak Grove: La., U.S.A. 90 F9
Oakham: Leics., England 27 U14
Oak Hill: Ohio, U.S.A. 88 K6
Oak Hill: W. Va., U.S.A. 88 L7
Oakington: Cambs., Eng. 25 W15
Oakland: Calif., U.S.A. 93 C5
Oakland: Md., U.S.A. 89 M6
Oakland: Nebr., U.S.A. 92 H4
Oakland City: Ind., U.S.A. 88 H6
Oaklands: N.S.W., Austl. 71 G10
Oakleigh: Vict., Australia 71 F11
Oakley: Bucks., England 25 T16
Oakley: Hants., England 25 T17
Oakley: Idaho, U.S.A. 92 E4
Oakley, Great: Essex, Eng. 25 Y16
Oakley, Great: Northants., England 25 U15
Oak Park: *city*, Ill., U.S.A. 88 H5
Oak Ridge: Tenn., U.S.A. 88 J7
Oakville: La., U.S.A. 90 *Ins.*
Oakville: Ont., Canada 89 M4
Oakworth: W. Yorks., Eng. 27 S12
Oamaru: South I., N.Z. 70 N17
Oami: Japan 63 g3
Oasis: *Dept.*, Algeria (*cap.* Ouargla) 78 E4
Oathlaw: Tayside, Scotland 29 Q6
Oatlands: S. Africa 75 F6
Oatlands: Tas., Australia 68 H8
Oatman: Ariz., U.S.A. 93 E6
Oaxaca: Mexico 86 K14
Ob´: *riv.*, U.S.S.R. 48 h5
Ob´, G. of: U.S.S.R. 48 J4
Oba: Ont., Canada 88 J1
Oba: *i.*, New Hebrides 67 N5
Obama: Japan 63 d3
Oban: Nigeria 81 F3
Oban: Sask., Canada 92 F2
Oban: Stewart I., New Zealand 71 M18
Oban: Strath., Scotland 29 L7
Obatogamau Lake: Que., Canada 89 O1
Obbia: Somalia 79 R18
Obdach: Austria 41 U8
Obeh: Afghanistan 58 K8
Oberá: Argentina 96 D2
Ober Aargau: *geog. reg.*, Switzerland 40 N8
Oberammergau: (*famous for its decennial 'Passion Play'*), W. Germany 41 R8
Oberbayern: *Dist.*, Bavaria, West Germany 41 R8
Oberfranken: *Dist.*, Bavaria, West Germany 45 R5
Ober-Grafendorf: Austria 41 V7
Ober-Haching: W. Germany 41 R7
Ober Harz: *mtns.*, Germany 45 Q4
Oberhausen: W. Germany 44 M4
Ober Hollabrunn: Austria 41 W7
Oberholzer: Trans., S. Afr. 74 *Lins.*
Oberkirch: W. Germany 40 O7
Oberlin: Ohio, U.S.A. 88 K5
Oberndorf: W. Germany 40 O7
Oberndorf: W. Germany 40 O7
Oberon: N.S.W., Australia 71 H9
Oberpfalz: *Dist.*, Bavaria, West Germany 41 R6
Oberstdorf: W. Germany 40 Q8
Oberstein: W. Germany 44 N6
Ober Traubling: W. Germany 41 S7
Obertrum: Austria 41 T8
Oberursel: W. Germany 44 O5
Obervellach: Austria 41 T9
Oberwald: Switzerland 40 O9
Oberwart: Austria 41 W8
Ober Zeiring: Austria 41 U8
Obetim: Nigeria 81 F3

Obi: *i.*, Vietnam 64 D5
Obidos: Brazil 94 F4
Obidos: Portugal 35 B17
Obihiro: Japan 63 ZZ6
Obi Is.: Moluccas, Indon. 61 K12
Obion: & *riv.*, Tenn., U.S.A. 90 G7
Oblarn: Austria 41 T8
Obluch´ye: U.S.S.R. 63 Y5
OBO: Haut-M'Bomou, Central African Rep. 76 C1
Obobogorap: S. Africa 74 D3
Obock: Djibouti 79 Q17
Obolo: Nigeria 81 F3
Obor: U.S.S.R. 63 Z5
Oborniki: Poland 45 W3
Oboyan´: U.S.S.R. 50 E4
Obra: *riv.*, Poland 45 V3
Obrenovac: Yugoslavia 39 R14
O'Briensbridge: Clare, Repub. of Ireland 31 D14
Obrovac: Yugoslavia 41 V11
Obruk: Turkey 56 C2
Observatory Cay: *reef*, Austl. 69 J3
Obu: Japan 63 e3
Obuasi: Ghana 80 D3
Obubra: Nigeria 81 F3
Ocala: Fla., U.S.A. 91 K11
Ocampo: Chihuahua, Mex. 93 F7
Ocampo: Coahuila, Mexico 93 G7
Ocaña: Colombia 94 C2
Ocaña: Spain 35 E17
Occhiobello: Italy 41 R11
Occidental, Cordillera: *mtns.*, Colombia 94 B5
Ocean Cape: Alaska, U.S.A. 84 F6
Ocean City: Md., U.S.A. 89 O6
Ocean City: N.J., U.S.A. 89 P6
Ocean Falls: B.C., Canada 92 B2
Ocean I.: (Br.), Gilbert Is. 67 N2
Oceanographer Fracture Zone: N. Atlantic Ocean 8 35N 40W
Ochagavia: Spain 37 D13
Ochakov: Ukraine 50 D5
Ochemchiri: Georgia, U.S.S.R. 50 F6
Ochiai: Japan 63 c3
Ochil Hills: Tayside, Scotland 29 O7
Ochiltree: Strath., Scotland 29 N9
Ochlockonee: *riv.*, Fla., U.S.A. 91 K10
Ochsenfurt: W. Germany 45 Q6
Ochtrup: W. Germany 44 N3
Ocilla: Ga., U.S.A. 91 K10
Ock: *riv.*, Berks., England 23 K9
Ockelbo: Sweden 47 P6
Ockendon, S.: Essex, Eng. 25 W16
Ockies: S. Africa 74 D5
Ockley: Surrey, England 25 V17
Ocland: Romania 43 T13
Ocmulgee: *riv.*, Ga., U.S.A. 91 K9
Ocna Mari: Romania 39 T14
Ocó: Guinea-Bissau 80 B2
Oconee: *riv.*, Ga., U.S.A. 91 K9
Oconomowoc: Wis., U.S.A. 88 G4
Oconto: Wis., U.S.A. 88 H3
Oconto Falls: *city*, Wis., U.S.A. 88 G3
Ocotal: Nicaragua 86 L15
Ocotlán: Mexico 86 j13
Ocracoke Inlet: N.C., U.S.A. 91 O8
Octodurus: Roman settlement at Martigny, Switz. 40 N9
Ocumare del Tuy: Venez. 94 D1
Ocussi: Timor, Indonesia 65 G8
Oda: Ghana 80 D3
Ódádhahraun: *lava field*, Iceland 46 e4
Odate: Japan 63 ZZ6
Odawara: Japan 63 f3
Odda: Norway 47 K6
Oddobo: Ethiopia 79 Q17
Oddur: Somalia 79 Q19
Odelzhausen: W. Germany 41 R7
Odemira: Portugal 35 B18
Ödemiş: Turkey 39 V17
Odenbull: N. Frisian Is., W. Germany 44 O1
Odendaalsrus: O.F.S., S. Africa 75 *Ins.*
Odenkirchen: W. Germany 44 M4
Odense: Funen, Denmark 47 M9
Odenwald: *hills*, W. Germany 44 P6
Oder (Odra): *riv.*, E. Ger./Pol. 42 O10
Oderberg: E. Germany 45 U3
Oderzo: Italy 41 S10
Odeshög: Sweden 47 O7
Odessa: Mo., U.S.A. 90 E6
Odessa: Tex., U.S.A. 93 G6
Odessa: Ukraine 50 D5
Odessa: Wash., U.S.A. 92 D3
Odessus: Greek city at Varna, Bulgaria 39 U15
Odienné: Ivory Coast 80 C3
Odiham: Hants., England 25 U17
Odongk: Cambodia 64 C4
Odoorn: Netherlands 44 M3
Odorhei: Romania 43 T13
Odra (Oder): *riv.*, Poland 43 P11
Odstock: Wilts., England 25 S17
Odweina: Somalia 79 R18
Odžaci: Yugoslavia 39 Q14
Odzala: Congo 81 G4
Odzi: Rhodesia 77 D6
Oea: Phoenician and Roman city at Tripoli 32 E5
Oebistelde: E. Germany 45 Q3
Oeiras: Brazil 94 J5
Oelsnitz: E. Germany 45 S5
Oelwein: Iowa, U.S.A. 88 F4
Oeniadae: Greek city on coast W. of mouth of Achelous river, SW. of Aitolikón, Greece 39 R17
Oeno I.: (Br.), S. Pacific Ocean 7 25S 135W
Oenoe: fort of W. Attica near frontier with *Boeotia* about 12 miles SSE. of Thebes. 39 S17
Oenophyta: ancient village of E. *Boeotia* near frontier of *Attica* about 10 miles S. of Chalcis 39 S17
Oescus: Roman camp on Danube near confluence with Golem Iskr, Bulg. 39 T15
Oeta: *mtn.* rising from Spercheus valley, 17 miles SW. of Lamia, Greece 39 S17
Oetling: Argentina 96 C2
Of: Turkey 57 G1
Ofanto: *riv.*, Italy 38 O16
Ofin: *riv.*, Ghana 80 D3
Offa: Nigeria 81 E3
Offaly: *Co.*, Repub. of Irel. (*cap.* Tullamore) 31 F13
Offenbach: W. Germany 44 O5
Offenburg: W. Germany 40 N7
Offley, Great: Herts., England 25 V16
Offranville: France 36 G5
Ofot Fiord: Norway 46 P2

Ofude: Uganda 76 D2
Ogaden: *geog. reg.*, Eth. 79 Q18
Ogaki: Honshu, Japan 63 e3
Ogallala: Nebr., U.S.A. 92 G4
Ogarino: U.S.S.R. 50 G3
Ogasawara Arch. (Bonin Is.): (Jap.), Pacific O. 60 N6
Ogbomosho: Nigeria 81 E3
Ogbourne St. George: Wilts., England 25 S17
Oğdem: Turkey 57 G1
Ogden: Utah, U.S.A. 92 E4
Ogdensburg: N.Y., U.S.A. 89 O3
Ogeechee: *riv.*, Ga., U.S.A. 91 K9
Ogema: Sask., Canada 92 G3
Ogenbargen: W. Germany 44 N2
Ogilvie Range: Canada 84 F5
Oglio: *riv.*, Italy 40 P10
Ogliuga: *i.*, Aleutians 84 *Ins.*
Ogmore: Queens., Australia 70 H4
Ognon: *riv.*, France 40 L8
Ogo: *geog. reg.*, Somalia 79 R18
Ogoja: Nigeria 81 F3
Ogooué: *riv.*, Congo/Gabon 81 G5
Ogooué-Ivindo: *Reg.*, Gabon (*cap.* Makokou) 81 G4
Ogooué-Lolo: *Reg.*, Gabon (*cap.* Koula-Moutou) 81 G5
Ogooué-Maritime: *Reg.*, Gabon (*cap.* Port Gentil) 81 F5
Ogr: Sudan 79 K7
Ogre: Latvia, U.S.S.R. 47 T8
Ogulin: Yugoslavia 41 V10
Oguma: Nigeria 81 F3
Ogumi: Nigeria 81 F3
Ogun: *riv.*, Nigeria 81 E3
Ogun: *State*, Nigeria (*cap.* Abeokuta) 81 E3
Oguni: Japan 63 f1
Ogur: Uganda 76 D2
Ogurchinskiy I.: Caspian Sea 50 H7
Oguta: Nigeria 81 F3
Ohai: South I., N.Z. 71 L17
Ohakune: North I., N.Z. 70 P14
Ohau, Lake: South I., N.Z. 70 M17
Ohio: *riv.*, U.S.A. 88 G7
Ohio: *State*, U.S.A. (*cap.* Columbus) 88 K5
Ohopuho: S.W. Africa 73 G13
Ohrdruf: E. Germany 45 Q5
Ohře (Eger): *riv.*, Czech. 45 U5
Ohrid: Yugoslavia 39 R16
Ohrid Lake: Yugo./Alb. 39 R16
Ohrigstad: Trans., S. Africa 75 J2
Ohura: North I., N.Z. 70 P14
Oi: Japan 63 e3
Oiapoque: Brazil 94 G3
Oiapoque: *riv.*, Fr. Guiana/Brazil 94 G3
Oich, Loch: Highl., Scot. 28 M5
Oie, I´: France 37 D9
Oigh-Sgeir: *i.*, Inner Hebr., Scotland 28 H6
Oil City: Pa., U.S.A. 89 M5
Oildale: Calif., U.S.A. 93 D5
Oilgate: Wex., Repub. of Ireland 31 H15
Oilton: Okla., U.S.A. 90 C7
Oim: Chinghai, China 62 R7
Oise: *Dept. & riv.*, France (*cap.* Beauvais) 36 H6
Oisemont: France 36 G6
Oissel: France 36 G6
OITA: & *Pref.*, Japan 63 b4
Ojinaga: Mexico 93 G7
Ojo de Agua: Argentina 96 C2
Ojos del Salado: *mtn.*, Chile 96 B2
Ojung: Sweden 47 O6
Oka: Japan 63 e3
Oka: *riv.* (Upper Tunguska), U.S.S.R. 49 M7
Oka: *riv.* (Volga), U.S.S.R. 50 F3
Okaba: Indonesia 69 F1
Okahandja: & *Dist.*, SW. Africa 74 B1
Okaihau: North I., N.Z. 70 O12
Okanagan Lake: B.C., Can. 92 D2
Okanagan Mtns.: B.C., Can. 92 C3
Okanda Plat.: Gabon 81 G5
Okano: *riv.*, Gabon 81 G4
Okanogan: & *riv.*, Wash., U.S.A. 92 D3
Okány: Hungary 43 R13
Okarito: South I., N.Z. 70 N16
Okavango Basin: *geog. reg.*, Botswana 73 H9
Okaya: Japan 63 f2
OKAYAMA: & *Pref.*, Japan 63 c3
Okazaki: Japan 63 e3
Okeechobee: & *lake*, Fla., U.S.A. 91 L12
Okeene: Okla., U.S.A. 90 B7
Okefinokee Swamp: Ga., U.S.A. 91 K10
Okehampton: Devon, Eng. 24 N18
Oke Iho: Nigeria 81 E3
Okemah: Okla., U.S.A. 90 C8
Okene: Nigeria 81 F3
Okha: Gujarat, India 58 L10
Okha: U.S.S.R. 49 Q7
Okhaldhunga: Nepal 59 P9
Okhansk: U.S.S.R. 50 J3
Okhota: *riv.*, U.S.S.R. 49 Q5
Okhotsk: & *sea*, U.S.S.R. 49 Q6
Okhta: U.S.S.R. 46 W4
Oki: Buru, Indonesia 65 H7
Okiep: S. Africa 74 B4
Okigwi: Nigeria 81 F3
Oki Is.: Japan 63 Y7
Okinawa: *i. & group*, Ryukyu Is. 63 X9
Okino Erabu: *i.*, Ryukyu Is. 63 X9
Okitipupa: Nigeria 81 E3
OKLAHOMA: *State*, U.S.A. (*cap.* Oklahoma City) 90 C8
OKLAHOMA CITY: Okla., U.S.A. 90 C8
Okmulgee: Okla., U.S.A. 90 D8
Oko: *wadi*, Sudan 54 E10
Okondja: Gabon 81 G5
Okoshi: Japan 63 e3
Okotoks: Alta., Canada 92 E2
Okovango: *riv.*, Angola/S.W. Africa 77 B6
Okoyo: Congo 81 H5
Okpara: *riv.*, Benin/Nigeria 81 E3
Okřísky: Czechoslovakia 45 V6
Okt'abr'sk: Kazakh., U.S.S.R. 50 J5
Oktabr'skoy Revolyutsii I.: Severnaya Zemlya, Arctic O. 49 L2
Oktyabr'skoye: Chelyabinsk', U.S.S.R. 51 K4
Oktyabr'skoye: Tyumen, U.S.S.R. 51 L2
Oku: Okinawa, Ryukyu Is. 63 X9
Okuchi: Japan 63 b4
Okuru: South I., N.Z. 70 M16
Okuta: Nigeria 81 E3
Okwa: *riv.*, Botswana 77 B7
Ólafsfjördhur: Iceland 46 d3
Öland: *i.*, Sweden 47 P8
Olary: S. Australia 71 D9
Olasan: Ethiopia 79 R18

Olathe—Ouarzazate 173

Olathe: Kans., U.S.A. 90 D6
Olavarría: Argentina 96 C4
Oława: Poland 43 P11
Olbernhau: E. Germany 45 T5
Olbia: Greek city on left bank of estuary S. of Nikolayev, U.S.S.R. 33 J2
Olbramkostel: Czech. 45 V7
Old Aberdeen: Grampian, Scotland 28 R5
Old Baldy: mtn., see Wrightson, Mt.
Old Bolingbroke: Lincs., England 27 W13
Oldbury: West Midlands, England 24 R15
Oldbury upon Severn: Avon, England 24 Q16
Old Castile: old Prov., Spain 35 D16
Oldcastle: Meath, Repub. of Ireland 30 G12
Old Cleeve: Som., England 24 P17
Old Crow: Yukon, Canada 84 F4
Old Deer: Gram., Scotland 28 R4
Oldeani: Tanzania 76 E3
Oldebroek: Netherlands 44 L3
Oldenburg: Lower Saxony, W. Germany 44 O2
Oldenburg: Schleswig-Holstein, W. Germany 45 Q1
Oldenburg: Dist., Lower Saxony, West Germany 44 O2
Oldenhorn: mtn., Switz. 40 N9
Oldenzaal: Netherlands 44 M3
Old Gumbiro: Tanzania 77 E5
Oldham: Gt. Man., Eng. 27 R12
Oldhamstocks: Loth., Scot. 29 R8
Old Harbour: Jamaica 86 Ins.
Old Head of Kinsale: cape, Cork, Repub. of Ireland 31 D16
Old Hickory: Tenn., U.S.A. 88 H7
Oldland: Avon, England 24 R17
Old Leake: Lincs., England 27 W13
Old Leighlin: Carlow, Repub. of Ireland 31 G14
Old Man, The: mtn., Cumbria, England 26 P11
Old Man on his Back Plat.: Sask., Canada 92 F3
Oldmeldrum: Gram., Scot. 28 R5
Old Molopo: riv., S. Africa 74 D4
Olds: Alta., Canada 92 E2
Oldshore: High., Scotland 28 L3
Oldsum: N. Frisian Is., W. Germany 44 O1
Old Tati: Botswana 77 C7
Oldtown: Dublin, Repub. of Ireland 30 J12
Old Town: Maine, U.S.A. 89 R3
Olean: N.Y., U.S.A. 89 M4
Oleggio: Italy 40 O10
Olekma: riv., U.S.S.R. 49 O6
Olekminsk: U.S.S.R. 49 O5
Olenek: U.S.S.R. 49 N4
Olenek: riv., U.S.S.R. 49 O3
Olenek Bay: U.S.S.R. 49 O3
Olen'ya: U.S.S.R. 46 X2
Oléron, Île d': i., France 37 D10
Olesnica: Poland 43 P11
Olesno: Poland 43 Q11
Olevsk: Ukraine 43 U11
Olfen: W. Germany 44 N4
Ol'ga: U.S.S.R. 63 Z6
Olga Lake: Que., Canada 89 N1
Olhava: Finland 46 T4
Oli: riv., Nigeria 81 E3
Olib: i., Yugoslavia 41 U11
Olicana: Roman name of Ilkley, W. Yorks., England 27 S12
Olifants: riv., Cape Prov., S. Africa 74 C5
Olifants: riv., Trans., S. Afr. 75 J2
Olifant's Drift: Trans., S. Afr. 75 G2
Olifantshoek: S. Africa 74 E3
Olifant's Point: cape, S. Afr. 74 Ins.
Olimar: Uruguay 96 E3
Olinda: Pernambuco, Braz. 94 L5
Oling Hu: lake, China 62 S9
Olio: Queens., Australia 69 G4
Olisipo: Roman town and port at Lisbon, Portugal 35 B17
Oliva, Cordillera de: range, Argentina 96 B2
Oliva de Jerez: Spain 35 C17
Olivares: Spain 35 E17
Olive Hill: Ky., U.S.A. 88 K6
Oliveira: Brazil 95 J8
Olivenza: Spain 35 C17
Olivet: France 36 G8
Olkusz: Poland 43 Q11
Ollague: Chile 95 D8
Ollague, Volc.: Chile 95 D8
Ollerton: Notts., England 27 T13
Olliergues: France 37 J10
Ollila: Finland 46 U2
Ollita, Cordillera de: range, Argentina 96 A3
Olmedo: Spain 35 D16
Olmutz: German name of Czechoslovak town Olomouc 43 P12
Olney: Bucks., England 25 U15
Olney: Ill., U.S.A. 88 G6
Olney: Tex., U.S.A. 90 B9
Oloko: Nigeria 81 F3
Ololi: Congo 81 G5
Olomouc: Czechoslovakia 43 P12
Olonzac: France 37 H12
Oloron-Ste.-Marie: France 37 E12
Olot: Spain 35 H15
Olovo: Yugoslavia 39 Q14
Olovyannaya: U.S.S.R. 49 n7
Olpae: Greek city at E. end of G. of Amvrakia, Grc. 39 R17
Olpe: W. Germany 44 N4
OLSZTYN: & Prov., Poland 43 R10
Olt: riv., Romania 39 T14
Olten: Switzerland 40 N8
Oltenia: Prov., Romania 39 S14
Olteniţa: Romania 39 U14
Olteţ: riv., Romania 43 T14
Oltu: Turkey 57 G1
O'luan, Cape: Taiwan 63 W10
Olutanga: i., Philippines 64 G5
Olvera: Spain 35 D18
Olveston: Avon, England 24 Q16
OLYMPIA: Wash., U.S.A. 92 C3
Olympia: ancient Greek shrine in river Alpheus valley, about 20 miles E. of Katakolon, Greece 39 R18
Olympic Nat. Park: Wash., U.S.A. 92 C3
Olympus: mtn., Greece 39 S16
Olynthus: Greek city about 8 miles inland from head of G. of Toroni, Greece 39 S16
Olyutorskiy Bay: U.S.S.R. 49 s5
Om': riv., U.S.S.R. 51 N3
Oma: U.S.S.R. 48 f4
Omachi: Japan 63 e2
Omae, Cape: Japan 63 f3
OMAGH: Tyr., N. Ireland 30 G10
Omaha: Nebr., U.S.A. 92 H4
'Oman: Sultanate 55 J11
Cap.: Muscat
Area: 82,000 sq. miles (212,380 sq. km.)
Pop.: 678,000 (1971 E)
'Oman, G. of: Arabian Sea 55 J10
Omara: Kenya 76 E3
Omaruru: S.W. Africa 73 H14
Ombabika: Ont., Canada 85 L7
Ombai Str.: Indonesia 65 H8
Ombaia: Gabon 81 G5
Ombambo: S.W. Africa 73 G13
Ombella-M'Poko: Pref., Cen. Afr. Rep. (cap. Bimbo) 76 A1
Ombersley: Hereford & Worcester, England 24 R15
Ombu Gompa: Tibet, China 62 R8
Ombwe: Zaire 76 C3
Omdraaisvlei: S. Africa 74 E5
Omdurman: Sudan 54 D11
Omeath: Louth, Repub. of Ireland 30 J11
Omegna: Italy 40 O10
Omein: Ethiopia 79 Q18
Omeo: Vict., Australia 71 G11
Omi: Japan 63 e2
Omigawa: Japan 63 g3
Omineca: riv., B.C., Canada 92 B1
Omišalj: Yugoslavia 41 U10
Omitara: S.W. Africa 74 C1
Omiya: Japan 63 f3
Omizo: Japan 63 e3
Ommen: Netherlands 44 M3
Omo: riv., Ethiopia 76 E1
Omolon: riv., U.S.S.R. 49 r4
Omoloy: riv., U.S.S.R. 49 o4
Omonville: France 36 D6
Omortag: Bulgaria 39 U15
OMSK: & Reg., U.S.S.R. 51 M3
Omu: Japan 63 ZZ6
Omu: Kirin, China 63 X6
Omura: Japan 63 a4
Omuta: Japan 63 b4
Omutinskiy: U.S.S.R. 51 L3
Omutninsk: U.S.S.R. 50 H3
On (Heliopolis): Egyptian city site NNW. of Cairo 56 B6
Ona: riv., Khakass, U.S.S.R. 51 Q4
Ona: riv., Krasnoyarsk, U.S.S.R. 51 R3
Onamia: Minn., U.S.A. 88 E2
Onan: Celebes 65 F7
Onancock: Va., U.S.A. 89 O7
Onanis: S.W. Africa 74 A1
Onaping Lake: Ont., Can. 88 L2
Onarga: Ill., U.S.A. 88 G5
Oncativo: Argentina 96 C3
Onchan: I. of Man, U.K. 26 N11
Onchiota: N.Y., U.S.A. 89 O3
Ondangua: S.W. Africa 73 H13
Onder Ongeluk: S. Africa 74 E4
Onderstedorings: S. Africa 74 D5
Ondo: Nigeria 81 E3
Ondo: State, Nigeria (cap. Akure) 81 E3
Ondolean: Celebes 65 G7
Ondor Khan: Mongolia 62 U5
Onega: U.S.S.R. 48 e5
Onega, Lake: U.S.S.R. 50 E2
Onega: riv., U.S.S.R. 50 E2
Onehunga: North I., N.Z. 70 P13
Oneida: Tenn., U.S.A. 88 J7
Oneida Lake: N.Y., U.S.A. 89 O4
O'Neill: Nebr., U.S.A. 92 H4
Onekotan I.: Kuril Is. 60 P2
Oneonta: Ala., U.S.A. 91 H9
Oneonta: N.Y., U.S.A. 89 O4
Ongers: riv., S. Africa 74 E5
Ongerup: W. Australia 68 B6
Ongjin: S. Korea 63 X7
Ongoka: Zaire 76 C3
Ongole: Andhra Pradesh, India 58 O11
Onguati: S.W. Africa 74 A1
Onguday: U.S.S.R. 51 P4
Oni: Georgia, U.S.S.R. 50 F6
Onib Mines: Sudan 54 E10
Onibury: Salop, England 24 Q15
Onich: Highland, Scotland 29 L6
Onitsha: Nigeria 81 F3
Onjongni: N. Korea 63 X7
Onkhor: Somalia 79 R17
Onnela: Finland 46 U2
Onnour: Chad 78 H6
Ono: Aichi, Japan 63 e3
Ono: Fukui, Japan 63 e3
Ono: Gifu, Japan 63 e3
Onoda: Japan 63 b4
Ono-i-lau: i., Fiji Is. 67 Q6
Onolimbu: Nias, Sumatra 65 B6
Onomichi: Japan 63 c3
Onon: riv., U.S.S.R. 49 N7
Ononi: Japan 63 g2
Onotoa: i., Gilbert Is. 67 P2
Onpo: Kwangtung, China 62 U10
Onseepkans: S. Africa 74 C4
Onslow: W. Australia 68 B4
Onslow Bay: N.C., U.S.A. 91 N8
Ontario: Oreg., U.S.A. 92 D2
Ontario: Prov., Canada (cap. Toronto) 85 L7
Ontario, Lake: Can./U.S.A. 89 N4
Onteng: Equatorial Guinea 81 G4
Onteniente: Spain 35 F17
Onto Lake: Finland 46 V4
Ontonagon: Mich., U.S.A. 88 G2
Ontong Java Is. (Lord Howe Atoll): Solomon Is. 67 L3
Onvane: Gabon 81 G4
Onzain: France 36 G8
Oobagooma: W. Australia 68 C3
Oodnadatta: S. Australia 69 F5
O'okiep: S. Africa 74 B4
Oola: Lim., Repub. of Irel. 31 E14
Ooldea: S. Australia 68 E6
Oostende (Ostend): Belg. 36 H4
Oosterhesselen: Neth. 44 M3
Oosterhout: Netherlands 44 K4
Oosthaven: Sumatra 65 D8
Oostmalle: Belgium 44 K4
Ootacamund: Tamil Nadu, India 58 N12
Ootsa Lake: town, B.C., Can. 92 B2
Opala: Zaire 76 B3
Opari: Sudan 76 D2
Opasatika: Ont., Canada 88 K1
Opatija: Yugoslavia 41 U10
Opatovice: Czechoslovakia 45 V5
Opatow: Poland 43 R11
Opava: Czechoslovakia 43 P12
Opazatika Lake: Ont., Can. 88 K1
Opelika: Ala., U.S.A. 91 J9
Opelousas: La., U.S.A. 90 E10
Opeongo Lake: Ont., Can. 89 M3
Opheim: Mont., U.S.A. 92 F3
Ophir: Alaska, U.S.A. 84 D5
Ophir: South I., N.Z. 70 M17
Ophthalmia Range: W. Australia 68 B4
Opienge: Zaire 76 C2
Opland: Co., Norway (cap. Lillehammer) 47 L6
Opobo: & riv., Nigeria 81 F4
Opochka: U.S.S.R. 47 V8
Opoczno: Poland 43 R11
Opodepe: Mexico 93 E7
OPOLE: & Prov., Poland 43 P11
Opononi: North I., N.Z. 70 O12
OPORTO (Porto): Douro, Portugal 35 B16
Opotiki: North I., N.Z. 70 Q14
Opouma: Congo 81 H4
Opp: Ala., U.S.A. 91 H10
Oppenau: W. Germany 40 O7
Oppenheim: W. Germany 44 O6
Opponitz: Austria 41 U8
Optand: Sweden 46 O5
Opunake: North I., N.Z. 70 O14
Oquendo: Philippines 64 G4
Ora: Italy 41 R9
Ora Banda: W. Australia 68 C6
Oradea: Romania 43 R13
Oradour-sur-Vayres: France 37 F10
Oraefajökull: mtn., Iceland 46 e4
Orai: Uttar Pradesh, India 58 N9
Oraison: France 40 L12
Orallo: Queens., Australia 70 H6
Oramar: Turkey 57 J3
ORAN: & Dept., Algeria 35 F19
Oran: Argentina 96 C1
Orange: France 37 K11
Orange: N.S.W., Australia 71 H9
Orange: Tex., U.S.A. 90 E10
Orange: Va., U.S.A. 89 M6
Orange: riv., S. Africa 74 B4
Orangeburg: S.C., U.S.A. 91 L9
Orange-Fish Tunnel: O.F.S., S. Africa 75 F5
Orange Free State: Prov., S. Africa (cap. Bloemfontein) 75 G4
Orange Range: Indonesia 61 M12
Orangeville: Ont., Canada 88 L4
Orange Walk: Belize 86 Ins.
Oranienburg: E. Germany 45 T3
Oranjefontein: Trans., S. Afr. 75 G1
Oranjemund: SW. Africa 74 B4
Oranjeville: O.F.S., S. Africa 75 H3
Oranmore: Galway, Repub. of Ireland 31 D13
Orapa: Botswana 77 C7
Oras: Philippines 64 H4
Orasul Stalin see Braşov.
Oraviţa: Romania 39 R14
Orawia: South I., N.Z. 71 L18
Orba: riv., Italy 40 O11
Orbe: Switzerland 40 M9
Orbec: France 36 F6
Orbetello: Italy 38 M15
Orbieu: riv., France 37 H12
Orbost: Vict., Australia 71 H11
Orbyhus: Sweden 47 P6
Orcadas: rsch. stn., Antarctica 9 65S 45W
Orcera: Spain 35 E17
Orchies: France 36 J5
Orchomenus: Greek city at W. end of Lake Copais, about 24 miles NW. of Thebes 39 S17
Orchomenus: Greek city about 18 miles NW. of Tripolis, Greece 39 S18
Orchy, Glen: Strath., Scot. 29 M7
Orco: riv., Italy 40 N10
Orcop: Hereford & Worcester, England 24 Q16
Ord: Inner Hebr., Scotland 28 K5
Ord: Nebr., U.S.A. 92 H4
Ord: riv., W. Australia 68 D3
Ord, Mount: W. Australia 68 D3
Orde, El: Argentina 96 B4
Ordie: Grampian, Scotland 28 Q5
Ording: W. Germany 44 O1
Ordos Plat.: Inner Mongolia, China 62 T7
ORDU: & Prov., Turkey 56 E1
Ordubad: Azerbaydzhan, U.S.S.R. 57 J2
Orduña: Spain 35 E15
Ordynskoye: U.S.S.R. 51 O4
ORDZHONIKIDZE: North Ossetia, U.S.S.R. 50 F6
Ore: riv., Sweden 46 Q4
Orealla: Guyana 87 e8
OREBRO: & Co., Sweden 47 O7
Oredezh: U.S.S.R. 50 D3
Oregon: Ill., U.S.A. 88 G4
Oregon: State, U.S.A. (cap. Salem) 92 C4
Oregon City: Wash., U.S.A. 92 C3
Oregrund: Sweden 47 Q6
Orekhov: Ukraine 50 E5
Orekhovo: Bulgaria 39 S15
Orekhovo-Zuyevo: U.S.S.R. 50 E3
OREL: Orlov, U.S.S.R. 50 E4
Orellana: Peru 94 B5
Orellana, Embalse de: res., Spain 35 D17
Orem: Utah, U.S.A. 93 E4
Oren: Turkey 39 U18
ORENBURG (Chkalov): & Reg. U.S.S.R. 50 J4
Orense: Argentina 96 D4
ORENSE: & Prov., Spain 35 C15
Orepuki: South I., N.Z. 71 L18
Orestias: Greece 39 U16
Øre Sund: str., Den./Swed. 47 M9
Oretani: ancient Spanish tribe of upper Guadiana valley 35 E16
Orford: Suff., England 25 Z15
Organa: Spain 35 G15
Organ Pipe Cactus Nat. Mon. Ariz., U.S.A. 93 E6
Orgaz: Spain 35 E17
Orgelet: France 40 L9
Orgères: France 36 G7
Orgeyev: Moldavia, U.S.S.R. 50 C5
Orgiva: Spain 35 E18
Orgon: France 37 L12
Orhaneli: Turkey 56 A2
Orhangazi: Turkey 56 A1
Orhon: riv., Mongolia 62 S5
Orhy, Pic d': mtn., Pyrenees 37 D13
Orick: Calif., U.S.A. 92 C4
Oriental, Cordillera: range, Colombia 94 C3
Orih Lake: Finland 46 V5
Orihuela: Spain 35 F17
Orille, La: Mexico 86 j14
Orillia: Ont., Canada 89 M3
Orimattila: Finland 47 T6
Orinoco: riv., Venezuela 94 E2
Orinoco Delta: geog. reg., Venezuela 87 c6
Orissa: State, India (cap. Bhubaneswar) 59 O10
Oristano: & gulf, Sardinia 38 L17
Orivesi: Finland 47 T6
Oriximina: Brazil 94 F4
Orizaba: Mexico 86 K14
Orkla: riv., Norway 46 L5
Orkney: Is. & Admin., Scotland (cap. Kirkwall) 28 Ins.
Orlando: Fla., U.S.A. 91 L11
Orlando: Trans., S. Africa 74 Ins.
Orleanais: Prov., France 34 G13
ORLEANS: Loiret, France 36 G8
Orleans, Canal: France 36 H8
Orleans, Forêt d': geog. reg., France 36 G8
Orléans, Île d': i., Que., Canada 89 Q2
Orléansville: see El Asnam.
Orleton: Hereford & Worcester, England 24 Q15
Orlické Hory: mtns., Czech. 45 W5
Orlik: U.S.S.R. 49 I7
Orlov: Reg., U.S.S.R. (cap. Orel) 50 E4
Ormara: Baluchistan, Pak. 58 K9
Ormea: Italy 40 N11
Ormesby: Cleve., Eng. 26 T10
Ormiston: Loth., Scotland 29 Q8
Ormoc: Philippines 64 G4
Ormond: Fla., U.S.A. 91 L11
Ormož: Yugoslavia 41 W9
Ormskirk: Lancs., England 27 Q12
Ornain: riv., France 36 L7
Ornans: France 40 M8
Orne: riv. & Dept., France (cap. Alençon) 36 E7
Ørnes: Norway 46 N3
Orneta: Poland 43 R9
Orno: i., Sweden 47 Q7
Örnsköldsvik: Sweden 46 Q5
Orochen: U.S.S.R. 49 o6
Orocué: Colombia 94 C3
Orofino: Idaho, U.S.A. 92 D3
Orokolo: New Guinea 69 H1
Oronsay: i., Inner Hebr., Scotland 29 J7
Orontes (Nahr el Assi): riv., Syria 56 E4
Oropesa: Spain 35 D17
Oropus: ancient Greek village N. of Mt. Parnis on coast opposite Néa Psará, Greece 39 S17
Oroquieta: Mindanao, Phil. 64 G5
Orosei, G. of: Sardinia 38 L16
Orosháza: Hungary 43 R13
Oroville: Calif., U.S.A. 93 C5
Oroville: Wash., U.S.A. 92 D3
Oroya, La: Peru 94 B6
Orphir: Mainland, Orkney Is., Scotland 28 P2
Orrin: riv., High., Scot. 28 M4
Orrin, Glen: High., Scot. 28 M4
Orrisdale: I. of Man, U.K. 26 M11
Orroroo: S. Australia 71 C9
Orrskog: Sweden 47 P6
Orsa: Sweden 47 O6
Orsennes: France 37 G9
Orsett: Essex, England 25 W16
Orsha: Byelorussia 50 D4
Orsières: Switzerland 40 N9
Orsk: U.S.S.R. 50 J4
Orşova: Romania 39 S14
Ørsted: Denmark 47 M8
Orston: Notts., England 27 U14
Orta: Italy 40 O10
Ortenburg: W. Germany 44 P5
Orthez: France 37 E12
Ortigueira: Spain 35 C15
Orting: Wash., U.S.A. 92 C3
Ortiz: Mexico 93 E7
Ortles: mtn., Italy 40 Q9
Ortli: Austria 41 W7
Orton: Cumbria, England 26 Q11
Ortona: Italy 38 O15
Ortonville: Minn., U.S.A. 92 H3
Ortrand: E. Germany 45 T4
Orträsk: Sweden 46 Q4
Oruro: Bolivia 94 D7
Orust: i., Sweden 47 M7
Orvieto: Italy 38 N15
Orwell: Cambs., England 25 V15
Orwell: riv., Suff., England 25 Y15
Os: Norway 46 M5
Osage: Iowa, U.S.A. 88 E4
Osage: riv., Kans., U.S.A. 90 D6
Osage City: Kans., U.S.A. 90 D6
OSAKA: & Pref., Japan 63 d3
Osaka: Gifu, Japan 63 e3
Osaka Bay: Japan 63 d3
Osakis: Minn., U.S.A. 92 H3
Osawatomie: Kans., U.S.A. 90 D6
Osbournby: Lincs., England 27 V14
Osceola: Ark., U.S.A. 88 G8
Osceola: Iowa, U.S.A. 88 E5
Osceola: Mo., U.S.A. 90 E6
Osceola: Nebr., U.S.A. 92 H4
Oschatz: E. Germany 45 T4
Oschersleben: E. Germany 45 R3
Oschiri: Sardinia 38 L16
Osen: Norway 46 M4
Osetia, North, A.S.S. Repub.: U.S.S.R. (cap. Ordzhonikidze) 50 F6
Osetia, South, A.S.S. Repub.: U.S.S.R. (cap. Tskhinvali) 50 F6
Osh: Kirgiz., U.S.S.R. 51 M6
Oshawa: Ont., Canada 89 M4
Oshi: Japan 63 f2
Oshio: Japan 63 d3
Oshkosh: Wis., U.S.A. 88 G3
Oshmyany: Byelorussia 47 T9
Oshogbo: Nigeria 81 E3
Oshwe: Zaire 76 A3
Osijek: Yugoslavia 39 Q14
Osilo: Sardinia 38 L16
Osimo: Italy 41 T12
Osingen: W. Germany 45 Q3
Osinniki: U.S.S.R. 51 P4
Osinovo: U.S.S.R. 51 P2
Osipovichi: Byelorussia 43 V10
Oskaloosa: Iowa, U.S.A. 88 E5
Oskarshamn: Sweden 47 P8
Oskarström: Sweden 47 N8
Oskelaneo: Que., Canada 89 O1
Oskoba: U.S.S.R. 49 M5
Oskol: riv., U.S.S.R. 50 E5
Oslava: riv., Czech. 45 W6
OSLO: & fiord, Norway 47 M7
Osmanabad: Maharashtra, India 58 N11
Osmancik: Turkey 56 D1
Osmaniye: Turkey 56 E3
Osmanlar: Turkey (Dardan. Inset) 20 Ins.
Osmotherley: N. Yorks., Eng. 26 T11
Osnabrück: W. Germany 44 O3
Osnabrück: Dist., Lower Saxony, West Germany 44 N3
Osnaburgh House: Ont., Canada 92 J2
Osno: Poland 45 U3
Osor: Yugoslavia 41 U11
Osorio: Brazil 96 E2
Osorno: Chile 95 C12
Osorno: Spain 35 D15
Osprey Reef: Australia 69 H2
Osroene: ancient name of district in NW. Mesopotamia opposite Commagene between rivers Euphrates and Khabur (E. Turkey) 56 F3
Oss: Netherlands 44 L4
Ossa: mtn. (1981 m) NE of Larisa, Thessaly, Greece 39 S17
Ossabaw: i., Ga., U.S.A. 91 L10
Osse: riv., Nigeria 81 F3
Osséle: Congo 81 H5
Osseo: Wis., U.S.A. 88 F3
Ossett: W. Yorks., England 27 S12
Ossiacher See: lake, Austria 41 T9
Ossian, Loch: High., Scot. 29 M6
Ossining: N.Y., U.S.A. 89 P5
Ostbevern: W. Germany 44 N3
Oste: riv., W. Germany 44 P2
Ostend (Oostende): Belgium 36 H4
Osterburg: E. Germany 45 R3
Osterburken: W. Germany 44 P6
Öster Dal: riv., Sweden 47 N6
Osterfeld: E. Germany 45 R4
Östergötland: Co., Sweden (cap. Linköping) 47 O7
Osterhofen: W. Germany 41 T7
Osterholz-Scharmbeck: W. Germany 44 O2
Østerø: i., Faeroe Is. (Dan.) 46 h5
Osterode: E. Germany 45 Q4
Osterøy: i., Norway 47 J6
ÖSTERSUND: Jamtland, Sweden 46 O5
Østfold: Co., Norway (cap. Moss) 47 M7
Osthammar: Sweden 47 Q6
Osthofen: W. Germany 44 O6
Ostia: Italy 38 N16
Ostiglia: Italy 41 R10
Östra Kvarken: str., Swed./Finland 46 R5
OSTRAVA: Severomoravsky, Czechoslovakia 43 Q12
Oštrelj: Yugoslavia 41 W11
Ostróda: Poland 43 Q10
Ostrog: Ukraine 43 U11
Ostrogozhsk: U.S.S.R. 50 E4
Ostrołęka: Poland 43 R10
Ostropol: Ukraine 43 U12
Ostrov: Czechoslovakia 45 S5
Ostrov: Romania 39 V14
Ostrov: U.S.S.R. 47 V8
Ostrovnoye: U.S.S.R. 49 S4
Ostrowiec: Poland 43 R11
Ostrów Mazowiecka: Poland 43 R10
Ostrów Wielkopolski: Pol. 43 P11
Ostrožac: Yugoslavia 41 V11
Ostrzeszów: Poland 43 P11
Ostuni: Italy 38 P16
Osugi: Japan 63 c4
Osumi Is.: Japan 63 Y8
Osuna: Spain 35 D18
Oswaldtwistle: Lancs., England 27 R12
Oswego: Kans., U.S.A. 90 D7
Oswego: N.Y., U.S.A. 89 N4
Oswestry: Salop, England 27 P14
Oświęcim: Poland 43 Q11
Ota: Gumma, Japan 63 f2
Ota: Yamaguchi, Japan 63 b3
Otago: Dist., South I., N.Z. (cap. Dunedin) 70 M17
Otago Penin.: South I., N.Z. 71 N17
Otaki: Japan 63 g3
Otaki: North I., N.Z. 70 P15
Otaru: Japan 63 ZZ6
Otatal, Cerro: mtn., Mexico 93 E7
Otava: riv., Czechoslovakia 45 T6
Otavalo: Ecuador 94 B3
Otavi: S.W. Africa 77 A6
Otepää: Estonia, U.S.S.R. 47 U7
Otford: Kent, England 25 W17
Othe, Forêt d': geog. reg., France 36 J7
Othery: Som., England 24 Q17
Othona: Roman fort at Bradwell on Sea, Essex, Eng. 25 X16
Othonoi: i., Ionian Is. (Grc.) 39 Q17
Oti: riv., Ghana/Togo 80 E2
Otjihavera: S.W. Africa 74 B1
Otjivero: S.W. Africa 74 B1
Otjiwarongo: S.W. Africa 73 H14
Otley: Suff., England 25 Y15
Otley: W. Yorks., England 27 S12
Ot Moor: Oxon., England 25 T16
Otočac: Yugoslavia 41 V11
Otoka: Yugoslavia 41 W11
Otorohanga: North I., N.Z. 70 P14
Otra: riv., Norway 47 K7
Otranto: Italy 39 Q16
Otranto, Str. of: Italy/Alb. 39 Q16
Otsego: Mich., U.S.A. 88 J4
Otsu: Ibaraki, Japan 63 g2
OTSU: Shiga, Japan 63 d3
Otta: & riv., Norway 47 L6
Ottawa: Ill., U.S.A. 88 G5
Ottawa: Kans., U.S.A. 90 D6
Ottawa: Ohio, U.S.A. 88 J5
OTTAWA: Ont., Canada 89 O3
Ottawa: riv., Canada 89 N2
Ottawa Is.: Canada 84 I6
Ottenby: Öland, Sweden 47 P8
Otter: riv., Devon, England 24 P18
Otter: riv., Norway 47 K7
Otterburn: Northumb., Eng. 26 R9
Otter Ferry: village, Strathclyde, Scotland 29 L7
Otterham: Corn., England 24 M18
Otter Head: cape, Ont., Can. 88 H1
Otterndorf: W. Germany 44 O2
Otterøy: i., Norway 46 K5
Otter Rock: North Channel 29 J8
Otterswick: Yell, Shetland Is. 28 Ins.
Otterton: Devon, England 24 P18
Ottery: C.P., S. Africa 74 Ins.
Ottery St. Mary: Devon, England 24 P18
Ottingen: W. Germany 40 Q7
Ottone: Italy 40 P11
Ottoshoop: Trans., S. Africa 75 F2
Ottringham: Humb., Eng. 27 V12
Ottumwa: Iowa, U.S.A. 88 E5
Ottweiler: Saarland, W. Ger. 44 N6
Otun: Nigeria 81 F3
Oturkpo: Nigeria 81 F3
Otur-Kyuyel': U.S.S.R. 49 Q4
Otway, Cape: Vict., Austl. 71 E12
Otwock: Poland 43 R10
Otyimbingue: S.W. Africa 74 B1
Otz: & riv., Austria 41 Q8
Ötztal Alps: Austria 41 Q9
Ouachita: riv., Ark./La., U.S.A. 90 E9
Ouachita Mtns.: Okla./Ark., U.S.A. 90 D8
Ouadai: geog. reg., Chad 79 J7
Ouadda: Cen. Afr. Rep. 76 B1
Ouaddai: Pref., Chad (cap. Abeché) 79 J7
Ouadou: riv., Mali/Maur. 80 B1
OUAGADOUGOU: Upper Volta 80 D2
OUAHIGOUYA: Nord, Upper Volta 80 D2
Ouaka: Pref., Cen. Afr. Rep. (cap. Bambari) 76 B1
Ouaka: riv., Cen. Afr. Rep. 76 B1
Oualata: Mauritania 78 C6
Ouamé: Niger 81 F2
Ouanda Djallé: Cen. Afr. Rep. 79 J8
Ouango: Cen. Afr. Rep. 76 B2
Ouangolodougou: Ivory Coast 80 C3
Ouanary: Fr. Guiana 94 G3
Ouanne: riv., France 36 J8
Ouarakoro: Mali 80 C2
OUARGLA: Oasis, Algeria 78 F3
Ouarpa: riv., Cen. Afr. Rep. 76 B1
OUARZAZATE: & Prov., Morocco 80 K8

For Abbreviations see list on p.113. Italic type, e.g. Ephesus, refers to historical names not on maps. Capital letters, e.g. MADRID, show capitals of countries; small capital letters, e.g. CADIZ, show capitals of provinces, etc. General notes p.116.

Oubangui (Ubangi): *riv.*, Africa **76** A2
Ouberg: S. Africa **75** F6
Oucques: France **36** G8
Ouddorp: Netherlands **44** J4
Oudëika: Mali **78** D6
Oudenaarde: Belgium **44** J5
Oudenbosch: Netherlands **44** K4
Oude Tonge: Netherlands **44** K4
Oudjda: Morocco **80** L8
Oudtshoorn: & *Dist.*, S. Afr. **74** E6
Oued, El: Algeria **32** D5
Oued Aïssa: Algeria **80** L9
Oued-Rhiou: Algeria **35** G19
Oued Taria: Algeria **35** G19
Oued Zem: Morocco **80** K8
Oueiba: *well*, Chad **79** J6
Ouellé: Ivory Coast **80** D3
Ouémé: *riv.*, Benin 81 E3
Ouessant, Ile d' (Ushant): *i.*, France **36** A7
Ouesse: Benin 81 E3
OUESSO: Sangha, Congo **81** H4
Ouest: *Reg.*, Cameroun (*cap.* Bafoussam) **81** G3
Ouest: *Dept.*, Ivory Coast (*cap.* Man) **80** C3
Ouezzane: Morocco **80** K8
Ougarta: Algeria **80** L9
Oughter, Lough: Cavan, Repub. of Ireland **30** G11
Oughterard: Galway, Repub. of Ireland **31** C13
Ougrée: Belgium **44** L5
Ouham: *Pref. & riv.*, Cen. Afr. Rep. (*cap.* Bossangoa) **81** H3
Ouham-Pendé: *Pref.*, Cen. Afr. Rep. (*cap.* Bozoum) **81** H3
Ouidah: Benin 81 E3
Ouistreham: France **36** E6
OUJDA: & *Prov.*, Morocco **80** L8
Oujeft: Mauritania **78** B6
Oulchy-le-Château: France **36** J6
Oullins: France **37** K10
Oulton: Cumbria, England **26** P10
Oulton: W. Yorks., England **27** T12
OULU (Uleåborg): & *Prov.*, Finland **46** T4
Oulu: *lake & riv.*, Finland **46** U4
Oulx: Italy **40** M10
Oum Chalouba: Chad **79** J6
Oumé: Ivory Coast **80** C3
Oum er Rbia: *riv.*, Morocco **80** K8
Oum Hadjer: Chad **78** H7
Oum Hadjer: *watercourse*, Chad **79** J6
Ounane: Algeria **78** F4
Ounas: *riv.*, Finland **46** T3
Ou Neua: Laos **64** C2
Oundle: Northants., Eng. **25** V15
Ounianga Kebir: *well*, Chad **79** J6
Ounianga Sérir: *well*, Chad **79** J6
Ouoroni: Mali **80** C2
Ouplaas: S. Africa **74** E6
Ourém: Brazil **94** H4
Ouria: Guinea **80** B3
Ouricuri: Brazil **94** J5
Ourinhos: Brazil **96** F1
Ouro Fino: Brazil **96** F1
Ouro Prêto: Brazil **94** J8
Ourthe: *riv.*, Belgium **44** L5
Ourville: France **36** F6
Ouse: *riv.*, E. Sussex, England **25** W18
Ouse: *riv.*, N. Yorks., Eng. **27** U12
Ouse, Great: *riv.*, England **25** W14
Ouse, Little: *riv.*, England **25** W15
Ousel: *riv.*, Bucks./Beds., England **25** U16
Oussekh, El: Algeria **32** C5
Oust: *riv.*, France **36** C8
Outarville: France **36** H7
Outeniqua Mtns.: S. Africa **74** E6
Outer Hebrides: *is.*, Scotland **28** G4
Outer Skerries: *rocks*, Shetland Is., Scotland **28** *Ins.*
Outjo: S.W. Africa **73** H14
Outlook: Sask., Canada **92** F2
Outokumpu: Finland **46** V5
Outram: South I., N.Z. **71** N17
Outtrim: Vict., Australia **71** F12
Outwell: Norf., England **25** W14
Ouvèze: *riv.*, France **37** L11
Ouyen: Vict., Australia **71** E10
Ouzouer: France **36** G8
Ouzouer-sur-Loire: France **36** H8
Ovacik: Turkey **56** C3
Ovada: Italy **40** O11
Ovalau: *i.*, Fiji Is. **67** P5
Ovalle: Chile **96** A3
Ovambo: *tribal area*, S.W. Africa **73** H13
Ovar: Portugal **35** B16
Ovens: *riv.*, Vict., Australia **71** G11
Over: Ches., England **27** Q13
Overath: W. Germany **44** N5
Øverbygd: Norway **46** Q2
Overflakkee: *i.*, Neth. **44** K4
Overijssel: *Prov.*, Netherlands (*cap.* Zwolle) **44** M3
Överkalix: Sweden **46** S3
Övermark: Finland **46** R5
Overpelt: Belgium **44** L4
Overseal: Derby., England **27** S14
Oversee: W. Germany **44** P1
Overstrand: Norf., England **25** Y14
Overton: Clwyd, Wales **27** Q14
Overton: Hants., England **25** T17
Overton: Lancs., England **27** Q11
Overton: Tex., U.S.A. **90** D9
Övertorneå: Sweden **46** S3
Överum: Sweden **47** P8
Ovidiopol': Ukraine **39** V13
OVIEDO: & *Prov.*, Spain **35** D15
Oviglio: Italy **40** O11
Oviks Mtns.: Sweden **46** N5
Ovilava: Roman settlement at Wels, Austria **40** U7
Øvre Rendal: Norway **47** M6
Ovruch: Ukraine **43** V11
Owaka: South I., N.Z. **71** M18
OWANDO: Likonala-Moussaka, Congo 81 H5
Owashi: Japan **63** e3
Owatonna: Minn., U.S.A. **88** E3
Owego: N.Y., U.S.A. **89** N4
Owel, Lough: Westmeath, Repub. of Ireland **30** G12
Owen: Wis., U.S.A. **88** F3
Owen: *i.*, Burma **59** R12
Owen Fracture Zone: Indian Ocean **9** 10N 55E
Owen, Mt: North I., N.Z. **70** O15
Owencarrow: *riv.*, Don., Repub. of Ireland **30** F9
Owen Falls: Uganda **76** D2
Owenkilew: *riv.*, Tyr., N. Ireland **30** G10
Owenmore: *riv.*, Mayo, Repub. of Ireland **30** B11
Owenmore: *riv.*, Sligo, Repub. of Ireland **30** D11
Owensboro: Ky., U.S.A. **88** H7
Owens Creek: *town*, Queens., Australia **70** H3
Owen Sound: *city*, Ont., **Canada 88** L3
Owen Stanley Range: New Guinea **69** H1
Owermoigne: Dorset, Eng. **24** R18
OWERRI: Imo, Nigeria 81 F3
Owning: Kilk., Repub. of Ireland **31** G15
Owo: Nigeria **81** F3
Owosso: Mich., U.S.A. **88** J4
Owraman: Iran **57** K4
Owschlag: W. Germany **44** P1
Owston Ferry: *village*, Humberside, England **27** U13
Owyhee: Nev., U.S.A. **92** D4
Owyhee: *riv.*, U.S.A. **92** D4
Owyhee Dam: & *res.*, Oreg., U.S.A. **92** D4
Oxbow: Sask., Canada **92** G3
Oxelösund: Sweden **47** P7
Oxenhope: W. Yorks., Eng. **27** S12
OXFORD: & *Co.*, England **25** T16
Oxford: Miss., U.S.A. **90** G8
Oxford: N.Y., U.S.A. **89** O4
Oxford: N.C., U.S.A. **89** M7
Oxford: N.S., Canada **89** U3
Oxford: South I., N.Z. **70** O16
Oxford House: Man., Canada **92** H2
Oxford Lake: Man., Canada **92** H2
Oxhill: War., England **25** S15
Oxley: N.S.W., Australia **71** F10
Ox Mtns. (Slieve Gamph): Sligo, Repub. of Ireland **30** D11
Oxnam: Borders, Scotland **29** R9
Oxnard: Calif., U.S.A. **93** C6
Oxton: Borders, Scotland **29** Q8
Oxton: Notts., England **27** T13
Oxus (Amu): *riv.*, U.S.S.R. **51** K7
Oxyrhynchus: ancient Egyptian village, site of papyrus-finds, beyond Bahr Yusuf canal about due W. of Beni Mazar, Egypt **54** D9
Oya: Sarawak, Malaysia **65** E6
Oyama: Shizuoka, Japan **63** f3
Oyama: Tochigi, Japan **63** f2
Øye: Norway **46** L5
OYEM: Woleu-N'Tem, Gabon **81** G4
Oykel: *riv.*, High., Scot. **28** M4
Oykel, Glen: High., Scot. **28** M3
Oykel, Strath: *valley*, High., Scotland **28** M4
Oykell Bridge: High., Scotland **28** M4
Oymyakon: U.S.S.R. **49** Q5
Oyne: Grampian, Scotland **28** Q5
Oyo: Nigeria **81** E3
Oyo: *State*, Nigeria (*cap.* Ibadan) 81 E3
Oyonnax: France **40** L9
Oyster Haven: *bay*, Cork, Repub. of Ireland **31** E16
Özalp: Turkey **57** J2
Ozarichi: Byelorussia **43** V10
Ozark: Ala., U.S.A. **91** J10
Ozark: Ark., U.S.A. **90** E8
Ozark: Mo., U.S.A. **88** E7
Ozark Plat.: Mo., U.S.A. **88** E7
Ozarks, Lake of the: Mo., U.S.A. **88** E6
Ózd: Hungary **43** R12
Ozerko: U.S.S.R. **46** X2
Ozernoye: U.S.S.R. **49** r7
Ozery: U.S.S.R. **50** E4
Ozieri: Sardinia **38** L16
Ozmancik: Turkey **56** D1
Ozona: Tex., U.S.A. **93** G6
Ozorków: Poland **43** Q11
Ozuki: Japan **63** b3

PA-AN: Kawthule, Burma **59** R11
Paan (Batang): Tibet, China **62** R8
Paarl: & *Dist.*, S. Africa **74** C6
Paauilau: Hawaiian Is. **83** d2
Pabbay: *i.* (*S. of Barra*), Outer Hebr., Scotland **28** G6
Pabbay: *i.* (*W. of Harris*), Outer Hebr., Scotland **28** G4
Pabianice: Poland **43** Q11
Pabna: Bangladesh **59** P10
Pacaraima, Sierra: *mtns.*, Venezuela **94** E3
Pachai: Kweichow, China **62** T9
Pachalla: Sudan **76** D1
Pacaltsdorp: S. Africa **74** E7
Pachbhadra: Rajasthan, India **58** M9
Pacheca: Brazil **96** E3
Pachino: Sicily **38** O18
Pachmarhi: Madhya Pradesh, India **58** N10
Pachu: Sinkiang, China **51** N7
Pachuca: Mexico **86** K13
Pachung: Szechwan, China **62** T8
Pacific: Mo., U.S.A. **88** F6
Pacific Grove: Calif., U.S.A. **93** C5
Pacitan: Java 65 E8
Pacov: Czechoslovakia **45** V6
Pacy: France **36** G6
Padam: Jammu & Kashmir **58** N8
Padang: Anambas Is., Indonesia **65** D6
Padang: Sumatra **65** C7
Padang: *i.*, Sumatra **65** C6
Padangsidimpuan: Sum. **65** B6
Padang Tikar: *i.*, Borneo **65** D7
Padasjoki: Finland **47** T6
Padborg: Denmark **44** P1
Padbury: Bucks., England **25** U16
Paddagat: S. Africa **74** C5
Padene: Yugoslavia **41** W11
Paderborn: W. Germany **44** O4
Padiham: Lancs., England **27** R12
Padilla: Bolivia **94** E7
Padilla: Mexico **86** K13
Padina: Yugoslavia **39** R14
Padlei: N.W.T., Canada **84** K5
Padova (Padua): Italy **41** R10
Padron: Spain **35** B15
Padside: N. Yorks., England **27** S11
Padstow: Corn., England **24** M18
Padua (Padova): Italy **41** R10
Paducah: Ky., U.S.A. **88** G7
Paducah: Tex., U.S.A. **90** A8
Padus: Roman name of river Po, Italy **38** M14
Paeligni: ancient tribe of district around Sulmona, Italy **38** N15
Paeroa: North I., N.Z. **70** P13
Paesana: Italy **40** N11
Paestum: Latin colony of Rome on coast of Tyrrhenian Sea about 25 miles SE. of Salerno, Italy **38** O16
Pafuri: Mozambique **75** J1
Pafuri: *riv.*, Trans., S. Africa **75** J1
Pag: & *i.*, Yugoslavia **41** V11
Pagalu (Annobon): *i.*, (Equatorial Guinea), G. of Guinea **81** F5
Pagan: *i.*, Mariana Is. **61** O8
Pagasae: Greek city and port on west side of inlet S. of Volos, Greece **39** S17
Pagasae, G. of: ancient name of large gulf S. of Volos, Greece **39** S17
Pagatan: Borneo **65** F7
Pageralam: Sumatra **65** C7
Pagny: France **40** M7
Pagoda Point: *cape*, Burma **59** Q11
Pagona: New Guinea **69** G1
PAGO PAGO: American Samoa **70** *Ins.*
Pagosa Springs: Colo., U.S.A. **93** F5
Pagoumene: New Caledonia **67** M6
Pahandut: Borneo **65** E7
Pahang: *riv.*, Malaya, Malaysia **65** c12
Pahang: *State*, Malaya, Malaysia, (*cap.* Kuantan) **65** c12
Pahiatua: North I., N.Z. **70** P15
Pahlevi Enzeli: Iran **57** L3
Pahokee: Fla., U.S.A. **91** L12
Pahute Mesa: *mtns.*, Nev., U.S.A. **93** D5
Paible: Outer Hebr., Scot. **28** G4
Paicheng: Kirin, China **63** W5
Paicheng: Sinkiang, China **51** O6
Paichuan: Heilungkiang, China **63** X5
Paichuan: Sinkiang, China **62** R6
Paierh Hu: *lake*, Inner Mongolia, China **62** V5
Paignton: Devon, England **24** O19
Paiho: Shensi, China **62** U8
Paijanne Lake: Finland **47** T6
Pailin: Cambodia 64 C4
Pailton: War., England **25** T15
Paimakwan (Kanghsien); Kansu, China **62** T8
Paimbœuf: France **36** C8
Paimpol: France **36** B7
Painan: Sumatra **65** C7
Painel: Brazil **96** E2
Painesville: Ohio, U.S.A. **88** L5
Painscastle: Powys, Wales **24** P15
Painswick: Glos., England **24** R16
Painted Desert: Ariz., U.S.A. **93** E5
Painted Post: *city*, N.Y., U.S.A. **89** N4
Paintsville: Ky., U.S.A. **88** K7
Paisiang: Hopeh, China **62** U7
Paisley: Oreg., U.S.A. **92** C4
Paisley: Strath., Scotland **29** N8
Paita: Peru **94** A5
Paitingtzu: Kansu, China **62** R6
Paja: & *riv.*, Panama **94** *Ins.*
Pajala: Sweden **46** S3
Paka: Malaya, Malaysia **65** c11
Pakala: Andhra Pradesh, India **58** N12
Pakanbaru: Sumatra **65** C6
Pakaraima Mtns.: Guyana **87** c7
Pakefield: Suff., England **25** Z15
Pakhtusovo Camp: U.S.S.R. **48** g3
Pakhuis: S. Africa **74** C6

Pakistan: *Republic* **58** L9
Cap.: Islamabad
Area: 342,750 sq. miles (887,723 sq. km.)
Pop.: 54,014,000 (*1970E*)
The area & population figures include the Pakistani-held part of Jammu and Kashmir.

Pak Langu: Thailand **65** a10
Paklay: Laos **64** C3
Pako: Tibet, China **58** O8
Pakokku: Burma **59** R10
Pakpattan: Punjab, Pak. **58** M8
Pakrac: Yugoslavia **38** P14
Paks: Hungary **43** Q13
Paksé: Laos **64** D3
Paksha: Kwangtung, China **62** U10
Pak Tha: Laos **64** C2
Paktia: *prov.*, Afghanistan (*cap.* Gardez) **55** L8
Paku: Celebes **65** G7
Pakwach: Uganda **76** D2
Pala: Central African Rep. **76** B1
Pala: Chad **81** G3
Palabuhanratu: Java **65** D8
Palacios: Tex., U.S.A. **90** C11
Pala de Lena: Spain **35** D15
Palaeopolis: Samothrace, *see* Pirgos.
Palafrugell: Spain **35** H16
Palaiokhóra: Crete **39** S19
Palaiseau: France **36** H7
Palala: *riv.*, Trans., S. Africa **75** H1
Palamcottah: Tamil Nadu, India **58** N13
Palamós: Spain **35** H16
Palanan: Luzon, Phil. **64** G3
Palanduz: Iran **57** L4
Palanga: Lithuania, U.S.S.R. **47** R9
Palangan: Iran **57** K4
Palangkaraya: Borneo 65 E7
Palanpur: Gujarat, India **58** M10
Palapye: Botswana **75** G1
Palatka: Fla., U.S.A. **91** L11
Palau: Sardinia **38** L16
Palau Is.: Caroline Is. **61** L10
Palauk: Burma **59** R12
Palavas: France **37** J12
Palaw: Burma **59** R12
Palawan: *i.*, Philippines **64** F4
Palazzolo: Italy **40** P10
Palazzolo: Sicily **38** O18
Palazzuolo: Italy **41** R12
Palbe: Ghana **80** D3
Pal'diski: Estonia, U.S.S.R. **47** T7
Paleisheuwel: S. Africa **74** C6
Palel: Manipur, India **59** Q10
Paleleh: Celebes **65** G6
Palembang: Sumatra **65** C7
PALENCIA: & *Prov.*, Spain **35** D15
Palermo: Argentina **96** C1
PALERMO: Sicily **38** N17
Palestine: Tex., U.S.A. **90** D10
Palestine: *geog. reg.*, SW. Asia **56** D6
Paletwa: Burma **59** Q10
Palghat: Tamil Nadu, India **58** N12
Palhoça: Brazil **96** F2
Pali: Rajasthan, India **58** M9
Palikun (Barkol): Sinkiang, China **62** Q6
Palimé: Togo **80** E3
Palinyuchi: Inner Mongolia, China **62** V6
Palisade: Nev., U.S.A. **92** D4
Palitana: Gujarat, India **58** M10
Palkino: U.S.S.R. **47** U8
Palk Str.: Sri Lanka/India **58** N13
Palla: Botswana **75** G1
Palla Bianca: *mtn.*, Italy **41** Q9
Pallanza: Italy **40** O10
Palla Road: *see* Dinokwe
Pallas Grean: Lim., Repub. of Ireland **31** E14
Pallaskenry: Lim., Repub. of Ireland **31** D14
Pallas-Ounastunturin National Park: Finland **46** S2
Pallasovka: U.S.S.R. **50** G4
Pallastunturi: Finland **46** T2
Pallene: Greek name of Kassandra penin., Greece **39** S17
Pallice, La: France **37** D9
Pallier: New Hebrides **67** N4
Palling: Norf., England **25** Z14
Pallisa: Uganda **76** D2
Palliser: *cape & bay*, North I., New Zealand **70** P15
Palluau: France **37** D9
PALMA: Maj., Balearic Is. **35** H17
Palma: Mozambique **77** F5
Palma, La: Panama **94** B2
Palma, La: Spain **35** C18
Palma, La: *i.*, Canary Is. **78** A4
Palmanova: Italy **41** T10
Palmar, El: Venezuela **87** c7
Palmares: Pernambuco, Brazil **94** K5
Palmares: Rio Grande do Sul, Brazil **96** E3
Palmas: Brazil **96** E2
Palmas, Cape: Liberia **80** C4
Palmas, G. of: Sardinia **38** L17
Palmas, Las: Argentina **96** D2
PALMAS, LAS: Canary Is. **78** A4
Palm Beach: *city*, Fla., U.S.A. **91** L12
Palmeira: Alagoas, Brazil **94** K5
Palmeira: Rio Grande do Sul, Brazil **96** E2
Palmental: S.W. Africa **74** A1
Palmer: Alaska, U.S.A. **84** E5
Palmer: *riv.*, N. Territ., Australia **68** E4
Palmer: *riv.*, Queens., Austl. **69** G3
Palmer Land: Antarctica **9** 75S 65W
Palmer Station: *rsch. stn.*, Antarctica **9** 65S 65W
Palmerston: Ont., Canada **88** L4
Palmerston: South I., N.Z. **71** N17
Palmerston Is. (Avarua): Cook Is. **70** *Ins.*
Palmerston North: North I., New Zealand **70** P15
Palmerstown: Mayo, Repub. of Ireland **30** C11
Palmerton: Pa., U.S.A. **89** O5
Palmerton: S. Africa **75** H5
Palmerville: Queens., Austl. **69** G3
Palmetto: Fla., U.S.A. **91** K12
Palmi: Italy **38** O17
Palmietfontein: Cape Prov., S. Africa **75** G5
Palmietfontein: Trans., S. Afr. **75** G3
Palmira: Colombia **94** B3
Palm I.: Queens., Australia **70** G2
Palmito, El: Mexico **93** G7
Palmwoods: Queens., Austl. **70** K6
Palmyra: Mo., U.S.A. **88** F6
Palmyra: N.Y., U.S.A. **89** N4
Palmyra: O.F.S., S. Africa **75** G4
Palmyra (Tadmor): Syria **56** F4
Palmyra I.: (U.S.A.), N. Pacific Ocean **7** 05N 165W
Palmyras Point: *cape*, India **59** P10
Palnackie: Dumfries & Galloway, Scotland **29** O10
Palni: Tamil Nadu, India **58** N12
Palnure: Dumfries & Galloway, Scotland **29** N10
Palo Alto: Calif., U.S.A. **93** C5
Paloe: Celebes **65** F7
Paloë: *i.*, Indonesia **65** G8
Paloh: Borneo **65** D6
Palomar, Mount: Calif., U.S.A. **93** D6
Palomas, Las: Spain (Gib. *Inset*) **32** *Ins.*
Palopo: Celebes **65** G7
Palos, C. de: *cape*, Spain **35** F18
Palo Santo: Argentina **96** D2
Palouse: Wash., U.S.A. **92** D3
Palpa: Peru **94** C6
Palparara: Queens., Austl. **69** G4
Pålsboda: Sweden **47** O7
Paltamo: Finland **46** U4
Palu: Celebes **65** F7
Palu: Turkey **56** F2
Paluan: Philippines **64** G4
Palung: Chinghai, China **62** R7
Paluzza: Italy **41** T9
Pama: Upper Volta **80** E2
Pamachic: Mexico **93** F7
Pambula: N.S.W., Austl. **71** H11
Pamekasan: Madura, Indon. **65** E8
Pameungpeuk: Java **65** D8
Pamiers: France **37** G12
Pamirs: *mtns.*, Tadzhik., U.S.S.R. **51** M7
Pamlico Sound: N.C., U.S.A. **91** N8
Pampa: Tex., U.S.A. **90** A8
Pampa de la Salinas: Arg. **96** B3
Pampanua: Celebes **65** G7
Pampa Peñon: Chile **96** B1
Pampas de la Plata: Arg. **96** C3
Pamphylia: ancient name of central coastal region of southern Turkey centring round Antalya **56** B3
Pamplona: Colombia **94** C2
PAMPLONA: Navarra, Spain **37** D13
Pampoenpoort: S. Africa **74** E5
Pamu: Kwangsi Chuang, China **62** T10
Pamyati: U.S.S.R. **51** Q3
Pana: Ill., U.S.A. **88** G6
Panaca: Nev., U.S.A. **93** E5
Panache, Lake: Ont., Can. **88** L2
Panactum: fort of NW. *Attica* near frontier with Boeotia about 12 miles SSE. of Thebes. **39** S17
Panagyurishte: Bulgaria **39** T15
Panaji: Goa, Daman & Diu, India 58 M11
Panaitan I., Java, Indon. **65** D8

Panama: *Republic* **87** L16
Cap.: Panama
Area: 29,306 sq. miles (75,902 sq. km.)
Pop.: 1,523,000 (*1971 E*)

PANAMA: Panama **94** *Ins.*

Panama Canal Zone: to be incorporated into Panama by 1999

Panama City: Fla., U.S.A. **91** J10
Panamint Mtns.: Calif., U.S.A. **93** D5
Panaon: *i.*, Philippines **64** H5
Panarea: *i.*, Lipari Is. (It.) **38** O17
Panaro: *riv.*, Italy **41** R11
Pana Tinani: *i.*, New Guinea **69** J2
Panay: *i.* & *gulf.*, Phil. **64** G4
Panbeguwa: Nigeria **81** F2
Pančevo: Yugoslavia **39** R14
Panciu: Romania **39** U14
Pandan: Catanduanes I., Philippines **64** G4
Pandan: Panay, Phil. **64** G4
Pandassan: Sabah, Malaysia **65** F5
Pan de Azucar: Chile **96** A2
Pan de Azucar: Uruguay **96** D3
Pandharpur: Maharashtra, India **58** N11
Pando: Uruguay **96** D3
Panevezhis: Lithuania, U.S.S.R. **47** T9
Panfilov: Kazakh., U.S.S.R. **51** O6
Panfilovo: U.S.S.R. **50** F4
Panga: Zaïre **76** C2
Pangala: Congo **81** G5
Pangani: Tanzania **76** E4
Pangani (Ruvu): *riv.*, Tanzania **76** E3
Pangbourne: Berks., England **25** T17
Pangi: Zaïre **76** C3
Pangkajene: Celebes 65 F7
Pangkalanbrandan: Sumatra **65** B6
Pangkalpinang: Bangka, Indonesia **65** D7
Pangkiang: Inner Mongolia, China **62** U6
Panglong: Burma **59** R10
Pangnirtung: N.W.T., Can. **85** N4
Pangong Range: China/India **58** N8
Pangta: Tibet, China **62** R8
Pangto: Tibet, China **59** Q8
Pantoja: Peru **94** B4
Panguitch: Utah, U.S.A. **93** E5
Panguma: Sierra Leone **80** B3
Pangururan: Sumatra **65** B6
Pangutaran Group: *is.*, Phil. **65** G5
Pangyurishche: Bulgaria **39** T15
Panhsien: Kweichow, China **62** S9
Panion: ancient Syrian city at Baniyas, Damascus, Syr. **56** D5
Panipat: Haryana, India **58** N9
Panissières: France **37** K10
Panjang: *i.*, Vietnam 64 C5
Panjgur: Baluchistan, Pakistan **58** K9
PANJIM: Goa, Daman & Diu., India **58** M11
Pankop: Trans., S. Afr. **75** H2
Pankrat'yev I.: U.S.S.R. **48** g2
Pankshin: Nigeria **81** F3
Panna: Madhya Pradesh, India **58** O10
Pannal: N. Yorks., England **27** S12
Panne, La: Belgium **36** H4
Pannonia: Roman province of eastern Austria and western Hungary bounded by Danube, foothills south of Sava, and a line drawn south from about Vienna **42** O13
Panopah: Borneo **65** E7
Panormus: Sicel and Roman town at Palermo, Sicily **38** N17
Panshan: Liaoning, China **63** W6
Panshih: Kirin, China **63** X6
Pantar: *i.*, Indonesia **65** G8
Pantellaria: *i.*, Italy **38** N18
Panticapaeum: Greek city on W. coast of Kerch strait, U.S.S.R. **33** K2
Pánuco: Coahuila, Mexico **93** G7
Pánuco: Vera Cruz, Mexico **86** K13
Panulcillo: Chile **96** A3
Panyalili: Celebes 65 G7
Panzi: Zaïre **76** A4
Paochang: Inner Mongolia, China **62** V6
Paofeng: Honan, China **62** U8
Paoki: Shensi, China **62** T8
Paola: Italy **38** P17
Paola: Kans., U.S.A. **90** D6
Paoli: Ind., U.S.A. **88** H6
Paoning (Langchung): Szechwan, China **62** T8
Paoshan (Yungchang): Yunnan, China **62** R9
Paoteh: Shansi, China **62** U7
Paoting (Chingyuan): Hopeh, China **62** V7
Paotow: Inner Mongolia, China **62** U6
Paotsing: Hunan, China **62** T9
Paotsing: Heilungkiang, China **63** Y5
Pap: Sudan **76** D1
Pápa: Hungary **43** P13
Papakura: North I., N.Z. **70** P13
Papal States: formerly an independent area ruled by the Papal See including Rome, Bologna, and Ancona, Italy **38** N15
Papantla: Mexico **86** K13
Papar: Sabah, Malaysia **65** F5
Paparoa Range: South I., New Zealand **70** N16
Papa Stour: *i.*, Shetland Is. Scotland **28** *Ins.*
Papa Westray: *i.*, Orkney Is., Scotland **28** *Ins.*
PAPEETE: Society Is. **83** f3
Papenburg: W. Germany **44** N2
Paphlagonia: ancient name for mountainous district of northern Turkey from *Bithynia* to region of Sinop **56** C1
Paphos: Cyprus **56** C4
Papkuil: S. Africa **74** E4
Paposo: Chile **96** A2
Pappenheim: W. Germany **41** Q7
Paps, The: *mtn.*, Kerry, Repub. of Ireland **31** C15
Paps of Jura: *mtns.*, Scotland **29** J8

Papua New Guinea: *Independent State* **69** H1
***Cap.*: Port Moresby**
Area: 183,540 sq. miles (475,369 sq. km.)
Pop.: 2,481,000 (*1971 E*)

Papua, G of: New Guinea **69** G1
Papudo: Chile **96** A3
Paquet: Newf., Canada **85** v2
Pará: *see* Belém.
Pará: *State*, Brazil (*cap.* Belém) **94** G4
Parabel': U.S.S.R. **51** O3
Paracel Is.: S. China Sea **64** E3
Parachilna: S. Australia **71** C8
Parachinar: NW. Front. Prov., Pakistan **58** M8
Paraćin: Yugoslavia **39** R15
Paracatu: Brazil **94** H7
Parado: Sumbawa, Indon. **65** F8
Paragould: Ark., U.S.A. **88** F7
Paragua: *riv.*, Venezuela **94** E2
Paraguaçu: Brazil **96** E1
Paraguari: Paraguay **96** D2

Paraguay: *Republic* **94/5**
Cap.: Asunción
Area: 157,047 sq. miles (406,752 sq. km.)
Pop.: 2,466,000 (*1971 E*)

Paraguay: *riv.*, Paraguay **95** F9
Paraiba: *riv.*, Brazil **96** F1
Paraiba: *State*, Brazil (*cap.* João Pessoa) **94** K5
Paraingkareha: Indonesia **65** G8
Paraiso: Mexico **86** k14

Paraiso—Petaluma 175

Paraiso: Panama 94 Ins.
Paraisopolis: Brazil 96 F1
Parakhino-Poddub'ye: U.S.S.R. 50 D3
PARAKOU: Nord-Est, Benin 81 F3
PARAMARIBO: Surinam 94 F2
Paramillo: mtn., Colombia 94 B2
Paramirim: Brazil 94 J6
Paramushir I.: Kuril Is. 60 Q1
PARANÁ: & riv., Entre Rios, Argentina 96 C3
Paranã: Brazil 94 H6
Parana: State, Brazil (cap. Curitiba) 96 E1
Paranagua: Brazil 96 F2
Paranaiba: Brazil 94 G7
Paranapanema: riv., Brazil 96 E1
Paranapiacaba, Serra da: mtns. Brazil 96 F1
Paranestion: Greece 39 T16
Parang: Philippines 65 G5
Paraoa: i., Tuamotu Arch. 83 g3
Parati: Brazil 96 G1
Paratinga: Brazil 94 J6
Paray-le-Monial: France 37 K9
Parbati: riv., India 58 N10
Parbhani: Maharashtra, India 58 N11
Parbold: Lancs., England 27 Q12
Parchim: E. Germany 45 R2
Parczew: Poland 43 S11
Pardo: riv., Mato Grosso, Brazil 95 G8
Pardo: riv., São Paulo, Braz. 96 F1
Pardubice: Czechoslovakia 45 V5
Parece Vela: i., Pacific O. 61 M7
Parecis, Serra Dos: mtns., Brazil 94 E6
Paren: U.S.S.R. 49 S5
Parent: Que., Canada 89 O2
Parent, Lac: Que., Canada 89 N1
Parepare: Celebes 65 F7
Parfenovo: U.S.S.R. 51 O4
Parga: Greece 39 R17
Paria: gulf & penin., Ven. 87 b5
Pariaguán: Venezuela 94 E2
Pariaman: Sumatra 65 C7
Parichi: Byelorussia 43 V10
Parigi: Celebes 65 G7
Parigne-l'Évêque: France 36 F8
Parika: Guyana 87 d7
Parilla: S. Australia 71 D10
Parilli: Sudan 76 D1
Parintins: Brazil 94 F4
Paris: Ark., U.S.A. 90 E8
PARIS: France 36 H7
Paris: Idaho, U.S.A. 92 E4
Paris: Ill., U.S.A. 88 H6
Paris: Ky., U.S.A. 88 J6
Paris: Mo., U.S.A. 88 E6
Paris: Ont., Canada 88 L4
Paris: Tenn., U.S.A. 88 G7
Paris: Tex., U.S.A. 90 D9
Parisienne, Ile: i., Ont., Can 88 J2
Parium: Greek city on S. coast of Sea of Marmara, about 25 miles E. of Lapseki, Turkey 39 U16
Park: dist., Outer Hebr., Scotland 28 H4
Parkano: Finland 47 S5
Parker: Ariz., U.S.A. 93 E6
Parker: S. Dak., U.S.A. 92 H4
Parker Dam: Ariz., U.S.A. 93 E6
Parkersburg: W. Va., U.S.A. 88 L6
Parkes: N.S.W., Australia 71 H9
Park Falls: city, Wis., U.S.A. 88 F3
Parkham: Devon, England 24 N18
Parkin: Ark., U.S.A. 90 F8
Parknasilla: Kerry, Repub. of Ireland 31 B16
Park Range: Colo., U.S.A. 93 F4
Park Rapids: city, Minn., U.S.A. 88 D2
Park River: N. Dak., U.S.A. 92 H3
Parkston: S. Dak., U.S.A. 92 H4
Parla Kimedi: Orissa, India 59 O11
Parma: Idaho, U.S.A. 92 D4
Parma: Italy 40 Q11
Parma: Ohio, U.S.A. 88 L5
Parnaguá: Brazil 94 J6
Parnaiba: Brazil 94 J4
Parnaiba: riv., Brazil 94 H5
Parnarama: Brazil 94 J5
Parnassos: mtn., Greece 39 S17
Parnassus: South I., N.Z. 70 O16
Parndarna: S. Australia 71 B10
Parnis: mtn., Greece 39 S17
Paro: Bhutan 59 P9
Paroo: riv., Queens., Austl. 71 F7
Paropamisadae: ancient Greek name of Hindu Kush range 58 L8
Paro Pamisus Ra.: Afghan. 58 K8
Paros: & i., Cyclades (Grc.) 39 T18
Parowan: Utah, U.S.A. 93 E5
Parracombe: Devon, Eng. 24 O17
Parral: Chile 96 A4
Parramatta: N.S.W., Austl. 71 J9
Parras: Mexico 93 G7
Parrett: riv., Som., England 24 Q17
Parris Island: city, S.C., U.S.A. 91 L9
Parrsboro: N.S., Canada 89 T3
Parry, Cape: Greenland 85 r3
Parry, Cape: N.W.T., Can. 84 g3
Parry Bay: N.W.T., Canada 85 l4
Parry Is.: N.W.T., Canada 84 J2
Parry Sound: city, Ont., Canada 88 L3
Parsberg: W. Germany 45 R6
Parsęta: riv., Poland 45 W2
Parsnip: riv., B.C., Canada 92 C1
Parsons: Kansas, U.S.A. 90 D7
Parsons: W. Va., U.S.A. 89 M6
Parsonstown (Birr): Offaly, Repub. of Ireland 31 F13
Partê Mtn.: Sweden 46 P3
Partenkirchen: W. Germany 41 R8
Parthenay: France 37 E9
Parthia: ancient country SE. of Caspian Sea and an ancient empire which extended from the Indus to the Euphrates 55 J7
Partinico: Sicily 38 N17
Partizansk: U.S.S.R. 63 Y6
Parton: Dumfries & Galloway, Scotland 29 N9
Partry: Mayo, Repub. of Ireland 30 C12
Partry Mtns: Mayo, Repub. of Ireland 30 C12
Paru: riv., Brazil 94 G4
Paru de Oeste: riv., Brazil 94 F4
Parwan: prov., Afghanistan (cap. Charikar) 55 L8
Parwan: riv., India 58 N10
Parwich: Derby., England 27 S13
Parys: O.F.S., S. Africa 75 G3
Pas: France 36 H5
Pas, The: Man., Canada 92 G2
Pasadena: Calif., U.S.A. 93 D6
Pasadena: Tex., U.S.A. 90 D11
Pasargadae: ancient Persian city about 50 miles NNE. of Shiraz Iran 55 H8
Pascagoula: Miss., U.S.A. 90 G10
Paşcani: Romania 43 U13
Pasco: Wash., U.S.A. 92 D3
Pasco, Cerro de: town, Peru 94 B6
Pas-de-Calais: Dept., France (cap. Arras) 36 G5
Pasewalk: E. Germany 45 T2
Pashkovo: U.S.S.R. 63 Y5
Pasighat: Arunachal Pradesh, India 59 R9
Pasing: W. Germany 41 R7
Pasiputih: Sumatra 65 B6
Pas-i-Radak: Iran 55 H9
Pasir Mas: Malaya, Malaysia 65 c10
Pasirpengarajan: Sumatra 65 C6
Pasir Puteh: Malaya, Malaysia 65 c11
Pašman: i., Yugoslavia 41 V12
Pasni: Baluchistan, Pak. 58 K9
Paso de Indios: Argentina 95 D12
Paso de los Libres: Arg. 96 D2
Paso de los Toros (Santa Isabel): Uruguay 96 D3
Paso Robles: Calif., U.S.A. 93 C5
Pasqua: Sask., Canada 92 F2
Pasquia Hills: Sask., Can. 92 G2
Passage: Wat., Repub. of Ireland 31 H15
Passage West: Cork, Repub. of Ireland 31 E16
Passaic: N.J., U.S.A. 89 O5
Passamaquoddy Bay: N.B., Canada 89 S3
Passau: W. Germany 41 T7
Passchendaele: & battlefield, Belgium 36 J5
Pass Christian: Miss., U.S.A. 90 G10
Passero, Cape: Sicily 38 O18
Passo Fundo: Brazil 96 E2
Passos: Brazil 94 H8
Passu Keah: reef, Paracel Is. 64 E3
Passuteng Hu: lake, Sinkiang, China 51 P6
Passy: France 40 M10
Pasto: Columbia 94 B3
Paston: Northants., England 27 V14
Pastora Peak: Ariz., U.S.A. 93 F5
Pastrana: Spain 35 E16
Pasur: Turkey 57 G2
Pasuruan: Java 65 E8
Pasvik: riv., Nor./U.S.S.R. 46 V2
Paszto: Hungary 43 Q13
Patagonia: geog. reg., Arg. 95 C13
Patan: Gujarat, India 58 M10
Patan: Nepal 59 P9
Patangan: Iran 57 K4
Patas: Peru 94 B5
Patavium: Roman city at Padua, Italy 41 R10
Patay: France 36 G7
Patchewollock: Vict., Austl. 71 E10
Patchogue: N.Y., U.S.A. 89 P5
Patchway: Avon, England 24 Q16
Patea: North I., N.Z. 70 P14
Pategi: Nigeria 81 F3
Pateley Bridge: N. Yorkshire, England 27 S11
Patensie: S. Africa 75 F6
Paterno: Sicily 38 O18
Paternoster Is.: Indon. 65 F8
Paterson: N.J., U.S.A. 89 O5
Paterson: N.S.W., Australia 71 J9
Pathankot: Punjab, India 58 N8
Pathfinder Dam: Wyo., U.S.A. 92 F4
Pathfinder Reservoir: Wyo., U.S.A. 92 F4
Pathhead: Lothian, Scot. 29 Q8
Path of Condie: Tay., Scot. 29 P7
Patiala: Punjab, India 58 N8
Patmos: i., Dodecanese (Grc.) 39 U18
PATNA: Bihar, India 59 P9
Patna: Strathclyde, Scotland 29 M9
Patnos: Turkey 57 H2
Patos: Minas Gerais, Brazil 94 H7
Patos: Paraiba, Brazil 94 K5
Patos, Los: riv., Argentina 96 B3
Patos, Lago dos: Brazil 96 E3
Patquia: Argentina 96 B3
Patras (Patrai): & gulf, Grc. 39 R17
Patreksfjordhur: Iceland 46 b4
Patrick: I. of Man, U.K. 26 M11
Patrington: Humb., England 27 V12
Patrocinio: Brazil 94 H7
Patsiven: U.S.S.R. 46 W2
Patta I.: Kenya 76 F3
Pattani: & State, Thailand 65 b10
Pattergassen: Austria 41 T9
Patterson: La., U.S.A. 90 F11
Patti: Sicily 38 O17
Pattijoki: Finland 46 T4
Pattingham: Staffs., England 27 R14
Patu: Brazil 94 K5
Patutahi: North I., N.Z. 70 Q14
PAU: Pyrénées-Atlantiques, Fr. 37 E12
Paucartambo: Peru 94 C6
Pau dos Ferros: Brazil 94 K5
Pauillac: France 37 E10
Pauini: Brazil 94 D5
Pauk: Burma 59 Q10
Paul: Corn., England 25 K19
Paulding: Ohio, U.S.A. 88 J5
Paulistana: Brazil 94 J5
Paul Pietersburg: & Dist., Natal, S. Africa 75 J3
Paul Roux: O.F.S., S. Africa 75 G4
Paulsberg: mtns., S. Africa 74 Ins.
Pauls Valley: city, Okla., U.S.A. 90 C8
Paungde: Burma 59 R11
Pauri: Uttar Pradesh, India 58 N8
Pauto: riv., Colombia 94 C2
Pavia: Italy 40 P10
Pavia d'Udine: Italy 41 T10
Pavilosta: Latvia, U.S.S.R. 47 R8
PAVLODAR: & Reg., Kazakh., U.S.S.R. 51 N4
Pavlogradka: U.S.S.R. 51 M4
Pavlov: U.S.S.R. 50 F3
Pavlovo: U.S.S.R. 49 n5
Pavlovsk: Altai, U.S.S.R. 51 O4
Pavlovsk: Voronezh, U.S.S.R. 50 F4
Pavullo: Italy 41 Q11
Pawan: riv., Borneo 65 E7
Pawhuska: Okla., U.S.A. 90 C7
Pawnee: Okla., U.S.A. 90 C7
Pawnee City: Nebr., U.S.A. 93 H4
Paw Paw: Mich., U.S.A. 88 J4
Pawtucket: R.I., U.S.A. 89 Q5
Pax Iulia: Roman town at Beja, Portugal 35 C17
Paxoi: i., Ionian Is. (Grc.) 39 R17
Paxson: Alaska, U.S.A. 84 E5
Paxton: Ill., U.S.A. 88 G5
Paxton: Nebr., U.S.A. 92 G4
Payakumbuh: Sumatra 65 C7
Payas: Turkey 56 E3
Payde: Estonia, U.S.S.R. 47 T7
Payen: Heilungkiang, China 63 X5
Payenhala: Inner Mongolia, China 63 W5
Payerne: Switzerland 40 M9
Payette: Idaho, U.S.A. 92 D4
Payne, Lake: Que., Canada 85 m6
Payne Bay: town, Que., Can. 85 m5
Paynesville: Liberia 80 B3
Payor: Senegal 80 B2
Payrac: France 37 G11
Paysandu: Uruguay 96 D3
Pays d'Albret: geog. reg., Fr. 34 F14
Pays de Caux: geog. reg., Fr. 36 F6
Payson: Utah, U.S.A. 93 E4
Payturma: U.S.S.R. 49 I3
Payun: mtn., Argentina 96 B4
PAZ, LA: Bolivia 94 D7
Paz, La: Entre Rios, Arg. 96 D3
Paz, La: Mendoza, Arg. 96 B3
Pazar: Turkey 57 G1
Pazarcık: Turkey 56 E3
Pazin: Yugoslavia 41 T10
Pe: Burma 59 R12
Pea: riv., Ala., U.S.A. 91 H10
Peabody: Kans., U.S.A. 90 C6
Peace: riv., Alta./B.C., Can. 92 D1
Peacehaven: E. Sussex, Eng. 25 V18
Peace River: Alta., Canada 92 D1
Péage, Le: France 37 K10
Peak District: Derby., Eng. 27 S13
Peak District National Park: Derby., England 27 S13
Peak Downs Mine: Queens., Australia 70 H4
Peak, The: town, N.S.W., Australia 71 F8
Peake Deep: N. Atlantic Ocean 8 40N 25W
Peak Hill: town, N.S.W., Australia 71 H9
Peale, Mount: Utah, U.S.A. 93 F5
Pearl: Ont., Canada 88 G1
Pearl: riv., Miss., U.S.A. 90 G10
Pearl Harbor: Hawaiian Is. 83 c2
Pearl River I.: La., U.S.A. 90 Ins.
Pearsall: Tex., U.S.A. 90 B11
Pearston: & Dist., S. Africa 75 F6
Peary Chan.: N.W.T., Can. 84 j2
Peary Land: Greenland 85 q1
Pease: riv., Texas, U.S.A. 90 B8
Peasemore: Berks., England 25 T17
Peasmarsh: E. Sussex, Eng. 25 X18
Peat Inn: Fife, Scotland 29 Q7
Pebane: Mozambique 77 E6
Pébo: Central African Rep. 76 A1
Pec: Yugoslavia 39 R15
Peccioli: Italy 41 Q12
Peghenga (Petsamo): U.S.S.R. 46 W2
Pechora: riv., U.S.S.R. 48 g4
Pechori: U.S.S.R. 47 U8
Pecos: N. Mex., U.S.A. 93 F5
Pecos: Tex., U.S.A. 93 G6
Pecos: riv., N. Mex./Tex., U.S.A. 93 G6
Pecs: Hungary 43 Q13
Peddie: & Dist., S. Africa 75 G6
Pedernales: Venezuela 94 E2
Pedreias: Brazil 94 J4
Pedro II: Brazil 94 J4
Pedro, Point: cape, Sri Lanka 58 O13
Pedro Afonso: Brazil 94 H5
Pedro Antonio Santos: Mex. (Honduras. Inset) 86 Ins.
Pedro Juan Caballero: Paraguay 95 F8
Pedro Luro: Argentina 96 C4
Pedro Miguel: & riv., Pan. 94 Ins.
Pedum: ancient Latin city about 4 miles S. of Tivoli (Tibur) 38 N16
Peebinga: S. Australia 71 D10
Peebles: Borders, Scotland 29 P8
Peebles: Sask., Canada 92 G2
Peechelba: Vict., Australia 71 G11
Pee Dee: riv., S.C./N.C., U.S.A. 91 M9
Peekshill: N.Y., U.S.A. 89 P5
Peel: I. of Man, U.K. 26 M11
Peel: marsh, Netherlands 44 L4
Peel: riv., Canada 84 F4
Peel Fell: mtn., Northumb., England 26 Q9
Peel Point: cape, N.W.T., Canada 84 h3
Peene: riv., E. Germany 45 S2
Peenemünde: E. Germany 45 T1
Peer: Belgium 44 L4
Peerless Lake: Alta., Canada 92 E1
Pegae: ancient port NW. of Megara on G. of Corinth 39 S17
Pegasus Bay: South I., N.Z. 70 O16
Peggau: Austria 41 V8
Pegnitz: W. Germany 45 R6
Pego: Spain 35 F17
Pegswood: Northumb., Eng. 26 S9
Pegu: Burma 59 R11
Pegu: State, Burma (cap. Rangoon) 59 R11
Pegu Yoma: range, Burma 59 R11
Peh: riv., China 62 U10
Pehanchen: see Peian.
Pehčevo: Yugoslavia 39 S16
Pehchen: Liaoning, China 63 W6
Pehpiao: Liaoning, China 63 W6
Pehuajo: Argentina 96 C4
Peian (Pehanchen): Heilungkiang, China 63 X5
Peihai: Kwangsi Chuang, China 62 T10
Peine: W. Germany 45 Q3
PEIPING: see Peking.
Peipus, Lake (Lake Chud): U.S.S.R. 47 U7
Peita: riv., China 62 R7
Peiting: W. Germany 41 Q8
Peitz: E. Germany 45 U4
Peixe: Brazil 94 H6
Pejantan: i., Indonesia 65 D6
Pekalongan: Java 65 D8
Pekan: Malaya, Malaysia 65 c12
Pekin: Ill., U.S.A. 88 G5
PEKING (Peiping): & Municipality, China 62 V7
Pekkala: Finland 46 U3
Pelada, La: Argentina 96 C3
Pelagruža: is., Yugoslavia 38 P15
Pelaihari: Borneo 65 E7
Peleduy: U.S.S.R. 49 N6
Pelee: i., Ont., Canada 88 K5
Pelee Point: cape, Ont., Can. 88 K5
Peleliu: Palau Is. 61 L10
Peleng: str. & i., Banggai Is., Indonesia 65 G7
Pelham: Ga., U.S.A. 91 J10
Pelhřimov: Czechoslovakia 45 V6
Pelican Lake: Minn., U.S.A. 88 E1
Pelican Point: cape, SW. Afr. 74 A1
Pelin: Kweichow, China 62 T9
Pelion: mtn. (1615 m) rising immediately NE. of Volos, Greece 39 S17
Pelješac: penin., Yugoslavia 38 P15
Pelkosenniemi: Finland 46 U3
Pella: Iowa, U.S.A. 88 E5
Pella: Italy 40 O10
Pella: Nigeria 81 G2
Pella: S. Africa 74 C4
Pella: city of ancient Israel E. of river Jordan about 10 miles NW. of Ajlun, Jordan 55 b2
Pellegrino: Italy 40 P11
Pellegrue: France 37 F11
Pellerin, Le: France 36 D8
Pellworm: i., N. Frisian Is., W. Germany 44 O1
Pelly: riv., Canada 84 f5
Peloponnese (Morea): reg., Greece 39 S18
Pelotas: Brazil 96 E3
Pelotas: riv., Brazil 96 E2
Peltovuoma: Finland 46 T2
Pelugot: Israel 55 a3
Pelusium: Graeco-Roman city at most easterly mouth of Nile between Port Said and B. of Tina, Egypt (Suez Canal Inset) 32 Ins.
Pelvoux, Mont: France 40 M11
Pelym: riv., U.S.S.R. 51 K2
Pelynt: Corn., England 24 M19
Pelzer: S.C., U.S.A. 91 K8
Pemalang: Java 65 D8
Pemanggil: i., Malaya, Malaysia 65 d12
Pemaquid Pt.: Maine, U.S.A. 89 R4
Pematangsiantar: Sumatra 65 B6
PEMBA: Cabo Delgado, Moz. 77 F5
Pemba: Zambia 77 C6
Pemba I.: Zanzibar 76 E4
Pemberton: B.C., Canada 92 C2
Pemberton: Queens., Austl. 70 K5
Pemberton: W. Australia 68 B6
Pembina: riv., Alta., Canada 84 k6
Pembina Mtns.: Can./U.S.A. 92 H3
Pembrey: Dyfed, Wales 24 N16
Pembridge: Hereford & Worcester, England 24 Q15
Pembroke: Dyfed, Wales 24 M16
Pembroke: Ont., Canada 89 N3
Pembroke, Cape: Canada 85 I5
Pembroke Coast National Park: Dyfed, Wales 24 L16
Pembroke Dock: Dyfed, Wales 24 M16
Pembuang: Borneo 65 E7
Pemuco: Chile 96 A4
Peñafiel: Portugal 35 B16
Peñafiel: Spain 35 D16
Penally: Dyfed, Wales 24 M16
Peña Negra, Sierra de: mtns., Spain 35 C15
Penang: see Pinang.
Penapolis: Brazil 95 G8
Peñaranda de Bracamonte: Spain 35 D16
Penarik: Natuna Is., Indon. 65 D6
Peñarroya: Spain 35 D17
Penarth: S. Glam., Wales 24 P17
Peñás, Cape: Spain 35 D15
Peñas, Punta: Venezuela 87 c5
Penas Gulf: Chile 95 C13
Penboyr: Dyfed, Wales 24 N16
Pencader: Dyfed, Wales 24 N16
Pencaitland: Loth., Scotland 29 Q8
Pencarreg: Dyfed, Wales 24 N15
Pende: riv., Chad 81 H3
Pendeen: Corn., England 25 K19
Pendembu: Sierra Leone 80 B3
Pendleton: Oreg., U.S.A. 92 D3
Pendock: Hereford & Worcester, England 24 R16
Pend Oreille Lake: Idaho, U.S.A. 92 E3
Penedo: Brazil 94 K6
Penestin: France 36 C8
Peneus (Pinios): river flowing into Aegean at Stomion, Greece 39 S17
Pengam Moors: airfield, S. Glam., Wales 24 P17
Pengan: Szechwan, China 62 T8
Penganga: riv., India 58 N11
P'eng-chia: i., Taiwan 63 W9
Penge: Zaire 76 B4
Penglai: Shantung, China 63 W7
Pengshui: Szechwan, China 62 T9
Penhalonga: Rhodesia 77 D6
Peniche: Portugal 35 B17
Penicuik: Lothian, Scotland 29 P8
Penida: i., Indonesia 65 F8
Penifiler: Inner Hebr., Scot. 28 J5
Peñiscola: Spain 35 G16
Penistone: S. Yorks., England 27 S12
Penjbarar: Iran 57 K5
Penjwin: Iraq 57 J4
Penketh: Lancs., England 27 Q13
Penki: Liaoning, China 63 W6
Penkridge: Staffs., England 27 R14
Penllech: Gwynedd, Wales 27 M14
Penmachno: Gwynedd, Wales 27 O13
Penmaenmawr: Gwyn, Wales 27 O13
Penmarch: France 36 A8
Penmarch, Pointe de: cape, France 36 A8
Pennabilli: Italy 41 S12
Pennal: Gwynedd, Wales 27 O14
Pennan: Grampian, Scotland 28 R4
Pennapolis: Brazil 95 G8
Penne: Italy 38 N15
Penner: riv., Andhra Pradesh, India 58 N12
Pennine Alps: Switz./Italy 40 N10
Pennine Chain: range, England 26 R10
Pennsboro: W. Va., U.S.A. 88 L6
Pennsylvania: State, U.S.A. (cap. Harrisburg) 89 M5
Penn Yan: N.Y., U.S.A. 89 N4
Peno: U.S.S.R. 50 D3
Penobscot: riv., Maine, U.S.A. 89 R3
Penola: S. Australia 71 D11
Peñon, El: Argentina 96 B2
Penong: S. Australia 68 E6
Penpont: Dumfries & Galloway, Scotland 29 O9
Penrhyndeudraeth: Gwynedd, Wales 27 N14
Penrith: Cumbria, England 26 Q10
Penrith: N.S.W., Australia 71 J9
Penruddock: Cumbria, England 26 Q10
Penryn: Corn., England 24 L19
Pensacola: Fla., U.S.A. 91 H10
Pensacola Bay: Fla., U.S.A. 91 H10
Pensacola Mts.: Antarctica 9 85S 60W
Pensarn: Clwyd, Wales 27 O13
Pensford: Avon, England 24 Q17
Penshurst: Kent, England 25 W17
Penshurst: Vict., Australia 71 E11
Pensiangan: Sabah, Malaysia 65 F6
Pensilva: Corn., England 24 N19
Pentecost: i., New Hebrides 67 N5
Penticton: B.C., Canada 92 D3
Pentland: Queens., Austl. 69 H4
Pentland Firth: Orkney Is./Scotland 28 P2
Pentland Hills: Strathclyde/Lothian, Scotland 29 P8
Pentland Skerries: Orkney Is., Scotland 28 Q2
Pentraeth: Gwynedd, Wales 27 N13
Pentre Foelas: Clwyd, Wales 27 O13
Pentrich: Derby., England 27 T13
Penuguan: Sumatra 65 C7
Penwith: penin., Corn., England 25 K19
Penybont: Powys, Wales 24 P15
Pen-y-Ghent: mtn., N. Yorks., England 26 R11
Pen-y-groes: Gwyn., Wales 27 N13
PENZA: & Reg., U.S.S.R. 50 F4
Penzance: Corn., England 25 K19
Penzberg: W. Germany 41 R8
Penzhina: gulf & riv., U.S.S.R. 49 S5
Penzhino: U.S.S.R. 49 s5
Penzlin: E. Germany 45 T2
Peoria: Ill., U.S.A. 88 G5
Pepani: riv., S. Africa 74 E2
Peparethus: ancient Greek name of island Skópelos, Aegean Sea 39 S17
Pepel: Sierra Leone 80 B3
Peplos: Greece 39 U16
Peqin: Albania 39 Q16
Pequiri: riv., Brazil 96 E1
Pequot Lakes: city, Minn., U.S.A. 88 D2
Pera: Turkey (Dardan. Inset) 20 Ins.
Peraea: Hellenistic name of region about 15 miles deep E. of Jordan between approximately Ajlun and Libb, Jordan 55 b2
Pera Head: cape, Queens., Australia 69 G2
Peraiba, Monte: Austr./It. 41 S9
Perak: riv., Malaya, Malaysia 65 b11
Perak: State, Malaya, Malaysia (cap. Ipoh) 65 b11
Perala: Finland 46 R5
Peralta: Spain 35 F15
Peraposio: Finland 46 U3
Percé: Que., Canada 89 T1
Percy: France 36 D7
Percy Is.: Queens., Australia 70 J3
Perdeberg: O.F.S., S. Africa 75 F4
Perdekop: Trans., S. Africa 75 H3
Perdu, Mont: Spain/France 37 F13
Perechin: Ukraine 43 S12
Pereginskoye: Ukraine 43 T12
Pereira: Colombia 94 B3
Perejil I.: Morocco (Gib. Inset) 32 Ins.
Perello: Spain 35 G16
Pereslavl'-Zalesskiy: U.S.S.R. 50 E3
Pereyaslav: Ukraine 50 D4
Pereyaslavka: U.S.S.R. 63 Y5
Perez: Chile 96 B2
Perg: Austria 41 U7
Pergamino: Argentina 96 C3
Pergine: Italy 41 R9
Pergola: Italy 41 S12
Perham: Minn., U.S.A. 92 H3
Perhentian Is.: Malaya, Malaysia 65 C5
Perhon: riv., Finland 46 S5
Peri: riv., Turkey 57 G2
Peribonca: riv., Canada 89 Q1
Perico: Argentina 96 B1
Periers: France 36 D6
Perigord: geog. reg., France 37 F10
PÉRIGUEUX: Dordogne, Fr. 37 F10
Perim I.: Yemen P.D.R., Red Sea 54 F12
Perinthus: Greek city on N. coast of sea of Marmara at Ereğli, Turkey 39 U16
Perito Moreno: Argentina 95 C13
Periyakulam: Tamil Nadu, India 58 N12
Perlach: W. Germany 41 R7
Perlas, Las: Nicaragua 87 I15
Perleberg: E. Germany 45 R2
Perlis: State, Malaya, Malaysia (cap. Kangar) 65 b10
Perm (Molotov): & Reg., U.S.S.R. 50 J3
Permanggil: i., Malaya, Malaysia 65 d12
Pernambuco: State, Brazil (cap. Recife) 94 K5
Pernatty Lag.: S. Australia 71 B8
Pernio: Finland 47 S6
Peronne: France 36 H6
Perosa Argentina: Italy 40 N11
Peros Banhos: i., (Br. Indian Ocean Territ.), Indian Ocean 19 0 70E
PERPIGNAN: Pyrénées-Orientales, France 37 H13
Perranporth: Corn., England 24 L19
Perranzabuloe: Corn., Eng. 24 L19
Perrhaebia: mountainous district between Kalabaka and Elasson, Greece 39 R17
Perron: Que., Canada 89 N1
Perros-Guirec: France 36 B7
Perrott, South: Dorset, Eng. 24 Q18
Perry: Fla., U.S.A. 91 K10
Perry: Iowa, U.S.A. 88 D5
Perry: N.Y., U.S.A. 89 M4
Perry: Okla., U.S.A. 90 C7
Perryton: Tex., U.S.A. 90 A7
Perryville: Alaska, U.S.A. 84 D6
Perryville: Mo., U.S.A. 88 G7
Persepolis: ancient Persian capital about 30 miles NE. of Shiraz, Iran 55 H9
Pershore: Hereford & Worcester, England 24 R15
Persian Gulf: SW. Asia 55 H9
Pertek: Turkey 56 F2
Perth: Ont., Canada 89 N3
Perth: Tayside, Scotland 29 P7
PERTH: W. Australia 68 B6
Perth Amboy: N.J., U.S.A. 89 O5
Pertuis: France 40 L12
Pertuis Breton: str., France 37 D9
Pertuis d'Antioche: str., Fr. 37 D9

Peru: Republic 94 B5
Cap.: Lima
Area: 496,222 sq. miles (1,285,215 sq. km.)
Pop.: 13,567,939 (1972 C)

Peru: Ill., U.S.A. 88 G5
Peru: Ind., U.S.A. 88 H5
Peru Basin: S. Pacific Ocean 7 15S 95W
Peru-Chile Trench: S. Pacific Ocean 7 25S 75W
PERUGIA: Umbria, Italy 38 N15
Peruibe: Brazil 96 F1
Perušic: Yugoslavia 41 V11
Peruwelz: Belgium 44 J5
Pervencheres: France 36 F7
Perveri: Turkey 57 H3
Pervomaysk: Ukraine 50 D5
Perwez: Belgium 44 K5
Pesaro: Italy 41 S12
Pescadores Is.: Taiwan 62 V10
Pescara: Italy 38 O15
Pescarolo: Italy 40 Q10
Peschanaye: U.S.S.R. 50 G5
Peschanoye: Kazakh., U.S.S.R. 51 N4
Peschici: Italy 38 P16
Peschiera: Italy 41 Q10
Pescia: Italy 41 Q12
Pe Shan: range, Sinkiang, China 62 Q6
PESHAWAR: NW. Front. Prov., Pakistan 58 M8
Pesh Khabur (Faish Khabur): Iraq 57 H3
Peshkopi: Albania 39 R16
Pesmes: France 40 L8
Pesqueira: Brazil 94 K5
Pesquerio: riv., Mexico 93 H7
Pessac: France 37 E11
Pessene: Mozambique 75 K2
Pessinus: Celtic settlement of Galatia about 10 miles SE. of Sivrihisar, Turkey 56 B2
Pestovo: U.S.S.R. 50 E3
Petah Tiqva: Israel 55 a2
Petaluma: Calif., U.S.A. 93 C5

For Abbreviations see list on p.113. Italic type, e.g. *Ephesus*, refers to historical names not on maps. Capital letters, e.g. MADRID, show capitals of countries; small capital letters, e.g. CADIZ, show capitals of provinces, etc. General notes p.116.

176 Petange—Pocking

Petange: Luxembourg 44 L6
Petatlán: Mexico 86 j14
Petauke: Zambia 77 D5
Peterbell: Ont., Canada 88 K1
Peterborough: Cambs., England 27 V14
Peterborough: N.H., U.S.A. 89 Q4
Peterborough: Ont., Can. 89 M3
Peterborough: S. Australia 71 C9
Peterchurch: Hereford & Worcester, England 24 Q15
Peterculter: Gram., Scotland 28 R5
Peterhead: Gram., Scotland 28 S4
Peterlee: Dur., England 26 T10
Petermann Range: Austl. 68 D5
Petermanns Glac.: Grnld. 85 O1
Petermanns Peak: Grnld. 85 R3
Peter Pond Lake: Sask., Canada 92 F1
Petersburg: Alaska, U.S.A. 84 f6
Petersburg: Ill., U.S.A. 88 G5
Petersburg: Ind., U.S.A. 88 H6
Petersburg: S. Africa 75 F6
Petersburg: Va., U.S.A. 89 N7
Petersburg: W. Va., U.S.A. 89 M6
Petersdorf: W. Germany 45 R1
Petersfield: Hants., England 25 U17
Petersfield: Jamaica 86 *Ins.*
Petershausen: W. Germany 41 R7
Peterson Bay: *settlement*, N.W.T., Canada 84 K4
Peterstal: W. Germany 40 O7
Peterstow: Hereford & Worcester, England 24 Q16
Petertavy: Devon, England 24 N18
Petham: Kent, England 25 Y17
Petherton, North: Som., Eng. 24 P17
Petherton, South: Som., Eng. 24 Q18
Petherwin, South: Corn., England 24 N18
Petit Bois: *i.*, Miss., U.S.A. 90 G10
Petit François: Fr. Guiana 94 G3
Petit Morin: *riv.*, France 36 J7
Petit St. Bernard, Col du: *pass*, France/Italy 40 M10
Peto: Mexico 86 L13
Petone: North I., N.Z. 70 P15
Petorca: Chile 96 A3
Petoskey: Mich., U.S.A. 88 J3
Petra: rock-carved capital of Nabateans in Wadi Araba, Jordan 56 D6
Petrel: *rsch. stn.*, Antarctica 9 65S 60W
Petreto: Corsica 38 L16
Petrich: Bulgaria 39 S16
Petrie Reef: Loyalty Is. 67 M5
Petrified Forest Nat. Mon.: Ariz., U.S.A. 93 F5
Petrikov: Byelorussia 43 V10
Petrikovka: Ukraine 50 D5
Petrinja: Yugoslavia 41 W10
Petrodvorets: U.S.S.R. 47 V7
Petrograd: name of Leningrad between 1914 and 1924, U.S.S.R. 50 D3
Petrokrepost': U.S.S.R. 47 W7
Petrolia: Ont., Canada 88 K4
Petrolina: Brazil 94 J5
Petronell: Austria 41 W7
Petropavlovsk-Kamchatskiy: Khabarovsk, U.S.S.R. 49 r7
PETROPAVLOVSK: North Kazakhstan, U.S.S.R. 51 L4
Petropolis: Brazil 96 G1
Petroşani: Romania 43 S14
Petroşita: Romania 43 T14
Petrovac: Yugoslavia 39 R14
Petrovgrad (Zrenjanin): Yugoslavia 39 R14
Petrovsk: U.S.S.R. 60 F1
Petrovsk: Saratov, U.S.S.R. 50 G4
PETROZAVODSK: Karelian A.S.S. Rep., U.S.S.R. 50 D2
Petrusburg: O.F.S., S. Africa 75 F4
Petrus Steyn: O.F.S., S. Afr. 75 H3
Petrusville: S. Africa 75 F5
Petsamo (Pechenga): U.S.S.R. 46 W2
Pettau: German name of Yugoslav town Ptuj 41 V9
Pettigoe: Don./Ferm., Ireland 30 F10
Petukhovo: U.S.S.R. 51 L3
Petworth: W. Sussex, Eng. 25 U18
Peu: Santa Cruz Is., Pacific O. 67 N4
Peuerbach: Austria 41 T7
Peumo: Chile 96 A3
Pevek: U.S.S.R. 49 T4
Pevensey: E. Sussex, Eng. 25 W18
Pevensey Levels: E. Sussex, England 25 W18
Pewsey: & *val.*, Wilts., Eng. 25 S17
Pewsum: W. Germany 44 N2
Peyrano: Argentina 96 C3
Peyrat-le-Château: France 37 G10
Peyrehorade: France 37 D12
Peyreleau: France 37 J11
Peyrolles: France 40 L12
Pezenas: France 37 J12
Pezos, Los: Chile 96 A2
Pfaffenhausen: W. Germany 40 Q7
Pfaffenhofen: W. Germany 41 R7
Pfälzer Bergland: *mtns.*, W. Germany 44 N6
Pfälzer Wald: *mtns.*, W. Ger. 44 N6
Pfarrkirchen: W. Germany 41 S7
Pfeffenhausen: W. Germany 41 R7
Pforzheim: W. Germany 40 O7
Pfullendorf: W. Germany 40 P8
Pfullingen: W. Germany 40 P7
Pfungstadt: W. Germany 44 O6
Phak Pang: Thailand 64 C3
Phalan: Laos 64 D3
Phalerum: ancient harbour of Athens E. of Piraeus. 39 S18
Phalodi: Rajasthan, India 58 M9
Phalsbourg: France 40 N7
Phangan: *i.*, Thailand 64 C5
Phangnga: Thailand 64 B5
Phanom Dongrak: *range*, Thailand 64 C4
Phan Rang: Vietnam 64 D4
Phan Thiêt: Vietnam 64 D4
Phari Dzong: Tibet, China 59 P9
Pharos: penin.; in ancient times an island and site of a great lighthouse near Alexandria, Egypt 56 B6
Pharsalus: Greek city at SE. end of plain about 30 miles S. of Larisa, Greece 39 S17
Phaselis: Greek city on W. coast of G. of Antalya about 20 miles N. of C. Kelidonya, Turkey 56 B3
Phatnitikon: Greek name of Damietta arm of Nile, Egypt 56 B6
Phatthalung: Thailand 64 C5
Phej Buri: Thailand 64 B4
Phelps, Lake: N.C., U.S.A. 91 N8
Phenix City: Ala., U.S.A. 91 J9
Phetchabun: Thailand 64 C3
Phiafay: Laos 64 D4
Philadelphia: Miss., U.S.A. 90 G9
Philadelphia: Pa., U.S.A. 89 O6
Philadelphia: S. Africa 74 C6
Philadelphia: Graeco-Roman city on river Gediz at Alaşehir, Turkey 39 U17
Philadelphia: Graeco-Roman city NE. of El Faiyum, Egypt 54 D9
Philae: Graeco-Roman city on island in Nile just above 1st Cataract, Egypt 54 D10
Philip: S. Dak., U.S.A. 92 G4
Philippeville: Belgium 44 K5
Philippi: Macedonian and Roman city in plain NW. of Kavalla, Greece 39 T16
Philippines: *Republic* 64/5
Cap.: Quezon City
Area: 115,707 sq. miles (299,681 sq. km.)
Pop.: 39,769,000 (*1972 E*)
Philippine Sea: Pacific O. 61 L8
Philippine Trench: Philippine Sea 7 05N 125E
Philippi Settlement: Bahamas 91 M12
Philippopolis: *see* Plovdiv.
Philippolis: & *Dist.*, O.F.S., S. Africa 75 F5
Philipsburg: Mont., U.S.A. 92 E3
Philipsburg: Pa., U.S.A. 89 M5
Philipsburg: St. Martin I., Lesser Antilles 87 b1
Philippsburg: W. Germany 44 O6
Philipstown: Offaly, Repub. of Ireland 31 G13
Philipstown: & *Dist.*, S. Afr. 73 F5
Philistia: classical name of part of SW. Palestine which was occupied by the Philistines, now belonging to Egypt and Israel 55 a3
Philleigh: Corn., England 24 M19
Phillips: Wis., U.S.A. 88 F3
Phillips Bay: N.W.T., Can. 85 L1
Phillipsburg: N.J., U.S.A. 89 O5
Phitsanulok: Thailand 64 C3
PHNOM PENH: Cambodia 64 C4
Phocaea: Greek city at Foça at N. end of Izmir G., Tur. 39 U17
Phocis: ancient Greek district including valley N. and E. of Levadhia and stretching past Mt. Parnassos to G. of Corinth 39 S17
Phoenicia: classical name of area occupied by the Phoenicians on the Mediterranean coast, Lebanon 56 D5
PHOENIX: Ariz., U.S.A. 93 E6
Phoenix I.: Phoenix Islands 7 05S 175W
Phoenix Is.: (Br.), S. Pacific Ocean 7 05S 175W
Phoenixville: Pa., U.S.A. 89 O5
Phokwani: Trans., S. Africa 75 H2
Phopagaon: Nepal 59 O9
Phoune Thong: Laos 64 D3
Phrae: Thailand 64 C3
Phudien: Vietnam 64 D3
Phuket: Thailand 64 B5
Phuket (Thalang) I.: Thailand 64 B5
Phulbani: Orissa, India 59 O10
Phuloc: Vietnam 64 D5
Phumi Krek: Cambodia 64 D4
Phumi Toek Chou: Cambodia 64 C4
Phunhuan: Vietnam 64 D4
Phuoc Lê: Vietnam 64 D4
Phuoc Long: Vietnam 64 D5
Phuquoc: *i.*, Vietnam 64 C4
Phuyen: Vietnam 64 D4
Phyle: village of central *Attica* about 14 miles N. of Athens 38 S17
Piacenza: Italy 40 P10
Piadena: Italy 40 Q10
Pialba: Queens., Australia 70 K5
Pianezza: Italy 40 N10
Piangil: Vict., Australia 71 E10
Pianoro: Italy 41 R11
Pianosa: *i.* (It.), Adriatic Sea 38 O15
Pianosa: *i.* (It.), Tyrrhenian Sea 38 M15
Piatra Neamţ: Romania 43 U13
Piaui: *State*, Brazil (*cap.* Teresina) 94 J5
Piave: *riv.*, Italy 41 S10
Piazza Armerina: Sicily 38 O18
Piazzolo: Italy 41 Q9
Pibor Post: Sudan 76 D1
Pic: *riv.*, Ont., Canada 88 H1
Picardy: *Prov.*, France 34 H12
Picayune: Miss., U.S.A. 90 G10
Pic de Tio: *mtn.*, Guinea 80 C3
Picenum: ancient district comprising Abruzzi and Southern Marche, Italy 38 N15
Pichanal: Argentina 96 C1
Picher: Okla., U.S.A. 90 D7
Pichieh: Kweichow, China 62 T9
Pichilemu: Chile 96 A3
Pickerel Lake: Ont., Canada 88 F1
Pickering: & *val.*, N. Yorks., England 26 U11
Pickersgill: Guyana 87 d7
Pickhill: N. Yorks., England 26 T11
Pickle Crow: Ont., Canada 85 k7
Pickwick Dam: Tenn., U.S.A. 90 G8
Pickwick Landing Reservoir: Tenn./Ala., U.S.A. 90 G8
Pico: *i.*, Azores Is. 78 *Ins.*
Picola: Vict., Australia 71 F10
Picos: Brazil 94 J5
Picton: N.S.W., Australia 71 J10
Picton: Ont., Canada 89 N4
Picton: South I., N.Z. 70 P15
Picton: N. Yorks., England 26 T11
Pictou: & *i.*, N.S., Canada 89 U3
Piddington: Northants., England 25 U15
Piddle: *riv.*, Dorset, Eng. 24 R18
Piddletrenthide: Dorset, Eng. 24 R18
Piedade: Brazil 96 F1
Piedimonte: Italy 38 O16
Piedimulera: Italy 40 O9
Piedmont: Ala., U.S.A. 91 J9
Piedmont: Mo., U.S.A. 88 F7
Piedmont: S.C., U.S.A. 91 K8
Piedmont: *Reg.*, Italy (*cap.* Turin (Torino)) 40 N11
Piedra Blanca: *i.*, Phil. 64 G4
Piedrabuena: Spain 35 D17
Piedrahita: Spain 35 D16
Piedras, Las: Uruguay 96 D3
Piedras Negras: Mexico 93 G7
Piedra Sola: Uruguay 96 D3
Pie I.: Ont., Canada 88 G1
Pieksämäki: Finland 46 U5
Pielis Lake: Finland 46 V5
Piemonte: *see* Piedmont.
Pienaarsrivier: Trans., S. Africa 75 H2
Pienaarsvlei: S. Africa 74 E6
Piercebridge: Dur., England 26 S10
Pierce City: Mo., U.S.A. 90 D7
Pierlat: Central African Republic 76 B1
Pierowall: Orkney Is., Scotland 28 *Ins.*
Pierre: France 37 L9
PIERRE: S. Dak., U.S.A. 92 G4
Pierre-Buffière: France 37 G10
Pierrefitte-Nestalas: France 37 E13
Pierrefort: France 37 H11
Pierrelatte: France 37 K11
Pierreville: Que., Canada 89 P2
Piešťany: Czechoslovakia 43 P12
Pieske Lake: Sweden 46 P3
Pietarsaari (Jacobstadt): Finland 46 S5
PIETERMARITZBURG: Natal, S. Africa 75 J4
Pietersburg: & *Dist.*, Trans., S. Africa 75 H1
Pietramala: Italy 41 R11
Pietrasanta: Italy 40 Q12
Piet Retief: & *Dist.*, Trans., S. Africa 75 J3
Pieux, Les: France 36 D6
Pieve di Cadore: Italy 41 S9
Pieve di Teco: Italy 40 N11
Pievepelago: Italy 40 Q11
Pieve San Stefano: Italy 41 S12
Pigeon: *riv.*, U.S.A./Can. 88 F1
Pigeon Lake: Ont., Canada 89 M3
Piggot: Ark., U.S.A. 88 F7
Piggs Peak: Swaziland 75 J2
Pignans: France 40 M12
Pigüé: Argentina 96 C4
Pihsien: Kiangsu, China 62 V8
Pihtipudas: Finland 46 T5
Piippola: Finland 46 T4
Pijijiapan: Mexico 86 k14
Pikes Peak: Colo., U.S.A. 93 F5
Piketberg: & *Dist.*, S. Africa 74 C6
Pikeville: Ky., U.S.A. 88 K7
Pikow: Kansu, China 62 T8
Pikwitonei: Man., Canada 92 H1
Pila: Argentina 96 D4
Piła: Poland 43 P10
Pilão Arcado: Brazil 94 J6
Pilar: Argentina 96 C3
Pilar: Brazil 96 F1
Pilar: Paraguay 96 D2
Pilas: *i.*, Philippines 65 G5
Pilcaniyeu: Argentina 95 C12
Pilcomayo: *riv.*, S. America 95 E8
Pilcomayo Nat. Park: Argentina 96 D2
Pile: Karpathos, Dodec. 39 U19
Pilgrim's Rest: & *Dist.*, Trans., S. Africa 75 J2
Pili: Cos, Dodecanese 39 U18
Pilica: *riv.*, Poland 43 R11
Pil'khyn: U.S.S.R. 49 t4
Pill: Avon, England 24 Q17
Pillau (Baltiysk): U.S.S.R. 47 Q9
Pilleth: Powys, Wales 24 P15
Pilliga: N.S.W., Australia 71 H8
Pilling: Lancs., England 27 Q12
Pillinger: Tas., Australia 68 H8
Pillowell: Glos., England 24 Q16
Pilltown: Wat., Repub. of Irel. 31 F16
Pilon: *riv.*, Mexico 90 B13
Pilos: Greece 39 R18
Pilottown: La., U.S.A. 90 *Ins.*
PILSEN (Plzeň): Západočeský, Czech. 45 T6
Piltene: Latvia, U.S.S.R. 47 R8
Pilton: Som., England 24 Q17
Pimba: S. Australia 71 B8
Pimperne: Dorset, England 24 R18
Pina: *riv.*, Panama 94 *Ins.*
Pinacate: *mtn.*, Mexico 93 E6
Pinaki: *i.*, Tuamotu Arch. 83 h3
Pinamalayan: Philippines 64 G4
PINANG: Pinang, Malaysia 65 b11
Pinang: *i.* & *State*, Malaya, Malaysia (*cap.* Pinang) 65 b11
Pinarbaşi: Turkey 56 E2
Pinar del Rio: Cuba 87 I13
Pinas: Argentina 96 B3
Pinchbeck: Lincs., England 27 V14
Pincher Creek: *town*, Alta., Canada 92 E3
Pinckneyville: Ill., U.S.A. 88 G6
Pińczów: Poland 43 R11
Pindamonhangaba: Brazil 96 F1
Pindus Mtns.: Greece 39 R16
Pine Bluff: Ark., U.S.A. 90 E8
Pine Bluffs: Wyo., U.S.A. 92 G4
Pine City: Minn., U.S.A. 88 E3
Pine Creek: *town*, N. Territ., Australia 68 E2
Pinega: U.S.S.R. 48 F5
Pinega: *riv.*, U.S.S.R. 50 G2
Pinehill: Queens., Australia 70 G4
Pinehouse Lake: Sask., Canada 92 F1
Pinehurst: N.C., U.S.A. 91 M8
Pineland: Tex., U.S.A. 90 E10
Pinelands: C.P., S. Africa 74 *Ins.*
Pine River: *city*, Minn., U.S.A. 88 D2
Pinerolo: Italy 40 N11
Pines, I. of: Cuba 87 I13
Pinetown: & *Dist.*, Natal, S. Africa 75 J4
Pineville: Ky., U.S.A. 88 K7
Pineville: La., U.S.A. 90 E10
Piney: France 36 K7
Piney Buttes: *mtns.*, Mont., U.S.A. 92 F3
Ping: *riv.*, Thailand 64 B3
Pinga: Zaire 76 C3
Pingchuan: Hopeh, China 62 V6
Pingelly: W. Australia 68 B6
Pingin: W. Australia 68 C6
Pingkiang: Hunan, China 62 U9
Pingku: Hopeh, China 62 V6
Pingliang: Kansu, China 62 T7
Pinglo: Kwangsi Chuang, China 62 U10
Pinglo: Ninghsia Hui, China 62 T7
Pinglu: Shansi, China 62 U7
Pinglu: Shansi, China 62 U8
Pingnam, Kwangsi Chuang, China 62 U10
Pingnan: Fukien, China 62 V9
Pingrup: W. Australia 68 B6
Pingshan: Hopeh, China 62 U7
Pingsiang: Kiangsi, China 62 U9
Pingting: Shansi, China 62 U7
Pingtu: Shantung, China 62 V7
Ping-tung: Taiwan 63 W10
Pingwu (Lungan): Szechwan, China 62 S8
Pingyang: Chekiang, China 63 W9
Pingyao: Shansi, China 62 U7
Pingyun: Kwangtung, China 62 V10
Pinheiro: Maranhão, Brazil 94 H4
Pinheiro Machado: Rio Grande do Sul, Brazil 96 E3
Pinhel: Portugal 35 C16
Pini: *i.*, Sumatra 65 B6
Piniós: *riv.*, Greece 39 R17
Pinjarra: W. Australia 68 B6
Pinkafeld: Austria 41 W8
Pinkiang (Harbin): Heilungkiang, China 63 X5
Pinkie Clough: battlefield on W. side of river Esk opposite Dalkeith, Lothian, Scotland 29 P8
Pinlaung: Burma 59 R10
Pinlebu: Burma 59 R10
Pinmore: Strath., Scotland 29 M9
Pinnacles: N.S.W., Austl. 71 D9
Pinnaroo: S. Australia 71 D10
Pinneberg: W. Germany 45 P2
Pinnes, Cape: Greece 39 T16
Pinopolis Reservoir: *see* Moultrie, Lake.
Pinrang: Celebes: 65 F7
Pins, Ile des: Loyalty Is. 67 N6
Pinsk: Byelorussia 43 U10
Pintado, El: Argentina 96 C1
Pintados: Chile 94 D8
Pinto: Argentina 96 C2
Pinzano al Tagliamento: It. 41 S9
Pinzolo: Italy 41 Q9
Pioche: Nev., U.S.A. 93 E5
Piombino: Italy 38 M15
Pioneer Fracture Zone: N. Pacific Ocean 7 35N 140W
Pioneer Mtns.: Mont., U.S.A. 92 E3
Pionsat: France 37 H9
Piotrków: Poland 43 Q11
Piove di Sacco: Italy 41 S10
Piovene: Italy 41 R10
Pipar: Rajasthan, India 58 M9
Pipestone: Minn., U.S.A. 92 H4
Pipestone: *riv.*, Ont., Canada 92 J2
Pipinas, Las: Argentina 96 D4
Pipriac: France 36 D8
Piqua: Ohio, U.S.A. 88 J5
Piracicaba: & *riv.*, Brazil 96 F1
Piracuruca: Brazil 94 J4
Piraeus (Piraievs): Greece 39 S18
Pirai: Brazil 96 F1
Piraju: Brazil 96 F1
Pir Ali: Iran 57 L5
Pirámide, Cerro: *mtn.*, Chile 95 C13
Piran: Yugoslavia 41 T10
Piranė: Argentina 96 D2
Piranhas: Brazil 94 K5
Pirapora: Brazil 94 J7
Pirassununga: Brazil 96 F1
Piratini: Brazil 96 E3
Pirbright: Surrey, England 25 U17
Pirdop: Bulgaria 39 T15
Pirenópolis: Brazil 94 H7
Pirgos: Crete 39 T19
Pirgos: Elis, Greece 39 R18
Pirgos: Laconia, Greece 39 S18
Pirgos: Samothrace, Greece 39 T16
Pirgos: Thira, Cyclades 39 T18
Piriac: France 36 C8
Piriapolis: Uruguay 96 D3
Pirie: S. Africa 75 G6
Pirin Mtns.: Bulgaria 39 S16
Piripiri: Brazil 94 J4
Pirmasens: W. Germany 44 N6
Pirna: E. Germany 45 T5
Pirnmill: Strath., Scotland 29 L8
Pirojpur: Bangladesh 59 P10
Pirot: Yugoslavia 39 S15
Pirovac: Yugoslavia 41 V12
Pirtleville, Ariz., U.S.A. 93 F6
Piru: Moluccas, Indonesia 61 K12
Pityatin: Ukraine 50 D4
Pisa: Italy 40 Q12
Pisagua: Chile 94 C7
Pisarovina: Yugoslavia 41 V10
Pisciotta: Italy 38 O16
Pisco: Peru 94 B6
Písek: Czechoslovakia 45 U6
Pisgah: Biblical name of mtn. W. of *Mt. Nebo* and 6 miles NW. of Madaba, Jordan 55 b3
Pisha: Sinkiang, China 51 O7
Pishan (Guma): Sinkiang, China 51 N7
Pishin: Baluchistan, Pak. 58 L8
Pishin: Iran 55 K9
Pisidia: ancient name of mountainous district of southern Turkey between *Galatia* and *Pamphylia* around Akşehir 56 B3
Pisogne: Italy 40 Q10
Pissos: France 37 E11
Pisticci: Italy 38 P16
Pisto: Finland 46 V4
Pistoia: Italy 41 Q12
Pisz: Poland 43 R10
Pit: *riv.*, Calif., U.S.A. 92 C4
PITA: & *Reg.*, Guinea 80 B2
Pital: Mexico 86 k14
Pitanga: Brazil 96 E1
Pitanguí: Brazil 94 J7
Pitapunga, Lake: N.S.W., Australia 71 E10
Pitcairn I.: (Br.), Pacific O. (*cap.* Adamstown) 7 30S 130W
Pitcairly: Tay., Scotland 29 P6
Pite: *riv.*, Sweden 46 R4
Piteå: Sweden 46 R4
Piteşti: Romania 39 T14
Pithion: Greece 39 U16
Pithiviers: France 36 H7
Pitiquito: Mexico 93 E6
Pitkyaranta: Karelian A.S.S. Rep., U.S.S.R. 47 W6
Pitlochry: Tay., Scotland 29 O6
Pitscottie: Fife, Scotland 29 Q7
Pitsea: Essex, England 25 W16
Pitsligo, New: Gram., Scot. 28 R4
Pittenweem: Fife, Scotland 29 Q7
Pitt I.: B.C., Canada 92 B2
Pittsburg: Kans., U.S.A. 90 D7
Pittsburg: Tex., U.S.A. 90 D9
Pittsburgh: Pa., U.S.A. 89 M5
Pittsfield: Ill., U.S.A. 88 F6
Pittsfield: Maine, U.S.A. 89 R3
Pittsfield: Mass., U.S.A. 89 P4
Pittston: Pa., U.S.A. 89 O5
Pittsworth: Queens., Austl. 70 J6
Pitu: Moluccas, Indonesia 61 K11
Pity Me: *village*, Dur., Eng. 26 S10
Piua Petri: Romania 39 U14
Piura: Peru 94 A5
Piuthan: Nepal 59 O9
Piva: *riv.*, Yugoslavia 39 Q15
Pizzighettone: Italy 40 P10
P. K. le Roux Dam.: O.F.S./C.P., South Africa 75 F4
Plabennec: France 36 A7
Placentia: & *bay*, Newf., Can. 85 v3
Placentia: Roman colony at Piacenza, Italy 40 P10
Placerville: Calif., U.S.A. 93 C5
Placetas: Cuba 87 M13
Plaidy: Gram., Scotland 28 R4
Plain Dealing: La., U.S.A. 90 E9
Plainfield: N.J., U.S.A. 89 O5
Plainview: Minn., U.S.A. 88 E3
Plainview: Tex., U.S.A. 93 G6
Plampang: Sumbawa, Indonesia 65 F8
Plan: Italy 41 R9
Planá: Czechoslovakia 45 S6
Planaltina: Brazil 94 H7
Planasia: Roman name of island of Pianosa 38 M15
Plancoët: France 36 C7
Plano: Tex., U.S.A. 90 C9
Plantaurel, Montagnes du: *mtns.*, France 37 G12
Plant City: Fla., U.S.A. 91 K11
Plaquemine: La., U.S.A. 90 F10
Plasencia: Spain 35 C16
Plashetts: Northumb., Eng. 26 Q9
Plaski: Yugoslavia 41 V10
Plassey: village where Clive defeated the Bengal army in 1757, N. of Calcutta, Bengal, India 59 P10
Plast: U.S.S.R. 51 K4
Plastun: U.S.S.R. 63 Z6
Plasy: Czechoslovakia 45 T6
Plata: *hill*, Spain (Gib. *Inset*) 32 *Ins.*
PLATA, LA: Buenos Aires, Argentina 96 D3
Plata, Pampas de la: *plains*, Argentina 96 C3
Plataeae: Greek city of SE. *Boeotia* about 8 miles S. of Thebes 39 S17
Platani: *riv.*, Sicily 38 N18
Platbakkies: S. Africa 74 C5
Plate: *riv.*, Arg./Uruguay 96 D3
Plateau: *State*, Nigeria (*cap.* Jos) 81 F3
Plati: Greece 39 S16
Platinum: Alaska, U.S.A. 84 c6
Platrand: Trans., S. Africa 75 H3
Platte: S. Dak., U.S.A. 92 H4
Platte: *riv.*, Nebr., U.S.A. 92 H4
Platteville: Wis., U.S.A. 88 F4
Plattling: W. Germany 41 S7
Platt Nat. Park: Okla., U.S.A. 90 C8
Plattsburg: N.Y., U.S.A. 89 P3
Plau: E. Germany 45 S2
Plaue: E. Germany 45 Q5
Plauen: E. Germany 45 S5
Plauer Canal: E. Germany 45 R3
Plauer See: *lake*, Neubrandenburg, E. Germany 45 S2
Plauer See: *lake*, Potsdam, E. Germany 45 S3
Plav: Yugoslavia 39 Q15
Pļaviņas: Latvia, U.S.S.R. 47 T8
Plavnica: Yugoslavia 39 Q15
Plavsk: U.S.S.R. 50 E4
Playgreen Lake: Man., Can. 92 H2
Plaza Huincul: Argentina 96 B4
Pleasant Hill: Mo., U.S.A. 90 D6
Pleasanton: Kans., U.S.A. 90 D6
Pleasanton: Tex., U.S.A. 90 B11
Pleasantville: N.J., U.S.A. 89 O6
Pléaux: France 37 H10
Pleiku: Vietnam 64 D4
Pleine-Fougères: France 36 D7
Plelan: France 36 C7
Plemet: France 36 C7
Pleneuf: France 36 C7
Pleniţa: Romania 39 S14
Plenty, Bay of: North I., New Zealand 70 Q13
Plentywood: Mont., U.S.A. 92 G3
Plérin: France 36 C7
Plesetsk: U.S.S.R. 50 F2
Pleshchenitsy, Byelorussia 47 U9
Pleso-Kurya: U.S.S.R. 51 O4
Plessisville: Que., Canada 89 Q2
Plestin-les-Greves: France 36 B7
Pleszew: Poland 43 P11
Pletipi Lake: Que., Canada 85 m7
Plettenburg: W. Germany 44 N4
Plettenburg Bay: *town*, S. Africa 74 E7
Pleubian: France 36 B7
Pleumartin: France 37 F9
Pleurtuit: France 36 C7
Pleven: Bulgaria 39 T15
Plevenon: France 36 C7
Pleyben: France 36 B7
Plitvice: Yugoslavia 41 V11
Plješi Mtns.: Yugoslavia 41 V11
Pljevlja: Yugoslavia 39 Q15
Płock: Poland 43 Q10
Plockton: Highland, Scot. 28 K5
Ploëmeur: France 36 B8
Ploërdut: France 36 B7
Ploërmel: France 36 C8
Ploeşti: Romania 39 U14
Ploeuc: France 36 C7
Plomarion: Lesbos, Greece 39 U17
Plomb du Cantal: *mtn.*, Fr. 37 H10
Plombières: France 40 M8
Plomin: Yugoslavia 41 U10
Plön: W. Germany 45 Q1
Płońsk: Poland 43 R10
Płoty: Poland 45 V2
Plouagat: France 36 B7
Plouaret: France 36 B7
Plouay: France 36 B8
Ploudalmézeau: France 36 A7
Plouescat: France 36 A7
Plouézec: France 36 C7
Plougasnou: France 36 B7
Plougastel-Daoulas: France 36 A7
Plouguenast: France 36 C7
Plouguerneau: France 36 A7
Plouha: France 36 C7
Plouhinec: France 36 A7
Plouigneau: France 36 B7
Plounevez-Lochrist: France 36 A7
PLOVDIV (Philippopolis): & *Prov.*, Bulgaria 39 T15
Plozévet: France 36 A8
Pluckley: Kent, England 25 X17
Plumas, Las: Argentina 95 D12
Plumb Bridge: Tyr., N. Irel. 30 G10
Plumbland: Cumbria, Eng. 26 P10
Plum I.: N.Y., U.S.A. 89 P5
Plumpton: E. Sussex, England 25 V18
Plumpton Wall: Cumbria, Eng. 26 Q10
Plumstead: S. Africa 74 *Ins.*
Plumtree: Notts., England 27 T14
Plumtree: Rhodesia 77 C7
Plunge: Lithuania, U.S.S.R. 47 R9
Pluvigner: France 36 B8
Plyavinyas: Latvia, U.S.S.R. 47 T8
Plym: *riv.*, Devon, England 24 N19
Plymouth: Devon, England 24 N19
Plymouth: Ind., U.S.A. 88 H5
Plymouth: Mass., U.S.A. 89 Q5
PLYMOUTH: Montserrat, Leeward Is. 87 b2
Plymouth: N.H., U.S.A. 89 Q4
Plymouth: N.C., U.S.A. 91 N8
Plymouth: Vt., U.S.A. 89 P4
Plymouth: Windward Is. 87 c5
Plymouth: Wis., U.S.A. 88 H4
Plympton: Devon, England 24 N19
Plynlimon Fawr: *mtn.*, Dyfed, Wales 24 O15
Plyussa: *riv.*, U.S.S.R. 47 V7
Plzeň (Pilsen): Czech. 45 T6
Po: Upper Volta 80 D2
Po: *riv.*, Italy 41 R11
Pobé: Benin 81 E3
Pobé: Upper Volta 80 D2
Poběžovice: Czechoslovakia 45 S6
Pobla de Lillet, La: Spain 35 G15
Pobla de Segur: Spain 35 G15
Pocahontas: Ark., U.S.A. 88 F7
Pocatello: Idaho, U.S.A. 92 E4
Pochep: U.S.S.R. 50 D4
Pöchlarn: Austria 41 V7
Pocitos: Argentina 96 B1
Pocking: W. Germany 41 T7

Pocklington—Powys 177

Pocklington: Humberside, England 27 U12
Poções: Brazil 94 J6
Pocomoke City: Md., U.S.A. 89 O6
Poconé: Brazil 94 F7
Poços de Caldas: Brazil 96 F1
Podbořany: Czechoslovakia 45 T5
Poděbrady: Czechoslovakia 45 V5
Po delle Tolle: *riv.*, Italy 41 S11
Podgaytsy: Ukraine 43 T12
Podgrad: Yugoslavia 41 U10
Po di Goro: *riv.*, Italy 41 S11
Podivín: Czechoslovakia 41 W7
Podkagernaya: U.S.S.R. 49 S5
Podkamennaya-Tunguska: U.S.S.R. 51 Q2
Podkamennaya (Stony) Tunguska: *riv.*, U.S.S.R. 49 L5
Podlasie: *geog. reg.*, Poland 43 S10
Podmokly: Czechoslovakia 45 U5
Podol'sk: U.S.S.R. 50 E3
Podor: Senegal 80 B1
Podul Iloaei: Romania 43 U13
Poel: *i.*, E. Germany 45 R1
Poeninae Alpes: Roman name for Pennine Alps 40 N10
Poenina Vallis: Roman name for district of Valais, Switzerland 40 N9
Poetovio: Roman camp, later colony, at Ptuj, Yugo. 41 V9
Pofadder: S. Africa 74 C4
Poggendorf: E. Germany 45 T1
Poggibonsi: Italy 41 R12
Poggio Renatico: Italy 41 R11
Poghdar: Afghanistan 58 K8
Pogradec: Albania 39 R16
Po Hai (Chihli), G. of: China 62 V7
Pohang: S. Korea 63 X7
Pohjois-Karjala: *Prov.*, Finland (*cap.* Joensuu) 46 V5
Pohořelice: Czechoslovakia 41 W7
Pohsien: Anhwei, China 62 V8
Point à la Hache: La., U.S.A. 90 *Ins.*
Pointe à Pitre: Guadeloupe 87 c2
POINTE NOIRE: Congo 81 G5
Point Hope: *town*, Alaska, U.S.A. 84 C4
Point Lake: N.W.T., Canada 84 h4
Point Lay: *settlement*, Alaska, U.S.A. 88 c4
Point Pleasant: *city*, W. Va., U.S.A. 88 K6
Poire-sur-Vie, Le: France 37 D9
Poirino: Italy 40 N11
Poisson Blanc, Lac: Que., Canada 89 O2
Poissy: France 36 H7
POITIERS: Vienne, France 37 F9
Poitou: *Prov.*, France 34 F13
Poix: France 36 G6
Poix-Terron: France 36 K6
Pokaran: Rajasthan, India 58 M9
Pokataroo: N.S.W., Austl. 71 H7
Pokhara: Nepal 59 O9
Pokka: Finland 46 T2
Poko: Zaïre 76 C2
Pokochang Ho: *riv.*, Tibet, China 59 P8
Pokotu: Inner Mongolia, China 63 W5
Pokrovka: Kirgiz., U.S.S.R. 51 N6
Pokupsko: Yugoslavia 41 V10
Pokur: U.S.S.R. 51 N2
Pola (Pula): Yugoslavia 41 T11

Poland: *Republic* **42/3**
Cap.: Warsaw
Area: 120,359 sq. miles (311,730 sq. km.)
Pop.: 33,107,000 (*1972 E*)

Polanow: Poland 45 W1
Polatane: Turkey 56 F1
Polatli: Turkey 56 C2
Polcura: Chile 96 A4
Połczyn Zdrój: Poland 45 W2
Polden Hills: Som., Eng. 24 Q17
Polder, NE. & SW.: Ijsselmeer, Netherlands 44 L3
Polegate: E. Sussex, England 25 W18
Polela: *Dist.*, Natal, S. Africa 75 H4
Polesella: Italy 41 R11
Polessk: U.S.S.R. 47 R9
Polesworth: War., England 27 S14
Polevskoy: U.S.S.R. 51 K3
Polglass: Highland, Scot. 28 L3
Poli: Cameroun 81 G3
Poli: Heilungkiang, China 63 Y5
Policastro, G. of: Italy 38 Q17
Police: Czechoslovakia 45 W5
Polička: Czechoslovakia 45 W6
Poligny: France 40 L9
Polikhnitos: Lesbos, Greece 39 U17
Polillo: & *is.*, Philippines 64 G4
Polis: Cyprus 56 C4
Polivinka: U.S.S.R. 50 J3
Poliyiros: Greece 39 S16
Poljane: Yugoslavia 41 U9
Pollachi: Tamil Nadu, India 58 N12
Pollensa: Balearic Is. 35 H17
Pollington: Humb., England 27 T12
Polmak: Norway 46 V1
Polnovat: U.S.S.R. 51 L2
Polo: Ill., U.S.A. 88 G5
Polonnoye: Ukraine 43 U11
Polossu: Tibet, China 62 R8
Polotane: Turkey 56 F1
Polotsk: Byelorussia 50 C3
Polperro: Corn., England 24 M19
Polsham: Som., England 24 Q17
Polson: Mont., U.S.A. 92 E3
Poltava: Ukraine 50 D5
Poltavka: U.S.S.R. 51 M4
Polubny: Czechoslovakia 45 V5
Poludino: Kazakh., U.S.S.R. 51 L4
Polwarth: Borders, Scot. 29 R8
Polyarnyy: U.S.S.R. 46 X2
Polynesia: *geog. reg.*, Pacific Ocean 7
Poma: Argentina 96 B1
Poman: Argentina 96 B2
Pomba: *riv.*, Brazil 96 G1
Pombal: Brazil 94 K5
Pombal: Portugal 35 B17
Pomene: Mozambique 77 E7
Pomerania: *geog. reg.*, E. Ger./Poland 42 O10
Pomeranian Bay: E. Ger./Pol. 45 U1
Pomeroy: Ohio, U.S.A. 88 K6
Pomeroy: Tyr., N. Ireland 30 H10
Pomeroy: Wash., U.S.A. 92 D3
Pomona: Calif., U.S.A. 93 D6
Pomona: Queens., Australia 70 K6
Pomona: S.W. Africa 74 A3
Pomorie: Bulgaria 39 U15
Pompaelo: Roman town at Pamplona, Spain 35 F15
Pompano Beach: Fla., U.S.A. 91 L12
Pompei: Roman city near southern face of Mt. Vesuvius, Italy 38 O16
Pompeiopolis: Graeco-Roman city at Taşkopru, Turkey 56 D1
Pompeiopolis: Graeco-Roman city on Mersin bay about 2 miles SW. of Mersin, Turkey 56 D3
Pomyt: U.S.S.R. 51 L2
Ponape: *i.*, Caroline Islands 7 05N 155E
Ponca: Nebr., U.S.A. 92 H4
Ponca City: Okla., U.S.A. 90 C7
Ponce: Puerto Rico 87 N14
Ponce de Leon Bay: Fla., U.S.A. 91 L13
Ponchatoula: La., U.S.A. 90 F10
Pond Creek: *city*, Okla., U.S.A. 90 C7
Pondicherry: India 58 N12
Pond Inlet: *town*, N.W.T., Canada 85 M3
Pondoland: *geog. reg.*, S. Afr. 75 H5
Pondosa: Calif., U.S.A. 92 C4
Ponérihouen: New Caledonia, Pacific Ocean 67 N6
Ponferrada: Spain 35 C15
Pongaroa: North I., N.Z. 70 Q15
Pongo: *riv.*, Sudan 76 C1
Pongola: *riv.*, Natal, S. Africa 75 J3
Pongola: *riv.*, Trans., S. Afr. 75 G1
Poniec: Poland 45 W4
Ponnani: Tamil Nadu, India 58 N12
Ponomarevka: U.S.S.R. 50 H4
Ponorogo: Java 65 E8
Ponoy: Karelian A.S.S. Rep., U.S.S.R. 48 F4
Pons: France 37 E10
Pons: Spain 35 G16
Pons Aelii: Roman bridge and fort of Hadrian's Wall on river Tyne at Newcastle, Northumb., Eng. 26 S10
Pontacq: France 37 E12
PONTA DELGADA: São Miguel I., Azores Is., Portugal 78 *Ins.*
Ponta Grossa: Brazil 96 E2
Pontailler: France 40 L8
Pont-à-Mousson: France 40 M7
Ponta Porã: Brazil 95 F8
Pontardawe: W. Glam., Wales 24 O16
Pontardulais: W. Glam., Wales 24 N16
Pontarlier: France 40 M9
Pontassieve: Italy 41 R12
Pontaubault: France 36 D7
Pont-Audemer: France 36 F6
Pontamur: France 37 H10
Pont-Aven: France 36 B8
Pont Canavese: Italy 40 N10
Pontchartrain, Lake: La., U.S.A. 90 F10
Pont Château: France 36 C8
Pont-Croix: France 36 A7
Pont-d'Ain: France 40 L9
Pont-de-Beauvoisin: France 40 L10
Pont-de-l'Arche: France 36 G6
Pont-de-Roide: France 40 M8
Pont-de-Salars: France 37 H11
Pont-de-Veyle: France 37 K9
Pont du Chetiff (Sidi bel Atar): Algeria 35 G18
Ponte: Italy 40 P9
Pontebba: Italy 41 T9
Ponte da Barca: Portugal 35 B16
Ponte dell' Olio: Italy 40 P11
Pontedera: Italy 40 Q12
Ponte di Legno: Italy 40 Q9
Pontefract: W. Yorks., Eng. 27 T12
Ponteix: Sask., Canada 92 F3
Ponteland: Northumb., England 26 S9
Ponte Leccia: Corsica 38 L15
Ponte Nova: Brazil 94 J8
Pont-en-Royans: France 40 L10
Ponterwyd: Dyfed, Wales 25 O15
Ponte San Martino: Italy 40 N10
Ponte San Pietro: Italy 40 P10
Pontesbury: Salop, England 27 Q14
PONTEVEDRA: & *Prov.*, Spain 35 B15
Pont-Faverger: France 36 K6
Pontgibaud: France 37 H10
Pontiac: Ill., U.S.A. 88 G5
Pontiac: Mich., U.S.A. 88 K4
Pontianak: Borneo 65 D7
Pontian Besar: Malaya, Malaysia 65 c13
Pontine Is.: Italy 38 N16
Pontivy: France 36 C7
Pont-l'Abbé: France 36 A8
Pont-l'Évêque: France 36 F6
Pontlottyn: Mid Glam., Wales 24 P16
Pontnewydd: Gwent, Wales 24 P16
PONTOISE: Val-d'Oise, France 36 H6
Ponton, Great: Lincs., Eng. 27 U14
Pontoon: Mayo, Repub. of Ireland 30 C12
Pontorson: France 36 D7
Pontotoc: Mass., U.S.A. 90 G8
Pontoux: France 37 E12
Pontremoli: Italy 40 P11
Pontresina: Switzerland 40 P9
Pontrieux: France 36 B7
Pontrilas: Hereford & Worcester, England 24 Q16
Pont-St.-Esprit: France 37 K11
Pont-sur-Yonne: France 36 J7
Pontus: ancient name of district of Turkey E. of *Paphlagonia* on Black Sea coast 56 D1
Pontvallain: France 36 F8
Pontypool: Gwent, Wales 24 P16
Pontypridd: Mid Glam., Wales 24 P16
Pool: W. Yorks., England 27 S12
Poole: Dorset, England 24 S18
Poolewe: High., Scot. 28 K4
Pooley Bridge: Cumbria, England 26 Q10
Pool Malebo (Stanley Pool): *lake*, River Congo (Zaire) 81 H5
Pool of Muckhart: *village*, Tayside, Scotland 29 O7
Poona: *see* Pune
Poonboon (Stony Crossing): N.S.W., Australia 71 E10
Pooncarie: N.S.W., Austl. 71 E9
Poopó, Lake: Bolivia 94 D7
Poor Knights I.: N.Z. 70 P12
Poorman: Alaska, U.S.A. 84 D5
Poortjie: S. Africa 74 E5
Popakai: Surinam 94 F3
Popayán: Colombia 94 B3
Poperinghe: Belgium 36 H5
Popigay: U.S.S.R. 49 N3
Poplar: Mont., U.S.A. 92 F3
Poplar Bluff: Mo., U.S.A. 88 F7
Poplar Hill: Ont., Canada 92 J2
Poplarville: Miss., U.S.A. 90 G10
Popocatepetl: *volc.*, Mexico 86 K14
Popokabaka: Zaïre 88 H6
Popoli: Italy 38 N15
Popovo: Bulgaria 39 U15
Poppleton, Nether: N. Yorks., England 27 S12
Poprad: Czechoslovakia 43 R12
Porali: *riv.*, Baluchistan, Pak. 58 L9
Porangahau: North I., N.Z. 70 Q15
Porbandar: Gujarat, India 58 L10
Porcher, I.: B.C., Canada 92 A2
Porcupine: *riv.*, Alaska, U.S.A. 84 e4
Porcupine Mtn.: Sask./Man., Canada 92 G2
Pordic: France 36 C7
Poreč: Yugoslavia 41 T10
Poretskoye: U.S.S.R. 50 G3
Porga: Benin 80 E2
Pori (Björneborg): Finland 47 R6
Poritsk: Ukraine 43 T11
Porjus: Sweden 46 Q3
Porkhov: U.S.S.R. 50 C3
Porkkala: Finland 47 T7
Porlamar: Venezuela 94 E1
Porlock: Som., England 24 O17
Pornic: France 36 C8
Pornichet: France 36 C8
Porolissum: Roman town about 10 miles E. of Zalău, Romania 43 S13
Poronaysk: U.S.S.R. 49 Q8
Porpac: Hungary 41 W8
Porquerolles, Île de: *i.*, Îles de Hyères, France 40 M12
Porrentruy: Switzerland 40 N8
Porreta Terme: Italy 41 Q11
Porsanger Fiord: Norway 46 T1
Porsgrunn: Norway 47 L7
Porspoder: France 36 A7
Porsuk: *riv.*, Turkey 56 B2
Port: Louth, Repub. of Irel. 30 J12
Portachuelo: Bolivia 94 E7
Portacloy: Mayo, Repub. of Ireland 30 B11
Port Adelaide: S. Australia 71 C10
Portadown: Armagh, N. Irel. 30 J11
Portaferry: Down, N. Irel. 30 K11
Portage: Pa., U.S.A. 89 M5
Portage: Wis., U.S.A. 88 G4
Portage du Fort: Que., Can. 89 N3
Portage la Prairie: Man., Canada 92 H2
Portageville: Mo., U.S.A. 88 G7
Portal, El: Calif., U.S.A. 93 D5
Port Alberni: B.C., Canada 92 C3
Port Albert: Vict., Australia 71 G12
PORTALEGRE: Alto Alentejo, Portugal 35 C17
Portales: N. Mex., U.S.A. 93 G6
Port Alfred: Que., Canada 89 Q1
Port Alfred: S. Africa 75 G6
Port Alice: B.C., Canada 92 B2
Port Allan: O.F.S., S. Afr. 75 G4
Port Allegany: Pa., U.S.A. 89 M5
Port Allen: La., U.S.A. 90 F10
Port Alma: Queens., Austl. 70 J4
Port Angeles: Wash., U.S.A. 92 C3
Port Ann: *village*, Strathclyde, Scotland 29 L7
Port Antonio: Jamaica 86 *Ins.*
Port Appin: Strath., Scot. 29 L6
Portarlington: Laois/Offaly, Repub. of Ireland 31 G13
Port Arthur: La., U.S.A. 90 E11
Port Arthur: Tas., Australia 68 H8
Port Arthur: Tex., U.S.A. 90 E11
Port Askaig: Inner Hebr., Scotland 29 J8
Port Augusta: S. Australia 71 B9
Port-au-Port Penin.: Newf., Canada 85 t2
PORT-AU-PRINCE: Haiti 87 m14
Port Austin: Mich., U.S.A. 88 K3
Port-aux-Basques: Newf., Canada 85 t3
Portavogie: Down, N. Irel. 30 K11
Portbail: France 36 D6
Port Ballintrae: Antrim, N. Ireland 30 H9
Port Bannatyne: Strathclyde, Scotland 29 L8
Port Beaufort: S. Africa 74 D7
Port Bell: Uganda 76 D2
Port Bergé: Malagasy Rep. 73 O13
PORT BLAIR: Andaman & Nicobar Is. 59 Q12
Port Bordon: P.E.I., Canada 89 U2
Port Bou: Spain 37 J13
Port Bouet: Ivory Coast 80 D3
Port Brabant (Tuktoyaktuk): N.W.T., Canada 84 f4
Port Broughton: S. Austl. 71 B9
Port Burwell: Que., Canada 85 n5
Port Campbell: Vict., Austl. 71 E12
Port Chalmers: South I., N.Z. 71 N17
Port Charlotte: Inner Hebr., Scotland 29 J8
Port Chester: N.Y., U.S.A. 89 P5
Port Clinton: Ohio, U.S.A. 88 K5
Port Clinton: *harbour*, Queens., Australia 70 J4
Port Colborne: Ont., Can. 89 M4
Port Cros, Île de: *i.*, Îles de Hyères, France 40 M12
Port Curtis: Queens., Austl. 70 J4
Port Daniel: Que., Canada 89 T1
Port-de-Bouc: France 37 K12
Port de Paix: Haiti 87 m14
Port-de-Piles, Le: France 36 F9
Port Dickson: Malaya, Malaysia 65 b12
Port Dinorwic: Gwyn., Wales 27 N13
Port Douglas: Queens., Australia 69 H3
Port Dover: Ont., Canada 88 L4
Port Durnford: Natal, S. Afr. 75 J4
Port Eads: La., U.S.A. 90 *Ins.*
Port Edwards: Wis., U.S.A. 88 G3
Portel: Brazil 94 G4
Port Elgin: N.B., Canada 89 T2
Port Elizabeth: S. Africa 75 F6
Port Ellen: Inner Hebr., Scotland 29 J8
Port Elphinstone: Grampian, Scotland 28 R5
Porteña: Argentina 96 C3
Port Erin: I. of Man., U.K. 26 M11
Port Erroll: Gram., Scotland 28 S5
Porterville: Calif., U.S.A. 93 D5
Porterville: S. Africa 74 C6
Portesham: Dorset, England 24 Q18
Portessie: Gram., Scotland 28 Q4
Port Essington: B.C., Can. 92 B2
Port Etienne: *see* Nouadhibou.
Port-Eynon: West Glam., Wales 24 N16
Portezuelo: Chile 96 A2
Port Fairy: Vict., Australia 71 E12
Port Fu'ad: Egypt (Suez Canal *Inset*) 32 *Ins.*
PORT GENTIL: Ogooué-Maritime, Gabon 81 F5
Port Germein: S. Australia 71 C9
Port Gibson: Miss., U.S.A. 90 F10
Port Glasgow: Strath., Scot. 29 M8
Portglenone: Antrim, N. Irel. 30 J10
Portgordon: Gram., Scotland 28 P4
PORT HARCOURT: Rivers, Nigeria 81 F4
Port Hardy: B.C., Canada 92 B2
Port Harrison: *see* Inoucdjouac.
Port Hawkesbury: Cape Breton I., Canada 89 V3
Porthcawl: Mid Glam., Wales 24 O17
Port Hedland: W. Australia 68 B4
Port Henry: N.Y., U.S.A. 89 P3
Porthleven: Cornwall, England 25 L19
Port Hood: Cape Breton I., Canada 89 V2
Port Hope: Ont., Canada 89 M4
Porthtowan: Corn., England 24 L19
Port Huron: Mich., U.S.A. 88 K4
Port Il'yicha: Azerbaydzhan, U.S.S.R. 57 L2
Portimão: Portugal 35 B18
Portimo: Finland 46 U3
Portinnisherrich: Strathclyde, Scotland 29 L7
Port Isaac: Corn., England 24 M18
Portishead: Avon, England 24 Q17
Port Jackson: N.S.W., Australia 71 J9
Port Jervis: N.Y., U.S.A. 89 O5
Port Kelang: Malaya, Malaysia 65 b12
Port Kembla: N.S.W., Austl. 71 J10
Port Kennedy: Thursday I., Queens., Australia 69 G2
Portknockie: Gram., Scotland 28 Q4
Portland: Ind., U.S.A. 88 J5
Portland: Maine, U.S.A. 89 Q4
Portland: Mich., U.S.A. 88 J4
Portland: N.S.W., Australia 71 H9
Portland: Oreg., U.S.A. 92 C3
Portland: Tenn., U.S.A. 88 H7
Portland: Vict., Australia 71 D12
Portland, Isle of: Dorset, England 24 R18
Portland Bill: *cape*, Dorset, England 24 R18
Portland Promontory: Que., Canada 85 M6
Portland Reef: Tuamotu Arch. 83 h4
PORT LAOISE (Maryborough): Laois, Repub. of Ireland 31 G13
Port Lavaca: Tex., U.S.A. 90 C11
Portlaw: Wat., Repub. of Ireland 31 G15
Portlethen: Gram., Scotland 28 R5
Port Lincoln: S. Australia 70 A10
Port Logan: Dumfries & Galloway, Scotland 29 M10
Port Loko: Sierra Leone 80 B3
Port MacDonnell: S. Austl. 71 D12
Port Macquarie: N.S.W., Australia 71 K8
Portmadoc: Gwynedd, Wales 27 N14
Portmagee: Kerry, Repub. of Ireland 31 A16
Portmahomack: High., Scot. 28 O4
Port Maria: Jamaica 86 *Ins.*
Portmarnock: Dublin, Repub. of Ireland 30 J13
Port Menier: Que., Canada 85 n8
Port Morant: Jamaica 86 *Ins.*
PORT MORESBY: Papua New Guinea 69 H1
Portmuck: Antrim, N. Irel. 30 K10
Portnacroish: Strath., Scot. 29 L6
Portnahaven: Inner Hebr., Scotland 29 H8
Port Neches: Tex., U.S.A. 90 E11
Port Nelson: Man., Canada 92 J1
Port Nolloth: S. Africa 74 B4
Port-Nouveau-Quebec: Que., Canada 85 N6
Porto: Corsica 38 L15
Porto (Oporto): Douro, Portugal 35 B16
PÔRTO ALEGRE: Rio Grande do Sul, Brazil 96 E3
Porto Alexandre: Angola 73 G13
Porto Amboim: Angola 73 G12
PORTO AMÉLIA: *see* PEMBA
Portobello: Lothian, Scot. 29 P8
Porto Botte: Sardinia 38 L17
Pôrto Britânia: Brazil 96 E1
Pôrto Camargo (Pôrto Xavier): Brazil 96 E1
Porto Ceresio: Italy 40 O10
Porto Civitanova: Italy 38 N15
Pôrto Dantas: Brazil 96 E2
Porto d'Ascoli: Italy 38 N15
Pôrto de Mos: Portugal 35 B17
Pôrto de Móz: Brazil 94 G4
Porto di Malamocco: Italy 41 S10
Porto dos Cajueiros: Brazil 94 H6
Porto Empedocle: Sicily 38 N18
Pôrto Esperança: Brazil 94 F7
Porto Farina: Tunisia 38 M18
Portoferraio: Elba, Italy 38 M15
Portofino: Italy 40 P11
Port of Menteith: Central, Scotland 29 N7
PORT-OF-SPAIN: Trinidad 87 c5
Porto Garibaldi: Italy 41 S11
Porto Grande: Cape Verde Is. 78 *Ins.*
Portogruaro: Italy 41 S10
Pôrto Guaíra: Brazil 96 E1
Portola: Calif., U.S.A. 93 C5
Porto Lago: Greece 39 T16
Pôrto Lucena: Brazil 96 E2
Portomaggiore: Italy 41 R11
Pôrto Mendes: Brazil 96 E1
Pôrto Murtinho: Brazil 95 F8
Porton: Wilts., England 25 S17
Pôrto Nacional: Brazil 94 H6
PORTO NOVO: Benin 81 E3
Pôrto Occulto: Brazil 96 E1
Porto Recanati: Italy 41 T12
Porto San Stefano: Italy 38 M15
Pôrto Santa Helena: Brazil 96 E1
Porto Santo: *i.*, (Port.), Atl. O. 78 A3
Pôrto São José: Brazil 96 E1
Portoscuso: Sardinia 38 L17
Pôrto Seguro: Brazil 94 K7
Porto Tolle: Italy 41 S11
Porto Torres: Sardinia 38 L16
Pôrto União: Brazil 96 E2
Pôrto Válter: Brazil 94 C5
Porto Vecchio: & *gulf*, Corsica 38 L16
PÔRTO VELHO: Rondônia, Brazil 94 E5
Portovenere: Italy 40 P11
Portoviejo: Ecuador 94 A4
Pôrto Xavier: *see* Pôrto Camargo.
Portpatrick: Dumfries & Galloway, Scotland 29 L10
Port Perry: Ont., Canada 89 M3
Port Phillip Bay: Vict., Austl. 71 F12
Port Pirie: S. Australia 71 C9
Port Radium: N.W.T., Can. 84 H4
Portreath: Corn., England 24 L19
Portree: Inner Hebr., Scot. 28 J5
Portroe: Tip., Rep. of Ireland 31 E14
Port Royal Sound: S.C., U.S.A. 91 L9
Portrush: Antrim, N. Ireland 30 H9
Port Safaga: Egypt 54 D9
Port Said: Egypt (Suez Canal *Inset*) 32 *Ins.*
Port St. Joe: Fla., U.S.A. 91 J11
Port St. Johns: *see* Umzimvubu
Port St. Louis: France 37 K12
Port St. Mary: *village*, I. of Man, U.K. 26 M11
Portsalon: Don., Repub. of Ireland 30 F9
Port Samson: W. Austl. 68 B4
Port Saunders: Newf., Can. 85 u1
Port Shepstone: & *Dist.*, Natal, S. Africa 75 J5
Port Simpson: B.C., Canada 92 A2
Portskewett: Gwent, Wales 24 Q16
Portslade: W. Sussex, England 25 V18
Portsmouth: Dominica, Windward Is. 87 c3
Portsmouth: Hants., Eng. 25 T18
Portsmouth: N.H., U.S.A. 89 Q4
Portsmouth: Ohio, U.S.A. 88 K6
Portsmouth: Va., U.S.A. 89 N7
Portsonachan: Strath., Scot. 29 L7
Portsoy: Grampian, Scotland 28 Q4
Port Stanley: Ont., Canada 88 L4
Portstewart: Lon., N. Irel. 30 H9
PORT SUDAN: Red Sea, Sudan 54 E11
Port Sulphur: La., U.S.A. 90 *Ins.*
Port Talbot: W. Glam., Wales 24 O16
Port Tampa: Fla., U.S.A. 91 K12
Port Taufiq: Egypt (Suez Canal *Inset*) 32 *Ins.*
Port Townsend: Wash., U.S.A. 92 C3

Portugal: *Republic* **35 B17**
Cap.: Lisbon (Lisboa)
Area: 35,340 sq. miles (91,531 sq. km.)
Pop.: 8,668,267 (*1970 C*)

Portugalia: Angola 76 B4
Portuguese Timor: now incorporated into Indonesia
Portumna: Galway, Repub. of Ireland 31 E13
Port-Vendres: France 37 J13
Port Victoria: S. Australia 71 B10
Port Vladimir: U.S.S.R. 46 X2
Port Wakefield: S. Australia 71 C10
Port Weld: Malaya, Malaysia 65 b11
Port William: Dumfries & Galloway, Scotland 29 M10
Portyerrock: Dumfries & Galloway, Scotland 29 N10
Porus: Jamaica 86 *Ins.*
Porvenir: Chile 95 C14
Porvenir, El: Tex., U.S.A. 93 F6
Porvoo (Borga): Finland 47 T6
POSADAS: Misiones, Arg. 96 D2
Posadas: Spain 35 D18
Poseh: Kwangsi Chuang, China 62 T10
Poshan: Shantung, China 62 V7
Poshva: U.S.S.R. 50 J3
Posi: Yunnan, China 62 S10
Posidonia: Greek colony in S. Campania, later known as *Paestum* (q.v.). 38 O16
Pösing: W. Germany 45 S6
Posio: Finland 46 V3
Poso: & *lake*, Celebes 65 G7
Posof: Turkey 57 H1
Possel: Cen. Afr. Rep. 76 A1
Possneck: E. Germany 45 R5
Possum Kingdom Reservoir: Tex., U.S.A. 90 B9
Post: Tex., U.S.A. 93 G6
Postavy: Byelorussia 47 U9
Poste-de-la-Baleine: Que., Canada 85 M6
Poste Maurice Cortier (Bidon 5): Algeria 78 E5
Postillon Is.: Indonesia 65 F8
Postmasburg: S. Africa 74 E4
Postojna: Yugoslavia 41 U10
Potaissa: Roman colony at Turda, Romania 43 S13
Potamos: Andikithira, Grc. 39 S19
Potaro Landing: Guyana 87 d8
Potash: La., U.S.A. 90 *Ins.*
Potchefstroom: & *Dist.*, Trans., S. Africa 75 G3
Poteau: Okla., U.S.A. 90 D8
Poteet: Tex., U.S.A. 90 B11
POTENZA: Basilicata, Italy 38 O16
Potenza: The Marches, Italy 41 T12
Poteque: Mozambique 75 K2
Potes: Spain 35 D15
Potfontein: S. Africa 75 F5
Potgietersrus: & *Dist.*, Trans., S. Africa 75 H2
Poti: Georgia, U.S.S.R. 50 F6
Potidaea: Greek city on isthmus at head of Kassándra pensinsula, Greece 39 S16
Potiskum: Nigeria 81 G2
Potlatch: Idaho, U.S.A. 92 D3
Potomac: *riv.*, U.S.A. 89 N6
Potosi: Bolivia 94 D7
Potosi: Mo., U.S.A. 88 F7
Pototan: Panay, Philippines 64 G4
Potrerillos: Chile 96 B2
Potrincourt Lake: Que., Can. 89 O1
Potro, Cerro del: Chile/Arg. 96 B2
POTSDAM: & *Dist.*, E. Germany 45 T3
Potsdam: N.Y., U.S.A. 89 O3
Potsdam: S. Africa 75 G6
Potter Hanworth: Lincs., England 27 V13
Potter Heigham: Norf., England 25 Z14
Potters Bar: Herts., Eng. 25 V16
Pottmes: W. Germany 41 R7
Potton: Beds., England 25 V15
Pottsdown: Pa., U.S.A. 89 O5
Pottsville: Pa., U.S.A. 89 N5
Pottuvil: Sri Lanka 58 O13
Pouancé: France 36 D8
Pouce Coupé: B.C., Canada 92 C1
Poughkeepsie: N.Y., U.S.A. 89 P5
Pouilly: France 36 H8
Pouilly-en-Auxois: France 36 K8
Pouilly-sous-Charlieu: Fr. 37 K9
Poulton le Fylde: Lancs., England 27 P12
Poundstock: Corn., England 24 M18
Poupan: S. Africa 75 F5
Pouso Alegre: Brazil 96 F1
Poussé: Cameroun 81 G2
Poussu: Finland 46 V4
Poutrincourt L.: Que., Can. 89 O1
Pouzauges: France 37 E9
Povijana: Yugoslavia 41 V11
Póvoa de Varzim: Portugal 35 B16
Povungnituk: Que., Canada 85 M6
Powassan: Ont., Canada 89 M2
Powder: *riv.*, U.S.A. 92 F4
Powell: Wyo., U.S.A. 92 F4
Powell, Lake: Ariz./Utah, U.S.A. 93 E5
Powick: Hereford & Worcester, England 24 R15
Powys: *Co.*, Wales (*co. town* Llandrindod Wells) 24 P15

For Abbreviations see list on p.113. Italic type, e.g. *Ephesus*, refers to historical names not on maps. Capital letters, e.g. MADRID, show capitals of countries; small capital letters, e.g. CADIZ, show capitals of provinces, etc. General notes p.116.

178 Powys, Vale of—Queanbeyan

Powys, Vale of: Powys, Wales **27** P14
Powys Castle: Powys, Wales **27** P14
Poxoreu: Brazil **94** G7
Poyang (Jaochow): Kiangsi, China **62** V9
Poyang, Lake: Kiangsi, China **62** V9
Poyntzpass: Armagh, N. Irel. **30** J11
Poyraz: Turkey (Bosporus. *Inset)* **20** *Ins.*
Poza de la Sal: Spain **35** E15
Pozanti: Turkey **56** D3
Požarevac: Yugoslavia **39** R14
Požega: Croatia, Yugo. **38** P14
Požega: Serbia, Yugoslavia **39** R15
Pozhva: U.S.S.R. **50** J3
POZNAŃ: & *Prov.*, Poland **43** P10
Pozo Almonte: Chile **94** D8
Pozoblanco: Spain **35** D17
Pozos: Mexico **86** j13
Pozzuoli: Italy **38** O16
Pra: *riv.*, Ghana **80** D3
Pracchia: Italy **41** Q11
Prachatice: Czechoslovakia **45** T6
Prachin Buri: Thailand **64** C4
Prachuap Khirikhan: Thailand **64** B4
Pradelles: France **37** J11
Prades: France **37** H13
Præneste: ancient Latin city, later Roman colony, about 23 miles ESE. of Rome. **38** N16
Prägarten: Austria **41** U7
Pragersko: Yugoslavia **41** V9
PRAGUE (Praha): Siredočesky, Czech. **45** U5
Prahovo: Romania **39** S14
Prai: Malaya, Malaysia **65** b11
PRAIA: Cape Verde Is. **78** *Ins.*
Praid: Romania **43** T13
Prainha: Brazil **94** G4
Prairie: Queens., Australia **69** G4
Prairie City: Oreg., U.S.A. **92** D4
Prairie Dog Town Fork: *riv.*, Tex./Okla., U.S.A. **90** A8
Prairie du Chien: *city*, Wis., U.S.A. **88** F4
Pralognan: France **40** M10
Pran Buri: Thailand **64** B4
Prata: Brazil **94** H7
Pratas: *i.*, (China), S. China Sea **64** F2
Prato: Italy **41** R12
Pratolino: Italy **41** R12
Pratomagno: *valley*, Italy **41** R12
Prats-de-Mollo: France **37** H13
Pratt: Kans., U.S.A. **90** B7
Pravia: Spain **35** C15
Prawle Point: *cape*, Devon, England **24** O19
Prazzo: Italy **40** N11
Pre: Cambodia 64 D4
Préchac: France **37** E11
Précy: France **36** K8
Predazzo: Italy **41** R9
Predgornoye: Kazakh., U.S.S.R. **51** O4
Predivinsk: U.S.S.R. **51** Q3
Preeceville: Sask., Canada **92** G2
Pré-en-Pail: France **36** E7
Prees: Salop, England **27** Q14
Preesall: Lancs., England **27** Q12
Preetz: W. Germany **45** Q1
Préfailles: France **36** C8
Pregolya: *riv.*, U.S.S.R. **47** R9
Preignac: France **37** E11
Preko: Yugoslavia **41** V11
Přelouč: Czechoslovakia **45** V5
Prémery: France **36** J8
Premuda: *i.*, Yugoslavia **41** U11
Prenai: Lithuania, U.S.S.R. **47** S9
Prenzlau: E. Germany **45** T2
Preparis: *i.*, (India), Indian Ocean **59** Q12
Preparis North Chan.: Indian O. **59** Q11
Preparis South Chan.: Indian O. **59** Q12
Prerov: Czechoslovakia **43** P12
Prerow: E. Germany **45** S1
Pré St. Didier: Italy **40** M10
Presanella, Cima: *mtn.*, Italy **41** Q9
Prescot: Mers., England **27** Q13
Prescott: Ariz., U.S.A. **93** E6
Prescott: Ark., U.S.A. **90** E9
Prescott: Ont., Canada **89** O3
Preseglie: Italy **40** Q10
Presevo: Yugoslavia **39** R15
Presidencia Roca: Arg. **96** D2
Presidente de la Plaza: Arg. **96** D2
Presidente Dutra: Brazil **94** J5
Presidente Epitácio: Brazil **95** G8
Presidente Frei: *rsch. stn.*, Antarctica **9** 65S 60W
Presidente Prudente: Brazil **95** G8
Presidente Roque Sáenz Peña: Argentina **96** C2
Président Thiers Reef: Austral Is. **83** f4
Presidio: Tex., U.S.A. **93** G7
Preslav: Bulgaria **39** U15
Presnogor'kovka: U.S.S.R. **51** L4
Prešov: Czechoslovakia **43** R12
Prespa Lake: Yugoslavia/Greece/Albania **39** R16
Presque Isle: *city*, Maine, U.S.A. **89** R2
Pressac: France **37** F9
Pressath: W. Germany **44** R6
Pressburg: German name of Czechoslovak town of Bratislava **43** P12
Prestatyn: Clwyd, Wales **27** P13
Prestbury: Ches., England **27** R13
Prestbury: Glos., England **24** R16
Prestea: Ghana **80** D3
Presteigne: Powys, Wales **24** P15
Přeštice: Czechoslovakia **45** T6
Preston: Herts., England **25** V16
Preston: Humb., England **27** V12
Preston: Idaho, U.S.A. **92** E4
PRESTON: Lancs., England **27** Q12
Preston: Leics., England **27** U14
Preston: Mo., U.S.A. **88** E7
Preston Candover: Hants., England **25** T17
Preston on the Hill: Ches., England **27** Q13
Prestonpans: Loth., Scot. **29** Q8
Prestonsburg: Ky., U.S.A. **88** K7
Prestwich: Gt. Man., Eng. **27** R12
Prestwick: Strath., Scotland **29** M9
Prestwick: *airfield*, Strathclyde, Scotland **29** M8
Prestwood: Bucks., England **25** U16
PRETORIA: & *Dist.*, Trans., S. Africa **75** H2
Pretoria North: Trans., S. Africa **75** H2
Pretoriuskop: Trans., S. Africa **75** J2
Preuilly-sur-Claise: France **37** F9
Prevalje: Yugoslavia **41** U9
Preveza: Greece **39** R17
Prezid: Yugoslavia **41** U10
Pribilof Is.: (U.S.A.), Bering Sea **84** C6
Pribinjć: Yugoslavia **38** P14
Priboj: Yugoslavia **39** Q15
Pribram: Czechoslovakia **45** U6
Price, Cape: Andaman Is. **59** Q12
Prich': & *riv.*, Byelorussia **43** V10
Prichard: Ala., U.S.A. **90** G10
Prickwillow: Cambs., Eng. **25** W15
Priego: Spain **34** E16
Priekule: Latvia, U.S.S.R. **47** R8
Prien: W. Germany **41** S8
Priene: Greek city on right bank of river *Maeander* (Menderes) about 5 miles N. of its mouth, Turkey **39** U18
Prieska: & *Dist.*, S. Africa **74** E4
Priest River: Idaho, U.S.A. **92** D3
Prijedor: Yugoslavia **38** P14
Prijepolje: Yugoslavia **39** Q15
Prikumsk: U.S.S.R. **50** F6
Prilep: Yugoslavia **39** R16
Priluki: Ukraine **50** D4
Přimda: Czechoslovakia **45** S6
Primeiras I.: Mozambique **77** E6
Primero: *riv.*, Argentina **96** C3
Primis: ancient Ethiopian, later Roman, fort about 75 miles N. of Wadi Halfa. **54** D10
Primorsk: U.S.S.R. **47** V6
Primorsk: *Terr.*, U.S.S.R. (*cap.* Vladivostok) **63** Y6
Primrose Lake: Sask., Can. **92** F2
Prince Albert: Sask., Canada **92** F2
Prince Albert: & *Dist.*, S. Africa **74** E6
Prince Albert Nat. Park: Sask., Canada **92** F2
Prince Albert Penin.: N.W.T., Canada **84** H3
Prince Albert Road: S. Afr. **74** D6
Prince Albert Sound: N.W.T., Canada **84** H3
Prince Alfred, Cape: N.W.T., Canada **84** g3
Prince Alfred's Hamlet: S. Afr. **74** C6
Prince Charles I.: N.W.T., Canada **85** M4
Prince Edward I.: *Prov.*, Canada (*cap.* Charlottetown) **89** U2
Prince Edward Is.: (S. Afr.), Indian Ocean **9** 50S 35E
Prince Edward I. Nat. Park: P.E.I., Canada **89** U2
Prince George: B.C., Can. **92** C2
Prince Gustaf Adolf Sea: N.W.T., Canada **84** J2
Prince of Wales I.: Alaska, U.S.A. **84** f6
Prince of Wales I.: Australia **69** G2
Prince of Wales I.: N.W.T., Canada **84** K3
Prince of Wales Str.: N.W.T., Canada **84** H3
Prince Patrick I.: N.W.T., Canada **84** g2
Prince Regent Inlet: N.W.T., Canada **85** k3
Prince Rupert: B.C., Can. **91** A2
Princes Risborough: Bucks., England **25** U16
Princess Anne: Md., U.S.A. **89** O6
Princess Royal I.: B.C., Can. **92** B2
Princes Town: Trinidad **87** c5
Princeton: B.C., Canada **92** C3
Princeton: Ill., U.S.A. **88** G5
Princeton: Ind., U.S.A. **88** H6
Princeton: Ky., U.S.A. **88** H7
Princeton: Minn., U.S.A. **88** E3
Princeton: Mo., U.S.A. **93** J4
Princeton: N.J., U.S.A. **89** O5
Princeton: W. Va., U.S.A. **88** L7
Princetown: Devon, Eng. **24** O18
Prince William Sound: Alaska, U.S.A. **84** E5
Princhester: Queens., Austl. **70** J4
Principe: *i.* G. of Guinea [*cap.* (with São Tomé) São Tomé] **81** F4
Prineville: Oreg., U.S.A. **92** C4
Prinzapolca: Nicaragua **87** I15
Priors Marston: War., Eng. **25** T15
Priozernyy: Kazakh., U.S.S.R. **51** O5
Priozersk: U.S.S.R. **47** W6
Pripet (Pripyat): *riv.*, U.S.S.R. **50** D4
Pripet Marshes: U.S.S.R. **43** U10
Prishibinskoe: Azerbaydzhan, U.S.S.R. **57** L2
Priština: Yugoslavia **39** R15
Pritech: Kazakh., U.S.S.R. **51** M4
Pritzerbe: E. Germany **45** S3
Pritzwalk: E. Germany **45** S2
PRIVAS: Ardèche, France **37** K11
Privelzhye: U.S.S.R. **50** G4
Privol'noye: Ukraine **50** D5
Priyutnoye: U.S.S.R. **50** F5
Prizren: Yugoslavia **39** R15
Prizzi: Sicily **38** N18
Prnjavor: Yugoslavia **38** P14
Probolinggo: Java **65** E8
Probus: Corn., England **24** M19
Proctor: Minn., U.S.A. **88** E2
Proctor Point: *cape*, La., U.S.A. **90** *Ins.*
Progreso: Mexico **86** L13
Progreso, El: Guatemala **86** k14
Progresso: Brazil **94** C5
Prokhladnyy: U.S.S.R. **50** F6
Prokopyevsk: U.S.S.R. **51** P4
Prokuplje: Yugoslavia **39** R15
Proletariy: U.S.S.R. **50** D3
Propontis: ancient name for the S. of Marmara, Tur. **39** V16
Propriá: Brazil **94** K6
Propriano: Corsica **38** L16
Prorer Bay: Rügen, E. Germany **45** T1
Proserpine: Queens., Austl. **70** H3
Prosna: *riv.*, Poland **43** P11
Prosopitis: Greek name of upper section of Nile Delta in angle between Rosetta and Damietta arms, Egypt **56** B6
Prosperous: Kild., Repub. of Ireland **31** H13
Prosser: Wash., U.S.A. **92** D3
Prostějov: Czechoslovakia **43** P12
Proston: Queens., Australia **70** J6
Protea: Trans., S. Africa **74** M *Ins.*
Protem: S. Africa **74** D7
Protivín: Czechoslovakia **45** U6
Prouille: France **37** H12
Provadiya: Bulgaria **39** U15
Prøven: Greenland **85** O3
Provence: *Prov.*, France **34** K15
Provence Alps: France **40** L12
Providence: Ky., U.S.A. **88** H7
PROVIDENCE: R.I., U.S.A. **89** Q5
Providence: Utah, U.S.A. **92** E4
Providence, Cape: N.W.T., Canada **84** h3
Providence, Cape: South I., New Zealand **71** L18
Providence Mtns.: Calif., U.S.A. **93** D6
Providencia: *i.*, (Col.), Caribbean Sea **87** I15
Provincetown: Mass., U.S.A. **89** Q4
Provins: France **36** J7
Provo: Utah, U.S.A. **93** E4
Provost: Alta., Canada **92** E2
Prudentópolis: Brazil **96** E2
Prudhoe: Northumb., Eng. **26** S10
Prudnik: Poland **43** Q11
Prüm: & *riv.*, W. Germany **44** M5
Prusa: Graeco-Roman city at Bursa, Turkey **39** V16
Pruszków: Poland **43** R10
Prut: *riv.*, U.S.S.R./Rom. **33** H2
Pruzhany: Byelorussia **43** T10
Przasnysz: Poland **43** R10
Przedborz: Poland **43** Q11
Przemków: Poland **45** V4
Przemyśl: Poland **43** S12
Przeworsk: Poland **43** S11
Przewoz: Poland **45** U4
Przheval'sk: Kirgiz., U.S.S.R. **51** N6
Psara: *i.*, Greece **39** T17
Pskent: Uzbek., U.S.S.R. **51** L6
PSKOV: & *Reg.*, U.S.S.R. **50** C3
Pskov, Lake: U.S.S.R. **47** U7
Pszczyna: Poland **43** Q12
Ptolemais: Greece **39** R16
Ptuj: Yugoslavia **41** V9
Puah: I.: Celebes **65** G7
Puan: Argentina **96** C4
Pucallpa: Peru **94** C5
Pucheng: Fukien, China **62** V9
Puchow: Shansi, China **62** U8
Puck: Poland **43** Q9
Puckaun: Tip., Repub. of Irel. **31** E14
Pucklechurch: Avon, England **24** R17
Pudasjärvi: Finland **46** U4
Puddington: Devon, Eng. **24** O18
Puddletown: Dorset, Eng. **24** R18
Pudimoe: S. Africa **75** F3
Pudozh: U.S.S.R. **50** E2
Pudsey: W. Yorks., England **27** S12
Pudu: Sumatra **65** C7
Pudukkottai: Tamil Nadu, India **58** N12
Puebla: Mexico **86** K14
Puebla, La: Spain **35** D17
Puebla de Alcocer: Spain **35** D17
Puebla de Sanabria: Spain **35** C15
Pueblo: Colo., U.S.A. **93** G5
Pueblo Hundido: Chile **96** A2
Pueblo Nuevo: Venezuela **94** D1
Puelches: Argentina **96** B4
Puenteareas: Spain **35** B15
Puente del Arzobispo, El: Spain **35** D17
Puentedeume: Spain **35** B15
Puente la-Reina: Spain **37** D13
Puerh (Ningerh): Yunnan, China **62** S10
Puerto Aisén: Chile **95** C13
Puerto Angel: Mexico **86** K14
Puerto Arista: Mexico **86** k14
Puerto Asis: Colombia **94** B3
Puerto Ayacucho: Venezuela **94** D2
Puerto Barrios. Guatemala (Honduras *Inset*) **86** *Ins.*
Puerto Belgrano: Argentina **96** C4
Puerto Bermejo: Argentina **96** D2
Puerto Bermúdez: Peru **94** C6
Puerto Berrio: Colombia **94** C2
Puerto Cabello: Venezuela **94** D1
Puerto Cabezas: Nicaragua **87** I15
Puerto Cabo Gracias a Dios: Nicaragua **87** I15
Puerto Capaz: Morocco **35** D19
Puerto Carreño: Colombia **94** D2
Puerto Casado: Paraguay **95** F8
Puerto Chicama: Peru **94** B5
Puerto Coig: Argentina **95** D14
Puerto Cooper: Paraguay **96** D1
Puerto Cortés: Honduras **86** *Ins.*
Puerto Cumarebo: Ven. **94** D1
Puerto Dalmacia: Argentina **96** D2
Puerto de Cabras: Canary Is. **78** B4
Puerto de Chorrera: Panama **94** *Ins.*
Puerto de la Paloma: Uruguay **96** E3
Puerto de Lobos: Mexico **93** E6
Puerto de Santa Maria: Sp. **35** C18
Puerto Deseado: Argentina **95** D13
Puerto Gaiba: Bolivia **94** F7
Puerto Grether: Bolivia **94** E7
Puerto Guarani: Paraguay **95** F8
Puerto Heath: Bolivia **94** D6
Puerto Iguazú: Paraguay **96** E2
Puerto la Cruz: Venezuela **94** E1
Puerto Limón: Costa Rica **87** I15
Puertollano: Spain **35** D17
Puerto Lobos: Argentina **95** D12
Puerto Madryn: Argentina **95** D12
Puerto Maldonado: Peru **94** D6
Puerto México (Coatzacoalcos): Mexico **86** k14
Puerto Montt: Chile **95** C12
Puerto Morazán: Nicaragua **86** L15
Puerto Morelos: Mexico **86** L13
Puerto Natales: Chile **95** C14
Puerto Ocampo: Argentina **96** D2
Puerto Padre: Panama **94** *Ins.*
Puerto Peñasco: Mexico **93** E6
Puerto Pilon: Panama **94** *Ins.*
Puerto Pinasco: Paraguay **95** F8
Puerto Pirámides: Argentina **95** E12
Puerto Piray: Argentina **96** E2
Puerto Plata: Dominican Rep. **87** m14
Puerto Princesa: Palawan, Phil. **64** F5

Puerto Rico: *Commonwealth associated with U.S.A.* **87** N14
Cap.: San Juan
Area: 3,435 sq. miles
(8,897 sq. km.)
Pop.: 2,794,000 (*1972 E*)

Puerto Rico Trench: N. Atlantic Ocean **8** 20N 70W
Puerto Santa Maria: Spain **35** C18
Puerto Sastre: Paraguay **95** F8
Puerto Siles: Bolivia **94** D6
Puerto Suarez: Bolivia **94** F7
Puerto Trinidad: Panama **94** *Ins.*
Puerto Varas: Chile **95** C12
Puerto Victoria: Peru **94** C5
Puerto Wilches: Colombia **94** C2
Pueşti: Romania **39** U13
Pugachev: U.S.S.R. **50** G4
Puget Sound: Wash., U.S.A. **92** C3
Puget-Thénier: France **40** M12
Puglia: *see* Apulia.
Puhoi: North I., N.Z. **70** P13
Puhoso: Finland **46** U4
Puhsien: Shansi, China **62** U7
Puigcerdá: Spain **35** G15
Puigmal: *mtn.*, Pyrenees **37** H13
Puigreig: Spain **35** G16
Puiseaux: France **36** H7
Puivert: France **37** H13
Pujada Bay: Mindanao, Phil. **65** H5
Pujehun: Sierra Leone **80** B3
Pujon Reservoir: N. Korea **63** X6
Pukaki: South I., N.Z. **70** N17
Puka Puka: *i.*, Tuamotu Arch. **83** h2
Pukaruha: *i.*, Tuamotu Arch. **83** h3
Pukchong: N. Korea **63** X6
Pukekohe: North I., N.Z. **70** P13
Pukemiro: North I., N.Z. **70** P13
Pukeuri Junction: South I., New Zealand **70** N17
Pukow: Kiangsu, China **62** V8
Pula (Pola): Yugoslavia **41** T11
Pula, Cape: Sardinia **38** L17
Pulacayo: Bolivia **94** D8
Pulan: Tibet, China **58** O8
Pulanduta: Philippines **64** G4
Pulanów: Poland **45** W1
Pulaski: N.Y., U.S.A. **89** N4
Pulaski: Tenn., U.S.A. **91** H8
Pulaski: Va., U.S.A. **88** L7
Pulaski: Wis., U.S.A. **88** G3
Puławy: Poland **43** R11
Pulborough: W. Sussex, Eng. **25** U18
Pulham: Norf., England **25** Y15
Pulicat Lake: Andhra Pradesh, India **58** O12
Pulkkila: Finland **46** T4
Pullman: Wash., U.S.A. **92** D3
Pulo Anna: *i.*, Caroline Is. **61** L11
Pulozero: U.S.S.R. **46** X2
Pułtusk: Poland **43** R10
Pülümür: Turkey **56** F2
Pulungki: Kansu, China **62** R6
Puma: Tanzania **76** D3
Pumasillo: *mtn.*, Peru **94** C6
Puná I.: Ecuador **94** A4
Punakha: Bhutan **59** P9
Punch: Jammu & Kashmir **58** M8
Puncheston: Dyfed, Wales **24** M16
Punda Maria: Trans., S. Afr. **75** J1
Pundu: Borneo **65** E7
Pune (Poona): Maharashtra, India 58 M11
Pungsan: N. Korea **63** X6
Punjab: *State*, India (*cap.* Chandigarh) **58** N8
Punjab: *Prov.*, Pakistan (*cap.* Lahore) **58** M8
Punkaharju: Finland **47** V6
Puno: Peru **94** C7
Punta Alta: Agentina **96** C4
Punta Arenas (Magallanes): Chile **95** C14
Punta Argentera: *mtn.*, Italy **40** N11
Punta Colorada: Chile **96** A2
Punta de Diaz: Chile **96** A2
Punta de los Llanos: Arg. **96** B3
Punta de Vacas: Argentina **96** B3
Punta Gorda: Belize **86** *Ins.*
Punta Gorda: Fla., U.S.A. **91** K12
Puntarenas: Costa Rica **86** I15
Punxsutawney: Pa., U.S.A. **89** M5
Puolanka: Finland **46** U4
Puponga: South I., N.Z. **70** O15
Pupuya, Nevado: *mtn.*, Bol. **94** D6
Puquio: Peru **94** C6
Puquios: Chile **96** B2
Pur: *riv.*, U.S.S.R. **48** j4
Purbeck, Isle of: *penin.*, Dorset, England **24** R18
Purcell: Okla., U.S.A. **90** C8
Purcell Mtns.: Mont., U.S.A. **92** D3
Purchena: Spain **35** E18
Purdy Is.: Bismarck Arch. **66** J2
Purfleet: Essex, England **25** W17
Purgatoire: *riv.*, Colo., U.S.A. **93** G5
Puri: Orissa, India **59** P11
Purisima, La: Mexico **93** E7
Puriton: Som., England **24** Q17
Purleigh: Essex, England **25** X16
Purmerend: Netherlands **44** K3
Purnamoota: N.S.W., Austl. **71** D8
Purnea: Bihar, India **59** P9
Pursat: Cambodia 64 C4
Purston Jaglin: W. Yorks., Eng. **27** T12
Purukcahu: Borneo 65 E7
Purulia: W. Bengal, India **59** P10
Purús: *riv.*, Brazil **94** E5
Pŭrvomay: Bulgaria **39** T15
Purwodadi: Java **65** E8
Puryong: N. Korea **63** X6
Pusa: Sarawak, Malaysia **65** E6
Pusad: Maharashtra, India **58** N11
Pusan: S. Korea **63** X7
Pusha: Sinkiang, China **51** N7
Pushkin: U.S.S.R. **47** W7
Pushkino: Azerbaydzhan, U.S.S.R. **57** L2
Pusht-i-Kuh: *range*, Iran **57** K5
Puskitamika Lake: Que., Can. **89** N1
Püspökladány: Hungary **43** R13
Putaendo: Chile **96** A3
Putanges: France **36** E7
Putao: Burma 59 R9
Putbus: E. Germany **45** T1
Putehachi: Inner Mongolia, China **63** W5
Puteoli: Roman colony and fort about 6 miles W. of centre of Naples, Italy **38** O16
Putfontein: Trans., S. Africa **74** N*Ins.*
Putford, East: Devon, Eng. **24** N18
Putford, West: Devon, Eng. **24** N18
Putien (Hingwa): Fukien, China **62** V9
Puting, Cape: Borneo **65** E7
Putlitz: E. Germany **45** S2
Putnam: Conn., U.S.A. **89** Q5
Putnok: Hungary **43** R12
Putoran Mtns.: U.S.S.R. **49** I4
Putsonderwater: S. Africa **74** D4
Puttalam: Sri Lanka **58** N13
Putten: *i.*, Netherlands **44** K4
Putumayo: *riv.*, Peru **94** C4
Pütürge: Turkey **56** F2
Putussibau: Borneo **65** E6
Puula Lake: Finland **47** U6
Puxton: Avon, England **24** Q17
PUY, LE: Haute-Loire, Fr. **37** J10
Puyallup: Wash., U.S.A. **92** C3
Puy-de-Dôme: *Dept.*, France (*cap.* Clermont-Ferrand). **37** J10
Puy-Guillaume: France **37** J10
Puyko: U.S.S.R. **48** h4
Puylaroque: France **37** G11
Puylaurens: France **37** H12
Puyoô: France **37** E12
Pweto: Zaïre **76** C4
Pwllheli: Gwynedd, Wales **27** N14
Pyandzh (Oxus): *riv.*, Afghanistan/U.S.S.R. **51** M7
Pyapon: Burma **59** R11
Pyarnu: & *riv.*, Estonia, U.S.S.R. **47** T7
Pyarnu Bay: Estonia, U.S.S.R. **47** T7
Pyatigorsk: U.S.S.R. **50** F6
Pyatikhatki: Ukraine **50** D5
Pyatkovo: U.S.S.R. **51** L3
Pyavozero, Lake: Karelian A.S.S. Rep., U.S.S.R. **46** W3
Pyawbwe: Burma **59** R10
Pyhä Lake: Oulu, Finland **46** T5
Pyhä Lake: Turku Pori, Fin. **47** S6
Pyhä Lake: Vaasa, Finland **46** T5
Pyhäntä: Finland **46** U4
Pyinmana: Burma **59** R11
Pyle: Mid Glam., Wales **24** O16
Pymatuning Reservoir: Pa., U.S.A. **88** L5
PYONGYANG: North Korea **63** X7
Pyramid Hill: *town*, Vict., Australia **71** F11
Pyramids: *antiquities*, Egypt **56** B7
Pyrennes: *mtns.*, Spain/France **34** G1
Pyrénées-Atlantiques: *Dept.*, France (*cap.* Pau) **37** E12
Pyrénées-Orientales: *Dept.*, France (*cap.* Perpignan) **37** H13
Pyrmont: W. Germany **44** P4
Pyrzyce: Poland **45** U2
Pyshma: *riv.*, U.S.S.R. **51** L3
Pytalovo: U.S.S.R. **47** U8
Pytchley: Northants., Eng. **25** U15
Pyu: Burma **59** R11
Pyworthy: Devon, England **24** N18

Qabagh: Iran **57** L3
Qabr Hud: Hadhramaut, Yemen P.D.R. **55** G11
Qachas Nek: & *Dist.*, Lesotho **75** H5
Qadhima: Saudi Arabia **54** E10
Qaf: Saudi Arabia **56** E6
Qagssimiut: Greenland **85** P5
QAHIRA, EL (Cairo): Egypt **56** B6
Qahma: Saudi Arabia **54** F11
Qahtan: *tribal area*, Saudi Arabia **54** F10
Qai'iya: Saudi Arabia **54** F10
Qaim: Iraq **57** G4
Qain: Iran **55** J8
Qais: *i.*, Persian Gulf **55** H9
Qaisar: Afghanistan **58** K7
Qaisuma: Saudi Arabia **54** F9
Qaiyara: Iraq **57** H4
Qajar: Iran **57** L4
Qala Bist: Afghanistan **58** K8
Qal'a Dizeh: Iraq **57** J3
QALA NAU: Badghis, Afghanistan **58** K7
Qala Panja: Afghanistan **51** M7
Qal'a Salih: Iraq **57** K6
Qala Shahar: Afghanistan **58** L7
Qal'a Sikar: Iraq **57** K6
Qal'at Akhdar: Sau. Arab. **54** E9
Qal'at Dab'a: Jordan **56** E6
Qal'at Mu'adhdham: Saudi Arabia **54** E9
Qal'at Mudawwara: Saudi Arabia **54** E9
Qal'at Ruhaiya: Sau. Arabia **54** E9
Qal'at Saura: Saudi Arabia **54** E9
Qal'eh Darreh: Iran **57** K2
Qal'eh Hulilan: Iran **57** K5
Qal'eh Husainiyeh: Iran **57** K5
Qaleh-i-Kang: Afghanistan **58** K8
Qal'eh-i-Shahid: Iran **57** L5
Qal'eh Salboteh: Iran **57** L5
Qalqiliya: Jordan **55** a2
Qalyûb: Egypt **56** B6
Qameshliya: Syria **57** G3
Qana: Saudi Arabia **54** F9
Qantara East, El.: Egypt (Suez Canal. *Inset*) **32** *Ins.*
Qantara, El: Egypt (Suez Canal. *Inset*) **32** Ins.
Qara: Egypt **54** C9
Qara: Saudi Arabia **54** F9
Qara: *riv.*, Iran **55** G7
Qarani: *well*, Saudi Arabia **55** J10
Qarasai: Sinkiang, China **51** O7
Qara Tepe: Iraq **57** J4
Qardam: Saudi Arabia **55** H11
Qarghaliq: *see* Yehcheng.
Qariya: Saudi Arabia **54** G11
Qariya 'Ulya: Saudi Arabia **55** G9
Qarra: *tribe*, Oman **55** H11
Qârûn, Lake: Egypt **56** B7
Qaryatein: Syria **56** E4
Qasab: Iraq **57** H3
Qasaiwara: *well*, Sau. Arab. **55** H10
Qasim: *geog. reg.*, Sau. Arab. **54** F9
Qasr, El: Egypt **54** C9
Qasr Abu Ghar: Iraq **57** K6
Qasr al Khubbaz: Iraq **57** H5
Qasr Amij: Iraq **57** G5
Qasr as Subiya: Kuwait **57** L7
Qasr Azraq: Jordan **56** E6
Qasr Farafra: Egypt **54** C9
Qasr Helqum: *ruin*, Iraq **57** G5
Qasr-i-Shirin: Iran **57** J4
Qasr Kharane: Jordan **56** E6
Qasr Naba: Iraq **57** K6
Qasrqand: Iran **55** K9
Qassâsîn: Egypt (Suez Canal *Inset)* **32** *Ins.*
Qa'taba: Yemen **54** F12

Qatar: *Sheikhdom* **55** H9
Cap.: Doha
Area: 4,000 sq. miles
(10,360 sq. km.)
Pop.: 100,000 (*1969 E*)

Qatif: Saudi Arabia **55** G9
Qatrana: Jordan **56** E6
Qattara Depression: Egypt **54** C7
Qena: & *wadi*, Egypt **54** D9
Qila Saifullah: Baluchistan, Pakistan **58** L8
Qishm: & *i.*, Persian Gulf **55** J9
Qishn: Yemen P.D.R. **55** H11
Qizan: Saudi Arabia **54** F11
Qizil: *riv.*, Iran **57** K3
Qizil Kya: Iran **57** K3
Qohord-e Pain: Iran **57** L4
Qomul (Hami): Sinkiang, China **62** Q6
Qormi (Curmi): Malta **32** *Ins.*
Qôrnoq: Greenland **85** o5
Qoshlash Langar: Sinkiang, China **51** O7
Quadring: Lincs., England **27** V14
Quad Tlelat: Algeria **35** F19
Quainton: Bucks., England **25** U16
Quakenbrück: W. Germany **44** N3
Quakertown: Pa., U.S.A. **89** O5
Quambatook: Vict., Austl. **71** E10
Quambone: N.S.W., Austl. **71** G8
Quanah: Tex., U.S.A. **90** B8
Quanary: Fr. Guiana **94** G3
Quangngai: Vietnam 64 D3
Quangtri: Vietnam 64 D3
Quangyên: Vietnam 64 D2
Quan Long: Vietnam 64 D5
Quantico: Va., U.S.A. **89** N6
Quantocks, The: *hills*, Som., England **24** P17
Quantoxhead, East: Som., England **24** P17
Qu'Appelle: & *riv.*, Sask., Canada **92** G2
Quarai: & *riv.*, Brazil **96** D3
Quarantine: La., U.S.A. **90** *Ins.*
Quarff: Mainland, Shetland Is. **28** *Ins.*
Quarndon: Derby., England **27** S14
Quarré-les-Tombes: France **36** J8
Quarter: Strath., Scotland **29** N8
Quartu San Elena: Sardinia **38** L17
Quatford: Salop, England **27** R14
Quatre Bras: Belgium **44** K5
Quatt: Salop, England **24** R15
Qubba: Saudi Arabia **54** F9
Quchan: Iran **55** J7
Queanbeyan: N.S.W., Australia **71** H10

Québec—Redcross 179

QUÉBEC: Que., Canada (cap. Québec) 89 Q2
Québec: Prov., Canada 85 m7
Quebracho: Uruguay 96 D3
Quebrachos: Argentina 96 C2
Qued El Abtal: Algeria 35 G19
Quedlinburg: E. Germany 45 R4
Queen Adelaide Arch.: is., Chile 95 C14
Queen Bess, Mount: B.C., Canada 92 C2
Queenborough: I. of Sheppey, England 25 X17
Queen Charlotte: & is., B.C., Canada 84 f7
Queen Charlotte Sound: B.C., Canada 84 f7
Queen Charlotte Str.: B.C., Canada 92 B2
Queen Elizabeth Islands: N.W.T., Canada 84/85
Queen Elizabeth National Park: Central, Scotland 29 M7
Queen Maud Gulf: N.W.T., Canada 84 K4
Queen Maud Land: Antarctica 9 75S 00
Queensberry: mtn., Dumfries & Galloway, Scotland 29 O9
Queensbury: W. Yorks., Eng. 27 S12
Queenscliff: Vict., Australia 71 F12
Queensferry: Loth., Scotland 29 P8
Queen's Head: Salop, Eng. 27 Q14
Queensland: State, Australia (cap. Brisbane) 70 H5
Queenstown (Cobh): Cork, Repub. of Ireland 31 E16
Queenstown: & Dist., S. Afr. 75 G5
Queenstown: South I., N.Z. 70 M17
Queenstown: Tas., Australia 68 H8
Queguay: Uruguay 96 D3
Quela: Angola 73 H11
QUELIMANE: Zambezia, Mozambique 77 E6
Quelo: Angola 81 G6
Quelpart (Cheju) I.: S. Korea 63 X8
Quembo: riv., Angola 77 A5
Quemoy: Fukien, China 62 V10
Quemu Quemu: Argentina 96 C4
Quendon: Essex, England 25 W16
Que Que: Rhodesia 77 C6
Quercianella: Italy 40 Q12
Querétaro: Mexico 86 j13
Querfurt: E. Germany 45 R4
Quérigut: France 37 H13
Quernmore: Lancs., Eng. 27 Q11
Querrien: France 36 B8
Quesnel: & lake, B.C., Can. 92 C2
Questa: N. Mex., U.S.A. 93 F5
Questembert: France 36 C8
Quetico: Ont., Canada 88 F1
Quetico Prov. Park: Ont., Canada 88 F1
QUETTA: Baluchistan, Pak. 58 L8
Quettehou: France 36 D6
Quévilly, Le Petit: France 36 G6
Quezaltenango: Guatemala 86 k15
QUEZON CITY: Luzon, Phil. 64 G4
Quhes: Albania 39 R16
Quiaca, La: Argentina 95 D8
Quibala: Angola 73 G12
Quibaxi: Angola 73 G11
Quibdó: Colombia 94 B2
Quibell: Ont., Canada 92 J3
Quiberon: & bay, France 36 B8
Quickborn: W. Germany 45 P2
Quiindy: Paraguay 96 D2
Quila: Mexico 93 F8
Quilengues: Angola 73 G12
Quillabamba: Peru 94 C6
Quillacollo: Bolivia 94 D7
Quillagua: Chile 95 D8
Quillaicillo: Chile 96 A3
Quillan: France 37 H13
Quillebeuf: France 36 F6
Quill Lakes: Sask., Canada 92 G2
Quillota: Chile 96 A3
Quilon: Kerala, India 58 N13
Quilpie: Queens., Australia 70 F6
Quilpué: Chile 96 A3
Quilty: Clare, Repub. of Ireland 31 C14
Quimerch: France 36 A7
Quimili: Argentina 96 C2
QUIMPER: Finistère, France 36 A8
Quimperlé: France 36 B8
Quin: Clare, Repub. of Ireland 31 D14
Quinag: mtn., High., Scot. 28 L3
Quincy: Fla., U.S.A. 91 J10
Quincy: Ill., U.S.A. 88 F6
Quincy: Mass., U.S.A. 89 Q4
Quindalup: W. Australia 68 B6
Quines: Argentina 96 B3
Quinga: Mozambique 77 F6
Quingey: France 40 L8
Quinhagak: Alaska, U.S.A. 84 c6
Qui Nhon: Vietnam 64 D4
Quinjama: Angola 77 B5
Quintana de la Serena: Spain 35 D17
Quintanar de la Orden: Sp. 35 E17
Quinter: Kans., U.S.A. 93 G5
Quintero: Chile 96 A3
Quintin: France 36 C7
Quinto: riv., Argentina 96 C3
Quinzau: Angola 73 G11
Quinze, Lac des: Que., Can. 89 M2
Quionga: Mozambique 77 F5
Quipapá: Brazil 94 K5
Quipungo: Angola 73 G12
Quirihue: Chile 96 A4
Quirima: Angola 77 A5
Quirindi: N.S.W., Australia 71 J8
Quiroga: Spain 35 C15
Quissanga: Mozambique 77 F5
Quissico: Mozambique 77 D7
Quitapa: Angola 77 A5
Quitaro: riv., Guyana 87 d9
Quita Sueño: i., (U.S.A./Col.), Caribbean Sea 87 I15
Quiterajo: Mozambique 77 F5
Quitilipi: Argentina 96 C2
QUITO: Ecuador 94 B4
Quiur: Iran 57 L4
Quixadá: Brazil 94 K4
Quixeramobim: Brazil 94 K5
Qum: & riv., Iran 55 H8
Qumbu: S. Africa 75 H5
Qunfidha: Saudi Arabia 54 F11
Quoich, Loch: High., Scot. 28 L5
Quorn: S. Australia 71 C9
Quorndon: Leics., England 27 T14
Quoyloo: Mainland, Orkney Is., Scotland 28 P2
Qur, Shaib: wadi, Sau. Arab. 57 G6
Qurna: Iraq 57 K6
Qurveh: Iran 57 K4
Qus: Egypt 54 D9
Qusaiba: Saudi Arabia 54 F9
Qusaima: Egypt 56 D6
Qusair: Iraq 57 J6
Qusaiyir: (Qusair): Yemen P.D.R. 55 H12
Quseir: Egypt 54 D9
Qusibeh: Iran 57 L6
Qutain: Saudi Arabia 54 G10
Qutdligssat: Greenland 85 o3
Quteife: Syria 56 E5
Quthing: & Dist., Lesotho 75 G5
Qutur: riv., Iran 57 J2
Quwai'iya: Saudi Arabia 54 G10
Quwair: Iraq 57 H3

Raahe: Finland 46 T4
Rääkkylä: Finland 46 V5
Raalte: Netherlands 44 M3
Raas: i., Indonesia 65 E8
Raasay: i., Inner Hebr., Scot. 28 K5
Raasay, Sound of: Inner Hebr., Scotland 28 J4
Rab: & i., Yugoslavia 41 U11
Raba: Sumbawa, Indonesia 65 F8
Raba: riv., Hungary/Austria 43 P13
Rabade: Spain 35 C15
Rabahidvég: Hungary 41 W8
Rabai: Kenya 76 E3
Rabak: Sudan 54 D12
Rabastens: France 37 F12
Rabat (Victoria): Gozo, Malta 32 Ins.
Rabat: Malta 32 Ins.
RABAT: & Pref., Morocco 80 K8
Rabat Kila: Iran 55 K9
Rabaul: New Britain, Bismarck Arch. 67 K2
Rabigh: Saudi Arabia 54 E10
Rabka: Poland 43 Q12
Raccoon Point: cape, La., U.S.A. 90 F11
Raccourci, Lake: La., U.S.A. 90 Ins.
Race, Cape: Newf., Canada 85 w3
Rach Gia: Vietnam 64 D4
Racibórz: Poland 43 Q11
Racine: Wis., U.S.A. 88 H4
Rackenford: Devon, Eng. 24 O18
Rackeve: Hungary 43 Q13
Rackwick: Orkney Is., Scot. 28 P2
Rada: Yemen 54 F12
Rădăuţi: Romania 43 T13
Radcliffe: Gt. Man., England 27 R12
Radde: U.S.S.R. 63 Y5
Radeberg: E. Germany 45 T4
Radebeul: E. Germany 45 T4
Radegast: E. Germany 45 S4
Radevormwald: W. Germany 44 N4
Radew: riv., Poland 45 W1
Radford: Va., U.S.A. 88 L7
Radhanpur: Gujarat, India 58 M10
Radibor: E. Germany 45 U4
Radium Hill: S. Australia 71 D9
Radjik: Bangka, Indonesia 65 D7
Radlett: Herts., England 25 V16
Radlinski, Mt.: Antarctica 9 85S 110W
Radlje ob Dravi (Marenburg): Yugoslavia 41 V9
Radnage: Bucks., England 25 U16
Radnevo: Bulgaria 39 T15
Radnice: Czechoslovakia 45 T6
Radnor Forest: Powys, Wales 24 P15
Radolfzell: W. Germany 40 O8
Radom: Poland 43 R11
Radomir: Bulgaria 39 S15
Radomsko: Poland 43 Q11
Radomyshl': Ukraine 43 V11
Radostov: Byelorussia 43 T11
Radoviš: Yugoslavia 39 S16
Radovljica: Yugoslavia 41 U9
Radstadt: Austria 41 T8
Radstock: Avon, England 24 R17
Radvilishkis: Lithuania, U.S.S.R. 47 S9
Radville: Sask., Canada 92 G3
Radway: War., England 24 T15
Radzymin: Poland 43 R10
Radzyń: Poland 43 S11
Rae Bareli: Uttar Prad., Ind. 58 O9
Raeford: N.C., U.S.A. 91 M8
Rae Isthmus: N.W.T., Can. 85 L4
Raesfeld: W. Germany 44 M4
Raeside, Lake: W. Australia 68 C5
Raetia (Rhaetia): Roman province comprising Austrian Tyrol and Vorarlberg with parts of Bavaria and Switzerland 42 M13
Raetihi: North I., N.Z. 70 P14
Rafaela: Argentina 96 C3
Rafah: Egypt 55 a3
Rafai: Central African Rep. 76 B2
Rafford: Gram., Scotland 28 O4
Rafha: Saudi Arabia 54 F9
Rafid: Jordan 55 b2
Rafnseyri: Iceland 46 b4
Rafsanjan: Iran 55 J8
Raga: Sudan 76 C1
Ragang Volc.: Mindanao, Philippines 64 G5
Ragaz, Bad: Switzerland 40 P9
Ragged I.: Maine, U.S.A. 89 R4
Raglan: Gwent, Wales 24 Q16
Raglan: North I., N.Z. 70 P13
Ragstone Ridge: hills, Kent, England 25 W17
Ragusa: Sicily 38 O18
Ragusa (Dubrovnik): Yugoslavia 39 Q15
Raha: Celebes 65 G7
Rahab: desert, Iraq 57 J6
Rahad: riv., Sudan 54 D12
Rahad el Berdi: Sudan 79 J7
Rahaliya: Iraq 57 H5
Raharney: Westmeath, Repub. of Ireland 30 G12
Raheita: Ethiopia 79 Q17
Rahouia: Algeria 35 G19
Raiatea: i., Society Is. 83 e3
Raices: Argentina 96 D3
Raichur: Karnataka, India 58 N11
Raida: Yemen P.D.R. 54 G12
Raidjua: i., Indonesia 65 G9
Raigarh: Madhya Pradesh, India 59 O10
Raiis: Saudi Arabia 54 E10
Rain: W. Germany 41 Q7
Rainbow: Vict., Australia 71 D10
Rainelle: W. Va., U.S.A. 88 L7
Rainford: Mers., England 27 Q13
Rainham: Kent, England 25 X17
Rainier: Oreg., U.S.A. 92 C3
Rainier, Mount: Wash., U.S.A. 92 C3
Rainy: riv., Minn., U.S.A. 88 D1
Rainy Lake: Canada/U.S.A. 88 E1
Rainy River: town, Ont., Can. 88 D1
Raipur: Madhya Pradesh, India 58 O10
Rairakhol: Orissa, India 59 O10
Rait: Tayside, Scotland 29 P7
Raivavae: i., Austral Is. 83 f4
Raja: mtn., Borneo 65 E7
Rajahmundry: Andhra Pradesh, India 58 O11
Rajang: & riv., Sarawak, Malaysia 65 E6
Rajanpur: Punjab, Pak. 58 M9
Rajasthan: State, India (cap. Jaipur) 58 M9
Raj Buri: Thailand 64 B4
Rajgarh: Rajasthan, India 58 N9
Rajkot: Gujarat, India 58 M10
Raj Nandgaon: Madhya Pradesh, India 59 O10
Rajpipla: Gujarat, India 58 M10
Rajpur: Madhya Pradesh, India 58 M10
Rajshahi: Bangladesh 59 P10
Raju: Syria 56 E3
Rajur: Maharashtra, India 58 N10
Rajura: Maharashtra, India 58 N11
Rakai: Uganda 76 D3
Rakaposhi: mtn., Jammu & Kashmir 58 M7
Rake Street: Mayo, Repub. of Ireland 30 C11
Rakhovo: Ukraine 43 T12
Rakhyut: Oman 55 H11
Rakitnoye: U.S.S.R. 50 E4
Rakke: Estonia, U.S.S.R. 47 U7
Rakkejaur: Sweden 46 Q4
Rakkestad: Norway 47 M7
Rakops: Botswana 77 B7
Rakovnik: Czechoslovakia 45 T5
Rakuku: Botswana 77 B6
Rakusha: Kazakh., U.S.S.R. 50 H5
Rakvere: Estonia, U.S.S.R. 47 U7
RALEIGH: N.C., U.S.A. 91 M8
Raleigh Bay: N.C., U.S.A. 91 N8
Ralls: Tex., U.S.A. 93 G6
Rama: Nicaragua 86 I15
Ramadi: Iraq 57 H5
Ramallah: Jordan 55 b3
Ramallo: Argentina 96 C3
Ramanathapuram: Tamil Nadu, India 58 N13
Ramasaig: Inner Hebr., Scot. 28 H5
Ramat-Gan: Israel 55 a2
Ramatlhabama: Trans., S. Africa 75 F2
Rambervillers: France 40 M7
Rambla, La: Spain 35 D18
Rambouillet: France 36 G7
Rambutyo: i., Admiralty Is. 66 J2
Ramea Is.: Newf., Canada 85 u3
Rame Head: cape, Corn., England 24 N19
Ramerupt: France 36 K7
Ram Hormuz: Iran 57 L6
Ramillies: & battlefield, Belgium 44 K5
Ramishk: Iran 55 J9
Ramiat Ghafa: sand reg., Saudi Arabia 55 J10
Ramiat Hamra: sand reg., Saudi Arabia 55 H10
Ramle: Israel 55 a3
Ramnad: Tamil Nadu, India 58 N13
Ramnagar: Uttar Pradesh, India 59 O9
Râmnicu Sărat: Romania 39 U14
Râmnicu Vâlcea: Romania 39 T14
Ramor, Lough: Cavan, Repub. of Ireland 30 G12
Ramoth Ammon: cap. of kingdom of Ammon (q.v.) now called 'Amman 55 b3
Ramoth-Gilead: city of ancient Israel 10 miles SW. of Dera'a, Syria and 10 miles ESE of Irbid, Jordan 56 E5
Ramotswa: Botswana 75 F2
Rampart: Alaska, U.S.A. 84 d4
Rampur: Himachal Pradesh, India 58 N8
Rampur: Uttar Pradesh, India 58 N9
Ramree: & i., Burma 59 Q11
Ramsay Lake: Ont., Can. 88 K2
Ramsbottom: Gt. Man., Eng. 27 R12
Ramsbury: Wilts., England 25 S17
Ramsele: Sweden 46 P5
Ramsey: Essex, England 25 Y16
Ramsey: Cambs., England 25 V15
Ramsey: & bay, I. of Man, United Kingdom 26 N11
Ramsey I.: Wales 24 L16
Ramsey St. Mary's: Cambridgeshire, England 25 V15
Ramsgate: Kent, England 25 Y17
Ramsgate: Tas., Australia 68 H8
Ramsgill: N. Yorks., Eng. 26 S11
Ramsgrange: Wex., Repub. of Ireland 31 H15
Ramsjö: Sweden 47 O5
Ranai: Natuna Is., Indon. 65 D6
Ranau: Sabah, Malaysia 65 F5
Rancagua: Chile 96 A3
Rance: riv., France 36 C7
Ranchi: Bihar, India 59 P10
Rand: N.S.W., Australia 71 G10
Randalstown: Antrim, N. Ireland 30 J10
Randan: France 37 J9
Randers: Denmark 47 M8
Randfontein: Trans., S. Afr., 74 M Ins.
Randi Lake: Sweden 46 Q3
Randolph: Vt., U.S.A. 89 P4
Randow: riv., E. Germany 45 U2
Råneå: Sweden 46 S4
Ranfurly: South I., N.Z. 70 N17
Rangal: Queens., Australia 70 H4
Rangas, Cape: Celebes 65 F7
Rangeley: & lake, Maine, U.S.A. 89 Q3
Ranger: Tex., U.S.A. 90 B9
Ranger Lake: Ont., Canada 88 K2
Rangia: Assam, India 59 Q9
Rangiora: South I., N.Z. 70 O16
Rangiroa: i., Tuamotu Arch. 83 f3
Rangitaiki: & riv., North I., New Zealand 70 Q14
Rangitata: riv., South I., New Zealand 70 N16
Rangitikei: riv., North I., New Zealand 70 Q14
Rangkasbitung: Java 65 D8
RANGOON: Pegu, Burma 59 R11
Rangpur: Bangladesh 59 P9
Rania: Iraq 57 J3
Ranibennur: Maharashtra, India 58 N12
Ranikhet: Uttar Prad., Ind. 58 N9
Rankaia: riv., South I., N.Z. 70 N16
Rankine: N. Territ., Austl. 69 F3
Rankin Inlet: N.W.T., Canada 85 k5
Rankin's Springs: N.S.W., Australia 71 G9
Rankinston: Strath., Scot. 29 N9
Rannes: Queens., Australia 70 J5
Rannoch: dist. & loch, Tayside, Scotland 29 N6
Rannoch Moor: Strathclyde/Tayside, Scotland 29 M6
Rann of Kutch: marsh, Gujarat, India 58 L10
Rannon: New Hebrides 67 N5
Rano: Nigeria 81 F2
Ranskill: Notts., England 27 T13
Rantauparapat: Sumatra 65 B6
Rantoul: Ill., U.S.A. 88 G5
Rantsila: Finland 46 T4
Ranua: Finland 46 U4
Ranya: Saudi Arabia 54 F10
Raon-l'Étape: France 40 M7
Raoui Erg: desert, Algeria 80 L9
Raoul Is., Kermadec Is., Pacific O. 67 Q7
Rapa: i., Austral Is. 83 g5
Rapallo: Italy 40 P11
Rapang: Celebes 65 F7
Raphoe: Don., Repub. of Ireland 30 F10
Rapid City: S. Dak., U.S.A. 92 G4
Rapla: Estonia, U.S.S.R. 47 T7
Rappahannock: riv., Va., U.S.A. 89 N6
Rapperswil: Switzerland 40 O8
Raqi: well, Oman 55 J10
RAQQA: & Prov., Syria 56 F4
Raquette Lake: N.Y., U.S.A. 89 O4
Raraka: i., Tuamotu Arch. 83 g3
Raroia: i., Tuamotu Arch. 83 g3
Rarotonga: i., Cook Is. 70 Ins.
Rarwino: Poland 45 V2
Rasa: i., Philippine Sea 60 L7
Ras Abu Madd: cape, Saudi Arabia 54 E10
Ras al Ardh: cape, Kuwait 57 L7
Ras al Hadd: cape, Oman 55 J10
Ras al Khaimah: U.A.E. 55 J9
Ras Alula: cape, Somalia 79 S17
Ras Bargan: cape, Iran 57 L7
Ras Banas: Egypt 54 E10
Ras Baridi: cape, Saudi Arabia 54 E10
Ras Binnah: cape, Somalia 79 S17
Raše Channel: inlet, Yugoslavia 41 U11
Ras Dashan: mtn., Ethiopia 54 E12
Ras el' Ain: Syria 57 G3
Ras el Hilal: cape, Libya 33 G5
Râs el 'Ish: Egypt (Suez Canal Inset) 32 Ins.
Ras el Kanayis: cape, Egypt 54 C8
Ras el Keil: cape, Somalia 79 R18
Ras-El-Ma: Algeria 80 L8
Ras el Ma: Mali 80 D1
Ras el Milh: cape, Libya 33 H5
Ras et Tin: cape, Libya 33 G5
Raseynyay: Lithuania, U.S.S.R. 47 S9
Ras Fartak: cape, Yemen P.D.R. 55 H11
Ras Fastah: cape, Iran 55 K9
Ras Gabah: cape, Somalia 79 S18
Râs Ghârib: cape, Egypt 54 D9
Rashad: Sudan 79 L7
Ras Hafun: cape, Somalia 79 S17
Rasharkin: Antrim, N. Irel. 30 J10
Rashid: tribe, Saudi Arabia 55 H11
Ras Imran: cape, Saudi Arab. 79 Q17
Raška: Yugoslavia 39 R15
Raskelf: N. Yorks., England 26 T11
Ras Khanzira: cape, Somalia 79 R17
Ras Mabber: cape, Somalia 79 S18
Ras Malan: cape, Baluchistan, Pakistan 58 L9
Ras Masandam: cape, Saudi Arabia 55 J9
Ras Mohammed: cape, Sinai Penin., Egypt 54 D9
Ras Muari: cape, Sind, Pakistan 58 L10
Rason, Lake: W. Australia 68 C5
Ras Ormara: cape, Baluchistan, Pakistan 58 K9
Ras Puzim: cape, Iran 55 K9
Ras Rakan: cape, Qatar 55 H9
Ras Rashidi: cape, Iran 55 K9
Rass: Saudi Arabia 54 F9
Rasskazovo: U.S.S.R. 50 F4
Ras Sura: cape, Somalia 79 R17
Ras Tanura: Saudi Arabia 55 H9
Rastatt: W. Germany 40 O7
Råsto (Lainio): riv., Sweden 46 R2
Råsto Lake: Sweden 46 R2
Rataje: Czechoslovakia 45 U6
Ratangarh: Rajasthan, India 58 M9
Ratby: Leics., England 27 T14
Ratelpoort: S. Africa 74 B4
Rath: Offaly, Repub. of Irel. 31 F13
Rathangan: Kild., Repub. of Ireland 31 H13
Rathcabban: Tip., Repub. of Ireland 31 E13
Rathcool: Cork, Repub. of Ireland 31 D15
Rathcoole: Dublin, Repub. of Ireland 31 J13
Rathcormack: Cork, Repub. of Ireland 31 E15
Rathdowney: Laois, Repub. of Ireland 31 F14
Rathdrum: Wick., Repub. of Ireland 31 J14
Rathen: Gram., Scotland 28 S4
Rathenow: E. Germany 45 S3
Rathfarnham: Dublin, Repub. of Ireland 31 J14
Rathfeigh: Meath, Repub. of Ireland 30 J12
Rathfryland: Down, N. Irel. 30 J11
Rathgormac: Wat., Repub. of Ireland 31 G15
Rathkeale: Lim., Repub. of Ireland 31 D14
Rathkenny: Meath, Repub. of Ireland 30 H12
Rathlackan: Mayo, Repub. of Ireland 30 C11
Rathlin I.: N. Ireland 30 J9
Rathlin Sound: Rathlin I./Antrim, N. Ireland 29 J9
Rathluirc (Charleville): Cork, Repub. of Ireland 31 D15
Rathmelton: Don., R. of Irel. 30 F9
Rathmolyon: Meath, Repub. of Ireland 30 H13
Rathmore: Kerry, Repub. of Ireland 31 C15
Rathmullan: Don., Repub. of Ireland 30 F9
Rathnew: Wick., Repub. of Irel. 31 J14
Ratho: Lothian, Scotland 29 P8
Rathowen: Westmeath, Repub. of Ireland 30 F12
Rathvilly: Carlow, Repub. of Ireland 31 H14
Ratingen: W. Germany 44 M4
Rat Is.: Aleutians 84 a7
Ratlam: Madhya Pradesh, India 58 N10
Ratnagiri: Maharashtra, India 58 M11
Ratnapura: Sri Lanka 58 O13
Ratno: Ukraine 43 T11
Ratoath: Meath, Repub. of Ireland 30 J12
Ratodi: Botswana 75 G1
Raton: N. Mex., U.S.A. 93 G5
Rat Rapids: town, Ont., Can. 92 J2
Ratta: U.S.S.R. 48 K5
Ratten: Austria 41 V8
Rattenberg: Austria 41 R8
Rattray: Tayside, Scotland 29 P6
Rattray Head: cape, Grampian, Scotland 28 S4
Rättvik: Sweden 47 O6
Ratz, Mount: B.C., Canada 84 f6
Ratzeburg: W. Germany 45 Q2
Ratzlingen: E. Germany 45 R3
Raub: Malaya, Malaysia 65 b12
Rauch: Argentina 96 D4
Rauen: E. Germany 45 U3
Raufarhöfn: Iceland 46 f3
Raufoss: Norway 47 M6
Raukokore: North I., N.Z. 70 Q13
Raukumara Range: North I., New Zealand 70 R13
Rauma: Finland 47 R6
Raunds: Northants., Eng. 25 U15
Rauschenberg: W. Germany 44 O5
Raushan: Saudi Arabia 54 F10
Rautas: Sweden 46 Q2
Rautavaara: Finland 46 V5
Rautenbach: S. Africa 75 F6
Rautio: Finland 46 T4
Ravahere: i., Tuamotu Arch. 83 g3
Ravar: Iran 55 J8
Rava-Russkaya: Ukraine 43 S11
Ravenglass: Cumbria, Eng. 26 P11
Raveningham: Norf., Eng. 25 Z14
Ravenna: Italy 41 S11
Ravenna: Nebr., U.S.A. 92 H4
Ravensburg: W. Germany 40 P8
Ravensklip: Trans., S. Afr. 74 N Ins.
Ravensthorpe: W. Australia 68 C6
Ravenstonedale: Cumbria, England 26 R11
Ravenswood: Queens., Australia 70 G3
Ravensworth: N. Yorks., Eng. 26 S11
Ravi: riv., India/Pakistan 58 M8
Ravn, Cape: Greenland 85 R4
Rawalpindi: Punjab, Pakistan 58 M8
Rawa Mazowiecko: Poland 43 R11
Rawan: Iran 57 L4
Rawang: Malaya, Malaysia 65 b12
Rawang: Tibet, China 58 O8
Rawansir: Iran 57 K4
Rawcliffe: Humb., England 27 U12
Rawene: North I., N.Z. 70 O12
Rawicz: Poland 45 W4
Rawlinna: W. Australia 68 D6
Rawlins: Wyo., U.S.A. 92 F4
Rawmarsh: S. Yorks., Eng. 27 T13
RAWSON: Chubut, Arg. 95 D12
Rawsonville: S. Africa 74 C6
Rawtenstall: Lancs., Eng. 27 R12
Raxaul: Bihar, India 59 O9
Ray: N. Dak., U.S.A. 92 G3
Rayadrug: Andhra Pradesh, India 58 N12
Rayleigh: Essex, England 24 X16
Raymond: Alta., Canada 92 E3
Raymond: Que., Canada 89 Q2
Raymond: Wash., U.S.A. 92 C3
Raymond Terrace: N.S.W., Australia 71 J9
Raymondville: Texas, U.S.A. 90 C12
Rayne: La., U.S.A. 90 E10
Rayones: Mexico 93 G7
Rayong: Thailand 64 C4
Raystown Branch: riv., Pa., U.S.A. 89 M5
Rayton: Trans., S. Africa 75 H2
Rayville: La., U.S.A. 90 F9
Raz, Pointe du: cape, France 36 A7
Razan: Iran 57 L4
Razdol'noye: U.S.S.R. 63 Y6
Razelm, Lake: Romania 39 V14
Razgrad: Bulgaria 39 U15
Razgul'noye: Kazakh., U.S.S.R. 51 L4
Ražice: Czechoslovakia 45 U6
Razlog: Bulgaria 39 S16
Razmak: NW. Front. Prov., Pakistan 58 L8
Ré, Île de: i., France 37 D9
Readford: Yukon, Canada 84 F5
READING: Berks., England 25 U17
Reading: Pa., U.S.A. 89 O5
Read's Drift: S. Africa 74 E4
Real, El: Panama 94 B2
Realicó: Argentina 96 C4
Réalmont: France 37 H12
Réam: Cambodia 64 C4
Reanascreena: Cork, Repub. of Ireland 31 C16
Réao: i., Tuamotu Arch. 83 h3
Rear Cross: Tip., Repub. of Ireland 31 E14
Rearsby: Leics., England 27 T14
Reate: Roman city at Rieti, Italy 38 N15
Reay: Highland, Scotland 28 O2
Reay Forest: High., Scot. 28 M3
Rebiana: well, Libya 79 J5
Rebnes Lake: Sweden 46 P3
Reboly: Karelian A.S.S. Rep., U.S.S.R. 46 W5
Rebun: i., Japan 63 ZZ5
Recalde: Argentina 96 C4
Recanati: Italy 41 T12
Recaş: Romania 39 R14
Recco: Italy 40 P11
Recess: Galway, Repub. of Ireland 31 B13
Recey-sur-Ource: France 36 K8
Recherche Arch.: W. Austl. 68 C6
Rechitsa: Byelorussia 50 D4
Rećica: Yugoslavia 41 V10
RECIFE: Pernambuco, Brazil 94 K5
Recife, Cape: S. Africa 75 F7
Recinto: Chile 96 A4
Recke: W. Germany 44 N3
Recklinghausen: W. Germany 44 N4
Recknitz: riv., E. Germany 45 S2
Reconquista: Argentina 96 D2
Recovery Glacier: Antarctica 9 85S 30W
Recreo: Argentina 96 B2
Rector: Ark., U.S.A. 88 F7
Reculver: Kent, England 25 Y17
Red: riv., Minn./N. Dak., U.S.A. 93 H3
Red: riv., U.S.A. 90 E10
Red (Rouge & Yuan): riv., China/N. Vietnam 62 S10
Redang: i., Malaya, Malaysia 65 C5
Red Basin: geog. reg., Szechwan, China 62 T8
Red Bay: city, Ala., U.S.A. 90 G8
Red Bluff: Calif., U.S.A. 92 C4
Redbourn: Herts., England 25 V16
Redbridge: Gt. Ldn., England 25 W16
Red Bud: Ill., U.S.A. 88 G6
Redcar: Cleve., England 26 T10
Redcliff: Alta., Canada 92 E2
Red Cliff: Guyana 87 e9
Redcliffe: Queens., Australia 70 K6
Red Cliffs: Vict., Australia 71 E10
Red Cloud: Nebr., U.S.A. 93 H4
Redcross: Wick., Repub. of Ireland 31 J14

For Abbreviations see list on p.113. Italic type, e.g. *Ephesus*, refers to historical names not on maps. Capital letters, e.g. MADRID, show capitals of countries; small capital letters, e.g. CADIZ, show capitals of provinces, etc. General notes p.116.

180 Red Deer—Rock

Red Deer: Alta., Canada **92** E2
Red Deer: *riv.*, Sask., Can. **92** E2
Red Deer: *riv.*, Sask./Man., Canada **92** G2
Reddersburg: & *Dist.*, O.F.S., S. Africa **75** G4
Redding: Calif., U.S.A. **92** C4
Reddish: Gt. Man., England **27** R13
Redditch: Hereford & Worcester, England **24** S15
Redelinghuys: S. Africa **74** C6
Redenção: Brazil **94** K4
Redesdale: *val.*, Northumb., England **26** R9
Redesdale: Vict., Australia **71** F11
Redesmouth: Northumb., England **26** R9
Redfield: S. Dak., U.S.A. **92** H4
Redgrave: Suff., England **25** X15
Redhill: S. Australia **71** C9
Redhill: Surrey, England **25** V17
Red Hill: Vict., Austl. **70** F12
Redhills: Cavan, Repub. of Irel. **30** G11
Red Hills: Kans., U.S.A. **90** B7
Redics: Hungary **41** W9
Red Indian, Lake: Newf., Canada **85** u2
Red Lake: *town*, Ont., Can. **92** J2
Red Lake Falls: *city*, Minn., U.S.A. **92** H3
Red Lion: Pa., U.S.A. **89** N6
Red Lodge: Mont., U.S.A. **92** F3
Redlynch: Wilts., England **25** S18
Redon: France **36** C8
Redondela: Spain **35** B15
Redondo: Portugal **35** C17
Red Pass: *town*, B.C., Can. **92** D2
Redruth: Corn., England **24** L19
Red Sea: Asia/Africa **54** E10
Red Sea: *prov.*, Sudan. (*cap.* Port Sudan) **55** D10
Red Tank: Panama **94** *Ins.*
Red Volta: *riv.*, Upper Volta **80** D2
Redwater: Alta., Canada **92** E2
Red Wharf Bay: Gwynedd, Wales **27** N13
Redwick: Avon, England **24** Q16
Redwick: Gwent, Wales **24** Q16
Red Wing: Minn., U.S.A. **88** E3
Redwood City: Calif., U.S.A. **93** C5
Ree, Lough: Repub. of Irel. **30** F12
Reed City: Mich., U.S.A. **88** J4
Reeder: N. Dak., U.S.A. **92** G3
Reedham: Norf., England **25** Z14
Reedsburg: Wis., U.S.A. **88** F4
Reedville: Va., U.S.A. **89** N7
Reedy Glacier: Antarctica **9** 90S 140W
Reefton: South I., N.Z. **70** N16
Reepham: Lincs., England **27** V13
Reepham: Norf., England **25** Y14
Reeth: N. Yorks., England **26** S11
Refahiye: Turkey **56** F2
Reftele: Sweden **47** N8
Refugio: Tex., U.S.A. **90** C11
Rega: *riv.*, Poland **45** V2
Regar: Tadzhik., U.S.S.R. **51** L7
Regen: W. Germany **41** T7
Regen: *riv.*, W. Germany **45** S6
Regensburg: W. Germany **45** S6
Reggane: Algeria **78** E4
Reggio: La., U.S.A. **90** *Ins.*
Reggio di Calabria: Italy **38** O17
Reggio nell' Emilia: Italy **40** Q11
Reghin: Romania **43** T13
Regina: Fr. Guiana **94** G3
REGINA: Sask., Canada **92** G2
Regina: Roman fort at Regensburg, W. Germany **40** S6
Registan: *geog. reg.*, Afghan. **58** K8
Registro do Araguaia: Brazil **94** G7
Regone: Mozambique **77** E6
Regueibat: *geog. reg.*, Mauritania **78** B4
Reguengos: Portugal **35** C17
Regulbium: Roman fort at Reculver, Kent, England **25** Y17
Rehanli: Turkey **56** E3
Rehau: W. Germany **45** S5
Rehna: E. Germany **45** R2
Rehoboth: & *Dist.*, S.W. Afr. **74** B1
Rehovot: Israel **55** a3
Rei Bouba: Cameroun **81** G3
Reichenau: Austria **41** V8
Reichenbach: E. Germany **45** S5
Reichenfels: Austria **41** U8
Reichenhall: W. Germany **41** S8
Reichertshofen: W. Germany **41** R7
Reid River: Queens., Austl. **70** G2
Reidsville: N.C., U.S.A. **89** M7
Reiff: Highland, Scotland **28** L3
Reigate: Surrey, England **25** V17
Reims: France **36** K6
Reinberg: E. Germany **45** T1
Reindeer, Lake: Man., Can. **92** G1
Reindeer Depot: N.W.T., Canada **84** f4
Reine, La: Que., Canada **89** M1
Reinosa: Spain **35** D15
Reira: Sudan **54** D11
Reisa: *riv.*, Norway **46** R2
Reiss: High., Scotland **28** P3
Reit im Winkl: W. Germany **41** S8
Reitoru: *i.*, Tuamotu Arch. **83** g3
Reitz: & *Dist.*, O.F.S., S. Afr. **75** H3
Rekareka: *i.*, Tuamotu Arch. **83** g3
Rekinniki: U.S.S.R. **49** S5
Reliance: N.W.T., Canada **84** J5
Relizane: Algeria **35** G19
Remansão: Brazil **94** H4
Remanso: Brazil **94** J5
Rembang: Java **65** E8
Remchis: Algeria **35** F19
Remedios: Panama **87** I16
Remels: W. Germany **44** N2
Remi: Gallic tribe with centre at Reims, France **36** K6
Remich: Luxembourg **44** M6
Remiremont: France **40** M7
Remontnoye: U.S.S.R. **50** F5
Remoulins: France **37** K12
Rems: *riv.*, W. Germany **40** P7
Remscheid: W. Germany **44** N4
Rena: Norway **47** M6
Renaison: France **37** J9
Renaze: France **36** D8
Renca: Argentina **96** B3
Renchen: W. Germany **40** O7
Rendova: *i.*, Solomon Is. **67** L3
Rendsburg: W. Germany **44** P1
Renfrew: Ont., Canada **89** N3
Renfrew: Strath., Scotland **29** N8
Rengat: Sumatra **65** C7
Rengo: Chile **96** A3
Reni: Ukraine **39** V14
Renigunta: Andhra Pradesh, India **58** N12
Renkum: Netherlands **44** L4
Renland: *geog. reg.*, Grnld. **85** r3
Renmark: S. Australia **71** D10
Rennell I.: Coral Sea **67** M4
RENNES: Ille-et-Vilaine, France **36** D7
Rennington: Northumb., England **26** S9
Rennweg: Austria **41** T8
Reno: Nev., U.S.A. **93** D5
Reno: *riv.*, Italy **41** R11
Renoster: *riv.*, O.F.S., S. Africa **75** G3
Renovo: Pa., U.S.A. **89** N5
Rensburg: Trans., S. Africa **74** N*Ins*
Rensselaer: Ind., U.S.A. **88** H5
Rensselaer: N.Y., U.S.A. **89** P4
Renteria: Spain **37** D12
Renton: Wash., U.S.A. **92** C3
Reo: Flores, Indonesia 65 G8
Reposaari: Finland **47** R6
Repton: Derby., England **27** S14
Republic: Mich., U.S.A. **88** H2
Republic: Wash., U.S.A. **92** D3
Republican: *riv.*, U.S.A. **93** G4
Repulse Bay: *settlement*, N.W.T., Canada **85** L4
Repulse Bay: Queens., Austl. **70** H3
Requena: Peru **94** C5
Requena: Spain **35** F17
Reşadiye: Turkey **56** E1
Resafe: Arabian fortress and Roman remains, Syria **56** F4
Resele: Sweden **46** P5
Resen: Yugoslavia **39** R16
Resende: Brazil **96** G1
RESHT: Gilan, Iran **57** L3
Resia: Italy **41** T9
Residencia: Trans., S. Africa **74** M *Ins.*
RESISTENCIA: Chaco, Arg. **96** D2
Reşiţa: Romania **43** R14
Resko: Poland **45** V2
Resko, Lake: Poland **45** V1
Resolution I.: New Zealand **71** L17
Resolution I.: N.W.T., Can. **85** n5
Resolven: W. Glam., Wales **24** O16
Resort, Loch: Outer Hebrides, Scotland **28** G3
Ressano Garcia: Moz. **75** K2
Ressons: France **36** H6
Ressons-sur-Matz: France **36** H6
Reston: Borders, Scotland **29** R8
Retamito: Argentina **96** B3
Retford, East: Notts., Eng. **27** U13
Rethel: France **36** K6
Rethem: W. Germany **44** P3
Rethimnon: Crete **39** T19
Retiers: France **36** D8
Retreat: S. Africa **74** *Ins.*
Retsag: Hungary **43** Q13
Rettendon: Essex, England **25** X16
Retz: Austria **41** T7
Reuben: Israelite tribe which inhabited region E. of Dead Sea and N. of river *Arnon*, Jordan **55** b3
Reuilly: France **36** H8

Reunion: *Fr. overseas dept.* **19** 20S 50E
Cap.: St. Denis
Area: 970 sq. miles (2,512 sq. km.)
Pop.: 466,000 (*1972 E*)

Reus: Spain **35** G16
Reusel: Netherlands **44** L4
Reuss: *riv.*, Switzerland **40** O8
Reutlingen: W. Germany **40** P7
Reutte: Austria **41** Q8
REVEL (Tallinn): Estonia, U.S.S.R. **47** T7
Revel: France **37** G12
Revello: Italy **40** N11
Revelstoke: B.C., Canada **92** D2
Reventason: Peru **94** A5
Revermont: *geog. reg.*, Fr. **40** L9
Revigny: France **36** K7
Revilla Gigedo Is.: (Mex.), Pacific O. **86** h14
Revin: France **36** K6
Revubuè: *riv.*, Mozambique **77** D6
Rewa: Madhya Pradesh, India **58** O10
Rewanui: South I., N.Z. **70** N16
Rewari: Haryana, India **58** N9
Rexburg: Idaho, U.S.A. **92** E4
Rexton: Mich., U.S.A. **88** J2
Reykholt: Iceland **46** C4
Reykjahlidh: Iceland **46** e4
Reykjanes Ridge: N. Atlantic Ocean **8** 55N 35W
REYKJAVIK: Iceland **46** c4
Reynoldston: W. Glam., Wales **24** N16
Reynosa: Mexico **90** B12
Rēzekne: Latvia, U.S.S.R. **47** U8
Rēznas Lake: Latvia, U.S.S.R. **47** U8
Rgotina: Yugoslavia **39** S14
Rhaetia: see *Raetia*
Rhaetian Alps: Switzerland **40** P9
Rhagae: former capital of Median Empire, also called *Ragae* and *Rageo*, on site of modern Tehran, Iran **55** H7
Rhamnus: Greek village of NE. *Attica* on the coast about 8 miles NE. of Marathon **39** S17
Rhayader: Powys, Wales **24** O15
Rhede: W. Germany **44** N2
Rheden: Netherlands **44** M3
Rheinbach: W. Germany **44** M5
Rheinburg: W. Germany **44** M4
Rheindahlen: W. Germany **44** M4
Rheine: W. Germany **44** N3
Rheinhessen-Pfalz: *Dist.*, Rhineland-Palatinate, West Germany **44** N6
Rheinsberg: E. Germany **45** S2
Rheneia: island about ¼ mile W. of *Delos* and 2 miles W. of Mikonos, Aegean Sea **39** T18
Rhenen: Netherlands **44** L4
Rhergo: Mali **80** D1
Rheydt: W. Germany **44** M4
Rhiconich: Highland, Scot. **28** M3
Rhinau: France **40** N7
Rhine: *riv.*, W. Germany **44** M4
Rhinelander: Wis., U.S.A. **88** G3
Rhineland-Palatinate: *State*, W. Germany (*cap.* Mainz) **44** N5
Rhins (of Galloway), The: *dist.*, Dumf. & Gall., Scotland **29** L10
Rhinns of Kells: *dist.*, Dumf. & Gall., Scotland **29** N9
Rhinns Point: *cape*, Inner Hebr., Scotland **29** J8
Rhinocolura: ancient fort at El 'Arish, Egypt **56** C6
Rhinog Fawr: *mtn.*, Gwynedd, Wales **27** O14
Rhinow: E. Germany **45** S3
Rhin Ruppiner Canal: E. Ger. **45** S3
Rhir, Cape: Morocco **80** K8
Rhium: promontory on S. side of narrows between G. of Patras and G. of Corinth, Greece **39** R17
Rhodanus: Roman name of river Rhône **37** K11
Rhode: Offaly, Repub. of Ireland **31** G13
Rhode Island: *State*, U.S.A. (*cap.* Providence) **89** Q5
Rhodes: Dodecanese, Greece **39** V18
Rhodes: S. Africa **75** G5
Rhodes (Rodhos): *i.*, Dodecanese, Greece **39** U18

Rhodesia (Zimbabwe): ***unilaterally declared independence from U.K. 1965* 77 C6**
Cap.: Salisbury
Area: 150,333 sq. miles (389,362 sq. km.)
Pop.: 5,690,000 (*1972 E*)

Rhodes Memorial: Cape Town, S. Africa **74** *Ins.*
Rhodope Mtns.: Bulgaria **39** T16
Rhondda: & *val.*, Mid Glam., Wales **24** P16
Rhône: *Dept.*, France (*cap.* Lyon) **37** K9
Rhône: *riv.*, France **37** K11
Rhône Canal: France **40** N7
Rhoose: S. Glam., Wales **24** P17
Rhoscolyn: Gwynedd, Wales **27** M13
Rhosllanerchrugog: Clwyd, Wales **27** P13
Rhosneigr: Gwynedd, Wales **27** M13
Rhossili: W. Glam., Wales **24** N16
Rhu: Strathclyde, Scotland **29** M7
Rhuddlan: Clwyd, Wales **27** P13
Rhum: *i. & sound*, Inner Hebr., Scotland **28** J6
Rhunahaorine: Strath., Scot. **29** K8
Rhyl: Clwyd, Wales **27** P13
Rhymney: Mid Glam., Wales **24** P16
Rhyndacus: Greek name of river Simav, Turkey **39** V17
Rhynie: Grampian, Scotland **28** Q5
Riang: Arunachal Pradesh, India **59** Q9
Riaño: Spain **35** D15
Riasi: Jammu & Kashmir **58** M8
Riau Arch.: Indonesia **65** C6
Riaza: Spain **35** E16
Ribadeo: Spain **35** C15
Ribadesella: Spain **35** D15
Ribadleh: Ethiopia **79** R18
Ribatejo: *Prov.*, Portugal (*cap.* Santarem) **35** B17
Ribaue: Mozambique **77** E5
Ribble: *riv.*, England **27** Q12
Ribble Head: N. Yorks., Eng. **26** R11
Ribblesdale: *val.*, Lancs./N. Yorks., England **27** R12
Ribchester: see *Bremetennacum*
Ribe: Denmark **47** L9
Ribeauville: France **40** N7
Ribeira: & *riv.*, Brazil **96** F1
Ribeirão Prêto: Brazil **96** F1
Ribemont: France **36** J6
Riberac: France **37** F10
Riberalta: Bolivia **94** D6
Ribi: Papua/New Guinea **66** J3
Rib Lake: *city*, Wis., U.S.A. **88** F3
Rib Mtn.: Wis., U.S.A. **88** G3
Ribnica: Yugoslavia **41** U10
Ribnitz: E. Germany **45** S1
Řicany: Czechoslovakia **45** U6
Riccall: N. Yorks., England **27** T12
Riccarton: Borders, Scotland **29** Q9
Riccarton: South I., N.Z. **70** O16
Riccarton: Strath., Scotland **29** M8
Riccione: Italy **41** S12
Rice Lake: *city*, Wis., U.S.A. **88** F3
Riceys, Les: France **36** K8
Rich: Morocco **80** L8
Richards, Cape: N.W.T., Canada **85** M1
Richard's Bay: *town & bay*, Natal, S. Africa **75** K4
Richborough: Kent, Eng. **25** Y17
Richelieu: France **36** F8
Richelieu: *riv.*, Que., Can. **89** P3
Richfield: Utah, U.S.A. **93** E5
Richford: Vt., U.S.A. **89** P3
Richhill: Armagh, N. Irel. **30** H11
Rich Hill: *city*, Mo., U.S.A. **90** D6
Richibucto: N.B., Canada **89** T2
Richie's Arch.: Andaman Is. **59** Q12
Richland: Oreg., U.S.A. **92** D4
Richland: Wash., U.S.A. **92** D3
Richland Center: Wis., U.S.A. **88** F4
Richlands: Va., U.S.A. **88** L7
Richmond: Calif., U.S.A. **93** C5
Richmond: & *Dist.*, Cape Prov., S. Africa **74** E5
Richmond: Gt. Ldn., England **25** V17
Richmond: Ind., U.S.A. **88** J6
Richmond: Ky., U.S.A. **88** J7
Richmond: Maine, U.S.A. **89** R3
Richmond: Mo., U.S.A. **90** E6
Richmond: & *Dist.*, Natal, S. Africa **75** J4
Richmond: N.S.W., Austl. **71** J9
Richmond: N. Yorks., England **26** S11
Richmond: Ont., Canada **89** O3
Richmond: Oreg., U.S.A. **92** C4
Richmond: Que., Canada **89** P3
Richmond: Queens., Austl. **69** G4
Richmond: South I., N.Z. **70** O15
Richmond: Tex., U.S.A. **90** D11
RICHMOND: Va., U.S.A. **89** N7
Richmond Gulf: Que., Can. **85** M6
Richwood: W. Va., U.S.A. **88** L6
Rickmansworth: Herts., Eng. **25** V16
Riddings: Cumbria, England **26** Q9
Riddle: Idaho, U.S.A. **92** D4
Rideau Lake: Ont., Canada **89** N3
Ridgelands: Queens., Austl. **70** J4
Ridgetown: Ont., Canada **88** L4
Ridgewell: Essex, England **25** X15
Ridgway: Pa., U.S.A. **89** M5
Riding Mill: Northumb., Eng. **26** S10
Riding Mtn.: Man., Canada **92** G2
Riding Mtn. Nat. Park: Man., Canada **92** G2
Ridsdale: Northumb., Eng. **26** R9
Riebeek East: S. Africa **75** G6
Ried: Austria **41** T7
Riedenburg: W. Germany **41** R7
Ried in Tirol: Austria **40** Q8
Riedlingen: W. Germany **40** P7
Rieneck: W. Germany **44** P5
Riesa: E. Germany **45** T4
Riesi: Sicily **38** O18
Riet: *riv.*, O.F.S., S. Africa **75** F4
Riet: *riv.*, Trans., S. Africa **74** N*Ins.*
Rietberg: W. Germany **44** O4
Rietbron: S. Africa **74** E6
Rietfontein: S. Africa **74** D3
Rietgat: O.F.S., S. Africa **75** G3
Rieti: Italy **38** N15
Rietpoel: S. Africa **74** C7
Rietvlei: S. Africa **75** H5
Rieumes: France **37** G12
Rieupeyroux: France **37** H11
Rieutort: France **37** J11
Rievaulx Abbey: N. Yorks., England **26** T11
Riez: France **40** M12
Rift Valley: *Reg.*, Kenya (*cap.* Nakuru) **76** E2
RIGA: Latvia, U.S.S.R. **47** T8
Riga, G. of: Latvia, U.S.S.R. **47** S8
Rigai: *well*, Saudi Arabia **57** K7
Rigby: Idaho, U.S.A. **92** E4
Rignac: France **37** H11
Rigolet: Newf., Canada **85** O7
Rig Rig: Chad **81** G2
Rigside: Strath., Scotland **29** O8
Riihimaki: Finland **47** T6
Rijeka (Fiume): Yugoslavia **41** U10
Rijswijk: Netherlands **44** K3
Rikita: Sudan **76** C1
Rila Mtns.: Bulgaria **39** S15
Rille: France **36** F8
Rillington: Humberside, England **26** U11
Rimatara: *i.*, Austral Is. **83** e4
Rimavska Sobota: Czech. **43** R12
Rimbo: Sweden **47** Q7
Rime: *watercourse*, Chad **78** H7
Rimini: Italy **41** S11
Rimogne: France **36** K6
Rimouski: Que., Canada **89** R1
Rinca: *i.*, Indonesia 65 F8
Rincon: N. Mex., U.S.A. **93** F6
Rinconada: Argentina **96** B1
Rincon Peak: N. Mex., U.S.A. **93** F5
Rindal: Norway **46** L5
Rineanna: Clare, Repub. of Ireland **31** D14
Ring: Wat., Repub. of Ireland **31** F15
Ringas: Rajasthan, India 58 N9
Ringebu: Norway **47** M6
Ringerike: Norway **47** M6
Ringkøbing: & *fiord*, Den. **47** L8
Ringmer: E. Sussex, England **25** W18
Ringsaker: Norway **47** M6
Ringsend: Lon., N. Ireland **30** H9
Ringstead: Norf., England **25** X14
Ringsted: Zealand, Den. **47** M9
Ringstorp: Sweden **47** O7
Ringvassøy: *i.*, Norway **46** O2
Ringway: *airfield*, England **27** R13
Ringwood: Dorset, England **25** S18
Ringwood: Vict., Australia **71** F11
Ringwould: Kent, England **25** Y17
Rinteln: W. Germany **44** P3
Rinvyle: Galway, Repub. of Ireland **30** B12
Rio Azul: Brazil **96** E2
Riobamba: Ecuador **94** B4
Rio BRANCO: Acre, Brazil **94** D5
Rio Branco: Parana, Braz. **96** F2
Rio Branco: Uruguay **96** E3
Rio Bueno: Jamaica **86** *Ins.*
Rio Claro: Brazil **96** F1
Rio Colorado: Argentina **96** C4
Rio Cuarto: Argentina **96** C3
Rio de Contas: Brazil **94** J6
RIO DE JANEIRO: Guanabara, Brazil **96** G1
Rio de Janeiro: *State*, Brazil (*cap.* Niteroi) **96** G1
Rio del Rey: Cameroun **81** F4
Rio do Sul: Brazil **96** F2
Rio Gallegos: Santa Cruz, Argentina **95** D14
Rio Grande: Argentina **95** D14
Rio Grande: Brazil **96** E3
Rio Grande: Mexico **86** j13
Rio Grande: *riv.*, U.S.A./Mexico **93** G7
Rio Grande City: Tex., U.S.A. **90** B12
Rio Grande do Norte: *State*, Brazil (*cap.* Natal) **94** K5
Rio Grande do Sul: *State*, Brazil (*cap.* Pôrto Alegre) **96** E2
Rio Grande Rise: S. Atlantic Ocean **8** 35S 40W
Riohacha: Colombia **94** C1
Rio Hondo: Argentina **96** C2
RIOJA, LA: & *State*, Arg. **96** B2
Rioja, La: Chile **96** B1
Riom: France **37** J10
Riomes-Montagne: France **37** H10
Rio Muerto: Argentina **96** C2
Rio Mulatos: Bolivia **94** D7
Rion: France **37** E12
Rio Negro: Brazil **96** F2
Rio Negro: *Prov.*, Arg. (*cap.* Viedma) **95** D12
Rionero in Vulture: Italy **38** O16
Rio Pardo: Mato Grosso, Brazil **94** G8
Rio Pardo: Minas Gerais, Brazil **94** J7
Rio Pardo: Rio Grande do Sul, Brazil **96** E2
Rio Pomba: Brazil **96** F1
Rio Segundo: Argentina **96** C3
Riosucio: Colombia **94** B2
Riouw Arch.: *see* Riau.
Rio Verde: Brazil **94** G7
Ripats: Sweden **46** R3
Ripe: E. Sussex, England **25** W18
Ripley: Derby., England **27** T13
Ripley: Miss., U.S.A. **90** G8
Ripley: N. Yorks., England **27** S11
Ripley: Ohio, U.S.A. **88** K6
Ripley: Surrey, England **25** V17
Ripley: Tenn., U.S.A. **90** G8
Ripley: W. Va., U.S.A. **88** L6
Ripoll: Spain **35** H15
Ripon: N. Yorks., England **26** S11
Ripon: S. Africa **75** F6
Ripon: Wis., U.S.A. **88** G4
Ripon Falls: Uganda **76** D2
Rippingale: Lincs., England **27** V14
Ripponden: W. Yorks., Eng. **27** R12
Riqai: *well*, Saudi Arabia **57** K7
Risalpur: NW. Front. Prov., Pakistan **58** M8
Risan: Yugoslavia **39** Q15
Risbäck: Sweden **46** O4
Risby: Suff., England **25** X15
Risca: Gwent, Wales **24** P16
Riscle: France **37** E12
Riseley: Beds., England **25** V15
Risha: *wadi*, Saudi Arabia **54** F9
Rishiri: *i.*, Japan **63** ZZ5
Rishon le Zion: Israel **55** a3
Rishton: Lancs., England **27** R12
Rishworth: W. Yorks., England **27** S12
Rising Sun: Ind., U.S.A. **88** J6
Risle: *riv.*, France **36** F6
Risør: Norway **47** L7
Rissani: Morocco **80** L8
Rissington, Great: Glos., England **25** S16
Ristijärvi: Finland **46** V4
Ristikent: U.S.S.R. **46** W2
Risut: Oman **55** H11
Ritchie Falls: S. Africa **74** C4
Ritchie's Arch.: Andaman Is. **59** Q12
Ritenbenk: Greenland **85** o4
Ritter, Mount: Calif., U.S.A. **93** D5
Ritva: Finland **46** U4
Ritzville: Wash., U.S.A. **92** D3
Riva: Italy **41** Q10
Rivadavia: Buenos Aires, Argentina **96** C4
Rivadavia: Chile **96** A2
Rivadavia: Mendoza, Arg. **96** B3
Rivadavia: Salta, Argentina **96** C1
Rival: France **37** L10
Rival: *riv.*, France **37** L10
Rivalkoy: Turkey **56** A1
Rivarolo: Italy **40** N10
Rivas: Nicaragua **86** L15
Rive-de-Gier: France **37** K10
Rivera: Argentina **96** C4
Rivera: Uruguay **96** D3
River Cess: Liberia **80** C3
Riverchapel: Wex., Repub. of Ireland **31** J14
River Falls: *city*, Wis., U.S.A. **88** E3
Rivergaro: Italy **40** P11
Riverhead: N.Y., U.S.A. **89** P5
Riverhurst: Sask., Canada **92** F2
Riverina: *geog. reg.*, N.S.W., Australia **71** F10
River Plate: *est.*, Argentina **96** D3
Rivers: Man., Canada **92** G2
Rivers: *state*, Nigeria (*cap.* Port Harcourt) **81** F4
Riversdale: & *Dist.*, S. Afr. **74** D7
Riverside: Calif., U.S.A. **93** D6
Riverside: Wyo., U.S.A. **92** F4
Rivers Inlet: *town*, B.C., Can. **92** B2
Riversleigh: Queens., Austl. **69** F3
Riverstick: Cork, Repub. of Ireland **31** E16
Riverstown: Sligo, Repub. of Ireland **30** E11
Riverton: Man., Canada **92** H2
Riverton: S. Africa **75** F4
Riverton: S. Australia **71** C10
Riverton: South I., N.Z. **71** M18
Riverton: Wyo., U.S.A. **92** F4
River View: Va., U.S.A. **91** N7
Rivesaltes: France **37** H13
Riviera di Levante: *coast*, It. **40** P11
Riviera di Ponente: *coast*, It. **40** O12
Riviere a Pierre: Que., Can. **89** P2
Riviere au Renard: Que., Canada **89** T1
Riviere du Loup: Que., Can. **89** R2
Riviere du Moulin: Que., Canada **89** Q1
Rivoli: Italy **40** N10
Rivoli: hill on right bank of Adige about 3 miles N. of S. Ambrogio, Italy **41** Q10
RIYADH: Saudi Arabia **54** G10
Riyaq: Lebanon **56** E5
RIZAIYEH (Urmia): Azerbaijan-e Bakhtari, Iran **57** J3
RIZE: & *Prov.*, Turkey **57** G1
Rize Mtns.: Turkey **57** G1
Rizokarpasa: Cyprus **56** D4
Rizzuto, Cape: Italy **38** P17
Rjukan: Norway **47** L7
Rö: Loyalty Is. **67** N6
Roa: Norway **47** M6
Roa: Spain **35** E16
Roade: Northants., England **25** U15
Roadford: Clare, Repub. of Ireland **31** C13
Roadside: Gram., Scotland **28** R6
Roag, Loch: Outer Hebr., Scotland **28** H3
Roan: Norway **46** M4
Roandji: Cen. Afr. Rep. **76** B1
Roanne: France **37** K9
Roanoke: Ala., U.S.A. **91** J9
Roanoke: Va., U.S.A. **89** M7
Roanoke: *riv.*, Va./N.C., U.S.A. **89** N7
Roanoke I., N.C., U.S.A. **91** O8
Roanoke Rapids: *city*, N.C., U.S.A. **89** N7
Roaringwater Bay: Cork, Repub. of Ireland **31** C16
Roatán I.: Honduras **86** L14
Robben I.: S. Africa **74** C6
Robbinsdale: Minn., U.S.A. **88** E3
Robbio: Italy **40** O10
Robe: S. Australia **71** C11
Robe: *riv.*, Mayo, Repub. of Ireland **30** C12
Röbel: E. Germany **45** S2
Robert Brown, Cape: Can. **85** l4
Roberton: Bord., Scotland **29** Q9
Roberton: Strath., Scotland **29** O8
Robertsbridge: E. Sussex, England **25** W18
Robertsfors: Sweden **46** R4
Robertsganj: Uttar Pradesh, India **59** O10
Robertson: & *Dist.*, S. Afr. **74** C6
ROBERTSPORT: Grand Cape Mount, Liberia **80** B3
Robertstown: Kild., Repub. of Ireland **31** H13
Robertstown: S. Australia **71** C9
Roberval: Que., Canada **89** P1
Robeson Chan.: Grnld./Can. **85** n1
Robin Hood's Bay: *village*, N. Yorks., England **26** U11
Robinson: Ill., U.S.A. **88** H6
Robinson: Trans., S. Africa **74** M*Ins.*
Robinson Crusoe: *i.*, Juan Fernandez Is., Chile **95** B10
Robinson Gorge National Park: Queens., Australia **70** H5
Robinson Ranges: W. Austl. **68** B5
Robinvale: Vict., Australia **71** E10
Robla, La: Spain **35** D15
Roblin: Man., Canada **92** G2
Roborough: Devon, England **24** N18
Robson, Mount: B.C., Can. **92** D2
Robstown: Tex., U.S.A. **90** C12
Roca, La: Spain **35** C17
Rocas: *i.*, Brazil **94** L4
Rocca San Casciano: Italy **41** R11
Rocester: Staffs., England **27** S14
Roch: Dyfed, Wales **24** L16
Rocha: Uruguay **96** E3
Rochdale: Gt. Man., England **27** R12
Roche: Corn., England **24** M19
Roche, La: France **40** M9
Roche-Bernard, La: France **36** C8
Roche-Chalais, La: France **37** F10
Rochechouart: France **37** F10
Rochedale: Queens., Austl. **69** F4
Rochefort: Belgium **44** L5
Rochefort-en-Terre: France **36** C8
Rochefort-Montagne: Fr. **37** H10
Rochefort-sur-Mer: France **37** E10
Rochefoucauld, La: France **37** F10
Rochelle: Ill., U.S.A. **88** G5
ROCHELLE, LA: Charente-Maritime, France **37** D9
Rocheservière: France **36** D9
Rochester: Ind., U.S.A. **88** H5
Rochester: Kent, England **25** X17
Rochester: Minn., U.S.A. **88** E3
Rochester: N.H., U.S.A. **89** Q4
Rochester: N.Y., U.S.A. **89** N4
Rochester: Northumb., Eng. **26** R9
Rochester: Vict., Australia **71** F11
ROCHE-SUR-YON, LA: Vendée, France **37** D9
Rochford: Essex, England **25** X16
Rochfortbridge: Westmeath, Repub. of Ireland **31** G13
Rock, The: N.S.W., Austl. **71** G10
Rock: *riv.*, U.S.A. **88** G4

For Abbreviations see list on p.113. Italic type, e.g. *Ephesus*, refers to historical names not on maps. Capital letters, e.g. MADRID, show capitals of countries; small capital letters, e.g. CADIZ, show capitals of provinces, etc. General notes p.116.

Rockall—Ryukyu Is. 181

Rockall: i., (Br.), Atlantic O. (Lat. 57° 30' N., Long. 14° W.) 20
Rockall Plateau: N. Atlantic Ocean 8 55N 20W
Rockbeare: Devon, England 24 P18
Rock Chapel: Cork, Repub. of Ireland 31 C15
Rockcliffe: Cumbria, Eng. 26 P10
Rockcorry: Monaghan, Repub. of Ireland 30 G11
Rockdale: Tex., U.S.A. 90 C10
Rockefeller Plateau: Antarctica 9 80S 145W
Rock Falls: city, Ill., U.S.A. 88 G5
Rockford: Ill., U.S.A. 88 G4
Rockford: Iowa, U.S.A. 88 E4
Rockglen: Sask., Canada 92 F3
Rockhampton: Queens., Australia 70 J4
Rockhampton Downs: N. Territ., Australia 69 F3
Rockill: Lim., Repub. of Ireland 31 D15
Rock Hill: city, S.C., U.S.A. 91 L8
Rockingham: Northants., England 27 U14
Rockingham: N.C., U.S.A. 91 M8
Rockingham: W. Australia 68 B6
Rock Island: city, Ill., U.S.A. 88 F5
Rockland: Maine, U.S.A. 89 R3
Rocklands Reservoir: Vict., Australia 71 D11
Rockmart: Ga., U.S.A. 91 J8
Rockmills: Cork, Repub. of Ireland 31 E15
Rockport: Ind., U.S.A. 88 H7
Rockport: Ont., Canada 89 O3
Rockport: Tex., U.S.A. 90 C11
Rock Rapids: Iowa, U.S.A. 92 H4
Rocksprings: Tex., U.S.A. 93 G6
Rock Springs: Wyo., U.S.A. 92 F4
Rockstone: Guyana 87 d7
Rockville: Ind., U.S.A. 88 H6
Rockville: Md., U.S.A. 89 N6
Rockwell City: Iowa, U.S.A. 92 J4
Rockwood: Maine, U.S.A. 89 R3
Rocky Ford: Colo., U.S.A. 93 G5
Rocky Mount: city, Va., U.S.A. 89 M7
Rocky Mount: city, N.C., U.S.A. 91 N8
Rocky Mtn. Nat Park: Colo., U.S.A. 93 F4
Rocky Mtns.: N. America 92 C2
Rocky Mt. House: Alta., Can. 92 E2
Rocroi: France 36 K6
Röda: Egypt 56 B7
Roda: salt lake, Syria 57 G4
Roda, La: Spain 35 E17
Rødberg: Norway 47 L6
Rødby: Denmark 47 M9
Roddickton: Newf., Can. 85 u1
Rodel: Outer Hebr., Scot. 28 H4
Roden: Netherlands 44 M2
Rodenberg: W. Germany 44 P3
Rodeo: Argentina 96 B3
RODEZ: Aveyron, France 37 H11
Rodhos (Rhodes): i., Dodec., Greece 39 U18
Roding: W. Germany 45 S6
Roding: riv., Essex, England 25 W16
Rodings, The: dist., Essex, England 23 W16
Rodlin: E. Germany 45 T2
Rodna: Romania 43 T13
Rodora: Trans., S. Africa 74 Ins.
Rodriguez: i., (Mauritius), Indian Ocean 19 10S 60E
Rodriguez Fracture Zone: Indian Ocean 9 20S 65E
Roebourne: W. Australia 68 B4
Roe Isthmus: N.W.T., Can. 85 L4
Roermond: Netherlands 44 L4
Roeselare: Belgium 44 J5
Roes Welcome Sound: N.W.T., Canada 85 L5
Rogachev: Byelorussia 50 D4
Rogaland: Co., Norway (cap. Stavanger) 47 K7
Rogart: Highland, Scotland 28 N3
Rogatec: Yugoslavia 41 V9
Rogatica: Yugoslavia 39 Q15
Rogatin: Ukraine 43 T12
Rogers: Ark., U.S.A. 90 D7
Rogers, Mount: Va., U.S.A. 88 L7
Rogers City: Mich., U.S.A. 88 K3
Roggeveld Mtns.: S. Africa 74 D6
Rogiet: Gwent, Wales 24 Q16
Rognac: France 37 L12
Rognan: Norway 46 O3
Rohan: France 36 C7
Rohr: Austria 41 U7
Rohrbach: Austria 41 T7
Rohrbach: France 44 N6
Rohri: Sind, Pakistan 58 L9
Roi Et: Thailand 64 C3
Roisel: France 36 J6
Roja: Argentina 96 C3
Rojdåfors: Sweden 47 N6
Rojden: Sweden 47 N6
Rokeby: Durham, England 26 S10
Rokel: riv., Sierra Leone 80 B3
Rokishkis: Lithuania, U.S.S.R. 47 T9
Rokitno: Ukraine 43 U11
Rokko (Lu-chiang): Taiwan 63 W10
Rokugo, Cape: Japan 63 e2
Rokycany: Czechoslovakia 45 T6
Røldal: Norway 47 K7
Roldan: Argentina 96 C3
Rolfe: Iowa, U.S.A. 92 J4
Rolfsøy: i., Norway 46 S1
Rolla: Mo., U.S.A. 88 F7
Rolla: N. Dak., U.S.A. 92 H3
Rollag: Norway 47 L6
Rolle: Switzerland 40 M9
Rolleston: Notts., England 27 U13
Rolleston: Queens., Austl. 70 H5
Rollingstone: Queens., Austl. 70 G2
Rolo: Italy 41 Q11
Rolvenden: Kent, England 25 X17
Roma: Gotland, Sweden 47 Q8
ROMA (Rome): Italy 38 N16
Roma: Queens., Australia 70 H6
Roma: i., Indonesia 55 H8
Romagnano: Italy 40 O10
Romain, Cape: S.C., U.S.A. 91 M9
Romaldkirk: N. Yorks., England 26 R10
Roma-Los Saenz: Mexico 90 B12
Roman: Romania 43 U13
Roman: U.S.S.R. 49 N5
Romana, La: Dominican Rep. 87 N14
Roman Apennines: mtns., Italy 38 N15
Romanche Fracture Zone: Atlantic Ocean 8 0 20W
Romani: Egypt 56 C6

Romania: Republic 33 G2
Cap.: Bucharest (Bucureşti)
Area: 91,699 sq. miles (237,500 sq. km.)
Pop.: 20,470,000 (1971 E)

Romano, Cape: Fla., U.S.A. 91 L13
Romanovka: U.S.S.R. 49 N7
Romanovskaya: U.S.S.R. 50 F5
Roman Rock: i., S. Africa 74 Ins.
Romans: France 37 L10
Romanshorn: Switzerland 40 P8
Romanzof, Cape: Alaska, U.S.A. 84 C5
Romblon: Philippines 64 G4
Rome: Ga., U.S.A. 91 J8
ROME (Roma): Italy 38 N16
Rome: N.Y., U.S.A. 89 O4
Romiley: Gt. Man., England 27 R13
Romilly-sur-Seine: France 36 J7
Romkimy: U.S.S.R. 51 O2
Romney: W. Va., U.S.A. 89 M6
Romney, New: Kent, Eng. 25 X18
Romney Marsh: Kent, England 25 X17
Romny: Ukraine 50 D4
Rømø: i., Denmark 47 L9
Romodanovo: U.S.S.R. 50 G4
Romont: Switzerland 40 M9
Romorantin: France 36 G8
Romsey: Hants., England 25 S18
Romsey: Vict., Australia 71 F11
Ron: Vietnam 64 D3
Rona: i., Inner Hebr., Scot. 28 K4
Rona, North: i., Scotland 28 K2
Ronaldsay, North & South: is., Orkney Is., Scotland 28 Ins.
Ronaldsway: airfield, I. of Man, United Kingdom 26 M11
Ronas Hill: Mainland, Shetland Is. 28 Ins.
Ronay: i., Outer Hebr., Scotland 28 G5
Roncador Cay: i., (U.S.A./Col.), Caribbean Sea 87 I15
Roncesvalles: Spain 37 D12
Ronceverte: W. Va., U.S.A. 88 L7
Ronchi: Italy 41 T10
Ronco: riv., Italy 41 S11
Ronco Scrivia: Italy 40 O11
Ronda: Spain 35 D18
Rondawel: Trans., S. Africa 75 G2
Ronde: i., Grenadines, Windward Is. 87 c4
Rondebosch: S. Africa 74 Ins.
Rondônia: Territ., Brazil (cap. Pôrto Velho) 94 E6
Rondonópolis: Brazil 94 G7
Rong: i., Cambodia 64 C4
Ronge, Lac La: Sask., Can. 92 G1
Rønne: Bornholm, Denmark 47 O9
Ronne Ice Shelf: Antarctica 9 80S 60W
Ronneby: Sweden 47 O8
Ron Phibun: Thailand 64 B5
Ronse: Belgium 44 J5
Roodepoort: Trans., S. Afr. 74 M Ins.
Roodhouse: Ill., U.S.A. 88 F6
Roof Butte: mtn., Ariz., U.S.A. 93 F5
Rooibank: S.W. Africa 74 A1
Rooiberg: S. Africa 74 C5
Rooigrond: S. Africa 75 F2
Rooikop: Trans., S. Afr. 74 N Ins.
Rooiwerf: S. Africa 74 D6
Rookhope: Durham, Eng. 26 R10
Roorkee: Uttar Pradesh, India 58 N9
Roos: Humb., England 27 V12
Roosendaal: Netherlands 44 K4
Roosenekal: Trans., S. Afr. 75 H2
Roosevelt: Minn., U.S.A. 88 D1
Roosevelt: Utah, U.S.A. 93 F4
Roosevelt Island: Antarctica 9 80S 165W
Roosevelt Reservoir: Ariz., U.S.A. 93 E6
Roosevelt Reservoir: Wash., U.S.A. 92 D3
Roosky: Leit., Repub. of Ireland 30 F12
Roos Senekal: Trans., S. Afr. 75 H2
Ropazhi: Latvia, U.S.S.R. 47 T8
Roper: riv., N. Territ., Austl. 68 E2
Roper Mission Station: N. Territ., Australia 68 E2
Ropley: Hants., England 25 T17
Ropp: Nigeria 81 F3
Ropsley: Lincs., England 27 U14
Roque: Panama 94 Ins.
Roquefort: Aveyron, France 37 H12
Roquefort: Landes, France 37 E11
Roquemaure: France 37 K11
Roques, Los: is., Venezuela 94 D1
Roquevaire: France 40 L12
Rora Head: cape, Orkney Is., Scotland 28 P2
Roraima: Territ., Brazil (cap. Boa Vista) 94 E3
Roraima: mtn., Guy./Ven. 87 c8
Røros: Norway 46 M5
Rorschach: Switzerland 40 P8
Rorstad: Norway 46 O3
Rørvik: Norway 46 M4
Rosa: Argentina 95 C13
Rosa: Zambia 77 D4
Rosa, Cape: Algeria 38 L18
Rosa, Monte: Switz./Italy 40 N10
Rosapenna: Don., Repub. of Ireland 30 F9
Rosarinho: Brazil 94 F4
Rosario: Argentina 96 C3
Rosario: Chile 96 A1
Rosario: Durango, Mexico 93 F7
Rosario: Lower Calif., Mex. 93 D6
Rosário: Maranhão, Brazil 94 J4
Rosario: Paraguay 96 D1
Rosário: Rio Grande do Sul, Brazil 96 E3
Rosario: Sinaloa, Mexico 86 J13
Rosario: Uruguay 96 D3
Rosario de la Frontera: Arg. 96 C2
Rosario de Lerma: Arg. 96 B1
Rosario del Tama: Arg. 96 B3
Rosário Oéste: Brazil 94 F6
Rosario Tala: Argentina 96 D3
Rosas: & gulf, Spain 35 H15
Rosas, Las: Argentina 96 C3
Rosbercon: Kilk., Repub. of Ireland 31 H15
Roscoff: France 36 B7
Roscommon: Mich., U.S.A. 88 J3
ROSCOMMON: & Co., Repub. of Ireland 30 E12
Roscrea: Tip., Repub. of Ireland 31 F14
ROSEAU: Dominica, Windward Is. 87 c3
Roseau: N. Dak., U.S.A. 92 H3
Rosebank: C.P., S. Africa 74 Ins.
Rose Blanche: Newf., Can. 85 t3
Rosebud: Tex., U.S.A. 90 C10
Roseburg: Oreg., U.S.A. 92 C4
Rosedale: Miss., U.S.A. 90 F9
Rosedale: Queens., Austl. 70 J5
Rosedale: Vict., Australia 71 G12
Rosedale Abbey: village, N. Yorks., England 26 U11
Rosegreen: Tip., Repub. of Ireland 31 F15
Rosehearty: Grampian, Scot. 28 R4
Roseires: Sudan 79 L7
Rose I.: Bahamas 91 N13
Rose I.: Samoa 70 Ins.
Rosemarket: Dyfed, Wales 24 M16
Rosemarkie: High., Scot. 28 N4
Rosenallis: Laois, Repub. of Ireland 31 G13
Rosenbach: Austria 41 U9
Rosenberg: Tex., U.S.A. 90 D11
Rosenberg: Sweden 47 N7
Rosendael: France 36 H4
Rosendal: O.F.S., S. Africa 75 G4
Rosenheim: W. Germany 41 S8
Rose Point: cape, N.S., Can. 89 T3
Rosetown: Sask., Canada 92 F2
Rosetta: Egypt 56 B6
Roseville: Calif., U.S.A. 93 C5
Roseville: Ill., U.S.A. 88 F5
Rosewood: N. Territ., Austl. 68 D3
Rosewood: Queens., Austl. 70 K6
Rosh Pinna: Israel 55 b2
Rosiclare: Ill., U.S.A. 88 G7
Rosières: France 36 H6
Rosignano Marittimo: Italy 40 Q12
Rosignol: Guyana 87 e7
Roşiori de Vede: Romania 43 T14
Rositsa: Bulgaria 39 U15
Roskilde: Zealand, Den. 47 N9
Roskow: E. Germany 45 S3
Røs Lake: Norway 46 O4
Roslavl': U.S.S.R. 50 D4
Roslea: Ferm., N. Ireland 30 G11
Rosley: Cumbria, England 26 P10
Roslin: Lothian, Scotland 29 P8
Roslyn: Wash., U.S.A. 92 C3
Rosmead: S. Africa 75 F5
Rosneath: Strath., Scotland 29 M7
Rosporden: France 36 B8
Ross: Here. & Worcs., Eng. 24 Q16
Ross: South I., N.Z. 70 N16
Ross: i., Burma 59 R12
Ross, New: Wex., Repub. of Ireland 31 H15
Rossano: Italy 38 P17
Ross-Carbery: Cork, Repub. of Ireland 31 C16
Rosseau, Lac: Ont., Canada 89 M3
Rossel: i., New Guinea 69 J2
Rosses, The: dist., Don., Repub. of Ireland 30 E10
Rosses Point: village, Sligo, Repub. of Ireland 30 D11
Rossett: Clwyd, Wales 27 Q13
Ross Ice Shelf: Antarctica 9 85S 180
Rossignol, Lake: N.S., Can. 89 T3
Rossington: S. Yorks., Eng. 27 T13
Rossinver: Leit./Sligo, Repub. of Ireland 30 E11
Ross I.: Antarctica 90 80S 165E
Rossland: B.C., Canada 92 D3
Rosslare: & harb., Wex., Repub. of Ireland 31 J15
Rosslau: E. Germany 45 S4
Rossmore: Cork, Repub. of Ireland 31 D16
Rosso: Senegal 80 A1
Rosso, Cap: cape, Corsica 38 L15
Ross of Mull: penin., Inner Hebr., Scotland 29 J7
Rosson: Sweden 46 P5
Rossosh: U.S.S.R. 50 E4
Ross Port: Mayo, Repub. of Ireland 30 B11
Ross River: Yukon, Canada 84 f5
Ross Sea: Antarctica 9 80S 180
Rossville: Ga., U.S.A. 91 J8
Rossville: Ill., U.S.A. 88 H5
Rostellan: Cork, Repub. of Ireland 31 E16
Rosthern: Sask., Canada 92 F2
ROSTOCK: & Dist., E. Germany 45 S1
ROSTOV: & Reg., U.S.S.R. 50 E5
Rostov: Yaroslavsk, U.S.S.R. 50 E3
Rostrenen: France 36 B7
Rostrevor: Down, N. Irel. 30 J11
Rosvassbukt: Norway 46 O4
Roswell: N. Mex., U.S.A. 93 G6
Rosyth: Fife, Scotland 29 P7
Rota: i., Mariana Is. 61 O9
Rotan: Tex., U.S.A. 90 A9
Rotenburg: W. Germany 44 P2
Roth: W. Germany 45 R6
Rötha: E. Germany 45 S4
Rothbury: Northants., Eng. 26 S9
Rothenburg: W. Germany 45 Q6
Rother: riv., Derby./S. Yorks., England 27 T13
Rother: riv., E. Sussex, Eng. 25 X18
Rother: riv., W. Sussex, Eng. 25 U18
Rotherfield: E. Sussex, Eng. 24 W17
Rotherham: S. Yorks., Eng. 27 T13
Rothes: Grampian, Scotland 28 P4
Rothesay: Strath., Scotland 29 L8
Rothiemay: Gram., Scotland 28 Q4
Rothienorman: Gram., Scot. 28 R5
Rothsay: N.B., Canada 89 T3
Rothsay Forest: England 26 S9
Rothwell: Lincs., England 27 V13
Rothwell: Northants., Eng. 25 U15
Rothwell: W. Yorks., England 27 T12
Roti: i. & str., Indonesia 65 G9
Roto: N.S.W., Australia 71 F9
Rotondella: Italy 38 P16
Rotorua: North I., N.Z. 70 Q14
Rottenburg: W. Germany 40 O7
Rottenstone Lake: Sask., Can. 92 G1
Rotterdam: Netherlands 44 K4
Röttingen: W. Germany 45 P6
Rottnest I.: W. Australia 68 B6
Rottweil: W. Germany 40 O7
Rotuma: i. (Br.), Pacific O. 67 P4
Rotz: W. Germany 45 S6
Roubaix: France 36 J5
Roudnice: Czechoslovakia 45 U5
ROUEN: Seine-Maritime, Fr. 36 G6
Rouffach: France 40 N8
Rougé: France 36 D8
Rouge: riv., Vietnam 64 C2
Rouge: riv., Que., Canada 89 O2
Rough Castle: fort on Antonine Wall about 2 miles W. of Falkirk, Central, Scot. 29 O7
Roughton: Norf., England 25 Y14
Roughty: riv., Kerry, Repub. of Ireland 31 B16
Rouiba: Algeria 35 H18
Rouillac: France 37 E10
Rouina: Algeria 35 G18
Roujan: France 37 J12
Roulers: see Roeselare.
Roumania: see Romania.
Roundfort: Mayo, Repub. of Ireland 30 C12
Round Mount: mtn., N.S.W., Australia 71 K8
Round Mountain: city, Nev., U.S.A. 93 D5
Roundstone: Galway, Repub. of Ireland 31 B13
Roundup: Mont., U.S.A. 92 F3
Roundwood: Wick., Repub. of Ireland 31 J13
Rounton, West: N. Yorks., England 26 T11
Roura: Fr. Guiana 94 G3
Rousay: i., Orkney Is., Scot. 28 Ins.
Rouses Point: N.Y., U.S.A. 89 P3
Rousky: Tyr., N. Ireland 30 G10
Roussillon: Prov., France 35 H15
Rouvroy: France 36 H5
Rouxville: & Dist., O.F.S., S. Africa 75 G5
Rouyn: Que., Canada 89 M1
ROVANIEMI: Lappi, Finland 46 T3
Rovato: Italy 40 P10
Roven'ki: Ukraine 50 E5
Rovereto: Italy 41 R10
Rovershagen: E. Germany 45 S1
Rovigo: Italy 41 R10
Rovinj: Yugoslavia 41 T10
Rovkul'skoye, Lake: Karelian A.S.S. Rep., U.S.S.R. 46 W4
Rovno: Ukraine 43 U11
Rovnoye: U.S.S.R. 50 G4
Rowad: i., Syria 56 D4
Rowanburn: Dumfries & Galloway, Scotland 29 Q9
Rowanduz: see Ruwandiz.
Rowena: N.S.W., Australia 71 H7
Rower, The: Kilk., Repub. of Ireland 31 H15
Rowington: War., England 25 S15
Rowley Shoals: W. Austl. 68 B3
Rowsley, Great: Derby., England 27 S13
Roxboro: N.C., U.S.A. 89 M7
Roxburgh: Bord., Scotland 29 R8
Roxburgh: South I., N.Z. 71 M17
Roxo, Cape: Senegal 80 A2
Roxton: Beds., England 25 V15
Roxwell: Essex, England 25 W16
Roy: N. Mex., U.S.A. 93 G5
Roy, Glen: High., Scotland 28 M6
Roya: Latvia, U.S.S.R. 47 S8
Royal Charlotte Reef: S. China Sea 64 E5
Royale, Isle: Mich., U.S.A. 88 G1
Royal Oak: Mich., U.S.A. 88 K4
Royan: France 37 D10
Roybridge: High., Scotland 28 M6
Roye: France 36 H6
Royere: France 37 G10
Roy Hill: W. Australia 68 C4
Royston: Herts., England 25 V15
Royston: W. Yorks., England 27 T12
Roysville: Liberia 80 B3
Royton: Gt. Man., England 27 R12
Rożaj: Yugoslavia 39 R15
Rozbork: Poland 45 V3
Rozel: Jersey, Chan. Is. 25 Ins.
Rozhishche: Ukraine 43 T11
Rożmitál: Czechoslovakia 45 T6
Rożňava: Czechoslovakia 43 R12
Rozoy-sur-Serre: France 36 K6
Rozvadov: Czechoslovakia 45 S6
Rozwadow: Poland 43 S11
Rushchevo: U.S.S.R. 50 F4
Ruabon: Clwyd, Wales 27 P14
Ruaha, Great: riv., Tanzania 76 E4
Ruaha National Park: Tanzania 76 D4
Ruahine Range: North I., New Zealand 70 Q14
Ruan Minor: Corn., Eng. 25 L19
Ruapehu: mtn., North I., New Zealand 70 P14
Ruapuke I.: New Zealand 71 M18
Ruatoria: North I., N.Z. 70 R13
Ruawai: North I., N.Z. 70 O13
Rub' al Khali: desert, Saudi Arabia 55 G11
Rubha Hunish: pt., Inner Hebr., Scotland 28 J4
Rubha Mhail: pt., Inner Hebr., Scotland 29 J8
Rubha Reidh: pt., Highland, Scotland 28 K4
Rubi: riv., Zaïre 76 C2
Rubia, La: Argentina 96 C3
Rubico: Roman name of river reaching Adriatic Sea 10 miles NW. of Rimini, Italy 41 S11
Rubona: Uganda 76 D2
Rubtsovsk: U.S.S.R. 51 O4
Rubuga: Tanzania 76 D4
Ruby: Alaska, U.S.A. 84 D5
Rudall: S. Australia 71 B9
Rudbar: Afghanistan 58 K8
Rudbar: Iran 57 L3
Rudby: N. Yorks., England 26 T11
Ruddington: Notts., Eng. 27 T14
Ruden: i., E. Germany 45 T1
Rudenau: S.W. Africa 74 B1
Rudensk: Byelorussia 43 U10
Rudersdorf: E. Germany 45 T3
Rudgwick: W. Sussex, Eng. 25 V17
Rudham, East: Norf., Eng. 25 X14
Rud-i-Sar: Iran 57 M3
Rud-i-Shur: riv., Iran 55 J8
Rudki: Ukraine 43 S12
Rudkøbing: Denmark 47 M9
Rudnichnyy: U.S.S.R. 50 H3
Rudnya: U.S.S.R. 50 D4
Rudolf, Lake: see Turkana, Lake
Rudolstadt: E. Germany 45 R5
Rudston: Humb., England 27 V11
Rudyard: Mich., U.S.A. 88 J2
Rue: France 36 G5
Ruelle: France 37 F10
Rufa'a: Sudan 54 D12
Ruffec: France 37 F9
Rufford: Lancs., England 27 Q12
Rufiji: riv., Tanzania 76 E4
Rufino: Argentina 96 C3
Rufunsa: Zambia 77 C6
Rugby: N. Dak., U.S.A. 92 H3
Rugby: War., England 25 T15
Rugeley: Staffs., England 27 S14
Rügen: i., E. Germany 45 T1
Rugles: France 36 F7
Rugsund: Norway 46 J6
Ruhengeri: Rwanda 76 C3
Ruhla: E. Germany 45 Q5
Ruhland: E. Germany 45 T4
Ruhr: riv., W. Germany 44 N4
Rūjiena: Latvia, U.S.S.R. 47 T8
Rukungire: Uganda 76 C3
Rukwa: Reg., Tanzania (cap. Sumbawanga) 76 D4
Rukwa, Lake: Tanzania 76 D4
Ruma: Yugoslavia 39 Q14
Rumah: Saudi Arabia 54 G9
Rumaila: well, Iraq 57 K6
Rumaitha: Iraq 57 J6
Rumana: Iraq 57 H4
Rumania: see Romania.
Rumbek: Sudan 76 C1
Rumbia: Celebes 65 G6
Rumblingbridge: Tayside, Scotland 29 O7
Rumburgh: Suff., England 25 Y15
Rumburk: Czechoslovakia 45 U5
Rumelifeneri: Turkey (Bosporus Inset) 20 Ins.
Rumford: Maine, U.S.A. 89 Q3
Rumelihisari: Turkey (Bosporus Inset) 20 Ins.
Rumilly: France 40 L10
Rum Jungle: N. Terr., Austl. 68 E2
Rumma: wadi, Saudi Arabia 54 F9
Rumney: S. Glam., Wales 24 P16
Rumoi: Japan 63 ZZ6
Rumuruti: Kenya 76 E2
Runanga: South I., N.Z. 70 N16
Runcorn: Ches., England 27 Q13
Runduma: i., Indonesia 65 G8
Rungu: Zaïre 76 C2
Rungwa: & riv., Tanzania 76 D4
Runkel: W. Germany 44 O5
Runnymede: a meadow on the right bank of the Thames where King John signed the Magna Carta in 1215; 2 miles W. of Staines, Gt. Ldn., England 25 U17
Runswick: N. Yorks., England 26 U10
Runtu: S.W. Africa 77 A6
Ruovesi: Finland 47 T6
Rupa: Arunachal Pradesh, India 59 Q9
Rupanyup: Vict., Australia 71 E11
Rupat: i., Sumatra 65 C6
Rupea: Romania 43 T13
Rupert: Idaho, U.S.A. 92 E4
Rupununi: riv., Guyana 87 d9
Rur: riv., W. Germany 44 M5
Rurrenabaque: Bolivia 94 D6
Rurutu: i., Austral Is. 83 e4
Rusambo: Rhodesia 77 D6
Rusape: Rhodesia 77 D6
Ruse (Ruschuk): Bulgaria 39 U15
Rush: Dublin, Repub. of Ireland 30 J12
Rushall: W. Mid., England 27 S14
Rushan: Tadzhik., U.S.S.R. 51 M7
Rushden: Northants., England 25 U15
Rushen: dist., I. of Man, United Kingdom 26 M11
Rushford: Minn., U.S.A. 88 F4
Rushkar: Iran 55 J8
Rushton Marsh: Staffs., England 27 R13
Rushville: Ill., U.S.A. 88 F5
Rushville: Ind., U.S.A. 88 J6
Rushworth: Vict., Australia 71 F11
Rusk: Tex., U.S.A. 90 D10
Russell: Kans., U.S.A. 90 B6
Russell: Man., Canada 92 G2
Russell: North I., N.Z. 70 P12
Russell Is.: Solomon Is. 67 L3
Russell Point: cape, N.W.T., Canada 84 h3
Russellville: Ala., U.S.A. 91 H8
Russellville: Ark., U.S.A. 90 E8
Russellville: Ky., U.S.A. 88 H7
Russi: Italy 41 S11
Russia: see Union of Soviet Socialist Republics.
Russian Mission: Alaska, U.S.A. 84 c5
Russian Soviet Federal Socialist Republic: U.S.S.R. (cap. Moscow) 50/51
Rust: Austria 41 W8
Rustak: Afghanistan 51 L7
Rust de Winterdam: lake, Trans., S. Africa 75 H2
Rustenburg: & Dist., S. Afr. 75 G2
Rustig: O.F.S., S. Africa 75 G3
Rustington: W. Sussex, Eng. 25 V18
Ruston: La., U.S.A. 90 E9
Ruswarp: N. Yorks., England 26 U11
Rutaimi: well, Iraq 57 G4
Rutana: Burundi 76 D3
Rutba: Iraq 57 G5
Rute: Spain 35 D18
Ruteng: Flores, Indon. 65 G8
Ruthenia: geog. reg., Ukraine 43 S12
Rutherfordton: N.C., U.S.A. 88 L8
Rutherglen: Strath., Scot. 29 N8
Rutherglen: Vict., Australia 71 G11
Ruthin: Clwyd, Wales 27 P13
Ruthven: Tayside, Scotland 29 P6
Ruthwell: Dumfries & Galloway, Scotland 29 P10
Rüti: Switzerland 40 O8
Rutland: Vt., U.S.A. 89 P4
Rutland: i., Andaman Is. 59 Q12
Rutqa: wadi, Iraq 57 G5
Rutshuru: Zaïre 76 C3
Rutter: Ont., Canada 88 L2
Ruurlo: Netherlands 44 M3
Ruvu: Coast, Tanzania 76 E4
Ruvu: Tanga, Tanzania 76 E3
Ruvu (Pangani): riv., Tanzania 76 E3
Ruvuma: Reg., Tanzania (cap. Songea) 77 E5
Ruvuma: riv., Tanzania/Mozambique 77 E5
Ruwaidha: Saudi Arabia 54 F10
Ruwais: U.A.E. 55 H10
Ruwalla: tribal area, Saudi Arabia 56 F6
Ruwandiz: Iraq 57 J3
Ruweiba: Sudan 54 C11
Ruwenzori: mtn. & range, Zaïre/Uganda 76 C2
Ruyena: Latvia, U.S.S.R. 47 T8
Ruyigi: Burundi 76 D3
Ruyton of the Eleven Towns: Salop, England 27 Q14
Ruzayevka: U.S.S.R. 50 G4
Ruzhany: Byelorussia 43 T10
Ružomberok: Czech. 43 Q12

Rwanda: Republic 76 C3
Cap.: Kigali
Area: 10,169 sq. miles (26,338 sq. km.)
Pop.: 3,827,000 (1971 E)

Rwasamaire: Uganda 76 D3
Ryan, Loch: Dumfries & Galloway, Scotland 29 L10
RYAZAN': & Reg., U.S.S.R. 50 E4
Ryazhsk: U.S.S.R. 50 F4
Rybachiy Penin.: U.S.S.R. 46 X2
Rybach'ye: Kirgiz., U.S.S.R. 51 N6
Rybáře: Czechoslovakia 45 S5
Rybinsk: U.S.S.R. 50 E3
Rybinsk Reservoir: U.S.S.R. 50 E3
Rybnik: Poland 43 Q11
Ryburgh, Great: Norf., Eng. 25 X14
Ryde: I. of Wight, England 25 T18
Rye: E. Sussex, England 25 X18
Rye: riv., N. Yorks., England 26 T11
Ryhall: Leics., England 27 V14
Ryhill: W. Yorks., England 27 T12
Ryhope: Tyne & Wear, England 26 T10
Rylane: Cork, Repub. of Ireland 31 D16
Ryl'sk: U.S.S.R. 50 D4
Rylstone: N.S.W., Australia 71 H9
Rylstone: N. Yorks., England 27 R11
Rypin: Poland 43 Q10
Rysen: Netherlands 44 M3
Rysum: W. Germany 44 N2
Ryswick (Ryswyk): town on road between The Hague and Delft, Netherlands 44 K3
Ryton: Tyne & Wear, England 26 S10
Ryukyu (Nansei) Is.: (Jap.), E. China Sea (cap. Naha) 63 X9

182 Ryukyu Trench—St. Pierre-Église

Ryukyu Trench: Philippine Sea 7 25N 130E
Ryumgaard: Denmark 47 M8
Rzepin: Poland 45 U3
Rzeszów: & Prov., Poland 43 R11
Rzhev: U.S.S.R. 50 D3

Saaduela: Ethiopia 79 Q17
Saager: Austria 41 U9
Saale: riv., E. Germany 45 R4
Saaler Bodden: bay, E. Ger. 45 S1
Saales: France 40 N7
Saalfeld: E. Germany 45 R5
Saalfelden: Austria 41 S8
Saane: riv., Switzerland 40 N9
Saanen: Switzerland 40 N9
Saar: riv., Saarland, W. Ger. 44 M6
Saarbrücken: Saarland, W. Germany 44 N6
Saarburg: W. Germany 44 M6
Saaremaa I.: U.S.S.R. 50 B3
Saarijärvi: Finland 46 T5
Saari Selkä: mtns., Fin. 46 T2
Saarland: Prov., W. Germany (cap. Saarbrücken) 44 M6
Saarlautern: Saarland, W. Germany 44 M6
Saarlouis: Saarland, W. Ger. 44 M6
Saarmund: E. Germany 45 T3
Saavedra: Argentina 96 C4
Saavedra: Chile 96 A4
Saba: i. (Neth.), Lesser Antilles 87 b2
Saba: (Biblical *Sheba*) ancient state in S. Arabia, with its capital at Marib, Yemen 54 G11
Saba'a: rly. station, Egypt (Suez Canal. Inset) 32 Ins.
Šabac: Yugoslavia 39 Q14
Sabadell: Spain 35 H16
Sabah: State, Malaysia (cap. Kota Kinabalu) 65 F6
Sábana, La: Argentina 96 D2
Sabanalarga: Colombia 94 C1
Sabang: Celebes 65 F6
Sabassé: Upper Volta 80 D2
Sabatinus: Roman name of L. Bracciano, Italy 38 N15
Sabaudia: Italy 38 N16
Sab' Biyar: Syria 56 E5
Sabden: Lancs., England 27 R12
Sabha: wadi, Saudi Arabia 55 G10
Sabie: & Dist., Mozambique 75 K2
Sabie: & riv., Trans., S. Afr. 75 J2
Sabile: Latvia, U.S.S.R. 47 S8
Sabinal: Mexico 93 F6
Sabinal: Tex., U.S.A. 90 B11
Sabinas: Mexico 93 G7
Sabinas Hidalgo: Mexico 93 G7
Sabine: Tex., U.S.A. 90 E11
Sabine: riv., U.S.A. 90 E10
Sabine, Mt.: Antarctica 9 75S 165E
Sabine Lake: Tex./La., U.S.A. 90 E11
Sabini: ancient tribe in hills to NE. of Rome as far as Terni. 38 N15
Sabini Mtns.: Italy 38 N15
Sabinov: Czechoslovakia 43 R12
Sabiote: Spain 35 E17
Sabirabad: Azerbaydzhan, U.S.S.R. 57 L2
Sabkha Mijura: salt lake, Saudi Arabia 55 H10
Sabkha Mutti: salt lake, United Arab Emirates 55 H10
Sablayan: Philippines 64 G4
Sable, Cape: Fla., U.S.A. 91 L13
Sable, Cape: N.S., Canada 89 T4
Sable I.: N.S., Canada 87 O9
Sable Is.: La., U.S.A. 90 Ins.
Sable Is.: Marquesas Is. 83 g1
Sables: riv., Que., Canada 89 Q1
Sablé-sur-Sarthe: France 36 E8
Sablon, Point du: cape, Fr. 37 K12
Sabon Birni: Nigeria 81 F2
Sabór: riv., Portugal 35 C16
Sabrat(h)a: Punic and Roman city on N. African coast about 50 miles W. of Tripoli 32 E5
Sabres: France 37 E11
Sabrina: Roman name of river Severn, England 24 R16
Sabtang: i., Philippines 64 G2
Sabya: Saudi Arabia 54 F11
Sabzawar (Shīn Dand): Afghanistan 58 K8
Sabzawar: Iran 55 J7
Sac: riv., Mo., U.S.A. 90 E7
Sacandaga Res.: N.Y., U.S.A. 89 O4
Sacedón: Spain 35 E16
Sachigo: riv., Ont., Canada 92 J2
Sachigo Lake: Ont., Canada 92 J2
Sachsen: see Saxony.
Sachsenburg: Austria 41 T9
Sacile: Italy 41 S10
Sackets Harbor: N.Y., U.S.A. 89 N4
Säckingen: W. Germany 40 N8
Sackville: N.B., Canada 89 T3
Saco: Maine, U.S.A. 89 Q4
Saco: Mont., U.S.A. 92 F3
SACRAMENTO: Calif., U.S.A. 93 C5
Sacramento: riv., Calif., U.S.A. 92 C4
Sacramento Mtns.: N. Mex., U.S.A. 93 F6
Sacratif, Cape: Spain 35 E18
Sacriston: Durham, England 26 S10
Sacrum promuntorium: Roman name of C. St. Vincent, Portugal 35 B18
Săcueni: Romania 43 S13
Sa'da: Yemen 54 F11
Sádaba: Spain 35 F15
SÁ DE BANDEIRA: see LUBANGO
Sadani: Tanzania 76 E4
Sadao: Thailand 65 b10
Saddell: Strath., Scotland 29 K8
Saddleworth: Gt. Manchester, Eng. 27 R12
Sadiola: Mali 80 B2
Sadiya: Assam., India 59 R9
Sado: i., Japan 63 f1
Sado: riv., Portugal 35 B17
Sadon: Burma 59 R9
Sadovoye: U.S.S.R. 50 F5
Sädva Lake: Sweden 46 P3
Sae: i., New Guinea 66 J2
Sæby: Denmark 47 M8
Saeki: Japan 63 b4
Safa: Saudi Arabia 54 G9
Safad: Israel 55 b2
Safakulevo: U.S.S.R. 51 K3
Safaniya: oil site, Saudi Arab. 55 G9
Safed Koh: range, Afghan./Pakistan 58 M8
Safety: Alaska, U.S.A. 84 c5
Säffle: Sweden 47 N7
Safford: Ariz., U.S.A. 93 F6
Saffron Waldon: Essex, Eng. 25 W15
SAFI: & Prov., Morocco 80 K8
Safita: Syria 56 E4
Safranbolu: Turkey 56 C1
Saga: Indonesia 61 L12
SAGA: & Pref., Japan 63 b4
SAGAING: & State, Burma 59 R10
Sagak, Cape: Aleutians 84 C7
Sagami Bay: Japan 63 f3
Sagar: Karnataka, India 58 N12
Sagara: Japan 63 f3
Sagawitchewan: Man., Can. 92 J2
Sag Fiord: Norway 46 O3
Sag Harbor: N.Y., U.S.A. 89 P5
Saginaw: Mich., U.S.A. 88 K4
Saginaw Bay: Mich., U.S.A. 88 K4
Sagiz: Kazakh., U.S.S.R. 50 J5
Sagone, Golfe de: gulf, Cors. 38 L15
Sagra, La: mtn., Spain 35 E18
Sagres: Portugal 35 B18
Sagritz: Austria 41 S9
Sagua la Grande: Cuba 87 I13
Saguaro Nat. Mon.: Ariz., U.S.A. 93 E6
Saguenay: riv., Que., Can. 89 Q1
Sagunto: Spain 35 F17
Sagyndyk, Cape: Caspian Sea 50 H6
Sahagún: Spain 35 D15
Sahara Desert: N. Africa 78 D5
Saharan Atlas: range, Alg. 80 L8
Saharanpur: Uttar Pradesh, India 58 N9
Sahba: wadi, Saudi Arabia 55 G10
Sahiliya: Iraq 57 H5
Sahiwal: Punjab, Pakistan 58 M8
Sahma: sand reg., Sau. Arab. 55 J10
Sahneh: Iran 57 K4
Sahuaripa: Mexico 93 F7
Šahy: Czechoslovakia 43 Q12
Sai: Japan 63 ZZ6
Saibai: i., Queens., Austl. 69 G1
SAÏDA: & Dept., Algeria 80 M8
Saida (Sidon): Lebanon 56 D5
Saidabad: Iran 55 J9
Said Bundas: Sudan 76 B1
Saidu: N.W. Front. Prov., Pak. 58 M8
Saighan: Afghanistan 58 L7
Saigo: Oki Is., Japan 63 Y7
Saigon: see Ho Chi Minh City
Saihut: Yemen, P.D.R. 55 H11
Saijo: Ehime, Japan 63 c4
Saijo: Hiroshima, Japan 63 c3
Saillans: France 37 L11
Saimaa Lake: Finland 47 U6
Saimarreh: riv., Iran 57 K5
Saimbeyli: Turkey 56 E2
Saindak: Baluchistan, Pak. 58 K9
Sain Diz: Iran 57 K3
Sain Shanda: Mongolia 62 U6
St. Abb's: & head, Borders, Scotland 29 R8
Ste. Adresse: France 36 F6
St. Aegyd: Austria 41 V8
St. Affrique: France 37 H12
St. Agapit: Que., Canada 89 Q2
St. Agathe des Monts: Que., Canada 89 O2
St. Agnan: France 37 G10
St. Agnes: Corn., England 24 L19
St. Agnes: i., Scilly Is., Eng. 25 J19
St. Agrève: France 37 K10
St. Aignan: France 36 G8
St. Aignan-sur-Roë: France 36 D8
St. Aimé: Algeria 35 G19
St. Alban: France 37 J11
St. Albans: & val., Herts., England 25 V16
St. Albans: Newf., Canada 85 v3
St. Albans: Vt., U.S.A. 89 P3
St. Albans: W. Va., U.S.A. 88 L6
St. Albans Head: cape, Dorset, England 24 R18
St. Amand: France 36 J8
St. Amand-de-Vendôme: Fr. 36 G8
St. Amand-Mont-Rond: Fr. 37 H9
St. Amans-Soult: France 37 H12
St. Amarin: France 40 N8
St. Ambroix: France 37 K11
St. Amour: France 40 L9
St. Andrä: Austria 41 U9
St. André: & plain, France 36 G7
St. André: Que., Canada 89 R2
St. André-de-Cubzac: Fr. 37 E11
St. Andrew: Windward Is. 87 c4
St. Andrew Bay: Fla., U.S.A. 91 J10
St. Andrews: Fife, Scotland 29 Q7
St. Andrews: N.B., Canada 89 S3
St. Annaland: Neth. 44 K4
St. Anne: Alderney, Channel Is. 25 Ins.
St. Anne: Ill., U.S.A. 88 H5
Ste. Anne de Beaupré: Que., Canada 89 Q2
Ste. Anne de Portneuf (Hamilton Cove): Que., Canada 89 R1
Ste. Anne des Monts: city, Que., Canada 89 S1
Ste. Anne du Lac: city, Que., Canada 89 O2
St. Anne's: Lancs., England 27 P12
St. Annes: Queens., Australia 70 G3
St. Ann's Bay: town, Jamaica 86 Ins.
St. Ann's Head: cape, Dyfed, Wales 24 L16
St. Anthony: Idaho, U.S.A. 92 E4
St. Anthony: Newf., Canada 85 v1
St. Anton: Austria 40 Q8
St. Antonin: France 37 G11
St. Arnaud: Vict., Australia 71 E11
St. Asaph: Clwyd, Wales 27 P13
St. Astier: France 37 F10
St. Aubin: Jersey, Chan. Is. 25 Ins.
St. Aubin-du-Cormier: Fr. 36 D7
St. Augustin: Que., Can. 85 t1
St. Augustine: Fla., U.S.A. 91 L11
St. Aulaye: France 37 F10
St. Austell: & bay, Corn., Eng. 24 M19
St. Avold: France 44 M6
St. Bartholomew: i., (Fr.), Lesser Antilles 87 b2
St. Bathans: South I., N.Z. 70 M17
St. Beauzély: France 37 H11
St. Bees: Cumbria, England 26 O11
St. Bees Head: cape, Cumbria, England 26 O10
St. Benin-d'Azy: France 36 J9
St. Benoît: France 37 G9
St. Bernard: La., U.S.A. 90 Ins.
St. Bernard, Great: pass, Switzerland/Italy 40 N10
St. Bernard, Little: pass, France/Italy 40 M10
St. Blazey: Corn., England 24 M19
St. Blin: France 40 L7
St. Boniface: Man., Canada 92 H3
St. Bonnet: France 40 M11
St. Bonnet-le-Froid: France 37 K10
ST. BOSWELLS: Borders, Scot. 29 Q8
St. Boswells: see Newtown St. Boswells.
St. Brelade's: Jersey, Channel Is. 25 Ins.
St. Breward: Corn., England 24 M18
St. Briavels: Glos., England 24 Q16
St. Brides: bay, Dyfed, Wales 24 L16
St. Bride's Major: Mid Glam., Wales 24 O17
ST. BRIEUC: Côtes-du-Nord, France 36 C7
St. Buryan: Cornwall, England 25 K19
St. Calais: France 36 F8
St. Cast: France 36 C7
St. Catharines: Ont., Can. 89 M4
St. Catherine, Lake: La., U.S.A. 90 Ins.
St. Catherines: Strath., Scot. 29 L7
St. Catherines: i., Ga., U.S.A. 91 L10
St. Catherine's Point: cape, I. of Wight, England 25 T18
St. Cernin: France 37 H10
St. Chamond: France 37 K10
St. Charles: Mo., U.S.A. 88 F6
St. Chef: France 40 L10
St. Chély: France 37 H11
St. Chély-d'Apcher: France 37 J11
St. Chinian: France 37 H12

St. Christopher-Nevis-Anguilla: *Br. associated state* 87 b2
Cap.: Basseterre
Area: 118 sq. miles (306 sq. km.)
Pop.: 58,000 (*1971 E*)

St. Ciers: France 37 E10
St. Clair: Mich., U.S.A. 88 K4
St. Clair: Mo., U.S.A. 88 F6
St. Clair, Lake: Can./U.S.A. 88 K4
St. Claud: France 37 F10
St. Claude: France 40 L9
St. Clears: Dyfed, Wales 24 N16
St. Cleer: Corn., England 24 N19
St. Cloud: Minn., U.S.A. 88 D3
Saint Coeur de Marie: Que., Canada 89 Q1
St. Columb Major: Corn., England 24 M19
St. Columb Minor: Corn., England 24 L19
St. Combs: Gram., Scot. 28 S4
St. Cosme-de-Vair: France 36 F7
Ste. Croix: France 37 G12
St Croix (Santa Cruz): i. (U.S.A.), Lesser Antilles 87 a2
Ste. Croix: Switzerland 40 M9
St Croix: riv., Can./U.S.A. 89 S3
St. Croix: riv., Wis./Minn., U.S.A. 88 E3
St. Croix Falls: city, Wis., U.S.A. 88 E3
St. Cyprien: France 37 G11
St. Cyr: riv., Que., Canada 89 O1
St. Cyrus: Gram., Scotland 29 R6
St. Dalmas: France 40 M11
St. David's: Dyfed, Wales 24 L16
St. David's Head: cape, Dyfed, Wales 24 L16
St. David's I.: Bermudas 87 Ins.
St. David (Mapia) Is.: Indonesia 61 L11
St. Day: Corn., England 24 L19
St. Denis: France 36 H7
St. Dennis: Corn., England 24 M19
St. Didier: France 37 K10
St. Dié: France 40 M7
St. Dizier: France 36 K7
St. Dogmaels: Dyfed, Wales 24 M15
St. Donat: France 37 K10
St. Donat's: S. Glam., Wales 24 O17
St. Elias, Mount: Alaska, U.S.A. 84 e5
St. Elias Mtns.: Canada 84 F5
St. Elie: Fr. Guiana 94 G3
St. Eloy: France 37 H9
Ste. Enimie: France 37 J11
St. Erme: Corn., England 24 L19
St. Erth: Corn., England 25 L19
Saintes: France 37 E10
St. Étienne: Alpes de Haute Provence, Fr. 40 L11
ST. ÉTIENNE: Loire, France 37 K10
St. Étienne-de-Montluc: France 36 D8
St. Eustatius: i., Leeward Is. 87 b2
St. Evariste: Que., Canada 89 Q3
St. Faith's: Natal, S. Africa 75 J5
St. Fargeau: France 36 J8
St. Felicien: Que., Canada 89 P1
St. Fergus: Gram., Scotland 28 S4
Saintfield: Down, N. Ireland 30 K11
St. Fillans: Tay., Scotland 29 N7
St. Finan's Bay: Kerry, Repub. of Ireland 31 A16
St. Firmin: France 40 M11
St. Florent-des-Bois: France 37 D9
St. Florentin: France 36 J7
St. Florent-le-Vieil: France 36 D8
St. Florent-sur-Cher: France 36 H9
St. Flour: France 37 J10
St. Flovier: France 36 G9
Ste. Fortunade: France 37 G10
Ste. Foy: France 37 K10
Ste. Foy-la-Grande: France 37 F11
St. Francis: Maine, U.S.A. 89 R2
St. Francis: riv., Que., Can. 89 P3
St. Francis: riv., U.S.A. 88 F7
St. Francis, Cape: S. Africa 75 F7
St. Francis, Lake: Que., Can. 89 Q3
St. Francis Bay: S.W. Africa 74 A2
St. Francis Mtns.: Mo., U.S.A. 88 F7
St. Francois de Boundji: Congo 81 H5
St. Fulgent: France 36 D9
St. Gabriel: Que., Canada 89 P2
ST. GALLEN: & canton, Switz. 40 P8
St. Gallenkirch: Austria 40 P8
St. Galmier: France 37 K10
St. Gaudens: France 37 F12
Ste. Gauburge: France 36 F7
St. Gaultier: France 37 G9
St. Geniez: France 37 H11
St. Genix: France 40 L10
St. George: Bermudas 87 Ins.
St. George: N.B., Canada 89 S3
St. George: Queens., Austl. 70 H7
St. George: S.C., U.S.A. 91 L9
St. George: Utah, U.S.A. 93 E5
St. George: i., Fla., U.S.A. 91 J11
St. George: i., Pribilof Is., Alaska, U.S.A. 84 C6
St. George, Cape: Fla., U.S.A. 91 J11
St. George, G. of: Argentina 95 D13
St. George, Point: cape, Calif., U.S.A. 92 C4
ST. GEORGE'S: Grenada, Windward Is., 87 c4
St George's: & bay, Newf., Canada 85 t2
St. George's Chan.: Repub. of Ireland/Wales 31 J15
St. Georges de Didonne: Fr. 37 D10
St. George's I.: Bermudas 87 Ins.
St. Germain: France 36 H7
St. Germain-des-Fosses: Fr. 37 J9
St. Germain-du-Bois: France 37 L9
St. Germain-Lembron: Fr. 37 J10
St. Germans: Corn., England 24 N19
St. Gervais: Haute-Savoie, France 40 M10
St. Gervais: Hérault, France 37 J12
St. Gervais: Puy-de-Dôme, France 37 H9
St. Géry: France 37 G11
St. Gildas, Pointe de: cape, France 36 C8
St. Gildas-des-Bois: France 36 C8
St. Gilgen: Austria 41 T8
St. Gilles: France 37 K12
St. Gilles-sur-Vie: France 37 D9
St. Girons: France 37 G13
St. Girons-en-Maresin: Fr. 37 D12
St. Goar: W. Germany 44 N5
St. Goran: Corn., England 24 M19
St. Gotthard Pass: Switz. 40 O9
St. Govan's Head: Dyfed, Wales 24 M16
St. Guénolé: France 36 A8
St. Harmon: Powys, Wales 24 P15
St. Helena: i., (Br.), S. Atlantic Ocean 8 20S 10W
St. Helena Bay: S. Africa 74 C6
St. Helenafontein: S. Africa 74 C6
St. Helena Sound: S.C., U.S.A. 91 L9
Ste. Hélène: France 37 E11
St. Helen's: I. of Wight, Eng. 25 T18
St. Helens: Mers., England 27 Q13
St. Helens: Oreg., U.S.A. 92 C3
St. Helen's: Tas., Australia 68 H8
ST. HELIER: Jersey, Chan. Is. 25 Ins.
Ste. Hermine: France 37 D9
St. Hilaire-du-Harcouet: Fr. 36 D7
St. Hilary: S. Glam., Wales 24 P17
St. Hippolyte: France 40 M8
St. Hippolyte-du-Fort: Fr. 37 J12
St. Hubert: Belgium 44 L5
St. Hyacinthe: Que., Canada 89 P3
St. Ignace: Mich., U.S.A. 88 J3
St. Ignace, Isle: Ont., Can. 88 H1
St. Imier: Switzerland 40 N8
St. Ingbert: Saarland, W. Ger. 44 N6
St. Ives: Cambs., England 25 V15
St. Ives: & bay, Corn., Eng. 25 L19
St. Jacobiparochie: Neth. 44 L2
St. Jakob: Austria 41 S9
St. James: Minn., U.S.A. 88 D4
St. James: S. Africa 74 Ins.
St. Jean: Fr. Guiana 94 G2
St. Jean: Que., Canada 89 P3
St. Jean-d'Angély: France 37 E10
St. Jean-de-Bournay: France 40 L10
St. Jean-de-Daye: France 36 D6
St. Jean-de-Losne: France 36 L8
St. Jean-de-Luz: France 37 D12
St. Jean-de-Maurienne: Fr. 40 M10
St. Jean-de-Monts: France 37 C9
St. Jean-du-Gard: France 37 J11
St. Jean-Pied-de-Port: Fr. 37 D12
St. Jérôme: Que., Canada 89 O3
St. Jérôme (Metabetchouan): Que., Canada 89 Q1
St. Johann: Styria, Austria 41 U8
St. Johann: Tyrol, Austria 41 S8
St. John: Kans., U.S.A. 90 B7
Saint John: N.B., Canada 89 S3
St. John: i., Virgin Is. 87 a1
St. John: riv., Can./U.S.A. 89 S3
St. John: riv., Liberia 80 C3
St. John, Lake: Que., Can. 89 P1
St. John Beckermet: Cumbria, England 26 O11
St. John I. (Changchuan): Kwangtung, China 62 U10
ST. JOHN'S: Antigua, Leeward Is. 87 c2
St. Johns: Ariz., U.S.A. 93 F6
St. John's: I. of Man, U.K. 26 M11
St. John's: Jersey, Chan. Is. 25 Ins.
St. Johns: Mich., U.S.A. 88 J4
ST. JOHN'S: Newf., Canada 84 w3
St. Johns: riv., Fla., U.S.A. 91 L11
St. John's I.: Red Sea 54 E10
St. Johnsbury: Vt., U.S.A. 89 P3
St. John's Chapel: Durham, England 26 R10
St. John's Point: cape Don., Repub. of Ireland 30 D10
St. John's Point: cape, Down, N. Ireland 30 K11
St. Johnstown: Don., Repub. of Ireland 30 G10
St. Joseph: Dominica, Windward Is. 87 c3
St. Joseph: Mich., U.S.A. 88 H4
St. Joseph: Mo., U.S.A. 93 J4
St. Joseph: Que., Canada 89 Q2
St. Joseph: riv., (Lake Erie). U.S.A. 88 J5
St. Joseph: riv., U.S.A. 88 J4
St. Joseph Bay: Fla., U.S.A. 91 J11
St. Joseph d'Alma: Que., Canada 89 Q1
St. Joseph I.: Ont., Canada 88 K2
St. Josse: France 36 G5
St. Jovite: Que., Canada 89 O2
St. Julien: France 40 M9
St. Julien-de-Vouvantes: Fr. 36 D8
St. Julien-du-Sault: France 36 J7
St. Julien-Lars: France 37 F9
St. Junien: France 37 F10
St. Just: Corn., England 25 K19
St. Just-en-Chaussée: France 36 H6
St. Justin: France 37 E12
St. Keverne: Corn., England 24 L19
St. Kew: Corn., England 24 M18
St. Kilda: South I., N.Z. 71 N17
St. Kilda: i., (Scot.), Atlantic O. 22 C3
St. Kitts (St. Christopher): i., Leeward Is. (cap. Basseterre) 87 b2
St. Lambert-du-Lattay: France 36 E8
St. Laurent: Gard, France 37 K12
St. Laurent: Gironde, France 37 E10
St. Laurent: Jura, France 40 L9
St. Laurent-de-la-Salanque: France 37 H13
St. Lawrence: Queens., Australia 70 H4
St. Lawrence: riv., Canada/U.S.A. 89 R1
St. Lawrence, G. of: Can. 89 U2
St. Lawrence I.: (U.S.A.), Bering Sea 84 b5
St. Leonard: France 37 G10
St. Leonard: N.B., Canada 89 S2
St. Leonards: E. Sussex, Eng. 25 X18
St. Leonhard: Carinthia, Austria 41 U9
St. Leonhard: Tyrol, Austria 41 Q8
St. Levan: Corn., England 25 K19
St. Lô: Manche, France 36 D6
St. Louis: Mo., U.S.A. 88 F6
ST. LOUIS: Fleuve, Senegal 80 A1
St. Louis: riv., Minn., U.S.A. 88 E2
St. Loup: Deux-Sèvres, Fr. 37 E9
St. Loup: Haute-Saône, Fr. 40 M8
St. Lucia: bay & lake, Natal, S. Africa 75 K4

St. Lucia: *Br. associated state* 87 c4
Cap.: Castries
Area: 238 sq. miles (616 sq. km.)
Pop.: 103,000 (*1971 E*)

St. Lucia Game Reserve: Natal, S. Africa 75 K4
St. Luke: i., Mergui Arch., Burma 59 R12
St. Lys: France 37 G12
St. Magnus Bay: Shetland Is. 28 Ins.
St. Maixent: France 37 E9
St. Malo: & gulf, France 36 C7
St. Malo-de-la-Lande: Fr. 36 D6
St. Mamelin: France 36 H5
St. Marc: Haiti 87 m14
St. Marcellin: France 40 L10
St. Margarets: Dublin, Repub. of Ireland 30 J13
St. Margaret's at Cliffe: Kent, England 25 Y17
St. Margaret's Hope: Orkney Is. 28 Q2
St. Maria: Switzerland 40 Q9
Ste. Marie: Que., Canada 89 Q2
Ste. Marie, Cape: Malagasy Rep. 73 N15
Ste. Marie-aux-Mines: Fr. 40 N7
Ste. Marie I.: Malagasy Rep. 73 O13
St. Marien: France 37 H9
Stes. Maries, Les: France 37 K12
St. Maries: Idaho, U.S.A. 92 D3
St. Marks: I. of Man, U.K. 26 M11
St. Mark's: S. Africa 75 G6
St. Mars-la-Jaille: France 36 D8
St. Martin: Austria 41 W8
St. Martin: Cher, France 36 H8
St. Martin: Pyrénées-Atlantiques, France 37 D12
St. Martin: i., (Fr. & Neth.), Lesser Antilles 87 b1
St. Martin, Lake: Man., Canada 92 H2
St. Martin-de-Ré: Île de Ré, France 37 D9
St. Martin's: Guernsey, Channel Is. 25 Ins.
St. Martin's: Jersey, Chan. Is. 25 Ins.
St. Martins: N.B., Canada 89 T3
St. Martin's: Salop, Eng. 27 P14
St. Martin's: i., Scilly Is., Eng. 25 J19
St. Martinville: La., U.S.A. 90 F10
St. Mary Bay: N.S., Canada 89 S3
St. Mary in the Marsh: Kent, England 25 X17
St. Mary's: Jersey, Chan. Is. 25 Ins.
St. Mary's: Kans., U.S.A. 90 C6
St. Mary's: Orkney Is. 28 Q2
St. Mary's: Tas., Australia 68 H8
St. Mary's: W. Va., U.S.A. 88 L6
St. Mary's: i., Scilly Is., Eng. 25 J19
St. Mary's: riv., N.S., Can. 89 U3
St. Mary's Bay: Newf., Can. 85 w3
St. Mathieu: France 37 F10
St. Mathurin: France 36 E8
St. Matthew: i., Mergui Arch., Burma 59 R12
St. Matthew I., (U.S.A.), Bering Sea 85 b5
St. Matthews: S.C., U.S.A. 91 L9
St. Maughans: Gwent, Wales 24 Q16
St. Maur: France 36 H7
St. Maure: France 36 F8
St. Maurice: France 40 M8
St. Maurice: Switzerland 40 N9
St. Maurice: riv., Que., Can. 89 P2
St. Mawes: Corn., England 24 L19
St. Mawgan: Corn., England 24 M19
Ste. maxime: France 40 M12
St. Maximin: France 40 L12
St. Méen: France 36 C7
Ste. Menehould: France 36 K6
Ste. Mère-Église: France 36 D6
St. Merryn: Corn., England 25 M18
St. Michael: Alaska, U.S.A. 84 c5
St. Michael: Burgenland, Austria 41 W8
St. Michael: Salzburg, Austr. 41 T8
St. Michel: France 40 M10
St. Michel des Saints: Que., Canada 89 P2
St. Mihiel: France 36 L7
St. Moïse: Que., Canada 89 S1
St. Monance: Fife, Scotland 29 Q7
St. Moritz: Switzerland 40 P9
St. Nazaire: France 36 C8
St. Neot: Corn., England 24 M19
St. Neots: Cambs., England 25 V15
St. Nicholas: Dyfed, Wales 24 L16
St. Nicholas at Wade: Kent, England 25 Y17
St. Nicolas (Sint Niklaas): Belgium 44 K4
St. Niklaus: Switzerland 40 N9
St. Ninians: Central, Scot. 29 O7
St. Omer: France 36 H5
Saintonge: Prov., France 34 F14
St. Osyth: Essex, England 25 Y16
St. Palais: Charente-Inférieure, France 37 D10
St. Palais: Pyrénées-Atlantiques, France 37 D12
St. Pardoux: France 37 F10
St. Paterne: Indre-et-Loire, France 36 F8
St. Paterne: Sarthe, France 36 F7
St. Patrickswell: Lim., Republic of Ireland 31 D14
St. Paul: Alpes de Haute Provence, Fr. 40 M11
St. Paul: Alta., Canada 92 E2
St. Paul: Austria 41 U9
St. Paul: Fr. Guiana 94 G3
ST. PAUL: Minn., U.S.A. 88 E3
St. Paul: Nebr., U.S.A. 92 H4
St. Paul: Pyrénées-Orientales: France 37 H13
St. Paul: i., (Fr.), Indian Ocean 9 40S 75E
St. Paul: i., Pribilof Is., Alaska, U.S.A. 84 C6
St. Paul: riv., Liberia 80 B3
St. Paul, Cape: Ghana 80 E3
St. Paulien: France 37 J10
St. Paul Rocks: (Brazil), N. Atlantic Ocean 8 00 30W
St. Pauls: N.C., U.S.A. 91 M8
St. Paul's Bay: village, Malta 32 Ins.
Ste. Pazanne: France 36 D8
St. Pé: France 37 E12
St. Péray: France 37 K11
St. Père-en-Retz: France 36 C8
St. Peter's: Jersey, Chan. Is. 25 Ins.
St. Peter: Minn., U.S.A. 88 E3
St. Peter: Yugoslavia 41 U10
St. Peter, Lake: Que., Can. 89 P2
St. Peter, Point: cape, Que., Canada 89 T1
ST. PETER PORT: Guernsey, Channel Is. 25 Ins.
St. Petersburg: Fla., U.S.A. 91 K12
St. Petersburg: name of former capital of Russia, now Leningrad, U.S.S.R. 50 D3
St. Pierre: Jersey, Chan. Is. 25 Ins.
St. Pierre: Martinique, Windward Is. 87 c
St. Pierre-d'Albigny: France 40 M10
St. Pierre-d'Oléron: France 37 D10
St. Pierre-Église: France 36 D6

St. Pierre-en-Port—San Juan Bautista 183

St. Pierre-en-Port: France **36** F6
St. Pierre I.: (Fr.), N. America. [*cap.* (with Miquelon) St. Pierre] **85** u3
St. Pierre-le-Moutier: France **37** J9
St. Pierre-Quilbignon: Fr. **36** A7
St. Pierre-sur-Dives: France **36** E6
St. Pinnock: Corn., England **24** M19
St. Pois: France **36** D7
St. Poix: France **36** D8
St. Pol: France **36** H5
St. Pol-de-Léon: France **36** A7
St. Pol-sur-Mer: France **36** H4
St. Polten: Austria **41** V7
St. Pons: France **37** H12
St. Porchaire: France **37** E10
St. Pourçain: France **37** J9
St. Quentin: France **36** J6
St. Quentin, Pointe de: *cape*, France **35** G5
St. Rambert-d'Albon: Fr. **37** K10
St. Raphaël: France **40** M12
St. Raphaël: Que., Canada **89** Q2
St. Raymond: Que., Can. **89** Q2
St. Rémy: France **37** K12
St. Rémy-en-Bouzemort: France **36** K7
St. Rémy-sur-Durolle: Fr. **37** J10
St. Renan: France **36** A7
St. Rhémy: Italy **40** N10
St. Rome-de-Tarn: France **37** H11
St. Rose: La., U.S.A. **90** *Ins.*
St. Sampson: Guernsey, Channel Is. **25** *Ins.*
St. Saulge: France **36** J8
St. Sauveur: Alpes Maritimes, France **40** N11
St. Sauveur: Yonne, France **36** J8
St. Sauveur-Lendelin: Fr. **36** D6
St. Sauveur-le-Vicomte: Fr. **36** D6
St. Savin: Gironde, France **37** E10
St. Savin: Vienne, France **37** F9
St. Savine: France **36** K7
St. Sebastian Bay: S. Africa **74** D7
St. Seine-l'Abbaye: France **36** K8
St. Sernin-sur-Rance: Fr. **37** H12
St. Servan: France **36** D7
St. Sever: France **37** E12
St. Siméon: Que., Canada **89** R2
St. Simons: *i.*, Ga., U.S.A. **91** L10
St. Stephen (*N. of Launceston*), Corn., England **24** N18
St. Stephen: (*on river Fal*), Corn., England **24** M19
St. Stephen: N. B., Canada **89** S3
St. Stephen: S.C., U.S.A. **91** M9
St. Sulpice: France **37** G12
St. Sulpice-Laurière: France **37** G9
St. Symphorien: France **37** E11
St. Symphorien sur Coise: France **37** K10
St. Teath: Corn., England **24** M18
Ste. Thérèse: Que., Canada **89** P3
St. Thomas: Ont., Canada **88** L4
St. Thomas: *i.*, (U.S.A.), Lesser Antilles **87** a1
St. Tite: Que., Canada **89** P2
St. Trojan: France **37** D10
St. Trond: *see* Sint Truden.
St. Tropez: France **40** M12
St. Tropez, Golfe de: *gulf*, France **40** M12
St. Ursanne: Switzerland **40** N8
St. Vaast-la-Hougue: France **36** D6
St. Valéry-en-Caux: France **36** F6
St. Valéry-sur-Somme: Fr. **36** G5
St. Vallier: Ardèche, France **37** K10
St. Varent: France **36** E9
St. Veit: Carinthia, Austria **41** U9
St. Veit: Salzburg, Austria **41** T8
St. Vigeans: Tayside, Scot. **29** Q6

St. Vincent: *Br. associated state* **87** c4
Cap.: Kingstown
Area: 250 sq. miles (648 sq. km.)
Pop.: 90.000 (*1971 E*)

St. Vincent, Cape: Portugal **35** B18
St. Vincent, Gulf: S. Austl. **71** C10
St. Vincent-de-Tyrosse: Fr. **37** D12
St. Vith: Belgium **44** M5
St. Vivien: France **37** D10
St. Walburg: Sask., Canada **92** F2
St. Wendel: Saarland, W. Ger. **44** N6
St. Weonards: Hereford & Worcester, England **24** Q16
St. Yorre: France **37** J9
St. Yrieix: France **37** G10
Saio: Ethiopia **76** D1
Saipan: *i.*, Mariana Is. (*cap. of* Pacific Ocean Trust Terr.) **61** O8
Saiqal: Iraq **57** K6
Sais: Ancient Egyptian city on E. bank of Rosetta mouth of Nile, about 20 miles ESE. of Damanhur, Egypt **56** B6
Saison: *riv.*, France **37** E12
Saissac: France **37** H12
Saitama: *Pref.*, Japan (*cap.* Urawa) **63** f3
Saivomoutka: Sweden **46** S2
Saiwun (Sai'un): Yemen P.D.R. **55** G11
Sajama, Nev. de: Bolivia **94** D7
Sak (S. Africa): *see* Zak.
Sak: *riv.*, Thailand **64** C3
Saka: Kenya **76** E3
Saka: Tibet, China **59** P9
Sakai: Osaka, Japan **63** d3
Sakai: Tottori, Japan **63** c3
Sakaide: Japan **63** c3
Sakaka: Saudi Arabia **54** F9
Sakakawea, Lake: N. Dak., U.S.A. **92** G3
Sakala: *i.*, Indonesia **65** F8
Sakamachi: Japan **63** f1
Sakami: *riv.*. Canada **85** M7
Sakania: Zaïre **77** C5
Sakari: Japan **63** ZZ7
Sakarya: *Prov.*, Turkey (*cap.* Adapazari) **56** B1
Sakarya: *riv.*, Turkey **56** B1
Sakashita: Japan **63** e3
Sakata: Japan **63** Z7
Sakawa: Japan **63** c4
Sakbayème: Cameroun **81** G4
Sake: Zaïre **76** C3
Sakhalin: *i. & bay*, U.S.S.R. **49** Q7
Sakiri: Central African Rep. **76** B1
Sakishima Group: *is.* (Jap.), E. China Sea **63** W10
Sakon Nakhon: Thailand **64** C3
Sakrivier: S. Africa **74** D5
Saksaul'skiy: Kazakh., U.S.S.R. **51** K5
Sakurai: Japan **63** d3
Säkylä: Finland **47** S6
Sal: *i.*, Cape Verde Is. **78** *Ins.*
Šala: Czechoslovakia **43** P12
Sala: Sweden **47** P7
Salabangka Is.: Celebes **65** G7
Sala Consilina: Italy **38** O16
Saladillo: Buenos Aires, Argentina **96** D4
Saladillo: San Luis, Arg. **96** B3
Saladillo: *riv.*, Argentina **96** C2
Salado: *riv.*, Buenos Aires, Argentina **96** D4
Salado: *riv.*, Chile **96** A2
Salado: *riv.*, Mexico **90** B12
Salado: *riv.*, San Luis/Mendoza, Argentina **96** B3
Salado: *riv.*, Santa Fé, Arg. **96** C2
Salado, El: Mexico **93** G8
Salaga: Ghana **80** D3
Salaga: Liberia **80** C3
Salagle: Somalia **79** N9
Salahiya: Syria **57** G4
Salahuddin: Iraq **57** J3
Salahuddin: *Prov.*, Iraq **57** H4
Salair: U.S.S.R. **51** P4
Salal: *well*, Chad **81** H2
Salala: Sudan **54** F10
Salala: Oman **55** H11
Salamanca: Chile **96** A3
Salamanca: N.Y., U.S.A. **89** M4
SALAMANCA: & *Prov.*, Sp. **35** D16
Salamanga: Mozambique **75** K3
Salamat: *Pref.*, Chad (*cap.* Am-Timan) **79** J7
Salamatabad: Iran **57** K4
Salamaua: New Guinea **66** J3
Salamis: island opposite Piraeus at NE. end of Saronic G., Greece. **39** S18
Salamis: Greek city about 6 miles north of Famagusta, Cyprus **56** C4
Salas: Spain **35** C15
Salas de los Infantes: Spain **35** E15
Salatsgriva: Latvia, U.S.S.R. **47** T8
Salaverry: Peru **94** B5
Salavina: Argentina **96** C2
Salawati: *i.*, W. Irian, Indon. **61** L12
Salayar: *i., & str.*, Indonesia **65** G8
Sala y Gomez: *i.*, (Chile), S. Pacific Ocean **7** 30S 110W
Sala y Gomez Ridge: S. Pacific Ocean **7** 30S 100W
SALAZAR: Cuanza Norte, Angola **73** G11
Salbris: France **36** H8
Salcombe: Devon, England **24** O19
Saldaña: Spain **35** D15
Saldanha: & *bay*, S Africa **74** B6
Saldus: Latvia, U.S.S.R. **47** S8
Sale: Gt. Man., England **27** R13
Salé: Morocco **80** K8
Sale: Vict., Australia **71** G12
Salekhard: U.S.S.R. **48** h4
Salem: Ark., U.S.A. **90** F7
Salem: Ill., U.S.A. **88** G6
Salem: Ind., U.S.A. **88** H6
Salem: Tamil Nadu, India **58** N12
Salem: Mass., U.S.A. **89** Q4
Salem: Mo., U.S.A. **88** F7
Salem: N.J., U.S.A. **89** O6
Salem: Ohio, U.S.A. **88** L5
SALEM: Oreg., U.S.A. **92** C4
Salem: S. Africa **75** G6
Salem: Va., U.S.A. **88** L7
Salemboe Is.: Indonesia **65** E8
Salemi: Sicily **38** N18
Salen: Highland, Scotland **29** K6
Salen: Inner Hebr., Scotland **29** K6
Sälen: Sweden **47** N6
Salernes: France **40** M12
Salerno: & *gulf*, Italy **38** O16
Salers: France **37** H10
Salesbury: Lancs., England **27** R12
Salfit: Jordan **55** b2
Salford: Beds., England **25** U15
Salford: Gt. Man., England **27** R13
Salgótarján: Hungary **43** Q12
Salhouse: Norf., England **25** Y14
Salies: France **37** E12
Salignac: France **37** G11
Salihabad: Iran **57** K5
Salihli: Turkey **39** V17
Salim: Afghanistan **58** L8
Salima: Malawi **77** D5
Salina: Kans., U.S.A. **90** C6
Salina: Utah, U.S.A. **93** E5
Salina: *i.*, Lipari Is. (It.) **38** O17
Salina Cruz: Mexico **86** K14
Salinas: Bolivia **94** D7
Salinas: Brazil **94** J7
Salinas: Ecuador **94** A4
Salinas: *riv.*, Calif., U.S.A. **93** C5
Salinas, Cape: Majorca **35** H17
Salinas, Pampa de las: *salt pan*, Argentina **96** B3
Salinas Grandes: *salt pan*, Argentina **96** C2
Saline: Fife, Scotland **29** O7
Saline: *riv.*, Ark., U.S.A. **90** E9
Salinitas: Chile **96** B2
Salinópolis: Brazil **94** H4
Salins: France **40** L9
Salins, Les: France **40** M12
SALISBURY: Mashonaland South, Rhodesia **77** D6
Salisbury: Md., U.S.A. **89** O6
Salisbury: Mo., U.S.A. **88** E6
Salisbury: N.H., U.S.A. **89** Q4
Salisbury: N.C., U.S.A. **91** L8
Salisbury: S. Australia **71** C10
Salisbury: Wilts., England **25** S17
Salisbury Downs: N.S.W., Australia **71** E7
Salisbury I.: Canada **85** M5
Salisbury Plain: Wilts., Eng. **24** S17
Salisbury Sound: Alaska, U.S.A. **84** F6
Salkeld, Great: Cumbria, England **26** Q10
Salkhad: Syria **56** E5
Salla: Finland **46** V3
Sallanches: France **40** M10
Sallins: Kild., Repub. of Irel. **31** H13
Salliquello: Argentina **96** C4
Sallisaw: Okla., U.S.A. **90** D8
Sallom: Sudan **54** E11
Sallyana: Nepal **58** O9
Sallybrook: Cork, Repub. of Ireland **31** E16
Salman: Iraq **57** J6
Salm I.: Franz Josef Land **48** g2
Sal'miyarvi: U.S.S.R. **46** W2
Salmon: Mont., U.S.A. **92** E3
Salmon: *riv.*, Idaho, U.S.A. **92** D3
Salmon: *riv.*, N.B., Canada **89** T2
Salmon Arm: B.C., Canada **92** D2
Salmon Gums: W. Australia **68** C6
Salmon River Mtns.: Idaho, U.S.A. **92** D4
Salmünster: W. Germany **44** P5
Salo: Finland **47** S6
Salo: Italy **40** Q10
Salonae: Roman town at Split, W. Yugoslavia **38** P15
Salon-de-Provence: France **37** L12
Salonga: *riv.*, Zaïre **76** B3
Salonica (Thessaloniki): Greece **39** S16
Salonta: Romania **43** R13
Salop: *Co.*, England (*co. town* Shrewsbury) **27** Q14
Salou, Cape: Spain **35** G16
Saloum: *riv.*, Senegal **80** A2
Sal Rei: Cape Verde Is. **78** *Ins.*
Salsacate: Argentina **96** B3
Salses: France **37** H13
Sal'sk: U.S.S.R. **50** F5
Salso: *riv.*, Sicily **38** N18
Salsomaggiore: Italy **40** P11
SALT: Al Balqa, Jordan **55** b2
Salt: *riv.*, Ariz., U.S.A. **93** E6
Salt: *riv.*, Mo., U.S.A. **88** E6
Salt: *riv.*, S. Africa **74** E6
SALTA: & *Prov.*, Argentina **96** B1
Saltaire: S. Africa **75** F6
Saltash: Corn., England **24** N19
Saltburn by the Sea: Cleveland, England **26** U10
Saltcoats: Sask., Canada **92** G2
Saltcoats: Strath, Scotland **29** M8
Saltee Is.: Repub. of Ireland **31** H15
Saltfjellet National Park: Norway **46** O3
Saltfleet: Lincs., England **27** W13
Salt Fork: *riv.*, Kans./Okla., U.S.A. **90** C7
Salt Fork,: *riv.*, Tex./Okla., U.S.A. **90** A8
Salthill: Galway, Repub. of Ireland **31** C13
SALTILLO: Coahuila, Mexico **93** G7
SALT LAKE CITY: Utah, U.S.A. **93** E4
Salt Lakes: *lake*, W. Austl. **68** B5
Saltmills: Wex., Repub. of Ireland **31** H15
Salto: Uruguay **96** D3
Salto, El: Mexico **86** J13
Salto Grande: Brazil **96** F1
Salton Sea: Calif., U.S.A. **93** D6
Saltoro: *mtn.*, Jammu & Kashmir **58** N7
Saltoun: Loth., Scotland **29** Q8
Saltpond: Ghana **80** D3
Salt Range: Punjab, Pak. **58** M8
Saltville: Va., U.S.A. **88** L7
Saluda: *riv.*, S.C., U.S.A. **91** K8
Saludecio: Italy **41** S12
Salur: Andhra Pradesh, India **59** O11
Saluzzo: Italy **40** N11
SALVADOR: (Bahia): Bahia, Brazil **94** K6
Salvador, Lake: La., U.S.A. **90** *Ins.*
Salvator Rossa National Park: Queens., Australia **70** G5
Salvage Is.: (Port.), Atl. O. **78** A3
Salvetat, La: France **37** H12
Salviac: France **37** G11
Salvore: Yugoslavia **41** T10
Salwa: Saudi Arabia **55** H10
Salween: *riv.*, China/Burma **59** R10
Sal'yany: Azerbaydzhan, U.S.S.R. **57** L2
Salzach: *riv.*, Austria **41** T8
Salzbergen: W. Germany **44** N3
Salzbrunn: S.W. Africa **74** B2
SALZBURG: & *Prov.*, Austr. **41** T8
Salzgitter: W. Germany **45** Q3
Salzkotten: W. Germany **44** O4
Salzwedel: E. Germany **45** R3
Sama: U.S.S.R. **51** K2
Šamac: Yugoslavia **39** Q14
Samad: Oman **55** J10
Samah: Hainan, China **62** T11
Samakh: Israel **55** b2
Samal: *i.*, Philippines **65** H5
Samales Group: *is.*, Phil. **65** G5
Samalut: Egypt **54** D9
Sama Markala: Mali **80** C2
Samandağ: Turkey **56** D3
Samangan: *prov.*, Afghanistan (*cap.* Haibak) **55** L7
Samar: *i.*, Philippines **64** H4
Samara: *riv.*, U.S.S.R. **50** H4
Samarai: *i.*, New Guinea **69** J2
Samarga: U.S.S.R. **63** Z5
Samaria: Israelite city near *Sebustiyeh*, NW. of Nablus, Jordan **55** b2
Samarinda: Borneo: **65** F7
Samarka: U.S.S.R. **63** Y6
Samarkand: Uzbek, U.S.S.R. **51** L7
Samarobriva: Roman name of Gallic centre at Amiens, France **36** H6
Samarra: Iraq **57** H4
Samarra: *riv.*, U.S.S.R. **50** H4
Samastipur: Bihar, India **59** P9
Samawa: Iraq **57** J6
Samaza: Ivory Coast **80** D3
Samba: Zaïre **76** B2
Sambalpur: Orissa, India **59** O10
Sambar, Cape: Borneo **65** E7
Sambas: Borneo **65** D6
Sambava: Malagasy Rep. **73** O12
Sambhal: Uttar Pradesh, India **58** N9
Samboja: Borneo **65** F7
Sambolabo: Cameroun **81** G3
Sambor: Cambodia **64** D4
Sambor: Ukraine **43** S12
Sambre: *riv.*, Belgium **44** K5
Sambrogo: Upper Volta **80** D2
Samburg: U.S.S.R. **48** j4
Samburu Game Reserve: Kenya **76** E2
Samchok: S. Korea **63** X7
Same: Tanzania **76** E3
Samer: France **36** G5
Sammar: Morocco **35** E19
Samnan: *see* Semnan.
Samnium: ancient district of southern Appennines, extending between Isernia and Benevento, Italy **38** O16
Samnua: Laos **64** C2
Samoa: *see* **American Samoa & Western Samoa.**
Samobor: Yugoslavia **41** V10
Samoded: U.S.S.R. **50** F2
Samoëns: France **40** M9
Samokhvalovichi: Byelorussia **43** U10
Samokov: Bulgaria **39** S15
Samoroguan: Upper Volta **80** D2
Šamorin: Czechoslovakia **43** P12
Sámos: *i.*, Greece **39** U18
Samosata: Roman camp and city at Samsat, on S. border of Malatya, Turkey **56** F3
Samothrace (Samothráki): *i.*, Greece **39** T16
Sampacho: Argentina **96** C3
Sampanahan: Borneo **65** F7
Sampit: & *riv.*, Borneo **65** E7
Sampit Bay: Borneo **65** E7
Sampwe: Zaïre **77** C4
Samra: Saudi Arabia **54** F9
Samrah: Turkey **57** G3
Sam Rayburn Res.: Tex., U.S.A. **90** D10
Samro Lake: U.S.S.R. **47** V7
Samsat: Turkey **56** F3
Samsø: *i.*, Denmark **47** M9
Samson: Ala., U.S.A. **91** H10
SAMSUN: & *Prov.*, Turkey **56** E1
Samtens: E. Germany **45** T1
Samtredia: Georgia, U.S.S.R. **57** H1
Samui: *i.*, Thailand **64** C5
Samus': U.S.S.R. **51** O3
Samut Songkhram: Thailand **64** C4
San: Mali **80** D2
San: *riv.*, Cambodia **64** D4
San: *riv.*, Poland **43** S12
SAN'A: Yemen **54** F11
Sana: *riv.*, Yugoslavia **38** P14
Sanae: *rsch. stn.*, Antarctica **9** 75S 05W
Sanaga: *riv.*, Cameroun **81** G4
San Agata di Militello: Sicily **38** O17
Sanak Is.: Alaska, U.S.A. **84** c7
San Ambrogio: Italy **41** Q10
San Ambrosio: *i.*, Chile **95** B9
Sanana: & *i.*, Indonesia **65** H7
SANANDAJ: Kurdestan, Iran **57** K4
San Andrés: *i.*, Carib. Sea **87** I15
San Andres Mtns.: N. Mex., U.S.A. **93** F6
San Andrés Tuxtla: *see* Tuxtla, Mexico.
San Angelo: Italy **40** P10
San Angelo: Tex., U.S.A. **93** G6
San Angelo in Vado: Italy **41** S12
San Antioco: Sardinia **38** L17
San Antonio: Antofagasta, Chile **96** B1
San Antonio: Argentina **96** B2
San Antonio: Atacama, Chile **96** A2
San Antonio: Belize **86** *Ins.*
San Antonio: Santiago, Chile **96** A3
San Antonio: Tex., U.S.A. **90** B11
San Antonio: *riv.*, Tex., U.S.A. **90** C11
San Antonio, Cape: Arg. **96** D4
San Antonio, Cape: Cuba **86** I13
San Antonio Abad: Iviza, Balearic Is. **35** G17
San Antonio Bay: Tex., U.S.A. **90** C11
San Antonio de los Cobres: Argentina **96** B1
San Antonio Mount: Mexico **93** F6
San Antonio Oeste: Arg. **95** E12
San Antonio Peak: Calif., U.S.A. **93** D6
San Arcangelo de Romagna: Italy **41** S11
Sanau: *well*, Yemen P.D.R. **55** H11
San Augustin, Cape: Mindanao, Philippines **65** H5
San Augustine: Tex., U.S.A. **90** D10
San Bartolo: Chile **96** B1
San Bartolomeo: Italy **38** O16
San Benedetto: Italy **38** N15
San Benedicto: *i.*, (Mex.), Pacific O. **86** h14
San Benito: Tex., U.S.A. **90** C12
San Bernardino: Calif., U.S.A. **93** D6
San Bernardino: Paraguay **96** D2
San Bernardino Mtns.: Calif., U.S.A. **93** D6
San Bernardino Pass: Switz. **40** P9
San Bernardo: Chile **96** A3
San Blas, Cape: Fla., U.S.A. **91** J11
San Borja: Bolivia **94** D6
San Braz de Alportel: Port. **35** C18
San Buenaventura: Mex. **93** G7
San Camilo: Argentina **96** C1
San Carlos: Amazonas, Ven. **94** D3
San Carlos: Chile **96** A4
San Carlos: Coahuila, Mex. **93** G7
San Carlos: Cojedes, Ven. **94** D2
San Carlos: Mendoza, Arg. **96** B3
San Carlos: Philippines **64** G4
San Carlos: Salta, Argentina **96** B2
San Carlos: Uruguay **96** E3
San Carlos de Bariloche: Arg. **95** C12
San Carlos de la Rápita: Sp. **35** G16
San Carlos Lake: Ariz., U.S.A. **93** E6
San Casciano in Val di Pesa: Italy **41** R12
Sancergues: France **36** H8
Sancerre: France **36** H8
Sancha: Kansu, China **62** T8
Sanchez: Mexico **93** F7
Sánchez: Dominican Rep. **87** N14
San Clemente: Spain **35** E17
San Clemente: *i.*, Calif., U.S.A. **93** D6
Sancoins: France **37** H9
San Cosme: Paraguay **96** D2
San Cristóbal: Argentina **96** C3
San Cristobal: Solomon Is. **67** M4
San Cristóbal: Venezuela **94** C2
Sancti Spiritus: Cuba **87** M13
Sand: *i.*, Wis., U.S.A. **88** F2
Sand: *riv.*, O.F.S., S. Africa **75** *Ins.*
Sand: *riv.*, Wakkerstroom, Trans., S. Africa **75** H3
Sand: *riv.*, Zoutpansberg, Trans., S. Africa **75** H1
Sanda: *i.*, Strath., Scotland **29** K9
Sandakan: Sabah, Malaysia **65** F5
Sandal Magna: W. Yorks., England **27** T12
Sandane: Norway **47** K6
Sandanski: Bulgaria **39** S16
Sandarne: Sweden **47** P6
Sanday: *i.*, Orkney Is. **20** *Ins.*
Sandbach: Ches., England **27** R13
Sandbäckshult: Sweden **47** P8
Sandbank: Strath., Scotland **28** M8
Sandbult: Trans., S. Afr. **75** G1
Sand Cay: *reef*, Australia **69** H3
Sanddøla: *riv.*, Norway **46** N4
Sandefjord: Norway **47** M7
Sanderson: Tex., U.S.A. **93** G6
Sanderston: S. Australia **71** C10
Sandfisch Bay: S.W. Africa **74** A1
Sandflats: S. Africa **75** F6
Sandfontein: S.W. Africa **77** A7
Sandford: Devon, England **24** O18
Sandgate: Kent, England **25** Y17
Sandgate: Queens., Austl. **70** K6
Sandhaven: Gram., Scotland **28** R4
Sandhead: Dumfries & Galloway, Scotland **29** M10
Sandhurst: Berks., England **25** U17
Sandhurst: Kent, England **25** X17
Sandia: Peru **94** D6
Sandia Peak: N. Mex., U.S.A. **93** F5
San Diego: Calif., U.S.A. **93** D6
San Diego: Tex., U.S.A. **90** B12
San Diego, Cape: Argentina **95** D14
Sandıklı: Turkey **56** B2
Sandila: Uttar Pradesh, India **58** O9
Sanding: *i.*, Mentawai Is., Indonesia **65** C7
Sandlings, The: *dist.*, Suff., England **25** Y15
Sandnes: Norway **47** J7
Sandness: Mainland, Shetland Is. **28** *Ins.*
Sandnessjøen: Norway **46** N4
Sandø: *i.*, Faeroe Is. (Dan.) **46** h6
Sandoa: Zaïre **77** B4
Sandomierz: Poland **43** R11
Sandon: Staffs., England **27** R14
Sandover: *riv.*, N. Territ., Australia **69** F4
Sandoway: Burma **59** Q11
Sandown: I. of Wight, Eng. **25** T18
Sandpoint: Idaho, U.S.A. **92** D3
Sandray: *i.*, Outer Hebr., Scotland **28** G6
Sandringham: Norf., Eng. **25** X14
Sandsend: N. Yorks., Eng. **26** U10
Sand Springs: *city*, Okla., U.S.A. **90** C7
Sandspruit: Trans., S. Africa **75** H3
Sandstone: Minn., U.S.A. **88** E2
Sandstone: W. Australia **68** B5
Sandträsk: Sweden **46** R3
Sandur: Iceland **46** b4
Sandusky: Mich., U.S.A. **88** K4
Sandusky: Ohio, U.S.A. **88** K5
Sandvig: Bornholm, Den. **47** O9
Sandviken: Sweden **47** P6
Sandvlakte: S. Africa **75** F6
Sandvliet: O.F.S., S. Africa **75** H3
Sandwich: Ill., U.S.A. **88** G5
Sandwich: Kent, England **25** Y17
Sandwich Bay: Newf., Can. **84** O7
Sandwick: Mainland, Shetland Is. **28** *Ins.*
Sandy: Beds., England **28** V15
Sandy Cape: Fraser I., Queens., Australia **70** K5
Sandy Hook: *penin.*, N.J., U.S.A. **89** P5
Sandy Is.: Chesterfield Is. **67** M5
Sandy Lake: *town*, Ont., Canada **92** J2
San Enrique: Argentina **96** C4
San Estanislao: Paraguay **96** D1
San Estebán: *i.*, Mexico **93** E7
San Estevão: Portugal **35** B17
San Felice: Italy **41** R11
San Felipe: Chile **96** A3
San Felipe: Venezuela **94** D1
San Feliú de Guixols: Spain **35** H16
San Feliú de Llobregat: Sp. **35** H16
San Félix: Venezuela **94** E2
San Félix: *i.* (Chile), Pac. O. **95** A9
San Fernando: Chile **96** A3
San Fernando: (*N. of Manila*), Luzon, Philippines **64** G3
San Fernando: (*on W. coast*), Luzon, Philippines **64** G3
San Fernando: Lower California, Mexico **93** D6
San Fernando: & *riv.*, Tamaulipas, Mexico **90** B13
San Fernando: Spain **35** C18
San Fernando: Trinidad **87** c5
San Fernando: Venezuela **94** D2
San Fernando de Atabapo: Venezuela **94** D3
San Fiora: Italy **38** M15
Sanford: Fla., U.S.A. **91** L11
Sanford: Maine, U.S.A. **89** Q4
Sanford: N.C., U.S.A. **91** M8
Sanford: *riv.*, W. Australia **68** B5
Sanford, Mount: Alaska, U.S.A. **84** e5
San Francisco: Calif., U.S.A. **93** C5
San Francisco: Córdoba, Argentina **96** C3
San Francisco (San Francisco del Chanar): Córdoba, Argentina **96** C2
San Francisco: San Luis, Argentina **96** B3
San Francisco: *riv.*, Arg. **96** B1
San Francisco, Cape: Ec. **94** A3
San Francisco de Conchos: Mexico **93** F7
San Francisco del Oro: Mex. **93** F7
San Francisco del Rincon: Mexico **86** j13
San Francisco de Macoris: Dominican Rep. **87** m14
San Francisco Peaks: *mtns.*, Ariz., U.S.A. **93** E5
Sanga: Upper Volta **80** E2
Sanga: Mozambique **77** E5
San Gabriel: Ecuador **94** B3
San Gabriel Mtns.: Calif., U.S.A. **93** D6
Sangama: Tanzania **76** D4
Sangamner: Maharashtra, India **58** M11
Sangamon: *riv.*, Ill., U.S.A. **88** G6
Sangar: Afghanistan **58** L8
Sangar: U.S.S.R. **49** o5
Sangareddipet: Andhra Pradesh, India **58** N11
Sangasso: Mali **80** C2
Sangchih: Hunan, China **62** U9
Sangeang: *i.*, Indonesia **65** F8
Sanger: Calif., U.S.A. **93** D5
Sangerhausen: E. Germany **45** R4
Sanggau: Borneo **65** E6
Sangha: *riv.*, Congo **81** H4
Sangihe I.: & *is.*, Indonesia **65** H6
Sang-i-Masha: Afghanistan **58** L8
San Gimignano: Italy **41** Q12
San Giorgio di Nogaro: Italy **41** T10
San Giovanni-Bianco: Italy **40** P10
San Giovanni in Fiore: Italy **38** P17
San Giovanni Valdarno: Italy **41** R12
Sangird: Iran **55** J7
Sangju: S. Korea **63** X7
Sangkan: *riv.*, China **62** U7
Sangkulirang: Borneo **65** F6
Sangli: Maharashtra, India **58** M11
Sangmélima: Cameroun **81** G4
Sangmissoq: Greenland **85** p6
Sangre de Cristo Mtns.: Colo./N. Mex., U.S.A. **93** F5
San Gregorio: Uruguay **96** D3
Sangre Grande: Trinidad **87** c5
Sangro: *riv.*, Italy **38** O15
Sanguesa: Spain **35** F15
Sangwa: Zaïre **76** C4
Sañico: Argentina **95** C12
Sanibel I.: Fla., U.S.A. **91** K12
San Ignacio: Argentina **96** D2
San Ignacio: Beni, Bolivia **94** D6
San Ignacio: Santa Cruz, Bolivia **94** E7
San Ignacio: Mexico **93** E7
San Ignacio: Paraguay **96** D2
San Ilario: Italy **40** Q11
Sanish: N. Dak., U.S.A. **92** G3
Sanitatas: S.W. Africa **73** G13
Sanitz: E. Germany **45** S1
San Jacinto Peak: Calif., U.S.A. **93** D6
San Jaime: *see* J. B. Arruabarrena.
San Javier: Bolivia **94** E7
San Javier: Chile **96** A4
San Javier: Misiones, Arg. **96** D2
San Javier: Santa Fé, Arg. **96** D3
San Javier: *riv.*, Arg. **96** D2
Sanjo: Japan **63** f2
San João: Portugal **35** C16
San Joaquin: Brazil **94** E6
San Joaquin Valley: Calif., U.S.A. **93** C5
San Jorge, G. of: Spain **35** G16
San José: Bolivia **94** E7
San Jose: Calif., U.S.A. **93** C5
SAN JOSÉ: Costa Rica **86** I16
San José: Guatemala **86** k15
San José: Luzon, Phil. **64** G3
San José: Mindoro, Phil. **64** G4
San José: *i.*, Mexico **93** E7
San José de Amacuro: Ven. **94** E2
San José de Feliciano: Arg. **96** D3
San José del Boquéron: Arg. **96** C2
San José del Cabo: Mexico **93** F8
San José del Guaviare: Col. **94** C3
San José de Mayo: Uruguay **96** D3
SAN JUAN: & *Prov.*, Arg. **96** B3
San Juan: Morocco **80** L7
SAN JUAN: Puerto Rico **87** a1
San Juan: *riv.*, Colo., U.S.A. **93** F5
San Juan Bautista: Iviza, Balearic Is. **35** G17
San Juan Bautista: Paraguay **96** D2

184 San Juan de Guadalupe—Sayr Usa

San Juan de Guadalupe: Mexico 93 G8
San Juan del Norte (Grey Town): Nicaragua 87 I15
San Juan de los Moros: Venezuela 94 D2
San Juan del Rio: Mexico 93 G8
San Juan Mtns.: Colo., U.S.A. 93 F5
San Julián: Argentina 95 D13
San Justo: Argentina 96 C3
Sankaram: riv., Gu./Mali 80 C2
Sankiang: Kwangsi Chuang, China 62 T9
Sankuru: riv., Zaire 76 B3
San Lázaro, Sierra de: Mex. 93 E8
San Leonardo: Italy 41 R9
San Lorenzo: Argentina 96 C3
San Lorenzo: Bolivia 95 E8
San Lorenzo: Venezuela 94 C2
San Lorenzo: i., Mexico 93 E7
Sanlúcar de Barrameda: Sp. 35 C18
San Lucas: Bolivia 94 D8
San Lucas, Cape: Mexico 93 F8
San Luis: & Prov., Arg. 96 B3
San Luis: Corrientes, Arg. 96 D2
San Luis: Cuba 87 M13
San Luis: Guatemala (Hond. Inset) 86 Ins.
San Luis: Mexico 93 E6
San Luis del Cordero: Mex. 93 G7
San Luis Obispo: Calif., U.S.A. 93 C5
San Luis Potosí: Mexico 86 j13
Sanluri: Sardinia 38 L17
San Marcello Pistoiese: Italy 41 Q11
San Marcial: Mexico 93 E7
San Marcial: N. Mex., U.S.A. 93 F6
San Marco, Cape: Sardinia 38 L17
San Marco in Lamis: Italy 38 O16
San Marcos: Colombia 94 B2
San Marcos: Tex., U.S.A. 90 C11
San Marcos: i., Mexico 93 E7

San Marino: *Republic* 41 S12
Cap.: San Marino
Area: 24 sq. miles (62 sq. km.)
Pop.: 18,000 (*1971 E*)

San Martín: Catamarca, Argentina 96 B2
San Martín Corrientes, Arg. see Yapeyú.
San Martín: Mendoza, Arg. 96 B3
San Martín: Neuquén, Arg. 95 C12
San Martín: San Luis, Arg. 96 B3
San Martín, Lake: Arg. 95 C13
San Martín de Valdeiglesias: Spain 35 D16
San Mateo: Venezuela 94 E2
San Mateo: mtn., N. Mex., U.S.A. 93 F6
San Matías, G.: Argentina 95 E12
San Maura (Levkás): i., Ionian Is. (Grc.) 39 R17
San Miguel: El Salvador 86 L15
San Miguel: i., Calif., U.S.A. 93 C6
San Miguel: i., Panama 94 B2
San Miguel: riv., Brazil 94 E6
San Miguel Is.: Philippines 64 F5
San Miguel: riv., Bolivia 94 E6
San Miguel Is.: Philippines 64 F5
San Miniato: Italy 41 Q12
San Narciso: Luzon, Phil. 64 G4
Sannazzaro: Italy 40 O10
San Nicandro Garganico: Italy 38 O16
San Nicolás: Argentina 96 C3
San Nicolas: i., Calif., U.S.A. 93 D6
Sanniquellie: Nimba, Liberia 80 C3
San Pedro: Buenos Aires, Argentina 96 D3
San Pedro: Calif., U.S.A. 93 D6
San Pedro: Córdoba, Arg. 96 B3
San Pedro: Ivory Coast 80 C4
San Pedro: Jujuy, Argentina 96 C1
San Pedro: Mexico 93 E7
San Pedro: Misiones, Arg. 96 E2
San Pedro: Paraguay 96 D1
San Pedro: Peru 94 B5
San Pedro: Venezuela 94 F2
San Pedro de Atacama: Chile 96 B1
San Pedro de las Colonias: Mexico 93 G7
San Pedro del Paraná: Paraguay 96 D2
San Pedro del Pinatar: Spain 35 F18
San Pedro de Macorís: Dominican Rep. 89 N14
San Pedro do Sul: Portugal 35 B16
San Pedro Sula: Honduras 86 L14
San Pietro: i., Sardinia 38 L17
San Polo: Italy 40 Q11
Sanquhar: Dumfries & Galloway, Scotland 29 O9
San Rafael: Argentina 96 B3
San Rafael: Calif., U.S.A. 93 C5
San Rafael: Mexico 93 G7
San Remo: Italy 40 N12
San Roque: Argentina 96 D2
San Roque: Brazil 96 F1
San Roque: Spain (Gib. Inset) 32 Ins.
San Saba: riv., Tex., U.S.A. 90 B10
San Salvador: Argentina 96 D3
SAN SALVADOR: El Salvador 86 L15
San Salvador (Watling): i., Bahamas 87 m13
Sansane Haoussa: Niger 81 E2
Sansane Mango: Togo 80 E2
San Sebastián: Argentina 95 D14
San Sebastián: Canary Is. 78 A4
San Sebastian: Guipuzcoa, Spain 36 D12
San Sebastião, Cape: Moz. 77 E7
Sansepolcro: Italy 41 S12
San Severo: Italy 38 O16
Sanshui: Kwangtung, China 62 U10
Sansoy: U.S.S.R. 63 Y6
San Stefano: small port where treaty which ended the Russo-Turkish War was signed in 1878, W. of Istanbul, Turkey 39 V16
San Stefano d'Aveto: Italy 40 P11
San Stefano di Cadore: Italy 41 S9
Santa Agueda: Mexico 93 E7
Santa Ana: Argentina 96 B2
Santa Ana: Bolivia 94 D6
Santa Ana: Calif., U.S.A. 93 D6
Santa Ana: El Salvador 86 L15
Santa Ana: Mexico 93 E6
Santa Anita: Mexico 93 F8
Santa Anna: Tex., U.S.A. 90 B10
Santa Barbara: Argentina 96 C1
Santa Bárbara: Brazil 96 E2
Santa Bárbara: Mexico 93 F7
Santa Barbara: & i., Calif., U.S.A. 93 D6
Santa Catalina: i., Calif., U.S.A. 93 D6
Santa Catalina: i., Mexico 93 E7
Santa Catalina, G. of: Calif., U.S.A. 93 D6
Santa Catarina: State, Brazil (cap. Florianópolis) 96 E2
Santa Catarina I.: Brazil 96 F2
Santa Clara: Cuba 87 M13
Santa Clara: Mexico 93 G8
Santa Clara: i., Juan Fernández Is. (Chile) 95 B10
Santa Cruz: Argentina 95 D14
Santa Cruz: Bolivia 94 E7
Santa Cruz: Calif., U.S.A. 93 C5
Santa Cruz: Chile 96 A3
Santa Cruz: Jamaica 86 Ins.
Santa Cruz: Luzon, Phil. 64 G4
Santa Cruz: Mexico 93 E6
Santa Cruz: Mindanao, Phil. 65 H5
Santa Cruz: Rio Grande do Norte, Brazil 94 K5
Santa Cruz: Rio Grande do Sul, Brazil 96 E2
Santa Cruz: São Paulo, Braz. 96 F1
Santa Cruz: i., Calif., U.S.A. 93 D6
Santa Cruz (St. Croix): i. (U.S.A.), Lesser Antilles 87 a2
Santa Cruz: Prov., Argentina (cap. Rio Gallegos) 95 D13
Santa Cruz de la Zarza: Sp. 35 E17
Santa Cruz del Sur: Cuba 87 M13
Santa Cruz de Tenerife: & Prov., Canary Islands 78 A4
Santa Cruz Is.: (Br.), Pac. O. 67 N4
Santa Dona di Piave: Italy 41 S10
Santa Elena: Argentina 96 D3
Santa Elena: Panama 94 Ins.
Santa Elena: Venezuela 94 E3
Santa Elena, Cape: C.R. 86 L15
Santa Eufemia, G. of: Italy 38 P17
Santa Fé: & Prov., Arg. 96 C3
Santa Fé: Brazil 94 D4
Santa Fe: N. Mex., U.S.A. 93 F5
Santa Fé: Spain 35 E18
Santa Fé: see Marcelino.
Santa Filomena: Brazil 94 H5
Santa Genoveva: mtn., Mex. 93 E8
Santai: Szechwan, China 62 T8
Santa Inés I.: Chile 95 C14
Santa Isabel: Brazil 94 E4
Santa Isabel: Equatorial Guinea see Malabo.
Santa Isabel: La Pampa, Argentina 96 B4
Santa Isabel: Santa Fé, Arg. 96 C3
Santa Isabel: i., Solomon Is. 67 L3
Santa Izabel: Brazil 96 E3
Santa Justina: Argentina 96 C2
Santa Lucia: Uruguay 96 D3
Santa Lucia Range: Calif., U.S.A. 93 C5
Santa Margarita: i., Mexico 93 E8
Santa Maria: Argentina 96 B2
Santa Maria: Brazil 96 E2
Santa Maria: Calif., U.S.A. 93 C6
Santa Maria: Cape Verde Is. 78 Ins.
Santa Maria: i., Azores 78 Ins.
Santa Maria: i., New Hebr. 67 N4
Santa Maria: lake, Mexico 93 F6
Santa Maria: riv., Arg. 96 B2
Santa Maria, Cape: Angola 73 G12
Santa Maria, Cape: Portugal 35 C18
Santa Maria de Boa Vista: Brazil 94 K5
Santa Maria di Leuca, Cape: Italy 39 Q17
Santa Maria Madalena: Brazil 96 G1
Santa Marta: Colombia 94 C1
Santa Monica: Calif., U.S.A. 93 D6
Santana, Coxilha de: mtns., Uruguay/Brazil 96 D3
Santan: Borneo 65 F7
Sântana: Romania 43 R13
Sant' Ana da Boa Vista: Brazil 96 E3
Santana, Coxilha de: mtns., Uruguay/Brazil 96 D3
Santana do Ipanema: Brazil 94 K5
Santander: & Prov., Spain 35 E15
Santander Jiménez: Mexico 90 B13
Santañy: Majorca, Balearic Is. 35 H17
Santaochen: Heilungkiang, China 63 X5
Santa Paula: Calif., U.S.A. 93 D6
Santarém: Brazil 94 G4
Santarém: Ribatejo, Port. 35 B17
Santa Rita: N. Mex., U.S.A. 93 F6
Santa Rita: Panama 94 Ins.
Santa Rita do Weil: Brazil 94 D4
Santa Rosa: Bolivia 94 D6
Santa Rosa: Brazil 96 E2
Santa Rosa: Calif., U.S.A. 93 C5
Santa Rosa: Córdoba, Arg. 96 C3
Santa Rosa: Honduras 86 L15
Santa Rosa: La Pampa, Argentina 96 C4
Santa Rosa: N. Mex., U.S.A. 93 G6
Santa Rosa: Panama 94 Ins.
Santa Rosa: San Luis, Arg. 96 B3
Santa Rosa: i., Calif., U.S.A. 93 C6
Santa Rosa I. Nat. Mon.: i., Fla., U.S.A. 91 H10
Santa Rosalia: Mexico 93 E7
Santa Rosalia Mtns.: Nev., U.S.A. 92 D4
Santa Rosa Reef: Mariana Is. 61 N9
Santa Teresa: Mexico 90 C13
Santa Vitória do Palmar: Brazil 96 E3
Santee: riv., S.C., U.S.A. 91 M9
Santee Reservoir: see Marion, Lake.
San Telmo: Mexico 93 D6
Santerno: riv., Italy 41 R11
Santeuil: France 36 G7
Santhia: Italy 40 O10
Santi: Malawi 77 D5
SANTIAGO: Chile 96 A3
Santiago: Dominican Rep. 87 m14
Santiago: Mexico 93 F8
Santiago: Spain 35 B15
Santiago: riv., Mexico 86 j13
Santiago de Cuba: Cuba 87 M13
Santiago del Estero: & Prov., Argentina 96 C2
Santiago do Boqueirão: Brazil 96 D2
Santiago do Cacém: Port. 35 B17
Santiago Ixcuintla: Mexico 86 J13
Santiaguillo, Lago de: Mex. 93 F8
Santigi: Celebes 65 G6
Santillana: Spain 35 D15
San Tirana: Italy 40 O10
Santo Amaro: Brazil 94 K6
Santo André: Brazil 96 F1
Santo Angelo: Brazil 96 E2
Santo Antão: C. Verde Is. 78 Ins.
Santo Antônio: Guaporé, Brazil 94 E5
Santo Antônio: Rio Grande do Norte, Brazil 94 K5
Santo Antônio de Balsas: Brazil 94 H5
Santo Antônio do Içá: Braz. 94 D4
Santo Antônio do Leverger: Brazil 94 F7
Santo Antônio do Patrulha: Brazil 96 E2
Santo Antonio do Zaïre: Angola 81 G6
Santo Domingo: Costa Rica 87 I16
SANTO DOMINGO: Dominican Republic 87 N14
Santo Domingo: Mexico 93 D6
Santones: Gallic tribe with centre at Saintes, France 37 E10
Santos: Brazil 96 F1
Santos de Maimona, Los: Spain 35 C17
Santos Dumont: Brazil 96 G1
Santo Tomás: Mexico 93 D6
Santo Tomé de Guayana: Venezuela 94 E2
Santry: Dublin, Repub. of Ireland 31 J13
San Valentin, Cerro: mtns., Chile 95 C13
Sanvic: France 36 F6
San Vicente: Chile 96 A3
San Vicente: Colombia 94 C3
San Vicente: El Salvador 86 L15
San Vicente: Mexico 93 D6
San Vicente: Spain 35 D15
San Vicino: mtn., Italy 41 T12
Sanvignes: France 37 K9
San Vito: Italy 41 S10
San Vito, Cape: Sicily 38 N17
Sanyati: riv., Rhodesia 77 C6
San Ysidro: Calif., U.S.A. 93 D6
Sanyuan: Shensi, China 62 T8
Sanza Pombo: Angola 73 H11
São Antonio: Principe, G. of Guinea 81 F4
São Benedito: Brazil 94 J4
São Bento: Maranhão, Braz. 94 J4
São Bento: Santa Catarina, Brazil 96 F2
São Borja: Brazil 96 D2
São Carlos: Brazil 96 F1
São Domingos: Brazil 94 H6
São Felipe: Brazil 94 D3
São Felix: Brazil 94 K6
São Francisco: Minas Gerais, Brazil 94 J7
São Francisco: riv., Brazil 94 J5
São Francisco do Sul: Braz. 96 F2
São Gabriel: Rio Grande do Sul, Brazil 96 E3
São Gonçalo: Brazil 96 F1
Sao Hill: Tanzania 76 E4
São Jerônimo: Brazil 96 E2
São João: Brazil 96 F1
São João da Bôa Vista: Braz. 96 F1
São João da Barra: Brazil 95 J8
São João del Rei: Brazil 96 G1
São João do Araguaia: Brazil 94 H5
São João do Piauí: Brazil 94 J5
São Joaquim: Santa Catarina, Brazil 96 F2
São Joaquim: São Paulo, Brazil 94 H8
São Jorge: i., Azores 78 Ins.
São José: Amazonas, Brazil 94 D4
São José: Santa Catarina, Brazil 96 F2
São José de Mipibu: Brazil 94 K5
São José do Egito: Brazil 94 K5
São José do Norte: Brazil 96 E3
São José do Rio Prêto: Brazil 94 H8
São Leopoldo: Brazil 96 E2
São Lourenço: Minas Gerais, Brazil 96 G1
São Lourenço: Rio Grande do Sul, Brazil 96 E3
São Luís: Maranhão: Brazil 94 J4
São Luís Gonzaga: Brazil 96 E2
São Manuel: Brazil 96 F1
São Mateus: Espírito Santo, Brazil 94 K7
São Mateus: Paraná, Braz. 96 E2
São Miguel: i., Azores Is. 78 Ins.
Saône: riv., France 37 K9
Saône-et-Loire: Dept., Fr. (cap. Mâcon) 37 K9
São Nicolau: i., Cape Verde Is. 78 Ins.
São Paulo: & State, Brazil 96 F1
São Paulo de Olivença: Braz. 94 D4
São Pedro: Brazil 96 F1
São Pedro do Piauí: Brazil 94 J5
São Raimundo Nonato: Brazil 94 J5
São Salvador do Congo: Zaire, Angola 81 G6
São Sebastião: Rio Grande do Sul, Brazil 96 E3
São Sebastião: & i., São Paulo, Brazil 96 F1
São Sebastião do Paraíso: Brazil 96 F1
São Sepé: Brazil 96 E3
São Simão: Brazil 96 F1
São Tiago: i., Cape Verde Is. 78 Ins.
São Tomé: & i., G. of Guinea 81 F4
Saouai: Mizoram, India 59 Q10
Saoura: Dept., Algeria (cap. Béchar) 78 D4
Saoura: riv., Algeria 80 L9
São Vicente: Brazil 96 F1
São Vicente: i., Cape Verde Is. 78 Ins.
São Vicente Ferrer: Brazil 94 J4
Sapai: Greece 39 T16
Sapala: Upper Volta 80 D2
Sapaleri: mtn., Argentina/Chile 96 B1
Sapanca: Turkey 56 B1
Sapele: Nigeria 81 F3
Sapelo: i., Ga., U.S.A. 91 L10
Sape Str.: Indonesia 65 F8
Saphane: Turkey 56 A2
Sapientza: i., Greece 39 R18
Šapjane: Yugoslavia 41 U10
Saposoa: Peru 94 B5
Sappisadsi: Sweden 46 R3
Sapporo: Japan 63 ZZ6
Sapri: Italy 38 O16
Sapudi: i., Indonesia 65 E8
Sapulpa: Okla., U.S.A. 90 C8
Saqqiz: Iran 57 K3
Sar: Oman 55 J10
Sara: Upper Volta 80 D2
Sara: riv., Chad 81 H3
Sarab: Iran 57 K3
Sarafutsu: Japan 63 ZZ5
Saragossa (Zaragoza): Zaragoza, Spain 35 F16
Saraguro: Ecuador 94 B4
Sarai: U.S.S.R. 50 F4
Sarajärvi: Finland 46 U4
Sarajevo: Bosnia-Hercegovina, Yugoslavia 39 Q15
Saraktask: U.S.S.R. 50 J4
Sarala: Mali 80 C2
Sarala: U.S.S.R. 51 P4
Saramon: France 37 F12
Saranac Lake: city, N.Y., U.S.A. 89 O3
Saranac Lakes: N.Y., U.S.A. 89 O3
Saranda: Tanzania 76 D4
Sarandë: Albania 39 R17
Sarandi: Brazil 96 E2
Sarandí del Yí: Uruguay 96 D3
Sarangani Bay: & is., Mindanao, Philippines 65 H5
Sarangarh: Madhya Pradesh, India 59 O10
Saransk: Mordov, U.S.S.R. 50 G4
Sarapul: U.S.S.R. 50 H3
Sarasota: Fla., U.S.A. 91 K12
Sarata: Ukraine 39 V13
Saratoga: Wyo., U.S.A. 92 F4
Saratoga Springs: city, N.Y., U.S.A. 89 P4
Saratov: & Reg., U.S.S.R. 50 G4
Saravane: Laos 64 D3
Sarawak: State, Malaysia (cap. Kuching) 65 E6
Saray: Turkey 39 U16
Saraycik: Turkey (Dardan. Inset) 20 Ins.
Saraykoy: Turkey 56 A3
Sarbaz: Iran 55 K9
Sarbisheh: Iran 55 J8
Sárbogárd: Hungary 43 Q13
Sarclet: Highland, Scotland 28 P3
Sarco: Chile 96 A2
Sardakova: U.S.S.R. 51 N2
Sardarshahr: Rajasthan, India 58 M9
Sardasht: Iran 57 J3
Sardes: Lydian, later Graeco-Roman, city about 5 miles W. of Salihli, Turkey 39 V17
Sardinia: i., (It). Medit. Sea (cap. Cagliari) 38 L17
Sardis: & res., Miss., U.S.A. 90 G8
Sardloq: Greenland 85 P5
Sardobsk: U.S.S.R. 50 F4
Sareks National Park: Sweden 46 P3
Sarektjäkko: mtn., Sweden 46 P3
Sarema: i., Estonia, U.S.S.R. 47 S7
Sarentino: Italy 41 R9
Sarera Bay: West Irian, Indonesia 61 M12
Sarga: Upper Volta 80 D2
Sargans: Switzerland 40 P8
Sargasso Sea: N. Atlantic Ocean 8 25N 70W
Sargodha: Punjab, Pak. 58 M8
Sarh: Moyen-Chari, Chad 81 H3
Sari: Mazandaran, Iran 55 H7
Saric: Mexico 93 E6
Sarich, Cape: U.S.S.R. 50 D6
Sar-i-Chashma: Afghan. 58 L8
Sarigan: i., Mariana Is. 61 O8
Sarigöl: Turkey 56 A2
Sarikai: Sarawak, Malaysia 65 E6
Sarıkamış: Turkey 57 H1
Sar-i-Kul: Iran 57 L5
Sariman: Borneo 65 E7
Sarina: Queens., Australia 70 H3
Sariñena: Spain 35 F16
Sar-i-Pul: Afghanistan 51 L7
Sar-i-Pul: Iran 57 J4
Sariwon: N. Korea 63 X7
Sariyer: Turkey (Bosporus. Inset) 20 Ins.
Sariz: Iran 55 J8
Sark: i., Channel Is. 25 Ins.
Sarkhani: Iran 57 K2
Şarkişla: Turkey 56 E2
Şarköy: Turkey 39 U16
Sarlat: France 37 G11
Sarliac: France 37 F10
Sarmizegethusa: Dacian capital later Roman colony at Gredistje about 15 miles SW. of Hațeg, Romania 43 S14
Sar Mtns.: Yugo./Alb. 39 R15
Särna: Sweden 47 N6
Sarnen: Switzerland 40 O9
Sarnia: Ont., Canada 88 K4
Sarnico: Italy 40 P10
Sarny: Ukraine 43 U11
Särö: Sweden 47 M8
Saronic G.: Greece 39 S18
Saronno: Italy 40 P10
Saros, G. of: Turkey (Dardan. Inset) 20 Ins.
Sarpsborg: Norway 47 M7
Sarqaq: Greenland 85 o3
Sarra: well, Libya 79 J5
Sarralbe: France 40 N7
Sarrar: Saudi Arabia 55 G9
Sarrebourg: France 40 N7
Sarreguemines: France 44 N6
Sarre-Union: France 40 N7
Sarriá: Spain 35 C15
Sarstedt: W. Germany 45 P3
Sartène: Corsica 38 L16
Sarthe: Dept., France (cap. Le Mans) 37 F7
Sarthe: riv., France 36 E8
Sartilly: France 36 D7
Satirana: Italy 40 O10
Sartyn'ya: U.S.S.R. 51 K2
Sarvar: Hungary 43 P13
Sarvistan: Iran 55 H9
Saryagach: Kazakh., U.S.S.R. 51 L6
Sary-Ozek: Kazakh., U.S.S.R. 51 N6
Sarysu: riv., U.S.S.R. 51 L5
Sarzeau: France 36 C8
Sarzeh: Iran 55 J9
Sasak: Sumatra 65 B6
Sasaram: Bihar, India 59 O10
Sasd: Hungary 43 Q13
Sasebo: Japan 63 a4
Saser Kangri: mtn., Jammu & Kashmir 58 N8
Sashiki: Japan 63 b4
Saskylakh: U.S.S.R. 49 N3
Saskatchewan: Prov., Can. (cap. Regina) 92 F2
Saskatchewan: riv., Man./Sask., Canada 92 G2
Saskatoon: Sask., Canada 92 F2
Sasolburg: O.F.S., S. Africa 75 G3
Sasovo: U.S.S.R. 50 F4
Sassabaneh: Ethiopia 79 Q18
Sassandra: Ivory Coast 80 C4
Sassandra: riv., Ivory Coast 80 C3
Sassari: Sardinia 38 L16
Sassnitz: E. Germany 45 T1
Sasso: Emilia Romagna, Italy 41 R11
Sassoferrato: Italy 41 S12
Sasstown: Liberia 80 C4
Sassuolo: Italy 41 Q11
Sastre: Argentina 96 C3
Sata, Cape: Japan 63 Y8
Satadougou: Mali 80 B2
Şatak: Turkey 57 H2
Satala: Roman camp and city at Erzincan, Turkey 56 F2
Satara: Maharashtra, India 58 M11
Satara: Trans., S. Africa 75 J2
Satellite Bay: N.W.T., Can. 84 H2
Säter: Sweden 47 O6
Satevo: Mexico 93 F7
Satırlar: Turkey 56 A3
Satley: Durham, England 26 S10
Satna: Madhya Pradesh, India 58 O10
Sátoraljaújhely: Hungary 43 R12
Satpura Range: India 58 N10
Sattledt: Austria 41 U7
Satu Mare: Romania 43 S13
Satumma: Ethiopia 76 E1
Satun: & Prov., Thailand 65 b10
Satyga: U.S.S.R. 51 K3
Sauce: Argentina 96 D3
Sauces, Los: Chile 96 A4
Sauchen: Gram., Scotland 28 R5
Sauda: Norway 47 K7
Saude: Brazil 94 J6

Saudi Arabia: *Kingdom* 54/5
Cap.: Riyadh
Area: 873,000 sq. miles (2,261,070 sq. km.)
Pop.: 7,965,000 (*1971 E*)

Sauer: S. Africa 74 C6
Sauerland: geog. reg., W. Ger. 44 N4
Saughall: Ches., England 27 Q13
Saugor: Madhya Pradesh, India 58 N10
Saugues: France 37 J11
Saujbulagh (Mehabad): Iran 57 J3
Saujon: France 37 E10
Sauk Centre: Minn., U.S.A. 88 D3
Sauk Rapids: city, Minn., U.S.A. 88 D3
Sauldre: riv., France 36 H8
Saulgau: W. Germany 40 P7
Saulieu: France 36 K8
Saulkrasti: Latvia, U.S.S.R. 47 T8
Sault au Cochon: riv., Que., Canada 89 R1
Sault Ste. Marie: Mich., U.S.A. 88 J2
Sault Ste. Marie: Ont., Can. 88 J2
Saulx: France 40 M8
Saulxures: France 40 M8
Saum: Hadhramaut, Yemen P.D.R. 55 G11
Saumarez Reef: Australia 69 J4
Saumlaki: Tanimbar Is., Indonesia 61 L13
Saumur: France 36 E8
Saundersfoot: Dyfed, Wales 24 M16
Saurashtra: (now absorbed in Maharashtra, State), India.
Sausu: Celebes 65 G7
Sautar: Angola 77 A5
Sauternes: France 37 E11
Sauveterre: Gironde, France 37 E11
Sauveterre: Pyrénées-Atlantiques, France 37 E12
Sauzet: France 37 G11
Sauzé-Vaussais: France 37 F9
Sauzon: Belle Île, France 36 B8
Sava: riv., Yugoslavia 39 Q14
Savage: Mont., U.S.A. 92 G3
Savaii: i., W. Samoa 70 Ins.
Savalou: Benin 81 E3
Savanna: Ill., U.S.A. 88 F4
Savannah: Ga., U.S.A. 91 L9
Savannah: Tenn., U.S.A. 90 G8
Savannah: riv., Ga./S.C., U.S.A. 91 L9
Savannah Beach: city, Ga., U.S.A. 91 L10
Savannakhet: Laos 64 C3
Savanna la Mar: Jamaica 86 Ins.
Savant Lake: town, Ont., Canada 92 J2
Savantvadi: Maharashtra, India 58 M11
Savaria: Roman colony at Szombathely, Hungary 41 W8
Săvârşin: Romania 43 S13
Savastepe: Turkey 39 U17
Savé: Benin 81 E3
Save: riv., France 37 G12
Save: riv., Mozambique 77 D7
Saveh: Iran 57 M4
Şavenay: France 36 D8
Săveni: Romania 43 U13
Saverdun: France 37 G12
Savernake Forest: Wilts., England 25 S17
Saverne: France 40 N7
Savigliano: Italy 40 N11
Savigny: France 36 F8
Savines: France 40 M11
Savinobor: U.S.S.R. 50 J2
Savio: riv., Italy 41 S11
Savitaipale: Finland 47 U6
Savnik: Yugoslavia 39 Q15
Savoie: Dept., France (cap. Chambéry) 40 M10
Savona: Italy 40 O11
Savonlinna: Finland 47 V6
Savoonga: St. Lawrence I., Bering Sea 84 b5
Savoy: Prov., France 34 K14
Savoy Alps: France 40 M10
Şavşat: Turkey 57 H1
Sävsjö: Sweden 47 O8
Sävsjöström: Sweden 47 O8
Savu (Sawu): i., Indonesia 65 G9
Savudrija Pt.: cape, Yugoslavia 41 T10
Savukoski: Finland 46 V3
Savur: Turkey 57 G3
Savu Sea: Indonesia 65 G8
Saw: Burma 59 Q10
Sawab: wadi, Iraq 56 F5
Sawah: Borneo 65 F6
Sawai Madhopur: Rajasthan, India 58 N9
Sawangtungko: Mentawai Is., Indonesia 65 C7
Sawankhalok: Thailand 64 B3
Sawara: Japan 63 g3
Sawbridgeworth: Herts., England 25 W16
Sawel Mtn.: Lon./Tyr., N. Ireland 30 G10
Sawi: Thailand 64 B4
Sawmills: Rhodesia 77 C6
Sawtooth Mtns.: U.S.A. 92 D4
Sawtry: Cambs., England 25 V15
Sawu (Savu): i., Indonesia 65 G9
Saxa Rubra: Roman settlement near right bank of Tiber about 7 miles N. of Rome 38 N16
Saxby: riv., Queens., Austl. 69 G3
Saxby All Saints: Humb., England 27 V12
Saxilby: Lincs., England 27 U13
Saxlingham Nethergate: Norf., England 25 Y14
Saxmundham: Suff., Eng. 25 Y15
Saxton: N. Yorks., England 27 T12
Saxton: Pa., U.S.A. 89 M5
Say: Niger 81 E2
Sayal: well, Chad 78 H6
Sayán: Peru 94 B6
Sayan, Eastern: mtns., U.S.S.R. 49 I7
Sayan, Western: mtns., U.S.S.R. 49 L7
Sayat: Turkmen., U.S.S.R. 51 K7
Sayda-Guba: U.S.S.R. 46 X2
Sayo: Japan 63 d3
Sayre: Okla., U.S.A. 90 B8
Sayre: Pa., U.S.A. 89 N5
Sayr Usa: Mongolia 62 T6

Sazan: *i.,* Albania 39 Q16
Sázava: *riv.,* Czechoslovakia 45 V6
Sazh: *riv.,* Byelorussia 50 D4
Sba: Algeria 78 D4
Sbeitla: Tunisia 32 D4
Scaër: France 36 B7
Sca Fell: *mtn.,* Cumb., Eng. 26 P11
Scalasaig: Colonsay, Scot. 29 J7
Scalby: N. Yorks., England 26 V11
Scalea: Italy 38 O17
Scaleby: Cumbria, England 26 Q10
Scalford: Leics., England 27 U14
Scallabis: Roman town at Santarém, Portugal 35 B17
Scalloway: Shetland Is. 28 *Ins.*
Scalpay: *i.,* Inner Hebr., Scotland 28 K5
Scalpay: *i.,* Outer Hebr., Scotland 28 H4
Scamadale, Loch: Strathclyde, Scotland 29 L7
Scamander: river flowing into sea near *Sigeum,* opposite Cape Helles, Turkey 39 U17
Scamblesby: Lincs., Eng. 27 V13
Scânteia: Romania 43 U13
Scapa Flow: *harbour,* Orkney Is. 28 P2
Scarba: *i.,* Scotland 29 K7
Scarbantia: Roman town at Sopron, Hungary 41 W8
Scarborough: C.P., S. Africa 74 *Ins.*
Scarborough: N. Yorks., Eng. 26 V11
Scarborough: Tobago, Windward Is. 87 c5
Scarborough Shoal: S. China Sea 64 F3
Scarfskerry: High., Scot. 28 P2
Scariff I.: Repub. of Ireland 31 A16
Scarinish: Inner Hebr., Scot. 29 H7
Scarle, North: Lincs., Eng. 27 U13
Scarp: *i.,* Outer Hebr., Scot. 28 G3
Scarperia: Italy 41 R11
Scarriff: Clare, Repub. of Ireland 31 D14
Scartaglin: Kerry, Repub. of Ireland 31 C15
Scarva: Down, N. Ireland 30 J11
Scatari I.: Cape Breton I., Canada 89 V3
Scavaig, Loch: Inner Hebr., Scotland 28 J5
Sceaux: France 36 H7
Schaale: *riv.,* E. Germany 45 Q2
Schaal See: *lake,* E. & W. Germany 45 Q2
Schaerbeek: Belgium 44 K5
SCHAFFHAUSEN: & *Canton,* Switzerland 40 O8
Schagen: Netherlands 44 K3
Schapen: W. Germany 44 N3
Scharding: Austria 41 T7
Scharhörn: *i.,* W. Germany 44 O2
Scharrel: W. Germany 44 N2
Scheerpoort: Trans., S. Afr. 75 G2
Scheessel: W. Germany 44 P2
Scheibbs: Austria 41 V7
Scheinfeld: W. Germany 45 Q6
Scheldt: *riv.,* Belgium 44 J5
Schelklingen: W. Germany 40 P7
Schenectady: N.Y., U.S.A. 89 P4
Scherfede: E. Germany 44 P4
Schermbeck: W. Germany 44 M4
Schiedam: Netherlands 44 K4
Schiehallion: *mtn.,* Tayside, Scotland 29 N6
Schiermonnikoog: *i.,* W. Frisian Is., Netherlands 44 M2
Schiers: Switzerland 40 P9
Schifferstadt: W. Germany 44 O6
Schillig: W. Germany 44 O2
Schiltach: W. Germany 40 O7
Schio: Italy 41 R10
Schirmeck: France 40 N7
Schkeuditz: E. Germany 45 S4
Schleiden: W. Germany 44 M5
Schleitheim: Switzerland 40 O8
Schleiz: E. Germany 45 R5
Schleswig: W. Germany 44 P1
Schleswig-Holstein: *State,* W. Germany (*cap.* Kiel) 45 P2
Schleusingen: E. Germany 45 Q5
Schlieben: E. Germany 45 T4
Schlitz: W. Germany 44 P5
Schlön: E. Germany 45 S2
Schluchtern: W. Germany 44 P5
Schlusselfeld: W. Germany 45 Q6
Schmalkalden: E. Germany 45 Q5
Schmallenburg: W. Germany 44 O4
Schmidmuhlen: W. Germany 45 S6
Schmölln: Leipzig, E. Germany 45 S5
Schmölln: Neubrandenburg, E. Germany 45 U2
Schneeberg: E. Germany 45 S5
Schopf, Mt.: Antarctica 9 85S 120W
Schofield: Wis., U.S.A. 88 G3
Schole Bank: Channel Is. 25 *Ins.*
Schollmach: W. Germany 41 T7
Schomberg: W. Germany 40 O7
Schönau: W. Germany 40 N8
Schönbach: Czechoslovakia 45 S5
Schönberg: Rostock, E. Germany 45 Q2
Schönberg: Schleswig-Holstein, W. Germany 45 Q1
Schönebeck: E. Germany 45 R3
Schongau: W. Germany 41 Q8
Schöningen: W. Germany 45 Q3
Schoombee: S. Africa 75 F5
Schoonhoven: Netherlands 44 K4
Schopfheim: W. Germany 40 N8
Schoppenstedt: W. Germany 45 Q3
Schotten: W. Germany 44 P5
Schouten Is.: W. Irian, Indonesia 61 M12
Schouwen: *i.,* Netherlands 44 J4
Schramberg: W. Germany 40 O7
Schrankogl: *mtn.,* Austria 41 R8
Schraplau: E. Germany 45 R4
Schreiber: Ont., Canada 88 H1
Schrobenhausen: W. Germany 41 R7
Schruns: Austria 40 P8
Schubelbach: Switzerland 40 O8
Schulenburg: W. Germany 45 P3
Schulenburg: Tex., U.S.A. 90 C11
Schull: Cork, Repub. of Irel. 31 B16
Schuls: Switzerland 40 Q9
Schulzendorf: E. Germany 45 U3
Schuttorf: W. Germany 44 N3
Schuyler: Va., U.S.A. 89 M7
Schuylkill: *riv.,* Pa., U.S.A. 89 O5
Schwaan: E. Germany 45 S2
Schwabach: W. Germany 45 R6
Schwaben: *Dist.,* Bavaria, West Germany 40 Q8
Schwäbisch Gmünd: West Germany 45 P7
Schwabmünchen: W. Germany 41 Q7
Schwandorf: W. Germany 45 S6
Schwanebeck: E. Germany 45 R4
Schwanenstadt: Austria 41 T7
Schwaner Mtns.: Borneo 65 E7
Schwarmstedt: W. Germany 44 P3

Schwarzach: Austria 41 T8
Schwarze Elster: *riv.,* E. Germany 45 T4
Schwarzenbach: W. Germany 45 R5
Schwarzenbek: W. Germany 45 Q2
Schwarzenburg: E. Germany 45 S5
Schwarzenburg: Switzerland 40 N9
Schwaz: Austria 41 R8
Schwedt: E. Germany 45 U2
Schweich: W. Germany 44 M6
Schweinfurt: W. Germany 45 Q5
Schweizer-Reneke: & *Dist.,* Trans., S. Africa 75 F3
Schwelm: E. Germany 45 R2
Schwenningen: W. Germany 40 O7
Schwepnitz: E. Germany 45 T4
SCHWERIN: & *Dist.,* E. Germany 45 R2
Schwerin See: *lake,* E. Ger. 45 R2
Schwieloch: E. Germany 45 U3
SCHWYZ: & *Canton,* Switz. 40 O8
Sciacca: Sicily 38 N18
Scie, La: Newf., Canada 85 v2
Scilly, Isles of: England 25 J19
Scilly Is.: Society Is. 83 e3
Scinawa Lubin: Poland 45 W4
Scione: Greek city about 10 miles E. of *Mende* on S. coast of Kassándra peninsula, Greece 39 S16
Scioto: *riv.,* Ohio, U.S.A. 88 K6
Scobey: Mont., U.S.A. 92 F3
Scodra: Roman town at Shkodër, N. Albania 39 Q15
Scole: Norf., England 25 Y15
Scolus: Greek city E. of Boeotia, about 6 miles SE. of Thiva, Greece 39 S17
Scone: N.S.W., Australia 71 J9
Scone, New: Tay., Scotland 29 P7
Scoresby Land: Greenland 85 r3
Scoresby Sound: Greenland 85 r3
Scoresbysund: Greenland 85 r3
Scorno, Pta. dello: *cape,* Asinara, Sardinia 38 L16
Scorton: N. Yorks., England 26 S11
Scotforth: Lancs., England 27 Q11
Scothern: Lincs., England 27 V13
Scotia Ridge: S. Atlantic Ocean 8 55S 45W
Scotia Sea: Southern Ocean 8 60S 50W
Scotland: United Kingdom (*cap.* Edinburgh) 28-9
Scotland Neck: N.C., U.S.A. 89 N7
Scotstown: High., Scotland 29 K6
Scotstown: Monaghan, Repub. of Ireland 30 G11
Scotstown: Que., Canada 89 Q3
Scott, Cape: B.C., Canada 84 G7
Scott, Mount: Oreg., U.S.A. 92 C4
Scott Base: *rsch. stn.,* Antarctica 9 80S 165E
Scottburgh: Natal, S. Africa 75 J5
Scott City: Kans., U.S.A. 90 A6
Scotter: Lincs., England 27 U13
Scott Inlet: N.W.T., Canada 85 m3
Scotton: Lincs., England 27 U13
Scott Reef: Australia 68 C2
Scottsbluff: Nebr., U.S.A. 92 G4
Scottsboro: Ala., U.S.A. 91 H8
Scottsburg: Ind., U.S.A. 88 J6
Scottsdale: Tas., Australia 68 H8
Scottville: Mich., U.S.A. 88 H4
Scottville: Queens., Austl. 70 G3
Scourie: High., Scotland 28 L3
Scousburgh: Mainland, Shetland Is. 28 *Ins.*
Scrabby: Cavan, Repub. of Ireland 30 F12
Scrabster: High., Scotland 28 O2
Scranton: Pa., U.S.A. 89 O5
Scridain, Loch: Inner Hebr., Scotland 29 J7
Scrivia: *riv.,* Italy 40 O11
Scruton: N. Yorks., England 26 S11
Scugog, Lake: Ont., Canada 89 M3
Sculthorpe: Norf., England 25 X14
Scunthorpe: Humb., England 27 U12
Scurdie Ness: *cape,* Tayside, Scot. 29 S6
Scurrival Point: *cape,* Outer Hebr., Scotland 28 G5
Scutari (Shkodër): Albania 39 Q15
Scutari (Üsküdar): Turkey (Bosporus. *Inset*) 20 *Ins.*
Scyllaeum: promontory at E. tip of *Argolis.* 39 S18
Scythopolis: Hellenistic city near Beisan, Israel (*see also* under *Beth-shan*) 55 b2
Seacow: *riv.,* S. Africa 75 F5
Seaflower Str.: Mentawai Is., Indonesia 65 B7
Seaford: Del., U.S.A. 89 O6
Seaford: E. Sussex, England 25 W18
Seaforth, Loch: Outer Hebr., Scotland 28 H4
Seagraves: Tex., U.S.A. 93 G6
Seaham Harbour: Dur., Eng. 26 T10
Seahorse Point: *cape,* Can. 85 I5
Seahouses: Northumb., Eng. 26 S8
Sea I.: Ga., U.S.A. 91 L10
Seal, Cape: S. Africa 74 E7
Sealga, Loch na: Highland, Scotland 28 I4
Sea Lake: *town,* Vict., Austl. 71 E10
Sealy: Tex., U.S.A. 90 C11
Seamer: N. Yorks., England 26 T11
Seamill: Strath., Scotland 28 M8
Sea Point: *cape,* S. Africa 74 *Ins.*
Searcy: Ark., U.S.A. 90 F8
Searsport: Maine, U.S.A. 89 R3
Seascale: Cumbria, England 26 P11
Seaside: Oreg., U.S.A. 92 C3
Seaton: Devon, England 24 P18
Seaton Delaval: Northumb., England 26 S9
Seaton Ross: Humberside, Eng. 27 U12
Seaton Sluice: Northumb., England 26 T9
Seattle: Wash., U.S.A. 92 C3
Seaview: I. of Wight, Eng. 25 T18
Seaview Range: Queens., Australia 69 H3
Seba: Savu I., Indon. 65 G9
Sebakung: Borneo 65 F7
Sebastian Vizcaino Bay: Mexico 93 E7
Sebatik: *i.,* Borneo 65 F6
Sebba: Upper Volta 80 E2
Sebei: Dist., Uganda (*cap.* Kapchorwa) 76 D2
Sebennitikon: Greek name of Nile mouth emerging from E. end of L. Burullus, Egypt 56 B6
Sebersdorf: Austria 41 V8
Sebeş: Romania 43 S14
Sebewaing: Mich., U.S.A. 88 K4
Sebezh: U.S.S.R. 50 C3
SEBHA: & *Prov.,* Libya 78 G4
Sebinkarahisar: Turkey 56 F1
Sebinus: Roman name of L. Iseo, Italy 40 Q10
Sebiş: Romania 43 S13

Sebkra Azzel Matti: *salt lake,* Algeria 78 E4
Sebkra Mekerrhane: *salt lake,* Algeria 78 E4
Sebkra Oum El Drouss Telli: *salt lake,* Mauritania 78 B5
Seblat: Sumatra 65 C7
Sebnitz: E. Germany 45 U5
Sebou: *riv.,* Morocco 80 K8
Sebring: Fla., U.S.A. 91 L12
Sebu: Mindanao, Phil. 65 G5
Sebuku: Borneo 65 F7
Secchia: *riv.,* Italy 41 Q11
Sechura: & *desert,* Peru 94 A5
Seclin: France 36 H5
Secondigny: France 37 E9
Secretary I.: N.Z. 70 L17
Secunderabad: Andhra Pradesh, India 58 N11
Sedalia: Mo., U.S.A. 88 E6
Sedan: France 36 K6
Sedan: Kans., U.S.A. 90 C7
Sedan: S. Australia 71 C10
Sedano: Spain 35 E15
Sedbergh: Cumbria, England 26 Q11
Sedd-el-Bahr (Seddül Bahır): Turkey (Dardan. *Inset*) 20 *Ins.*
Seddonville: South I., N.Z. 70 O15
Seddül Bahır: Turkey (Dardan. *Inset*) 20 *Ins.*
Sedgefield: Durham, Eng. 26 T10
Sedgemoor: battlefield about 1 mile N. of Westonzoyland, England 24 Q17
Sedgley: W. Mid., England 27 R14
Sedičany: Czechoslovakia 45 U6
Sedlec: Czechoslovakia 45 U6
Sedlescombe: E. Sussex, Eng. 25 X18
Sédrata: Algeria 32 D4
Seefeld: Austria 41 R8
Seeheim: S.W. Africa 74 B3
Seeis: S.W. Africa 74 B1
Seelow: E. Germany 45 U3
Sées: France 36 F7
Seesen: W. Germany 45 Q4
Seetaler Alps: Austria 41 U8
Sefadu: Sierra Leone 80 A7
Seferihisar: Turkey 39 U17
Sefid: *riv.,* Iran 57 L3
Sefkat: Turkey 56 F2
Sefrou: Morocco 80 L8
Segamat: Malaya, Malaysia 65 c12
Segbana: Benin 81 E2
Segborough: Benin 81 E3
Segedunum: Roman fort at end of Hadrian's Wall at Wallsend, Northumb., England 26 S10
Segesta: Sicel, later Roman city, on foothills about 10 miles S. of Castellammare, Sicily 38 N18
Segezha: Karelian A.S.S.R., U.S.S.R. 48 E5
Seghill: Northumb., Eng. 26 S9
Segontia: Roman town at Sigüenza, Spain 35 E16
Segontium: Roman fort at Caernarvon, Wales 27 N13
Segorbe: Spain 35 F17
SÉGOU: & *Reg.,* Mali 80 C2
SEGOVIA: & *Prov.,* Spain 35 D16
Segovia: *riv.,* Honduras 86 I 15
Segré: France 36 E8
Segre: *riv.,* Spain 35 G15
Seguam: *i. & passage,* Aleutians 84 b7
Séguéla: Ivory Coast 80 C3
Seguin: Tex., U.S.A. 90 C11
Segundo: *riv.,* Argentina 96 C3
Segura: *riv.,* Spain 35 F17
Sehlabathebe: Lesotho 75 H4
Sehore: Madhya Pradesh, India 58 N10
Sehwan: Sind, Pakistan 58 L9
Seiches: France 36 E8
Seifand Maeimou: *well,* Mali 80 B1
Seighford: Staffs., England 27 R14
Seignosse: France 37 D12
Seikpyu: Burma 59 Q10
Seil: *i.,* Scotland 29 K7
Seille: *riv.,* France 37 L9
Sein, Île de: *i.,* France 36 A7
Seinäjoki: Finland 46 S5
Seine: *riv.,* France 36 G6
Seine: *riv.,* Ont., Canada 88 E1
Seine, Baie de la: *bay,* France 36 E6
Seine-et-Marne: *Dept.,* Fr. (*cap.* Melun) 36 H7
Seine-Maritime: *Dept.,* Fr. (*cap.* Rouen) 36 F6
Seini: Romania 43 S13
Seira (Hsilo): Taiwan 63 W10
Sekadau: Borneo 54 E6
Seke: Tanzania 76 D3
Sekenke: Tanzania 76 D3
Sekibi: *i.* (Jap.), E. China Sea 63 W9
Sekima: Borneo 65 E7
Sekiyama: Japan 63 I2
Sekkiret: Niger 78 F6
SEKONDI: Western, Ghana 80 D4
Sela: Norway 46 M4
Selama: Malaya, Malaysia 65 b11
Selangor: *riv.,* Malaya, Malaysia 65 b12
Selangor: *State,* Malaya, Malaysia (*cap.* Shah Alam) 65 b12
Selatan: Cape: Borneo 65 E7
Selatpandjang: Sumatra 65 C6
Selçuk: Turkey 39 U18
Selborne: Hants., England 25 U17
Selbu Lake: Norway 46 M5
Selby: N. Yorks., England 27 T12
Seldovia: Alaska, U.S.A. 84 d6
Sele: *riv.,* Italy 38 O16
Selemiya: Syria 56 E4
Selenga: *riv.,* Mongolia/U.S.S.R. 49 M8
Selenter See: *lake,* W. Ger. 45 Q1
Selestat: France 40 N7
Selety: *riv.,* U.S.S.R. 51 M4
Selety-Tengiz, Lake: Kazakh., U.S.S.R. 51 M4
Seleuceia in Pieria: ancient port of Antakya at mouth of Orontes, Turkey 56 E3
Seleuceia-on-Tigris: Hellenistic city immediately opposite *Ctesiphon,* Iraq 57 J5
SÉLIBABY: Guidimaka, Mauritania 80 B1
Seligenstadt: W. Germany 44 O5
Seliger, Lake: U.S.S.R. 50 D3
Selima Oasis: Sudan 54 C10
Selimiye: Turkey 39 U18
Selinus: Greek city on coast about 5 miles E. of C. Granitola, Sicily 38 N18
Seliyarova: U.S.S.R. 51 M2
Selizhárovo: U.S.S.R. 50 D3
Seljord: Norway 47 L7
Selkirk: Borders, Scotland 29 Q8
Selkirk: Man., Canada 92 H1
Selkirk Mtns.: B.C., Canada 92 D2

Sellasia: ancient Greek village about 8 miles N. of Spárti, Greece 39 S18
Selles-sur-Cher: France 36 G8
Sellheim: Queens., Australia 70 G3
Sellières: France 40 L9
Sellindge: Kent, England 25 X17
Selling: Kent, England 25 X17
Selma: Ala., U.S.A. 91 H9
Selma: Calif., U.S.A. 93 D5
Selma: N.C., U.S.A. 91 M8
Selmer: Tenn., U.S.A. 90 G8
Selong: Lombok, Indon. 65 F8
Selongey: France 40 L8
Selsey: W. Sussex, England 25 U18
Selsey Bill: *cape,* W. Sussex, England 25 U18
Selston: Notts., England 27 T13
Seiters: W. Germany 44 N5
Seltz: France 40 O7
Selukwe: Rhodesia 77 D6
Sélune: *riv.,* France 36 D7
Selva: Argentina 96 C2
Selvas: *for.,* Brazil 94 E5
Selworthy: Som., England 24 O17
Selwyn: Queens., Australia 69 G4
Selwyn Range: B.C., Can. 92 D2
Selwyn Range: Queens., Australia 69 G4
Selymbria: Greek city on N. side of Sea of Marmara at Silivri, İstanbul, Turkey 39 V16
Selzthal: Austria 41 U8
Semarang: Java 65 E8
Semau: *i.,* Indonesia 65 G9
Sembe: Congo 81 G4
Sembilan Is.: Malaya, Malaysia 65 b11
Semdinli: Turkey 57 J3
Semenov: U.S.S.R. 50 F3
Semënovka: U.S.S.R. 50 G4
Sëmerë: Benin 81 E3
Semeru: *mtn.,* Java 65 E8
Semic: Yugoslavia 41 V10
Semichi Is.: Aleutians 84 A7
Seminoe Reservoir: & *dam,* Wyo., U.S.A. 92 F4
Seminole: Okla., U.S.A. 90 C8
Semiozernyy: Kazakh., U.S.S.R. 51 K4
SEMIPALATINSK: & *Reg.,* Kazakh., U.S.S.R. 51 O4
Semirara Is.: Philippines 64 G4
Semisopochnoi: *i.,* Aleutians 84 a7
Semiyarka: Kazakh., U.S.S.R. 51 N4
Semiz-Bugu: Kazakh., U.S.S.R. 51 M4
Semki: Ukraine 43 U12
Semley: Wilts., England 24 R17
Semna: Sudan 54 D10
Semnan: Iran 55 H7
Semois: *riv.,* Belgium 44 L6
Semondans: Zaire 76 A3
Semporna: Sabah, Malaysia 65 F6
Semuda: Borneo 65 F7
Semur: France 36 K8
Sena: Mozambique 77 D6
Seña, La: Argentina 96 D5
Sena Madureira: Brazil 94 D5
Senanga: Zambia 77 B6
Sénarport: France 36 G6
Senas: France 37 L12
Senatobia: Miss., U.S.A. 90 G8
Sendai: Kagoshima, Japan 63 b5
SENDAI: Miyagi, Japan 63 g1
Sendenhorst: W. Germany 44 N4
Sendlingsrott: S. Africa 74 B4
Seneca: Oreg., U.S.A. 92 D4
Seneca: S.C., U.S.A. 91 K8
Seneca Lake: N.Y., U.S.A. 89 N4
Seneffe: Belgium 44 K5

Senegal: *Republic* 80 A2
Cap. Dakar
Area: 76,124 sq. miles
(197,161 sq. km.)
Pop.: 4,022,000 *(1971 E)*

Senegal: *riv.,* Senegal/Mauritania 80 A1
Senegal Oriental: *Reg.,* Senegal (*cap.* Tambacounda) 80 B2
Senekal: & *Dist.,* O.F.S., S. Africa 75 G4
Senetosa, Cap: *cape,* Cors. 38 L16
Senftenberg: E. Germany 45 U4
Sengalia: Italy 41 T12
Sentinel Range: Antarctica 9 80S 90W
Senj: Yugoslavia 41 U11
Senjen: *i.,* Norway 46 P2
Senkaku Is.: (Jap.), E. China Sea 63 W9
Senkobo: Zambia 77 C6
Senlis: France 36 H6
Sennar: Sudan 54 D12
Senne: *riv.,* Belgium 44 K5
Senneh: *see* Sanandaj
Sennen: Corn., England 25 K19
Senneterre: Que., Canada 89 N1
Senneville: France 36 F6
Senny Bridge: *Powys,* Wales 24 O16
Senonches: France 36 G7
Senones: Gallic tribe with centre at Sens, France 36 J7
Sénoudebou: Senegal 80 B2
Senoželce: Yugoslavia 41 U10
Sens: France 36 J7
Sens-de-Bretagne: France 36 D7
Senta: Yugoslavia 39 R14
Şenyurt: Turkey 57 G3
Seo de Urgel: Spain 35 G15
Seoni: Madhya Pradesh, India 58 N10
SEOUL (Kyongsong): S. Korea 63 X7
Sepang: Borneo 65 E6
Sepanjang: *i.,* Indonesia 65 F8
Sepasu: Borneo 65 F6
Sepik: *riv.,* New Guinea 66 H2
Sepolno: Poland 43 P10
Sepone: Laos 64 D3
Septouba: *riv.,* Brazil 94 F7
Sepphoris: Herodian city about 4 miles N. of Nazareth, Israel 55 b2
Sept Îles: Que., Canada 85 N7
Sepulveda: Spain 35 E16
Sequana: Roman name of river Seine, France 36 Q6
Sequani: Gallic tribe in Haut-Saône and Haut-Rhin, France 40 M8
Sequeros: Spain 35 C16
Sequoia Nat. Park: Calif., U.S.A. 93 D5
Seradino: Argentina 96 C3
Serafimovich: U.S.S.R. 50 F5
Seraing: Belgium 44 L5
Serakhs: Turkmen., U.S.S.R. 51 K7
Serang: Java 65 D8

Serapeum: Egypt (Suez Canal *Inset*) 32 *Ins.*
Serasan: *i.,* Indonesia 65 D6
Seraya: Syria 56 D4
Serbia: *Repub.,* Yugo. [*cap.* Beograd (Belgrade)] 39 R14
Serbja: *see* Serbia.
Sercaia: Romania 39 U13
Serdeles: Libya 78 G4
Serdelesgatam Spain 35 E16
Serdica: Roman town at Sofia, Bulgaria 39 S15
Serebun: Inner Mongolia, China 62 U6
Sered: Czechoslovakia 43 P12
Seredka: U.S.S.R. 47 V7
Seregno: Italy 40 P10
Séreilhac: France 37 G10
Serein: *riv.,* France 36 J8
SEREMBAN: Negri Sembilan, Malaya, Malaysia 65 b12
Serengeti Nat. Park: Tanzania 76 D3
Serenje: Zambia 77 D5
Serenli: Somalia 79 N9
Seret: *riv.,* Ukraine 43 T12
Serfontein: O.F.S., S. Africa 75 G3
Sergach: U.S.S.R. 50 G3
Sergelen (Dolonn): Mongolia 62 T5
Sergines: France 36 J7
Sergipe: *State,* Brazil (*cap.* Aracaju) 94 K6
Sergiyevsky: U.S.S.R. 50 H3
Seria: Brunei 65 E6
Serian: Sarawak, Malaysia 65 E6
Sérifos: *i.,* Cyclades 39 T18
Sérignac: France 36 B7
Sérignan: France 37 J2
Serik: Turkey 56 B3
Seringapatam (Srirangapatnam): Karnataka, India 58 M12
Seringapatam Reef: Austl. 68 C2
Serio: *riv.,* Italy 40 P10
Serir of Kalanshu: *plat.,* Libya 79 J4
Serivia: *riv.,* Italy 40 O11
Sermaize-les-Bains: France 36 K7
Sermata: *i.,* Indonesia 68 D1
Sermide: Italy 41 R11
Sernyy-Zavod: Turkmen., U.S.S.R. 50 J7
Serodino: Argentina 96 C3
Seroei: W. Irian, Indonesia 61 M12
Serouenout: Algeria 78 F5
Serov: U.S.S.R. 51 K3
SEROWE: Central, Botswana 75 G1
Serpa: Portugal 35 C18
SERPA PINTO: Cuando-Cubango, Angola 77 A5
Serpents Mouth: Venezuela 87 c5
Serpukhov: U.S.S.R. 50 E3
Serqueux: France 36 G6
Serquigny: France 36 F6
Serrai: Greece 39 S16
Serrana Bank: *i.,* Carib. Sea 87 I15
Serranias del Burro: *mtns.,* Mexico 93 G7
Serra San Bruno: Italy 38 P17
Serrat, Cape: Tunisia 38 L18
Serra Talhada: Brazil 94 K5
Serre: *riv.,* France 36 J6
Serres: France 40 L11
Serrezuela: Argentina 96 B3
Serrières: France 37 K10
Serrinha: Brazil 96 F2
Sérro: Brazil 94 J7
Sertã: Portugal 35 B17
Sertânia: Brazil 94 K5
Sertão: *geog. reg.,* Brazil 94 K5
Serule: Botswana 77 C7
Serutu: Borneo 65 D7
Servia: Greece 39 S16
Serviceton: Vict., Australia 71 D11
Sesajap Lama: Borneo 65 F6
Sese Is.: Lake Victoria, Uganda 76 D3
Sesheke: Zambia 77 B6
Sesimbra: Portugal 35 B17
Seskinore: Tyr., N. Ireland 30 G10
Sessa: Angola 77 B5
Sessok: Flores, Indonesia 65 G8
Sestos: Greek city on W. side of narrowest point of Dardanelles near Eceabat, Turkey 39 U16
Sestri: Italy 40 O11
Sestri Levante: Italy 40 P11
Sestroretsk: U.S.S.R. 47 V6
Sestrunj: *i.,* Yugoslavia 41 V11
Setaka: Japan 63 b4
Setana: Japan 63 Z6
Sete: France 37 J12
Sete Quedas (Guaira Falls): Brazil 96 E1
Setia: Roman colony in foothills about 37 miles SE. of Rome. 38 N16
SETIF: & *Dept.,* Algeria 35 J18
Setiu: Malaya, Malaysia 65 c11
Setlagodi: S. Africa 75 F3
Seto: Aichi, Japan 63 e3
SETTAT: & *Prov.,* Morocco 80 K8
Sette Cama: Gabon 81 F5
Setting Lake: Man., Canada 92 H1
Settle: N. Yorks., England 27 R11
Settrington: N. Yorks., Eng. 27 U11
Setubal: & *bay,* Portugal 35 B17
Seudre: *riv.,* France 37 E10
Seugne: *riv.,* France 37 E10
Seul, Lake: Ont., Canada 92 J2
Seul Choix Point: *cape,* Mich., U.S.A. 88 J3
Seulimeum: Sumatra 65 B5
Seurre: France 36 L8
Sevan: & *lake,* Armenia, U.S.S.R. 57 J1
Sevastapol': U.S.S.R. 50 D6
Sevatt Ambo: Sudan 76 D1
Seven: *riv.,* N. Yorks., Eng. 26 U11
Seven Heads: *cape,* Cork, Repub. of Ireland 31 D16
Seven Islands: *town,* Que., Canada 85 N7
Sevenoaks: Kent, England 25 W17
Sevenoaks: Natal, S. Africa 75 J4
Seven Sisters: W. Glam., Wales 24 O16
Seven Sisters Mount: B.C., Canada 92 B2
Seven Stones: *rocks,* England 25 J19
Severac-le-Château: France 37 J11
Severn: *riv.,* Canada 85 L6
Severn: *riv.,* England/Wales 24 R16
Severn: *riv.,* N.S.W., Austl. 71 J7
Severn, Mouth of the: *est.,* England/Wales 24 Q17
Severnaya Zemlya (North Land): *is.* (U.S.S.R.), Arctic O. 49 I2
Severn Tunnel: Glos./Gwent, England/Wales 24 Q17
Severočeský: *Reg.,* Czechoslovakia (*cap.* Ustí) 45 U5
Severomoravsky: *Reg.,* Czechoslovakia (*cap.* Ostrava) 43 P12
Severo-Yenisseyskiy: U.S.S.R. 51 Q2
Sevi: U.S.S.R. 49 L7

186 Sevier Desert—Sidi Kacem

Sevier Desert: Utah, U.S.A. 93 E5
SEVILLA: & Prov., Spain 35 D18
Sevketiye: Turkey (Dardan. Inset) 20 Ins.
Sèvre: (Nantaise), riv., Fr. 36 E9
Sèvre (Niortaise), riv., Fr. 37 E9
Sèvres: France 36 H7
Sevron: riv., France 37 L9
Sewa: riv., Sierra Leone 80 B3
Seward: Alaska, U.S.A. 84 E5
Seward: Nebr., U.S.A. 93 H4
Seward Penin.: Alaska, U.S.A. 84 c4
Sewell: Chile 96 A3

Seychelles: *Republic* 19 O 50E
Cap.: Victoria
Area: 145 sq. miles (376 sq. km.)
Pop.: 52,650 (1971 C)

Seychelles Mauritius Plateau: Indian Ocean 9 15S 60E
Seydhisfjördhur: Iceland 46 f4
Seydişehir: Turkey 56 B3
Seyfe, Lake: Turkey 56 D2
SEYHAN (Adana): Adana, Turkey 56 D3
Seyhan: riv., Turkey 56 D3
Seyhit: riv., Turkey 56 B2
Seyitgazi: Turkey 56 B2
Seymour: Ind., U.S.A. 88 J6
Seymour: S. Africa 75 G6
Seymour: Tex., U.S.A. 90 B9
Seymour: Vict., Australia 71 F11
Seymour: Wis., U.S.A. 88 G3
Seyne: France 40 M11
Seyne-sur-Mer, La: France 40 L12
Seyssel: France 40 L10
Sežana: Yugoslavia 41 T10
Sézanne: France 36 J7
Sfântu Gheorghe: Romania 39 T14
Sfax: Tunisia 32 E5
Sfinári: Crete 39 S19
's-GRAVENHAGE (The Hague): Netherlands 44 K3
Sgùrr a'Chaorachain: mtn., Highland, Scotland 28 L5
Sgùrr a'Choire Ghlais: mtn., Western Highlands, Scot. 28 M5
Sgùrr Alasdair: mtn., Inner Hebr., Scotland 28 J5
Sgùrr Bàn: mtn., Highland, Scotland 28 L4
Sgùrr Fhuaran: mtn., Highland, Scotland 28 L5
Sgùrr Mòr: mtn., Highland, Scotland 28 L4
Sgùrr na Ciche: mtn., Highland, Scotland 28 L5
Sgùrr na Lapaich: mtn., Highland, Scotland 28 L5
Sgùrr Ruadh: mtn., Highland, Scotland 28 L4
Shaba: Prov., Zaïre (cap. Lubumbashi) 77 C5
Shaba Gompa: Tibet, China 59 P8
SHABANI: Matabeleland South, Rhodesia 77 D7
Shabikha: well, Iraq 57 H6
Shabla: Bulgaria 39 V15
Shabunda: Zaïre 76 C3
Shabwa: Yemen P.D.R. 54 G11
Shackleton Ice Shelf: Antarctica 9 70S 95E
Shackleton Range: Antarctica 9 85S 30W
Shader: Outer Hebr., Scot. 28 J3
Shadgan: Iran 57 L6
Shadrinsk: U.S.S.R. 51 K3
Shafter: Nev., U.S.A. 92 E4
Shaftesbury: Dorset, Eng. 24 R17
Shagan: Kazakh., U.S.S.R. 50 J5
Shagham: well, Yemen P.D.R. 55 G11
Shag Rocks: (Br.), Atlantic Ocean 95 J14
Shah: riv., Iran 57 L3
Shahabad: Iran 57 K4
Shahabad: Uttar Pradesh, India 58 N9
Shahba: Syria 56 E5
Shah Dad: Iran 55 J8
Shahdadkot: Sind, Pak. 58 L9
Shahdol: Madhya Pradesh, India 58 O10
Shahhat: Libya 79 J3
Shahi: i., Lake Urmia, Iran 57 J3
Shahidan: Iraq 57 J3
Shahin Dazh: Iran 57 K3
Shahjahanpur: Uttar Pradesh, India 58 N9
Shahjui: Afghanistan 58 L8
Shahpur: Iran 57 J2
Shahr-i-Babak: Iran 55 J8
Shahr-i-Tajan: see Sari.
Shahriza: Iran 55 H8
Shahr Kurd: Iran 55 H8
Shahrud: Iran 55 J7
Shahrukh: Iran 55 K8
Shahsawar: Iran 55 H7
Shahsien: Fukien, China 62 V9
Shaibara: i. (Sau. Arab.), Red Sea 54 E9
Shaikabad: Afghanistan 58 L8
Shaikh Ghadhban: Iran 57 L6
Shaikh Sa'ad: Iraq 57 K5
Shaikh Shu'aib: i., Persian G. 55 H9
Shaikh 'Uthman: Yemen P.D.R. 54 F12
Shaim: U.S.S.R. 51 K2
Shaira: Yemen 54 F11
Shajapur: Madhya Pradesh, India 58 N10
Shakhova, Cape: Azerbaydzhan, U.S.S.R. 57 M1
Shakhrisyabz: Uzbek., U.S.S.R. 51 L7
Shakhty: U.S.S.R. 50 F5
Shakhun'ya: U.S.S.R. 50 G3
Shakhyar: Sinkiang, China 51 O6
Shaki: Nigeria 81 E3
Shakopee: Minn., U.S.A. 88 E3
Shakyay: Lithuania, U.S.S.R. 47 S9
Shala, Lake: Ethiopia 76 E1
Shalbourne: Wilts., England 25 S17
Shalfleet: I. of Wight, England 25 T18
Shaliko: Sinkiang, China 51 O6
Shalinskoye: U.S.S.R. 51 Q3
Shalkar: Himachal Pradesh, India 58 N8
Shallufa, El: Egypt (Suez Canal Inset) 32 Ins.
Shalya: U.S.S.R. 50 J3
Shalym: U.S.S.R. 51 P4
Shama: riv., Tanzania 76 D4
Shamattawa: Man., Canada 92 J1
Shambe: Sudan 76 D1
Shambles: sandbank, Eng., 24 R19
Shamil: Iran 55 J9
Shamiya: desert, Iraq 57 K6
Shamkhor: Azerbaydzhan, U.S.S.R. 57 K1
Shammar: tribal area, Sau. Arab./Iraq 54 F9
Shammar: tribal area, Syria/Iraq 57 G4
Shamokin: Pa., U.S.A. 89 N5
Shamrock: Fla., U.S.A. 91 K11
Shamrock: Tex., U.S.A. 90 A8
Shamva: Rhodesia 77 D6
Shanagarry: Cork, Repub. of Ireland 31 E16
Shanagolden: Lim., Repub. of Ireland 31 C14
Shanballymore: Cork, Repub. of Ireland 31 E15
Shandak: Iran 55 K9
Shandon: Strath., Scotland 29 M7
Shangalowe: Zaïre 77 C5
Shangani: & riv., Rhodesia 77 C6
Shangcheng: Honan, China 62 V8
Shang-chih: Heilungkiang, China 63 X5
SHANGHAI: & Municipality, China 63 W8
Shangjao: Kiangsi, China 62 V9
Shangkao: Kiangsi, China 62 U9
Shangkiu: Honan, China 62 V8
Shangnan: Shensi, China 62 U8
Shangshui: Honan, China 62 U8
Shangtu: riv., Hopeh 62 V6
Shangugu: Rwanda 76 C3
Shangyiu: Kiangsi, China 62 U9
Shanhotun: Heilungkiang, China 63 X6
Shanhsien: Shantung, China 62 V8
Shanklin: I. of Wight, Eng. 25 T18
Shanna: well, Saudi Arabia 55 H11
Shannon: i., Greenland 85 S2
Shannon: riv., Repub. of Irel. 31 E13
Shannon, Mouth of the: est., Repub. of Ireland 31 B15
Shannon Airport: Clare, Repub. of Ireland 31 D14
Shannonbridge: Offaly, Repub. of Ireland 31 E13
Shansi: Prov., China [cap. Taiyüan (Yangku)] 62 U7
Shan States: Burma (cap. Taunggyi) 59 R10
Shantan: Kansu, China 62 S7
Shantar Is., U.S.S.R. 49 p6
Shantung: Prov., China (cap. Tsinan) 62 V7
Shanwa: Tanzania 76 D3
Shanyang: Shensi, China 62 T8
Shaohing: Chekiang, China 63 W8
Shaokuan (Kukong): Kwangtung, China 62 U10
Shaowu: Fukien, China 62 V9
Shaoyang: Hunan, China 62 U9
Shap: Cumbria, England 27 Q10
Shap Fells: Cumbria, England 26 Q10
Shapinsay: i., Orkney Is. 28 Ins.
Shaqa: Saudi Arabia 54 F11
Shaqra: (Shuqra): Yemen P.D.R. 54 G12
Shaqra: Saudi Arabia 54 G9
Shara: riv., Inner Mongolia, China 62 V6
Shara: riv., Sinkiang, China 62 R7
Sharadurdu: Inner Mongolia, China 62 S6
Sharamura: Inner Mongolia, China 62 V5
Sharapoy Koshki I.: U.S.S.R. 48 h3
Shardin: Iran 57 L6
Share: Nigeria 81 E3
Shargorod: Ukraine 43 V12
Shari: Japan 63 ZZ6
Shari, Lake: Iraq 57 J4
Sharifabad: Iran 55 J7
Sharifkhaneh: Iran 57 J2
Sharjah: U.A.E. 55 J9
Shark Bay: W. Australia 68 A5
Sharkh: Oman 55 J10
Sharnbrook: Beds., England 25 U15
Sharon: Pa., U.S.A. 88 L5
Sharon: Biblical name of coastal plain extending N. from Jaffa, Israel 55 a2
Sharon Springs: Kans., U.S.A. 93 G5
Sharoy: U.S.S.R. 50 G6
Sharpness: Glos., England 24 R16
Sharqat (Asshur): Iraq 57 H4
Shar'ya: U.S.S.R. 50 G3
Shashi: riv., Rhod./Bots. 77 C7
Shasi: Hupeh, China 62 U8
Shassengue: Angola 73 H12
Shasta, Mount: volc., Calif., U.S.A. 92 C4
Shasta Dam: Calif., U.S.A. 92 C4
Shatosze: Szechwan, China 62 T8
Shatra: Iraq 57 K6
Shatsk: U.S.S.R. 50 F4
Shatsky Rise: N. Pacific Ocean 7 30N 155E
Shatt, El: Egypt (Suez Canal. Inset) 32 Ins.
Shatt al Arab: riv., Iraq/Iran 57 K6
Shattuck: Okla., U.S.A. 90 B7
Shaumyani: Georgia, U.S.S.R. 57 J1
Shaumyanovsk: Azerbaydzhan, U.S.S.R. 57 K1
Shaunavon: Sask., Canada 92 F3
Shaw: Gt. Man., England 27 R12
Shaw: Miss., U.S.A. 90 F9
Shaw: riv., W. Australia 68 B4
Shawano: Wis., U.S.A. 88 G3
Shawbost, North: Outer Hebr., Scotland 28 H3
Shawbury: Salop, England 27 Q14
Shawinigan Falls: Que., Can. 89 P2
Shaw I.: Queens., Australia 70 H3
Shawnee: Okla., U.S.A. 90 C8
Shchekur'ya: U.S.S.R. 48 H5
Shchors: Ukraine 50 D4
Shchuchin: Byelorussia 43 T10
Shchuchinsk: Kazakh., U.S.S.R. 51 M4
Shebandowan Lake: Ont., Canada 88 F1
Shebbear: Devon, England 24 N18
Sheboygan: Wis., U.S.A. 88 H4
Sheboygan Falls: city, Wis., U.S.A. 88 H4
Shechem: Canaanite city near Nablus, Jordan 55 b2
Sheddings, The: Antrim, N. Ireland 30 J10
Shediac: N.B., Canada 89 T2
Sheehy: mtn., Cork, Repub. of Ireland 31 C16
Sheelin, Lough: Repub. of Ireland 30 G12
Sheep Haven: bay, Don., Repub. of Ireland 30 F9
Sheepmoor: Trans., S. Afr. 75 J3
Sheep's Head (Muntervary Head): cape, Cork, Repub. of Ireland 31 B16
Sheepwash: Devon, England 24 N18
Sheerness: I. of Sheppey, England 25 X17
Sheet Harbour: N.S., Can. 89 U3
Sheffield: Ala., U.S.A. 91 H8
Sheffield: South I., N.Z. 70 O16
SHEFFIELD: S. Yorks., England 27 T13
Shefford: Beds., England 25 V15
Shehsien: Honan, China 62 U7
Sheigra: High., Scotland 28 L3
Sheikh: Somalia 79 R18
Sheikhupura: Punjab, Pak. 58 M8
Sheik Hussein: Ethiopia 76 F1
Shekak: riv., Ont., Canada 88 J1
Sheki: Azerbaydzhan, U.S.S.R. 57 K1
Shekar Dzong: Tibet, China 59 P9
Sheklung: Kwangtung, China 62 U10
Shelbina: Mo., U.S.A. 88 E6
Shelbourne: Vict., Australia 71 F11
Shelburne: N.S., Canada 89 T4
Shelburne: Ont., Canada 88 L3
Shelby: Mich., U.S.A. 88 H4
Shelby: Miss., U.S.A. 90 F9
Shelby: Mont., U.S.A. 92 E3
Shelby: N.C., U.S.A. 91 L8
Shelby: Ohio, U.S.A. 88 K5
Shelbyville: Ill., U.S.A. 88 G6
Shelbyville: Ind., U.S.A. 88 J6
Shelbyville: Ky., U.S.A. 88 J6
Shelbyville: Tenn., U.S.A. 91 H8
Sheldon: Iowa, U.S.A. 92 H4
Sheldwich: Kent, England 25 X17
Shelekhov Bay: U.S.S.R. 49 r5
Shelfield: W. Mid., England 27 S14
Shelford: Cambs., England 25 W15
Shelikof Str.: Alaska, U.S.A. 84 d6
Shellal: Egypt 54 D10
Shell Beach: city, La., U.S.A. 90 Ins.
Shellbrook: Sask., Canada 92 F2
Shellem: Nigeria 81 G3
Shelley: Idaho, U.S.A. 92 E4
Shell Harbour: N.S.W., Australia 71 J10
Shell I.: La., U.S.A. 90 Ins.
Shelton: Alaska, U.S.A. 84 c4
Shelton: Wash., U.S.A. 92 C3
Shelui: Tanzania 76 D3
Shemakha: Azerbaydzhan, U.S.S.R. 57 L1
Shemek: Libya 32 E5
Shemonaikha: Kazakh., U.S.S.R. 51 O4
Shenandoah: Iowa, U.S.A. 92 H4
Shenandoah: Pa., U.S.A. 89 N5
Shenandoah: Va., U.S.A. 89 M6
Shenandoah: riv., Va., U.S.A. 89 M6
Shenandoah Nat. Park: Va., U.S.A. 89 M6
Shendam: Nigeria 81 F3
Shendi: Sudan 54 D11
Shëngjini: Albania 39 Q16
Shenkiu: Honan, China 62 V8
Shenkursk: U.S.S.R. 50 F2
Shenmu: Shensi, China 62 U7
Shensi: Prov., China [cap. Sian (Ch'ang-an)] 62 T8
Shenstone: Staffs., England 27 S14
Shentsa: Tibet, China 59 P8
Shenyang (Mukden): Liaoning, China 63 W6
Sheopur: Madhya Pradesh, India 58 N9
Shepetovka: Ukraine 43 U11
Shepherd Bay: N.W.T., Can. 84 K4
Shepherdswell: Kent, Eng. 25 Y17
Shepparton: Vict., Austl. 71 F11
Sheppey, Isle of: Kent, Eng. 25 X17
Shepreth: Cambs., England 25 W15
Shepshed: Leics., England 27 T14
Shepton Mallet: Som., Eng. 24 Q17
Sherada: Ethiopia 76 E1
Sherarat: tribal area, Saudi Arabia 56 F6
Sherbakul': U.S.S.R. 51 M4
Sherborne: Dorset, England 24 Q18
Sherborne St. John: Hants., England 25 T17
Sherbro I.: Sierra Leone 80 B3
Sherbrooke: N.S., Canada 89 U3
Sherbrooke: Que., Canada 89 Q3
Sherburn: Dur., England 26 T10
Sherburn: N. Yorks., England 26 U11
Sherburn in Elmet: N. Yorks., England 27 T12
Shercock: Cavan, Repub. of Ireland 30 H11
Shere: Surrey, England 25 V17
Shereik: Sudan 54 D11
Shergi: i., Kerkenna Is., Tunisia 32 E5
Sheridan: Ark., U.S.A. 90 E8
Sheridan: Wyo., U.S.A. 92 F4
Sheriff Hales: Salop, Eng. 27 R14
Sheriff Hutton: N. Yorks., England 27 U11
Sheriffmuir: battlefield about 3 miles NNE. of Dunblane, Tayside, Scotland 29 O7
Sheringham: Norf., England 25 Y14
Sherington: Bucks., Eng. 25 U15
Sherkin I.: Repub. of Ireland 31 C17
Sherlovaya Gora: U.S.S.R. 49 n7
Sherman: Tex., U.S.A. 90 C9
Sherman Mills: city, Maine, U.S.A. 89 R3
Sherridon: Man., Canada 92 G1
Shershera: Ethiopia 76 E1
Sherstobitovo: U.S.S.R. 51 N3
Sherston: Wilts., England 24 R16
's-HERTOGENBOSCH: North Brabant, Netherlands 44 L4
Sherwood Forest : Notts., England 27 T13
Sheshader: Outer Hebrides, Scotland 28 J3
Shetland: is. & Admin., Scotland (cap. Lerwick) 28 Ins.
Shewa: Prov., Ethiopia (cap. Addis Ababa) 79 M8
Sheyenne: riv., N. Dak., U.S.A. 92 H3
Shiant: is & sound, Outer Hebr., Scotland 28 J4
Shiashkotan I.: Kuril Is. 60 P2
Shibam: Hadhramaut, Yemen P.D.R. 55 G11
SHIBARGHAN: Jowzjan, Afghanistan 55 L7
Shibata: Japan 63 f2
Shibeli: riv., Ethiopia 76 F1
Shibeli: riv., Somal./Eth. 79 Q18
Shibetsu: Japan 63 YY6
Shibîn El Kôm: Egypt 56 B6
Shibli: Iran 57 K3
Shibuya: Japan 63 f3
Shickshock Mtns., Que., Canada 89 S1
Shiel, Loch: Highland/Strathclyde, Scotland 29 K6
Shieldaig: High., Scot. 28 K4
Shifnal: Salop, England 27 R14
Shiga: Pref., Japan (cap. Otsu) 63 e3
Shigatse: see Jihkatse.
Shihchan: Inner Mongolia, China 49 o7
Shihcheng: Kiangsi, China 62 V9
Shihchi: Tibet, China 62 R8
Shihchu: Szechwan, China 62 T8
SHIHKIACHWANG: Hopeh, China 63 U7
Shihku: Yunnan, China 62 R9
Shihnan (Enshih): Hupeh, China 62 T8
Shihping: Yunnan, China 62 S10
Shihr: Yemen P.D.R. 55 G12
Shihtao: Shantung, China 63 W7
Shihthsien: Kweichow, China 62 T9
Shihtsung: Yunnan, China 62 S10
Shikama: Japan 63 d3
Shikarpur: Sind, Pakistan 58 L9
Shikoku: i., Japan 63 c4
Shilbottle: Northumb., Eng. 26 S9
Shildon: Durham, England 26 S10
Shilka: U.S.S.R. 49 n7
Shilka: riv., U.S.S.R. 49 N7
Shillave: Ethiopia 79 Q18
Shillay: i., Outer Hebr., Scot. 28 G4
Shillelagh: Wick., Repub. of Ireland 31 H14
SHILLONG: Meghalaya, India (also cap. of Assam) 59 Q9
Shilobane: Trans., S. Africa 75 J2
Shiloh: sanctuary of ancient Israel about 9 miles S. by W. of Nablus (Shechem), Israel 55 b2
Shilongol: Inner Mongolia, China 62 V6
Shilute: Lithuania, U.S.S.R. 47 R9
Shimabara: & gulf, Japan 63 b4
Shimane: Pref., Japan (cap. Matsue) 63 c3
Shimanovskiy: U.S.S.R. 49 o7
Shima Penin.: Japan 63 e3
Shimentzu: Inner Mongolia, China 63 W5
Shimminato: Japan 63 e2
Shimizu: Kochi, Japan 63 c4
Shimizu: Shizuoka, Japan 63 f3
Shimoda: Kochi, Japan 63 c4
Shimoda: Shizuoka, Japan 63 f3
Shimodate: Japan 63 f2
Shimoga: Karnataka, India 58 N12
Shimoni: Kenya 76 E3
Shimonoseki: Japan 63 b4
Shimpek: Kazakh., U.S.S.R. 51 M6
Shin: riv., High., Scot. 28 N4
Shin, Loch: High., Scot. 28 M3
Shinafiya: Iraq 57 J6
Shinar: biblical name of Southern Babylonia. Possibly corruption of the name Sumer: also called Chaldea, now southern Iraq 57 K6
Shinas: Oman 55 J10
Shinchiku (Hsinchu): Taiwan, 63 W10
Shincliffe: Dur., England 26 S10
Shin Dand (Sabzawar): Afghanistan 58 K8
Shiner: Tex., U.S.A. 90 C11
Shingbwiyang: Burma 59 R9
Shingu: Japan 63 d4
Shingwedzi: Trans., S.Afr. 75 J1
Shingwedzi: riv., Mozam./S. Afr. 75 J1
Shinji: Japan 63 c3
Shinjo: Japan 63 ZZ7
Shinkolobwe: Zaïre 77 C5
Shinrone: Offaly, Repub. of Ireland 31 F14
Shinsi: Kansu, China 62 S8
Shintaku: Nigeria 81 F3
SHINYANGA: & Reg., Tanzania 76 D3
Shiobara: Japan 63 f2
Shio no Point: cape, Japan 63 d4
Ship: i., Miss., U.S.A. 90 G10
Shipdham: Norf., England 25 X14
Shipki Pass: China/India 58 N8
Shipley: W. Yorks., England 27 S12
Shippensburg: Pa., U.S.A. 89 N5
Shippigan: & i., N.B., Can. 89 T2
Shipston on Stour: War., England 25 S15
Shipton: Glos., England 24 S16
Shipton under Wychwood: Oxon., England 25 S16
Shirabad: Uzbek., U.S.S.R. 51 L7
Shirakawa: Fukushima, Japan 63 g2
Shirakawa: Gifu, Japan 63 e2
SHIRAZ: Fars, Iran 55 H9
Shirbîn: Egypt 56 B6
Shiré: riv., Malawi 77 E6
Shirebrook: Derby., England 27 T13
Shirenewton: Gwent Wales 24 Q16
Shirensu: Iran 57 L4
Shiretoko, Cape: Japan 63 YY6
Shiriya, Cape: Japan 63 ZZ6
Shiroishi: Japan 63 g1
Shirotori: Japan 63 e3
Shirwell: Devon, England 24 N17
Shishaldin: volc., Aleutians 84 c7
Shishigi: Japan 63 a4
Shishmaref: Alaska, U.S.A. 84 C4
Shisur: Oman 55 H11
Shitembo: Angola 73 H12
Shithatha: Iraq 57 H5
Shiu Hoshih: Sinkiang, China 51 p6
Shivpuri: Madhya Pradesh, India 58 N9
Shiwa Ngandu: Zambia 77 D5
SHIZUOKA: & Pref., Japan 63 f3
Shkodër (Scutari); & lake, Albania 39 Q15
Shkotovo: U.S.S.R. 63 Y6
Shmidt I.: Severnaya Zemlya, Arctic O. 49 L1
Shoa: geog. reg., Ethiopia 79 M8
Shoa Ghimirra: Ethiopia 76 E1
Shoalhaven: riv., N.S.W., Australia 71 J10
Shoal Lake: town, Man., Canada 92 G2
Shoal Water Bay: Queens., Australia 70 J4
Shoan Is.: S. Korea 63 X8
Shobdon: Hereford & Worcester, England 24 Q15
Shodo: i., Japan 63 d3
Shoeburyness: Essex, Eng. 25 X16
Shohsien: Shansi, China 62 U7
Shoin: Japan 63 e2
Shoka (Changchun): Taiwan 63 W10
Sholapur: Maharashtra, India 58 N11
Shoreham: Kent, England 25 W17
Shoreham by Sea: W. Sussex, England 25 V18
Shorkot Road: Punjab, Pakistan 58 M8
Shortland Is.: Solomon Is. 67 L3
Shorwell: I. of Wight, England 25 T18
Shoshone: Idaho, U.S.A. 92 E4
Shoshone: Wyo., U.S.A. 92 F4
Shoshone Basin: Wyo., U.S.A. 92 F4
Shoshone Mtns.: Nev., U.S.A. 93 D5
Shotley Bridge: village, Dur., England 26 S10
Shotley Gate: Suff., England 25 Y16
Shotover: Queens., Austl. 70 H5
Shottermill: Surrey, England 25 U17
Shotton: Durham, England 26 T10
Shotts: Strath., Scotland 29 O8
Shouldham: Norf., England 25 W14
Showa: Tibet, China 62 R9
Showyang: Shansi, China 62 U7
Shpikov: Ukraine 43 V12
Shpola: Ukraine 50 D5
Shrawardine: Salop, Eng. 27 Q14
Shreveport: La., U.S.A. 90 E9
Shrewsbury: La., U.S.A. 90 Ins.
Shrewsbury: Salop, Eng. 27 Q14
Shrewton: Wilts., England 24 S17
Shrivenham: Oxon., Eng. 25 S16
Shrule: Galway, Repub. of Ireland 30 C12
Shu'aiba: Iraq 57 K6
Shubar-Kuduk: Kazakh., U.S.S.R. 50 J5
Shuikow: Fukien, China 62 V9
Shulan: Kirin, China 63 X6
Shuleh: riv., China 62 R6
Shumagin Is.: Alaska, U.S.A. 84 c7
Shumerlya: U.S.S.R. 50 G3
Shumikha: U.S.S.R. 51 K3
Shuna: i., Scotland 29 K7
Shunchang: Fukien, China 62 V9
Shungnak: Alaska, U.S.A. 84 D4
Shunking (Nanchung): Szechwan, China 62 T8
Shunyi: Peking Municipality, China 62 V6
Shuqra: Yemen P.D.R. 79 R17
Shur: riv., Iran 55 J8
Shura: Iraq 57 H4
Shuraabad: Azerbaydzhan, U.S.S.R. 57 L1
Shurgaz: Iran 55 J9
Shurma: U.S.S.R. 50 H3
Shuru: Iran 55 J8
Shush: Iran 57 L5
Shusha: Azerbaydzhan, U.S.S.R. 57 K2
Shushal: Jammu & Kashmir 58 N8
Shushartie: B.C., Canada 92 B2
Shushi Is.: S. Korea 63 X8
Shushong: Botswana 75 G1
Shushtar: Iran 57 L5
Shushwap Lake: B.C., Can. 92 D2
Shusp: Iran 55 J8
Shuya: U.S.S.R. 50 F3
Shuyang: Kiangsu, China 62 V8
Shuzenji: Japan 63 f3
Shvenchėnis: Lithuania, U.S.S.R. 47 U9
Shwangcheng: Heilungkiang, China 63 X5
Shwangliao: Inner Mongolia, China 63 W6
Shwangshan: Kirin, China 63 W6
Shwangyang: Kirin, China 63 X6
Shwebo: Burma 59 R10
Shwegu: Burma 59 R10
Shwegun: Burma 59 R11
Shwegyin: Burma 59 R11
Shweli: riv., China/Burma 59 R10
Shyaulyay: Lithuania, U.S.S.R. 47 S9
Shyok: Jammu & Kashmir 58 N8
Si: riv., China 62 U10
Si: riv., Thailand 64 C3
Siaga: Celebes 65 G6
Siaho: Kansu, China 62 S7
Siahrud: Iran 57 L3
Siah Vashan: Iran 57 L4
Siakow: Kansu, China 62 S7
Siak Sri Indrapura: Sum. 65 C6
Siefa: Poland 43 S10
Sialkot: Punjab, Pak. 58 M8
Siam: see Thailand.
Siam., G. of: SE. Asia 64 C4
Sian: Kirin, China 63 X6
SIAN (Ch'ang-an): Shensi, China 62 T8
Siang: riv., Hunan, China 62 U9
Siang: riv., Kwangsi Chuang, China 62 T10
Siangshan: Chekiang, China 63 W9
Siangsiang: Hunan, China 62 U9
Siangtan: Hunan, China 62 U9
Siangyang: Hupeh, China 62 U8
Siangyin: Hunan, China 62 U9
Siánori: Mexico 93 F7
Siantan: i., Anambas Is., Indonesia 65 D6
Siaohoying: Szechwan, China 62 S8
Siapu (Funing): Fukien, China 63 W9
Siargao: i., Philippines 64 H5
Siaton: Philippines 64 G5
Siatsing: Shantung, China 62 V7
Siatsun: Shantung, China 63 W7
Siau: i., Sangihe Is., Indon. 65 H6
Sib: Iran 55 K9
Sibayi, Lake: Natal, S. Afr. 75 K3
Šibenik: Yugoslavia 38 O15
Siberia: geog. reg., U.S.S.R. 49
Siberut: i. & str., Mentawai Is., Indonesia 65 B7
Sibi: Baluchistan, Pakistan 58 L9
Sibigo: Simeuluë, Sumatra 65 B6
Sibiryakov I.: U.S.S.R. 48 j3
Sibiti: Congo 81 G5
Sibiu: Romania 39 T14
Sible Hedingham: Essex, England 25 X16
Sibley Prov. Park: Ont., Canada 88 G1
Sibo: Sweden 47 P6
Siboa: Celebes 65 G6
Sibigo: Simeuluë, Sumatra 65 B6
Sibolga: Sumatra 65 B6
Sibsagar: Assam, India 59 Q9
Sibsey: Lincs., England 27 W13
Sibu: Sarawak, Malaysia 65 E6
Sibu: i., Malaya, Malaysia 65 d12
Sibuguey Bay: Mindanao, Philippines 64 G5
Sibuko: Mindanao, Phil. 64 G5
SIBUT: Kémo-Gribingui: Cen. Afr. Rep. 76 A1
Sibuti: Sarawak, Malaysia 65 E6
Sibutu: i & str., Borneo 65 F6
Sibuyan: i. & sea, Phil. 64 G4
Sichon: Thailand 64 B5
Sichwan: Honan, China 62 U8
Sicié, Cap: cape, France 40 L12
Sicilian Chan.: Sicily/Tunisia 38 M18
Sicily: i. & Reg., Italy (cap. Palermo) 38 N18
Sicuani: Peru 94 C6
Šid: Yugoslavia 39 Q14
Sidamo: geog. reg., Ethiopia 76 E1
Sidamo: Prov., Ethiopia (cap. Yirga Alam) 79 M9
Sidara: Yemen P.D.R. 55 G12
Sidbury: Devon, England 24 P18
Sidbury: S. Africa 75 G6
Side: ancient Greek port about 3 miles SW. of Manavgat, Turkey 56 B3
Sideby: Finland 47 R5
Siderno Marina: Italy 38 P17
Sidheros, Cape: Crete 39 U19
Sidhirokastron: Greece 39 S16
Sidhpur: Gujarat, India 58 M10
Sidi Aissa: Algeria 35 H19
Sidi Barrani: Egypt 54 C8
Sidi Bel Abbès: Algeria 35 F19
Sidi Bennour: Morocco 80 K8
Sidi Ifni: Morocco 80 J9
Sidi Kacem: Morocco 80 K8

For Abbreviations see list on p.113. Italic type, e.g. *Ephesus*, refers to historical names not on maps. Capital letters, e.g. MADRID, show capitals of countries; small capital letters, e.g. CADIZ, show capitals of provinces, etc. General notes p.116.

Sidikalang—Sneek 187

Sidikalang: Sumatra 65 B6
Sidi M'Hamid Ben Ali: Algeria 35 G18
Sidi Tha'am: Yemen 54 F11
Sidlaw Hills: Tayside, Scotland 29 P6
Sidmouth: Devon, England 24 P18
Sidney: Mont., U.S.A. 92 G3
Sidney: Nebr., U.S.A. 92 G4
Sidney: N.Y., U.S.A. 89 O4
Sidney: Ohio, U.S.A. 88 J5
Sidoktaya: Burma 59 Q10
Sidon (Saida): Lebanon 56 D5
Sidorovsk: U.S.S.R. 48 K4
Sidra, G. of: Libya 33 F5
Siebenbäu: W. Germany 45 Q2
Siebenlehn: E. Germany 45 T4
Siecq: France 37 E10
Siedenburg: W. Germany 44 O3
Siedlce: Poland 43 S10
Sieg: riv., W. Germany 44 N5
Siegburg: W. Germany 44 N5
Siegen: W. Germany 44 O5
Siemiatycze: Poland 43 S10
Siempang: Cambodia 64 D4
Siemreap: Cambodia 64 C4
Siena: Italy 38 M15
Sienhsien: Hopeh, China 62 V7
Sienning: Hupeh, China 62 U9
Sieppijärvi: Finland 46 T3
Sieradz: Poland 43 Q11
Sierpc: Poland 43 Q10
Sierra Blanca: mtn., N. Mex., U.S.A. 93 F6
Sierra Blanca: town, Tex., U.S.A. 93 F6
Sierra Colorado: town, Arg. 95 D12
Sierra del Carmen Nat. Park: Mexico 93 G7
Sierra de San Pedro Martin Nat. Park: Mexico 93 D6
Sierra Gorda: town, Chile 96 B1

Sierra Leone: Republic 80 B3
Cap.: Freetown
Area: 27,925 sq. miles (72,326 sq. km.)
Pop.: 2,600,000 (1971 E)

Sierra Leone Basin: N. Atlantic Ocean 8 05N 20W
Sierra Madre: ranges, Mex., see Eastern, Western, & Southern Sierra Madre.
Sierra Mojada: town, Mexico 93 G7
Sierra Morena: mtns., Spain 35 D17
Sierra Nevada: mtns., Arg./Chile 96 B2
Sierra Nevada: mtns., Calif., U.S.A. 93 D5
Sierra Nevada: mtns., Spain 35 E18
Sierra Nevada de Cocuy: mtns., Colombia 94 C2
Sierre: Switzerland 40 N9
Sietow: E. Germany 45 S2
Sievi: Finland 46 T5
Sifeng: Liaoning, China 63 W6
Sifengkow: Hopeh, China 62 V6
Sif Fatima: Algeria 78 F3
Sifié: Ivory Coast 80 C3
Sifnos: i., Cyclades 39 T18
Sifton: Man., Canada 92 G2
Sig: Algeria 35 F19
Sigean: France 37 H12
Sigep: Mentawai Is., Indon. 65 B7
Sigerfjord: Vesterålen, Nor. 46 O2
Sigeum: Greek city at SW. entrance to Dardanelles on Çanakkale side, Turkey 39 U16
Siggiewi: Malta 32 Ins.
Sigglesthorne: Humb., Eng. 27 V12
Sighet: Romania 43 S13
Sighişoara: Romania 43 T13
Sigillo: Italy 41 S12
Sigli: Sumatra 65 B5
Siglufjördhur: Iceland 46 d3
Sigmaringen: W. Germany 40 P7
Signau: Switzerland 40 N9
Signia: ancient Latin city in hills about 28 miles SE. of Rome. 38 N16
Signy Island: rsch. stn., Antarctica 9 65S 50W
Signy-l'Abbaye: France 36 K6
Sigoisoinan: Mentawai Is., Indonesia 65 B7
Sigoulès: France 37 F11
Sigourney: Iowa, U.S.A. 88 E5
Sigsbee Knolls: Gulf of Mexico 8 20N 95W
Sigsig: Ecuador 94 B4
Sigtuna: Sweden 47 P7
Sigüenza: Spain 35 E16
SIGUIRI: & Reg., Guinea 80 C2
Sigulda: Latvia, U.S.S.R. 47 T8
Sihawal: Madhya Pradesh, Ind. 58 O10
Sihlengi: S. Africa 75 J3
Sihsien: Anhwei, China 62 V9
Sihsien: Shansi, China 62 U7
Sihwa: Honan, China 62 U8
Siika: riv., Finland 46 T4
Siikainen: Finland 47 R6
Siikajoki: Finland 46 T4
Siilinjärvi: Finland 46 U5
SIIRT: & Prov., Turkey 57 G3
Sijalila Hills: Rhodesia 77 C6
Sijani: well, Saudi Arabia 55 H11
Sik: Malaya, Malaysia 65 b11
Sikang: (now absorbed in Szechwan, Prov.), China 62 R8
Sikar: Rajasthan, India 58 N9
SIKASSO: & Reg., Mali 80 C2
Sikea: Greece 39 S18
Sikeston: Mo., U.S.A. 88 G7
Sikhote Alin Range: U.S.S.R. 63 Z5
Sikhukhuza: Trans., S. Afr. 75 J2
Sikinos: i., Cyclades 39 T18
Sikionia: Greece 39 S17
Sikkim: State, India (cap. Gantok) 59 P9
Siklós: Hungary 43 Q14
Sikotan: i., Kuril Is. 63 YY6
Siktyakh: U.S.S.R. 49 O3
Siku: Kansu, China 62 S8
Sikwani: Botswana 75 G2
Sil: riv., Spain 35 C15
Sila: United Arab Emirates 55 H10
Silame: Nigeria 81 E2
Silandro: Italy 41 Q9
Silba: i., Yugoslavia 41 U11
Silchar: Assam, India 59 Q10
Silchester: Hants., England 25 T17
Şile: Turkey 56 A1
Sileby: Leics., England 27 T14
Silecroft: Cumbria, England 26 P11
Siler City: N.C., U.S.A. 91 M8
Silesia: geog. reg., Poland 43 P11
Silgarhi Doti: Nepal 58 O9
Silhuas: Peru 94 B5
Sili: Upper Volta 80 D2
Siliao (Liao): riv., Inner Mongolia, China 63 W6
Silifke: Turkey 56 C3
Siliguri: W. Bengal, India 59 P9
Silil: Somalia 79 Q17
Siliqua: Sardinia 38 L17
Silistra: Bulgaria 39 U14
Silivri: Turkey 39 V16
Siljan Lake: Sweden 47 O6
Silkeborg: Denmark 47 L8
Silksworth: Tyne and Wear, England 26 T10
Sillajhuay, Cordillera de: mtn., Chile 94 D7
Silleiro, Cape: Spain 35 B15
Sillé-le-Guillaume: France 36 E7
Sillerud: Sweden 47 N7
Silloth: Cumbria, England 26 P10
Siloam Springs: Ark., U.S.A. 90 D7
Silogui: Mentawai Is., Indonesia 65 B7
Silsbee: Tex., U.S.A. 90 D10
Silsden: W. Yorks., England 27 S12
Siltou: well, Niger 81 H1
Siluko: Nigeria 81 F3
Silvan: Turkey 57 G2
Silvânia: Brazil 94 H7
Silvaplana: Switzerland 40 P9
SILVA PORTO: Bié, Angola 73 H12
Silver City: Idaho, U.S.A. 92 D4
Silver City: Nev., U.S.A. 93 D5
Silver City: N. Mex., U.S.A. 93 F6
Silver City: Panama 94 Ins.
Silver Creek: city, N.Y., U.S.A. 89 M4
Silverdale: Lancs., England 26 Q11
Silver End: Essex, England 25 X16
Silver Lake: city, Oreg., U.S.A. 92 C4
Silvermine Mtns.: Tip., Repub. of Ireland 31 E14
Silverstone: Northants., England 25 U15
Silverton: Colo., U.S.A. 93 F5
Silverton: Devon, England 24 P18
Silverton: N.S.W., Austl. 71 D8
Silverton: Oreg., U.S.A. 92 C3
Silvertown: Ga., U.S.A. 91 J9
Silves: Portugal 35 B18
Silz: Austria 41 Q8
Simaleke Hilir: Mentawai Is., Indonesia 65 B7
Simanggang: Sarawak, Malaysia 65 E6
Simard, Lac: Que., Canada 89 M2
Simatang: i., Celebes 65 G6
Simav: & riv., Turkey 39 V17
Simba: Zaïre 76 B2
Simbillâwein: Egypt 56 B6
Simbo: Tabora, Tanzania 76 D3
Simbo: Kigoma, Tanzania 76 C3
Simcoe: Ont., Canada 88 L4
Simcoe, Lake: Ont., Canada 89 M3
Simeuluë: i., Sumatra 65 B6
SIMFEROPOL': Crimea, U.S.S.R. 50 D6
Simi: i., Dodecanese 39 U18
Simiti: Colombia 94 C2
SIMLA: Himachal Pradesh, India 58 N8
Simleul Silvaniel: Romania 43 S13
Simmelsdorf: W. Germany 45 R6
Simmern: W. Germany 44 N6
Simo: Finland 46 T4
Simoca: Argentina 96 B2
Simois: river flowing N. into Dardanelles about 4 miles E. of Aegean entrance, Turkey 39 U17
Simo Lake: Finland 46 U3
Simonburn: Northumb., England 26 R9
Simonsbath: Som., England 24 O17
Simonsburg: W. Germany 44 O1
Simonstown: S. Africa 74 Ins.
Simpang: Sumatra 65 C7
Simpele: Finland 47 V6
Simplicio Mendes: Brazil 94 J5
Simplon: & pass, Switz. 40 O9
Simpson Desert: N. Territ., Australia 69 F4
Simrishamn: Sweden 47 O9
Simunjan: Sarawak, Malaysia 65 E6
Simushir I.: Kuril Is. 60 P2
Sinabang: Simeuluë, Sum. 65 B6
Sinadogo: Somalia 79 R18
Sinai, Mt. (Jebel Katherina): Egypt 54 D9
Sinaia: Romania 39 T14
Sinai Penin.: Egypt 56 C6
Sinaloa: & State, Mexico (cap. Culiacán) 93 F7
Sinamba: Zambia 77 C6
Sinauen: Libya 32 E5
Sinbo: Burma 59 R10
Sincelejo: Colombia 94 B2
Sinchang: Chekiang, China 63 W9
Sinchao: Inner Mongolia, China 62 T7
Sincheng: Honan, China 62 U8
Sinchon: N. Korea 63 X7
Sinclair's Bay: High., Scot. 28 P2
Sin Cowe: reef, S. China Sea 64 E5
Sind: Prov., Pakistan (cap. Karachi) 58 L9
Sindangan: Mindanao, Phil. 64 G5
Sindangbarang: Java 65 D8
Sindara: Gabon 81 G5
Sinde: Zambia 77 C6
Sindhuli Garhi: Nepal 59 P9
Sindi: Estonia, U.S.S.R. 47 T7
Sindırgi: Turkey 39 V17
Sindjai: Celebes 65 G8
Sines: & cape, Portugal 35 B18
Sine-Saloum: Reg., Senegal (cap. Kaolack) 80 A2
Sinettä: Finland 46 T3
Sinfra: Ivory Coast 80 C3
Sing: Thailand 64 C4
Singa: Sudan 54 D12

Singapore: Republic 65 e13
Cap.: Singapore
Area: 225 sq. miles (583 sq. km.)
Pop.: 2,147,000 (1972 E)

SINGAPORE: Singapore 65 c13
Singara: ancient city of Mesopotamia, later Roman camp at Balad Sinjar, Iraq 57 G3
Singaraja: Bali, Indonesia 65 F8
Singatoka: Viti Levu, Fiji Is. 67 P5
Singen: W. Germany 40 O8
SINGIDA: & Reg., Tanzania 76 D3
Singidunum: Roman camp at Belgrade, Yugoslavia 39 R14
Singitikós, G. of: Greece 39 T16
Singkaling Hkamti: Burma 59 R9
Singkang: Celebes 65 G7
Singkawang: Borneo 65 D6
Singkep: i., Indonesia 65 C7
Singkuang: Sumatra 65 B6
Singleton: N.S.W., Austl. 71 J9
Singleton: W. Sussex, Eng. 25 U18
Singora (Songkhla): Thai. 64 C5
Singtal: Hopeh, China 62 U7
Singu: Burma 59 R10
Singuélé: Cen. Afr. Rep. 76 B1
Sinhsien: Shansi, China 62 U7
Sinhwa: Hunan, China 62 U9
SINING (Hsining): Chinghai, China 62 S7
Siniscola: Sardinia 38 L16
Siniyvir: Ukraine 43 S12
Sinj: Yugoslavia 38 P15
Sinjar: Iraq 57 G3
Sinkat: Sudan 54 E11
Sinkiang: Shansi, China 62 U7
Sinkiang Uighur Auton. Reg.: China (cap. Urumchi) 51 O6
Sinlumkaba: Burma 59 R10
Sinmin: Liaoning, China 63 W6
Sinnamary: Fr. Guiana 94 G2
Sinning: Hunan, China 62 U9
Sinnûris: Egypt 56 B7
Sinoe: Co., Liberia (co. town Greenville) 80 C3
Sinoe: riv., Liberia 80 C3
SINOIA: Mashonaland North, Rhodesia 77 D6
SINOP: & Prov., Turkey 56 D1
Sinpin: Liaoning, China 63 X6
Sinpu: Kwangtung, China 62 V10
Sinsheim: W. Germany 44 O6
Sintai: Shantung, China 62 V7
Sîntana: Romania 39 R13
Sint Andries: Belgium 44 J4
Sintang: Borneo 65 E6
Sintien: Hunan, China 62 U9
Sint Niklaas: Belgium 44 K4
Sinton: Tex., U.S.A. 90 C11
Sintra: Portugal 35 B17
Sintsai: Honan, China 62 V8
Sint Truiden: Belgium 44 L5
Sintu: Kwangsi Chuang, China 62 U10
Sinuiju: N. Korea 63 W6
Sinujif: Somalia 79 R18
Sinyang: Honan, China 62 U8
Sinyeh: Honan, China 62 U8
Sinzig: W. Germany 44 N5
Siófok: Hungary 43 Q13
Sioma: Zambia 77 B6
Sion: France 36 D8
SION: Valais, Switzerland 40 N9
Sionascaig, Loch: Highland, Scotland 28 L3
Sion Mills: Tyr., N. Ireland 30 G10
Siorac: France 37 F11
Sioule: riv., France 37 J9
Sioux City: Iowa, U.S.A. 92 H4
Sioux Falls: city, S. Dak., U.S.A. 92 H4
Sioux Lookout: Ont., Can. 92 J2
Siphae: Greek city of S. Boeotia on N. coast of G. of Corinth about 18 miles SE. of Thebes. 39 S17
Siphaqeni: Transkei, S. Africa 75 H5
Siple Mt.: Antarctica 9 75S 130W
Sipora: i., Mentawai Is., Indonesia 65 B7
Sipotele Sucevei: Romania 43 T13
Sippar: ancient city, biblical Sepharvaim, N. of Babylon, Iraq 57 J5
Siquijor: i., Philippines 64 G5
Sir: New Guinea 69 G1
Sira (Siros): i., Cyclades, Greece 39 S16
Sira: riv., Norway 47 K7
Sir Abu Nu'air: Persian Gulf 55 H9
Sirajganj: Bangladesh 59 P10
Sir Alexander, Mount: B.C., Canada 92 C2
Şiran: Turkey 56 F1
Sir Bani Yas: i., Persian Gulf 55 H10
Sir Creek: inlet, India/Pak. 58 L10
Siret: riv., Romania 43 U13
Sirhan, Wadi: depression, Saudi Arabia 56 E6
Siri: Ethiopia 76 E1
Şiria: Romania 43 R13
Širik, Cape: Sarawak, Malaysia 65 E6
Širinec Kriz: Yugoslavia 41 W10
Siris: Greek city on G. of Taranto about 25 miles SW. of Metaponto, Italy 38 P16
Sir James McBrien: mtn., N.W.T., Canada 84 G5
Sir Joseph Bank Group: is., S. Australia 71 B10
Sirmium: Roman camp at Sremska Mitrovica, Yugo. 39 Q14
Sırnak: Turkey 57 H3
Sirohi: Rajasthan, India 58 M10
Sirombu: Nias, Sumatra 65 B6
Sironj: Rajasthan, India 58 N10
Siros (Ermoupolis): Cyclades, Greece 39 S16
Siros (Sira): i., Cyclades, Grc. 39 S16
Sirra: wadi, Saudi Arabia 54 G10
Sirsa: Haryana, India 58 N9
Sirte: Libya 33 F5
Sirtica: dist., Libya 78 H3
Şirvan: Turkey 57 H2
Sirvice: Turkey 56 F2
Sirwan: Iraq 57 J4
Sir Wilfred Laurier, Mt.: Can. 84 H7
Sisak: Yugoslavia 38 P14
Siscia: Roman camp at Sisak, Yugoslavia 41 W10
Sisili: riv., Ghana 80 D2
Sisophon: Cambodia 64 C4
Sissach: Switzerland 40 N8
Sisseton: S. Dak., U.S.A. 92 H3
Sissonne: France 36 J6
Sistan: geog. reg., Iran/Afghanistan 55 K8
Sisteron: France 40 L11
Sistersville: W. Va., U.S.A. 88 L6
Sitamau: Madhya Pradesh, India 58 N10
Sitapur: Uttar Pradesh, India 58 O9
Siteki: Swaziland 75 J3
Sitges: Spain 35 G16
Sithonia: penin., Greece 39 S16
Sitia: Crete 39 U19
Sitidgi Lake: N.W.T., Can. 84 f4
Sítio da Abadia: Brazil 94 H6
Sitka: Alaska, U.S.A. 84 F6
Sitkin, Great: i., Aleutians 84 B7
Sitkin, Little: i., Aleutians 84 a7
Sitra: depression, Egypt 54 C9
Sittang: riv., Burma 59 R11
Sittard: Netherlands 44 L4
Sittingbourne: Kent, Eng. 25 X17
SITTWE (Akyab): Arakan, Burma 59 Q11
Situbondo: Java 65 E8
Siushan: Szechwan, China 62 T9
Siushui: Kiangsi, China 62 U9
Siuyen: Liaoning, China 63 W6
Sivaki: U.S.S.R. 49 o7
Sivand: Iran 55 H8
SIVAS: & Prov., Turkey 56 E2
Siverek: Turkey 56 F3
Sivrice: Turkey 56 F2
Sivrihisar: Turkey 56 B2
Siwa: Celebes 65 G7
Siwa: Egypt 54 C9
Siwalik Range: India 58 N8
Siwan: Bihar, India 59 O9
Sixmilebridge: Clare, Repub. of Ireland 31 D14
Sixmilecross: Tyr., N. Irel. 30 G10
Sixt: Haute-Savoie, France 40 M9
Sizun: France 36 A7
Sjaelland: see Zealand.
Sjenica: Yugoslavia 39 R15
Sjougdnäs: Sweden 46 O4
Skadovsk: Ukraine 50 D5
Skaelskør: Zealand, Den. 47 M9
Skaer Fiord: Greenland 85 S2
Skaftafell: Iceland 46 e4
Skaga Fiord: Iceland 46 d3
Skagaströnd: Iceland 46 c4
Skagen: Denmark 47 M8
Skagerrak: str., Nor./Den. 47 L8
Skagway: Alaska, U.S.A. 84 F6
Skala: Ukraine 43 U12
Skalar: Iceland 46 f3
Skälder Bay: Sweden 47 N8
Skalka Lake: Sweden 46 Q3
Skånland: Norway 46 P2
Skänninge: Sweden 47 O7
Skansen: Greenland 85 o4
Skara: Sweden 47 N7
Skaraborg: Co., Sweden (cap. Mariestad) 47 N7
Skarda: i., Yugoslavia 41 U11
Skardu: Jammu & Kashmir 58 N7
Skarnes: Norway 47 M6
Skarżysko: Poland 43 R11
Skateraw: Gram., Scotland 28 R5
Skaw, The: cape, Denmark 47 M8
Skeena: riv., B.C., Canada 92 B2
Skeffling: Humb., England 27 W12
Skeggjastadhir: Iceland 46 f3
Skegness: Lincs., England 27 W13
Skeldon: Guyana 87 e8
Skellefte: riv., Sweden 46 Q4
Skellefteå: Sweden 46 R4
Skellig Rocks: Repub. of Ireland 31 A16
Skellingthorpe: Lincs., Eng. 27 U13
Skelmanthorpe: W. Yorks., England 27 S12
Skelmersdale: town, Lancs., England 27 Q12
Skelmorlie: Strath., Scotland 29 M8
Skelton: Cumbria, England 26 Q10
Skelton: Cleve., England 26 U10
Skendleby: Lincs., England 27 W13
Skene: Sweden 47 N8
Skenfrith: Gwent, Wales 24 Q16
Skern: Denmark 47 L9
Skerries: Dublin, Repub. of Ireland 30 J12
Skerry Bank: Scotland 28 N2
Skerryvore: rock, Inner Hebr., Scotland 29 G7
Skhiza: i., Greece 39 R18
Ski: Norway 47 M7
Skiathos: i., N. Sporades 39 S17
Skiatook: Okla., U.S.A. 90 C7
Skibbereen: Cork, Repub. of Ireland 31 C16
Skibotn: Norway 46 R2
Skiddaw: mtn., Cumb., Eng. 26 P10
Skidel: Byelorussia 43 S10
SKIEN: Telemark, Norway 47 L7
Skierniewice: Poland 43 R11
Skikda: Algeria 32 D4
Skillingfors: Sweden 47 N7
Skiønstå: Norway 46 O3
Skipness: Strath., Scotland 29 L8
Skipsea: Humb., England 27 V12
Skipton: N. Yorks., England 27 R12
Skipton: Vict., Australia 71 E11
Skirlaugh: Humb., England 27 V12
Skirling: Borders, Scotland 29 P8
Skiros: i., N. Sporades 39 T17
Skirwith: Cumbria, England 26 Q10
Skive: Denmark 47 L8
Skjalfanda: riv., Iceland 46 e4
Skjold: Norway 47 J7
Skjöldöfsstadhir: Iceland 46 f4
Skofja Loka: Yugoslavia 41 U9
Skoganvarre: Norway 46 T2
Skokholm I.: Dyfed, Wales 24 L16
Skol'ye: Ukraine 43 S12
Skomer I.: Dyfed, Wales 24 L16
Skópelos: i., N. Sporades 39 S17
Skopin: U.S.S.R. 50 E4
SKOPJEG: Macedonia, Yugo. 39 R15
Skorodnoye: U.S.S.R. 50 E4
Skotousa: Greece 39 S16
Skotterud: Norway 47 N7
Skövde: Sweden 47 N7
Skovorodino: U.S.S.R. 49 O7
Skowhegan: Maine, U.S.A. 89 R3
Skrad: Yugoslavia 41 U10
Skradin: Yugoslavia 38 O15
Skreen: Sligo, Repub. of Irel. 30 D11
Skreen: Wex., Repub. of Irel. 31 J15
Skreia: Norway 47 M6
Skudeneshavn: Norway 47 J7
Skulerud: Norway 47 M7
Skuø: i., Faeroe Is. 46 h6
Skuodas: Lithuania, U.S.S.R. 47 R8
Skushuban: Somalia 79 S17
Skuteč: Czechoslovakia 45 W6
Skútustadhir: Iceland 46 e4
Skwierzyna: Poland 45 V3
Skye, I. of: Inner Hebr., Scot. 28 J5
Slack: site of Roman fort about 1 mile N. of Hebden Bridge, England 27 S12
Slagelse: Zealand, Denmark 47 M9
Slaggyford: Northumb., Eng. 26 Q10
Slaidburn: Lancs., England 27 R12
Slaithwaite: W. Yorks., Eng. 27 S12
Slaley: Northumb., England 26 R10
Slamannan: Central, Scot. 29 O8
Slamet: mtn., Java 65 D8
Slane: Meath, Repub. of Ireland 30 H12
Slaney: riv., Wex./Carlow, Repub. of Ireland 31 H15
Slănic: Romania 39 T14
Slantsy: U.S.S.R. 47 V7
Slaný: Czechoslovakia 45 U5
Slapton: Devon, England 24 O19
Slate Is.: Ont., Canada 88 H1
Slater: Mo., U.S.A. 88 E6
Slatina: Romania 39 T14
Slaugham: W. Sussex, Eng. 25 V17
Slave: riv., Canada 84 h6
Slave Coast: Nigeria 81 E3
Slave Lake, Great: Alta., Canada 84 h5
Slave Lake, Lesser: Alta., Canada 92 E1
Slăveni: Romania 39 T14
Slavgorod: U.S.S.R. 51 N4
Slavkov: Czechoslovakia 43 P12
Slavonia: geog. reg., Yugo. 33 F2
Slavonice: Czechoslovakia 45 V7
Slavuta: Ukraine 43 U11
Slavyansk: Ukraine 50 E5
Sława: Poland 45 W4
Sławno: Poland 43 P9
Slayton: Minn., U.S.A. 92 H4
Sleaford: Lincs., England 27 V14
Slea Head: cape, Kerry, Repub. of Ireland 31 A15
Sleat: penin., Inner Hebr., Scotland 28 K5
Sleat, Sound of: I. of Skye/Scotland 28 K5
Sledmere: Humb., England 27 U11
Sleeper Is.: Canada 84 I6
Sleeping Bear Pt.: U.S.A. 88 H3
Sleighford: Staffs., Eng. 27 R14
Sleights: N. Yorks., England 26 U11
Sleitmute: Alaska, U.S.A. 84 D5
Slessor Glacier: Antarctica 9 80S 30W
Slidell: La., U.S.A. 90 G10
Slide Mtn: N.Y., U.S.A. 89 O5
Sliedrecht: Netherlands 44 K4
Sliema: Malta 32 Ins.
Slieve Anierin: mtn., Leit., Repub. of Ireland 30 F11
Slieve Aughty Mtns.: Galway/Clare, Repub. of Ireland 31 D13
Slieve Beagh: hill, Tyr./Ferm., N. Ireland 30 G11
Slieve Bernagh: mtns., Clare, Repub. of Ireland 31 D14
Slieve Bloom Mtns.: Laois/Offaly, Repub. of Ireland 31 F13
Slieve Car: mtn., Mayo, Repub. of Ireland 30 B11
Slieve Donard: mtn., Down, N. Ireland 30 K11
Slievefelim Mtns.: Lim., Repub. of Ireland 31 E14
Slieve Gallion: hill, Lon., N. Ireland 30 H10
Slieve Gamph (Ox Mtns.): Sligo, Repub. of Ireland 30 D11
Slieve Mish Mtns.: Kerry, Repub. of Ireland 31 B15
Slieve Miskish Mtns.: Cork, Repub. of Ireland 31 A16
Slieve More: mtn., Achill I., Repub. of Ireland 30 A11
Slievenaman: mtn., Tip., Repub. of Ireland 31 F15
Slieve Snaght: mtn., Don., Repub. of Ireland 30 G9
SLIGO: & Co., Repub. of Ireland 30 E11
Sligo Bay: Repub. of Ireland 30 D11
Slim: Malaya, Malaysia 65 b12
Slindon: W. Sussex, England 25 U18
Slinfold: W. Sussex, England 25 V17
Slingsby: N. Yorks., England 26 U11
Slioch: mtn., High., Scot. 28 L4
Slite: Gotland, Sweden 47 Q8
Sliven: Bulgaria 39 U15
Slivnitsa: Bulgaria 39 S15
Slobodskoy: U.S.S.R. 50 H3
Slobozia: Romania 39 U14
Slocan: B.C., Canada 92 D3
Sloka: Latvia, U.S.S.R. 47 S8
Slonim: Byelorussia 43 T10
Slonta: Libya 33 G5
Slootdorp: Netherlands 44 K3
Slough: Berkshire, England 25 U16
Slovakia: Territ., Czech. 43 Q12
Slovechno: Ukraine 43 V11
Slovenia: Repub., Yugo. (cap. Ljubljana) 41 U9
Slovenija: see Slovenia.
Slovenj Gradec: Yugo. 41 V9
Slovenska Bistrica: Yugo. 41 V9
Slovenske Gorice: hills, Yugoslavia 41 V9
Słubice: Poland 45 U3
Sluch': riv., Ukraine 43 U11
Sluis: Netherlands 44 J4
Slunj: Yugoslavia 41 V10
Słupsk: Poland 43 P9
Slutsk: Byelorussia 43 U10
Slyne Head: i., Galway, Repub. of Ireland 31 A13
Slyudyanka: U.S.S.R. 49 M7
Smackover: Ark., U.S.A. 90 E9
Smailholm: Bord., Scotland 29 Q8
Smallburgh: Norf., England 25 Y14
Small Point: cape, Maine, U.S.A. 89 R4
Smara: Spanish Sahara 78 B4
Smarden: Kent, England 25 X17
Smeaton: N. Yorks., England 27 T12
Smeaton, Great: N. Yorks., England 26 T11
Smederevo: Yugoslavia 39 R14
Smeeth: Kent, England 25 X17
Smela: Ukraine 50 D5
Smetanina: U.S.S.R. 51 Q3
Smethwick: W. Mid., England 24 S15
Smidovich: U.S.S.R. 63 Y5
Smilovichi: Byelorussia 43 U10
Smiltene: Latvia, U.S.S.R. 47 T8
Smith (Mirror Landing): Alta., U.S.A. 92 E1
Smith Bay: Greenland/Can. 85 M2
Smith Bay: Alaska, U.S.A. 84 d3
Smithborough: Monaghan, Repub. of Ireland 30 G11
Smith Center: Kans., U.S.A. 93 H5
Smithers: B.C., Canada 92 B2
Smithfield: Cumb., England 26 Q10
Smithfield: & Dist., O.F.S., S. Africa 75 G5
Smithfield: Utah, U.S.A. 92 E4
Smiths Falls: Ont., Canada 89 N3
Smithton: Tas., Australia 68 H8
Smithtown: N.S.W., Austl. 71 K8
Smithville: Tex., U.S.A. 90 C10
Smitswinkel Bay: S. Africa 74 Ins.
Smoky: riv., Alta., Canada 92 D2
Smoky Cape: N.S., Canada 89 V2
Smoky Hill: riv., Kans., U.S.A. 93 H5
Smoky Hills: Kans., U.S.A. 93 H5
Smoky Lake: town, Alta., Canada 92 E2
Smøla: i., Norway 46 K5
SMOLENSK: & Reg., U.S.S.R. 50 D4
Smolenskoye: U.S.S.R. 51 P4
Smolevichi: Byelorussia 43 V9
Smolyan: Bulgaria 39 T16
Smooth Rock Falls: city, Ont., Canada 88 L1
Smoothstone Lake: Sask., Canada 92 F2
Smorgon': Byelorussia 47 U9
Smyrna (izmir): Turkey 39 U17
Snæfell: mtn., Iceland 46 f4
Snaefell: mtn., I. of Man, United Kingdom 26 N11
Snæfellsjökull: mtn., Iceland 46 b4
Snainton: N. Yorks., England 26 U11
Snaith: Humb., England 27 T12
Snake: riv., Wash., U.S.A. 92 D3
Snake Lake: see Pinehouse Lake.
Snake Range: Nev., U.S.A. 93 E5
Snake River Canyon: Oreg./Idaho, U.S.A. 92 D3
Snake River Plain: Idaho, U.S.A. 92 E4
Snape: N. Yorks., England 26 S11
Snåsa: Norway 46 N4
Sneek: Netherlands 44 L2

For Abbreviations see list on p.113. Italic type, e.g. Ephesus, refers to historical names not on maps. Capital letters, e.g. MADRID, show capitals of countries; small capital letters, e.g. CADIZ, show capitals of provinces, etc. General notes p.116.

188 Sneem—Spratly I.

Sneem: Kerry, Repub. of Ireland 31 B16
Sneeuberg Range: S. Afr. 75 F5
Snežnik, Mount: Yugo. 41 U10
Snina: Czechoslovakia 43 S12
Snizort, Loch: Inner Hebr., Scotland 28 H4
Snodland: Kent, England 25 W17
Snøhetta: *mtn.*, Norway 46 L5
Snohomish: Wash., U.S.A. 92 C3
Snowdon: *mtn.*, Gwyn., Wales 27 N13
Snowdon: *mtn.*, South I., New Zealand 70 O15
Snowdonia Nat. Park: Gwynedd, Wales 27 O14
Snowdrift: N.W.T., Canada 84 h5
Snowflake: Ariz., U.S.A. 93 E6
Snow Hill: Md., U.S.A. 89 O6
Snowtown: S. Australia 71 C9
Snowy: *riv.*, Vict./N.S.W., Australia 71 H11
Snowy Mts.: Vict./N.S.W., Australia 71 H11
Snyatyn: Ukraine 43 T12
Snyder: Tex., U.S.A. 93 G6
Soalala: Malagasy Rep. 73 O13
Soave: Italy 41 R10
Soay: *i.*, Inner Hebr., Scot. 28 J5
Soba: Nigeria 81 F2
Sobat: *riv.*, Ethiopia/Sudan 79 L8
Sobernheim: W. Germany 44 N6
Soběslav: Czechoslovakia 45 U6
Sobieszów (Hermsdorf): Poland 45 V5
Sobolevo: U.S.S.R. 49 r7
Sobotka: Czechoslovakia 45 V5
Sobozo: Niger 78 G5
Sobrado: Brazil 94 G5
Sobral: Brazil 94 J4
Sobrance: Czechoslovakia 43 S12
Sochaczew: Poland 43 R10
Soche (Yarkand): Sinkiang, China 51 N7
Sochi: U.S.S.R. 50 E6
Social Circle: Ga., U.S.A. 91 K9
Society Is.: (Fr.), Pacific O. (*cap.* Papeete) 83 e3
Socola: La., U.S.A. 90 *Ins.*
Socompa: *volc.*, Chile 96 B1
Socompa, Porto de: *pass.*, Chile 96 B1
Socorro: Brazil 96 F1
Socorro: Colombia 94 C2
Socorro: N. Mex., U.S.A. 93 F6
Socorro: *i.* (Mex.), Pacific O. 86 h14
Socotra: *i.* (Yemen P.D.R.), Indian O. 79 P7
Soctrang: Vietnam 64 D5
Soda Mtns.: Libya 78 H4
Sodankylä: Finland 46 U3
Soda Springs: Idaho, U.S.A. 92 E4
Soddu: Ethiopia 76 E1
Söderhamn: Sweden 47 P6
Söderköping: Sweden 47 P7
Södermanland: *Co.*, Sweden (*cap.* Nyköping) 47 P7
Södertalje: Sweden 47 P7
Sodiri: Sudan 54 C12
Soebatsfontein: S. Africa 74 B5
Soekmekaar: Trans., S. Afr. 75 H1
Soest: W. Germany 44 O4
Soest: Netherlands 44 L3
Sofala: Botswana 75 G1
Sofala & Manica: *Prov.*, Moz. (*cap.* Beira) 77 D6
SOFIA (Sofiya): Bulgaria 39 S15
Sofiysk: U.S.S.R. 49 P7
Soga: Tanzania 76 E4
Sogamoso: Colombia 94 C2
Sogata: Ethiopia 76 E1
Sögel: W. Germany 44 N3
Sogne Fiord: Norway 47 J6
Sogn og Fjordane: *Co.*, Nor. (*cap.* Leikanger) 47 K6
Soğut: Turkey 56 B1
Söğut, Lake, Turkey 56 A3
Sohag: Egypt 54 D9
Soham: Cambs., England 25 W15
Sohana: Solomon Is. 67 K3
Sohol: Senegal 80 B2
Soignies: Belgium 44 K5
Soin: Upper Volta 80 D2
Soissons: France 36 J6
Soitué: Argentina 96 B4
Sokal': Ukraine 43 T11
Söke: Turkey 39 U18
Sokndal: Norway 47 K7
Sokode: Togo 80 E3
Sokol: U.S.S.R. 50 F3
Sokółka: Poland 43 S10
Sokolo: Mali 80 C2
Sokolovac: Yugoslavia 41 W9
Sokołów: Poland 43 S10
SOKOTO: & *State*, Nigeria 81 F2
Sokuluk: Kirgiz., U.S.S.R. 51 M6
Solá: Argentina 96 D3
Solai: Kenya 76 E2
Solčava: Yugoslavia 41 U9
Sol de Maio: Brazil 96 E2
Sölden: Austria 41 R8
Sol'dy: U.S.S.R. 50 D3
Soledad: Argentina 96 C3
Soledade: Brazil 96 E2
Solent, The: *str.*, I. of Wight/England 25 T18
Solenzara: Corsica 38 L16
Solesmes: France 36 J5
Solf: Finland 46 R5
Solferino: battlefield about 5 miles NE. of Castiglione delle Stiviere, Italy 40 Q10
Sol Haud: *geog. reg.*, Somalia 79 R18
Solihull: W. Mid., England 25 S15
Solikamsk: U.S.S.R. 50 J3
Solimões (Amazon): *riv.*, Brazil 94 D4
Solingen: W. Germany 44 N4
Solkon: U.S.S.R. 49 q4
Sollas: Outer Hebr., Scot. 28 G4
Sollefteå: Sweden 46 P5
Sóller: Maj., Balearic Is. 35 H17
Sollia: Norway 47 M6
Sollum: & *gulf*, Egypt 54 C8
Solna: Sweden 47 P7
Solo (Surakarta): Java 65 E8
Solodniki: U.S.S.R. 50 G5
Sologne: *geog. reg.*, France 36 H8
Solok: Sumatra 65 C7
Solomon: *riv.*, Kans., U.S.A. 90 C6
Solomon Is.: *Br. protectorate* Pacific O. (*cap.* Honiara) 67 L3
Solomon Rise: Pacific Ocean 7 O 155E
Soloneshnoye: U.S.S.R. 51 O4
Solon Springs: *city*, Wis., U.S.A. 88 F2
Solor: *i.*, Indonesia 65 G8
SOLOTHURN: & *Canton*, Switzerland 40 N8
Solo-Tyube: Kazakh., U.S.S.R. 51 L6
Solre-le-Château: France 36 K5
Solsona: Spain 35 G16
Solta: *i.*, Yugoslavia 38 P15
Soltau: W. Germany 45 P3
Solton: U.S.S.R. 51 P4
Soluk: Libya 33 G5
Solund: *i.*, Norway 47 J6
Solunshan: Inner Mongolia, China 63 W5
Solva: Dyfed, Wales 24 L16
Sölvesborg: Sweden 47 O8
Solway Firth: England/Scotland 26 O10
SOLWEZI: North-Western, Zambia 77 C5
Sol-Yeletsk: U.S.S.R. 50 J4
Soma: Turkey 39 U17
Somain: France 36 J5

Somalia: *Republic* 79 *Ins.*
Cap.: Mogadiscio
Area: 246,155 sq. miles (637,541 sq. km.)
Pop.: 2,941,000 (*1972 E*)

Somali Basin: Indian Ocean 9 O 50E
Sombernon: France 36 K8
Sombor: Yugoslavia 39 Q14
Sombrero: *i.* (Br.), Virgin Is. 87 b1
Şomcuta Mare: Romania 43 S13
Somercotes, North: Lincs., England 27 W13
Somero: Finland 47 S6
Somerset: Ky., U.S.A. 88 J7
Somerset: *Co.*, England (*co. town* Taunton) 24 P17
Somerset East: & *Dist.*, S. Africa 75 F6
Somerset I.: Bermudas 87 *Ins.*
Somerset I.: N.W.T., Canada 84 k3
Somerset West: & *Dist.*, S. Africa 74 C7
Somersham: Cambs., Eng. 25 V15
Somerton: Som., England 24 Q17
Somerton: *airfield*, I. of Wight, England 25 T18
Somerville: Tenn., U.S.A. 90 G8
Somerville: Tex., U.S.A. 90 C10
Someş: *riv.*, Romania 43 S13
Someşu: *riv.*, Romania 43 S13
Somkele: Natal, S. Africa 75 K4
Sommariva: Italy 40 N11
Somme: *Dept.*, France (*cap.* Amiens) 36 H6
Somme: *riv.*, France 36 G5
Sommen Lake: Sweden 47 O8
Sommepy: France 36 K6
Sömmerda: E. Germany 45 R4
Somme-Tourbe: France 36 K6
Sommières: France 37 K12
Sompeta: Andhra Pradesh, India 59 O11
Sompuis: France 36 K7
Son: *riv.*, India 59 O10
Sona: Panama 87 I16
Soncino: Italy 40 P10
Sønderborg: Denmark 47 L9
Sonderhausen: E. Germany 45 Q4
Søndre Strømfjord: Grnld. 85 o4
Sondrio: Italy 40 P9
Sonepat: Haryana, India 58 N9
Sonepur: Orissa, India 59 O10
Song: Nigeria 81 G3
Song: Sarawak, Malaysia 65 E6
Song: Thailand 64 C3
Songarh: Gujarat, India 58 M10
Sông-can: Vietnam 64 D4
SONGEA: Ruvuma, Tanzania 77 E5
Songelskiy: U.S.S.R. 46 W2
Songeons: France 36 G6
Songkhla (Singora): Thailand 64 C5
Songkhla: *State*, Thailand 65 b10
Songhone: Laos 64 D3
Songololo: Zaire 81 G6
Songo Songo I.: Tanzania 77 E4
Songwe: Malawi 77 D4
Sonhat: Madhya Pradesh, India 59 O10
Sonkajärvi: Finland 46 U5
Sonkovo: U.S.S.R. 50 E3
Son La: Vietnam 64 C2
Sonmiani: & *bay*, Baluchistan, Pakistan 58 L9
Sonneberg: E. Germany 45 R5
Sonntag: Austria 40 P8
Sonobe: Japan 63 d3
Sonoita: Mexico 93 E6
Sononder: S. Africa 74 D4
Sonora: Calif., U.S.A. 93 C5
Sonora: Tex., U.S.A. 93 G6
Sonora: *State & riv.*, Mexico (*cap.* Hermosillo) 93 E7
Sonskiy: U.S.S.R. 51 Q4
Sonsón: Colombia 94 B2
Sonsonate: El Salvador 86 L15
Sonsorol: *i.*, Caroline Is. 61 L10
Sonstraal: S. Africa 74 E3
Sontay: Vietnam 64 D2
Sonthofen: W. Germany 40 Q8
Sontra: W. Germany 45 P4
Soon Wald: *mtns.*, W. Ger. 44 N6
Sopka Klyuchevskaya: *mtn.*, Kamchatka, U.S.S.R. 49 S6
Sopley: Dorset, England 25 S18
Sopot: Poland 43 Q9
Soppero: Sweden 46 R2
Sopron: Hungary 43 P13
Sora: Italy 38 N16
Sora: ancient Latin city on river Liri about 55 miles ESE. of Rome 38 N16
Soracte: mtn. about 25 miles N. of Rome overlooking right bank of Tiber. 38 N15
Sorata: Bolivia 94 D7
Sorbas: Spain 35 E18
Sorbie: Dumf. & Gall., Scot. 29 N10
Sorbiodunum: Roman Settlement at Old Sarum about 2m. N. of Salisbury, Eng. 25 S17
Sorbygden: Sweden 46 P5
Sordwana Bay: S. Africa 75 K3
Sore: France 37 E11
Sorel: Que., Canada 89 P2
Sorell: Tas., Australia 68 H8
Soresina: Italy 40 P10
Sørfjord: Norway 46 N3
Sørflatanger: Norway 46 M4
Sorges: France 37 F10
Sorgono: Sardinia 38 L16
Sorgun: Turkey 56 D2
SORIA: & *Prov.*, Spain 35 E16
Soriano: Uruguay 96 D3
Sorido: Schouten Is., Indonesia 61 M12
Sorisdale: Inner Hebr., Scot. 29 J6
Sorkhekan: Iran 57 L5
Sorkjosen: Norway 46 R2
Sørli: Norway 46 N4
Sorn: Strath., Scotland 29 N8
Sorocaba: Brazil 96 F1
Sorochinsk: U.S.S.R. 50 H4
Sørøen: *i.*, Norway 46 S1
Soroki: Moldavia, U.S.S.R. 43 V12
Sorokino: U.S.S.R. 51 P4
Sorol: *i.*, Caroline Is. 61 N10
Soromesi's: Botswana 77 B6
Sorong: West Irian, Indonesia 61 L12
Soroti: Uganda 76 D2
Sørøysundet: *sound* Norway 46 S1
Sorraia: *riv.*, Portugal 35 B17
Sorrento: Italy 38 O16
Sorrento: Vict., Australia 71 F12
Sorsele: Sweden 46 P4
Sorso: Sardinia 38 L16
Sorsogon: Luzon, Phil. 64 G4
Sort: Spain 35 G15
Sortavala: Karelian A.S.S. Rep., U.S.S.R. 47 W6
Sortland: Vesterålen, Nor. 46 O2
Sør Trøndelag: *Co.*, Norway (*cap.* Trondheim) 46 M5
Sörup: W. Germany 44 P1
Sorvatine: Sweden 47 N5
Sos: Spain 35 F15
Sosan: S. Korea 63 X7
Sošice: Yugoslavia 41 V10
Sosneado: *mtn.*, Argentina 96 B3
Sosnovo: U.S.S.R. 47 W6
Sosnovoborsk: U.S.S.R. 50 G4
Sosnowiec: Poland 43 Q11
Sosoktu: Inner Mongolia, China 62 S6
Sospel: France 40 N12
Sosso: Central African Rep. 81 H4
Sossus Vlei: *lake*, S.W. Afr. 74 A2
Šoštanj: Yugoslavia 41 V9
Sos'va: U.S.S.R. 51 K3
Sos'va, North: *riv.*, U.S.S.R. 51 K2
Sos'vinskaya Kul'tbaza: U.S.S.R. 51 K2
Sota: *riv.*, Benin 81 E2
Sotik: Kenya 76 D3
Sotkamo: Finland 46 V4
Soto: Argentina 96 B3
Sotra: *i.*, Norway 47 J6
Sottevast: France 36 D6
Sotteville-les-Rouen: France 36 G6
Sotuba Barrage: Niger Riv., Mali 80 C2
Souab: *wadi*, Syria 57 G4
Soual: France 37 H12
Souan Ké: Congo 81 G4
Soubré: Ivory Coast 80 C3
Souffiay: Congo 81 G4
Souflion: Greece 39 U16
Soufrière: St. Lucia, Windward Is. 87 c4
Sougueta: Guinea 80 B2
Sougueur: Algeria 35 G19
Souillac: France 37 G11
Souk Ahras: Algeria 38 K18
Souk el Arba: Morocco 80 K8
Souk el Arba: Tunisia *see* Jendouba
Souk el Khemis: Tunisia 38 L18
Souk Jemaa des Oulad Abbou: Morocco 80 K8
Soukouralla: Guinea 80 C3
Soulac: France 37 D10
Soulby: Cumbria, England 26 R11
Soultz: France 40 N7
Soummam: *riv.*, Algeria 35 J18
Sounfat: Mali 78 E5
Sountellane: *well*, Niger 81 G1
Souppes: France 36 H7
Soure: Brazil 94 H4
Sour El Ghozlane: Algeria 35 H18
Souris: Man., Canada 92 G3
Souris: P.E.I., Canada 89 U2
Souris: *riv.*, N. Dak., U.S.A. 92 G3
Sour Lake: *city*, Tex., U.S.A. 90 D10
Sournia: France 37 H13
Sous: *riv.*, Morocco 80 K8
Sousceyrac: France 37 H11
Sousel: Brazil 94 G4
Sousel: Portugal 35 C17
SOUSSE: & *Governorate*, Tunisia 38 M19
Soustons: France 37 D12
Souterraine, La: France 37 G9
South: *Dist.*, Botswana 75 G2

South Africa: *Republic* 74/5
Cap.: Pretoria
Legislative Cap.: Cape Town
Area: 471,819 sq. miles (1,222,011 sq. km.)
Pop.: 22,092,000 (*1971 E*)

Southam: War., England 25 T15
Southampton: Hants., Eng. 25 T18
Southampton: Ont., Canada 88 L3
Southampton: *i.* & *cape*, Can. 85 l5
South Andaman: *i.*, Andaman Is. 59 Q12
South Atlantic Ocean 8
South Auckland—Bay of Plenty: *Dist.*, N.I., New Zealand (*cap.* Hamilton) 70 P14
South Australia: *State*, Austl. (*cap.* Adelaide) 69 F6
South Australian Basin: S. Pacific Ocean 7 40S 120E
South Bank: Cleve., Yorks. 26 T10
South Barrule: *hill*, I. of Man, U.K. 26 M11
South Baymouth: Ont., Canada 88 K3
South Bend: Ind., U.S.A. 88 H5
South Bend: Wash., U.S.A. 92 C3
South Benfleet: Essex, England 25 X16
South Berwick: Maine, U.S.A. 89 Q4
South Beveland: *i.*, Neth. 44 J4
South Blackwater: Queens., Australia 70 H5
Southborough: Kent, Eng. 25 W17
South Boston: Va., U.S.A. 89 M7
South Brent: Devon, Eng. 24 O19
Southbridge: South I., N.Z. 70 O16
South Buganda: *Dist.*, Uganda 76 D2
South Cape: Spitsbergen 48 c2
South Cape: Stewart I., N.Z. 71 L18
South Carolina: *State*, U.S.A. (*cap.* Columbia) 91 L9
South Cave: *village*, Humb., England 27 U12
South Charleston: Va., U.S.A. 88 L6
South Charlton: Northumb., England 26 S9
South China Sea: SE. Asia 64 E4
South Clifton: Notts., Eng. 27 U13
South Creake: Norf., Eng. 25 X14
South Dakota: *State*, U.S.A. (*cap.* Pierre) 92 G4
South Dorset Downs: *hills*, Dorset, England 24 R18
South Downs: *hills*, E./W. Sussex, England 25 U18
South Dvina: *riv.*, U.S.S.R. 48 d6
South East Cape: Tas., Austl. 68 H8
Southeast Cape: Vict., Austl. 71 G12
Southeast Indian Basin 9 35S 105E
Southeast Indian Ridge: Indian Ocean 9 45S 90E
Southeast Pacific Basin: S. Pacific Ocean 9 65S 110W
Southeast Pass: La., U.S.A. 90 *Ins.*
Southend: Strath., Scotland 29 K9
Southend on Sea: Essex, England 25 X16
Southern: *Dist.*, Uganda 76 D2
Southern: *Prov.*, Sierra Leone (*cap.* Bo) 80 B3
Southern: *Prov.*, Zambia (*cap.* Maramba) 77 C6
Southern Alps: *range*, South I., New Zealand 70 N16
Southern Cross: W. Australia 68 B6
Southern Indian Lake: Man., Canada 92 H1
Southern Ocean 9
Southern Pines: N.C., U.S.A. 91 M8
Southern Region: Sudan (*cap.* Juba) 76
Southern Sierra Madre: *range*, Mexico 86 K14
Southern Uplands: *mtns.*, Scotland 29 N9
Southery: Norf., England 25 W14
South Esk: *riv.*, Tay., Scot. 29 Q6
South Fiji Basin: S. Pacific Ocean 7 30S 175E
South Foreland: *cape*, Kent, England 25 Y17
South Fulton: Tenn., U.S.A. 88 G7
South Gamboa: Panama 94 *Ins.*
South Gate: Dyfed, Wales 24 N15
South Georgia: *i.*, (Br.), Atlantic Ocean 95 K14
South Glamorgan: *Co.*, Wales (*co. town* Cardiff) 24 P17
South Hafun Bay: Somalia 79 S17
South Hams: *dist.*, Devon, Eng. 24 O19
South Harris: *dist.*, Outer Hebr., Scotland 28 H4
South Haven: Mich., U.S.A. 88 H4
South Hayling: Hants., Eng. 25 U18
South Hetton: Durham, Eng. 26 T10
South Hill: Va., U.S.A. 89 M7
Southhills: *town*, Natal, S. Africa 75 J5
South Holland: *Prov.*, Neth. (*cap.* The Hague) 44 K3
South Honshu Ridge: N. Pacific Ocean 7 15N 140E
South Horr: Kenya 76 E2
South Indian Basin: Southern Ocean 9 60S 55E
South I.: New Zealand 70 N16
South Kirkby: W. Yorks., Eng. 27 T12

South Korea: *Republic* 63 X7
Cap.: Seoul
Area: 38,031 sq. miles (98,500 sq. km.)
Pop.: 33,265,000 (*1972 E*)

South Kvaløy: *i.*, Norway 46 Q2
South Lake Eyre: *lake*, S. Australia 69 F5
Southland: *Dist.*, South I., N.Z. (*cap.* Invercargill) 71 L17
South Luconia Shoals: S. China Sea 65 E5
South Magnetic Pole: Antarctica 9 70S 135E
South Marutea: *i.*, Tuamotu Arch. 83 h4
South Milwaukee: Wis., U.S.A. 88 H4
South Milton: Devon, England 24 O19
South Mimms: Herts., England 25 V16
Southminster: Essex, Eng. 25 X16
South Molton: Devon, Eng. 24 O17
South Moor: *town*, Dur., England 26 S10
South Morar: *dist.*, High., Scotland 28 K6
South Nahanni: *riv.*, Canada 84 G5
South Natuna Is.: Indon. 65 D6
South Ockendon: Essex, England 25 W16
South Orkney Is.: Southern Ocean 9 65S 50W
South Osetia: *Auton. Reg.*, Georgia, U.S.S.R. (*cap.* Tskhinvali) 50 F6
South Pacific Ocean 7
South Pagai: *i.*, Mentawai Is., Indonesia 65 C7
South Perrott: Dorset, Eng. 24 Q18
South Petherton: Som., Eng. 24 Q18
South Petherwin: Corn., Eng. 24 N18
South Pittsburg: Tenn., U.S.A. 91 J8
South Point: *cape*, Mich., U.S.A. 88 K3
South Pole: Antarctica 9 90S
South Porcupine: Ont., Can. 88 L1
Southport: Mers., England 27 P12
Southport: N.C., U.S.A. 91 M9
Southport: N. Territ., Austl. 68 E2
Southport: Queens., Austl. 70 K6
South Portland: Maine, U.S.A. 89 Q4
South Riding Rock: *i.*, Bahamas 91 M13
South Ronaldsay: *i.*, Orkney Is. 28 Q2
South St. Paul: Minn., U.S.A. 88 E3
South Sandwich Trench: Southern Ocean 8 60S 25W
South Saskatchewan: *riv.*, Alta./Sask., Canada 92 F2
South Shetland Is.: Antarctica 9 65S 65W
SOUTH SHIELDS: Tyne & Wear, England 26 T10
South Sioux City: Nebr., U.S.A. 92 H4
South Sound: Repub. of Ireland 31 C13
South Stoke: Oxon., England 25 T16
South Taranaki Bight: North I., New Zealand 70 P14
South Tyne: *riv.*, Northumb., England 26 R10
South Udde: *cape*, Öland, Sweden 47 P8
South Uist: *i.*, Outer Hebr., Scotland 28 G5

South Vietnam: *see* **Vietnam**

Southwark: Gt. Ldn., England 25 V17
Southwell: Notts., England 27 U13
South Wellesley I.: Queens., Australia 69 F3

South-West Africa (Namibia): UN Trust Territory administered by S. Africa 73 H14
Cap.: Windhoek
Area: 318,261 sq. miles (824,296 sq. km.)
Pop.: 650,000 (*1971 E*)

South West Cay: *i.*, (U.S.A./Col.), Caribbean Sea 87 I15
Southwest Indian Basin: Indian Ocean 9 35S 65E
Southwest Indian Ridge: Indian Ocean 9 35S 50E
Southwest Pacific Basin: S. Pacific Ocean 7 35S 150W
Southwest Pass: La., U.S.A. 90 *Ins.*
Southwick: Tyne & Wear, England 26 T10
Southwick: Hants., England 25 T18
South Wingfield: Derby., England 27 T13
South Witham: Lincs., England 27 U14
Southwold: Suff., England 25 Z15
Southwood: Queens., Austl. 70 H6
South Wootton: Norf., England 25 W14
South Yorkshire: *Metropolitan Co.*, England (*co. town* Sheffield) 27 T11
South Zeal: Devon, England 24 O18
Soutpan: O.F.S., S. Africa 75 G4
Souvenir: Fr. Guiana 94 G3
Souvigny: France 37 J9
Souza: Brazil 94 K5
Soven: Argentina 96 B3
Sovetsk (Tilsit): U.S.S.R. 47 R9
Sovetsk: Kirov, U.S.S.R. 50 G3
Sovetskoye: U.S.S.R. 50 G4
Soviet Harbour: U.S.S.R. 49 Q8
Soviet Union: *see* **Union of Soviet Socialist Republics.**
Sowerby: N. Yorks., England 26 T11
Sowerby Bridge: W. Yorks., England 27 S12
Soya (La Perouse) Str.: U.S.S.R./Japan 63 ZZ5
Soyopa: Mexico 93 F7
Sozh: *riv.*, U.S.S.R. 50 D4
Sozopol: Bulgaria 39 U15
Spa: Belgium 44 L5

Spain: *Monarchy* 35
Cap.: Madrid
Area: 194,883 sq. miles (504,747 sq. km.)
Pop.: 34,134,000 (*1971 E*)

Spalato: Italian name for town of Split, on coast of Yugoslavia 38 P15
Spalding: Lincs., England 25 V14
Spalding: S. Australia 71 C9
Spaldwick: Cambs., England 25 V15
Spandau: E. Germany 45 T3
Spångenäs: Sweden 47 P8
Spanish: *riv.*, Ont., Canada 88 L2
Spanish Guinea *see* **Equatorial Guinea.**

Spanish Sahara: *see* **Western Sahara**
Spanish Town: Jamaica 86 *Ins.*
Sparkford: Som., England 24 Q17
Sparks: Nev., U.S.A. 93 D5
Sparta: Ga., U.S.A. 91 K9
Sparta (Spárti): Greece 39 S18
Sparta: Ill., U.S.A. 88 G6
Sparta: Mich., U.S.A. 88 J4
Sparta: Tenn., U.S.A. 91 J8
Sparta: Wis., U.S.A. 88 F4
Spartanburg: S.C., U.S.A. 91 L8
Spartel, Cape: Morocco (Gib. *Inset*) 32 *Ins.*
Spárti: Greece 39 S18
Spartivento, Cape: Italy 38 P18
Spartivento, Cape: Sardinia 38 L17
Spas-Demensk: U.S.S.R. 50 D4
Spassk: U.S.S.R. 63 Y6
Spasskoye: Kazakh., U.S.S.R. 51 L4
Spatha, Cape: Crete 39 S19
Spean, Glen: High., Scotland 28 M6
Spean Bridge: High., Scotland 28 M6
Spearfish: S. Dak., U.S.A. 92 G4
Spearman: Tex., U.S.A. 90 A7
Speedwell, Cape: U.S.S.R. 48 G2
Speeton: N. Yorks., England 26 V11
Speke: *airfield*, Mers., Eng. 27 Q13
Speke Gulf: Lake Victoria 76 D3
Spelonken: Trans., S. Africa 75 J1
Spencer: Ind., U.S.A. 88 H6
Spencer: Iowa, U.S.A. 92 H4
Spencer: W. Va., U.S.A. 88 L6
Spencer, Cape: Alaska, U.S.A. 84 F6
Spencer, Cape: S. Australia 71 B10
Spencer's Gulf: S. Australia 71 B10
Spence's Bridge: B.C., Can. 92 C2
Spennymoor: Durham, England 26 S10
Spenser Mtns.: South I., New Zealand 70 O16
Spercheus: river flowing S. of Lamia into G. of *Malis*, Greece 39 S17
Sperrin Mtns.: Tyr., N. Ireland 30 H10
Spessart: *hills*, W. Germany 44 P6
Spetsai: *i.*, Greece 39 S18
Spettisbury: Dorset, Eng. 24 R18
Spey: *riv.*, Gram., Scotland 28 P4
Spey, Strath: *val.*, Highland/Grampian, Scotland 28 O5
Speyer: W. Germany 44 O6
Spezia, La: Italy 40 P11
Sphacteria: island in bay of Navarino, separated by narrow channel from peninsula of Pilos, Greece 39 R18
Spicer Is.: Canada 85 M4
Spiddle: Galway, Repub. of Ireland 31 C13
Spieka: W. Germany 44 O2
Spiekeroog: *i.*, E. Frisian Is., W. Germany 44 N2
Spiez: Switzerland 40 N9
Spigno: Italy 40 O11
Spilimbergo: Italy 41 S9
Spilsby: Lincs., England 27 W13
Spinazzola: Italy 38 P16
Spincourt: France 36 L6
Spion Kop: *mtn.*, Natal, S. Africa 75 H4
Spirit Lake: *city*, Idaho, U.S.A. 92 D3
Spirit River: *town*, Alta., Canada 92 D1
Spirovo: U.S.S.R. 50 E3
Spišská Nová Ves: Czech. 43 R12
Spithead: *str.*, I. of Wight/England 25 T18
Spitsbergen (Svalbard): *is.* (Nor.) Arctic O. (*cap.* Longyearbyen) 48 c2
Spitskop: S. Africa 75 F4
Spittal: Austria 41 T9
Spittal: Dyfed, Wales 24 M16
Spittal of Glenshee: Tayside, Scotland 29 P6
Spitz: Austria 41 V7
Split: Yugoslavia 38 P15
Split Lake: Man., Canada 92 H1
Splugen Pass: Switz./Italy 40 P9
Spofforth: N. Yorks., England 27 T12
Spokane: Wash., U.S.A. 92 D3
Spoleto: Italy 38 N15
Spondon: Derby., England 27 T14
Spooner: Wis., U.S.A. 88 F3
Sporades (Dodecanese): *is.*, Greece 39 U18
Sporades, Northern: *is.*, Grc. 39 T17
Sporyy Navook, Cape: U.S.S.R. 48 h2
Sprague: Wash., U.S.A. 92 D3
Spratly I.: S. China Sea 64 E5

Spray—Sucre 189

Spray: N.C., U.S.A. **89** M7
Spree: *riv.*, E. Germany **45** T3
Spremberg: E. Germany **45** U4
Sprenge: W. Germany **45** Q1
Spresiano: Italy **41** S10
Spreyton: Devon, England **24** O18
Sprigg: S. Africa **74** D4
Springbok: S. Africa **74** B4
Springbok Flats: Trans., S. Africa **75** H2
Springburn: South I., N.Z. **70** N16
Spring City: Tenn., U.S.A. **91** J8
Springdale: Ark., U.S.A. **90** D7
Springdale: Newf., Canada **85** u2
Springe: W. Germany **44** P3
Springer: N. Mex., U.S.A. **93** G5
Springerville: Ariz., U.S.A. **93** F6
Springfield: Colo., U.S.A. **93** G5
Springfield: Fife, Scotland **29** P7
SPRINGFIELD: Ill., U.S.A. **88** G6
Springfield: Ky., U.S.A. **88** J7
Springfield: Mass., U.S.A. **89** P4
Springfield: Minn., U.S.A. **92** J4
Springfield: Mo., U.S.A. **88** E7
Springfield: Ohio, U.S.A. **88** K6
Springfield: Oreg., U.S.A. **92** C4
Springfield: South I., N.Z. **70** N16
Springfield: Tenn., U.S.A. **88** H7
Springfield: Vt., U.S.A. **89** P4
Springfield Place-Lake View: Mich., U.S.A. **88** J4
Springfontein: O.F.S., S. Afr. **75** F5
Springhill: La., U.S.A. **90** E9
Springhill: N.S., Canada **89** T3
Springlands: Guyana **87** e7
Spring Mtns.: Nev., U.S.A. **93** D5
Springs: Trans., S. Africa **74** N *Ins.*
Springs: *Dist.*, Trans., S. Africa **75** H3
Springsure: Queens., Austl. **70** H5
Spring Valley: *town*, Minn., U.S.A. **88** E4
Spring Valley: *town*, S. Afr. **75** G6
Springville: N.Y., U.S.A. **89** M4
Springville: Utah, U.S.A. **93** E4
Sprowston: Norf., England **25** Y14
Spruce Mount: Nev., U.S.A. **93** E4
Spur: Tex., U.S.A. **93** G6
Spurn Head: *cape*, Humberside, England **27** W12
Squamish: B.C., Canada **92** C3
Squillace: & *gulf*, Italy **38** P17
Srakay: Lithuania, U.S.S.R. **47** T9
Srebrnica: Yugoslavia **39** Q14
Sredets: Bulgaria **39** U15
Sredne Kolymsk: U.S.S.R. **49** R4
Śrem: Poland **45** W3
Sremska Mitrovica: Yugo. **39** Q14
Srepnica: Poland **45** U2
Srepok: *riv.*, Cambodia **64** D4
Sretensk: U.S.S.R. **49** n7
Sri Buat: *i.*, Malaya, Malaysia **65** c12

Sri Lanka: *Republic* **58** O13
Cap.: Colombo
Area: 25,322 sq. miles
(65,584 sq. km.)
Pop.: 12,711,143 (*1971 C*)

SRINAGAR: *summer cap. of Indian held territory*, Jammu & Kashmir **58** M8
Sri Racha: Thailand **64** C4
Srivilliputtur: Tamil Nadu, India **58** N13
Srnetica: Yugoslavia **38** P14
Środa: Poland **43** P10
Środa Śląska: Poland **45** W4
Staber Huk: *cape*, Fehmarn, W. Germany **45** R1
Stack, Loch: High., Scot. **28** M3
Stack Skerry: *rock*, Scotland **28** N2
Stacks Mtns.: Kerry, Repub. of Ireland **31** B15
Stade: W. Germany **44** P2
Stade: *Dist.*, Lower Saxony, West Germany **44** O2
Stadharholskirkja: Iceland **46** c4
Stadhastadhur: Iceland **46** b4
Stadhur: Iceland **46** c4
Stadl: Austria **41** T8
Stadskanaal: Netherlands **44** M3
Stadthagen: W. Germany **44** P3
Stadtilm: E. Germany **45** R5
Stadtlauringen: W. Germany **45** Q5
Stadtoldendorf: W. Germany **44** P4
Stadtroda: E. Germany **45** R5
Staffa: *i.*, Inner Hebr., Scot. **29** J7
Stäffelstein: W. Germany **45** R5
Staffin: Inner Hebr., Scot. **28** J4
Stafford: Kans., U.S.A. **90** B7
STAFFORD: Staffs., England **27** R14
Staffordshire: *Co.*, England (*co. town* Stafford) **27** R14
Stagno: Italy **40** Q12
Staierdorf Anina: Romania **39** R14
Staincross: W. Yorks., Eng. **27** S12
Staindrop: Durham, Eng. **26** S10
Staines: Gt. Ldn., England **25** U17
Stainforth: N. Yorks., England **27** R11
Stainforth: S. Yorks., England **27** T12
Stainland: W. Yorks., Eng. **27** S12
Stainmore: *dist.*, Cumbria/Durham, England **26** R10
Stainton: Cleve., England **26** T10
Staintondale: *village*, N. Yorks., England **26** V11
Stainz: Austria **41** V9
Staithes: Cleve., England **26** U10
Stake, Hill of: Strath., Scot. **29** M8
Stalać: Yugoslavia **39** R15
Stålboga: Sweden **47** P7
Stalbridge: Dorset, England **24** R18
Stalham: Norf., England **25** Z14
Ställdalen: Sweden **47** O7
Stallworthy, Cape: N.W.T., Canada **84** k1
Stalon: Sweden **46** O4
Stalonäs: Sweden **46** O4
Stalybridge: Ches., England **27** R13
Stamford: Conn., U.S.A. **89** P5
Stamford: Lincs., England **25** V14
Stamford: N.Y., U.S.A. **89** O4
Stamford: Queens., Austl. **69** G4
Stamford: Tex., U.S.A. **90** B9
Stamford Bridge: Humb., England **27** U12
Stamfordham: Northumb., England **26** S9
Stamps: Ark., U.S.A. **90** E9
Stamullin: Meath, Repub. of Ireland **30** J12
Stanchik: U.S.S.R. **49** R3
Standerton: & *Dist.*, Trans., S. Africa **75** H3
Standish: Gt. Man., Eng. **27** Q12
Standlake: Oxon., England **25** T16
Standon: Herts., England **25** W16
Standon: Staffs., England **27** R14
Stanford: Ky., U.S.A. **88** J7
Stanford: Mont., U.S.A. **92** E3
Stanford: S. Africa **74** C7
Stanford in the Vale: Oxon., England **25** S16
Stange: Norway **47** M6
Stanger: Natal, S. Africa **75** J4
Stangfjord: Norway **47** J6
Stanghella: Italy **41** R10
Stanhope: Durham, Eng. **26** R10
Stanley: Durham, England **26** S10
STANLEY: Falkland Is. (Br.) **95** F14
Stanley: N. Dak., U.S.A. **92** G3
Stanley: Tayside, Scotland **29** P7
Stanley: Tas., Australia **68** H8
Stanley: Wis., U.S.A. **88** F3
Stanley: W. Yorks., England **27** T12
Stanley Falls: *see* Boyoma Falls
Stanley Pool: *lake, see* Pool Malebo.
Stanleyville: *see* Kisangani.
Stann Creek: *town*, Belize **86** *Ins.*
Stannington: Northumb., England **26** S9
Stannum: N.S.W., Austl. **71** J7
Stanovoy Range: U.S.S.R. **49** o6
STANS: Unterwalden, Switz. **40** O9
Stansbury: S. Australia **71** B10
Stansted: Essex, England **25** W16
Stanthorpe: Queens., Austl. **71** J7
Stanton: Nebr., U.S.A. **92** H4
Stanton: N. Dak., U.S.A. **92** G3
Stanton: N.W.T., Canada **84** G4
Stanton: Suff., England **25** X15
Stanton Harcourt: Oxon., England **25** T16
Stanton upon Hine Heath: Salop, England **27** Q14
Stanway: Glos., England **24** S16
Stanwix: site of fort of Hadrian's Wall on N. bank of river Eden opposite Carlisle, England **26** Q10
Stapleford: Notts., England **27** T14
Stapleford: Wilts., England **24** S17
Stapleford Abbots: Essex, England **25** W16
Staple Hill: Som., England **24** P18
Staplehurst: Kent, England **25** X17
Staples: Minn., U.S.A. **88** D2
Stara Gradiška: Yugoslavia **38** P14
Stara Pazova: Yugoslavia **39** R14
Staraya Russa: U.S.S.R. **50** D3
Stara Zagora: Bulgaria **39** T15
Starcross: Devon, England **24** P18
Stargard: E. Germany **45** T2
Stargard: Poland **45** V2
Starigrad: Yugoslavia **41** U11
Staritsa: U.S.S.R. **50** E3
Starke: Fla., U.S.A. **91** K11
Starkville: Miss., U.S.A. **90** G9
Starnberg: W. Germany **41** R7
Starobei'sk: Ukraine **50** E5
Starobin: Byelorussia **43** U10
Starodub: U.S.S.R. **50** D4
Starogard: Poland **43** Q10
Starokonstantinov: Ukraine **43** U12
Staro Orekhovo: Bulgaria **39** U15
Start Point: *cape*, Devon, England **24** O19
Start Point: *cape*, Orkney Is., Scotland **28** *Ins.*
Stary Sącz: Poland **43** R12
Staryy Biryuzyak: U.S.S.R. **50** G6
Staryy Chartoriysk: Ukraine **43** T11
Staryy Dorogi: Byelorussia **43** V10
Staryy Oskol: U.S.S.R. **50** E4
Staryy Sambor: Ukraine **43** S12
Staryy Tuguz: Kazakh., U.S.S.R. **51** K5
Stassfurt: E. Germany **45** R4
Staszów: Poland **43** R11
State College: Pa., U.S.A. **89** N5
Staten I.: Argentina **95** E14
Statesboro: Ga., U.S.A. **91** L9
Statesville: N.C., U.S.A. **91** L8
Stathern: Leics., England **27** U14
Staufen: Bavaria, W. Germany **40** Q8
Staufen: Baden Württemberg, W. Germany **40** N8
Staufenberg: W. Germany **44** O5
Staughton, Great: Cambs., England **25** V15
Staunton: Glos., England **24** R16
Staunton: Ill., U.S.A. **88** G6
Staunton: Va., U.S.A. **89** M6
STAVANGER: Rogaland, Nor. **47** J7
Staveley: Derby., England **27** T13
Staveley: N. Yorks., England **28** T11
Stavelot: Belgium **44** L5
Stavenhagen: E. Germany **45** S2
Staveren: Netherlands **44** L3
Stavern: Norway **47** M7
Staverton: Northants., Eng. **25** T15
STAVROPOL': & *Territ.*, U.S.S.R. **50** F5
Stawell: Vict., Australia **71** E11
Staxigoe: High., Scotland **28** P3
Stayton: Oreg., U.S.A. **92** C4
Steamboat Springs: *city*, Colo., U.S.A. **93** F4
Stearns: Ky., U.S.A. **88** J7
Stebbing: Essex, England **25** W16
Steeg: Austria **41** T8
Steele: Mo., U.S.A. **88** G7
Steelpoort: Trans., S. Africa **75** J2
Steelpoort: *riv.*, Trans., S. Africa **75** H2
Steenbokpan: O.F.S., S. Africa **75** F3
Steens Mt.: Oreg., U.S.A. **92** D4
Steenstrups Glac.: Grnld. **85** o2
Steeping, Little: Lincs., Eng. **27** W13
Steeping: *riv.*, Lincs., Eng. **27** W13
Steeple: Essex, England **25** X16
Steeple Bumpstead: Essex, England **25** W15
Steeple Claydon: Bucks., England **25** U16
Steeple Morden: Cambs., England **25** V15
Steep Rock: *town*, Man., Canada **92** H2
Steep Rock Lake: Ont., Can. **88** E1
Steeton: N. Yorks., England **27** S12
Stefanie, Lake: Ethiopia **76** E2
Stegelitz: E. Germany **45** R3
Stegi: *see* Siteki
Steiermark: *see* Styria
Steigerwald: *mtns.*, W. Germany **45** Q6
Steimbke: W. Germany **44** P3
Steinach: E. Germany **45** R5
Steinach: Styria, Austria **41** U8
Steinach: Tirol, Austria **41** R8
Steinau: W. Germany **44** O2
Steinbach: Man., Canada **92** H3
Steinbach: W. Germany **40** O7
Steinfeld: W. Germany **44** O3
Steinfeld: *geog. reg.*, Austria **41** W8
Steinfort: Luxembourg **44** L6
Steinhagen: E. Germany **45** S1
Steinhausen: S.W. Africa **77** A7
Steinheim: W. Germany **44** P4
Steinhudersee: *lake*, W. Ger. **44** P3
STEINKJER: Nord-Trøndelag, Norway **46** M4
Steinkopf: S. Africa **74** B4
Stekene: Belgium **44** K4
Stellarton: N.S., Canada **89** U3
Stellenbosch: & *Dist.*, S. Afr. **74** C6
Stelvio National Park: Italy **40** Q9
Stelvio Pass: Switz./Italy **40** Q9
Stemshaug: Norway **46** L5
Stenay: France **36** L6
Stendal: E. Germany **45** R3
Stenhousemuir: Central, Scotland **29** O7
Stenico: Italy **41** Q9
Stenness, Loch of: Mainland, Orkney Is. **28** P2
Stensele: Sweden **46** P4
Stenton: Loth., Scotland **29** Q8
Stepan': Ukraine **43** U11
STEPANAKERT: Nagorno-Karabakh, Azerbaydzhan, U.S.S.R. **57** K2
Stepanavan: Armenia, U.S.S.R. **57** J1
Stepaside: Dublin, Repub. of Ireland **31** J13
Stephenville: Newf., Canada **85** t2
Stephenville: Tex., U.S.A. **90** B9
Stepnyak: Kazakh., U.S.S.R. **51** M4
Sterea Hellas: *reg.*, Greece **39** S17
Sterkspruit: S. Africa **75** G5
Sterkstroom: & *Dist.*, S. Afr. **75** G5
Sterlibashevo: U.S.S.R. **50** J4
Sterling: Colo., U.S.A. **93** G4
Sterling: Ill., U.S.A. **88** G5
Sterling City: Tex., U.S.A. **93** G6
Sterlitamak: U.S.S.R. **50** J4
Sternberg: E. Germany **45** R2
Šternbeck: Czechoslovakia **43** P12
STETTIN (Szczecin): & *Prov.*, Poland **45** U2
Stettiner Haff: *lag.*, Poland/E. Germany **45** U2
Stettler: Alta., Canada **92** E2
Steubenville: Ohio, U.S.A. **88** L5
Stevenage: Herts., England **25** V16
Stevens: Alaska, U.S.A. **84** E4
Stevenson: Ala., U.S.A. **91** J8
Stevens Point: *city*, Wis., U.S.A. **88** G3
Stevenston: Strath., Scot. **29** M8
Steventon: Oxon., England **25** T16
Stewart: B.C., Canada **92** B1
Stewart: *riv.*, Canada **84** f5
Stewart I.: New Zealand **71** L18
Stewart Is.: Solomon Is. **67** M3
Stewarton: Strath., Scotland **29** M8
Stewart River: *settlement*, Yukon, Canada **84** F5
Stewartstown: Tyr., N. Irel. **30** H10
Stewart Town: Jamaica **86** *Ins.*
Stewkley: Bucks., England **25** U16
Steyning: W. Sussex, England **25** V18
Steynsburg: & *Dist.*, S. Afr. **75** F5
Steynsrus: O.F.S., S. Africa **75** G3
Steyr: Austria **41** U7
Steytlerville: & *Dist.*, S. Afr. **75** F6
Stia: Italy **41** R12
Stibb Cross: Devon, Eng. **24** N18
Stichill: Bord., Scotland **29** R8
Sticker: Corn., England **24** M19
Stickford: Lincs., England **27** W13
Stickney: Lincs., England **27** W13
Stiffkey: Norf., England **25** X14
Stigler: Okla., U.S.A. **90** D8
Stikine Mtns.: B.C., Canada **84** f5
Stilis: Greece **39** S17
Still Bay: *town*, S. Africa **74** D7
Stillington: N. Yorks., Eng. **27** T11
Stillwater: Minn., U.S.A. **88** E3
Stillwater: Okla., U.S.A. **90** C7
Stilton: Cambs., England **25** V15
Stilwell: Okla., U.S.A. **90** D8
Stinchar: *riv.*, Strath., Scot. **29** M9
Stinkfontein: S. Africa **74** B4
Štip: Yugoslavia **39** S16
Stirling: Central, Scotland **29** O7
Stirling Range: *mtns.*, W. Australia **68** B6
Stithians: Corn., England **24** L19
Stjernøy: *i.*, Norway **46** S1
Stobo: Borders, Scotland **29** P8
Stockach: W. Germany **40** P8
Stockbridge: Hants., England **25** T17
Stockenstrom: *Dist.*, S. Afr. **75** G6
Stockerau: Austria **41** W7
STOCKHOLM: & *Co.*, Sweden **47** Q7
Stockinbingal: N.S.W., Austl. **71** G10
Stockingford: War., England **27** S14
Stockland: Devon, England **24** P18
Stockport: Gt. Man., England **27** R13
Stocksbridge: S. Yorks., Eng. **27** S13
Stocksfield: Northumb., Eng. **26** S10
Stockton: Calif., U.S.A. **93** C5
Stockton: Ill., U.S.A. **88** F4
Stockton: N.S.W., Austl. **71** J9
Stockton on Tees: Cleveland, England **26** T10
Stockton Plat.: Tex., U.S.A. **93** G6
Stockwith: Notts., England **27** U13
Stoer: & *cape*, High., Scot. **28** L3
Stoffberg: Trans., S. Africa **75** H2
Stogursey: Som., England **24** P17
Stoke: Kent, England **25** X17
Stoke, South: Oxon., Eng. **25** T16
Stoke by Nayland: Suff., England **25** X16
Stoke Climsland: Corn., Eng. **24** N18
Stoke Ferry: Norf., England **25** X14
Stoke Gabriel: Devon, Eng. **24** O19
Stoke Goldington: Bucks., England **25** U15
Stokeinteignhead: Devon, England **24** O18
Stoke Mandeville: Bucks., England **25** U16
Stokenchurch: Bucks., Eng. **25** U16
Stoke on Trent: Staffs., Eng. **27** R13
Stoke Prior: Hereford & Worcester, England **24** R15
Stokesay: Salop, England **24** Q15
Stokesley: N. Yorks., England **26** T11
Stokkseyri: Iceland **46** c5
Stoksund: Norway **46** M4
Štolac: Yugoslavia **38** P15
Stolberg: W. Germany **44** M5
Stolbtsy: Byelorussia **43** U10
Stolin: Byelorussia **43** U11
Stollberg: E. Germany **45** S5
Stolzenfels: S.W. Africa **74** C4
Stómion: Greece **39** S17
Stone: Bucks., England **25** U16
Stone: Glos., England **24** R16
Stone: Staffs., England **27** R14
Stonefield: Mayo, Repub. of Ireland **30** B11
Stonehaven: Gram., Scot. **28** R6
Stonehenge: Queens., Austl. **69** G4
Stonehenge: Wilts., England **25** S17
Stonehouse: Glos., England **24** R16
Stonehouse: Strath., Scotland **29** O8
Stoneykirk: Dumfries & Galloway, Scotland **29** M10
Stoney Stanton: Leics., Eng. **27** T14
Stoneywood: Grampian, Scot. **28** R5
Stongfjord: Norway **47** J6
Stonington Island: *rsch. stn.*, Antarctica **9** 70S 70W
Stonybreck: Shetland Is., Scotland **28** *Ins.*
Stony Crossing (Poonboon): N.S.W., Australia **71** E10
Stonyford: Kilk., Repub. of Ireland **31** G14
Stony Lake: Ont., Canada **89** M3
Stony Rapids: *town*, Sask., Canada **84** J6
Stony Stratford: Bucks., Eng. **25** U15
Stony Tunguska: *riv.*, U.S.S.R. **49** L5
Stopsley: Beds., England **25** V16
Stör: *riv.*, W. Germany **44** P2
Stora Lule Lake: Sweden **46** Q3
Stora Sjöfallet National Park: Sweden **46** P3
Storavan Lake: Sweden **46** Q4
Stord: *i.*, Norway **47** J7
Store Koldewey: *i.*, Grnld. **85** S2
Storelvdal: Norway **47** M6
Storfors: Sweden **47** O7
Storjorm: *lake*, Sweden **46** O4
Storkåge: Sweden **46** R4
Storkerson Bay: N.W.T., Canada **84** g3
Storkmarknes: Norway **46** O2
Storkow: E. Germany **45** T3
Storlien: Sweden **46** N5
Stormberg: S. Africa **75** G5
Storm Berg: *range*, S. Africa **75** G5
Stormont: *dist.*, Tay., Scot. **29** O6
Storms River: *town*, S. Africa **74** E6
Stormsvlei: S. Africa **74** D7
Stornäs: Sweden **46** O4
STORNOWAY: Western Isles, Scotland **28** J3
Stórolfshvoll: Iceland **46** c5
Storozhinets: Ukraine **43** T12
Storr, The: *mtn.*, Inner Hebr., Scotland **28** J4
Storrington: W. Sussex, Eng. **25** V18
Storsjö: Sweden **46** N5
Storsjön: *lake*, Sweden **46** O5
Stort: *riv.*, Essex/Herts., Eng. **25** W16
Storuman: Sweden **46** P4
Stor Uman, Lake: Sweden **46** P4
Storvik: Sweden **47** P6
Storvindeln Lake: Sweden **46** P4
Stotel: W. Germany **44** O2
Stotfold: Beds., England **25** V15
Stottesdon: Salop, England **24** R15
Stoughton: W. Sussex, Eng. **25** U18
Stoughton: Wis., U.S.A. **88** G4
Stour: *riv.*, Dorset, England **24** S18
Stour: *riv.*, Suff./Essex, Eng. **25** X15
Stour, Great: *riv.*, Kent, Eng. **25** Y17
Stourbridge: W. Mid., Eng. **24** R15
Stourport: Hereford & Worcester, England **24** R15
Støvring: Denmark **47** L8
Stow: Lincs., England **27** U13
Stow: Borders, Scotland **29** Q8
Stowlangtoft: Suff., England **25** X15
Stowmarket: Suff., England **25** X15
Stow on the Wold: Glos., England **25** S16
Stoyba: U.S.S.R. **49** P7
Strabane: Tyr., N. Ireland **30** G10
Strachan: Gram., Scotland **28** Q5
Strachur: Strath., Scotland **29** L7
Stradbally: Kerry, Repub. of Ireland **31** A15
Stradbally: Laois, Repub. of Ireland **31** G13
Stradbally: Wat., Repub. of Ireland **31** G15
Stradbroke: Suff., England **25** Y15
Stradella: Italy **40** P10
Stradishall: Suff., England **25** X15
Stradone: Cavan, Repub. of Ireland **30** G12
Straffan: Kild., Repub. of Ireland **31** H13
Strahan: Tas., Australia **68** H8
Straiton: Strath., Scotland **29** M9
Strakonice: Czechoslovakia **45** T6
Stralsund: E. Germany **45** T1
Strand: Hedmark, Norway **47** M6
Strand: Rogaland, Norway **47** J7
Strand: S. Africa **74** C7
Stranda: Norway **46** K5
Strandhill: Sligo, Repub. of Ireland **30** D11
Strandzha: Bulgaria **39** U15
Strang: I. of Man, U.K. **26** M11
Strangford: & *lough*, Down, N. Ireland **30** K11
Strängnäs: Sweden **47** P7
Stranocum: Antrim, N. Irel. **30** J9
Stranorlar: Don., Repub. of Ireland **30** F10
Stranraer: Dumfries & Galloway, Scotland **29** L10
STRASBOURG: Bas-Rhin, Fr. **40** N7
Strasbourg: Sask., Canada **92** G2
Strasburg: Colo., U.S.A. **93** G5
Strasburg: E. Germany **45** T2
Strasburg: N. Dak., U.S.A. **92** G3
Strass: Austria **41** V9
Strassburg: Austria **41** U9
Strassebersbach: W. Germany **44** O5
Stratfield Mortimer: Berks., England **25** T17
Stratford: North I., N.Z. **70** P14
Stratford: Ont., Canada **88** L4
Stratford: Vict., Australia **71** G11
Stratford: Wick., Repub. of Ireland **31** H14
Stratford on Avon: War., England **25** S15
Stratford St. Mary: Essex, England **25** X16
Strathalbyn: S. Australia **71** C10
Strathan: High., Scotland **28** L6
Strathaven: Strath., Scot. **29** N8
Strathblane: Central, Scot. **29** N8
Strathbogie: *dist.*, Grampian, Scotland **28** Q5
Strathclyde: *Reg.*, Scotland (*cap.* Glasgow) **29** M8
Strathcona Prov. Park: B.C., Canada **92** B3
Strathdon: Gram., Scotland **28** P5
Strathdon: *val.*, Gram., Scot. **28** Q5
Strathearn: *val.*, Tayside, Scotland **29** O7
Strathkanaird: High., Scot. **28** L4
Strathmiglo: Fife, Scotland **29** P7
Strathmore: Alta., Canada **92** E2
Strathmore: *val.*, Tay., Scot. **29** Q6
Strathpeffer: High., Scot. **28** M4
Strathroy: Ont., Canada **88** L4
Strathy: & *cape*, Highland, Scotland **28** O2
Strathy: *riv.*, High., Scot. **28** N3
Strathyre: Central, Scotland **29** N7
Stratton: Colo., U.S.A. **93** G5
Stratton: Corn., England **24** M18
Stratton: Maine, U.S.A. **89** Q3
Stratton Audley: Oxon., Eng. **25** T16
Stratton, Long: Norf., Eng. **25** Y15
Stratus: Greek city of *Acarnania* on *Achelous* river about due west of Agrinion, Greece **39** R17
Straube: S.W. Africa **74** C2
Straubing: W. Germany **41** S7
Straumbui: Norway **47** M6
Strausberg: E. Germany **45** T3
Strawberry Mount: Oreg., U.S.A. **92** D4
Stráž: Czechoslovakia **45** S6
Strazhitza: Bulgaria **39** T15
Streatley: Beds., England **25** V16
Streator: Ill., U.S.A. **88** G5
Stredočesky: *Reg.*, Czechoslovakia [*cap.* Prague (Praha)] **45** U6
Středoslovenský: *Reg.*, Czechoslovakia (*cap.* Banska Bystrica) 43 Q12
Street: Som., England **24** Q17
Street: Westmeath, Repub. of Ireland **30** G12
Strehaia: Romania **39** S14
Strehla: E. Germany **45** T4
Strelka: (*on riv. Chunya*), U.S.S.R. **49** M5
Strelka: (*on riv. Yenisey*), U.S.S.R. **51** Q3
Strensall: N. Yorks., England **27** T11
Stresa: Italy **40** O10
Stretford: Gt. Man., England **27** R13
Stretham: Cambs., England **25** W15
Stretton: Ches., England **27** Q13
Stretton: Leics., England **27** U14
Stříbrná Skalice: Czech. **45** U6
Stříbné Hory: Czech. **45** T6
Stříbro: Czechoslovakia **45** T6
Strichen: Gram., Scotland **28** R4
Strickland, Great: Cumbria, England **26** Q10
Strimon, G. of: Greece **39** S16
Stringtown: Okla., U.S.A. **90** C8
Strmica: Yugoslavia **41** W11
Strofádhes: *is.*, Ionian Is. **39** R18
Ströhen: W. Germany **44** O3
Strokestown: Rosc., Repub. of Ireland **30** E12
Ström: Sweden **47** P6
Stroma: *i.*, Scotland **28** P2
Strömbacka: Sweden **47** P6
Stromberg: W. Germany **44** N6
Stromboli: *volc.*, Lipari Is. **38** O17
Stromeferry: High., Scot. **28** K5
Stromness: Mainland, Orkney Is. **28** P2
Strømø: *i.*, Faeroe Is. **46** h5
Strömstad: Sweden **47** M7
Strömsund: Sweden **46** O5
Ströms Vattudal: *valley*, Sweden **46** O4
Strongoli: Italy **38** P17
Stronsay: *i.*, Orkney Is., Scot. **28** *Ins.*
Stronsay Firth: Orkney Is., Scotland **28** Q1
Strontian: High., Scotland **29** K6
Strood: Kent, England **25** W17
Stroomen, Cape: Celebes **65** G6
Stroove: Don., Repub. of Ireland **30** H9
Stropkov: Czechoslovakia **43** R12
Stroud: Glos., England **24** R16
Stroud: N.S.W., Australia **71** J9
Stroudsburg: Pa., U.S.A. **89** O5
Stroża: Poland **45** W4
Struan: Tayside, Scotland **29** O6
Strücklingen: W. Germany **44** N2
Struer: Denmark **47** L8
Struga: Yugoslavia **39** R16
Strugi-Krasnyye: U.S.S.R. **47** V7
Struma: *riv.*, Bulgaria/Grc. **39** S16
Strumble Head: *cape*, Dyfed, Wales **24** L15
Strumica: Yugoslavia **39** S16
Struy: Highland, Scotland **28** M5
Strydenburg: S. Africa **74** E4
Stryków: Poland **43** Q11
Strzmon: Greek name for river Struma **39** S16
Stryy: Ukraine **43** S12
Strzegom: Poland **45** W5
Strzelce Krajne: Poland **45** V3
Strzelin: Poland **43** P11
Strzelno: Poland **43** Q10
Strzyżow: Poland **43** R12
Stuart: Fla., U.S.A. **91** L12
Stuart: Iowa, U.S.A. **92** J4
Stuart: Va., U.S.A. **88** L7
Stuartfield: Gram., Scotland **28** R4
Stuart Lake: B.C., Canada **92** C2
Stub Alps: Austria **41** U8
Stuben: Austria **40** Q8
Studland: Dorset, England **24** S18
Studley: War., England **24** S15
Stühlingen: W. Germany **40** O8
Stungtrang: Cambodia **64** D4
Stungtreng: Cambodia **64** D4
Stupava: Czechoslovakia **41** X7
Stura: *riv.*, Piedmont (N.), Italy **40** N10
Stura: *riv.*, Piedmont (S.), It. **40** N11
Sturgeon: *riv.*, Ont., Canada **88** L2
Sturgeon Bay: *city*, Wis., U.S.A. **88** H3
Sturgeon Falls: *city*, Ont., Canada **89** M2
Sturgis: Ky., U.S.A. **88** H7
Sturgis: Mich., U.S.A. **88** J5
Sturgis: S. Dak., U.S.A. **92** G4
Sturminster Marshall: Dorset, England **24** R18
Sturminster Newton: Dorset, England **24** R18
Sturry: Kent, England **25** Y17
Sturt Creek: *town & river*, W. Australia **68** D3
Sturt Desert: S. Austl./Queens., Australia **69** G5
Sturton: Lincs., England **27** U13
Sturt Vale: S. Australia **71** D9
Stutterheim: & *Dist.*, S. Afr. **75** G6
Stuttgart: Ark., U.S.A. **90** F8
STUTTGART: Baden-Württemberg, W. Germany **40** P7
Stutton: Suff., England **25** Y16
Stuurman: S. Africa **74** D5
Stviga: Byelorussia **43** U10
Styr': *riv.*, Ukraine **43** T11
Styra: Greek city of S. Euboea on coast opposite Marathón. **39** T17
Styria: *Prov.*, Austria (*cap.* Graz) **41** U8
Suabina: New Guinea **69** H2
Suai: Sarawak, Malaysia **65** E6
Suakin: Sudan **54** E11
Suala Selka: *mtns.*, Finland **46** T2
Suancheng (Ningkwo): Anhwei, China **62** V8
Suanhan: Szechwan, China **62** T8
Suanhwa: Hopeh, China **62** V6
Suari Selka: *mtns.*, Fin./U.S.S.R. **46** V2
Subai & Suhul: *tribal area*, Saudi Arabia **54** F10
Subashi: Iran **57** L4
Subi: *i.*, Indonesia **65** D6
Subiaco: Italy **38** N16
Subi Reef: S. China Sea **64** E4
Sublaqueum: Roman city at Subiaco, Italy. **38** N16
Subotica: Yugoslavia **39** Q13
Succoth: city of ancient Israel to E. of river Jordan about 18 miles WSW. of Jerash, Jordan **55** b2
Suceava: Romania **43** U13
Sucha: Poland **43** Q12
Suchdol: Czechoslovakia **45** U7
Suchow (Kiuchuan): Kansu, China **62** R7
Suchow (Tungshan): Kiangsu, China **62** V8
Suchow (Wuhsien): Kiangsu, China **63** W8
Sucia: *riv.*, Panama **94** *Ins.*
Suck: *riv.*, Rosc./Galway, Repub. of Ireland **31** E13
Sucre: Bolivia **94** D7

For Abbreviations see list on p.113. Italic type, e.g. *Ephesus*, refers to historical names not on maps. Capital letters, e.g. MADRID show capitals of countries; small capital letters, e.g. CADIZ, show capitals of provinces, etc. General notes p.116.

190 Suda—Tagliamento

Suda: *riv.*, U.S.S.R. **50** E3
Sud: *Dept.*, Benin (*cap.* Cotonou) **81** E3
Sud: *Dept.*, Ivory Coast (*cap.* Abidjan) **80** C3
Sudair: Saudi Arabia **54** G9

Sudan: *Republic* **79** K7
Cap.: Khartoum
Area: 967,491 sq. miles (2,505,802 sq. km.)
Pop.: 16,489,000 (*1972 E*)

Südbaden: *Dist.*, Baden Württemberg, West Germany **40** O8
Sudbury: Derby., England **27** S14
Sudbury: Ont., Canada **88** L2
Sudbury: Suff., England **25** X15
Sudd, The: *geog. reg.*, Sudan **76** C1
Suddie: Guyana **87** d7
Sud-Est: *Dept.*, Benin (*cap.* Porto-Novo) **81** E3
Sudetenland: *geog. reg.*, Czechoslovakia **42** O11
Sudeten Mtns.: Czech./Pol. **45** V5
Sudogda: U.S.S.R. **50** F3
Sud-Ouest: *Reg.*, Cameroun (*cap.* Buea) **81** F3
Sud-Ouest: *Dept.*, Benin (*cap.* Athiémé) **81** E3
Sud-Ouest: *Dept.*, Upper Volta (*cap.* Gaoua) **80** D2
Süd-Perd: *cape*, Rügen, E. Germany **45** T1
Südwürttemberg-Hohenzollern: *Dist.*, Baden Württemberg, West Germany **40** P7
Sudzha: U.S.S.R. **50** E4
Sue: *riv.*, Sudan **76** C1
Sueca: Spain **35** F17
Sue Peak: Tex., U.S.A. **93** G7
Sueyoshi: Japan **63** b5
Suez: *& canal*, Egypt **32** *Ins.*
Suez, G. of: Egypt **54** D9
Sufaina: Saudi Arabia **54** F10
Suffolk: Va., U.S.A. **89** N7
Suffolk: *Co.*, England (*co. town* Ipswich) **25** Y15
Sufian: Iran **57** K2
Sufu (Kashgar): Sinkiang, China **51** N7
Sugar Creek: *city*, Mo., U.S.A. **90** D6
Sugar Land: Tex., U.S.A. **90** D11
Sugarloaf Point: N.S.W., Australia **71** K9
Suget Pass: Sinkiang, China **58** N9
Suğla, Lake: Turkey **56** B3
Sugut, Cape: Sabah, Malaysia **65** F5
Suhar: Oman **55** J10
SUHL: *& Dist.*, E. Germany **45** Q5
Suhr: *riv.*, Switzerland **40** O8
Suhrabad: Iran **57** J2
Suhsien: Anhwei, China **62** V8
Suichung: Liaoning, China **63** W6
Suichwan: Kiangsi, China **62** U9
Suihsien: Hupeh, China **62** U8
Suihwa: Heilungkiang, China **63** X5
Suikai: Kwangtung, China **62** U10
Suikiang: Yunnan, China **62** S9
Suileng: Heilungkiang, China **63** X5
Suilven: *mtn.*, High., Scot. **28** L3
Suining: Hunan, China **62** T9
Suipin: Heilungkiang, China **63** Y5
Suippes: France **36** K6
Suir: *riv.*, Repub. of Ireland **31** F15
Suiteh: Shensi, China **62** U7
Suiting (Tahsien): Szechwan, China **62** T8
Suiyang: Kweichow, China **62** T9
Sujica: Yugoslavia **38** P15
Sukabumi: Java **65** D8
Sukadana: Borneo **65** D7
Sukadana: Sumatra **65** D8
Sukagawa: Japan **63** g2
Sukamara: Borneo **65** E7
Sukaraja: Borneo **65** E7
Sukau: Sabah, Malaysia **65** F5
Sukeva: Finland **46** U5
Sukhana: U.S.S.R. **49** n4
Sukhanovka: U.S.S.R. **49** p7
Sukhe-Bator: Mongolia **49** m7
Sukhona: *riv.*, U.S.S.R. **50** F3
SUKHUMI: Abkhaz, U.S.S.R. **50** F6
Sukkertoppen: Greenland **85** o4
Sukkur: Sind, Pakistan **58** L9
Suknne: Syria **56** F4
Sukothai: Thailand **64** B3
Sukow: Shansi, China **62** U7
Sukpay Datani: U.S.S.R. **63** Z5
Sulaiman Range: Pakistan **58** L9
SULAIMANIYA: *& Prov.*, Iraq **57** J4
Sulaimiya: Saudi Arabia **54** G10
Sula Is.: Indonesia **65** H7
Sulaiyil: Saudi Arabia **54** G10
Sula Sgeir: *rocks*, Scotland **28** J2
Sulawesi (Celebes): Indonesia **65** G7
Sulby: I. of Man, U.K. **26** N11
Sulechow: Poland **45** V3
Sulęcin: Poland **45** V3
Sule Skerry: *rock*, Scotland **28** N2
Sulgen: Switzerland **40** P8
Sulgrave: Northants., Eng. **25** T15
Suliki: Sumatra **65** C7
Sulina: Romania **39** V14
Sulingen: W. Germany **44** O3
Suliskey Bank: Outer Hebr., Scotland **28** J2
Sulitjelma: Norway **46** P3
Sullana: Peru **94** A4
Sullivan: Ill., U.S.A. **88** G6
Sullivan: Ind., U.S.A. **88** H6
Sullivan: *i.*, Mergui Arch., Burma **59** R12
Sully: France **36** H8
Sulmona: Italy **38** N15
Sulphur: La., U.S.A. **90** E10
Sulphur: Okla., U.S.A. **90** C8
Sulphur: *riv.*, Tex., U.S.A. **90** D9
Sulphur Springs: *city*, Tex., U.S.A. **90** D9
Sultanabad: Iran **55** J7
Sultanabad (Arak): Iran **57** L4
Sultan-Bent: Turkmen., U.S.S.R. **51** K7
Sultan Hamud: Kenya **76** E3
Sultanhisar: Turkey **39** V18
Sultaniçe: Turkey (Dardan. *Inset*) **20** *Ins.*
Sultaniyeh: Iran **57** L3
Sultan Mtns.: Turkey **56** B2
Sultanpur: Uttar Pradesh, India **58** O9
Sulu Arch.: Philippines **65** G5
Sulu Sea: Philippines **64** F5
Sulyukta: Kirgiz., U.S.S.R. **51** L7
Sulzbach: W. Germany **45** R6
Sumalata: Celebes **65** G6
Sumatra: *i.*, Indonesia **65** C7
Šumava: *mtns.*, Czech. **41** T7
Sumba: *i. & str.*, Indonesia **65** F8
Sumbawa: *& i.*, Indonesia **65** F8
SUMBAWANGA: Rukwa, Tanzania **76** D4
Sumbay: Peru **94** C7
Sumbu Game Reserve: Zambia **77** D4
Sumburgh Head: *cape*, Shetland Is. **28** *Ins.*
Sumbuya: Sierra Leone **80** B3
Sümeg: Hungary **43** P13
Sumenep: Madura, Indon. **65** E8
Sumer: southern Babylonia, land occupied by Sumerians prior to the incursion of the Semites, now Southern Iraq **57** K6
Summan: *plain*, Sau. Arab. **54** G9
Summer Bridge: *village*, N. Yorks., England **27** S11
Summer Isles: Highland, Scotland **28** L3
Summer Lake: Oreg., U.S.A. **92** C4
Summerside: P.E.I., Canada **89** U2
Summerville: S.C., U.S.A. **91** L9
Summit: Alaska, U.S.A. **84** E5
Summit: Panama **94** *Ins.*
Summit Peak: Colo., U.S.A. **93** F5
Sumner: Iowa, U.S.A. **88** E4
Sumoto: Japan **63** d3
Sumpangbinangai: Celebes **65** F7
Šumperk: Czechoslovakia **43** P12
Sumprabum: Burma **59** R9
Sumter: S.C. U.S.A. **91** L9
Sumy: Ukraine **50** D4
Sunagawa: Japan **63** ZZ6
Sunaisala: *salt lake*, Iraq **57** G4
Sunart: *dist. & loch*, High., Scotland **29** K6
Sunbury: Pa., U.S.A. **89** N5
Sunbury: Vict., Australia **71** F11
Suncho Corral: Argentina **96** C2
Sunchon: N. Korea **63** X7
Sunchow (Kweiping): Kwangsi Chuang, China **62** U10
Suncook: N.H., U.S.A. **89** Q4
Sundance: Wyo., U.S.A. **92** G4
Sundarbans: *geog. reg.*, Bengal, India **59** P10
Sundargarh: Orissa, India **59** O10
Sunda Str.: Indonesia **65** D8
Sundays: *riv.*, S. Africa **75** F6
Sundbyberg: Sweden **47** P7
Sunderby: Sweden **46** R4
Sunderland: Tyne & Wear, England **26** T10
Sunderland, North: Northumb., England **26** S8
Sundern: W. Germany **44** O4
Sundra: Trans., S. Africa **74** O *Ins.*
Sundre: Gotland, Sweden **47** Q8
Sundridge: Kent, England **25** W17
Sundridge: Ont., Canada **89** M3
Sundsvall: Sweden **46** P5
Sungaibuntu: Java **65** D8
Sungaikakap: Borneo **65** D7
Sungailiat: Bangka, Indon. **65** D7
Sungailimau: Sumatra **65** C7
Sungaipenu: Sumatra **65** C7
Sungari: *riv.*, Heilungkiang/Kirin, China **63** Y5
Sungari Reservoir: Kirin, China **63** X6
Sungei Lembing: Malaya, Malaysia **65** c12
Sungei Patani: Malaya, Malaysia **65** b11
Sungei Renggam: Malaya, Malaysia **65** b12
Sungfow: Hupeh, China **62** U8
Sungguminasa: Celebes **65** F8
Sunghsien: Honan, China **62** U8
Sunghur: Iran **57** K4
Sungkiang: Kiangsu, China **63** W8
Sungkiang: *Prov.* (absorbed in Heilungkiang) China
Sungming: Yunnan, China **62** S9
Sungtao: Kweichow, China **62** T9
Sungtze: Hupeh, China **62** U8
Sungurlu: Turkey **56** D1
Sunho: Heilungkiang, China **63** X5
Sunium: promontory at S. tip of *Attica* **39** T18
Sunja: Yugoslavia **41** W10
Sunk Island: *village*, Humberside, England **27** V12
Sunndalsøra: Norway **46** L5
Sunne: Sweden **47** N7
Sunningdale: Berks., Eng. **25** U17
Sunnyside: Utah, U.S.A. **93** E5
Sunnyside: Wash., U.S.A. **92** C3
Sunrise: Alaska, U.S.A. **84** E5
Sunshine: Vict., Australia **71** F11
Suntien: Yunnan, China **62** S9
Suntsar: Baluchistan, Pakistan **58** K9
Sunwu: Heilungkiang, China **63** X5
Sunyang: Shensi, China **62** T8
SUNYANI: Brong-Ahafo, Ghana **80** D3
Sunyi: Kwangtung, China **62** U10
Suo (Suao): Taiwan **63** W10
Suo Gulf: Japan **63** b4
Suomussalmi: Finland **46** V4
Suonenjoki: Finland **46** U5
Suonne Lake: Finland **47** U6
Suordakh: U.S.S.R. **49** p4
Suorva: Sweden **46** Q3
Superior: Ariz., U.S.A. **93** E6
Superior: Nebr., U.S.A. **93** H4
Superior: Wis., U.S.A. **88** E2
Superior: Wyo., U.S.A. **92** F4
Superior, Lake: Can./U.S.A. **88** H2
Suphan: Thailand **64** C4
Suphan: *mtn.*, Turkey **57** H2
Supu: Hunan, China **62** U9
Supung Dam: Yalu Riv., Liaoning, China/N. Korea **63** X6
Suq 'Anam: Yemen **54** F11
Suq Ash Shuyukh: Iraq **57** K6
Suqayq Dajjah: Iraq **57** K6
Sur (Tyre): Lebanon **55** b1
Sur: Oman **55** J10
Sur, Point: *cape*, Calif., U.S.A. **93** C5
Sura: U.S.S.R. **48** f5
Sura: *riv.*, U.S.S.R. **50** G4
Sura: Syrian city and Roman camp at Hammam, Syria **56** F4
Surab: Baluchistan, Pakistan **58** L9
Surabaya: Java **65** E8
Surakarta (Solo): Java **65** E8
Surama: Guyana **87** d8
Suran: *riv.*, France **37** L9
Surat: Gujarat, India **58** M10
Surat: Queens., Australia **70** H6
Suratgarh: Rajasthan, India **58** M9
Surazh: U.S.S.R. **50** D4
Surdon: France **36** F7
Surdulica: Yugoslavia **39** S15
Sure: *riv.*, Luxembourg **44** L6
Surendranagar: Gujarat, India **58** M10
Surgères: France **37** E9
Surghak: Sinkiang, China **51** O7
Surgut: U.S.S.R. **51** M2
Surhavac-Ljubijat: Yugo. **41** W11
Suri: W. Bengal, India **59** P10
Surigao: *& str.*, Mindinao, Philippines **64** H5
Surin: Thailand **64** C4

Surinam: *Republic* **94** F3
Cap.: Paramaribo
Area: 63,251 sq. miles (163,820 sq. km.)
Pop.: 406,000 (*1971 E*)

Surkhob: *riv.*, U.S.S.R. **51** L7
Surmaq: Iran **55** H8
Sürmene: Turkey **57** G1
Surovikino: U.S.S.R. **50** F5
Surprise Lake: Que., Canada **89** O1
Surrey: *Co.*, England (*co. town* Kingston) **25** V17
Surrey: *Prov.*, Jamaica **86** *Ins.*
Sursee: Switzerland **40** O8
Sursk: U.S.S.R. **50** G4
Surtsey: *i.*, Iceland **46** c5
Sürüç: Turkey **56** F3
Surud, Mount: Somalia **79** R17
Suruga Bay: Japan **63** f3
Surukh: Iran **57** L4
Surulangun: Sumatra **65** C7
Surup: Philippines **65** H5
Surzur: France **36** C8
Süs: Switzerland **40** Q9
Susa: Italy **40** N10
Susa: Persian and Elamite capital. Site at Shush SW. of Dizful, Iran **57** L5
Sušac: *i.*, Yugoslavia **38** P15
Sušak: Yugoslavia **38** O14
Susak: *i.*, Yugoslavia **41** U11
Susaki: Japan **63** c4
Susami: Japan **63** d4
Suşehri: Turkey **56** F1
Sušice: Czechoslovakia **45** T6
Susitna: Alaska, U.S.A. **84** d5
Susitna: *riv.*, Alaska, U.S.A. **84** E5
Suslonger: U.S.S.R. **50** G3
Susquehanna: Pa., U.S.A. **89** O5
Susquehanna: *riv.*, Pa./Md., U.S.A. **89** N6
Susques: Argentina **96** B1
Sussex: N.B., Canada **89** T3
Sussex: *see* Sussex, East & West.
Sussex, East: *Co.*, England (*co. town* Lewes) **25** W18
Sussex, Vale of: E./W. Sussex, England **25** V18
Sussex, West: *Co.*, England (*co. town* Chichester) **25** U18
Susurluk: Turkey **39** V17
Sutherland: N.S.W., Austl. **71** J10
Sutherland: Sask., Canada **92** F2
Sutherland: *& Dist.*, S. Afr. **74** D6
Sutherland Range: W. Austl. **68** D5
Sutlej: *riv.*, Pakistan/India **58** M9
Sutsien: Kiangsu, China **62** V8
Sutterton: Lincs., England **27** V14
Sutton: Gt. Ldn., England **25** V17
Sutton: Nebr., U.S.A. **93** H4
Sutton: S. Africa **74** E3
Sutton: W. Sussex, England **25** U18
Sutton, Little: Ches., Eng. **27** Q13
Sutton Bridge: Lincs., Eng. **25** W14
Sutton Coldfield: W. Midlands, England **27** S14
Sutton in Ashfield: Notts., England **27** T13
Sutton on Hull: Humb., Eng. **27** V12
Sutton on Sea: Lincs., Eng. **27** W13
Sutton on the Forest: N. Yorkshire, England **27** T11
Sutton on Trent: Notts., England **27** U13
Sutton St. James: Lincs., England **25** W14
Sutton St. Nicholas: Hereford & Worcester, England **24** Q15
Sutton Scotney: Hants., Eng. **25** T17
Sutton upon Derwent: N. Yorkshire, England **27** U12
Sutton Valence: Kent, Eng. **25** X17
Suttor: *riv.*, Queens., Austl. **70** G3
Suttsu: Japan **63** ZZ6
Sutun: Tibet, China **62** R9
Suure-Yani: Estonia, U.S.S.R. **47** T7
SUVA: Fiji Is. **67** P5
Suvainiškis: Latvia, U.S.S.R. **47** T8
Suvasvesi: *lake*, Finland **46** V5
Suvla: Bay S. of Cape Suvla on Gallipoli penin., Turkey **20** *Ins.*
Suvla, Cape: Turkey (Dardan. *Inset.*) **20** *Ins.*
Suwa: Japan **63** f2
Suwaih: Oman **55** J10
Suwaira: Iraq **57** J5
Suwairiqiya: Saudi Arabia **54** F10
Suwałki: Poland **43** S9
Suwannaphum: Thailand **64** C3
Suwannee: *riv.*, Fla., U.S.A. **91** K11
Suwanwari: Thailand **64** D3
Suwar: Syria **57** G4
SUWEIDA: *& Prov.*, Syria **56** E5
Suwen: Kwangtung, China **62** U10
Suwon: S. Korea **63** X7
Suzak: Kazakh., U.S.S.R. **51** L6
Suze, La: France **36** F8
Suzuka Mtns., Japan **63** e3
Suzzara: Italy **41** Q11
Svalbard (Spitsbergen): *is.* (Nor.), Arctic O. (*cap.* Longyearbyen) **48** c2
Svalbardh: Iceland **46** f3
Svanstein: Sweden **46** S3
Svappavaara: Sweden **46** R3
Svarteborg: Sweden **47** M7
Svatkia: *riv.*, Czechoslovakia **45** W6
Svatovo: Ukraine **50** E5
Svätý Jur: Czechoslovakia **41** X7
Svay Rieng: Cambodia **64** D4
Sveagruva: Spitsbergen **48** c2
Svealand: *geog. reg.*, Sweden **47** O7
Svedala: Sweden **47** N9
Sveg: Sweden **47** O5
Svelvik: Norway **47** M7
Svendborg: Denmark **47** M9
Svenstavik: Sweden **46** O5
Sventoji: *riv.*, Lithuania, U.S.S.R. **47** T9
SVERDLOVSK: *& Reg.*, U.S.S.R. **51** K3
Sverdrup: *is. & chan.*, N.W.T., Canada **84** K2
Sverdrup I.: U.S.S.R. **48** j3
Svetac: *i.*, Yugoslavia **38** O15
Sveti Ivan Zabno: Yugo. **41** W10
Sveti Ivan Zelina: Yugo. **41** W10
Sveti Juraj: Yugoslavia **41** U11
Sveti Peter: Yugoslavia **41** V9
Světlá: Czechoslovakia **45** V6
Svetlogorsk: U.S.S.R. **47** R9
Svetlyy: U.S.S.R. **49** n6
Svetogorsk: U.S.S.R. **47** V6
Svetozarevo: Yugoslavia **39** R15
Svilajnac: Yugoslavia **39** R14
Svilengrad: Bulgaria **39** U16
Svinø: *i.*, Faeroe Is. **46** h5
Svir'stroy: U.S.S.R. **50** D2
Svishchtov: Bulgaria **39** T15
Svitávka: Czechoslovakia **45** W6
Svitavy: Czechoslovakia **45** W6
Svobodnyy: U.S.S.R. **59** o7
Svolvær: Lofoten Is., Nor. **46** O2
Svratka: *riv.*, Czech. **45** W6
Svyatitsa: Byelorussia **43** U10
Swabian Jura: *plat.*, W. Ger. **40** P7
Swadlincote: Derby., Eng. **27** S14
Swaffham: Norf., England **25** X14
Swaffham Prior: Cambs., England **25** W15
Swainby: N. Yorks., England **26** T11
Swain Reefs: Great Barrier Reef, Australia **70** K3
Swainsboro: Ga., U.S.A. **91** K9
Swain's I.: Tokelau Is. **70** *Ins.*
Swakop: *riv.*, S.W. Africa **74** A1
Swakopmund: *& Dist.*, S.W. Africa **74** A1
Swalcliffe: Oxon., England **25** T15
Swale: *riv.*, N. Yorks., Eng. **26** S11
Swaledale: *val.*, N. Yorkshire, England **26** S11
Swallow Is.: (Br.), Pacific O. **67** N3
Swallow Reef: S. China Sea **64** E5
Swan: *riv.*, W. Austl. **68** B6
Swanage: Dorset, England **24** S18
Swan Hill: *town*, Vict., Austl. **71** E10
Swan Is.: Caribbean Sea **86** L14
Swan Lake: Man., Canada **92** G2
Swan Lake: Minn., U.S.A. **88** D3
Swanlinbar: Cavan, Repub. of Ireland **30** F11
Swannington: Norf., Eng. **25** Y14
Swan Range: Mont., U.S.A. **92** E3
Swan River: Man., Canada **92** G2
Swanscombe: Kent, England **25** W17
SWANSEA: W. Glamorgan, Wales **24** O16
Swansea: Tas., Australia **68** H8
Swansea Bay: W. Glamorgan, Wales **24** O16
Swans I.: Maine, U.S.A. **89** R3
Swanton Morley: Norf., Eng. **25** X14
Swardeston: Norf., England **25** Y14
Swartberg, Groot: *range*, S. Africa **74** E6
Swartfontein: Trans., S. Afr. **75** G2
Swastika: Ont., Canada **88** L1
Swaton: Lincs., England **27** V14
Swatow: Kwangtung, China **62** V10
Swatragh: Lon., N. Ireland **30** H10
Swavesey: Cambs., England **25** V15
Swawel: S. Africa **74** D5
Sway: Hants., England **25** S18
Swaycheck: Cambodia **64** C4
Swayfield: Lincs., England **27** U14

Swaziland: *Kingdom* **75** J3
Cap.: Mbabane
Area: 6,705 sq. miles (17,366 sq. km.)
Pop.: 421,000 (*1971 E*)

Sweden: *Kingdom* **46/7**
Cap.: Stockholm
Area: 173,665 sq. miles (449,792 sq. km.)
Pop.: 8,131,000 (*1972 E*)

Swedru: Ghana **80** D3
Sween, Loch: Strath., Scotland **29** K8
Sweet Springs: Mo., U.S.A. **88** E6
Sweetwater: Tenn., U.S.A. **91** J8
Sweetwater: Tex., U.S.A. **90** A9
Sweetwater: *riv.*, Wyo., U.S.A. **92** F4
Sweetwater Canal: Egypt **32** *Ins.*
Sweileh: Jordan **55** b2
Swellendam: *& Dist.*, S. Afr. **74** D7
Swempoort: S. Africa **75** G5
Świbowina: Poland **45** V2
Świdnica: Poland **45** W5
Świdwin: Poland **45** V2
Świebodzin: Poland **45** V3
Świetlino: Poland **45** W1
Swift Current: Sask., Canada **92** F2
Swilly: *lough & riv.*, Don., Repub. of Ireland **30** F9
Swimbridge: Devon, England **24** O17
Swinburne: O.F.S., S. Africa **75** H4
Swinburne, Cape: N.W.T., Canada **84** j3
Swinderby: Lincs., England **27** U13
Swindon: Wilts., England **25** S16
Swinefleet: Humb., England **27** U12
Swineford: Mayo, Repub. of Ireland **30** D12
Swineshead: Beds., England **25** V15
Swineshead: Lincs., England **27** V14
Swinford: Leics., England **25** T15
Swinoujście: Poland **45** U2
Swinton: Borders, Scotland **29** R8
Swinton: Gt. Man., England **27** R12
Swinton: S. Yorks., England **27** T13

Switzerland: *Republic* **40** O9
Cap.: Bern
Area: 15,941 sq. miles (41,287 sq. km.)
Pop.: 6,311,000 (*1971 E*)

Swona: *i.*, Orkney Is. **28** P2
Swords: Dublin, Repub. of Ireland **30** J13
Syas'stroy: U.S.S.R. **50** D2
Sybaris: Greek city at mouth of Crati river at SW. corner of G. of Taranto, Italy **38** P17
Sybil Point: *cape*, Kerry, Repub. of Ireland **31** A15
Sycamore: Ill., U.S.A. **88** G5
Sychevka: U.S.S.R. **50** D3
Sycow: Poland **43** P11
Syderø: *i.*, Faeroe Is. **46** h6
Sydney: N.S., Canada **89** V2
SYDNEY: N.S.W., Australia **71** J9
Sydney Mines: N.S., Can. **89** V2
Sydprøven: Greenland **85** P5
Syene: ancient Egyptian city and Roman camp at Aswan, Egypt **54** D10
Syke: W. Germany **44** O3
SYKTYVKAR: Komi, U.S.S.R. **50** H2
Sylacauga: Ala., U.S.A. **91** H9
Sylhet: Bangladesh **59** Q10
Sylt: *i.*, N. Frisian Is., W. Germany **44** O1
Sylvania: Ga., U.S.A. **91** L9
Sylvan Lake: *town*, Alta., Canada **92** E2
Sylvester: Ga., U.S.A. **91** K10
Sym: *& riv.*, U.S.S.R. **51** P2
Symi: *i.*, Dodecanese **39** U18
Symington: Strath., Scotland **29** M8
Symington: Strath., Scotland **29** O8
Synnada: Phrygian, later Graeco-Roman city at Afyonkarahisar, Turkey **56** B2
Syr: *riv.*, U.S.S.R. **51** L6
Syracuse: Kans., U.S.A. **93** G5
Syracuse: N.Y., U.S.A. **89** N4
Syracuse: Sicily **38** O18
Syresham: Northants., England **25** T15

Syria: *Republic* **56** F4
Cap.: Damascus
Area: 71,498 sq. miles (185,180 sq. km.)
Pop.: 6,661,000 (*1972 E*)

Syriam: Burma **59** R11
Syrian Desert (Hamad): SW. Asia **56** F5
Syrtis Maior: Roman name of G. of Sidra **33** F5
Syrtis Minor: ancient name for G. of Gabès off Tunisia **32** E5
Syssleback: Sweden **47** N6
Syston: Leics., England **27** T14
Syston: Lincs., England **27** U14
Syvde: Norway **46** J5
Syzran': U.S.S.R. **50** G4
Szamotuły: Poland **45** W3
Szarvas: Hungary **43** R13
Szczebrzeszyn: Poland **43** S11
SZCZECIN (Stettin): *& Prov.*, Poland **45** U2
Szczecinek: Poland **43** P10
Szczytno: Poland **43** R10
Szecheng (Lingyun): Kwangsi Chuang, China **62** T10
Szechwan: *Prov.*, China [*cap.* Chengtu (Hwayang)] **62** S8
Szeged: Hungary **43** R13
Szeghalom: Hungary **43** R13
Székesfehérvár: Hungary **43** Q13
Szekszárd: Hungary **43** Q13
Szemao: Yunnan, China **62** S10
Szeming (Amoy): Fukien, China **62** V10
Szenan: Kweichow, China **62** T9
Szengen: Kwangsi Chuang (N.), China **62** T10
Szengen: Kwangsi Chuang (S.), China **62** T10
Szentendre: Hungary **43** Q13
Szentes: Hungary **43** R13
Szent Gotthárd: Hungary **41** W9
Szeping: Liaoning, China **63** W6
Szigetvár: Hungary **43** P13
Szolnok: Hungary **43** R13
Szombathely: Vas, Hung. **43** P13
Szprotawa: Poland **45** V4
Szushiherhhao: Inner Mongolia, China **63** W5

Taaibosspruit: Trans., S. Afr. **74** L *Ins.*
Taal: Luzon, Philippines **64** G4
Taarstedt: W. Germany **44** P1
Taba: Saudi Arabia **54** F9
Tabaco: Luzon, Philippines **64** G4
Tabadian: Senegal **80** B2
Tabala: Niger **81** E2
Tabankort: Mali **78** E6
Tabankulu: S. Afr. **75** H5
Tabar Is.: Bismarck Arch. **67** K2
Tabarem: *well*, Niger **81** E2
Tabarka: Tunisia **38** L18
Tabas: Iran **55** J8
Tabas: Iran **55** K8
Tabbaghaj: Iran **57** K3
Tabelbala: Algeria **80** L9
Taber: Alta., Canada **92** E3
Tabiteuea: *i.*, Gilbert Is. **67** O2
Tablas: *i.*, Philippines **64** G4
Tablas, Las: Panama **87** I16
Table Mount: *& bay*, S. Africa **74** *Ins.*
Taboga Island: Pan. **94** *Ins.*
Taboguilla Island: Pan. **94** *Ins.*
Tábor: Czechoslovakia **45** U6
Tabor: biblical name of mtn. E. of Nazareth and SW. of Lake Tiberias, Israel **55** b2
TABORA: *& Reg.*, Tanzania **76** D4
Tabor City: N.C., U.S.A. **91** M8
Tabory: U.S.S.R. **51** K3
Tabou: Ivory Coast **80** C4
TABRIZ: Azerbaijan-e Khavari, Iran **57** K2
Tabuk: Saudi Arabia **54** E9
Tabut: Yemen P.D.R. **55** H11
Tacalé: Brazil **94** G3
Tacheng: Sinkiang, China **51** O5
Tachikawa: Japan **63** f3
Tachia: Taiwan **63** W10
Tachov: Czechoslovakia **45** S6
Tachuan: Kansu, China **62** R6
Tacloban: Philippines **64** G4
Tacna: Peru **94** C7
Tacoma: Wash., U.S.A. **92** C3
Taconic Range: *mtns.*, N.Y., U.S.A. **89** P4
Taco Pozo: Argentina **96** C2
Tacora: *mtn.*, Peru **94** C7
Tacuarembó: Uruguay **96** D3
Tacuati: Paraguay **96** D1
Tacutu: *riv.*, Guyana **87** d9
Tadcaster: N. Yorks., England **27** T12
Taddington: Derby., Eng. **27** S13
Tademait Hamada: *plat.*, *Algeria* **78** E4
Tadhau: *well*, Oman **55** H11
Tadjerouine: Tunisia **38** L19
Tadjoura: *& gulf*, Djibouti **79** Q17
Fr. Terr. of **79** Q17
Tadley: Hants., England **25** T17
Tadmor (Palmyra): Syria **56** F4
Tadoussac: Que., Canada **89** R1
Tadzhikistan: *S.S. Repub.*, U.S.S.R. (*cap.* Dushanbe) **51** L7
Taegu: S. Korea **63** X7
Taehuksan: *i.*, S. Korea **63** X8
Taejon: S. Korea **63** X7
Taenarum: ancient Greek name of Cape Matapan, Greece **39** S18
Taenga: *i.*, Tuamotu Arch. **83** g3
Taerh-hanmaoming-anlienhochi: Inner Mongolia, China **62** U6
Taerhhanwangfu: Inner Mongolia, China **63** W6
Taf: *riv.*, Dyfed, Wales **24** M16
Tafalla: Spain **35** F15
Tafang: Kweichow, China **62** T9
Tafassaset: *watercourse*, Algeria/Niger **78** F5
Tafersit: Morocco **35** E19
Taff: *riv.*, Mid Glam., Wales **24** P16
Taff's Well: Mid Glam., Wales **24** P16
Tafiré: Ivory Coast **80** C3
Tafnidilt: Morocco **80** J9
Taft: Calif., U.S.A. **93** D5
Tafwap: Nicobar Is. **59** Q13
Taganrog: *& gulf*, U.S.S.R. **50** E5
Tagant: *Dist.*, Mauritania (*cap.* Tidjikja) **78** B6
Tagbilaran: Philippines **64** G5
Taggafadi: Niger **78** F6
Taggia: Italy **40** N12
Taghmon: Wex., Repub. of Ireland **31** H15
Tagliamento: *riv.*, Italy **41** S9

For Abbreviations see list on p.113. Italic type, e.g. *Ephesus*, refers to historical names not on maps. Capital letters, e.g. MADRID, show capitals of countries; small capital letters, e.g. CADIZ, show capitals of provinces, etc. General notes p.116.

Taglio di Porto Vico—Tayinloan 191

Taglio di Porto Vico: Italy 41 S10
Tagoat: Wex., Repub. of Ireland 31 J15
Tagoudit: Morocco 80 K9
Tagremaret: Algeria 35 G19
Tagua, La: Colombia 94 C3
Taguatinga: Brazil 94 H6
Taguchi: Japan 63 e3
Taguerzimt: Western Sahara 78 B5
Tagula: *i.*, New Guinea 69 J2
Tagus: *riv.*, Spain/Portugal 35 C17
Tahaa: Society Is. 83 e3
Tahakopa: South I., N.Z. 71 M18
Tahan: *mtn.*, Malaya, Malaysia 65 c11
Tahanea: *i.*, Tuamotu Arch. 83 g3
Tahat: *mtn.*, Algeria 78 F5
Tahiti: *i.*, Society Is. 83 f3
Tahivilla: Spain (Gib. *Inset*) 32 *Ins.*
Tahlequah: Okla., U.S.A. 90 D8
Tahoe, Lake: Nev., U.S.A. 93 D5
TAHOUA: *& Dept.*, Niger 81 F2
Tahsien (Suiting): Szechwan, China 62 T8
Tahta: Egypt 54 D9
Tahuata: *i.*, Marquesas Is. 83 h2
Tahulandang: *i.*, Sangihe Is., Indonesia 65 H6
Tahuna: Sangihe Is., Indon. 65 H6
Tai: Ivory Coast 80 C3
Tai, Lake: China 63 W8
Taian: Shantung, China 62 V7
Taibe: *see* Taiyiba.
Taichao: Tibet, China 59 Q8
Taichow (Linhai): Chekiang, China 63 W9
Taichu (Taichung): Taiwan 63 W10
Taif: Saudi Arabia 54 F10
Taihape: North I., N.Z. 70 P14
Taiho: Anhwei, China 62 V8
Taihoku (Taiwan): *see* Taipeh.
Taihsien: Shansi, China 62 U7
Taihu: Anhwei, China 62 V8
Taiji: Japan 63 d4
Taiki: Japan 63 ZZ6
Taikintala: Inner Mongolia, China 63 W5
Taiku: Shansi, China 62 U7
Taikung: Kweichow, China 62 T9
Tailai: Heilungkiang, China 63 W5
Tailan: Afghanistan 58 K7
Taileleo: Mentawai Is., Indonesia 65 B7
Tailem Bend: S. Australia 71 C10
Taim: Brazil 96 E3
Taima: Saudi Arabia 54 E9
Tain: Highland, Scot. 28 N4
Tainan: Taiwan 63 W10
Tainaron (Matapan), Cape: Greece 39 S18
Taining: Fukien, China 62 V9
Tai-o-Hae: Marquesas Is. 83 g1
Taipale: Finland 46 V5
T'AI-PEI (Taipeh): Taiwan 63 W9
Taiping (Chungtso): Kwangsi Chuang, China 62 T10
Taiping: Perak, Malaya, Malaysia 65 b11
Taipingchwan: Kirin, China 63 W6
Tairua: North I., N.Z. 70 P13
Tais: Sumatra 65 C7
Taisha: Japan 63 c3
Taisho (Ta-chuang): Taiwan 63 W10
Taishun: Chekiang, China 62 V9
Taitao Penin.: Chile 95 C13
Taito (Tai-tung): Taiwan 63 W10
Taivalkoski: Finland 46 V4

Taiwan (Formosa): *Republic* 63 W10
Cap.: T'ai-pei
Area: 13,592 sq. miles (35,203 sq. km.)
Pop.: 14,500,000 (*1971 E*)

Taiwara: Afghanistan 58 K8
Taiyiba: Jordan 55 b2
TAIYUAN (Yangku): Shansi, China 62 U7
TA'IZ: Yemen 54 F12
Tajima: Japan 63 f2
Tajimi: Japan 63 e3
Tajumulco: *volc.*, Guatemala 86 k14
Tak: Thailand 64 B3
Takab: Iran 57 K3
Takabba: Kenya 76 F2
Takachu: Botswana 77 B7
Takada: Japan 63 f2
Takahama: Fukui, Japan 63 d3
Takahama: Ishikawa, Japan 63 e2
Takahashi: Japan 63 c3
Takaka: South I., N.Z. 70 O15
Takalar: Celebes 65 F8
TAKAMATSU: Kagawa, Japan 63 d3
Takanabe: Japan 63 b4
Takanameba: Cameroun 81 G4
Takao (Kaohsiung): Taiwan 63 W10
Takaoka: Japan 63 e2
Takapoto: *i.*, Tuamotu Arch. 83 f2
Takaroa: *i.*, Tuamotu Arch. 83 g2
Takasaki: Honshu, Japan 63 f2
Takata: Japan 63 b4
Takatsu: Japan 63 b3
Takatsuki: Japan 63 d3
Takaungu: Kenya 76 E3
Takaw: Burma 59 R10
Takayama: Japan 63 e2
Takayu: Japan 63 g2
Tak Bai: Thailand 65 c10
Take: Nigeria 81 F3
Takefu: Japan 63 e3
Takehara: Japan 63 c3
Takeno: Japan 63 d3
Takeo: Cambodia 64 C4
Takeo: Japan 63 b4
Take Shima (Liancourt Rocks): Sea of Japan 63 Y7
Takhadid: *well*, Iraq 57 J7
Takhar: *Prov.*, Afghanistan 55 L7
Takhing: Kwangtung, China 62 U10
Takholo: U.S.S.R. 63 Z5
Takht: Iran 57 K3
Takhta-Bazar: Turkmen., U.S.S.R. 51 K7
Takhtabrod: Kazakh., U.S.S.R. 51 L4
Takhta-Kupyr: Uzbek., U.S.S.R. 51 K6
Takht-i-Sulaiman: *mtn.*, Baluchistan/N.W. Front. Prov., Pak. 58 L8
Takieta: Niger 81 F2
Takihara: Japan 63 e3
Takikawa: Japan 63 ZZ6
Takingeun: Sumatra 65 B6
Takistan: Iran 57 L3
Takkaze: *riv.*, Ethiopia 54 E12
Takla Lake: B.C., Canada 92 B1
Takla Makan: *desert*, Sinkiang, China 51 O7
Takoradi: Ghana 80 D4
Takotna: Alaska, U.S.A. 84 D5
Taktak: Iraq 57 J4
Taku: Tientsin Municipality, China 62 V7
Takua Pa: Thailand 64 B5
Takuin: Yunnan, China 62 S9
Takum: Nigeria 81 F3
Takumé: *i.*, Tuamotu Arch. 83 g3
Takut: Burma 59 R10
Takutea: *i.*, Cook Is. 70 *Ins.*
Tala: Chinghai, China 62 R7
Talai: Kirin, China 63 W5
Talaimanaar: Sri Lanka 58 N13
Talangrimbo: Sumatra 65 D7
Talara: Peru 94 A4
Talasea: New Britain, Bismarck Arch. 67 K3
Talass: Kirgiz., U.S.S.R. 51 M6
Talat: Thailand 64 C3
Talaton: Devon, England 24 P18
Talaud Is.: Indonesia 65 H6
Talavera de la Reina: Spain 35 D17
Talbot: Vict., Australia 71 E11
Talbot, Cape: W. Australia 68 D2
Talbot Inlet: N.W.T., Can. 85 M2
Talca: Chile 96 A4
Talcahuano: Chile 96 A4
TALDY-KURGAN: *& Reg.*, Kazakh., U.S.S.R. 51 N5
Taleh: Somalia 79 R18
Talgar: Kirgiz., U.S.S.R. 51 N6
Talgarth: Powys, Wales 24 P16
Tali: Shensi, China 62 T8
Tali: Yunnan, China 62 S9
Taliabu: *i.*, Sula Is., Indon. 65 G7
Talibon: Philippines 64 G4
Talima: Brazil 94 G3
Talisayan: Mindanao, Phil. 64 G5
Talise: *i.*, Celebes 65 H6
Talish Range: *mtns.*, Iran 57 L3
Talisker: Inner Hebr., Scot. 28 J5
Taliwang: Sumbawa, Indon. 65 F8
Tal-i-Zangu, Iran 57 L5
Talkeetna: Alaska, U.S.A. 84 E5
Talkha: Egypt 56 B6
Talkheh: *riv.*, Iran 57 J3
Talladale: High., Scot. 28 L4
Talladega: Ala., U.S.A. 91 H9
Tallaght: Dublin, Repub. of Ireland 31 J13
TALLAHASSEE: Fla., U.S.A. 91 J10
Tallahatchie: *riv.*, Miss., U.S.A. 90 G8
Tallangatta: Vict., Australia 71 G11
Tallanstown: Louth, Repub. of Ireland 30 H12
Tallapoosa: Ga., U.S.A. 91 J9
Tallapoosa: *riv.*, Ala./Ga., U.S.A. 91 J9
Tallard: France 40 M11
Tallåsen: Sweden 47 P6
Tallassee: Ala., U.S.A. 91 J9
Tallata Mafara: Nigeria 81 F2
Talley: Dyfed, Wales 24 O16
TALLINN (Revel): Estonia, U.S.S.R. 47 T7
Tallow: Wat., Repub. of Irel. 31 E15
Tallulah: La., U.S.A. 90 F9
Tălmaciu: Romania 39 T14
Tal'menka: U.S.S.R. 51 O4
Talmont: France 37 D9
Tal'noye: Ukraine 50 D5
Talo: Yunnan, China 59 R10
Talodi: Sudan 79 L7
Talok: Borneo 65 F6
Talquin Lake: Fla., U.S.A. 91 J10
Talsint: Morocco 80 L8
Talsy: Latvia, U.S.S.R. 47 S8
Taltal: Chile 96 A2
Taltal: *riv.*, Chile 96 B2
Taltson River: N.W.T., Can. 84 h5
Talu: Sumatra 65 B6
Taluban: Thailand 65 b10
Taludaa: Celebes 65 G6
Taluk: Sumatra 65 C7
Talvik: Norway 46 S1
Talwood: Queens., Australia 71 H7
Talybont: Dyfed, Wales 24 O15
Talyllyn: Gwynedd, Wales 27 O14
Tama: Iowa, U.S.A. 88 E5
Tamak: U.S.S.R. 49 T5
TAMALE: Northern, Ghana 80 D3
Tamale Port: Ghana 80 D3
Tamaliyeh: Iran 57 L5
Tamana: *i.*, Gilbert Is., Pacific Ocean 67 P2
Tamanar: Morocco 80 K8
Taman Negara: *Nat. Park*, Malaya, Malaysia 65 c11
Tamano: Japan 63 c3
Tamanrasset: Algeria 78 F5
Tamanrasset: *watercourse*, Algeria 78 E5
Tamanthi: Burma 59 R9
Tamaqua: Pa., U.S.A. 89 O5
Tamar: *riv.*, Devon/Corn., England 24 N18
Tamashima: Japan 63 c3
Tamási: Hungary 43 Q13
TAMATAVE: *& Prov.*, Malagasy Rep. 73 O13
Tamaulipas: *State*, Mexico (*cap.* Ciudad Victoria) 93 H8
Tamaya: Chile 96 A3
Tamazula: Mexico 93 F7
Tamazunchale: Mexico 86 K13
Tamba Dabatou: Guinea 80 B2
Tamba, La: Guinea 80 B2
Tambach: Kenya 76 E2
TAMBACOUNDA: Senegal Oriental, Senegal 80 B2
Tambawel: Nigeria 81 E2
Tambelan Is.: Indonesia 65 D6
Tambellup: W. Australia 68 B6
Tamberias: Argentina 96 B3
Tambey: U.S.S.R. 48 J3
Tambilahan: Sumatra 65 C7
Tambo: Queens., Australia 70 G5
Tambo: *riv.*, Vict., Australia 71 G11
Tambolongan: *i.*, Indonesia 65 G8
Tamboritha, Mount: Vict., Australia 71 G11
TAMBOV: *& Reg.*, U.S.S.R. 50 F4
Tambre: *riv.*, Spain 35 B15
Tambura: Sudan 76 C1
Tamchak (Machuan): *riv.*, Tibet, China 59 P9
Tamdy-Bulak: Uzbek., U.S.S.R. 51 K6
Tamega: *riv.*, Portugal 35 C16
Tamel Aike: Argentina 95 C13
Tamera: Tunisia 38 L18
Tamerton Foliot: Devon, England 24 N19
Tamgak Mtns: Niger 78 F6
Tamgue Massif: *range*, Guinea 80 B2
Tamil Nadu: *State*, India (*cap.* Madras) 58 N12
Tamim: *Prov.*, Iraq 57 J4
Tamiš: *riv.*, Romania/Yugoslavia 39 R14
Tamis: *well*, Saudi Arabia 55 G11
Tamise: *see* Tamsche.
Tamky: Vietnam 64 D3
Tamlelt Plain: Morocco 80 L8
Tammerfors (Tampere): Fin. 47 S6
Tammisaari: Finland 47 S7
Tampa: Fla., U.S.A. 91 K12
Tampa Bay: Fla., U.S.A. 91 K12
Tampere (Tammerfors): Finland 47 S6
Tampico: Mexico 86 K13
Tampin: Malaya, Malaysia 65 c12
Tamra: Saudi Arabia 54 G10
Tamridah: Socotra 79 P7
Tamtsak Bulak: Mongolia 60 H2
Tamu: Burma 59 Q10
Tamworth: N.S.W., Austl. 71 J8
Tamworth: Staff., England 27 S14
Tana: Norway 46 V1
Tana: *i.*, New Hebrides 67 N5
Tana: *riv.*, Ghana 80 D3
Tana: *riv.*, Kenya 76 E3
Tana: *riv.*, Norway/Finland 46 U2
Tana, Lake: Ethiopia 79 M7
Tanabe: Japan 63 d4
Tanabu: Japan 63 ZZ6
Tanacross: Alaska, U.S.A. 84 e5
Tana Fiord: Norway 46 V1
Tanaga: *i.*, Aleutians 84 B7
Tanagra: Greek city of NE. *Boeotia* about 15 miles E. of Thebes. 39 S17
Tanahbala: *i.*, Sumatra 65 B7
Tanahdjampea: *i.*, Indonesia 65 G8
Tanahgrogot: Borneo 65 F7
Tanahmasa: *i.*, Sumatra 65 B7
Tanak, Cape: Aleutians 84 C7
Tanakeke I.: Celebes 65 F8
Tanakpur: Uttar Pradesh, India 58 O9
Tanamerah: W. Irian, Indonesia 66 H3
Tanana: Alaska, U.S.A. 84 d4
TANANARIVE: *see* ANTANANARIVO
Tanaro: *riv.*, Italy 40 N11
Tanchon: N. Korea 63 X6
Tanchow: Kwangsi Chuang, China 62 T9
Tanda: Uttar Pradesh, India 59 O9
Țăndărei: Romania 39 U14
Tandaue: Angola 77 A6
Tanderagee: Armagh, N. Ireland 30 J11
Tandil: Argentina 96 D4
Tandjile: *Pref.*, Chad (*cap.* Lai) 81 H3
Tando Adam: Sind, Pak. 58 L9
Tandou, Lake: N.S.W., Austl. 71 E9
Taneatua: North I., N.Z. 70 Q14
Tanega: *i.*, Osumi Is., Japan 63 Y8
Tanezrouft: *geog. reg.*, Alg. 78 E5
Tanfeng: Shensi, China 62 T8
TANGA: *& Reg.*, Tanzania 76 E4
Tangail: Bangladesh 59 P10
Tanga Is., Bismarck Arch. 67 K2
Tanganyika, Lake: E. Africa 76 C4
Tangar (Hwangyuan): Chinghai, China 62 S7
Tangaza: Nigeria 81 E2
Tangen: Norway 47 M6
Tangerhütte: E. Germany 45 R3
Tangermünde: E. Germany 45 R3
TANGIER: *& Prov.*, Morocco 80 B7
Tangier, Bay of: Morocco (Gib. *Inset*) 32 *Ins.*
Tang-i-Magas: Iran 57 L5
Tanglha Range: Tibet, China 59 P8
Tangkulayumu Hu: *lake*, Tibet, China 59 P8
Tangorin: Queens., Austl. 69 G4
Tang Pass: Tibet, China 59 Q8
Tangshan: Hopeh, China 62 V7
Tangshan: Kiangsu, China 62 V8
Tangtu: Anhwei, China 62 V8
Tanguieta: Benin 81 E2
Tanguy: U.S.S.R. 49 M6
Tangyan: Burma 59 R10
Tangyuan: Heilungkiang, China 63 X5
Tanhsien: Hainan, China 62 T11
Tanhua: Finland 46 U3
Tanigumi: Japan 63 e3
Tanimbar Is.: Indonesia 61 L13
Tanis (*Avaris*): Egyptian city near modern *San*, 25 miles NE. of Faqus, Egypt 56 B6
Tanitikon: Greek name of Nile mouth emerging at E. end of L. Manzala, Egypt 56 B6
Tanjong Malim: Malaya, Malaysia 65 b12
Tanjore (Thanjavur): Tamil Nadu, India 58 N12
Tanjung: Borneo 65 F7
Tanjung Balai: Riau Arch., Indonesia 65 e3
Tanjungbalai: Sumatra 65 B6
Tanjungenim: Sumatra 65 C7
Tanjungkarang-Telukbetung: Sumatra 65 D8
Tanjungpandan: Billiton, Indonesia 65 D7
Tanjungpinang: Riau Arch., Indonesia 65 s13
Tanjungpusu: Borneo 65 F7
Tanjungredeb: Borneo 65 F6
Tanjungselor: Boreno 65 F6
Tank: NW. Front. Prov., Pakistan 58 M8
Tankapirtti: Finland 46 U2
Tankiang: Kweichow, China 62 T9
Tanleng: Szechwan, China 62 S9
Tanlinh: S. Vietnam 64 D4
Tann: W. Germany 45 Q5
Tanna: E. Germany 45 R5
Tannadice: Tay., Scotland 29 Q6
Tannas: Sweden 46 N5
Tannenberg: battlefield about 20 m. E of Lubawa, Pol. 43 R10
Tanout: Niger 81 F2
Tanpa: Tibet, China 62 S8
Tân Phong: Vietnam 64 D4
Tanqua: *riv.*, S. Africa 74 c6
Tanque: Mexico 93 G7
Tansing: Nepal 59 O9
Tansui (Tanshui): Taiwan 63 W9
Tansyk: Kazakh., U.S.S.R. 51 N5
Tanta: Egypt 56 B6
Tantabin: Burma 59 R11
Tantanoola: Australia 71 D11
Tantow: E. Germany 45 U2
Tanuf: Oman 55 J10
Tanun: Yemen P.D.R. 55 H11
Tanunda: S. Australia 71 C10

Tanzania: *Republic* 76 D4
Cap.: Dodoma
Area: 362,820 sq. miles (939,704 sq. km.)
Pop.: 13,996,000 (*1972 E*)

Tao: *riv.*, China 62 U9
Taofu: Tibet, China 62 S8
Taohsien: Hunan, China 62 U9
Taolaichao: Kirin, China 63 X6
Taolakopa: Tibet, China 59 P8
Taonan: Kirin, China 63 W5
Taormina: Sicily 38 O18
Taos: N. Mex., U.S.A. 93 F5
Taosha: Kansu, China 62 S7
Taoudenni: Mali 78 D5
Taourirt: Algeria 78 E4
Taourirt: Morocco 80 L8
Taouz: Morocco 80 L8
Tapa: Estonia, U.S.S.R. 47 T7
Tapachula: Mexico 86 k15
Tapah: Malaya, Malaysia 65 b11
Tapa Is.: Sumatra 65 B6
Tapajós: *riv.*, Brazil 94 F5
Tapaktuan: Sumatra 65 B6
Tapan: Sumatra 65 C7
Tapanui: South I., N.Z. 71 M17
Tapa Shan: *range*, China 62 T8
Taperoá: Brazil 94 K6
Tapeta: Liberia 80 C3
Tapis: *mtn.*, Malaya, Malaysia 65 c11
Tapolca: Hungary 43 P13
Tappahannock: Va., U.S.A. 89 N7
Tapti: *riv.*, India 58 M10
Tapuaenuku: *mtn.*, South I., New Zealand 70 O16
Tapul Group: *is.*, Philippines 65 G5
Taquara: Brazil 96 E2
Taquari: *riv.*, Mato Grosso, Brazil 94 F7
Taquari: Rio Grande do Sul, Brazil 96 E2
Tara: *& hill*, Meath, Repub. of Ireland 30 H12
Tara: Queens., Australia 70 J6
Tara: U.S.S.R. 51 M3
Tara: Zambia 77 C6
Tara: *riv.*, U.S.S.R. 51 N3
Tara: *riv.*, Yugoslavia 39 Q15
Taranga I.: N.I., New Zealand 70 P12
Tarabuco: Bolivia 94 D7
Tarabulus esh Sham (Tripoli): Lebanon 56 D4
Tarabya: Turkey (Bosporus *Inset*) 20 *Ins.*
Taradale: North I., N.Z. 70 Q14
Tarag el 'Aalab: *geog. reg.*, Syrian Desert 56 F5
Tarago: N.S.W., Australia 71 H10
Tarakan: Borneo 65 F6
Taraki: Japan 63 b4
Tarakliya: Moldavia, U.S.S.R. 39 V14
Taralga: N.S.W., Australia 71 H10
Tarana: N.S.W., Australia 71 H9
Taranaki: *Dist.*, North I., N.Z. (*cap.* New Plymouth) 70 P14
Tarancon: Spain 35 E16
Tarändo: Sweden 46 S3
Tarangire Game Reserve: Tanzania 76 E3
Tarangole: Sudan 76 D2
Taransay: *i.*, Outer Hebr., Scotland 28 G4
Taranto: Italy 38 P16
Taranto, G. of: Italy 38 P17
Tarapacá: Chile 94 D7
Tarare: France 37 K10
Tararua Range: North I., New Zealand 70 P15
Tarascon: Ariège, France 37 G13
Tarascon: Bouches-du-Rhône, France 37 K12
Tarat: Algeria 78 F4
Tarauacá: Brazil 94 C5
TARAWA: *i.*, Gilbert Is. 67 O1
Tarawera: North I., N.Z. 70 Q14
Tarazit Mtns.: Niger 78 F5
Tarazona: Spain 35 F16
Tarbagatay Mtns.: Kazakh., U.S.S.R. 51 O5
Tarbat Ness: *cape*, Highland, Scotland 28 O4
Tarbert: Kerry, Repub. of Ireland 31 C14
Tarbert: Outer Hebr., Scotland 28 H4
Tarbert: Strath., Scotland 29 L8
Tarbert, East & West Loch: Outer Hebr., Scotland 28 H4
Tarbert, Loch: Inner Hebr., Scotland 29 J8
TARBES: Hautes-Pyrenées, France 37 F12
Tarbet: Strath., Scotland 29 M7
Tarbolton: Strath., Scotland 29 N8
Tarboro: N.C., U.S.A. 91 N8
Tarcento: Italy 41 T9
Tarcoola: S. Australia 68 E6
Tarcoon: N.S.W., Australia 71 G8
Tardenois: *hills*, France 36 J6
Tardets: France 37 E12
Tardoire: *riv.*, France 37 F10
Taree: N.S.W., Australia 71 K8
Tarfa: *wadi*, Egypt 54 D9
TARFAYA: *& Prov.*, Morocco 78 B4
Tarfside: Tayside, Scotland 28 Q6
Targuist: Morocco 35 D19
Târgu Frumos: Romania 43 U13
Târgu Jiu: Romania 39 S14
Târgu Mureș: Romania 43 T13
Târgu Ocna: Romania 43 U13
Târgu Săcuesc: Romania 39 U14
Tarhit: Algeria 80 L8
Tarhuna: Libya 32 E5
Tarifa: Spain (Gib. *Inset*) 32 Ins.
Tarija: Bolivia 95 E8
Tarija: *riv.*, Bolivia 96 C1
Tarikere: Karnataka, India 58 N12
Tarim: Hadhramaut, Yemen P.D.R. 55 G11
Tarim: *riv.*, Sinkiang, China 55 O6
Tarime: Tanzania 76 D3
Taritatu: *riv.*, Indonesia 61 M12
Tarjanne Lake: Finland 47 S5
Tarka: Niger 81 F2
Tarka: *Dist.*, S. Africa 75 G5
Tarkastad: S. Africa 75 G5
Tarkhankut, Cape: U.S.S.R. 50 D5
Tarko-Sale: U.S.S.R. 48 j5
Tarkwa: Ghana 80 D3
Tarlac: Luzon, Philippines 64 G3
Tarland: Gram., Scotland 28 Q5
Tarleton: Lancs., England 27 Q12
Tarma: Peru 94 B6
Tarn: *Dept. & riv.*, France (*cap.* Albi) 37 H12
Tärna: Sweden 46 O4
Târnava: *riv.*, Romania 43 T13
Tarn-et-Garonne: *Dept.*, Fr. (*cap.* Montauban) 37 G11
Tarnobrzeg: Poland 43 R11
Tarnova: *mtns.*, Yugoslavia 41 T10
Tarnow: Poland 43 R11
Tärnsjö: Sweden 47 P6
Taro: Burma 59 R9
Tarong: Queens., Australia 70 J6
Taroom: Queens., Australia 70 H5
Taroudant: Morocco 80 K8
Tarpon Springs: Fla., U.S.A. 91 K11
Tarporley: Ches., England 27 Q13
Tarracina: (mod. Terracina), Roman colony on coast about 12 miles E. of Cape Circeo, Italy 38 N16
Tarraco: Roman town at Tarragona, Spain 35 G16
Tarraconensis: Roman province of N. and E. Spain, comprising the whole peninsula except *Baetica* and *Lusitania* 35
TARRAGONA: *& Prov.*, Spain 35 G16
Tarrant City: Ala., U.S.A. 91 H9
Tarrant Gunville: Dorset, England 24 R18
Tarrasa: Spain 35 H16
Tárrega: Spain 35 G16
Tarsatica: Roman town at Rijeka, Yugoslavia 39 O14
Tarskavaig: Inner Hebr., Scotland 28 K5
Tarso Muri: *mtn.*, Libya 78 H5
Tarsus: Turkey 56 D3
Tartary, Gulf of: U.S.S.R. 49 Q8
Tartas: France 37 E12
Tartu: Estonia, U.S.S.R. 47 U7
TARTUS: *& Prov.*, Syria 56 D4
Tarutao: *i.*, Thailand 65 a10
Tarutung: Sumatra 65 B6
Tarves: Gram., Scotland 28 R5
Tarvin: Ches., England 27 Q13
Tarvisio: Italy 41 T9
Taryn: Kazakh., U.S.S.R. 51 N6
Taşanli: Turkey 56 A2
Taschereau: Que., Canada 89 M1
Tasek Dampar: *lake*, Malaya, Malaysia 65 c12
Taseko, Mount: B.C., Can. 92 C2
Taşeli: *range*, Turkey 56 C3
Taseyevo: U.S.S.R. 51 Q3
Tashauz: Turkmen., U.S.S.R. 50 J6
TASHKENT: Uzbekistan, U.S.S.R. 51 L6
Tashkumyr: Kirgiz., U.S.S.R. 51 M6
Tash Qurghan: Sinkiang, China 51 N7
Tashtyp: U.S.S.R. 51 P4
Tasikmalaya: Java 65 D8
Tasiussaq: Greenland 85 O3
Tasker: *well*, Niger 81 G1
Taşköpru: Turkey 56 D1
Taşliçay: Turkey 57 H2
Tasman: U.S.S.R. 49 R5
Tasman, Mount: South I., New Zealand 70 N16
Tasmania: *i. & State*, Austl. (*cap.* Hobart) 68 *Ins.*
Tasman Mtns.: *& bay*, South I., New Zealand 70 O15
Tasman Sea: Australasia 67 M9
Tășnad: Romania 43 S13
Tassaro: Italy 40 P11
Tassili-n-Ajjer: *plat.*, Alg. 78 F4
Tassili Oua-n-Ahaggar: *plat.*, Algeria 78 E5
Tata: Morocco 80 K9
Tataba: Solomon Is. 67 L3
Tatabánya: Hungary 43 Q13
Tatakoto: *i.*, Tuamotu Arch. 83 h3
Tatamagouche: N.S., Can. 89 U3
Tatar: A.S.S. Rep.: U.S.S.R. (*cap.* Kazan') 50 H3
Tatar Pazardzhik: Bulgaria 39 T15
Tatarsk: U.S.S.R. 51 N3
Tatars Pass: Ukraine 43 T12
Tate: Ga., U.S.A. 91 J8
Tateno: Japan 63 b4
Tateyama: Japan 63 f3
Tathlina, Lake: N.W.T., Can. 84 H5
Tathlith: *wadi*, Saudi Arabia 54 F10
Tatien: Fukien, China 62 V9
Tatla Lake: *city*, B.C., Can. 92 C2
Tatnam, Cape: Man., Can. 85 K6
Tatong: Vict., Australia 71 G11
Tatry: *mtns.*, Czech./Pol. 43 Q12
Tatsienlu (Kangting): Szechwan, China 62 S8
Tatsing: Kansu, China 62 S7
Tatta: Sind, Pakistan 58 L10
Tattenhall: Ches., England 27 Q13
Tattershall: Lincs., England 27 V13
Tattingstone: Suff., England 25 Y16
Tatu (Ting): *riv.*, China 62 S8
Tatui: Brazil 96 F1
Tatum: N. Mex., U.S.A. 93 G6
Tatung: Shansi, China 62 U6
Tatung: *riv.*, China 62 S7
Tatura: Vict., Australia 71 F11
Tatvan: Turkey 57 H2
Tau: *i.*, Samoa 70 *Ins.*
Tauá: Brazil 94 J5
Taubaté: Brazil 96 F1
Tauber: *riv.*, W. Germany 45 P6
Tauberbischofsheim: W. Ger. 44 P6
Tauere: *i.*, Tuamotu Arch. 83 g3
Tauern National Park: Austria 41 S8
Taufkirchen: W. Germany 41 S7
Tauk: Iraq 57 J4
Taumarunui: North I., N.Z. 70 P14
Taumaturgo: Brazil 94 C5
Taum Sauk Mount: Mo., U.S.A. 88 F7
Taung: *& Dist.*, S. Africa 75 F3
Taungdwingyi: Burma 59 R10
TAUNGGYI: Shan, Burma 59 R10
Taungup: Burma 59 Q11
Taunton: Mass., U.S.A. 89 Q5
TAUNTON: Som., England 24 P17
Taunton Deane, Vale of: Som., England 24 P17
Taunus: *mtns.*, W. Germany 44 O5
Tauorga: *& salt lake*, Libya 33 F5
Taupo: North I., N.Z. 70 Q14
Taupo, Lake: North I., N.Z. 70 P14
Taurage: Lithuania, U.S.S.R. 47 S9
Tauranga: North I., N.Z. 70 Q13
Taureau, Lac: Que., Can. 89 P2
Tauromenium: Greek and Roman city at Taormina, Sicily 38 O18
Taurus (Toros) Mtns.: Tur. 56 C3
Taushkan: *riv.*, Sinkiang, China 51 N6
Tauste: Spain 35 F16
Tauters: Italy 41 R9
Tauu: *i.*, Solomon Is. 67 L2
Tauves: France 37 H10
Tauz: Azerbaydzhan, U.S.S.R. 56 J1
Tavani: N.W.T., Canada 84 k5
Tavaputs Plateau, East: Utah, U.S.A. 93 F5
Tavas: Turkey 56 A3
Tavda: U.S.S.R. 51 L3
Tavda: *riv.*, U.S.S.R. 51 K3
Taveta: Kenya 76 E3
Taveta: Tanzania 77 E4
Taveuni: *i.*, Fiji Is. 67 Q5
Tavira: Portugal 35 C18
Tavistock: Devon, England 24 N18
Tavistock: Ont., Canada 88 L4
Tavolara: *i.*, Sardinia 38 L16
Tavolzhan: Kazakh., U.S.S.R. 51 N4
Tavoy: *& i.*, Burma 59 R12
Tavoy Point: *cape*, Burma 59 R12
Tavsanli: Turkey 56 A2
Tavua: Viti Levu, Fiji Is. 67 P5
Taw: *riv.*, Devon, England 24 O18
Tawas City: Mich., U.S.A. 88 K3
Tawau: Sabah, Malaysia 65 F6
Tawitawi: *i.*, Sulu Arch., Philippines 65 G5
Tawny: Don., Repub. of Ireland 30 F9
Tawton, North: Devon, Eng. 24 O18
Taxenbach: Austria 41 S8
Tay: *riv.*, Tayside, Scotland 29 O6
Tay, Firth of: Scotland 29 Q7
Tay, Loch: Tay., Scotland 29 N6
Tayabamba: Peru 94 B5
Tayaokow: Liaoning, China 63 W6
Tayfur: Turkey (Dardan. *Inset*) 20 *Ins.*
Tayga: U.S.S.R. 49 I 6
Tayinloan: Strath., Scotland 29 K8

192 Taylakovy—Tiburon

Taylakovy: U.S.S.R. **51** M3
Taylor: Texas, U.S.A. **90** C10
Taylor, Mount: N. Mex., U.S.A. **93** F5
Taylorville: Ill., U.S.A. **88** G6
Taymyr, Lake: U.S.S.R. **49** M3
Taymyra: *riv.*, U.S.S.R. **49** I 3
Taymyr Penin.: & *bay*, U.S.S.R. **49** M2
Tayninh: Vietnam 64 D4
Taynuilt: Strath., Scotland **29** L7
Tayport: Fife, Scotland **29** Q7
Tayshet: U.S.S.R. **51** R3
Tayshir: Mongolia **62** R5
Tayside: *Reg.*, Scotland (*cap.* Dundee) **29** O6
Taytay: Palawan, Philippines **64** F4
Tayu: Java **65** E8
Tayu (Nanan): Kiangsi, China **62** U9
Tayung: Hunan, China **62** U9
Tayung: Kwangtung, China **63** *Ins.*
Tayvallich: Strath., Scotland **29** K7
Taz: *penin. & bay*, U.S.S.R. **48** j4
Taz: *riv.*, U.S.S.R. **48** K4
TAZA: & *Prov.*, Morocco **80** L8
Taza Khurmatli: Iraq **57** J4
Tazenakht: Morocco **80** K8
Tazizilet: *wadi*, Niger **78** F6
Tazy: U.S.S.R. **49** N6
TBILISI (Tiflis): Georgia, U.S.S.R. **57** J1
T'boop: S. Africa **74** C5
Tchad (Chad), Lake: Chad **81** G2
Tchagen: Chad **81** H2
Tchaourou: Benin 81 E3
TCHIBANGA: Nyanga, Gabon **81** G5
TCHIEN: Grand Gedeh, Liberia **80** C3
Tczew: Poland **43** Q9
Teaca: Romania **43** T13
Teague: Texas, U.S.A. **90** C10
Tealby: Lincs., England **27** V13
Tean: Staffs., England **27** S14
Te Anau: *lake*, South I., N.Z. **70** L17
Teangue: Inner Hebr., Scot. **28** K5
Teano Range: W. Australia **68** B4
Teapa: Mexico **86** k14
Te Araroa: North I., N.Z. **70** R13
Te Aroha: North I., N.Z. **70** P13
Te Awamutu: North I., N.Z. **70** P14
Tebay: Cumbria, England **26** Q11
Tébessa: Algeria **38** L19
Tebicuary: *riv.*, Paraguay **96** D2
Tebingtinggi: (*North*), Sum. **65** B6
Tebingtinggi: (*South*), Sum. **65** B7
Tebourba: Tunisia **38** L18
Teboursouk: Tunisia **38** L18
Tech: *riv.*, France **37** H13
Tecka: Argentina **95** C12
Tecomán: Mexico **86** j14
Tecpan: Mexico **86** j14
Tecuci: Romania **39** U14
Tecumseh: Okla., U.S.A. **90** C8
Ted: Somalia **79** Q19
Tedburn St. Mary: Devon, England **24** O18
Tedzhen: Turkmen., U.S.S.R. **51** K7
Tedzhen: *riv.*, U.S.S.R./Iran **51** K7
Teelin: Don., Repub. of Ireland **30** D10
Tees: *riv.*, Durham/Cleveland, England **26** S10
Teesdale: *valley*, Durham, England **26** R10
TEESSIDE: Cleveland, England **26** T10
Tefé: Brazil **94** E4
Tefenni: Turkey **56** A3
Tegal: Java **65** D8
Tegea: Greek city about 3 miles SSE. of Tripolis, Grc. **39** S18
Tegel: E. Germany **45** T3
Tegerhi: Libya **78** G5
Tegina: Nigeria **81** F2
Tego: Queens., Australia **71** G7
TEGUCIGALPA: Honduras **86** L15
Tegul'det: U.S.S.R. **51** P3
Tehachapi Mtns.: Calif., U.S.A. **93** D6
Tehhing: Kiangsi, China **62** V9
Tehhwei: Kirin, China **63** X6
Tehini: Ivory Coast **80** D3
Tehko: Tibet, China **62** R8
TEHRAN: Iran **55** H7
Tehri: Uttar Pradesh, India **58** N8
Tehsien: Shantung, China **62** V7
Tehtsin: Tibet, China **62** R9
Tehtu: Heilungkiang, China **63** X5
Tehuacán: Mexico **86** K14
Tehuantepec: Mexico **86** K14
Tehuantepec: *isthmus and gulf*, Mexico **86** K14
Tehumardi: Estonia, U.S.S.R. **47** S7
Teian (Anlu): Hupeh, China **62** U8
Teifi: *riv.*, Wales **24** M15
Teign: *riv.*, Devon, England **24** O18
Teignmouth: Devon, Eng. **24** P18
Teil, Le: France **37** K11
Teinho: Kwangtung, China **63** *Ins.*
Teith: *riv.*, Tayside, Scotland **29** N7
Teiuş: Romania **43** S13
Te Kaha: North I., N.Z. **70** Q13
Tekapo: *lake*, South I., New Zealand **70** N16
Te Karaka: North I., N.Z. **70** Q14
Te Kauwhata: North I., N.Z. **70** P13
Te Kawa: North I., N.Z. **70** P14
Tekax: Mexico **86** L13
Tekely: Kazakh., U.S.S.R. **51** N6
Tekes: *riv.*, *see* Tekossu.
TEKIRDAĞ: & *Prov.*, Turkey **39** U16
Tekkali: Andhra Pradesh, India **59** O11
Tekoa: Wash., U.S.A. **92** D3
Tekokota: *i.*, Tuamotu Arch. **83** g3
Tekossu: & *riv.*, Sinkiang, China **51** O6
Te Kuiti: North I., N.Z. **70** P14
Tel Afar: Iraq **57** H3
Telahsi: Chinghai, China **59** Q8
Telanipura: Sumatra **65** C7
Telavi: Georgia, U.S.S.R. **57** J1
TEL AVIV-JAFFA: Israel **55** a2
Tel'bes: U.S.S.R. **51** P4
Telč: Czechoslovakia **45** V6
Telegraph Creek: B.C., Can. **84** f6
Telekhany: Byelorussia **43** T10
Telemark: *Co.*, Norway (*cap.* Skien) **47** L7
Telén: Argentina **96** B4
Telescope Peak: Calif., U.S.A. **93** D5
Teles Pires: *riv.*, Brazil **94** F5
Telford: Salop, England **27** R14
Telfs: Austria **41** R8
Telgte: W. Germany **44** N4
TÉLIMÉLÉ: & *Reg.*, Guinea **80** B2
Tel Kalakh: Syria **56** E4
Tel Kochek: Syria **57** H3
Tell City: Ind., U.S.A. **88** H7
Tel-el-Amarna: site of city in ancient Egypt on right bank of Nile near Mallawi **54** D9
Tell-el-Kebîr: Egypt **56** B6
Teller: Alaska, U.S.A. **84** C4
Tell Hum: modern site of *Capernaum* **55** b2
Tellicherry: Tamil Nadu, India **58** N12
Tello: Argentina **96** B3
Telluride: Colo., U.S.A. **93** F5
Telok Anson: Malaya, Malaysia **65** b11
Telok Datok: Malaya, Malaysia **65** b12
Telouet: Morocco **80** K8
Telsen: Argentina **95** D12
Telšiai: Lithuania, U.S.S.R. **47** S9
Telukbutun: Natuna Is. **65** D6
Telukdalem: Nias, Indonesia **65** B6
Tel Uwainat: Iraq **57** H3
Tema: Ghana **80** D3
Temangan: Malaya, Malaysia **65** c11
Temasint: Algeria **78** F5
Tematangei: Tuamotu Arch. **83** g4
Temax: Mexico **86** L13
Temba: *riv.*, Nigeria **81** G3
Tembenchi: U.S.S.R. **49** I 4
Temblador: Venezuela **94** E2
Tembuland: *geog. reg.*, S. Africa **75** H5
Teme: *riv.*, England **24** R15
Temerin: Yugoslavia **39** Q14
Temerloh: Malaya, Malaysia **65** c12
Temse: Belgium **44** K4
Temesvár: Hungarian name of town Timişoara, Romania **43** R14
Temir: Kazakh., U.S.S.R. **50** J5
Temir-Tau: Kazakh., U.S.S.R. **51** M4
Temir-Tau: Kemerovo, U.S.S.R. **51** P4
Témiscouata, Lac: Que., Canada **89** R2
Temma: Tasmania **68** G8
Temmes: Finland **46** T4
Temnikov: U.S.S.R. **50** F4
Temora: N.S.W., Australia **71** G10
Temósachic: Mexico **93** F7
Tempe: Ariz., U.S.A. **93** E6
Tempe: O.F.S., S. Africa **75** G4
Tempe: valley S. of Olympus through which river Piniós flows, Greece **39** S17
Tempe Downs: N. Territory, Australia **68** E4
Tempio: Sardinia **38** L16
Templand: Dumfries & Galloway, Scotland **29** P9
Temple: Lothian, Scotland **29** P8
Temple: Texas, U.S.A. **90** C10
Temple Combe: Som., Eng. **24** R18
Templeglentan: Lim., Repub. of Ireland **31** C15
Templemore: Tip., Repub. of Ireland **31** F14
Templenoe: Kerry, Repub. of Ireland **31** B16
Templepatrick: Antrim, N. Ireland **30** J10
Templeton: Devon, England **24** O18
Templeton: Dyfed, Wales **24** M16
Templetouhy: Tip., Repub. of Ireland **31** F14
Templin: E. Germany **45** T2
Tempo: Ferm., N. Ireland **30** G11
Temryuk: U.S.S.R. **50** E5
Temuco: Chile **96** A4
Temuka: South I., N.Z. **70** N17
Tena: Ecuador **94** B4
Tenali: Andhra Pradesh, India **58** O11
Tenararo: *i.*, Tuamotu Arch. **83** h4
Ténarunga: *i.*, Tuamotu Arch. **83** h4
Tenasserim: Burma **59** R12
Tenasserim: *State*, Burma (*cap.* Moulmein) **59** R12
Tenasserim, Great: *riv.*, Burma/Thailand **59** R12
Tenbury: Here. & Worcs., Eng. **24** Q15
Tenby: Dyfed, Wales **24** M16
Tence: France **37** K10
Tench I.: Bismarck Arch. **67** K2
Tende: France **40** N11
Ten Degree Chan.: Indian O. **59** Q13
Tendel: Mauritania **78** B6
Tendelti: Sudan **54** D12
Tendrara: Morocco **80** L8
Tendring: Essex, England **25** Y16
Tenedos: ancient Greek name of island Bozcaada, off Çanakkale, Turkey **39** U17
Ténékert: Mali **78** E6
Ténéré: *geog. reg.*, Niger **78** G6
Tenerife: *i.*, Canary Is. **78** A4
Ténès: Algeria **35** G18
Tengchung (Tengyueh): Yunnan, China **62** R9
Tengchwan: Yunnan, China **62** S9
Tenggarong: Borneo **65** F7
Tenggol: *i.*, Malaya, Malaysia **65** c11
Tenghsien: Honan, China **62** U8
Tenghsien: Shantung, China **62** V7
Tengiz, Lake: Kazakh., U.S.S.R. **51** L4
Tengkiu: Hainan, China **62** T11
Tengkow: Inner Mongolia, China **62** T7
Tengréla: Ivory Coast **80** C2
Tengyueh (Tengchung): Yunnan, China **62** R9
Teniente Matienzo: *rsch. stn.*, Antarctica **9** 65S 65W
Tenkasi: Tamil Nadu, India **58** N13
Tenke: (*NW. of Likasi*), Zaïre **77** C5
Tenke: (*S. of Likasi*), Zaïre **77** C5
TENKODOGO: Centre-Est, Upper Volta 80 D2
Tennant Creek: *town*, N. Territory, Australia **68** E3
Tennessee: *riv.*, U.S.A. **91** J8
Tennessee: *State*, U.S.A. (*cap.* Nashville) **88** H8
Tennille: Ga., U.S.A. **91** K9
Tenochtitlán: capital of the Aztec Empire, captured by the Spanish in 1521. Site at México City, Mexico **86** K14
Tenom: Sabah, Malaysia **65** F5
Tenosique: Mexico **86** k14
Tenryu: *riv.*, Japan **63** e3
Tensift: *riv.*, Morocco **80** K8
Tenterden: Kent, England **25** X17
Tenterfield: N.S.W., Austl. **71** K7
Ten Thousand Islands: Fla., U.S.A. **91** L13
Teodolina: Argentina **96** C3
Teófilo Otôni: Brazil **94** J7
Teos: Greek city on headland on NE. shore of gulf E. of Koraka Cape, Turkey **39** U17
Teotepec, Cerro: Mexico **86** j14
Tepa: Babar Is., Indonesia **61** K1
Tepehuanes: Mexico **93** F7
Tepeköy: Turkey **57** G2
Tepelenë: Albania **39** R16
Tepic: Mexico **86** j13
Teplaya Gora: U.S.S.R. **50** J3
Teplice-Sanov: Czech. **45** T5
Te Puke: North I., N.Z. **70** Q13
Teques, Los: Venezuela **94** D1
Ter: *riv.*, Spain **35** H16
Téra: Niger **80** E2
Terakeka: Sudan **76** D1
Teramo: Italy **38** N15
Terampa: Anambas Is., Indonesia **65** D6
Terang: Vict., Australia **71** E12
Ter Apel: Netherlands **44** N3
Teratak: Borneo **65** E7
Tercan: Turkey **57** G2
Terceira: *i.*, Azores **78** *Ins.*
Teregova: Romania **39** S14
Terenga: U.S.S.R. **50** G4
Terenure: Dublin, Repub. of Ireland **31** J13
Teren'-Uzyak: Kazakh., U.S.S.R. **51** K6
Teresa Cristina: Brazil **96** E1
TERESINA: Piauí, Brazil **94** J5
Teressa: *i.*, Nicobar Is. **59** Q13
Terewah, Lake: N.S.W., Australia **71** G7
Tergeste: Roman city at Trieste, Italy **41** T10
Tergnier: France **36** J6
Terhazza: *ruin*, Mali **78** C5
Terkama: Chad **79** J7
Terling: Essex, England **25** X16
Terme: Turkey **56** E1
Terme di Valdieri: Italy **40** N11
Termet: *well*, Niger **81** G1
Termez: Uzbek., U.S.S.R. **51** L7
Termini: Sicily **38** N18
Termoli: Italy **38** O16
Termon: Mayo, Repub. of Ireland **30** A11
Termonde: *see* Dendermonde.
Termonfeckin: Louth, Repub. of Ireland **30** J12
Termunten: Netherlands **44** N2
Ternate: Moluccas, Indon. **61** K11
Ternberg: Austria **41** U8
Terneuzen: Netherlands **44** J4
Terney: U.S.S.R. **63** Z5
Terni: Italy **38** N15
Ternopol': Ukraine **43** T12
Terowie: S. Australia **71** C9
Terpeniya Bay: U.S.S.R. **49** Q8
Terrace: B.C., Canada **92** B2
Terracina: Italy **38** N16
Terra Firma: Botswana **74** E2
Terralba: Sardinia **38** L17
Terranova: Sardinia **38** L16
Terrasson: France **37** G10
Terrebonne: Que., Canada **89** P3
Terrebonne Bay: La., U.S.A. **90** F11
Terre Haute: Ind., U.S.A. **88** H6
Terrell: Tex., U.S.A. **90** C9
Terrington: Norf., England **25** W14
Terrington: N. Yorks., Eng. **27** U11
Terror, Mt.: Antarctica **9** 80S 165E
Terry: Mont., U.S.A. **92** F3
Terryglass: Tip., Repub. of Ireland **31** E13
Ters-Akkan: *riv.*, U.S.S.R. **51** L4
Terschelling: *i.*, W. Frisian Is. **44** L2
Tertenia: Sardinia **38** L17
Terter: *riv.*, Azerbaydzhan, U.S.S.R. **57** K1
TERUEL: & *Prov.*, Spain **35** F16
Terumon: Sumatra **65** B6
Tervola: Finland **46** T3
Tesechoacán: Mexico **86** K14
Teshi: *riv.*, Nigeria **81** E3
Teshio: & *riv.*, Japan **63** ZZ6
Teslin: Yukon, Canada **84** f5
Teslin: *riv.*, Canada **84** f5
Tesnou: Algeria **78** E5
Tessalit: Mali **78** E5
Tessaoua: Niger **81** F2
Tessenberg: Austria **41** S9
Tessenei: Ethiopia **54** E11
Tessin: E. Germany **45** S1
Test: *riv.*, Hants., England **25** T17
Teste de Buch, La: France **37** D11
Testour: Tunisia **38** L18
Têt: *riv.*, France **37** H13
Tetbury: Glos., England **24** R16
TETE: & *Dist.*, Mozambique **77** D6
Téterchen: France **44** M6
Teterev: *riv.*, Ukraine **43** V11
Teterow: E. Germany **45** S2
Teteven: Bulgaria **39** T15
Tetford: Lincs., England **27** W13
Tetiaroa: *i.*, Society Is. **83** f3
Tetney: Lincs., England **27** V13
Teton: *riv.*, Mont., U.S.A. **92** E3
Tetovo: Yugoslavia **39** R15
Tetsworth: Oxon., England **25** T16
Tettenhall: W. Mid., England **27** R14
Tettnang: W. Germany **40** P8
TETUÁN: & *Prov.*, Morocco **80** K7
Tetyushi: U.S.S.R. **50** G4
Teuco: *riv.*, Argentina **96** C1
Teufelsbach: S.W. Africa **74** B1
Teulada: & *cape*, Sardinia **38** L17
Teupitz: E. Germany **45** T3
Teurnia: Roman town about 5 miles NW. of Spittal, Austria **41** T9
Teuschnitz: W. Germany **45** R5
Teutoburger Wald: W. Germany **44** O4
Teviot: S. Africa **75** F5
Teviot: *riv.*, Bord., Scotland **29** R8
Teviotdale, *val.*, Bord., Scot. **29** Q9
Teviothead: Bord., Scotland **29** Q9
Tevriz: U.S.S.R. **51** M3
Tew, Great: Oxon., England **25** T16
Tewane: Botswana **75** G1
Tewkesbury: Glos., England **24** R16
Texarkana: Tex., U.S.A. **90** D9
Texas: Queens., Australia **71** J7
Texas: *State*, U.S.A. (*cap.* Austin) **93** H6
Texas City: Tex., U.S.A. **90** D11
Texel: *i.*, W. Frisian Is. **44** K2
Texoma, Lake: Okla., U.S.A. **90** C9
Teyateyaneng: & *Dist.*, Lesotho **75** G4
Tezin: Afghanistan **58** L8
Tezpur: Assam, India **59** Q9
Thabana Ntlenyana: *mtn.*, Lesotho **75** H4
Thaba Nchu: & *Dist.*, O.F.S. S. Africa **75** G4
Thabazimbi: Transvaal, S. Africa **75** G2
Thabeikkyin: Burma **59** R10
Tha Deua: Laos **64** C3
Thadiq: Saudi Arabia **54** G9
Thahin: Thailand **64** C4
Thaibinh: Vietnam **64** D2

Thailand: *Kingdom* **64** C3
Cap.: Bangkok (Krung Thep)
Area: 198,455 sq. miles (513,998 sq. km.)
Pop.: 35,335,000 (*1971 E*)

Thai Muang: Thailand **64** B5
Thainguyen: Vietnam **64** D2
Thakham: Thailand **64** B5
Thakhek: Laos **64** C3
Thakwaneng: S. Africa **75** F3
Thal: NW. Front. Prov. Pakistan **58** M8
Thala: Tunisia **38** L19
Thalang (Phuket) I.: Thailand **64** B5
Thalatborivat: Cambodia 64 D4
Thallon: Queens., Australia **71** H7
Thamami: Saudi Arabia **54** F9
Thame: Oxon., England **25** U16
Thame: *riv.*, Oxon./Bucks., England **25** T16
Thames: North I., N.Z. **70** P13
Thames: *riv.*, England **25** U16
Thames: *riv.*, Ont., Canada **88** L4
Thamsbrück: E. Germany **45** Q4
Thamshavn: Norway **46** L5
Thamud: *well*, Yemen P.D.R. **55** H11
Thamugadi: Roman town at *Timgad*, about 20 miles E. of *Lambaesis* (q.v.) **32** D4
Thana: Maharashtra, India **58** M11
Thandaung: Burma **59** R11
Thane: Queens., Australia **70** J7
Thanet: Isle of: *dist.*, Kent, England **25** Y17
Thangool: Queens., Australia **70** J5
Thanh Hoa: Vietnam **64** B3
Thann: France **40** N8
Thanjavur: Tamil Nadu, India **58** N12
Thannhausen: W. Germany **40** Q7
Thaon-les-Vosges: France **36** M7
Thapsacus: ancient Syrian city on right bank of Euphrates, about 12 miles SE. of Meskene, Syria **56** F4
Thapsus: Roman town at most southerly point of G. of Hammamet about 10 miles N. of Mahdia, Tunisia **38** M19
Thar Desert: *see* Gt. Indian Desert.
Thargomindah: Queens., Australia **70** E6
Tharrawaddy: Burma **59** R11
Tharthar: *wadi*, Iraq **57** H4
Tha Song Yang: Thailand **64** B3
Thásos: *i. & str.*, Greece **39** T16
Thatcham: Berks., England **25** T17
Thatcher: Ariz., U.S.A. **93** F6
Thaton: Burma **59** R11
Thaungdut: Burma **59** Q10
Thawatti: Burma **59** R11
Thaxted: Essex, England **25** W16
Thaya (Dyje): *riv.*, Czech./Austria **41** V7
Thayer: Mo., U.S.A. **88** F7
Thayetmyo: Burma **59** R11
Thazi: Burma **59** R10
Theba: Ariz., U.S.A. **93** E6
Thebes (Thivai): Greece **39** S17
Thebes (No): ancient Egyptian city on right bank of Upper Nile near Luxor, Egypt **54** D9
Thedford: Nebr., U.S.A. **92** G4
Theebine: Queens., Austl. **70** K5
Theil, Le: France **36** F7
Theiss: German name of river Tisza, Hungary and Yugoslavia **43** R14
Thelon: *riv. & game sanctuary*, Canada **84** j5
Themar: E. Germany **45** Q5
Themed: Egypt **56** D7
Thénezay: France **37** E9
Thenon: France **37** G10
Theodore: Queens., Austl. **70** J5
Therezopolis: Brazil **96** F2
Therma: Greek city on E. coast of inlet S. of Salonica, Greece **39** S16
Thérmai, G. of: Greece **39** S16
Thermiá (Kithnos): *i.*, Grc. **39** T18
Thermopolis: Wyo., U.S.A. **92** F4
Thermopylae: pass between mtns. and Gulf of *Malis* (gulf E. of Lamia and W. of N. Euboea), Greece **39** S17
Thesiger Bay: N.W.T., Can. **84** g3
Thespiae: Greek city of central *Boeotia* about 8 miles W. of Thebes **39** S17
Thessalia: *see* Thessaly.
Thessalon: Ont., Canada **88** K2
Thessaloniki: Greece **39** S16
Thessaly: *Reg.*, Greece **39** S17
Thetford: Norf., England **25** X15
Thetford Mines: *city*, Que., Canada **89** Q2
Theunissen: O.F.S., S. Africa **75** G4
The Vale: N.S.W., Australia **71** E9
Theveste: Punic town, later Roman Camp, at Tebessa, Algeria **38** L19
Thiaucourt: France **40** L7
Thiberville: France **36** F6
Thibodaux: La., U.S.A. **90** F11
Thiéblemont-Farémont: Fr. **36** K7
Thief River Falls: *city*, Minn., U.S.A. **92** H3
Thielt: *see* Tielt.
Thiene: Italy **41** R10
Thiérache: *geog. reg.*, France **36** J6
Thiers: France **37** J10
THIÈS: & *Reg.*, Senegal **80** A2
Thika: Kenya **76** E3
Thillot, Le: France **40** M8
Thimerais: *geog. reg.*, Fr. **36** G7
THIMPHU: Bhutan **59** P9
Thingeyri: Iceland **46** b4
Thingvellir: Iceland **46** c4
Thio: Ethiopia **54** F12
Thionville: France **44** M6
Thi Qar: *Prov.*, Iraq **57** K6
Thira: *i.*, Cyclades **39** T18
Thirkleby: N. Yorks., England **26** T11
Thirlmere: *lake*, Cumb., Eng. **26** P10
Thiron: France **36** G7
Thirsk: N. Yorks., England **26** T11
Thirty One Mile Lake: Que., Canada **89** O2
Thisted: Denmark **47** L8
Thistil Fiord: Iceland **46** h3
Thistle Creek: *settlement*, Yukon, Canada **84** F5
Thistle I.: S. Australia **71** B10
Thitu: *reef*, S. China Sea **64** E4
Thivai: *see* Thebes.
Thivars: France **36** G7
Thiviers: France **37** F10
Thizy: France **37** K9
Thjórsá: *riv.*, Iceland **46** d4
Thoen: Thailand **64** B3
Thomas: Okla., U.S.A. **90** B8
Thomas Street: *village*, Rosc., Repub. of Ireland **30** E13
Thomaston: Ga., U.S.A. **91** J9
Thomaston: Maine, U.S.A. **89** R3
Thomaston: N.B., Canada **89** S3
Thomastown: Kilk., Repub. of Ireland **31** G14
Thomasville: Ala., U.S.A. **91** H10
Thomasville: Ga., U.S.A. **91** K10
Thomasville: N.C., U.S.A. **91** L8
Thompson: *riv.*, Iowa, U.S.A. **88** E5
Thompson: Man., Canada **92** H1
Thomson's Falls: *see* Nyahururu
Thomson: Ga., U.S.A. **91** K9
Thomson: riv., Queens., Australia **69** G4
Thônes: France **40** M10
Thönglabakki: Iceland **46** d3
Thonon: France **40** M9
Thorame-Haute: France **40** M11
Thoré: *riv.*, France **37** H12
Thoreno: France **40** M12
Thoresby, North: Lincs., England **27** V13
Thorhout: Belgium **44** J4
Thorigny: France **36** J7
Thörl: Austria **41** V8
Thornaby on Tees: Cleveland, England **26** T10
Thornborough: Bucks., Eng. **25** U15
Thornbury: Avon, England **24** Q16
Thornbury: South I., N.Z. **71** M18
Thorndon: Suff., England **25** Y15
Thorne: S. Yorks., England **27** U12
Thorner: W. Yorks., England **27** T12
Thorney: Cambs., England **25** V14
Thornhill: Dumf. & Gall., Scot. **29** O9
Thornhill: Central, Scotland **29** N7
Thornhill: W. Yorks., England **27** S12
Thornley: Durham, England **26** T10
Thornton: Ches., England **27** Q13
Thornton: Fife, Scotland **29** P7
Thornton: Lancs., England **27** P12
Thornton: N. Yorks., England **27** R12
Thornton Cleveleys: Lancs., England **27** P12
Thornton Dale: *village*, N. Yorkshire, England **26** U11
Thornton le Beans: N. Yorkshire, England **26** T11
Thornville: Natal, S. Africa **75** J4
Thorpdale: Vict., Australia **71** G12
Thorpe: Derby., England **27** S13
Thorpe le Soken: Essex, Eng. **25** Y16
Thorpe on the Hill: Lincs., England **27** U13
Thorpe Thewles: Cleveland, England **26** T10
Thorrington: Essex, England **25** Y16
THORSHAVN: Strömö, Faeroe Is. **46** h5
Thorverton: Devon, England **24** O18
Thouars: France **36** E9
Thouet: *riv.*, France **37** E9
Thousand Islands: Canada/U.S.A. **89** N3
Thrace: *Reg.*, Greece **39** T16
Thráki: *see* Thrace.
Thrapston: Northants., England **25** U15
Three Anchor Bay: S. Africa **74** Ins.
Three Bridges: W. Sussex, Eng. **25** V17
Three Cities, The: Malta **32** *Ins.*
Three Forks: Mont., U.S.A. **92** E3
Three Hills: *town*, Alta., Canada **92** E2
Three Kings Is.: N.Z. **67** O8
Three Points: *cape*, Ghana **80** D4
Three Rivers: *city*, Tex., U.S.A. **90** B11
Three Sisters: S. Africa **74** E5
Three Springs: W. Australia **68** B5
Threlkeld: Cumbria, Eng. **26** P10
Threshfield: N. Yorks., Eng. **27** R11
Thria: Greek village and plain in *W. Attica* about 3 miles NE. of Eleusis **39** S17
Thropton: Northumb., England **68** C5
Thrumster: High., Scotland **28** P3
Thuin: Belgium **44** K5
Thuir: France **37** H13
Thulaima: Saudi Arabia **54** G10
Thule: Greenland **85** N2
Thule: *mtn.*, N.W.T., Can. **85** M3
Thumby: W. Germany **45** P1
Thun: & *lake*, Switzerland **40** N9
Thunder Bay: Mich., U.S.A. **88** K3
Thunder Bay: & *town*, Ont., Canada **88** G1
Thunkar: Bhutan **59** Q9
Thuqaib Pools: Saudi Arabia **54** G10
Thur: *riv.*, Switzerland **40** O8
Thurcroft: S. Yorks., England **27** T13
Thurgau: *Canton*, Switz. (*cap.* Frauenfeld) **40** P8
Thurii: Greek city near mouth of *Crathis* river, about 10 miles N. of Corigliano Calabro, Italy **38** P17
Thuringer Wald: *mtns.*, E. Germany **45** Q5
Thürkow: E. Germany **45** S2
Thurlby: Lincs., England **27** V14
Thurles: Tip., Repub. of Ireland **31** F14
Thurlow, Great: Suff., Eng. **25** W15
Thurlow Dam: Ala., U.S.A. **91** J9
Thurlow Downs: N.S.W., Australia **71** E7
Thurmaston: Leics., Eng. **27** T14
Thurrock: *see* Grays Thurrock.
Thursby: Cumbria, England **26** P10
Thursday I.: Queens., Austl. **69** G2
Thursley: Surrey, England **25** U17
Thurso: Highland, Scotland **28** O2
Thurso: *riv.*, High., Scotland **28** P2
Thurston I.: Antarctica **9** 75S 100W
Thurton: Norf., England **25** Y14
Thury-Harcourt: France **36** E7
Thusis: Switzerland **40** P9
Thyateira: city of ancient *Lydia*, now in ruins near Akhisar, Turkey **39** U17
Thyou: Upper Volta **80** D2
TIARET: & *Dept.*, Algeria **35** G19
Tiaro: Queens., Australia **70** K5
Tiaski: Senegal **80** B1
Tiassale: Ivory Coast **80** D3
Tibaga: Upper Volta **80** E2
Tibagi: & *riv.*, Brazil **96** E1
Tibanefontein: Trans., S. Africa **75** H1
Tibati: Cameroun **81** G3
Tibbermore: High., Scotland **29** O7
Tibberton: Glos., England **24** R16
Tibberton: Salop, England **27** R14
Tibenham: Norf., England **25** Y15
Tiber: *riv.*, Italy **38** N16
Tiberias: Israel **55** b2
Tiberias, Lake (Sea of Galilee): Israel **55** b2
Tibesti: *highlands*, Chad **78** H5
Tibesti Serir: *plat.*, Libya **78** H5
Tibet: *Autonomous Region*, China (*cap.* Lhasa) **59** —
Tibiscum: Roman town at Caransebeş, Romania **43** S14
Tibnin: Lebanon **55** b1
Tiboku Falls: Guyana **87** d8
Tibooburra: N.S.W., Austl. **71** E7
Tibro: Sweden **47** O7
Tibshelf: Derby., England **27** T13
Tibur: ancient Latin city at Tivoli, Latium, Italy. **38** N16
Tiburon: Haiti **87** m14

For Abbreviations see list on p.113. Italic type, e.g. *Ephesus*, refers to historical names not on maps. Capital letters, e.g. MADRID, show capitals of countries; small capital letters, e.g. CADIZ, show capitals of provinces, etc. General notes p.116.

Tiburón—Torver 193

Tiburon: *i.*, Mexico **93** E7
Ticao: *i.*, Philippines **64** G4
Ticehurst: E. Sussex, England **25** W17
Tichitt: Mauritania **78** C6
Ticino: *Canton*, Switzerland (*cap.* Bellinzona) **40** O9
Ticino: *riv.*, Italy **40** O10
Ticinum: Roman city at Pavia, Italy **40** P10
Tickalara: Queens., Austl. **71** E7
Tickera: S. Australia **71** B9
Tickhill: S. Yorks., England **27** T13
Ticonderoga: N.Y., U.S.A. **89** P4
Tidaholm: Sweden **47** N7
Tiddim: Burma **59** Q10
Tideford: Corn., England **24** N19
Tideswell: Derby., England **27** S13
TIDJIKJA: Tagant, Mauritania **78** B6
Tidworth: Wilts., England **25** S17
Tiebissou: Ivory Coast **80** C3
Tiefencastel: Switzerland **40** P9
Tiehli: Heilungkiang, China **63** X5
Tiehling: Liaoning, China **63** W6
Tieio: Ivory Coast **80** C3
Tiékongoba: Mali **80** C2
Tiel: Netherlands **44** L4
Tielt: Belgium **44** J5
Tieme: Ivory Coast **80** C3
Tiémou: Ivory Coast **80** C3
Tienchang: Anhwei, China **62** V8
Tienchen: Shansi, China **62** U6
Tiencheng: Kwangtung, China **62** U10
Tienen: Belgium **44** K5
Tiengssu: Kwangsi Chuang, China **62** T9
Tienho: Kwangsi Chuang, China **62** T10
Tienpao: Kwangsi Chuang, China **62** T10
Tien Shan: *range*, Sinkiang, China **51** O6
Tienshui: Kansu, China **62** T8
Tientsin: Tientsin Municipality, China **62** V7
Tienyen: Vietnam 64 D2
Tierce: France **36** E8
Tiermas: Spain **35** F15
Tierp: Sweden **47** P6
Tierra Amarilla: Chile **96** A2
Tierra Amarilla: N. Mex., U.S.A. **93** F5
Tierra del Fuego: *i. & Territ.*, Chile Argentina (*cap. of Argentinian Territ.* Ushuaia) **95** D14
Tietar: *riv.*, Spain **35** D17
Tiete: *riv.* Brazil **96** F1
Tiffauges: France **38** D8
Tiffin: Ohio, U.S.A. **88** K5
TIFLIS (Tbilisi): Georgia, U.S.S.R. **57** J1
Tifore: *i.*, Indonesia **65** H6
Tifton: Ga., U.S.A. **91** K10
Tifu: Buru, Indonesia **65** H7
Tigăneşti: Romania **39** U14
Tiger Is.: Indonesia **65** G8
Tighnabruaich: Strath., Scot. **29** L8
Tigieglo: Somalia **79** Q19
Tigil': U.S.S.R. **49** r6
Tignere: Cameroun **81** G3
Tignes: *res.*, France **40** M10
Tignish: P.E.I., Canada **89** T2
Tigre: Ethiopia (*cap.* Makale) **79** M7
Tigre: *riv.*, Ecuador/Peru **94** B4
Tigre, El: Venezuela **94** E2
Tigres, Los: Argentina **96** C2
Tigris: *riv.*, Iraq/Turkey **57** J5
Tiguila: Mali **80** D2
Tigzirt-sur-Mer: Algeria **35** J18
Tihama: *geog. reg.*, Saudi Arabia **54** F11
Tijesno: Yugoslavia **41** V12
Tijoca: Brazil **94** H4
Tijuana: Mexico **93** D6
Tijucas: Brazil **96** F2
Tikanau: *i.*, Tuamotu Arch. **83** f2
Tikamgarh: Vindhya Pradesh, India **59** N10
Tikane: S.W. Africa **74** A1
Tikei: *i.*, Tuamotu Arch. **83** g2
Tikhoretsk: U.S.S.R. **50** F5
Tikhvin: U.S.S.R. **50** D3
Tikopia: Santa Cruz Is., Pacific Ocean **67** N4
Tikrit: Iraq **57** H4
Tikshozero, Lake: Karelian A.S.S.R., U.S.S.R. **46** W3
Tiksi: U.S.S.R. **49** o3
Tiladummati Atoll: Maldive Is. **58** M13
Tilamuta: Celebes **65** G6
Tilburg: Netherlands **44** L4
Tilbury: Essex, England **25** W17
Tilcara: Argentina **96** B1
Tileagd: Romania **43** S13
Tilemsi: *watercourse*, Mali **78** E6
Tilichiki: U.S.S.R. **49** s5
Tilin: Burma **59** Q10
Till: *riv.*, Northumb., Eng. **26** R8
Tillabery: Niger **81** E2
Tillamook: Oreg., U.S.A. **92** C3
Tillanchong: *i.*, Nicobar Is. **59** Q13
Tille: *riv.*, France **36** L8
Tiller, Lake: N.C., U.S.A. **91** L8
Tilley: Alta., Canada **92** E2
Tillicoultry: Central, Scot. **29** O7
Tillingham: Essex, England **25** X16
Tillonsburg: Ont., Canada **88** L4
Tilly: France **36** L6
Tillyfourie: Gram., Scotland **28** Q5
Tilly-sur-Seulles: France **36** E6
Tilney St. Lawrence: Norf., England **25** W14
Tilokhar: Bihar, India **59** O10
Tilos: *i.*, Dodecanese **39** U18
Tilshead: Wilts., England **24** S17
Tilstock: Salop, England **27** Q14
Tiltagara: N.S.W., Austl. **71** F8
Tiltil: Chile **96** A3
Tilzit (Sovetsk): U.S.S.R. **47** R9
Tim: U.S.S.R. **50** E4
Timagami, Lake: Ont., Can **88** L2
Timahoe: Kild., Repub. of Ireland **31** H13
Timaru: South I., N.Z. **70** N17
Timasheyskaya: U.S.S.R. **50** E5
Timbalier: *i. & bay*, La., U.S.A. **90** F1
Timbalier I., East: La., U.S.A. **90** *Ins.*
Timbedra: Mauritania **80** C1
Timber Lake: *town*, S. Dak., U.S.A. **92** G3
Timberland: Lincs., Eng. **27** V13
Timberscombe: Som., Eng. **24** P17
Timbo: Guinea **80** B2
Timboon: Vict., Australia **71** E12
Timbuktu (Tombouctou): Mali **80** D1
Timdjaouine: Algeria **78** E5
Timerein: Sudan **54** E11
Timimoun: Algeria **80** M9
Timis: *riv.*, Romania/Yugoslavia **39** R14
Timiskaming: Que., Canada **89** M2
Timiskaming, Lake: Ont./Que., Canada **89** M2
Timişoara: Romania **39** R14
Timkovichi: Byelorussia **43** U10
Timmins: Ont., Canada **88** L1
Ti-m-Missao: Algeria **78** E5
Timmonsville: S.C., U.S.A. **91** M8
Timmoudi: Algeria **80** L9
Timoe: Tuamotu Arch. **83** h4
Timoleague: Cork, Repub. of Ireland **31** D16
Timor: *i.*, (Indon./Port.), SE. Asia **65** G8
Timor Sea: Australia **68** D2
Timote: Argentina **96** C4
Timpah: Borneo **65** E7
Timpson: Tex., U.S.A. **90** D10
Timsâh, Lake: Egypt (Suez Canal *Inset*) **32** *Ins.*
Timur: Kazakh., U.S.S.R. **51** L6
Tina: *riv.*, S. Africa **75** H5
Tina, Bay of: Egypt **56** c6
Tinaca Point: *cape*, Mindanao, Philippines **65** H5
Tinahely: Wick., Repub. of Ireland **31** J14
Tinajones: *riv.*, Panama **94** *Ins.*
Tinambung: Celebes **65** F7
Tinca: Romania **43** R13
Tinchebray: France **36** E7
Tin City: Alaska, U.S.A. **84** C4
Tindouf: Algeria **78** C4
Ti-n-Ekkart: *well*, Mali **81** E1
Tineo: Spain **35** C15
Ting (Tatu): *riv.*, China **62** S8
Tingan: Hainan, China **62** U11
Tingcho: Tibet, China **58** O8
Tingchow (Changting): Fukien, China **62** V9
Tingewick: Bucks., England **25** T16
Tinggi: *i.*, Malaya, Malaysia **65** d12
Tingha: N.S.W., Australia **71** J7
Tinghing: Hopeh, China **62** V7
Tinghir: Morocco **80** K8
Tinghsien: Hopeh, China **62** U7
Tingis: Roman name of Tangier **35** D19
Tingkye: Tibet, China **59** P9
Tinglev: Denmark **47** L9
Tingo Maria: Peru **94** B5
Tingoora: Queens., Australia **70** J6
Tingpien: Shensi, China **62** T7
Tingri: Tibet, China **59** P9
Tingsin (Maomu): Kansu, China **62** R6
Tingsryd: Sweden **47** O8
Tingyuan: Anhwei, China **62** V8
Tinian: *i.*, Mariana Is. **61** O8
Tinie: Upper Volta **80** D2
Tinjoub: *oasis*, Algeria **80** K9
Tinkisso: *riv.*, Guinea **80** C2
Tinnevelly (Tirunelveli): Tamil Nadu, India **58** N13
Tinniswood, Mt.: B.C., Can. **92** C2
Tinn Lake: Norway **47** L7
Tinnoset: Norway **47** L7
Tinogasta: Argentina **96** B2
Tinombo: Celebes: **65** G6
Tinos: & *i.*, Cyclades **39** T18
Tiñosa, Cape: Spain **35** F18
Tinrhert Hamada: *plat.*, Alg. **78** F4
Tinsley: S. Yorks., England **27** T13
Ti-n-Tadjane: Algeria **78** E5
Tintagel: Corn., England **24** M18
Tintane: *well*, Mauritania **78** A5
Tinteniac: France **36** D7
Tintern: *abbey*, Gwent, Wales **24** Q16
Tintina: Argentina **96** C2
Tintinara: S. Australia **71** D10
Tinto: Cameroun **81** F3
Tintwistle: Derby., Eng. **27** S13
Tinwald: South I., N.Z. **70** N16
Tinye: Upper Volta **80** D2
Tio, Pic de: *mtn.*, Guinea **80** C3
Tiogo: La., U.S.A. **90** E10
Tioman: *i.*, Malaya, Malaysia **65** d12
Tione: Italy **41** Q9
Tioro, Str.: Celebes **65** G7
Tipasa: Algeria **35** H18
Tiphsah: biblical name of ancient *Thapsacus*, near Raqqa, Syria **56** F4
Tipperary: Tip., Repub. of Ireland **31** E15
Tipperary: *Co.*, Repub. of Ireland (*cap. of S. Riding*, Clonmel; *cap. of N. Riding*, Nenagh) **31** F14
Tipton: Ind., U.S.A. **88** H5
Tipton: Iowa, U.S.A. **88** F5
Tipton: Okla., U.S.A. **90** B8
Tipton: W. Mid., England **27** R14
Tipton, Mount: Ariz., U.S.A. **93** E5
Tipton St. John's: Devon, England **24** P18
Tiptree: Essex, England **25** X16
TIRANE (Tirana): Albania **39** Q16
Tirano: Italy **40** Q9
Tiras Plat: S.W. Africa **74** B3
Tiraspol': Moldavia, U.S.S.R. **50** C5
Tire: Turkey **39** U17
Tirebolu: Turkey **56** F1
Tiree: *airfield*, Inner Hebrides, Scotland **29** H7
Tiree: *i.*, Inner Hebr., Scot. **29** H6
Tiree Passage: *chan.*, Inner Hebr., Scotland **29** H7
Tirga More: *mtn.*, Outer Hebrides, Scotland **28** H4
Tirich Mir: *mtn.*, Pakistan **58** M7
Tiris-Zemmour: *Dist.*, Mauritania (*cap.* F'Derik) **78** B5
Tirlemont: *see* Tienen.
Tirley: Glos., England **24** R16
Tirlyanski: U.S.S.R. **50** J4
Tirnavos: Greece **39** S17
Tirol: *see* Tyrol.
Tir-Phil: Mid. Glam., Wales **24** P16
Tirschenreuth: W. Germany **45** S6
Tirso: *riv.*, Sardinia **38** L16
Tiruchendur: Tamil Nadu, India **58** N13
Tiruchchirapalli: Tamil Nadu, India **58** N12
Tirunelveli: Tamil Nadu, India **58** N13
Tirupati: Andhra Pradesh, India **58** N12
Tiruppattur: Tamil Nadu, India **58** N12
Tiruvannamalai: Tamil Nadu, India **58** N12
Tiryns: ancient city about 2½ miles N. of Navplion, Greece **39** S18
Tirzah: city of ancient *Israel* in valley NE. of Nablus, Israel, exact site unknown **55** b2
Tisa'a: *rly. station*, Egypt (Suez Canal. *Inset*) **32** *Ins.*
Tisbury: Wilts., England **24** R17
Tisdale: Sask., Canada **92** G2
Tisjeh: *well*, Somalia **79** R17
Tiskovac: Yugoslavia **41** W11
Tišnov: Czechoslovakia **45** W6
Tissemsilt: Algeria **35** G19
Tista: *riv.*, India/Bangladesh **59** P9
Tisza: *riv.*, Yugo./Hung. **43** R14
Tit: Algeria **78** E4
Tit: Algeria **78** F5
Titaf: Algeria **78** D4
Titchfield: Hants., England **25** T18
Titchmarsh: Northants., England **25** V15
Titel: Yugoslavia **39** R14
Titicaca, Lake: Bolivia/Peru **94** D7
Titley: Here. & Worcs., Eng. **24** Q15
Titlis: *mtn.*, Switzerland **40** O9
TITOGRAD: Montenegro, Yugoslavia **39** Q15
Titovo Užice: Yugoslavia **39** Q15
Titov Veles: Yugoslavia **39** R16
Titsey: site of Roman villa about 2½ miles W. of Westerham, border of Kent and Surrey, England **25** W17
Tittmoning: W. Germany **41** S7
Titule: Zaire **76** C2
Titusville: Fla., U.S.A. **91** L11
Titusville: Pa., U.S.A. **89** M5
Tiumpan Head: *cape*, Outer Hebr., Scotland **28** J3
Tivaouane: Senegal **80** A2
Tiverton: Devon, England **24** P18
Tivetshall St. Margaret: Norf., England **25** Y15
Tivoli: Italy **38** N16
Tivyside: *val.*, Dyfed, Wales **24** N15
Tizard: *reef*, S. China Sea **64** E4
Tizi: Algeria **35** G19
Tizimin: Mexico **86** L13
Tizi Ouzou: & *Dept.*, Algeria **35** J18
Tiznit: Morocco **80** K9
Tjalang: *see* Calang
Tjåmotes: Sweden **46** Q3
Tjeggelvas Lake: Sweden **46** P3
Tjeldsund: Norway **46** P2
Tjidjulang: *see* Cijulang
Tjilitjap: *see* Cilicap
Tjirebon: *see* Cirebon
Tjolotjo: Rhodesia **77** C6
Tjörn: Iceland **46** c4
Tjorn: *i.*, Sweden **47** M7
Tjummarum: Netherlands **44** L2
Tlahualilo de Zaragoza: Mexico **93** G7
Tlaring: S. Africa **75** F3
Tlaxcala: Mexico **86** K14
Tlaxiaco: Mexico **86** K14
TLEMCEN: & *Dept.*, Algeria **80** L8
Tlyarata: U.S.S.R. **50** G6
Tmolus: chain of mtns. between rivers *Hermus* (Gediz) and *Cayster*, Tur. **39** U17
Tnihaia: Algeria **78** D5
To: Upper Volta **80** D2
To: *i.*, Japan **63** f3
To: *riv.*, China **62** T9
Toango (Toungo): Nigeria **78** G8
Toano: Va., U.S.A. **89** N7
Toau: *i.*, Tuamotu Arch. **83** f3
Toay: Argentina **96** C4
Toba: Japan **63** e3
Toba, Lake: Sumatra **65** B6
Tobago: *i.*, Trinidad & Tobago **87** c5
Tobarra: Spain **35** F17
Tobelo: Moluccas, Indon. **61** K11
Tobermore: Lon., N. Irel. **30** H10
Tobermory: Inner Hebr., Scotland **29** J6
Tobermory: Ont., Canada **88** L3
Tobermory: Queens., Austl. **70** E6
Toberonochy: Luing, Strathclyde, Scotland **29** K7
Tobi: *i.*, Honshu, Japan **63** Z7
Tobi: *i.*, Pacific O. **61** L11
Tobique: N.B., Canada **89** S2
Toboali: Bangka, Indonesia **65** D7
Tobol: *riv.*, U.S.S.R. **51** L3
Toboli: Celebes **65** G7
Tobol'sk: U.S.S.R. **51** L3
Tobruk: Libya **33** G5
Tocantinopolis: Brazil **94** H5
Tocatins: *riv.*, Brazil **94** H4
Toccoa: Ga., U.S.A. **91** K8
Tochapu Shan: *mtn.*, Tibet, China **58** O8
Tochiang: Sinkiang, China **48** k10
Tochigi: *Pref.*, Japan (*cap.* Utsunomiya) **63** f2
Tocksfors: Sweden **47** M7
Tockwith: N. Yorks., Eng. **27** T12
Toconao: Chile **96** B1
Tocopilla: Chile **95** C8
Tocorpuri: *mtn.*, Bolivia **96** B1
Tocra: Libya **33** G5
Tocumwal: N.S.W., Austl. **71** F10
Toddington: Beds., England **25** U16
Todeli: Sula Is., Indonesia **65** G7
Todenyang: Kenya **76** E2
Todi: Italy **38** N15
Todmorden: S. Australia **68** E5
Todmorden: W. Yorks., Eng. **27** R12
Todtnau: W. Germany **40** N8
Toe Head: Cork, Repub. of Ireland **31** C17
Toe Head: Harris, Scot. **28** G4
Toeslaan: S. Africa **74** D4
Tofield: Alta., Canada **92** E2
Tofua: *i.*, Tonga **67** R5
Togane: Japan **63** g3
Toghraqbulaq: China **62** Q6
Togi: Japan **63** e2
Togian Is.: Celebes **65** G7

Togo: *Republic* **80** E3
Cap.: Lome
Area: 21,853 sq. miles
(56,599 sq. km.)
Pop.: 1,960,000 (*1972 E*)

Toguchin: U.S.S.R. **51** O3
Toguzak: *riv.*, U.S.S.R. **51** K4
Tohen: Somalia **79** S17
Tohma: *riv.*, Turkey **56** E2
Tohmajarvi: Finland **46** W5
Tohopekaliga L.: Fla., U.S.A. **91** L11
Toi Lake: Finland **46** S5
Toili: Celebes **65** G7
Toinya: Sudan **76** C1
Toise River: *town*, S. Africa **75** G6
Tojo: Celebes 65 G7
Tojo: Japan **63** c3
Tokaanu: North I., N.Z. **70** P14
Tokai: S. Africa **74** *Ins.*
Tokaj: Hungary **43** R12
Tokamachi: Japan **63** f2
Tokanui: South I., N.Z. **71** M18
Tokar: Sudan **54** E11
Tokara Is.: Ryukyu Is. **63** X9
Tokarevka: Kazakh., U.S.S.R. **51** M4
TOKAT: & *Prov.*, Turkey **56** E1
Toke: Celebes **65** G7
Tokelau (Union) Is.: (N.Z.), Pacific O. **70** *Ins.*
Tokhumtu: Sinkiang, China **51** O6
Toki: Japan **63** e3
Tokmak: Kirgiz., U.S.S.R. **51** N6
Toko (Tungchiang): Taiwan **63** W10
Tokosun: Sinkiang, China **51** P6
Tokotan: Uruppu, Kuril Is. **63** YY5
Tokoto: Inner Mongolia, China **62** U6
Toktogul: Kirgiz., U.S.S.R. **51** M6
Toktoyaktuk (Port Brabant): N.W.T. Canada **84** f4
Tokuno: *i.*, Ryukyu Is. **63** X9
TOKUSHIMA: & *Pref.*, Japan **63** d3
Tokuyama: Japan **63** b3
TOKYO: & *Pref.*, Japan **63** f3
Tolaga Bay: *town*, North I., New Zealand **70** R14
Tolarno: N.S.W., Australia **71** E9
Tolbukhin: Bulgaria **39** U15
Toledo: Chile **96** A2
Toledo: Ohio, U.S.A. **88** K5
Toledo: Oreg., U.S.A. **92** C4
TOLEDO: & *Prov.*, Spain **35** D17
Toledo, Montes de: *mtns.*, Spain **35** C17
Toledo Bend Res.: La., U.S.A. **90** E10
Tolen: *i.*, Netherlands **44** K4
Toletum: Roman town at Toledo (central Spain) **35** D17
Tolga: Algeria **32** D5
Tolima: *mtn.*, Colombia **94** B3
Tolitoli: Celebes **65** G6
Tolkkinen: Finland **46** U4
Tollense See: *lake*, E. Ger. **45** T2
Tollerton: N. Yorks., Eng. **27** T11
Tollesbury: Essex, England **25** X16
Tolleshunt d'Arcy: Essex, England **25** X16
Tolmeta: Libya **33** G5
Tolmezzo: Italy **41** T9
Tolmin: Yugoslavia **41** T9
Tolob: Mainland, Shetland Is. **28** *Ins.*
Tolong: Philippines **64** G5
Tolosa: Spain **37** C12
Tolosa: Roman city at Toulouse, France **37** G12
Tolpuddle: Dorset, Eng. **24** R18
Tolsta, North: Outer Hebr., Scotland **28** J3
Tolstachoelish: Outer Hebr., Scotland **28** H3
Tolsta Head: *cape*, Outer Hebr., Scotland **28** J3
Tolstoy, Cape: U.S.S.R. **49** r6
Tolten: Chile **95** C11
Toluca: Mexico **86** K14
Tolun: Inner Mongolia, China **62** V6
Tol'yatti: U.S.S.R. **50** G4
Tolz: W. Germany **41** R8
Tom': *riv.*, U.S.S.R. **51** P4
Toma: Ethiopia **79** Q18
Tomah: Wis., U.S.A. **88** F4
Tomahawk: Wis., U.S.A. **88** G3
Tomakomai: Japan **63** ZZ6
Tomakovka: Ukraine **50** D5
Tomar: Portugal **35** B17
Tomari: Japan **63** e2
Tomari: U.S.S.R. **63** ZZ5
Tomaszow: Lodz, Poland **43** R11
Tomaszow: Lublin, Poland **43** S11
Tomaszow Mazowiecki: Pol. **43** R11
Tomatin: High., Scotland **28** O5
Tomatlan: Mexico **86** J14
Tombe: Sudan **76** D1
Tombetsu: Japan **63** ZZ5
Tombigbee: *riv.*, Miss./Ala., U.S.A. **90** G10
Tomboco: Angola **73** G11
Tombouctou (Timbuktu): Mali **80** D1
Tomdoun: Highland, Scotland **28** L5
Tome: Chile **96** A4
Tomea: *i.*, Tukangbesi Is., Indonesia **65** G8
Tomelilla: Sweden **47** N9
Tomelloso: Spain **35** E17
Tomen-y-Mur: site of Roman fort about 2 miles miles S. of Ffestiniog, Gwyn., Wales **27** O14
Tomgraney: Clare, Repub. of Ireland **31** D14
Tomi: Greek city on Black Sea at Constanța, Dobrogea, Romania **39** V14
Tomich: High., Scotland **28** M5
Tomini, G. of: Celebes **65** G7
Tomintoul: Gram., Scotland **28** P5
Tomioka: Japan **63** g2
Tomma: *i.*, Norway **46** N3
Tommot: U.S.S.R. **49** o6
Tomnavoulin: Gram., Scot. **28** P5
Tomo: *riv.*, Colombia **94** D2
Tomochic: Mexico **93** F7
Tomooku: Japan **63** d4
Tompkins: Sask., Canada **92** F2
Tompkinsville: Ky., U.S.A. **88** J7
Tompo: U.S.S.R. **49** p5
Tom Price: W. Australia **68** B4
Tom Price, Mount: W. Australia **68** B4
TOMSK & *Reg.* U.S.S.R. **51** O3
Tonachic: Mexico **93** F7
Tonala: Mexico **86** k14
Tonantins: Brazil **94** D4
Tonbridge: Kent, England **25** W17
Tønder: Denmark **47** L9
Tondo: Zaire **78** H10
Tone: *riv.*, Japan **63** g3
Tone: *riv.*, Som., England **24** P7

Tonga: *Kingdom* **67** R6
Cap.: Nukualofa
Area: 270 sq. miles
(699 sq. km.)
Pop.: 92,000 (*1972 E*)

Tonga: Sudan **79** L8
Tongaat: Natal, S. Africa **75** J4
Tonganoxie: Kans., U.S.A. **90** D6
Tongaporutu: North I., N.Z. **70** P14
Tongatabu: *i.*, Tonga **67** R6
Tonga Trench: S. Pacific Ocean **7** 25S 175W
Tongchon: N. Korea **63** X7
Tongeren: Belgium **44** L5
Tongjoson, Gulf: N. Korea **63** X7
Tongland: Dumf. & Gall., Scot. **29** N10
Tongoy: Chile **96** A3
Tongsa Dzong: Bhutan **59** Q9
Tongue: & *loch*, Highland, Scotland **28** N3
Tongue: *riv.*, Mont./Wyo., U.S.A. **92** F3
Tonichi: Mexico **93** F7
Tonj: Sudan **76** C1
Tonj (Ibba): *riv.*, Sudan **76** C1
Tonk: Rajasthan, India **58** N9
Tonkawa: Okla., U.S.A. **90** C7
Tonkin, G. of: S. China Sea **64** D3
Tonkon Point: *cape*, Hainan, China **62** U11
Tonle Sap: *lake*, Cambodia 64 C4
Tonlerepou: Laos **64** D4
Tonnay-Boutonne: France **37** E10
Tonnay-Charente: France **37** E10
Tonneins: France **37** F11
Tonnerre: France **36** J8
Tönning: W. Germany **44** O1
Tonopah: Nev., U.S.A. **93** D5
Tonrekshin: Kazakh., U.S.S.R. **50** H5
TØNSBERG: Vestfold, Nor. **47** M7
Tonstad: Norway **47** K7
Tonyduff: Cavan, Repub. of Ireland **30** G12
Toodyay: W. Australia **68** B6
Tooele: Utah, U.S.A. **93** E4
Toogoolawah: Queens., Australia **70** K6
Toolebuc: Queens., Austl. **69** G4
Tooligie: S. Australia **71** A9
Toolondo: Vict., Australia **71** D11
Toombeola: Galway, Repub. of Ireland **31** B13
Toome: Antrim, N. Ireland **30** J10
Toompine: Queens., Austl. **70** F6
Toomyvara: Tip., Repub. of Ireland **31** E14
Toora: Vict., Australia **71** G12
Tooraweenah: N.S.W., Australia **71** H8
Toosa: Sweden **47** P7
Toowoomba: Queens., Australia **70** J6
Topalu: Romania **39** V14
Topcliffe: N. Yorks., Eng. **26** T11
TOPEKA: Kans., U.S.A. **90** D6
Tophouse: South I., N.Z. **70** O15
Toplice: Yugoslavia **41** V10
Toplița: Romania **43** T13
Topolčane: Yugoslavia **39** R16
Topolčany: Czechoslovakia **43** Q12
Topol'noye: U.S.S.R. **51** O4
Topolobampo: Mexico **93** F7
Topolovgrad: Bulgaria **39** U15
Topozero Lake: Karelian A.S.S.Rep., U.S.S.R. **46** W4
Toppenish: Wash., U.S.A. **92** C3
Toprakkale: Turkey **56** E3
Topsham: Devon, England **24** P18
Topuchatsung: Tibet, China **59** P9
Topusko: Yugoslavia **41** V10
Toquzak: *riv.*, U.S.S.R. **51** K4
Tor: Sinai Penin., Egypt **54** D9
Torata: New Guinea **69** G1
Torbali: Turkey **39** U17
Torbat-e Jam: Iran **55** K7
Tor Bay: Devon, England **24** O19
Torbay: Devon, England **24** P19
Torbay: Newf., Canada **85** w3
Torchin: Ukraine **43** T11
Torch Lake: Mich., U.S.A. **88** J3
Tørdal: Norway **47** L7
Tordesillas: Spain **35** D16
Töre: Sweden **46** S4
Töreboda: Sweden **47** O7
Torekov: Sweden **47** N8
Torena, Monte: Italy **40** Q9
Torfou: France **36** D8
Torgau: E. Germany **45** S4
Torgelow: E. Germany **45** U2
Torgilsbu: Greenland **85** p5
Torhout: Belgium **44** J4
Torigni: France **36** E6
Toriñana, Cape: Spain **35** B15
TORINO (Turin): Piedmont, Italy **40** N10
Torit: Sudan **76** D2
Torma: Finland **46** T4
Tormarton: Avon, England **24** R17
Tormes: *riv.*, Spain **35** C16
Tornado, Mount: B.C./Alta., Canada **92** E3
Torne: *riv.*, Sweden/Finland **46** T3
Torne Lake: Sweden **46** Q2
Torngat Mtns.: Newf., Can. **85** n6
Tornio: Finland **46** T4
Tornow: Poland **45** U3
Tornquist: Argentina **96** C4
Toro: Spain **35** D16
Torodi: Niger **81** E2
Törökszentmiklos: Hungary **43** R13
Torone: Greek city on W. side of Sithonia Penin., Greece **39** S16
Toroni, G. of: Greece **39** S16
Toronto: N.S.W., Australia **71** J9
TORONTO: Ont., Canada **89** M4
Toronto, Lake: Mexico **93** F7
Toropets: U.S.S.R. **50** D3
Toro Point: *cape*, Panama **94** *Ins.*
Tororo: Uganda 76 D2
Toros (Taurus) Mtns.: Tur. **56** C3
Torpa: Norway **47** M6
Torphichen: Loth., Scot. **29** O8
Torphins: Gram., Scotland **28** Q5
Torpoint: Corn., England **24** N19
Torpshammar: Sweden **46** P5
Torquay: Devon, England **24** O19
Torralba: Spain **35** E16
Torran Rocks: Scotland **29** J7
Torre Annunziata: Italy **38** O16
Torreblanca: Spain **35** G16
Torrecilla en Cameros: Sp. **35** E15
Torrelaguna: Spain **35** E16
Torrelavega: Spain **35** D15
Torremolinos: Spain **35** D18
Torrens, Lake: S. Australia **71** B8
Torrente: Spain **35** F17
Torreon: Mexico **93** G7
Torre Pellice: Italy **40** N11
Tôrres: Brazil **96** F2
Torres: Mexico **93** E7
Torres Is.: New Hebrides **67** N4
Torres Novas: Portugal **35** B17
Torres Strait: Queens., Austl. **69** G2
Torres Vedras: Portugal **35** B17
Torrevieja: Spain **35** F18
Torrey: Utah, U.S.A. **93** E5
Torridge: *riv.*, Devon, Eng. **24** N18
Torridon: & *loch*, Highland, Scotland **28** K4
Torriglia: Italy **40** P11
Torrijos: Spain **35** D17
Torrington: Conn., U.S.A. **89** P5
Torrington: Wyo., U.S.A. **92** G4
Torrington, Great: Devon, England **24** N18
Torrisholme: Lancs., Eng. **27** Q11
Torrön Lake: Sweden **46** N5
Torrowangee: N.S.W., Austl. **71** D8
Torrox: Spain **35** E18
Torryburn: Fife, Scotland **29** O7
Torsby: Sweden **47** N6
Torthorwald: Dumfries & Galloway, Scotland **29** O9
Tortola: *i.*, Virgin Is. **87** a1
Tortoli: Sardinia **38** L17
Tortona: Italy **40** O11
Tortorici: Sicily **38** O17
Tortosa: & *cape*, Spain **35** G16
Tortuga: *i.*, Mexico **93** E7
Tortuga, La: *i.*, Venezuela **94** D1
Tortum: Turkey **57** G1
Toruń: Poland **43** Q10
Torup: Sweden **47** N8
Tôrva: Estonia, U.S.S.R. **47** T7
Torver: Cumbria, England **26** P11

For Abbreviations see list on p.113. Italic type, e.g. *Ephesus*, refers to historical names not on maps. Capital letters, e.g. MADRID, show capitals of countries; small capital letters, e.g. CADIZ, show capitals of provinces, etc. General notes p.116.

194 Tory I.—Tungamah

Tory I.: Repub. of Ireland 30 E9
Torzhok: U.S.S.R. 50 D3
Tosa Bay: Japan 63 c4
Toscaig: High., Scot. 28 K5
Toscana: see Tuscany
Tosen: & fiord, Norway 46 N4
Tosno: U.S.S.R. 50 D3
Tossa: Spain 35 H16
Tosso: Nigeria 81 G3
Tostado: Argentina 96 C2
Tostedt: W. Germany 44 P2
Tostuya: U.S.S.R. 49 N3
Tosu Nor: lake, China 62 R7
Tosya: Turkey 56 D1
Totak Lake: Norway 47 L7
Totana: Spain 35 F18
Toteng: Botswana 77 B7
Totes Gebirge: mtns., Austr. 41 T8
Totham, Great: Essex, Eng. 25 X16
Totland: I. of Wight, Eng. 25 S18
Tot'ma: U.S.S.R. 50 F2
Totnes: Devon, England 24 O19
Totora: Bolivia 94 D7
Totoya: i., Fiji Is. 67 Q5
Tottenham: N.S.W., Austl. 71 G9
Tottington: Gt. Man., England 27 R12
Tottington: Norf., England 25 X14
Totton: Hants., England 25 T18
TOTTORI: & Pref., Japan 63 d3
Touba: Ivory Coast 80 C3
Touba: Senegal 80 A2
Toucy: France 36 J8
Toufourine: Mali 78 D5
Tougan: Upper Volta 80 D2
Touggourt: Algeria 78 F3
Tougouri: Upper Volta 80 D2
TOUGUE: & Reg., Guinea 80 B2
Toukoundia: Guinea 80 B2
Toul: France 40 L7
Toulepleu: Ivory Coast 80 C3
Toulon: Saône-et-Loire, Fr. 37 K9
Toulon: Var, France 40 L12
TOULOUSE: Haute-Garonne, France 37 G12
Toumodi: Ivory Coast 80 D3
Touna: Mali 80 C1
Toungo: Nigeria 78 G8
Toungoo: Burma 59 R11
Touques: riv., France 36 F6
Tourakom: Laos 64 C3
Tourcoing: France 36 J5
Tour-du-Pin, La: France 40 L10
Tourlaville: France 36 D6
Tourloti: Crete 39 T19
Tourmakeady: Mayo, Repub. of Ireland 30 C12
Tournai: Belgium 44 J5
Tournan: France 36 H7
Tournon: Ardèche, France 37 K10
Tournon: Indre, France 37 F9
Tournon: Lot-et-Garonne, France 37 G11
Tournus: France 37 K9
Touros: Brazil 94 K5
Touroumbane: Mauritania 80 c1
TOURS: Indre-et-Loire, Fr. 36 F8
Touws River: S. Africa 74 D6
Towakaima: Guyana 87 d7
Towanda: Pa., U.S.A. 89 N5
Towang: Arunachal Pradesh, India 59 Q9
Towari: Celebes 65 G7
Towcester: Northants., Eng. 25 U15
Tower Hamlets: Gt. Ldn., England 25 V16
Towie: Grampian, Scotland 28 Q5
Tow Law: Durham, Eng. 26 S10
Towner: N. Dak., U.S.A. 92 G3
Townhill: Fife, Scotland 29 P7
Townsend: Mont., U.S.A. 92 E3
Townshend I.: Queens., Australia 70 J4
Townsville: Queens., Austl. 70 G2
Towshan: Kwangtung, China 62 U10
Towton: battlefield about 2 miles S. of Tadcaster, N. Yorkshire, England 27 T12
Towuti, Lake: Celebes 65 G7
Towy: riv., Dyfed, Wales 24 N16
Toxandria: Roman name of area between Scheldt and Meuse, Belgium 34 J11
Toyah: Tex., U.S.A. 93 G6
TOYAMA: & Pref., Japan 63 e2
Toyama Bay: Japan 63 e2
Toyohashi: Japan 63 e3
Toyokawa: Japan 63 e3
Toyonaka: Japan 63 d3
Toyono: Japan 63 f2
Toyooka: Japan 63 d3
Tozanlı: riv., Turkey 56 E1
Tozeur: Tunisia 32 D5
Traben Trarbach: W. Ger. 44 N6
TRABZON: & Prov., Turkey 56 F1
Tracadie: N.B., Canada 89 T2
Trachonitis: ancient Greek name of district in N. of Jebel Druz, NW. of Shahba, Syria 56 E5
Tracy: Minn., U.S.A. 92 H4
Tracy City: Tenn., U.S.A. 91 J8
Traer: Iowa, U.S.A. 88 E4
Trafalgar: Vict., Australia 71 G12
Trafalgar, Cape: Spain 35 C18
Traiguen: Chile 96 A4
Trail: B.C., Canada 92 D3
Traill I.: Greenland 85 r3
Traismauer: Austria 41 V7
TRALEE: & bay, Kerry, Repub. of Ireland 31 B15
Tralles: Greek city at Aydın 39 U18
Tramore: & bay, Wat., Repub. of Ireland 31 G15
Tranås: Sweden 47 O7
Trancas: Argentina 96 B2
Tranche, La: France 37 D9
Tranent: Loth., Scotland 29 Q8
Trang: Thailand 64 B5
Trangan: i., Aru Is., Indon. 61 L13
Trangie: N.S.W., Australia 71 G9
Trangsviken: Sweden 46 O5
Trani: Italy 38 P16
Transantarctic Mts.: Antarctica 9 80S 145E
Transcona: Man., Canada 93 H3
Transito, El: Chile 96 A2
Transkei: Bantustan, S. Afr. 75 H6
Transvaal: Prov., S. Africa (cap. Pretoria) 75 H2
Transylvanian Alps: Rom. 39 S14
Trapani: Sicily 38 N18
Trapezus: Greek city at town of Trabzon, Turkey 56 F1
Trapper Peak: Mont., U.S.A. 92 E3
Traquair: Borders, Scot. 29 P8
Traralgon: Vict., Australia 71 G12
Trarza: Dist., Mauritania (cap. Nouakchott) 78 A6
Trarza: geog. reg., Maur. 78 A6
Trasimeno, Lake: Italy 38 M15
Tras-os-Montes: Angola 77 A5
Tras os Montes: Prov., Portugal (cap. Vila Real) 35 C16
Traun: & riv., Austria 41 U7
Traunsee: lake, Austria 41 T8
Traunstein: W. Germany 41 S8
Traveller's Lake: N.S.W., Australia 71 D9
Travemünde: W. Germany 45 Q2
Traverse City: Mich., U.S.A. 88 J3
Travinh: Vietnam 64 D5
Travis, Lake: Tex., U.S.A. 90 B10
Travnik: Yugoslavia 38 P14
Trawsfynydd: Gwyn., Wales 27 O14
Trbanj: Yugoslavia 41 V11
Trbovlje: Yugoslavia 41 V9
Tre Is.: Vietnam 64 D4
Treasury (Mono) Is.: Solomon Is. 67 L3
Třeban: Czechoslovakia 45 U6
Trebbia: riv., Italy 40 P11
Trebbin: E. Germany 45 T3
Třebechovice: Czech. 45 W5
Trebeurden: France 36 B7
Třebíč: Czechoslovakia 45 V6
Trebinje: Yugoslavia 39 Q15
Trebišov: Czechoslovakia 43 R12
Trebnje: Yugoslavia 41 V10
Trebol, El: Argentina 96 C3
Třeboň: Czechoslovakia 45 U6
Treboul: France 36 A7
Trecastle: Powys, Wales 24 O16
Tredegar: Gwent, Wales 24 P16
Treene: riv., W. Germany 44 P1
Trefeglwys: Powys, Wales 24 O15
Treffurt: E. Germany 45 Q4
Trefonen: Salop, England 27 P14
Tregaron: Dyfed, Wales 24 O15
Tregnago: Italy 41 R10
Tregoney: Corn., England 24 M19
Tregrosse Islets: Australia 69 J3
Tregynon: Powys, Wales 27 P14
Treharris: Mid Glam., Wales 24 P16
Trehörningsjö: Sweden 46 Q5
Treig, Loch: High., Scotland 29 M6
Treignac: France 37 G10
Treinta-y-Tres: Uruguay 96 E3
Trekelano: Queens., Austl. 69 F4
Trélazé: France 36 E8
Trelew: Argentina 95 D12
Trelleborg: Sweden 47 N9
Trelleck: Gwent, Wales 24 Q16
Tremadoc: Gwynedd, Wales 27 N14
Tremblade, La: France 37 D10
Trembleur Lake: B.C., Can. 92 C2
Trembovlya: Ukraine 43 T12
Tremiti Is.: Italy 38 O15
Třemošná: Czechoslovakia 45 T6
Tremp: Spain 35 G15
Trenche: riv., Que., Canada 89 P1
Trenčín: Czechoslovakia 43 Q12
Trengganu: State, Malaya, Malaysia (cap. Kuala Trengganu) 65 c11
Trenque Lauquen: Argentina 96 C4
Trent: riv., England 27 U12
Trent: riv., Ont., Canada 89 N3
Trent, Vale of: Staffs., England 27 S14
Trentham: Staffs., England 27 R14
Trentham: Vict., Australia 71 F11
Trentino-Alto Adige: Reg., Italy (cap. Trento) 41 R9
Trentishoe: Devon, England 24 O17
TRENTO: Trentino-Alto Adige, Italy 41 R9
Trenton: Mo., U.S.A. 88 E5
Trenton: Nebr., U.S.A. 93 G4
TRENTON: N.J., U.S.A. 89 O5
Trenton: Ont., Canada 89 N3
Trenton: Tenn., U.S.A. 90 G8
Treorchy: Mid Glam., Wales 24 P16
Trepassey: Newf., Canada 85 w3
Treport, Le: France 36 G5
Treptow: E. Germany 45 T2
Trerus: tributary meeting right bank of Liri about 5 miles SE. of Ceccano, Italy 38 N16
Tres Arboles: Uruguay 96 D3
Tres Arroyos: Argentina 96 C4
Três Casas: Brazil 94 E5
Tresco: i., Scilly Is. 25 J19
Trescore Balneario: Italy 40 P10
Tres Cruces: mtn., Argentina/Chile 96 B2
Tres Forcas, Cape: Morocco 80 L7
Três Forquilhas: Brazil 96 E2
Treshnish Isles: Inner Hebr., Scotland 29 J6
Três Lagoas: Brazil 94 G8
Tres Lomas: see Jose Maria Blanco, Argentina 96 C4
Tres Marias Is.: Mexico 86 J13
Tresmeer: Corn., England 24 N18
Três Passos: Brazil 96 E2
Tres Picos: Argentina 96 C4
Três Pontas: Brazil 96 F1
Tres Puntas, Cape: Arg. 95 D13
Três Rios: Brazil 96 G1
Tresta: Mainland, Shetland Is. 28 Ins.
Tres Tabernæ: Roman station about 30 miles SE. of Rome 38 N16
Trets: France 40 L12
Tretten: Norway 47 M6
Treuchtlingen: W. Germany 41 Q7
Treuenbrietzen: E. Germany 45 S3
Treurfontein: see Coligny
Treveri: Gallic tribe with centre at Trier, W. Germany 44 M6
Treves (Trier): W. Germany 44 M6
Trevières: France 36 E6
Treviglio: Italy 40 P10
Trevignon, Pointe de: cape, France 36 B8
Treviso: Italy 41 S10
Trevor: Gwynedd, Wales 27 N14
Trevose Head: cape, Corn., England 24 L18
Trévoux: France 37 K10
Treysa: W. Germany 44 P5
Trgovishche: Bulgaria 39 U15
Triang: Malaya, Malaysia 65 c12
Triangle, The: geog. reg., Burma 59 R9
Triberg: W. Germany 40 O7
Tribsees: E. Germany 45 S1
Tricase: Italy 39 Q17
Trichardt: Trans., S. Africa 75 H3
Trichiana: Italy 41 S9
Trichinopoly: see Tiruchirappalli
Trichur: Kerala, India 58 N12
Trida: N.S.W., Australia 71 F9
Trident: reef, S. China Sea 64 E4
Tridentina: see Trentino-Alto Adige
Trident Peak: Nev., U.S.A. 92 D4
Tridentum: Roman city at Trento, Italy 41 R9
Trie: France 37 F12
Triebel: Poland 45 U4
Trieben: Austria 41 U8
Trier (Treves): W. Germany 44 M6
Trier: Dist., Rhineland-Palatinate, West Germany 44 M6
Triesdorf: W. Germany 45 Q6
TRIESTE: Friuli-Venezia Giulia, Italy 41 T10
Trieste, G. of: Adriatic Sea 41 T10
Trifonia: U.S.S.R. 46 W2
Triglav: mtn., Yugoslavia 41 T9
Trikeri Str.: Greece 39 S17
Trikhonis, Lake: Greece 39 R17
Trikkala: Greece 39 R17
Trikomo: Cyprus 56 C4
Trillick: Tyr., N. Ireland 30 G11
Trim: Meath, Repub. of Ireland 30 H12
Trimdon: Dur., England 26 T10
Trimingham: Norf., Eng. 25 Y14
Trimley: Suff., England 25 Y16
Trimontium: Roman fort at Newstead on river Tweed 1 mile E. of Melrose, Scotland 29 Q8
Trimouille, La: France 37 G9
Trinafour: Tay., Scotland 29 N6
Trincheras: Mexico 93 G7
Trincomalee: Sri Lanka 58 O13
Tring: Herts., England 25 U16
Trinidad: Bolivia 94 E6
Trinidad: Colo., U.S.A. 93 G5
Trinidad: Cuba 87 M13
Trinidad: Paraguay 96 D2
Trinidad: Uruguay 96 D3
Trinidad Bay: Panama 94 Ins.
Trinidad I.: Argentina 96 C4
Trinidad: i., S. Atlantic Ocean 8 25S 30W
Trinidad: i., Trinidad & Tobago 87 c5

Trinidad & Tobago: *Republic* 87 c5
Cap.: Port-of-Spain
Area: 1,980 sq. miles (5,128 sq. km.)
Pop.: 1,030,000 (1971 E)

Trinité: Martinique, Windward Is 87 c3
Trinity: Newf., Canada 85 w2
Trinity: & riv., Tex., U.S.A. 90 D10
Trinity: riv., Calif., U.S.A. 92 C4
Trinity Is.: Alaska, U.S.A. 84 d6
Trinkitat: Sudan 54 E11
Trino: Italy 40 O10
Trion: Ga., U.S.A. 91 J8
Triphylia: coastal plain S. of river Alpheus, Greece 39 R18
Tripodiscus: ancient village in territory of Megara 39 S17
Tripoli (Tarabulus): Lebanon 56 D4
TRIPOLI: & Prov., Libya 32 E5
Tripolis: Greece 39 S18
Tripolitania: Prov., Libya 32 E5
Triptis: E. Germany 45 R5
Tripura: Union Territory, India (cap. Agartala) 59 Q10
Trischen: i., W. Germany 44 O1
Tristan da Cunha: i., (Br.), S. Atlantic Ocean 8 40S 05W
Triton: i., Paracel Is. 64 E3
Trittau: W. Germany 45 Q2
Triunfo: Brazil 96 E2
Triunfo, El: Mexico 93 E8
TRIVANDRUM: Kerala, India 58 N13
Trn: Bulgaria 39 S15
Trnava: Czechoslovakia 43 P12
Trnovo (Turnovo): Bulg. 39 T15
Trnovo: Yugoslavia 39 Q15
Troarn: France 36 E6
Trobriand Is.: New Guinea 69 J1
Troesmis: Roman camp on river Danube at Iglitza about 10 miles E. of Brăila, Romania 39 V14
Troezen: Greek city about 3 miles S. of foot of Methana promontory in E. of Argolis about 30 miles E. of Nauplia 39 S18
Trogir: Yugoslavia 38 P15
Trois Evêches, Les: mtn., France 40 M11
Trois Pistoles: Que., Canada 89 R1
Trois Rivieres: Que., Canada 89 P2
Trois Vierges: Luxembourg 44 L5
Troitsk: U.S.S.R. 51 K4
Troitskiy: U.S.S.R. 51 K3
Troitsko-Pecharsk: U.S.S.R. 50 J2
Troitskoye: Altai, U.S.S.R. 51 O4
Troitskoye: Khabarovsk, U.S.S.R. 49 p8
Trollhattan: Sweden 47 N7
Trombetas: riv., Brazil 94 F4
Trombudo: Brazil 96 F2
Tromelin: i., (Fr.), Indian Ocean 19 10S 50E
Trompsburg: & Dist., O.F.S., S. Africa 75 F5
Troms: Co., Norway (cap. Tromsø) 46 Q2
TROMSØ: Troms, Norway 46 Q2
Trona: Calif., U.S.A. 93 D5
Tronador: mtn., Chile 95 C12
TRONDHEIM: & fiord, Sør Trøndelag, Norway 46 M5
Tronoh: Malaya, Malaysia 65 b11
Tronto: riv., Italy 38 N15
Troodos: mtn., Cyprus 56 C4
Troon: Corn., England 25 L19
Troon: Strath., Scotland 29 M8
Tropea: Italy 38 O17
Trosa: Sweden 47 P7
Trossachs: dist., Central, Scotland 29 N7
Trostberg: W. Germany 41 S7
Trotternish: dist., Inner Hebr., Scotland 28 J4
Trotuş: riv., Romania 43 U13
Troutbeck: Cumbria, Eng. 26 Q11
Trout Creek: town, Ont., Canada 89 M3
Trout Lake: N.W.T., Can. 84 H5
Trout Lake: town, Ont., Canada 92 K2
Trouville: France 36 F6
TROWBRIDGE: Wilts., Eng. 24 R17
Troy: Ala., U.S.A. 91 J10
Troy: Mo., U.S.A. 88 F6
Troy: N.Y., U.S.A. 89 P4
Troy: N.C., U.S.A. 91 M8
Troy: Ohio, U.S.A. 88 J5
Troy: prehistoric site at Hissarlık about 4 miles SE. of entrance to Dardanelles on Çanakkale side, Turkey 39 U17
Troyan: Bulgaria 39 T15
Troyanov: Ukraine 43 V11
TROYES: Aube, France 36 K7
Trstena: Czechoslovakia 43 Q12
Trubchevsk: U.S.S.R. 50 D4
Truchas Peak: N. Mex., U.S.A. 93 F5
Trucial Coast: U.A.E. 55 H10
Trucial States: see United Arab Emirates
Trujillo: Honduras 86 L14
Trujillo: Peru 94 B5
Trujillo: Spain 35 D17
Trujillo: Venezuela 94 C2
Truk Is.: Caroline Islands 7 05N 150E
Trumann: Ark., U.S.A. 90 F8
Trumpington: Cambs., Eng. 25 W15
Trun: France 36 F7
Trundle: N.S.W., Australia 71 G9
Truns: Switzerland 40 O9
TRURO: Corn., England 24 L19
Truro: N.S., Canada 89 U3
Truro: S. Australia 71 C10
Trusham: Devon, England 24 O18
Truth or Consequences: N. Mex., U.S.A. 93 F6
Trutnov: Czechoslovakia 45 V5
Tryavna: Bulgaria 39 T15
Truyère: riv., France 37 H11
Tryon: N.C., U.S.A. 91 K8
Tryphena: Great Barrier I., New Zealand 70 P13
Trysil: Norway 47 N6
Trysil (Klar): riv., Norway 47 M6
Trzcianka: Poland 43 P10
Trzebiatow: Poland 45 V1
Trzebisz: Poland 45 U2
Trzebnica: Poland 43 P11
Tsagan Sanji: Sinkiang, China 62 Q6
Tsageri: Georgia, U.S.S.R. 50 F6
Tsaidam Swamps: Chingai, China 62 Q7
Tasala Apopka, Lake: Fla., U.S.A. 91 K11
Tsanga: Tibet, China 62 S8
Tsanghsien: Hopeh, China 62 V7
Tsangpo: riv., Tibet, China 59 Q9
Tsangwu (Wuchow): Kwangsi, China 62 U10
Tsaobis: S.W. Africa 74 A1
Tsaratanana: Malagasy Rep. 73 O13
Tsarevo: Bulgaria 39 U15
Tsaski: Nigeria 81 F2
Tsau: Botswana 77 B7
Tsavo: Kenya 76 E3
Tsavo National Park: Kenya 76 E3
Tsechung: Szechwan, China 62 S9
Tsela: Tibet, China 59 Q9
Tselinograd: & Reg., Kazakh., U.S.S.R. 51 M4
Tselo: Sinkiang, China 51 O7
Tsenchi: Kwangsi Chuang, China 62 U10
Tsengshing: Kwangtung, China 62 U10
Tsentral'nyy: U.S.S.R. 51 P3
Tses: S.W. Africa 74 C2
Tsesis: Latvia, U.S.S.R. 47 T8
Tsetserliq: Mongolia 62 S6
TSHABONG: Kgalagadi, Botswana 74 E3
Tshane: Botswana 77 B7
Tshangalele, Lake: Zaïre 77 C5
Tshela: Zaïre 81 G6
Tshikapa: Zaïre 76 B4
Tshilenge: Zaïre 76 B4
Tshinsenda: Zaïre 77 C5
Tshofa: Zaïre 76 C4
Tshuapa: riv., Zaïre 76 B3
Tsian: Kirin, China 63 X6
Tsienan: Hopeh, China 62 V6
Tsihombe: Malagasy Rep. 73 O15
Tsinan: Kansu, China 62 T8
TSINAN: Shantung, China 62 V7
Tsincheng: Shansi, China 62 U7
Tsingchen: Shantung, China 62 V7
Tsinghai: see Chinghai
Tsing Hai (Koko Nor): lake, China 62 S7
Tsinghsien: Hopeh, China 62 V7
Tsinghsien: Hunan, China 62 T9
Tsingi: Kwangsi Chuang, China 62 T10
Tsingkiang: Kiangsi, China 62 V9
Tsingkiang (Hwaiyin): Kiangsu, China 62 V8
Tsingkien: Shensi, China 62 U7
Tsingkow: Kiangsu, China 62 V8
Tsingmai (Kimkang): Hainan, China 62 T11
Tsingpien: Shensi, China 62 T7
Tsingshen: Szechwan, China 62 S9
Tsingtao: Shantung, China 63 W7
Tsingyuan: Kansu, China 62 S7
Tsingyuan: Liaoning, China 63 X6
Tsingyun: Kwangtung, China 62 U10
Tsining: Inner Mongolia, China 62 U6
Tsining: Shantung, China 62 V7
Tsinkiang (Chuanchow): Fukien, China 62 V10
Tsinling Shan: range, China 62 T8
Tsintsabis: S.W. Africa 77 A6
Tsinyang: Honan, China 62 U7
Tsitsihar (Lungkiang): Heilungkiang, China 63 W5
TSKHINVALI: South Ossetia, Georgia, U.S.S.R. 50 F6
Tsochuan: Shansi, China 62 U7
Tsolo: S. Africa 75 H5
Tsomo: S. Africa 75 G6
Tsu: Mie, Japan 63 e3
Tsuchiura: Japan 63 g2
Tsuda: Japan 63 d3
Tsuge: Japan 63 e3
Tsukinoki: riv., Japan 63 g2
Tsukumi: Japan 63 b4
Tsumeb: S.W. Africa 77 A6
Tsumis: S.W. Africa 74 B1
Tsumu: Tibet, China 59 Q9
Tsungjen: Kiangsi, China 62 V9
Tsungming: Kiangsu, China 63 W8
Tsungyang: Hupeh, China 62 U9
Tsungyi: Kiangsi, China 62 U9
Tsunhochit Wangfu: Inner Mongolia, China 62 V6
Tsunhwa: Hopeh, China 62 V6
Tsuni: Kweichow, China 62 T9
Tsuno: Japan 63 b4
Tsuruga: Japan 63 e3
Tsurumi, Cape: Japan 63 c4
Tsuruoka: Japan 63 Z7
Tsushima: Japan 63 e3
Tsushima: is. & str., Japan 63 X8
Tsuwano: Japan 63 b3
Tsuyama: Japan 63 d3
Tsuyung: Yunnan, China 62 S9
Tsymlyanskaya: U.S.S.R. 50 F5
Tsyp-Navolok: U.S.S.R. 46 X2
Tsyr: Ukraine 43 T11
Tu: New Britain, Bismarck Arch. 67 K3
Tua: Zaïre 73 H10
Tuakau: North I., N.Z. 70 P13
Tual: Kai Is., Indonesia 61 L13
Tuam: Galway, Repub. of Ireland 30 D12
Tuamotu (Low) Arch.: (Fr.), Pacific O. 83 g3
Tuan: Kwangsi Chuang, China 62 T10
Tuao: Luzon, Philippines 64 G3
Tuapse: U.S.S.R. 50 E6
Tuaran: Sabah, Malaysia 65 F5
Tuatapere: South I., N.Z. 71 L18
Tuath, Loch: Inner Hebr., Scotland 29 J6
Tuba City: Ariz., U.S.A. 93 E5
Tubal: wadi, Iraq 57 G5
Tuban: Java 65 E8
Tubarão: Brazil 96 F2
Tubau: Sarawak, Malaysia 65 E6
Tubbataha Reefs: Phil. 64 F5
Tubber: Galway, Repub. of Ireland 31 D13
Tubbercurry: Sligo, Repub. of Ireland 30 D11
Tubingen: Baden-Württemberg, W. Germany 40 P7
Tubinskiy: U.S.S.R. 50 J4
Tubuai: i., Austral Is. 83 f4
Tubuai (Austral) Is.: (Fr.), Pacific O. 83 f4
Tubuia: i., Society Is. 83 e3
Tucacas: Venezuela 94 D1
Tucavaca: Bolivia 94 f7
Tucci: Roman town at Martos, Spain 35 E18
Tuchan: France 37 H13
Tuchentgze: Inner Mongolia, China 62 V6
Tuchola: Poland 43 P10
Tuckerton: N.J., U.S.A. 89 O6
Tucson: Ariz., U.S.A. 93 E6
TUCUMAN: & Prov., Arg. 96 B2
Tucumcari: N. Mex., U.S.A. 93 G5
Tucumcari Mount: N. Mex., U.S.A. 93 G5
Tucunuco: Argentina 96 B3
Tucupita: Venezuela 94 E2
Tucuruí: Brazil 94 H4
Tuddenham: Suff., England 25 X15
Tudela: Spain 35 F15
Tuder: Roman city at Todi, Italy 38 N15
Tudhoe: Durham, England 26 S10
Tuella: riv., Portugal 35 C16
Tuerhpote: Heilungkiang, China 63 W5
Tuffé: France 36 F7
Tufi: New Guinea 69 H1
Tufts Abyssal Plain: N. Pacific Ocean 7 45N 145W
Tuğ: Turkey 57 H2
Tugela: & Dist., Natal, S. Africa 75 J4
Tugela: riv., Natal, S. Africa 75 J4
Tug Fork: riv., U.S.A. 88 K7
Tugssâq: Greenland 85 O3
Tuguegarao: Luzon, Phil. 64 G3
Tugur: U.S.S.R. 49 p7
Tuhkala: Finland 46 V3
Tuilungteching: Tibet, China 59 Q8
Tuinplaas: Trans., S. Africa 75 H2
Tuisarkan: Iran 57 L4
Tukangbesi Is.: Indonesia 65 G8
Tuktoyaktuk: N.W.T., Can. 84 f4
Tukum: Latvia, U.S.S.R. 47 S8
Tukuyu: Tanzania 77 D4
Tukzar: Afghanistan 58 L7
Tula: Hidalgo, Mexico 86 K13
Tula: Tamaulipas, Mexico 86 K13
TULA: & Reg., U.S.S.R. 50 E4
Tulagi: Solomon Is. 67 M3
Tulak: Afghanistan 58 K8
Tulan: Chinghai, China 62 R7
Tulare: & lake, Calif., U.S.A. 93 D5
Tularosa: N. Mex., U.S.A. 93 F6
Tulbagh: & Dist., S. Africa 74 C6
Tulcan: Ecuador 94 B3
Tulcea: Romania 39 V14
Tul'chin: Ukraine 43 V12
TULEAR: & Prov., Malagasy Rep. 73 N14
Tuli: Rhodesia 77 C7
Tuli Block: Dist., Botswana 75 G1
Tulia: Tex., U.S.A. 93 G6
Tulin: U.S.S.R. 49 M7
Tulkarm: Jordan 55 b2
Tulla: Clare, Repub. of Irel. 31 D14
Tullaghoge: Tyr., N. Ireland 30 H10
Tullahoma: Tenn., U.S.A. 91 H8
Tullamore: N.S.W., Australia 71 G9
TULLAMORE: Offaly, Repub. of Ireland 31 G13
Tullaroan: Kilk., Repub. of Ireland 31 G14
TULLE: Correze, France 37 G10
Tullibigeal: N.S.W., Austl. 71 G9
Tullins: France 40 L10
Tulln: Austria 41 W7
Tulloch: Highland, Scotland 28 M6
Tullogher: Kilk., Repub. of Ireland 31 G15
Tullow: Carlow, Repub. of Ireland 31 H14
Tully: Queens., Australia 69 H3
Tully: Rosc., Repub. of Irel. 30 E12
Tullyallen: Louth, Repub. of Ireland 30 J12
Tullycanna: Wex., Repub. of Ireland 31 H15
Tullylease: Cork, Repub. of Ireland 31 D15
Tullynessle: Gram., Scotland 28 Q5
Tullyvin: Cavan, Repub. of Ireland 30 G11
Tuloma: riv., U.S.S.R. 46 X2
Tulpfontein: S. Africa 74 C6
Tulsa: Okla., U.S.A. 90 D7
Tulsequah: B.C., Canada 84 f6
Tulsk: Rosc., Repub. of Ireland 30 E12
Tulua: Colombia 94 B3
Tulufan (Turfan): Sinkiang, China 51 P6
Tulun: U.S.S.R. 49 M7
Tulungagung: Java 65 E8
Tumaco: Colombia 94 B3
Tumba, Lake: Zaïre 81 H5
Tumbarumba: N.S.W., Australia 71 H10
Tumbaya: Argentina 96 B1
Tumbe: Zaïre 76 B3
Tumbes: Peru 94 A4
Tumby Bay: town, S. Austl. 71 B10
Tumentze: Kirin, China 63 Y6
Tumeremo: Venezuela 94 E2
Tumereng: Guyana 87 c7
Tumkur: Karnataka, India 58 N12
Tummel: riv. & loch, Tayside, Scotland 29 O6
Tummel Bridge: Tay., Scot. 29 N6
Tumpat: Malaya, Malaysia 65 c10
Tumu: Ghana 80 D2
Tumucumaque, Serra de: range, Brazil 94 G3
Tumut: & riv., N.S.W., Australia 71 H10
Tuna: Gujarat, India 58 M10
Tunbridge Wells: Kent, England 25 W17
TUNCELI: & Prov., Turkey 56 F2
Tundubai: well, Sudan 54 C11
Tunduma: Tanzania 77 D4
Tunduru: Tanzania 77 E5
Tundzha: riv., Bulgaria 39 T15
Tung: riv., China 62 U10
Tungabhadra: riv., India 58 N11
Tungamah: Vict., Australia 71 F11

Tungan: Hunan, China **62** U9
Tungcheng: Anhwei, China **62** V8
Tungchu: Tibet, China **59** Q9
Tungchwan (Huitse): Yunnan, China **62** S9
Tunghai (Hsin-hai-lien): Kiangsu, China **62** V8
Tunghai: Yunnan, China **62** S10
Tungho: Heilungkiang, China **63** X5
Tunghwa: Kirin, China **63** X6
Tungjen: Chinghai, China **62** S7
Tungjen: Kweichow, China **62** T9
Tungkiang: Heilungkiang, China **63** Y5
Tungkiang: Szechwan, China **62** T8
Tungkwan: Shensi, China **62** U8
Tungkwang: Hopeh, China **62** V7
Tunglan: Kwangsi Chuang, China **62** T10
Tungliao: Inner Mongolia, China **63** W6
Tunglu: Chekiang, China **62** V9
Tungning: Heilungkiang, China **63** Y6
Tungokochen: U.S.S.R. **49** n7
Tungpeh: Honan, China **62** U8
Tungshan: Fukien, China **62** V10
Tungshan (Suchow): Kiangsu, China **62** V8
Tungsheng: Inner Mongolia, China **62** T7
Tungsiang: Kiangsi, China **62** V9
Tungtai: Kiangsu, China **63** W8
Tung Ting, Lake: Hunan, China **62** U9
Tunguska, Lower: *riv.*, U.S.S.R. **49** m5
Tunguska, Stony: *riv.*, U.S.S.R. **49** L5
Tunguska, Upper: *riv.*, U.S.S.R. **49** M6
Tungwei: Kansu, China **62** T7
Tungwuchumuchin: Inner Mongolia, China **62** V5
Tunhwang: Kansu, China **62** Q6
Tunica: Miss., U.S.A. **90** F8
TUNIS & *Governorate*: Tunisia **38** M18
Tunis, Gulf of: Tunisia **38** M18

Tunisia: *Republic* **32** D5
Cap.: Tunis
Area: 63,378 sq. miles
(164,149 sq. km.)
Pop.: 5,137,000 *(1970 E)*

Tunja: Colombia **94** C2
Tunn Lake: Norway **46** N4
Tunstall: Lancs., England **26** Q11
Tunstall: Staffs., England **27** R13
Tunstall: Suff., England **25** Y15
Tunuyan: & *riv.*, Argentina **96** B3
Tuongduong: Vietnam **64** C3
Tuora: U.S.S.R. **49** o6
Tuostakh: U.S.S.R. **49** p4
Tupā: Brazil **95** G8
Tupaciguara: Brazil **94** H7
Tupelo: Miss., U.S.A. **90** G8
Tupik: U.S.S.R. **49** n7
Tupper Lake: *city*, N.Y., U.S.A. **89** O3
Tupton, New: Derby., Eng. **27** T13
Tupungato: Argentina **96** B3
Tupungato: *mtn.*, Argentina/Chile **96** B3
Tuque, La: Que., Canada **89** P2
Tura: Meghalaya, India **59** O9
Tura: U.S.S.R. **49** M5
Tura: *riv.*, U.S.S.R. **51** K3
Turaba: & *wadi*, Hijaz, Saudi Arabia **54** F10
Turaba: Najd, Saudi Arabia **54** F9
Turaif: *pump. sta.*, Saudi Arabia **56** F6
Turanian Plain: Kazakh., U.S.S.R. **51** K6
Tura Rin: Queens., Australia **70** J6
Turbat: Baluchistan, Pak. **58** K9
Turbat-i-Haidari: Iran **55** J7
Turbo: Colombia **94** B2
Turckheim: France **40** N7
Turda: Romania **43** S13
Turda: *well*, Sudan **79** K7
Turdetani: ancient Spanish tribe of Guadalquivir valley **35** D18
Tureia: *i.*, Tuamotu Arch. **83** h4
Tureh: Iran **57** L4
Turek: Poland **43** Q10
Tureta: Nigeria **81** F2
Turfan: see Tulufan
Turgay: Tselinograd, Kazakh., U.S.S.R. **51** M4
TURGAY: & *Reg.* & *riv.*, Kustanay, Kazakh., U.S.S.R. **51** K5
Turgeon: *riv.*, Canada **89** M1
Turgovishte: Romania **39** U15
Turgutlu: Turkey **39** U17
Turhal: Turkey **56** E1
Turiaçu: & *riv.*, Brazil **94** H4
TURIN (Torino): Piedmont, Italy **40** N10
Turinsk: U.S.S.R. **51** K3
Turinskaya Sloboda: U.S.S.R. **51** K3
Turka: Ukraine **43** S12
Turkana, Lake: E. Africa **76** E2
Turkestan: Kazakh., U.S.S.R. **51** L6
Turkestan: *geog. reg.*, Central Asia **52 —**

Turkey: *Republic* **54** E7
Cap.: Ankara
Area: 301,380 sq. miles
(780,574 sq. km.)
Pop.: 37,010,000 *(1972 E)*

Turkmanchai: Iran **57** K3
Turkmenistan: S.S. Rep., U.S.S.R. *(cap.* Ashkhabad) **51** K7
Turks Is.: (Br.) W. Indies *[cap* (with *Caicos)* Grand Turk] **87** m13
Turks Is., Passage: W. Indies **87** m13
TURKU (Åbo): *Prov.*, Finland **47** S6
Turku ja Pori: *Prov.*, Finland *(cap.* Turku) **47** S6
Turkwell: *riv.*, Kenya **76** E2
Turlough: Mayo, Repub. of Ireland **30** C12
Turmus 'Aiya: Jordan **55** b2
Turnau: Austria **41** V8
Turnberry: Strath., Scotland **29** M9
Turnditch: Derby., England **27** S13
Turneffe Is.: Belize **86** *Ins*
Turner I.: Greenland **85** r4
Turner Valley: *town*, Alta., Canada **92** E2
Turnhouse: *airfield*, Lothian, Scotland **29** P8
Turnor Lake: Sask., Can. **92** F1
Turnu Măgurele: Romania **39** T15
Turnu Roşu: Romania **39** T14
Turnu Severin: Romania **39** S14
Turriff: Gram., Scotland **28** R4
Tursamäe: Estonia, U.S.S.R. **47** U7

Tursaq: Iraq **57** J5
Tursun: Turkey (Dardan. *Inset)* **20** *Ins.*
Turtkul': Uzbek., U.S.S.R. **51** K6
Turtle: *riv.*, Ont., Canada **88** E1
Turtle Bay: Mexico **93** E7
Turtleford: Sask., Canada **92** F2
Turtle Is.: (Indon.), BanJa Sea **61** K13
Turtle Is.: Celebes **65** G7
Turtle Mtns.: Canada/U.S.A. **92** G3
Turton: Lancs., England **27** R12
Turua: North I., N.Z. **70** P13
Turukta: U.S.S.R. **49** N5
Turun: Iran **55** J7
Turut: Iran **55** J7
Turzovka: Czechoslovakia **43** Q12
Tuscaloosa: Ala., U.S.A. **91** H9
Tuscany: *Reg.*, Italy *(cap.* Florence) **38** M15
Tuscarora: Nev., U.S.A. **92** D4
Tuscola: Ill., U.S.A. **88** G6
Tuscola: Tex., U.S.A. **90** B9
Tusculum: ancient Latin city near Frascati, Italy. **38** N16
Tuscumbia: Ala., U.S.A. **91** H8
Tushan: Kweichow, China **62** T9
Tuskar Rock: *i.*, Repub. of Ireland **31** J15
Tuskegee: Ala., U.S.A. **91** J9
Tusun: Egypt (Suez Canal *Inset)* **32** *Ins.*
Tut: Iran **55** H8
Tutagu: Sinkiang, China **62** Q6
Tutbury: Staffs., England **27** S14
Tuticorin: Tamil Nadu, India **58** N13
Tutin: Yugoslavia **39** R15
Tutrakan: Bulgaria **39** U14
Tuttlingen: W. Germany **40** O8
Tutubu: Tanzania **76** D4
Tutuila: *i.*, Samoa **70** *Ins.*
Tuva A.S.S. Rep.: U.S.S.R. *(cap.* Kyzyl) **49** L7
Tuvalu: *is.,* (Br.) Pacific Ocean *(cap.* Funafuti) **67** P3
Tuwairifa: *well*, Sau. Arab. **55** G10
Tuxer Vorberge: Austria **41** R8
Tuxford: Notts., England **27** U13
Tuxpan: Nayarit, Mexico **86** J13
Tuxpan: Vera Cruz, Mexico **86** K13
Tuxtla: Mexico **86** K14
Tuxtla Gutierrez: Mexico **86** k14
Tuy: Spain **35** B15
Tuyên Quang: Vietnam **64** D2
Tuyhoa: Vietnam **64** D4
Tuyong: Thailand **65** b10
Tuz, Lake: Turkey **56** C2
Tuz: Lake: Turkey **56** C2
Tuz Khurmatli: Iraq **57** J4
Tuzla: Yugoslavia **39** Q14
Tuzluca: Turkey **57** H1
Tvärån: Sweden **46** R4
Tvedestrand: Norway **47** L7
Tveitsund: Norway **47** L7
Tvŭrditsa: Bulgaria **39** T15
Twante: Burma **59** R11
Tweed: Ont., Canada **89** N3
Tweed: *riv.*, Scot./Eng. **26** R8
Tweeddale: *val.*, Bord., Scot. **29** Q8
Tweed Heads: N.S.W., Australia **70** K7
Tweedmouth: Northumb., England **26** S8
Twee Rivieren: C.P. S. Africa **74** D3
Tweedsmuir Prov. Park: B.C., Canada **92** B2
Tweeling: O.F.S., S. Africa **75** H3
Twelve Pins, The: *mtn.*, Galway, Repub. of Irel. **30** B12
Twillingate: Newf., Canada **85** V2
Twin Falls: *city*, Idaho, U.S.A. **92** E4
Twistringen: W. Germany **44** O3
Two Bridges: Devon, Eng. **24** O18
Two Dales: *village*, Derby., England **27** S13
Two Harbors: Minn., U.S.A. **88** F2
Twomileborris: Tip., Repub. of Ireland **31** F14
Two Rivers: *city*, Wis., U.S.A. **88** H3
Two Thumb Range: South I., New Zealand **70** N16
Two Waters: S. Africa **75** F6
Twyford: Berks., England **25** U17
Twyford: Hants., England **25** T17
Twyford: Leics., England **27** U14
Twynholm: Dumfries & Galloway, Scotland **29** N10
Tyborøn: Denmark **47** L8
Tychany: U.S.S.R. **49** I5
Tychy: Poland **43** Q11
Tydd St. Giles: Cambs., England **25** W14
Tydd St. Mary: Lincs., Eng. **25** W14
Tygda: U.S.S.R. **49** o7
Tyldesley: Gt. Man., England **27** R12
Tyler: Tex., U.S.A. **90** D9
Tylertown: Miss., U.S.A. **90** F10
Tym: *riv.*, U.S.S.R. **51** O3
Tyn: Czechoslovakia **45** U6
Tynagh: Galway, Repub. of Ireland **31** E13
Tyndall: S. Dak., U.S.A. **92** H4
Tyndinskiy: U.S.S.R. **49** O6
Tyndrum: Central, Scotland **29** M7
Tyne: *riv.*, Loth., Scot. **29** Q8
Tyne, North: *riv.*, Northumb., England **26** R9
Tyne, South: *riv.*, Northumb., England **26** R10
Tyne and Wear: *Metropolitan Co.*, England *(co. town* South Shields) **26** S10
Tyne Gap: Northumb., Eng. **26** R10
Tynemouth: Tyne & Wear, England **26** T9
Tynewydd: Mid Glam., Wales **24** O16
Tyniště: Czechoslovakia **45** W5
Tynset: Norway **46** M5
Tyras: Greek name of river Dniester **33** H7
Tyre (Sur): Lebanon **55** b1
Tyri Fiord: Norway **47** M6
Tyrol (Tirol): *Prov.*, Austria *(cap.* Innsbruck) **41** R8
Tyrone: Pa., U.S.A. **89** M5
Tyrone: *Co.*, N. Ireland *(cap.* Omagh) **30** G10
Tyrrell, Lake: Vict., Austl. **71** E10
Tyrrellspass: Westmeath, Repub. of Ireland **31** G13
Tyrrhenian Sea: S. Europe **38** M17
Tysoe: War., England **25** S15
Tyssedal: Norway **47** J6
Tytherley: Hants., England **25** S17
Tyubelyakh: U.S.S.R. **49** Q4
Tyukalinsk: U.S.S.R. **51** M3
Tyulyapsy: U.S.S.R. **51** P3
TYUMEN': & *Reg.*, U.S.S.R. **51** L3

Tyumen: *riv.*, N. Korea/China **63** X6
Tyung: *riv.*, U.S.S.R. **49** n4
Tyup: Kirgiz., U.S.S.R. **51** N6
Tywardreath: Corn., England **24** M19
Tywyn: Gwynedd, Wales **27** N14
Tzaneen: Trans., S. Africa **75** J1
Tzehsien: Hopeh, China **62** U7
Tzeki: Kiangsi, China **62** V9
Tzekwei: Hupeh, China **62** U8
Tzeli: Hunan, China **62** U9
Tzetung: Szechwan, China **62** T8
Tzeya: *riv.*, China **62** V7
Tzeyang (Yenchow): Shantung, China **62** V7
Tzu: *riv.*, China **62** U9

Ua-Huka: *i.*, Marquesas Is. **83** h1
Ua Pu: *i.*, Marquesas Is. **83** g1
Uarini: Brazil **94** D4
Uati: Brazil **94** D5
Uatumā: *riv.*, Brazil **94** F4
Uaupes: Brazil **94** D4
Uba: Brazil **96** G1
Ubagan: *riv.*, U.S.S.R. **51** L4
Ubaira: Brazil **94** K6
Ubangi (Oubangui): *riv.*, Zaire/Cen. Afr. Rep. **76** A2
UBARI: & *Prov.*, Libya **78** G4
Ubatuba: Brazil **96** F1
Ube: Japan **63** b4
Ubeda: Spain **35** E17
Uberaba: Brazil **94** H7
Uberlândia: Brazil **94** H7
Uberlingen: W. Germany **40** P8
Ubiaja: Nigeria **81** F3
Ubinskoye: U.S.S.R. **51** N3
Ubinskoye, Lake: U.S.S.R. **51** O3
Uboljatna: Reservoir: Thailand **64** C3
Ubombo: & *Dist.*, Natal, S. Africa **75** K3
Ubon Ratchathani: Thailand **64** C3
Ubort': *riv.*, Byelorussia **43** V11
Ubsa Nor: *lake*, Mongolia **51** Q4
Uch-Aral: Kazakh., U.S.S.R. **51** O5
Uchiko: Japan **63** c4
Uchi Lake: *town*, Ont., Can. **92** J2
Uchino: Japan **63** f2
Uchte: W. Germany **44** O3
Uchur: *riv.*, U.S.S.R. **49** P6
Ucker: *riv.*, E. Germany **45** S2
Uckeritz: E. Germany **45** U2
Uckermark: *geog. reg.*, E. Germany **42** N10
Uckermunde: E. Germany **45** U2
Uckfield: E. Sussex, England **25** W18
Uckro: E. Germany **45** T4
Udaipur: Rajasthan, India **58** M10
Udaipur Garhi: Nepal **59** P9
Udayagiri: Andhra Pradesh, India **58** N12
Udbina: Yugoslavia **41** V11
Uddevalla: Sweden **47** M7
Udd Lake: Sweden **46** P4
Uden: Netherlands **44** L4
Udenes: Norway **47** M6
Udhampur: Jammu & Kashmir **58** N8
Udine: Italy **41** T9
Udinense: Italy **41** T9
Udlice: Czechoslovakia **45** T5
Udmurt A.S.S. Rep.: U.S.S.R. *(cap.* Izhevsk) **50** H3
Udny: Grampian, Scotland **28** R5
Udon Thani (Mak Khaeng): Thailand **64** C3
Udskoye: U.S.S.R. **49** P7
Udzha: U.S.S.R. **49** n3
Udzhari: Azerbaydzhan, U.S.S.R. **57** K1
Ueda: Honshu, Japan **63** f2
UELE: *riv.*, Zaire **76** B2
Uelen: U.S.S.R. **84** C4
Uel'kal: U.S.S.R. **49** U4
Uene: *riv.*, Zaire **76** C2
Ueno: Japan **63** e3
UFA: Bashkir, U.S.S.R. **50** J4
Ufa: *riv.*, U.S.S.R. **50** J3
Uffculme: Devon, England **24** P18
Uffeln: W. Germany **44** N3
Uffenheim: W. Germany **45** Q6
Uffington: Oxon., England **25** S16
Ufford: Suff., England **25** Y15
Ugalla: *riv.*, Tanzania **76** D4

Uganda: *Republic* **76** D2
Cap.: Kampala
Area: 91,134 sq. miles
(236,037 sq. km.)
Pop.: 10,462,000 *(1972 E)*

Ugarit: ancient city. Site at *Ras Shamra*, N. of Latakia, Syria **56** D4
Ugashik: Alaska, U.S.A. **84** D6
Ughelli: Nigeria **81** F3
Ugie: S. Africa **75** H5
Ugie: *riv.*, Gram., Scotland **28** S4
Ugijar: Spain **35** E18
Ugines: France **40** M10
Uglegorsk: U.S.S.R. **49** Q8
Uglovaya: U.S.S.R. **49** o7
Ugnov: Ukraine **43** S11
Ugthorpe: N. Yorks., Eng. **26** U11
Ugut: U.S.S.R. **51** M2
Uhlava: *riv.*, Czechoslovakia **45** T6
Uhrichsville: Ohio, U.S.A. **88** L5
Uhu: Solomon Is. **67** M3
Uibis: S.W. Africa **74** B2
Uig: Inner Hebr., Scotland **28** J4
Uig: Outer Hebr., Scotland **28** G3
Uige: Angola **73** H11
Uige: *Prov.*, Angola *(cap.* Carmona) **73** H11
Uil: Kazakh., U.S.S.R. **50** H5
Uil: *riv.*, U.S.S.R. **50** H5
Uimaniemi: Finland **46** T3
Uinta Mtns.: Utah, U.S.A. **93** E4
Uist, North: *i.*, Outer Hebr., Scotland **28** G4
Uist, South: *i.*, Outer Hebr., Scotland **28** G5
Uitenhage: & *Dist.*, S. Africa **75** F6
Uithoorn: Netherlands **44** K3
Uithuizermeden: Neth. **44** M2
Ujae: *i.*, Marshall Is. **63** d2
Ujak: Sudan **76** D1
Uji Is.: Japan **63** X8
Ujjar: Spain **35** E18
Ujiji: Tanzania **76** C3
Ujjain: Madhya Pradesh, India **58** N10
Ujpest: Hungary **43** Q13
Ujscie: Poland **43** P9
Ujung Pandang: & *Strait*, Celebes **65** F8
Uka: & *bay*, U.S.S.R. **49** S6
Ukamas: S.W. Africa **74** C4
Ukerewe I.: Lake Victoria **76** D3
Ukhrul: Manipur, India **59** Q9
Ukhta: U.S.S.R. **50** H2

Ukiah: Calif., U.S.A. **93** C5
Ukmerge: Lithuania, U.S.S.R. **47** T9
Ukraine S.S. Repub.: U.S.S.R. *(cap.* Kiev) **50** D5
'Ula: Saudi Arabia **54** E9
Ulak: *i.*, Aleutians **84** B7
Ulam: Queens., Australia **70** J4
Ulan: *riv.*, China **59** Q8
ULAN BATOR (Urga): Mongolia **62** T5
Ulan Chonchi: Inner Mongolia, China **62** S6
Ulangom: Mongolia **51** Q5
Ularunda: Queens., Austl. **70** G6
Ulawa: *i.*, Solomon Is. **67** M3
Ulaya: Tanzania **76** E4
Ul'banskiy Bay: U.S.S.R. **49** p7
Ulbster: High., Scotland **28** P3
Ulceby: Humb., England **27** V12
Ulchin: S. Korea **63** X7
Ulcinj: Yugoslavia **39** Q16
Uldale: Cumbria, England **26** P10
ULEÅBORG (Oulu): Oulu, Fin. **46** T4
Ulee Lheue: Sumatra **65** H5
Ulgham: Northumb., Eng. **26** S9
Uliastay (Jibhalanta): Mongolia **62** R5
Ulindi: *riv.*, Zaire **76** C3
Ulithi: *i.*, Caroline Is. **61** M10
Ulja: Yugoslavia **41** V11
Ulla: *riv.*, Spain **35** B15
Ulladulla: N.S.W., Australia **71** J10
Ullapool: High., Scotland **28** L4
Ullared: Sweden **47** N8
Ullatti: Sweden **46** R3
Ulldecona: Spain **35** G16
Ulleskelf: N. Yorks., England **27** T12
Ullesthorpe: Leics., England **25** T15
Ullock: Cumbria, England **26** P10
Ullswater: *lake*, Cumbria, England **26** Q10
Ulludag National Park: Turkey **39** V16
Ullung: *i.*, S. Korea **63** Y7
Ulm: W. Germany **40** P7
Ulma: *riv.*, U.S.S.R. **49** o7
Ulricehamn: Sweden **47** N8
Ulrum: Netherlands **44** M2
Ulsan: S. Korea **63** X7
Uls Fiord: Norway **46** Q2
Ulster: *Prov.*, Ireland **30** F11
Ulster Canal: N. Ireland/Repub. of Ireland **30** H11
Ultima: Vict., Australia **71** E10
Ulu Baker: *mtn.*, Malaya, Malaysia **65** c11
Ulubey: Turkey **56** A2
Uluborlu: Turkey **56** B3
Uludağ: *mtn.*, Turkey **56** A1
Ulukişla: Turkey **56** D3
Ulundi: Natal, S. Africa **75** J4
Ulutau: & *mtns.*, Kazakh., U.S.S.R. **51** L5
Ulva: *i.*, Inner Hebr., Scot. **29** J7
Ulverston: Cumbria, Eng. **26** P11
Ulverstone: Tas., Australia **68** H8
'Ulya: Saudi Arabia **55** G9
Ul'yanovka: Ukraine **50** D4
UL'YANOVSK: & *Reg.*, U.S.S.R. **50** G4
Ulzburg: W. Germany **45** P2
Ulzen: W. Germany **45** Q3
Umag: Yugoslavia **41** T10
Uman': Ukraine **50** D5
Umanak: & *fiord*, Greenland **85** o3
Umarkot: Sind, Pakistan **58** L9
Umbeluzi: *riv.*, Swaziland **75** K3
Umbertide: Italy **38** N15
Umboi: *i.*, New Guinea **66** J3
Umbria: *Reg.*, Italy *(cap.* Perugia) **38** N15
Ume: *riv.*, Sweden **46** Q4
UMEÅ: Västerbotten, Sweden **46** R5
Umfolozi: *Dist.*, Natal, S. Afr. **75** J4
Umfolozi, Black & White: *riv.*, Natal, S. Africa **75** J4
Umfolozi Game Reserve: Natal, S. Africa **75** J4
Umfors: Sweden **46** O4
Umfuli: *riv.*, Rhodesia **77** C6
Umgeni: *Dist.* & *riv.*, Natal, S. Africa **75** J4
Umhlali: Natal, S. Africa **75** J4
Umiat: Alaska, U.S.A. **84** d4
Umkomaas: & *riv.*, Natal, S. Africa **75** J5
Umkondo: *riv.*, Swaziland **75** J3
Umm al Qawain: U.A.E. **55** J9
Umm Dam: Sudan **54** D12
Umm el Abid: Libya **78** H4
Umm Hagar: Ethiopia **54** E12
Umm Lahai: *well*, Sudan **79** K6
Umm Lajj: Saudi Arabia **54** E9
Umm Qeis: Jordan **55** b2
Umm Qurein: Sudan **54** C11
Umm Rakh: Saudi Arabia **54** E9
Umm Rasas: Masira I., Oman **55** J10
Umm Ruwaba: Sudan **54** D12
Umm Samim: *salt lake*, Saudi Arabia **55** J10
Umm Wajid: Saudi Arabia **54** G9
Umm Zamul: *well*, Saudi Arabia **55** J10
Umnak: *i.*, Aleutians **84** C7
Umnäs: Sweden **46** P4
Umniati: *riv.*, Rhodesia **77** D6
Umpqua: *riv.*, Oreg., U.S.A. **92** C4
Umraniye: Turkey **56** B2
Umred: Maharashtra, India **58** N10
Umsinga: & *Dist.*, Natal, S. Africa **75** J4
Umsweswe: Rhodesia **77** C6
UMTALI: Manicaland, Rhodesia **77** D6
Umtata: S. Africa **75** H5
Umtata: *riv.*, S. Africa **75** H5
Umuahia: Nigeria **81** F3
Umurbey: Turkey (Dardan. *Inset)* **20** *Ins.*
Umvoti: *Dist.* & *riv.*, Natal, S. Africa **75** J4
Umvuma: Rhodesia **77** D6
Umzimkulu: S. Africa **75** H5
Umzimkulu: *riv.*, S. Africa **75** H5
Umzimvubu: *riv.*, Transkei, S. Africa **75** H5
Umzinto: & *Dist.*, Natal, S. Africa **75** J5
Una: U.S.S.R. **48** e5
Una: *riv.*, Yugoslavia **39** P14
Unadhsdalur: Iceland **46** b3
Unalakleet: Alaska, U.S.A. **84** c5
Unalaska: *i.*, Aleutians **84** C7
Unango: Mozambique **77** E5
Unauna: *i.*, Celebes **65** G7
Uncia: Bolivia **94** D7
Uncocua: Angola **73** G13
Uncompahgre Peak: Colo., U.S.A. **93** F5
Uncompahgre Plat.: Colo., U.S.A. **93** F5

Underberg: Natal, S. Africa **75** H4
Underbool: Vict., Australia **71** D10
Undu, Cape: Sumba, Indon. **65** G9
Undva: Estonia, U.S.S.R. **47** S7
Unecha: U.S.S.R. **50** D6
Unga: Alaska, U.S.A. **84** c6
Ungarie: N.S.W., Australia **71** G9
Ungarra: S. Australia **71** B9
Ungava Bay: Que., Canada **85** N6
Ungava Penin.: Que., Can. **85** M5
Ungeny: Moldavia, U.S.S.R. **43** V12
Unggi: N. Korea **63** Y6
União: Brazil **94** J4
União da Vitoria: Brazil **96** E2
Unije: *i.*, Yugoslavia **41** U11
Unimak: *i., & passage,* Aleutians **84** c7
Union: Argentina **96** B4
Union: Chile **96** B1
Union: Mo., U.S.A. **88** F6
Union: Oreg., U.S.A. **92** D3
Union: S.C., U.S.A. **91** L8
Union: Trans., S. Africa **74** *Nins.*
Union: *i.*, Grenadines, Windward Is. **87** c4
Union, Cape: N.W.T., Can. **85** n1
Union, La: Chile **95** C12
Union, La: Mexico **86** j14
Union, La: Salvador **86** L15
Union City: Ind., U.S.A. **88** J5
Union City: Pa., U.S.A. **89** M5
Union City: Tenn., U.S.A. **88** G7
Uniondale: & *Dist.*, S. Africa **74** E6
Uniondale Road: S. Africa **74** E6
Unionhall: Cork, Repub. of Ireland **31** C16
Union (Tokelau) Is.: (N.Z.), Pacific O. **70** *Ins.*

Union of Soviet Socialist Republics 48/9
Cap.: Moscow
Area: 8,647,250 sq. miles
(22,396,378 sq. km.)
Pop.: 246,309,000 *(1972 E)*

Union Springs: *city*, Ala., U.S.A. **91** J9
Uniontown: Ala., U.S.A. **91** H9
Uniontown: Pa., U.S.A. **89** M6
Unionville: Mo., U.S.A. **88** E5

United Arab Emirates 55 H10
Cap.: Abu Dhabi
Area: 32,000 sq. miles
(82,880 sq. km.)
Pop.: 197,000 *(1971 E)*

United Kingdom of Great Britain and Northern Ireland 22/3
Cap.: London
Area: 94,214 sq. miles
(244,014 sq. km.)
Pop.: 55,348,957 *(1971 C)*

United States of America:
Republic **86/7**
Cap.: Washington D.C.
Area: 3,628,150 sq. miles
(9,396,909 sq. km.)
Pop.: 208,500,000 *(1972 E)*

United States Range: Can. **85** M1
Unity: Sask., Canada **92** F2
Unna: W. Germany **44** N4
Unnao: Uttar Pradesh, Ind. **58** O9
Unsang, Cape: Sabah, Malaysia **65** F5
Unst: *i.*, Shetland Is. **28** *Ins.*
Unstone: Derby., England **27** T13
Unstrut: *riv.*, E. Germany **45** R4
Unterfranken: *Dist.*, Bavaria, West Germany **45** Q5
Unter Gänserndorf: Austria **41** W7
Unter Harz: *mtns.*, E. Ger. **45** R4
Unterluss: W. Germany **45** Q3
Unterwalden: *Canton*, Switz. *(caps.* Sarnen *and* Stans) **40** O9
Unye: Turkey **56** E1
Unzha: *riv.*, U.S.S.R. **50** F3
Uozu: Japan **63** e2
Upata: Venezuela **94** E2
Upavon: Wilts., England **25** S17
Upemba, Lake: Zaire **77** C4
Upemba National Park: Zaire **77** C4
Upernavik: Greenland **85** O3
Uphall: Lothian, Scotland **29** O8
Upham: Hants., England **25** T18
Uphill: Avon, England **24** Q17
Upholland: Lancs., England **27** Q12
Upington: S. Africa **74** D4
Uplawmoor: Strath., Scot. **29** N8
Upolu: *i.*, W. Samoa **70** *Ins.*
Upper: *Reg.*, Ghana *(cap.* Bolgatanga) **80** D2
Upper Arrow Lake: B.C., Canada **92** D2
Upper Arley: Hereford & Worcester, England **24** R15
Upper Austria: *Prov.*, Austr. *(cap.* Linz) **41** T7
Upperchurch: Tip., Repub. of Ireland **31** E14
Upper Gumar: Somalia **79** Q18
Upper Juba: *Reg.*, Somalia *(cap.* Isha Baidoa) **79** Q19
Upper Lake: Calif., U.S.A. **92** C4
Upper Lough Erne: Ferm., N. Ireland **30** F11
Upper Marlboro: Md., U.S.A. **89** N6
Upper Musquodoboit: Nova Scotia, Canada **89** U3
Upper Nile: *Prov.*, Sudan *(cap.* Malakal) **76** D1
Upper Red Lake: Minn., U.S.A. **88** D1
Upper Sandusky: Ohio, U.S.A. **88** K5
Upper Seal, Lake: Que., Canada **85** m6
Upper Thames Valley: England **25** S16
Upper Tunguska: *riv.*, U.S.S.R. **49** M6

Upper Volta: *Republic* **80** D2
Cap.: Ouagadougou
Area: 105,869 sq. miles
(274,201 sq. km.)
Pop.: 5,491,000 *(1971 E)*

Upper Yarra Reservoir: Vict., Australia **71** F11
Uppingham: Leics., England **27** U14
UPPSALA: & *Co.*, Sweden **47** P7
Upshi: Jammu & Kashmir **58** N8
Upton: Oxon., England **25** T16
Upton: Wyo., U.S.A. **92** G4
Upton upon Severn: Hereford & Worcester, England **24** R15

Upwey: Dorset, England **24** R18
Upwood: Cambs., England **25** V15
Uqair: Saudi Arabia **55** H9
Ur: Sumerian city. Site at *Maiyar*, Iraq **57** K6
Uraga: Japan **63** f3
Urakawa: Japan **63** ZZ6
Ural: *hill*, N.S.W., Australia **71** G9
Ural: *riv.*, U.S.S.R. **50** H4
Uralla: N.S.W., Australia **71** J8
Ural Mtns.: U.S.S.R. **50** J3
URAL'SK: & *Reg.*, Kazakhstan, U.S.S.R. **50** H4
Urambo: Tanzania **76** D4
Urana: N.S.W., Australia **71** G10
Urandangie: Queens., Austl. **69** F4
Urandi: Brazil **94** J6
Urangan: Queens., Austl. **70** K5
Uranquinty: N.S.W., Austl. **71** G10
Uraricoera: *riv.*, Brazil **94** E3
Urartu: Assyrian name of Ararat and region of Turkey/Iran/Armenia, U.S.S.R. **57** J2
Ura-Tyube: Tadzhik., U.S.S.R. **51** L7
URAWA: Saitama, Japan **63** f3
Urbana: Ill., U.S.A. **88** G5
Urbana: Ohio, U.S.A. **88** K5
Urbania: Italy **41** S12
Urbino: Italy **41** S12
Urchfont: Wilts., England **24** S17
Urcos: Peru **94** C6
Urda: Kazakh., U.S.S.R. **50** G5
Urdingen: W. Germany **44** M4
Urdos: France **37** E13
Urdzhar: Kazakh., U.S.S.R. **51** O5
Ure: *riv.*, N. Yorks., England **26** S11
Urech'ye: Byelorussia **43** U10
Uren': U.S.S.R. **50** G3
Ures: Mexico **93** E7
Urewera National Park: N.I., New Zealand **79** Q14
URFA: & *Prov.*, Turkey **56** F3
Urfahr: Austria **41** U7
Urga: *see* Ulan Bator.
Urgel, Llanos de: *geog. reg.*, Spain **35** G16
Urgench: Uzbek., U.S.S.R. **51** K6
Urgeseti: Sinkiang, China **62** Q6
Urgun: Afghanistan **58** L8
Urgup: Turkey **56** D2
Urgut: Uzbek., U.S.S.R. **51** L7
Uribia: Colombia **94** C1
Urimbrin: Queens., Austl. **70** E7
Urique: Mexico **93** F7
Urisino: N.S.W., Australia **71** E7
Urjala: Finland **47** S6
Urk: Netherlands **44** L3
Urkarakh: U.S.S.R. **50** G6
Urla: Turkey **39** U17
Urlaur: Mayo, Repub. of Ireland **30** D12
Urlingford: Kilk., Repub. of Ireland **31** F14
Urmia (Rizaiyeh): Iran **57** J3
Urmia, Lake: Iran **57** J3
Urmston: Gt. Man., England **27** R13
Urosevac: Yugoslavia **39** R15
Urquhart: Gram., Scotland **28** P4
Ursat'yevskaya: Uzbek., U.S.S.R. **51** L6
Ursk: U.S.S.R. **51** P4
Urso: Roman colony at Osuna, Spain **35** D18
Urt: France **37** D12
Urtam: U.S.S.R. **51** O3
Uruachic: Mexico **93** F7
Uruapan: Mexico **86** j14
Urucara: Brazil **94** F4
Uruçuí: Brazil **94** J5
Urucurituba: Brazil **94** F4
Uruguaiana: Brazil **96** D2

Uruguay: *Republic* **96** D3
Cap. Montevideo
Area: 68,548 sq. miles (177,539 sq. km.)
Pop. 2,921,000 (1971 E)

Uruguay: *riv.*, Argentina **96** D3
Urumchi: *see* Wulumuchi.
Urunga: N.S.W., Australia **71** K8
Urungu: *riv.*, Sinkiang, China **51** P5
Urup: i., Kuril Is. **63** YY5
'Uruq bin Tamaisha: *sand reg.*, Saudi Arabia **55** H10
'Uruq Shaiba': *sand reg.*, Saudi Arabia **55** H10
'Uruq Zaza: *sand reg.*, Saudi Arabia **55** G11
Urussanga: Brazil **96** F2
Uruwira: Tanzania **76** D4
Uruzgan: *prov.*, Afghanistan **58** L8
Uryupinsk: U.S.S.R. **50** F4
Urziceni: Romania **39** U14
Usagara: Tanzania **76** D3
Usak: & *Prov.*, Turkey **56** A2
Usakos: S.W. Africa **74** A1
Usce: Yugoslavia **39** R15
Usedom: E. Germany **45** T2
Useko: Tanzania **76** D4
Usetsu: Japan **63** e2
Usfan: Saudi Arabia **54** E10
Ushakov I.: (U.S.S.R.) Arctic O. **48** J1
Ushant (Ile d'Ouessant): i., France **36** A7
Ushnuiyeh: Iran **57** J3
Ushomir: Ukraine **43** V11
Ushtarinan: Iran **57** L4
Ushtarinan Kuh: *mtn.*, Iran **57** L5
Ush-Tobe: Kazakh., U.S.S.R. **51** N5
USHUAIA: Tierra del Fuego, Argentina **95** D14
Usimbe: Tanzania **76** E4
Usingen: W. Germany **44** O5
Usk: & *riv.*, Gwent, Wales **24** Q16
Uskub: Turkish name of Yugoslav town Skopje **39** R15
Uskudar (Scutari): Turkey (Bosporus. *inset*) **20** *Ins*
Uslar: W. Germany **44** P4
Usman': U.S.S.R. **50** E4
Usoke: Tanzania **76** D4
Usol'ye: U.S.S.R. **49** M7
Usovo: Ukraine **43** V11
Uspenskiy: Kazakh., U.S.S.R. **51** M5
Ussel: France **37** H10
Ussuriysk: U.S.S.R. **63** Y6
Ust'-Belaya: U.S.S.R. **49** T4
Ust'-Bol'sheretsk: U.S.S.R. **49** r7
Ust'-Bukhtarma: Kazakh., U.S.S.R. **51** O5
Uštěk: Czechoslovakia **45** U5
Uster: Switzerland **40** O8
Ustí: Severočesky, Czechoslovakia **45** W6
Ustibovo: Byelorussia **43** T10
Ustica: i., Tyrrhenian Sea **38** N17
Ustí-nad-Labem: Czech. **45** U5
Ustjoki: Finland **46** U2
Ust'-Kamchatsk: U.S.S.R. **49** S6

Ust'-KAMENOGORSK: East Kazakhstan, U.S.S.R. **51** O5
Ust'-Karsk: U.S.S.R. **49** n7
Ust'-Katav: U.S.S.R. **50** J4
Ust'-Kozhva: U.S.S.R. **48** g4
Ust'-Kut: U.S.S.R. **49** m6
Ust'-Labinsk: U.S.S.R. **50** E5
Ust'-Luga: U.S.S.R. **47** V7
Ust'-Nyukzha: U.S.S.R. **49** O6
Ust'-Staritsa: U.S.S.R. **51** O3
Ust'-Tarka: U.S.S.R. **51** N3
Ust'-Tsil'ma: U.S.S.R. **48** G4
Ust'-Ulagan: U.S.S.R. **51** P4
Ust'-Urt Plat.: Uzbek., U.S.S.R. **50** J6
Ust' Usa: U.S.S.R. **48** g4
Ust'-Uyskoye: U.S.S.R. **51** K4
Ust'-Voya: U.S.S.R. **48** g5
Ust'-Vym': U.S.S.R. **50** H2
Ust'-ye: U.S.S.R. **50** E3
Ust'ye Girvas: U.S.S.R. **46** W2
Ust'ye Lola: U.S.S.R. **46** W2
Usu: i., Indonesia **65** G9
Usuki: Japan **63** b4
Usumbura: *see* Bujumbura.
Usure: Tanzania **76** D3
Usutu: *riv.*, Swaziland **75** J3
Usworth: Tyne & Wear, England **26** S10
Uta: Japan **63** b3
Utah: *State*, U.S.A. (*cap.* Salt Lake City) **93** E5
Utah Lake: Utah, U.S.A. **93** E4
Utena: Lithuania, U.S.S.R. **47** T9
Utengule: Tanzania **77** E4
Utete: Tanzania **76** E4
Utevka: U.S.S.R. **50** H4
Uthai Thani: Thailand **64** C3
Utiariti: Brazil **94** F6
Utica: N.Y. U.S.A. **89** O4
Utica: Punic and Roman city on G. of Tunis near Porto Farina, Tunisia **33** M18
Utiel: Spain **35** F17
Utikuma Lake: Alta., Can. **92** D1
Utila I.: Honduras **86** *Ins.*
Uto: Japan **63** b4
Utokho: Inner Mongolia, China **62** N6
Utrecht: & *Dist.*, Natal, S. Africa **75** J3
UTRECHT: & *Prov.*, Neth. **44** L3
Utrera: Spain **35** D18
UTSUNOMIYA: Tochigi, Japan **63** f2
Uttaradit: Thailand **64** C3
Uttar Pradesh (United Provinces): *State*, India (*cap.* Lucknow) **58** O9
Uttoxeter: Staffs., England **27** S14
Utum Po: Thailand **64** C4
Utuncha: U.S.S.R. **49** Q3
Utupua: i., Santa Cruz Is., Pacific O. **67** N4
Utze: W. Germany **45** Q3
Uusikaupunki: Finland **47** R6
Uusimaa: *Prov.*, Finland (*cap.* Helsinki) **47** T6
Uvaia: Brazil **96** E2
Uvalde: Tex., U.S.A. **90** B11
Uvea: i., Loyalty Is. **67** N6
Uvea: i., Wallis Is., Pac. O. **67** Q4
Uvinza: Tanzania **76** D4
Uvira: Zaire **76** C3
Uvkusigssat: Greenland **85** o3
'Uwaim: Saudi Arabia **54** F9
'Uwaina: *well*, Saudi Arabia **55** G9
Uwajima: Japan **63** c4
Uwet: Nigeria **81** F3
Uxellodunum: Roman name of Gallic fort at *Puy d'Issolu* on river Dordogne SE. of Martel, Fr. **37** G11
Uxmal: ruined Maya city in Southern Yucatán, Mexico **86** L14
Uyak: Alaska, U.S.A. **84** d6
Uyar: U.S.S.R. **51** Q3
Uyeasound: Shetland Is. **28** *Ins.*
Uyedineniye I.: U.S.S.R. **48** K2
Uyo: Nigeria **81** F3
Uyskoye: U.S.S.R. **51** K4
Uyu: *riv.*, Burma **59** R9
'Uyun: Saudi Arabia **54** F9
Uyuni: Bolivia **94** D8
Uzbekistan: S.S. Rep., U.S.S.R. (*cap.* Tashkent) **51** K5
Uzda: Byelorussia **43** U10
Uzel: France **36** C7
Uzerche: France **37** G10
Uzès: France **37** K11
Uzh: *riv.*, Ukraine **43** V11
Uzhgorod: Ukraine **43** S12
Uzhur: U.S.S.R. **51** P3
Uzmaston: Dyfed, Wales **24** M16
Uzun-Agach: Kazakh., U.S.S.R. **51** N6
Uzunkopru: Turkey **39** U16
Uzunyayla: *geog. reg.*, Tur. **56** E2

Vaagø: i., Faeroe Is. **40** h5
Vaag: *riv.*, S. Africa **75** G3
Vaal: *riv.*, S. Africa **75** F4
Vaala: Finland **46** U4
Vaalbank Dam: S. Africa **75** H3
Vaaldam Nature Reserve: Trans., S. Africa **75** H3
Vaalfontein: S. Africa **74** C5
Vaalgras: S.W. Africa **74** B1
Vaalhoek: Trans., S. Africa **75** J2
Vaalwater: Trans., S. Africa **75** H2
VAASA (Vasa): & *Prov.*, Fin. **46** R5
Vac: Hungary **43** Q13
Vacaria: Brazil **96** E2
Vacation Station: *rsch. stn.*, Antarctica **9** 80S 160E
Vacation Village: Bahamas **91** M12
Vandalia: Ill., U.S.A. **88** G6
Vandalia: Mo., U.S.A. **88** F5
Vaccaei: ancient Spanish tribe of area around Salamanca, Spain **35** D16
Vaccarès, Étang de: *lag.*, Fr. **37** K12
Vacha: E. Germany **45** Q5
Vacy: N.S.W., Australia **71** J9
Vadodara (Baroda): Gujarat, India **58** M10
Vadsø: Finnmark, Norway **46** V1
Vadstena: Sweden **47** O7
VADUZ: Liechtenstein **40** P8
Værøn: Norway **46** M5
Vaga: *riv.*, U.S.S.R. **50** F3
Vaganski: *mtn.*, Yugoslavia **41** V11
Vagay: U.S.S.R. **51** L3
Vaggeryd: Sweden **47** O8
Vågs Fiord: Norway **46** P2
Vah: *riv.*, Czechoslovakia **43** P12
Vahitahi: i., Tuamotu Arch. **83** h3
Vaiges: France **36** E7
Vaihingen: W. Germany **44** O7
Vailly: Aisne, France **36** J6
Vailly: Cher, France **36** J8
Vairaatea: i., Tuamotu Arch. **83** h3
Vaire: France **37** D9
Vaison: France **37** L11
Vaitupu: i., Tuvalu **67** P3
Vakh: *riv.*, U.S.S.R. **51** N2
Valaam: i., L. Ladoga, U.S.S.R. **47** W6
Valais: *Canton*, Switzerland (*cap.* Sion) **40** N9
Valamaz: U.S.S.R. **50** H3

Val Brillant: Que., Canada **89** S1
Valcheta: Argentina **95** D12
Val-d'Ajol, Le: France **40** M8
Valdecañas, Embalse de: *res.*, Spain **35** D17
Valdemárpils: Latvia, U.S.S.R. **47** S8
Valdemarsvik: Sweden **47** P7
Val-d'Oise: *Dept.*, France (*cap.* Pontoise) **36** G6
Valdepeñas: Spain **35** E17
Valderrobres: Spain **35** G16
Valdes Penin.: Argentina **95** E12
Valdez: Alaska, U.S.A. **84** E5
Valdivia: Chile **95** C11
Valdivia: Colombia **94** C2
Valdobbiadene: Italy **41** R10
Val d'Or: Que., Canada **89** N1
Valdosta: Ga., U.S.A. **91** K10
Vale: Oreg., U.S.A. **92** D4
Vale, The (Til Til): N.S.W., Australia **71** E9
Valença: Bahia, Brazil **94** K6
Valença: Piauí, Brazil **94** J5
Valençay: France **36** G8
Valence: Gers, France **37** F12
Valence: Tarn-et-Garonne, Fr. **37** F11
VALENCE-SUR-RHÔNE: Drôme, France **37** K11
VALENCIA: & *Prov.* (old & new), Spain **35** F17
Valencia: Venezuela **94** D1
Valencia de Alcántara: Spain **35** C17
Valencia de Don Juan: Spain **35** D15
Valencia, G. of: Spain **35** G17
Valenciennes: France **36** J5
Váleni de Munte: Romania **39** U14
Valensole: France **40** L12
Valentia I.: Repub. of Irel. **31** A16
Valentin: U.S.S.R. **63** Y6
Valentine: Nebr., U.S.A. **92** G4
Valenza: Italy **40** O10
Valerio: Mexico **93** F7
Valeyrac: France **37** E10
Valga: Estonia, U.S.S.R. **47** U8
Valier: Mont., U.S.A. **92** E3
Valipirtti: Finland **46** V3
Valjevo: Yugoslavia **39** Q14
Val'karay: U.S.S.R. **49** t4
Valkeakoski: Finland **47** T6
Valladolid: Mexico **86** L13
VALLADOLID: & *Prov.*, Spain **35** D16
Vallage: *geog. reg.*, France **36** K7
Vallecas: Spain **35** E16
Valle de la Pascua: Venezuela **94** D2
Valle de Zaragoza: Mexico **93** F7
Valle Fertil: Argentina **96** B3
Valle Grande: Bolivia **94** E7
Vallejo: Calif., U.S.A. **93** C5
Vallenar: Chile **96** A2
Valletjies: S. Africa **74** D6
VALLETTA: Malta **32** *Ins*
Valley: & *airfield*, Gwynedd, Wales **27** M13
Valley City: N. Dak., U.S.A. **92** H3
Valleyfield: Que., Canada **89** O3
Valli dei Signori: Italy **41** R10
Vallières: France **37** H10
Vallimanca: *riv.*, Arg. **96** C4
Vallon: France **37** K11
Vallonise: France **40** M11
Vallorbe: Switzerland **40** M9
Valls: Spain **35** G16
Val Marie: Sask., Canada **92** F3
Valmaseda: Spain **35** E15
Valmiera: Latvia, U.S.S.R. **47** T8
Valmont: France **36** F6
Valmy: Algeria **35** F14
Valmy: battlefield about 15 miles E. of Suippes, France **36** K6
Valognes: France **36** D6
Valona (Vlone): Albania **39** Q16
Valoria la Buena: Spain **35** D16
Valparaiso: Chile **96** A3
Valparaiso: Ind., U.S.A. **88** H5
Valréas: France **37** K11
Vals: France **37** K11
Vals: Switzerland **40** P9
Vals: *riv.*, O.F.S., S. Africa **75** G3
Vals, Cape: W. Irian, Indonesia **61** M13
Val Tellina: *val.*, Italy **40** P9
Valthjofsstadhir: Iceland **46** f4
Valtimo: Finland **46** V5
Valtournanche: Italy **40** N10
Valtura: Yugoslavia **41** T11
Valuyki: U.S.S.R. **50** E4
Val Venosta: *val.*, Italy **41** Q9
Valverde: Canary Is. **78** A4
Valverde del Camino: Spain **35** C18
Vammala: Finland **47** S6
Vamos: Crete **39** T19
VAN: & *Prov.*, Turkey **57** H2
Van, Lake: Turkey **57** H2
Van Alstyne: Tex., U.S.A. **90** C9
Vanavana: i., Tuamotu Arch. **83** h4
Vanavara: U.S.S.R. **49** M5
Van Buren: Ark., U.S.A. **90** D8
Van Buren: Maine, U.S.A. **89** S2
Vanceboro: Maine, U.S.A. **89** S3
Vanceburg: Ky., U.S.A. **88** K6
Vanch: Tadzhik., U.S.S.R. **51** M7
Vancouver: B.C., Canada **92** C3
Vancouver: Wash., U.S.A. **92** C3
Vancouver Is.: B.C., Canada **92** B3
Vancouver, Mount: Canada/U.S.A. **84** F5
Vanda Station: *rsch. stn.*, Antarctica **9** 80S 160E
Vandalia: Ill., U.S.A. **88** G6
Vandalia: Mo., U.S.A. **88** F5
Vanderhoof: B.C., Canada **92** C2
Van Diemen, Cape: Austl. **68** E2
Van Diemen Gulf: Australia **68** E2
Van Dieman's Land: former name of Tasmania, Austl. **68** *Ins.*
Vandoies: Italy **41** R9
Vedea: *riv.*, Romania **39** T14
Vedia: Argentina **96** C3
Veendam: Netherlands **44** M2
Veenendaal: Netherlands **44** L3
Veenwouden: Netherlands **44** L2
Vefsna Fiord: & *riv.*, Norway **46** N4
Vega: & i., Norway **46** M4
Vega, La: Dominican Repub. **87** m14
Vega Fiord: Norway **46** M4
Vegesack: W. Germany **44** O2
Vegreville: Alta., Canada **92** E2
Vehmaa: Finland **47** R6
Veii: ancient town of S. Etruria about 9 miles NNW. of Rome **38** N15
Veinticinco de Mayo: Buenos Aires, Argentina **96** C4
Veinticinco de Mayo: La Pampa, Argentina **96** B4
Veisali: Solomon Is. **67** L3
Vejer de la Frontera: Spain (Gib. *inset*) **32** *Ins*
Vejle: Denmark **47** L9
Vejprty: Czechoslovakia **45** T5
Vela: Argentina **96** D4
Velay, Monts du: France **37** J10
Velázquez: Uruguay **96** E3
Velburg: W. Germany **45** R6

Velden: W. Germany **45** R6
Velddrif: S. Africa **74** C6
Velebit Mtns.: Yugoslavia **41** V11
Velebitski Chan.: *str.*, Yugoslavia **41** U10
Veleia: Roman city about 10 miles W. of Bardi, Emilia Romagna, Italy **40** P11
Velestinon: Greece **39** S17
Velez, D.: Argentina **96** C3
Velez Malaga: Spain **35** D18
Velez Rubio: Spain **35** E18
Velfjord: Norway **46** N4
Velgast: E. Germany **45** S1
Velika Gorica: Yugoslavia **41** W10
Velika Mtns.: Yugoslavia **41** U10
Velikaya: U.S.S.R. **49** t5
Velikaya: *riv.*, U.S.S.R. **47** V8
Velikaya Kema: U.S.S.R. **63** Z5
Veliki Popovic: Yugoslavia **39** R14
Velikiye Luki: U.S.S.R. **50** D3
Velikiy Ustyug: U.S.S.R. **50** G2
Velikodolinskoye: Ukraine **39** V13
Veliko Turnovo: Bulgaria **39** T15
Velingara: Senegal **80** B2
Velizh: U.S.S.R. **50** D3
Veljun: Yugoslavia **41** V10
Velke Bytce: Czechoslovakia **45** W6
Velke Mezirici: Czech. **43** P12
Vel'ky-Berezny: Czech. **43** S12
Vella Lavella: i., Solomon Is. **67** L3
Vellaunodunum: Roman name of Gallic centre at Montargis, France **36** H8
Vellberg: W. Germany **45** P6
Velletri: Italy **38** N16
Vellore: Tamil Nadu, India **58** N12
Velluire: France **37** E9
Velosnes: France **36** L6
Velp: Netherlands **44** L3
Velva: N. Dak., U.S.A. **92** G3
Vem: Denmark **47** L8
Vemdalen: Sweden **46** N5
Venacher, Loch: Central, Scotland **29** N7
Venado Tuerto: Argentina **96** C3
Venafrum: Roman city about 10 miles E. of Cassino, It. **38** N16
Venarey: France **36** K8
Vence: France **40** N12
Venceslau Braz: Brazil **96** F1
Vendas Novas: Portugal **35** B17
Vendee: *Dept.*, France (*cap.* La Roche-sur-Yon) **37** D9
Vendenheim: France **40** N7
Vendeuvre-sur-Barse: France **36** K7
Vendœuvres: France **37** G9
Vendôme: France **36** G8
Vendrell: Spain **35** G16
Veneti: Gallic tribe in area of Morbihan, France **36** C8
Venetian Alps: Italy **41** S9
Veneto: *Reg.*, Italy (*cap.* Venice) **41** S10
VENEZIA (Venice): Veneto, Italy **41** S10

Venezuela: *Republic* **94** D2
Cap. Caracas
Area: 352,143 sq. miles (912,050 sq. km.)
Pop.: 10,721,522 (1971 C)

Venezuela, G. of: Venezuela **94** C1
Venezuelan Basin: Caribbean Sea **8** 10N 70W
Vengerovo: U.S.S.R. **51** N3
Veniaminofa Volc.: Alaska, U.S.A. **84** D6
VENICE (Venezia): Veneto, Italy **41** S10
Venice: La., U.S.A. **90** *Ins.*
Venice, G. of: Italy **41** S10
Vénissieux: France **37** K10
Venkatagiri: Andhra Pradesh, India **58** N12
Venlo: Netherlands **44** M4
Venraai: Netherlands **44** L4
Venta: *riv.*, U.S.S.R. **47** S8
Venta Belgarum: Romano-British town at Winchester, Hants., England **25** T17
Venta Icenorum: Romano-British town at Caister about 3 miles S. of Norwich, Norf., England **25** Y14
Ventana, Punta de la: *cape*, Mexico **93** F8
Venta Silurum: Romano-British town at Caerwent about 2 miles NW. of Portskewett, Gwent, Wales **24** Q16
Ventersburg: & *Dist.*, O.F.S., S. Africa **75** G4
Ventersdorp: & *Dist.*, Trans., S. Africa **75** G3
Venterstad: & *Dist.*, S. Afr. **75** F5
Ventil-Kynok: U.S.S.R. **51** O2
Ventimiglia: Italy **40** N12
Ventnor: I. of Wight, Eng. **25** T18
Ventotene: i., Italy **38** N16
Ventry: Kerry, Repub. of Ireland **31** A15
Ventspils: Latvia, U.S.S.R. **47** R8
Ventura: Calif., U.S.A. **93** D6
Vaygach I.: U.S.S.R. **48** g3
Vazec: Czechoslovakia **43** Q12
Vcherayshe: Ukraine **43** V12
Vecaki: Latvia, U.S.S.R. **47** T8
Vechel: Netherlands **44** L4
Vecht: *riv.*, Netherlands **44** M3
Vechta: W. Germany **44** O3
Vecilla, La: Spain **35** D15
Vectis: Roman name of I. of Wight, England **25** T18
Vedea: *riv.*, Romania **39** T14
Venusia: Roman city near site of Rionera in Vulture, Italy **38** O16
Vera: Argentina **96** C3
Vera: Spain **35** F18
Vera, Lake: Paraguay **96** D2
Veracruz: Mexico **86** K14
Veranópolis: Brazil **96** E2
Veraval: Gujarat, India **58** M10
Verbanus: Roman name of L. Maggiore, Italy **40** O10
Verbilki: U.S.S.R. **50** E3
Vercel: France **40** M8
Vercelli: Italy **40** O10
Verdal: Norway **46** N5
Verde, Cape: Senegal **80** A2
Verde: W. Germany **44** P3
Verde Penin.: Argentina **96** C4
Verdigris: *riv.*, Kans./Okla., U.S.A. **90** D7
Verdon: *riv.*, France **40** M12
Verdun: Le: France **37** D10
Verdun: France **36** L6
Verdun-sur-le-Doubs: Fr. **37** L9
Vereeniging: & *Dist.*, Trans., S. Africa **75** G3
Vereshchagino: U.S.S.R. **50** H3
Veretski Pass: Ukraine **43** S12
Verette: La., U.S.A. **90** *Ins.*
Verga, Cape: Guinea **80** B2
Vergara: Spain **35** E15
Vergara: Uruguay **96** E3
Vergato: Italy **41** R11
Vergennes: Vt., U.S.A. **89** P3
Verin: Spain **35** C16
Verissimo Sarmento: Angola **76** B4
Verkeerdevlei: O.F.S., S. Afr. **75** G4

Verkhnaya Chebula: U.S.S.R. 51 P3
Verkhnaya Sinyachikha: U.S.S.R. 51 K3
Verkhnaya Toyma: U.S.S.R. 50 G2
Verkhnaya Tura: U.S.S.R. 50 J3
Verkhneural'sk: U.S.S.R. 50 J4
Verkhniy Baskunchak: U.S.S.R. 50 G5
Verkhniy Kigi: U.S.S.R. 50 J3
Verkhniy Mamon: U.S.S.R. 50 F4
Verkhniy Talin: Armenia, U.S.S.R. 57 H1
Verkhoyansk: U.S.S.R. 49 P4
Verkhoyansk Range: U.S.S.R. 49 o4
Vermaaklikheid: S. Africa 74 D7
Vermaas: Trans., S. Africa 75 F3
Vermandois: *geog. reg.*, Fr. 36 J6
Vermenton: France 36 J8
Vermilion: Alta., Canada 92 E2
Vermilion Bay: La., U.S.A. 90 E11
Vermilion Lake: Minn., U.S.A. 88 E2
Vermillion: S. Dak., U.S.A. 92 H4
Vermillion Bay: *town*, Ont., Canada 92 J3
Vermont: Trans., S. Africa 75 J2
Vermont: *State*, U.S.A. *(cap.* Montpelier) 89 P3
Vern: France 36 E8
Vernal: Utah, U.S.A. 93 F4
Vernarède, La: France 37 J11
Vernazza: Italy 40 P11
Verneuil: France 36 F7
Verneukpan: *lake*, S. Africa 74 D4
Vernon: B.C., Canada 92 D2
Vernon: France 36 G6
Vernon: Tex., U.S.A. 90 B8
Vernoux: France 37 K11
Verny: France 44 M6
Vero Beach: *city*, Fla., U.S.A. 91 L12
Verolanuova: Italy 40 Q10
Verona: Italy 41 Q10
Vérroia: Greece 39 S16
Versailles: Ky., U.S.A. 88 J6
Versailles: Mo., U.S.A. 88 E6
VERSAILLES: Yvelines, France 36 H7
Versmold: W. Germany 44 O3
Verteillac: France 37 F10
Verterae: Roman name of Brough, Cumbria, Eng. 26 R10
Vertou-les-Sorinières: Fr. 36 D8
Vertus: France 36 K7
Verulam: Natal, S. Africa 75 J4
Verulamium: British, later Roman, town at St. Albans, Herts., England 25 V16
Verviers: Belgium 44 L5
Vervins: France 36 J6
Verwig: Dyfed, Wales 24 M15
Verwood: Dorset, England 25 S18
Veryan: Corn., England 24 M19
Verzone: Italy 41 T9
Verzy: France 36 K6
Vesanto: Finland 46 U5
Veseli: Bohemia, Czech. 42 O12
Veseli: Moravia, Czech. 43 P12
Veshenskaya: U.S.S.R. 50 F5
Vesontio: Roman name of settlement at Besançon, France 40 M8
VESOUL: Haute-Saône, Fr. 40 M8
Vesta: Costa Rica 87 I16
Vest Agder: *Co.*, Norway *(cap.* Kristiansand) 47 K7
Vesterålen: *is.*, Norway 46 O2
Vest Fiord: Norway 46 O2
Vestfold: *Co.*, Norway *(cap.* Tønsberg) 47 M7
Vestmannaeyjar: *i.*, Iceland 46 c5
Vestvågøy: *i.*, Lofoten Is. 46 N2
Vesuvius: *volc.*, Italy 38 O16
Veszprém: Hungary 43 P13
Vet: *riv.*, O.F.S., S. Africa 75 G4
Vetera: Roman camp at *Xanten* on Rhine opposite Wesel, W. Germany 44 M4
Vetlanda: Sweden 47 O8
Vetluga: & *riv.*, U.S.S.R. 50 G3
Vetren: Bulgaria 39 T15
Vetto: Italy 40 Q11
Veules-les-Roses: France 36 F6
Veurne: Belgium 36 H4
Veuve, La: France 36 K6
Vevey: Switzerland 40 M9
Veynes: France 40 L11
Veys, Baie des: France 36 D6
Vézelay: France 36 J8
Vézelise: France 40 M7
Vézere: *riv.*, France 37 G9
Vezirkopru: Turkey 56 D1
Via Appia: Roman road running SE. from Rome to coast at *Tarracina* (q.v.) and thence to Capua, Benevento, and Brindisi 38 N16
Via Aurelia: Roman road leading W. from Rome and up W. coast of Italy. 38
Viacha: Bolivia 94 D7
Viadana: Italy 40 Q11
Via Flaminia: Roman road leading N. from Rome to *Ariminum* (Rimini) 38 N15
Via Latina: Roman road running approximately Rome-Cassino-Capua 38 N16
Viamonte: Argentina 96 C3
Viana do Alentejo: Portugal 35 C17
Viana do Castelo: Portugal 35 B16
Vianen: Netherlands 44 L4
Via Praenestina: Roman road leading E. by S. from Rome. 38 N14
Viareggio: Italy 40 Q12
Via Tiburtina: Roman road leading E. from Rome to *Tibur* (Tivoli). 38 N16
Viaur: *riv.*, France 37 H11
Viborg: Denmark 47 L8
Vibo Valentia: Italy 38 P17
Vibraye: France 36 F7
Vicarstown: Laois, Repub. of Ireland 31 G13
Vicdessos: France 37 G13
Vicecomodoro Marambio: *rsch. stn.*, Antarctica 9 65S 60W
Vicenza: Italy 41 R10
Vicetia: Roman city at Vicenza, Italy 41 R10
Vich: Spain 35 H16
Vichuquen: Chile 96 A3
Vichy: France 37 J9
Vicksburg: Ariz., U.S.A. 93 E6
Vicksburg: Mich., U.S.A. 88 J4
Vicksburg: Miss., U.S.A. 90 F9
Vic-le-Comte: France 37 J10
Vico: Corsica 38 L15
Vic-sur-Cère: France 37 H11
Victor Harbour: S. Austl. 71 C10
Victoria: Argentina 96 C3
VICTORIA: B.C., Canada 92 C3

Victoria: Chile 96 A4
Victoria (Rabat): Gozo, Malta 32 *Ins.*
VICTORIA: Hong Kong 62 U10
Victoria: Cameroun 81 F4
Victoria: Tex., U.S.A. 90 C11
Victoria: Va., U.S.A. 89 M7
Victoria: *riv.*, N. Territ., Australia 68 E3
Victoria: *Prov.*, Rhodesia *(cap.* Fort Victoria) 77 D7
Victoria, Lac: Que., Canada 89 N2
Victoria, Lake: E. Africa 76 D3
Victoria, Lake: N.S.W., Australia 71 D9
Victoria, Mount: Burma 59 Q10
Victoria Beach: Man., Can. 92 H2
Victoria East: *Dist.*, S. Africa 75 G6
Victoria Falls: Rhod./Zam. 77 C6
Victoria Fiord: Greenland 85 o1
Victoria Harbour: Ont., Can. 89 M3
Victoria I.: Franz Josef Land 48 E1
Victoria I.: N.W.T., Canada 84 h3
Victoria Land: Antarctica 9 75S 155E
Victoria Point: *cape*, Burma 59 R12
Victoria River Downs: N. Territ., Australia 68 E3
Victoriaville: Que., Canada 89 Q2
Victoria West: & *Dist.*, S. Africa 74 E5
Victorica: Argentina 96 B4
Victorino de la Plaza: Arg. 96 C4
Vicuña: Chile 96 A3
Vida: Romania 39 T14
Vidalia: Ga., U.S.A. 91 K9
Vidalia: La., U.S.A. 90 F10
Vidauban: France 40 M12
Viderø: *i.*, Faeroe Is. 46 h5
Vidin: Bulgaria 39 S15
Vidisha: Madhya Pradesh, India 58 N10
Vidlin: Mainland, Shetland Is. 28 *Ins.*
Vidourle: *riv.*, France 37 J12
Viechtach: Germany 45 S6
VIEDMA: Rio Negro, Arg. 95 E12
Viedma, Lake: Argentina 95 C13
Viejo: *riv.*, Panama 94 *Ins.*
Viella: Spain 35 G15
Vielle-Aure: France 37 F13
Vielmur: France 37 H12
Vielsalm: Belgium 44 L5
VIENNA (Wien): Austria 41 W7
Vienna: Ga., U.S.A. 91 K9
Vienna: *Prov.*, Austria 41 W7
Vienne: France 37 K10
Vienne: *Dept.*, France *(cap.* Poitiers) 37 F9
Vienne: *riv.*, France 36 F8
Vien Poukha: Laos 64 C2
VIENTIANE: Laos 64 C3
Vieques (Crab I.): U.S.A.), Lesser Antilles 87 a1
Vierema: Finland 46 U5
Vierfontein: O.F.S., S. Afr. 75 G3
Viersen: W. Germany 44 M4
Vierzon: France 36 H8
Viesca: Mexico 93 G7
Vieste: Italy 38 P16

Vietnam: *Republic* 64 D3
Cap.: Hanoi
Area: 129,623 sq. miles (335,767 sq. km.)
Pop.: 40,404,000 *(1971 E)*

Vigan: Luzon, Philippines 64 G3
Vigeois: France 37 G10
Vigevano: Italy 40 O10
Vigia: Brazil 94 H4
Vignory: France 36 L7
Vigo: Spain 35 B15
Vihanti: Finland 46 T4
Vihiers: France 36 E8
Viiksinselkä, Lake: Karelian A.S.S. Rep., U.S.S.R. 46 W5
Viipuri (Vyborg): U.S.S.R. 47 V6
Vijayawada: Andhra Pradesh, India 58 O11
Vijosë: *riv.*, Albania 39 Q16
Vik: Iceland 46 d5
Viker: Norway 47 M6
Vikersund: Norway 47 L7
Vikna: *i.*, Norway 46 M4
Vikøyri: Norway 47 K6
Vikulov: Cape: U.S.S.R. 48 H3
Vikulovo: U.S.S.R. 51 M3
VILA: New Hebrides 67 N5
Vila Armindo Monteira: Timor 65 H8
Villa Arriaga: Angola 73 G12
Vila Bittencourt (Narino): Brazil 94 D4
VILA CABRAL: see LICHINGA
Vila Caldas Xavier: Moz. 77 D5
Vila Coutinho: Moz. 77 D5
Vila da Maganja: Mozambique 77 E6
Vila da Ponte: Angola 73 H12
VILA DE JOÃO BELO: see XAI-XAI
Vila de Manatuto: Timor 65 H8
Vila do Conde: Portugal 35 B16
Vila Fontes: Mozambique 77 E6
Vila Franca de Xira: Port. 35 B17
Vila Gamito: Mozambique 77 D5
Vila General Carmona: Timor 65 H8
Vila Gomes da Costa: Mozambique 77 D7
Vila Gouveia: Mozambique 77 D6
Vila Junqueiro: Mozambique 77 E6
Vilaka: Latvia, U.S.S.R. 47 U8
Viliane: *riv.*, France 36 D8
Vila Luiza: Mozambique 75 K2
Vila Machado: Mozambique 77 D6
Vila Manica: Mozambique 77 D6
Vila Mariano Machado: Ang. 73 G12
Vila Mouzinho: Mozambique 77 D5
Vila Murtinho: Brazil 94 D6
Vilanculos: Mozambique 77 E7
Vila Nova de Cerveira: Port. 35 B16
Vila Nova de Famílicão: Portugal 35 B16
Vila Nova de Malaca: Timor 65 H8
Vila Nova de Milfontes: Portugal 35 B18
Vila Nova do Seles: Angola 73 G12
Vila Paiva de Andrada: Mozambique 77 D6
Vila Pereira d'Eça: Angola 73 H13
Vila Pery: see Manica
VILA REAL: Tras os Montes, Portugal 35 C16
Viña Real de Santo António: Portugal 35 C18
Vilar Formoso: Portugal 35 C16
Vila Salazar: Timor 65 H8

Vila Siqueira: Brazil 96 E3
Vila Teixeira da Silva: Ang. 73 H12
Vila Teixeira de Sousa: Ang. 77 B5
Vila Vasco da Gama: Moz. 77 D5
Vila Velha de Rodão: Portugal 35 C17
Vilbel, Bad: W. Germany 44 O5
Vilelas: Argentina 96 C2
Vileyka: Byelorussia 47 U9
Vilhelmina: Sweden 46 P4
Vilhena: Brazil 94 E6
Viliga: U.S.S.R. 49 r5
Viliya: *riv.*, Byelorussia 47 U9
Viljandi: Estonia, Austr. 41 U7
Viljoenskroon: S. Africa 75 G3
Vilkovo: Ukraine 39 V14
Villa Ahumada: Mexico 93 F6
Villa Allende: Mexico 93 G7
Villa Ángela: Argentina 96 C2
Villa Bella: Bolivia 94 D6
Villa Bens: see Tarfaya
Villa Berthet: Argentina 96 C2
Villablino: Spain 35 C15
Villa Brana: Argentina 96 C2
Villa Bustos: Argentina 96 C2
Villa Cañas: Argentina 96 C3
Villacañas: Spain 35 E17
Villacarrillo: Spain 35 E17
Villa Cisneros: see Dakhla
Villa Coronado: Mexico 93 F7
Villada: Spain 35 D15
Villa del Rosario: Argentina 96 C3
Villa de Maria: Argentina 96 C2
Villa de Méndez: Mexico 90 B13
Villadiego: Spain 35 D15
Villa Dolores: Argentina 96 B3
Villa Federal: Argentina 96 D3
Villa Franca: Paraguay 96 D2
Villafranca: Spain 35 C15
Villafranca del Cid: Spain 35 F16
Villa García: Mexico 93 G7
Villagrán: Mexico 93 H8
Villa Hayes: Paraguay 96 D2
Villa Hermosa: Mexico 86 k14
Villa Huidobro: Argentina 96 C3
Villaines-la-Juhel: France 36 E7
Villa Iris: Argentina 96 C4
Villajoyosa: Spain 35 F17
Villalba: Spain 35 C15
Villaldama: Mexico 93 G7
Villalonga: Argentina 95 E11
Villalpando: Spain 35 D16
Villa Madero: Mexico 93 G8
Villa María: Argentina 96 C3
Villa Montes: Bolivia 94 E8
Villandraut: France 37 E11
Villa Nora: Trans., S. Africa 75 H1
Villanova: Rhodes, Dodec. 39 V18
Villanova d'Asti: Italy 40 N11
Villa Nueva: Argentina 96 C3
Villanueva: Mexico 86 j13
Villanueva de Córdoba: Sp. 35 D17
Villanueva de la Serena: Sp. 35 D17
Villa Ocampo: Durango, Mexico 93 F7
Villa Oliva: Paraguay 96 D2
Villapourçon: France 36 J9
Villaputzu: Sardinia 38 L17
Villarcayo: Spain 35 E15
Villar del Arzobispo: Spain 35 F17
Villa Rey: Paraguay 96 D1
Villarica: Chile 95 C11
Villarrica: Paraguay 96 D2
Villarrobledo: Spain 35 E17
Villars: France 37 L9
Villa San Giovanni: Italy 38 O17
Villa San Martin: Argentina 96 C2
Villa Unión: Argentina 96 B2
Villa Valeria: Argentina 96 C3
Villavicencio: Columbia 94 C3
Villazón: Bolivia 95 D8
Ville: France 40 N7
Villebaudon: France 36 D7
Villebois-Lavalette: France 37 F10
Villedieu: Indre, France 37 G9
Villedieu: Manche, France 36 D7
Ville-en-Tardenois: France 36 J6
Villefranche: Alpes Maritimes, France 40 N12
Villefranche: Aveyron, Fr. 37 H11
Villefranche: Haute-Garonne, France 37 G12
Villefranche-de-Conflent: France 37 H13
Villefranche-sur-Saône: Fr. 37 K10
Villemur: France 37 G12
Villena: Spain 35 F17
Villenauxe: France 36 J7
Villeneuve-de-Marsan: Fr. 37 E12
Villeneuve-l'Archevêque: Fr. 36 J7
Villeneuve-sur-Lot: France 37 F11
Villeneuve-sur-Yonne: Fr. 36 J7
Ville Platte: La., U.S.A. 90 E10
Villers-Bretonneux: France 36 H6
Villers-Cotterêts: France 36 J6
Villersexel: France 40 M8
Villers-sur-Mer: France 36 E6
Ville-sur-Tourbe: France 36 K6
Villeurbanne: France 37 K10
Villiers: O.F.S., S. Africa 75 H3
Villiersdorp: S. Africa 74 C6
Villiers-St.-Georges: France 36 J7
Villierstown: Wat., Repub.of Ireland 31 F15
Villingen: W. Germany 40 O7
Villo Duca d'Abruzzi: Somalia 79 R19
Villupuram: Tamil Nadu, India 58 N12
Vilminore: Italy 40 Q10
Vilna: Alta., Canada 92 E2
VILNIUS (Wilno): Lithuania, U.S.S.R. 47 T9
Vilos, Los: Chile 96 A3
Vilppula: Finland 47 T5
Vilsbiburg: W. Germany 41 S7
Vilsen: W. Germany 44 O3
Vilshofen: W. Germany 41 T7
Vilvoorde: Belgium 44 K5
Vilyaka: Latvia, U.S.S.R. 47 U8
Vil'yandi: Estonia, U.S.S.R. 47 T7
Vilyui: *riv.*, U.S.S.R. 49 O5
Vilyuy Mtns.: U.S.S.R. 49 N4
Vilyuysk: U.S.S.R. 49 O5
Vimercate: Italy 40 P10
Vimiero: town on Atlantic coast about 5 miles NE. of Torres Vedras, Portugal 35 B17
Viminacium: Roman camp on Danube about 5 miles E. of confluence with Morava at *Kostolatz*, Yugo. 39 R14
Vimmerby: Sweden 47 O8
Vimoutiers: France 36 F7
Vimy Ridge: battlefield N. of Arras, France 36 H5
Vizcaino, Sierra: *mtns.*, Mexico 93 E7
Vizcaino Desert: Mexico 93 E7
Vizcaya: *Prov.*, Spain *(cap.* Bilbao) 35 E15
Vize: Turkey 39 U16

Vinca: France 37 H13
Vincennes: Ind., U.S.A. 88 H6
Vinces: Ecuador 94 B4
Vinchina: Argentina 96 B2
Vindel: *riv.*, Sweden 46 Q4
Vindelicia: ancient name for district of *Raetia* centred round Augsburg, W. Germany 41 Q7
Vindeln: Sweden 46 Q4
Vindhya Pradesh: (absorbed in Madhya Pradesh), Ind. 58
Vindhya Range: India 58 N10
Vindobona: Roman camp and town at Vienna, Austr. 41 W7
Vindolanda: Roman fort S. of Hadrian's Wall at *Chesterholme*, about 1½ miles N. of Henshaw, Northumb., England 26 R10
Vindonissa: Roman camp at *Windisch*, about 15 miles S. of confluence of rivers Rhine and Aare, N. Switz. 40 O8
Vinegar Hill: battlefield about 2 miles NE. of Enniscorthy, Wex., Repub. of Ireland 31 H14
Vinga: Romania 43 R13
Vingåker: Sweden 47 O7
Vinh: Vietnam 64 D3
Vinh Loi: Vietnam 64 D5
Vinhlong: Vietnam 64 D4
Vinica: Croatia, Yugoslavia 41 W9
Vinica: Slovenia, Yugoslavia 41 V10
Vinita: Okla., U.S.A. 90 D7
Vinkovci: Yugoslavia 39 Q14
Vinnitsa: Ukraine 43 V12
Vinon: France 40 L12
Vinovium: Roman fort at *Binchester* about 1 mile N. of Bishop Auckland, Durham, England 26 S10
Vinton: Iowa, U.S.A. 88 E4
Vinton: La., U.S.A. 90 E10
Viöl: W. Germany 44 P1
Violet Town: Vict., Austl. 71 F11
Vipava: Yugoslavia 41 V9
Vipiteno: Italy 41 R9
Vipos: Argentina 96 B2
Viqueque: Timor 65 H8
Vir: *i.*, Yugoslavia 41 V11
Virac: Philippines 64 G4
Viramgam: Gujarat, India 58 M10
Viranşehir: Turkey 56 F3
Virbalis: Lithuania, U.S.S.R. 47 S9
Virden: Ill., U.S.A. 88 G6
Virden: Man., Canada 92 G3
Vire: France 36 E7
Vire: *riv.*, France 36 D6
Virginia: Cavan, Repub. of Ireland 30 G12
Virginia: Ill., U.S.A. 88 F6
Virginia: Minn., U.S.A. 88 E2
Virginia: O.F.S., S. Africa 75 *Ins.*
Virginia: *State*, U.S.A. *(cap.* Richmond) 89 M7
Virginia Beach: Va., U.S.A. 89 O7
Virgin Gorda: *i.*, (Br.), Virgin Is. 87 b1
Virgin Is.: (Br.), West Indies *(cap.* Road Town) 87 a1
Virgin Is.: (U.S.A.), West Indies *(cap.* Charlotte Amalie) 87 a1
Virieu-le-Grand: France 40 L10
Virihaure Lake: Sweden 46 P3
Virisen Lake: Sweden 46 O4
Viróchey: Cambodia 64 D4
Viroconium: Cornoviorum: Roman city at *Wroxeter* on river Severn about 5 miles ESE. of Shrewsbury, Salop, England 27 Q14
Viroqua: Wis., U.S.A. 88 F4
Virovitica: Yugoslavia 39 P14
Vir Pazar: Yugoslavia 39 Q15
Virrat: Finland 47 T5
Virserum: Sweden 47 O8
Virtaniemi: U.S.S.R. 46 V2
Virtasalmi: Finland 46 U5
Virton: Belgium 44 L6
Virtsu: Estonia, U.S.S.R. 47 S7
Virunga Nat. Park: Zaire 76 C3
Virunum: Roman town mid-way between St. Veit and Klagenfurt, Austria 41 U9
Vis: *i.*, Yugoslavia 38 P15
Visalia: Calif., U.S.A. 93 D5
Visayan Sea: Philippines 64 G4
VISBY: Gotland, Sweden 47 Q8
Viscount Melville Sd.: Can. 84 J3
Visé: Belgium 44 L5
Višegrad: Yugoslavia 39 Q15
VISEU: Beira Alta, Portugal 35 C16
Viseu: Brazil 94 H4
Vishakapatnam: Andhra Pradesh, India 59 O11
Vislanda: Sweden 47 O8
Višnja Gora: Yugoslavia 41 V10
Višnjan: Yugoslavia 41 T10
Viso, Monte: Italy 40 N11
Visoko: Yugoslavia 39 Q15
Visp: Switzerland 40 N9
Visselhövede: W. Germany 44 P3
Vistula (Wisła): *riv.*, Poland 43 Q10
Vitebsk: Byelorussia 50 D3
Viterbo: Italy 38 N15
Vitichi: Bolivia 94 D8
Vitigudino: Spain 35 C16
Viti Levu: *i.*, Fiji Is. 67 P5
Vitim: U.S.S.R. 49 N6
Vitim: *riv.*, U.S.S.R. 49 n6
Vitis: Austria 41 V7
Vitória: Espírito Santo, Brazil 95 J8
Vitória: Alava, Spain 35 E15
Vitória da Conquista: Brazil 94 J6
Vitória do Mearim: Brazil 94 J4
Vitório do Xingu: Brazil 94 G4
Vitre: France 36 D7
Vitry-en-Artois: France 36 H5
Vitry-le-François: France 36 K7
Vittangi: Sweden 46 R3
Vitte: Hiddensee, E. Ger. 45 T1
Vitteaux: France 36 K8
Vittel: France 40 L7
Vittoria: Sicily 38 O18
Vittorio Veneto: Italy 41 S10
Vitvattnet: Sweden 46 S3
Vityaz Trench: S. Pacific Ocean 7 15S 170E
Vivero: Spain 35 C15
Vivi: U.S.S.R. 49 L5
Vivian: La., U.S.A. 90 E9
Viviers: France 37 K11
Viviez: France 37 H11
Vivonne: France 37 F9
Vivorata: Argentina 96 D4
Vivunki: Sweden 46 S3
Vizagapatam: see Vishakapatnam

Vize I.: (U.S.S.R.), Arctic Ocean 48 j2
Vizianagaram: Andhra Pradesh, India 59 O11
Vizille: France 40 L10
Vizille: Romania 39 U14
Vizovice: Czechoslovakia 43 P12
Vizzini: Sicily 38 O18
Vlaardingen: Netherlands 44 K4
VLADIMIR: & *Reg.*, U.S.S.R. 50 F3
Vladimirovskiy: Kazakh., U.S.S.R. 51 K4
Vladimir-Volynskiy: Ukraine 43 T11
VLADIVOSTOK: Primorsk, U.S.S.R. 63 Y6
Vlaklaagte: S. Africa 74 E6
Vlakte: Trans., S. Africa 75 H2
Vlasim: Czechoslovakia 45 U6
Vlei: *riv.*, O.F.S., S. Africa 75 H3
Vlieland: *i.*, W. Frisian Is. 44 K2
Vlissingen (Flushing): Walcheren, Netherlands 44 J4
Vlonë (Valona): Albania 39 Q16
Vltava (Moldau): *riv.*, Czech. 45 U5
Vöcklabruck: Austria 41 T7
Vöcklamarkt: Austria 41 T7
Vocontii: Gallic tribe in area between rivers Isère and Durance, France 40 L11
Vodlozero, Lake: U.S.S.R. 50 E2
Vodňany: Czechoslovakia 45 U6
Vodochody: Czechoslovakia 45 U5
Voe: Mainland, Shetland Is. 28 *Ins.*
Voelrivier: S. Africa 75 F6
Vogels Berg: *mtn.*, W. Ger. 44 P5
Voghera: Italy 40 P11
Vohémar: Malagasy Rep. 73 O12
Vohenstrauss: W. Germany 45 S6
Voi: Kenya 76 E3
Void: France 40 L7
VOINJAMA: Loffa, Liberia 80 C3
Voiron: France 40 L10
Voislova: Romania 39 S14
Voitsberg: Austria 41 V8
Vojm: *lake*, Sweden 46 P4
Vojnik: Yugoslavia 41 V9
Vokhma: U.S.S.R. 50 G3
Voknavolok: Karelian A.S.S. Rep., U.S.S.R. 46 W4
Volary: Czechoslovakia 45 T7
Volcae Arecomisci: Gallic tribe with centre at Nîmes, France 37 K12
Volcae Tectosages: Gallic tribe in area between Toulouse and Narbonne, France 37 H12
Volcán, El: Chile 96 A3
Volcano (Kazan) Is.: (Jap.) Pacific O. 60 N7
Volchansk: Ukraine 50 E4
Volchikha: U.S.S.R. 51 O4
Volga: *riv.*, U.S.S.R. 50 F15
VOLGOGRAD (Stalingrad): & *Reg.*, U.S.S.R. 50 F5
Volissós: Chios, Greece 39 T17
Völkermarkt: Austria 41 U9
Volkhov: U.S.S.R. 50 D3
Volklingen: Saarland, W. Germany 44 M6
Volkmarsen: W. Germany 44 P4
Volkovysk: Byelorussia 43 T10
Volksrust: Trans., S. Africa 75 H3
Vollenhove: Netherlands 44 L3
Volnovakha: Ukraine 50 E5
Vol'noye: U.S.S.R. 50 G5
Volochayevka Zaya: U.S.S.R. 63 Y5
Volochisk: Ukraine 43 U12
Volodarsk: Ukraine 43 V12
Volodarskoye: Kazakh., U.S.S.R. 51 L4
VOLOGDA: & *Reg.*, U.S.S.R. 50 E3
Volokolamsk: U.S.S.R. 50 E3
Volonne: France 40 M11
Volontirovka: Moldavia, U.S.S.R. 39 V13
Volos: Greece 39 S17
Volosovo: U.S.S.R. 47 V7
Volozhin: Byelorussia 47 U9
Volpedo: Italy 40 O11
Volsci: ancient tribe of S. Latium. 38 N14
Volsiniensis: Roman name of L. Bolsena, Italy 38 M15
Vol'sk: U.S.S.R. 50 G4
Volstruispoort: S. Africa 74 E5
Volta: Italy 40 Q10
Volta: *riv.*, Ghana 80 E3
Volta: *Reg.*, Ghana *(cap.* Ho) 80 E3
Volta, Lake: Ghana 80 D3
Volta Noire: *Dept.*, Upper Volta *(cap.* Dédougou) 80 D2
Volta Redonda: Brazil 96 G1
Voltas, Cape: S. Africa 74 B4
Volterra: Italy 41 Q12
Volturno: *riv.*, Italy 38 N16
Volubilis: Roman town about 30 miles W. of Fez, Mor. 80 L8
Volvic: France 37 J10
Volynë: *Dept.*, France *(cap.* Épinal) 40 M7
Volyniya Podolsk Plat.: Ukraine 50 C5
Vom: Nigeria 81 F3
Vondeling: S. Africa 74 E6
Vónitsa: Greece 39 R17
Vonne: *riv.*, France 37 F9
Vopna Fiord: Iceland 46 f4
Vopnafjordhur: Iceland 46 f4
Vorarlberg: *Prov.*, Austria *(cap.* Bregenz) 40 P8
Vordingborg: Zealand, Denmark 47 M9
Voreppe: France 40 L10
Vorey: France 37 J10
Vorkuta: U.S.S.R. 48 H4
Vormsi: *i.*, Estonia, U.S.S.R. 47 S7
Vorokhta: Ukraine 43 T12
VORONEZH: & *Reg.*, U.S.S.R. 50 E4
Voronovitsa: Ukraine 43 V12
Voronovo: Byelorussia 43 T10
Voroshilovgrad: Ukraine 50 E5
Vorrë: Albania 39 Q16
Vorroi: Crete 39 T19
Vørterkaka Nunatak: Antarctica 9 75S 25E
Võru: Estonia, U.S.S.R. 47 U8
Vosburg: S. Africa 74 E5
Vosges: *Dept.*, France *(cap.* Épinal) 40 M7
Vosges Mtns.: France 40 N7
Voskresenskoye: U.S.S.R. 50 G3
Vöslau: Austria 41 W8
Voss: Norway 47 K6
Vostok: *rsch. stn.*, Antarctica 9 80S 105E
Vostok I.: Pacific O. 83 e2
Votice: Czechoslovakia 45 U6
Votkinsk: U.S.S.R. 50 H3
Votuporanga: Brazil 96 F1
Voum: *riv.*, Cameroun 81 F4
Vouvant: France 37 E9
Vouvray: France 36 F8
Vouziers: France 36 K6
Voves: France 36 G7

198 Vowchurch—Webster City

Vowchurch: Hereford & Worcester, England 24 Q15
Voxna: & riv., Sweden 47 O6
Voynitsa: Karelian A.S.S.Rep., U.S.S.R. 46 W4
Vozhe, Lake: U.S.S.R. 50 E2
Vozhega: U.S.S.R. 50 F2
Vozhgora: U.S.S.R. 48 f5
Voznesensk: Ukraine 50 D5
Voznesen'ye: U.S.S.R. 50 E2
Vrana: Yugoslavia 41 V12
Vranje: Yugoslavia 39 R15
Vransko: Yugoslavia 41 U9
Vratsa: Bulgaria 39 S15
Vrbas: Yugoslavia 39 Q14
Vrbnik: Krk, Yugoslavia 41 U10
Vrbovec: Yugoslavia 41 W10
Vrchovina Českomoravská: mtns., Czechoslovakia 45 V6
Vrchovina Lužická: mtns., Czechoslovakia 45 V5
Vrede: & Dist., O.F.S., S. Africa 75 H3
Vredefort: & Dist., O.F.S., S. Africa 75 G3
Vreden: W. Germany 44 M3
Vredenburg: S. Africa 74 B6
Vreed-en-Hoop: Guyana 87 d7
Vreysrus: Trans., S. Africa 74 Lins.
Vrgin Most: Yugoslavia 41 V10
Vrhnika: Yugoslavia 41 U10
Vrhovine: Yugoslavia 41 V11
Vries: Netherlands 44 M2
Vrigne-aux-Bois: France 36 K6
Vron: France 36 G5
Vršac: Yugoslavia 39 R14
Vrsar: Yugoslavia 41 T10
Vrtoče: Yugoslavia 41 W11
Vrútky: Czechoslovakia 43 Q12
Vryburg: & Dist., S. Africa 75 F3
Vryheid: & Dist., Natal, S. Africa 75 J3
Všetaty: Czechoslovakia 45 U5
Vsetin: Czechoslovakia 43 P12
Vučitrn: Yugoslavia 39 R15
Vukovar: Yugoslavia 39 Q14
Vulcano: i., Lipari Is. 38 O17
Vulcan Rock: i., S. Africa 74 Ins.
Vũng Tàu: cape, Vietnam 64 D4
Vuojärvi: Finland 46 U3
Vuoksi Lake: U.S.S.R. 47 V6
Vuolvo Lake: Sweden 46 Q3
Vuontisjärvi: Finland 46 T2
Vuopieniemi: Finland 46 V2
Vuotoso: Finland 46 U2
Vura: Uganda 76 D2
Vŭrbitsa: Bulgaria 39 U15
Vyartsilya: Karelian A.S.S.Rep., U.S.S.R. 46 W5
Vyatka: riv., U.S.S.R. 50 G3
Vyazemskiy: U.S.S.R. 63 Y5
Vyaz'ma: U.S.S.R. 50 D3
Vyborg (Viipuri): U.S.S.R. 47 V6
Vychegda: riv., U.S.S.R. 50 G2
Východoslovenský: Reg., Czechoslovakia (cap. Košice) 43 R12
Vydrino: U.S.S.R. 51 R3
Vyksa: U.S.S.R. 50 F3
Vym': riv., U.S.S.R. 50 H2
Vyri: Estonia 47 U8
Vyrnwy, Lake: Powys, Wales 27 O14
Vyshka: Turkmen., U.S.S.R. 50 H7
Vyshniy Volochek: U.S.S.R. 50 D3
Vyškov: Czechoslovakia 43 P12
Vysoké Myto: Czech. 45 W6
Vysokovsk: U.S.S.R. 50 E3
Vysotsk: Ukraine 43 U11
Vyšší Brod: Czechoslovakia 41 U7
Vytegra: U.S.S.R. 50 E2

Wa: Ghana 80 D2
Waal: riv., Netherlands 44 L4
Wabash: Ind., U.S.A. 88 J5
Wabash: riv., U.S.A. 88 H6
Wabasha: Minn., U.S.A. 88 E3
Wabatongushi Lake: Ont., Canada 88 J1
Wabeno: Wis., U.S.A. 88 G3
Wabowden: Man., Canada 92 H1
Wabra: Saudi Arabia 54 G9
Wąbrzeźno: Poland 43 Q10
Wabuk Point: cape, Ont., Canada 85 l 6
Waco: Tex., U.S.A. 90 C10
Waco, Lake: Tex., U.S.A. 90 C10
Wadayama: Japan 63 d3
Wad Banda: Sudan 79 K7
Waddan: Libya 33 F6
Wadden Zee: bay, Neth. 44 L2
Waddesdon: Bucks., Eng. 25 U16
Waddington: Lincs., Eng. 27 U13
Waddingham: Lincs., Eng. 27 U13
Waddington, Mount: B.C., Canada 92 B2
Wadebridge: Corn., England 24 M18
Wadena: Minn., U.S.A. 88 D2
Wadena: Sask., Canada 92 G2
Wadenhoe: Northants., Eng. 25 U15
Wadern: Saarland, W. Ger. 44 M6
Wadersloh: W. Germany 44 O4
Wadesboro: N.C., U.S.A. 91 L8
Wad Hamid: Sudan 54 D11
Wadhurst: E. Sussex, Eng. 25 W17
Wadi: Karnataka, India 58 N11
Wadian: geog. reg., Saudi Arabia 57 G6
Wadi Halfa: Sudan 54 D10
WAD MEDANI: Blue Nile, Sudan 54 D12
Wadworth: S. Yorks., Eng. 27 T13
Waesch, Mt.: Antarctica 9 80S 130W
Wafania: Zaire 76 B3
Wagenaarskraal: S. Africa 74 E5
Wagenfeld: W. Germany 44 O3
Wageningen: Netherlands 44 L4
Wager Bay: N.W.T., Can. 85 L4
Wager Bay: settlement, N.W.T., Canada 84 k4
Wagga Wagga: N.S.W., Australia 71 G10
Waghai: Gujarat, India 58 M10
Wagin: W. Australia 68 B6
Waging: W. Germany 41 S8
Wagner: S. Dak., U.S.A. 92 H4
Wagoner: Okla., U.S.A. 90 D8
Wagon Mound: N. Mex., U.S.A. 93 G5
Wagram: battlefield about 12 miles NE. of Vienna, Austria 43 P12
Wagrowiec: Poland 43 P10
Wagsa: well, Iraq 57 H6
Wahai: Moluccas, Indon. 61 K12
Wahiba: tribe, Oman 55 J10
Wahlstatt: village in Silesia where Germans fought and checked Mongols in 1241, a few miles S. of Legnica (Liegnitz), Wrocław, Poland 45 W4
Wahpeton: N. Dak., U.S.A. 92 H3
Waialua: Hawaiian Is. 83 b2
Waianae: Hawaiian Is. 83 b2
Waiau: & riv., South I., N.Z. 70 O16
Waiblingen: W. Germany 40 P7
Waidhofen: N.W. of Vienna, Austria 41 V7
Waidhofen: S.W. of Vienna, Austria 41 U8
Waigama: W. Irian, Indon. 61 K12
Waigeo: i., W. Irian, Indon. 61 L12
Waiheke I.: New Zealand 70 P13
Waihi: North I., N.Z. 70 P13
Waihopo: North I., N.Z. 70 O12
Waika: Zaire 76 C3
Waikabubak: Sumba, Indon. 65 F8
Waikaia: South I., N.Z. 71 M17
Waikaka: South I., N.Z., 71 M17
Waikato: riv., North I., New Zealand 70 P13
Waikawa: South I., N.Z., 71 M18
Waikerie: S. Australia 71 C10
Waikouaiti: South I., N.Z. 71 N17
Wailuku: Hawaiian Is. 83 c2
Waimanalo: Hawaiian Is. 83 c2
Waimangaroa: South I., New Zealand 70 N15
Waimate: South I., N.Z. 70 N17
Waimea: Hawaiian Is. 83 b2
Wainfleet All Saints: Lincs., England 27 W13
Wainganga: riv., India 58 N10
Waingapu: Sumba, Indon. 65 G8
Waini: riv., Guyana 87 d7
Waini Point: cape, Guyana 87 d6
Wainwright: Alaska, U.S.A. 84 D3
Wainwright: Alta., Canada 92 E2
Waiotapu: North I., N.Z. 70 Q14
Waipara: South I., N.Z. 70 O16
Waipawa: North I., N.Z. 70 Q14
Waipio: Hawaiian Is. 83 d2
Waipiro: North I., N.Z. 70 R14
Waipu: North I., N.Z. 70 P12
Waipukurau: North I., N.Z. 70 Q15
Wairau: riv., South I., N.Z. 70 O15
Wairoa: North I., N.Z. 70 Q14
Wais: Iran 57 L6
Waitaha: South I., N.Z. 70 N16
Waitaki: riv., South I., N.Z. 70 N17
Waitangi: Chatham Is. 67 Q10
Waitangi: North I., N.Z. 70 P12
Waitara: North I., N.Z. 70 P14
Waitsburg: Wash., U.S.A. 92 D3
Waiuku: North I., N.Z. 70 P13
Waiyeung: Kwangtung, China 62 U10
Wajale: Somalia 79 Q18
Wajh: Saudi Arabia 54 E9
Wajima: Japan 63 e2
Wajir: Kenya 76 F2
Wak, El: Kenya 76 F2
Waka: Ethiopia 76 E1
Wakasa: Japan 63 d3
Wakasa Bay: Honshu, Japan 63 d3
Wakatipu, Lake: South I., New Zealand 70 M17
Wakaw: Sask., Canada 92 F2
WAKAYAMA: & Pref., Japan 63 d3
Wake: Japan 63 d3
Wake I.: (U.S.A.), N. Pacific Ocean 7 15N 165E
Wakeeney: Kans., U.S.A. 93 H5
Wakefield: Mich., U.S.A. 88 G2
Wakefield: Que., Canada 89 O3
WAKEFIELD: W. Yorks., Eng. 27 T12
Wake Forest: city, N.C., U.S.A. 91 M8
Wakeham: see Maricourt.
Wakering, Great: Essex, Eng. 25 X16
Wakes Colne: Essex, Eng. 25 X16
Wakhan: geog. reg., Afghan. 51 M7
Waki: Japan 63 d3
Wakin: Tibet, China 62 S9
Wakkanai: Japan 63 ZZ5
Wakkerstroom: & Dist., Trans., S. Africa 75 J3
Wakool: N.S.W., Australia 71 F10
Walberswick: Suff., England 25 Z15
Wałbrzych: Poland 45 W5
Walcha: N.S.W., Australia 71 J8
Walcheren: i., Netherlands 44 J4
Walcot: Lincs., England 27 V13
Walcourt: Belgium 44 K5
Wałcz: Poland 45 W2
Wald: Austria 41 U8
Waldbröhl: W. Germany 44 N5
Waldburg Range: W. Austl. 68 B4
Waldeck: W. Germany 44 P4
Walden: N.Y., U.S.A. 89 O5
Waldheim: E. Germany 45 T4
Waldhöhe: S.W. Africa 77 A7
Waldia: Ethiopia 79 M7
Waldkappel: W. Germany 45 P4
Waldoboro: Maine, U.S.A. 89 R3
Waldron: Ark., U.S.A. 90 D8
Waldsee: W. Germany 40 P8
Waldshut: W. Germany 40 O8
Walea Strait: Celebes 65 G7
Walej, Shaib: wadi, Iraq 56 F5
Walen, Lake: Switzerland 40 P8
Wales: Alaska, U.S.A. 84 C4
Wales: United Kingdom (cap. Cardiff) 24
Walferdange: Luxembourg 44 M6
Walgau: geog. reg. Austria 40 P8
Walgett: N.S.W., Australia 71 H8
Walgrave: Northants., Eng. 25 U15
Walhalla: S.C., U.S.A. 91 K8
Walhalla: Vict., Australia 71 G11
Walikale: Zaire 76 C3
Walkden: Gt. Man., England 27 R12
Walker: Minn., U.S.A. 88 D2
Walker Bay: S. Africa 74 C7
Walker Lake: Nev., U.S.A. 93 D5
Walkern: Herts., England 25 V16
Walkerton: Ont., Canada 88 L3
Walkraal: Cape Prov., S. Africa 74 D5
Wall: Northumb., England 26 R9
Wallace: Idaho, U.S.A. 92 D3
Wallaceburg: Ont., Canada 88 K4
Wallachia: geog. reg., Rom. 43 T14
Wallal: Queens., Australia 70 G6
Wallangarra: Queens., Austl. 71 J7
Wallaroo: S. Australia 71 B9
Wallasey: Mers., England 27 P13
Walla Walla: N.S.W., Austl. 71 G10
Walla Walla: Wash., U.S.A. 92 D3
Walldürn: W. Germany 44 P6
Wallekraal: S. Africa 74 B5
Wallendbeen: N.S.W., Austl. 71 H10
Wallerawang: N.S.W., Austl. 71 J9
Wallingford: Oxon., Eng. 25 T16
Wallis Is.: (Fr.), Pacific O. [cap. (with Futuna) Mata Utu] 67 Q4
Wallowa Mtns.: Oreg., U.S.A. 92 D3
Walls: Mainland, Shetland Is. 28 Ins.
Wallsend: Tyne & Wear, England 26 S10
Walluku: Maui, Hawaiian Is. 83 c2
Wallumbilla: Queens., Austl. 70 H6
Walmer: Kent, England 25 Y17
Walmer: S. Africa 75 F7
Walney I.: Cumbria, England 26 P11
Walnut Cove: city, N.C., U.S.A. 88 L7
Walnut Ridge: city, Ark., U.S.A. 88 F7
Walpeup: Vict., Australia 71 E10
Walpole: Norf., England 24 W14
Walpole: i., Loyalty Is. 67 N6
Walpole, North: N.H., U.S.A. 89 P4
Walsall: W. Mid., England 27 S14
Walsden: W. Yorks., England 27 R12
Walsenburg: Colo., U.S.A. 93 G5
Walsham, North: Norf., England 25 Y14
Walsham le Willows: Suff., England 25 X15
Walsingham: Durham, Eng. 26 S10
Walsingham, Little: Norf., England 25 X14
Walsingham, Cape: N.W.T., Canada 85 n4
Walsoken: Norf., England 25 W14
Walsoorden: Netherlands 44 K4
Walsrode: W. Germany 44 P3
Walterboro: S.C., U.S.A. 91 L9
Walters: Okla., U.S.A. 90 B8
Walterhausen: E. Germany 45 Q5
Waltham: Humb., England 27 V12
Waltham: Que., Canada 89 N3
Waltham, Great: Essex, Eng. 25 W16
Waltham Abbey: town, Essex, England 25 W16
Waltham Forest: borough, Gt. Ldn., England 25 V16
Waltham on the Wolds: Leics., England 27 U14
Walton: Cumbria, England 26 Q10
Walton: N.Y., U.S.A. 89 O4
Walton le Dale: Lancs., Eng. 27 Q12
Walton-on-Thames: Surrey, England 25 V17
Walton on the Naze: Essex, England 25 Y16
Walton West: Dyfed, Wales 24 L16
Walvis Bay: town, S. Africa 74 A1
Walvis Bay: Dist., SW. Africa (administered from Walvis Bay, S. Africa) 74 A1
Walvis Ridge: S. Atlantic Ocean 8 30S 00
Walwale: Ghana 80 D2
Wamba: Zaire 76 C2
Wamba: Nigeria 81 F3
Wamba: riv., Zaire 81 H5
Wamego: Kans., U.S.A. 90 C6
Wamgasi: Buru, Indonesia 65 H7
Wami: riv., Tanzania 76 E4
Wamlana: Buru, Indon. 65 H7
Wamsasi: Buru, Indon. 65 H7
Wamsisi: Buru, Indonesia 65 H7
Wanaaring: N.S.W., Austl. 71 F7
Wanaka: & lake, South I., New Zealand 70 M17
Wanapiri: W. Irian, Indon. 61 M12
Wanapitei: riv., Ont., Can. 88 L2
Wanapitei Lake: Ont., Can. 88 L2
Wanbi: S. Australia 71 D10
Wanchese: N.C., U.S.A. 91 O8
Wanchuan (Kalgan): Inner Mongolia, China 62 U6
Wandaik: Guyana 87 d8
Wandels Sea: Greenland 85 S1
Wandiwash: Tamil Nadu, India 58 N12
Wandoan: Queens., Austl. 70 H6
Wandsworth: Gt. Ldn., England 25 V17
Wang: riv., Thailand 64 B3
Wanganella: N.S.W., Austl. 71 F10
Wanganui: & riv., North I., New Zealand 70 P14
Wangaratta: Vict., Australia 71 G11
Wangching: Kirin, China 63 X6
Wangen: W. Germany 40 P8
Wangen: Switzerland 40 N8
Wangerooge: i., E. Frisian Is. 44 N2
Wangiwangi: i., Tukangbesi Is., Indonesia 65 G8
Wangkung: Inner Mongolia, China 62 V5
Wangkwei: Heilungkiang, China 63 X5
Wangyehmiao: see Wulanhaote
Wanhsien: Kansu, China 62 T7
Wanhsien: Szechwan, China 62 T8
Wanie Rukula: Zaire 76 C2
Wanjung: Shansi, China 62 U7
Wankaner: Gujarat, India 58 M10
Wankendorf: W. Germany 45 Q1
Wankie: Rhodesia 77 C6
Wankie National Park: Rhodesia 77 C6
Wanko South: Queens., Australia 70 F6
Wanle Wen: Somalia 79 Q19
Wanlockhead: Dumfries & Galloway, Scotland 29 O9
Wanme: W. Irian, Indon. 29 O9
Wansbeck: riv., Northumb., England 26 S9
Wansford: Northants., Eng. 25 V14
Wanshan (Ladrone) Is.: Kwangtung, China 62 U10
Wanstrow: Som., England 24 R17
Wantage: Oxon., England 25 T16
Wantsai: Kiangsi, China 62 U9
Waorschoot: Belgium 44 J4
Wapakoneta: Ohio, U.S.A. 88 J5
Wapello: Iowa, U.S.A. 88 F5
Wapi: Laos 64 D3
Wapiti: riv., B.C./Alta., Can. 92 D2
Wappapello Reservoir: Mo., U.S.A. 88 F7
Wappenham: Northants., England 25 T15
War: Uganda 76 D2
War: W. Va., U.S.A. 88 L7
Warandab: Ethiopia 79 Q18
Warangal: Andhra Pradesh, India 58 N11
Waranga Res.: Vict., Austl. 71 F1
Waratah: Tasmania 68 H8
Waratah Bay: S. Australia 71 G12
Warboys: Cambs., England 25 V15
Warbstow: Corn., England 24 M18
Warburg: W. Germany 44 P4
Warburton: Vict., Australia 71 F11
Warburton: riv., S. Austl. 69 F5
Warburton Ra.: W. Austl. 68 D5
Warcop: Cumbria, England 26 R10
Ward: South I., N.Z. 70 P15
Ward: riv., Queens., Austl. 70 G6
Wardeglo: Kenya 76 F2
Warden: O.F.S., S. Africa 75 H3
Wardere: Ethiopia 79 R18
Wardha: Maharashtra, India 58 N10
Ward Hill: Hay, Orkney Is. 28 P2
Wardington: Oxon., Eng. 25 T15
Wardour, Vale of: Wilts., England 24 S17
Ware: B.C., Canada 84 G6
Ware: Herts., England 25 V16
Waregem: Belgium 44 J5
Wareham: Dorset, England 24 R18
Warehorne: Kent, England 25 X17
Waren: E. Germany 45 S2
Waren: W. Irian, Indon. 61 L12
Warendorf: W. Germany 44 O4
Ware Shoals: S.C., U.S.A. 91 K8
Warfum: Netherlands 44 M2
Wargalla: well, Somalia 79 R18
Wargrave: Berks., England 25 U17
Warhenholz: W. Germany 45 Q3
Warialda: N.S.W., Australia 71 J7
Warin: E. Germany 45 R2
Waringsford: Down, N. Irel. 30 J11
Waringstown: Down, N. Ireland 30 J11
Wark: Northumb., England 26 R9
Warka: Poland 43 R11
Warkworth: North I., N.Z. 70 P13
Warkworth: Northumb., England 26 S9
Warlingham: Surrey, Eng. 25 V17
Warman: Sask., Canada 92 F2
Warmbad: & Dist., S.W. Africa 74 C4
Warm Baths: Trans., S. Afr. 75 H2
Warminster: Wilts., England 24 R17
Warm Springs: city, Nev., U.S.A. 93 D5
Warm Springs: city, Va., U.S.A. 89 M6
Warnemünde: E. Germany 45 S1
Warner Range: Calif./Oreg., U.S.A. 92 C4
Warnham: W. Sussex, Eng. 25 V17
Warnow: riv., E. Germany 45 S2
Warooka: S. Australia 71 B10
Warra: Queens., Australia 70 J6
Warracknabeal: Vict., Austl. 71 E11
Warragamba Reservoir: N.S.W., Australia 71 J9
Warragul: Vict., Australia 71 F12
Warra Hailu: Ethiopia 79 M7
Warramboo: S. Australia 71 A9
Warraweena: N.S.W., Austl. 71 G7
Warrego: riv., Queens., Australia 70 F6
Warrego Range: Queens., Australia 69 H5
Warren: Ark., U.S.A. 90 E9
Warren: Minn., U.S.A. 92 H3
Warren: N.S.W., Australia 71 G8
Warren: Ohio, U.S.A. 88 L5
Warren: Pa., U.S.A. 89 M5
Warren Landing: Man., Canada 92 H2
Warrenpoint: Down, N. Ireland 30 J11
Warrensburg: Mo., U.S.A. 90 E6
Warrensburg: N.Y., U.S.A. 89 P4
Warrenton: Mo., U.S.A. 88 F6
Warrenton: N.C., U.S.A. 89 M7
Warrenton: S. Africa 75 F4
Warrenton: Va., U.S.A. 89 N6
Warri: Nigeria 81 F3
Warrington: Fla., U.S.A. 91 H10
Warrington: Lancs., Eng. 27 Q13
Warrinilla: Queens., Austl. 70 H5
Warrnambool: Vict., Austl. 71 E12
Warroad: Minn., U.S.A. 88 D1
Warrong: Queens., Australia 70 G5
Warrumbungle National Park: N.S.W., Australia 71 H8
Warsaw: Ind., U.S.A. 88 J5
Warsaw: Mo., U.S.A. 88 E6
Warsaw: N.Y., U.S.A. 89 M4
Warsaw: N.C., U.S.A. 91 M8
WARSAW (Warszawa): & Prov., Poland 43 R10
Warsaw: Va., U.S.A. 89 N7
Warse: Moluccas, Indonesia 61 L12
Warsop: Notts., England 27 T13
Warstade: W. Germany 44 P2
Warstein: W. Germany 44 O4
WARSZAWA (Warsaw): Poland 43 R10
Warta: Poland 43 Q11
Warta: riv., Poland 45 W3
Warter: Humb., England 27 U12
Wartling: E. Sussex, England 25 W18
Waru: Moluccas, Indonesia 61 L12
Waruf: Ethiopia 79 Q17
Warwick: Cumbria, England 26 Q10
WARWICK: & Co., England 25 S15
Warwick: Queens., Austl. 70 J7
Warwick: R.I., U.S.A. 89 Q5
Wasatch Plat.: Utah, U.S.A. 93 E5
Wasatch Range: Idaho/Utah, U.S.A. 92 E4
Wasbank: Natal, S. Africa 75 J4
Wasbister: Orkney Is. 28 Ins.
Wasco: Calif., U.S.A. 93 D5
Wasdale: Cumbria, England 26 P11
Wasdale Head: Cumb., Eng. 26 P11
Wase: riv., Nigeria 81 F3
Waseca: Minn., U.S.A. 88 E3
Wasekameo Lake: Sask., Canada 92 F1
Wash, The: bay, England 25 W14
Washago: Ont., Canada 89 M3
Washbrook: Suff., England 25 Y15
Washburn: Maine, U.S.A. 89 R2
Washburn: N. Dak., U.S.A. 92 G3
Washburn: Wis., U.S.A. 88 F2
Washburn, Mount: Wyo., U.S.A. 92 E4
Washford: Som., England 24 P17
WASHINGTON: D.C., U.S.A. 89 N6
Washington: Ga., U.S.A. 91 K9
Washington: Ind., U.S.A. 88 H6
Washington: Iowa, U.S.A. 88 F5
Washington: Kans., U.S.A. 93 H5
Washington: Mo., U.S.A. 88 F6
Washington: N.C., U.S.A. 91 N8
Washington: Ohio, U.S.A. 88 K6
Washington: Pa., U.S.A. 88 L5
Washington: Tyne & Wear, England 26 S10
Washington: W. Sussex, Eng. 25 V18
Washington: i., Wis., U.S.A. 88 H3
Washington: State, U.S.A. (cap. Olympia) 92 C3
Washington, Mount: N.H., U.S.A. 89 Q3
Washington Land: Grnld. 85 n1
Washir: Afghanistan 58 K8
Washita: riv., U.S.A. 93 H5
Wasigny: France 36 K6
Wasit: Prov., Iraq 57 J5
Wasit: Yemen P.D.R. 54 G12
Wasit: Oman 55 J10
Wąsosz: Poland 45 W4
Wąsowa: Poland 45 W2
Wasselonne: France 40 N7
Wassenaar: Netherlands 44 K3
Wasserburg: W. Germany 41 S7
Wassertrüdingen: W. Ger. 45 Q6
Wassy: France 36 K7
Wasta, El: Egypt 54 D9
Wa States: Burma 59 R10
Wasungen: E. Germany 45 Q5
Waswanipi Lake: Que., Can. 89 N1
Watampone: Celebes 65 G7
Watchet: Som., England 24 P17
Watenstedt: see Salzgitter.
Waterbeach: Cambs., Eng. 25 W15
Waterbeck: Dumfries & Galloway, Scotland 29 P9
Waterberg: S.W. Africa 77 A7
Waterberg: Dist., Trans., S. Africa 75 H2
Waterbury: Conn., U.S.A. 89 P5
Waterbury: Vt., U.S.A. 89 P3
Wateree: riv., S.C., U.S.A. 91 L8
Wateree Res: S.C., U.S.A. 91 L8
Waterfall: Cork, Repub. of Ireland 31 D16
Waterford: S. Africa 75 F6
WATERFORD: & Co., Repub. of Ireland 31 G15
Waterford Harbour: Wat./Wex., Repub. of Ireland 31 H15
Watergrasshill: Cork, Repub. of Ireland 31 E15
Waterhen Lake: Man., Can. 92 H2
Waterhouses: Durham, Eng. 26 S10
Wateringbury: Kent, Eng. 25 W17
Waterklip: S. Africa 74 C5
Waterkloof: O.F.S., S. Afr. 75 F5
Waterloo: Ala., U.S.A. 88 G8
Waterloo: Belgium 44 K5
Waterloo: Ill., U.S.A. 88 F6
Waterloo: Iowa, U.S.A. 88 E4
Waterloo: Ont., Canada 88 L4
Waterloo: Que., Canada 89 P3
Waterloo: Sierra Leone 80 B3
Waterlooville: Hants., Eng. 25 T18
Waterside: Strath., Scot. 29 N9
Waterton & Glacier International Peace Parks: U.S.A./Canada 92 E3
Watertown: N.Y., U.S.A. 89 O4
Watertown: S. Dak., U.S.A. 92 H4
Watertown: Wis., U.S.A. 88 G4
Waterval: riv., Trans., S. Afr. 75 H3
Waterval-Bo: Trans., S. Africa 75 J2
Water Valley: city, Miss., U.S.A. 90 G8
Waterville: Kerry, Repub. of Ireland 31 A16
Waterville: Maine, U.S.A. 89 R3
Waterways: Alta., Canada 92 E1
Watford: Herts., England 25 V16
Watford City: N. Dak., U.S.A. 92 G3
Wath: N. Yorks., England 27 S11
Wath upon Dearne: S. Yorks., England 27 T13
Watkins Glen: city, N.Y., U.S.A. 89 N4
Watlington: Norf., England 25 W14
Watlington: Oxon., England 25 T16
Watnam: Kwangtung, China 62 U10
Watonga: Okla., U.S.A. 90 B8
Watrous: Sask., Canada 92 F2
Watsa: Zaire 76 C2
Wateska: Ill., U.S.A. 88 H5
Watsi-Kengo: Zaire 76 B3
Watson: Sask., Canada 92 G2
Watson: Utah, U.S.A. 93 F5
Watson Lake: town, Yukon, Canada 84 G5
Watten: High., Scotland 28 P3
Watten, Loch: High., Scot. 28 P3
Watthana: Thailand 64 C4
Watton: Norf., England 25 X14
Watton: Staffs., England 27 R14
Watton at Stone: Herts., England 25 V16
Watts Bar Dam: Tenn., U.S.A. 91 J8
Watts Bar Reservoir: Tenn., U.S.A. 91 J8
Wattwil: Switzerland 40 P8
Watubela Is.: Indonesia 61 L12
WAU: & riv., Bahr el-Ghazal Sudan 76 C1
Waubra: Vict., Australia 71 E11
Wauchope: N.S.W., Austl. 71 K8
Wauchula: Fla., U.S.A. 91 L12
Wau el Kebir: Libya 78 H4
Wau en Namus: Libya 78 H5
Waukaringa: S. Australia 71 C9
Waukegan: Ill., U.S.A. 88 H4
Waukesha: Wis., U.S.A. 88 G4
Waukon: Iowa, U.S.A. 88 F4
Waunfawr: Gwynedd, Wales 27 N13
Waupaca: Wis., U.S.A. 88 G3
Waupun: Wis., U.S.A. 88 G4
Wauraltee: S. Australia 71 B10
Waurika: Okla., U.S.A. 90 C8
Wausau: Wis., U.S.A. 88 G3
Wauseon: Ohio, U.S.A. 88 J5
Wausaukee: Wis., U.S.A. 88 H3
Wautoma: Wis., U.S.A. 88 G3
Wauwatosa: Wis., U.S.A. 88 G4
Wave Hill: town, N. Territ., Australia 68 E3
Wavendon: Bucks., England 25 U15
Waveney: riv., Norf./Suff., England 25 Z15
Waverley: North I., N.Z. 70 P14
Waverley: S. Africa 75 G5
Waverly: Iowa, U.S.A. 88 E4
Waverly: N.Y., U.S.A. 89 N4
Waverly: Ohio, U.S.A. 88 K6
Waverly: Tenn., U.S.A. 88 H7
Waverly: Va., U.S.A. 89 N7
Wavre: Belgium 44 K5
Wawa: Ont., Canada 88 J1
Wawne: Humb., England 27 V12
Waxahachie: Tex., U.S.A. 90 C9
Way, Lake: W. Australia 68 C5
Wayabulo: Moluccas, Indonesia 61 K11
Waycross: Ga., U.S.A. 91 K10
Wayen Torrai: Inner Mongolia, China 62 S6
Wayland: Ky., U.S.A. 88 K7
Wayland: Mich., U.S.A. 88 J4
Waynesboro: Ga., U.S.A. 91 K9
Waynesboro: Miss., U.S.A. 90 G10
Waynesboro: Pa., U.S.A. 89 N6
Waynesboro: Va., U.S.A. 89 M6
Waynesburg: Pa., U.S.A. 88 L6
Waynesville: N.C., U.S.A. 91 K8
Waza: Afghanistan 58 L8
Wazirabad: Punjab, Pak. 58 M8
We: i., Indonesia 64 B5
Weald, The: dist., E./W. Sussex /Kent, England 25 W17
Weald Bassett, North: Essex 25 W16
Wear: riv., Durham, Eng. 26 S10
Weardale: val., Durham, England 26 R10
Wear Head: Durham, Eng. 26 R10
Weasenham: Norf., England 25 X14
Weatherford: Okla., U.S.A. 90 B8
Weatherford: Tex., U.S.A. 90 C9
Weaver: riv., Ches., England 27 Q13
Weaverham: Ches., England 27 Q13
Weaverthorpe: N. Yorks., Eng. 27 U11
Weaverville: Calif., U.S.A. 92 C4
Web: Ethiopia 76 E2
Webb City: Mo., U.S.A. 90 D7
Weber: North I., N.Z. 70 Q15
Webster: S. Dak., U.S.A. 92 H3
Webster City: Iowa, U.S.A. 88 E4

For Abbreviations see list on p.113. Italic type, e.g. Ephesus, refers to historical names not on maps. Capital letters, e.g. MADRID, show capitals of countries; small capital letters, e.g. CADIZ, show capitals of provinces, etc. General notes p.116.

Webster Groves—Wilbarston 199

Webster Groves: city, Mo., U.S.A. 88 F6
Webster Springs: W. Va., U.S.A. 88 L6
Wecthalle: N.S.W., Australia 71 G9
Weda: Moluccas, Indon. 61 K11
Wedan: New Guinea 69 J2
Wedde: Netherlands 44 N2
Weddell Sea: Southern Ocean 9 75S 40W
Wedderburn: Vict., Austl. 71 E11
Wedder Hill: Strathclyde, Scotland 29 N8
Weddingstedt: W. Germany 44 P1
Wedgeport: N.S., Canada 89 T4
Wedmore: Som., England 24 Q17
Wednesbury: W. Mid., Eng. 27 R14
Wedoodoo: W. Australia 68 D6
Weebo: W. Australia 68 C5
Weed: Calif., U.S.A. 92 C4
Weedon: Que., Canada 89 Q3
Weedon Bec: Northants., England 25 T15
Week St. Mary: Corn., Eng. 24 N18
Weeley: Essex, England 25 Y16
Weem: Tayside, Scotland 29 O6
Weenen: & Dist., Natal, S. Africa 75 J4
Weerd: Netherlands 44 L4
Weeting: Norf., England 25 X15
Weetzen: W. Germany 44 P3
Wee Waa: N.S.W., Austl. 71 H8
Wegdraai: S. Africa 74 D4
Węgorzyno: Poland 45 V2
Wegscheid: W. Germany 41 T7
Wehdel: W. Germany 44 O2
Weheka: South I., N.Z. 70 M16
Wei: riv., Hopeh/Shantung, China 62 U7
Wei: riv., Shensi, China 62 T8
Weichang: Hopeh, China 62 V6
Weichow: i., China 62 T10
Weida: E. Germany 45 S5
Weiden: W. Germany 45 S6
Weihai: Shantung, China 63 W7
Weiho: Heilungkiang, China 63 X6
Weihsien: Shantung, China 62 V7
Weilburg: W. Germany 44 O5
Weilheim: Baden-Württemberg, W. Germany 40 P7
Weilheim: Bavaria, W. Ger. 41 R8
Weimar: E. Germany 45 R5
Weinfelden: Switzerland 40 P8
Weingarten: W. Germany 40 P8
Weinheim: W. Germany 44 O6
Weining: Kweichow, China 62 S9
Weinstetten: W. Germany 40 Q7
Weir: riv., Queens., Austl. 71 H7
Weir River: town, Man., Canada 92 J1
Weirton: W. Va., U.S.A. 88 L5
Weiser: Idaho, U.S.A. 92 D4
Weishan: Yunnan, China 62 S9
Weisi: Yunnan, China 62 R9
Weismain: W. Germany 45 R5
Weissbach in Lechtal: Austr. 40 Q8
Weissenburg: W. Germany 45 Q6
Weissenfels: E. Germany 45 R4
Weissenkirchen: Austria 41 V7
Weisshorn: mtn., Switz. 40 N9
Weisswasser: E. Germany 45 U4
Weitensfeld: Austria 41 U9
Weitra: Austria 41 U7
Weiz: Austria 41 V8
Wejherowo: Poland 43 Q9
Welbedacht Dam: O.F.S., S. Africa 75 G4
Welbourn Hill: town, S. Australia 68 E5
Welby: Lincs., England 27 U14
Welch: W. Va., U.S.A. 88 L7
Welden: W. Germany 41 Q7
Weldon: Northants., Eng. 25 U15
Weldon: N.C., U.S.A. 89 N7
Weléga: Prov., Ethiopia (cap. Nakamti) 79 M8
Welford: Northants., Eng. 25 T15
Welgedag: Trans., S. Africa 74 N Ins.
Welgelee: O.F.S., S. Africa 75 Ins.
Welgevonden: S. Africa 75 F6
Welkom: O.F.S., S. Africa 75 Ins.
Welland: Ont., Canada 89 M4
Welland: Here. & Worcs., Eng. 24 R15
Welland: riv., England 27 V14
Wellesbourne Mountford: War., England 25 S15
Wellesley Is.: Queens., Australia 69 F3
Well Found: S. Africa 75 F6
Wellingborough: Northants., England 25 U15
Wellington: Here. & Worcs., Eng. 24 Q15
Wellington: Kans., U.S.A. 90 C7
Wellington: N.S.W., Austl. 71 H9
WELLINGTON: & Dist., North I., New Zealand 70 P15
Wellington: Ont., Canada 89 N4
Wellington: Salop, England 27 Q14
Wellington: Som., England 24 P18
Wellington: S. Africa 74 C6
Wellington: S. Australia 71 C10
Wellington: Tex., U.S.A. 90 A8
Wellington, Lake: Vict., Australia 71 G12
Wellington Heath: Hereford & Worcester, England 24 R15
Wellington I.: Chile 95 C13
Wellow: Notts., England 27 T13
Wellow, West: Hants., Eng. 25 S18
Wells: B.C., Canada 92 C2
Wells: Minn., U.S.A. 88 E4
Wells: Som., England 24 Q17
Wells, Lake: W. Australia 68 C5
Wellsboro: Pa., U.S.A. 89 N5
Wellsburg: Ohio, U.S.A. 88 L5
Wellsford: North I., N.Z. 70 P13
Wells-Gray Prov. Park: B.C., Canada 92 D2
Wells next the Sea: Norf., England 25 X14
Wellston: Ohio, U.S.A. 88 K6
Wellsville: Mo., U.S.A. 88 F6
Wellsville: N.Y., U.S.A. 89 N4
Wefna: riv., Poland 43 P10
Welnetham: Suff., England 25 X15
Welney: Norf., England 25 W14
Wèlo: Prov., Ethiopia (cap. Dessye) 79 N7
Welo: Somalia 79 R18
Wels: Austria 41 U7
Welsh: La., U.S.A. 90 E10
Welshampton: Salop, Eng. 27 Q14
Welshpool: Powys., Wales 27 P14
Welton: Lincs., England 27 V13
Welverdiend: Trans., S. Afr. 74 L Ins.
Welwyn: Herts., England 25 V16
Welwyn Garden City: Herts., England 25 V16
Wem: Salop, England 27 Q14
Wema: Zaire 76 B3
Wembere: riv., Tanzania 76 D3
Wembury: Devon, England 24 N19
Wemyss, East: Fife, Scotland 29 P7
Wemyss Bay: village, Strathclyde, Scotland 29 M8
Wenatchee: Wash., U.S.A. 92 C3
Wenchang: Hainan, China 62 U11
Wenchi: Ghana 80 D3
Wenchow (Yungkia): Chekiang, China 63 W9
Wendeburg: W. Germany 45 Q3
Wendel: Calif., U.S.A. 92 C4
Wendelstein: W. Germany 45 R6
Wendisch Buchholz: E. Ger. 45 T3
Wendover: Bucks., England 25 U16
Wendron: & moor, Corn., England 25 L19
Wenebegon Lake: Ont., Can. 88 K2
Wengniutechi: Inner Mongolia, China 62 V6
Wengpo: Tibet, China 59 P8
Wenhaston: Suff., England 25 Z15
Wenholthausen: W. Germany 44 O4
Wenhsien: Kansu, China 62 S8
Wenlock: riv., Australia 69 G2
Wenlock Edge: Salop, Eng. 27 Q14
Wenshan (Kaihwa): Yunnan, China 62 S10
Wensleydale: val., N. Yorks., England 26 R11
Wensum: riv., Norf., Eng. 25 Y14
Wenteng: Shantung, China 63 W7
Wentworth: N.S.W., Austl. 71 D10
Wentworth: S. Yorks., Eng. 27 T13
Wenvoe: S. Glam., Wales 24 P17
Weobley: Here. & Worcs., Eng. 24 Q15
Wepener: & Dist., O.F.S., S. Africa 75 G4
Werben: E. Germany 45 R3
Werbig: E. Germany 45 U3
Werdau: E. Germany 45 S5
Werder: E. Germany 45 S3
Werl: W. Germany 44 N4
Werlte: W. Germany 44 N3
Wermelskirchen: W. Germany 44 N4
Wernberg: W. Germany 45 S6
Werneck: W. Germany 45 Q6
Wernigerode: E. Germany 45 Q4
Werra: riv., E. Germany 45 Q5
Werribee: Vict., Australia 71 F11
Werrington: Northants., England 27 V14
Werris Creek: town, N.S.W., Australia 71 J8
Wertheim: W. Germany 44 P6
Wertingen: W. Germany 41 Q7
Wervicq: Belgium 44 J5
Wesel: W. Germany 44 M4
Weser: riv., W. Germany 44 P3
Weser Gebirge: hills, W. Ger. 44 P3
Wesiri: Wetar, Indonesia 65 H8
Weslaco: Texas, U.S.A. 90 C12
Wesleyville: Newf., Canada 85 w2
Wesleyville: Pa., U.S.A. 89 M4
Wessel, Cape: Australia 69 F2
Wesselburen: W. Germany 44 O1
Wessel Is.: Australia 69 F2
Wesselsbron: O.F.S., S. Afr. 75 G3
Wessex: kingdom of Saxon England comprising originally most of Wiltshire, Berkshire, Hampshire, and Dorset 25 S17
Wessington Springs: city, S. Dak., U.S.A. 92 H4
West: Tex., U.S.A. 90 C10
West Aberthaw: S. Glam., Wales 24 P17
West Allis: Wis., U.S.A. 88 G4
West Ashby: Lincs., Eng. 27 V13
West Atlantic-Indian Basin: Southern Ocean 8 65S 20W
West Auckland: Dur., Eng. 26 S10
West Australian Basin: Indian Ocean 9 20S 95E
West Bagborough: Som., England 24 P17
West Bank: Inner Hebr., Scotland 29 H8
West Barns: Lothian, Scot. 29 Q8
West Bay: village, Dorset, England 24 Q18
West Bay: La., U.S.A. 90 Ins.
West Beckham: Norf., Eng. 25 Y14
West Bend: Wis., U.S.A. 88 G4
West Bengal: State, India (cap. Calcutta) 59 P10
West Bergholt: Essex, Eng. 25 X16
West Berlin: West Germany 45 T3
West Beskids: mtns., Czech./Poland 43 Q12
Westbourne: W. Sussex, Eng. 25 U18
West Branch: Mich., U.S.A. 88 J3
West Branch (Susquehanna Riv.): riv., Pa., U.S.A. 89 N5
West Bridgford: Notts., Eng. 27 T14
West Bromwich: W. Mid., Eng. 27 R14
Westbrook: Hereford & Worcester, England 24 P15
West Burra: i., Shetland Is. 28 Ins.
Westbury: Bucks., England 25 T15
Westbury: Salop, England 27 Q14
Westbury: Som., England 24 Q17
Westbury: Wilts., England 24 R17
Westbury on Severn: Glos., England 24 R16
West Butterwick: Humberside, England 27 U12
Westby: N.S.W., Australia 71 G10
Westby: Wis., U.S.A. 88 F4
West Calder: Lothian, Scot. 29 O8
West Caroline Basin: N. Pacific Ocean 7 00 135E
West Chevington: Northumb., England 26 S9
West Chiltington: W. Sussex, England 25 V18
West Chungking: Szechwan, China 62 S8
West Columbia: Tex., U.S.A. 90 D11
West Dean: W. Sussex, England 25 U18
West des Moines: riv., Iowa/Minn., U.S.A. 88 E4
West Down: Devon, Eng. 24 N17
West Dvina: riv., U.S.S.R. 47 T8
West End Settlement: Bahamas 91 M12
Westerburg: W. Germany 44 N5
Westerdale: village, N. Yorks., England 26 U11
Westerham: Kent, England 25 W17
Westerland: N. Frisian Is. 44 O1
Westerly: R.I., U.S.A. 89 Q5
Wester Markelsdorf: Fehmarn, W. Germany 45 R1
Westermill: Orkney Is. 28 Q2
Western: Dist., Uganda 76 D2
Western: Reg., Ghana (cap. Sekondi) 80 D3
Western: Reg., Kenya (cap. Kakamega) 76 D2
Western: Prov., Zambia (cap. Mongu) 77 B6
Western Australia: State, Australia (cap. Perth) 68
Western Desert: Egypt 54 C9
Western Ghats: hills, India 58 M11
Western Highlands: mtns., Scotland 28 L5
Western Isles: is. & Admin., Scotland (cap. Stornoway) 28 G4
Western Port: bay, Vict., Australia 71 F12
Western Reef: S. China Sea 64 E4

Western Sahara Territory administered by Morocco & Mauretania 78 B4
Cap.: El Aaiun
Area: 102,703 sq. miles (266,001 sq. km.)
Pop.: 76,425 (1970 C)

Western Samoa: Kingdom
Cap.: Apia
Area: 1,133 sq. miles (2,934 sq. km.)
Pop.: 143,547 (1971 C)

Western Sayan Mtns.: U.S.S.R. 51 Q4
Western Sierra Madre: range, Mexico 93 F7
Wester Ross: geog. reg., Highland, Scotland 28 L4
Westerstede: W. Germany 44 N2
Westerwald: mtns., W. Germany 44 N5
West European Basin: N. Atlantic Ocean 8 45N 20W
West Falkland: i., Falkland Is. 95 E14
West Felton: Salop, Eng. 27 Q14
Westfield: High., Scotland 28 O2
Westfield: Mass., U.S.A. 89 P4
Westfield: N.Y., U.S.A. 89 M4
West Firle: E. Sussex, Eng. 25 W18
West Flanders: Prov., Belg. (cap. Bruges) 36 H5
West Fork (Trinity Riv.): riv., Tex., U.S.A. 90 B9
West Frankfort: Ill., U.S.A. 88 G7
West Frisian Is.: Neth. 44 L2
Westgate on Sea: Kent, Eng. 25 Y17

West Germany: Federal Republic 42 L11
Cap.: Bonn
Area: 95,815 sq. miles (248,161 sq. km.)
Pop.: 59,534,000 (1971 E)

West Glamorgan: Co., Wales (co. town Swansea) 24 O16
West Haddon: Northants., England 25 T15
West Hallam: Derby., Eng. 27 T14
West Harptree: Avon, Eng. 24 Q17
West Helena: Ark., U.S.A. 88 E8
West Heslerton: N. Yorks., Eng. 26 U11
West Hoathly: W. Sussex, Eng. 25 V17
Westhoughton: Gt. Man., Eng. 27 Q12
West Ice Shelf: Antarctica 9 70S 80E
West Ilsley: Berks., England 25 T16
West Irian: Prov., Indonesia (cap. Joyapura) 61 N12
Westkapelle: Walcheren, Netherlands 44 J4
West Kilbride: Strath., Scot. 29 M8
West Kirby: Mers., England 27 P13
West Lafayette: Ind., U.S.A. 88 H5
West Lake: Reg., Tanzania (cap. Bukoba) 76 D3
Westland: Dist., South I., N.Z. (cap. Greymouth) 70 N16
Westland National Park: S.I., New Zealand 70 N16
West Langwell: Highland, Scotland 28 N3
Westleigh: O.F.S., S. Africa 75 G3
Westleton: Suff., England 25 Z15
West Liberty: Iowa, U.S.A. 88 F5
West Linton: Borders, Scot. 29 P8
West Loch Tarbert: Strath., Scotland 29 K8
West Loch Tarbert: bay, Outer Hebr., Scotland 28 H4
Westlock: Alta., Canada 92 E2
West Looe: Corn., England 24 N19
West Lorne: Ont., Canada 88 L4
West Lulworth: Dorset, Eng. 24 R18
West Malling: Kent, Eng. 25 W17
West Malvern: Hereford & Worcester, Eng. 24 R15
West Mariana Basin: N. Pacific Ocean 7 15N 135E
Westmeath: Co., Repub. of Ireland (cap. Mullingar) 30 F12
West Memphis: Ark., U.S.A. 90 F8
West Meon: Hants., England 25 T17
West Mersea: Essex, Eng. 25 X16
West Midlands: Metropolitan Co., England (co. town Wolverhampton) 27 S15
Westmill: Herts., England 25 V16
Westminster: Gt. Ldn., England 25 V16
Westminster: Md., U.S.A. 89 N6
Westminster: S.C., U.S.A. 91 K8
West Monroe: La., U.S.A. 90 E9
West Moors: village, Dorset, England 25 S18
Westnewton: Cumbria, Eng. 26 P10
West Nicholson: Rhodesia 77 C7
Weston: Sabah, Malaysia 65 F5
Weston: Ont., Canada 89 M4
Weston: Avon, England 24 R17
Weston: W. Va., U.S.A. 88 L6
Westonaria: Trans., S. Africa 74 MIns.
Westoning: Beds., England 25 U16
Weston super Mare: Avon, England 24 Q17
Weston under Penyard: Gwent, Wales 24 Q16
Weston Underwood: Derby., England 27 S14
Weston upon Trent: Staffs., England 27 R14
Westonzoyland: Som., Eng. 24 Q17
West Palm Beach: city, Fla., U.S.A. 91 L12
West Plains: Mo., U.S.A. 88 F7
West Point: Ga., U.S.A. 91 J9
West Point: Miss., U.S.A. 90 G9
Westpoint: Nebr., U.S.A. 92 H4
West Point: Va., U.S.A. 89 N7
West Point: cape, Jamaica 86 Ins.
West Point: cape, Que., Can. 85 n8
Westport: Mayo, Repub. of Ireland 30 B12
Westport: Ont., Canada 89 N3
Westport: South I., N.Z. 70 N15
West Putford: Devon, Eng. 24 N18
Westray: i., Orkney Is. 28 Ins.
Westray Firth: Orkney Is. 28 Ins.
West Road: riv., B.C., Can. 92 C2
West Rounton: N. Yorks., England 26 T11
Westruther: Borders, Scot. 29 Q8
West Scotia Basin: Southern Ocean 8 60S 60W
West Siberian Plain: U.S.S.R. 51 M3
West Spitsbergen: i., Spits. 48 c2
West Sussex: Co., Eng. (co. town Chichester) 25 U18
West Terschelling: Terschelling, W. Frisian Is. 44 L2
West Union: Iowa, U.S.A. 88 F4
Westville: Ill., U.S.A. 88 H5
Westville: N.S., Canada 89 U3
West Virginia: State, U.S.A. (cap. Charleston) 88 L6
West Vlaanderen: see West Flanders
West Walton Highway: Norf., England 25 W14
Westwego: La., U.S.A. 90 Ins.
West Wellow: Hants., Eng. 25 S18
West Wittering: W. Sussex, England 25 U18
Westwood: Calif., U.S.A. 92 C4
Westwood: Queens., Austl. 70 J4
West Wratting: Cambs., Eng. 25 W15
West Wyalong: N.S.W., Australia 71 G9
West Wycombe: Bucks., Eng. 25 U16
West York: reef, S. China Sea 64 F4
West Yorkshire: Metropolitan Co., England (co. town Wakefield) 27 S12
Wetar: i., Indonesia 65 H8
Wetaskiwin: Alta., Canada 92 E2
Wete: Tanzania 76 E3
Wetheral: Cumbria, England 26 Q10
Wetherby: W. Yorks., England 27 T12
Wethersfield: Essex, Eng. 25 X16
Wetter: W. Germany 44 O5
Wetteren: Belgium 44 J5
Wettin: E. Germany 45 R4
Wetton: Staffs., England 27 S13
Wetumka: Okla., U.S.A. 90 C8
Wetumpka: Ala., U.S.A. 91 H9
Wetwang: Humb., England 27 U11
Wetzlar: W. Germany 44 O5
Wewak: New Guinea 66 H2
Wewoka: Okla., U.S.A. 90 C8
WEXFORD: & Co., Repub. of Ireland 31 J15
Wexford Harbour: & bay, Wex., Repub. of Ireland 31 J15
Wey: riv., Surrey/Hants., Eng. 25 U17
Weybridge: Surrey, England 25 V17
Weyburn: Sask., Canada 92 G3
Weyhill: Hants., England 25 S17
Weymouth: Dorset, England 24 R18
Weymouth: N.S., Canada 89 T3
Whaddon: Glos., England 24 R16
Whakatane: North I., N.Z. 70 Q13
Whaleback, Mount: W. Australia 68 B4
Whale Cay: i., Bahamas 91 N13
Whale I.: North I., N.Z. 70 Q13
Whale River: Que., Canada 85 N6
Whaley Bridge: Derby., Eng. 27 S13
Whalsay: i., Shetland Is. 28 Ins.
Whalton: Northumb., Eng. 26 S9
Whangape: North I., N.Z. 70 O12
WHANGAREI: Northland, North I., N.Z. 70 P12
Whaplode: Lincs., Eng. 27 V14
Whaplode Drove: Lincs., England 25 V14
Wharanui: South I., N.Z. 70 P15
Wharfe: riv., N./W. Yorks., Eng. 27 S12
Wharfedale: val., N. Yorks., England 27 R11
Wharton: Tex., U.S.A. 90 C11
Wharton Basin: Indian Ocean 9 20S 105E
Whauphill: Dumfries & Galloway, Scotland 29 N10
Wheathill: Ferm., N. Ireland 30 F11
Wheatland: Wyo., U.S.A. 92 G4
Wheatley: Oxon., England 25 T16
Wheatley, North: Notts., England 27 U13
Wheeler Dam: Ala., U.S.A. 91 H8
Wheeler Peak: Nev., U.S.A. 93 E5
Wheeler Peak: N. Mex., U.S.A. 93 F5
Wheeling: W. Va., U.S.A. 88 L5
Wheelock: Ches., England 27 R13
Wheldrake: N. Yorks., Eng. 27 U12
Whernside: mtn., Cumbria/N. Yorks., England 26 R11
Whickham: Tyne & Wear, England 26 S10
Whiddy I.: Repub. of Irel. 31 B16
Whimple: Devon, England 24 P18
Whipsnade: Beds., England 25 U16
Whissonsett: Norf., England 25 X14
Whistler: Ala., U.S.A. 90 G10
Whitbeck: Cumbria, England 26 P11
Whitburn: Tyne & Wear, England 26 T10
Whitburn: Lothian, Scot. 29 O8
Whitby: Ches., England 27 Q13
Whitby: N. Yorks., England 26 U11
Whitby: Ont., Canada 89 M4
Whitchurch: Avon, England 24 Q17
Whitchurch: Bucks., Eng. 25 U16
Whitchurch: Devon, Eng. 24 N18
Whitchurch: Hants., Eng. 25 T17
Whitchurch: Salop, England 27 Q14
Whitchurch: S. Glam., Wales 24 P16
White: riv., Ind., U.S.A. 88 H6
White: riv., Mo./Ark., U.S.A. 90 F8
White: riv., N. Dak., U.S.A. 92 G4
White: riv., Ont., Canada 88 J1
White: riv., Tex., U.S.A. 93 G6
White: riv., Yukon, Canada 84 F5
Whiteabbey: Antrim, N. Ireland 30 K10
Whiteadder: riv., Bord., Scot. 22 J5
White Bay: Newf., Canada 85 u1
White Castle: La., U.S.A. 90 F10
Whitechurch: Wex., Repub. of Ireland 31 H15
White Cliffs: N.S.W., Austl. 71 E8
White Coomb: mtn., Dumfries & Galloway, Scotland 29 P9
White Court: Alta., Canada 92 D2
Whitefish: Mont., U.S.A. 92 E3
Whitefish Point: cape, Mich., U.S.A. 88 J2
Whitefish Range: Mont., U.S.A. 92 E3
Whitegate: Clare, Repub. of Ireland 31 E14
Whitegate: Cork, Repub. of Ireland 31 E16
White Hall: Ill., U.S.A. 88 F6
Whitehall: Kilk., Repub. of Ireland 31 G14
Whitehall: Mich., U.S.A. 88 H4
Whitehall: Stronsay, Orkney Islands 28 Ins.
Whitehall: Wis., U.S.A. 88 F3
Whitehaven: Cumbria, Eng. 26 O10
Whitehead: Antrim, N. Irel. 30 K10
Whitehills: Gram., Scotland 28 Q4
WHITEHORSE: Yukon, Canada 84 F5
White Horse, Vale of: Oxon., England 25 T16
Whitehouse: Antrim, N. Irel. 30 K10
White I.: New Zealand 70 Q13
Whitekirk: Lothian, Scot. 29 Q7
White Lake: La., U.S.A. 90 E11
White Lake: Ont., Canada 88 J1
White Mtns.: Calif., U.S.A. 93 D5
White Mtns.: N.H., U.S.A. 89 Q3
Whiten Head: cape, Highland, Scotland 28 M2
White Nile: riv. & Prov., Sudan (cap. Ed Dueim) 79 L7
White Oil Springs: Iran 57 L6
White Otter Lake: Ont., Can. 88 F1
Whiteparish: Wilts., Eng. 25 S17
White Pine Peak: Nev., U.S.A. 93 D5
White Plains: N.Y., U.S.A. 89 P5
White River: Ont., Canada 88 J1
White River: S. Dak., U.S.A. 92 G4
White River: Trans., S. Afr. 75 J2
White River Junction: Vt., U.S.A. 89 P4
White River Valley: Nev., U.S.A. 93 D5
White Roding: Essex, Eng. 25 W16
White Russia: see Byelorussian S.S. Republic
Whites: O.F.S., S. Africa 75 Ins.
White Salmon: Wash., U.S.A. 92 C3
White Sands Nat. Mon.: N. Mex., U.S.A. 93 F6
White Sea: U.S.S.R. 48 e4
Whiteshell Prov. Park: Man., Can. 92 H2
Whites Town: Louth, Repub. of Ireland 30 J12
White Umfolozi: riv., Natal, S. Africa 75 J4
Whiteville: N.C., U.S.A. 91 M8
White Volta: riv., Upper Volta 80 D2
Whitewater: Wis., U.S.A. 88 G4
Whitewater Baldy: mtn., N. Mex., U.S.A. 93 F6
Whitewood: Sask., Canada 92 G2
Whitfield: Northumb., Eng. 26 R10
Whitfield: Vict., Australia 71 G11
Whithorn: Dumfries & Galloway, Scotland 29 N10
Whitianga: North I., N.Z. 70 P13
Whiting: Ind., U.S.A. 88 H5
Whiting Bay: village, Strathclyde, Scotland 29 L9
Whitland: Dyfed, Wales 24 M16
Whitletts: Strath., Scotland 29 M9
Whitley: Berks., England 25 U17
Whitley Bay: town, Tyne & Wear, England 26 T9
Whitmire: S.C., U.S.A. 91 L8
Whitney: Here. & Worcs., Eng. 24 P15
Whitney, Mount: Calif., U.S.A. 93 D5
Whitsome: Bord., Scot. 29 R8
Whitstable: Kent, England 25 Y17
Whitsunday I.: Queens., Australia 70 H3
Whittingham: Northumb., England 26 S9
Whittington: Derby., Eng. 27 T13
Whittington: Lancs., Eng. 26 Q11
Whittington: Salop, England 27 P14
Whittington, Great: Northumb., England 26 S9
Whittlesea: S. Africa 75 G6
Whittlesea: Vict., Australia 71 F11
Whittlesey: Cambs., Eng. 25 V14
Whitton: N.S.W., Australia 71 G10
Whitton: Suff., England 25 Y15
Whitwell: Derby., England 27 T13
Whitwell: I. of Wight, Eng. 25 T18
Whitwell: Tenn., U.S.A. 91 J8
Whitwick: Leics., England 27 T14
Whitworth: Lancs., England 27 R12
Whixall: Salop, England 27 Q14
Wholdaia, Lake: N.W.T., Canada 84 j5
Whyalla: S. Australia 71 B9
Whyjonta: N.S.W., Austl. 71 E7
Wiang Phrao: Thailand 64 B3
Wiang Tai: Thailand 64 B3
Wiarton: Ont., Canada 88 L3
Wiawso: Ghana 80 D3
Wiay: i., Outer Hebr., Scot. 28 G5
Wibaux: Mont., U.S.A. 92 G3
Wichabai: Guyana 87 d9
Wichita: Kans., U.S.A. 90 C7
Wichita, Lake: Tex., U.S.A. 90 B9
Wichita Falls: city, Tex., U.S.A. 90 B9
Wichita Mtns.: Okla., U.S.A. 90 B8
Wick: High., Scotland 28 P3
Wick: riv., High., Scotland 28 P3
Wicken: Cambs., England 25 W15
Wickenburg: Ariz., U.S.A. 93 E6
Wickford: Essex, England 25 X16
Wickham: Hants., England 25 T18
Wickhambrook: Suff., Eng. 25 X15
Wickham Market: Suff., England 25 Y15
WICKLOW: & Co., Repub. of Ireland 31 J14
Wicklow Head: cape, Wick., Repub of Ireland 31 J14
Wicklow Mtns.: Repub. of Ireland 31 J13
Wickwar: Avon, England 24 R16
Widdrington: Northumb., England 26 S9
Widecombe in the Moor: Devon, England 24 O18
Wide Firth: Orkney Is. 28 P1
Widemouth Bay: Corn., England 24 M18
Widford: Herts., England 25 W16
Widgeegoara: Queens., Australia 71 G7
Widgemooltha: W. Austl. 68 C6
Widiya: well, Saudi Arabia 54 G11
Widnes: Cheshire, England 27 Q13
Wiedenbrück: W. Germany 44 O4
Wielichowo: Poland 45 W3
Wielun: Poland 43 Q11
WIEN (Vienna): Austria 41 W7
Wiener Neustadt: Austria 41 W8
Wieprz: riv., Poland 43 S11
Wieren: W. Germany 45 Q3
Wieringen: Netherlands 44 K3
Wierum: Netherlands 44 L2
Wieruszów: Poland 43 Q11
Wierzbnik: Poland 43 R11
WIESBADEN: Hesse, W. Ger. 44 O5
Wiesede: W. Germany 44 N2
Wieselburg: Austria 41 V7
Wiesenburg: E. Germany 45 S3
Wiesloch: W. Germany 44 O6
Wietze: W. Germany 45 P3
Wigan: Lancs., England 27 Q12
Wigginton: Staffs., England 27 S14
Wigglesworth: Lancs., Eng. 27 R12
Wigh el Kebir, El: Libya 78 H5
Wighton: Norf., England 25 X14
Wigmore: Hereford & Worcester, England 24 Q15
Wigston Magna: Leic., Eng. 27 T14
Wigton: Cumbria, England 26 P10
Wigtown: & bay, Dumfries & Galloway, Scotland 29 N10
Wijk aan Zee: Netherlands 44 K3
Wik: W. Germany 45 Q1
Wil: Switzerland 40 P8
Wilbarston: Northants., England 25 U15

For Abbreviations see list on p.113. Italic type, e.g. *Ephesus*, refers to historical names not on maps. Capital letters, e.g. MADRID, show capitals of countries; small capital letters, e.g. CADIZ, show capitals of provinces, etc. General notes p.116.

200 Wilber—Yadrin

Wilber: Nebr., U.S.A. 93 H4
Wilberfoss: Humb., England 27 U12
Wilbraham, Great: Cambs., England 25 W15
Wilbur: Wash., U.S.A. 92 D3
Wilburton: Okla., U.S.A. 90 D8
Wilby: Northants., England 25 U15
Wilcannia: N.S.W., Austl. 71 E8
Wilczek Land: i., Franz Josef Land 48 H1
Wildalpen: Austria 41 U8
Wildbad: W. Germany 40 O7
Wildberg: Potsdam, E. Germany 45 S3
Wildberg: Baden-Württemberg, W. Germany 40 O7
Wildeshausen: W. Germany 44 O3
Wildhorn: mtn., Switzerland 40 N9
Wildon: Austria 41 V9
Wild Spitze: mtn., Austria 41 Q9
Wildstrubel: mtn., Switz. 40 N9
Wildwood: Calif., U.S.A. 92 C4
Wildwood: Fla., U.S.A. 91 K11
Wilfersdorf: Austria 41 W7
Wilge: riv., O.F.S., S. Afr. 75 H3
Wilge: riv., Trans., S. Africa 75 H2
Wilhelm, Mt.: New Guinea 66 H3
Wilhemina Pk.: W. Irian, Indonesia 66 G2
Wilhelmshaven: W. Germany 44 O2
Wilkes-Barre: Pa., U.S.A. 89 O5
Wilkesboro: N.C., U.S.A. 88 L7
Wilkes Land: Antarctica 9 70S 110E
Wilkhaven: High., Scot. 28 O4
Wilkie: Sask., Canada 92 F2
Wilkins Sound: N.W.T., Canada 84 h2
Wilkinstown: Meath, Repub. of Ireland 30 H12
Willard: N. Mex., U.S.A. 93 F6
Willard: Ohio, U.S.A. 88 K5
Willaston: Ches., England 27 R13
Willebroek: Belgium 44 K4
WILLEMSTAD: Netherlands Antilles 94 D1
Willemstad: Netherlands 44 K4
Willenhall: W. Mid., England 27 R14
Willeroo: N. Territ., Austl. 68 E3
Willesborough: Kent, Eng. 25 X17
Williams: Ariz., U.S.A. 93 E5
Williams: W. Australia 68 B6
Williamsburg: Ky., U.S.A. 88 J7
Williamsburg: Va., U.S.A. 91 N7
Williams I.: Bahamas 91 M13
Williams Lake: town, B.C., Canada 92 C2
Williamson: W. Va., U.S.A. 88 K7
Williamsport: Pa., U.S.A. 89 N5
Williamston: Mich., U.S.A. 88 J4
Williamston: N.C., U.S.A. 91 N8
Williamston: S.C., U.S.A. 91 K8
Williamstown: Galway, Repub. of Ireland 30 D12
Williamstown: S. Australia 71 C10
Willimantic: Conn., U.S.A. 89 P5
Willingdale Doe: Essex, Eng. 25 W16
Willingdon: E. Sussex, Eng. 25 W18
Willingen: W. Germany 44 O4
Willingham: Cambs., Eng. 25 W15
Willingham: Lincs., England 27 U13
Willington: Derby., Eng. 27 S14
Willington: Durham, Eng. 26 S10
Willisau: Switzerland 40 N8
Willis Islets: Australia 69 J3
Williston: N. Dak., U.S.A. 92 G3
Williston: & Dist., S. Africa 74 D5
Williston, Lake: British Columbia, Canada 92 C1
Williton: Som., England 24 P17
Willits: Calif., U.S.A. 93 C5
Willmore Wilderness Prov. Park: Alta., Canada 92 D2
Willochra: S. Australia 71 C9
Willoughby: Lincs., England 27 W13
Willoughby: O.F.S., S. Afr. 75 G5
Willoughby: War., England 25 T15
Willoughby, Cape: S. Austl. 71 C10
Willoughby on the Wolds: Notts., England 27 T14
Willoughton: Lincs., Eng. 27 U13
Willow Bunch: Sask., Can. 92 F3
Willowmore: & Dist., S. Afr. 74 E6
Willow Run: Mich., U.S.A. 88 K4
Willows, The: S. Africa 75 F5
Willow South: Alaska, U.S.A. 84 d5
Willow Springs: city, Mo., U.S.A. 88 F7
Willowvale: see Gatyana
Wills River: Queens., Austl. 69 F4
Willunga: S. Australia 71 C10
Wilmette: Ill., U.S.A. 88 H4
Wilmington: Del., U.S.A. 89 O6
Wilmington: Ill., U.S.A. 88 G5
Wilmington: N.C., U.S.A. 91 N8
Wilmington: Ohio, U.S.A. 88 K6
Wilmington: S. Australia 71 C9
Wilmslow: Ches., England 27 R13
Wilnecote: War., England 27 S14
WILNO (Vil'nyus): Lithuania, U.S.S.R. 47 T9
Wilsden: W. Yorks., England 27 S12
Wilsdruff: E. Germany 45 T4
Wilsford: Lincs., England 27 V14
Wilson: Ark., U.S.A. 90 F8
Wilson: N.C., U.S.A. 91 N8
Wilson: Okla., U.S.A. 90 C8
Wilson: riv., Queens., Austl. 69 G5
Wilson: riv., W. Australia 68 D3
Wilson, Cape: Canada 85 l4
Wilson, Mount: Colo., U.S.A. 93 F5
Wilson City: Bahamas 91 N12
Wilson Dam: Ala., U.S.A. 91 H8
Wilson's Promontory: Vict., Australia 71 G12
Wilsontown: Strath., Scot. 29 O8
Wilton: Borders, Scotland 29 Q9
Wilton: Maine, U.S.A. 89 Q3
Wilton: N. Dak., U.S.A. 92 G3
Wilton: N. Yorks., England 26 U11
Wilton: Wilts., England 25 S17
Wilton: riv., N. Territ., Austl. 68 E2
Wiltshire: Co., England (co. town Trowbridge) 25 S17
Wiltz: Luxembourg 44 L6
Wiluna: W. Australia 68 C5
Wimblington: Cambs., Eng. 25 W15
Wimborne Minster: Dorset, England 24 S18
Wimereux: France 36 G5
Wimpole: Cambs., England 25 V15
Wina: riv., Cameroun 81 G3
Winamac: Ind., U.S.A. 88 H5
Winan: Saudi Arabia 55 G9
Winburg: & Dist., O.F.S., S. Africa 75 G4
Wincanton: Som., England 24 R17
Winch, East: Norf., Eng. 25 X14
Wincham: Ches., England 27 R13
Winchcombe: Glos., Eng. 24 S16
Winchelsea: E. Sussex, Eng. 25 X18
Winchelsea: Vict., Australia 71 F12
WINCHESTER: Hants., Eng. 25 T17
Winchester: Ill., U.S.A. 88 F6
Winchester: Ind., U.S.A. 88 J5
Winchester: Ky., U.S.A. 88 J7
Winchester: Tenn., U.S.A. 91 H8
Winchester: Va., U.S.A. 89 M6
Windber: Pa., U.S.A. 89 M5
Windecken: W. Germany 44 O5
Winder: Ga., U.S.A. 91 K9
Windera: Queens., Australia 70 J6
Windermere: & lake, Cumbria, England 26 Q11
Windermere Lake: Ont., Canada 88 K2
Windgap: Kilk., Repub. of Ireland 31 G15
WINDHOEK: & Dist., S.W. Africa 74 B1
Windigo Lake: town, Ontario, Can. 92 J2
Windischgarsten: Austria 41 U8
Windosa: Queens., Austl. 69 G5
Wind River Ra.: Wyo., U.S.A. 92 F4
Windrush: riv., England 25 S16
Windsheim: W. Germany 45 Q6
Windsor: Berks., England 25 U17
Windsor: Mo., U.S.A. 88 E6
Windsor: Newf., Canada 85 v2
Windsor: N.S.W., Australia 71 J9
Windsor: N.C., U.S.A. 91 N8
Windsor: N.S., Canada 89 T3
Windsor: Ont., Canada 88 K4
Windsor: Vt., U.S.A. 89 P4
Windsor Great Park: Berks., England 25 U17
Windsorton: S. Africa 75 F4
Windward Is.: W. Indies 87 c4
Windward Passage: Cuba/Haiti 87 m13
Winfarthing: Norf., England 25 Y15
Winfield: Alta., Canada 92 E2
Winfield: Kans., U.S.A. 90 C7
Winford: Avon, England 24 Q17
Wing: Bucks., England 25 U16
Wingate: Durham, England 26 T10
Wingates: Northumb., Eng. 26 S9
Wingfield, South: Derby., England 27 T13
Wingham: Kent, England 25 Y17
Wingham: N.S.W., Austl. 71 K8
Wingham: Ont., Canada 88 L4
Wingles: France 36 H5
Winifreda: Argentina 96 C4
Winisk: Ont., Canada 85 L6
Winisk: riv., Canada 85 L7
Wink: Tex., U.S.A. 93 G6
Winkel: Netherlands 44 K3
Winkleigh: Devon, England 24 O18
Winkler: Man., Canada 92 H3
Winneba: Ghana 80 D3
Winnebago, Lake: Wis., U.S.A. 88 G4
Winnemucca: Nev., U.S.A. 92 D4
Winner: S. Dak., U.S.A. 92 H4
Winnetka: Ill., U.S.A. 88 H4
Winnett: Mont., U.S.A. 92 F3
Winnfield: La., U.S.A. 90 E10
Winnibigoshish Lake: Minn., U.S.A. 88 D2
Winning Pool: W. Australia 68 A4
WINNIPEG: Man., Canada 92 H3
Winnipeg, Lake: Man., Can. 92 H2
Winnipegosis: & lake, Man., Canada 92 H2
Winnipesaukee, Lake: N.H., U.S.A. 89 Q4
Winnsboro: La., U.S.A. 90 F9
Winnsboro: S.C., U.S.A. 91 L8
Winnsboro: Tex., U.S.A. 90 D9
Winona: Minn., U.S.A. 88 F3
Winona: Miss., U.S.A. 90 G9
Winooski: Vt., U.S.A. 89 P3
Winschoten: Netherlands 44 N2
Winscombe: Avon, England 24 Q17
Winsford: Ches., England 27 Q13
Winsford: Som., England 24 O17
Winsham: Som., England 24 Q18
Winsley: Wilts., England 24 R17
Winslow: Ariz., U.S.A. 93 E5
Winslow: Bucks., England 25 U16
Winslow: Maine, U.S.A. 89 R3
Winster: Derby., England 27 S13
Winstone: Glos., England 24 R16
Winston-Salem: N.C., U.S.A. 88 L7
Winterberg: W. Germany 44 O4
Winterborne Abbas: Dorset, England 24 Q18
Winterborne Stickland: Dorset, England 24 R18
Winterfeld: E. Germany 45 R3
Winter Garden: city, Fla., U.S.A. 91 L11
Winter Harbour: bay, N.W.T., Canada 84 h3
Winter Haven: Fla., U.S.A. 91 L11
Winteringham: Humb., Eng. 27 U12
Winter Park: city, Fla., U.S.A. 91 L11
Winters: Tex., U.S.A. 90 B10
Winterset: Iowa, U.S.A. 88 D5
Winterswijk: Netherlands 44 M4
Winterthur: Switzerland 40 O8
Winterton: Humb., England 27 U12
Winterton: Natal, S. Africa 75 H4
Winterton: Norf., England 25 Z14
Winthrop: Minn., U.S.A. 88 D3
Winton: N.C., U.S.A. 89 N7
Winton: Queens., Austl. 69 G4
Winton: S. Africa 74 E3
Winton: South I., N.Z. 71 M18
Winton: Cumbria, England 26 R11
Wirksworth: Derby., Eng. 27 S13
Wirrabara: S. Australia 71 C9
Wirral: penin., Mers., Eng. 27 P13
Wirrega: S. Australia 71 D11
Wirrulla: S. Australia 68 E6
Wisbech: Cambs., England 25 W14
Wisborough Green: W. Sussex, England 25 U17
Wiscasset: Maine, U.S.A. 89 R3
Wisconsin: riv., Wis., U.S.A. 88 G4
Wisconsin: State, U.S.A. (cap. Madison) 88 F3
Wisconsin Dells: city, Wis., U.S.A. 88 G4
Wisconsin Rapids: city, Wis., U.S.A. 88 G3
Wiseman: Alaska, U.S.A. 84 E4
Wishaw: Strath., Scotland 29 O8
Wishek: N. Dak., U.S.A. 92 H3
Wishford, Great: Wilts., England 25 S17
Wisfa (Vistula): riv., Poland 43 Q10
Wislany Zaliv: gulf, Poland/U.S.S.R. 47 Q9
Wisłoka: riv., Poland 43 R12
Wismar: Guyana 87 d7
Wismar: & bay, E. Germany 45 R2
Wisp Hill: Dumf. & Gall./Bord., Scotland 29 Q9
Wissant: France 36 G5
Wissembourg: France 44 N6
Wissey: riv., Norf., England 25 W14
Wissingen: W. Germany 44 O3
Wistanstow: Salop, Eng. 24 Q15
Wiston: Dyfed, Wales 24 M16
Wistow: Cambs., England 25 V15
Wistow: N. Yorks., England 27 T12
Witagron: Surinam 94 F2
Witbank: & Dist., Trans., S. Africa 75 H2
Witberge: mtns., S. Africa 75 G5
Witbooisvlai: S.W. Africa 74 C2
Witchford: Cambs., Eng. 25 W15
Witchampton: Dorset, Eng. 24 R18
Witdraai: S. Africa 74 D3
Witham: Essex, England 25 X16
Witham: riv., Lincs., Eng. 27 V13
Witham, South: Lincs., Eng. 27 U14
Witham Friary: Som., Eng. 24 R17
Witheridge: Devon, England 24 O18
Withern: Lincs., England 27 W13
Withernsea: Humb., Eng. 27 W12
Withersfield: Queens., Austl. 70 G4
Withersfield: Suff., England 25 W15
Withiel: Corn., England 24 M19
Withington: Glos., England 24 S16
Withington: Hereford & Worcester, England 24 Q15
Withnell: Lancs., England 27 Q12
Withypool: Som., England 24 O17
Witkoms: S. Africa 74 D3
Witkop: Albert Dist., Cape Prov., S. Africa 75 G5
Witkop: Gordonia Dist., Cape Prov., S. Africa 74 D3
Witley: Surrey, England 25 U17
Witley, Great & Little: Hereford & Worcester, England 24 R15
Witmos: S. Africa 75 F6
Witney: Oxon., England 25 T16
Witpoortjie: Trans., S. Afr. 74 M Ins.
Witputs: S.W. Africa 74 B3
Wit Sands Bay: S. Africa 74 Ins.
Witsieshoek: O.F.S., S. Afr. 75 H4
Wittelsheim: France 40 N8
Witten: W. Germany 44 N4
Wittenberg: E. Germany 45 S4
Wittenberge: E. Germany 45 R2
Wittenburg: E. Germany 45 R2
Wittering, West: W. Sussex, England 25 U18
Wittingen: W. Germany 45 Q3
Wittlich: W. Germany 44 M6
Witton, East: N. Yorks., England 26 S11
Witton Gilbert: Durham, England 26 S10
Witton le Wear: Durham, England 26 S10
Wittstock: E. Germany 45 S2
Witu: Kenya 76 F3
Witvlei: (E. of Saltzbrunn), S.W. Africa 74 C2
Witvlei: (E. of Windhoek) S.W. Africa 77 A7
Witwaters Rand: ridge, Trans., S. Africa 74 M Ins.
Witzenhausen: W. Germany 45 P4
Wiveliscombe: Som., Eng. 24 P17
Wivenhoe: Essex, England 25 X16
Wix: Essex, England 25 Y16
Wkra: riv., Poland 43 R10
Wlen (Lähn): Poland 45 V4
Włocławek: Poland 43 Q10
Włodawa: Poland 43 S11
Włoszczowa: Poland 43 Q11
Woburn: Beds., England 25 U16
Woburn Sands: Bucks., Eng. 25 U15
Wodehouse: Dist., S. Africa 75 G5
Wodesha: Ethiopia 76 E1
Wodonga: Vict., Australia 71 G11
Woerden: Netherlands 44 K3
Woerth: France 40 N7
Wogeo: i., New Guinea 66 H2
Wokam: i., Aru Is., Indon. 61 L13
Woking: Surrey, England 25 U17
Wokingham: Berks., Eng. 25 U17
Woldegk: E. Germany 45 T2
Wold Newton: Humb., Eng. 26 V11
Wolen-N'Tem: Reg., Gabon (cap. Oyem) 81 G4
Wolf: riv., Wis., U.S.A. 88 G3
Wolfcreek: Oreg., U.S.A. 92 C4
Wolfeboro: N.H., U.S.A. 89 Q4
Wolfenbuttel: W. Germany 45 Q3
Wolferton: Norf., England 25 W14
Wolfhagen: W. Germany 44 P4
Wolfhill: Tayside, Scotland 29 P7
Wolf Lake: Yukon, Canada 84 f5
Wolf Point: city, Mont., U.S.A. 92 F3
Wolfratshausen: W. Germany 41 R8
Wolf Rock: England 25 K19
Wolfsberg: Austria 41 U9
Wolfsburg: West Germany 45 Q3
Wolfville: N.S., Canada 89 T3
Wolgast: E. Germany 45 T1
Wolhusen: Switzerland 40 O8
Wolin: Poland 45 U2
Wollaston: Northants., England 25 U15
Wollaston: Salop, England 27 Q14
Wollaston, Cape: N.W.T., Canada 84 H3
Wollaston Foreland: Grnld. 85 S3
Wollaston Is.: Chile 95 D15
Wollaston Lake: Sask., Can. 92 G1
Wollaston Penin.: N.W.T., Canada 84 h4
Wollaton: Notts., England 27 T14
Wollogorang: N. Territ., Australia 69 F3
Wollongong: N.S.W., Austl. 71 J10
Wolmaransstad: & Dist., Trans., S. Africa 75 F3
Wolmirstedt: E. Germany 45 R3
Wolo: Celebes 65 G7
Wołów: Poland 45 W4
Wolseley: Sask., Canada 92 G2
Wolseley: S. Africa 74 C6
Wolseley: S. Australia 71 D11
Wolsingham: Durham, Eng. 26 S10
Wolstanton: Staffs., Eng. 27 R13
Wolstenholme: Que., Canada 85 M5
Wolston: W. Mid., England 25 T15
Wolsztyn: Poland 45 W3
Wolthausen: W. Germany 45 P3
Woluwe St. Pierre: Belgium 44 K5
Wolvedans: S. Africa 74 D6
Wolvega: Netherlands 55 M3
WOLVERHAMPTON: W. Mid., England 27 R14
Wolverine: Mich., U.S.A. 88 J3
Wolverton: Bucks., England 25 U15
Wolvey: War., England 25 T15
Wolviston: Cleve., Eng. 26 T10
Wolwehoek: O.F.S., S. Afr. 75 H3
Womalilla: Queens., Austl. 70 G6
Wombourn: Staffs., England 27 R14
Wombwell: S. Yorks., Eng. 27 T12
Womersley: N. Yorks., Eng. 27 T12
Wondai: Queens., Australia 70 J6
Wonderfontein: Trans., S. Africa 75 H2
Wonderfontein: riv., Trans., S. Africa 74 L Ins.
Wonderkop: O.F.S., S. Afr. 75 G3
Wonju: S. Korea 63 X7
Wonominta: N.S.W., Austl. 71 E8
Wonreli: Kisar I., Indon. 65 H8
Wonsan: N. Korea 63 X7
Wonthaggi: Vict., Australia 71 F12
Wooburn: Bucks., England 25 U16
Wood: S. Dak., U.S.A. 92 G4
Woodbridge: Suff., England 25 Y15
Wood Buffalo Nat. Park: Alta., Canada 84 h6
Woodburn: N.S.W., Austl. 71 K7
Woodburn: Oreg., U.S.A. 92 C3
Woodenbridge: Wick., Repub. of Ireland 31 J14
Woodend: Vict., Australia 71 F11
Woodford: Galway, Repub. of Ireland 31 E13
Woodford: Queens., Austl. 70 K6
Woodgreen: N. Territ., Australia 68 E4
Woodhall Spa: Lincs., Eng. 27 V13
Woodland: Durham, Eng. 26 S10
Woodlark (Murua): i., New Guinea 69 J1
Woodplumpton: Lancs., Eng. 27 Q12
Woodroffe, Mount: South Australia 68 E5
Woods, Lake of the: Can./U.S.A. 92 J3
Woodsboro: Tex., U.S.A. 90 C11
Woodsfield: Ohio, U.S.A. 88 L6
Woods Hole: Mass., U.S.A. 89 Q5
Woodside: Gram., Scotland 28 R5
Woodside: S. Australia 71 C10
Woodside: Vict., Australia 71 G12
Woodstock: Ill., U.S.A. 88 G4
Woodstock: N.B., Canada 89 S2
Woodstock: N.S.W., Austl. 71 H9
Woodstock: Ont., Canada 88 L4
Woodstock: Oxon., England 25 T16
Woodstock: (Burke), Queens., Australia 69 G3
Woodstock: (Gregory North), Queens., Australia 69 G4
Woodstock: S. Africa 74 Ins.
Woodstock: Va., U.S.A. 89 M6
Woodstock: Vt., U.S.A. 89 P4
Woodsville: N.H., U.S.A. 89 P3
Woodville: Derby., England 27 S14
Woodville: Miss., U.S.A. 90 F10
Woodville: North I., N.Z. 70 P15
Woodville: Tex., U.S.A. 90 D10
Woodward: Okla., U.S.A. 90 B7
Wookey: Som., England 24 Q17
Wool: Dorset, England 24 R18
Woolacombe: Devon, Eng. 24 N17
Wooler: Northumb., Eng. 26 R8
Woolfardisworthy: Devon, England 24 N18
Woolgoolga: N.S.W., Austl. 71 K8
Woolhampton: Berks., Eng. 25 T17
Woolpit: Suff., England 25 X15
Woolsthorpe: Lincs., Eng. 27 U14
Woomelang: Vict., Austl. 71 E10
Woomera: S. Australia 71 B8
Woonsocket: R.I., U.S.A. 89 Q5
Woonsocket: S. Dak., U.S.A. 92 H4
Wooramel: W. Australia 68 A5
Wooramel: riv., W. Austl. 68 B5
Woore: Salop, England 27 R14
Woorinen: Vict., Australia 71 E10
Wooroolin: Queens., Austl. 70 J6
Wooster: Ohio, U.S.A. 88 L5
Woosung: Kiangsu, China 63 W8
Wootton: Humb., England 27 V12
Wootton: Northants., Eng. 25 U15
Wootton, North: Norf., Eng. 25 W14
Wootton, South: Norf., Eng. 25 W14
Wootton Bassett: Wilts., England 24 S16
Wootton Wawen: War., England 25 S15
Worbis: E. Germany 45 Q4
WORCESTER: Hereford & Worcester, England 24 R15
Worcester: & Dist., S. Africa 74 C6
Worcester: Mass., U.S.A. 89 Q4
Worfield: Salop, England 27 R14
Wörgl: Austria 41 S8
Workington: Cumbria, Eng. 26 O10
Worksop: Notts., England 27 T13
Workum: Netherlands 44 L3
Worlaby: Humb., England 27 V12
Worland: Wyo., U.S.A. 92 F4
Worleston: Ches., England 27 Q13
Worlington, East: Devon, England 24 O18
Worlingworth: Suff., Eng. 25 Y15
Wormbridge: Hereford & Worcester, England 24 Q16
Wormhoudt: France 36 H5
Wormit: Fife, Scotland 29 Q7
Worms: W. Germany 44 O6
Worms Head: cape, W. Glam., Wales 24 N16
Worsbrough: S. Yorks., England 27 T12
Wortel: S. Africa 74 C4
Worth: W. Germany 45 S6
Worth: Kent, England 25 Y17
Worth, Lake: Tex., U.S.A. 90 C9
Worthen: Salop, England 27 Q14
Worther See: lake, Austria 41 U9
Worthing: W. Sussex, Eng. 25 V18
Worthington: Leics., Eng. 27 T14
Worthington: Minn., U.S.A. 92 H4
Wotton under Edge: Glos., England 24 R16
Wouldham: Kent, England 25 W17
Wour: Chad, 78 H5
Wowan: Queens., Australia 70 J4
Wowoni: i., Celebes 65 G7
Woy Woy: N.S.W., Austl. 71 J9
Wragby: Lincs., England 27 V13
Wrangel I.: East Siberian Sea 49 U3
Wrangell: Alaska, U.S.A. 84 f6
Wrangell Mtns., Alaska, U.S.A. 84 e5
Wrangle: Lincs., England 27 W13
Wrath, Cape: High., Scot. 28 L2
Wratting, West: Cambs., England 25 W15
Wray: Colo., U.S.A. 93 G4
Wreay: Cumbria, England 26 Q10
Wreck Reef: Australia 69 K4
Wrekin, The: hill, Salop, England 27 Q14
Wrelton: N. Yorks., England 26 U11
Wrentham: Suff., England 25 Z15
Wretham: Norf., England 25 X15
Wrexham: Clwyd, Wales 27 Q13
Wriezen: E. Germany 45 U3
Wright Peak: mtn., Antarctica 9 75S 95W
Wrightson, Mt.: Ariz., U.S.A. 93 E6
Wrightsville: Ga., U.S.A. 91 K9
Wrightville: N.S.W., Austl. 71 F8
Wrigley: N.W.T., Canada 84 g5
Wrington: Avon, England 24 Q17
Writtle: Essex, England 25 W16
Wrockwardine: Salop, Eng. 27 Q14
Wrockwardine Wood: Salop, England 27 R14
WROCŁAW (Breslau): & Prov., Poland 43 P11
Wronki: Poland 45 W3
Wroot: Humb., England 27 U12
Wrotham: Kent, England 25 W17
Wrottesley, Cape: N.W.T., Canada 84 g3
Wroughton: Wilts., England 25 S16
Wroxeter: Salop, England 27 Q14
Wroxham: Norf., England 25 Y14
Wroxton: Oxon., England 25 T15
Wrzesnia: Poland 43 P10
Wrzosowo: Poland 45 V1
Wschowa: Poland 45 W4
Wu: riv., China 62 T9
Wubin: W. Australia 68 B6
Wuchang: (part of Wuhan), Hupeh, China 62 U8
Wuchang: Heilungkiang, China 63 X6
Wuchow (Tsangwu): Kwangsi, China 62 U10
Wudham: Oman 55 J10
Wufeng: Hupeh, China 62 U8
Wuhan: Hupeh, China 62 U8
Wuhing: Chekiang, China 63 W8
Wuhsien: see Suchow
Wuhsuan: Kwangsi Chuang, China 62 T10
Wuhu: Anhwei, China 62 V8
Wukang: Chekiang, China 62 V8
Wukang: Hunan, China 62 U9
Wukari: Nigeria 81 F3
Wukunoerh: Inner Mongolia, China 62 V5
Wulanhaote (Wangyehmiao): Inner Mongolia, China 63 W5
Wulfersdorf: E. Germany 45 S2
Wuli: Kwangsi Chuang, China 62 T10
Wulukomushih Ling: mtn., Tibet, China 59 P7
WULUMUCHI (Urumchi): Sinkiang Uighur Auton. Reg., China 51 P6
Wulunku Hu: lake, Sinkiang, China 51 P5
Wum: Cameroun 81 G3
Wuning: Kiangsi, China 62 V9
Wunstorf: W. Germany 44 P3
Wuntho: Burma 59 R10
Wupatki Nat. Mon.: Ariz., U.S.A. 93 E5
Wupper: riv., W. Germany 44 N4
Wuppertal: W. Germany 44 N4
Wuppertal: S. Africa 74 C6
Würmsee: lake, W. Germany 41 R8
Wurno: Nigeria 81 F2
Württemberg-Hohenzollern: Prov., (now absorbed in Baden-Württemberg, Prov.) W. Germany 40 O7
Würzburg: W. Germany 45 P6
Wurzen: E. Germany 45 S4
Wushan: Szechwan, China 62 T8
Wushih: Sinkiang, China 51 N6
Wustrow: E. Germany 45 S1
Wusu: Sinkiang, China 51 O6
Wutai: Shansi, China 62 U7
Wuting: Yunnan, China 62 S9
Wutsin: Kiangsu, China 62 V8
Wuvulu: i., New Guinea 66 H2
Wuwei: Anhwei, China 62 V8
Wuwei (Liangchow): Kansu, China 62 S7
Wu Yi Shan: mtns., China 62 V9
Wuyuan: Kiangsi, China 62 V9
Wuyuan: Inner Mongolia, China 62 T6
Wuyun: Heilungkiang, China 63 X5
Wyaaba: riv., Queens., Austl. 69 G3
Wyandotte: Mich., U.S.A. 88 K4
Wyandra: Queens., Austl. 70 G6
Wyangala Reservoir: N.S.W., Australia 71 H8
Wycheproof: Vict., Austl. 71 E11
Wycombe, High & West: Bucks., England 25 U16
Wye: Kent, England 25 X17
Wye: riv., England/Wales 24 Q16
Wyk: W. Germany 44 O1
Wyke: W. Yorks., England 27 S12
Wykeham: N. Yorks., Eng. 26 U11
Wyke Regis: Dorset, England 24 R18
Wylam: Northumb., Eng. 29 S10
Wylye: & riv., Wilts., England 24 S17
Wymeswold: Leics., Eng. 27 T14
Wymondham: Leics., Eng. 27 U14
Wymondham: Norf., Eng. 25 Y14
Wynberg: S. Africa 74 Ins.
Wyndham: South I., N.Z. 71 M18
Wyndham: W. Australia 68 D3
Wynne: Ark., U.S.A. 90 F8
Wynne Wood: city, Okla., U.S.A. 90 C8
Wynnum: Queens., Austl. 70 K6
Wynyard: Sask., Canada 92 G2
Wynyard: Tas., Australia 68 H8
Wyoming: State, U.S.A. (cap. Cheyenne) 92 F4
Wyoming Basin: Wyo., U.S.A. 92 F4
Wyoming Range: Wyo., U.S.A. 92 E4
Wyong: N.S.W., Australia 71 J9
Wyperfeld National Park: Vict., Australia 71 D10
Wyreema: Queens., Austl. 70 J6
Wyrzysk: Poland 43 P10
Wysokie Mazowieckie: Pol. 43 S10
Wyszków: Poland 43 R10
Wythall: Here. & Worcs., Eng. 24 S15
Wythburn: Cumbria, Eng. 26 P10
Wytheville: Va., U.S.A. 88 L7

Xa Cassau: Angola 77 B4
XAI-XAI: Gaza, Mozambique 75 K2
Xalanga: S. Africa 75 G5
Xánthi: Greece 39 T16
Xanxerê: Brazil 96 E2
Xapuri: Brazil 94 D6
Xenia: Ohio, U.S.A. 88 K6
Xhora: Transkei, S. Africa 75 H5
Xiengkhouang: Laos 64 C3
Xilókastron: Greece 39 S17
Xingu: riv., Brazil 94 G4
Xirokhori (Istiaia): Euboea, Greece 39 S17
Xuka Drift: S. Africa 75 H5

Yaamba: Queens., Austl. 70 J4
Yaan: Szechwan, China 62 S9
Yaapeet: Vict., Australia 71 E10
Yabassi: Cameroun 81 G4
Yablonovyy Range: U.S.S.R. 49 N7
Yacamunda: Queens., Austl. 70 G3
Yackandandah: Vict., Austl. 71 G11
Yacuiba: Bolivia 95 E8
Yadgir: Karnataka, India 58 N11
Yadkin: riv., N.C., U.S.A. 88 L7
Yadrin: U.S.S.R. 50 G3

For Abbreviations see list on p.113. Italic type, e.g. *Ephesus*, refers to historical names not on maps. Capital letters, e.g. MADRID, show capitals of countries; small capital letters, e.g. CADIZ, show capitals of provinces, etc. General notes p.116.

Yaerhnocha Hu: lake, Tibet, China 59 P8
Yaeyama Group: is. (Jap.), China Sea 63 W10
Yafforth: N. Yorks., England 26 T11
Yagareh: Somalia 79 R18
Yagyl-Yakh: riv., U.S.S.R. 51 N3
Yahia: Thailand 65 b10
Yahila: Zaïre 76 B2
Yahisuli: Zaïre 76 B3
Yahk: B.C., Canada 92 D3
Yahuma: Zaïre 76 B2
Yaita: Japan 63 f2
Yaizu: Japan 63 f3
Yakata: Zaïre 76 B2
Yakiang: Tibet, China 62 S8
Yakima: Wash., U.S.A. 92 C3
Yako: Upper Volta 80 D2
Yakoma: Zaïre 76 B2
Yakoruda: Bulgaria 39 S15
Yaksha: U.S.S.R. 50 J2
Yaku: i., Osumi Is., Japan 63 Y8
Yakuluku: Zaïre 76 C2
Yakut A.S.S. Republic: U.S.S.R. (cap. Yakutsk) 49 o5
Yakutat: & bay, Alaska, U.S.A. 84 F6
YAKUTSK: Yakut, U.S.S.R. 49 o5
Yala: & State, Thailand 65 b10
Yalding: Kent, England 25 W17
Yale: B.C., Canada 92 C3
Yale: Mich., U.S.A. 88 K4
Yale: Okla., U.S.A. 90 C7
Yale Point: mtn., Ariz., U.S.A. 93 E5
Yalgoo: W. Australia 68 B5
Yalinga: Cen. Afr. Rep. 76 B1
Yalleroi: Queens., Australia 69 H4
Yallingup: W. Australia 68 B6
Yallourn: Vict., Australia 71 G12
Yalobusha: riv., U.S.A. 90 F9
Yalova: Kocaeli, Turkey 56 A1
Yalova: Tekirdağ, Turkey (Dardan. Inset) 20 Ins.
Yalpunga: N.S.W., Austl. 71 E7
Yalta: U.S.S.R. 50 D6
Yalu: Inner Mongolia, China 63 W5
Yalu: riv., N. Korea/China 63 X6
Yalung (Nya): riv., China 62 R8
Yalutorovsk: U.S.S.R. 51 L3
Yalvaç: Turkey 56 B2
Yamada: Honshu, Japan 63 ZZ7
Yamada: Kyushu, Japan 63 b4
YAMAGATA: Pref., Japan 63 g1
YAMAGUCHI: & Pref., Japan 63 b3
Yamala: Queens., Australia 70 H4
Yamal Penin.: U.S.S.R. 48 h3
Yamanaka: Japan 63 e2
Yamanashi: Pref., Japan (cap. Kofu) 63 f3
Yamase: Japan 63 d3
Yamatu: Sinkiang, China 51 O5
Yamazaki: Japan 63 d3
Yamba: Ethiopia 76 E1
Yamba: N.S.W., Australia 71 K7
Yambata: Zaïre 76 B2
Yambe: W. Irian, Indonesia 61 L12
Yambering: Guinea 80 B2
Yambio: Sudan 76 C2
Yambol: Bulgaria 39 U15
Yambuya: Zaïre 76 B2
Yamdena: i., Tanimbar Is., Indonesia 61 L13
Yamethin: Burma 59 R10
Y'Ami: i., Philippines 64 G2
Yamia: Niger 81 G2
Yamma Yamma, Lake: Queens., Australia 69 G5
Yampa: riv., Colo., U.S.A. 93 F4
Yampi Sound: W. Australia 68 C3
Yampol': (Kamenets-Podol'skiy Reg.), Ukraine 43 U12
Yampol': (Vinnitsa Reg.), Ukraine 43 V12
Yamsk: U.S.S.R. 49 R6
Yamuna (Jumna): riv., India 58 O9
Yana: Sierra Leone 80 B3
Yana: riv., U.S.S.R. 49 p3
Yanac: Vict., Australia 71 D11
Yanam: Andhra Pradesh, India 58 O11
Yanaul: U.S.S.R. 50 H3
Yanbu': Saudi Arabia 54 E10
Yancannia: N.S.W., Austl. 71 E8
Yanco: N.S.W., Australia 71 G10
Yandina: Queens., Australia 70 K6
Yandogay: U.S.S.R. 49 u4
Yandunburra: Queens., Australia 70 F7
Yanga: Central African Rep. 76 B1
Yangambi: Zaïre 76 B2
Yangchoyung Ho: lake, Tibet, China 59 Q9
Yanghsien: Shensi, China 62 T8
Yangi-Yul: Uzbek., U.S.S.R. 51 L6
Yangkao: Shansi, China 62 U6
YANGKU (Taiyuan): Shansi, China 62 U7
Yanglin: Yunnan, China 62 S9
Yangouéré: geog. reg., Central African Republic 81 H4
Yangtze: riv., China 63 W8
Yangyang: N. Korea 63 X7
Yang Yang: Senegal 80 A1
Yanis'yarvi: & lake, Karelian A.S.S. Rep., U.S.S.R. 46 W6
Yankton: S. Dak., U.S.A. 92 H4
Yanna: Queens., Australia 70 G6
Yannina (Ioannina): Greece 39 R17
Yanonge: Zaïre 76 B2
Yantabulla: N.S.W., Austl. 71 F7
Yany-Kurgan: Kazakh., U.S.S.R. 51 L6
Yao: Chad 81 H2
Yaoan: Yunnan, China 62 S9
Yaohsien: Shensi, China 62 T8
Yaotsup: Japan 63 e3
YAOUNDE: Cameroun 81 G4
Yap: i., Caroline Is. 61 M10
Yapen: i., W. Irian, Indonesia 61 M12
Yapeyu (San Martin): Argentina 96 D2
Yaqui: riv., Mexico 93 F7
Yaraka: Queens., Australia 69 G4
Yaransk: U.S.S.R. 50 G3
Yarburgh: Lincs., England 27 W13
Yarcombe: Devon, England 24 P18
Yarda: Chad 78 H6
Yardley Hastings: Northants., England 25 U15
Yare: riv., Norf., England 25 Y14
Yaremcha: Ukraine 43 T12
Yarensk: U.S.S.R. 50 G2
Yarim: Yemen 54 F12
Yaritagua: Venezuela 94 D1
Yarkand (Soche): Sinkiang, China 51 N7
Yarkino: U.S.S.R. 51 R3
Yarm: Cleve., England 26 T10
Yarmolintsy: Ukraine 43 U12
Yarmouth: I. of Wight, England 25 T18

Yarmouth: N.S., Canada 89 S4
Yarmouth: Queens., Australia 70 G6
Yarmouth, Gt.: Norf., Eng. 25 Z14
Yarnscombe: Devon, Eng. 24 N18
YAROSLAVL': & Reg., U.S.S.R. 50 E3
Yaroslavsk: Reg., U.S.S.R. (cap. Yaroslavl') 50 E3
Yarra: riv., Vict., Austl. 71 F11
Yarram: Vict., Australia 71 G12
Yarraman: Queens., Austl. 70 K6
Yarrawonga: Vict., Austl. 71 F11
Yarronvale: Queens., Austl. 70 F6
Yarrow: & riv., Bord., Scot. 29 P8
Yartenga: Upper Volta 80 D2
Yartsevo: U.S.S.R. 50 D3
Yarva-Yani: Estonia, U.S.S.R. 47 T7
Yary: Fr. Guiana 94 G3
Yasawa Group: is., Fiji Is. 67 P5
Yasel'da: riv., Byelorussia 43 T10
Yashbum: Yemen P.D.R. 54 G12
Yasin: Gilgit, Jammu & Kashmir 58 M7
Yasinya: Ukraine 43 T12
Yasothan: Thailand 64 C3
Yass: N.S.W., Australia 71 H10
Yassås: Norway 46 N4
Yasu: Japan 63 e3
Yasun, Cape: Turkey 56 E1
Yat: Niger 78 G5
Yatağan: Turkey 39 V18
Yatakala: Upper Volta 80 E2
Yates Center: Kans., U.S.A. 90 D7
Yathkyed Lake: N.W.T., Canada 84 K5
Yatsushiro: & bay, Japan 63 b4
Yatta: Jordan 55 b3
Yatta Plat.: Kenya 76 E3
Yattendon: Berks., England 25 T17
Yatton: Avon, England 24 Q17
Yatton (Keynell): Wilts., England 24 R17
Yauca: Peru 94 C7
Yauri: Peru 94 C6
Yavari: riv., Brazil/Peru 94 C4
Yavaros: Mexico 93 F7
Yavne (Yibna): Israel 55 a3
Yavorov: Ukraine 43 S12
Yawatahama: Japan 63 c4
Yaxley: Cambs., England 25 V14
Yaya: U.S.S.R. 51 P3
Yayladagi: Turkey 56 E4
Yazdan: Iran 55 K8
Yazd-e Khvast: Iran 55 H8
Yazoo: riv., Miss., U.S.A. 90 F9
Yazoo City: Miss., U.S.A. 90 F9
Ybbs: Austria 41 V7
Ychoux: France 37 E11
Ye: Burma 59 R11
Yea: Vict., Australia 71 F11
Yeadon: W. Yorks., England 27 S12
Yealmpton: Devon, Eng. 24 N19
Yebyu: Burma 59 R12
Yecla: Spain 35 F17
Yecora: Mexico 93 F7
Yedseram: riv., Nigeria 81 G2
Yeelanna: S. Australia 71 A10
Yefremov: U.S.S.R. 50 E4
Yegendybulak: Kazakh., U.S.S.R. 51 N5
Yegor'yevsk: U.S.S.R. 50 E3
Yehcheng (Qarghaliq): Sinkiang, China 51 N7
Yehchih: Yunnan, China 62 R9
Yehgunkou: Sinkiang, China 51 P6
Yehsien: Shantung, China 62 V7
Yei: Sudan 76 D2
Yeji: Ghana 80 D3
Yekabpils: Latvia, U.S.S.R. 47 T8
Yekia: well, Chad 81 H1
Yelabuga: U.S.S.R. 50 H3
Yelan': U.S.S.R. 50 F4
Yelan-Kolenovskiy: U.S.S.R. 50 F4
Yelarbon: Queens., Austl. 71 J7
Yele: Sierra Leone 80 B3
Yelets: U.S.S.R. 50 E4
Yelgava: Latvia, U.S.S.R. 47 S8
Yelizarovo: U.S.S.R. 51 L2
Yelizavety, Cape: U.S.S.R. 49 Q7
Yell: i., Shetland Is., Scot. 28 Ins.
Yellandu: Andhra Pradesh, India 58 O11
Yellow (Hwang): riv., China 62 S7
Yellowhead Pass: B.C./Alta., Canada 92 D2
YELLOWKNIFE: N.W.T., Can. 84 h5
Yellow Mount: town, N.S.W., Australia 71 G9
Yellow Sea: China 63 W7
Yellowstone: riv., Mont., U.S.A. 92 F3
Yellowstone Lake: Wyo., U.S.A. 92 E4
Yellowstone Nat. Park: Wyo., U.S.A. 92 E4
Yellville: Ark., U.S.A. 88 E7
Yel'nya: U.S.S.R. 50 D4
Yel'sk: Byelorussia 43 V11
Yeltes: riv., Spain 35 C16
Yelvertoft: Northants., Eng. 25 T15
Yelverton: Devon, England 24 N19
Yelwa: Nigeria 81 E2
Yemanzhelinka: U.S.S.R. 51 K4

Yemen: Republic 54 F11
Cap.: San'a
Area: 75,290 sq. miles
(195,001 sq. km.)
Pop.: 6,062,000 (1972 E)

Yemen People's Democratic Republic 54 G12
Cap.: Aden
Area: 111,000 sq. miles
(287,490 sq. km.)
Pop.: 1,475,000 (1971 E)

Yen: Malaya, Malaysia 65 b11
Yenakiyevo: Ukraine 50 E5
Yenan (Fushih): Shensi, China 62 T7
YENANGYAUNG: Magwe, Burma 59 Q10
Yen Bai: Vietnam 64 C2
Yencheng: Shensi, China 62 U7
Yencheng: Honan, China 62 U8
Yencheng: Kiangsu, China 63 W8
Yencheng: see Qarghaliq
Yenchow (Tzeyang): Shantung, China 62 V7
Yenda: N.S.W., Australia 71 G10
Yendi: Ghana 80 D3
Yengan: Burma 59 R10
Yeni: Niger 81 E2
Yenice: Turkey 39 U17
Yenice: riv., Turkey 56 E2
Yenikoy: Istanbul, Turkey (Bosporus Inset) 20 Ins.
Yenikoy: Tekirdağ, Turkey (Dardan. Inset) 20 Ins.
Yenişehir: Turkey 56 A1
Yenisey: riv., U.S.S.R. 48 k5
Yenisey, G. of: U.S.S.R. 48 K3

Yeniseysk: U.S.S.R. 51 Q3
Yenki: Kirin, China 63 X6
Yenki (Kara-Shahr): Sinkiang, China 51 P6
Yenne: France 40 L10
Yenotayevsk: U.S.S.R. 50 G5
Yenping: Fukien, China 62 V9
Yenshan: Hopeh, China 62 V7
Yenshow: Heilungkiang, China 63 X5
Yentai: Shantung, China 63 W7
Yentsing: Tibet, China 62 R9
Yentsing: Yunnan, China 62 S9
Yentun: Sinkiang, China 62 Q6
Yeo, Lake: W. Australia 68 C5
Yeola: Maharashtra, India 58 M10
Yeotmal: Maharashtra, India 58 N10
Yeoval: N.S.W., Australia 71 H9
Yeovil: Som., England 24 Q18
Yeppoon: Queens., Austl. 70 J4
Yeraki: Greece 39 S18
Yerba Buena: Chile 96 A2
Yerbent: Turkmen., U.S.S.R. 50 J7
Yercaud: Tamil Nadu, India 58 N12
YEREVAN (Erivan): Armenia, U.S.S.R. 57 J1
Yerington: Nev., U.S.A. 93 D5
Yerkoy: Turkey 56 D2
Yerlisu: Turkey (Dardan. Inset) 20 Ins.
Yermakovskoye: U.S.S.R. 51 Q4
Yerofey Pavlovich: U.S.S.R. 49 O7
Yerong Creek: town, N.S.W., Australia 71 G10
Yeropol: U.S.S.R. 49 s4
Yershov: U.S.S.R. 50 G4
Yerupaja: mtn., Peru 94 B6
Yerville: France 36 F6
Yeşil: riv., Turkey 56 E1
Yessey: U.S.S.R. 49 M4
Yeste: Spain 35 E17
Yestratovskiy: U.S.S.R. 50 E4
Yetholm: Borders, Scotland 29 R8
Yetman: N.S.W., Australia 71 J7
Yetminster: Dorset, England 24 Q18
Ye-u: Burma 59 R10
Yeu, Île d': i., France 37 C9
Yeungchun: Kwangtung, China 62 U10
Yeungkong: Kwangtung, China 62 U10
Yevlakh: Azerbaydzhan, U.S.S.R. 57 K1
Yevpatoriya: U.S.S.R. 50 D5
Yevseyevo: U.S.S.R. 49 R4
Yeya: riv., U.S.S.R. 50 F5
Yeysk: U.S.S.R. 50 E5
YEZD: & Governorate, Iran 55 H8
Yffiniac: France 36 C7
Y-Gaer: site of Roman fort, about 3 miles W. of Brecon, Powys, Wales 24 P16
Yhu: Paraguay 96 D1
Yi: riv., Uruguay 96 D3
Yialousa: Cyprus 56 D4
Yiannitsá: Greece 39 S16
Yibna (Yavne): Israel 55 a3
Yihsien: Hopeh, China 62 V7
Yildizeli: Turkey 56 E2
Yilliminning: W. Australia 68 B6
Yin-ch'uan (Ninghsia): Ninghsia Hui, China 62 T7
Yingchiapate: Sinkiang, China 51 O6
Yinghsien: Shansi, China 62 U7
Yingkow (Newchwang): Liaoning, China 63 W6
Yingpanshan: Szechwan, China 62 T9
Yingshan: Hupeh, China 62 V8
Yingtak: Kwangtung, China 62 U10
Yinkanie: S. Australia 71 D10
Yinmabin: Burma 59 Q10
Yinnietharra: W. Australia 68 B4
Yin Shan: range, Inner Mongolia, China 62 T6
Yirol: Sudan 76 D1
Yithion: Greece 39 S18
Yitu: Shantung, China 62 V7
Yiwul: Yunnan, China 62 S10
Yiyang: Hunan, China 62 U9
Yli-li: Finland 46 T4
Ylikitha, Lake: Finland 46 V3
Ylitornio: Finland 46 S3
Ylivieska: Finland 46 T4
Ylivuokki: Finland 46 V4
Ymanskraal: S. Africa 74 C6
Ymers I.: Greenland 85 r3
Yoakum: Tex., U.S.A. 90 C11
Yochow (Yoyang): Hunan, China 62 U9
Yogyakarta: Java, Indonesia 65 E8
Yoichi: Japan 62 ZZ6
Yoju: S. Korea 63 X7
Yokadouma: Cameroun 81 H4
Yokaichiba: Japan 63 g3
Yokkaichi: Japan 63 e3
Yoko: Cameroun 81 G3
YOKOHAMA: Kanagawa, Jap. 63 f3
Yokosuka: Japan 63 f3
Yokote: Japan 63 ZZ7
Yola: Japan 63 d3
Yola: Gongola, Nigeria 81 G3
Yolçati: Turkey 56 F2
Yolombo: Zaïre 76 B3
Yom: riv., Thailand 64 C3
YOMOU: & Reg., Guinea 80 C3
Yonago: Japan 63 c3
Yongama: Zaïre 76 B3
Yongampo: N. Korea 63 W7
Yongchon: S. Korea 63 X7
Yongdok: S. Korea 63 X7
Yonghung: N. Korea 63 X7
Yong Peng: Malaya, Malaysia 65 c12
Yongwol: S. Korea 63 X7
Yonkers: N.Y., U.S.A. 89 P5
Yonne: Dept., France (cap. Auxerre) 36 J8
Yonne: riv., France 36 J7
Yora: riv., U.S.S.R. 57 J1
Yorii: Japan 63 f2
York: Ala., U.S.A. 90 G9
York: Man., Canada 92 J1
York: Nebr., U.S.A. 93 H4
YORK: N. Yorks., England 27 T12
York: Pa., U.S.A. 89 N6
York: S.C., U.S.A. 91 L8
York: W. Australia 68 B6
York, Cape: Australia 69 G2
York, Vale of: North Yorkshire, Eng. 26 T11
Yorke Penin.: S. Australia 71 B10
Yorketown: S. Australia 71 B10
York Moors, North: North Yorkshire, England 26 U11
Yorkshire Dales Nat. Park: N. Yorks., England 26 R11
Yorkshire Wolds: hills, Humberside/North Yorkshire; Eng. 27 U11-

Yorkton: Sask., Canada 92 G2
Yorktown: Tex., U.S.A. 90 C11
Yoruba: geog. reg., Nigeria 81 E3
Yosemite Nat. Park: Calif., U.S.A. 93 D5
Yoshida: Hiroshima, Japan 63 c3
Yoshida: Niigata, Japan 63 f2
Yoshida: Yamanashi, Japan 63 f3
Yoshino: riv., Japan 63 c4
Yoshinobu: Japan 63 c4
YOSHKAR-OLA: Mari, U.S.S.R. 50 G3
Yosu: South Korea 63 X8
Youanmi: W. Australia 68 B5
Youghal: & bay, Cork, Repub. of Ireland 31 F16
Youghioghenny: riv., Pa., U.S.A. 89 M6
Youkou: Ivory Coast 80 C3
Youkounkoun: Guinea 80 B2
Youlgreave: Derby., Eng. 27 S13
Youmba: Congo 81 H4
Young: N.S.W., Australia 71 H10
Young: Sask., Canada 92 F2
Young Nunataks: Antarctica 9 70S 50E
Youngstown: Alta., Canada 92 E2
Youngstown: Ohio, U.S.A. 88 L5
Youssoufia: Morocco 80 K8
Yoxford: Suff., England 25 Z15
Yoxhall: Staffs, England 27 S14
Yoyang (Yochow): Hunan, China 62 U9
YOZGAT: & Prov., Turkey 56 D2
Ypala: Ghana 80 D3
Ypane: riv., Paraguay 96 D1
Ypres (Ieper): Belgium 36 H5
Ypsilanti: Mich., U.S.A. 88 K4
Yreka: Calif., U.S.A. 92 C4
Ysbyty Ystwyth: Dyfed, Wales 24 O15
Yscloskey: La., U.S.A. 90 Ins.
Ysgubor-y-Coed: Dyfed, Wales 27 O14
Ysleta: Tex., U.S.A. 93 F6
Yssingeaux: France 37 K10
Ystad: Sweden 47 N9
Ystalyfera: West Glamorgan, Wales 24 O16
Ystradgynlais: Powys, Wales 24 O16
Ystrad Meurig: Dyfed, Wales 24 O15
Ystwyth: riv., Dyfed, Wales 24 O15
Ythan: riv., Grampian, Scotland 28 R5
Ytre Ådal: Norway 47 M6
Ytteran: Sweden 46 O5
Yuan: riv., Hunan, China 62 U9
Yuan (Rouge): riv., Yunnan, China 62 S10
Yuanan: Hupeh, China 62 U8
Yuanchow (Chihkiang): Hunan, China 62 T9
Yuankiang: Honan, China 62 U9
Yuanku: Honan, China 62 U7
Yuanling: Hunan, China 62 U9
Yuanmow: Yunnan, China 62 S9
Yubetsu: Japan 63 ZZ6
Yubo: Sudan 76 C1
Yucatan: penin. & chan., Mexico 86 L13
Yucatan Basin: Caribbean Sea 8 20N 85W
Yudnapinna: S. Australia 71 B9
Yüerhlai: Heilungkiang, China 63 Y5
Yugan: riv., U.S.S.R. 51 M3

Yugoslavia: Republic 38/9
Cap.: Belgrade
Area: 98,766 sq. miles
(255,804 sq. km.)
Pop.: 20,811,000 (1972 E)

Yuhang: Chekiang, China 62 V8
Yuhsien: Honan, China 62 U8
Yuhsien: Hopeh, China 62 U7
Yukagir Plat.: U.S.S.R. 49 r4
Yukari: Iran 57 K2
Yuki: Fukien, China 62 V9
Yukon: riv., Alaska, U.S.A. 84 d4
Yukon: Territ., Canada (cap. Whitehorse) 84 F5
Yule: riv., W. Australia 68 B4
Yuli: Nigeria 81 G3
Yulin: Kwangsi Chuang, China 62 U10
Yulin: Shensi, China 62 T7
Yuma: Ariz., U.S.A. 93 E6
Yuma: Colo., U.S.A. 93 G4
Yumbel: Chile 96 A4
Yumen: Kansu, China 62 R6
Yumoto: Japan 63 g2
Yumurtalik: Turkey 56 D3
Yuna: W. Australia 68 B5
Yunaska: i., Aleutians 84 b7
Yuncheng: Shantung, China 62 V7
Yungan: Fukien, China 62 V9
Yungas: las: mtns., Bolivia 94 D7
Yungay: Antofagasta, Chile 96 B1
Yungay: Nuble, Chile 96 A4
Yungchang (Paoshan): Yunnan, China 62 R9
Yungchun: Fukien, China 62 V9
Yungera: Vict., Australia 71 E10
Yungfu: Kwangsi Chuang, China 62 T10
Yungjen: Yunnan, China 62 S9
Yungning: Yunnan, China 62 S9
Yungsheng: Yunnan, China 62 S9
Yungshun: Hunan, China 62 T9
Yungsiu: Kiangsi, China 62 V9
Yungtai: Fukien, China 62 V9
Yungting: see Enteng
Yunhsien: Hupeh, China 62 U8
Yunhsien: Yunnan, China 62 S9
Yunhwo: Chekiang, China 62 V9
Yunkwei Plateau: China 62 T9
Yunnan: Prov., China (cap. Kunming) 62 S9
Yunsi: Hupeh, China 62 U8
Yunsiao: Fukien, China 62 V10
Yunta: S. Australia 71 C9
Yura: Japan 63 d4
Yurga: U.S.S.R. 51 P3
Yurimaguas: Peru 94 B5
Yur'yevets: U.S.S.R. 50 F3
Yur'yev-Pol'skiy: U.S.S.R. 50 E3
Yushu: Kirin, China 63 X6
Yushu (Jyekundo): Chinghai, China 62 R8
Yutien (Keriya): Sinkiang, China 51 O7
Yuty: Paraguay 96 D2
Yuwang: Ninghsia Hui, China 62 T7
Yuyang: Szechwan, China 62 T9
Yuyao: Chekiang, China 63 W8

Yuyu: Shansi, China 62 U6
Yuzawa: Japan 63 f2
Yuzha: U.S.S.R. 50 F3
Yuzhno-Sakhalinsk: U.S.S.R. 63 ZZ5
Yuzhnov: U.S.S.R. 50 D4
Yvelines: Dept., France (cap. Versailles) 36 G7
Yverdon: Switzerland 40 M9
Yvetot: France 36 F6
Ywathit: Burma 59 R11
Yzeure: France 37 J9

Zaandam: Netherlands 44 K3
Zab, Great: riv., Iraq/Turkey 57 H3
Zab, Little: riv., Iraq 57 H4
Zabid: Yemen 54 F12
Zabok: Yugoslavia 41 V9
Zabrze: Poland 43 Q11
Zabul: Prov., Afghanistan (cap. Kalat-i-Ghilzai) 55 L8
Zabul (Nasratabad): Iran 58 K8
Zacapa: Guatemala 86 L14
ZACATECAS: Mexico 86 j13
Zacatecas: State, Mexico 93 G8
Zacler: Czechoslovakia 45 V5
Zadar: & chan., Yugoslavia 41 V11
Zafarobad: Tadzhik., U.S.S.R. 51 L7
Zafra: Spain 35 C17
Zaga: Yugoslavia 41 T9
Zagan: Poland 44 V4
Zagazig: Egypt 56 B6
Zaghedah: Iran 57 L5
Zaghouan: Tunisia 38 M18
Zagnandao: Benin 81 E3
Zagora: Morocco 80 K8
Zagorsk: U.S.S.R. 50 E3
ZAGREB: Croatia, Yugo. 41 V10
Zagros Mtns.: Iran 57 K5
Zagubica: Yugoslavia 39 R14
Zagvozd: Yugoslavia 38 P15
Zahara: Spain (Gib. Inset) 32 Ins.
Zahebre: Ivory Coast 80 C3
ZAHIDAN (Duzdab): Baluchistan & Sistan, Iran 55 K9
Zahle: Lebanon 56 D5
Zaholi: Iran 55 K9
Zaid: Saudi Arabia 54 E10
Zaiddiya: Yemen 54 F11
Zaindeh: riv., Iran 55 H8

Zaïre: Republic 73 J10
Cap.: Kinshasa
Area: 905,063 sq. miles
(2,344,113 sq. km.)
Pop.: 22,860,000 (1972 E)

Zaire: Prov., Angola (cap. São Salvador do Congo) 81 G6
Zaire (Congo): riv., Zaïre 76 B2
Zaječar: Yugoslavia 39 S15
Zak: riv., S. Africa 74 D5
Zaka: Rhodesia 77 D7
Zakbayéme: Cameroun 81 G4
Zakho: Iraq 57 H3
Zakinthos (Zante): i., Ionian Is. 39 R18
Zako: Central African Rep. 76 B1
Zako: Tibet, China 62 R8
Zakopane: Poland 43 Q12
Zakouma National Park: Chad 73 J7
Zakroczym: Poland 43 R10
Zakros: Crete 39 U19
Zala: Co., Hungary (cap. Zalaegerszeg) 41 W9
Zalaegerszeg: Hungary 41 W9
Zalakomár: Hungary 43 P13
Zalalövo: Hungary 41 W9
Zalău: Romania 43 S13
Żalec: Yugoslavia 41 V9
Zaleshchiki: Ukraine 43 T12
Zalingei: Sudan 79 J7
Zaltbommel: Netherlands 44 L4
Zamakh: well, Yemen P.D.R. 55 G11
Żamberk: Czechoslovakia 45 W5
Zambezi: riv., Mozam./Rh. 77 D6
Zambezia: Dist., Mozam. (cap. Quelimane) 77 E6

Zambia: Republic 77 C6
Cap.: Lusaka
Area: 290,724 sq. miles
(752,975 sq. km.)
Pop.: 4,515,000 (1972 E)

Zamboanga: Philippines 65 G5
Zambrow: Poland 42 S10
Zamfara: riv., Nigeria 81 F2
ZAMORA: & Prov., Spain 35 D16
Zamora: Poland 43 S11
Zam'yany: U.S.S.R. 50 G5
Zanaga: Congo 81 G5
Zandvoort: Netherlands 44 K3
Zanesville: Ohio, U.S.A. 88 L6
Zangadi: Chad 81 G3
Zanjon: riv., Argentina 96 B3
Zante: riv., Argentina 96 B3
Zante (Zakinthos): i., Ionian Is. 39 R18
Zanthus: W. Australia 68 C6
ZANZIBAR: & i., Tanzania 76 E4
Zaouiet El-Kahla: Algeria 78 F4
Zaozerny: U.S.S.R. 51 Q3
Zapadnaya Dvina: U.S.S.R. 50 D3
Zapadočesky: Reg., Czechoslovakia (cap. Pilsen (Plzeň)) 45 T6
Zapadoslovensky: Reg., Czechoslovakia (cap. Bratislava) 43 P12
Zapala: Argentina 96 A4
Zapaleri: mtn., Bol./Arg. 96 B1
Zape, El: Mexico 93 F7
Zaporozh'ye: Ukraine 50 E5
Zara: Turkey 56 E2
Zaragoza: Colombia 94 C2
Zaragoza: Mexico 93 G7
ZARAGOZA (Saragossa): & Prov., Spain 35 F16
Zaranj: Iran 55 J8
Zaranou: Ivory Coast 80 D3
Zarasay: Lithuania, U.S.S.R. 47 U9
Zárate: Argentina 96 D3
Zarauz: Spain 37 C12
Zaraysk: U.S.S.R. 50 E4
Zaraza: Venezuela 94 D2
Zardeh Kuh: mtn., Iran 55 H8
Zari: Nigeria 81 G2
Zaria: Nigeria 81 F2
Zarin: riv., Iran 57 L4
Zarineh: riv., Iran 57 K3
Zaris: S.W. Africa 74 B2
Zărnești: Romania 39 T14
Zarqa: riv., Jordan 55 b2
Zarqa (Jabbok): riv., Jordan 55 b2
Zarrinabad: Iran 57 L3
Żary: Poland 45 V4
Zarzis: Tunisia 32 E5